*Insider Trading
and the Stock Market*

HENRY G. MANNE

Insider Trading
and the Stock Market

THE FREE PRESS, New York
Collier-Macmillan Limited, London

To my Mother and Father

Preface

PROBABLY no aspect of modern corporate life has been more roundly condemned than insider trading. Few people, even moderately well-informed about corporate affairs, can have failed to have heard some of this criticism. And none, it may be guessed, has heard this practice praised. The present work does, however, largely defend insider trading. And whether the reader agrees with the ultimate conclusion or not, he can hardly fail to recognize that the question is a complex and difficult one, deserving serious study rather than pat answers and off-hand solutions.

The major effort of this book is to offer an objective scheme of analysis, useful in describing and predicting the various effects of insider trading. The tone of this work is quite different from most of the previous literature. That literature, discussed in the first chapter, has been socially valuable in establishing a moral standard and a set of attitudes about corporate executives' conduct. The importance of this contribution should certainly not be ignored or belittled. Moral and ethical business standards have played a substantial role in the development of several areas of American business conduct. And one need only examine the unhappy consequences of dishonorable behavior by businessmen in certain underdeveloped economies to realize the commercial importance of a sense of responsibility and fair dealing.

But valuable as such attitudes may be, it is nonetheless imperative that we be willing to discuss various business practices objectively and disinterestedly. For no matter how useful an area or a practice may be as a vehicle for expression of moral concern, there is no substitute for the careful analysis necessary for formulating social policy. It is a fundamental weakness of most discussions of insider trading that they never push beyond a sense of moral outrage.

Our common law courts, with their sometime genius for insight and wisdom in dealing with extremely complex issues, seem to have handled the problem of insider trading in a practical and sensible fashion. They recognized that there may be dangers to certain noninsiders attendant upon insider trading. By and large, the courts seem to have sensed these dangers and erected prophylactic barriers where possible. This legal background is discussed in Chapter II, and a justification for the common law rules, usually unarticulated in judicial opinions, is offered. There were, however, some problems with which these courts were not equipped to deal. Courts can act only on the parties before them in individual cases, and, as a practical matter of policing, this may be too inefficient or too costly to give the total protection needed. Thus it was generally believed that Congressional action was required to deal with certain specific forms of stock manipulation and with short-term insider trading. But at no time did Congress adopt a thoroughgoing and absolute prohibition on insider trading. Nor does such a rule exist at the date of this writing.

The last statement may surprise may readers. The implications of many recent newspaper stories in connection with the celebrated case of *Securities and Exchange Commission v. Texas Gulf Sulphur Co.* are that insider trading is illegal and that the purpose of that litigation is to prove whether the defendants are guilty of the practice. But that simply is not so. The real significance of the case lies in the rules that the courts *will* adopt. The question of what the Texas Gulf Sulphur officials did or do not do is of relatively little consequence compared to the fundamental legal rule against insider trading that the SEC is asking the courts to approve.

Nonetheless, new rules on insider trading have been developing at a rapid rate in the past five years. This legal development has not, however, been accompanied by parallel advances in the theory or analysis of this trading. A surprisingly large number of significant questions have hitherto gone unnoticed or untreated. For example, some of the issues or phenomena now discussed for the first time include: the various techniques for insider trading other than the direct and immediate use of information in the stock market; the extent to which these practices actually occur in America; the actual effect of insider trading on stock market price movements; how barring or allowing insider trading would effect specific classes of individuals trading in the stock market, specifically short-term traders and long-term investors; whether the rewards of insider trading flow to the individuals who in some sense are responsible for producing the news; the distinctive features of inside information as a possible form of compensation for innovational activities in large corporations; the feasibility of preventing insider trading and the costs involved; and, finally, the possibilities and propriety of insider trading by government officials.

This book is offered primarily as a theoretical treatment of this fascinating subject. The reader will notice at many points a caveat to the effect that data on a particular point are needed but presently unavailable. Perhaps it is not the least contribution of this work that these areas are specified and analyzed. This is not to suggest, however, that empirical research is the only acceptable mode of proof in this area. Hopefully, the reader will find the conclusions convincing even though many are based on hypothesis. In this sense, however, these conclusions are tentative, and when all the data have been gathered, many of them may have to be modified.

Certainly the time has arrived for the Securities and Exchange Commission to establish a research office with responsibility for investigating issues like the ones raised in this book. Such agencies as the SEC were created and originally defended on the supposition that the regulation would be done by experts, knowledgeable and sophisticated about the area in their charge. But this expertise has frequently been notably absent. It is interesting to observe that the current position of the SEC, in the area of insider trading, is that the courts, with the aid of the Commission as a party litigant, are best equipped to guide this legal development. Thus no guidelines on insider trading have been issued by the SEC. The courts, in turn, show signs of assuming the SEC's expertise from their role in the litigation. Thus, while professing its faith in a common law development of this area, the SEC substantially influences the direction of that change.

This book should furnish the Commission with an outline or guide for the conduct of the research it should be doing in this area. Hopefully, this research work will be begun before definitive and possibly damaging judicial holdings appear.

A word would seem to be in order about what may be the most common form of criticism of this book. From previous encounters it has appeared that thoughtful critics are largely concerned with the possibility that insider trading will put corporate managers in a conflict of interest position with shareholders. Undoubtedly, one can find specific instances of fraud, deceit, and manipulation that could be prevented by an effective rule against insider trading. But the important question that must be considered is whether the outlawing of all insider trading is the most appropriate sanction for this undesirable conduct. The answer seems to be in the negative, since traditional modes of administrative and criminal law enforcement are probably more appropriate and may be more efficient for dealing with these problems. At any rate, the burden of proof should rest on those who believe that drastic treatment is required. The time has come for the opponents of insider trading to justify their position with more than a few isolated scare stories.

My greatest debt for this work is to my students in seminars and classes in corporation law at The George Washington University, where I first began work on this subject. They have been at once my most ardent supporters and most severe critics. Several of these former students performed well as research assistants; and I should like especially to acknowledge the excellent help I received from Stuart M. Fischbein, Donn K. Jenkins, Steven A. Karsch, Timothy G. Greene, Morton H. Press, Matthew Rosen, and Radcliffe Welles. I also received extremely valuable suggestions, ideas, and criticisms from Armen A. Alchian, Joseph Aschheim, Joseph Bishop, Vartkes L. Broussalian, Eugene V. Rostow, and J. Fred Weston. Needless to say, none of the named individuals bears any responsibility for errors or weaknesses in this work. Mrs. Ella Louise Belk was my secretarial mainstay and a delight to work with. Parts of this book were earlier submitted to the Yale Law School in partial fulfillment of the requirements for the Degree of Doctor of the Science of Law.

I might add that the appearance of this book at a time when the Texas Gulf Sulphur litigation is much in the news is entirely coincidental. Early drafts of this work were completed, in substantially their present form, long before that action was brought. The book is entirely my own independent work and I have no connection, financial, legal or otherwise, with Texas Gulf Sulphur or any of the litigants in that case or any other case dealing with insider trading.

Henry G. Manne

Washington, D.C.
March 1966

Contents

X. OBJECTIONS TO INFORMATION AS COMPENSATION

Fraudulent Manipulation. The Intentional Creation of Bad News. Delay in Disclosures. Stock Pools. Profits from Bad News. The Nature of Competition for Entrepreneurs. Profiting by Wrong Persons.

XI. THE PROBLEMS OF PUBLIC AND PRIVATE POLICING

Outsiders with Valuable Information. The Arbitrary Approach to Enforcement. Enforcement Techniques. The "Stop-Trading" Approach. Internal Policing.

XII. A POSTSCRIPT ON GOVERNMENT

How Government Officials May Get Inside Information. News of Corporate Mergers. Government Procurement. The Special Position of Congressmen. The Misleading Emphasis on Stock Ownership. The Pros and Cons of Government Insider Trading. Executive Views on Insider Trading. Proposed Legislation. Approaches to Reform.

I

Background

PRIOR TO THE year 1910 no one had ever publicly questioned the morality of corporate officers, directors, and employees trading in the shares of corporations. There are several reasons why attitudes began to change early in the twentieth century. Part of the reason was simply a time lag between the dramatic, almost revolutionary development of the large publicly held corporation in the last quarter of the nineteenth century and the recognition of all the problems created by this institution. The functional relationship of shareholders in the corporation to each other had changed dramatically. No longer was it possible for each shareholder to demand in a personal and imperative way that his business associates deal with him fairly. In small enterprises social and psychological forces operate to maintain desirable interpersonal relationships, and individual policing is relatively easy and inexpensive. But these factors were missing in the large corporation with publicly traded shares. An open market for shares, with its greater assurance of liquidity for apprehensive shareholders, was the functional substitute for the older approach. Being less well understood than familiar forms, the open market has never been fully trusted, even by lawyers whose special province has always been the resolution of interpersonal conflicts.

The popular concept of morality in business in the late nineteenth century was very different from that of today. One need only read the classic descriptive works[1] to understand the change. Today an announcement that insiders are dealing in their company's shares is sufficient to cause an almost audible gasp of public indignation. And yet in a survey by the New York *Times* in 1915,[2] 90 per cent of business executives interviewed admitted to trading regularly in their own company's shares. Today a comparable survey might find a few individuals admitting these transactions, but in all probability the percentage would be near zero.[3]

Law and Economics

FROM THE BEGINNING the subject of insider trading has been almost exclusively the province of lawyers and law professors. There is a rich economic literature that may be drawn on for understanding the problems, but economists, almost to the man, have remained silent on this specific question. In recent years, however, the legal literature has developed apace—in quantity, if not in quality. This fact has had a noticeable influence on developments in the whole area. The fundamental approach of lawyers to issues such as this one is quite different from that of economists. The lawyers' approach to most questions reflects the centuries-old tradition of viewing problems in the context of a case or lawsuit, the arena for settling disputes between two live, human beings. Indeed, much of the common law (which is most of American law prior to the twentieth century) is the formalization of rules governing individuals in their personal relationships. Perhaps the only important exceptions to this statement in the common law are the archaic rules of real property and the uniquely developed commercial law.

Thus when lawyers, judges, and law professors are faced with issues of broad social or economic consequences, their tendency is to approach the subject with relationships between specific individuals in mind. Their acceptance or rejection of a practice will reflect their notion of the fairness of the transaction simply from the point of view of the two individuals involved. It is not difficult to see why lawyers have generally concluded that there is something unfair (primarily in the sense of "unequal") about insiders with undisclosed good news buying shares from existing shareholders.

Economists think with a different tradition behind them. Theirs is perhaps the most scientific of the social sciences. Here the word *scientific* must connote objectivity and moral detachment, as well as systematic verification of results. Economists tend to view any controversy as reflecting a platonic, ideal conflict. The question for an economist is rarely one of the mutual fairness of a transaction between individual parties. He is not a specialist in matters of individual morality. *Fairness* ordinarily connotes to economists the propriety of allocation of resources or income among large, distinguishable bodies or groups of individuals. To the economist individuals are a fungible commodity, each substitutable for another. The economist, viewing the issue of insider trading, will ask how all shareholders are affected financially by the practice, whether it results in a desirable allocation of resources, and whether the return to insiders reflects a competitive or a monopoly gain.

Until fairly recent years, economic theory did not offer the necessary tools for dealing with this topic. Indeed only one major work has specifically dealt with information as a commodity.[4] Yet no market analysis of valuable information is possible without isolating it in this way. The absence of any accepted economic tools for analyzing this subject made the insider-trading area a fertile one for the lawyers' equity approach with its overtones of fairness and morality. Indeed, it is one of the greatest virtues of our legal system that it performs this function when scientific explanation is lacking. But, as we develop greater understanding of underlying phenomena, the equity approach may become less appropriate for the solution to new legal issues.

The theory of the entrepreneur, the second major area of economic analysis that may be drawn on in analyzing insider trading, is perhaps more familiar to economists than is information theory. Here a rich economic literature exists, the pioneering work on which is largely associated with the names of Joseph Schumpeter and Frank Knight. Indeed, the present work is in large part an application of the theories of these two economists to the modern question of insider trading. As Schumpeter suggested, innovation is simply a new combination of existing factors.

Early Analysis of Insider Trading

THE ARGUMENTS against insider trading, interestingly enough, are not very old. Professor A. A. Berle, in an important statement on the subject in 1927,[5] gives the honor of being first in line to Professor H. L. Wilgus for his 1910 article[6] collecting the existing cases and commenting on the then fresh U.S. Supreme Court decision in *Strong* v. *Repide*.[7] Wilgus discussed the minority of cases that concluded that certain types of insider trading should not be allowed, but these cases, as was pointed out in a later article,[8] could probably have been decided on the basis of common-law fraud or deceit.

After reviewing the case holdings, Wilgus concluded that for a director to "take advantage of his position to secure the profits that all have won, offends the moral sense; no shareholder expects to be so treated by the director he selects; no director would urge his friends to select him for that reason; that the law yet allows him to do this, does more to discourage legitimate investment in corporate shares than almost anything else, and allows the fiction of corporate entity to obstruct instead of advance justice."[9] This quote constitutes almost the full extent of analysis in Professor Wilgus' article, which Berle seventeen years later said was the "most effectively expounded" statement of the position.[10] Wilgus did at least suggest the necessity of some argument beyond "offense to the moral sense." But, like most other arguments in this field, Professor Wilgus' were largely statements of conclusions. He offers no evidence, logical or empirical, to back them up.[11] His allegations are important, however, and they will be dealt with in this book. Special attention will be given in Chapter VII to the charge that legitimate investment is discouraged by allowing insider trading.

To Berle, the "ablest exponent" of the opposing position was Robert Walker in 1923.[12] Again, however, the quality of the analysis is disappointing. Walker's principal argument was that the weight of precedent was on his side. Further, to oppose the moral position of his opponents, Walker criticized the courts for "leaving the safe human ground of fraud or deceit" and "establishing an abstract obligation, a commandment or ethical principle."[13] Walker offered some concrete arguments as well. For instance, he suggested that the rule proposed by Wilgus would catch those directors who were buying shares merely for investment and not speculating on inside information. And Wilgus, charged Walker, overlooked the fact that many outside stockholders were as smart as or smarter than the insiders with whom they dealt. These arguments seem disingenuous at best, but Walker did not really seem too concerned about the whole affair. He believed that most of the judicial sympathy with the minority rule he opposed occurred in states that were not financially important and that chartered few or no publicly held corporations. His argument was primarily directed against a broad fiduciary rule applicable in all cases of insider trading, including trading in listed securities. He approved a somewhat liberal application of the common-law fraud rule, and by implication he anticipated the modern notion of a fiduciary duty among shareholders in closely held corporations.[14]

Berle's
Position

By 1927 Professor Berle indicated the desirability of converging two proposals then being made in the literature about corporations. One of these was the fiduciary concept proposed by Wilgus. The other was the concept of publicity of corporate financial accounts, generally associated with the name of Berle's mentor, William Z. Ripley,[15] and with that of Louis D. Brandeis.[16] Berle saw this convergence as the most appropriate answer to Walker's contention that a fiduciary relationship made no sense in anonymous transactions over a stock exchange. Now, Berle pointed out, the mechanical problems were solved. Regular disclosure about corporate affairs should be made before the insiders begin their trading.[17] In this way, problems of policing insiders would be minimized, while other market traders get the full value of the corporate information.

It is well-known history that the Ripley-Brandeis-Berle proposals for publicity of corporate accounts became an important feature of the Securities Exchange Act of 1934.[18] Berle was not explicit on how he would treat the use of special information, not a part of regularly published corporate accounts, that might provide the basis for corporate insiders' trading in listed securities. The implications are quite clear, however, that he sided with Professor Wilgus on this point, and Berle also attempted to justify his position.

> With neither power nor information, the stockholder becomes merely the beneficiary—*cestui*—of the corporate management. Deprive him of any right by way of fiduciary relation, and the business of investing in stocks becomes too hazardous to continue. More specifically, a corporate management which, as individuals, chooses to enter the open market and which at the same time exercises control over the release of information concerning corporate affairs, can deal with the current value of its securities, if not at pleasure, at least with tremendous effect; and the liquid value of the corporate securities held by the stock-

holder becomes a matter which the corporate management itself can determine.[19]

The assumption in the first sentence of this passage—that shareholders have *no* information—can never be wholly true. Shareholders certainly know how large a dividend they are receiving, and, at least in the case of listed securities, they can know the current and past market value of their own and others' securities.[20] If indeed they had no information, their status as *cestuis que trust* might be complete, but complete ignorance does not follow from the failure of an insider to disclose particular pieces of information on which he bases his trading. Furthermore, by suggesting the total dependence of shareholders on the insiders' information, Berle implies quite unfairly that shareholders are motivated solely by trading profits and not by long-term capital gains or dividends.[21]

Berle's second quoted sentence, suggesting that trading is "too hazardous to continue" without a fiduciary duty, can mean one of two things. It can mean that the risks of such trading are so great to outside shareholders that they will leave the market—a result that we do not want. But this cannot be completely true, or the shareholders whom Berle was seeking to protect would not be in existence at the time he wrote. That is, if the risk was in fact too hazardous for some individuals to assume consciously (and no one suggests that the shareholders of the period were unaware that insiders were allowed to trade freely), presumably those individuals were not shareholders. But shareholders were willing to assume these risks, consciously and in large numbers. Since they were there, "too hazardous to continue" cannot refer to the existence of outside shareholders in the market.

Alternatively, the statement might refer to particular individuals who stay out of the market because they feel that insider trading increases their risk of loss. The problem then would lie in the decrease in market liquidity resulting from the smaller number of individual traders. But Berle has no evidence to substantiate this proposition. In the first place, it is possible that insiders who are trading add more liquidity than they frighten away. More important, however, the argument assumes that insider trading actually increases the risk of loss to outside shareholders. As we shall see in Chapter VII, it is doubtful that this is generally true. Furthermore, to the extent that insider trading does in certain instances injure some particular individuals, unidentifiable in advance, financial advantages flowing to all shareholders more than compensate for this loss.

It is possible that behind Berle's thinking was the "bumpkin" theory of outside shareholders. That is, these people should be treated somewhat as wards in chancery or profligates who would waste their valuable assets while their needy families starve and languish at home. No one, it must be acknowledged, has explicitly made this argument.

In the last part of his argument, Berle may have been implying some relationship between insider trading and the danger of manipulation of corporate affairs. Certainly this relationship was frequently alluded to in the congressional hearings[22] on the Securities and Exchange Act of 1934. But again this causal relationship should not be assumed. As we shall see in the discussion in Chapter X, only very rarely is there any reason to believe that insider traders have an incentive to manage corporate affairs contrary to the interests of all shareholders.

The 1933–1934 Congressional Hearings

To THE POLITICALLY uninitiated it might seem that there exists one treasure trove of analysis of insider trading. For weeks and months during 1933 and 1934, in some of the most spectacular legislative hearings ever held in Washington, the greats of the financial, industrial, and commercial communities were put through searing examinations of their practices. In the Senate hearings many important and famous men willingly or grudgingly conceded that they traded in the stock market with inside information. The Senate Committee on Banking and Currency and its chief counsel, Ferdinand Pecora, waxed indignant. But one looks in vain for an analysis as to why this trading was deemed evil. No one could deny that prior to 1933 insider trading, both in promotional stocks and existing issues, occurred regularly. But the bankers and executives involved were not the proper witnesses to make a logical case for a strong rule against insider trading. The witnesses should have been Berle, Brandeis, and others who maintained the undesirability of the practice.

For one brief moment during the course of the 1933 Senate hearings, one such witness testified on insider trading. Thomas G. Corcoran, one of the draftsmen of the bill under consideration, stated in reference to the present Section 16(b) of the Securities Exchange Act:

> That [Section 16(b)] is to prevent directors receiving the benefits of short-term speculative swings on the securities of their own companies, because of inside information. The profit of such transaction under the bill would go to the corporation. You hold the director, irrespective of any intention or expectation to sell the security within six months after, because it will be absolutely impossible to prove the existence of such intention or expectation, and you have to have this crude rule of thumb, because you cannot undertake the burden of having to prove that the director intended, at the time he bought, to get out on a short swing.[23]

Corcoran noted a few moments later that the New York Stock Exchange was aware of "these evils, and despairing of effective prosecutions under the laws of all States . . . have [*sic*] urged that this situation be cured by the passage of a Federal law governing the incorporation of companies."[24] As Corcoran characterized it, the objection of the stock exchange to "these provisions is that they put a heavier burden on listed companies, because the directors of such companies cannot cheat their stockholders, than it does on unlisted companies, which will still be in the position where the directors can cheat their stockholders."

Senator Thomas Gore of Oklahoma asked Corcoran if the Section was "aimed at the general evil of officers and directors rigging their stock up and down, and squeezing out their own stockholders."[25] Corcoran replied that it was, and that was the end of the discussion of what was wrong with insider trading. Even so, Senator Gore's implication that Section 16(b) was designed to prevent fraud and manipulation has not been accepted by courts or commentators, and other Sections of the Act were explicitly stated to be for that purpose.[26]

The 1934 Report of the Senate committee stated:

> Among the most vicious practices unearthed at the hearings before the subcommittee was the flagrant betrayal of their fiduciary duties by directors and officers of corporations who used their positions of trust and confidential information which came to them in such positions, to aid them in their market activities. Closely allied to this type of abuse was the unscrupulous employment of inside information by large stockholders who, while not directors and officers, exercised sufficient control over the destinies of their companies to enable them to acquire and profit by information not available to others.[27]

The House Report was simply more of the same: "Men charged with the administration of others' money must not use inside information for their own advantage."[28] Why not? We are never told. To call insider trading a breach of a fiduciary duty was simply conclusionary, as there was no law prior to 1934 generally considering it to be such. And to say that the practice was vicious or unscrupulous was also not a reasoned answer. Worse than that, the emotional tone of the arguments probably intimidated anyone who tried to defend the practice or even make cogent inquiries.

Recent Discussions

THE LOW QUALITY of analysis found in the 1933–1934 hearings and reports has characterized subsequent investigations into the subject as well. In 1963 the Special Study of Securities Markets of the SEC begged the same questions as did the earlier efforts.[29] After stating that the keystone of the entire structure of federal securities legislation was disclosure and pointing out that Section 16 was consistent with this disclosure philosophy, the Study forthwith recommended the extension of this Section to securities not previously covered. This approach was fundamentally that of the New York Stock Exchange in 1933, that is, that the only thing wrong with rules against insider trading is that they did not cover unlisted as well as listed stocks. This time Congress obliged.[30]

At one point the Special Study was almost led into some analysis of insider trading. While considering the question of broker-dealers who sit on corporate boards of directors, the Study noted the complexities faced when information gained from this position was used either personally or for customers to whom a fiduciary obligation was owed.[31] But that problem, complex as the Special Study said it was, was not carefully analyzed or, for that matter, really faced at all. With an almost audible sigh of relief that such an alternative was available, the Special Study concluded that this was "the kind of area in which the self-regulatory agencies, with support from governmental agencies where violations of legal duties are involved, can be instrumental in defining and effectuating higher ethical standards."[32] The matter then was left up to the SEC by the Special Study.

Actually since the early attempts to deal with the subject of corporate insider trading, the matter has generally been assumed to be closed. In 1961, Professor Louis Loss could state that the "purpose of §16(b)—prevention of the unfair use of information by corporate insiders—does not, of course, admit of dispute."[33] And a young SEC lawyer, writing in a law review in 1964, stated that "the policy in favor of providing public investors with all available information that might be material to their investment decisions—a policy too obvious to require further elaboration—far outweighs any policy in favor of allowing corporate insiders to trade freely, *on the basis of inside information*, in the securities of their corporations—a policy for which it is difficult to conceive of any justification."[34]

Cary's
Position

OTHER STATEMENTS to similar effect, though far more influential, have come from Professor William Cary, who was Chairman of the SEC from 1961 to 1965.[35] On no less than four different occasions during his tenure as chairman, Professor Cary concluded that full disclosure is so important that insiders who could not disclose material facts about corporate affairs should forego any transaction in the stock at that time, for whatever reason the transaction might be entered into. In his opinion, *In the Matter of Cady, Roberts & Co.*, Cary states: "So many times that citation is unnecessary, we have indicated that the purchase and sale of securities is a field in special need of regulation for the protection of investors."[36] Cary further states that the SEC "antifraud provisions[37] are not intended as a specification of particular acts or practices which constitute fraud, but rather are designed to encompass the infinite variety of devices by which *undue advantage* [italics mine] may be taken of investors and others."[38]

Apparently among the infinite variety of devices by which undue advantage may be taken of investors is the use of valuable information in insider trading. Although in this opinion Cary did not state why insider trading was unfair, on other occasions he has attempted to explain why he felt it was an evil.

> A manager should receive corporate information not for his own personal emolument, but to assist the corporation in its operations. The use of inside information by a director or other manager to trade in shares is the securing of additional compensation in a covert fashion, and should be condemned. (It further, of course, infects the integrity of the market.)[39]

Close analysis of this statement is certainly required. Cary implies that managers have contracted for a specific compensation and that they have no claim on anything else of value from the corporation.[40] If there were in fact some prohibition in the employment contract, or in existing law, against all forms of insider trading, then indeed it would be fair to make this statement as quoted. But this statement was not a correct description of the law on the subject, nor was it offered as such. It was offered as a logical argument for a change in the existing rules.

The phrase "securing of additional compensation" implies that the insider is recovering more than he has contracted for. But this is a question of his employment-contract terms—express, implied, or omitted—and what the law on insider trading was at the time he entered into his employment contract. If there are no prohibitions other than Section 16(b) of the 1934 Act and some liberalized fraud concepts operating, then there can be no implied provision prohibiting the insider from trading in his employer's shares when he possesses "inside information." If there is no provision, expressed or implied, in the contract forbidding this share trading, it cannot be said to be proscribed by the contract. And it cannot be assumed that silence on such a topic implies proscription. Strong reasons should be advanced for so restricting insiders by implication. Cary's statement displays conviction but not proof.

As a further mark of Cary's strong feelings on this subject, we should notice that insider trading (that is, trading with information not publicly disclosed) allows covert compensation and "infects the integrity of the market." Trading with inside information does appear to be covert; we shall see that as a practical matter this must be so. But this is a long way from suggesting that shareholders are unaware that corporate insiders trade in the securities market. That proposition, if true, would certainly be the most frightening thing yet discovered about public participation in the stock market. Finally, we are told neither what the "integrity of the market" is nor how insider trading infects it.

Cary was obviously troubled by his own strong insistence that insider trading was wrong. In another place he does attempt to justify his position. He states:

> I should like to suggest reasons for compelling disclosure on a broad basis. First, should not any corporation in whose shares there is a public interest, be required to disclose all material information? Secondly, corporate managements themselves seem to suggest that the modern corporation has a duty to disclose everything to almost everybody. Quite frequently we read the following in a company annual report:
>
> > In addition, [a corporation] has civic responsibilities to the various communities where its affiliates operate, financial responsibilities to the educational institutions from which it draws many of its key employees, and—under many categories—responsibilities to governments.
>
> If the company really believes, and says, it has a responsibility to these numerous groups, must it not at least account to these groups by full disclosure?
>
> Finally, another reason for disclosure is the continuing and increasing relationships of many corporations with the government (both federal and local). They are frequently dependent on government contracts, financing, etc. Does not this tend to give these corporations a special character? I would suggest that these government contacts impose on management most serious responsibilities. These contacts with the agencies of the public are perhaps a strong reason for disclosure to the public. They further suggest the need for management voluntarily to pursue higher standards or be confronted with a Congressional investigation and subsequent demand to do so.[41]

Apart from the obvious *non sequitur* in the third paragraph and the rather threatening tone of the last, the argument for disclosure still seems to miss a crucial point about insider trading. Cary confuses two different concepts of disclosure in the quoted passage. One is the actual announcement of various activities, as required by law. The other, with which we are immediately concerned, is disclosure of information *before it is traded upon by insiders*. Ultimately, most information used by insiders is disclosed; otherwise the insiders may make no profit from it. But the question of insider trading requires concern only with the *timing* of a disclosure, not its ultimate occurrence. And the proper time for any disclosure will vary with the purpose for which it is being made. Since these purposes, some of which are listed by Cary, show great variety, it is illogical to conclude that one disclosure time is appropriate for all. Further, the mere fact that disclosure is required for one specific purpose tells us nothing about whether it should be made at another time for a different purpose.

Conclusion

THIS EXERCISE could be continued indefinitely. Over and over one finds statements that insider trading without disclosure is indefensible and unfair, that shareholders are being duped or defrauded, that undue advantage is taken of them, and that they are being subjected to unfair risk. We are told that business ethics must be improved, that shareholders do not expect their managers to trade before disclosure, and that it is a violation of their fiduciary duty to trade in this fashion.

All of these can be lumped under the general heading of "it's just not right" propositions,[42] and, if repetition were a form of scientific proof, undoubtedly the case against insider trading would long ago have been proved. Unfortunately, however, these disputations have merely served to conceal the fact that in the literature on insider trading almost no careful analysis of the subject exists.[43] This is not to say that moral standards do not play an important role in the business community. Indeed, unless there is broad-based agreement on various standards of ethical conduct, free markets do not seem to function very effectively. But no amount of moral exhortation can substitute for the rigorous analysis necessary to understand the problem of insider trading. If we can understand the institutions, practices and consequences of insider trading, we may then make more appropriate moral judgments.

II

The Traditional Legal Context

THE COMMON LAW on insider trading reflects a fundamental tension characteristic of American corporation law. This tension results from the law's effort to cover both large, publicly held corporations and small, closely held ones with one set of rules. Most of our traditional corporate legal norms, both statutory and common law, were designed for the large corporation. Indeed, most of them developed during the era when the corporate form was rarely used for smaller business associations. As the corporate form became popular for small ventures and began to replace the familiar partnership, pressures on these legal rules intensified.[1]

The legal attitude toward protection of shareholders in large corporations has clearly reflected the free-market philosophy underlying our corporation laws. With an active and open market for corporate shares, there is little for law and courts to do. Aggrieved shareholders can sell their shares at the market price, and this price will be determined by the total market's appraisal of the worth of the securities. The identity of individuals participating in such a market need not be known, since market forces will determine the price. Because corporate managers are assumed to operate the business consistent with the interests of the shareholders, presumably there is little danger to other shareholders because insiders are trading.

It is not surprising then that prior to 1909 the overwhelming number of states that had considered the matter concluded that there was no obligation on the part of an insider buying shares to disclose information known only to him. This was the so-called majority rule, holding that directors and officers of a corporation may deal at arm's length with the company's shareholders. This is still termed the majority rule, though it is no longer that in fact.

The only limitation on insiders purchasing shares in a majority-rule state is the one operating on any contracting party at common law: He could not retain any gains resulting from fraud. But fraud cases are extremely difficult to prove. There must normally be an affirmative misrepresentation. It must be recognized as such by its perpetrator and relied upon as true by the victim. The latter's reliance must be reasonable under the circumstances, and he must prove actual damages. Some of these elements are extremely difficult to prove in a normal stock-exchange transaction. The insider will ordinarily not make any statement. Consequently the affirmative misrepresentation will not appear. Further, the courts have held that in an exchange transaction it was not reasonable for an outsider to rely upon silence as an indication that the status quo would continue. The common-law-fraud doctrine seemed tailor-made for a laissez-faire, market economy in which few restraints on business dealing were evident.

The Minority Rule

ONLY THREE STATES early declined the majority rule. Georgia in 1903[2] and Kansas in 1904[3] adopted the *minority rule*, and Nebraska followed in 1916.[4] It is interesting to note that in 1911

Kansas became the first state to adopt a Blue-Sky Law, requiring full and truthful disclosures in the public *sale* of securities. The minority rule created a fiduciary relationship between corporate directors and officers on the one hand and selling shareholders on the other. Under this rule full disclosure of all relevant facts was required before the fiduciary could deal with his beneficiary. Legal analogies were found in the relationships between a trustee and his beneficiary, between a principal and an agent, and among the members of a partnership. However, since one had to own shares to gain the protective relationship, only share purchases by insiders from existing shareholders and not sales to outsiders were covered by the rule. Blue-Sky Laws do, of course, cover many sales to outsiders, including many sales by corporate insiders in so-called secondary offerings.

The fiduciary relationship is an equitable concept signifying that a special degree of care or concern must be demonstrated by the fiduciary for the beneficiary. It is usually counterposed to the notion of an arm's-length transaction, the prototype of which is the sale in an open market to a perfect stranger. Fiduciary duties are generally found to exist when the relationship of the parties precludes the desirability of arm's-length dealing. The most obvious case is that of one individual entrusted with the property of another to manage it in the latter's interest. This trustee may not then deal with the owner in relation to the property as if they were strangers in the marketplace. If, for instance, the trustee wishes to buy the property for himself, his interest is in conflict with that of the owner, and the fiduciary duty requires full disclosure on his part. If this is not forthcoming, he will not be allowed to realize any profit from his breach of duty. And in his regular management of trust property, the trustee is subject to constant overseeing by courts of equity.

An employment contract also creates a fiduciary relationship. An agent, among other duties, must deal fairly with his principal, refrain from developing competing interests, preserve his principal's business secrets and make full disclosure of any self-interest in dealing with his principal.[5] These rules are basically employment-contract provisions implied by law. They are implied because contracting parties rarely spell out such ideas explicitly, though both parties would probably have agreed in advance to their desirability.

It is, of course, quite possible to provide explicitly for full disclosure or some other aspect of fiduciary duty even when the law would not imply it. Somewhat surprising, there is only one reported case of a provision of this kind being used.[6] In that case, each of the two shareholders agreed to "give to the other party full information of all transactions relating to the business of the corporation. . . ." The parties also agreed to divulge "any information . . . which may be conducive to the profitable operation of the corporation." This is an extremely unusual provision, but the court showed no hesitation or difficulty in enforcing it when the defendant purchased the plaintiff's shares without disclosing the negotiation of a very profitable lease. Provisions of this sort, whether in articles of incorporation or in separate shareholders' agreements, could be extremely valuable planning devices for small corporations. Surprisingly, they are almost unknown to attorneys or businessmen.[7]

Strict fiduciary standards have long been applied to the dealings of one partner with another. Business relationships of two, three, or more individuals, working closely together and relying heavily on the integrity of each other, probably function more satisfactorily because the law implies the fiduciary obligation. The dependencies are too great and the relationships too personal to allow reliance solely on the disciplinary forces of the market. Consequently, partnership law implied the fiduciary standard in every partnership contract. This provision operated as an open invitation for equity courts to oversee and supervise the relationships of partners. A famous quotation from Judge Benjamin Cardozo epitomizes the standards required.

> Joint adventurers, like copartners, owe to one another, while the enterprise continues, the duty of the finest loyalty. Many forms of conduct permissible in a workaday world for those act-

ing at arm's length, are forbidden to those bound by fiduciary ties. A trustee is held to something stricter than the morals of the market place. Not honesty alone, but the punctilio of an honor the most sensitive, is then the standard of behavior. . . .[8]

The Special-Facts Rule

So LONG as the corporate form was used only for enterprises with large numbers of nonmanaging shareholders, the problem of insider trading never seemed important. During the period of special chartering of corporations, some direct surveillance and control of the use of the corporate form was possible.[9] But by 1875 this period had ended and general incorporation acts available to a minimum of three incorporators prevailed in every state. By 1900 the proliferation of small corporations had begun, although it was not until the 1940's with their substantial income-tax rates that the form became extremely popular for small businesses. By 1909 the need for some coalescence of the majority and minority rules had become clear, and in that year the Supreme Court of the United States decided _Strong_ v. _Repide_.[10]

The defendant in that case was the general manager of a corporation which owned land in the Philippine Islands. He owned approximately 75 per cent of the shares and acted with complete authority to negotiate the sale of the company's lands to the United States government. During the course of these negotiations, the defendant, through an agent who did not identify his principal, approached the plaintiff to buy her small, minority interest. Because of the government's failure to police guerrilla activity in the area, the land had become nearly worthless, and the plaintiff sold her shares for approximately one tenth of their value after the government purchase.

The Court found that the plaintiff would not have sold if she had known that the defendant was the purchaser. The Court stated that the matter could not be determined simply by the bare relationship existing between a director and a shareholder. "That the defendant was a director of the corporation is but one of the facts upon which the liability is asserted, the existence of all the others in addition making such a combination as rendered it the plain duty of the defendant to speak."[11] The Court laid heavy stress on the affirmative steps taken to conceal the identity of the defendant, speaking of this as "strong evidence of fraud." And the fact that a pending sale of surrounding lands to the government was a matter of common gossip in newspaper stories was brushed aside, as only the defendant was in a position to know accurately the state of negotiations.

Thus was born the so-called special-facts rule, which is without question the prevailing approach in the states today.[12] This rule is a long way from a thoroughgoing prohibition on insider trading. For example, no case has ever found an insider liable for a transaction that took place over an organized stock exchange. This seems to be an implicit recognition by common-law courts that specific regulation is needed only in those instances when an active market for corporate securities does not guarantee to shareholders sufficient protection against fraud. A leading case[13] recognized this fact implicitly when it stated that mere silence does not usually amount to a breach of duty. "Purchases and sales of stock dealt in on the stock exchange are commonly impersonal affairs. . . . Business of that nature is a matter to be governed by practical rules. Fiduciary obligations of directors ought not to be made so onerous that men of experience and ability will be deterred from accepting such office."[14] The Court did recognize that parties may stand in such relation to each other that an equitable responsibility arises to communicate facts, but the implication was clear that such a relationship would be difficult to find in the normal stock-exchange transaction.

The special-facts rule seems to require some relationship between the parties indicating a substantial danger of fraud.[15] The courts might, therefore, compare the financial sophistication of the parties and, if the disparity is too great, give the plaintiff the benefit of the rule. Reasonable reliance by the shareholder on the insider's intimation of assistance might also be considered. Many cases granting relief involve a director's seeking out the individual shareholder to induce a sale of his securities. And cases involving so-called incorporated partnerships, where two parties hold all shares of the corporation, are not uncommon. The conditions discussed are generally characteristic of closely held corporations, where the opportunities for subtle misstatements or misleading acts are often very great, though the proof of fraud may be extremely difficult. It does appear, therefore, that courts in their application of the special-facts rule have attempted to limit it to those cases in which the possibility of undue influence was greatest.

Another variable in the special-facts equation is the information withheld. Matters of opinion, as opposed to fact, are not covered, though half-truths are, once disclosure is begun. The failure to disclose any significant information may be the basis for liability, but the likelihood of liability seems greater if the undisclosed information involves a merger, consolidation, dissolution, or sale of substantially all of the corporation's assets.[16]

There is one final indication that the special-facts rule developed as a substitute for market protection when the market is not operating effectively. Only existing shareholders who sell shares to insiders receive any protection from the rule. Outsiders buying from insiders are never covered. It can be argued that the outsider has the world to choose from in making his purchases. Thus he does have the protection of the marketplace in his transactions. Ordinarily he will not stand in a peculiar relationship to a corporate insider raising the dangers of subtle fraud. The existing shareholder, on the other hand, is frequently locked in. No active market for his shares exists, and he may be especially susceptible to the pessimistic sales pitch of an insider.

The common-law approach to insider's trading in the shares of large corporations with listed securities was clear. No doctrine of common law impeded their trading with undisclosed information. As the Supreme Judicial Court of Massachusetts in *Goodwin*

v. *Agassiz* stated: "Law in its sanctions is not coextensive with morality. It cannot undertake to put all parties to every contract on an equality as to knowledge, experience, skill and shrewdness. It cannot undertake to relieve against hard bargains made between competent parties without fraud."[17]

Brophy v. Cities Service Co.

THE CASES DISCUSSED up to this point have all involved an allegation of injury by an individual shareholder in a private action to recover damages. Somewhat different are the cases proceeding from the theory that the stock trading has injured the corporation, thus allowing a corporate rather than an individual recovery. Only the Securities Exchange Act of 1934 and one common-law case have ever maintained this position. The case, *Brophy* v. *Cities Service Co.*,[18] decided by the Delaware Court of Chancery in 1949, has never been cited on the merits in any subsequent case. Its facts are somewhat novel, and the opinion is far from convincing.

In that case a Mr. Kennedy, the confidential secretary of the president of Cities Service oil company, was privy to information concerning the corporation's purchases of its own shares in the open market. He would purchase before and sell after completion of the corporation's projected transactions. The court reasoned that the information belonged to the corporation and that it was a violation of his fiduciary duty to the corporation for Kennedy to use this property for his own benefit. In answer to the argument that no damage to the corporation was shown—presumably because his share purchases were not large enough to affect the market price—the court said that no damages need be shown when a beneficiary is merely recovering illicit profits made by his fiduciary.

It can be inferred from the opinion that Kennedy had not been expressly authorized by a competent officer to trade in the corporation's shares. If such permission had been given, it could certainly have been argued forcefully that his profits constituted part of his compensation under his employment contract. There is, however, some mystery about the facts. We are told that four directors of the corporation had previously been joined in the same action and that they had been dropped as defendants. But we are not told why they were dropped. Conceivably, the court viewed the entire transaction as a conspiracy to avoid liability under Section 16(b) of the Securities Exchange Act. If this is so, however, there is no mention of it in the opinion.

But it is not difficult, logically, to imply a trading prohibition from all the surrounding facts. There is always an implied provision in any employment contract that the employee will not act on his own self-interest to the detriment of his employer. We need only find some injury to the corporation from Kennedy's transactions. The court stated that it could not infer loss to the corporation from the general allegations in the complaint. And yet these allegations were sufficient to allow the court to deduce the necessary conclusion: the defendant's purchases must have damaged the corporation. A consideration of the effects of share purchases by the corporation and Kennedy will show why this is so.

As a corporation proceeds with its purchases, the price of the stock will rise. This rise will continue until the projected number of shares has been purchased. Any unusual purchases made before the corporation begins its buying will simply push the projected price curve of corporate purchases that much higher. The corporation lost the opportunity to buy in those shares that Kennedy purchased at the lower price. The loss to the corporation was the difference between what Kennedy paid for his shares and what the corporation paid for its last purchase of the same number of shares. Thus, no matter how small Kennedy's purchases were and how insignificant the effect of his purchases was on market price, if corporate purchases increase the market price, the corporation was damaged by Kennedy's trading.

Unfortunately, the court in the *Brophy* case did not engage in any analysis of potential loss. It merely characterized Kennedy's position as being confidential and concluded that he could not, therefore, profit by his information. If the court had offered a sound analysis, the case could not be deemed to create a general rule against insider trading. Subsequent judicial disregard of the opinion strongly suggests dissatisfaction with the opinion as written. The result in the *Brophy* case does seem correct, but no convincing reason was offered by the judge for his conclusion.[19]

Section 16(b) of the Securities Exchange Act of 1934

IN AN EXPLICIT effort to equalize the bargaining position of insiders and other market investors, Congress adopted Section 16(b) of the Securities Exchange Act of 1934,[20] termed the *insiders' short-swing profit rule*. The Section was not designed to protect corporate shareholders in what might be considered their contract expectations. Indeed, a shareholder who sold to an insider liable under the Act still has only his common-law protections. The Section was designed only to prevent insiders from profiting from inside information, and the inhibiting device chosen was not a suit by the injured shareholder but rather a suit by the corporation or a derivative suit on its behalf. Prior to the 1964 amendments, the provisions of Section 16 applied only to the insiders of corporations that had an equity security registered on an exchange. Since 1964, however, they apply to any corporation engaged in interstate commerce or whose securities are traded through the mails if it has total assets exceeding $1 million and five hundred or more record holders of an equity security.[21]

At first glance Section 16 would seem to be an effective device for preventing insider trading. Insiders are required by 16(a) to report any changes in their holdings of corporate securities, and this information is readily available to lawyers attracted by the promise of relatively large and easy fees.[22] The proof required for a successful 16(b) prosecution is the height of simplicity. The plaintiff need merely show that during any six-month period the insider sold corporate securities at a higher price than he paid during the same period. A variety of procedural problems have arisen,[23] but the courts have generally shown considerable sympathy with the stated congressional policy in their interpretation of the Act.[24]

But with all these advantages, Section 16 has still probably not had an appreciable effect on the total amount gained by insiders as a result of their possessing inside information. There are two fundamental reasons why this is so. The statute has no effect on any attempt to make profits at the end of a six-month period. Since securities must be held for six months in order to qualify for capital-gains treatment under the Internal Revenue Code, many corporate insiders, buying before disclosure of important information, would hold them for the six-month period in any event. If shares have been held for six months, sales may be made without violating the Section. Short sales by insiders, however, are always prohibited.

But there is a second and far more fundamental reason why Section 16 cannot be effective in preventing insider trading. The coverage of the Section is limited to specifically designated insiders trading in the securities of the corporation to which they bear the specified relationship. The Section touches upon only one of the several methods by which valuable information may be exploited.

For instance, the prohibition of the Section does not necessarily cover trading in the securities of a controlled subsidiary by an officer, director, or 10 per cent shareholder in the parent company if the individual trading is not an officer, director, or 10 per cent shareholder of the subsidiary. It would seem that only if the individual actually controls the parent corporation would he be considered the beneficial owner of the control shares for purposes of the 10 per cent limitation.[25]

Much more important, however, the entire, complex system

for the exchange of information to other individuals is left completely untouched by the Section because it covers only immediate uses of information by insiders buying and selling securities. As Professor Louis Loss says: "There is also no guarantee against evasion by mutual 'back-scratching' of insiders in different corporations, or by trading through relatives or friends."[26] However, it should not be denied that the Section has had considerable influence in forming the moral values voiced and held by the business community.

Blau v. Lehman

THAT THE SEC has long chafed under the restrictive applicability of Section 16 is illustrated by the 1962 decision in *Blau v. Lehman*.[27] This was the Supreme Court's first opportunity to construe Section 16(b) of the 1934 Act. The case involved a partner in the investment-banking firm of Lehman Brothers—a Mr. Thomas, who had succeeded another Lehman partner, John Hertz, on the board of directors of the Tide Water Associated Oil Company. The banking firm, according to the opinion, using information generally available to the public and without consulting Thomas, bought and sold Tide Water shares and realized a short-swing profit. The petitioner, and the Securities Exchange Commission as *amicus curiae*, argued that the firm of Lehman Brothers was a director of the corporation within the meaning of the Act and that consequently the entire profits of the banking firm, and not merely the partnership share of Thomas, should be recovered by the corporation. The Court concluded that the partnership could be liable if it had designated or deputized an individual to be its representative on a board or if he was active in making partnership trading decisions. But such liability did not automatically follow in the case at hand.

The Court was unimpressed with the argument of the petitioner and the Commission that the Section should be extended to include anyone realizing short-swing profits that might be based on inside information. The Court noted that Congress had considered and rejected draft provisions extending the Section's liability to anyone, insider or not, "to whom such unlawful disclosure" was made. Furthermore, Congress had left the Act unamended after a 1952 Court of Appeals case[28] limited the Act to the designated insiders. The Court said: "Congress . . . might amend § 16(b) if the Commission would present to it the policy arguments it has presented to us, but we think that Congress is the proper agency to change an interpretation of the Act unbroken since its passage, if the change is to be made."[29]

The core of the opinion involves defining the word *director*. This word is defined in the Act to include "any person performing similar functions" to those of a director, and the statutory definition of *person* includes a partnership.[30] But the Court refused to apply the entity theory of partnership,[31] under which any partner's act would be the act of the partnership. They concluded that the definitional sections allow a partnership to be treated as an entity but do not require it in every case. They held that Congress did not intend that partnerships be included automatically whenever one partner was a statutory insider.

In his dissenting opinion, Justice William O. Douglas, while berating the pursuit of the entity-aggregate will-o'-the-wisp, concluded that it was easier in this case "to make this partnership a 'director' for purposes of § 16 than to hold the opposite."[32] He was particularly disturbed by what seemed to him to be the exclusion of the most important segment of the financial community from the coverage of Section 16(b). Justice Douglas then went on to repeat the usual arguments about the abuses of trading in inside information. His opinion is replete with such words as *fiduciaries, vicious, predatory,* and *flagrant betrayal.* He reminds us again of Brandeis' admonitions and the fact that the hearings leading to the Securities Exchange Act of 1934 were filled with stories of personal gain by insiders. (For the full text of the *Blau v. Lehman* opinion, see the Appendix, pages 195–205.)

A Rationalization
of Section 16(b)

THE MAJORITY OPINION in the *Blau* case is in the tradition of pre-existing law on the subject of insider trading. It was Douglas who missed the point of Congress' refusal to outlaw all insider trading. The touchstone in all prior law, statutory or common law, was the concept of fraud, not fiduciary duty. Section 16(b) can be rationalized as an antimanipulation device but not as an effective prohibition of insider trading. It cannot succeed at the latter task, but it may be quite effective for the former. Since insiders are left free to exchange their information, the Section may have had little economic effect. On the other hand, because the Section dictates that information *must* be exchanged in most instances before it can be used, insiders will have little incentive to manipulate corporate affairs for their own trading purposes and contrary to the interest of all shareholders.[33] It is one thing to manipulate corporate affairs when the insider can quickly exploit this information by himself. It is quite another matter to engage in manipulation for the immediate benefit of a third person. If manipulation of corporate affairs for trading purposes does occur in American corporations, Section 16(b) has probably been an effective device for minimizing it.

Neither legislative history nor the subsequent literature on the Section has viewed Section 16 as another of the antimanipulation devices Congress included in the 1934 Act.[34] But Congress' refusal to include a general prohibition on insider trading and its apparent concern with deceptive practices suggests that this explanation of Section 16 may be correct. The Supreme Court's opinion in *Blau* v. *Lehman* is consistent with this explanation. The opinion is, like the common-law cases traced back to *Strong* v. *Repide*, logical and respectable. Section 16 filled what may have been an important gap in the law's treatment of insider dealing, and the *Blau* decision limited that Section to serving this antimanipulation purpose.

The defeat for the Securities and Exchange Commission was unmistakable. The Commission's plea for an assumption of guilt was met by the Supreme Court's demand for specific evidence that the director might be involved in a scheme that the Section was designed to prevent. As is often true, effective law in an area turns on questions of the burden of proof. So long as there is no presumption of wrongdoing when information exchanges are possible, the job of policing Section 16(b) will remain extremely difficult. The *Blau* opinion signaled the limit to which the SEC could push the Section. But long before this limit was set, a new, more radical, and far less defensible development was well under way.

III

Developments Under SEC Rule 10b-5

As THE Supreme Court reminded us in *Blau* v. *Lehman,* Congress expressly declined to adopt a broad rule against all trading with inside information. In Section 17(a) of the Securities Act of 1933, Congress did provide a stringent antifraud rule in connection with the sale of securities. From its context and legislative history, this Section appears to have been designed as a catchall for undesirable stock promotional practices not otherwise covered in the Act.[1] In 1936, Congress amended the Securities Exchange Act of 1934 to include a general antideception section, now Section 15(c)(1), applicable to brokers and dealers in their purchases or sales of over-the-counter stocks.[2] This Section gave the Securities and Exchange Commission broad powers to make rules for the regulation of broker-dealers, perhaps broad enough to prohibit insider trading in unlisted securities, though this has never been done explicitly.[3]

The 1934 Act also contains a general provision, Section 10(b), dealing with purchases or sales of securities. This Section makes it unlawful:

> To use or employ, in connection with the purchase or sale of any security registered on a national securities exchange or any

security not so registered, any manipulative or deceptive device or contrivance in contravention of such rules and regulations as the Commission may prescribe as necessary or appropriate in the public interest or for the protection of investors.

Again, the legislative history of this Section, though very meager, suggests that Congress recognized the possibility of manipulative or deceptive devices other than those specifically treated in Section 9 of the Act.[4] It is under this Section 10 that the major legal developments prohibiting insider trading have occurred.

In 1942, rebuffed in its legislative effort to extend Section 17(a) of the 1933 Act to purchases as well as to sales of securities,[5] the Commission promulgated Rule X-10B-5.[6] This Rule is a combination of the jurisdictional coverage of Section 10(b) of the 1934 Act ("any person" and "purchase or sale") with the substantive aspects of Section 17(a) of the 1933 Act. The Rule, like its parent statutory Sections, is not remarkable for its clarity, logic, organization or precision.

It shall be unlawful for any person, directly or indirectly, by the use of any means or instrumentality of interstate commerce, or of the mails, or of any facility of any national securities exchange,

(1) to employ any device, scheme, or artifice to defraud,

(2) to make any untrue statement of a material fact or to omit to state a material fact necessary in order to make the statements made, in the light of the circumstances under which they were made, not misleading, or

(3) to engage in any act, practice, or course of business which operates or would operate as a fraud or deceit upon any person, in connection with the purchase or sale of any security.

Litigation Under
Rule 10b–5

RULE 10b-5 was born of one section aimed at fraudulent stock issues and another aimed largely at deceptions by brokers. Consequently, it is not surprising that for the first five years after its promulgation, about its only use was in broker-dealer disciplinary actions by the SEC. The first judicial recognition of its applicability to insider trading in a private civil action came in 1947.[7] And it was another five years before a truly important decision occurred, in *Speed* v. *Transamerica Corp.*[8]

In the *Speed* case a tobacco company had a cigarette-tobacco inventory that had greatly appreciated in value during World War II, and this was common knowledge in financial and tobacco circles. It was not known, however, that the controlling shareholder had devised a liquidation plan whereby this appreciated value could be realized in spite of price controls on cigarettes. It was the controlling shareholder's failure to disclose to the plaintiff minority shareholder his intention to liquidate the corporation under this plan that a Federal District Court considered actionable. Without knowledge of the plan, knowledge that tobacco inventories had appreciated, was not important. Judge Paul Leahy referred to 10b-5 as follows:

> The rule is clear. It is unlawful for an insider, such as a majority stockholder, to purchase the stock of minority stockholders without disclosing material facts affecting the value of the stock, known to the majority stockholder by virtue of his inside position but not known to the selling minority stockholders, which information would have affected the judgment of the sellers. The duty of disclosure stems from the necessity of preventing a corporate insider from utilizing his position to take unfair advantage of the uninformed minority stockholders. It is an attempt to provide some degree of equalization of bargaining positions in order that the minority may exercise an informed judgment in any such transaction. Some courts have called this a fiduciary duty while others state it is a duty imposed by the "special circumstances." One of the primary purposes of the Securities Exchange Act of 1934 . . . was to outlaw the use of inside information by corporate officers and principal stockholders for their own financial advantage to the detriment of uninformed public security holders.[9]

Judge Leahy's language clearly went beyond anything suggested in earlier cases. It might be noted, however, that this was still not a transaction across an exchange, and it did involve the sale of substantially all the assets of the corporation. And, most important, Transamerica had approached the minority share-holders personally to make an offer for their shares. Thus it is not surprising that many commentators, even after the *Speed* case, continued to believe that Rule 10b-5 was basically designed only to extend the special-facts rule of *Strong* v. *Repide* to all cases involving security transactions within interstate commerce.[10] Most of the provisions of the Securities Exchange Act of 1934 applied only to corporations with securities registered on an exchange.[11] Rule 10b-5, however, like Section 10(b) of the Act, applied to "any person" so long as the transaction fell within the purview of congressional powers.

Some Unanswered Questions

AFTER THE *Speed* decision the pace of 10b-5 civil actions involving insider trading began to quicken,[12] until in 1965 it reached almost flood proportions.[13] This mushrooming volume of cases does not, however, represent a coherent development of the law. Only in June, 1964, for example, did the Supreme Court of the United States apparently decide that a private right of action is permitted by the Act.[14] Many, many issues remain unsettled. The basic validity of the promulgation of Rule 10b-5 has not been carefully tested. Its applicability to nonbroker-dealers has not even been questioned. Many issues raised by the fraud-fiduciary duty dichotomy are in doubt. For instance, the cases disagree on the necessity for *scienter*, or knowledge by the defendant that a misrepresentation is being made; the necessity for reliance by the plaintiff, with the subordinate question of whether he must show "due care" in relying; the necessity for "some semblance of privity," that is, some relationship between the alleged violator of the rule and the plaintiff; whether damages need to be shown (generally true on a fraud theory) or whether the defendant's profits may be recovered (characteristic of fiduciary-duty actions); and the necessity that the undisclosed information be material.[15]

Other questions peculiar to the use of undisclosed information abound. Are customers for whom a broker buys with inside information liable? Is the danger of liability greater for directors than for others who receive undisclosed news? May tips and rumors be played with impunity, or is there a danger if they prove true? Are security analysts in danger if a theory proves correct? Can insiders ever purge themselves of all inside information? Any thoroughgoing restriction on insider trading raises all these questions and more. But the decided cases have barely begun to raise the questions, and already the answers are in hopeless confusion.

In the Matter of
Cady, Roberts & Co.

UNDOUBTEDLY THE MOST important opinion up until 1966 under Rule 10b-5 is a 1961 opinion by the Securities and Exchange Commission, *In the Matter of Cady, Roberts & Co.*[16] This was an action to discipline a broker and his firm for a violation of Rule 10b-5; it did not involve any issue of money damages for aggrieved stock buyers.

A registered representative of Cady, Roberts, J. Cheever Cowdin, was a director of the Curtiss-Wright Corporation. There had been a great rise in the price of that company's shares as a result of considerable ballyhoo about a new engine under development. Shortly thereafter, the board of directors substantially cut the dividend of the company. During the period of rising prices, a broker and partner in Cady, Roberts, Robert M. Gintel, had been buying shares for approximately thirty discretionary accounts of firm customers, one of whom was his wife. The day before the dividend was cut, he began selling shares from these discretionary accounts. In the two days before the transactions in question he had sold over half these holdings.

After the dividend decision by the board of directors, the meeting was recessed. Cowdin telephoned a message for Gintel that the dividend had been cut. Upon receiving this information,

Gintel entered substantial sell orders for some[17] of his discretionary accounts, and he sold a substantial block of shares short for
some accounts.

The dividend action occurred at approximately 11:00 A.M.,
at which time the standard authorization for transmission of this
information to the New York Stock Exchange was given. For
reasons never explained, but presumed to be inadvertent, the
New York Stock Exchange did not receive this information for
nearly one-and-a-half hours. The Dow Jones financial news service was not given the information for approximately forty-five
minutes, again presumedly through inadvertence.

Regardless of the reasons for those delays, the associates of
Cady, Roberts & Company acted with alacrity and efficiency.
Gintel's orders were executed fifteen and eighteen minutes, respectively, after the dividend action. The stock, needless to say,
plummeted on the later publication of the news. Gintel's actions
were found to be a willful violation of Section 17(a) of the
Securities Act of 1933, of 10(b) of the Securities Exchange Act
of 1934, and of Rule 10b-5.

In his opinion in *Cady, Roberts*, Chairman Cary stated that
liability under 10b-5 rests on two principal elements: "the existence of a relationship giving access, directly or indirectly, to
information intended to be available only for a corporate purpose
and not for the personal benefit of anyone, and second, the inherent unfairness involved where a party takes advantage of such
information knowing it is unavailable to those with whom he is
dealing." Presumably both these elements and not merely the latter
must appear to establish liability, since Chairman Cary states further: "our task here is to identify those persons who are in a
special relationship with a company and privy to its internal affairs, and thereby suffer correlative duties in trading in its securities."

The Commission had no difficulty in finding the requisite
special relationship existing between Curtiss-Wright, Cowdin,
Gintel, and Cady, Roberts.[18] But the prohibition on trading was

extended to those selling for discretionary accounts managed for third parties with no special relationship with the company.[19]

The Commission clearly rejected the suggestion, made in a variety of ways by the respondents, that Rule 10b-5 was not intended to extend beyond the special-facts rule in state law. For instance, the special-facts rule is limited to shareholders selling to insiders and does not extend to those buying from them. Further, as indicated previously, no special-facts case ever found liability in a transaction over an exchange, and some "semblance of privity" always had to be shown. The Commission replied that cases under the common-law special-facts rule had no relevance here, since purchasers as well as buyers over an exchange were intended to be protected by the Act, and that privity was not required in an action by the Commission to discipline a broker.[20]

The opinion in *Cady, Roberts* is important for several reasons. It laid to final rest the belief that Rule 10b-5 was still circumscribed by the older special-facts approach. The case itself involves only a disciplinary action by the Commission against a broker, but the underlying logic would certainly seem applicable to a private civil action. And even though the opinion requires the existence of some "special relationship" giving access to information, its general tone as an attack on all insider trading was unmistakable. This opinion undoubtedly provided a good part of the confidence with which the SEC took its next and most radical step. (For the full text of *Cady, Roberts,* see the Appendix, pages 206–213.)

Texas Gulf Sulphur Company

IN APRIL, 1965, the SEC brought insider trading to the public's attention with the most dramatic disclosure since the Pecora hearings in 1933. *SEC* v. *Texas Gulf Sulphur Company* became the focus of attention for the whole subject of insider trading. This case, which went to trial on May 9, 1966, presents in almost classic terms all of the factors that must be considered in a comprehensive treatment of insider trading. The resolution of the questions in this case may determine the law in this field for many years to come. This case is so important and so illustrative of the fundamental issues involved in insider trading that a summary of the available facts is presented here.[21]

The Texas Gulf Sulphur Company was founded in 1909 and taken over in 1916 by Bernard Baruch, J. P. Morgan and other financial interests. Until the mid-1950's, Texas Gulf was the world's leading producer of sulphur. By this time, however, several factors had combined to depress the price of Texas Gulf stock. The world demand for sulphur was very low, and Texas Gulf was a one-product company. Texas Gulf had lost many millions of dollars in unsuccessful efforts to develop new sulphur deposits. Younger corporations with less complacent management were making successful bids for a growing share of the sulphur market.

In 1959 a new team of managers took over the direction of Texas Gulf's affairs. The company embarked on a venturesome and imaginative program of diversification, exploration, and development. The company entered the booming potash and phosphate fields and pioneered the development of an important new mining process for sulphur. As part of the Company's ambitious program of prospecting for mineral deposits, a company geologist, in a helicopter equipped with magnetic surveying equipment, discovered the first sign of valuable new deposits in Timmins, Ontario, in 1959. It was not until some time in late 1963, however, that the company made the first drilling that indicated the possible presence of a rich vein of copper and zinc. This was the famous Timmins ore find, presently estimated to contain 55 million tons of copper, zinc, and silver.

When the first successful drill-hole was completed, the geologist in charge instituted tight security measures for his crew. No one was allowed to leave the camp site. Various schemes, such as fake drill cores and the removal of the drilling rig to another location, were employed to prevent the truth from leaking out. It is alleged by the SEC that at this time the geologist called the president of the company in New York. The SEC's complaint further alleges that from this time until April 16, 1964, various officers, directors, and employees of the company, knowing this information and the fact that it had not been released to the public, bought shares on the open market, bought calls on the company shares, or were given stock options by the company. Another list of individuals, not connected officially with the company, were named in the SEC's complaint as having received information about the find and having purchased shares of Texas Gulf before public disclosure. These persons were not made defendants in the suit, although some have been named in subsequent private civil actions.

By March, 1964, New York and Washington, and undoubtedly other areas of the United States and Canada, were rife with rumors about Texas Gulf Sulphur. The price of the shares had risen from $17.375 on November 10, 1963, to $29.375 by mid-April, 1964. It subsequently reached a high of 71 in the period before the SEC's suit was filed on April 19, 1965.

On April 12, 1964, the company announced that it was indeed prospecting in the Timmins area but that preliminary indications were that more drilling would be required for proper evaluation of this prospect. The announcement continued: "The drilling to date has not been conclusive, but the statements made by many outside quarters are unreliable and include information and figures that are not available to Texas Gulf." The rumors were termed "unreliable" and "premature and possibly misleading" and were said to have originated with speculators not connected with the company. But on April 16, 1964, four days later, Texas Gulf officials announced a "major ore discovery" of about twenty-five million tons of copper, zinc, and silver. These officials subsequently explained that, as of April 12, only one good core had been discovered, whereas by the 16th there were seven cores that accurately indicated the extent of the discovery. Company officials have also claimed that the April 12 statement resulted from careful consideration of the entire situation. While not wanting to mislead the public with any unproved claims, they also did not want the public misled by rumors. As soon as the facts were available, the statement of April 16 was made.

Among the defendants was a director, Thomas G. Lamont, who was also a director of the Morgan Guaranty Bank. He was not initially charged with purchasing any shares for himself, but rather with having caused the bank to purchase Texas Gulf stock for various clients for whom Morgan Guaranty acted as trustee or agent, including a hospital and the bank's own employees' profit-sharing fund. Lamont is alleged merely to have advised an official at Morgan Guaranty on the 16th to "look at the news ticker for news pertaining to Texas Gulf." Lamont also claimed that the information had been released earlier by a Canadian mining paper.

Another party who was named as having traded on the inside information but was not sued as a defendant was Herbert Klotz, then an assistant secretary of the Department of Commerce. Klotz, previously associated with a Washington, D.C., investment banking house, forthwith resigned from his government position. He claimed that his only source of information was a secretary in the Department of Commerce who was a family friend of the Texas Gulf geologist at Timmins. Klotz said he noticed heavy trading with a price increase and, therefore, played the tip. The geologist admitted recommending Texas Gulf stock to friends based on the general improvement in the company's affairs, but he maintains that he told no outsiders about the discovery at Timmins.

In April of 1965, the Securities and Exchange Commission filed suit in the United States District Court for the Southern District of New York against Texas Gulf Sulphur Company and a number of individual defendants. The complaint itemizes purchases of shares and calls or the receipt of stock options by the defendants between November 12, 1963, the discovery date, and April 16, 1964. Each of the many paragraphs of the complaint stated that the individuals acted on "knowledge and information of material facts . . . not generally known to the investing public . . . without disclosing to the seller the aforementioned material facts." Interspersed chronologically with allegations of purchases by defendants are a series of allegations relating to purchases by third persons informed about the discovery by a named defendant.

After describing the allegedly misleading press release of April 12, 1964, and the correct announcement on April 16, the complaint alleges that during this period "numerous stockholders of defendant TEXAS GULF sold their shares of defendant TEXAS GULF stock at prices at which they would not have sold their shares, had they known the material facts which were known to, but not made available to them by, defendant TEXAS GULF." This suggests the possibility of liability of the corporation to these shareholders, perhaps in civil actions as there is no prayer for damages from the company.[22] The complaint indicates that during the relevant time period, defendants purchased an aggregate of 9,100 shares of Texas Gulf Sulphur stock and calls on 5,200 shares and that they received options to purchase an aggregate of 31,200 shares.[23] During the same period, persons who allegedly bought on the advice of defendants purchased 12,100 shares and calls on 14,100 shares. This indicates that 21,200 shares were purchased and 50,500 shares were covered by options or calls during the relevant time period. The 21,200 shares represent less than 10 per cent of the approximately 261,000 shares traded during the twenty-two-week period in question. In the ensuing three weeks after the announcement was made, purchases totaled approximately 557,000 shares, and the price approximately doubled.

The SEC prayed for several kinds of equitable relief. First, they asked that the individual defendants be enjoined from violating Rule 10b-5 in the following ways:

(a) engaging in the purchase and sale of securities on the basis of information with respect to material facts relating to defendant TEXAS GULF acquired by said defendants in the course of their corporate duties or employment with defendant TEXAS GULF which information had not been made available to defendant TEXAS GULF, its stockholders and other public investors; (b) making available such information, directly or indirectly, to other persons for the purpose of permitting or allowing such other persons to benefit from the receipt of such information through the purchase and sale of securities; and (c) engaging in other conduct of similar purport and object.

Next, the SEC requested an order directing certain of the named defendants "to offer rescission to the person from whom each of these defendants purchased stock and options or calls to purchase TEXAS GULF stock during the period from November 12, 1963, to April 17, 1964." The Commission also demanded restitution by certain named defendants to the individuals who sold stock to parties advised by the defendants. That is, the sellers to those receiving information from the insiders would receive restitution directly from the insider, not from the purchaser of the stock. The SEC also requested the cancellation of unexercised stock options and the return of profits or stock if they had been exercised.[24] And finally, the SEC requested that Texas Gulf Sulphur be permanently enjoined from disseminating false or misleading statements concerning its activities.

Several things must be noted about the SEC's prayer. The first remedy is limited to defendants' trading on facts learned "in the course of their corporate duties or employment." They are enjoined either from using this information directly in the market or from passing this information along to other individuals. Individual defendants who purchased shares are to offer rescission to the individuals from whom they purchased and restitution to those from whom their friends purchased. The corporation, however, is not charged in this complaint with any financial responsibility to those who relied on its statements.

The prayer for restitution to individuals selling to those who bought on the advice of insiders is most peculiar. The complaint does not even limit this liability to cases of sales to first-level advisees. Texas Gulf's geologist at Timmins is alleged to have advised a Miss Atkinson, a secretary in the Department of Commerce, who in turn told two individuals, whose shares are also included in the request-for-restitution order. One of these two was Assistant Secretary of Commerce Herbert Klotz, who is alleged merely to have worked in the same office as Miss Atkinson. There is no attempt to include individuals advised by second-level advisees, though it is well-known that these did exist.

In going beyond liability to the persons who sold to insiders, the SEC has perhaps made the most unusual proposal. Clearly, the number of shares an advisee purchases or causes others to purchase cannot be controlled by the insider. Thus, as the advisee and his friends become richer, it is more and more in their power to bankrupt the insider-adviser if civil actions are brought against him by those who sold to the advisees. It may well be that advisees will also be made liable for rescission or restitution by the opposite party to their particular transactions, but this too is very troublesome. There must be some limits to this notion. A certain number of fundamentally unreliable tips will in fact prove to be correct. It would be the height of absurdity to hold speculators on low-reliability advice liable on the few occasions when their gambles paid off. But it would seem equally strange to make the insider who told the first outsider an insurer for every seller's loss.[25]

Some question might also be raised about the SEC's paternalistic concern with the sellers of calls to corporate insiders. From all indications, the individuals who make markets in puts and calls are among the most sophisticated market traders in existence. It is probably safe to say that their sophistication about market transactions exceeds that of their self-appointed protector, the SEC. While a number of individual stock sellers have brought private actions against the Texas Gulf insiders, some members of the put and call industry in New York might be somewhat embarrassed at even being included in the SEC's protective complaint. These firms or individuals would not ordinarily bring an action against insiders for purchasing calls with undisclosed information. It is a safe bet that call dealers are well aware that insiders constitute a substantial number of their customers and that they do not buy calls on their own company's stock without some information or highly reliable belief that has not been disclosed in the market. If the dealers are uneasy about the risks they are taking, it is simple enough for them to cover their own sales of calls by buying the stock in the market or by selling a put.[26] It might have been more sensible for the SEC to have treated these call brokers in the same way as advisees of the insiders. That is, the Commission might have demanded restitution for any individuals who sold shares to these call brokers rather than for the brokers themselves.

If law is to perform its function in our society, it must conform to new problems and even new attitudes. But it is crucial that courts know precisely what issues are involved before they make changes with important social, political, or economic consequences. There is in today's literature, however, very little analysis helpful to a court or a legislature asked to resolve the issues posed by the *Texas Gulf Sulphur* case. The SEC has shown little disposition to do the necessary study, though presumably that is why specialized agencies were created.[27]

The Market For Valuable Information: An Introduction

IN MANY RESPECTS the entire stock market is a complex arrangement for the marketing of information. In an investment market characterized by great risk a high premium will normally be paid for reliable information. In a market more stable and less subject to fluctuations, the difference in rate of return to the more-informed and the less-informed participants becomes smaller. The market for United States government bonds illustrates this kind of relatively stable market. As a market is subjected to more uncertainty, information about the possibility of change and its actual occurrence become more valuable. The different amounts of profit of different individuals will reflect their different degrees of sophistication and the reliability of their information. The stock market is, par excellence, the arbiter of the value of information.

The information necessary for successful investment or trading in the stock market is a fairly complex matter. It is not, as is almost true of Government bonds, simply a matter of knowing what return is offered. First, there are two broad categories of information which must be distinguished. The first of these comprehends what might be called financial sophistication, and the second involves the specific bits of data representing news of change. The first category may be likened to the knowledge of a static or unchanging system. Its content is simply knowledge of all relevant events of the past.[1] There may be large differences of opinion about the meaning or even the occurrence of these past events, but all the information that can be made available is included in this category.

Information in the second category reflects the existence of change. It is information that, in a realistic sense, cannot be predicted in advance, even in a probability sense. To the extent that a particular bit of information can be predicted, its value lies in the first category rather than in the second. As we shall see, however, neither type of information can be successfully exploited without the other. And it should also be observed that this dichotomy of what we shall term *first-* and *second-category information* is a construct designed solely to aid in the exposition of various facets of the insider-trading question. The distinction is not a necessary one for other purposes, and actually distinguishing between the categories might be extremely difficult or impossible in many instances. Nonetheless, the theoretical distinction is important for present purposes, because it allows us to understand why different techniques for marketing information have developed.

First-Category Information

SEVERAL LEVELS of first-category information must be considered. The most fundamental level includes knowledge of the existence and nature of the stock market, alternative forms of investment, how to deal with stock brokers, how individual circumstances may dictate different investment or financial policies, the various tax consequences of different choices, and the basic institutional arrangements of the economy. The next level covers the fundamentals of finance and includes basic sophistication about balance sheets, income statements, stock market reports, and financial news generally.

A higher level of information in the first category is knowledge of the manner in which specific events that may occur in the world affect the stock market. For example, we should include here knowledge of how the following events would affect the stock market: a change in Federal Reserve Board interest policies, either restricting or expanding the amount of credit; a change in the tax laws, perhaps affecting capital-gains treatment or depreciation allowances; international developments that may affect both the supply of and demand for different commodities.

At the next higher level it must be understood how various changes, such as those just listed, will affect not only the stock market in general but particular industries and particular companies. For instance, knowledge of how the announcement of a huge iron-ore discovery will affect market price may be necessary to evaluate the find properly. Knowledge of conditions in the electric-power industry will certainly be crucial to evaluating information about nuclear-power generators. And knowledge of a huge order from a foreign country may be worthless if it is not known whether sufficient bottoms are available for shipment.

Sophistication about conditions in an industry or a particular company is not as easily acquired as are the lower levels of sophistication. The more fundamental information may be had simply by paying the tuition costs at a university or by reading a book or newspapers. Occasionally the mere expenditure of time observing the world will be sufficient. But knowledge of particular industries and companies is not so cheaply come by. Typically it is gained as a by-product of employment within the industry or the company.

This education is not ordinarily hidden or confidential, but full sophistication about an industry is peculiarly available to those within it and rarely available to those on the outside. This is perhaps even more true of particular companies than it is of whole industries, because knowledge of the value of specific bits of information is less circumscribed by unknown details at the industry level than it is within a particular company. Knowledge that the demand for steel is up appreciably can be exploited by buying stock in all steel companies, even though some individual companies may not participate in the gain, perhaps because, unlike other companies, they are already operating at full capacity.

First-category education or sophistication about an industry or a firm cannot generally be considered inside information in the sense we shall use that term. It may be purchased in a variety of ways, and as already noted, it may be gained as part of an employment contract.[2] Securities analysts and investment advisers are in the business of collecting this kind of information in order to sell it, preanalyzed or not, to their customers. This information is frequently available in trade journals, the financial press, and in published data about particular companies, including the monthly 8-K reports that must be filed with the Securities and Exchange Commission. To a considerable extent the principal costs necessary to gain this kind of information are those involved in collecting it, storing it, and transmitting it to the ultimate purchaser. There is, however, little loss in its value if it is known to everyone, and small gain if it is known to only a few.

A Case Study in the Marketing of First-Category Information

THE CASE of *Securities and Exchange Commission* v. *Capital Gains Research Bureau, Inc.*[3] involves an overt market for first-category information. There is no suggestion that inside information was involved. The Capital Gains Research Bureau, Inc., was an investment advisory service that engaged in a practice known in the trade as *scalping*. The advisory firm purchased a company's shares for its own account shortly before recommending the same security to its clients without disclosure of its own interest. Then the firm would sell upon a rise in market price following the recommendation.[4] The SEC sought an injunction under Section 206 of the Investment Advisers Act of 1940, alleging that scalping "operated as a fraud or deceit" upon firm clients. The phrase *operates as a fraud* is given the same broad meaning it regularly receives in interpretations of Rule 10b-5. There is no evidence mentioned in the opinion that the advisory firm may have been engaged in manipulative practices such as touting stocks contrary to the adviser's belief or attempting to raise prices artificially in order to unload holdings at a profit. The Supreme Court's opinion, written by Mr. Justice Arthur Goldberg, emphasized that under the standard of fraud that Congress enacted in the 1940 Act, it was not necessary to show any dishonesty or intent to defraud. As he stated several times, the fundamental purpose of the Act was to achieve a "high standard of business ethics in the securities industry."[5]

Justice Goldberg examined select bits of testimony given in the hearings leading to the adoption of the Investment Advisers Act of 1940. These statements by members of the investment-advisory industry condemned investment counselors' trading in securities in which their clients were interested.[6] A report of the SEC on practices of investment companies concluded that "all conflicts of interest between the investment counsel and the client" should be removed.[7] Both the SEC and investment advisers condemned affiliations by investment advisers with investment bankers or corporations. Their stress was "not limited to deliberate or conscious impediments to objectivity"; the emphasis was said to be on "subconscious motivation."[8]

Perhaps Goldberg was naive in accepting the statements of competitors in an industry as to the meaning of high business ethics. Even from the carefully selected evidence included in the *Capital Gains* opinion, it seems that the Investment Advisers Act of 1940 may have been designed, consciously or unconsciously, to prevent competition in the investment-advisory industry. Cries of unethical conduct by competitors should be treated with a severe dose of skepticism. They are a common sign of requests for government aid in subduing obstreperous competitors.[9]

Justice Goldberg did find it incumbent on himself to establish an hypothesis under which scalping might injure clients. This is his explanation:

> An adviser who, like respondents, secretly trades on the market effect of his own recommendation may be motivated—consciously or unconsciously—to recommend a given security not because of its potential for long-run price increase (which would profit the client), but because of its potential for short-run price increase in response to anticipated activity from the recommendation (which would profit the adviser). An investor seeking the advice of a registered investment adviser must, if the legislative purpose is to be served, be permitted to evaluate such overlapping motivations, through appropriate disclosure, in deciding whether an adviser is serving "two masters" or only one, "especially . . . if one of the masters happens to be economic self-interest." *U.S.* v. *Mississippi Valley Co.*, 364 U.S. 520, 549.[10]

The last sentence is the heart of the opinion, and yet it leaves much explanation to be desired. Goldberg seems to be saying that there are two possible reasons why prices may increase after a recommendation. The first of these is that the recommendation is based on solid fact and that the price increase will stick, thus allowing the advisee to realize a long-term gain. The alternative is that the price rises merely because of the recommendation, and it will not stick because truth will out and the price will drop back. Disclosure of stock purchases by the advisory firm will, according to Goldberg's logic, allow the investor to evaluate these possibilities. Aside from the dubiousness of the last proposition and the fact that there was no evidence whatever that Capital Gains Research Bureau, Inc., acted in bad faith in its recommendations, it is essential in analyzing the practice of scalping to recognize certain aspects of the market for valuable information. (The text of the *SEC* v. *Capital Gains* opinion may be found in the Appendix, pages 214–227.)

Let us assume that the stock recommendation was made in the good-faith belief that it was true and that the investment adviser took a prior position in the security with the intention of selling after his recommendation was made. For example, the adviser may have concluded that the stock of a given company should increase from 50 to 52. But he may realize that others will not share his confidence and that the total number of shares he can cause his clients to purchase is only sufficient to raise the price of the security from 50 to 51½. Assuming that his recommendation is correct, or merely that he has confidence that it is, he must believe that there is an additional profit to be made by purchasing shares in this corporation. If he waits to purchase shares until after he has made his recommendation to his customers, the information will be given to others and the price will quickly reach 52. His customers, on the average, will still have realized something less than the full $2 gain, though presumably they are satisfied with the value they are receiving. Unless they can resell the advice, they are indifferent whether the adviser or various third persons using his information realize additional profit.

The analysis is not altered in any important respect if we conclude that the customers themselves could have realized the additional profit. Whether the unpaid-for additional value goes to third parties or to his clients is a matter of indifference to the investment adviser. He will be concerned to make sure that his customers are satisfied with his service, but he will be equally concerned to prevent them or others from receiving his service for less than it is worth to them. Thus it may be true that he takes a market gain at the expense of his customers. However, this conclusion in no way implies that he has done anything wrong, and any attempt on the part of courts or others to determine whether information buyers are receiving full value must necessarily end up in a morass of indeterminacy.

Failure of the investment adviser to disclose to his customers that he has taken a position does not imply that they have been misled in any way that damages them, since they have no way of knowing in advance the value of the bits of information they have purchased. If they are satisfied in retrospect and continue to deal with the same information seller, there is no basis for saying that they have been harmed. For this reason a simple "label" requirement indicating that the adviser may be trading in his recommended stocks[11] seems in no way harmful, although it probably adds nothing to the knowledge that customers in this market really want. Performance will speak far louder than labels.

Second-Category Information

WE TURN NEXT to second-category information, that is, knowledge of specific events or of the probability of future events that will ultimately cause a change in share prices. This information may or may not be inside information, as we shall use that term, because the distinction is purely a functional one depending on how the news is treated. For example, a disclosure in the newspapers that the government is about to step up procurement of aircraft represents a change from previous conditions. This is a specific bit of information which, if properly understood, has a value in the marketplace. But it cannot be considered inside information if it is publicized to all interested parties before it is acted upon in the stock market. This remains true even though opinions will differ about the impact of the order upon particular companies. Non-inside, second-category information might typically include news of such matters as government financial, tax, and credit policies; changes in the general market demand for a specific product; nationalization of foreign holdings by proclamation; loss of an important plant or building as a result of fire or natural causes; and other matters that in the ordinary course of events can be known to outsiders just as quickly as they will be known to officials within affected industries or companies.

Often non-inside news of important changes affecting stock

prices will be published in general newspapers, the financial press or trade journals as soon as it is available. And certain portions of this information may be discovered simultaneously by many interested parties, thus preventing any one individual from making a substantial profit from it. An example would be a general upturn in the demand for steel recognized by officials in many different steel companies at about the same time. This information may have some small trading value, but, for reasons we shall examine in Chapter VII, it is very unlikely that any substantial amount of true insider trading will be based on it. This kind of information rather quickly becomes first-category information and is reflected in the market value of affected stocks.

To constitute the inside information that is the subject of this book, two conditions seem necessary. The event must be one that, if all other factors were held constant, would substantially affect the price of a company's shares. But the news must also be capable of physical exploitation in the market by some individuals before the matter becomes public knowledge. That is, it must be possible for some individual or select group of individuals to buy or sell shares before the effect of the news has been substantially reflected in the market.

Certain events or developments lend themselves peculiarly to exploitation by insiders. Not surprisingly, many of these are items that corporate employees or others close to the corporation will have produced. Higher earnings or the concommitant dividend increase are clear examples. New products or inventions, new ore discoveries, oil finds, or successful marketing or management techniques also will generally be known first to those in the company responsible for the development. And news of merger offers, tender-bids, or important contracts, though perhaps originating with an outsider, will also be partially within the control of corporate officials.

Inside information may cover knowledge of the probability of a particular occurrence, as well as knowledge of an actual occurrence. Thus, as an executive is approached about a merger that he believes can be effectuated on profitable terms, he has valuable information even though the certainty of occurrence is less than 100 per cent. The value of his information must, in fact, be discounted by the probability of nonoccurrence. This explains why insiders may frequently make investments that do not yield a quick capital gain. Nonetheless, if the decision is based on some specific knowledge, then no matter how uncertain it is that a benefit will be realized or how much judgment or first-category information is involved in the conclusion, an element of true inside information will be present.[12]

There are still other reasons why insiders may not realize 100 per cent of the potential value of a bit of information. Insiders often do not have exclusive control of inside information. Not all the information that insiders do control is necessarily of their own making. Knowledge of an important contract or take-over bid is automatically shared with at least one other party. And many significant pieces of information are windfalls to the individuals who first learn of them. For instance, by virtue of the explorations of one mining company in an area, the value of neighboring holdings may appreciate tremendously. This fact may be successfully exploited in the stock market before the news is publicized. Unexpected adverse developments may likewise constitute the content of true inside information. Again the only test is the purely functional one of whether the news can be exploited in the stock market before it becomes first-category information.

Although the point will be discussed at some length in the next chapters, it should be noted now that stockholders in a corporation do not have to be aware of developments in order to share the benefits. Ultimately the information will be reflected in a higher share price. So long as they hold their shares and do not sell before this happens, the information will become first-category information and work to their benefit. But to exploit second-category information, one must either buy the stock or pass the information to someone else who will buy the stock. In either case, the share price will increase in an amount determined by the value of the information. At that point the information becomes first-category information, and anyone remaining an investor will, through this process, have realized the value with no additional expenditure of money or time.

Thus the value of first-category information may be acquired at almost no cost. But the acquisition of second-category information is a very different story. It normally cannot be acquired without cost, and hot tips are usually worth what is paid for them. But because the value of second-category information tends to be highly ephemeral, its acquisition and transmission are quite complex. The next three chapters are concerned with the institutional and analytical aspects of the market for this information.

V

Mechanisms for Marketing Inside Information

In the last chapter we distinguished several different types of valuable information and examined certain of the mechanisms available for its profitable exploitation. In this chapter we will deal with those institutionalized marketing devices that are peculiarly appropriate for exploiting true inside information. Unfortunately it is extremely difficult to find helpful and reliable data in this area. One of the reasons is the reticence of insiders and others to talk about what today may be illegal activity. Gone is the day when 90 per cent of corporate directors interviewed in a newspaper poll would state that they speculated in the stocks of their own company. Now polite businessmen simply do not discuss the matter, and it is deemed bad taste in some circles even to mention it.

But all of the difficulty does not lie in the reticence of insiders to talk about their market transactions. A more fundamental difficulty may be their failure to understand that they are in fact engaging in this kind of activity. The truth of certain economic relationships is often not recognized by the parties involved. Luckily for them, understanding is not a prerequisite to gain.[1]

As was suggested in the last chapter, there are fundamentally three different ways in which valuable information about stock market prices may be profitably exploited. The first of these, direct sale for money, is of almost no practical importance in connection with pure inside information. Although there are no cases directly on the point, it is very likely that a court would hold the direct sale of insider information by an insider to be a breach of fiduciary duty. Perhaps the closest legal analogy would lie in those cases holding that a sale of corporate office without a transfer of control is illegal,[2] even though analytically the two situations bear little resemblance. In each case there is a sale of something peculiarly associated with the corporation itself. More important, in each case the intangible is something not normally sold in this fashion. There are other cases involving the sale or transmission of valuable information, such as trade secrets sold to competitors or customer lists sold or used by a former employee. The law is generally quite clear in prohibiting these practices,[3] and these cases might be relied upon to prevent sales of stock-market information. However, the harm to the employer is readily apparent in these cases, but it is not with the sale of inside information.

Exploiting Information
by Stock Purchases

THE SECOND METHOD by which the value of information may be exploited is by buying stocks.[4] Interestingly enough, a purchase of stock can have precisely the same effect as a direct sale of the information. In any normal sale, in which all interests in the item sold are transferred to a buyer, there is no value left to the seller. He has exchanged any claim to that value for something else, which to him is of equivalent or higher value. So it is in the stock market. As those with valuable information purchase shares, *ipso facto*, they tend to make the price or value of all shares rise. Assuming perfect knowledge on their part and that all other variables affecting price remain constant, insiders would continue to buy shares until the aggregate market price of all outstanding shares has increased by an amount equal to the value of the information.[5]

At this point, the information itself has become valueless. Its disclosure will add nothing to the market price (assuming other holders will understand its value). The knowledgeable individuals buying stock before this price is reached have, therefore, in a real sense disposed of the value of their information in exchange for an appreciation in the value of their shares. At the same time, the market value of the shares held by people who may know nothing whatever of the new information has increased. The insider has, in effect, transferred part of the value of his information to the public. Anyone holding shares in the company has now benefited proportionately by this underlying reality whether he has particular knowledge of it or not.

The transaction described is not, in any ordinary sense, a sale of the information. To constitute a sale, those receiving the benefit of the item sold (here, the information) would have to give up something in return. But the benefit of this information is available at no additional cost to those who hold their shares.[6] This results because there has been a creation of new value. The insiders' gain is not made at the expense of anyone. The occasionally voiced objection to insider trading—that someone must be losing the specific money the insiders make—is not true in any relevant sense. The fallacy results from a failure to analyze adequately the nature of the insiders' gain and the fact that the shareholders participate in the new value in proportion to their shareholdings.

A simple analogy may help clarify the point. If an individual makes an invention and secures a patent on it, he is protected in his ownership of the information involved in the patent. He may now sell this information directly, either by licensing others to use his patent or by an outright sale of the patent itself. But, consider an individual who has developed a valuable idea on which no patent is obtainable. Occasionally such ideas are directly marketable, though the law provides little protection for non-patentable ideas.[7] If direct marketing of the idea itself is not feasible, the holder has two alternatives. He may either suppress the idea, or he may secure a right in some marketable property to which the value of the idea can be attached. Thus, if his idea is that there is a huge demand for an item he calls *hula-hoops,* and hula-hoops are nonpatentable, he may go into the business of selling circular tubes of plastic. Others will undoubtedly follow if his idea is successful, and he consequently earns less than he would make if the idea had been patentable. Nonetheless, he has exchanged the value of his information or idea for the increased value of the property (in this case, plastic tubing) to which the information value has been attached.

Basically the same phenomenon occurs in the case of scientists and research workers who have agreed as part of their employment contract that all patents belong to the company. This common provision would seem at first glance to prevent the inventor from benefiting financially—apart from any bonuses his company may give him—from significant discoveries he makes. But if the invention is important enough to affect the market value of the company's shares, the inventor may secure a part of the value of his invention by purchasing shares of his employer's stock. Even if the inventor has no proprietary interest in the patent, he may be able to secure for himself a large part of the value of his invention, if he moves quickly enough in the stock market. This phenomenon will be discussed in more detail in the next chapter.

Information Exchanges

THERE IS STILL a third mechanism for marketing valuable inside information. Ultimately any information will be exploited by a purchase of shares, but a different market for information exists at a more preliminary stage. Just as the direct sale of information is logically possible, so information may be exchanged before it is acted upon by a share purchase or sale. An exchange or barter system has some advantage over either direct sales of information or insider share purchases, since the first is probably illegal and the second is somewhat constrained by various legal rules and moral precepts. It is probable that a market for the exchange of valuable information operates on a large scale in the United States. Aspects of this market have been examined, investigated, discussed, and even litigated on countless occasions. And yet, only rarely in the voluminous literature in learned journals, congressional hearings, SEC studies, and reported cases has it ever been noted that a simple economic exchange phenomenon is involved.[8] This rare recognition has not been sufficient to dispel the confusion surrounding this basic notion.

The exchange or barter system for valuable information operates in ways ranging from the most informal to the most sophisticated, complex, and highly institutionalized. The most informal level would comprehend, for example, two executives who are members of the same golf club. One may be a director of an automobile-manufacturing company and the other a director of a steel company. Over the years it would not be unusual at all for these two friends to give each other information, or advice based on reliable information, about their respective companies. If the two companies generated approximately the same quantity of valuable information over a period of years, measured in dollar terms, each of the men might be made better off financially by this practice, even though they did not recognize it as an exchange. The direct use of insider information for short-swing profits on listed securities was made illegal in 1934. But a careful study might reveal that the estates of executives in the companies covered were built up, not by ownership of their own company's shares but rather from trading in the shares of several other companies. The necessary data would not be difficult to obtain from tax returns, and yet the existing research in this area has not produced a single helpful statistic.[9]

Problems with a
Barter Market

THERE ARE numerous difficulties in even simple bartering. It is very cumbersome and not apt to be satisfactory to both parties over a period of time. Each party may feel that he is giving more than he is receiving. And if one individual tries to ration the flow of information to his friend, he is apt to find that they are engaged in an implicit bargaining situation that neither party relishes or quite understands. It is not likely that memberships in country clubs, golf foursomes, or other voluntary social groups are determined by a one-for-one exchange of valuable information. But cultural, religious, political, moral, and economic attitudes and values are constantly exchanged through such mechanisms. It is neither crass nor undemocratic to suggest that individuals, in choosing their voluntary associations, will look for individuals with whom the exchange of these values will not be one-sided. Valuable business information is simply another of the factors that, either consciously or unconsciously, may be included in the equation.

Barter is an inefficient method of exchange, and often it cannot be done on a large enough scale to allow the full exploitation of certain kinds of information. In the fellow-golfers example, one of the two executives might know a certain bit of information sufficient to make the price of his company's shares rise from 50 to 55. Before announcing this information to anyone not already privy to it, he would exploit it to the fullest extent of his own financial abilities. However, this may not be sufficient to account for the full value implicit in the information. He may, for instance, only be able to account for a rise in the stock-market price from 50 to 51. If he turns the balance of the value over to his golfing acquaintances, they may only be able to raise the price to 52. There would still be substantial value in the information, and it is not reasonable to assume, *a priori*, that individuals are willing to lose such a valuable commodity or give it away when efficient exchange devices are readily available.

If an insider chooses to distribute valuable information on the informal basis suggested, he runs into some additional difficulties. There will often be a time lag before he can reach his friends, and during this time the information, usually a very volatile commodity, may be fully exploited by others who have it. Also, the friends will tell their friends, and the information may spread very quickly. Thus, with each additional disclosure, the first executive's control over the remaining value of the information may be lost very rapidly.

Selection of Corporate Directors

A SOMEWHAT REFINED version of the golfers' exchange may explain the selection of certain individuals to sit on boards of directors. The reason for many of these appointments has long been one of the nagging academic questions about the business world.[10] Without for a moment suggesting that there are not myriad other factors that enter into these selections, it is interesting to note the possibility of using such appointments as information-exchange devices. In effect, the party with whom the exchange relation is sought is made a kind of "junior insider," placed there primarily to capitalize on his position for his own benefit. By virtue of his being a director, this individual will normally be privy to considerable information about the company and perhaps its industry. If, incidentally, he brings valuable skill to the running of the company, so much the better. Admittedly, all appointments cannot be explained on this basis. It is possible, however, that careful empirical research might establish many directorships as information-exchange appointments.[11]

Another question about directors that has long troubled scholars in the field is: Why do directors not direct?[12] We may now offer a strong hypothesis. To the extent that appointments are made in order to make valuable information available to directors, we should not expect those directors to direct. Nor should we even expect them to be very interested in most corporate affairs. Interest on their part might signify either a demand for more information than the director "deserves" or a threat to the present control group. Too much interest from outside directors must frequently result in a termination of the relationship. There should be little mystery as to why many directors do not direct.

The same concept of an exchange of information may help to explain and perhaps soften the old criticism of the famous stock pools of the 1920's and earlier. Most pools had a great many corporate executives and directors among their members. Typically these individuals were privy to advance inside information about a corporation. Most pools came into existence when there were prospects of a merger, a favorable earning statement, or other encouraging news.[13] If the manager of the pool were also the insider with valuable information, the pool became not only an efficient device for disseminating information but also a foolproof way of policing the information the pool sought to exploit. The pool was possibly the most efficient device ever discovered for the exchange of valuable information. Unfortunately, the device lent itself easily to fraudulent market manipulation,[14] and the anti-manipulation provisions of the Securities and Exchange Act of 1934 were the result.[15]

A Clearinghouse for Information

As WE HAVE SEEN, the individual or individuals initially possessing valuable information are rarely able to exploit fully the value of that information by purchases in the stock market or by direct sales of the information. They may be left with information that others, who are able to exploit it, would like to have. If these latter individuals at other times have information they cannot exploit directly, the necessary conditions for a beneficial exchange exist, and we should expect the exchange to occur. As we have seen, this can be done informally and on a small scale by direct barter. For the large-scale exchange mechanisms, however, we shall have to look elsewhere.

Basically what is needed for the effective functioning of this market is some sort of clearinghouse operation. This clearinghouse would have to perform at least four distinguishable functions. It would have to be a repository of valuable information or its value. The clearinghouse might, in this respect, be viewed as an information retailer who buys wholesale. Secondly, whoever performs this clearinghouse function should be in a position to determine which individuals are entitled to share in the value of information collected. That is, the functionary should be able to identify those individuals who, as a result of "depositing" valuable information, have gained some claim against the total pool. And, naturally, he should also be able to determine the amount of the claim held by these parties. Presumably, over some period of time the amount any individual might claim from the pool would be determined by the amount of information he has furnished. Finally, some method should be available for assuring that the people withdrawing information or its value are in fact entitled to it and that there is no substantial leakage to those who are not entitled.

Is anyone or any institution performing all of these functions in the modern American economy? A firm answer cannot be given to this question, as too many of the details would be or are carefully guarded secrets. But one group is certainly in a position to perform the functions mentioned if it wishes. The special relationship of investment bankers, underwriters, and large brokerage houses to the American corporation has long been a subject of controversy, analysis, and even litigation.[16] These multifaceted organizations undoubtedly perform many different services for American businesses. They are financial advisers, management counselors, executive and director finders, merger arrangers, underwriters, and many other things. They may be, in addition, the clearinghouses par excellence for valuable information. Let us examine then how these functionaries (for convenience we shall refer to them simply as investment bankers[17]) can perform the functions necessary for operating a clearinghouse for information.

Investment Bankers As Information Repositories

A SUCCESSFUL CLEARINGHOUSE should be able to receive and store the necessary information. One method of doing this we have already mentioned: the placement of representatives on corporate boards of directors. Although this practice may not be as common as it was in years gone by, the figures are still impressive. The SEC's Special Study[18] reported that 1,471 registered broker-dealer firms stated that members were directors of one or more publicly traded companies. Of this number, 101 were represented on the boards of at least ten companies. Lehman Brothers led the list with directorships on fifty-eight listed and twenty-three over-the-counter companies.

But these figures do not tell the whole story, as it is not necessary for representatives of these firms to be directors in order to gain information. As the SEC's Special Study states:

> It should also be pointed out that underwriting firms, whether or not they have a representative on a company's board of directors, often retain a special relationship which enables them to obtain information concerning the company which the general public does not have. In the first place, the requirement in an underwriting agreement of regular financial reports to the managing underwriters, as distinguished from the general body of stockholders, may give a firm a considerable advantage in the market. Secondly, a firm with an underwriting relationship is likely to be among the first to be advised of any corporate developments.[19]

Today it is generally believed that the position of investment bankers in controlling large corporations is substantially weaker than it was thirty years ago. Some writers declare that control has passed from banker hands into management hands.[20] Whether or not this is true in any meaningful sense, it cannot be denied that investment bankers remain one of the important creative forces in American business. Whether their actions take the form of arranging a merger, financing important new industrial developments, or arranging the spin-off of an unprofitable subsidiary, they are privy at an early stage to important information. The illustrations could be continued at length. Regardless of the power of management, the investment-banking fraternity is uniquely situated to be a repository of valuable information and to serve the first of the four functions necessary for an information clearinghouse.

Investment Bankers As Distributors of Information

THE NEXT FUNCTION is that of determining who is entitled to share in the value of information produced. There are several ways in which investment-banking houses may perform this function. If a house controls a given corporation or exercises substantial influence, it will be able to name members to the corporation's board of directors. These need not be members of the firm itself but rather individuals whom the bankers recognize as entitled to share in valuable information. It must be repeated that there are many other reasons why a particular individual may be named to a board of directors, but one factor likely to be considered is whether or not the individual chosen should be given access to the information normally available to directors.[21]

The function of deciding who is entitled to information may be quite complex. The problem is compounded by the unlikelihood that actual books would be kept today. The old pools undoubtedly did just that. The problem is one of knowing who is responsible for having "deposited" valuable information previously with the bankers. No simple answer will ordinarily be available. It may be almost impossible to know, for example, who

actually engineered a certain merger or who was responsible for
the bankers' knowing about new industrial developments. The
bankers must of necessity have close, personal associations with
corporations and their executives in order to perform this function. The decision-making involved in these selections will be
more demanding of experience and wisdom than of bookkeeping
abilities.

The necessary bookkeeping becomes even more complicated
when we consider the third function: determining how much
"credit" particular individuals are entitled to. Again subtle, complex, and difficult questions arise. The market for valuable information is by no means a precise one in which it is easy to put
a dollar figure on the information received and that disclosed.
Rough and inexact approximations must constantly be made. The
process is perhaps more one of artistry than of science or bookkeeping. Yet the whole complex market for inside information
depends on the successful performance of this function.

Some of the factors preventing a precise distribution of valuable information may be readily imagined. Identical kinds and
quality of information may occur at different stages of overall
stock-market changes. What appear to be bits of information of
the same value may give profits in one case and losses in another.
Some information, very easily obtained or requiring little or no
effort on its developer's part, may be worth considerably more
than information resulting from a lifetime of hard work. The
developer of the latter may often feel that he has established a
considerable claim against clearinghouse balances. Furthermore,
different individuals will have different financial abilities to utilize
information given them. Decisions will, therefore, have to be
made as to whether an "account" should be credited with the
objective value of the information given or the value to the
recipient of the information used. Each of these problems demand
subtle computations and expert diplomacy. Clearly, the relationship of investment bankers to corporate executives must be one
of great trust and confidence.[22] And it should not be difficult to

understand why documentation and empirical data are difficult to obtain in this area.

Priority
Lists

THE COMPLEX PROCESS described is facilitated by two well-known devices. The first of these, the so-called *priority* or *preferred list*, is simply a list of names of individuals to be preferred in receiving specific bits of information or advice to buy certain stocks. These have been discussed for years,[23] but rarely has it been recognized that these lists may serve a function as broad as that suggested by this analysis. At one point in the 1934 Senate Hearings on Stock Exchange Practices, Ferdinand Pecora, the chief counsel of the committee, suggested that names on priority lists were those of corporate executives whose companies dealt with a particular banking house, and he suggested that the individuals listed kept the banking house informed of corporate affairs.[24] The banker being questioned was indignant at the suggestion that information was being bought and sold, although he and the writers on the subject have failed to offer a plausible alternative explanation.[25] Clearly, names do not appear on these lists merely because the individuals are good friends of the banking house.

Under outdated or outlawed underwriting practices, differing numbers of bargain shares were offered to different individuals.[26] This allowed a rather precise pay-off, as the exact amount being distributed could be known in advance. That technique could only be used with new issues and would have only limited utility today—if it is legal at all.[27] The modern version of the priority list contains names of people who will be told particular bits of information or advised to buy certain shares. Each of these techniques raises problems, however, as there is no way to control the further disclosure of the information. Advice to buy shares would seem to give more protection than disclosure of information, though the information itself may be considered less reliable by the recipients, because it is more difficult to confirm.

Considerable sophistication can be added to the priority list technique by the use of various lists. The most important list—or lists, if different combinations of recipients are desired—will usually contain the names of individuals who have been or are currently most instrumental in generating information. Other lists will form a descending pyramid, as the larger number of individuals with smaller claims are assigned their appropriate places on lower priority lists. Such a system could engender considerable incentive to get to the top list. But if this essentially market device is to perform the function alleged for it, those spaces must be reserved for individuals whose contributions are greatest.

Discretionary Accounts

PROBABLY MORE EFFICIENT than priority lists as an information-exchange control device is the so-called *discretionary account*. This is nothing more than a deposit of money with a broker who is given full discretion to buy or sell any shares for the account. Surprisingly little has been written about these accounts in the present connection. It is commonly recognized that most trust funds are at the same time discretionary accounts, and it has occasionally been complained that discretionary accounts lend themselves to "churning," or excessive trading to build up commissions.[28] Apart from these matters, neither of which concerns us here, the most common statement by brokers and bankers is that they really prefer not to have discretionary accounts and that they do not accept them as a matter of common practice.[29] Investment advisers other than brokers sell investment advice for a fee,[30] but brokers and bankers do not as a general rule handle discretionary accounts for a fee. It would appear that this service may be reserved for customers who pay in a form other than cash, because the existence of discretionary accounts with no advisory-fee charge is well known on Wall Street. The SEC's Special Study makes no mention of these accounts.

Nothing about discretionary accounts appeared in the 1933 congressional hearings either, possibly because they may not have been used then. The pool was a far more efficient device and would frequently have served the same purpose as the discretionary account. With the outlawing of pools in 1934, a tolerable substitute may have been found in the discretionary account. It would be interesting to know if their popularity is a post-1934 matter, but again the investigators seem to have been asking the wrong questions.

The discretionary account, for which the broker has broad powers to invest a specified amount of money at his discretion and to buy and sell securities, has several advantages over priority lists. These accounts are especially suitable for dealing in information whose value will be exploited rapidly in the market. The broker can enter the necessary transactions at once, without having to contact his principals. This advantage is not so important if the information can be withheld for a while, but often that cannot be done. A perfect illustration of this point is provided by *In the Matter of Cady, Roberts & Co.* There, it will be recalled, the inside information was that the company had passed a dividend. The broker, Gintel, was able to sell out his discretionary accounts in Curtiss-Wright shares very quickly and even to go short for those accounts. Had he been delayed as much as an hour, the entire operation might have been unsuccessful. If he had used priority lists to identify the same individuals and communicate with them, they would undoubtedly have gained less profits as a group, and many would have been left out altogether.

Insider trading in especially volatile information, like dividend news, has been increasingly attacked by the SEC and regulated by the New York Stock Exchange. Therefore, the popularity of discretionary accounts may be declining. But still other advantages to the discretionary account must be considered for an accurate appraisal of their usefulness. As we have seen, the priority list requires either that a particular bit of information be disclosed or that customers be advised to buy without any indication of why. If the information is disclosed—a process never required by discretionary accounts—there is no efficient way of policing the further distribution of this information by individuals on the list. Also, if only the information is disclosed, the bankers have no way of determining how skillfully the individual will evaluate the information nor how many shares he will purchase. All of these difficulties disappear if discretionary accounts are used.

With discretionary accounts the market for valuable information begins to approach an automaticity unusual in barter markets. This is not to say that the system works perfectly, or that there are no leaks in the information channels, or that mistakes will not be made—the pools were undoubtedly more efficient. But, for large-scale bartering of volatile information with the necessity of some policing, this device is probably the best available. Where policing problems do not loom large, either because the news will not be disclosed for a long time or because quick dissemination to a large number of people is desired, the priority list is the more efficient device.[31]

In comparison to the total trading in a given stock, the number of transactions based on discretionary accounts and priority lists may be quite small. Most insiders will not plan to sell out within six months, and therefore direct purchases will still be widely used—unless the courts make that illegal or the stock exchanges are successful in hampering it. Informal exchanges or gifts of valuable information may play a larger role than is commonly recognized. But, most important, as we shall see in Chapter VII, the total amount of short-swing, insider trading is itself likely to be quite small. A large fraction of this trading, however, may be accounted for by priority lists and discretionary accounts.

The important proposition of this chapter is that the market for valuable information described actually exists. Some of the evidence to establish this point is a bit dated to be sure, but recent studies indicate no fundamental changes. And, if empirical evidence is lacking, we can fall back on logical inference. Then the case for the existence of this market is very strong. It would be extraordinary if the vast riches regularly available in the form of valuable information were simply lost by astute businessmen like sand sifting through their open hands. Until convincing evidence to the contrary is available, we should assume that this market exists and is efficiently maintained by important functionaries in the financial community.

VI

Market Effects of Different Trading Rules

IN CHAPTER VII we shall observe the effect of alternative legal rules regarding insider trading upon specific individuals in the market. After that we shall consider whether a rule allowing insiders to trade in corporate securities is or is not generally beneficial to all shareholders. First, however, it is important to understand the more general market effects of different trading rules. We shall investigate three different rules. The first is the rule of completely free trading by insiders. The second is the rule of no insider trading. The third, important only for analytic purposes, is a rule that would allow insiders to trade only in puts and calls or to receive stock options from their company, but not to exploit information directly by buying and selling shares.

To aid in comparing the effects of these different rules, certain simplifying assumptions will be made. We shall assume that we can know precisely the number of points a given stock will move up or down on the disclosure of good or bad news. And, to continue with the illustration used earlier, we shall consider the case of a share selling at 50, with good news worth five points. That is, the total market value of the information is $5 times the total number of shares outstanding. Under any of the three rules we shall consider, the ultimate effect must be to cause an increase in share price from 50 to 55. And we shall assume that no external circumstances other than those relating to the inside information operate to change the price of the stock.

Practical Limits on Exploitation of Inside Information

It is important to recognize some facts about the extent to which market exploitation of information is feasible. If an individual wished to exploit the full value of a certain piece of information, it would seem that he would have to purchase every share of the company's stock. Only in this fashion could he gain that part of the value of the information that would adhere to each share of stock. Actual instances of direct purchases of all shares are quite rare in publicly traded companies, though mergers may accomplish the same thing. In these cases we can say that the purchaser has information about the company's potential under his control. His belief that he can manage the company more profitably is the valuable inside information, and, by purchasing all the shares, he may realize the full value of that information.[1]

But even if purchasing all the shares of a company's stock were practicable, it could not guarantee the realization of the full value of the information. Factors other than those known in the market will affect sellers' decisions to sell. The purchase price has to be sufficient to overcome a range of subjective individual preferences that, in our example, would make it impossible normally to buy all of the company's shares at a price of 50.[2] Clearly, a market price of 50 does not signify that all shares of the company can be bought at that price. And yet anything paid in excess of 50 for these shares reduces the market value of the information to that extent, because we are assuming that the price will rise only to 55.

The purchase of a small percentage of the outstanding shares of a company's stock will often be sufficient to raise the market price to the level indicated by the information. In a company with ten million shares outstanding, the purchase of fifty thousand shares might be sufficient to raise the quoted price of the shares from 50 to 55.[3] Here the indicated value of the information is $50 million, but, assuming an average purchase price of 52 for the insiders, the gain is only $150,000.[4] If an insider buys in excess of fifty thousand shares, he is no longer trading on his inside information but rather he is hoping for market misinterpretation of the news when it appears. As we shall see in the next chapter, this may not be illogical, but these later purchases will be made with considerably less certainty than the earlier ones. In the ensuing discussion, when we refer to an insider exploiting the full value of the information, the reference is only to his purchasing enough shares to raise the current market price of the shares to the point indicated by the value of the new information, not to his recovering the actual value of the information. In fact, however, even this kind of full exploitation is rare.

Individuals receiving valuable information about the companies whose shares are actively traded often will not be able to capture the full value of that information for themselves. Information is often more mercurial than mercury. In many instances it is impossible to prevent its rapid dissemination to others. The time period that insiders have to capture the fresh information may occasionally be as small as minutes,[5] although in some cases of really substantial news the period will be considerably longer.[6] The insiders' problem may be insufficient capital or unavailable credit within the necessary time period. Or the difficulty may take the form of his unwillingness or inability to liquidate present holdings in order to exploit the new knowledge.[7]

The insider is also faced with a considerable amount of uncertainty. In the first place, his own knowledge will rarely be perfect, and he cannot know the extent to which others in possession of the same information have already been buying. He cannot know precisely the effect of his and other purchases on the price of the company shares since other factors may be operating to accentuate their effect or counteract it. Finally, there is no absolute certainty in the stock market even for insiders; the discovery of an important new sulphur deposit may be followed closely by a collapse of sulphur prices.

These are uncertainties with which even the most knowledgeable insider must contend. Thus many individuals are not willing to risk their entire fortune on what often appears to be a fairly sure thing.[8] Furthermore, insiders may choose not to trade at all on small bits of information that they can afford to exploit fully. The smaller the per-share value of the inside information, the larger will the effects of other market uncertainties appear. The closer the current price is to the anticipated price, the less likely are insiders to buy the stock.

Free-Trading Rule

WE ARE NOW in a position to describe graphically the process of a price change under a rule of free insider trading. We shall assume that corporate insiders are free to use undisclosed information in any way they see fit. They may exploit it directly themselves, they may tell friends, or they may do both of these things. We will, however, assume that no calls will be purchased nor stock options issued.[9] As we shall see, this is a simplifying assumption that in no way detracts from the logic of the analysis.

Beginning with the stable price of 50, we should expect the price to rise slowly as the first few insiders begin to make their purchases. But additional people now begin to buy the stock, as they believe that they are in possession of valuable information.

Their number increases by some logarithmic function, and the effect can be shown by an exponential curve, or ramp function, flattening out at 55, as illustrated in Figure 1.

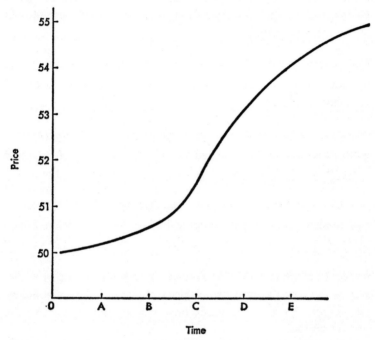

FIGURE 1. Simple Price Rise with Insider Trading

The shape of this curve will vary, even for one particular stock, with many different factors. We have already noted the problem of knowing the supply schedule for the stock. The kind and quality of information involved will be important. And some bits of news will travel much faster than others. Perhaps more important will be the pattern of insiders' distribution of different kinds of information. If this pattern is always the same for particular types of recurring information, such as earnings reports or new government contracts, the coefficient that will describe the exponential curve will be a constant. If this is so, and if it is possible to discover this constant, projection of some price changes of shares might be feasible. The statistical refinements necessary to prove and utilize this thesis would be extraordinarily complex. But there are some indications of this kind of price-change dependency, and these indications have not been explained in any other way.[10]

Few price changes ever result in a pure ramp-function curve. Rather, as we shall explain, the curve begins in the fashion just described, probably begins to show tremors at some point before reaching 55 but nonetheless continues above that point to, say, 58. It may then drop back to 53, go back to 56, back down to 54½, and then lose any further noticeable effect from the news. This oscillation effect can be likened to a ripple in a pond. If the pond is very still, a ripple can be followed all the way to the shore. But if several people are throwing pebbles into the same pond and creating a variety of ripples, then the oscillations from one pebble will tend to disappear or become indistinguishable from others before the first ones actually reach the shore. The effect of new information on the stock-market price in our illustration will tend to disappear while oscillating around the $55 line, but other forces may well carry the actual stock price above or below this figure. (See Figure 2.) Those changes, however, are not relevant to the present discussion.

We are now in a position to explain in more detail the entire effect of a given piece of market information under the rule of free insider trading. The curve will begin to rise in exponential fashion simply because an increasing number of people will receive the information and rely upon it over a period of time. But for reasons already examined, insiders will become less certain of profits as the price approaches that indicated by the value of the news. At some point before the stock reaches its heights, some of the original purchasers will either sell or stop their own purchasing even though the total number of purchasers may still be increasing. We have assumed that no other changes are occurring to affect the price of this share, but naturally the traders in our il-

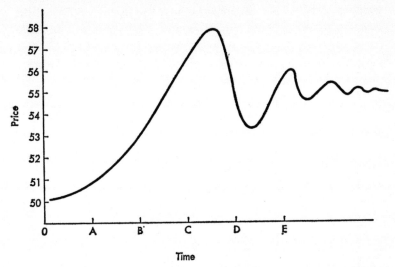

FIGURE 2. Price Rise with Insider Trading and Consequent Effects

lustration cannot know that such changes will not occur. The effect of this may or may not be noticeable as a tremor, but at least it portends the larger oscillations that will follow.

Physical
Analogies

As INFORMATION originating with one or a few people is disseminated to a larger number, the effect on the market is analogous to the laws governing friction and kinetic energy. As the information moves from its original source at an exponential rate to more and more people, it will become increasingly difficult to stop it precisely at the $55 line. This might occur if the information reflects a specific, ascertainable, nonrepeating addition to value, as in the case of a tender-bid or a tax refund.

Many individuals, seeing that the stock is selling at, say, 52 and realizing that there is at least $3 of value left in the information, will put in orders to purchase. But, because there is a time lag before orders are executed[11] or because too many people had the same information at the same time, the information may actually be worth only two points. Nonetheless, the effect of the buy orders anticipating a three-point rise will be sufficient to carry the price of the share beyond the $55 point.

Time lags in the transmission of and action upon information are probably the major factors involved in the oscillation phenomenon. There are, however, other kinds of interferences operating as well, and here analogues borrowed from modern communication theory will help to explain the economics of information. Basically the three influences at work are the stock-market analogues of the concepts of *attenuation, noise,* and *distortion.*

The concept of attenuation has already been referred to. The ripple in the still pond presents a perfect analogue to the spread of information. This time, however, we must enlarge our hypothetical pool in order to understand the situation, for, no matter how still a pool, if it is large enough we will not be able to discern the wave effect at the shore. Frank Knight has stated the matter in economic terms: "When the idea becomes common property it is like any other superabundant element in production, a free good and no longer a productive factor in the effective economic sense."[12] A corollary of this statement is that the more people who have a bit of information, the less it is worth.[13]

As the price increases there is a deterioration in the "quality" of buyers, that is, there will be more buyers who cannot have a high degree of confidence in the reliability of their information, and their mode of behavior in the stock market may tend to be more erratic than that of insiders. As we have seen, the value of the original information is now approaching zero, though the market may carry the price beyond that indicated by the value of the information. Unless the insider is also willing to purchase shares based on so-called technical rather than fundamental factors, we should not ordinarily expect to find him among those buying at these higher reaches. Indeed, it is a safe assumption that few executives appear as buyers in this phase of a stock rise. It is interesting that the first group of purchasers of Texas Gulf Sulphur stock after November, 1963, purchased at prices ranging from 17 to 27,[14] although a month after their last purchase the stock sold as high as $58.

Another kind of imperfection that prevents the perfect transmission of information in the marketplace is analogous to the communications concept of noise. In a crowded room with a number of people speaking at once, it is often difficult to listen to one particular conversation. Other words, phrases, and sounds constantly intrude and blank out the sought-after conversation.[15] Similarly, in the market for valuable information, though one may be straining to hear only reliable news, one continually hears a veritable babble of rumors, hot tips, suggestions, and leads. Straining out the reliable from the unreliable is extremely difficult and in many cases, especially for smaller shareholders, literally impossible to do with any degree of confidence. The effect of this is to make one wary of all information, including that which actually is perfectly true. We must, therefore, discount the reliability of everything we hear, including what are, in fact, the true reports. At the same time we also tend to give a certain degree of credibility to other reports because we cannot know for sure that they are not among the reliable ones. The entire matter of gathering information becomes a subtle problem in statistics and probabilities.

The third kind of interference, distortion, is familiar to lawyers. The notion is similar to the policy underlying the inadmissibility of hearsay evidence. As information is transferred from one individual to another, distortions in the actual message transmitted necessarily occur. Some of these distortions result from mechanical defects in the system of communication. Others can be explained in psychological terms, as different people gain different mental images from the same external stimulus. Distortion also results from the varying degrees of sophistication with which an individual can treat a given bit of information. The accountant, upon learning that a company is shifting from FIFO to a LIFO system of inventory accounting, may quickly recognize that a smaller net-income figure will result. The layman with no accounting background may not infer anything from this disclosure. This sort of difference in reaction—and the examples could be multiplied indefinitely—will always prevent perfectly smooth transitions to new price levels.

Those who trade with least certainty will tend to predominate in number near the top of the price curve generated by the inside information. Various time lags, attenuation, noise, and distortion will all dictate that they discount the truth of their information to a larger extent than insiders do. Movements in stock prices caused by their transactions will tend to be exaggerated as they buy too late and sell too early, judged by the ideal of perfect information. Since they have some information, however, their transactions will tend to move up and down within some limits, and, because ultimately the inside information is disclosed, the movement will probably tend to oscillate around the $55 line, with the price movements generated by the $5 per share bit of news eventually becoming indistinguishable from other factors.

No-Insider-Trading Rule

THE NEXT RULE we shall examine is that of no insider trading. Some preliminary refinements are necessary, as there can be many variations of the no-trading rule. The most important point is that it takes time for most disclosures of information to have a full impact upon the market, even though we exclude inside traders. That is, we cannot assume that the moment a particular piece of information is disclosed, the price will immediately jump from 50 to 55. We have already described some of the reasons for a time lag in the dissemination of information. But with full public disclosure, much of this time lag will be compensated for by the increased number of people who will be trading. The speed with which information can be disseminated on the broad tape or in the *Wall Street Journal* is very fast as compared to the word-of-mouth technique implied by our discussion of free insider trading. With a rule of full disclosure, the period required for total dissemination and market reflection of news will rarely exceed a few hours. In many cases, minutes will be adequate.

There are alternative ways to isolate the market effect of a perfect no-insider-trading rule. First we may assume that insiders will not be allowed to trade in the market until the full effect of the disclosure has occurred. That is, using our familiar illustration, even though the disclosure occurred at 50, insiders would be prevented from trading until the shares had reached a price of 55. Although such a rule would be extremely difficult to police and no one has proposed it as a practical matter, something of this sort would be necessary to insure that insiders did not continue to gain some advantage by their position. If the insider is allowed to buy at 50½ after disclosure, we have really accomplished very little over a rule allowing him to purchase at 50 before disclosure.[16] It should be clear that an effective rule against insider trading would require that insiders abstain from trading during some period after public disclosure.

Whether we exclude insiders from immediate postdisclosure trading or not, the rate of increase in price will be quite steep. In fact the absence of insiders may be hardly noticeable, as they will be so few in number compared to outside traders and because the trading results of effective disclosure will generally swamp the market. In either event, as illustrated by Figure 3, the rate of price increase will generally be quite a bit steeper than would be the case when insiders can trade freely before public disclosure.

An alternative assumption letting us isolate the result of an effective rule against insider trading is more realistic than assuming a delay in insider trading after disclosure. This assumption probably gives a more accurate reflection of what would happen

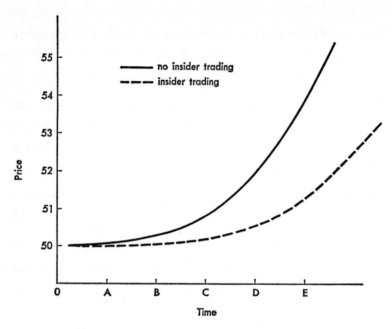

FIGURE 3.   General Comparison of Insider Trading and No Insider
Trading Rules

in the stock market if insider trading were prohibited. This time
we shall assume that *all* trading in shares will be stopped just before disclosure of important information and not resumed again
until the information has been disseminated and understood. With
this assumption there is no problem of insider trading after public
disclosure, because no one can trade during the relevant period.
This technique is actually in limited use today for reasons not
unrelated to our present considerations.[17]

The effect of such a rule is dramatic. No longer will we find
an exponential curve; the exponent is now infinity, and the line
is absolutely vertical. That is, no transactions will occur between
the price of 50, when the disclosure is made, and the final price
of 55. The effect of this rule is illustrated graphically in Figure 4.
If prices always change in accordance with such a step function,

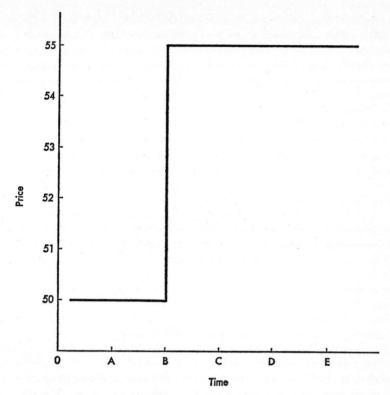

FIGURE 4. Trading Prevented Until Full Dissemination of Information

a graph of prices over a period of time would look like a series of plateaus of irregular width and height.

There are many practical difficulties with the assumption that all trading will be stopped for a period of time. The first problem is knowing when to stop trading. This difficulty is mitigated in theory by our assumption that no insider trading has occurred in the period before disclosure. In practice, of course, it would not be so easy. The other difficulty is knowing when to resume full trading. Theoretically, a regulatory authority would sanction trading when the information had been fully disseminated and understood. Again there are practical difficulties in knowing when this moment occurs, but we shall assume for now that it can be done.

It should now be clear that any rules designed to prohibit insider trading will, on the average, generate much steeper price increases than will the free-trading rule. In fact, when the most effective device possible to prevent insider trading is utilized— the suspension of all trading—the slope of the price curve is infinitely steep, that is, vertical. In comparing the effects of these different rules on individual traders in the market, we shall deal with these two extremes, the relatively shallow exponential curve derived from the free-trading rule and the vertical, step-function result of preventing insider trading. It should be kept in mind, however, that these are theoretical abstractions, descriptive only in an average and generalized sense.

Options and Calls

THE LAST RULE we shall examine is that allowing insiders to receive stock options from their company or to buy puts or calls. The *call* is simply an option to buy shares at a stated price at a specified future time. If the insider knows bad news that will cause a downturn in the share price, then he can take a *put*, or an option to sell at a stated price at some time in the future. No one has proposed such a rule as the one we are considering, and it appears to have little independent justification. But it will aid us in properly analyzing the subject of insider trading. The purchase of a call "at the market" or the taking of an option to buy later at the present market price provides perhaps the cheapest means for an individual to realize profits from an anticipated price rise. This method is in fact used today but rarely as the sole means of exploiting inside information.

The general market effect of a rule allowing insiders to take options or calls is, ironically, almost identical in its market effect to the rule allowing no insider trading. If we assume that the cost of the option or call is borne by the insider and not by the corporation and that it is not known that insiders are taking options or calls, the fact of issuance should not cause the slightest tremor in the market price of the corporation's shares. The seller of the option may have to cover later by delivering shares, but that will occur after the news has been released and can have no effect on the earlier market price.[18]

After the information has been disclosed, the call, per share, will appreciate in value by an amount equal to the per-share value of the information. If insiders are free only to buy calls[19] and if the information is released at the same time that it would be with no insider trading, no shareholder or potential shareholder in this corporation has been affected in any way by an insider's transactions. Insiders may be enabled to gain the full value of the information, minus the cost of the call, but no shareholder has less than he would have had under the rule of no insider trading. This point may seem quite startling to some readers, as it suggests, quite properly, that insiders can fully benefit by inside information without injury to any shareholder of the corporation.

It would seem at first glance that the last statement would have to be qualified if the call seller were also a shareholder in the corporation. That is, even though the individual acted in two separate capacities, a shareholder of the corporation would be injured if he sold a call to insiders. However, to the extent that the call seller is covered by ownership of shares, he cannot lose money on his transaction with the insider, because the loss on the call will be made up by the gain in his shares. True, he will not realize the gain that other shareholders will realize, but he has not lost as much as he would have by selling the shares outright at the time he sold the call.

VII

Effects of Different Legal Rules on Non-inside Traders

HAVING SEEN the general market effects different rules of law would produce, the ways in which information is disseminated in the market, and the interferences with smooth dissemination that exist, we can now begin to examine the effect different legal rules would have on particular individuals. Presumably the foundation of most objections to insider trading lies in the assumption of harm to outsiders. Ultimately the complaint must be that some individuals are being harmed by allowing insider trading. It is not enough simply to say that insider trading is unfair. If it is unfair, it must be unfair to somebody.

To understand whether anyone is injured—and if so, who— we might first compare the respective positions of the same individuals under the extreme rule of no insider trading and the other extreme of free trading by insiders. We will assume that the stock of our hypothetical corporation is selling at 50 and that no circumstances other than a piece of new information worth $5 will affect the price movement during the relevant time period.

The Demand Schedule
for Stocks

CERTAIN PECULIARITIES in the demand for stocks must first be examined. The demand for a share of stock is not the simple demand for one commodity. It is rather a complex demand both for that part of the underlying security about which everything is known (and whose market price fully reflects all prior knowledge) and for the value of information that will be assimilated into the known part in the future. For the first part of this package, the known security, the underlying demand schedule is probably no different from any other commodity sold in an extremely competitive market. The demand curve is completely elastic. Assuming no uncertainty, no differences in the amount of reliable information known to all traders, and no differences in their evaluation of this information, any of the shares in our illustration offered for sale below 50 would be immediately taken, and none offered above that price would be taken at all. This is true of the entire market; no distinction can be drawn between insiders and outsiders so far as this part of the demand for shares is involved.

As we turn to the second part of the security package, we must begin to distinguish between those who have reliable, accurate information and those who do not. The truth for most traders lies between these two extremes, but for simplicity of exposition, our analysis will proceed with a "know-it-all" and a "know-nothing" group of share traders. In the first group, those who know that they have reliable information, this information will be treated simply as any other commodity in a competitive market. That is, assuming that the information is worth $5 per share, individuals will take all they can of shares reflecting an information component being sold for less than $5. And these individuals will, as we noted in the last chapter, abstain when the price exceeds what they know the value to be.

The outs, the know-nothings, must now be divided into three separate groups: those whose market decisions will be a function of time, those whose decisions will be a function of the price of the security, and those whose decisions will reflect both factors. We are interested in the reactions to changes in time and price by those who now know only that the market price of the shares is 50.

Since the only two variables are time and price, transactions during the relevant time span for any reason other than a change in price are considered as time-function transactions. The relevant time period is basically the time it will take for complete market diffusion of new information. Most time-function transactions will occur because of external events that occurred during this period, which are not related to the price of the stock. Shareholders who bought or sold because of President John F. Kennedy's assassination would illustrate this concept. Also included here are transactions resulting from changed investment needs; a desire for more or less liquidity, higher dividends, or more growth; or a desire for more or less speculative securities. A large inheritance or the need for retirement income would be examples of changed financial circumstances dictating market transactions completely independent of the price of a particular company's shares. Death of a shareowner could be included in this category, as well as changes in government policies and economic events that affect the entire equity-capital market. There is no reason to believe that the distribution of these transactions will not be perfectly random over a long period of time; that is, there is no way to predict the occurrence of events that will cause time-function stock transactions.

We turn now to those shareholders whose transactions are a function of the price of the security. Again, these are individuals who know nothing about why the price is changing. They have no inside information, either about the company or the identity of those buying the shares. Some of these individuals will take a given price change as a signal or bit of information, while others will not. Those who do see a change as the equivalent of information will still disagree on the meaning of the signal, both as to its direction and its extent. Many of these individuals are "chartists," who trade on so-called technical factors and analyze graphic depictions of previous price movements. But, with a slight exception that we shall note, available data and studies indicate that this approach is unsuccessful. As indicated by the theory of market uncertainty,[1] the distribution of their transactions will be perfectly random in any statistically significant sample.

The group who do not take individual price changes as signals, if they are included in those trading during the relevant time period, may still take the *rate* of price change as a signal. Their transactions are a function of price change over time. Some will sell and some buy, either because the price level remained stable, because it changes slowly, or because it changes quickly. They also may be chartists, and, because they operate with total uncertainty, their transaction distribution will also tend to be random.[2]

We have now accounted for all individuals, both the know-it-alls and the know-nothings, who can be projected as traders during the time span with which we are concerned. There is no way of predicting how many transactions will occur, but it would seem normally to involve only a small fraction of the total number of outstanding shares. During the entire year 1964, with nearly nine billion shares listed on the New York Stock Exchange, only one and one-fourth billion or 14 per cent were traded.[3] On the average then only about .27 per cent of total shares are traded in a week. Many trades involve shares already counted in trades, whereas the shares not traded are only counted once. Thus the figure is actually overstated considerably.

The Brownian
Effect

THE EFFECT of having no know-it-alls, or insiders, in the market for some period of time would present a situation analogous to that described by the Brownian effect in physics. This phrase is used to describe the actions of gas molecules under pressure as they collide with and bounce off one another. These collisions are thought to occur with absolutely no pattern, and it is generally believed by scientists that these collisions represent perfect indeterminacy. The stock-market analogue of this phenomenon is generally referred to as a *random walk*,[4] and it can be illustrated as in Figure 5. If the random-walk theory of stock prices were

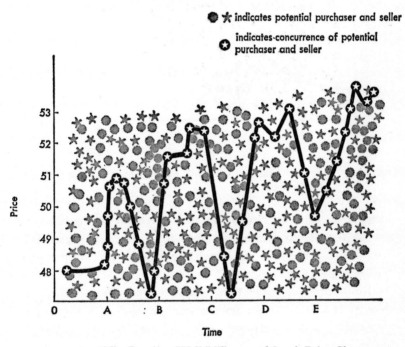

FIGURE 5. "The Random Walk" Theory of Stock Price Changes

completely correct, the direction and magnitude of price changes in shares would always be uncertain.[5] There would be no discernible dependence of one transaction price on the immediately preceding price. Such dependency can be introduced in the stock market only by an increase in knowledge. If this information requires time for full exploitation, we should not expect price

FIGURE 6. Effect of Insider Trading on Random Distribution of
            Transactions

changes to be fully random in their direction or extent. We
should, for reasons discussed in Chapter V, anticipate occasional,
very short periods during which the random-walk hypothesis
would not be valid.

Knowledgeable transactions will occur only sporadically and
even then may represent only a small fraction of transactions.
Their effect will be extremely small and very difficult to discern
statistically. However, using newer and highly complex methods
of statistical analysis, some economists report slight nonrandom
movements among stock prices.[6] No theoretical explanation for
this phenomenon has previously been offered, but the theory expounded here could explain both the general randomness of stock
prices and the occasional, slight nonrandomness.

As buyers with valuable information enter an otherwise randomly fluctuating market, their transactions will have a determi-
nable effect on share prices.[7] Even though a few know-nothing

transactions may continue to occur at varying prices, many that otherwise would have occurred at different prices will now appear on the price curve projected by the inside trader. Outside sellers will sell to the inside buyer when the price offered is more than the price outside buyers are offering. And some outside buyers and sellers, whose transactions are a function of price, will now buy from and sell to each other at a higher price. Thus many of the transactions occurring in random fashion prior to the entry into the market of insiders will now be drawn toward the insiders' transactions and tend to cluster with normal distribution around the price curve dictated by the dissemination of the new information. (See Figure 6.)

Effect of Allowing Insider Trading

WE ARE NOW in a position to explore the effects that different rules of law on insider trading would have on the market. Graphically, we can illustrate these by combining an illustration of the random distribution of buyers and sellers, with Figures 1 and 4 from the last chapter, showing the general market effects of different insider-trading rules. (See Figure 7.)

First we shall examine what happens to a select group of buyers and sellers of securities under the free-insider-trading rule. It will be noticed that various transactions will occur at different points along the line *OF*, which is generated by the transactions entered into when insider trading is allowed. This is not to suggest that some of the buyers, or indeed a great many of them, engaging in transactions between times *A* and *E* are not outsiders. But these transactions occur because they fall randomly at those points for reasons unrelated to the inside information. Some of the buyers may have taken the price rise as an indication that it would continue, but in no meaningful sense could they know this for a particular stock.

Undoubtedly, many of the sellers whose transactions occur on the line *OF* have sold to insiders. These sellers will have sold for

FIGURE 7. Comparison of Effects of Different Rules on Random Distribution of Transactions

reasons extraneous to the price change or because they took the price increase as a signal that it would continue no further. But, given the random distribution that will result from the ignorance of those who held stock at point *O*, some of them could be predicted in advance as potential sellers at various points along the line *OF*. However these individuals, whoever they turn out to be, are not unique or peculiar. Qualitatively they are no different from any of the other sellers, all outsiders, appearing anywhere in Figure 7. The same is true of those would-be sellers above or below the transaction line *OF* who will now receive the full value of the new information. The would-be buyers, who are not on the line *OF*, suffered a loss to the same extent.

What we have done is change the market conditions for the randomly distributed buyers and sellers. All actual transactions will now fall on the line *OF* generated by insiders. Some sales would have occurred at the same point without the infusion of insider buying. Other transactions, describing the fluctuating line *OH*, that would have occurred without the price change dictated by insiders, will not now occur. Those who would have been sellers are now better off. Those who would have been buyers are worse off to the same extent.

Some critics of insider trading must assume that the sellers on the line *OF* would not have lost money (or alternatively would have made money) if their buyers had not traded with inside information. But there is simply no way of knowing whether that statement is true or not. Without the insider trading one cannot assume that the price would have progressed from 50 to 55 along the line *OF*. If the inside information had not been developed at all, manifestly each of these sellers would have been worse off, because, assuming that everything else remains constant, his shares would have remained at a price of 50. He may or may not have sold, but there can be no question that $52.50 (the assumed average price on line *OF*) is worth more than $50. To the extent that any sale was more a function of the time period involved than it was of the price, these sellers are clearly better off with insider trading, assuming that good news would otherwise be released at time *E*.

It is possible to hypothesize conditions under which outsiders as a group are injured by insider trading. Since some of the buyers along the line *OF* are insiders and none of the sellers are, it might seem that on balance existing shareholders as a group are injured by insider trading. However, we would need additional evidence to reach that conclusion. Unless these same individuals would not have sold in the time period *AE* under the rule of no insider trading, they are still better off with insider trading, because they will receive more than 50 for their shares. On the average they should receive approximately 52½. To determine accurately the extent of harm to sellers under the insider-trading rule, we would have to know what those same sellers would do under the opposite rule. If sales are more frequently a function of price than of time, with the result that there will be more transactions along the line *OF* than would otherwise have occurred in the same time span *AE* without insider trading, and if that difference is great enough to compensate for the lower price received by sellers with no insider trading, then sellers, as a group, *are* in fact worse off with insider trading on good news.

Thus, there is both a plus and a minus for outside sellers from insider trading. The plus is the higher price received by those who would otherwise have sold at the stable, lower price, and the minus is the number of sales that now occur but which otherwise would not have occurred. It would be extremely difficult to obtain accurate data on this question, though we can make one safe assumption. Those sellers who lose will tend to be those whose trades are a function of price, and those who gain will tend to be those whose trades are a function of time only. When we consider good news, we know that the less frequently one sells shares the better he will fare.[8] There are reasons to assume that good news is more important than bad news for our purposes. First the long-term trend of stock prices is upward, so that, all other things being equal, occasions of good news should exceed those of bad. Perhaps more important, substantial good news seems often to develop quickly, as with news of a new product, a favorable merger offer or an important government contract. Bad news on the other hand may tend to unfold in more gradual fashion, or perhaps to be anticipated, as with a low earnings report or a dividend cut. Bad news may also more frequently be information affecting an entire industry and thus not be susceptible to insider trading at all.

If we limit our concern to the long-term investor rather than the short-swing share trader, there is little likelihood for injury from insider trading. The long-term investor is much less likely than the trader to sell because of price changes effected by insiders. He is more likely to become a seller because of changed financial circumstances or death. A strong argument can be made for limiting our concern to this group of shareholders, but, as we shall see, the effects will be small in any event.

The argument that insider trading may injure outsiders as a group can only hold if price changes occur more gradually with insider trading than without it. As a rule, this is probably true. But if the price curve were as steep with insider trading as without—as it is when insiders are only allowed to buy calls—no harm to outsiders could even be hypothesized. Because perfect enforecement of the full-disclosure rule does not and probably cannot exist, any possible harm to outsiders suggested by this discussion must be considerably discounted.

Effect on Outside Buyers and Sellers

BUT EVEN at this point we cannot conclude that outside sellers as a group lose with the rule of no insider trading. We still do not know the answer to the more relevant question of how all outsiders as a group fare under one rule as against the other. We must add to the plus side of the equation the gain resulting to noninsider buyers along the line *OF*, as these individuals are benefited to the same extent as insider buyers, if they hold their shares until time *E*. This factor must in turn be countered by subtracting the $5 benefit lost by all would-be buyers during the time period *AE* if there had been a rule of no insider trading.[9] So long as there are more outsider buyers along the line *OF* than there would be buyers along the $50 transaction line *OG*, this group of outsiders will prefer a rule of insider trading. Since the outsider buyers on *OF* will tend to be individuals who have taken a signal from the price rise, it is quite possible that their number may be relatively large. We do know that there will be more transactions by outside sellers along *OF* than by outside buyers, but we cannot know a priori that the difference will be large.

The conditions under which all stock-market outsiders as a group will lose under a rule of insider trading can be stated generally. We need only posit substantially more price-function trading than time-function trading with good news to get that result. But even though this represents a real, though indeterminate, loss to outsiders, it is not necessarily an overall economic loss to the community. To reach that conclusion would require the absurd assumption that insiders gain less than outsiders as a group lose. Even if the loss resulting to all outsiders from a rule of insider trading did approach the amount of gain by the insiders, the question of whether insider trading should be abandoned would by no means be answered. For, as we shall see, the ultimate question of economic desirability of insider trading involves far more than these hypothetical computations.

Timing of Disclosures

IF INSIDERS are allowed to exploit the value of information by purchasing calls, the time period for doing this will probably not be significantly different from the time period necessary to exploit the information under the free-trading rule. If, however, insiders are not allowed to benefit in any way from their information, it is conceivable that disclosure would occur at an earlier date. The implication from this is that if insider trading is allowed, insiders will release the information at a date more suited to their own interests. As some period of time is necessary for them to exploit their knowledge, it would seem that the information would generally be released later under the rule allowing insider trading than under the opposite rule. Only delay that actually enlarges the time period between development and disclosure should concern us. If the delay merely shifts the same time span to a later point, there will be no effect on outsiders as a group, even though a different set of individuals may be affected.

But the problem would not seem to be a serious one. Much information in a sense determines its own release date, and no alteration is feasible. A dividend declaration or the announcement of a development extraneous to the corporation, such as a tax refund, would be of this variety. In these cases it is still possible for insiders to exploit some of the value inherent in this information. There are cases in which delay will aid insiders in exploiting the value of the information. A great mining discovery, such as that of Texas Gulf Sulphur, higher earnings, or exceptional market acceptance of a new product, might be examples of this sort. But these delays may also be in the interest of the corporation. Texas Gulf Sulphur's first successful sample core at Timmins was known early in November of 1963, but it was not until April, 1964, that the company had succeeded in acquiring rights to other sections of land under which the vein ran. If the announcement had been made in November, 1963, it would certainly have been more expensive to acquire mineral rights in these other properties. The same is true with new products; the faster competitors get the word of success, the faster they will begin copying. Many subtleties and complexities in business may determine the timing of public reports.

It is very difficult to estimate the extent to which insider trading would effect the length of the predisclosure period, and empirical data would be extremely untrustworthy. On the one hand, insiders may often be unable to affect disclosure dates, and in many instances they will have no incentive to do so. Many techniques are available for exploiting information quickly, and often there will be no hurry. On the other hand, where time is needed, it is possible to delay disclosure. This is to the disadvantage of anyone selling within the period of additional delay. If, however, as will be argued in Chapter IX, inside information is an appropriate form of compensation for certain corporate functionaries, some control of disclosure timing may be necessary to assure that the device is effective.

The Shareholder's Contract Argument

A SOMEWHAT DIFFERENT argument against insider trading focuses on the alleged expectations of particular individuals rather than on the entire group of outsiders. The argument is that the sellers who do lose under the insider-trading rule invested with the expectation of receiving particular bits of good news. Having assumed the risk of news being bad, they should benefit from any desirable developments occurring during their tenure as shareholders.

But the expectation of most investors is probably different from that implied by this argument. Investors hope that their company will be well managed, and they anticipate sharing in the benefits of this efficiency. They do not, however, anticipate that they will be told news of specific events before it has affected the market price. Rather, they anticipate merely having their shares appreciate in value as a result of these events. By holding on to his shares, the investor will ultimately realize the value of any good news developed for his company. Few shareholders would want a rule requiring them to be informed in order to realize the benefit of new developments in their corporation. Most shareholders quite sensibly rely on the market mechanism to guarantee their sharing in the value of good news.

The argument also implies that any developments in a corporation's affairs will immediately affect share prices. Only in this way can developments be related to the period in which shares are held. But there is no feasible way of relating the benefits of particular bits of information to the ownership of shares in the company at particular moments. A share would have to be owned for the full life-and-death cycle of a company for this ever to be done precisely.

If the argument under discussion were carried to its logical extreme, there would be no such thing as a stock market. Anyone who fortuitously purchased shares just before an important announcement would have to pay the gain to his seller, who may have held the shares for the ten long years of unsuccessful exploration or research.[10] These are the very uncertainties that cannot be allocated in any scientific, or precise, or even rough fashion. The market allows individuals to assume whatever risks of this sort they wish, but they receive benefits only if their investment is continued and their shares are held at the time of disclosure or exploitation by those with the information.

The Outside,
Short-Term Trader

It seems appropriate to ask just what kind of trader might logically desire a rule preventing insiders from dealing in shares. Who stands to gain, financially or otherwise, by a rule barring insiders from trading? There is, of course, no recognizable or definable group who, under a full-disclosure rule, would pick up a set sum flowing to insiders under the free-trading rule. We are not dealing with a certain amount of money that can be rationally redistributed to different groups of individuals.[11]

The intelligent long-term investor, as we have seen, has substantially no interest in preventing his company's executives from trading in the company's shares. Apart from the advantage to him of this rather inexpensive form of compensation to the executives (a matter to be discussed in the chapters following), he would be indifferent as to the identity of those realizing the trading profits inherent in short-swing price movements. When the information has finally been disclosed or exploited, the long-term investor— the shareholder who holds on—receives the full value of the information developed by the executives of his corporation. Only by holding his shares does he actually guarantee the realization of this value, though at the same time he does incur the risk of suffering the effects of bad news. This, however, is precisely what the capital investor has agreed to do, and it conforms to the classical statements of the function of the capitalist. He will also be indifferent as to whether prices change gradually or fluctuate sharply, so long as the changes occur while he is a shareholder.

We have assumed that the typical investor-shareholder does not buy because he anticipates receiving specific, discrete bits of information. But another group of stock-market participants have a different interest. The individual who acts on information that he knows, or he has reason to know, is stale, unreliable, distorted, or given freely, hopes that it is true. He gambles against high odds that he can insinuate himself into the position of one who has reliable inside information. This kind of trader will ordinarily sell his shares when he has realized the assumed potential of his so-called hot tip. Thus his preference in the market is to receive the value of the good news directly rather than to participate indirectly in the ultimate market effects of the good news. In common parlance, he is a speculator and not an investor. To the extent that gambling psychology motivates his participation in the stock market, the speculator will favor a rule generating sharp fluctuations in stock prices over a rule allowing only gradual changes. Since he has gambled upon the possibility of exploiting good news, the quicker the result is known the better. He will prefer the excitement of sharp fluctuations and the possibility of winning or losing quickly. High peaks and low troughs over a short time period are precisely what stimulate and encourage him.[12]

As we have already seen, the prohibition of insider trading will protect the interests of this individual when there is good news. He will be injured by the same rule in the case of bad news, because he will bear the full brunt of it before he can get out of the market. But, if his psychology is the same as that of the gambler, he will be more encouraged by the possibility of gain than he will be discouraged by the same or even a higher probability of loss. As we shall see, no effective rule against insider trading is feasible, so the poor gambler may be additionally fooled into believing that the odds are better than they really are.

It is sometimes argued that the short-term traders in the market aid in maintaining liquidity. That is, their plentiful presence as ready buyers and sellers guarantees that shares may always be converted to cash and vice versa. Undoubtedly, liquidity is one of the crucial characteristics of a functioning securities market, but it undoubtedly overstates the case to credit this only to short-term traders. To the extent that one trader's transaction cancels another's, it is difficult to see how more than a marginal amount of liquidity is added. Furthermore, the insiders, while also performing a quasi-arbitrage function, provide additional liquidity for outsiders who wish to trade.

The Investor as a Trader

THUS FAR we have dealt with two extreme kinds of share purchasers, the pure speculator or trader and the pure investor or holder. At some point, however, every human investor must become a trader. Individuals cannot own shares in perpetuity, and death causes a change of ownership. At that moment, or at any other points at which ownership changes, the investor becomes a trader, and he may dispose of his shares the day before a bonanza is announced. But the investor-turned-trader may have sold and realized even less if insiders were not trading. More importantly, the longer a shareholder has held his shares, the less significant proportionately will be any gain lost to insiders the day before a piece of good news was publicly announced.

To illustrate this last point: if shares have risen over a period of five years from a price of 10 to a price of 50, the loss of two points as a result of not having inside information will not be very significant. But if the shares were bought the day before yesterday at 49 and sold today at 50, the failure to gain the two additional points seems quite important. Indeed, it means that the gain could have been tripled by holding on for a day. Thus it seems fair to conclude for a second time that the less frequently outside shareholders trade, the less they will lose as a result of the exploitation of valuable information by insiders. But the fact that the same individual may both hold and then trade stock does not justify a rule for investors when they turn into traders that we would not justify for the pure speculator.

The Rarity of Significant Inside Information

ANY UNDESERVED RISK to investors resulting from insider trading must, therefore, constitute a very small fraction of the total risk assumed by long-term investors. And when we realize that the development of significant information is not a very common occurrence, the matter reaches *de minimis* proportions. The kind of information causing a flurry in Texas Gulf Sulphur stock in early 1964 may, if we are very liberal in our estimate, occur on the average of once every ten years for each listed company.[13] Because, as we have seen, the time required for full exploitation of information by insiders is generally quite short, the odds against any long-term investor's being hurt by an insider trading on undisclosed information is almost infinitesimally small.[14] It is simply not enough to say that it may on occasion happen. The truth is that for any individual with whom we are concerned, the absolute odds in favor of his losing anything as a result of insider trading are so small as to be unworthy of serious concern.

This somewhat laborious discussion of what happens in the stock market does not constitute a strong argument *against* a proposal to bar all insider trading. Indeed it is not intended for that purpose at all, but merely to point out that no strong arguments along these lines are available in *defense* of such a proposal. The implication should be put to rest, however, that someone with an important interest is being deprived of his interest when insiders are allowed to trade.

But the debate is far from over. If this were as far as we could go, the entire issue would probably not be worth the time or effort spent upon it. However, the argument developed in the following three chapters is that a rule allowing insiders to trade freely may be fundamental to the survival of our corporate system. People pressing for the rule barring insider trading may inadvertently be tampering with one of the wellsprings of American prosperity.

VIII

The Entrepreneur in the
Large Corporation

ADAM SMITH was no great champion of the corporation. He felt
that a corporate manager's interest in the underlying property
was too attenuated for efficient management and the profit incentive too diluted for this form to be economically effective. He
thought that joint-stock companies were useful only if operations
were capable of being reduced to routine.[1] The Smith theory of
corporations was, paradoxically, not unlike that of Berle and
Means in *The Modern Corporation and Private Property*.[2] Each
of them complained that a separation of ownership and control
killed the incentive to profit that the sole proprietorship promoted. Smith's views in this matter were totally colored by his
observations of eighteenth-century business practices. In this
connection, he was undoubtedly more skilled as an observer than
as an economic theoretician. For Berle and Means, however, the
corrective evidence was actually close at hand.

Alfred Marshall, like Smith before him, felt that corporations
or joint-stock companies were best suited for insurance, banking,

and what we would call public-utility enterprises. Joint-stock companies, Marshall felt, "seldom have the enterprise, the energy, the unity of purpose and the quickness of action of a private business."[3] This made them particularly unsuited for "many branches of manufacture and of speculative commerce." Today we hardly question the efficiency of the corporate form, and in fact evidence of the corporation's efficiency in competitive endeavors was available long before 1920 when the eighth edition of Marshall's great *Principles of Economics* appeared. The mystique of the corporation apparently affected the outlook of great economists and lesser ones alike.

Frank Knight, in his classic *Risk, Uncertainty and Profit,*[4] has described certain fundamental errors in Adam Smith's theory and in the classical concept of competition and profit in general.[5] Knight suggests that Smith and others had seen as the dominant form of industry men using their own capital, hiring labor, and renting land from others. It seemed natural for them then to connect the income of the business manager with the ownership of capital.[6] Smith and the early classical economists envisioned what today we would term a perfectly competitive economic system, in which innovations and *profits*, in the technical, economic sense of the term, are missing.[7] Their model contained no element of ignorance or uncertainty. It is no wonder that the classical observations on corporations and the stock market, built as they were on the construct of perfect competition, are not helpful to us today.

Risk and Uncertainty

A MEANINGFUL THEORY of corporate enterprise and the role played by different individuals associated with the corporation is essential to understanding the peculiarities of insider trading. Some definitions are necessary at the outset. The first of these, the distinction between *risk* and *uncertainty*, is most closely associated in the history of economic thought with the work of Frank Knight. A slightly earlier work by Joseph Schumpeter, *The Theory of Economic Development*,[8] had already focused on this distinction for the special purpose of understanding the concept of entrepreneurship, to which we shall turn shortly.

Risk in this context refers to changes in value that may in some sense be said to be predictable. Even though we may not know the precise moment or even the quantity of gain or loss, a probability coefficient can still describe the risk of the event's occurring. To the extent that any rise or fall in value of property can be discounted by a known probability factor, its present value will in fact reflect that risk. This is most familiar to us through the concept of insurance, although the same phenomenon occurs in myriad ways in a complex market economy. Risk, for instance, is discounted in determining the present price of stocks. And though this price will also reflect the willingness or unwillingness of individuals to bear uncertainty, uncertainty as such cannot be discounted.

The assumption of risk is an economic service, and consequently it must be compensated. This compensation will be determined by familiar market forces in much the same way as any other market price. The assumption of risk does not give rise to *profit* in a competitive market system. Risk was a concept that Adam Smith did understand. He attributed to the capitalist, as his principal function, the assumption of this kind of risk. But in Adam Smith's system of pure competition, he presumed no great unforeseeable changes would occur, or at least he did not consider them to loom large in the affairs of men.

Uncertainty, as Knight describes it, relates to an entirely different phenomenon, though it is one inseparable from the affairs of men. The concept of uncertainty relates to the areas of men's ignorance, even in an approximate probability sense, of what the future holds. The invention of the internal-combustion engine reflected an unpredictable development having a great and unforeseeable impact on the value of men's labor, the value of existing productive facilities, and the prices of almost all commodities and services. Wars, weather, inventions, new merchandising techniques, changes in consumer preference, population shifts, and changes in birth rates may all illustrate Knight's idea of uncertainty. Any of these events may cause a rise or fall in the value of other properties whose utility depends in some fashion on this new event. If such events were merely insurable risks rather than pure uncertainties, any amount gained as a result would constitute the return for an assumption of risk but would not be profit. It is only when the rise in value results from an unpredictable event that we characterize the realized gain as profits. Anything else, including a payment for risk assumption, is either a part of the cost necessary to elicit production or supply in a competitive market or a part of monopoly rent (often referred to as *monopoly profits*).

Knight has often been criticized for pushing the distinction between risk and uncertainty too far. Clearly many of the phenomena he discusses as uncertainties can be insurable risks. The weather is perhaps the clearest example. And yet Knight's emphasis on the lack of reliable information is precisely the point needed for the present discussion. The difficulty is that Knight implied that there is an objective kind of uncertainty, an absolute lack of knowledge about the future. His concept of uncertainty is an ideal rather than a functional construct. However, our own interest is served by a purely functional definition of uncertainty. If a bit of information about the course of events can be made available only at a cost most men are unwilling to pay, we will treat this in the same way that Knight would treat pure uncertainty—although presumably Knight would not.

What may be risk from the point of view of the economy may be uncertainty for one individual. For our purposes, Knight's approach is helpful in emphasizing the fact that men do regularly act in ignorance of important variables and that there is a difference in the amount of ignorance or uncertainty with which different people operate. But the mere fact that one individual knows the risk he has assumed does not necessarily make the same matter any less uncertain for individuals without this information. Knight's distinction has considerable practical significance for our discussion.

Managers and Entrepreneurs

THE INTRODUCTION into economic thinking of the concepts of uncertainty and pure profits led in turn to another profound distinction, that between management and entrepreneurship. The distinction is spelled out carefully in both Knight's and Schumpeter's works. Both men recognize that managerial skill, in the abstract sense of an economic function or factor, is primarly a learnable, mechanical ability. Although the technical skills required for successful management may be very great and its market value very high, the fact remains that, within a fairly wide range, we know in advance what a manager is to do. To the extent that he is acting purely as a manager, his is not an innovating function. Because we know what the task entails, the service can be purchased like any commodity in the marketplace. A price, determined by the familiar laws of supply and demand, will be paid for the performance of this function.[9] There will still be many gradations and categories of this skill, each available at a different and commensurate price.

But the entrepreneur does not perform tasks that are in their detail predictable. Schumpeter describes the function of the entrepreneur:

> The carrying out of new combinations we call "enterprise"; the individuals whose function it is to carry them out we call "entrepreneurs." These concepts are at once broader and narrower than the usual. Broader, because in the first place we call entrepreneurs not only those "independent" businessmen in an exchange economy who are usually so designated, but all who actually fulfill the function by which we define the concept, even if they are, as is becoming the rule, "dependent" employees of a company, like

managers, members of boards of directors, and so forth, or even if
their actual power to perform the entrepreneurial function has
any other foundations, such as the control of a majority of shares.
As it is the carrying out of new combinations that constitutes the
entrepreneur, it is not necessary that he should be permanently
connected with an individual firm; many "financiers," "promoters," and so forth are not, and still they may be entrepreneurs
in our sense. On the other hand, our concept is narrower than the
traditional one in that it does not include all heads of firms or
managers or industrialists who merely may operate an established
business, but only those who actually perform that function.[10]

For Schumpeter the entrepreneur's function is to make new
combinations of productive factors, that is, to bring them together
in a new way. Routine business management is a critical function
in the successful operation of a corporation, but it will characterize the work of corporate executives *only after* productive factors have been successfully combined for the first time. Even
then, the entrepreneurial and the management functions are not
necessarily exclusive. Schumpeter suggests that an individual
starting his own business is an entrepeneur, but when he settles
down to running it as other people run their businesses, he is
merely managing.[11] It is "just as rare for anyone always to remain
an entrepreneur throughout the decades of his active life as it is
for a businessman never to have a moment in which he is an
entrepreneur, to however modest a degree."[12] Schumpeter later
made the point even more succinctly:

> The distinction between the entrepreneur and the mere head or
> manager of a firm who runs it on established lines or . . . between
> the entrepreneurial and the managerial function, is no more diffi-
> cult than the distinction between a workman and a landowner,
> who may also happen to form a composite economic personality
> called a farmer.[13]

Being an entrepreneur is a functional condition relating to
innovational activity and does not connote a status or class of persons. We cannot identify entrepreneurs as a separate social class,
as we might landowners or capitalists or labor. Furthermore, en-

trepreneurial activity itself is not always easy to identify or distinguish in advance. Schumpeter would distinguish entrepreneurs from inventors,[14] although he recognizes that the entrepreneur may also be an inventor just as he may also be a capitalist. Schumpeter's hesitancy in this regard stems from the fact that inventions must actually be carried into practice before profit is possible. It was the step of putting inventions into effect that Schumpeter saw as the entrepreneurial phase of invention. It is possible that Schumpeter was unfamiliar with the extent to which the exploitation of patents has long been routinized in the United States.

Capitalists and Entrepreneurs

THE THIRD important economic distinction is that between the entrepreneur and the capitalist. This is precisely the distinction Adam Smith and Berle and Means failed to make. In the economic arena of 1776, it was not easy to discern that the provision of capital and of entrepreneurial skill were two separate, specialized functions. In fact, at that time it was extremely rare for entrepreneurial services to be marketed in any way other than in a package with capital. Even today in common parlance, the word *entrepreneur* generally signifies the individual who starts his own business.[15] It was relatively easy to apply the concept of the entrepreneur to the traditional corporate promoter who raised money to found a business, which he might or might not then manage. Undoubtedly, these promoters were performing an entrepreneurial function,[16] but this usage served to focus our attention on the founding aspects of enterprise rather than on the necessity for continuing innovation.

A full understanding of the distinction between the entrepreneur and the capitalist requires detailed consideration of the characteristics of the remuneration received by the individuals in these two categories. As both Knight and Schumpeter point out, the capitalist has a function in even the most static and unprogressive kind of economy. No goods are permanent, and if the economy is to remain stable, provision must be made for replacement of depreciated facilities. The funds (or their goods counterpart) expended for this replacement purpose constitute capital, and the return on them is interest. In a stable, risk-free economy this interest would be an easily ascertainable figure determined by classically described market forces. But in that system there will be no return we can properly designate as profits to the capitalist or any other economic functionary. There can be no entrepreneur. Only the dynamic model of a competitive economy comprehends uncertainty about the future, and it is the existence of this uncertainty that gives rise to the concept of profits and the entrepreneur.

To Frank Knight we owe the origin of the concept of the entrepreneur as the "organizer of uncertainties." To Schumpeter the emphasis is more upon the entrepreneur as the creator of uncertainties, or the creator of the conditions necessary for true profit. To each of these economists and to many so-called "growth" economists today, it is the entrepreneur who sets progress in motion, not the capitalist.[17] The entrepreneur's relation to the capitalist is about the same as his relation to labor or the owner of land. As Schumpeter says, the entrepreneur is not the typical interest-receiver as Adam Smith may have seen him, because he is the typical interest-payer.[18]

The capitalist may be able to wrest from the entrepreneur a contract allowing the former to share in profits, but as Schumpeter remarked, "one must distinguish the economic nature of a return from what happens to it."[19] The return to the capitalist, though the amount may be indeterminate in advance, is still interest. The capitalist may even insist that he be allowed to risk his funds against the small probability of a large gain rather than against a high probability of a smaller gain. More prosaically, this choice today is between assuming the status of a bondholder or that of a common-stockholder. But the latter, as Schumpeter pointed out, functions as a creditor who is willing to forego the normal protections accorded that category of capital, in exchange for the right to share in profits.[20]

The Entrepreneur's Reward

THE ENTREPRENEUR as such, unlike the capitalist, is never the bearer of risk or uncertainty. Risk is borne only by those giving credit or otherwise extending capital. This may be the same individual as the entrepreneur, but the risk falls on him *as the capitalist* or as a possessor of goods, *not as an entrepreneur.*[21] Presumably Schumpeter would not even include the loss of time and energy as a risk to the entrepreneur as such. Knight is more explicit on this point; he assumes that the return to the entrepreneur is composed of two parts. The first is merely the ordinary wage for the labor performed, that is, the competitive rate of pay. The second part is true profit and is unrelated, in any normal market sense, to the work done.[22]

What then is the nature of the return to this upsetter of stable societies, this creator of disruptive forces? To both Knight and Schumpeter the answer to this question is precisely what is meant by the word *profit*. If the entrepreneur makes an economically successful new combination of factors, a surplus will be produced over and above the amount necessary merely to pay the present cost of component productive factors. In a static system, one without innovation, these costs would just be covered and no surplus would be produced. A surplus results because the new combination or innovation allows an existing producer to operate at a lower cost than previously, or it allows him to sell a new product at a price higher than the long-term equilibrium price. The entrepreneur buys the component factors of production at the old equilibrium price. Because he uses them either in a more productive or less costly way than do others who buy these same factors in the stable system, his use will produce a surplus over and above what other uses will create.

This surplus on occasion bears a relationship to the concept of monopoly rent or profit, and there may even be a coincidental identity. If the entrepreneur has no competitors when he introduces a new product, price will be determined according to the principles of monopoly. As he sells, he will realize what is generally termed monopoly profit. There is, in a fashion Marx did not imagine, a monopoly element in capitalist profits.[23] And yet the innovation and the monopoly are two distinct economic phenomena. Only the value of the innovation at the moment of creation reflects profit and the return to the entrepreneur. Subsequent income, though its amount may be determined according to the laws of monopoly pricing, is never profit in this sense. Even assuming that the monopoly position could be made permanent and secure against a price decline brought about by new competition, there can never be an additional return to the entrepreneur as such. "Profit from founding a business and permanent return are distinguished in practice; the former is the value of the monopoly, the latter is just the return from the monopoly condition."[24]

An illustration from the patent field will help make this point clear. An inventor who gets a patent monopoly may sell the patent or he may exploit it himself. If he sells it, all that he receives, in our sense, is entrepreneurial profit. The subsequent exploiter of the patent, though he will be charging a monoply price for the product, will only receive a competitive return for his investment. This same division of economic functions and returns will remain, *a fortiori*, if the inventor exploits the patent himself.

Another illustration of the distinction between profits and other returns is provided by the stock market. If an individual establishes a firm that has a patent monopoly and then sells his shares, he will receive approximately the present discounted value of all future monopoly profits the company is then expected to make. The company will continue to act as a monopoly after the sale of shares, but the return to the new shareowners will not in any sense contain a monopoly element. It will generally approximate the competitive rate of return on an investment of the size and type they have made.[25]

Entrepreneurial success is like monopoly (other than those protected by patents or other government grants) in still another way. It is rare that it can be made permanent. The entrepreneur rarely triumphs for himself alone. In almost all cases he creates a model or shows a way that can be copied. Others can and do follow him, first individuals and then perhaps hordes.[26] Copiers will continue to enter the industry until a new competitive equilibrium is created, that is, until again there is no surplus over cost because production has increased and price has declined. The copiers who enter the field before the full value of entrepreneurial innovation has been exploited will still realize some true profit, although the existence of the surplus may be extremely ephemeral. But the greatest profit will generally be made by the firm that is first with the new combination of factors.

This surplus-over-cost plays an extraordinarily important role in the Schumpeterian theory of economic development. Without this profit there would be no accumulation of wealth, because in a stable society the "non-consumption of profit is not saving in the proper sense, for it is not an encroachment upon the customary standard of life."[27] It is the entrepreneur's action that Schumpeter sees as the only important source of new wealth.

Entrepreneurial Motivation

As THE ENTREPRENEURIAL return is unpredictable, the theory needs some device to account for the available supply of entrepreneurial talent. The argument is perhaps more sociological than economic, and yet it is quite cogent. As Knight expresses it:

> The income of *any particular entrepreneur* will in general tend to be larger: (1) as he himself has ability, and good luck; but (2) perhaps more important as there is in the society a scarcity of self-confidence combined with the power to make effective guarantees

to employees. The abundance or scarcity of mere ability to manage business successfully exerts relatively little influence on profit;
the main thing is the rashness or timidity of entrepreneurs (actual
and potential) as a class in bidding up the prices of productive
services. Entrepreneur income, being residual, is determined by
the demand for these other services, which demand is a matter of
the self-confidence of entrepreneurs as a class, rather than upon a
demand for entrepreneur services in a direct sense. . . . The condition for large profits is a narrowly limited supply of high-grade
ability with a low general level of initiative as well as ability.[28]

For Schumpeter a similar line of reasoning leads him to conclude that the total amount of profit actually realized by an individual entrepreneur may be much greater than necessary to call
forth the entrepreneurial services that are actually operative. He
adds that the possibility of attaining the larger sum may work as
a stronger incentive than would be justified by multiplying the
amount by its coefficient of probability.[29] But he discounts the
importance of the incentive provided by some huge gains by
concluding that it is "quite clear" that the same amount of entrepreneurial service would be forthcoming if entrepreneurial profits
were smaller. Thus he is able to explain why "the entrepreneur
can be relatively so easily deprived of his profit and why the
'salaried' entrepreneur, for example the industrial manager who
frequently plays the entrepreneurial rôle, can generally be adequately remunerated with much less than the full amount of the
profit."[30]

But this point is not clear at all. In fact it portends, in a
manner we shall examine shortly, Schumpeter's most famous error: his prediction that the modern large corporate system could
not survive. At first, Schumpeter's point that large returns are
not a necessary incentive for entreprenurial effort seems correct.
The supply would appear to be determined solely by personal,
psychological forces. Entrepreneurs do appear in government and
in salaried positions, and the temperament for innovation may
turn up in such nonentrepreneurial professions as the clergy or

teaching. But surely these are the exceptions, and, though data would be difficult to obtain, the indications are that entrepreneurial talent tends to concentrate in those industries, professions, and positions providing the greatest potential for very substantial profits.

Entrepreneurial skill may not be allocated in a free economy in the same manner that potatoes or steel are. As Knight indicates, there are sociological and psychological variables in the equation. But the allocational aspects of market theory are not irrelevant, as Schumpeter seems to suggest. There will be *some* entrepreneurs willing to accept a salary, but that fact does not lead to Schumpeter's conclusion. Entrepreneurial skill will still be attracted by the possibility of high gain. In large American corporations one must ordinarily perform a kind of salaried apprenticeship before entrepreneurial rewards become available. But even the most bureaucratically minded person may begin to have original ideas if the possibility of large rewards is apparent.

It is undoubtedly true that entrepreneurs may be satisfied with "less than the full amount of the profit." Clearly, imitators and fast copiers will claim some of the full profit. But this is merely one of the conditions under which most entrepreneurs must operate. It might be added, too, that we can never know what the "full amount of the profit" is, as entrepreneurial profits are peculiarly difficult to separate from other kinds of return. But none of this proves the interesting implication of Schumpeter's statement: that no greater entrepreneurial activity will be forthcoming even if the rewards are allowed to go higher. If this were true, the plight of underdeveloped countries would be sad indeed, because it would imply that their economies already receive as much entrepreneurial skill as they ever will.[31] There is much that we do not yet know about entrepreneurial motivation. One thing, however, is clear. We do not know that allowing entrepreneurs to claim higher rewards will *not* produce more of this service.

New Firms
and Old

SCHUMPETER DID NOT believe that entrepreneurial skills could ever be appropriately utilized within the framework of the large, publicly held corporation. This is undoubtedly why his emphasis was generally on the "new firm" aspect of innovation. Even when he dealt with the subject of innovation within an existing firm, it was in terms of establishing a new enterprise. In a slightly obscure passage, whose importance has perhaps been overlooked, Schumpeter defined *new enterprises* to comprehend innovations by existing firms. This approach has some real advantages, but for Schumpeter it probably reflects his notion that new firms are the critical form of innovation. He simply did not think in terms of ongoing innovations in large, established firms. Schumpeter stated his point as follows:

> If the entrepreneur's strength is not exhausted on one project and yet he continues to carry on the same business, then he proceeds to *new changes which are always new enterprises according to our terminology*, [italics mine] often with means which he draws from his past profits. The process then appears to be different, but its nature is the same.[32]

But even then he went on to say that "new enterprises are mostly founded by new men and the old businesses sink into insignificance. . . . Even if an individual who previously carried on his business by annually repeating his part in the circular flow becomes an entrepreneur, no change takes place in the nature of the proceeding."[33] Thus he persisted in emphasizing the "new business firm" aspect of entrepreneurial activities.

In *The Theory of Economic Development* Schumpeter displays little familiarity with the workings of the modern company with widely diffused share ownership. His constant emphasis on the new establishment as the prime work of the entrepreneur is one aspect of this view, and his belief that entrepreneurs could be had for a salary is another. Unfortunately when the time came

for him to deal explicitly with this largely American development, he shaped his theory—and his prediction—of the corporation to fit his predilections. His misleading treatment of the
modern corporation leads us to a fascinating aspect of the subject
of insider trading.

Schumpeter's Theory of Modern Corporate Capitalism

SCHUMPETER BELIEVED, along with Knight, that without recurrent
entrepreneurial activity, any business would stagnate and collapse.
Time and the dynamic forces of competition wait for no man. It
is never sufficient for survival merely to manage a competitive
business in the purely technical sense. So long as other entrepreneurs exist, Schumpeter's circular flow or Knight's static
economy cannot exist. In the free-market system, one must run
very fast merely to stand still. This point is most carefully ar-
ticulated in Schumpeter's best-known book, *Capitalism, Socialism
and Democracy*.[34] There are three steps in the analysis: the dynamics of competition, the bureaucratization of business, and the
collapse.

Schumpeter's concept of competition is not that of an effete,
trifling game. To him competition is robust, enormous, cataclys-
mic, and revolutionary. Schumpeter's statement of competitive
reality makes the protestations of the Antitrust Division of the
Justice Department by comparison seem pale and futile—or
worse, wrong.

> In capitalist reality as distinguished from its textbook picture, it
> is not [price] competition which counts but the competition from
> the new commodity, the new technology, the new source of sup-
> ply, the new type of organization (the largest-scale unit of con-
> trol for instance)—competition which commands a decisive cost
> or quality advantage and which strikes not at the margins of the
> profits and the outputs of the existing firms but at their founda-
> tions and their very lives. This kind of competition is as much
> more effective than the other as a bombardment is in comparison
> with forcing a door, and so much more important that it becomes

a matter of comparative indifference whether competition in the ordinary sense functions more or less promptly; the powerful lever that in the long run expands output and brings down prices is in any case made of other stuff.

It is hardly necessary to point out that competition of the kind we now have in mind acts not only when in being but also when it is merely an ever-present threat. It disciplines before it attacks. The businessman feels himself to be in a competitive situation even if he is alone in his field or if, though not alone, he holds a position such that investigating government experts fail to see any effective competition between him and any other firms in the same or a neighboring field and in consequence conclude that his talk, under examination, about his competitive sorrows is all make-believe. In many cases, though not in all, this will in the long run enforce behavior very similar to the perfectly competitive pattern.[35]

At this point, however, Schumpeter's unfamiliarity with the large American corporation becomes evident. Here he seems to invent a theory to fit his preconceptions of a large corporation. Schumpeter concluded that progress-destroying bureaucratization was well under way on the American corporate scene.

This social function [entrepreneurship] is already losing importance and is bound to lose it at an accelerating rate in the future even if the economic process itself of which entrepreneurship was the prime mover went on unabated. For, on the one hand, it is much easier now than it has been in the past to do things that lie outside familiar routine—innovation itself is being reduced to routine. Technological progress is increasingly becoming the business of teams of trained specialists who turn out what is required and make it work in predictable ways. The romance of earlier commercial adventure is rapidly wearing away because so many more things can be strictly calculated that had of old to be visualized in a flash of genius.[36]

The effect of the routinization of innovation, Schumpeter believed, would be first to destroy the capitalist entrepreneurs as a class and finally, for lack of a champion, to destroy capitalism.

The perfectly bureaucratized giant industrial unit not only ousts the small or medium-sized firm and "expropriates" its owners, but in the end it also ousts the entrepreneur and expropriates the bourgeoisie as a class which in the process stands to lose not only its income but also what is infinitely more important, its function. The true pacemakers of socialism were not the intellectuals or agitators who preached it but the Vanderbilts, Carnegies and Rockefellers.[37]

The Basis of Schumpeter's Error

THIS CONCLUSION of Schumpeter's is perhaps the most criticized aspect of his entire system. Clearly the modern corporate system shows no sign of faltering. Innovation, inventions, and discovery are proceeding apace. Competitors of all sorts still feel so insecure and threatened that they beg for the government's protective wing. Companies rise and fall; industries disappear and new ones develop; personal fortunes are made, in big business and small, and fortunes are lost. Not much has changed in these regards in our dynamic milieu.

Innovation appears to have become routine, but the difficulty is perhaps only semantic. Clearly, corporations now finance research laboratories that pour out patents. But the development of organized research is surely an entrepreneurial success of the first order. Merely because certain kinds of technological research have been routinized, in no way shows that innovation has ceased. The development of organized research laboratories should stand as one of the major innovations of our era. It is sheer wistfulness to long for the attic inventor to do the same kind of inventing that laboratories full of scientists do better. Schumpeter's "romance of earlier commercial adventure" has in more ways than one been displaced by Du Pont's slogan, "The Romance of Chemistry." A new generation's romance may be only a smell in the nostrils of an older generation.

It is paradoxical that the man with whose name the concept of dynamic competition, the "perennial gale of creative destruction," is most associated should have reached these conclusions.

And yet, in spite of his occasional yearnings for small, family corporations[38] and some very amateurish psychologizing about men's attitudes towards tangible property,[39] Schumpeter left us with some important clues about this "disappearing" entrepreneur.

> We have seen that, normally, the modern businessman, whether entrepreneur or mere managing administrator, is of the executive type. From the logic of his position he acquires something of the psychology of the salaried employee working in a bureaucratic organization. Whether a stockholder or not, his will to fight and to hold on is not and cannot be what it was with the man who knew ownership and its responsibilities in the full-blooded sense of those words. His system of values and his conception of duty undergo a profound change. Mere stockholders of course have ceased to count at all—quite independently of the clipping of their share by a regulating and taxing state. Thus the modern corporation, although the product of the capitalist process, socializes the bourgeois mind; it relentlessly narrows the scope of capitalist motivation; not only that, it will eventually kill its roots.[40]

In this passage, Schumpeter suggests that the very personality type characteristic of entrepreneurs will disappear. And yet his explanation for this phenomenon is unclear and unconvincing. The entrepreneur "from the logic of his position ... acquires something of the psychology of the *salaried* [italics mine] employee. . . ."[41] Presumably "the logic of his position" refers to the bureaucratic atmosphere of a large corporation. But surely this does not infect everyone, as Schumpeter seems to suggest. The problem for the entrepreneur, the nonorganization man in the large company is simply to rise above the levels where bureaucratic organization is a necessity. But Schumpeter was still trying to fit every large corporate employee into his anachronistic view of large companies. Thus, he implies, as he had intimated years earlier, that corporate executives should only be paid a manager's form of compensation, that is, a salary. Schumpeter must have felt uneasy about the implications of this point, for he added the following amazing footnote to the passage quoted above.

Many people will deny this. This is due to the fact that they derive their impression from past history and from the slogans generated by past history during which the institutional change brought about by the big corporation had not yet asserted itself. Also they may think of the scope which corporate business used to give for illegal satisfactions of the capitalist motivation. But that would cut my way: the fact that *personal gain beyond salary and bonus cannot, in corporate business, be reaped by executives except by illegal or semi-illegal practices* [italics mine] shows precisely that the structural idea of the corporation is averse to it.[42]

Schumpeter believed that it was either illegal or immoral to compensate entrepreneurs within large corporations in an economically appropriate fashion. Probably the "illegal or semi-illegal" practices to which Schumpeter refers include trading on inside information. As his book was published in 1942, Schumpeter was probably familiar with Section 16(b) of the Securities and Exchange Act of 1934 and with the attitude towards insider trading of various writers. If this were true, he did not examine the economic premises upon which the charges against the practice were made.

Undoubtedly, if no way to reward the entrepreneur within a corporation exists, he will tend to disappear from the corporate scene. He will *seem*, as Schumpeter suggested, to have had his function routinized and his income turned into the ordinary manager's straight salary. One cannot quarrel with Schumpeter's prediction of what would happen to the large corporate system if the entrepreneur does disappear from the scene. The total bureaucratization of large private enterprises would almost necessarily ensue. The prediction for which Schumpeter has been so frequently criticized was closer to the mark than his critics realized. It follows quite logically from the compensation arrangement that Schumpeter mistakenly saw in the large corporation. His prediction might also follow in time if we abandoned our most effective system for rewarding entrepreneurs in the large corporations.

IX

Inside Information:
The Entrepreneur's Compensation

WE HAVE DEFINED the economic function of the entrepreneur and shown how this function may be critical for the survival of a firm in a competitive milieu. The most important variety of competition is not that of prices or product differentiation, each of which can be handled by pure managers, but rather the dynamic, radical, destructive competition of new products, new methods, or new organizations—all the handiwork of entrepreneurs. The pioneer theorists in this field probably overemphasized the importance of business founders and promoters as entrepreneurs and seriously underestimated the enormous entrepreneurial potential of large, modern corporations. A crucial theoretical difficulty has been finding an appropriate method of compensation for these services. Compensation for entrepreneurial services is not a simple matter. It differs from the interest paid the capitalist for risk-taking and the wage paid to the manager for providing a service that can be priced in advance in the market place. The special relationship between the entrepreneurial function and inside information remains to be examined.

In a system of small corporations and family businesses, entrepreneurial compensation is inextricably bound up with return for the capitalist and managerial functions. About the only time these can be separately computed occurs when a small-business founder sells out soon after establishing a successful venture. This is not analytically dissimilar to an inventor's selling his newly patented invention. The entrepreneurial return is also easy to isolate in the promotion of publicly held corporations. The amount is the value of the shares taken by the promoters at the time of promotion. The phrase *promoters' shares* is probably the only term in our vocabulary distinguishing a specific form of compensation for entrepreneurs.

Special Conditions for Entrepreneurial Compensation

IF LARGE, publicly held corporations are to survive, our theory implies the necessity of their retaining entrepreneurs. Thus, an appropriate form of compensation must be found for the special function these individuals perform. Many peculiarities distinguish innovational activity from the capitalist or the managerial function. Therefore, the method chosen for compensating entrepreneurs must meet a number of special conditions in order to be effective.

Clearly the method chosen must allow the individuals concerned to market the value of their special contributions. This cannot be the same compensation given managers, as some of these will perform entrepreneurial services and others will not. The difficulty, as noted previously, is that innovations may spring from almost any source, whether it be from an officer, director, lawyer, investment banker, or scientist working in a laboratory. Each of these functionaries will receive the normal compensation for the job for which he was hired. Ordinarily he will not be fired for failure to introduce radical innovations. He may enjoy considerable job security and an ever-rising annual income.[1] But what incentive does he have to perform the unusual or to revolutionize a company or an industry? Without some special device, the entrepreneur cannot in any meaningful sense market his service to a large corporation.

The compensation mechanism should not require a large, long-term financial investment by the entrepreneur. There should be a guarantee that anyone may sell entrepreneurial services.[2] Without such a guarantee, we should anticipate that entrepreneurial profits would be gained only by those wealthy enough to found their own businesses and exploit their own innovations. Clearly this condition is critical to the compensation of entrepreneurs in large corporations.

Perhaps the greatest peculiarity of a compensation scheme for entrepreneurs stems from the indeterminacy of results. True innovation cannot be predicted nor its value known before it has been thought of and made effective. True innovation cannot be planned and budgeted in advance. An individual cannot be hired to perform x amount of entrepreneurial service. He can be hired to work for a certain period of time with a title such as *entrepreneur*, but if this were regularly done, some job holders would receive handsome pay while producing no desirable results.

When functions previously considered entrepreneurial, such as inventing, are actually routinized, it is the program for routinization that constitutes the important innovation, not the anticipated discoveries. The prototype modern corporation represented a major entrepreneurial innovation. It superseded earlier, less efficient methods of organizing factors of production and has been widely copied since. But the first use of the modern corporate form was an innovation distinct from subsequent promotions of particular ventures. Subsequent promotions of publicly held companies required entrepreneurial skill, but those utilized a business form previously developed.

Salary and Bonus Modes
of Compensation

NEITHER SALARY nor bonuses meet the conditions we have stated for an appropriate form of compensation for entrepreneurs. There is little need to belabor the point that salary is inadequate for the task.[3] Salary is appropriate only to purchase a known service in the labor market. The parties to the agreement must have a fairly clear understanding of what the job entails and what the skill of the employee is relative to others in the same market.[4] This is equally true of the lowly bookkeeper and the president of the giant company. If it is known what job either is to do in order to maintain or improve the company's earnings, no innovational activity is being contracted for. An entrepreneurial decision may have been made by whoever hired him,[5] but this must be distinguished from the work the employee does.

The bonus would seem at first glance to meet most of the conditions necessary for compensating entrepreneurs. It is paid as an addition to normal salary, and the decision to pay a bonus can often be made after a successful innovation. It is important, however, to distinguish between the simple occasional bonus, not paid as part of a profit-sharing plan, and the more popular bonus plans in which the recipients and their percentage of profits are determined in advance.[6] The *introduction* of a profit-sharing plan may constitute pure entrepreneurial compensation, but only the value of the participation at exactly the time it is granted can constitute entrepreneurial compensation. The *operation* of this or any other profit-sharing plan fails to meet our necessary conditions. The effect of such a plan is to give the recipient a proprietary stake in the business. He is then an investor and a risk-taker, and his annual return will be that of a capitalist, regardless of how it is computed. The initial, discounted value of his participation in the plan may constitute entrepreneurial profits, but subsequent withdrawals will constitute interest on his investment.

The value of a profit-sharing plan, as of the time it is granted, is like the non-profit-sharing bonus, that is, the simple bonus given as a reward for good work on an *ad hoc* basis. If the recipient chooses to invest bonus money in the stock of the company, he has clearly become a capitalist investor. If the company pays the bonus in the form of stock, that relationship is also apparent. But there is no *economic* difference if the company gives the same individual a profit-sharing right whose value is the equivalent of the cash or stock they might have paid.[7]

The bonus scheme for compensating entrepreneurs has numerous drawbacks. Although courts do not easily overturn corporate compensation plans, the threat and the possibility of this happening always exist.[8] Furthermore, current SEC requirements require disclosure of all salaries and bonuses paid directors and certain officers in excess of $30,000, and many individuals do not want to disclose what may seem like astronomical figures. But most important, the bonus has to be decided upon unilaterally by someone other than the recipient. A certain degree of bargaining may occasionally occur, but the entrepreneur will tend to value his contribution to the company higher than others will. Furthermore, the bonus has to be determined on an annual basis, while the effects of any given innovation may be very prolonged. That makes it extremely difficult to assess accurately the value of any particular innovation.

Bonuses are not apt to be forthcoming in years when the company has actually lost money, even though the value of the innovation was substantial and without it the company might have shown greater losses. This suggests the final drawback to the use of profit-sharing bonuses to pay entrepreneurs—the extreme difficulty of determining corporate profits. Standard accounting techniques for determining profits simply cannot isolate the elements reflecting an entrepreneurial contribution. Profit-sharing plans tend to make employees emphasize current paper profits, as opposed to investments maximizing future returns.[9] Any profit-sharing plan, including bonuses, tends to give some incentive for entrepreneurial activity. But their tendency will be to induce the smaller kinds of innovations and cost-saving techniques rather than radical, major, dramatic developments. Unless we want to conclude that entrepreneurial activities are induced equally by a promise of large or small gains, we must look beyond bonuses and profit-sharing plans for entrepreneurial compensation.

Stock

Options

ONE METHOD by which the insider can gain part of the value he has produced is through stock options granted him before the valuable information has been disclosed. As we saw in Chapter VI, by exercising an option after disclosure, at the predisclosure price, the insider can claim precisely the per-share value of the information he has created. If no charge is made for the option, the gain represents pure profit.[10] The stock option appears then to be a desirable device for compensating entrepreneurial talent.

But there are serious drawbacks to using stock options as the sole or even major device for entrepreneurial compensation. Apart from the numerous conditions and restrictions on the use of stock options in the common law[11] and the Internal Revenue Code,[12] options must be granted prior to the innovation to serve the purpose at hand. If they are granted after the information is known but before disclosure, the economic effect is precisely that of a bonus equal to the anticipated gain, and all the valuation problems inherent in the bonus scheme are again present. But if the option is granted before the innovation, there is no way of knowing whether the potential gain is appropriate or not, because it will vary with the number of shares covered. This is not to say that such options will not induce any entrepreneurial activity. Manifestly, any proprietary interest, existing or contingent, will have some incentive effect. But the incentive is precisely the same as that to be gained from share ownership of the number of shares covered by the option, as the incentive will be commensurate with the absolute gain that can be realized and not with the potential percentage gain. Stock-option plans are more likely to provide a proper incentive for managers than for entrepreneurs.

The belief that stock options are not widely used for entrepreneurial compensation is difficult to substantiate, because from 1950 until 1964 there were very substantial tax advantages in the so-called restricted stock options. Apart from tax considerations, however, options are quite expensive for the corporation issuing them. The true cost to a corporation granting an option is precisely the same as the cost of an identical option purchased in a competitive call market. Indeed, corporations are free to cover their own option grants by purchasing calls on their own stock. In effect this may be happening when corporations buy their own shares in the market to use for stock options.[13] We know that generally the cost of a call "at the market" for six months and ten days is approximately 10 percent of the current market price of the shares.[14] But corporate stock options are usually granted for periods of up to five years, and we should anticipate the price of the longer option to be considerably more than the price of a six-month call; it may even approach the price of the underlying share.[15]

Stock options are inefficient devices for exploiting information because they are generally not mobile or liquid assets. To gain any tax advantage, they must be nontransferable, and many companies require the executive to hold the stock for a certain period of time after exercise.[16] Stock options are also not flexible devices for insiders' quick use. Shareholders usually ratify a stock-option plan before it becomes effective, and this can be very time-consuming. Discretion may be given in advance to directors or a salary committee to issue options pursuant to the plan. But even this requires some assessment in advance of the new development as to who will be entitled to what. Stock options are probably used on occasion to exploit inside information, but the device is too cumbersome and too expensive to be used frequently for that purpose.

Insider Trading

WITH EITHER bonuses or stock options, the employee is limited to a specific reward no matter how great his innovation. In the case of the options, the limit is posed by the number of shares optioned. The value of his contribution may far exceed the gain on these shares. There is no such limitation on the effectiveness of insider trading as compensation. As we have seen, even if the individual is unable to buy all the shares necessary to raise their price by the amount indicated by the value of his information, he may be able to bank his information and draw on it at a later time in the form of information about other shares.

Insider trading meets all the conditions for appropriately compensating entrepreneurs. It readily allows corporate entrepreneurs to market their innovations. As we have seen, this is not a direct marketing of the idea but rather a "sale" of information about an innovation. Thus, although we do not allow entrepreneurs a direct proprietary interest in their ideas, we can allow recovery for their ideas by permitting them to exploit information about the existence of the ideas in a market primarily based on information. In the next chapter we shall examine the reasons for believing that this market allocates appropriate returns to the particular individuals who have in fact performed an entrepreneurial function.

In order to exploit information, it is not essential that an individual hold any particular job or that he already have or make a large investment in the company. Only access to the new information and not status, position, or wealth will determine when an individual may be compensated by this method. He will generally have to make some investment of funds in order to exploit the information, even though the period of investment may be very short. However, assuming his willingness to disclose his information to someone else, credit should be available for this purpose, and he may at this point be introduced to financiers and bankers who will assist him in exploiting valuable information. If he already has his own funds, however, he will not have to make any disclosure to others.

There are strong similarities between the more traditional markets for entrepreneurial services and the market for inside information. Indeed an examination of these similarities should leave little doubt that the information market is merely a variant of the underlying market for entrepreneurial service. Schumpeter emphasized that the traditional entrepreneur must claim his remuneration before the forces of competition exercise their inexorable tendency to wipe out any surplus-over-costs. Now we may note the striking parallel between this point and one already examined in connection with the economics of information. As soon as information is transmitted by any of the methods described in Chapter V, it begins to lose its value. Ultimately, as Knight has pointed out, when it "becomes common property it is like any other superabundant element in production, a free good...." Thus, the modern corporate employee-entrepreneur, like his traditional counterpart, must move fast to claim the benefits of his innovation. Whether the competition be from copyists flooding into a new field or from other stock buyers pushing up the price, the entrepreneur ordinarily can cash in his special chips only if he moves quickly.

The traditional capitalist risks funds with the hope of substantial gain. Frequently this gain results because an entrepreneur has brought capital, management, and other resources together in a profitable fashion. The capitalist gains from the new combination, although, as Schumpeter points out, the nature of his return as interest is not basically changed by virtue of the fact that his investment has paid off.

When we compare the traditional relationship between the capitalist and the entrepreneur with the relationship between the inside trader and the long-term investor, another striking parallel becomes apparent. The investor gains as a result of the creation of good news, and this is reflected in the price of his shares. He participates in the new value created by an insider, just as the capitalist does vis-à-vis the traditional entrepreneur. The investor's return, unlike that of the insider who trades on his information, is compensation for the use of his funds and for his assumption of risk. The difference now is that the entrepreneur remains an employee of the company, where, hopefully, he will again produce a valuable innovation. One of the great advantages of the corporate form is that it allows a permanent employee to market the value of his entrepreneurial service alone. Because he need not have a proprietary interest in other property, he does not have to sell a separate asset in order to realize his profit.

Even if the insider simply buys shares and does not realize short-term gains by trading, he is no less like the traditional entrepreneur. The gain in the share value is his whether he realizes it immediately by a sale or holds it in the form of appreciated shares. In the latter case, he has merely opted to invest his insider profits as a capital investment. His function at that point changes, but this does not alter his prior status. He is then more like the inventor who establishes his own business in order to exploit his patent. He has changed roles, but neither of the functions he performs is changed in the process.

A major fallacy deriving from a failure to distinguish different functions is that the corporate insider should not be given any advantage over other investors in the corporation. This argument assumes that only the capitalist's kind of return is appropriate for anyone owning shares. It requires, of course, that funds already have been invested. This in turn means that funds must have been saved, borrowed, or inherited. Clearly an entrepreneur cannot guarantee his ability to participate in this way, nor is there any reason that we should demand that he combine the functions of entrepreneur and capitalist. And even if he did have sufficient funds to have made a prior investment, the egalitarian argument allows no special compensation for his entrepreneurial skill. It merely guarantees that the insider will have the same return on investment that other capitalists, who have contributed no valuable innovation, regularly enjoy as a result of the insider's successful activities. The insider is thus forced to share with all other shareholders the profit that otherwise he alone could have gained.[17]

A similar false notion is that no insider should receive compensation higher than the wage or salary expressly contracted for. This point would be well taken, as Knight has indicated, if entrepreneurial results were knowable and predictable. Compensation for this service would simply become a wage, with the same economic significance as that received by managers, technicians, and other suppliers of services in competitive markets. But no longer does the idea of a pure wage for entrepreneurs commend itself to our sense of logic. The major innovations in commercial and industrial history have not come from purely salaried employees.

Characteristics of the Entrepreneur

THE ULTIMATE DIFFICULTY in compensating the entrepreneur in large corporations may be a psychological one. He will tend to value his own potential for extraordinary gain at a higher figure than others would normally pay in advance. As Knight suggested, self-confidence is the hallmark of the entrepreneur, and his gain will be most spectacular when this quality is least available in others. He will probably not be a good organization man, satisfied with a reasonable salary and retirement benefits. We should anticipate that as business executives begin to rise above the level of the pure managers or technocrats or corporate bureaucrats, the form in which they receive their income will also begin to change. In fact it may on occasion be the sole mark of the rise to a new category. More and more of their income should come in the form of profits from trading in corporate shares to exploit information they have generated. As we know almost nothing about these practices, a vast amount of empirical research needs to be done in this area.[18]

There are peculiarities other than compensation that may help identify, describe, and understand the modern American entrepreneur. Berle and Means in *The Modern Corporation and Private Property* noted a phenomenon popularized under the rubric "separation of ownership and control." As applied to the large publicly held corporation, the term implied that those who ran the company, controlled its affairs, and charted its destiny had ceased to be the same individuals who owned the property. Berle and Means' work was replete with statistics showing that the shareholdings of directors of some of the largest corporations were very frequently meager or nonexistent.[19] The authors pointed to this fact as evidence that the modern corporation does not function consistently with the principles of traditional economics. Management, Berle and Means protested, did not have a claim to legitimacy, which existed when a family or an individual owned a controlling block of shares.[20]

We can now see that there is nothing peculiar about the phenomenon described at all. If the key executives of large corporations are also the principal performers of the entrepreneurial function, we should not necessarily anticipate that they would be large shareholders. Share trading, not share holding, will be the hallmark of the entrepreneur. This does not preclude the existence of older-style family businesses or those in which an individual doubles as entrepreneur and capitalist. But it should not be surprising to find a higher degree of specialization of these functions in large corporations. We should anticipate that key individuals in large corporations, those responsible for the progress and development of a business, would earn relatively more of their wealth by trading in corporate securities than by holding large blocks of shares. The phenomenon Berle and Means described does not have the significance usually ascribed to it. If share-trading offers more inducement to profitable operation than shareholding, we should not complain because management has substituted one for the other. The absence of a substantial, permanent ownership interest by corporate executives may be a clear indication that the modern corporate system is functioning properly.

Relation Between Corporate Size and Entrepreneurship

IN ONE RESPECT the theory advanced in this chapter coincides with Berle's and Schumpeter's views on the nature of top management in large corporations. As a corporation grows in absolute size and number of shareholders, the effect of a given development on share price becomes less and less, in absolute terms. For example, assume that an oil company with one million shares outstanding and total assets of $50 million discovers an oil pool worth five million dollars. This should cause the price of its shares to rise from 50 to approximately 55. The same discovery by a company with assets of $1 billion and twenty million shares outstanding might be so inconsequential as to have no effect whatever on the stock price. Theoretically, each share should rise by one quarter of a point, but, as we saw earlier, other market forces may easily counteract a quarter-point gain, whereas the certainty of realizing profits from a five-point gain is quite high.

If, as we have assumed, entrepreneurs want large gains and small risks, we should anticipate the true entrepreneurial personality to be more attracted to smaller corporations. There the greatest opportunities exist to make the proverbial killing. There is no reason to believe that some entrepreneurial skill and talent will not be found in large companies, but the competitive advantage lies with smaller ones. The smaller corporations we are referring to, however, may still be large enough to be listed on the New York Stock Exchange, and they must never be so small that their shares are not publicly traded. Otherwise the competitive advantage of publicly held corporations over close corporations in securing entrepreneurial talent would be lost.

If in fact small and medium-sized publicly held companies have the advantage noted over corporate giants, the implications are far-reaching. This could explain, for instance, why there is constant shifting among the positions of the top five hundred corporations in America.[21] It would further suggest that much of the concern with corporate size shown by writers and the Antitrust Division of the Department of Justice has been misplaced. For with size comes the relative inability to attract the highest quality of entrepreneurial, as opposed to managerial, skill. Small companies will naturally attract the individuals whose performance will make them grow.

To counteract this tendency and to induce potential entrepreneurs to remain with them, large companies would be expected to offer larger salaries and more attractive retirement plans than smaller companies. This may account for the correlation that has been found between salaries and size of companies.[22] The higher salary figures represent a cost to larger companies that smaller ones will not have to bear. Therefore, unless there are compensating economies of scale, the larger company is still at a competitive disadvantage compared to smaller ones.

There are reasons other than size why entrepreneurial skills may not be attracted to certain corporations. There are business corporations to which the very concept of the entrepreneur has no application. We have seen the importance of innovation for effective competition. But one critical aspect of the modern scheme of public-utility regulation is protection from competition. In exchange for this privilege, firms have their rates regulated. Their share prices tend to be stable, and there is little opportunity for quick trading gains. Not only is price competition impossible, but the more important creative destruction made famous by Schumpeter is also discouraged by rate regulation. Since a maximum rate of return on investment is prescribed, there is little chance for capturing in the stock market the actual value of great innovations. No rate regulation is perfect, however, and the regulatory scheme will ordinarily allow increased earnings—perhaps hidden—through small, cost-saving innovations. But the great inventive and dynamic developments associated with entrepreneurial success will rarely occur in firms that belong to efficiently regulated industries.[23]

We should therefore anticipate finding different personalities among the top executives of large and small companies and among those in regulated and nonregulated companies. The larger the company or the more regulated it is, the less likely are we to find the type of businessman commonly called a promoter, or an operator. The individual trying to boost himself socially and economically by his own bootstraps will find more opportunity to get rich quick in smaller concerns.

There is some empirical evidence that this is true. Economists have noted a higher incidence of certain minority-group members among the discernible entrepreneurial class.[24] A recent study indicates a small incidence of Jewish and Negro executives in regulated, as opposed to nonregulated, industries.[25] It is quite possible that this is true in larger, as opposed to smaller, corporations as well. But this need not indicate a higher incidence of anti-Semitism or racial prejudice in those companies.[26] We may be witnessing a subtle self-selection process, or, more accurately, a self-exclusion process dictated more by economic circumstances than has generally been recognized.

X

Objections to Information As Compensation

IT HAS BEEN suggested that insider trading increases the possibility of manipulation of stock prices.[1] To discuss this contention intelligently we must recognize that this manipulation may occur in several different ways. The first form of manipulation is the publication of untrue good or bad news with the intention that others in the stock market rely upon the statement. The second form of manipulation is the intentional production of bad news, again with the intention that it be relied upon in the stock market. The opposite of this, the intentional production of good news, is of course what corporate insiders are supposed to do, and it cannot be termed manipulative. The third form of manipulation is delaying the disclosure of either good or bad news (though honestly produced) for the purpose of allowing insiders more time to conduct profitable trading. A fourth form of manipulation, usually associated with pre-1934 stock-pool operations, is the buying and selling of stocks in order to create an artificial market price and an appearance of market activity.[2]

Fraudulent
Manipulation

THE FIRST TYPE of manipulation, the publication of untrue statements meant to be relied upon in the market, usually contains all the technical elements of common-law fraud.[3] This does not mean that it is desirable to leave the detection and policing of every case of fraud to individual shareholders showing damage. There will be clear economic savings in administrative regulation of this problem. Criminal sanctions also seem appropriate, and the experience in New York State has proved that vigorous enforcement of criminal sanctions can be effective in dealing with fraudulent manipulation. The attorney general of New York, operating under the simplest and shortest securities law in the country, regularly vies with the SEC, operating under the most complex and detailed system, for the prosecution of fraudulent stock manipulators. There is no indication that fraudulent manipulation presents such peculiar problems of policing that radical devices are necessary to accomplish the desired end. The appropriate criminal laws will be necessary in any event to deal with non-insiders who engage in fraudulent stock practices.

If insiders could in fact be prevented from trading in their company's shares or in information about their company, they would have no incentive to manipulate stock prices for trading purposes. But we cannot conclude from this that insider trading should never be allowed. For reasons that we shall examine in the next chapter, the effective policing of insider trading is extremely difficult, if not impossible. Therefore, some incentive to manipulation might always remain. But more important, outlawing all insider trading to prevent fraud is a shotgun approach to the problem. The danger is that most of the pellets will hit the wrong targets. And, to carry the ballistic simile further, this method may also be likened to using a cannon to kill a flea.

Entrepreneurs interested in a continuing flow of information on which to trade will have little incentive to manipulate stock prices. Insiders who generate false information in effect inflate their own currency. If such occurrences ever become known (and certainly discovery by the market is only a matter of time), the value of all information from the same source, the true and the untrue, will be discounted in the marketplace. That is, as soon as it is learned that insiders have fraudulently manipulated the stock of a particular company, all subsequent disclosures from that source will be treated with a certain degree of suspicion. True information normally worth ten points may only result in an eight-point rise upon first disclosure. The principal loser will be the insider who is compensated by short-term trading.

Most long-term investors will not be injured at all, as the market will ultimately reflect the full value of the true story. The entrepreneurs and some uninformed short-term speculators will lose the amount of the discount. When the first type of manipulation is viewed in this perspective, it seems doubtful that lying about corporate affairs for short-term trading purposes will be a popular pastime with many corporate executives. When it is further realized that sophisticated devices for detection of fraud, as well as suitable sanctions, are available to deal with this problem, its importance as an objection to insider trading almost vanishes.

It should at least be noted that insider trading may perform a valuable function that is the exact opposite of manipulation. If, for any reason, the current market price of a company's stock is known to be incorrect in terms of all available information, insiders will have an incentive to correct the market price of the stock. In time the truth will out,[4] and the price will change accordingly, whether insiders trade or not. Because this is so, anyone with information known to be correct will make money by stock-market transactions that force the price in the correct direction—in effect, by arbitrage. Given the importance of maintaining correct values on corporate securities,[5] we should perhaps be more concerned about rules preventing insiders from trading than with those raising some small possibility of artificial manipulation of prices.

The Intentional Creation
of Bad News

THE SECOND FORM of manipulation that might constitute an objection to insider trading is that insiders may intentionally create bad news in order to make stock-market profits. The objection basically is that insiders can make as much money trading on bad news as on good news and that therefore they will have as great an incentive to create bad news. But even though as much money can be made in the stock market from a specific bit of bad news as from good, there is vastly more incentive for insiders to produce good news than bad.

Most individuals in a position to make money from inside information will want to maintain that position and improve their future claims on valuable information. Nothing will succeed in that endeavor as much as the continued production of good news. There is no limit to the amount of good news the market can absorb, while bad news carries sharp constraints on its continued production. If too much bad news is created, the firm itself must inevitably fail and all trading cease. And even before that point is reached, other market forces operate to discipline creators of bad news. As the price of a corporation's shares drops relatively low, either an internal shakeup in management or a successful raid by an outsider is more likely to occur.[6] The preference for good news over bad has a very real economic basis.

There are also social and psychological pressures to produce good news rather than bad. Success is unquestionably part of the ethos of corporate executives, and bad news will be greeted with lowered esteem by the insider's colleagues, regardless of how much money is thereby made in the stock market. Success stories are repeated, not tales of failure. So while it is true that as much money can be made selling short as buying long, there can be little incentive for the intentional creation of bad news. Almost all of the vector forces operating on corporate insiders push in the direction of good news. The fact that money can be made on bad news is a neutral factor as far as incentive is concerned.

Delay in Disclosures

DELAYING DISCLOSURES to allow fuller exploitation of the value of the information may be the most serious form of manipulation. It is extremely difficult to find empirical proof that such practices do or do not occur. One aspect of the story of Texas Gulf Sulphur's find in Timmins, Ontario, illustrates the difficulty. The SEC implied in its complaint that the insiders delayed disclosure in order to have more time to exploit their information. On the face of it there is nothing implausible in this supposition. If publicity had been given the discovery in November, 1963, it is quite possible that none of the insiders' transactions between that date and April 16, 1964, would have occurred. But there is an equally plausible alternative explanation of the delay, which in no way implicates the insiders. As the corporation stated in its motion to dismiss the SEC's complaint against it,[7] the delay was necessary to gain mineral rights on adjacent properties and to discover the true extent of the ore vein. Certainly this was in the interest of all shareholders. Further, the delay avoided the possibility of misleading shareholders if the vein had not proved as large as it did.

For certain kinds of information little or no delay in disclosure is feasible. The date of dividend declarations is established without reference to the speed with which the information may be exploited in the market. Government contracts, changes in market conditions, and international developments will not normally be under the control of insiders for purposes of timing disclosure. Merger negotiations normally will be under their control, while announcements of proxy fights and many tender-bids will not.

But assuming that insiders can time disclosures in order to increase their own exploitation of information, it is still questionable whether the practice is objectionable. The answer to this turns on the acceptance or rejection of the general argument that entrepreneurs in large corporations should be compensated with information. If we accept the general argument, it follows that the timing of disclosure may be necessary in many cases to allow appropriate exploitation of the information. Clearly, as would have been true for Texas Gulf Sulphur, premature announcements can effectively prevent insiders from realizing more than a fraction of the value inherent in news. Devices for "banking" information may not function at all, because the value of the information may have been substantially exploited before it can be exchanged.

It is difficult to be specific about the relationship between the speed with which insiders can move in the case of different kinds of information and the speed they must employ to gain a substantial return. Manifestly, the faster they buy and cause the price to increase, the shorter becomes the period they will want to delay disclosure. Here again we find a surprising identity between the interests of insiders and outside shareholders. Assuming that we allow insider trading, it will be in the interest of both parties to have it done as quickly as possible. Thus, with free and open insider trading, we may find shorter delays in disclosure of new developments than we would if the practice were ineffectively or partially policed. The matter will turn largely on the speed with which different kinds of information may be exploited, but it is not inconceivable that the shortest average periods for disclosure will occur under a rule of completely free insider trading.

Stock
Pools

THE FINAL FORM of manipulation that might be associated with insider trading involves the artificial stimulation of the market in order to raise or lower the price of shares or merely to indicate heavy trading activity. This scheme is most commonly associated with the heyday of the stock pool in the 1920's. The Congressional Hearings on Stock Exchange Practices are replete with many instances of this occurrence,[8] and several provisions of the Act are specifically aimed at outlawing pools.[9] This form of manipulation seems comparable to the use of untrue statements. The untruths in this instance are aimed at stock traders who buy and sell on so-called *technical* factors rather than *fundamental* factors. The misleading assertion by the pool is that there was heavy buying in the shares, rather than a false claim that the company has discovered gold.

But a careful reading of the description of pool operations in the 1933 hearings reveals an unusual fact. The formation of many pools was associated with the actual occurrence of important developments in the corporation.[10] Furthermore, most of these pools gradually disseminated true information about the company. This strongly suggests that the pool, that alleged archvillain of the pre-1933 stock market, was an efficient device for exploiting information.[11] Furthermore, manipulation geared to outsiders' reliance on technical factors would appear to be highly risky. It is not surprising that there were few reported cases of manipulation being used successfully for fraudulent purposes.[12]

Profits from
Bad News

ANOTHER MAJOR CATEGORY of objections to insider trading is that the particular individuals trading are not the ones entitled to the information. This objection may take several different forms. The first is that insiders regularly profit from bad news as well as good. That is, even if they have not intentionally produced bad news in order to sell short, bad news does occur, and to allow the insider to capitalize on it is inequitable.[13] It is not an appropriate response, as it was when we were concerned with manipulation, to say that the insider has no incentive to produce bad news. Bad news may result from reasons far removed from the insider's intent. Nationalization of foreign properties, bad weather, a change in political administration, an accidental fire or explosion, or an important development by a competitor, all may be exploited by insiders.

This argument does not have to be limited to bad news. We can deal at the same time with the argument that the insider exploiting valuable information is not necessarily responsible for a great deal of the good news to which he has access. This is not to say that certain individuals are stealing information that would not come to them in the ordinary course of business; that problem will be dealt with in the next chapter. Rather, the argument is that it is unfair to allow the use of inside information by insiders who have not performed entrepreneurial services for the corporation.

The Nature of Competition
for Entrepreneurs

To ANSWER these very important contentions, we must refine our concept of entrepreneurial compensation. Heretofore we have assumed that the modern corporate innovator would exploit good news that he himself created. We have also assumed that the amount insiders could realize in the stock market because of their prior knowledge was a not-inappropriate return for innovational activity. This justification for insider trading would be sufficient if the modern, corporate insider-entrepreneur were the precise counterpart of the more traditional entrepreneur. But the older, simpler figure, classically illustrated by the corporate founder or promoter, could not make money on bad news. The founder of a business that promptly failed or the promoter of a corporation that never came into existence did not make any money functioning as an entrepreneur. This is consistent with Frank Knight's position that, on balance, America has received all of its entrepreneurial services free.[14] For the vast bulk of this service, there was simply no way to receive compensation.

With the advent of the large, publicly held corporation, however, the market for entrepreneurial services could be organized more efficiently. Now entrepreneurial services could be hired in the marketplace and not merely volunteered by corporate founders or promoters. By allowing the function of the entrepreneur to be performed by individuals exercising other jobs within the corporate structure, it became possible to hire entrepreneurial services, though valuable innovations might or might not be produced. The analogy of the hired research scientist who discovers nothing is apposite.

In the corporation individuals will be hired to perform a variety of functions at a market rate of return. Within fairly wide limits the individual will receive his compensation under the contract whether he performs his job well or not, though, if he does the job badly, he will ordinarily not be rehired when the contract expires. Advancement and security in large organizations normally do not require that the employee also be an entrepreneur. Therefore, the additional compensation provided by insider trading encourages this added activity, which also benefits the corporation.

But good or bad news can occur fortuitously or for reasons extraneous to the operation of the corporation. Insider trading on this information would not appear to benefit the corporation. Consideration of the market for entrepreneurial services, however, leads us to the opposite conclusion. Competition for entrepreneurs does not take the usual form of offering a specific amount of money. Rather, entrepreneurs will be attracted to those positions offering the greatest opportunity for them to make large, indefinite gains. These may result from good news or bad, intentionally or unintentionally created.

There will be no important loss to shareholders if insiders do trade on this news, and it will be possible, in an inexpensive way, to give entrepreneurs within the corporation a greater opportunity for gain. Because the cost to the corporation for this form of compensation is so low, competition among corporations for entrepreneurs would quickly force all of them to allow their insider-entrepreneurs to trade in bad news as well as good. And the corporate form of business organization, with publicly traded shares, would enjoy a competitive advantage in securing entrepreneurial services over noncorporate forms, where profits from bad news are impossible.

On the other hand, some competitive advantages lie with the smaller type of enterprise. The owner of a business or one who owns all the stock of a corporation *a fortiori* gains the full value of any developments for which he is responsible. But the modern corporate insider, as we saw in Chapter V, is rarely in a position to gain the full value of any news. Thus it is doubtful, even with the various exchange devices analyzed in Chapter V, that insiders in large corporations ever gain the full value of their own contributions. Trading on fortuitous or extraneous good news compensates to some extent for this loss.

Profiting by
Wrong Persons

THE LAST FORM of the "person-is-not-entitled" objection to insider trading is that individuals making insider profits are frequently far removed from a time or place or job in which they could perform any entrepreneurial service for the company. It is, however, extremely difficult to identify individuals performing the entrepreneurial function or to know the precise moment at which an individual performs an entrepreneurial act. The self-same act may constitute an entrepreneurial service in one company and a management function in another. Knight emphasized that the very selection of the right individuals to carry out management functions is a critical entrepreneurial job.[15] But this same activity in certain companies may constitute nothing more than a ritual or formality not requiring any fundamental exercise of discretion.

Directors, large shareholders, executives, lawyers, investment bankers, or many other individuals may, at one time or another, perform an entrepreneurial function. Most of the time, however, they will not be innovating. And for any particular development, many individuals may have made contributions. Who, among the lawyers, bankers, and executives involved, can be given full credit or the correct portions of credit for conceiving the desirability of a merger, searching out the most likely firm, and effectuating the desired plan? An entrepreneurial function has been performed, and the individuals involved will have some claim against the subsequent flow of inside information. But any attempt by an outsider to correlate the contribution and the reward on a one-for-one basis will probably fail. The contribution of an individual may be so subtle—so much a result simply of his being there—and yet so critical that we must be very cautious in concluding that no reward is deserved.

A variant of this objection is that some individuals, perhaps long retired from active participation in corporate affairs, still continue to receive the benefits of inside information. But this should occasion no surprise. In Chapter V we saw that insiders often find it desirable to utilize various information-exchange devices. These may also be used to postpone the time for using other information. Individuals may thus receive information later in exchange for their own earlier production that they could not or did not market directly. Many individuals, both for financial and tax reasons, will find it desirable to spread the return of information over as long a period as possible.

Individuals may also use information as gifts or payments to individuals not connected with the corporation. The most obvious example of this is the individual who gives information to his wife or children so that they may trade in the company's shares.[16] But their profits must be imputed to the insider himself. It is immaterial to an outside observer that an individual may choose to take his gain in the form of additional wealth for his children rather than for himself, or that he may choose to make a gift of it to anyone.

Information is not a free good, and we should not assume, without more information than we now possess, that its distribution is generally capricious, arbitrary, random, or uncontrolled. Rational, self-serving individuals will not blithely and willingly allow information of tremendous value to pass freely to individuals who have no valid claim upon it. The safer assumption is that individuals with the power to control the flow of valuable information do so rationally and allocate it in a market-like system of exchange, as explained in Chapter V. The insider-entrepreneur has more incentive than anyone else to prevent arbitrary payoffs, for he can lose more than anyone else. To find inside information in the hands of individuals with no apparent relationship to the company in question may demonstrate the effectiveness of the market in inside information rather than its ineffectiveness. But this private distribution system is not perfect, and there are leaks in the flow of valuable information. Internal policing of information is discussed in the next chapter.

XI

*The Problems of Public
and Private Policing*

INFORMATION IS one of the most easily transmitted of all commodities. To prevent its rapid dissemination while it has exchange value is extremely difficult. Any attempt to regulate or police a market in information confronts two obstacles. The first is the extremely difficult one of knowing which transactions to prevent. The second is the actual job of policing once the undesired transactions are identified.

Outsiders with Valuable Information

THROUGHOUT THIS WORK we have assumed that the critics of insider trading wish to prevent the exploitation of information that is not equally available to all traders in the market. As indicated in Chapter IV, this involves specific bits of undisclosed information about change and not information that may be derived or deduced from published data. This distinction, though important for the policing of insider trading, is extremely difficult to maintain in practice. From published figures on earnings and other financial data, an experienced securities analyst can often predict dividend increases, stock splits, and other financial events with a very high degree of accuracy. He may forecast these events before insiders, perhaps with no higher degree of confidence, know the same thing.

Other kinds of outside specialists will also trade in the stock market with information deduced from generally available sources. The management consultant who follows personnel changes, the industry specialist who knows the effects of government policies, or the lawyer who can predict the financial implications of changes in tax laws may trade with great confidence but without any undisclosed information. Furthermore, the services of many of these outside specialists are available to anyone willing to pay for them. Their price may be high, but no charge of unfairness can be leveled against trading based on this marketed advice. Another outside specialist is the business competitor. Executives of corporations in the same industry often recognize the impact of industrial changes on firms other than their own. New developments within one company may have a predictable effect on the profits of another company. The ensuing trading can be done with the same degree of reliability that characterizes the insider using true inside information.

Competitors are not the only ones who originate information before it is known to the insiders in the company whose shares are bought. A corporate executive changing his company's source of supply may cause a downturn in one company's shares and an increase in another's. These changes may be known to him before they are known to executives of either of the other companies. Government officials know the identity of a successful bidder before the various bidding companies have received the information. And myriad government officials other than contracting officers are in comparable positions. The internal revenue or antitrust lawyers who pass on mergers, the commissioners passing on rate changes, and the regulators allocating communications channels or commercial air routes are just a few of the government functionaries privy to inside information.

Another outsider who generates and exploits valuable information is the so-called corporate raider. Whether he functions through a proxy fight, a tender-bid, or a merger offer,[1] he knows his own intentions before they are known to the corporate insiders. His intention is frequently the important piece of undisclosed information,[2] but its disclosure would in many cases prevent his operation by making it too expensive. In other cases it may be more accurate to say that the raider's undisclosed information is merely his belief that he can manage the corporation better than the incumbent managers. In a proxy fight he will state this explicitly in an effort to convince other shareholders to believe him and vote for him. But if his strategy involves buying up shares as a prelude to a proxy fight or a merger, he will remain as silent as possible about his intentions.

A related situation involves purchases made by the corporation itself. If full disclosure were made of a corporation's intention to buy a certain number of shares, the stock price would immediately jump almost to the level indicated by the value of this news. All shares would have to be bought at this new market price, and the cost to the corporation for the same number of shares might be considerably greater than without disclosure.[3] But the action of the corporation buying without disclosure is the same—from shareholders' or traders' points of view—as an insider's buying shares when he knows undisclosed news.

The Arbitrary Approach
to Enforcement

THIS SHORT DISCUSSION of outsiders who may trade on reliable yet generally unknown information suggests the difficulties of identifying transactions to be proscribed. Yet, whatever arguments can be made for outlawing insider trading apply at least as strongly to these cases. Why then have the critics of "unfair" trading been almost exclusively concerned with insiders? One answer might be that the volume of trading before disclosure is greater in the case of insiders than outsiders. But we have no real evidence that this is true, and, in any event, it would still be only a partial answer because it acknowledges some "unfair" outsider trading.

Another answer has historical roots. When the first draft of the present Securities Exchange Act of 1934 was presented to Congress, Section 16 proscribed not only short-swing profits by insiders but disclosure to others and profiting by anyone to whom disclosure was made. Congress refused this broad coverage on the grounds that enforcement of such a provision was not feasible.[4] Attention was thus focused on the so-called *statutory insiders*—officers, directors, and beneficial holders of 10 per cent of an equity issue.

This definitional approach is heavy-handed and frequently arbitrary in its reach. But that merely puts it on a par with Section 16(b), described by one of its authors as a "crude rule of thumb."[5] This Section makes insiders named in Section 16(a) liable to the corporation for any profits made from buying and selling their company's securities within any six-month period. We should notice just how arbitrary this provision can be in operation. First, the six-month duration bears little relation to anything connected with insider trading. Obviously the capital-gains holding-period provision of the Internal Revenue Code offers considerable inducement to hold for that period. At some point before six months have elapsed, the influence of Section 16(b) is probably superfluous.

Even more damaging to insiders is the proscription of "any" profits from short-term trading. It makes no difference that the stocks appreciated for reasons the insider knew nothing about or that he may have been forced to sell for reasons totally unrelated to inside information. There are additional inequities in the operation of Section 16 as well.[6] Yet, we may still have some sympathy for this approach. It is dictated by the need to simplify enforcement and administration in what would otherwise be a phenomenally complex area.[7] It is no wonder that a way out was found in arbitrary rules of thumb. And it is no less wonder that the SEC, which today is trying to make its Rule 10b–5 into a general prohibition of insider trading, has not promulgated any rules or guidelines as to how this can be done.

Section 16 has probably not been very effective in securing its stated end. Over thirty years of litigation, hearings, and SEC regulation leave no doubt that the critics of insider trading are not satisfied. The whole tenor of recent legal developments, such as *Blau* v. *Lehman* and the *Texas Gulf Sulphur* case, indicates that the SEC feels that there is much ground left uncovered. The reasons are not hard to find.

Enforcement Techniques

As A FIRST step, the reporting requirements of Section 16(a), coupled with simple liability, seem like a step in the right direction. Criminal sanctions could be used to strengthen the effectiveness of enforcement. But if insiders find it necessary or profitable enough to do so, it is not difficult to escape detection. Shares held in street names, accounts of relatives and friends, secret accounts of all sorts, foreign brokers and bank accounts, and a host of other devices can make the job of discovering illicit inside trading extremely costly. Even the SEC, which has quite efficient discovery devices at its command, still relies largely on newspaper accounts of specific events to know when to begin a search. But there is no way of evaluating the degree of success they enjoy. As most corporate events do not receive the publicity of the Texas Gulf episode, the percentage of illicit transactions actually uncovered by police-detection methods could be very low.

But no one likes to commit even a quasi-criminal act, like a violation of Section 16(b), if he can accomplish the same end in legal fashion. Section 16(b) is strictly limited to trades in the shares of the insider's company. Other transactions and information trades are outside the scope of the Section. Some attempt might be made to broaden reporting requirements, but a reporting requirement is logical only in connection with trading in the shares of an insider's own company. Even if we required every insider of any company to report all his stock transactions—a gargantuan solution and not a very palatable one—it would still be impossible to distinguish profitable transactions properly entered into from those based on a trade of inside information. If these individuals are allowed to trade in any shares, it will be almost impossible to know when they are aided by inside information.[3]

These are the same individuals whose money is managed in discretionary accounts and whose names appear high on priority lists. They are the individuals named to the boards of directors of other corporations. They regularly follow the advice of their corporation's investment banker on what shares to buy. They may often be partners or limited partners in banking houses. Furthermore, these same executives will generally not hesitate to trade in the shares of other firms in their industry or of supplier or customer firms, even though the intelligence they bring to this trading is clearly gained by virtue of their own positions. And, finally, there are many direct methods for exchanging valuable information.

The mere listing of some of the myriad ways in which individuals can use information gained in the course of their corporate work shows how meaningless Section 16(b) is in preventing *all* insider trading. By focusing merely on one group of individuals trading in one particular company's shares, the Section becomes an open invitation to avoid its intended proscription. Many insiders, the public, and perhaps even the Securities and Exchange Commission are fooled by many of these subterfuges, but it is doubtful that determined corporate insiders have lost much money as a direct result of the Section.

Some additional techniques might improve the detection of insider trading. Each individual occupying an inside position could be paired off with individuals with whom he might be trading information. This pairing could be done by a detailed check of memberships in various organizations or of social engagements such as luncheon meetings, bridge games, and golf games or even by questionnaires about acquaintanceships. Special attention could be paid to individuals on interlocked boards of directors or the executives of companies who share the same investment bankers. The number of individuals to be covered would be extremely large, but computers might make the job feasible. Once these and many other pairings were programmed into a computer, it would be a relatively simple matter to detect some market transactions suggesting an exchange of information.

This kind of policing—intolerable as it must sound to anyone sensitive to gross invasions of privacy—would still not prove that any particular transaction was of the prohibited variety. It would merely raise a suspicion. Many transactions would not show up at all, as we have only programmed for pairs. The clearinghouse mechanism could easily provide, as it does, for multiparty exchanges that could not be discovered by this simple approach. Still other tools are available to the dedicated anti-inside trader. Discretionary accounts, priority lists, and interlocking boards of directors might be outlawed. The separation of investment banking and the brokerage business would also impede the smooth working of the market in information.[9] And every time any stock showed a substantial rise in price, large purchasers could be queried about their reasons for buying.

Even if all of this could be made effective, few would defend such a program. The administrative costs alone might be prohibitive. A much more important objection, however, is that such police-state tactics are simply intolerable. Spying on social meetings, computerized friendships, total disclosure of all financial affairs and decisions, the necessity to explain every profit—these are unthinkable in a civilized democracy. The costs, financially, morally, and politically, are too great, and we should never anticipate truly effective policing of insider trading by trying to ferret out every proscribed transaction as it occurs.

But this is precisely the direction in which the SEC seems to be moving. The implication of at least part of the complaint in the *Texas Gulf Sulphur* suit is that any trade known to be made before public disclosure of information violates SEC Rule 10b–5. It is one thing, however, to detect insider trading as widely publicized as that in the *Texas Gulf* case; it is another matter to administer this rule in a nondiscriminatory fashion. The SEC has ignored these dangers by relying on the courts to develop rules for it on a case-by-case basis.[10] Ultimately the enforcement difficulties remain, and they may be greater under this approach than they would be if the SEC faced up to the policing difficulties by promulgating detailed rules.

The "Stop-Trading" Approach

ULTIMATELY, THE ATTEMPT to pinpoint individual insiders and their proscribed transactions can lead to a radically different proposal. Such an attempt will not aim at preventing particular transactions or transactions by particular individuals. Rather, all trades by anyone can be stopped for some period of time before public disclosure of information. On occasion at present, the SEC and the stock exchanges, with the Commission's approval, do stop trading in a security.[11] The justifications usually offered for a trading suspension[12] could easily be extended to cover any news developments that might generate insider trading. The argument would be the same as that now used: time is needed for spectacular news to be disseminated and digested by the market to avoid wild fluctuations in price.

Implementation of this scheme in order to prevent insider trading would probably require close supervision of the affairs of every listed corporation. Trading in the company's stock could then be started and stopped as the supervisor saw the possibility of insiders' profiting by new developments. Such an approach might even seem to have an added advantage over other devices for preventing insider trading. Not only would insiders be prevented from exploiting their special knowledge, but speculation on tips by outsiders could also be prevented.

The consequences of such an extreme measure are hard to imagine. Even if the SEC displayed restraint in the exercise of such power, the operations of the capital market would undoubtedly be hampered. Public issues of new securities could not be underwritten with a high degree of confidence. The management of the entire stock market could in time pass from the hands of private investors and underwriters into the hands of government. Liquidity would be seriously lessened; and gross injustices would be done individuals wanting to sell their shares for reasons unrelated to insider trading. Most important, the market as a place for resolving differences of opinion and belief about economic values would lie shattered. Indeed, the amount of fortuitous gain and loss resulting from such a practice would be far greater than is likely under the rule of free insider trading on an open market.

Internal
Policing

BUT IF GOVERNMENT policing of insider trading is so difficult or so undesirable, it is reasonable to ask whether insiders can effectively police the information to which they are privy. In the previous chapter we theorized that the various information-exchange devices guarantee a rational allocation of values to individuals with some claim to information. Indeed, this assumption is crucial to the entire thesis of this book. But at first glance it would seem that the same reasons offered to show that government policing cannot be effective would apply to private policing.

However, for a variety of reasons, internal policing or allocation is quite different from the enforcement of government rules proscribing trading. In the first place, the scale upon which this policing must be done is quite small. It is generally sufficient for a company to instruct particular employees not to trade in its shares or to disclose valuable information to others. It would be a rare case in which continuous, successful, clandestine trading will go unnoticed. Eventually the office boy's Cadillac will show up in the company parking lot. And even if a decision to terminate an individual's employment is based on mere rumor or surmise of prohibited trading, private employers are generally free to terminate an employment relationship that is not to their liking.

It is interesting to note that the Canons of Ethics of the American Institute of Certified Public Accountants proscribe accountants' trading in the shares of corporate clients. No comparable provision appears in the Canons of Ethics of the American Bar Association. This does not mean that lawyers are always welcomed into the inner councils of corporate clients. Lawyers are sometimes instructed not to trade in a client company's shares. And law firms often have a policy against associates or members trading in clients' stock.

Various physical arrangements are available to corporations to assure the security of valuable information. For instance, it is possible to isolate bookkeepers and others who have access to valuable information until that information has been effectively exploited by others. When the first successful drilling core was identified by the chief geologist of Texas Gulf Sulphur at Timmins, Ontario, he ordered all workers to remain in the camp while word of the find was sent back to the home office. Oil geologists are regularly instructed to communicate to one individual in the home office by a predetermined code when the results of drilling are known. The list could undoubtedly be expanded. If the employee objects to these seeming indignities, there is no great social problem. He is free to seek another job where working conditions are more to his taste. These conditions for the protection of valuable information, like those relating to trade secrets, are simply a part of the terms of employment.

Undoubtedly there are numerous leaks in any private security system. Some of this is probably accepted by corporations as a matter of desirable employment relations. In many cases it will be tolerated because it is not important. Few subordinate employees in large corporations will be in a position to exploit information in any significant fashion. Attention can be focused on the few individuals who might be privy to valuable information and in a position to exploit it significantly. Probably many individuals who receive valuable information are those who are entitled to it by reason of their entrepreneurial contributions. Placement of individuals in particular jobs may constitute an important device by which entrepreneurs are compensated.

When we remember that insiders have the most to lose from indiscriminate disclosures of information affecting the market, their incentive to design appropriate policing devices is clear.[13] These devices may become so institutionalized that few overt actions to make information secure will be necessary. Strong moral strictures addressed to subordinate employees may have this effect. So may soundproof walls and doors with locks. Undoubtedly there are many more institutional arrangements to police information, even though their usefulness for that purpose may not be readily apparent.

The government's task, if it seeks to prevent insider trading, is far more difficult. The natural incentives and constraints are all against suppression of this trading, and simple institutional arrangements to prevent exploitation of information are difficult to conceive. The attempt to suppress the market in valuable information bears more resemblance to censorship and thought control than to attempts to suppress illicit transactions in drugs or whiskey. The suppression in one place of an undesired word or thought almost of necessity causes it to pop up in another place. Of all black markets, the one in ideas and knowledge is the most difficult to suppress.

XII

A Postscript on Government

IN OUR DISCUSSION of policing in the last chapter, we mentioned several types of outsiders who are frequently privy to valuable information about a corporation's shares. One class of these outsiders, government officials, is so large and so important that more detailed consideration is appropriate. Unquestionably the federal government is the largest producer of information capable of having a substantial effect on stock-market prices. And many corporate entrepreneurial developments will be known to government officials before the value has been exploited in the stock market by corporate insiders.

This last point may be illustrated by a corporation that discovers a huge new tin deposit in Bolivia. The discovery itself may represent successful entrepreneurial activity. But the ore cannot be mined unless heavy mining equipment unavailable in Bolivia is brought to the mining site, and without this equipment the discovery is worthless. The shipment of such equipment from the United States to most countries requires a permit or license

from the Department of Commerce, and the application for this
license requires the disclosure of considerable information.[1] It
takes little imagination, given the nature of the equipment, the
quantity, the consignor, and the consignee, to have some idea not
only of what has been discovered but how much. Even if the
government officials cannot deduce the necessary conclusions
from required disclosures of this sort, it is often possible that
these disclosures will serve as confirmation of other rumored
events. Or they may explain to an astute observer why the trading volume in this company's shares has been particularly high
in recent days.

How Government Officials
May Get Inside Information

BUT THIS purely hypothetical illustration does no more than illu-
minate one rather obscure aspect of the potential insider trading
by government officials. If we look at the principal kinds of
events that generally trigger large price changes in a company's
stock, it is surprising how many of them either originate with
the government or must be disclosed to the government. The
various categories of significant events causing a change in the
price of a company's shares may be broken down as follows:
(1) sharply increased earnings, dividend increases, stock splits,
and stock dividends; (2) a new product, an important patent, a
new development in marketing, and a radical change in consumer
preference; (3) public-utility rate changes and the granting of
franchises for communication channels or transportation routes;
(4) mergers, tender-bids, or proxy fights; and (5) large procurement contracts.

Generally, our first grouping—higher earnings, a dividend
increase, stock splits, and stock dividends—requires no notice to
government before the information can be fully exploited by
corporate insiders. Some special situations can be included in this
category, however. Frequently, higher or lower earnings may

result directly from government decisions. A tax refund may be approved days before the corporate taxpayer is actually notified. A contract-renegotiation board may uphold a contractor's claim. In early 1966, after various aluminum companies announced price increases, the government decreed the sale of some of its stockpiled aluminum. If this had been offered for sale at a low enough price, the news would surely have adversely affected the price of aluminum-company stocks. Other examples of this sort could also be mentioned, but generally this first category is less important than the others.

Ordinarily information about new products does not have to be disclosed to the government, but there are some dramatic exceptions. An obvious case requiring disclosure is that of new drugs, which must receive government approval before they may be sold commercially. In this case corporate insiders may first recognize the importance of a new development, but they cannot be certain that the product can be marketed. Thus the effect is to diminish the degree of certainty with which the corporate insiders may trade, though they will not be removed from the picture entirely. However, a different person will know about the development quite early, thus possibly lessening the corporate entrepreneur's return.

In some instances, government officials or employees may be the first to know that a new drug has been approved for marketing. To the extent that a government agency, such as the Food and Drug Administration or the National Institutes of Health, is either doing the research or granting licenses for the manufacture and testing of drugs, additional possibilities appear for profitable trading in drug-company stocks by the government officials involved. It is interesting to note that security analysts specializing in drug-industry stocks are regular visitors at these two agencies.

Some new products have commercial value only if the government agrees to purchase them. This would be peculiarly true of new weapons developed privately and offered to the Department of Defense. Again, as in the case of new drugs, no matter how optimistic the developers may be, uncertainty about value remains very high prior to government approval and purchase.

Patents, though issued by the government, seldom make government officials privy to valuable information. In the nature of present patent procedures, the filing of a patent application generally will not disclose any potential stock-market information not previously exploited. If any value remained unexploited, the idea would simply be kept secret rather than disclosed in a patent application.

Strangely enough, information on changes in consumer preference may be known first by government employees. The change may originate with the government. The clearest example in recent years occurred in connection with the cigarette cancer scare. Various government reports, notably those of the Surgeon General of the United States, always had a short-run effect on tobacco-company stocks. Short selling by anyone with advance knowledge of the contents of these reports could have brought handsome returns.

Somewhat related to government reports affecting the demand for a product are those government reports that affect supply. The most notable of these is the Department of the Interior's projection of the demand for petroleum products, which in turn is used as a factor in determining how much oil can be pumped from the ground in Texas. Closely tied to this kind of information is that regarding petroleum-import quotas, which has disparate effects on different companies. Other examples can be found in regulations affecting sugar and coffee imports.

Many activities of regulatory commissions provide possibilities for inside information. Various administrative agencies in Washington regulate the rates of public-utility companies. The Federal Power Commission has jurisdiction over the rates of natural-gas producers and electric-power companies in interstate commerce. The Federal Communications Commission regulates telephone, telegraph, and other communication systems' rates, and the Interstate Commerce Commission and the Civil Aeronautics Board do the same for railroads, airlines, and truckers. Each of these agencies has important additional powers. The Federal Power Commission may, for example, determine when a particular sales transaction between two companies brings these companies within its jurisdiction. They also pass on the validity of mergers involving regulated companies, as do each of the other agencies. The Federal Communications Commission has the power to allocate radio and television frequencies and to suspend licenses and force reorganizations of operating patterns. The list could be expanded to include numerous other agencies, departments, or offices with some kind of discretionary power over some phase of business.

News of Corporate Mergers

IN RECENT YEARS mergers have presented important opportunities for government officials to make or know important news. At least three and often more than four agencies of the federal government may receive advance notice of a planned merger. The first of these, the Internal Revenue Service, is all-important For some years few mergers that were not classified in advance as tax-free have been voluntarily entered. A tax-free merger merely signifies that the exchange of old securities for new will not be treated as a realization of ordinary income or capital gains. The cost to shareholders of a non-tax-free merger or reorganization is generally too high to warrant the transaction.

So important is this aspect of a corporate merger that the opinion of the Internal Revenue Service, as to whether a merger plan qualifies as tax-free, is often sought before public disclosure of a proposed merger. An IRS opinion may not be technically binding, but in practice it is usually the final word. A great variety of advance rulings on tax matters other than mergers could also be listed, although it is the merger that most frequently will affect the market price of shares.

Almost as important as tax considerations are the antitrust

implications of a merger. As mentioned, specialized regulatory agencies are often involved in early stages of merger negotiations, but the Antitrust Division of the Department of Justice and the Federal Trade Commission are most frequently in the picture. Each of these has long sought premerger-notification legislation from Congress, though this legislation has never been adopted.

Occasionally companies apply for an informal clearance with these agencies. These informal approvals have no legal sanction, though they are generally relied upon. But the politics of antitrust is quite different from that of the tax field. In most cases the parties to a merger do not seek preliminary approval from the FTC or the Justice Department because to do so is to invite disapproval and accelerate the agency's legal opposition to the projected merger. Nonetheless, important stock-market information may be generated by the agency's subsequent decision to oppose a merger or, in effect, sanction it by inaction. Whether we refer to advance notification of mergers or a suit brought after a merger has occurred, a potential gain from stock trading on this information is available.

For all the lengthy and unsuccessful legislative fights by the Justice Department and the Federal Trade Commission to receive premerger notification, the Securities and Exchange Commission, under its broad rule-making authority, may gain this power with no help from Congress. A proposed amendment to the present requirements for monthly reporting of significant developments (the 8K report) will require notification of agreement on the formal terms of a merger, even though shareholder votes and other conditions have not been fulfilled.[2] It remains to be seen how this would be enforced in practice, but the potential as a source of government information is great.

It should be added that, consistent with the overall SEC philosophy of disclosure, considerable amounts of information may have to be disclosed to the Commission. But rarely does information have to be disclosed before it could be fully exploited by corporate insiders. An important exception exists, however, for control fights. The SEC requires advance notice of the intention of management or of outsiders to solicit proxies, and normally this would have to be disclosed before share purchasing begins. Under a bill presently pending in Congress, the SEC would also be given substantial powers to regulate tender-bids and other devices for taking over control of corporations.[3] All in all, however, there does not seem to be too great an opportunity for trading in information disclosed to the SEC. There may be much less than in other important agencies of the federal government, and there is certainly more surveillance of the practice in the SEC than elsewhere.

Government Procurement

POPULAR ATTENTION to conflicts of interest in government has, for the most part, focused on military procurement. The reason is not hard to understand: the amounts of money involved may reach gigantic proportions. The recent contract awarded to the Lockheed Corporation, to build the first military order of the C-5A transport aircraft, totalled $2 billion and will probably be increased severalfold before all C-5A's have been procured. Presumably there will be additional private procurement of this aircraft as well. It is even more common that a single government contract to a small corporation may account for a substantial portion of the company's total earnings during the period of the contract.

Public fear in these matters stems from the danger that such large contracts may be awarded because there has been a payoff or because contracting personnel hold stock in the company awarded the contract. The public seems to equate these two.[4] The danger, in either case, is that the strength and efficiency of the government are being compromised. The real force behind the abhorrence of bribery is the actual or potential harm that may be done by government officials who deliberately choose "second best" for the country in order to pad their own pockets.

It has been pointed out by many commentators, notably Dean Bayless Manning,[5] that conflicts of interest from stock ownership do not constitute a serious problem in Washington. In fact, the steps taken to overcome this danger may have done considerable disservice to the cause of good government. There can be few individuals contemplating highranking government positions who would think of taking the job in order to increase the value of their stock holdings. On the other hand, many have shown their willingness to make the financial sacrifice of unloading their holdings in order to take these positions.

The danger that stock ownership in large companies will consciously or unconsciously affect government officials' contract choices has undoubtedly been wildly exaggerated. And the danger that stock trading may influence choices also seems small. At first glance stock trading would not seem to present any danger at all, since it would occur only after the decision had been made to grant the contract to a particular company. The fear of buying second best for the nation does not come immediately to mind, and some individuals may even defend this method of giving greater compensation to government officials.

But this does overlook the analysis offered earlier in this book. A given contract with a potential profit of $1 million would have no significant effect on the market price of shares of a company with annual earnings of $100 million. However, the same contract granted to a company with annual earnings of $1 million would have a dramatic impact. The direct danger of allowing government employees to trade in the shares of companies with whom they contract is that selections may be made partially or wholly on the basis of potential share-trading profits. But the potential damage to the country from this practice is probably not very great, and, if there were on balance positive advantages to be had from the practice, it could undoubtedly be tolerated. But, as we shall see below, there are other strong arguments against insider trading by government officials.

The Special Position
of Congressmen

CONGRESSMEN ARE peculiarly in a position to *receive* valuable market news, not *create* it. They are seldom in a position to originate information as there is little a congressman can do individually to effect a particular stock's price significantly. But the receipt of information may appear quite appropriate for congressmen. For one thing, congressmen must know what is going on so that they may legislate effectively, and information needed for legislative purposes may well be the same as that needed for profitable stock-market dealings.

The idea of paying congressmen money for a favor or a vote would undoubtedly be pure anathema to the overwhelming majority of them. This would constitute bribery and, in this blatantly illegal form, probably almost never occurs. Other devices for influencing legislators, such as campaign contributions or delivering blocks of votes, undoubtedly occur more often, though these practices cannot make congressmen wealthy.

Information is a different matter. Since most of our theorists on the subject treat it as though it were a free good, it is simply not part of our thinking to see the freely given tip as a payoff or bribe. We do not ordinarily talk or think about it in those terms. There is a feeling that the share buyer still risks his own money on the investment and that no one is really giving him anything. Undoubtedly some businessmen and government officials are more clever than that, but a great many probably do not see a stock market tip as a payoff. For those who do, there are various concealment devices available, including those discussed in Chapters V and VI.

Congressmen on certain committees and their aides could be focal points for receiving information produced or learned in all the various executive departments and agencies. Each department, agency, or office has at least one committee, and often one committee member, critical for the continued allocation of funds to that agency. Certain committees in Congress may, therefore, carry a higher price tag than others. This price tag would relate not to the political importance of the committee, as would be true of the Senate Foreign Relations Committee or the House Rules Committee, but rather to the financial opportunities presented by the assignment. The various executive agencies are certainly not above using pressures, cajolery, and valuable information to gain their requests from these committees. It would not be surprising then that certain congressmen would be informed very early of important administrative developments.

But, if information is used as a technique for influencing congressmen, individuals in key positions may command valuable information even when the news does not relate to matters of direct concern to the recipient. Just as a President may give political support to the pet project of a senator in exchange for his critical support on a matter of political importance to the President, there are other ways, too, that a President can reward the faithful. Valuable information may not be the least of these.

In this respect the President could function in a manner similar to that suggested for investment bankers in Chapter V. That is, he might act as a distributor of valuable information produced within the executive branch of the government. This information might be distributed in accord with past or anticipated value received from the recipients of the information. The theory of mutual advantage from exchange strongly implies that this relation, or some variant of it, is common.

The Misleading Emphasis on Stock Ownership

THE EMPHASIS on the necessity for an individual to disclose his stock holdings and to divest himself of them before assuming a government position has almost totally eclipsed concern with stock trading by government officials. In presidential and vice-presidential campaigns since 1952, all leading contenders have disclosed to the press certified statements of their net worth, including a list of securities and other assets owned or held in trust.[6] In 1953 Congress conducted its celebrated investigation of Charles Wilson's finances after his nomination as Secretary of Defense. Eventually he was forced to divest himself of a large block of General Motors stock.[7] Almost regularly since then we have heard of congressional inquiries into stock holdings of presidential appointees. The mere presence of a minescule potential for a conflict of interests seems sufficient to throw some investigators into paroxysms of moral indignation.

The point has been extremely well made by Dean Bayless Manning, that this obsession with stock ownership represents at best an exaggeration of a noble sentiment and at worst a serious hurdle for able personnel willing to serve in government in spite of a large financial sacrifice.[8] The conclusions reached in Dean Manning's studies on this subject do not seem open to serious dispute.

Insider trading, however, is a different matter. Unlike stock ownership, the dangers are not simply potential. Trading on inside information is what we may want to avoid, while it is never stock ownership per se that is deemed evil. Stock ownership is considered potentially harmful because it may warp or influence the judgment of government officials in connection with specific decisions they have to make. Very little attention has been paid, however, to the trading problem in studies of conflicts of interest among government personnel.[9] Stock ownership has been the principal concern of both academic and political investigators.

It is surprising, however, given the amount of potential profits available, that there is not a regular investigation of possible insider trading when important matters are disclosed by government officials. Stock-market price increases prior to government announcements affecting particular stocks can be easily noticed, though possibly only private individuals and not government officials account for this trading. In many instances, however, that seems highly improbable. Even though a particular government activity generates stock-market information of tremendous value,

there is usually no suspicion of insider trading by government
officials when disclosure of the event is made. Only rarely are
we treated by a newspaper columnist or government official to
the statement or even suggestion that insider trading is occurring.

Aside from extremely rare intimations in the press or a cause
célèbre such as the Texas Gulf affair,[10] there is no commonly
voiced suspicion that trading on inside information by high government officials is endemic in Washington. Interestingly enough,
when they are asked, many people in the government do not
deny that it occurs. Almost everyone has heard of someone else
trading with inside information or knows of someone who has
done so. Yet this news, available to anyone for the asking, is
usually left unexamined.

The Pros and Cons of Government Insider Trading

Two FUNDAMENTAL POINTS have been made here about corporate
insider trading. One is that no significant injury to corporate
investors can result from the practice, and the other is that insider
trading constitutes the most appropriate device for compensating
entrepreneurs in large corporations. The first of these two arguments holds true whether the person trading on inside information is in government or business. Indeed, if speedy exploitation
of information in the stock market is desirable, government employee's doing this would help accelerate price changes. It should
be recalled from Chapter VII, however, that on balance this
argument is largely neutral; it neither strongly favors nor dis-
favors insider trading.

The second part of the justification for insider trading in the
corporate sector, however, has no substantial application to government. The argument can be made that government employment is frequently not financially attractive and that insider
trading would encourage public service by able citizens otherwise
unwilling to make the necessary financial sacrifice. The motiva-
tional aspect of this argument may be correct, and it is not

unlikely that some officials have been so motivated. There would seem, however, to be overwhelming arguments, both theoretical and practical, against this justification.

The information on which government officials could trade would not ordinarily reflect entrepreneurial developments for which they are responsible. This is not to suggest that important innovations in government do not occur, nor that particular government decisions may not be of significant value to the shareholders of a given corporation. But we cannot define entrepreneurial activity in terms of any developments that will affect stock-market prices. Government innovations may injure a corporation economically as frequently as they benefit it. Very often the government official's news will have been reported to him rather than developed by him or anyone in government. And the most important innovations in government will generally have no effect on the stock market or the stock of any particular company.

We have no social, economic, or political interest in rewarding government officials simply for benefitting or injuring particular companies. Our interests are generally to the contrary and are quite the opposite of the economic interest society may have in rewarding corporate entrepreneurs. Survival of a business firm in a dynamic competitive economy demands a high degree of innovational activity. Insider trading has been justified as providing an important incentive for this desirable activity. But government officials, unless they are clearly representing private interests in their public capacities, do not play a significant role in this process of economic competition. Nor should we want activities of government officials to be aimed at the survival of any particular competing company.

Another difficulty with government insider trading relates to a point discussed in Chapter XI. There it was argued that the private allocation of valuable information will follow the dictates of market exchange and that serious leakages to the undeserving will be infrequent. However, myriad government reporting requirements may make private policing of information by corporate insiders very difficult. The net effect of requiring disclosure to unpoliced government officials may be to deprive corporate insiders of wealth they would otherwise attain and to deprive the shareholders of the benefits they would otherwise receive.

Another fundamental difficulty in allowing insider trading by government officials has already been mentioned. This is that important decisions, mainly in the area of government procurement, may be made with an eye to maximizing trading profits rather than serving the government's interest. This might occasionally be offered as an argument *for* insider trading by procurement officers. For the same contract, greater trading profits can ordinarily be made if the contract is given to the smaller of two competing companies. This does not seem, however, to be an appropriate device for dealing with problems of corporate size, and the dangers in this practice seem to outweigh any advantages.

But the principal evil inherent in government insider trading —and one that deserves much more attention than it has had—is the ease with which inside information can be utilized as a pay-off device. This potential has long gone almost unnoticed, and concealment is exceptionally easy. Most of the devices mentioned in Chapter V can be utilized by government officials as well as private executives. Effective enforcement of rules against insider trading will never be easy. But the job in government should be begun. The very fact that cases are known of both congressional and executive-branch employees utilizing stock-market information for private gain should be sufficient to warrant a thorough investigation.

Executive Views on Insider Trading

ON MAY 2, 1963, President Kennedy promulgated a presidential memorandum titled "Preventing Conflicts of Interest on the Part of Special Government Employees," addressed to all departments, agencies, and executive offices. His statement, though limited in application to temporary consultants or employees, is probably the first to notice officially the possibility of insider trading by government officials. It is also important for its implication that the practice occurs in significant amounts. The document states:

> *Insider Information.* The first principle of ethical behavior for the temporary or intermittent consultant or adviser is that he must refrain from any use of his public office which is motivated by, or gives the appearance of being motivated by, the desire for private gain for himself or other persons, including particularly those with whom he has family, business or financial ties. The fact that the desired gain, if it materializes, will not take place at the expense of the Government makes his action no less proper.
>
> An adviser or consultant must conduct himself in a manner devoid of the slightest suggestion that he is exploiting his Government employment for private advantage. Thus, a consultant or adviser must not, on the basis of any insider information, enter into speculation, or recommend speculation to members of his family or business associates, in commodities, land or the securities of any private company. He must obey this injunction even though his duties have no connection whatever with the Government programs or activities to avoid any appearance of acting on the basis of information obtained in the course of his Government work.[11]

There then followed in the same announcement a copy of the recently enacted, streamlined conflict-of-interest statute, pressure for which had come largely from the White House. Surprisingly, there is not one word in that statute that can be construed as applying to or disfavoring insider trading by government officials.

Very few government agencies had made any serious effort prior to 1966 to control insider trading. In 1960 careful examination showed that only three agencies had detailed any program for ferreting out insider trading by government employees and officials.[12] In one of these agencies, the Securities and Exchange Commission, specific provision in the statute creating the Commission makes unlawful the personal use of information filed with the Commission.[13] The SEC is certainly more sensitive to this question than any other agency and undoubtedly makes a continuing effort to prevent any abuse.[14] In most agencies with either detailed or simple prohibitions against unauthorized use of official information, sanctions for violation of the rules almost never appear.[15] And no agency other than the SEC has regularly shown itself eager to police its rules.

In May of 1965 President Johnson promulgated an executive order revoking all earlier orders and memoranda dealing with conflicts of interest.[16] Johnson's order directed the Civil Service Commission to issue regulations consistent with the standards of conduct prescribed in his order.

Pursuant to this order, the Civil Service Commission issued rules and regulations governing conduct of government employees in connection with information, as well as other subjects.[17] These rules contain at least two provisions relating to valuable information for regular government employees[18] and one provision for special or temporary employees.[19] As might be imagined, employees were directed not to use information obtained through government employment in their own financial affairs.

The Civil Service Commission's rules directed each agency head to issue regulations for that agency's employees prescribing standards of conduct and governing the reporting of financial interests. The Civil Service regulations themselves require all employees in a grade of GS-16 or higher, with certain exceptions, to submit a statement of financial interests. And this must be kept current on a quarterly basis.

By early 1966 only the Department of Justice had issued rules pursuant to the executive order.[20] Basically this department's regulations on inside trading simply follow those stated in the rules of the Civil Service Commission. It is quite likely that most agencies and departments will model their standards accordingly.

But net-worth statements and quarterly reporting of assets are inadequate tools for ferreting out many instances of insider trading. It is doubtful that government officials who trade in their own names or give information to close relatives would ever hold securities for any length of time. Furthermore, as government officials will often know the precise date on which disclosure of valuable information will be made, much of their trading could be very quick. A lot of trading can occur between points at which disclosure of holdings has to be made. And if accretions in assets between disclosure dates do not have to be explained, this form of disclosure might never turn up significant insider trading.

Of course, the mere fact that reporting is to be done quarterly does not indicate that inside traders would always have three months in which to realize their profits. On the average the maximum period for realizing profits before a new disclosure would be approximately six weeks. The rules would have been far more effective had they required immediate disclosure of any stock transactions or a statement of the source of all income.

Proposed Legislation

THE VARIOUS RULES and regulations referred to do have the virtue of being in existence while the most far-reaching legislative proposal is and may remain at a preliminary stage. In May of 1965, a bill "To promote public confidence in the integrity of Congress and the executive branch," was introduced by Senator Clifford P. Case of New Jersey.[21] This bill covers all members of Congress, candidates for Congress, and employees of the executive or legislative branch making in excess of $17,500 a year. These individuals are directed to file with the comptroller general a statement including, among other things, "the amount and source of each item of income... received by him or by him and his spouse jointly during the preceding calendar year which exceeds $100 in amount or value." He must also report "all dealings in securities or commodities by him, or by him and his spouse or by any person acting on his behalf or pursuant to his direction during the preceding calendar year."

The coverage of these sections could undoubtedly be broadened to include other forms of marketing information. But the really important aspect of the bill is that it is well-designed to put teeth into disclosure provisions. Annual reporting of income items will disclose even the shortest-term speculation, since the source of all items of income must be listed and not merely the amount and nature of assets as of a certain reporting date. It is possible that some of the bill's requirements are too onerous to be consistent with the goal of attracting able personnel into government positions; and there are other defects in the bill as well. But the greatest importance of this bill may lie in its recognition of the existence and nature of insider trading by government officials.

Approaches to Reform

ANOTHER UNIQUE feature of Senator Case's bill is the establishment of a Commission on Legislative Standards. This commission is directed to "conduct a thorough study of problems of conflicts of interest and of relations with executive and other agencies which confront Members of Congress with a view to devising and recommending measures and procedures to deal with such problems."[22] Such a commission, if properly directed, might be able to propose many effective devices for dealing with government insider trading. Arguably a less ambitious bill, merely to establish such an investigatory commission, would be more desirable for the present.

Certain conditions would probably have to be observed in order to develop a successful investigation of insider trading in government. The first and perhaps indispensable condition would be an agreement not to publicize particular cases uncovered. It is extremely unlikely that Congress would ever authorize an investigation that could conceivably embarrass most of its members as well as important figures in the executive branch. Second, to the extent that there have been violations of existing executive rules as well as the SEC's Rule 10b–5, a general immunity from any legal or administrative action should be declared in advance. This is consistent with the proposition that there has not been a general awareness of the evils inherent in government insider trading. More important, it is a practical necessity for accomplishing the stated goal.

Consideration should be given to treating valuable stock-market information in the same way we treat information classified for security purposes. There could be gradations of clearances and a "need-to-know" standard. Realistic security measures should be instituted, and records should be maintained of the names of individuals privy to specified kinds of information. This would facilitate discovery by spot-checking of trading when there has been a substantial price change in a particular stock.

At some point techniques for discovering government-employee trading may intrude on private trading. This is one of the costs of the frequently close relationship of government and private business today, and additional study should be given to that problem. Undoubtedly policing of government trading cannot be perfect, though it should be considerably easier than government policing of private insider trading.

Undoubtedly it will be difficult for many people to comprehend a justification of corporate insider trading and a strong condemnation of the same practice by government officials. The arguments on each side are complex, but that is not a sufficient basis for concluding that both cases alike must be either condemned or condoned. The distinction between private economic activity and government administration is both real and fundamental.

LIST OF CASES

Blau v. *Lehman*, 368 U.S. 403 (1962).

Boston & Maine R.R. Co. v. *Hillman*, CCH *Federal Securities Law Reporter*, par. 90,813 (S.D.N.Y., 1957).

Bosworth v. *Allen*, 168 N.Y. 157, 61 N.E. 163 (1901).

Bristol v. *Equitable Life Assurance Society of the U.S.*, 132 N.Y. 264, 30 N.E. 506 (1892).

Brophy v. *Cities Service Co.*, 31 Del. Ch. 241, 70 Atl. 2d 5 (1949).

In the Matter of Cady, Roberts & Co., SEC Release No. 6668, CCH *Federal Securities Law Reporter*, par. 76,803 (1961).

Colonial Laundries, Inc. v. *Henry*, 48 R.I. 332, 138 Atl. 47 (1927).

De Boy v. *Harris*, 207 Md. 212, 113 Atl. 2d 903 (1955).

E. I. DuPont de Nemours Power Co. v. *Masland*, 24 U.S. 100 (1917).

Essex Universal Corp. v. *Yates*, 305 Fed. 2d 572 (2d Cir., 1962).

Goodwin v. *Agassiz*, 283 Mass. 358, 186 N.E. 659 (1933).

Gratz v. *Claughton*, 187 Fed. 2d 46 (2d Cir., 1951).

Helms v. *Duckworth*, 249 Fed. 2d 482 (D.C.C.A., 1957).

Jacquith v. *Mason*, 99 Neb. 509, 156 N.W. 1041 (1916).

J. I. Case Co. v. *Borak*, 377 U.S. 426 (1964).

Kardon v. *National Gypsum Co.*, 73 Fed. Supp. 798 (D.C.E.D.Pa., 1947).

Kerbs v. *California Eastern Airways, Inc.*, 33 Del. Ch. 69, 90 Atl. 2d 652 (1952).

Lieberman v. *Becker*, 38 Del. Ch. 540, 155 Atl. 2d 596 (1954).

Meinhard v. *Salmon*, 249 N.Y. 458, 164 N.E. 545 (1928).

Mills v. *Sarjem Corp.*, 133 Fed. Supp. 753 (D.C.N.J., 1955).

Oliver v. *Oliver*, 118 Ga. 362, 45 S.E. 232 (1903).

Rattner v. *Lehman*, 193 Fed. 2d 564 (2d Cir., 1952).

Rogers v. *Hill*, 65 Fed. 2d 109 (2d Cir., 1932), *reversed* 289 U.S. 582 (1933).

Securities & Exchange Commission v. *Capital Gains Research Bureau, Inc.*, 375 U.S. 180 (1963).

Securities & Exchange Commission v. *Chenery Corp.*, 318 U.S. 80 (1943).

Securities & Exchange Commission v. *Chenery Corp.*, 332 U.S. 194 (1947).

Sher v. *Sandler*, 325 Mass. 348, 90 N.E. 2d 536 (1950).

Smolowe v. *Delendo Corp.*, 136 Fed. 2d 231, (2d Cir., 1943), *cert. denied*, 320 U.S. 751.

Speed v. *Transamerica Corp.*, 99 Fed. Supp. 808 (D.Del., 1951).

Steele v. *Louisville & Nashville Railroad Co.*, 323 U.S. 192, (1944).

Stein v. *Morris*, 120 Va., 390, 91 S.E. 177 (1917).

Steward v. *Harris*, 69 Kan. 498, 77 Pac. 277 (1904).

Strong v. *Repide*, 213 U.S. 419 (1909).

United States v. *Morgan*, 118 Fed. Supp. 621 (S.D.N.Y., 1953).

United States v. *Shindler*, 173 Fed. Supp. 393 (S.D.N.Y., 1959).

APPENDIX

SELECTED CASES

(All footnotes have been deleted.)

BLAU v. LEHMAN et al.

368 U.S. 403 (1962).

MR. JUSTICE BLACK delivered the opinion of the Court.

The petitioner Blau, a stockholder in Tide Water Associated Oil Company, brought this action in a United States District Court on behalf of the company under § 16(b) of the Securities Exchange Act of 1934 to recover with interest "short swing" profits, that is, profits earned within a six months' period by the purchase and sale of securities, alleged to have been "realized" by respondents in Tide Water securities dealings. Respondents are Lehman Brothers, a partnership engaged in investment banking, securities brokerage and in securities trading for its own account, and Joseph A. Thomas, a member of Lehman Brothers and a director of Tide Water. The complaint alleged that Lehman Brothers "deputed . . . Thomas, to represent its interests as a director on the Tide Water Board of Directors," and that within a period of six months in 1954 and 1955 Thomas, while representing the interests of Lehman Brothers as a director of Tide Water and "by reason of his special and inside knowledge of the affairs of Tide Water, advised and caused the defendants, Lehman Brothers, to purchase and sell 50,000 shares of . . . stock of Tide Water, realizing profits thereon which did not inure to and [were] not recovered by Tide Water."

The case was tried before a district judge without a jury. The evidence showed that Lehman Brothers had in fact earned profits out of short-swing transactions in Tide Water securities while Thomas was a director of that company. But as to the charges of deputization and wrongful use of "inside" information by Lehman Brothers, the evidence was in conflict.

195

First, there was testimony that respondent Thomas had succeeded Hertz, another Lehman partner, on the board of Tide Water; that Hertz had "joined Tidewater Company thinking it was going to be in the interests of Lehman Brothers"; and that he had suggested Thomas as his successor partly because it was in the interest of Lehman. There was also testimony, however, that Thomas, aside from having mentioned from time to time to some of his partners and other people that he thought Tide Water was "an attractive investment" and under "good" management, had never discussed the operating details of Tide Water affairs with any member of Lehman Brothers; that Lehman had bought the Tide Water securities without consulting Thomas and wholly on the basis of public announcements by Tide Water that common shareholders could thereafter convert their shares to a new cumulative preferred issue; that Thomas did not know of Lehman's intent to buy Tide Water stock until after the initial purchases had been made; that upon learning about the purchases he immediately notified Lehman that he must be excluded from "any risk of the purchase or any profit or loss from the subsequent sale"; and that this disclaimer was accepted by the firm.

From the foregoing and other testimony the District Court found that "there was no evidence that the firm of Lehman Brothers deputed Thomas to represent its interests as director on the board of Tide Water" and that there had been no actual use of inside information, Lehman Brothers having bought its Tide Water stock "solely on the basis of Tide Water's public announcements and without consulting Thomas."

On the basis of these findings the District Court refused to render a judgment, either against the partnership or against Thomas individually, for the $98,686.77 profits which it determined that Lehman Brothers had realized, holding:

> "The law is now well settled that the mere fact that a partner in Lehman Brothers was a director of Tide Water, at the time that Lehman Brothers had this short swing transaction in the stock of Tide Water, is not sufficient to make the partnership liable for the profits thereon, and that Thomas could not be held liable for the profits realized by the other partners from the firm's short swing transactions. Rattner v. Lehman, 2 Cir., 1952, 193 F.2d 564, 565, 567. This precise question was passed upon in the Rattner decision." 173 F. Supp. 590, 593.

Despite its recognition that Thomas had specifically waived his share of the Tide Water transaction profits, the trial court nevertheless held that within the meaning of § 16(b) Thomas had "realized" $3,893.41, his proportionate share of the profits of Lehman Brothers. The court consequently entered judgment against Thomas for that amount but refused to allow interest against him. On appeal, taken by both sides, the Court of Appeals for the Second Circuit adhered to the view it had taken in *Rattner* v. *Lehman,* 193 F.2d 564, and affirmed the District Court's judgment in all respects, Judge Clark dissenting. 286 F.2d 786. The Securities and Exchange Commission then sought leave from the Court of Appeals *en banc* to file an *amicus curiae* petition for rehearing urging the overruling of the *Rattner* case. The Commission's motion was denied, Judges Clark and Smith dissenting. We granted certiorari on the petition of Blau, filed on behalf of himself, other stockholders and Tide Water, and supported by the Commission. 366 U.S. 902. The questions presented by the petition are whether the courts below erred: (1) in refusing to render a judgment against the Lehman partnership for the $98,686.77 profits they were found to have "realized" from their "short-swing" transactions in Tide Water stock, (2) in refusing to render judgment against Thomas for the full $98,686.77 profits, and (3) in refusing to allow interest on the $3,893.41 recovery allowed against Thomas.

Petitioner apparently seeks to have us decide the questions presented as though he had proven the allegations of his complaint that Lehman Brothers actually deputized Thomas to represent its interests as a director of Tide Water, and that it was his advice and counsel based on his special and inside knowledge of Tide Water's affairs that caused Lehman Brothers to buy and sell Tide Water's stock. But the trial court found otherwise and the Court of Appeals affirmed these findings. Inferences could perhaps have been drawn from the evidence to support petitioner's charges, but examination of the record makes it clear to us that the findings of the two courts below were not clearly erroneous. Moreover, we cannot agree with the Commission that the courts' determinations of the disputed factual issues were conclusions of law rather than findings of fact. We must therefore decide whether Lehman Brothers, Thomas or both have an absolute liability under § 16(b) to pay over all profits made on Lehman's Tide Water stock dealings even though Thomas was not sitting on Tide Water's board to represent Lehman and even though the profits made by the partnership were on its own initiative, independently of any advice or "inside" knowledge given it by director Thomas.

First. The language of § 16 does not purport to impose its extraordinary liability on any "person," "fiduciary" or not, unless he or it is a "director," "officer" or "beneficial owner of more than 10 per-centum of any class of any equity security . . . which is registered on a national securities exchange." Lehman Brothers was neither an officer nor a 10% stockholder of Tide Water, but petitioner and the Commission contend that the Lehman partnership is or should be treated as a director under § 16(b).

(a) Although admittedly not "literally designated" as one, it is contended that Lehman is a director. No doubt Lehman Brothers, though a partnership, could for purposes of § 16 be a "director" of Tide Water and function through a deputy, since § 3(a)(9) of the Act provides that " 'person' means . . . partnership" and § 3(a)(7) that " 'director' means any director of a corporation or any person performing similar functions with respect to any organization, whether incorporated or unincorporated." Consequently, Lehman Brothers would be a "director" of Tide Water, if as petitioner's complaint charged Lehman actually functioned as a director through Thomas, who had been deputized by Lehman to perform a director's duties not for himself but for Lehman. But the findings of the two courts below, which we have accepted, preclude such a holding. It was Thomas, not Lehman Brothers as an entity, that was the director of Tide Water.

(b) It is next argued that the intent of § 3(a)(9) in defining "person" as including a partnership is to treat a partnership as an inseparable entity. Because Thomas, one member of this inseparable entity, is an "insider," it is contended that the whole partnership should be considered the "insider." But the obvious intent of § 3(a)(9), as the Commission apparently realizes, is merely to make it clear that a partnership can be treated as an entity under the statute, not that it must be. This affords no reason at all for construing the word "director" in § 16(b) as though it read "partnership of which the director is a member." And the fact that Congress provided in § 3(a)(9) for a partnership to be treated as an entity in its own right likewise offers no support for the argument that Congress wanted a partnership to be subject to all the responsibilities and financial burdens of its members in carrying on their other individual business activites.

(c) Both the petitioner and the Commission contend on policy grounds that the Lehman partnership should be held liable even though it is neither a director, officer, nor a 10% stockholder. Conceding that such an interpretation is not justified by the literal language of § 16(b) which plainly limits liability to directors, officers, and 10% stockholders, it is argued that we should expand § 16(b) to cover partnerships of which a director is a member in order to carry out the congressionally declared purpose of "preventing the unfair use of information which may have been obtained by such beneficial owner, director, or officer by reason of his relationship to the issuer. . . ." Failure to do so, it is argued, will leave a large and unintended loophole in the statute—one "substantially eliminating the great Wall Street trading firms from the statute's operation." 286 F.2d, at 799. These firms it is claimed will be able to evade the Act and take advantage of the "inside" information available to their members as insiders of countless corporations merely by trading "inside" information among the various partners.

The argument of petitioner and the Commission seems to go so far as to suggest that § 16(b)'s forfeiture of profits should be extended to include all persons realizing "short swing" profits who either act on the basis of "inside" information or have the possibility of "inside" information. One may agree that petitioner and the Commission present persuasive policy arguments that the Act should be broadened in this way to prevent "the unfair use of information" more effectively than can be accomplished by leaving the Act so as to require forfeiture of profits only by those specifically designated by Congress to suffer those losses. But this very broadening of the categories of persons on whom these liabilities are imposed by the language of § 16(b) was considered and rejected by Congress when it passed the Act. Drafts of provisions that eventually became § 16(b) not only would have made it unlawful for any director, officer or 10% stockholder to disclose any confidential information regarding registered securities, but also would have made all profits received by *anyone*, "insider" or not, "to whom such unlawful disclosure" had been made recoverable by the company.

Not only did Congress refuse to give § 16(b) the content we are now urged to put into it by interpretation, but with knowledge that in 1952 the Second Circuit Court of Appeals refused, in the *Rattner* case, to apply § 16(b) to Lehman Brothers in circumstances substantially like those here, Congress has left the Act as it was. And so far as the record shows this interpretation of § 16(b) was the view of the Commission until it intervened last year in this case. Indeed in the *Rattner* case the Court of Appeals relied in part on Commission Rule X-16A-3(b) which required insider-partners to report only the amount of their own holdings and not the amount of holdings by the partnership. While the Commission has since changed this rule to require disclosure of partnership holdings too, its official release explaining the change stated that the new rule was "not intended as a modification of the principles governing liability for short-swing transactions under Section 16(b) as set forth in the case of *Rattner* v. *Lehman.* . . ." Congress can and might amend § 16(b) if the Commission would present to it the policy arguments it has presented to us, but we think that Congress is the proper agency to change an interpretation of the Act unbroken since its passage, if the change is to be made.

Second. The petitioner and the Commission contend that Thomas should be required individually to pay to Tide Water the entire $98,686.77 profit Lehman Brothers realized on the ground that under partnership law he is co-owner of the entire undivided amount and has therefore "realized" it all. "[O]nly by holding the partner-director liable for the *entire* short-swing profits realized by his firm," it is urged, can "an effective prophylactic to the stated statutory policy . . . be fully enforced." But liability under § 16(b) is to be determined neither by general partnership law nor by adding to the "prophylactic" effect Congress itself clearly prescribed in § 16(b). That section leaves no room for judicial doubt that a director is to pay to his company only "any profit realized *by him*" from short-swing transactions. (Emphasis added.) It would be nothing but a fiction to say that Thomas "realized" all the profits earned by the partnership of which he was a member. It was not error to refuse to hold Thomas liable for profits he did not make.

Third. It is contended that both courts below erred in failing to allow interest on the recovery of Thomas' share of the partnership profits. Section 16(b) says nothing about interest one way or the other. This Court has said in a kindred situation that "interest is not recovered according to a rigid theory of compensation for money withheld, but is given in response to considerations of fairness. It is denied when its exaction would be inequitable." *Board of Commissioners* v. *United States,* 308 U.S. 343, 352. Both courts below denied interest here and we cannot say that the denial was either so unfair or so inequitable as to require us to upset it.

Affirmed.

MR. JUSTICE STEWART took no part in the disposition of this case.

MR. JUSTICE DOUGLAS, with whom THE CHIEF JUSTICE concurs, dissenting.

What the Court does today is substantially to eliminate "the great Wall Street trading firms" from the operation of § 16(b), as Judge Clark stated in his dissent in the Court of Appeals. 286 F.2d 786, 799.

This result follows because of the wide dispersion of partners of investment banking firms among our major corporations. Lehman Bros. has partners on 100 boards. Under today's ruling that firm can make a rich harvest on the "inside information" which § 16 of the Act covers because each partner need account only for his distributive share of the firm's profits on "inside information," the other partners keeping the balance. This is a mutilation of the Act.

If a partnership can be a "director" within the meaning of § 16(a), then "any profit realized by him," as those words are used in § 16(b), includes all the profits, not merely a portion of them, which the partnership realized on the "inside information." There is no basis in reason for saying a partnership cannot be a "director" for purposes of the Act. In *Rattner* v. *Lehman*, 193 F.2d 564, 567, Judge Learned Hand said he was "not prepared to say" that a partnership could not be considered a "director," adding "for some purposes the common law does treat a firm as a jural person." In his view a partnership might be a "director" within the meaning of § 16 if it "deputed a partner" to represent its interests. Yet formal designation is no more significant than informal approval. Everyone knows that the investment banking-corporation alliances are consciously constructed so as to increase the profits of the bankers. In partnership law a debate has long raged over whether a partnership is an entity or an aggregate. Pursuit of that will-o'-the-wisp is not profitable. For even New York with its aggregate theory recognizes that a partnership is or may be considered an entity for some purposes. It is easier to make this partnership a "director" for purposes of § 16 than to hold the opposite. Section 16(a) speaks of every "person" who is a "director." In § 3(a) (9) "person" is defined to include, *inter alia*, "a partnership." Thus, the purpose to subject a partnership to the provisions of § 16 need not turn on a strained reading of that section.

At the root of the present problem are the scope and degree of liability arising out of fiduciary relations. In modern times that liability has been strictly construed. The New York Court of Appeals, speaking through Chief Judge Cardozo in *Meinhard* v. *Salmon*, 249 N.Y. 458, 164 N.E. 545, held a joint adventurer to a higher standard than we insist upon today:

"Many forms of conduct permissible in a workaday world for those acting at arm's length, are forbidden to those bound by fiduciary ties. A trustee is held to something stricter than the morals of the market place. Not honesty alone, but the punctilio of an honor the most sensitive, is then the standard of behavior. As to this there has developed a tradition that is unbending and inveterate. Uncompromising rigidity has been the attitude of courts of equity when petitioned to undermine the rule of undivided loyalty by the 'disintegrating erosion' of particular exceptions (*Wendt* v. *Fischer*, 243 N.Y. 439, 444). Only thus has the level of conduct for fiduciaries been kept at a level higher than that trodden by the crowd. It will not consciously be lowered by any judgment of this court." 249 N.Y., at 464, 164 N.E., at 546.

In *Mosser* v. *Darrow*, 341 U.S. 267, we allowed a reorganization trustee to be surcharged $43,447.46 for profits made by his employees through trading in securities of subsidiaries of a bankrupt company. We made this ruling even though there was "no hint or proof that he has been corrupt or that he has any interest, present or future, in the profits he has permitted these employees to make." *Id.*, at 275. We said:

> "These strict prohibitions would serve little purpose if the trustee were free to authorize others to do what he is forbidden. While there is no charge of it here, it is obvious that this world open up opportunities for devious dealings in the name of others that the trustee could not conduct in his own. The motives of man are too complex for equity to separate in the case of its trustees the motive of acquiring efficient help from motives of favoring help, for any reason at all or from anticipation of counterfavors later to come. We think that which the trustee had no right to do he had no right to authorize, and that the transactions were as forbidden for benefit of others as they would have been on behalf of the trustee himself.
>
> "... equity has sought to limit difficult and delicate fact-finding tasks concerning its own trustee by precluding such transactions for the reason that their effect is often difficult to trace, and the prohibition is not merely against injuring the estate—it is against profiting out of the position of trust. That this has occurred, so far as the employees are concerned, is undenied." *Id.*, at 271–273.

It is said that the failure of Congress to take action to remedy the consequences of the *Rattner* case somehow or other shows a purpose on the part of Congress to infuse § 16 with the meaning that *Rattner* gave it. We took that course in *Toolson* v. *New York Yankees*, 346 U.S. 356, and adhered to a ruling the Court made in 1922 that baseball was not within the scope of the antitrust laws, because the business had been "left for thirty years to develop, on the understanding that it was not subject to" those laws. *Id.*, p. 357. Even then we had qualms and two Justices dissented. For what we said in *Girouard* v. *United*

States, 328 U.S. 61, 69, represents our usual attitude: "It is at best treacherous to find in congressional silence alone the adoption of a controlling rule of law." It is ironic to apply the *Toolson* principle here and thus sanction, as vested, a practice so notoriously unethical as profiting on inside information.

We forget much history when we give § 16 a strict and narrow construction. Brandeis in *Other People's Money* spoke of the office of "director" as "a happy hunting ground" for investment bankers. He said that "The goose that lays golden eggs has been considered a most valuable possession. But even more profitable is the privilege of taking the golden eggs laid by somebody else's goose. The investment bankers and their associates now enjoy that privilege." *Id.*, at 12.

The hearings that led to the Securities Exchange Act of 1934 are replete with episodes showing how insiders exploited for their personal gain "inside information" which came to them as fiduciaries and was therefore an asset of the entire body of security holders. The Senate Report labeled those practices as "predatory operations." S.Rep.No. 1455, 73d Cong., 2d Sess., p. 68. It said:

> "Among the most vicious practices unearthed at the hearings before the subcommittee was the flagrant betrayal of their fiduciary duties by directors and officers of corporations who used their positions of trust and the confidential information which came to them in such positions, to aid them in their market activities. Closely allied to this type of abuse was the unscrupulous employment of inside information by large stockholders who, while not directors and officers, exercised sufficient control over the destinies of their companies to enable them to acquire and profit by information not available to others." *Id.*, at 55. See also S.Rep.No. 792, 73d Cong., 2d Sess., p. 9.

The theory embodied in § 16 was the one Brandeis espoused. It was stated by Sam Rayburn as follows: "Men charged with the administration of other people's money must not use inside information for their own advantage." H.R. Rep.No. 1383, 73rd Cong., 2d Sess. 13.

What we do today allows all but one partner to share in the feast which the one places on the partnership table. They in turn can offer feasts to him in 99 other companies of which they are directors. 14 Stan. L. Rev. 192, 198. This result is a dilution of the fiduciary principle that Congress wrote into § 16 of the Act. It is, with all respect, a dilution that is possible only by a strained reading of the law. Until now, the courts have given this fiduciary principle a cordial reception. We should not leave to Congress the task of restoring the edifice that it erected and that we tear down.

APPENDIX TO OPINION OF MR. JUSTICE DOUGLAS

Lehman v. *Civil Aeronautics Board, supra,* 93 U.S. App. D.C., at 85–87, 209 F.2d, at 292–294.

"Petioner Lehman is a director of Pan American; petitioner Joseph A. Thomas is a director of National Airlines, Inc., and of American Export Lines, Inc.; petitioner Frederick L. Ehrman is a director of Continental Air Lines, Inc., and Mr. John D. Hertz is a director of Consolidated Vultee Aircraft Corporation. All the companies referred to are in the aeronautic field and so must have Board approval of the kind of interlocking relationships which are made unlawful unless approved. Messrs. Lehman, Thomas, Ehrman, Hertz, and others, are also members of Lehman Brothers, a partnership which, as previously pointed out, conducts an investment banking business.

"The Board held that an individual Lehman Brothers partner who is a director of a Section 409(a) company is a representative of another partner who is a director of another such company. The relationships thus found to exist were disapproved as to those involving Pan American and National; Pan American and American Export Lines; Pan American and Consolidated Vultee; National and Pan American; National and Consolidated Vultee; and Continental Air Lines and Consolidated Vultee. . . .

"More precisely the Board concluded that a Lehman Brothers partner who is director of an air carrier has a representative 'who represents such . . . director as . . . a director' in another Section 409(a) company if another Lehman Brothers partner is a director of the latter, coupled with the circumstances that he seeks on behalf of Lehman Brothers the security underwriting and merger negotiation services used by the company of which he is director. The underwriting of security issues and the conduct of merger negotiations constitute a substantial part of the business of Lehman Brothers, who have been employed for these purposes not infrequently by Section 409(a) companies. The partners feel free to solicit this business for their firm.

". . . But we must consider the facts of the case in the light of the purpose of Congress to keep the developing aviation industry free of unhealthy interlocking relationships, though this purpose must be carried out only as the statute provides. The relevant findings which point up the problem are not in dispute. The underwriting activities of Lehman Brothers is a substantial part of its business; substantial fees are also obtained by Lehman Brothers from merger negotiations.

Profits from the fees are shared by the partners. Section 409(a) companies, with Lehman Brothers partners as directors, need and use both types of services, and the partner directors seek such business for the partnership. In doing so they act as representatives of the partnership. It follows that they act as representatives of fellow partners, some of whom are directors of air carriers. Is this representation within the meaning of the statute? Does Mr. Thomas, to use his case as illustrative, who is a Lehman Brothers partner and also a director of National Airlines, represent, as director of National Airlines, Mr. Lehman, another Lehman Brothers partner and director of Pan American? We think that the affirmative answer of the Board should not be disturbed. For the situation comes to more than some community of interest and some sharing of common benefits as partners. The particular common interest and benefits are among directors of the regulated industry with respect to industry matters. The partnership link does not extend merely to a type of business remote from the aeronautical industry in which the partners are directors; it is with respect to business activities of air carriers and other aeronautical companies enumerated in Section 409(a). In these activities there is not only literal representation by one partner of another in partnership business but the particular partnership business is as well the business of aeronautical enterprises of which the partners are directors. When Mr. Thomas, again to illustrate, as director of National seeks to guide that company's underwriting business to Lehman Brothers he acts in the interest of and for the benefit of Mr. Lehman who is not only his underwriting partner but is also a director of an air carrier, Pan American. Mr. Lehman the partner is the same Mr. Lehman the director. The Board is not required to separate him into two personalities, as it were, and to say that Mr. Thomas represents him as a partner but not as a director, if, as is the case here, the representation is in regard to the carrying on of the affairs of Section 409(a) companies. The undoubted representation which grows out of the partnership we think follows into the directorships when the transactions engaged in are not only by the partners but concern companies regulated by the statute, of which the partners are directors. This is representation within not only the language but the meaning of the statute."

IN THE MATTER OF CADY, ROBERTS & Co.

Securities Exchange Act Release No. 6668
November 8, 1961.

CARY, CHAIRMAN: This is a case of first impression and one of signal importance in our administration of the federal securities acts. It involves a selling broker who executes a solicited order and sells for discretionary accounts (including that of his wife) upon an exchange. The crucial question is what are the duties of such a broker after receiving non-public information as to a company's dividend action from a director who is employed by the same brokerage firm.

These proceedings were instituted to determine whether Cady, Roberts & Co. ("registrant") and Robert M. Gintel ("Gintel"), the selling broker and a partner of the registrant, willfully violated the "anti-fraud" provisions of Section 10(b) of the Securities Exchange Act of 1934 ("Exchange Act") Rule 10b-5 issued under that Act, and Section 17(a) of the Securities Act of 1933 ("Securities Act") and, if so, whether any disciplinary action is necessary or appropriate in the public interest. The respondents have submitted an offer of settlement which essentially provides that the facts stipulated by respondents shall constitute the record in these proceedings for the purposes of determining the occurrence of a willful violation of the designated anti-fraud provisions and the entering of an appropriate order, on the condition that no sanction may be entered in excess of a suspension of Gintel for 20 days from the New York Stock Exchange.

The facts are as follows:

Early in November, 1959, Roy T. Hurley, then President and Chairman of the Board of Curtiss-Wright Corporation, invited 2,000 representatives of the press, the military and the financial and business communities to a public unveiling on November 23 of a new type of internal combustion engine being developed by the company. On November 24, 1959, press announcements concerning the new engine appeared in certain newspapers. On that day Curtiss-Wright stock was one of the most active issues on the New York Stock Exchange, closing at 35¼, up 3¼ on a volume of 88,700 shares. From November 6 through November 23, Gintel had purchased approximately 11,000 shares of Curtiss-Wright stock for about 30 discretionary accounts of customers of registrant. With the rise in the price on November 24, he began selling Curtiss-Wright shares for these accounts and sold on that day a total of 2,200 shares on the Exchange.

The activity in Curtiss-Wright stock on the Exchange continued the next morning, November 25, and the price rose to 40¾ a new high for the year. Gintel continued sales for the discretionary accounts and, between the opening of the market and about 11:00 A.M., he sold 4,300 shares.

On the morning of November 25 the Curtiss-Wright directors, including J. Cheever Cowdin ("Cowdin"), then a registered representative of registrant, met to consider, among other things, the declaration of a quarterly dividend. The company had paid a dividend, although not earned, of $.625 per share for each of the first three quarters of 1959. The Curtiss-Wright board, over the objections of Hurley, who favored declaration of a dividend at the same rate as in the prior quarters, approved a dividend for the fourth quarter at the reduced rate of $.375 per share. At approximately 11:00 A.M., the board authorized transmission of information of this action by telegram to the New York Stock Exchange. The Secretary of Curtiss-Wright immediately left the meeting room to arrange for this communication. There was a short delay in the transmission of the telegram because of a typing problem and the telegram, although transmitted to Western Union at 11:12 A.M., was not delivered to the Exchange until 12:29 P.M. It had been customary for the company also to advise the Dow Jones News Ticker of any dividend action. However, apparently through some mistake or inadvertence, the Wall Street Journal was not given the news until approximately 11:45 A.M. and the announcement did not appear on the Dow Jones ticker tape until 11:48 A.M.

Sometime after the dividend decision, there was a recess of the Curtiss-Wright directors' meeting, during which Cowdin telephoned registrant's office and left a message for Gintel that the dividend had been cut. Upon receiving this information, Gintel entered two sell orders for execution on the Exchange, one to sell 2,000 shares of Curtiss-Wright stock for ten accounts, and the other to sell short 5,000 shares for 11 accounts. Four hundred of the 5,000 shares were sold for three of Cowdin's customers. According to Cowdin, pursuant to directions from his clients, he had given instructions to Gintel to take profits on these 400 shares if the stock took a "run-up." These orders were executed at 11:15 and 11:18 A.M. at 40¼ and 40⅜, respectively.

When the dividend announcement appeared on the Dow Jones tape at 11:48 A.M., the Exchange was compelled to suspend trading in Curtiss-Wright because of the large number of sell orders. Trading in

Curtiss-Wright stock was resumed at 1:59 P.M. at 36½, ranged during the balance of the day between 34⅛ and 37, and closed at 34⅞.

Violation of Anti-Fraud Provisions

So many times that citation is unnecessary, we have indicated that the purchase and sale of securities is a field in special need of regulation for the protection of investors. To this end one of the major purposes of the securities acts is the prevention of fraud, manipulation or deception in connection with securities transactions. Consistent with this objective, Section 17(a) of the Securities Act, Section 10(b) of the Exchange Act and Rule 10b-5, issued under that section, are broad remedial provisions aimed at reaching misleading or deceptive activities, whether or not they are precisely and technically sufficient to sustain a common law action for fraud and deceit. Indeed, despite the decline in importance of a "federal rule" in the light of *Erie R. Co.* v. *Tomkins,* the securities acts may be said to have generated a wholly new and far-reaching body of federal corporation law.

* * *

These anti-fraud provisions are not intended as a specification of particular acts or practices which constitute fraud, but rather are designed to encompass the infinite variety of devices by which undue advantage may be taken of investors and others.

Section 17 and Rule 10b-5 apply to securities transactions by "any person." Misrepresentations will lie within their ambit, no matter who the speaker may be. An affirmative duty to disclose material information has been traditionally imposed on corporate "insiders," particularly officers, directors, or controlling stockholders. We, and the courts, have consistently held that insiders must disclose material facts which are known to them by virtue of their position but which are not known to persons with whom they deal and which, if known, would affect their investment judgment. Failure to make disclosure in these circumstances constitutes a violation of the anti-fraud provisions. If, on the other hand, disclosure prior to effecting a purchase or sale would be improper or unrealistic under the circumstances, we believe the alternative is to forego the transaction.

The ingredients are here and we accordingly find that Gintel willfully violated Sections 17(a) and 10(b) and Rule 10b-5. We also find a similar violation by the registrant, since the actions of Gintel, a member of registrant, in the course of his employment are to be regarded as actions of registrant itself. It was obvious that a reduction in the quarterly dividend by the board of directors was a material fact which could be expected to have an adverse impact on the market price of the company's stock. The rapidity with which Gintel acted upon receipt of the information confirms his own recognition of that conclusion.

We have already noted that the anti-fraud provisions are phrased in terms of "any person" and that a special obligation has been traditionally required of corporate insiders, e.g., officers, directors and controlling stockholders. These three groups, however, do not exhaust the classes of persons upon whom there is such an obligation. Analytically, the obligation rests on two principal elements; first, the existence of a relationship giving access, directly or indirectly, to information intended to be available only for a corporate purpose and not for the personal benefit of anyone, and second, the inherent unfairness involved where a party takes advantage of such information knowing it is unavailable to those with whom he is dealing. In considering these elements under the broad language of the anti-fraud provisions we are not to be circumscribed by fine distinctions and rigid classifications. Thus our task here is to identify those persons who are in a special relationship with a company and privy to its internal affairs, and thereby suffer correlative duties in trading in its securities. Intimacy demands restraint lest the uninformed be exploited.

The facts here impose on Gintel the responsibilities of those commonly referred to as "insiders." He received the information prior to its public release from a director of Curtis-Wright, Cowdin, who was associated with the registrant. Cowdin's relationship to the company clearly prohibited him from selling the securities affected by the information without disclosure. By logical sequence, it should prohibit Gintel, a partner of registrant. This prohibition extends not only over his own account, but to selling for discretionary accounts and soliciting and executing other orders. In somewhat analogous circumstances, we have charged a broker-dealer who effects securities transactions for an insider and who knows that the insider possesses non-public material information with the affirmative duty to make appropriate disclosures or dissociate himself from the transaction.

The three main subdivisions of Section 17 and Rule 10b-5 have been considered to be mutually supporting rather than mutually exclusive. Thus, a breach of duty of disclosure may be viewed as a device or scheme, an implied misrepresentation, and an act or practice, violative of all three subdivisions. Respondents argue that only clause (3) may be applicable here. We hold that, in these circumstances,

Gintel's conduct at least violated clause (3) as a practice which operated as a fraud or deceit upon the purchasers. Therefore, we need not decide the scope of clauses (1) and (2).

We cannot accept respondents' contention that an insider's responsibility is limited to existing stockholders and that he has no special duties when sales of securities are made to non-stockholders. This approach is too narrow. It ignores the plight of the buying public—wholly unprotected from the misuse of special information.

Neither the statutes nor Rule 10b-5 establish artificial walls of responsibility. Section 17 of the Securities Act explicitly states that it shall be unlawful for any person in the offer or sale of securities to do certain prescribed acts. Although the primary function of Rule 10b-5 was to extend a remedy to a defrauded seller, the courts and this Commission have held that it is also applicable to a defrauded buyer. There is no valid reason why persons who *purchase* stock from an officer, director or other person having the responsibilities of an "insider" should not have the same protection afforded by disclosure of special information as persons who *sell* stock to them. Whatever distinctions may have existed at common law based on the view that an officer or director may stand in a fiduciary relationship to existing stockholders from whom he purchases but not to members of the public to whom he sells, it is clearly not appropriate to introduce these into the broader anti-fraud concepts embodied in the securities acts.

Respondents further assert that they made no express representations and did not in any way manipulate the market, and urge that in a transaction on an exchange, there is no further duty such as may be required in a "face-to-face" transaction. We reject this suggestion. It would be anomalous indeed if the protection afforded by the anti-fraud provisions were withdrawn from transactions effected on exchanges, primary markets for securities transactions. If purchasers on an exchange had available material information known by a selling insider, we may assume that their investment judgment would be affected and their decision whether to buy might accordingly be modified. Consequently, any sales by the insider must await disclosure of the information.

Cases cited by respondents in which relief was denied to purchasers or sellers of securities in exchange transactions are distinguishable. The action here was instituted by the Commission, not by individuals. The cited cases concern private suits brought against insiders for violation of the anti-fraud rules. They suggest that the plaintiffs may not recover because there was lacking of "semblance of privity" since it was not shown that the buyers or sellers bought from or sold to the insiders. These cases have no relevance here as they concern the remedy of the buyer or seller *vis-a-vis* the insider. The absence of a remedy of the private litigant because of lack or privity does not absolve an insider from responsibility for fradulent conduct.

Respondents argue that any requirement that a broker-dealer in exchange transactions make disclosure of "adverse factors disclosed by his analysis" would create uncertainty and confusion as to the duties of those who are constantly acquiring and analyzing information about companies in which they or their clients are interested. Furthermore it is claimed, substantial practical difficulties would be presented as to the manner of making disclosures.

There should be no quandary on the facts here presented. While there may be a question as to the materiality and significance of some corporate facts and as to the necessity of their disclosure under particular circumstances, that is not this case. Corporate dividend action of the kind involved here is clearly recognizable as having a direct effect on the market value of securities and the judgment of investors. Moreover, knowledge of this action was not arrived at as a result of perceptive analysis of generally known facts, but was obtained from a director (and associate) during the time when respondents should have known that the board of directors of the issuer was taking steps to make the information publicly available but before it was actually announced.

Furthermore, the New York Stock Exchange has recognized that prompt disclosure of important corporate developments, including specifically dividend action, is essential for the benefit of stockholders and the investing public and has established explicit requirements and recommended procedures for the immediate public release of dividend information by issuers whose securities are listed on the Exchange. The practical problems envisaged by respondents in effecting appropriate disclosures in connection with transactions on the Exchange are easily avoided where, as here, all the registered broker-dealer need do is to keep out of the market until the established procedures for public release of the information are carried out instead of hastening to execute transactions in advance of, and in frustration of, the objectives of the release.

Finally, we do not accept respondents' contention that Gintel was merely carrying out a program of liquidating the holdings in his discretionary accounts—determined and embarked upon prior to his receipt of the dividend information. In this connection, it is further alleged that he had a fiduciary duty to these accounts to continue the sales, which overrode any obligations to unsolicited purchasers on the Exchange.

The record does not support the contention that Gintel's sales were merely a continuance of his prior schedule of liquidation. Upon receipt of the news of the dividend reduction, which Gintel knew was not public, he hastened to sell before the expected public announcement all of the Curtiss-Wright shares remaining in his discretionary accounts, contrary to his previous moderate rate of sales. In so doing, he also made short sales of securities which he then allocated to his wife's account and to the account of a customer whom he had never seen and with whom he had had no prior dealings. Moreover, while Gintel undoubtedly occupied a fiduciary relationship to his customers, this relationship could not justify any actions by him contrary to law. Even if we assume the existence of conflicting fiduciary obligations, there can be no doubt which is primary here. On these facts, clients may not expect of a broker the benefits of his inside information at the expense of the public generally. . . .

The Public Interest

All the surrounding circumstances and the state of mind of the participants may be taken into consideration in determining what sanctions should appropriately be imposed here.

It is clear that Gintel's conduct was willful in that he knew what he was doing. However, there is no evidence of a preconceived plan whereby Cowdin was to "leak" advance information of the dividend reduction so that Gintel could use it to advantage before the public announcement; on the contrary, the evidence points to the conclusion that Cowdin probably assumed, without thinking about it, that the dividend action was already a matter of public information and further that he called registrant's office to find out the effect of the dividend news upon the market. The record, moreover, indicates that Gintel's conduct was a spontaneous reaction to the dividend news, that he intended primarily to benefit existing clients of Cady, Roberts and Co. and that he acted on the spur of the moment and so quickly as to preclude the possibility of review by registrant or of his own more deliberate consideration of his responsibilities under the securities acts.

Gintel has been fined $3,000 by the New York Stock Exchange in connection with the instant transactions. The publication of this opinion, moreover, will in itself serve as a further sanction upon Gintel and registrant and will also induce a more careful observance of the requirements of the anti-fraud provisions in the area in question. Furthermore, registrant had no opportunity to prevent Gintel's spontaneous transactions and no contention has been made that its procedures for handling accounts did not meet proper standards. Under all the circumstances we conclude that the public interest and the protection of investors will be adequately and appropriately served if Gintel is suspended from the New York Stock Exchange for 20 days and if no sanction is imposed against the registrant. Accordingly, we accept respondent's offer of settlement.

An appropriate order will issue.

COMMISSIONERS WOODSIDE and COHEN join in the above opinion. COMMISSIONER FREAR dissents in part (see below).

FREAR, COMMISSIONER Dissenting in part. I agree that the facts disclosed by the record submitted in connection with the offer of settlement show willful violations of the anti-fraud provisions of the securities acts, and I concur in the views enunciated in the part of the Commission's Findings and Opinion dealing with such violation. However, in my opinion those facts and violations require the imposition of a greater sanction than the 20-day suspension of Gintel from membership on the New York Stock Exchange which is the maximum permitted under the offer of settlement, and I would accordingly reject the offer.

SECURITIES AND EXCHANGE COMMISSION v. CAPITAL GAINS RESEARCH BUREAU, INC., ET AL.
375 U.S. 180 (1963).

MR. JUSTICE GOLDBERG delivered the opinion of the Court.

We are called upon in this case to decide whether under the Investment Advisers Act of 1940 the Securities and Exchange Commission may obtain an injunction compelling a registered investment adviser to disclose to his clients a practice of purchasing shares of a security for his own account shortly before recommending that security for long-term investment and then immediately selling the shares at a profit upon the rise in the market price following the recommendation. The answer to this question turns on whether the practice—known in the trade as "scalping"—"operates as a fraud or deceit upon any client or prospective client" within the meaning of the Act. We hold that it does and the Commission may "enforce compliance" with the Act by obtaining an injunction requiring the adviser to make full disclosure of the practice to his clients.

The Commission brought this action against respondents in the United States District Court for the Southern District of New York. At the hearing on the application for a preliminary injunction, the following facts were established. Respondents publish two investment advisory services, one of which—"A Capital Gains Report"—is the subject of this proceeding. The Report is mailed monthly to approximately 5,000 subscribers who each pay an annual subscription price of $18. It carries the following description:

> "An Investment Service devoted exclusively to (1) The protection of investment capital. (2) The realization of a steady and attractive income therefrom. (3) The accumulation of CAPITAL GAINS thru the timely purchase of corporate equities that are proved to be undervalued."

Between March 15, 1960, and November 7, 1960, respondents, on six different occasions, purchased shares of a particular security shortly before recommending it in the Report for long-term investment. On each occasion, there was an increase in the market price and the volume of trading of the recommended security within a few days after the distribution of the Report. Immediately thereafter, respondents sold their shares of these securities at a profit. They did not disclose any aspect of these transactions to their clients or prospective clients.

On the basis of the above facts, the Commission requested a preliminary injunction as necessary to effectuate the purposes of the Investment Advisers Act of 1940. The injunction would have required respondents, in any future Report, to disclose the material facts concerning, *inter alia*, any purchase of recommended securities "within a very short period prior to the distribution of a recommendation . . . ," and "[t]he intent to sell and the sale of said securities . . . within a very short period after distribution of said recommendation. . . ."

The District Court denied the request for a preliminary injunction, holding that the words "fraud" and "deceit" are used in the Investment Advisers Act of 1940 "in their technical sense" and that the Commission had failed to show an intent to injure clients or an actual loss of money to clients. 191 F. Supp. 897. The Court of Appeals for the Second Circuit, sitting *en banc*, by a 5-to-4 vote accepted the District Court's limited construction of "fraud" and "deceit" and affirmed the denial of injunctive relief. 306 F. 2d 606. The majority concluded that no violation of the Act could be found absent proof that "any misstatements or false figures were contained in any of the bulletins"; or that "the investment advice was unsound"; or that "defendants were being bribed or paid to tout a stock contrary to their own beliefs"; or that "these bulletins were a scheme to get rid of worthless stock"; or that the recommendations were made "for the purpose of endeavoring artificially to raise the market so that [respondents] might unload [their] holdings at a profit." *Id.*, at 608–609. The four dissenting judges pointed out that "[t]he common-law doctrines of fraud and deceit grew up in a business climate very different from that involved in the sale of securities," and urged a broad remedial construction of the statute which would encompass respondents' conduct. *Id.*, at 614. We granted certiorari to consider the question of statutory construction because of its importance to the investing public and the financial community. 371 U. S. 967.

The decision in this case turns on whether Congress, in empowering the courts to enjoin any practice which operates "as a fraud or deceit upon any client or prospective client," intended to require the Commission to establish fraud and deceit "in their technical sense," including intent to injure and actual injury to clients, or whether Congress intended a broad remedial construction of the Act which would encompass nondisclosure of material facts. For resolution of this issue we consider the history and purpose of the Investment Advisers Act of 1940.

I.

The Investment Advisers Act of 1940 was the last in a series of Acts designed to eliminate certain abuses in the securities industry, abuses which were found to have contributed to the stock market crash of 1929 and the depression of the 1930's. It was preceded by the Securities Act of 1933, the Securities Exchange Act of 1934, the Public Utility Holding Company Act of 1935, the Trust Indenture Act of 1939, and the Investment Company Act of 1940. A fundamental purpose, common to these statutes, was to substitute a philosophy of full disclosure for the philosophy of *caveat emptor* and thus to achieve a high standard of business ethics in the securities industry. As we recently said in a related context, "It requires but little appreciation . . . of what happened in this country during the 1920's and 1930's to realize how essential it is that the highest ethical standards prevail" in every facet of the securities industry. *Silver* v. *New York Stock Exchange*, 373 U.S. 341, 366.

The Public Utility Holding Company Act of 1935 "authorized and directed" the Securities and Exchange Commission "to make a study of the functions and activities of investment trusts and investment companies. . . ." Pursuant to this mandate, the Commission made an exhaustive study and report which included consideration of investment counsel and investment advisory services. This aspect of the study and report culminated in the Investment Advisers Act of 1940.

The report reflects the attitude—shared by investment advisers and the Commission—that investment advisers could not "completely perform their basic function—furnishing to clients on a personal basis competent, unbiased, and continuous advice regarding the sound management of their investments—unless all conflicts of interest between the investment counsel and the client were removed." The report stressed that affiliations by investment advisers with investment bankers, or corporations might be "an impediment to a disinterested, objective, or critical attitude toward an investment by clients. . . ."

This concern was not limited to deliberate or conscious impediments to objectivity. Both the advisers and the Commission were well aware that whenever advice to a client might result in financial benefit to the adviser—other than the fee for his advice—"that advice to a client might in some way be tinged with that pecuniary interest [whether consciously or] subconsciously motivated. . . ." The report quoted one leading investment adviser who said that he "would put the emphasis . . . on subconscious" motivation in such situations.

It quoted a member of the Commission staff who suggested that a significant part of the problem was not the existence of a "deliberate intent" to obtain a financial advantage, but rather the existence "subconsciously [of] a prejudice" in favor of one's own financial interests. The report incorporated the Code of Ethics and Standards of Practice of one of the leading investment counsel associations, which contained the following canon:

> "[An investment adviser] should continuously occupy an impartial and disinterested position, as free as humanly possible from the *subtle* influence of prejudice, *conscious or unconscious;* he should scrupulously avoid any affiliation, or any act, which subjects his position to challenge in this respect." (Emphasis added.)

Other canons appended to the report announced the following guiding principles: that compensation for investment advice "should consist exclusively of direct charges to clients for services rendered"; that the adviser should devote his time "exclusively to the performance" of his advisory function; that he should not "share in profits" of his clients; and that he should not "directly or indirectly engage in any activity which may jeopardize [his] ability to render unbiased investment advice." These canons were adopted "to the end that the quality of services to be rendered by investment counselors may measure up to the high standards which the public has a right to expect and to demand."

One activity specifically mentioned and condemned by investment advisers who testified before the Commission was *"trading by investment counselors for their own account in securities in which their clients were interested. . . ."*

This study and report—authorized and directed by statute— culminated in the preparation and introduction by Senator Wagner of the bill which, with some changes, became the Investment Advisers Act of 1940. In its "declaration of policy" the original bill stated that

> "Upon the basis of facts disclosed by the record and report of the Securities and Exchange Commission . . . it is hereby declared that the national public interest and the interest of investors are adversely affected— . . . (4) when the business of investment advisers is so conducted as to defraud or mislead investors, or to enable such advisers to relieve themselves of their fiduciary obligations to their clients.
> "It is hereby declared that the policy and purposes of this title, in accordance with which the provisions of this title shall be interpreted, are to mitigate and, so far as is presently practicable to eliminate the abuses enumerated in this section." S. 3580, 76th Cong., 3d Sess., § 202.

Hearings were then held before Committees of both Houses of Congress. In describing their profession, leading investment advisers emphasized their relationship of "trust and confidence" with their clients and the importance of "strict limitations of [their right] to buy and sell securities in the normal way if there is any chance at all that to do so might seem to operate against the interests of clients and the public." The president of the Investment Counsel Association of America, the leading investment counsel association, testified that the

> "two fundamental principles upon which the pioneers in this new profession undertook to meet the growing need for unbiased investment information and guidance were, first, that they would limit their efforts and activities to the study of investment problems from the investor's standpoint, not engaging in any other activity, such as security selling or brokerage, which might directly or indirectly bias their investment judgment; and, second, that their remuneration for this work would consist solely of definite, professional fees fully disclosed in advance."

Although certain changes were made in the bill following the hearings, there is nothing to indicate an intent to alter the fundamental purposes of the legislation. The broad proscription against "any . . . practice . . . which operates . . . as a fraud or deceit upon any client or prospective client" remained in the bill from beginning to end. And the Committee Reports indicate a desire to preserve "the personalized character of the services of investment advisers," and to eliminate conflicts of interest between the investment adviser and the clients as safeguards both to "unsophisticated investors" and to "bona fide investment counsel." The Investment Advisers Act of 1940 thus reflects a congressional recognition "of the delicate fiduciary nature of an investment advisory relationship," as well as a congressional intent to eliminate, or at least to expose, all conflicts of interest which might incline an investment adviser—consciously or unconsciously—to render advice which was not disinterested. It would defeat the manifest purpose of the Investment Advisers Act of 1940 for us to hold, therefore, that Congress, in empowering the courts to enjoin any practice which operates "as a fraud or deceit," intended to require proof of intent to injure and actual injury to clients.

This conclusion moreover, is not in derogation of the common law of fraud, as the District Court and the majority of the Court of Appeals suggested. To the contrary, it finds support in the process by which the courts have adapted the common law of fraud to the

commercial transactions of our society. It is true that at common law
intent and injury have been deemed essential elements in a damage
suit between parties to an arm's-length transaction. But this is not
such an action. This is a suit for a preliminary injunction in which
the relief sought is, as the dissenting judges below characterized it, the
"mild prophylactic," 306 F. 2d, at 613, of requiring a fiduciary to disclose to his clients, not all his security holdings, but only his dealings
in recommended securities just before and after the issuance of his
recommendations.

The content of common-law fraud has not remained static as the
courts below seem to have assumed. It has varied, for example, with
the nature of the relief sought, the relationship between the parties,
and the merchandise in issue. It is not necessary in a suit for equitable
or prophylactic relief to establish all the elements required in a suit for
monetary damages.

> "Law had come to regard fraud . . . as primarily a tort, and hedged
> about with stingent requirements, the chief of which was a strong
> moral, or rather immoral element, while equity regarded it, as it had all
> along regarded it, as a conveniently comprehensive word for the expres-
> sion of a lapse from the high standard of conscientiousness that it
> exacted from any party occupying a certain contractual or fiduciary
> relation towards another party."

> "Fraud has a broader meaning in equity [than at law] and intention to
> defraud or to misrepresent is not a necessary element."

> "Fraud, indeed, in the sense of a court of equity properly includes
> all acts, omissions and concealments which involve a breach of legal or
> equitable duty, trust, or confidence, justly reposed, and are injurious
> to another, or by which an undue and unconscientious advantage is
> taken of another."

Nor is it necessary in a suit against a fiduciary, which Congress recognized the investment adviser to be, to establish all the elements required in a suit against a party to an arm's-length transaction. Courts
have imposed on a fiduciary an affirmative duty of "utmost good
faith, and full and fair disclosure of all material facts," as well as an
affirmative obligation "to employ reasonable care to avoid misleading" his clients. There has also been a growing recognition by
common-law courts that the doctrines of fraud and deceit which developed around transactions involving land and other tangible items
of wealth are ill-suited to the sale of such intangibles as advice and
securities, and that, accordingly, the doctrines must be adapted to the

merchandise in issue. The 1909 New York case of *Ridgely* v. *Keene,* 134 App. Div. 647, 119 N. Y. Supp. 451, illustrates this continuing development. An investment adviser who, like respondents, published an investment advisory service, agreed, for compensation, to influence his clients to buy shares in a certain security. He did not disclose the agreement to his client but sought "to excuse his conduct by asserting that . . . he honestly believed, that his subscribers would profit by his advice. . . ." The court, holding that "his belief in the soundness of his advice is wholly immaterial," declared the act in question "a palpable fraud."

We cannot assume that Congress, in enacting legislation to prevent fraudulent practices by investment advisers, was unaware of these developments in the common law of fraud. Thus, even if we were to agree with the courts below that Congress had intended, in effect, to codify the common law of fraud in the Investment Advisers Act of 1940, it would be logical to conclude that Congress codified the common law "remedially" as the courts had adapted it to the prevention of fraudulent securities transactions by fiduciaries, not "technically" as it has traditionally been applied in damage suits between parties to arm's-length transactions involving land and ordinary chattels.

The foregoing analysis of the judicial treatment of common-law fraud reinforces our conclusion that Congress, in empowering the courts to enjoin any practice which operates "as a fraud or deceit" upon a client, did not intend to require proof of intent to injure and actual injury to the client. Congress intended the Investment Advisers Act of 1940 to be construed like other securities legislation "enacted for the purpose of avoiding frauds," not technically and restrictively, but flexibly to effectuate its remedial purposes.

II.

We turn now to a consideration of whether the specific conduct here in issue was the type which Congress intended to reach in the Investment Advisers Act of 1940. It is arguable—indeed it was argued by "some investment counsel representatives" who testified before the Commission—that any "trading by investment counselors for their own account in securities in which their clients were interested . . ." creates a potential conflict of interest which must be eliminated. We need not go that far in this case, since here the Commission seeks only disclosure of a conflict of interests with significantly greater potential for abuse than in the situation described above. An adviser who, like respondents, secretly trades on the market effect of his own recommendation may be motivated—consciously or unconsciously—to recommend a given security not because of its potential for long-run price increase (which would profit the client), but because of its potential for short-run price increase in response to anticipated activity from the recommendation (which would profit the adviser). An investor seeking the advice of a registered investment adviser must, if the legislative purpose is to be served, be permitted to evaluate such overlapping motivations, through appropriate disclosure, in deciding whether an adviser is serving "two masters" or only one, "especially . . . if one of the masters happens to be economic self-interest." *United States* v. *Mississippi Valley Co.*, 364 U.S. 520, 549. Accordingly, we hold that the Investment Advisers Act of 1940 empowers the courts, upon a showing such as that made here, to require an adviser to make full and frank disclosure of his practice of trading on the effect of his recommendations.

III.

Respondents offer three basic arguments against this conclusion. They argue first that Congress could have made, but did not make, failure to disclose material facts unlawful in the Investment Advisers Act of 1940, as it did in the Securities Act of 1933, and that absent specific language, it should not be assumed that Congress intended to include failure to disclose in its general proscription of any practice which operates as a fraud or deceit. But considering the history and chronology of the statutes, this omission does not seem significant. The Securities Act of 1933 was the first experiment in federal regulation of the securities industry. It was understandable, therefore, for Congress, in declaring certain practices unlawful, to include both a general proscription against fradulent and deceptive practices and, out of an abundance of caution, a specific proscription against nondisclosure. It soon became clear, however, that the courts, aware of the previously outlined developments in the common law of fraud, were merging the proscription against nondisclosure into the general proscription against fraud, treating the former, in effect, as one variety of the latter. For example, in *Securities & Exchange Comm'n* v. *Torr*, 15 F. Supp. 315 (D.C.S.D.N.Y. 1936), rev'd on other grounds, 87 F. 2d 446, Judge Patterson held that suppression of information material to an evaluation of the disinterestedness of investment advice "operated as a deceit on purchasers," 15 F. Supp., at 317. Later cases also treated nondisclosure as one variety of fraud or deceit. In light of this, and in light of the evident purpose of the Investment Advisers Act of 1940 to substitute a philosophy of disclosure for the philosophy of *caveat emptor*, we cannot assume that the omission in the 1940 Act of a specific proscription against nondisclosure was intended to limit the application of the antifraud and antideceit provisions of the Act so as to render the Commission impotent to enjoin suppression of material facts. The more reasonable assumption, considering what had transpired between 1933 and 1940, is that Congress, in enacting the Investment Advisers Act of 1940 and proscribing any practice which operates "as a fraud or deceit," deemed a specific proscription against nondisclosure surplusage.

Respondents also argue that the 1960 amendment to the Investment Advisers Act of 1940 justifies a narrow interpretation of the original enactment. The amendment made two significant changes which are relevant here. "Manipulative" practices were added to the list of those specifically proscribed. There is nothing to suggest, however, that with respect to a requirement of disclosure, "manipulative" is any broader than fraudulent or deceptive. Nor is there any indication that by adding the new proscription Congress intended to narrow the scope of the original proscription. The new amendment also authorizes the Commission "by rules and regulations [to] define, and prescribe means reasonably designed to prevent, such acts, practices, and courses of business as are fraudulent, deceptive, or manipulative." The legislative history offers no indication, however, that Congress intended such rules to substitute for the "general and flexible" antifraud provisions which have long been considered necessary to control "the versatile inventions of fraud-doers." Moreover, the intent of Congress must be culled from the events surrounding the passage of the 1940 legislation. "[O]pinions attributed to a Congress twenty years after the event cannot be considered evidence of the intent of the Congress of 1940." *Securities & Exchange Comm'n* v. *Capital Gains Research Bureau, Inc.*, 306 F. 2d 606, 615 (dissenting opinion). See *United States* v. *Philadelphia Nat. Bank*, 374 U. S. 321, 348–349.

Respondents argue, finally, that their advice was "honest" in the sense that they believed it was sound and did not offer it for the purpose of furthering personal pecuniary objectives. This, of course, is but another way of putting the rejected argument that the elements of technical common-law fraud—particularly intent—must be established before an injunction requiring disclosure may be ordered. It is the practice itself, however, with its potential for abuse, which "operates as a fraud or deceit" within the meaning of the Act when relevant information is suppressed. The Investment Advisers Act of 1940 was "directed not only at dishonor, but also at conduct that tempts dishonor." *United States* v. *Mississippi Valley Co.*, 364 U. S. 520, 549. Failure to disclose material facts must be deemed fraud or deceit within its intended meaning, for, as the experience of the 1920's and 1930's amply reveals, the darkness and ignorance of commercial secrecy are the conditions upon which predatory practices best thrive. To impose upon the Securities and Exchange Commission the burden of showing deliberate dishonesty as a condition precedent to protecting investors through the prophylaxis of disclosure would effectively nullify the protective purposes of the statute. Reading the Act in light of its background we find no such requirement commanded. Neither the Commission nor the courts should be required "to separate the mental urges," *Peterson* v. *Greenville*, 373 U.S. 244, 248, of an investment adviser, for "[t]he motives of man are too complex . . . to separate. . . ." *Mosser* v. *Darrow*, 341 U. S. 267, 271. The statute, in recognition of the adviser's fiduciary relationship to his clients, requires that his advice be disinterested. To insure this it empowers the courts to require disclosure of material facts. It misconceives the purpose of the statute to confine its application to "dishonest" as opposed to "honest" motives. As Dean Shulman said in discussing the nature of securities transactions, what is required is "a picture not simply of the show window, but of the entire store . . . not simply truth in the statements volunteered, but disclosure." The high standards of business morality exacted by our laws regulating the securities industry do not permit an investment adviser to trade on the market effect of his own recommendations without fully and fairly revealing his personal interests in these recommendations to his clients.

Experience has shown that disclosure in such situations, while not onerous to the adviser, is needed to preserve the climate of fair dealing which is so essential to maintain public confidence in the securities industry and to preserve the economic health of the country.

The judgment of the Court of Appeals is reversed and the case is remanded to the District Court for proceedings consistent with this opinion.

Reversed and remanded.

Mr. Justice Douglas took no part in the consideration or decision of this case.

APPENDIX TO OPINION OF THE COURT

On one occasion respondents sold short some shares of a security immediately before stating in their Report that the security was overpriced. After the publication of the Report, respondents covered their short sales. Respondents' transactions are summarized by the Commission as follows:

Stock	Purchased	Purchase price	Recommended	Sold	Sale price	Profit
Continental Insurance Co. ...	3/15/60	47¾–47⅞	3/18/60	3/29/60	50⅛	$ 1,125.00
United Fruit Co.	5/13, 16, 19, 20/60	21¼ 22⅛	5/27/60	6/6, 7, 9, 10/60	23⅝–24½	10,725,00
Creole Petroleum Corp.	7/5, 14/60	25¼–28¾	7/15/60	7/20, 21, 22/60	27⅛–29	1,762.50
Hart, Schaffner & Marx ..	8/8/60	23	8/12/60	8/18, 22/60	24⅞–25¼	837.00
Union Pacfic	10/28, 31/60	25⅜–25⅝	11/1/60	11/7/60	27	1,757.00
Frank G. Shattuck Co.	10/11/60 (purchased calls)	16.83 (2.53 call cost, plus 14.30 option price)	10/14/60	10/25/60 (exercised calls and sold)	19½–20⅛	695.17
Chock Full O'Nuts	10/4/60 (sold short)	68¾–69 (sale price)	10/14/60 (disparaged)	10/24/60 (covered short sale)	62–62½ (purchase price)	2,772.33

Although some of the above figures relating to profits are disputed, respondents do not substantially contest the remaining figures.

224

Mr. Justice Harlan, dissenting.

I would affirm the judgment below substantially for the reasons given by Judge Moore in his opinion for the majority of the Court of Appeals sitting *en banc*, 306 F. 2d 606, and in his earlier opinion for the panel. 300 F. 2d 745. A few additional observations are in order.

Contrary to the majority, I do not read the Court of Appeals' *en banc* opinion as holding that either § 206(1) of the Investment Advisers Act of 1940, 54 Stat. 847 (prohibiting the employment of "any device, scheme, or artifice to defraud any client or prospective client"), or § 206(2), 54 Stat. 847 (prohibiting the engaging "in any transaction, practice, or course of business which operates as a fraud or deceit upon any client or prospective client"), is confined by traditional common law concepts of fraud and deceit. That court recognized that "federal securities laws are to be construed broadly to effectuate their remedial purpose." 306 F. 2d, at 608. It did not hold or intimate that proof of "intent to injure and actual injury to clients" (*ante*, p. 186) was necessary to make out a case under these sections of the statute. Rather it explicitly observed: "Nor can there be any serious dispute that a relationship of trust and confidence should exist between the advisor and the advised," *ibid.*, thus recognizing that no such proof was required. In effect the Court of Appeals simply held that the terms of the statute require, at least, some proof that an investment adviser's recommendations are not disinterested.

I think it clear that what was shown here would not make out a case of fraud or breach of fiduciary relationship under the most expansive concepts of common law or equitable principles. The nondisclosed facts indicate no more than that the respondents personally profited from the foreseeable reaction to sound and impartial investment advice.

The cases cited by the Court (*ante*, p. 198) are wide of the mark as even a skeletonized statement of them will show. In *Securities & Exchange Comm'n* v. *Torr*, 15 F. Supp. 315, reversed on other grounds, 87 F. 2d 446, defendants were in effect bribed to recommend a certain stock. Although it was not apparent that they lied in making their recommendations, it was plain that they were motivated to make them by the promise of reward. In the case before us, there is no vestige of proof that the reason for the recommendations was anything other than a belief in the soundness of the investment advice given.

Charles Hughes & Co. v. *Securities & Exchange Comm'n*, 139

F. 2d 434, involved sales of stock by customers' men to those ignorant
of the market value of the stocks at 16% to 41% above the over-the-
counter price. Defendant's employees must have known that the customers would have refused to buy had they been aware of the actual
market price.

The defendant in *Norris & Hirshberg, Inc.*, v. *Securities & Exchange Comm'n*, 85 U.S. App. D. C. 268, 177 F. 2d 228, dealt in
unlisted securities. Most of its customers believed that the firm was
acting only on their behalf and that its income was derived from commissions; in fact the firm bought from and sold to its customers, and
received its income from mark-ups and mark-downs. The nondisclosure of this basic relationship did not, the court stated, "necessarily
establish that petitioner violated the antifraud provisions of the Securities and Securities Exchange Acts." *Id.*, at 271, 177 F. 2d, at 231.
Defendant's trading practices, however, were found to establish such
a violation; an example of these was the buying of shares of stock
from one customer and the selling to another at a substantially higher
price on the same day. The opinion explicitly distinguishes between
what is necessary to prove common law fraud and the grounds under
securities legislation sufficient for revocation of a broker-dealer registration. *Id.*, at 273, 177 F. 2d, at 233.

Arleen Hughes v. *Securities & Exchange Comm'n*, 85 U. S. App.
D. C. 56, 174 F. 2d 969, concerned the revocation of the license of a
broker-dealer who also gave investment advice but failed to disclose
to customers both the best price at which the securities could be
bought in the open market and the price which she had paid for them.
Since the court expressly relied on language in statutes and regulations
making unlawful "any omission to state a material fact," *id.*, at 63,
174 F. 2d, at 976, this case hardly stands for the proposition that the
result would have been the same had such provisions been absent.

In *Speed* v. *Transamerica Corp.*, 235 F. 2d 369, the controlling
stockholder of a corporation made a public offer to buy stock, con-
cealing from the other shareholders information known to it as an
insider which indicated the real value of the stock to be considerably
greater than the price set by the public offer. Had shareholders been
aware of the concealment, they would undoubtedly have refused to
sell; as a consequence of selling they suffered ascertainable damages.

In *Archer* v. *Securities & Exchange Comm'n*, 133 F. 2d 795, defendant copartners of a company dealing in unlisted securities con-
cealed the name of Claude Westfall, who was found to be in control
of the business. Westfall was thereby enabled to defraud the cus-

tomers of the brokerage firm of Harris, Upham & Co., for which he worked as a trader. Securities of the customers of the latter firm were bought by defendants' company at under the market level, and defendants' company sold securities to the clients of Harris, Upham & Co. at prices above the market.

In all of these cases but *Arleen Hughes*, which turned on explicit provisions against nondisclosure, the concealment involved clearly reflected dishonest dealing that was vital to the consummation of the relevant transactions. No such factors are revealed by the record in the present case. It is apparent that the Court is able to achieve the result reached today only by construing these provisions of the Investment Advisers Act as it might a pure conflict of interest statute, cf. *United States* v. *Mississippi Valley Co.*, 364 U. S. 520, something which this particular legislation does not purport to be.

I can find nothing in the terms of the statute or in its legislative history which lends support to the absolute rule of disclosure now established by the Court. Apart from the other factors dealt with in the two opinions of the Court of Appeals, it seems to me especially significant that Congress in enacting the Investment Advisers Act did not include the express disclosure provision found in § 17(a)(2) of the Securities Act of 1933, 48 Stat. 84, even though it did carry over to the Advisers Act the comparable fraud and deceit provisions of the Securities Act. To attribute the presence of a disclosure provision in the earlier statute to an "abundance of caution" (*ante*, p. 198) and its omission in the later statute to a congressional belief that its inclusion would be "surplusage" (*ante*, p. 199) is for me a singularly unconvincing explanation of this controlling difference between the two statutes.

However salutary may be thought the disclosure rule now fashioned by the Court, I can find no authority for it either in the statute or in any regulation duly promulgated thereunder by the S. E. C. Only two Terms ago we refused to extend certain provisions of the Securities Exchange Act of 1934 to encompass "policy" considerations at least as cogent as those urged here by the S. E. C. *Blau* v. *Lehman*, 368 U. S. 403. The Court should have exercised the same wise judicial restraint in this case. This is particularly so at this interlocutory stage of the litigation. It is conceivable that at the trial the S. E. C. would have been able to make out a case under the statute construed according to its terms.

I respectfully dissent.

NOTES

Chapter I

1. The work which best conveys the ethos of the earlier epoch is Henry Clews, *Twenty-Eight Years in Wall Street* (New York: Irving Publishing Co., 1888).

2. *New York Times Annalist*, VI (1915), p. 65.

3. In a survey reported by Raymond C. Baumhart, S.J., "How Ethical Are Businessmen?", *Harvard Business Review* (July–August, 1961), p. 16, 42% of businessmen said they would buy shares in a company about to be acquired by their company under conditions indicating that the price would increase on announcement of the merger; 61% thought that other businessmen would buy under similar circumstances. At the time of this poll most businessmen would probably have believed such a practice to be legal because neither Section 16(b) of the Securities Exchange Act of 1934 nor Rule 10b-5 of the SEC would seem to have been applicable. Many refinements would be needed to make the cited poll meaningful. If businessmen were asked today "Do you trade regularly on inside information about your company?", the percentage answering affirmatively would undoubtedly be very small.

4. Perhaps the major breakthrough in developing an economic theory of information was made by Anthony Downs, *An Economic Theory of Democracy* (New York: Harper & Bros., 1957). See also James M. Buchanan and Gordon Tullock, *The Calculus of Consent* (Ann Arbor: University of Michigan Press, 1962). As far as the author is aware, however, the theory developed in Chapters IV–VII of this book is the first attempt to construct a systematic model for the most active market for valuable information, that is, the stock market. The works of Becker, Machlup, and Van Den Haag on the economics of education and knowledge are not directly relevant. Education bears a relationship to information analogous to that of transportation or storage to tangible commodities.

5. Adolf A. Berle, Jr., "Publicity of Accounts and Directors' Purchases of Stock," *Michigan Law Review*, XXV (1927), p. 827.

6. H. L. Wilgus, "Purchase of Shares of Corporation by a Director from a Shareholder," *Michigan Law Review*, VIII (1910), p. 267.

7. 213 U.S. 419 (1909).

8. Roberts Walker, "The Duty of Disclosure by a Director Purchasing Stock from His Stockholders," *Yale Law Journal*, XXXII (1923), p. 637. For some indication that this is still largely true, see Michael Conant, "Duties of Disclosure of Corporate Insiders Who Purchase Shares," *Cornell Law Quarterly*, XLVI (1961), p. 53.

9. Wilgus, *op. cit.*, p. 297.

10. Berle, *op. cit.*, p. 828.

11. An even less convincing example may be found in Clarence D. Laylin, "The Duty of a Director Purchasing Shares of Stock," *Yale Law Journal*, XXVII (1918), p. 731. Professor Laylin argued that, because shareholders ultimately receive dividends and directors declare dividends, the directors therefore owe a fiduciary duty to shareholders, and a fiduciary relationship precludes their buying shares without disclosing their inside information. The difficulty with Professor Laylin's syllogism is that his conclusions do not follow from his premises. He has suggested a very narrow application of the fiduciary-duty doctrine in the context of dividend distributions. Indeed, such cases can be found. But by no stretch of the imagination can it be said that there is *therefore* a broader fiduciary duty covering all aspects of the relationship between insiders and shareholders. This kind of reasoning, involving the fallacy of the undistributed middle, while it may serve certain purposes for common-law courts, should be carefully avoided in complex social or economic questions. It should be noted, in passing, that this approach precludes any protection for non-shareholders buying from corporate insiders.

12. Walker, *op. cit.*, p. 637.

13. *Ibid.*, p. 639.

14. See *Helms* v. *Duckworth*, 249 Fed. 2d 482 (D.C.C.A., 1957). The doctrine is by no means well-established, although several forces are presently converging for the development of such a rule. See Henry G. Manne's review of F. Hodge O'Neal and Jordan Derwin's *Expulsion or Oppression of Business Associates: "Squeeze-Outs" in Small Enterprises* in the *St. Louis University Law Journal*, VI (1961), p. 567.

15. William Z. Ripley, *Main Street and Wall Street* (Boston: Little, Brown & Co., 1927).

16. Louis D. Brandeis, *Other People's Money* (Washington, D.C.: National Home Library Foundation, 1933).

17. Berle, *op. cit.*, p. 827.

18. We still do not have a detailed history of the provisions of the 1934 Act. Ralph F. De Bedts, *The New Deal's SEC* (New York and London: Columbia University Press, 1964) gives the broad outlines, but a full intellectual and political history remains to be written.

19. Berle, *op. cit.*, pp. 830–31.

20. See Henry G. Manne, "Some Theoretical Aspects of Share Voting," *Columbia Law Review*, LXIV (1964), pp. 1434–44.

21. In his 1927 article in the *Michigan Law Review* (*op. cit.*), Berle cited Ripley's *Main Street and Wall Street* as supporting his idea that insider trading should be forbidden. A careful reading of Ripley's book (*op. cit.*, p. 205), however, discloses that his strongest reason for favoring full disclosure is his belief that companies that hide information have more speculative securities than those which do not. As we shall see in Chapter VI, this is a very questionable proposition. Even if it were completely true, it is not a strong argument. We are not told what "speculative securities" are, nor why they are bad. Furthermore, Ripley implied a causal connection between insider trading and rapid share-price fluctuations, with no attempt to substantiate this implication.

22. *Stock Exchange Practices, Hearings Before the Committee on Banking and Currency*, U.S. Senate, 73d Cong., 1st Sess., 1933 (10 volumes).

23. *Ibid.*, p. 6557.

24. *Ibid.*, p. 6559.

25. *Ibid.*

26. U.S. Senate Report No. 1455, 73d Cong., 2d Sess., 1934. Cf. Sections 9 and 10 of the 1934 Act. Section 16(b) begins with the words "for the purpose of preventing the unfair use of information which may have been obtained by such beneficial owner, director, or officer by reason of his relationship to the issuer. . . ." These introductory words are peculiar and it has been argued that these words are *limiting*, requiring some proof that the use of the information by an insider is in fact unfair. This contention was denied in *Smolowe* v. *Delendo Corp.*, 136 Fed. 2d 231, 236 (2d Cir., 1943), *cert. denied*, 320 U.S. 751. The denial is extensive and commonly accepted today as correct. The introductory words were said to aid constitutionality and

guide the SEC in its rule-making, but did not require a showing of unfairness or damage in every case otherwise covered by Section 16(b). See Louis Loss, Securities Regulation (Boston and Toronto: Little, Brown and Co., 1961) p. 1041.

27. *Ibid.*

28. H.R. Report No. 1383, 73d Cong., 2d Sess., 1934, p. 13.

29. *Report of Special Study of Securities Markets of the S.E.C.,* House Doc. No. 95, Part 3, 88th Cong., 1st Sess., 1963.

30. *Securities Acts Amendments of 1964,* 78 Stat. 565 (1964).

31. *Report of Special Study of Securities Markets of the S.E.C., op. cit.,* Part 1, pp. 438–39.

32. *Ibid.,* p. 440. "Self-regulatory agencies" would include the registered stock exchanges and the National Association of Securities Dealers.

33. Loss, *op. cit.,* p. 1088. The arguments against Section 16(b), even by representatives of the securities industry, are, according to Loss, directed against the method by which 16(b) seeks to achieve its purpose, not the purpose itself.

34. Michael Joseph, "Civil Liability Under Rule 10b-5—A Reply," *Northwestern University Law Review,* LIX (1964), p. 183.

35. *In the Matter of Cady, Roberts & Co.,* SEC Release No. 6668, *CCH Federal Securities Law Reporter* (1961), p. 81018; "Corporate Standards and Legal Rules," *California Law Review,* L (1962), p. 415; "The Direction of Management Responsibility," *The Business Lawyer,* XVIII (1962), p. 32; "Recent Developments in Securities Regulation," *Columbia Law Review,* LXIII (1963), p. 864. All of these are cited in David S. Ruder, "Pitfalls in the Development of a Federal Law of Corporations by Implications Through Rule 10b-5," *Northwestern University Law Review,* LIX (1964), p. 210.

36. *CCH Federal Securities Law Reporter* (1961), p. 81015.

37. There is a subtle borrowing from the general acceptability of common-law fraud rules in this choice of terms. None of the rather strict logic underlying the elements of common-law fraud can be found in the Commission's, or indeed many courts', interpretation of Rule 10b-5. Cf. William Prosser, *Handbook of the Law of Torts,* 3d ed. (St. Paul: West Publishing Co., 1964), p. 700.

38. *CCH Federal Securities Law Reporter* (1961), p. 81016.

39. *California Law Review,* L (1962), p. 415.

40. Cary himself has cited contradictory evidence when he noted that 42% of businessmen interviewed in the *Harvard Business Review* poll (cited in footnote 3) said they would buy shares of a company

being merged into theirs before public disclosure; 61% thought others would buy. Cary said this was a "surprising, and perhaps shocking, number of executives [who] feel that it is perfectly reasonable conduct to use inside information for their personal benefit." *The Business Lawyer*, XVIII (1962), p. 33.

41. *Ibid.*, p. 34.

42. This expression originated with an anonymous lady law student, who, during a classroom discussion of the subject, stamped her foot and angrily declaimed, "I don't care; it's just not right."

43. There are two exceptions to the rather bleak picture generally presented by the legal literature on insider trading. The first of these is Victor Brudney, "Insider Securities Dealings During Corporate Crises," *Michigan Law Review*, LXI (1962), p. 1. This is a thoughtful and analytical survey of many of the policy issues involved in the question of insider trading. Professor Brudney's strongest objections seem to be (1) the possibility of manipulation by insiders to maximize their trading profits and (2) the inappropriateness of inside information as a form of compensation. Each of these objections is discussed in Chapter X.

The author of the second work is both an economist and a lawyer, and it is not surprising that his conclusions differ somewhat from those of Berle or Cary. Professor Michael Conant has argued in "Duties of Disclosure of Corporate Insiders Who Purchase Shares," *Cornell Law Quarterly*, XLVI (1960), p. 53, that the value of this information belongs as a matter of traditional fiduciary-duty law to the corporation and not to the individual outside shareholder. Thus, he would extend the policy of Section 16(b) of the Securities and Exchange Act to cover all insider transactions, and the corporation would be entitled to recover the insider's profits. The law, however, does not bear out Professor Conant's position, and the one case he cites for it, the *Brophy* case, discussed in Chapter III, can easily be explained on other grounds.

But by far the most interesting aspect of Professor Conant's article is his statement (p. 57) of why we should *not* allow outsiders to recover profits from insiders with whom they have dealt:

> In the free market, the less informed party to the sale of a tangible item may inspect and ask questions. If the item sold is an intangible, he may ask questions. If he does not bother to inspect or ask questions, he has assumed the uncertainty that the other party may bargain with superior information. The corporate stockholder selling his shares to an officer or director is in such a position. The insider is likely to have

more information about the corporation's prospects than the ordinary shareholder. The shareholder is free to ask the insider for a summary of facts on which he bases his purchase. In this case, the law of fraud requires a complete answer by the insider, for speaking a half-truth under the circumstances would be equivalent to misrepresentation. If the shareholder does not bother to ask questions, he assumes the uncertainty that the insider may deal with superior knowledge.

Chapter II

1. Carlos D. Israels, "The Close Corporation and the Law," *Cornell Law Quarterly*, XXXIII (1948), p. 488; George D. Hornstein, "Stockholders' Agreements in the Closely Held Corporation," *Yale Law Journal*, LIX (1950), p. 1040; William L. Cary, "How Illinois Corporations May Enjoy Partnership Advantages, *Northwestern University Law Review*, XLVIII (1953), p. 427; and F. Hodge O'Neal, *Close Corporations* (Chicago: Callaghan & Co., 1958) 2 vols. Additional sources are cited in Ralph J. Baker and William L. Cary, *Cases and Materials on Corporations*, 3d ed. (Brooklyn: The Foundation Press, Inc., 1959).

2. *Oliver* v. *Oliver*, 118 Ga. 362, 45 S.E. 232 (1903).

3. *Stewart* v. *Harris*, 69 Kan. 498, 77 Pac. 277 (1904).

4. *Jacquith* v. *Mason*, 99 Neb. 509, 156 N.W. 1041 (1916).

5. American Law Institute, *Restatement of the Law Second*, Agency 2d (St. Paul: American Law Institute Publishers, 1958), Sections 387–98.

6. *Sher* v. *Sandler*, 325 Mass. 348, 90 N.E.2d 536 (1950). There have been at least two other kinds of situations in which courts deduced the existence of a fiduciary duty from extraneous private agreements. In *Helms* v. *Duckworth*, 249 Fed. 2d 482 (D.C.C.A., 1957), the court implied a fiduciary relationship from a survivor purchase agreement between the only two shareholders in a small corporation. In *DeBoy* v. *Harris*, 207 Md. 212, 113 Atl. 2d 903 (1955), the court found that the fiduciary relationship of a joint-venture partnership survived incorporation when there was no express dissolution of the partnership.

7. See Henry G. Manne's book review, *St. Louis University Law Journal*, VI (1961), p. 567.

8. *Meinhard* v. *Salmon*, 249 N.Y. 458, at p. 464, 164 N.E. 545, at p. 546, 62 A.L.R. 1 (1928).

9. For the best available discussion of legislative controls during the period of special chartering, as well as a superb corporation-law history, see John William Cadman, Jr., *The Corporation in New*

Jersey: Business and Politics, 1791–1875 (Cambridge, Mass.: Harvard University Press, 1949).

10. 213 U.S. 419 (1909).

11. *Strong* v. *Repide*, 213 U.S. 419, 431 (1909).

12. See Louis Loss, *Securities Regulation*, 2d ed. (Boston and Toronto: Little, Brown & Co., 1961), pp. 1446–48, with authorities cited. Other collections of cases may be found in Baker and Cary, *op. cit.*, pp. 553–63; and Michael Conant, "Duties of Disclosure of Corporate Insiders Who Purchase Shares," *Cornell Law Quarterly*, XLVI (1961), pp. 57–58.

13. *Goodwin* v. *Agassiz*, 283 Mass. 358, 186 N.E. 659 (1933). In this case the plaintiff, an experienced businessman, sold shares in a mining company over the Boston Stock Exchange to the defendants, who were officers and directors of the corporation. The insiders were buying because of their confidence in a new geological theory suggesting heavy copper deposits in an area in which the corporation was interested. Not long before this theory came to their attention, the company's previous explorations had proved unsuccessful, and this had been publicized in local newspapers. The court did not expressly hold that a transaction across an exchange always insulates insiders from liability. It merely found that in this case the circumstances did not indicate the need for special protection for the plaintiff.

14. *Ibid.*, p. 661.

15. For a cataloging of such circumstances, see F. Hodge O'Neal and Jordan Derwin, *Expulsion or Oppression of Business Associates: "Squeeze-Outs" in Small Enterprises* (Durham: Duke University Press, 1961). This book deals with a variety of problems in small businesses and not with the special-facts rule as such. It illustrates dramatically, however, the dangers for noncontrolling shareholders in smaller corporations with no active market for their securities.

16. See Baker and Cary, *op. cit.*, p. 560, and "Insider Liability Under Securities Exchange Act Rule 10b-5: The *Cady, Roberts* Doctrine," *University of Chicago Law Review*, XXX (1962), p. 124.

17. *Goodwin* v. *Agassiz*, 283 Mass. 358, at p. 363, 186 N.E. 659, at p. 661 (1933).

18. *Brophy* v. *Cities Service Co.*, 31 Del. Ch. 241, 70 Atl. 2d 5 (1949).

19. The *Brophy* case suggests an intriguing problem under Rule 10b-5, discussed in the next chapter. Cases have decided that corporations as well as individuals can violate the rule. Consequently, any

time a corporation goes unannounced into the market to purchase its own shares, and these purchases have the effect of raising the market price, a violation of 10b-5 might automatically follow. If, of course, the corporation announced in advance that it was going to purchase shares, the cost would be substantially greater, *as would the ultimate loss to those shareholders of the corporation who were not in the market to sell their shares.* See Chapter VI.

20. As amended to August 20, 1964:

> Section 16. (a) Every person who is directly or indirectly the beneficial owner of more than 10 per centum of any class of any equity security (other than an exempted security) which is registered pursuant to section 12 of this title, or who is a director or an officer of the issuer of such security, shall file, at the time of the registration of such security on a national securities exchange or by the effective date of a registration statement filed pursuant to section 12(g) of this title, or within ten days after he becomes such beneficial owner, director, or officer, a statement with the Commission (and, if such security is registered on a national securities exchange, also with the exchange) of the amount of all equity securities of such issuer of which he is the beneficial owner, and within ten days after the close of each calendar month thereafter, if there has been a change in such ownership during such month, shall file with the Commission (and if such security is registered on a national securities exchange, shall also file with the exchange), a statement indicating his ownership at the close of the calendar month and such changes in his ownership as have occurred during such calendar month.
>
> (b) For the purpose of preventing the unfair use of information which may have been obtained by such beneficial owner, director, or officer by reason of his relationship to the issuer, any profit realized by him from any purchase and sale, or any sale and purchase, of any equity security of such issuer (other than an exempted security) within any period of less than six months, unless such security was acquired in good faith in connection with a debt previously contracted, shall inure to and be recoverable by the issuer, irrespective of any intention on the part of such beneficial owner, director, or officer in entering into such transaction of holding the security purchased or of not repurchasing the security sold for a period exceeding six months. Suit to recover such profit may be instituted at law or in equity in any court of competent jurisdiction by the issuer, or by the owner of any security of the issuer in the name and in behalf of the issuer if the issuer shall fail or refuse to bring such suit within sixty days after request or shall fail diligently to prosecute the same thereafter; but no such suit shall be brought more than two years after the date such profit was realized.

This subsection shall not be construed to cover any transaction where such beneficial owner was not such both at the time of the purchase and sale, or the sale and purchase, of the security involved, or any transaction or transactions which the Commission by rules and regulations may exempt as not comprehended with the purpose of this subsection.

(c) It shall be unlawful for any such beneficial owner, director, or officer, directly or indirectly, to sell any equity security of such issuer (other than an exempted security), if the person selling the security or his principal (1) does not own the security sold, or (2) if owning the security does not deliver it against such sale within twenty days thereafter, or does not within five days after such sale deposit it in the mails or other usual channels of transportation; but no person shall be deemed to have violated this subsection if he proves that notwithstanding the exercise of good faith he was unable to make such delivery or deposit within such time, or that to do so would cause undue inconvenience or expense.

Subsections (d) and (e) provide certain exemptions for brokerage and arbitrage transactions. Certain relevant definitions appear in Section 3(a) of the 1934 Act:

(9) The term "person" means an individual, a corporation, a partnership, an association, a joint-stock company, a business trust, or an unincorporated organization.

(10) The term "security" means any note, stock, treasury stock, bond, debenture, certificate of interest or participation in any profit-sharing agreement or in any oil, gas, or other mineral royalty or lease, any collateral-trust certificate, pre-organization certificate or subscription, transferable share, investment contract, voting-trust certificate, certificate of deposit, for a security, or in general, any instrument commonly known as a "security"; or any certificate of interest or participation in, temporary or interim certificate for, receipt for, or warrant or right to subscribe to or purchase, any of the foregoing; but shall not include currency or any note, draft, bill of exchange, or banker's acceptance which has a maturity at the time of issuance of not exceeding nine months, exclusive of days of grace, or any renewal thereof the maturity of which is likewise limited.

(11) The term "equity security" means any stock or similar security; or any security convertible, with or without consideration, into such a security, or carrying any warrant or right to subscribe to or purchase such a security; or any such warrant or right; or any other security which the Commission shall deem to be of similar nature and consider necessary or appropriate, by such rules and regulations as it may prescribe in the public interest or for the protection of investors, to treat as an equity security. . . .

(13) The terms "buy" and "purchase" each include any contract to buy, purchase, or otherwise acquire.

(14) The terms "sale" and "sell" each include any contract to sell or otherwise dispose of.

21. *Securities Exchange Act of 1934,* Section 12 (g)(1)(A). The figure is actually 750 shareholders for approximately two years after the amendment was adopted and then it changes to 500. Sec. 12(g)(1)(B).

22. Loss, *op. cit.,* pp. 1051–55.

23. *Ibid.,* pp. 1044ff.

24. See, for example, *Smolowe* v. *Delendo Corp.,* 136 Fed. 2d 231 (2d Cir., 1943), and *Gratz* v. *Claughton,* 187 Fed. 2d 46 (2d Cir., 1951).

25. See *Opinion of the General Counsel,* Securities Exchange Act Release No. 1965 (1938) and *Boston & Maine R.R. Co.* v. *Hillman, CCH Federal Securities Law Reporter,* par. 90813 (S.D.N.Y., 1957). Perhaps in an effort to aid the SEC in "plugging" this hole, the New York Stock Exchange has recently forbidden directors of a listed company to own shares in a controlled subsidiary; see *Wall Street Journal* (Aug. 30, 1965), p. 22, col. 2. Clearly, under the doctrine of the *Blau* case, discussed later in this chapter, the Commission would have no authority to extend the application of 16(b) in this fashion. Presumably, however, the New York Stock Exchange is not limited by the same constraints that guide the SEC, as it is a private rule-making body. If the Exchange wins its current legislative fight to gain exemption from the antitrust laws, its status as a private rulemaker should be re-examined. Cf. *Steele* v. *Louisville & Nashville R.R. Co.,* 323 U.S. 192, especially at 198 (1944).

26. Loss, *op. cit.,* p. 1043.

27. 368 U.S. 403 (1962).

28. *Rattner* v. *Lehman,* 193 Fed. 2d 564 (2d Cir., 1952).

29. *Blau* v. *Lehman,* 368 U.S. 403, 413 (1962).

30. See definition Sec. 3(a)(9) in footnote 20.

31. See Floyd R. Mechem, *Elements of the Law of Partnership,* 2d ed. (Chicago: Callaghan and Co., 1920), pp. 8–13.

32. *Blau* v. *Lehman,* 368 U.S. 403, 416 (1962).

33. See Chapter X.

34. Senator Gore, as noted on p. 10, indicated his belief that 16(b) was an antimanipulation or antifraud provision. But this contention was specifically denied in *Smolowe* v. *Delendo Corp.,* 136 Fed. 2d 231 (2d Cir., 1943).

Chapter III

1. See Loss, *op. cit.*, p. 1423.

2. *Ibid.*, p. 1425.

3. Interestingly, Section 16(d) of the 1934 Act was amended in 1964 to exempt broker-dealers from the coverage of 16(b) when they are directors of companies for whose shares they maintain a market.

4. In fact this Section was originally numbered 9(c), but in a later draft it became 10(b). See Loss, *op. cit.*, p. 1424. Section 9 applies only to listed securities, and the move may have been aimed merely at authorizing rules against manipulative practices in over-the-counter stocks.

5. *Ibid.*, p. 1426.

6. *Code of Federal Regulations*, Vol. 17, Sec. 240.10b-5. This was originally promulgated as Rule X-10B-5 and is now simply Rule 10b-5.

7. *Kardon* v. *National Gypsum Co.*, 73 Fed. Supp. 798 (D.C.E.D. Pa., 1947).

8. 99 Fed. Supp. 808 (D. Del., 1951).

9. *Speed* v. *Transamerica Corp.*, 99 Fed. Supp. 808, 828–29 (D. Del., 1951).

10. Norman D. Lattin, *The Law of Corporations* (Brooklyn: The Foundation Press, Inc., 1959), p. 274–75.

11. This was changed in the 1964 amendments to cover any corporation with assets of $1 million and 750 shareholders operating in interstate commerce or whose securities are traded in interstate commerce or by use of the mails. The Securities Exchange Act of 1934, Sec. 12(g)(1)(A). By Sec. 12(g)(1)(B) the requirement for 750 shareholders is reduced to 500 after two years.

12. See David S. Ruder, "Civil Liability Under Rule 10b-5: Judicial Revision of Legislative Intent?", *Northwestern University Law Review*, LVII (1963), p. 627, and Appendix, p. 687. The acceleration of use of 10b-5 is dramatically illustrated by comparing Shepard's *United States Citations—Statutes, Edition Supplement 1943–1964* (covering cases until 1962) with the July, 1965, *Supplement.* In approximately the last two years 10b-5 has been cited in well over half again as many cases as it was in the previous twenty years of its existence.

13. See Daniel B. Posner, "Developments in Federal Securities Regulation," *The Business Lawyer*, XX (1965), p. 595.

14. *J. I. Case Co.* v. *Borak*, 377 U.S. 426 (1964). This case involved a civil action for an alleged violation of the SEC's proxy-solicitation rules promulgated under Section 14(a) of the Securities Exchange

Act. However, the broad language used in the opinion left no doubt that civil actions under Rule 10b-5 were approved as well. The Court, while noting that the statute makes no specific reference to a private right of action, concluded that "it is the duty of the courts to be alert to provide such remedies as are necessary to make effective the Congressional purpose."

15. Discussions of these and many other issues may be found in the following: Loss, *op. cit.*, pp. 1448–74; Posner, *op. cit.*; Ruder, "Pitfalls in the Development . . . ," *op. cit.*, p. 185; Daniel B. Posner, "Developments in Federal Securities Regulation," *The Business Lawyer*, XIX (1964), p. 593; Ruder, "Civil Liability Under Rule 10b-5 . . . ," *op. cit.*

16. *CCH Federal Securities Law Reporter* (1961), par. 76803.

17. The opinion makes no attempt to explain why Gintel did not sell out all of his discretionary accounts. For a possible explanation see Chapter V.

18. Query whether the Supreme Court in its subsequent opinion in *Blau* v. *Lehman* did not weaken the legal effect of the relationship so readily found incriminating by the Commission? It can be argued, however, that the necessary relationship under 10b-5 is a matter to be determined under all the existing circumstances, whereas the relationship necessary for liability under Section 16(b) is determined by the statute.

19. The Commission's ruling also prohibited soliciting and executing other orders. Query whether this means that if a customer of Cady, Roberts had at the precise moment but by sheer coincidence asked his broker Gintel to sell his Curtiss-Wright shares that Gintel would not be allowed to do so?

Another important and difficult question presented by the case is whether it is intended to have application to situations not involving such direct use of valuable information. If Gintel had merely called a friend at another brokerage house in no way connected with Curtiss-Wright and advised him to sell, would the second broker also be subject to disciplinary action?

20. This would seem to suggest that the Commission was setting up a different standard in an action to discipline a broker than would operate in a civil action for damages. Cf. "Broker Silence and Rule 10b-5: Expanding the Duty to Disclose," *Yale Law Journal*, LXXI (1962), p. 742. But see F. Arnold Daum and Howard W. Phillips, "The Implications of Cady, Roberts," *The Business Lawyer*, XVII (1962), p. 950. For an earlier argument that 10b-5 establishes a grada-

tion of duties with the most severe ones running against insiders and brokers but with rank outsiders left only with their common-law liabilities, see "The Prospects for Rule 10b-5: An Emerging Remedy for Defrauded Investors," *Yale Law Journal*, LIX (1950), p. 1143.

21. The sources for this summary of facts other than those specifically mentioned in the text are Robert Sheehan, "Great Day in the Morning for Texas Gulf Sulphur," *Fortune* (July, 1964), p. 137, and *The Wall Street Journal* (Eastern Edition), Mar. 9, 1965, p. 4, col. 2; Apr. 20, 1965, p. 3, col. 3; Apr. 21, 1965, p. 4, col. 2; Apr. 22, 1965, p. 28, col. 1; Apr. 23, 1965, p. 3, cols. 3–4; Apr. 27, 1965, p. 1, col. 8; July 8, 1965, p. 30, col. 2; July 9, 1965, p. 5, col. 1; and Aug. 4, 1965, p. 24, col. 2. It is interesting to note, according to the last cited report, that Texas Gulf and its officials defended their action primarily on the grounds that they were not engaged in insider trading, that the statement of Apr. 12, 1965, was necessary and correct under the circumstances, and that factors other than the Timmins strike affected the stock's price.

22. Civil actions against the corporation did in fact follow soon after the SEC's action. See *The Wall Street Journal*, Apr. 26, 1965, p. 5, col. 1. Some private actions were filed prior to the SEC's suit. See *The Wall Street Journal*, Apr. 21, 1965, p. 4, col. 2, and July 14, 1965, p. 1, col. 8.

23. Actually the number of shares purchased by the insiders seems small if they really intended to make a killing with inside information. This suggests one of three possibilities: the SEC has not yet uncovered all of the insiders' trading or giving of information to outsiders (see Chapters V and XI); or the insiders did not feel confident of the value of their information (see Chapters VI and VII); or these insiders simply were not trading on the Timmins information in any substantial amount.

24. Most of the company officials voluntarily returned to the company their stock options granted after Nov., 1964, or transferred to the company at cost the stock already taken under such options. See *The Wall Street Journal*, Aug. 4, 1965, p. 24, col. 2.

25. For additional analysis of the SEC's complaint and some astute observations about insider trading, See Jack M. Whitney II, "Section 10b-5: From Cady, Roberts to Texas Gulf: Matters of Disclosure." *The Business Lawyer*, XXI (1965), p. 193. Also see William H. Painter, "Inside Information: Growing Pains for the Development of Federal Corporation Law Under Rule 10b-5," *Columbia Law Review*, LXV (1965), p. 1361.

26. See Chapter VI.

27. See Ralph F. Fuchs, "Agency Development of Policy Through Rule-Making." *Northwestern University Law Review*, LIX (1965), p. 781, especially pp. 795ff. The SEC's actions in regard to Texas Gulf Sulphur call to mind that agency's much-criticized position in the second *Chenery* case, *Securities and Exchange Commission* v. *Chenery Corporation*, 332 U.S. 194 (1947). See especially Mr. Justice Robert Jackson's dissent, at 212–18. Also see *Securities and Exchange Commission* v. *Chenery Corporation*, 318 U.S. 80 (1943) and authorities cited in Fuchs, pp. 793–94. It is interesting to note in this connection that about six weeks before filing its complaint against Texas Gulf *et al.*, the SEC "deferred indefinitely" action on a proposed regulation to require disclosure of certain insider dealings. See *The Wall Street Journal*, Mar. 8, 1965, p. 3, col. 4. The SEC apparently does not feel that it is necessary to develop rules and regulations concerning insider trading. For the view that it is appropriate to have this field of law developed in a series of judicial determinations, see Arthur Fleischer, Jr., " 'Federal Corporation Law': An Assessment," *Harvard Law Review*, LXXVIII (1965), p. 1146.

Professor Loss has also implied that the SEC should not play solely the role of poor man's complainant. He said that "the Commission is in a peculiarly good position, since it is not bogged down entirely the way courts are in deciding only cases, to shepherd this development along, modulating the sanctions and then ultimately, from time to time, codifying the developments in statements of policy, which I think the courts would be delighted to have and would very largely respect." William L. Cary, Carlos Israels, and Louis Loss, "Recent Developments in Securities Regulation," *Columbia Law Review*, LXIII (1963), p. 867.

Chapter IV

1. In this respect the first-category of information may be analogized to a balance sheet that reflects all past financial occurrences. Second-category information, to follow the analogy through, would constitute events that would cause a change in the asset or liability entries in an existing balance sheet. A more apt analogy for first-category information is to the Schumpeterian stable economic system discussed in Chapter VIII.

2. In this respect it is similar to true inside information, which typically is initially acquired only by employees. But no one has ever suggested that the experience or sophistication gained from a job, apart

from trade secrets, cannot be exploited exclusively by the employee when he seeks to market its value by taking a higher-paying job. Probably jobs that allow the individual to invest part of the return in himself in this fashion pay less in tangible compensation than comparable jobs that do not. Furthermore, an individual may choose to work harder for the same pay in order to guarantee advancement. This too represents a form of investment, while the laggard may be said to be consuming the full value of his position currently.

3. 375 U.S. 180 (1963).

4. In the Supreme Court's opinion the last part of this sentence appears as "immediately selling the shares at a profit upon *the* [italics mine] rise in the market price following the recommendation." If the use of *the* rather than the indefinite article *a* was conscious, it implies the Court's belief that the rise resulted from the recommendation itself and not from the disclosure of first-category information about the company. But if the former is true, a species of real fraud is implied, though the Court explicitly denies that. But this *the* may be more indicative of what the Court really thought was happening than is the rest of the opinion.

5. *Securities and Exchange Commission* v. *Capital Gains Research Bureau, Inc.*, 375 U.S. 180, 186 (1963).

6. *Ibid.*, p. 189.

7. *Ibid.*, p. 187.

8. *Ibid.*, p. 188.

9. See Lawrence M. Friedman, "Freedom of Contract and Occupational Licensing 1890–1910: A Legal and Social Study," *California Law Review*, LIII (1965), p. 487, and Thomas G. Moore, "The Purpose of Licensing," *The Journal of Law and Economics*, IV (1961), p. 93.

10. *Securities and Exchange Commission* v. *Capital Gains Research Bureau, Inc.*, 375 U.S. 180, 196 (1963).

11. This appears to be all the SEC was asking for. *Securities and Exchange Commission* v. *Capital Gains Research Bureau, Inc.*, 375 U.S. 180, 181 (1963). The Court on p. 201 refers to "disclosure of material facts," which might conceivably be construed to require a statement not merely that scalping was involved but how many shares the advisory firm had purchased and whether it intended selling after a price rise.

12. This fact, that insider trading involves aspects of uncertainty and first-category as well as second-category information, necessarily complicates any effort to restrain trading in true inside information. See Chapter XI.

Chapter V

1. For examples of what may have been honest misunderstandings of the various institutional arrangements, see the testimony of George Whitney, a partner in the firm of J. P. Morgan & Co. in *Hearings Before the Committee on Banking and Currency of the United States Senate*, 73d Cong., 1st Sess., 1933, p. 172. For an interesting theoretical explanation of why understanding is not a prerequisite to gain, see Armen A. Alchian, "Uncertainty, Evolution, and Economic Theory," *Journal of Political Economy*, LVIII (1950), p. 211, reprinted in American Economics Association, *Readings in Industrial Organization and Public Policy*, Vol. VIII, eds., Richard B. Heflebower and George W. Stocking (Homewood, Ill.: Richard D. Irwin, Inc., 1958).

2. *Bosworth* v. *Allen*, 168 N.Y. 157, 61 N.E. 163 (1901); *Essex Universal Corporation* v. *Yates*, 305 Fed. 2d 572, 575 (2d Cir., 1962); Fletcher, *Cyclopedia Corporations*, Section 902 (Chicago: Callaghan and Co., 1954).

3. The classic cases are *E. I. du Pont De Nemours Powder Co.* v. *Masland*, 244 U.S. 100 (1917), a case involving a trade secret; *Colonial Laundries, Inc.* v. *Henry*, 48 R.I. 332, 138 Atl. 47 (1927), a case involving a customer list.

4. At many points in the ensuing discussion reference will be made only to the exploitation of good news and not to use of bad news. It is true, of course, that profits can be made by selling on bad news as easily as by buying on good, but at this point it is simply a matter of convenience to use only one illustration instead of two. In Chapters VI and X, where it is important to distinguish good from bad news, specific consideration will be given to each.

5. Aggregate price must, perforce, be measured by market price, but market price represents only the price of the marginally offered share. Only if the supply curve is completely elastic will the marginal price accurately reflect aggregate market price. That is, all shares would have to be offered at the same per-share price as the "next" share to be offered. But most supply curves can be assumed to have some inelasticity. And as no one's knowledge of the slope of the supply curve is perfect, the statement in the text (that insiders would buy until the aggregate market price of all outstanding shares has increased by an amount equal to the value of the information) represents only an ideal situation. The two would coincide in fact only when the outstanding shares would be offered at the market price and the information possessor purchased all of them. This may occasionally happen

with certain public tender-bids for shares. See Henry G. Manne, "Mergers and the Market for Corporate Control," *Journal of Political Economy*, LXXIII (1965), p. 116.

6. The statement is not completely accurate, as there is an opportunity cost involved in holding the shares, but for the long-term investor, this must be very small and probably negligible.

7. *Bristol* v. *Equitable Life Assurance Society of the U.S.*, 132 N.Y. 264, 30 N.E. 506 (1892); *Stein* v. *Morris*, 120 Va. 390, 91 S.E. 177 (1917). See also Harold C. Havighurst, "The Right to Compensation for an Idea," *Northwestern University Law Review* XLIX, (1954), p. 295, and William Prosser, *Handbook of the Law of Torts*, 3d ed., sec. 124 (St. Paul: West Publishing Co., 1964).

8. At many points during the Senate Hearings on Stock Exchange Practices in 1933, as well as in his book, *Wall Street Under Oath* (New York: Simon & Schuster, 1939), Ferdinand Pecora remarked that preferred lists and bargain shares seemed to evidence a reciprocity agreement among underwriters. However, these were merely innuendoes suggesting something evil rather than any attempt to understand a comprehensive market for information.

9. The New York Stock Exchange publishes annual figures in broad categories of those who own corporate shares, and the attention of most writers has focused on share ownership rather than on trading. See, for instance, Adolf A. Berle, Jr. and Gardiner C. Means, *The Modern Corporation and Private Property* (New York: The Macmillan Co., 1933), p. 51, and Lewis H. Kimmel, *Share Ownership in the United States* (Washington, D.C.: Brookings Institution, 1952). The SEC does maintain statistics on ownership and changes in ownership of their own companies' shares by corporate insiders. But for the reasons suggested in the text, such data is of little assistance in knowing the extent to which all stock trading reflects exploitation of undisclosed information. Cf. Louis Loss, *Securities Regulations* (Boston and Toronto: Little, Brown and Co., 1961), p. 1043.

10. Monopolistic collusion has been suggested as a possible explanation for many directors' appointments. See Louis D. Brandeis, *Other People's Money* (Washington: National Home Library Foundation, 1933), p. 35, and T.N.E.C., *Bureaucracy and Trusteeship in Large Corporations*, Monograph No. 11, 76th Cong., 3d Sess., 1940, pp. 6–8. This charge is more characteristic of the 1930's than of the 1960's, and, from what we know of how directors actually function, this would seem to be a crude and inefficient device for accomplishing the alleged

purpose. The charge has also been made that control over directorships has been used by investment bankers as an aid in maintaining a
monopoly position. See *United States* v. *Morgan,* 118 Fed. Supp. 621,
702 (S.D.N.Y., 1953).

11. Some of the raw data suggesting this hypothesis can be found
in two sources, the *Senate Hearings on Stock Exchange Practices in
1933, op. cit.,* and the SEC's *Special Study of Securities Markets,* Part
I, House Doc. No. 95, Part 1, 88th Cong., 1st Sess., 1963. In the first
source see, for example, pp. 29–33 for testimony and questioning of
J. P. Morgan and pp. 1208–09 for testimony and questioning of Otto
Kahn. In the *Special Study* see pp. 429–31 for discussion of directorships held by broker-dealers and their motives for going on boards.
The following from p. 429 is of interest:

> Of 4,964 firms replying to the questionnaire, 476 stated that members
> were directors of one or more companies whose stock was traded on an
> exchange, and 995 that they were directors of one or more companies
> whose stock was traded only over the counter. Many of these firms had
> only one or two directorships, but 101, including several of the largest
> underwriters and commission houses, were represented on the boards of
> at least 10 companies. For example, members of Bache & Co. were direc-
> tors of 23 listed and 29 over-the-counter companies; Kidder, Peabody &
> Co., 23 listed and 29 over-the-counter companies; Lehman Bros., 58
> listed and 23 over-the-counter companies; and Paine, Webber, Jackson
> & Curtis, 24 listed and 29 over-the-counter companies. In addition to
> these large, well established firms, several of the newer and smaller
> underwriting houses which specialized in bringing out new issues in
> recent years had members on the boards of directors of several over-
> the-counter companies. For example, Globus, Inc., had 17 such director-
> ships.

And consider the following from p. 433:

> The basic conflicts which are highlighted by the *Cady, Roberts* case
> stem from the fact that a director, by virtue of his office, may have
> access to corporate information not contemporaneously available to the
> general public. A representative of a broker-dealer sitting on the board
> of directors of a company may have difficulty resolving loyalties and
> duties to the company, his customers, and stockholders of the company
> who are not his customers. . . .
> Carl M. Loeb, Rhoades & Co. also tries to distinguish secret informa-
> tion which it receives through members who serve as directors, from
> that which may be disclosed. A partner of the firm told the Special
> Study:

I ascertain from management in most cases, or in all cases, if I am going to make this information available to anyone. I say, "Is this information available generally to any part of the investing public that wants to find it?"

* * * If that is the situation, I do not wait 6 months until the public report comes out on the company. If this is not secret information and you are sure this is information that would be available in like manner, you do not try to jump the market but, at the same time, you do not want to stand back and look stupid.

This is a very difficult area to move in. This is why we have this policy of not tying our trading department's hands with inside knowledge, because what is inside knowledge to me is already on the street in about 9 cases out of 10.

That is why we get the company to release the information as soon as possible, to remove the problem.

12. William O. Douglas, "Directors Who Do Not Direct," *Harvard Law Review*, XLVII (1934), p. 1305; Horace B. Samuel, *Shareholders' Money* (London: Sir Isaac Pitman & Sons, Ltd., 1933), p. 124.

13. Sen. Report No. 1455, 73d Cong., 2d Sess., 1934, p. 36.

14. Some of the reasons why pools could be easily converted into devices for fraudulent manipulation will become clearer in Chapter VII. Basically, the argument is that many outside shareholders respond to stock-price movements rather than to fundamental data about corporate affairs. Additional discussion of pools appears in Chapter X.

15. Sec. 9, *Securities Exchange Act of 1934*, as amended, 15 U.S.C. 78i (1965).

16. Brandeis, *op. cit.; Stock Exchange Practices, op cit.;* Roscoe T. Steffen, "The Investment Bankers' Case: Some Observations," *Yale Law Journal*, LXIV (1954), p. 169; William Dwight Whitney, "The Investment Bankers' Case—Including a Reply to Professor Steffen," *Yale Law Journal*, LXIV (1955), p. 319; Roscoe T. Steffen, "The Investment Bankers' Case: Observations in Rejoinder, *Yale Law Journal*, LXIV (1955), p. 863; William Dwight Whitney, "The Investment Bankers' Case: Surrejoinder," *Yale Law Journal*, LXIV (1955), p. 873; *United States* v. *Morgan*, 118 Fed. Supp. 621 (D.C.S.D.N.Y., 1953).

17. Merrill Lynch, Pierce, Fenner & Smith is the principal illustration of a firm ordinarily called a brokerage house but playing an increasingly important role in underwriting and other investment-banking functions. See T. A. Wise, *The Insiders* (New York: Doubleday & Co., Inc., n.d.), pp. 65–66.

18. Report of *Special Study of Securities Market of the SEC op. cit.*, Part 1, p. 429.

19. *Ibid.*, p. 433.

20. Robert A. Gordon, *Business Leadership in the Large Corporation* (Berkeley and Los Angeles: University of California Press, 1961), pp. 214–21; Andreas G. Papandreou, "Some Basic Problems in the Theory of the Firm," *A Survey of Contemporary Economics*, Vol. II, ed., Bernard F. Haley (Homewood, Ill.: Richard D. Irwin, Inc., 1952), p. 183.

21. This discussion has some implications for the subject of cumulative voting. Probably some of the opposition to cumulative voting stems from the fact that it requires a sharing of valuable information with someone not actually selected by those in control of the company.

22. Consider the following from *United States* v. *Morgan*, 118 Fed. Supp. 621, 817 (1953):

> But with a series of security issues, the saving in time and labor of the officers and employees of an issuer, which would have to be spent in teaching a new investment banker the intricacies of the business, and the financial setup of the company, are a matter of real consequence; and it must not be forgotten that many of the matters to be discussed are of such a character that company officials desire to have such conversations only with those whom they trust, and in whose integrity and competence they have complete confidence.

23. In *Wall Street Under Oath, op. cit.*, Pecora explained what he considered the origins of preferred lists. After stating that J. P. Morgan & Co. entered the business of underwriting common stocks in 1929 and that they did not want any implication of speculation associated with their name, he went on:

> But they decided that it was quite all right to offer the stock *privately*, to a select list of purchasers, "People that we know intimately, that we believe have enough knowledge of business and general conditions to know exactly what they are buying. . . ."

> This was the origin of the famous so-called "preferred lists" whose publication stirred the nation, and opened the eyes of millions of citizens to the hidden ways of Wall Street. In each case, stock was offered by J. P. Morgan & Company to the individuals on these lists at cost, or practically at cost. In each case the offer was made with full and irrefutable knowledge that there was, or would very shortly be, a public market for the stock at a much higher figure. In effect, it was the offer of a gift of very substantial dimensions (pp. 26–27).

Pecora also pointed out that there were almost 500 persons on one or the other of these "preferred lists." They included men exceedingly prominent in both business and government (pp. 28–29).

Naturally, the *Senate Hearings on Stock Exchange Practices in 1933* were replete with many references to these lists. Discussions of the subject begin on the following pages: 138, 145, 173, 177, 396, 401, 885, 1209, and 1232. The discussions usually involved Pecora's charge that these lists were used for "reciprocity" and the bankers' heated but unconvincing denials. It is perhaps fair to say, however, that no cogent analysis of the phenomenon exists anywhere in the *Hearings* or Pecora's book.

24. *Stock Exchange Practices, op. cit.,* pp. 62 and 814–15.

25. George Whitney of J. P. Morgan & Co. said that persons were put on such lists "as the result of continuing relations." *Ibid.,* p. 172. We are not told what these continuing relations are, nor did Pecora follow up on the subject.

26. See footnote 22, *supra.*

27. Section 16 of Schedule A of the Securities Act of 1933 requires that a registration statement include the price at which the security will be offered to the public "and any variation therefrom at which any portion of such security is proposed to be offered to any persons or classes of persons, other than the underwriters, naming them or specifying the class. A variation in price may be proposed prior to the date of the public offering of the security, but the Commission shall immediately be notified of such variation."

28. *Special Study of Securities Markets, op. cit.,* Part 1, p. 297.

29. See Douglas H. Bellemore, *Investments: Principals, Practices and Analysis* (New York: Simmons-Boardman Publishing Corp., 1962).

30. *Special Study of Securities Markets, op. cit.,* Part 1, p. 369. A few brokerage firms provide investment supervisory services, but most investment-counseling firms do not have custody of their clients' funds or securities. It is not hard to imagine a variety of business relationships between investment counselors and brokers, however. See *ibid,* p. 370.

31. Two additional factors may also occasionally dictate the use of priority lists rather than discretionary accounts. The latter may, first of all, be used only by brokers, whereas anyone regularly privy to valuable information may use the priority-list method of allocation. And discretionary accounts do require relinquishment of the personal use of the funds managed in the account, a step some individuals may be either unwilling or unable to take.

Chapter VI

1. *Speed* v. *Transamerica Corp.*, 99 Fed. Supp. 808 (D. Del. 1951) involved precisely this proposition, and the failure to disclose the intention of the stock purchaser was found to be a violation of SEC Rule 10b–5. There were independent grounds for finding a fiduciary duty, however, as the purchasers were already in control of the company. Cf. *Mills* v. *Sarjem Corp.*, 133 Fed. Supp. 753 (D.C.N.J. 1955) in which no violation of 10b–5 was found. *Speed* was distinguished, because the plan in *Mills* for purchasing control and liquidating was formulated by a complete outsider with no pre-existing fiduciary duty to the shareholders.

2. Henry G. Manne, "Some Theoretical Aspects of Share Voting," *Columbia Law Review*, LXIV (1964), p. 1435. As noted in footnote 4, Chapter V, there is usually some inelasticity in the supply curve.

3. Some explanation for the possibility of such a large leverage factor may be had by comparing the 9 billion shares listed on the New York Stock Exchange with the 1¼ billion shares traded in 1964, the Exchange's most active year. See *The Exchange*, XXVI, No. 7 (July, 1965), p. 1. This means that an average of only 5 million of the 9 billion outstanding shares are traded daily, or slightly more than .05%. The example in the text involves .5% of outstanding shares. The ratio of average trading to outstanding shares does, of course, vary with different companies.

4. This is, of course, a fairly extreme illustration. It indicates, however, that in companies with a low ratio of traded shares to outstanding shares, insider trading presents the least problem quantitatively. Frequently these are companies in which investor confidence in management is high or companies whose securities are considered of high-investment grade.

5. Cf. *In the Matter of Cady, Roberts & Co.*, SEC Release No. 6668, *CCH Federal Securities Law Reporter* (1961), p. 81018.

6. *Texas Gulf Sulphur* might involve that kind of situation.

7. Here tax considerations will frequently loom large. If the sale of securities would occur just short of six months after acquisition, the cost of foregoing a capital gain may be very substantial. Another common situation involves a pledge of securities physically in possession of the pledgee, with no right of substitution by the pledgor. Section 16(b) of the Securities Exchange Act of 1934 will present problems if the shares or the shares of the same class had been purchased within the preceding six months.

8. This may explain why the purchases by Texas Gulf insiders were not considerably greater than they were, although it is also possible that the SEC has not identified all the transactions resulting from the inside information.

9. There are some fairly strong reasons to believe that options and calls do not play an important role in insiders' trading. The seller of a call can, if he inquires, discover the identity of the purchaser. If he were to discover, for instance, that executives of U.S. Steel were buying calls on U.S. Steel's stock, prudence would dictate that he cover quickly by buying a matching number of U.S. Steel shares. He may in fact do more than cover, as he now has reliable information about the insiders' view of the company. In addition to purchasing shares, the dealer will undoubtedly raise the call price. This last factor is sufficient by itself to explain the difficulty insiders would have in exploiting valuable information on any large scale by the purchase of calls.

There is one additional reason why calls are not efficient devices for insiders to exploit their information. Sections 3a(10) and 3a(11) of the Securities Exchange Act of 1934 define a *security* and an *equity security* in such a way as to include a call. Thus changes in holdings by insiders must be reported, and any profits made by a purchase and sale of a call within six months may be recovered by the corporation under Section 16(b). Of course, short-term trading in calls is not prohibited by 16(b) to anyone not a statutory insider.

10. See Sidney S. Alexander, "Price Movements in Speculative Markets: Trends or Random Walks, No. 2," in *The Random Character of Stock Market Prices*, ed., Paul H. Cootner (Cambridge, Mass.: M.I.T. Press, 1964), p. 338, especially the conclusion, p. 369.

11. Except perhaps for specialists on the floor of an exchange.

12. Frank H. Knight, *Risk, Uncertainty and Profit* (Boston and New York: Houghton Mifflin Co., 1921), p. 342.

13. At least this corollary holds for the kind of information we are concerned with in this discussion. It is probably accurate as a broad generalization, but the proof would take longer than is warranted here.

14. Complaint, *S.E.C. v. Texas Gulf Sulphur Co.* Actually, aside from one defendant's purchase of 100 shares at 27 on Apr. 2, 1964, the highest price paid by this group was 25⅞.

15. See Colin Cherry, "The Cocktail Party Problem," *On Human Communication* (New York: Science Edition, Inc., 1961), pp. 277–78.

16. Par. 97 of the complaint in *S.E.C. v. Texas Gulf Sulphur Co.*

alleges that one defendant purchased or caused to be purchased 4,000 shares after information about the find was given to reporters but before it had reached the public. On the same day, Apr. 16, 1964, in perhaps the most celebrated transactions alleged in the complaint, Defendant Thomas S. Lamont advised a representative of the Morgan Guaranty Trust Co. "to 'watch the tape' for favorable news pertaining to Defendant TEXAS GULF." All of these transactions occurred in the price range of 31 to 33½. The stock closed that day at $37 and sold as high as $58 on Apr. 30 1964.

This discussion also suggests the role played by specialists and traders on the floor of the stock exchanges. As news is flashed on the broad tape—or as they hear it from other sources—they are physically in a position to trade on this information before it has been disseminated through the whole market. Specialists are, of course, presumed to stabilize the market by buying as prices go down and selling as prices go up. But a recent investigation of their activities in the days following the assassination of President Kennedy indicates that the lure of quick profits from valuable information may have been too much to resist. See *S.E.C. Study of Specialists and Floor Trader Activities on the New York Stock Exchange on November 22 to 26, 1963.* This study, dated Jan. 21, 1964, was submitted to Representative Staggers, Chairman of the House Subcommittee on Commerce and Finance of the Committee on Interstate and Foreign Commerce. For a description of the behavior of floor traders, see SEC's *Special Study of Securities Markets,* Part 2, House Doc. No. 95, Part 2, 88th Cong., 1st Sess., 1963.

17. See Chapter XI. Both the registered exchanges and the SEC have authority to suspend trading in a given security. The exchanges can only suspend trading through their facilities; the SEC has power to suspend exchange and over-the-counter transactions. The New York Stock Exchange and the SEC have utilized this device on numerous occasions. These suspensions may result from a failure to file required information with the SEC, as well as for reasons outside of the company's control such as an involuntary bankruptcy petition. Other reasons have included the death of an important official, fraud, and errors in financial data. For a collection of the cases see Louis Loss, *Securities Regulation* (Boston and Toronto: Little, Brown and Co., 1961), pp. 851–57.

18. To the extent that the call seller hedges and buys long himself, the effect would be the same as if the insiders went into the market

before disclosing the information. This effect should be assumed out of the present discussion in order to focus on the pure effect of the rule allowing insiders only to purchase calls or take options.

19. The more common case of stock options being granted to corporate executives will be considered in Chapter IX.

Chapter VII

1. For the fullest treatment of this fascinating topic, see the essays collected in *The Random Character of Stock Market Prices*, ed., Paul H. Cootner (Cambridge, Mass.: M.I.T. Press, 1964), hereafter cited as "Cootner." That market uncertainty will generate randomly distributed transactions was first argued theoretically by a French mathematician in 1900. See Louis Bachelier, "Theory of Speculation" in Cootner, p. 17.

2. The addition of *volume* as a variable in their computations would not seem to be significant for present purposes. See M. F. M. Osbourne, "Periodic Structure in the Brownian Motion of Stock Prices" in Cootner, p. 262.

3. *The Exchange*, XXVI, No. 6 (June, 1965) on the inside cover.

4. See Paul H. Cootner, "The Random Walk Hypothesis Re-examined," in Cootner, p. 189.

5. Cootner, *ibid.*, shows that a number of additional refinements could be added to this discussion. For the most part, these are quite technical and not immediately relevant to the theory advanced in the text. One point that should be mentioned is the existence of constraints or parameters on the area in which random movement occurs. One constraint is, of course, a bottom of zero. Stocks cannot have negative values. The other, and more important for practical purposes, is the constraint provided by the area of actual knowledge. Because of the known aspect of any stock, even the random price changes will tend to group in an area fairly close to some base line—in our example, the price of 50. This line will exercise a kind of gravitational pull on price, but this in no way contradicts the statement that price changes occur with no dependence on previous prices within the area of constraint. It simply means that the distribution of transactions will probably be statistically normal.

6. See Cootner, Part III.

7. See Henry G. Manne, "Mergers and the Market for Corporate Control," *Journal of Political Economy*, LXXIII (1965), p. 112, fn. 10.

8. For another analysis leading to the same conclusions, see Eugene

F. Fama, "Random Walks in Stock Market Prices," *Financial Analysts Journal*, XXI, No. 5 (Sept.-Oct., 1965), p. 55.

9. A leading securities lawyer, examining the question of who might be injured by insider trading, noted that it is "plausible that an anonymous prospective buyer is the person to complain rather than one of these random sellers. To such a prospective buyer, the defendant represented competition. Were the defendant not present, a lower bid might have been accepted by one of the hypothetical sellers." Jack M. Whitney II, "Section 10b-5: from Cady, Roberts to Texas Gulf: Matters of Disclosure," *The Business Lawyer*, XXI (1965), p. 201. Whitney did not, however, examine the impact of insider trading on all outsiders in the aggregate, and consequently his otherwise astute observations are quite incomplete.

10. In truth the shares may have been owned by a number of different individuals during the relevant time period so that the job of correlating gains and ownership would be even more difficult.

11. There would be a definite sum if we were considering corporate recovery of insiders' profits. If there were perfect enforcement of such a rule, however, insiders would have no incentive to trade. There would then be no profits for the corporation to recover. If corporate managers tried to maximize corporate income by trading for the corporation on inside information, our analysis from the point of view of outsiders would be the same as that under the rule of individual insider trading.

12. In this connection it is interesting to consider part of the famous discussion of the stock market which appears in John Maynard Keynes, *The General Theory of Employment Interest and Money* (London: Macmillan Co., Ltd., 1949), p. 157.

> Moreover, life is not long enough;—human nature desires quick results, there is a peculiar zest in making money quickly, and remoter gains are discounted by the average man at a very high rate. The game of professional investment is intolerably boring and overexacting to anyone who is entirely exempt from the gambling instinct; whilst he who has it must pay to this propensity the appropriate toll.

Unfortunately, in his discussion of different types of traders in the stock market Keynes seems to have limited himself to short-term speculators, who are presumed to be gambling, and long-term investors. There is no discussion of the role played by the informed short-term trader or the insider. The failure to recognize the influence of the latter participants led Keynes to conclude that the influence of the speculator would in the long run predominate over that of the informed investor. The stock market became for Keynes simply a casino which could not properly perform its capital allocating function. But, to the extent that informed short-term trading does occur, it is very likely that there is an important tendency in the stock market for share prices accurately and properly to reflect underlying values. And even though there will be fads and panics in particular stocks, or in the whole market at times, it does not follow that uninformed trading will predominate in the general determination of stock prices.

> There is reason to believe that intelligence rather than ignorance ultimately determines the course of individual share prices. Stock market decisions tend to be of the one-out-of-two-alternatives variety, such as buy or not buy, hold or sell, or put or call. To the extent that decisions on these questions are made by shareholders or potential shareholders operating without reliable information, over a period of time the decisions will tend to be randomly distributed and the effect will therefore be neutral. Decisions made by those with a higher degree of certainty will to that extent not meet a canceling effect since they will not be made on a random basis. Over some period of time it would seem that the average market price of a company's shares must be the "correct" one. Henry G. Manne, "Mergers and the Market for Corporate Control," *The Journal of Political Economy*, LXXIII, No. 2, April 1965, p. 112, n. 10.

13. The occurrence of any such event is, of course, completely unpredictable, but it is possible, looking over a previous period, to ascertain the average rate of occurrence. The Texas Gulf development seems to have caused more than a tripling of the stock price, though other factors may have been involved in this increase. In the postwar period, if we correct for price level changes, it is doubtful that specific corporate developments causing a 50% increase in a company's stock price over a short period of time have occurred on the average of once every ten years. In the text we have used a 10% increase, from 50 to 55, to illustrate the value of inside information. The discussion in Chapter IX will make it clear that most important instances of significant insider trading probably result from price changes in excess of 10%.

14. The Texas Gulf illustration is probably unusual in the length of the time period during which insiders traded before disclosure. Even that time period is approximately 1% of the time since the last previous important development in Texas Gulf's stock.

Chapter VIII

1. Adam Smith, *The Wealth of Nations*, ed., Edwin Cannan (New York: Modern Library, 1937), pp. 700 and 712-16.

2. (New York: The Macmillan Co., 1933), p. 343.

3. Alfred Marshall, *Principles of Economics*, 8th ed. (London: Macmillan & Co., Ltd., 1920), p. 604.

4. Frank H. Knight, *Risk, Uncertainty and Profit* (Boston and New York: Houghton Mifflin Co., 1921), hereinafter referred to as "Knight."

5. *Ibid.*, Chapter II.

6. There is an interesting paradox in the classical economists' view of the corporation. As the ensuing analysis will show, Smith failed to recognize the corporation as a vehicle for specialization of functions or the division of labor, a concept closely associated with his name. Marshall makes the same error. *Op. cit.*, p. 604.

7. Knight points out that Smith recognized profit as containing an element that was not merely interest on capital. Smith's exception differs from Knight's concept of profit resulting from uncertainty. It related more to the concept of insurable risk than of true uncertainty. Also see Marshall, *op. cit.*, pp. 293 and 604, where he implies an identity of the capitalist and the entrepreneur.

8. Joseph A. Schumpeter, *The Theory of Economic Development*, trans., Redvers Opie (Cambridge, Mass.: Harvard University Press, 1934), hereafter referred to as "Schumpeter TED." This work was first published in German in 1911, prior to Knight's 1916 doctoral thesis on uncertainty. It was revised into a second, English edition in 1926. Some minor modifications in the theory appeared in 1939 in Schumpeter's *Business Cycles*, ed., Rendigs Fels (New York, Toronto, London: McGraw-Hill Book Co., Inc., 1964).

9. There may still be some monopoly element in corporate managers' compensation. If the corporation itself is making any monopoly gain, it is quite possible that the managers are claiming part of it. Existing managers may also claim for themselves a substantial part of an amount equal to the entry costs of would-be competitors, though this is not technically a monopoly profit. See Henry G. Manne, "The 'Higher Criticism' of the Modern Corporation," *Columbia Law Review*, LXII (1962), pp. 404-06.

10. Schumpeter TED, pp. 74-75.

11. *Ibid.*, p. 78. Also see Edith Penrose, *The Growth of the Firm* (New York: John Wiley & Sons, Inc., 1959), p. 31. The reader is also

referred to Andreas G. Papandreou, "Some Basic Problems in the Theory of the Firm," *A Survey of Contemporary Economics,* Vol. II, ed., Bernard F. Haley (Homewood, Ill.: Richard D. Irwin, Inc., 1952), p. 214, for a distinction between the concept of the entrepreneur as a function and as an ideal type. The distinction is not very helpful. To the extent that Papandreou's ideal type, for example, a capitalist-entrepreneur, does not function as such, *vide* the capital-poor president of a large corporation, we should have to posit a new ideal type. The confusion can be avoided by always referring to the *function* of the entrepreneur when that word is used. The problem is a minor semantic one which has obscured more than it has clarified.

12. Schumpeter TED, p. 78.

13. Schumpeter, *Business Cycles, op. cit.,* p. 77.

14. Schumpeter TED, at p. 88.

15. It is equally interesting that the word *management* has the much broader suggestion of considerable entrepreneurial activity.

16. Cf. the examples used by Schumpeter in TED, p. 152, and *Business Cycles, op. cit.,* p. 78, with those used by Knight, p. 257.

Arthur Stone Dewing in his classic, *The Financial Policy of Corporations* (New York: The Ronald Press Co., 4th ed., 1946), Vol. I, p. 416, distinguishes the function of the inventor from that of the promoter. Dewing's emphasis is entirely on bringing different factors together to establish a new business. Thus he points out that promotion is different from "the administration of a business once it has started." *ibid.,* p. 416. But he never noted that the continuing entrepreneurial function is quite similar to that of the promoter. His description of the characteristics of the successful promoter, *ibid.* pp. 412–15, leaves no doubt, however, that Dewing's promoter can be the same man as Schumpeter's entrepreneur.

17. Peter T. Bauer and Basil S. Yamey, *The Economics of Under-Developed Countries* (Chicago: University of Chicago Press, 1957), and Colin Clark, "Growthmanship," *Intercollegiate Review,* Vol. I, No. 1 (Jan., 1965), p. 5.

18. Schumpeter TED, p. 180. For this entire discussion the interested reader is directed to Chapter IX in Knight's book and Chapter V in Schumpeter's.

19. Schumpeter TED, p. 144. As we shall see in the next chapter, this point of Schumpeter's is slightly misleading. In the modern, large corporation the capitalist investor does not actually wrest a part of the entrepreneur's profits from him. The accretion in the value of the

capitalist's holdings is analogous to the increase in the value of raw fibers after the introduction of the automatic loom. That is, the entrepreneur causes an increase in the marginal productivity of the production factors he uses. This is different from a sharing in the true profits of the entrepreneur, though this too occurs.

20. Schumpeter TED, p. 75.

21. *Ibid.*, p. 137.

22. Knight, p. 277. This dichotomy is consistent with what actually happens in large corporations, where innovators also hold salaried positions.

23. Schumpeter TED, p. 152.

24. *Ibid.* A similar distinction between profits and permanent, non-monopolistic returns is made by both Schumpeter and Knight. Cf. Schumpeter TED, p. 138, and Knight, p. 257.

25. Manne, *op. cit.*, p. 403.

26. Armen A. Alchian, "Uncertainty, Evolution and Economic Theory," *Journal of Political Economy*, LVIII (1950), p. 211, reprinted in American Economics Association, *Readings in Industrial Organization and Public Policy*, Vol. VIII, eds., Richard B. Heflebower and George W. Stocking (Homewood, Ill.: Richard D. Irwin, Inc., 1958), p. 207; and Knight, p. 170, fn. 1.

27. Schumpeter TED, p. 154.

28. Knight, p. 283–84.

29. Schumpter TED, p. 155; also see Milton Friedman and L. J. Savage, "The Utility Analysis of Choices Involving Risk," *Journal of Political Economy*, LVI (1948), p. 279, reprinted in *Landmarks in Political Economy*, Vol. 2, eds., Earl J. Hamilton, Albert Rees, and Harry G. Johnson (Chicago: University of Chicago Press, 1962), p. 297.

31. Bauer and Yamey, *op. cit.*, Chapter V.

32. Schumpeter TED, p. 136.

33. *Ibid.*

34. New York: Harper and Bros. Publishers, 1942.

35. *Ibid.*, p. 84–85.

36. *Ibid.*, p. 132.

37. *Ibid.*, p. 134.

38. *Ibid.*, p. 140.

39. *Ibid.*, p. 142.

40. *Ibid.*, p. 156.

41. *Ibid.*, p. 156.

42. *Ibid.*, pp. 156–57.

Chapter IX

1. Ironically this seems less true the higher the executive position. Presidents of many large companies have relatively little job security, and the lack of important innovations, when competitors are developing them, can certainly lead to early retirement. It may be that job promotions to the top are granted on the basis of actual and anticipated entrepreneurial performance and that the president is supposed to be much more than simply a co-ordinator.

2. This suggests an advantage for stock options different from those usually advanced. By giving options the company may enable executives to make trading profits they might otherwise be unable to finance.

3. It must be emphasized here that we are referring to the form of compensation and not the amount. Presumably, the figure can always be made large enough to attract anyone, but to raise salaries to this level would be very wasteful if alternative means for attracting entrepreneurs are available.

4. We are assuming that the parties know supply and demand conditions and are simply conforming to them by correctly classifying the job and the employee.

5. Knight, p. 342.

6. See George Thomas Washington and V. Henry Rothschild, II, *Compensating the Corporate Executive*, 3d ed. (New York: The Ronald Press Co., 1962), Vol. I, p. 84.

7. Courts have unfortunately complicated the law on bonuses by their failure to realize that, regardless of the names used, the bonus aspect of a profit-sharing plan is the value of the right when it is acquired. Any subsequent increase is simply a capital gain or interest. The leading opinion making this error was the dissent of Judge Thomas Swan in *Rogers* v. *Hill*, 65 Fed. 2d 109, 113 (2d Cir., 1932), *reversed*, 289 U.S. 582 (1933).

8. Washington and Rothschild, *op. cit.*, Chapter VIII.

9. See Armen A. Alchian and William R. Allen, *University Economics* (Belmont, Calif.: Wadsworth Publishing Co., Inc., 1964), p. 218.

10. It should be noted that this defense of stock options offers no justification for granting an option at less than the predisclosure market price of shares.

11. Washington and Rothschild, *op. cit.*, Vol. II, pp. 572–80. The Delaware Supreme Court, in a departure from the usual judicial hands-off policy toward compensation plans, has actually created a

number of specific legal tests for the validity of stock-option plans. The underlying rationale for this approach is the requirement that a corporation receive appropriate consideration for any compensation paid. Otherwise the payment will be treated as an invalid gift of corporate assets. See *Kerbs* v. *California Eastern Airways, Inc.*, 33 Del. Ch. 69, 90 Atl. 2d 652 (1952). Also see *Lieberman* v. *Becker*, 38 Del. Ch. 540, 155 Atl. 2d 596 (1954).

12. *Internal Revenue Code*, Sections 421–25 (1964). The most questionable aspect of these rules is the requirement that the stock be held for three years after exercise in order to receive capital-gains treatment. Prior to 1964, this period was six months, though it could not be less than two years after the option was granted. A reasonable feature, viewing the Internal Revenue Code as a scheme for the regulation of stock options, is the requirement that to qualify for special tax treatment the option must be granted at the market price. Options can be granted for up to five years, but they must be nontransferable.

As the *1964 House Ways and Means Committee Report* indicates, Congress viewed stock options as a device to make investors, not traders, out of employees. That report stated: "Your committee . . . decided to continue the stock option provision because it believes that it is good for the economy for management of various businesses to have a stake in their successful operation." *CCH Federal Tax Reporter*, 1966, Vol. 3, par. 2674.03, p. 33322. This view reflects the prevailing attitude that there are only managerial and capitalist functions to be performed in corporations. It overlooks the entrepreneurial function that may have provided the original impetus for stock options for select, key employees.

13. See *The Wall Street Journal*, June 30, 1965, p. 1, col. 8.

14. Richard J. Kruizenga, "Introduction to the Option Contract," Cootner, pp. 378–79.

15. An estimate of the difference in call prices for different time periods might be gained by valuing long-term conversion features in bonds or preferred stocks. But this is complicated by the redemption feature commonly appearing in the same securities and tending to prevent large premiums being paid for the conversion feature.

16. See George Thomas Washington and V. Henry Rothschild II, *op. cit.*, Vol. II, Chs. 15–16.

17. A fascinating parallel is provided by Schumpeter's analysis of what happens to the value of entrepreneurial activity in a pure communist state. See TED, pp. 144–52.

18. Unfortunately, even the most careful theoretical and empirical

works on executive compensation have assumed that salaries, bonuses, pensions, and stock options comprise the only forms of financial compensation of corporate employees. Because they fail to consider profits resulting from stock trading as a fundamental part of executive compensation, these models and statistical results are of little use. See Robin Marris, *The Economic Theory of 'Managerial' Capitalists* (New York: The Free Press 1964), Chapter 2, and David R. Roberts, *Executive Compensation* (New York: The Free Press, 1959).

19. Adolf A. Berle and Gardiner Means, *The Modern Corporation and Private Property* (New York: The Macmillan Co., 1933), p. 51. At a more mundane level, Louis Gilbert regularly harangues the executives of large corporations for their failure to own what he considers an appropriate number of shares. Louis D. and John J. Gilbert, *Twenty-Fifth Annual Report of Stockholder Activities at Corporation Meetings During 1964* (New York: Louis D. and John J. Gilbert, n.d.), pp. 171–72.

20. Berle later modified this position and concluded that management's claim to legitimacy was established by the excellence of its performance. Adolf A. Berle, *The 20th Century Capitalist Revolution* (New York: Harcourt, Brace & Co., 1954). Cf. Henry G. Manne, "The 'Higher Criticism' of the Modern Corporation," *Columbia Law Review*, LXII (1962), pp. 414–17.

21. See *Fortune* (July, 1965), p. 165.

22. Roberts, *op. cit.*, p. 50, states that "compensation is directly and quite closely related to size and that it probably has little independent connection with profitability." To Roberts compensation includes only salary, bonuses, and pension benefits.

23. This is not to say that these industries will stagnate. Innovation may simply come from without rather than from within. The diesel locomotive, the greatest advancement in modern railroading, was successfully promoted by General Motors, not the railroads.

24. Peter T. Bauer and Basil S. Yamey, *The Economics of Under-Developed Countries* (Chicago: University of Chicago Press, 1957), pp. 106–12. This section, entitled "The Foreign Entrepreneur," provides a fascinating discussion of this topic.

25. See report of study in *The New York Times* (Dec. 29, 1963) p. 1, col. 2. Vance Packard reports that utilities and heavy industries (presumably those characterized by very large corporations), including companies founded by Jews, have a low incidence of Jewish executives; see *The Pyramid Climbers* (New York: Fawcett World Library, 1962), p. 41.

26. See Armen A. Alchian and Reuben A. Kessel, "Competition, Monopoly, and the Pursuit of Money," *Aspects of Labor Economics —A Report of the National Bureau of Economic Research* (Princeton: Princeton University Press, 1962), pp. 164–70, for an alternative, though not contradictory, explanation of the same phenomenon in public utilities.

Chapter X

1. Adolf A. Berle, "Publicity of Accounts and Directors' Purchases of Stock," *Michigan Law Review,* XXV (1927), pp. 830–31; and Kenneth L. Yourd, "Trading in Securities by Directors, Officers and Stockholders: Section 16 of the Securities Exchange Act," *Michigan Law Review,* XXXVIII (1939), p. 133.

2. See James William Moore and Frank M. Wiseman, "Market Manipulation and the Exchange Act," *University of Chicago Law Review,* II (1934), p. 46.

3. William Prosser, *Handbook of the Law of Torts,* 3d ed. (St. Paul: West Publishing Co., 1964), p. 700; and Louis Loss, *Securities Regulation* (Boston and Toronto: Little, Brown & Co., 1961), pp. 1430ff.

4. See William J. Baumol, *The Stock Market and Economic Efficiency* (New York: Fordham University Press, 1965), Chapter III.

5. *Ibid.,* Chap. I.

6. Henry G. Manne, "Mergers and the Market for Corporate Control," *Journal of Political Economy,* LXXIII (1965), p. 110. This argument would seem to have little weight, however, when applied to the trading of a trustee in bankruptcy. See Stanley A. Kaplan, "Wolf v. Weinstein: Another Chapter on Insider Trading," *The Supreme Court Review, 1963,* ed., Philip B. Kurland (Chicago and London: University of Chicago Press, 1963), pp. 280ff.

7. Reported in *The Wall Street Journal,* July 9, 1965, p. 5, col. 1.

8. *Hearings Before the Senate Committee on Banking and Currency,* 73d Cong., 1st Sess., 1933, p. 3080ff. and 3245ff.; 2d Sess., 1934, pp. 6083ff.

9. Securities Exchange Act of 1934, Section 9.

10. U.S. Senate Report No. 1455, 73d Cong., 2d Sess., 1934, p. 36.

11. Pools would have a number of advantages for this purpose. If the pool manager was a knowledgeable corporate insider, he would not have to disclose the specific news to anyone. Participants could be invited on a mutual-exchange basis, as indicated in Chapter V. Policing problems would also be minimal. Research is needed on such ques-

tions as which pools succeeded, who managed pools, whether they disseminated true information, whether participants exchanged invitations, and whether specific bits of information were disclosed to participants.

Pools were not entirely without their defenders in the early 1930's. The position of R. W. Schabacker, *Stock Market Theory and Practice* (New York: B. C. Forbes Publishing Co., 1930), pp. 570–71, is similar to that offered in the text:

> The pool is thus a little more than an organization, on a scientific basis, of a group of "insiders." It is a group of men who are farsighted enough to see the potentiality of any stock and the logic of its eventually selling at the price and in the direction which the pool decides upon. All that the pool generally does, therefore, is to discount the future in a scientific way and hasten the market change which without organized action, might take 10 times as long to accomplish. . . .
> Economically the pool serves a worthy purpose of assisting the open market in evaluating correctly the true worth of the stock.

In the *1934 Senate Hearings on Stock Exchange Practices, op. cit.,* 73d Cong., 2d Sess., p. 6616, Richard Whitney, president of the New York Stock Exchange, offered this somewhat garbled but essentially logical defense of pools:

> I think the operation which we term now "manipulative" referred to by Mr. Pecora, where there is an endeavor to get great activity in the market by buying and selling, but through proper change of ownership, that that may well unfairly influence the market.
> I do think, however, that practically each and every case must rest on its own bottom. It is perfectly possible for an individual, or a joint account, or a pool, who believes that a security is selling below the level at which it should sell to buy that security in volume up to a point where they think the level is a proper one, and in doing so they are going to unquestionably influence the market, but in my opinion not unfairly.

12. Loss, *op. cit.,* pp. 1529–40. At p. 1538 Loss says that "before the mid-thirties, there was no American case of manipulation by trading alone. . . ."

13. Section 16(c) of the Securities Exchange Act of 1934 forbids the named insiders ever to sell stock in their companies short.

14. Knight, p. 364. He argues that entrepreneurs have almost always also been capitalists, in effect, financing their own entrepreneurial losses. Some such explanation is necessary in a system in which entrepreneurship is not a highly specialized function. A large corpo-

rate system, however, allows this specialization and its discrete compensation.

15. Knight, p. 310.

16. See discussion of "beneficial" ownership under the 16(b) prohibition on insider trading in Loss *op. cit.*, pp. 1100–01. Also see Stanley A. Kaplan, *op. cit.*, p. 305.

Chapter XI

1. These three methods for taking over control of a corporation are compared in Henry G. Manne, "Mergers and the Market for Corporate Control," *Journal of Political Economy*, LXXIII (1965), p. 110.

2. For a judicial holding that an outsider does not violate Rule 10b-5 by his failure to disclose this intention, see *Mills* v. *Sarjem Corp.*, 133 Fed. Supp. 753 (D.C.N.J. 1955).

3. See "Investing in Yourself," *The Wall Street Journal*, June 30, 1965, p. 1, col. 8. This article suggests that when publicly announced tender offers are used, the price is set about 20% above the current market price. However, this may still be cheaper than undisclosed purchasing when a large number of shares are to be bought in a short time.

4. For the legal history of this subject, see *Blau* v. *Lehman*, 368 U.S. 403, at p. 412 (1962).

5. See testimony of Thomas G. Corcoran in *Stock Exchange Practices, Hearings Before Senate Committee on Banking and Currency*, 73d Cong., 2d Sess., 1934, p. 6557.

6. See Louis Loss, *Securities Regulation* (Boston and Toronto: Little, Brown & Co., 1961), pp. 1037–1132, for a detailed treatment of enforcement problems.

7. Enforcement is facilitated by a requirement that the insiders defined in the Act report monthly any changes in their holdings of their company's securities. These reports are filed in Washington and in various regional offices of the SEC. The legal proceedings required to recover these profits for the corporation are extremely simple, and other shareholders and their lawyers stand ever ready to pounce on any insider's short-swing profits, whether accidently or intentionally realized. Enforcement is undoubtedly further facilitated by the business literature of the last fifty years. Legal rules and moral preachments have not been without their effect on insiders' consciences. Enforcement, however, is still very complex. For a full discussion of the legal problem encountered in connection with enforcement of

16(b), see Donald C. Cook and Myer Feldman, "Insider Trading Under the Securities Exchange Act," *Harvard Law Review*, LXVI (1953), p. 385.

8. Actually any rule which does not completely prevent stock trading or ownership by insiders will be only partially effective against the use of inside information. Although it may be possible to forbid sales or purchases of shares prior to public disclosure of important information, it is not possible to forbid the nonsale or the nonpurchase of shares. Yet knowing when not to sell or buy may on occasion be as valuable as knowing when to sell or buy. As insiders would have to own shares in order to "not sell," we might expect insiders to own more shares with a partially effective rule against insider trading than if there were no rule at all. During the period between the development of valuable information and its disclosure, the insider would know not to sell his shares. In the long run this knowledge would give him some advantage over other shareholders, though certainly not as great as he would have with a free-trading rule.

9. This was proposed in 1933 but was not adapted. See Ralph F. De Bedts, *The New Deal's SEC* (New York and London: Columbia University Press, 1964), pp. 61, 72, and 77.

10. See Arthur Fleischer, Jr., 'Federal Corporation Law': An Assessment," *Harvard Law Review*, LXXVIII (1965), p. 1146, and Michael Joseph, "Civil Liability Under Rule 10b-5—A Reply," *Northwestern University Law Review*, LIX (1964), p. 171, in which authors presently or formerly associated with the SEC defend this practice. It is criticized in David S. Ruder, "Pitfalls in the Development of a Federal Law of Corporations by Implication Through Rule 10b-5," *Northwestern University Law Review*, LIX (1964), p. 185. Curiously, none of these writers has defended or attacked the questionable practice of using a case-by-case approach instead of the Commission's broad rule-making powers to establish clear guidelines. Rule 10b-5 is *not* clear, and apparently was promulgated without notice and hearing for corporate insiders as affected parties. See Loss, *op. cit.*, p. 1427. An excellent discussion of this administrative law problem appears in Ralph F. Fuchs, "Agency Development of Policy Through Rule-Making," *Northwestern University Law Review*, LIX (1965), p. 781. See especially the cogent discussion (pp. 793–94) of legal and constitutional limitations on retroactively effective adjudicatory processes when prospectively applicable rule-making powers are available. Arguably, this issue is not raised by 10b-5, since the

sought-after adjudications are interpretations of a rule. But 10b-5 is not the kind of rule which Professor Fuchs is arguing for, as the context makes clear.

It might be added that there are still serious questions about the validity of 10b-5 as applied to all insider trading. The validity of the promulgation has been discussed and affirmatively sustained in only one district court opinion, *United States* v. *Shindler*, 173 Fed. Supp. 393 (S.D.N.Y. 1959), a criminal case involving alleged manipulation of stock prices, where only the Rule's invalidity as applied to *purchases* was argued. The Supreme Court's opinion in *Blau* v. *Lehman*, 368 U.S. 403 (1962), further weakens 10b-5's claim to validity. In that case the Court refused to hold a partnership as an insider under Section 16(b) because one partner was a director of the corporation in question. After reviewing the legislative history of the Section and Congress' refusal to have it apply to "anyone," the Court stated on p. 413: "Congress can and might amend § 16(b) if the Commission would present to it the policy arguments it has presented to us, but we think that Congress is the proper agency to change an interpretation of the Act unbroken since its passage, if the change is to be made." This admonishment to the Commission should presumably have some bearing on its attempt to surmount all the restrictive qualifications in 16(b) by making 10b-5 into even a broader provision than Congress refused in 1933. The case for the validity of 10b-5, construed as a thoroughgoing rule against insider trading, may be quite shaky.

11. Securities Exchange Act, Section 19(a)(2) allows suspension for up to twelve months or withdrawal of a registration "if the Commission finds that an issuer of such security has failed to comply with any provision of this title or the rules and regulations thereunder." Professor Loss has termed this remedy Draconian. Loss, *op. cit.*, p. 845. The Commission can also suspend trading for successive periods of up to ten days under Section 19(a) (4). For cases in which this power has been used, consult Loss, pp. 852ff. Section A16 of the *New York Stock Exchange Company Manual*, p. A–291, allows suspension of trading for "any action which substantially reduces . . . the value or amount of its securities."

12. See Loss, *op. cit.*, p. 854.

13. To the extent that insider trading by these individuals is not allowed, they have less incentive to police lower functionaries. Thus, the government's enforcement problems would probably be greater under such a rule than is indicated by the amount of insider trading presently occurring.

Chapter XII

1. 15 Code Fed. Reg., p. 39ff (1965).
2. CCH *Federal Securities Law Reporter*, Vol. 2, par. 31001 (Proposed 8K, Item 2).
3. S. 2731, 89th Cong., 1st Sess, 1965.
4. See Bayless Manning, "The Purity Potlatch: An Essay on Conflicts of Interest, American Government, and Moral Escalation," *Federal Bar Journal*, XXIV (1964), p. 239. Dean Manning thinks that the stockholding conflict of interest has "become a modern political obsession in this country" and that it should by no means be equated with bribery.
5. *Ibid.*, and also see The Association of the Bar of the City of New York Special Committee on the Federal Conflict of Interest Laws, *Conflict of Interest and Federal Service* (Cambridge: Harvard University Press, 1960), hereafter referred to as "Conflict of Interest and Federal Service." Dean Manning was staff director for this superb study. His article in the *Federal Bar Journal* is a colorful essay summarizing some of the findings of the special committee and presenting his own personal views on the subject. These two works must certainly stand as the cornerstone of any consideration of the classic forms of conflict of interest in government. Insider trading, unfortunately, is given rather brief consideration.
6. It is not really clear why this information is deemed relevant or interesting to voters. Undoubtedly, some of the popular demand for financial disclosure reflects idle curiosity about the financial affairs of important figures. These disclosures have told very little. Even apart from the complex accounting and valuation problems involved, publication seems aimed at disclosing the total size of a man's estate more than anything else. Occasionally, such disclosures give rise to an implication of possible conflict of interest, in which case certain securities will be sold or various interests put in trust.
7. For a detailed account of this and other congressional investigations on conflicts of interest from stockholdings, see *Conflict of Interest and Federal Service*, pp. 95–130.
8. Manning, *op. cit.*, pp. 248–49.
9. See *Conflict of Interest and Federal Service*, p. 238.
10. Even with all the fanfare given Herbert Klotz's insider trading in Texas Gulf Sulphur stock and his resignation, there remain many mysteries about the entire matter. It is interesting to note that Klotz was the undersecretary in charge of patronage appointments in the Department of Commerce. At the time of his resignation he was a

carryover from the Kennedy administration serving under a new secretary appointed by Johnson. Both Klotz and the SEC have claimed that a secretary in the department gave him his tip. She was reputedly a family friend of a Texas Gulf geologist in Timmins. Klotz claims that he noticed heavy buying on an upward price movement and, therefore, thought the tip was reliable.

Klotz is alleged to have made his purchases on Mar. 30 and 31, 1964, by which time rumors of the Texas Gulf discovery had already reached flood proportions in Washington. Clearly, all these rumors did not begin with a secretary in the Department of Commerce. There were undoubtedly other channels by which information about the find moved from Ontario or New York to Washington—channels reliable enough to be trusted by individuals who were not merely taking tips from secretaries.

11. *Preventing Conflicts of Interest on the Part of Special Government Employees*, The President's Memorandum of May 2, 1963 (Washington: U.S. Government Printing Office, 1963), pp. 8–9.

12. *Conflict of Interest and Federal Service*, p. 85.

13. Securities Exchange Act of 1934, Section 24(c).

14. See Securities and Exchange Commission, *Regulation Regarding Conduct of Members and Employees and Former Members and Employees of the Commission* (recirculated June 29, 1962).

15. *Conflict of Interest and Federal Service*, pp. 93–94.

16. Executive Order 11222, *Federal Register*, May 11, 1965, p. 6469.

17. *Federal Register*, Sept. 30, 1965, p. 12529.

18. *Ibid.*, Sections 735.204 (Financial Interests) and 735.206 (Misuse of Information).

19. *Ibid.*, Section 735.303 (Use of Inside Information).

20. *Federal Register*, Dec. 31, 1965, p. 17202.

21. S. 1877, 89th Cong., 1st Sess., 1965. Senators Maurine Neuberger, Joseph Clark, and Philip Hart joined Senator Case in introducing this bill.

22. *Ibid.*, Section 3(d).

Author Index*

* The reference in parentheses is the page number of the annotated citation from the Notes at the end of the volume.

Case Index

Subject Index

INVESTMENTS

INTRODUCTION TO ANALYSIS AND PLANNING

THIRD EDITION

BERNARD J. WINGER
RALPH R. FRASCA

University of Dayton

Prentice Hall
Englewood Cliffs, New Jersey 07632

Library of Congress Cataloging-in-Publication Data

Winger, Bernard J.
    Investments : introduction to analysis and planning / Bernard J.
Winger, Ralph R. Frasca.—3rd ed.
      p.   cm.
    Includes bibliographical references and index.
    ISBN 0-02-428613-3
    1. Investments.   I. Frasca, Ralph R.   II. Title.
HG4521.W488   1995
332.6—dc20   94-11016
                                                CIP

Editor: Leah Jewell
Assistant Editor: Teresa Cohan
Production Supervisor: Betsy Keefer
Production Manager: Lynn Pearlman
Text Designer: Anne Daly
Cover Art and Design: Viqui Maggio

 © 1995 by Prentice-Hall, Inc.
A Division of Simon & Schuster, Inc.
Englewood Cliffs, New Jersey 07632

Printed in the United States of America

10 9 8 7 6 5 4 3 2

ISBN 0-02-428613-3

PRENTICE-HALL INTERNATIONAL (UK) LIMITED, *London*
PRENTICE-HALL OF AUSTRALIA PTY. LIMITED, *Sydney*
PRENTICE-HALL CANADA, INC., *Toronto*
PRENTICE-HALL HISPANOAMERICANA, S.A., *Mexico*
PRENTICE-HALL OF INDIA PRIVATE LIMITED, *New Delhi*
PRENTICE-HALL OF JAPAN, INC., *Tokyo*
SIMON & SCHUSTER ASIA PTE. LTD., *Singapore*
EDITORA PRENTICE-HALL DO BRASIL, LTDA., *Rio de Janeiro*

Photo appearing on pages 1, 3, 31, 71, 107, and 131 courtesy of the American Stock Exchange.
Photo appearing on pages 176, 179, 217, and 261 courtesy of the New York Stock Exchange.

To Our Families

Preface

Our purpose in writing the third edition of *Investments: Introduction to Analysis and Planning* is the same as it was for the first edition: to help readers make intelligent and practical investment decisions. The text can be used successfully in a first investments course offered at four-year colleges or two-year institutions and in professional certification and continuing education programs. Our conversational tone and the publisher's excellent use of graphics and other visual presentations make the book lively and readable.

IMPORTANT CHARACTERISTICS OF THE TEXT

The text has certain features that most potential adopters like to consider before making a selection. The important characteristics are explained briefly.

A Planning Approach

The text features an integrated planning approach used over an investor's life. This approach focuses on goal setting, vehicle selection, performance evaluation with respect to stated goals, and portfolio modifications. Most successful investors follow this path, rather than one of periodic efforts to achieve a super return. While speculative activities are often illustrated, their potential risks are also clearly indicated along with their potential returns.

Decision-Making Perspective

The text focuses on individual investment decisions. Within this framework, the text has a greater analytical, rather than descriptive, tone. However, the analytical methods are designed for the capabilities of intended users. Both the math and statistics are elementary and fit the first investments course in practically all college curricula. (The text does not contain theorems or proofs, which are more appropriate in advanced classes.) Actually, an analytical approach works well in so-called lower-level courses because it is lively and maintains student interest.

Applications Orientation

The text features numerous applications of investment theory and strategies. These are contained in boxed features and chapter-end items, which the authors selected for timeliness and connection to topics discussed. This latter category includes *Review Questions, Problems and Projects,* and *Case Analyses*. Each chapter has two cases designed to illustrate the practical problems in investing. In addition, the cases and problems offer data manipulation exercises and analytical practice, particularly when they are used with the software available with the text. The review questions help students identify important topics and test their comprehension, while the projects (at least two to a chapter) indicate certain activities that bring students in contact with members of the investment community or direct them toward helpful library references.

Focus on Globalization, Ethical Issues, and Technology

International investment topics are integrated throughout the text in the various topical areas. Thus, for example, political risks are covered in the chapter dealing with investment risks (Chapter 4), and hedging exchange-rate risks with currency futures are explained in the chapter dealing with futures contracts (Chapter 13).

Ethical issues related to investing have been front-page news items in recent years, and names such as Michael Milken and Ivan Boesky have come to epitomize the so-called decade of greed—the 1980s. We have responded to the increasing importance of ethical issues by creating a boxed item called "A Question of Ethics," that deals with a controversial topic. The box presents an issue and two opposing sides, but it leaves resolution of the issue to the students. This format should provoke considerable student interest and spirited classroom discussion.

Clearly, investing has felt the impact of changes in information technology. Investors can utilize their personal computers to gather financial data, perform sophisticated analyses, and even execute trades. Topics involving the use of computers are discussed throughout the text, and the accompanying software provides students a hands-on experience with computer technology.

Real-World Examples

The text features discussions of actual, rather than "arm chair," investments. Some examples include an extensive analysis of the Mead Corporation in Chapters 6 and 7; and evaluation of Dreyer's convertible bond in Chapter 11; and an evaluation of IBM options in Chapter 12. Using real-world examples often leaves a few loose ends for instructors and students to resolve, but the excitement they bring to classroom discussions are well worth it.

CHANGES IN THE THIRD EDITION

A good investments text must change because its subject matter is in a constant state of flux. We have responded to market changes by revising both topical coverage and realtive emphasis. Changes in the third edition are overall in nature and specific-item directed. Each is explained in the following sections.

Overall Changes

There are five major overall changes designed to increase the text's effectiveness.

Enhanced Focus on Financial Planning.   Investing is only one part, albeit an important one, of financial planning. We have given a stronger focus to the investor's overall financial plan by creating a new chapter (Chapter 5), *Investments in the Overall Financial Plan,* that combines the important topics of liquidity management, debt management, life insurance planning, and retirement planning. The role of investments is highlighted clearly in each topic's discussion.

Increased Emphasis on Fundamental Analysis.   Continuing challenges to the efficient market hypothesis translate to growing support for finding undervalued equities. Fundamental analysis is the key to the valuation search; therefore, our treatment of the topic is expanded by including additional valuation material in the equity chapters.

Greater Recognition of the Investment Professional.   With the growing number of firms converting traditional retirement plans to voluntary plans, there is little doubt that the need for professional investment advice will increase considerably in the future. We have shaped certain discussions in the text to stimulate student interest in the direction of the investment professional. We also have included questions from previous CFA examinations that provide insights to the nature and rigor of the examination questions while simultaneously serving as a pretest for topics in the text.

Focused Boxed Items.   We have strengthened our boxed items by using three perspectives to focus the reader's attention: "Investment Insights," "Getting An Investment Edge," and "A Question of Ethics." The first perspective provides additional background on an important topic, the second perspective discusses ways that investors can reduce some investment costs or possibly increase returns, and the third perspective discusses ethical issues.

Improved Topical Integration.   There is an enhanced topical integration in the text that should help the instructor's presentations and topic assignments. All pooling arrangements are now covered in one chapter (Chapter

14) and the discussion of tangibles has been included in the real estate chapter (Chapter 15); also, preferred stock is now treated in the discussion of fixed income securities rather than in the section on equities. Overall, the text has been reduced from twenty to seventeen chapters, but without a material reduction in total topical coverage.

Specific Changes

Specific changes are detailed below.

1. Chapter 1 has been modified extensively. We have included a discussion of basic investment strategies and moved material on securities creation to Chapter 2, where it is integrated with the discussion of securities markets. Also, the treatment of federal income taxes has been thoroughly updated to reflect the 1993 Budget Reconciliation Act.

2. Chapter 3 has a broader discussion of time-value-of-money applications, and a new topic, seasonality and anomalies in stock returns, has been introduced.

3. Chapter 4's presentation of modern portfolio theory has been moved to the new chapter on portfolio management (Chapter 17). A new topic, the relationship of risk and time, has been introduced.

4. The discussion of life insurance as an investment vehicle has been enhanced in Chapter 5 by including the issue of how much life insurance is needed.

5. Chapter 6 has an intensified discussion (including an example, Pfizer) of growth as a key parameter in stock selection. Also, the discussion of valuation methods has been broadened to include multiple-of-earnings (or cash-flow) approaches.

6. Ratio analysis has been expanded in Chapter 7 with a discussion of profit margins; moreover, valuation of a company, Mead Corporation, includes a discussion of earnings and cash-flow approaches. A Standard and Poor's Research Report on Mead has been included at the end of the chapter to illustrate valuation methods and data.

7. In Chapter 9, a greater discussion of the topic of risk and return with fixed-income securities has been included along with more examples of reinvestment risks.

8. A new, major section on international bond investment has been added in Chapter 10, plus a discussion of Brady Bonds that have become popular recently. The discussion of preferred stock has been moved to this chapter and its coverage reduced.

9. Time premium on option contracts and premium decay over time are discussed in greater detail in Chapter 11. Also, discussion of two new securities, Dividend Enhanced Convertible Securities (DECs) and Preference Equity Redemption Cumulative Stock (PERCs), have been introduced.

10. Chapter 12 has been expanded to include options on futures contracts. The discussion of market-indexed certificates of deposit has also been broadened considerably.
11. Material on basis management and discussion of normal and inverted basis curves has been added to the topic of hedging with futures contracts in Chapter 13.
12. Chapter 14 has expanded coverage of international and global funds and, as noted above, all pooling arrangements have been included.
13. Real estate and other tangibles have been combined in Chapter 15. The discussion of the latter asset group has been shortened, although there is greater detail on the performance of goldmining stocks versus gold's price variablity.
14. Chapter 16 has been revised to provide greater coverage in two areas: integrating all investments into the portfolio plan and the usefulness of dollar cost averaging.
15. Chapter 17 is new to this edition, although some of its topics appeared in previous editions. Passive portfolio planning techniques and modifying portfolio positions (debt and equity) with derivative securities are completely new topics that have been added. The relative advantages and costs of using options versus futures contracts are also discussed.

PEDAGOGICAL FEATURES

We and the professionals at Macmillan have designed the text to be very teachable. Along with an informal writing style and the important characteristics noted above, adopters should find that the following items also enrich the teaching-learning environment.

Learning Objectives and Chapter Outline

Each chapter begins with an outline and a set of learning objectives. The outline helps students visualize a chapter as a whole entity and the objectives focus his or her attention on critical topics.

High-Impact Graphics

The text contains numerous graphics, making the student's comprehension easier and more interesting. There are both tables and figures (all are called exhibits, for ease of discussion). Many of the exhibits contain brief descriptions or highlight points making them self-contained learning tools.

Timely and Stimulating Boxed Items

As noted above, we have revised the boxed items to make them a truly integrated part of each chapter's subject matter. The boxes will stimulate student interest by showing investment activities in a practical setting and by challenging students to face controversial topics. We hope that instructors place greater emphasis on the boxes as pedagogical aids because they often provoke spirited discussions that enliven the classroom environment.

Strong Chapter-End Materials

As noted above each chapter contains two cases, at least two student projects, and numerous review questions and problems. This comprehensive coverage gives instructors a wide range of assignment material. Also, answers to the chapter-end problems and cases and part-end CFA examination questions appear in Appendix B at the end of the text.

A Flexible Teaching Outline

While we believe the text is covered easily in one quarter or semester, and while we feel the present flow of chapters is the most appropriate, instructors can make adjustments easily to meet their individual needs. If you prefer covering fixed-income securities before equities, simply cover Chapters 9 and 10 before Chapters 6, 7, and 8. Depending on students' backgrounds, Chapters 3 and 4 may be assigned as review chapters and not covered in detail in class. Similarly, Chapters 1 and 2 include considerable descriptive material that students can cover independently.

ANCILLIARY ITEMS

Instructors can use a number of ancilliary items as course aids. A discussion of each follows.

Instructor's Manual

An instructor's manual, prepared by the authors, is available. It contains a detailed topical outline, which helps instructors in planning lectures. The instructor's manual also contains comprehensive solutions to all chapter-end items, particularly the cases where additional insights are offered.

Test Bank

The authors have also prepared a comprehensive test bank that contains about 700 multiple-choice questions and 700 true-false questions. The questions have been written to test analytical and interpretative skills as well as material comprehension. Many questions are problem oriented, requiring calculations and analysis. The test bank is also available on a disk, which is very easy to use. Tests can be prepared in minutes with virtually no computer background or previous experience.

Computer Software

Adopters can request a disk that provides spreadsheet applications of many of the text problems involving extensive calculations. Programs include time-value-of-money applications, statistical analysis, beta calculation, Macaulay's duration coefficient, Black-Scholes option pricing, portfolio analysis, and others.

Also available on the disk are the yearly returns shown on the inside front and back covers of the text. These data can be used with spreadsheet programs for a variety of student projects, such as return projections or hypotheses testing.

The software with this edition is a substantial upgrade over the packages available with the previous editions. There are seventeen programs in total that can be used with only a minimal knowledge of spreadsheet basics. However, the mathematical formulas are left unhidden so that students can learn and use them in other applications if they wish.

ACKNOWLEDGMENTS

The dedication and efforts of many people are needed to complete a major textbook, and it is our pleasure to acknowledge those contributions. We are grateful to Macmillan for engaging the services of many excellent reviewers on previous editions: A. Frederic Banda, University of Akron; Cecil Bigelow, Mankato State University; Joseph Brandt, Incarnate World College; Jim Boyd, Louisiana State University; Joe B. Copeland, University of North Alabama; David J Crockett, Metropolitan State College; Ray Fernandez, Miami-Dade Community College; Cheryl A. McGaughy, Angelo State University; James R. Marchand, Radford University; Edward J. Pyatt, Hampton University; Donald Sorenson, University of Wisconsin—Whitewater; Davis Upton, Texas Tech University; and Howard R. Whitney, Franklin University.

We also wish to thank those reviewers who contributed to this edition: Joseph Brandt, Incarnate Word College; Cheryl A. McGaughy, Angelo State University; and Edward J. Pyatt, Hampton University.

We would like to thank our colleagues at the University of Dayton and in the Dayton-Cincinnati area for their help and support. Special thanks are due George Euskirchen, Thomas More College; Thomas E. Davidson, Thomas E. Davidson and Associates; and Patricia Decker, Fairleigh Dickinson.

Finally, we are deeply indebted to Denise Abbott and Teresa Cohan, Assistant Editor, for their assistance in the final stages of the text's development. We wish also to thank Betsy Keefer, Production Supervisor, and Barbara Hodgson, copyeditor, for their efforts in producing the text.

B. J. W.
R. R. F.

Contents

Understanding the Investment Process

Success in investing usually does not happen by chance, nor does it come quickly. All too often, beginners rush into an investment program without considering its risks in relation to its potential returns and without an understanding of the overall investment environment. The disappointments that often result can be avoided by taking the preliminary steps discussed in Part One.

Chapter 1 highlights the importance of having concrete investment goals and of trading off return and risk in selecting investments. It discusses investment planning, introduces specific investment vehicles, and explains basic investment strategies. Finally, it explains federal income tax considerations that investors should know.

Chapter 2 indicates how investments are created and highlights the functions of securities markets, explaining organized exchanges and the over-the-counter market. It also defines different types of stockbrokerage firms and the services they provide. The regulation of securities markets is explained within the context of legislation that has been enacted since 1933. Finally, the important task of finding investment information is discussed.

Chapter 3 deals primarily with time-value-of-money concepts that investors must understand if they are to evaluate returns of most investment alternatives. In addition, historical returns on key financial assets are shown.

Chapter 4 explains the nature of investment risk and shows how it is measured. The chapter highlights the importance of diversification and indicates how return correlations affect risk. It also presents risk statistics on key financial assets.

Chapter 5 discusses the relationship of investments within investors' personal financial plans. It explains liquidity and insurance needs and how they can be met and focuses on debt and retirement planning. The chapter emphasizes the importance of using appropriate investments throughout investors' lives.

CHAPTER ONE

Investors and Investments:
An Overview

After you finish this chapter, you will be able to:

- recognize that investors have different attitudes and try to achieve different investment goals.

- distinguish among the career opportunities available in investments and whether any appeal to you.

- understand the concept of investment and identify specific investment alternatives.

- understand what is meant by portfolio management and identify key steps in the investment process.

- understand the rate structure of the federal income tax and strategies to avoid taxes or defer them to later years.

- understand basic investment strategies that involve holding versus trading investments or defending against losses.

Investing is serious business. Indeed, the standard of living many people will enjoy (or tolerate) in the future may well depend on their investment success (or failure) today. If historical trends continue, we will probably rely less on the government or our employers to take care of our needs and more on our own initiative and planning. Successful investing is difficult, however. Prospective investors must first understand their investment personalities and be able to express their investment goals in specific, concrete terms. They also should become familiar with various investment alternatives and recognize certain tax avoidance and deferral techniques. Finally, investors should understand basic investment strategies.

INVESTOR PROFILES AND GOALS

Perhaps the best way for someone to start studying investing is to first study himself or herself. Do you want to be an active investor? Do you like taking risks? Are you looking for a current return, or are you willing to wait for price appreciation? After addressing these questions, you can concentrate on framing specific investment goals. And, you might consider seeking a career in the investments industry.

Investor Attitudes

Not everyone is alike in his or her investment personality or goals. Some people like to be actively involved in the investment process, while others prefer to sit on the sidelines. Some investors are willing to take high risks to achieve ambitious goals, while others are more conservative in outlook and prefer a more cautious approach. Finally, some invest to earn an immediate return, while others are content to defer their returns to later years.

Active management approach: investors select investments and make decisions when to buy and sell

Passive strategy: letting others make your investment decisions

Active Versus Passive Management   Individuals who prefer an **active management approach** select their own investments and decide when to buy and sell them. They also assume responsibility for reinvesting any cash returns the investments might generate. If you choose this approach, you should be prepared to devote a reasonable amount of time to do it properly. If you are unwilling to make such a commitment, then consider letting others manage most of your investments. A **passive strategy** can be as simple as limiting investments to mutual funds, or as involved as using a personal investment advisor. Actually, even passive strategies require some effort on the part of investors because they must choose *which* mutual fund or *what* investment advisory firm. Furthermore, after a choice is made, prudence dictates that they should review the fund's or advisor's performance on a fairly regular basis to determine if it is adequate and in line with investment goals. In reality, there is probably no such thing as a purely passive approach.

Disposition Toward Risk   Do you like to take risks? In hypothetical investment situations, many people say they do, but when they confront actual
risky choices with their own money at stake, they become very cautious.
Financial theory (and perhaps common sense) indicates that most investors
dislike risk, in the sense that we would prefer less of it rather than more in
trying to earn a given investment return. Anyone who operates contrarily
enjoys the thrill of the bet or of the game as much as she enjoys potential
winnings. Are there people like that? Sure, and you can find them at the
stockbroker's office as well as in Las Vegas. We assume they are the minority,
not the majority.

In studying investors, we identify three broad types—the **risk averter,**
the **risk seeker,** and the **risk-indifferent investor**—based on their behavior.

A risk averter is not one who never takes risks. He or she will take risks
but only when the return for doing so is sufficiently high. Line *A* in Exhibit 1.1
illustrates this point. It is called a risk-return line. The vertical axis shows
returns from various investments; the horizontal axis shows increasing
investment risk. The lines represent minimum returns each investor must
receive on an investment, given the degrees of risk indicated. Point *a,* for
example, shows the investor needs at least a 20% return to undertake an

Risk averter: requires
increasingly greater
returns for taking
greater risks

Risk seeker: requires
greater returns for
greater risks but
required increases in
return are less than
increases in risk

**Risk-indifferent
investor:** required return
increases are propor-
tional to increases in
risk

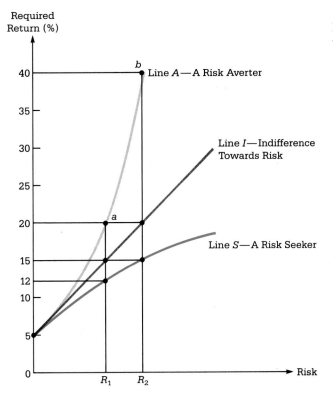

EXHIBIT 1.1
Investor attitudes
toward risk

investment with a risk level of R_1, while point b shows that a 40% return is required for risk level R_2. Although the required return doubled, the risk level shown at b is obviously not twice that shown at a. This line illustrates risk aversion: the investor requires ever-increasing returns to undertake increasingly risky investments.

Line S in Exhibit 1.1 shows a risk-return line for a risk seeker. At risk level R_1, this investor is content with a 12% return; at level R_2, the required return increases to only 15%. For a risk seeker, the increase in required return is always proportionately less than the increase in risk.

Line I shows a risk-indifferent investor's risk-return line. As you see, it lies between those of the risk averter and risk seeker. For this person, the increase in required return is always proportional to the increase in risk.

You may not be able to place yourself into any one of the three attitude categories on a consistent basis, and it isn't necessary to do so. In fact, many of us seem to be a bit of each, acting as risk averters when we buy insurance and acting as avid risk seekers when we buy state lottery tickets. The important point to learn is that every investor seeks some higher return as risk increases. Consequently, you as an investor must find a level of risk and return you feel comfortable with, which is called your **risk tolerance level.** If you are satisfied with nothing less than a sure thing, for example, you generally must be content with the lowest possible return, such as the 5% shown in Exhibit 1.1. Actually, finding your risk tolerance level may be a difficult task and not fully accomplished until you develop personal investment experiences. Although this text can't help identify your risk tolerance level, it can make you a better risk-aware investor by helping you in two important ways. It provides the tools:

Risk tolerance level: specific mix of risk and return that satisfies an investor

☐ to identify, measure, and understand risk determinants and
☐ to make reasonable estimates of how much additional return you can reasonably expect by taking greater risks.

Preference for Income Versus Price Appreciation   Income refers to interest, dividends, or other types of payment an investment might provide on a regular basis. Most bonds and many common stocks offer such returns. Other investments offer no income. The only way to profit from them is through price appreciation, which comes in the future. Investors may have to decide: Do they want investments with good income but not-so-good chances for price appreciation, or do they want investments with little or no income but good chances for growth? Different investors answer this question differently. Retirees, for example, usually favor income, while young people often look for growth opportunities.

Goals: The Reasons for Investing

If you are asked why you want to invest, you might say, "To make money, of course." Actually, it's not quite that simple. As we shall see throughout this text, there are numerous investment alternatives, all designed to make money. But how much money do you want to make, how fast, and with how much risk? If time isn't taken to answer these questions and pinpoint investment objectives, the odds are high that investment performance will be poor. Setting concrete, realistic investment goals is considered by many investment advisors to be the single most important step in the investment process. It sets the stage for many other investment decisions that eventually must be made. Below are some of the more important investment objectives.

Meeting Liquidity Needs   An asset is said to have **liquidity** when it can be converted to cash quickly with no loss in value. A savings account at a bank is extremely liquid; an acre of raw land held for future development is probably very illiquid. Practically everyone needs some degree of liquidity. We need it to even out irregular receipts of income and payment of expenses. We also like to have it in case of an emergency. So, some investments must be those that provide adequate liquidity. Although high yields are sought in these investments, yield is less important than accessibility to funds. Most investors will accept a lower yield for higher liquidity.

Liquidity: characteristic of an asset when it can be converted quickly to cash with no loss in value

Saving for a Large Expenditure   In many cases, we save and invest to accumulate sufficient funds for a future expenditure, such as a car or a house. Liquidity plays a less important role in these situations, particularly if the expenditure will not take place for a long time. Thus, an investor can take greater risks to earn higher returns, even though this might invite some inconveniences and lead to possible investment losses.

Retirement Planning   Retirement planning is, in many cases, the most critical investment objective. It is important because it influences the style and quality of our lives. Few people want to retire to an existence substantially inferior to the one they enjoyed during their working years. On the contrary, longer life expectancies and improved health have made many retirees seek a lifestyle that is better than what they had when they worked.

The long investment period that is usually involved in retirement planning permits greater flexibility in choosing investments for a retirement fund. In addition, certain income tax advantages can increase after-tax returns by a considerable amount. (These considerations are discussed in Chapter 5.) Retirement planning is done best when it is begun early in your career. If you are a recent college graduate, probably the last thing you want to hear is that you should begin investing for a retirement that takes place decades from now. However, the sooner and the more carefully you invest, the greater the retirement accumulation for a given dollar of savings. A dollar invested when you are 25 may be worth $10 or $20 invested when you are 45, particularly if you use appropriate tax shelters.

Speculating   Those investors fortunate enough to have satisfied tangible investment goals can then invest in more speculative ventures—if they wish. Investors at this stage have adequate funds to afford losses if investments perform poorly; they can also take considerably greater investment risks. Speculate in an oil exploration program if you wish, or start trading options or futures contracts. But don't invest in ignorance. Meeting speculation objectives often demands the greatest investment knowledge because of the wide array of investment alternatives.

Investment Professionals

Many people assist others in making investment decisions. They are considered investment professionals, or professional money managers. Some of the career opportunities in investments are detailed below.

Stockbroker (registered representative): helps investors trade securities; usually compensated through commissions

Stockbroker   A **stockbroker** (more appropriately called a **registered representative** of a stockbrokerage firm) deals with both individual and institutional investors, earning commissions for orders executed. As a stockbroker, you deal with the public, so selling skills are just as valuable as knowledge of investments. Most important, clients must have confidence in your ability to suggest appropriate investment alternatives and to help them manage their investment funds. Building a client base takes time, so don't expect a large income immediately. Successful brokers, however, often earn six-figure incomes. Indeed, according to the Securities Industry Association, the average retail broker earned $114,000 in 1992. So, if financial success is an important career objective, few professions offer potential monetary rewards as great as stockbrokering.

Security analyst: essentially a researcher who attempts to find attractive investment opportunities

Security Analyst   A **security analyst** is essentially a researcher who tries to determine which industries are attractive for investing and which securities are likely to do well in the future. Security analysts are employed by brokerage houses, mutual funds, insurance companies, and other financial institutions. Salaries are excellent, particularly for those who become CFAs (explained below), although they do not match the figures of successful stockbrokers.

Portfolio manager: typically works for a financial institution, making investments for the institution's clients

Portfolio Manager   A **portfolio manager** is typically employed by a mutual fund, insurance company, or commercial bank. He or she is responsible for investing large sums of money to achieve client goals. For example, you might work in the trust department of a commercial bank, managing a number of trust accounts. Compensation levels vary considerably among portfolio managers, depending primarily on the size of portfolios managed and the type of investing undertaken. A successful manager of a large mutual fund will also earn a six-figure income (or more).

Financial planner: helps people in all phases of financial planning, including investments

Financial Planner   Although financial planners advise clients in a number of areas, investments is often an important one. The **financial planner** might have his or her own practice but is more likely to be employed by a financial institution. Financial planners often sell a wide array of securities, but many specialize in limited partnerships or insurance-related financial products. Because of their activities in selling investments or offering invest-ment advice, many planners now must register with the Securities and Exchange Commission, as do stockbrokers. They also must obtain a license with the National Association of Securities Dealers. Financial planners enjoy high incomes, which depend on both fees and commissions on financial products they sell.

Investment Banker   **Investment bankers** are involved in the distribution of securities from issuers to buyers. They also serve as consultants in acquisi-tions and mergers. With often fascinating work and extraordinary compensa-tion, investment banking can be the epitome of success in investments. It is not unusual for someone to start at $60,000 a year immediately on graduation from a top MBA program, and he or she might be earning well over $100,000 two years later. Such positions are few, and they usually go to those with cre-dentials or connections. If you are intelligent and ambitious, though, don't think that landing such a position is beyond hope.

Investment banker: involved primarily in the distribution of securities

What background do you need for a career in investments? The follow-ing accomplishments will help you to be a success.

College Degrees   A college degree seems a prerequisite for many positions today, including those in the investment field. Any undergraduate degree is appropriate for becoming a stockbroker or financial planner, but a major in finance—or at least some courses in accounting, finance, and business—is best. If your sights are set on becoming a financial analyst, portfolio manager, or investment banker, then you will need more training in finance and busi-ness. An MBA or other appropriate master's degree is very helpful.

Certificates   The most appropriate certification is the Chartered Financial Analyst (CFA). You earn this designation by successfully completing a series of tests extending over a three-year period and by meeting other require-ments. For more information, write to the Association for Investment Management and Research, PO Box 3668, Charlottesville, VA 22903 (tele-phone 804-977-6600). Earning the CFA will enhance your career success if you want to become a financial analyst or portfolio manager. The testing is not easy but the rewards are worth the effort.

Many stockbrokers and financial planners are attempting to become Certified Financial Planners (CFPs). This certificate is awarded by The International Board of Certified Financial Planners, 5445 DTC Parkway, Englewood, CO 80111 (telephone 303-850-0333). A similar certificate—the Chartered Financial Consultant (ChFC)—is offered by the American College, 270 Bryn Mawr Avenue, Bryn Mawr, PA 19010. Financial planning is a rapidly growing area and one that is working hard to enhance its professionalism. The CFP and ChFC help considerably in this effort. They, too, are not easily earned, but having a certificate helps in demonstrating to clients your com-petence and integrity in the investments profession. As mentioned above, this may be crucial in developing a clientele.

THE CONCEPT OF INVESTMENT

Investment: tangible or intangible asset that provides a periodic return or has the potential to increase in value

Many people think of investments in a narrow sense. They consider stocks and bonds as investments but may not view their homes or savings accounts as such. Actually, an **investment** is any asset—tangible or intangible—that has the potential to provide a periodic return and/or to increase in value. This definition includes homes, savings accounts, and many other assets. You might buy a home for reasons other than profit, but the rent you save by owning and the potential for price appreciation clearly make it an investment. Exhibit 1.2 provides a summary of many important investment alternatives, and Exhibit 1.3 shows trends in individuals' financial asset holdings since 1980. As you see in Exhibit 1.3, mutual funds show a dramatic increase, while bank deposits and certificates of deposit (CDs) show a significant decline. By the way, the $8.0 trillion in 1993 works out to about $31,500 for every person in the United States—not a trivial amount and worth managing effectively!

Debt Instruments

Debt instrument: security that typically pays interest and makes its owner a creditor of the issuer

Many of our investments represent others' debt obligations. Businesses and governmental units borrow funds by selling debt instruments to the general public. If you own a **debt instrument,** you are a lender to the organization that issued it. This position gives you certain rights, an important one being that your claim to interest and repayment of principal comes before any payments to stockholders. Debt instruments are considered safer than many other investments, although it is dangerous to generalize; surely, the obligation of a weak or bankrupt issuer may not be worth much. You can categorize debt instruments in several ways, but perhaps the most useful is by maturity. There are short-, intermediate-, and long-term debt obligations. Most investors hold a wide array of debt instruments, and they are explained in Chapters 5, 9, and 10.

Short-term debt instrument: security with a maturity less than one year held primarily for liquidity purposes

Short-Term Debt Instruments   Short term means less than one year, so a short-term debt instrument will mature and be redeemed by its issuer within 12 months. Exhibit 1.2 shows a variety of often-held **short-term debt instruments.** It also shows that the most common reason for holding them is to meet liquidity needs, although they are often held as temporary investments whenever the long-term investment environment is uncertain and there is a strong feeling that interest rates might increase in the future. When held for this reason, the investor is described as looking for a temporary "parking place" for his or her cash.

Intermediate-term debt instrument: debt instrument with a maturity between one and ten years

Intermediate-Term Debt Instruments   An **intermediate-term debt instrument** is usually understood as one with a maturity between 1 and 10 years. Someone holding securities at the short end of this time span is proba-

EXHIBIT 1.2
Investment alternatives

Investment Vehicle	Examples	Reasons for Holding
I. DEBT INSTRUMENTS		
Short-term	Treasury bills, savings accounts, Series EE savings bonds, NOW accounts, money market accounts	Liquidity, temporary "parking place"
Intermediate-term	Treasury notes, nonnegotiable CDs, some government agency issues	Some liquidity, mostly earnings
Long-term	Treasury and corporate bonds, municipal bonds, agency bonds	Earnings with safety of principal
II. COMMON STOCKS		
Low-risk	PepsiCo, AT&T, Exxon, K-mart	Moderate growth, safety of principal
High-risk	Apple Computer, Amgen, Microsoft	Rapid growth
III. PREFERRED STOCK	ConEd 5% series, Sallie Mae $2.50 series	Income, safety of principal
IV. LEVERAGE-INHERENT SECURITIES		
Convertibles	Bally's 6%, USX 5 3/4%	Moderate income, growth with the common stock
Warrants	MGM, Federal National Mortgage	Quick capital appreciation
Put and call options	Individual stocks, market indexes, bonds, commodities	Quick capital appreciation, hedging
Futures contracts	Gold, corn, pork bellies, bonds, foreign currencies	Quick capital appreciation, hedging
V. POOLING ARRANGEMENTS	Mutual funds, investment trusts, limited partnerships	Various
VI. TANGIBLES	Real estate, collectibles, gold, precious gems	Hedge inflation

bly doing so to satisfy liquidity needs, while an investor at the long end is usually seeking income and sacrificing liquidity. Popular intermediate-term instruments are listed in Exhibit 1.2.

Long-Term Debt Instruments   A **long-term debt instrument** is one with a maturity greater than 10 years. As we shall see in Chapter 9, these instruments can be risky if they must be sold on short notice. Investors clearly give up liquidity when they purchase these debt instruments. The investment target is to earn a rate of return higher than that available with instruments of shorter maturities. Long-term debt alternatives are shown in Exhibit 1.2.

Long-term debt instrument: debt instrument with a maturity greater than ten years held primarily for income purposes

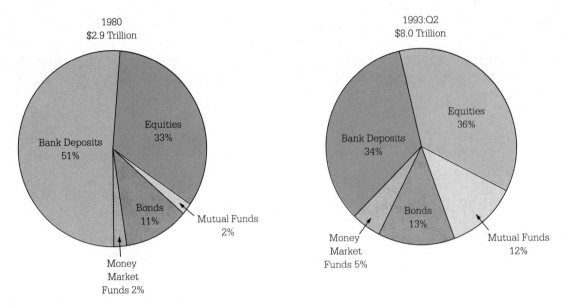

EXHIBIT 1.3
Major financial assets of individuals (Source: Securities Industry Association, *Trends,* vol. XIX, no. 8, December 14, 1993, p. 11.)

Common Stocks

Common stock: represents ownership interest in a corporation

A share of **common stock** represents an ownership (also called equity) interest in the corporation that issued it. As indicated above, a share of common stock is riskier than a debt instrument in the sense that its claims on assets or earnings are inferior. But, on the positive side, common stock has a residual claim on all assets or earnings that are left after creditors' interests have been satisfied. When you buy common stock, you are hoping this residual interest will grow over time as the corporation grows. That doesn't always happen, yet common stock can still be classified as low or medium risk and high risk. Common stock is an important investment vehicle. It is explained thoroughly in Chapters 6, 7, and 8.

Low- and Medium-Risk Common Stock   All common stock is inherently risky; thus, this classification has to do with degree of risk. A low-risk common stock can be thought of as one involving a minimal chance that the issuing corporation might go bankrupt in the foreseeable future. Exhibit 1.2 shows shares of Exxon and AT&T as examples. Stocks such as these are called "blue chips." Even though bankruptcy risk is small, shares of these companies are still very price-volatile and, hence, risky. An adequate portfolio of such stocks held for a sufficiently long period can minimize this price risk and produce substantial investment return.

BOX 1.1   INVESTMENT INSIGHTS

October 19, 1987: A Day of Financial Infamy

If you look at any stock market index, 1987 doesn't stand out as a particularly noteworthy year. The Dow Jones Industrials began it at 1,900 and ended at 1,935—a gain of about 2%—and the S&P 500 showed the same percentage increase. Look more closely at 1987, though, and you will find one of the most tumultuous years since indexes have been kept.

To begin with, the Dow was up to 2,740 by late August, a gain of 44%. Had the year ended then, it would have been one of the best years on record. Euphoria was everywhere, and although some analysts were warning of excesses, many were optimistic the bull market would continue. It didn't. Prices began softening in September but rallied toward the end of the month to close the Dow at around 2,650. But the slide continued in October, and at the close on Friday, October 16, the Dow stood at 2,246.

Then came Black Monday—October 19. When the day was over, the Dow's reading of 1,738 was almost unbelievable. It had lost 508 points! To put this in perspective, the supposedly great crash of October 29, 1929, saw the Dow lose 12.82% of its value, but the loss on Black Monday was 22.67%, almost twice as much. And the volume of shares traded—about 600 million on the New York Stock Exchange—was as remarkable as the price drop. On a normal day, volume is 250 million shares or so. You don't generally buy indexes; you buy specific stocks. Here is how a few fared: IBM, down $33 to $102 a share; USX, down $13 to $21 a share; and GM, down $13.13 to $53.87 a share. Imagine your nausea if your retirement nest egg was tied up in those three.

Do we know what caused the great crash? Not really. A government report (called the Brady Report) cited the heavy influence of two innovations: program trading and portfolio insurance. The evidence is hardly conclusive, though, and other researchers doubt these two practices were the primary causes. We may never know, just as we still do not know what caused the 1929 crash and the terrible depression that followed it.

High-Risk Common Stock   A high-risk common stock has a higher bankruptcy risk than the blue chips. These stocks indeed may be the Exxons and AT&Ts of the future, but be prepared for the worst if you buy them because many will not survive along the way. Again, an adequately diversified portfolio held long enough can lead to substantial investment return, and that is the only way these securities should ever be held.

Preferred Stocks

A **preferred stock** is a hybrid security; it has characteristics of both common stock and debt. It is like common stock in that it is equity and not debt. So its claims on assets and earnings come after those of all debtholders (but before

Preferred stock: called a hybrid security because it has characteristics of both debt and equity those of common stockholders). It is like debt in that it receives a fixed payment each year. In comparison to debt and common stock, preferred stock plays a much smaller role in most investors' portfolios. The reasons for this situation will be explained in Chapter 10.

Leverage-Inherent Securities

Leverage-inherent security: instrument with a built-in capacity to increase investment gain or loss

A **leverage-inherent security** is one that has a built-in capacity to increase investment gain or loss. By itself, leverage means increasing your investment holdings by borrowing. It's not hard to see that borrowed money invested in securities surely increases investment risk beyond what you have when you limit your investments to those for which you have adequate funds. The risk with a leverage-inherent security is not so clear but is no less real. Popular leverage-inherent securities are described below.

Corporate convertible security: instrument that can be converted into shares of common stock

Convertibles A **corporate convertible security**—bond or preferred stock—allows the holder to exchange it for a given number of shares of common stock. The idea is to have a security that pays a high rate of return while at the same time giving the investor a stake in the common stock through the conversion privilege. However, you pay a premium for such a privilege, which—all other factors being equal—increases your investment risk. Convertibles are covered in Chapter 11.

Warrant: instrument that gives its holder a right to buy shares of common stock at a set price over a given period

Warrants A **warrant** is issued by a corporation. It gives the holder a right to buy a given number of shares of the corporation's common stock at a set price for a given period. The investment appeal with warrants is that they usually sell at prices below the price of the common stock. By buying them instead of the common stock, you increase your ownership potential. However, if the price of the common stock is below the exercise price of a warrant at its maturity, the warrant will expire worthless, leading to a total loss for the investor. Warrants are explained in more detail in Chapter 11.

Call option: almost identical to a warrant except that it can be created by anyone

Put and Call Options A **call option** is almost identical to a warrant except it is not necessarily issued by a corporation and it has a much shorter life. A **put option** differs from a call option in that it gives the holder the right to sell, rather than buy, a given number of shares of stock. Many investment strategies involve options, and the important ones are explained in Chapter 12.

Put option: gives its holder the right to sell— rather than buy—shares of stock

Futures contract: obligation—not a right—to buy or sell some asset at a set price over a given period

Futures Contracts A **futures contract** is similar to an option but differs in one important respect: it is an obligation to buy or sell in the future at a price fixed today. Basically, these contracts are wagers on the future price of a commodity with the loser paying the winner the difference between the contract price and the actual price at maturity. Unless they are used in hedging situations, both put and call options and futures contracts may well be the riskiest investments you ever make. Be sure to read Chapters 12 and 13 before you even consider investing in them.

Pooling Arrangements

In a **pooling arrangement,** your investment dollar buys a diversified portfolio of securities or other assets. These arrangements are excellent whenever you lack adequate capital to achieve diversification on your own. In addition, many offer professional portfolio management. The most popular pooling arrangement is the mutual fund. Mutual funds and other pooling arrangements are discussed in Chapter 14.

Pooling arrangement: allows investors to pool their resources to gain diversification advantages

Real Estate and Other Tangibles

During periods of inflation, many investors look toward tangible assets as a means of hedging inflation's ill effects. Certain assets, such as gold and silver, collectibles, raw land, and income-producing real estate, are believed to be good hedging assets because their price increases are expected to match the inflation rate. Tangible assets are no less risky than the intangibles; in some respects, they are far riskier and require considerably more knowledge and expertise. Before considering an investment in any of them, you should read Chapter 15.

Portfolio Management

A **portfolio** is simply a collection of assets held simultaneously. If you own a home and household furnishings, jewelry, vested benefits in a retirement plan, and checking and savings accounts, you already have a portfolio. It may be bigger than you initially think. As you begin a program of investing, you should think of adding to this portfolio and how these additions will help you attain your investment objectives. For example, an important aspect of portfolio management is achieving adequate diversification. So, you may not want to increase your holdings of tangible assets if you already have a house and other tangibles; or, you might not want to own more long-term bonds if your employer's retirement plan is invested exclusively in such securities. In either of these cases, a common stock investment might be more suitable.

Portfolio: collection of assets held simultaneously

Another important aspect of portfolio management is determining when assets should be sold. Should you do this frequently, in an attempt to maximize your return over an investment cycle, or should you follow a more cautious buy-and-hold approach, changing the portfolio only when your investment goals change? Aspects of portfolio management are discussed later in this chapter, but the topic is covered in detail in Chapters 16 and 17.

Steps in Investment Planning

In a broad sense, **investment planning** is a strategy designed to manage an investor's wealth. As such, it must consider both preserving and increasing wealth. Successful planning follows a series of steps, as indicated in Exhibit 1.4. First, investors must determine their attitudes toward risk. Next, wealth

Investment planning: strategy for managing an investor's wealth

EXHIBIT 1.4
Steps in investment
planning

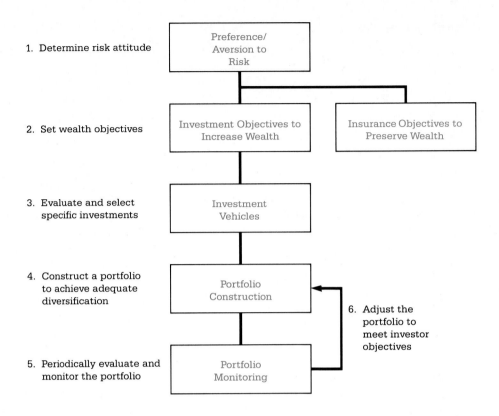

1. Determine risk attitude

2. Set wealth objectives

3. Evaluate and select
    specific investments

4. Construct a portfolio
    to achieve adequate
    diversification

5. Periodically evaluate and
    monitor the portfolio

6. Adjust the
    portfolio to
    meet investor
    objectives

objectives should be set. To protect existing wealth, adequate insurance coverage is usually necessary. Such coverage should protect against potential losses caused by accidents, illnesses, liability suits, and death. Indeed, investing without adequate insurance could be a very costly mistake.

To increase wealth, it is necessary to invest. After investment objectives are specified, the task of evaluating and then selecting specific investments begins. The need for adequate diversification must be considered when assets are selected. The resulting portfolio is periodically evaluated and monitored to determine if it is achieving investor objectives. If it is not, the portfolio must be adjusted, which might dictate selling some assets and purchasing others.

Let's consider the following example to illustrate the planning steps:

1. You decide that you have a moderately high risk tolerance level.
2. One of your wealth objectives is to accumulate at least $100,000 in 15 years to help your children through college.
3. You choose common stocks to achieve your goal, hoping their returns over the next 15 years will match their long-run average annual return of about 10%. Assuming this return is realized and you start investing immediately, you determine that you must invest about $2,900 each year to achieve the target (Chapter 3 shows you how to make this easy calculation).

4. Because you do not want to be a very active investor and because diversification is important, you choose a growth-oriented equity mutual fund as your investment vehicle.
5. The fund provides a year-end statement showing your investment's value; so you easily measure progress toward the goal.
6. Assume that through the first five years, the fund's performance falls short of the anticipated average annual return of 10%. This creates a serious problem, and to deal with it, you must decide to (a) increase the annual investment; or (b) shift your funds to a more aggressive mutual fund that might earn more than 10% over the remaining ten years; or (c) not achieve the target, which might mean your children will go to a less expensive college.

Your risk tolerance level set the stage for the rest of the process in the example. If you had a low risk tolerance level, you would have selected a less risky investment vehicle—for example, 15-year bank CDs with a guaranteed rate of 5%. In this case, you are assured of accumulating $100,000, but your annual investment must be $4,400 instead of $2,900. Finally, the assumed outcome in step 6 is a gloomy one. But your mutual fund might have averaged much better than 10%, making it possible for you to send your children to a pricey school or giving you an accumulation surplus to use elsewhere.

FEDERAL INCOME TAX CONSIDERATIONS

The federal income tax is a critical factor in investment decisions. The tax law is complex, and what is often worse, it is constantly changing. Few of us can become tax experts, but we can become familiar with the basic elements of the tax law that are important to investing.

A Progressive Rate Structure

The amount of income tax you pay depends on two factors: taxable income—which is called the tax base—and the tax rates applied to taxable income. In addition to knowing how to calculate your tax liability, you should be aware of your marginal tax rate.

Calculating Tax Liability   Federal income tax liability is determined by tax rates and taxable income. Taxable income is defined by the tax code, which is voluminous, complex, and constantly changing. The following discussion centers on tax rates; taxable income is discussed in the section on tax strategies. Exhibit 1.5 shows the 1993 rate structure for both individual and jointly filed tax returns. As you see, there are five rates to consider in determining tax liability. As an example calculation, if you are a single filer with $200,000 of taxable income, your tax liability is $61,772 [$31,172 + 0.36($200,000 − $115,000)].

BOX 1.2   GETTING AN INVESTMENT EDGE

Five Common Mistakes of Beginning Investors

MISTAKE 1: NO CLEAR COMPREHENSION OF RETURN AND RISK

How much return can I expect? Over what period of time? Subject to what risk? Know the answers to these crucial questions before you make an investment. Too many people have vague ideas about risk and return. Surveys consistently show a large number think that they should double their money with stocks in a year or two, which is virtually impossible to do consistently and difficult to do even occasionally. Others believe a doubling in 10 years is excellent, even though many investments have done this well. Some people believe that if they hold any stock long enough, it will eventually show a profit. (To dispel this foolish idea, you should see how many companies go bankrupt each year.) Others think stocks are so risky that they might lose everything invested in them. (Such a loss is almost impossible if the portfolio is reasonably diversified.) With hazy thinking like this, it's no wonder some investors lose heavily in the market and then view it as the world's largest organized crap game, whereas others are too timid to put their money anywhere that is not federally insured.

MISTAKE 2: USING A FRIEND OR RELATIVE AS AN INVESTMENT ADVISOR

If you are about to be graduated from college, you will be amazed at the number of friends you have in the securities or insurance business. (Some sell both.) A good percentage of these friends are former classmates who are learning their trade—on you. Select your broker or other advisor with the same care you exercise in finding a physician or an attorney. If your choice is a friend or relative, make it clear that when it comes to investing, the relationship is strictly professional. And don't rely on inside information or hot tips for investments. If your broker has any, he or she is probably in violation of the securities laws—and if you act on them, so are you.

MISTAKE 3: TRADING TOO FREQUENTLY

Beginning investors are often impatient. They buy a security, expecting an immediate price increase, and then hit the panic button if it doesn't materialize. Their anxiety is heightened by reading price quotations every day (or calling their broker every hour) and finding

---

Marginal tax rate: applies to additional taxable income

The Marginal Tax Rate   A **marginal tax rate** is the rate that applies to additional income. As indicated, the current tax law has five marginal rates: 15%, 28%, 31%, 36%, and 39.6%. The importance of the marginal rate is that it shows the amount of income that will be available to you out of an increase or a decrease in taxable income. For example, suppose Carol Clay's taxable income is $60,000. Suppose further that she is considering investing $50,000 out that prices of other stocks—ones they wanted to buy in the first place—are setting new highs. The solution? Sell the losers and buy the winners—right? Wrong! Over the long run, this investment approach enriches the broker and impoverishes you. As a rule of thumb, allow about 2% for commissions on the value of securities purchased *and* sold. If you buy and sell only twice a year, you dissipate 8% of your capital. Few investors can overcome a burden this huge and still show a respectable return. If your broker constantly calls with dumb slogans like, "Maybe it's time to take profits," or "Let's cut your losses short and let the profits run," you should look for a new broker.

MISTAKE 4: NOT ENOUGH DIVERSIFICATION

Much investment risk can be eliminated without sacrificing return through proper diversification. Yet surveys tell us that most investors hold fewer than five securities, with many holding only one or two. These investors are courting danger because even the bluest of the blue chips can go for years without showing a decent return. For that matter, so can a whole portfolio of blues. (From 1966 through 1981, you were better off in Treasury bills than in the 30 stocks that make up the Dow Jones Industrial Average.) To be adequately protected, you need a well-diversified portfolio, balanced across a wide array of different investments.

MISTAKE 5: NO CLEARLY FORMULATED INVESTMENT GOALS

This mistake is perhaps the most serious because it creates the environment that allows the others to flourish. If you know *why* you are investing, you will know better *how* to invest. Clearly established goals not only pinpoint investments likely to achieve them, but they also allow you to measure and evaluate performance. The question *"Am I achieving my goals?"* is concrete and measurable; the question *"Am I getting rich by investing?"* is surprisingly elusive. Until all securities you buy are eventually sold, you never really know how you are doing. Sure, you paid $90 for IBM and now it's only $45 a share, but you haven't lost anything because you haven't sold, and it will go back up. Logic like this makes every investor a winner—but don't try taking your winnings to a bank or living off of them.

in corporate bonds with a 10% annual pretax rate of return, or $5,000 of interest a year. Because this added interest income is still in the $53,500-to-$115,000 bracket, her marginal rate is 31%, and she will pay an additional $1,550 in taxes. Her after-tax return is $3,450 ($5,000 − $1,550) and her after-tax rate of return on the investment is 0.069 ($3,450/$50,000), or 6.9%.

EXHIBIT 1.5
1993 Tax rate schedules

Single — Schedule X			
If taxable income is	but not over	the tax is	of the amount over
$0	$22,100	. . . . .15%	$0
22,100	53,500	$3,315.00 + 28%	22,100
53,500	115,000	12,107.00 + 31%	53,500
115,000	250,000	31,172.00 + 36%	115,000
250,000	—————	79,772.00 + 39.6%	250,000
Married Filing Jointly or Qualifying Widow(er) — Schedule Y-1			
If taxable income is	but not over	the tax is	of the amount over
$0	$36,900	. . . . 15%	$0
36,900	89,150	$5,535.00 + 28%	36,900
89,150	140,000	20,165.00 + 31%	89,150
140,000	250,000	35,928.50 + 36%	140,000
250,000	—————	75,528.50 + 39.6%	250,000

A simpler method for calculating the after-tax return is shown below:

$$r' = (1.0 - MTR)r$$

where r' = the after-tax rate of return,

MTR = the marginal tax rate, and

r = the investment's pretax rate of return.

In Carol's case, we have: $0.069 = [(1.0 - 0.31) \times 0.10]$.

    You should see that the after-tax return to Carol will change if her taxable income is in a different tax bracket. For example, at $300,000 of taxable income, r' decreases to 6.04% $[(1.0 - 0.396) \times 0.10 = 0.0604]$.

Capital gains and losses: gains or losses when capital assets are sold at prices greater or less than their costs

Capital Gains and Capital Losses   **Capital gains and losses** result when investment assets, such as stocks and bonds, are sold at prices greater (capital gain) or less (capital loss) than their costs. Gains and losses are classified as short term if an asset is held one year or less and long term if it is held longer than one year. Short-term gains receive no special tax treatment, but long-term gains are given an advantage, in that the maximum applicable rate is 28%. So taxpayers with higher marginal rates have an incentive to earn long-term capital gains. For example, the tax savings on $10,000 of long-term gains to someone with a 39.6% marginal tax rate is $1,160 [$10,000 × (0.396 − 0.280)].

    Although all capital gains are taxable, you can deduct only $3,000 of capital losses (long or short term) in a tax year. So if you took, say, $12,000 of capital losses in 1993, only $3,000 can be deducted in that year; however, the remainder can be carried forward indefinitely and be deducted in future years. Also, losses can be used to offset gains. For example, suppose you earned $10,000 of capital gains in 1994. The unused portion of 1993's losses ($9,000) is used as an offset against 1994's gain; thus, you are taxed on only $1,000 of gains in 1994.

Tax Strategies

Although marginal tax rates were reduced substantially by the 1986 Tax Reform Act, they are still sufficiently high to encourage taxpayers to find ways to reduce their tax liabilities. Two broad strategies are used in this effort. The first is to avoid (not evade) paying taxes altogether, and the second is to defer paying them to a later time.

Tax Avoidance   **Tax avoidance** is a technique designed to eliminate the need to pay a tax. Avoidance techniques aren't always that easy to find. Three methods in investing, though, are widely used. The first is to invest in securities that pay nontaxable income—municipal bonds. Under the federal Constitution, an investment instrument of a state or local government cannot be taxed by the federal government. This provision establishes the tax-exempt status of state or locally issued bonds. It should be easy to see why people with high marginal tax rates prefer such bonds.

Tax avoidance: technique designed to eliminate the need to pay a tax

Suppose Carol Clay could invest in municipal bonds and earn a pre-tax rate of return of 8%. Should she do it, or should she invest in the corporate bonds? All other things held constant and assuming a 31% marginal tax rate, the municipals are the better investment. The pre-tax and after-tax rates on the municipals are the same, and this rate is higher than the after-tax rate of 6.9% on the corporate bonds of the previous example.

A second avoidance technique is to invest in a personal residence. If you meet certain conditions of age and residency, you are allowed a $125,000 exclusion of any gains on the sale of a personal residence. Moreover, you are free to defer any gains from sales until the $125,000 is reached. For example, suppose you buy a house for $20,000 and sell it 10 years later for $80,000. The $60,000 gain can be deferred *if* you purchase another house worth at least $80,000 within two years of the time the previous house is sold. Suppose you buy another house for $100,000, which you sell for $200,000 20 years later when you are over 55 years of age. Now, your total gains are $160,000 ($60,000 + $100,000), but $125,000 is excluded, leaving only $35,000 as taxable income. Put simply, it is hard to beat this tax advantage with other investments.

A third popular avoidance technique is to split income among family members, adding income to those members with low marginal rates and taking it away from those with high marginal rates. Frequently, this reallocation of income is accomplished by giving to children, in the form of outright gifts or through trusts. Only $1,000 of income from such transfers can receive favorable tax treatment. Income over this base amount is taxed at the parents' rate until the dependent reaches age 14; then it is taxed at his or her own rates. Although $1,000 of income is not considerable, it still is sufficiently large to make income splitting reasonably attractive. It often is used to accumulate funds for a child's college education.

Tax deferral: strategy designed to pay taxes in later years on income earned in current years

Deferring Income Taxes   **Tax deferral** means using various strategies that allow you to pay tax at a later time on income that you currently earn and that otherwise would be taxable. On the surface, deferral doesn't appear that attractive because you eventually must pay the tax. But don't underestimate the power of investing on a tax-deferred basis over long periods. We will examine this point in more detail in Chapter 5. If retirement income is one of your investment goals, it would probably be foolish not to use a deferral shelter, despite its possible shortcomings. Look on tax deferral as an interest-free loan from the government. Common sense tells us not to turn down interest-free loans unless the strings attached are particularly onerous.

BASIC INVESTMENT STRATEGIES

Although the planning steps indicated earlier in Exhibit 1.3 can help you achieve your goals, they do not indicate the basic strategies investors can use in this process. Should you simply buy and hold securities, or should you attempt to enhance return by trading them occasionally, or frequently? These issues are examined in this section.

Long-Term Investing

Long-term investing is often goal-directed—saving for retirement, for example. Even if the goal is simply wealth accumulation, many investors prefer to hold their investments for relatively long periods. Long-term investing works best when a well-conceived portfolio plan is established.

Buy-and-hold approach: strategy associated with long-term investing; once purchased, securities are seldom, if ever, sold

Long-term investing can be thought of as a **buy-and-hold approach.** We buy securities and hold them until there is some reason to sell, such as a need for cash. Although you might follow a buy-and-hold strategy in long-term investing, it is not necessary or even desirable that you do. Indeed, there may be instances when your portfolio should be adjusted by selling some securities and purchasing others. For example, suppose you are a cautious investor who wants a portfolio balanced equally among common stocks, bonds, and short-term securities. So you construct a portfolio accordingly. As time passes, your common stocks might increase substantially in value while the other two portfolio components show little change. The portfolio grows riskier as the common stock component increases in importance. Thus, to rebalance the portfolio, some stocks must be sold and the proceeds invested in the other components.

In addition to rebalancing to restore a risk level, portfolios also are often adjusted to take advantage of the tax law, as noted earlier. Also, changes may seem warranted within a portfolio component. Certain stocks that you purchased might not perform as you anticipated, leading you to sell them and acquire others. Or, your portfolio of bonds might take on different risk characteristics as time passes, again calling for action to restore a desired risk level. Finally, a long-term investment strategy must consider how current earnings of dividends and interest will be handled. Will they be withdrawn and used for purposes other than investing, or will they be reinvested? As portfolios grow over time, current earnings also grow, and the reinvestment problem increases in importance.

Short-Term Trading

As the name implies, **short-term trading** is a strategy that attempts to profit from short-term market volatility. This approach is called market timing. Short-term traders believe that they can forecast market movements because that is a prerequisite for success. Even if you are reasonably good at making such forecasts, you may not profit from frequent trading because transactions costs are usually high. Several studies have indicated that you must forecast future market directions with over 70% accuracy to benefit from trading on a year-to-year basis. Few investors achieve such accuracy levels.

Many beginning investors believe that they can forecast that well or that they can follow the advice of someone who supposedly can. Although there are numerous studies you might read to the contrary, the best advice is to try your approach on paper before you commit hard-earned savings. Allow sufficient time for the experiment and distinguish between luck and skill, particularly if you show extraordinary gains. For most of us, good luck usually ends sooner or later.

Short-term trading: strategy involving frequent trading that attempts to profit from market volatility

Exploiting Economic Cycles

Short-term trading is usually associated with market forecasting: you think the market will go up or down and you trade accordingly. A variant of this approach, called **sector rotation,** is designing an investment program to achieve maximum return over an economic—not a market—cycle. An economic cycle is rather long term (three to seven years, for example) and consists of four distinct phases: expansion, peak, contraction, and trough. As the economy goes, so go specific investments. Common stocks tend to do well through the expansion stage, perhaps peaking six months or so before the economic cycle peaks. Bonds are the security of choice in the trough, while short-term securities are favored during the contraction. By going from one to the other, investors supposedly will show better returns than they would by holding a portfolio equally weighted with the three and held throughout the entire economic cycle.

Sector rotation: strategy that trades different securities through the stages of an economic cycle

BOX 1.3   A QUESTION OF ETHICS

Is Investment Greed a Virtue or a Vice?

In the popular movie *Wall Street,* the corporate raider Gordon Gecko (played by Michael Douglas) delivers a scintillating oration at a shareholders' meeting in which he declares that greed is "good"; that it purifies the economic air, directing money and resources to where they are most productive. Gecko also defends the role of corporate raiders, who often dislodge bureaucratic management teams that are more concerned with maximizing their interests than with maximizing those of shareholders.

Gecko lays it on a bit thick, but his message is not terribly different from the economic advantages of a free enterprise system claimed by traditional neoclassic economists. Although few of us will ever rise to the role of corporate raider, each time we buy shares in a company we also cast our votes for resource allocation. So we, too, face an ethical issue: if we disapprove of a company's business interests or practices, should we buy the stock anyway if we think it's a good investment? Or, as a corollary view: should we invest only in companies that we think are socially responsible?

The socially responsive perspective to investing began in the 1980s. It grew out of a general dislike of a perceived overemphasis in society on material greed, epitomized by the Gordon Gecko character in fiction and Ivan Boesky in real life. So strong was antigreed sentiment that about a dozen mutual funds were created with the objective of investing in companies that exhibit socially responsive characteristics. So we have funds such as the Pax World Fund, the Shield Progressive Environment Fund, and the Right-Time Social Awareness Fund. Interestingly, some of these funds have earned rather decent returns for their investors.

Apparently, social awareness is not always antithetical with profit. A good example is Ben and Jerry's Ice Cream, a company well known for its community contributions as well as its fair treatment of employees, vendors, and customers. But the company also makes good products and enjoys a healthy and growing bottom line, which in turn has led to a growing stock price. Naturally, it's easy to be a social do-gooder when there's a gain in it, but what would Ben and Jerry investors do if the company's profits shrunk? Would they do the socially correct thing—continue to hold the stock?

It is unfortunate that a character like Gordon Gecko is used to portray profit-seeking investors. A better representative might be white- or blue-collar employees who must fund their own retirement plans because their employers can no longer afford to provide them traditional retirement packages. Should they choose social awareness funds, regardless of their performance? Perhaps the crucial issue is not if we should be socially responsible, but whether we best achieve that goal through our investment activities. Many people believe that social awareness investing may be an inefficient means to a desirable end.

The success of this approach rests squarely on your ability to forecast the four cycle phases. Virtually no one does this with consistent accuracy. A classic example is the most recent economic cycle that began its expansion phase in mid-1982. The peak for this cycle was forecasted by many "experts" in each year beginning in 1985. If you followed the cycle-exploitation approach, you probably sold your common stock holdings in 1985; as a result, you missed a substantial gain that took place between 1985 and the eventual peak in the cycle, which finally occurred in 1990.

Defending Against Potential Losses

Some investment strategies are primarily defensive; that is, they are designed to protect investor wealth. Life insurance is a good example, particularly so-called whole life policies that provide an investment return while simultaneously offering a large payout in the event of the insured's death. Although insuring is one way to protect wealth, **hedging** is another. A hedge arises when an investor establishes two offsetting positions at the same time. For example, suppose you are concerned that the value of a retirement nest egg might decrease substantially in a short period before your retirement. Assuming you will not sell the securities, an alternative would be to buy an option or a futures contract whose value moves in the opposite direction from your nest egg. If a loss does occur on your investments, an offsetting gain will be realized on the hedge instrument.

Hedging: strategy designed to limit losses, similar to insurance

SUMMARY

Investors have different attitudes and attempt to achieve different investment goals. Some investors are risk averters, others are risk seekers, and still others are risk-indifferent. Investment is undertaken for current liquidity, for a future expenditure, for retirement, or for speculation. Professional investors make investment decisions for others. They are employed in a number of positions in the investments industry.

Investments include short-, intermediate-, and long-term debt instruments, low-, medium-, and high-risk common stocks, preferred stocks, leverage-inherent securities, pooling arrangements, and real estate and other tangibles. Portfolio management considers adequate diversification and when securities should be bought or sold.

The federal income tax has a progressive rate structure with five possible rates: 15%, 28%, 31%, 36%, and 39.6%. Investors should know their marginal tax rates in making investment decisions. They also should be familiar with strategies for avoiding and deferring taxes.

Investors follow various investment strategies. Long-term investing considers a long time horizon and often is associated with an attempt to achieve specific goals. Short-term trading involves frequent trading activity and assumes investors can forecast market directions. It involves substantial transactions costs, and there is little evidence indicating investors achieve sufficient forecasting accuracy to make this strategy profitable. Exploiting economic cycles is a variant of short-term trading. It differs in that investors attempt to time their investments in tune with economic cycles. The strategy presumes investors can forecast economic cycles; there is little evidence supporting this premise.

KEY TERMS
(listed in order of appearance)

active management approach	preferred stock
passive strategy	leverage-inherent security
risk averter	corporate convertible security
risk seeker	warrant
risk-indifferent investor	call option
risk tolerance level	put option
liquidity	futures contract
stockbroker	pooling arrangement
security analyst	portfolio
portfolio manager	investment planning
financial planner	marginal tax rate
investment banker	capital gains and losses
investment	tax avoidance
debt instrument	tax deferral
short-term debt instrument	buy-and-hold approach
intermediate-term debt instrument	short-term trading
long-term debt instrument	sector rotation
common stock	hedging

REVIEW QUESTIONS

1. Distinguish between active and passive investment management approaches.
2. John, Tom, and Judy are three different types of investor. Each owns an investment that yields 10% a year. They are thinking of investing in another asset that has twice the risk of the one they own. If John is a risk averter, Tom a risk seeker, and Judy is risk indifferent, explain whether each might select the second investment if its expected return is 15%.
3. Explain a current return and a future return. Who might be interested primarily in the former? Who might choose the latter?
4. Identify four investment goals. Should you try to achieve all four goals at the same time, or should one or several come later? Explain.
5. Who are investment professionals? Discuss whether you think a career in investments appeals to you.
6. Define *investment* and then briefly identify the investment alternatives indicated in this chapter. How does a common stock differ from a corporate bond? What is meant by a leverage-inherent security?
7. What is a portfolio and what is portfolio management? Also, identify the key steps in investment planning. Which step may be the most important? Why?

8. Explain the following terms: *(a)* progressive rate structure, *(b)* marginal tax rate, *(c)* after-tax rate of return, *(d)* tax avoidance, and *(e)* tax deferral.
9. Explain the tax treatment of capital gains and losses.
10. Explain and discuss income tax advantages associated with a personal residence.
11. Explain and discuss income-splitting as a tax-avoidance technique.
12. Why is tax deferral referred to as an "interest-free loan" from the federal government?
13. Describe a long-term investment strategy. Does it necessarily mean a buy-and-hold approach is followed? Discuss at least three situations that might require portfolio changes.
14. Describe short-term trading. What basic assumption underlies the use of this strategy? Will the approach be successful if you can predict with just slightly better than 50% accuracy? Explain.
15. How does exploiting economic cycles differ from short-term trading? What basic assumption underlies the use of the former approach?
16. What is a defensive strategy? Discuss a situation where a defensive strategy might be appropriate.

---

1. Complete the following table, which indicates the relationships between required return and risk levels for three investor profiles: risk seeking (RS), risk averting (RA), and risk-indifferent (RI). Your entries should reflect estimated logical amounts.

PROBLEMS AND PROJECTS

Risk Level	Required Return		
	RS	RA	RI
0	6%	6%	6%
1	8	9	?
2	9	?	10
3	?	24	12

2. Maria Kelly has inherited $25,000 from her grandfather's will. Maria earns $30,000 a year from her job, is not married, and has virtually no debt obligations. She would like to receive some current income from her investments, but she also is interested in accumulating a nest egg for the future. Maria will tolerate a small portion of her portfolio invested speculatively, although she describes herself generally as a risk averter. Recommend specific investment types for Maria, indicating the amount you believe should be invested in each.
3. You anticipate having a 28% marginal tax rate in the upcoming year. Which investment do you prefer: a municipal bond yielding 9% or a corporate bond yielding 11%? Show your work and assume other characteristics of the bonds are not important.
4. John and Elaine Reston bought a house in 1972 for $40,000. In 1985, they sold this house for $110,000 and purchased another for $150,000. In 1995, the Restons sold this house for $300,000 and retired to an apartment in Florida. Determine the amount of taxable income, if any, from these transactions in 1972, 1985, and 1995. (Assume age and residency requirements are met.)

5. Determine the tax liability for a single filer, given the following taxable incomes: *(a)* $12,000, *(b)* $25,000, *(c)* $70,000, *(d)* $160,000, and *(e)* $400,000.
6. Determine the tax liability for a couple filing a joint return, given the following taxable incomes: *(a)* $22,000, *(b)* $50,000, *(c)* $120,000, *(d)* $200,000, and *(e)* $300,000.
7. *(Student Project)* Contact a local stockbrokerage firm and ask if they have any literature concerning career opportunities in investments. You can also ask for an interview to discuss the topic.
8. *(Student Project)* Think carefully of your major financial goals in life. Then, list them along with their monetary requirements. Finally, indicate the year you expect to achieve each goal. Save this information until you have studied Chapter 3; then you can work out a financial plan involving the time value of money.

CASE ANALYSES

1.1
An Investment Approach for the Schillers

Karen and Frank Schiller are a married couple with a joint income of over $100,000. Karen is 36 and Frank is 35, and they have three children: Mark (8), Cindy (6), and Bryan (2). The Schillers have saved about $28,000 in a savings account at their local bank, where they earn about 6% annually. Frank thinks they should invest the money in a relatively safe investment, such as long-term corporate bonds. Karen disagrees, arguing that they should invest in a few growth stocks that might double in value over several years. Karen believes they need high returns for two reasons: she is concerned that sufficient funds will not be available to help the children go to college, and she thinks their employers' retirement plans are inadequate. Although Frank likes the idea of doubling their money, he is skeptical and cautious because they know so little about stocks. He thinks that if they want greater risk, they should invest in real estate. He has seen a small place in their neighborhood that could be fixed up and rented.

Karen and Frank have asked your advice to help them invest. They heard you are taking a course on the subject and thought you might have some good tips. The Schillers will probably have a 31% marginal tax rate in the future.

Questions

a. What type of disposition toward risk do you think Karen and Frank have? Would it be useful if they could describe their risk tolerance to you—and to themselves? Discuss.
b. Do the Schillers have general ideas on why they are investing? Would it help if they made their objectives more concrete? Discuss.
c. The following table indicates potential returns and risks from various investment alternatives. Suppose the Schillers plan to save $10,000 a

year. Indicate how you think they should invest the funds in each of the next five years. Also, indicate how the $28,000 currently on hand should be invested.

Investment Alternative	Potential Return	Risk Index (10 = Highest)
Common stocks (broad portfolio)	12%	5
Corporate bonds	9	4
Residential real estate	8	3
Municipal bonds	8	4
Common stocks (growth)	15	7
Savings account	6	1

1.2 Tax Planning for Shirley Moreno's Investments

Shirley Moreno, a recent college graduate, has accepted a position as a chemist with a plastics manufacturer and will be moving to the Washington, D.C., area in the near future. Shirley has about $14,000 accumulated from previous summer jobs and gifts from her grandparents, and she wants to invest these funds along with monthly savings that should total $100. Shirley has virtually no understanding of investments.

Shirley's father has advised her to buy a condominium to save apartment rentals. Although this would take her entire $14,000 for a down payment on a $50,000 condo, she still could save the $100 a month. A real estate agent said that housing has been a good investment in the area, with prices increasing about 6% annually. A colleague at work thinks housing is an O.K. investment, but he believes Shirley will do much better in corporate bonds. He anticipates a 10% return here, and he urges Shirley to use their employer's tax deferral plan, called a 401(k) plan.

Shirley is considering investing in both the condo and the bonds. She thinks she also should have some kind of investment that provides immediate access to her funds in case of an emergency. Along this line, she is considering a money market savings account with a current yield of about 4%; however, she has read a magazine ad for a tax-free money market mutual fund offering 3%. Shirley probably will have a 28% marginal tax rate in the foreseeable future.

Questions

a. From a tax perspective, how does the condo investment differ from the bond investment? Suppose Shirley retires after 30 years. Assume her condo is now worth $285,000 and the bond fund is worth $245,000 (through monthly investments and reinvested interest). If Shirley sells the condo and withdraws completely from the bond fund, determine how much income tax she will owe from each event.

b. Which short-term investment seems more appropriate for Shirley? Explain.

c. Overall, how do you evaluate Shirley's investment approach? Discuss.

HELPFUL READING

Bajkowski, John. "Sector Rotation: Investing Based on the Economic Cycle." *AAII Journal,* March 1992, pp. 34–37.

Bogle, John C. "Investing in the 1990s: Remembrance of Things Past and Things Yet to Come." *The Journal of Portfolio Management,* Spring 1991, pp. 5–14.

Damato, Karen Slater. "Ten Lessons to Learn from Wall Street's Pros." *The Wall Street Journal,* January 8, 1993, p. C1.

Englander, Debra Wishik. "Financial Advice for Free." *Money,* November 1992, pp. 128–31.

Kritzman, Mark. "What Practitioners Need to Know about Utility." *Financial Analysts Journal,* May-June 1992, pp. 17–20.

Kuhn, Susan E. "Smart Strategies to Soothe the Sting of Higher Taxes." *Fortune,* September 20, 1993, pp. 27–29.

Maher, Maggy. "The New Investors." *Barron's,* August 30, 1993, p. 8.

Slater, Karen. "How to Avoid the Pitfalls in Picking a Financial Planner." *The Wall Street Journal,* July 9, 1992, p. C1.

Torres, Craig. "Computer Powerhouse of D.E. Shaw and Co. May Be Showing Wall Street's Direction." *The Wall Street Journal,* October 15, 1992, p. C1.

Tritch, Teresa. "Six Great Tax-Sheltered Investments." *Money,* May 1993, pp. 114–21.

CHAPTER TWO

The Investment Environment

After you finish this chapter, you will be able to:

- understand how investments are created and the difference between financial facilitation and financial intermediation.

- distinguish between primary and secondary markets and see how trading is conducted on organized exchanges and in the over-the-counter market.

- identify and evaluate factors important in selecting a stock-broker.

- recognize how legislation affects the securities markets.

- understand the mechanics of opening an account and making transactions, including the use of a margin account and the execution of short sales.

- identify sources of investment information.

People who are considering investing for the first time often find the process confusing and intimidating. They lack sufficient understanding of investment vehicles to construct their own portfolios, and many stockbrokers speak a language the prospective investors don't understand. Moreover, few investors are aware of their rights and protections provided by law. Experience being the best teacher, you probably will not gain a thorough understanding of the investment process until you actually invest. Nevertheless, much can be learned before you put your funds at risk. This chapter deals with many preinvestment procedures. It explains how primary and secondary markets work, what types of stockbrokerage firms are available, how to open an account and make transactions, and where to find investment information.

HOW INVESTMENTS ARE CREATED

On an average working day, business corporations and government units raise about $2 billion of new funds by issuing debt and equity instruments. As Exhibit 2.1 shows, in 1992, $502.2 billion was raised, most of it through the sale of bonds, and most of it by government units. Although this is a huge number, keep in mind it is only one year's production, and it is but a small increment added to the trillions of dollars' worth of all securities that have previously been issued. Moreover, this method of transferring funds involved only financial facilitation, not financial intermediation. Although our interest

EXHIBIT 2.1

Net funds raised in credit and equity markets in 1992 by nonfinancial organizations in billions of dollars. (Source: *Federal Reserve Bulletin*, July 1993)

U.S. Treasury debt		$303.8
U.S. agencies' debt		.2
Total federal debt		$304.0
Local government (tax-exempt) debt		53.3
Total government debt		$357.3
Corporate bonds		66.5
Total debt		$423.8
Corporate Equities (new issues)		
Common stock	$ 57.1	
Preferred stock	21.3	
Total equities		78.4
Total funds raised		$502.2
Government-raised	$357.3	
Corporate-raised	144.9	
Total	$502.2	

in investments is primarily with the former, it is important to distinguish between the two processes.

Financial Facilitation Versus Financial Intermediation

The term *financial intermediary* is used loosely to describe an institution that assists in transferring funds from those who have them (providers) to those who want to use them (users). An intermediary institution accepts funds from savers and in turn invests them elsewhere. Commercial banks, savings and loans, insurance companies, and mutual funds are examples of such institutions. As Exhibit 2.2 indicates, when you deposit your money in such an institution, you receive some evidence of ownership, such as a savings passbook (or a monthly statement) or an insurance policy, which also indicates the institution's liability to you. (Call it an IOU.) It is important to understand that your deposit in the bank is not merely loaned to someone else with the bank acting as an agent; rather, the bank creates a new asset with your funds—its loans to customers—and receives customers' IOUs as evidence of the loans. This process is **financial intermediation.**

In **financial facilitation,** the third party—in this case, an underwriter—assists in the distribution of specific securities issued by users of funds. For example, if IBM sells shares of its common stock, it does so through an investment banker, who buys the shares from IBM and resells them to investors who want to own IBM. To distinguish between the two, look at it this way: in financial intermediation, your asset (the deposit) creates another asset (the bank loan) and an offsetting IOU on the bank's part to return your money whenever you want; in financial facilitation, only one asset changes hands—from the issuer (IBM) to the underwriter and eventual-

Financial intermediation: system of transferring funds from providers to users that creates assets and liabilities for financial intermediaries, such as commercial banks

Financial facilitation: funds-transfer system involving an investment banker; no financial intermediaries are used

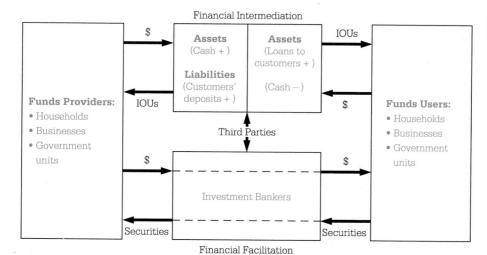

EXHIBIT 2.2
Flow of funds

ly to you (the investor). Moreover, this asset typically is a negotiable instrument, which means you can sell it easily, if you care to, and if someone wants to buy it. A deposit at a financial institution is not a negotiable instrument.

Underwriting: process whereby an investment banker guarantees a price on a security issue

Underwriting an Issue   **Underwriting** a new issue of common or preferred stocks or bonds is a process whereby an investment banker guarantees the issuing organization the sale of its securities at an agreed-on price. Underwriting is a marketing problem involving the distribution of thousands or millions of shares from the issuer to the final buyers. For large issues, the lead underwriter will involve other underwriting firms to form an **underwriting syndicate** (see Exhibit 2.3). Each underwriter forms selling groups that consist of individual brokerage firms whose registered representatives attempt to sell shares of the issue to their clients. If the issue is in demand, selling is easy; indeed, if demand exceeds a broker's supply, he must find some means for allocating shares among customers. Demand frequently is strong for shares of exciting new companies that are going public (making their shares available to the public for the first time). Underwriters earn their compensation through the so-called spread, which is the difference between the price guaranteed the issuing organization (say, $25 a share) and the selling price to investors (say, $26 a share). This means if you buy a new issue, you do not pay a commission to your broker. This feature appeals to many investors.

Underwriting syndicate: group of brokerage firms involved in underwriting large security issues

Selling on a Best-Effort Basis   If demand for an issue is weak, the representatives may have to exert considerable selling effort to move it. Keep in mind that underwriters are at risk from the time they guarantee a price to the issuer until the shares are finally sold. If they fail to sell the shares or sell

EXHIBIT 2.3
Underwriting a new
security issue

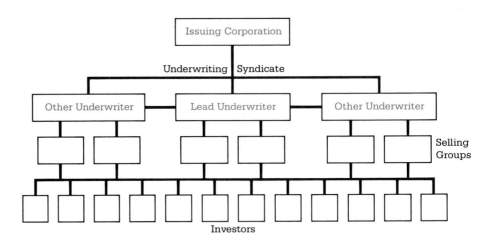

them below the guaranteed price, the underwriting will lead to losses. With some issues, these risks are so high that the investment banker will refuse to underwrite, agreeing to handle an issue only on a **best-effort basis**. This term means the underwriter will attempt to sell the issue and will receive a commission if he is successful. Companies with little public recognition might find this form of share distribution the only type available to them.

Private Placements   A **private placement** is a sale of securities (most often bonds) to a single buyer or a limited number of buyers (usually insurance companies). The private placement market formerly was used by small or risky companies that could not market a public issue. However, in recent years, large and successful companies have been turning to private placements. As a result, the dollar volume has increased substantially.

Market Participants

Exhibit 2.2 indicates the market participants: households, businesses, and government units. Their roles in financial markets are explained below.

Households   Households are individuals or families. All funds ultimately are provided by households because they are the owners of businesses and government units. However, for practical purposes, each of the three can provide investment funds during any given period. For example, a new bond issue by the U.S. Treasury last year might have been purchased by households (you), businesses (IBM), and government units (the Tennessee Valley Authority).

Businesses   Businesses are both providers and users of funds. In the latter capacity, they issue both debt and equity securities. Debt securities—bonds, notes, commercial paper, and others—are issued in the process of borrowing. Equity securities—common and preferred stock—are issued to provide investors fractional ownership interests in the business. If you buy IBM's bonds, you are its creditor; if you buy its stock, you are a part owner of the company.

Businesses also provide funds to other businesses and to government units, particularly the U.S. Treasury. Many businesses often have temporary excess funds they want to invest on a safe and liquid basis. Treasury securities with short maturities often are the most favored vehicles for this purpose.

Government Units   Many government units, ranging from the huge U.S. Treasury to the small local water authority, issue debt instruments to finance their operations. These instruments appeal to investors for various reasons. Treasury issues, as indicated above, are considered the safest of all investments, and local issues are popular because they avoid federal income taxes.

Best-effort basis: form of financial facilitation in which the investment banker attempts to sell an issue but does not guarantee its price

Private placement: sale of an issue to one or few buyers

SECURITIES MARKETS

Primary market: initial distribution of securities

A **primary market** refers to the initial distribution of securities as explained above. In a primary market, funds flow from providers (investors) to users. A **secondary market** comes into existence when investors want to sell the securities they acquired in the primary market. In this case, they sell to other investors, so funds flow from one investor to another. You should understand that transactions in secondary markets have nothing to do with the organization that issued the security initially. You might have purchased 100 shares of Intel at $100 a share through a public offering. At that time, Intel would have received $10,000. If you later sell the shares for $150 each, you do so in the secondary market, and the buyer pays $15,000 to you, not to Intel.

Secondary market: trading of previously issued securities

Practically all the trading activity you read and hear about occurs in the secondary market. Expressions such as "the market closed higher" describe prices in the secondary market. The existence of secondary markets is essential for the smooth functioning of primary markets. Being able to sell securities quickly and easily in the secondary market provides considerably greater demand for new issues than would otherwise be the case. Transactions in the secondary markets take place on organized exchanges or in the over-the-counter (OTC) market.

Capital market: trading of long-term securities

A **capital market** refers to the trading of securities with long-term maturities, primarily stocks and bonds; in contrast, a **money market** refers to the trading of short-term securities, such as U.S. Treasury bills. Capital markets are far more visible (and perhaps more important) to small investors, but we should not underestimate the size or importance of the money market. In total dollar value, it probably matches the capital market, and with modern communications technologies, it covers the globe and operates 24 hours a day.

Money market: trading of short-term securities

Organized Exchanges

Organized exchange: physical place where securities are traded

An **organized exchange** is most appropriately thought of as a place where buyers and sellers of securities physically meet to conduct trading activity. The primary advantage an organized exchange offers investors is that it creates a **continuous market,** which means you can always buy or sell a security at a competitively determined price that varies only slightly from one transaction to the next. Another advantage is that transactions can take place at minimum cost. If you had to hire someone to buy or sell securities for you and if an organized exchange didn't exist, your commission would be exorbitant and it would be difficult to know whether you paid or received a fair price for the securities. In contrast, all trades on certain organized exchanges are recorded almost the instant they are made. The trade price and number of shares traded are then displayed throughout the world by means of a computerized transmission network. If you visit a stockbroker's office or watch CNBC on cable TV, you will see the so-called tape, referring to

Continuous market: orderly trading of securities at competitively determined prices ticker tape, which was used to transmit information in the past. The tape moves continuously, showing each transaction taking place on the trading floor.

Stock Exchanges   The largest organized exchange is the New York Stock Exchange (NYSE). There are also the American Stock Exchange (the Amex) and 14 regional stock exchanges, the most important being the Pacific, Midwest, and Philadelphia exchanges. Companies choose to have their securities listed on an exchange and must meet minimum listing requirements to do so. The most stringent are those of the NYSE. The general rules for listing are:

1.   at least 1,100,000 shares held by the general public;
2.   at least 2,000 shareholders who own 100 or more shares;
3.   pretax incomes of at least $2,500,000 in the fiscal year before applying for a listing and no less than $2,000,000 in the two preceding years;
4.   a total market value of shares held by the public of at least $18,000,000; and
5.   net tangible assets of at least $18,000,000.

Organized exchanges account for about 55% of all equity shares traded (the other 45% are traded over the counter, which will be explained shortly); of this total, about 81% are traded on the NYSE, 7% on the Amex, and 12% on regional exchanges. As you see, the NYSE dominates trading of listed securities and so earns its nickname "the Big Board."

Other Securities and Other Exchanges   Other countries have national exchanges similar to the NYSE and the Amex in the United States. Canada, for example, has the Montreal Stock Exchange, the Toronto Stock Exchange, and the Canadian Stock Exchange. Important exchanges abroad include the Tokyo Stock Exchange (second in world dollar volume behind the NYSE) and the London Stock Exchange (third in world dollar volume). Other major stock exchanges are located in Frankfurt, Zurich, Paris, Sydney, and Hong Kong.

The major stock exchanges also trade other equity instruments (such as warrants and rights), bonds, and options. For example, the NYSE and the Amex list about 2,500 and 350 corporate bond issues, respectively. Options are traded on the Amex, the Pacific Stock Exchange, and the Philadelphia Stock Exchange. It should also be noted that the most important options exchange is the Chicago Board Options Exchange (CBOE).

Futures contracts are traded on a number of exchanges, both in the United States and in other countries. Dominant exchanges in the United States include the Chicago Board of Trade (CBOT); the Chicago Mercantile Exchange (CME) and its important division, the International Monetary Market (IMM); the Kansas City Board of Trade; and the New York Futures Exchange (NYFE), which is a subsidiary of the NYSE.

Order Execution on the NYSE

Organized exchanges are fascinating places to visit. What appears to be utter chaos is actually an efficient system for transferring billions of dollars' worth of securities each trading day. Exhibit 2.4 shows order execution on the NYSE and introduces its members who may be involved in the process. To be a member, you must buy or lease a "seat." Seat prices are determined by the demand for them, and they have varied considerably over time. For example, they hit a high of $515,000 in 1969, fell to $35,000 in 1977, and then rebounded to $1.1 million in 1987, right before the big crash on October 19, 1987. The price slumped to $575,000 in a sale in early 1993.

Commission brokers: brokers on organized exchanges employed by stockbrokerage firms

Commission Brokers   **Commission brokers** are employed by stockbrokerage firms. Assuming you deal with Merrill Lynch and have placed a market order to buy 100 shares of Xerox, your representative will transmit the order to one of Merrill Lynch's commission brokers on the floor of the exchange. Suppose that at the same time, someone else places an order to sell 100

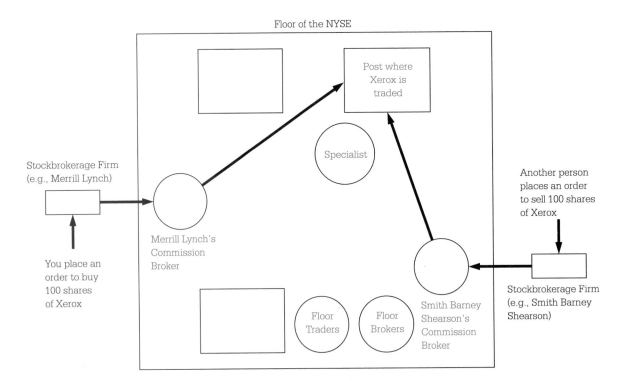

EXHIBIT 2.4
Diagram of a trade on the NYSE

shares of Xerox through her broker, Smith Barney Shearson. Both commission brokers would then go to the post where Xerox is traded. For an actively traded issue, such as Xerox, there will be a number of brokers and traders bidding to buy or sell shares. All of them will try to get the best possible price, either for their customers or for themselves. In effect, shares are auctioned to the highest bidders. (The NYSE and similar markets are thus called *auction markets*.) Perhaps the Merrill Lynch and Smith Barney Shearson brokers settle a trade at $50 a share. The entire transaction may be completed in less than two minutes.

Specialists **Specialists** play a number of critical roles in the trading process. They are expected to maintain an orderly and continuous market in the six or seven stocks assigned to them. To keep wide swings in price from occurring, they must buy or sell for their own accounts. For example, assume that when your commission broker arrives at Xerox's trading post, no other broker or trader is there to trade Xerox. Then it is the specialist's responsibility to trade. Another responsibility for the specialist is to maintain the limit books, which contain all limit orders clients have placed with their brokers. (Limit orders will be explained shortly.) Because of the inside information specialists have, it is possible for them to profit handsomely at the expense of outside investors. The NYSE, however, insists that customers' interests come first and specialists', second. This rule is monitored constantly for compliance and enforced rigorously because the integrity of the specialist is critical to maintaining customer confidence in the system.

Specialists: brokers on organized exchanges who perform critical functions, such as maintaining continuous markets

Floor Brokers and Floor Traders **Floor brokers** are not associated with any particular stockbrokerage firm but serve as independent operators. They assist commission brokers by executing orders on their behalf, for a fee. They also serve stockbrokerage firms that do not own seats on the floor. **Floor traders** operate strictly for themselves, hoping their position on the floor will help them trade stocks profitably.

Floor brokers: independent brokers who assist commission brokers

Floor traders: traders who operate strictly for themselves on an organized exchange

The Over-the-Counter Market

The **over-the-counter (OTC) market** refers to all security trading not conducted on organized exchanges. In most instances, it is a market that exists by virtue of telecommunications among stockbrokers. For example, suppose you want to buy shares of Apple Computer, an unlisted company. To do so, your broker uses her information terminal to determine if another brokerage house is "making a market" in Apple. (This means a broker holds an inventory of shares that are available for purchase by potential buyers.) Perhaps six such brokers are found, each offering to sell Apple at an ask price and buy it at a bid price. Because you are buying Apple, your broker is interested only in ask prices and will select the broker offering the lowest one, if there are differences.

Over-the-counter market: all security trading not conducted on organized exchanges

BOX 2.1   INVESTMENT INSIGHTS

Which Exchange Is Best? Depends on Who You Ask

Want to provoke an argument in the high-rise canyons of lower Manhattan? Just ask a group of traders whether it's better to trade stock on a traditional stock exchange or on the NASDAQ over-the-counter network.

"There is no comparison between an exchange with a floor and NASDAQ," asserts George Reichhelm, the president of the Amex Specialists Association. "Every time an investor buys or sells a stock on NASDAQ, he's the victim of a theft."

NASDAQ "market makers" at major brokerage firms vehemently disagree. The "theft"—the small commission a NASDAQ market maker earns on every trade—is simply the easiest way to pay the bills for trading stocks nationwide without a trading floor. The commissions are plenty fair, they insist. And the NASDAQ system is superior to a traditional stock exchange, they add, because far more dealers compete with each other to trade the same stocks and thus buy and sell them more aggressively.

Which side is right? The two approaches to trading stocks, while substantially different, are both superb. Each moves millions and millions of shares of stock a day with amazing speed and fairness. Nonetheless, NASDAQ gets the top ranking because it's far more automated and efficient.

For many companies, the NYSE no longer holds great allure. "Say we got listed on the New York Stock Exchange tomorrow," says Tom Meredith, the treasurer of Sun Microsystems, which remains happily ensconced on NASDAQ. "So what? For a company like us, there is absolutely no incentive to move."

A look at the differences between the two stock trading systems is instructive for shareholders and may make them feel more comfortable trading on NASDAQ.

The Big Board and the American Stock Exchange, unlike NASDAQ, rely on "specialists" to make their marketplaces function smoothly. Specialists, who are solely responsible for orchestrating the trading of specific stocks, must, for example, buy plummeting stocks to help break their fall.

In contrast, NASDAQ relies on its network of competing "market makers" to set prices for stocks and keep them trading briskly. They operate under less-rigorous rules than specialists, but the market making system works as well because of its competitive nature.

"If a market maker doesn't trade stocks consistently at or near the best prices, he won't get repeat business, and he knows that," says Douglas Parrillo, a senior vice president of the National Association of Securities Dealers, which operates NASDAQ.

SOURCE: Steve Kaufman, "Which Exchange Is Best? Depends Who You Ask." Knight-Ridder News Service, appearing in the *Dayton Daily News,* Smart Investor Section, Nov. 25, 1991, p. 16.

The OTC market accounts for about 45% of equity shares traded but dominates organized exchanges in two respects: it handles a far greater majority of individual stocks (about 30,000 versus about 3,000 on all the exchanges) and trades far more bonds. All government bonds and many corporate bonds (about 90%) trade OTC.

NASDAQ **NASDAQ** stands for National Association of Securities Dealers Automated Quotation System. It is a communication system that applies to about 3,500 actively traded OTC stocks. To be included, a company must meet certain requirements, similar to those imposed by organized exchanges but less stringent. The NASDAQ system allows buyers and sellers to locate each other quickly, as described above for Apple Computer. Without it, brokers must search for potential buying or selling dealers. The requirements imposed for firms to be part of the National Market System (NMS) are in addition to the basic NASDAQ requirements. NASDAQ/NMS firms have the benefit of up-to-the minute price and volume quotations, along with end-of-day price and volume data.

NASDAQ: communication system used to trade OTC securities

Market Segments The OTC market is extremely diverse and consists of three distinct segments. The first includes firms that meet the basic and NMS requirements; the second includes firms that meet the basic but not the NMS requirements; and the third consists of small firms that meet neither set of requirements. Price quotations for these firms are available only through the "pink sheets" published by the National Quotation Bureau.

The Third Market The **third market** refers to OTC trading of securities listed on an exchange. Large institutions frequently conduct such trades in an effort to avoid high commissions set by the exchanges. Participating brokerage houses are willing to reduce their fees because of the large volume of business transacted. Because regulated commissions (commission rates set by the exchanges) no longer exist, third market activity has decreased considerably.

Third market: OTC trading of exchange-listed securities

The Fourth Market The **fourth market** refers to trading activity conducted directly between buyer and seller without the assistance of a broker. Such trades involve a large number of shares of a large company with many millions of shares outstanding, such as General Motors. Suppose an investor owns 40,000 shares of GM. At $80 a share, the total market value is $3.2 million, and even a commission rate as small as 1% means a total commission of $64,000—$32,000 each for buyer and seller. Thus, it might pay investors to try to find each other without using a broker. Because buyers and sellers usually are large institutional investors, such as insurance companies, mutual funds, or retirement funds, it might be possible for a potential seller to locate a potential buyer through telephone inquiry or other means. Because of limited information, the size of the fourth market is not known, but many observers believe it is growing.

Fourth market: security trading unassisted by brokers

SELECTING A STOCKBROKER

Once you decide to invest, the next step is to choose a stockbroker. This step is important because the person you select may influence your investment decisions and certainly will charge you for services provided. This section explains services and charges; it also explains protections available to you under various laws and offers points to consider when choosing a broker.

Types of Stockbrokerage Firms

Stockbrokerage houses can be classified as full-service or limited-service firms. Services consist of two basic kinds: those related to order execution and those that are advisory.

Full-service firm: stock-brokerage firm offering a wide range of services, particularly security research and recommendations

Full-Service Firm   A **full-service firm** offers both order execution and a full range of advisory services. You probably can identify these firms by their slogans: "A Breed Apart" (Merrill Lynch) and "Rock Solid—Market Wise" (Prudential Securities). Full-service brokers spend a considerable amount of money on research, which they provide to their clients to help them make investment choices. This research often leads to recommendations to buy, hold, or sell specific securities; for example, a stock might be rated a "buy" for aggressive investors.

Full-service firms typically charge the highest commissions, but they may be lower if the transaction is small, as Exhibit 2.5 indicates. The high commissions are considered necessary to cover the expenses of research and other services provided, such as the extra advisory time representatives spend with clients. Although Exhibit 2.5 indicates commissions on stocks only, you should be aware that full-service brokers usually charge higher commissions for trading other securities, such as options, futures, warrants, and bonds. The rate structure is reasonably competitive within each brokerage class, although there are differences, as Exhibit 2.5 shows, and it makes sense to obtain commission information before selecting a broker.

EXHIBIT 2.5
Illustrative stockbrokerage commissions on common stock transactions

Transaction	Value of the Transaction	Commissions: $ and % of Value					
		Full-Service Broker		Well-Known Discounter		Smaller Discounter	
10 shares @ $35	$ 350	$ 18	5.1%	$ 35	10.0%	$25	7.1%
100 shares @ $35	3,500	$ 83	2.4%	$ 49	1.4%	$25	0.7%
500 shares @ $35	17,500	$263	1.5%	$114	0.7%	$68	0.4%

Exhibit 2.5 also indicates that commissions are quite low in relation to the amount invested, unless the order is fairly small. Keep in mind, however, that commissions are shown for only one transaction. If you trade stocks actively, turning over your holdings a number of times a year, your commissions can erode any trading profit you might earn. For example, suppose you use a full-service broker and buy and sell 100 shares at $35 on four occasions during the year. Total commissions will be $664 (8 × $83), or almost 19% of the funds invested. Few investors can overcome this commission burden, yet many beginning investors trade even more frequently—until they learn better or run out of funds.

Limited-Service Firm   A **limited-service firm** offers a limited range of investor services. Many such firms, called discounters, only execute orders. They make it clear that you are to make your own investment decisions; they do not provide investment advice. More often than not, the discounter you deal with is not located in your community, so all transactions are undertaken by telephone, using a toll-free number.

Limited-service firm: firm (called a discounter) that typically does not offer research but features low commissions

Within the past decade, a number of financial institutions, such as commercial banks and savings and loans, have entered the stockbrokerage business. Some offer limited investment advice; others have chosen to be strictly discounters. They appeal to investors who are reluctant to deal with an outside firm they have never seen; in effect, they are capitalizing on the trust and confidence people have in their local bankers. (That trust has grown thin in some instances in the wake of many failures and other financial problems.) Their commissions tend to be higher than other discounters and lower than full-service brokerage firms.

FACTORS TO CONSIDER IN SELECTING A BROKER

Because there are many brokerage firms from which to choose, how do you select one? There is no pat answer appropriate for every investor. You should consider the following factors in making a decision.

How Important Is Research?   Do you intend to use the recommendations a full-service broker provides, or do you plan to make your own investment decisions? If the latter situation is true, why do you want a full-service broker? Many investors start with one but find they become more independent over time. If that is the case, there is little reason to pay the higher commissions.

How Good Is Order Execution?   There is no evidence that discount brokers have poorer order execution than full-service firms. Each uses the organized exchanges and OTC markets in an identical manner and executes orders at the same prices and within the same lengths of time.

How Important Is the Representative's Advice? A salesperson of a full-service firm (the person you deal with and probably call "your broker") usually holds the title of registered representative or account executive. He has probably passed an examination and met other requirements to become licensed to sell securities and is qualified to explain investments to you and to consider their importance in relation to your stated investment objectives. If you are seeking investments offering high income, you can—and should— expect the representative to recommend appropriate securities to achieve the goal: bonds, for example, and not growth stocks. If this type of service is important, then a full-service broker should be selected.

How Frequently Will You Trade? Clearly, whether a full-service firm or a discounter is used, total commissions paid over a period of time depends on the number of transactions. As noted above, frequent trading may be prohibitively expensive. You should be aware, however, that commissions can be negotiated with many brokers. Active traders often receive discounts based on volume, but you might have to ask to receive them. Before selecting a broker, you should ask for commission information based on your estimate of activity. By all means, let the representative know that you are doing comparative shopping and that you expect to receive all available concessions. And keep in mind that discount firms also offer concessions.

> **Monthly investment plans:** offered by stock-brokerage firms; allow investors to make routine monthly investments into a preselected portfolio of securities

To avoid high commissions associated with small transactions and as a means of gaining good diversification, you should consider **monthly investment plans** offered by some brokers. These plans allow you to select securities in which you want to invest and then each month (or other period) you pay a set amount to the firm. In turn, the firm buys shares in your designated companies in the proportions you select. Commissions are relatively low, around 2%. Also be aware that many individual companies, such as IBM, offer **dividend reinvestment plans** (called DRIPs) that allow investors to receive additional shares of stock in lieu of cash dividends. The service charge with these plans is small, which makes them attractive vehicles for accumulating shares over time. Finally, some companies allow you to make your initial investment by purchasing shares directly from them, thus avoiding a broker altogether.

> **Dividend reinvestment plans:** offered by corporations; allow investors to use their dividends to buy additional stock

Resolving Disputes with Your Broker

If you deal with a stockbroker for any length of time, a dispute is almost inevitable. The most sensible way to resolve a problem is by discussing it with the broker and, hopefully, reaching an amicable agreement without involving formal procedures. If this method fails, you may have to choose either binding arbitration or litigation to settle the matter.

> **Binding arbitration:** method of settling broker-related disputes without involving litigation

In **binding arbitration,** a dispute is resolved by using an independent arbitrator. The term *binding* means that if you choose arbitration to resolve the dispute, you cannot later seek litigation if you are unhappy with the arbi-

BOX 2.2 GETTING AN INVESTMENT EDGE

What Is Binding Arbitration?

On the advice of a registered representative of a large brokerage company, an elderly couple invests most of their life savings—about $30,000—in bonds issued by a now-defunct energy company. They lose everything and appeal to the broker for compensation on the grounds the representative put them in an unsuitable investment. The company declines to make restitution—now what? In a growing number of cases, the answer is binding arbitration.

Investors with gripes such as the elderly couple's or those involving excessive trading (called "churning"), unauthorized transactions, or other misconduct can file a claim to have the dispute settled through binding arbitration. The process is quite simple and relatively inexpensive, with filing fees ranging from $25 to $1,000 (for disputes in excess of $500,000).

If a claim is less than $10,000, it is settled by one arbitrator who rules on the evidence provided by each side. Larger claims are heard by three-person panels in a formal hearing that is similar to a trial. Each side can be represented by an attorney, issue subpoenas, and cross-examine witnesses. If your claim goes to a hearing, expect to be on the "hot seat" with the opposing attorney trying to show that you were an intelligent investor, making your own investment decisions drawn from alternatives suggested by the representative. You must show that your losses were caused by the representative.

Establishing such evidence might be difficult if you do not keep accurate records of your communications with the representative. As usual, the best evidence is in written form; but you should keep a careful diary of verbal communications, such as tips or other forms of advice. Note the time and date and carefully record the nature of the conversation. In the past, punitive damages were not permitted in arbitration cases; however, that is no longer true, and large punitive awards were made in several high-visibility cases.

The alternative to arbitration is litigation. This route is expensive, and it is usually not advised if a claim is less than $200,000. You can get more information on arbitration from the NASD (33 Whitehall St., New York, NY 10004), the New York Stock Exchange (11 Wall Street, New York, NY 10006), and the American Arbitration Association (140 W. 51st St., New York, NY 10020).

trator's decision. Claims can be filed with the NYSE, Amex, the National Association of Securities Dealers (NASD), or the American Arbitration Association (AAA). (See Box 2.2 for more information about binding arbitration.) Claims settled in favor of investors have averaged a bit more than 50% of the total for claims filed with the exchanges and NASD, but the percentage is around 60% for claims filed with the AAA. The higher success factor for the AAA supports the contention that investors have a better chance with an arbitration panel that is not connected to the securities industry.

Litigation: settling a
broker-related dispute
through a lawsuit

Litigation is the typical common law process involving an alleged injured plaintiff seeking compensation from a defendant. The process can be expensive and not appropriate for resolving small claims. If you sign a typical customer agreement form when you open an account with a broker, you are probably waiving your right to litigation. Most agreements have clauses that require arbitration. You can void this clause if your broker agrees to it.

Regulation of Securities Markets

The nature of the securities industry has offered disreputable people considerable opportunities to defraud investors. Since 1933, important laws have been passed to protect investors; in addition, the industry has initiated reform through self-policing efforts. You have much greater protection now than in the past, but it would be a mistake to think fraud no longer exists or to believe losses you might suffer are the fault of your broker. It is important to know your rights and your obligations before you invest.

Securities Act of 1933:
legislation regulating
the issuance of new
securities

Prospectus: document
describing a new securi-
ty issue

The Securities Act of 1933   The **Securities Act of 1933** calls for full disclosure of new securities to be traded in interstate commerce. Such securities must be registered with the Securities and Exchange Commission (SEC), which approves their sale. To receive approval, the applicant must provide the SEC with economic and financial data relevant to the firm and the new offering. It does so in the form of a **prospectus.** After the SEC has determined that the prospectus represents adequate disclosure of all material information affecting the company's value and after the SEC has approved the registration, the company must provide the prospectus to any potential investor. Misrepresentation or fraud in preparing the prospectus can be the basis for lawsuits by investors and the SEC against the issuing corporation, its directors, stockbrokers handling the issue, and even public accountants who assisted in its preparation.

Stiff penalties and possible jail sentences have done much to provide investors with reliable and relevant prospectuses. However, SEC approval in no way assures the issue will be successful. Many new firms have prepared impeccably clean prospectuses and then gone into bankruptcy. The message is clear if you are considering investing: obtain a prospectus, read it thoroughly, particularly the section explaining risk factors, and believe what it says. Some investors seem to think a prospectus is a mere formality; it isn't. It is a helpful document and should be regarded as such.

**Securities Exchange
Act of 1934:** comprehen-
sive bill that regulates
all phases of the securi-
ties industry

The Securities Exchange Act of 1934   The **Securities Exchange Act of 1934** extended regulation to securities that had already been issued. With this provision, it brought under government regulation almost all aspects of the security markets. It required all securities traded on organized exchanges and the exchanges themselves to be registered with the SEC (which it established). It outlawed fraud and misrepresentation by anyone engaged in the sale of securities, including stockbrokers and their representatives. It forbade price manipulation, and it required registered firms to file with the SEC both a detailed annual report (called a **10-K Report**) and quarterly financial statements. It also stipulated that annual reports be provided to shareholders.

    The act also established guidelines for security trading by insiders, the intent being to prevent them from taking advantage of their privileged information. Initially, insiders were considered a firm's officers, employees, directors, or relatives of each. In recent years, the SEC has broadened its definition of *insider* to include practically anyone with information not available to the general public. In a noted case, a newspaper reporter was convicted under the law for providing advance information about news items subsequently printed in the paper.

The Maloney Act of 1938   The **Maloney Act of 1938** required trade associations in the securities industry to register with the SEC. Only one—the National Association of Securities Dealers (NASD)—has been formed and registered. The NASD is the self-regulating arm of the securities industry. It establishes and enforces a professional code of ethics and is responsible for testing and licensing dealers (noted earlier).

The Investment Company Act of 1940   The **Investment Company Act of 1940** brought regulation to investment companies, which we more frequently call mutual funds. Such companies are required to register with the SEC and provide shareholders with adequate information about the company's activities. A subsequent amendment to the act forbade paying excessive fees to fund advisors.

The Investment Advisors Act of 1940   The **Investment Advisors Act of 1940** requires anyone providing advice to investors (for a fee or other compensation) to register with the SEC and indicate his methods of investment analysis. The determination of who is an investment advisor has come under scrutiny in recent years because many products and services not usually thought of as investment-related are now being tailored in that direction. Two good cases in point deal with financial advisors and insurance agents. The former advise clients on a wide range of financial activities, including investments, while the latter sell policies that look like and pay out like investments. Should these professionals register as advisors? The trend in court cases seems to answer *yes*. As an investor, keep in mind that registration does not improve the quality of advice offered or in some other manner guarantee its usefulness. Some advisors advertise their registration, perhaps with the intent of impressing potential clients. Do not be impressed—virtually anyone with about $250 to pay the fee can register.

The Securities Investor Protection Act of 1970   The **Securities Investor Protection Act** protects investors from financial losses that might result

10-K Report: detailed financial report that must be filed with the Securities and Exchange Commission; also available to shareholders

Maloney Act of 1938: legislation requiring the registration of any trade group in the securities industry

Investment Company Act of 1940: legislation regulating investment companies

Investment Advisors Act of 1940: legislation regulating investment advisors

Securities Investor Protection Act: legislation that created the Securities Investor Protection Commission, which insures accounts with member brokers up to $500,000

from the failure of their broker. It created the Securities Investor Protection Corporation (SIPC), which insures an investor's account up to $500,000 for securities held and up to $100,000 in cash holdings. Most brokerage firms are members of the SIPC and contribute to its funding. It has been particularly helpful to discounters in their efforts to overcome investor reluctance to deal with out-of-town brokers.

Some investors believe the SIPC protection extends to any losses on securities they hold while a broker is in financial difficulty. This is not true. SIPC guarantees only that your securities eventually will be delivered to you or to another broker. Losses or gains during the time the failing firm's arrangements are being sorted out are the investor's. For example, SIPC only guarantees delivery of 100 shares of GM, if that is what you held with a failing broker; it does not guarantee a price for those shares. GM might have been worth $80 a share when your broker ceased to operate but be worth only $50 a share when you eventually have access to the shares.

OPENING AN ACCOUNT AND MAKING TRANSACTIONS

After you select a broker, the next step is to open an account. With it, you then can begin buying or selling securities.

Kinds of Accounts

Opening an account takes little time. If you are married, you should consider a joint account, with each spouse having authority to initiate orders. You can choose a cash account, margin account, discretionary account, or wrap account.

Cash account: account that requires payment within five working days for securities purchased

Cash Account   A **cash account** is similar to a charge account you might have with a retail establishment: you purchase securities and must pay for them within five working days after the day of purchase. (Holidays provide an extra day.) The same time frame applies when you sell: you then have five days to deliver the securities sold. Some brokers request an initial deposit before executing orders; others do not. Also, you can choose to have securities delivered to you or you can leave them with the broker in what is called a *street account*. This means the securities are registered in the broker's name.

Margin account: allows an investor to borrow from his broker, pledging securities as collateral

Margin Account   A **margin account** allows the broker, at your request, to borrow funds for you, pledging your securities as collateral for the loan. Each brokerage firm establishes a minimum amount (usually $2,000 to $3,000) to open a margin account, and the Board of Governors of the Federal Reserve System (the Fed) imposes an *initial margin requirement* based on the market value of securities purchased. This requirement varies, depending on the type of security purchased; for common and preferred stocks, it is 50% (many OTC stocks, however, cannot be margined because they supposedly lack collateral value); for warrants and high-quality bonds, it is 25%; and for Treasury and agency bonds, it is 5% of face value. In addition to the initial margin requirement, the Fed imposes a *maintenance margin requirement*. This means you must keep sufficient equity in your account so that it is at least 25% (for stocks) of the securities' market value. If your equity falls below this minimum, your broker is authorized to sell enough shares to restore the account to the initial margin requirement.

Most brokers impose a maintenance margin requirement slightly higher than the legal minimum. When this figure is touched, you get a margin call, which means you must either deposit additional funds to increase your equity or sell some of your shares. The mechanics of margin trading are shown in Exhibit 2.6. In this example, the investor received a margin call when the price of her shares declined to $28.57, she then deposited $571.50 with the broker, reducing his loan to $1,428.50 (which is the same amount as her equity).

You often are told that margin accounts are risky and should be avoided. Actually, they are no riskier than other lending arrangements. However, any loan increases risk. This is so because it allows you to magnify the amount of money invested, which is described as *leverage*. A greater investment means greater profits—or losses. Moreover, the broker charges interest on the loan, usually at the prime rate (the rate banks charge their most credit-worthy customers) plus one or two percentage points.

Other important characteristics of a margin account are the following:

☐ If your investments show profits, then your equity increases; you can either withdraw some of the excess equity or use it to acquire more securities.

☐ The margin requirements apply to your overall account; thus, surplus equity in some securities can offset deficient equity in others.

☐ You cannot take delivery on your shares; they must be held in the broker's street account.

Discretionary Account A **discretionary account** gives the broker powers of attorney, enabling her to conduct trades without seeking your prior approval. Such accounts are used by wealthy clients who want to turn over to the broker all investing activities. You should have the highest confidence in the broker's investment ability and integrity before considering such an account. Because of possible liability for misconduct, some stockbrokerage firms do not offer discretionary accounts.

> **Discretionary account:** gives a broker power of attorney to trade securities on an investor's behalf

Wrap Account A **wrap account** is established with a stockbroker but involves the use of a professional money manager who establishes and manages investors' portfolios, given their investment objectives. The stockbroker executes all trades arising from the manager's portfolio activities and pro-

> **Wrap account:** involves the services of a professional money manager who works with an investor's broker

EXHIBIT 2.6
The mechanics of a
margin account

Activity	Calculation
1. Investor deposits $2,000 and borrows $2,000 to purchase $4,000 of securities; she owns 100 shares of KLM at $40 a share.	Initial margin *(M)* can be used to leverage purchases *(P)*. At a margin requirement *(r)* of 0.5: $P = M/r = \$2,000/0.5 = \$4,000$
2. KLM's price falls. As it does, the investor's equity also falls. At $35 a share, her equity is down to $1,500. The broker's loan is still $2,000.	The investor's equity *(E)* is equal to the market value of securities *(V)* minus the broker's loan *(B)*; $E = V - B = \$3,500 - \$2,000 = \$1,500$
3. Finally, the price hits a point that triggers a margin call; this price is $28.57 a share.	The trigger point occurs when the investor's equity is equal to the maintenance margin requirement *(r′)* times the market value of the securities: $E = r'(V)$. If $r' = 0.3$, then $E = 0.3V$; but $E = (V - \$2,000)$ *So,* $(V - \$2,000) = 0.3V$ $0.7V = \$2,000$ $V = \$2,857$
4. The broker requires additional margin to restore the initial margin requirement of 0.5; the amount needed is $571.50.	A 0.5 requirement means E must equal $0.5V$. Since V is $2,857$, then $E = 0.5V$ $E = 0.5(\$2,857)$ $E = \$1,428.50$ Additional M = required E minus actual E Additional $M = \$1,428.50 - \$857.00$ $= \$571.50$
5. The broker charges interest for the month. (Note: interest is deducted automatically from your equity; however, it is ignored in step 4 for simplicity.)	Assuming the prime rate is 7% and the broker charges prime plus 2%: Interest $= (.09 \times \$2,000)/12$ $= \$180/12 = \$15$

vides quarterly performance reports for investors. Theoretically, the stockbroker is able to serve his clients more effectively by separating the investment function from the financial planning function. Another advantage supposedly arises from the money manager's superior investment skills.

Wrap accounts have grown considerably in importance, but they have several problems. First, a minimum investment often is $100,000, which eliminates small investors. Second, fees are high: the money manager usually gets 1% of funds invested and the broker typically adds another 1% or 2%; the manager must be good to overcome these charges. Third, there is little evidence that managers *are* that good. On balance, their performances are not appreciably better than those of mutual funds, which may have far lower fees.

Initiating a Position

After an account is opened, you can begin trading. Your first decision is whether you want to buy or sell securities. When you buy, you take a **long position;** when you sell securities that you do not already own, you take a **short position;** and when you sell securities you originally bought or buy securities you originally sold, you are **reversing a position.** Long positions seem natural to us because we associate investing with buying and holding securities. However, short positions, also called *short sales*, are common and no different from a long purchase as far as a broker is concerned.

A long position is taken if we think a security's price will increase (or if it provides us with income); a short position is appropriate if we believe its price will decrease. Buyers often are called "bulls," while sellers are referred to as "bears." Suppose you think IBM is overvalued at $150 a share and is likely to decrease in the future. You could place an order to short 100 shares of the stock at $150, hoping to reverse your position in the future after the price has fallen. The mechanics of the short sale are explained in Exhibit 2.7. Because sellers must use a margin account, margin is included in the illustration.

The SEC requires that all short sales be identified as such. Because of this requirement, the volume of short sales is compiled and reported in the financial press, such as the monthly report in *The Wall Street Journal*. Also, the SEC imposes the *up tick* rule, which means a short sale must be made on either an up tick or a zero tick (a tick refers to a price change). Consider the following string of prices for a stock: 25, 24, 24⅛, 24⅛, 24¼, 23⅞. Short sales could have taken place at 24⅛ and 24¼ (the two up ticks) but not 24 or 23⅞ (the two down ticks). The SEC created the up tick rule to reduce the possibility that short sellers could initiate a selling spree that might encompass the general public. After prices had fallen, the short sellers could step in and cover their positions at depressed prices.

Some people believe the broker imposes risks on the shareholders whose shares have been borrowed to complete the short sale. This is not so because of the margin protection. Actually, the broker's cash position is enhanced by both the short seller's margin deposit and the proceeds received from selling the securities. The disposition of interest earned on these amounts is left to the broker; some keep it, while some share it with clients who are active traders or who agree to lend their shares for short sale purposes. (These latter investors would have cash accounts, which require share-

Long position: buy securities, expecting price increases

Short position: sell securities not already owned, expecting price decreases

Reversing a position: sell if in a long position, buy if in a short position

EXHIBIT 2.7

Mechanics of a short sale

2. Broker *A* borrows 100 shares from Jane Doe and forwards them to Broker *B*.

3. Broker *B* sends John Roe 100 shares of IBM.

4. Broker *A* receives $15,000 from Broker *B*.

1. You place an order to short-sell 100 shares of IBM at $150 a share; you deposit $7,500 initial margin.

1a. John Roe places an order to buy 100 shares of IBM at $150 a share; he sends his check for $15,000 to Broker *B*.

QUESTIONS AND ANSWERS ON SHORT SALES

Q Can you withdraw the $15,000 from the short sale?
A No, your account is credited for the amount, but the funds are restricted.

Q Do you earn interest on the sale proceeds or any margin you put up?
A That depends. Some brokers share interest with active traders; it is earned by investors willing to lend their shares (Jane Doe), and by other brokers if they are the lenders. Most often it is kept by the broker. (Usually the borrowed shares come from the firm's street account.)

Q What if IBM pays a dividend while you are short? Who gets it—Jane Doe or John Roe?
A Each receives a dividend. IBM pays only one, so you must pay the other.

Q Who gets the voting rights?
A The shareholder of record, John Roe in the example. Jane Doe gave up voting rights when she allowed her shares to be loaned.

Q Suppose IBM's price increases to $170 a share; what happens?
A You lose, because you bet on a price decrease. In this case, your loss is $2,000 [($170 – $150) × 100].

Q Because you margined the short sale, can you get a margin call?
A Yes, in fact, with short sales your account is updated for current prices each day. (This is called *marking to market*.) At a price of $170, your equity percentage is only 32%. This figure is calculated as shown below:

$$\text{equity \%} = \left(\frac{\text{Initial Sales Amount} + \text{Initial Margin}}{\text{Current Market Value of Securities}} \right) - 1.0$$

$$\text{equity \%} = \left(\frac{\$15,000 + \$7,500}{\$170(100)} \right) - 1.0$$

$$\text{equity \%} = \left(\frac{\$22,500}{\$17,000} \right) - 1.0 = 1.32 - 1.0 = 0.32 \text{ or } 32\%$$

If the maintenance margin requirement is, say, 30%, you will get a margin call if IBM increases about another $3 a share.

Q Suppose IBM's price falls to $120 a share?
A You make a profit of $3,000 [($150 – $120) × 100].

Q Is there a time limit on a short sale?
A No, you can keep it forever–as long as you have enough margin.

holder approval. However, the broker can lend all shares held in the street account without prior approval.)

Finally, the short seller must pay any dividends declared by the company that issued the stock. At first glance, this seems a harsh penalty to pay for short selling. Actually, it isn't because the price of the stock in the market is automatically reduced by the amount of the dividend on the ex-dividend date. So the short seller breaks even: what is lost through the dividend payment is recouped by a gain on the short sale.

Placing Orders

With an account opened and a position taken, you can place a market order, a limit order, or a stop order. An order for 100 shares is called a *round lot,* while one for less than 100 shares is called an *odd lot.* You are charged a slightly higher commission for an odd-lot order.

Market Order A **market order** instructs your broker to buy or sell securities at the best possible price. At the time you make a transaction, the broker will give you the last price at which the security traded. For example, you might call wanting to sell 100 shares of Quaker Oats. The broker at a computer terminal will push the letters OAT (Quaker's trading symbol on the NYSE) and see a number, say, 49⅛ ($49.125). This information is given to you, and if you then give the instruction to sell at the market, your sell order will be placed. Within a minute or so, it will reach the floor of the NYSE and be executed at the best possible price for you. However, this price may not be 49⅛. It could be a bit higher or lower because of buying or selling pressure while your order is being processed. In a continuous market, you can expect any change to be minimal; for example, you might sell at 49¼ ($49.25).

Market order: order to buy or sell at the best price

Limit Order A **limit order** sets the price at which a transaction can take place. You could instruct the broker to buy Quaker at 49 ($49.00). This means your order will not be executed unless the price is less than or equal to $49.00. Limit orders remain in effect until they are either cancelled or executed. A day order, for example, terminates at the end of the day, while a good-till-cancelled order remains alive until cancelled. You might consider using limit orders when dealing in OTC securities with low trading activity. Their price swings during the order-processing period could be more dramatic than those of actively traded stocks.

Limit order: order to buy or sell at a set price

Stop Order A **stop order** (often referred to as a *stop-loss order*) is triggered by the market price of a security. It is used to protect profits or limit losses. Suppose you bought OAT at $20 a share and are quite pleased with the existing profit because it now sells for $50. Rather than selling and cashing in, you want to hold it because there is a chance its price could increase to $60. As a trade-off, you decide to place a stop order at $45 a share. If OAT increases in

Stop order: order triggered by the occurrence of a particular price

price, you simply place another stop order at a higher price and cancel the one at the lower price. If OAT's price falls and touches $45, your stop order becomes a market order. You will sell at the best possible price, which again may not be exactly $45.

Investors often use stop orders to relieve them of the task of watching their securities closely and making frequent buying and selling decisions. (You also can use a stop order to buy a security. The procedure is the same: when the trigger price is reached, a market order to buy is initiated. Short sellers often use stop orders in this manner to protect their profits.) Moreover, some investors believe they lack adequate discipline to initiate appropriate orders when a security's price is falling rapidly. The stop order makes the process mechanical—once the order is placed.

FINDING INVESTMENT INFORMATION

Most investment decisions require some research. Even if you decide to limit your investing to mutual funds or other pooling arrangements, you still must evaluate the alternative funds available. And if you make your own invest-ment decisions, your research must be ambitious. Information is the key to good research, and the sections to follow provide an overview of available sources. Additional sources are highlighted throughout the text with specific topics under discussion. For a summary of popular sources of investment information, see the Appendix at the end of this chapter.

Company Sources

As noted earlier, companies are required by the SEC to provide shareholders with annual and quarterly financial reports. Companies must also provide 10-K reports if they are requested. A 10-K report is a detailed compilation of a company's financial performance for the previous year. It presents the same data found in a company's annual financial report but may include other information not found there, such as asset depreciation methods or officer compensation levels.

Considerable information can be found in company reports. In addition to financial data, these documents contain discussions of past results and plans for the future. The corporate officers who provide these statements want to present their company in its most favorable light. Thus, caution is necessary.

To gain information more quickly, you might ask that your name be placed on a company's mailing list for press releases to financial analysts and other interested parties. Moreover, some investors call or write compa-nies, requesting information or clarification of certain topics that appear in financial reports. The success of this approach depends on the nature of your request and willingness of management to respond to it. You cannot expect that management will release privileged or sensitive information.

Government Sources

The federal government is a rich source of information about the overall economy and its component industries. Exhibit 2.8 indicates some of the more popular government publications. Most of these are available at university libraries or can be purchased through the Superintendent of Documents at rather nominal costs. Moreover, some of their economic series and analyses are now available on floppy disks. This is exceptionally convenient if you are using a personal computer in your research.

Monetary statistics and other useful information can be found in the *Federal Reserve Bulletin,* a monthly publication of the Federal Reserve System. It, too, is available at most libraries. Also, each of the 12 Federal Reserve banks offers free publications. You can write to them, asking to be placed on their mailing lists. Their addresses can be found in any issue of the *Bulletin.*

Investment Advisory Services

The three major investment advisory services are Standard and Poor's (S&P), Moody's, and Value Line. You should have no trouble finding most of them at your university and local libraries. They are extremely popular research sources and widely used by many investors. Exhibit 2.9 shows a research report for Mead Corporation from the Value Line *Survey.* It contains a consid-

---

Federal Government
To order, write: Superintendent of Documents
                      U.S. Government Printing Office
                      Washington, DC 20402

Business Conditions Digest	monthly
Business Statistics	biennial
Economic Indicators	monthly
Long Term Economic Growth	book
Statistical Abstract of the U.S.	annually
Survey of Current Business	monthly
U.S. Industrial Outlook	annually

Federal Reserve System
To order, write: Federal Reserve System
                      Board of Governors
                      Division of Administrative Services
                      Washington, DC 20551

Federal Reserve Bulletin	monthly
Annual Chart Book	annually

EXHIBIT 2.8
Government publications

EXHIBIT 2.9

Value Line report on Mead Corporation. (Source: *Value Line Investment Survey*, April 23, 1993, p. 932. Copyright 1993 by Value Line Publishing, Inc. All Rights Reserved; Reprinted by permission.)

erable amount of data, which will be more meaningful to you after you have read Chapters 6 and 7. Another useful advisory service is the Weisenberger *Survey of Investment Companies*. It reports information, including historical performances, on many mutual funds.

Investment newsletters form a different type of investment advisory service. Such newsletters are published by people who tout their skills at forecasting future security prices. They are expensive and their forecasting acumen is questionable. You can read the advertisements of some of these forecasters in each issue of *Barron's*. Read Chapter 8 before you decide to subscribe to one.

Newspapers and Magazines

Many investors find a considerable amount of information in newspapers and magazines. This information includes investment stories and articles that might stimulate your interest as well as financial data. Most of the newspapers and magazines mentioned below are available at libraries.

The Wall Street Journal *The Wall Street Journal is* published each work day. Many investors subscribe to the *Journal* or read it at their offices or libraries. It is not exclusively investment-oriented but rather covers a wide range of business and economic topics. Practically every issue has at least one story of relevance to most investors along with extensive price and trading information on a wide range of securities. It would be fruitless to attempt to describe this publication in detail; you simply must read an issue to appreciate its comprehensive coverage of investments. An interesting part of the *Journal* is its daily report on various market indicators, such as the Dow Jones Industrial Average (DJIA), shown in Exhibit 2.10. (Some of the information, such as a 200-day moving average, may be unfamiliar to you, but this is only temporary—until we cover Chapter 8.) The DJIA is perhaps the most widely watched market index in the United States because of its historical significance. Because it covers only 30 individual stocks, it is not considered a comprehensive market index. The S&P 500 Stock Index also has wide appeal and is far more representative of the overall market. It also differs in its method of computation, as you will learn in Chapter 3.

Barron's *Barron's,* a sister publication to the *Journal*, is published weekly and is exclusively investment-oriented. It has regular columns dealing with different aspects of investing and a market laboratory section in each issue. Additionally, it features stories on different companies, reports interviews with security analysts and other investment advisors, and offers refresher articles on different aspects of investing. If *Barron's* has a flaw, it would be its advertisements and some of its stories, which often lean to the sensational side of investing.

EXHIBIT 2.10

The DJIA and the S&P 500. (Reprinted with the permission of *Investor's Business Daily*, March 12, 1993.)

BOX 2.3   A QUESTION OF ETHICS

The Client-Broker Relationship: A Matter of Mutual Trust

A sound working relationship between a registered representative of a stockbrokerage firm and her clients rests largely on mutual trust. Clients must have assurance that their representatives are thoroughly familiar with their financial backgrounds, including their investment objectives, and that the representatives place their clients' interests above their own compensation incentives. Alternatively, representatives have a right to expect that clients will be honest with them, take a reasonable outlook on performance, and understand that representatives deserve compensation if they have performed their function professionally.

A question of ethics arises when either party strays from appropriate behavior. Our concern is not with flagrantly bad practices, such as account churning or outright lying and bad advice, but rather with less dramatic activities. Let's point the finger first at registered representatives.

Do you always initiate contacts with clients to improve their portfolios? Sure, your firm may be underwriting a security issue and you can get us in with no commission, but is the security appropriate for us? The same question applies to a stock your company has just put on its buy list. If you can't explain why your recommendation is suitable in our individual cases, then why did you call? Also, are you really recommending the best investments for us, or are you pushing products that generate high commissions? This is a particular problem with mutual funds, which are profitable to both you and your firm. If your company has a product of the month that you are supposed to push, will you refuse? Finally, can we expect that you are periodically monitoring our portfolio and realistically evaluating its performance? You are closer to the market than we are, and if some of our investments are not working well, tell us what to do. If there is a mutual trust between us, we'll appreciate your advice.

Now, let's view the situation from the representative's perspective. Why didn't you disclose all relevant financial information to me so that I could understand your situation? Instead, you kept several accounts with other brokers and didn't tell me. How was I supposed to know that you already were heavy into one investment and that more of it was not appropriate for your situation? And why do you take such a short-run view? Do you expect that every recommendation should immediately be profitable? You criticize me for allegedly wanting to churn your account, but aren't you the nervous one who constantly calls, suggesting that maybe we should sell this and buy that? Last, why do you ask for my help, use my firm's investment advice, and then place your orders with a discount broker?

On this last note, some observers believe that there is an inherent conflict in the compensation scheme (commissions) that always makes ethical behavior difficult. These people favor a fee-only system of compensation, although that has failed to gain widespread popularity in the financial planning industry.

Investor's Business Daily *Investor's Business Daily* (*IBD*) is a daily publication devoted exclusively to investment news. It provides full coverage of trading activity of stocks, bonds, options, futures, and mutual funds. *IBD* is similar to Section C of the *Journal* except that its coverage, in some respects, is more thorough. For example, it provides graphic displays of 30 stocks of interest on the NYSE, Amex, and OTC market each day; in addition, it highlights one company for extensive analysis, both graphic and in terms of the company's underlying fundamentals. If you are interested exclusively in investment news, you might consider *IBD* as an alternative to the *Journal*.

The Wall Street Transcript A weekly publication, *The Wall Street Transcript* is devoted exclusively to investments. It reports on speeches company executives make to security analysts and on other important corporate announcements. It also features research reports issued by security analysts and covers topics of interest to market technicians. It is expensive and may not be available at your university library. It has limited uses to the beginning investor and so is probably not worth its cost.

Magazines A number of good magazines provide investment information and ideas. *Forbes* is exclusively investment-oriented. Its stories and regular features usually are realistic in outlook, often forewarning investors of potential problems with various investments. Its annual survey of mutual funds is well worth the price of that issue.

Financial World is similar to *Forbes* but less extensive and perhaps less conservative in outlook. Although not a get-rich-quick magazine, it takes a more positive view than does *Forbes*.

Fortune magazine usually features in-depth articles on different companies or industries. These articles provide excellent background material but are not geared directly toward investing. Nevertheless, the articles are timely, as are the regular monthly columns.

Money magazine covers a wide range of financial planning topics, including investing. Its investment articles often provide personal investment stories—almost always of success—that are interesting and thought-provoking. After reading *Money*, you get the impression that becoming wealthy through investing is a simple task, involving little risk. More articles on investment failures would help temper that impression.

Computer Data Sources

Many investors are using personal computers (PCs) to assist them in making investment decisions or in managing and evaluating their portfolios. There are a number of data sources. For example, the Dow Jones News/Retrieval system is a vast source of information, ranging from 10-K extracts to transcripts of "Wall Street Week," the popular PBS weekly investment program.

Practically all investment advisory services, such as Value Line or S&P, offer investment information on diskette or over a telephone line. Indeed, so many sources are available that if you plan to use the computer in investing, you should consider subscribing to *Computerized Investing*. This bimonthly newsletter is published by the American Association of Individual Investors (AAII), a nonprofit organization of more than 130,000 members dedicated to helping people make better investment decisions (call (312) 280-0170 for information). The newsletter covers a wide range of computer data sources and investment applications; one issue during the year exceeds 600 pages and covers software and data bases exclusively.

The cost of software and access to data sources has declined substantially. Good programs are available for under $200, and good data sources are available for as little as $200 to $500 a year, perhaps less if you are satisfied with quarterly (rather than monthly or weekly) data. Assuming that you already own a computer, modem, and printer, the additional costs of computerized investing are reasonable; but if you first must purchase all this hardware, then the benefits are questionable. Finally, it would be a mistake to think that computerized investing will substantially improve your returns. Practically all professional investors use computerized methods and, as you will learn in Chapter 14, more than half of them fail to do as well as an unmanaged index. There is considerable hype in this area that investors should ignore.

Academic Journals

A number of academic journals cover research related to both investment theory and applications. Readers without a strong mathematical background will not thoroughly understand many of the articles. Even if you limit your reading to the introduction and summary-and-conclusions sections of some articles, you may still find useful investment insights. The following journals are most appropriate: *Journal of Finance, Journal of Financial and Quantitative Analysis, Financial Analysts Journal, Journal of Portfolio Management, Financial Management, The Financial Review, Journal of Financial Research,* and *The C.F.A. Digest*.

Most of these publications should be available at university libraries. A last journal worth mentioning is the *AAII Journal,* published by the AAII. Although not strictly an academic journal, it contains articles that are professionally prepared and useful to investors who plan to make their own investment decisions.

SUMMARY

Both financial facilitation and financial intermediation are involved in transferring funds from providers to users; however, only financial facilitation creates securities. Securities can be issued through an underwriting process or on a best-efforts basis.

A primary market refers to the initial distribution of securities, while a secondary market deals with trading of previously issued securities. Trading takes place on organized exchanges, such as the NYSE, and in the OTC market.

Stockbrokerage firms often are classified as either full-service or limited-service firms. Factors to consider in selecting a broker include the importance of research, the quality of order execution, and the value of a representative's advice. Securities markets are regulated extensively. Key pieces of legislation are the Securities Act of 1933, the Securities Exchange Act of 1934, the Maloney Act of 1938, the Investment Company Act of 1940, the Investment Advisors Act of 1940, and the Securities Investor Protection Act of 1970.

In dealing with a stockbroker, investors use cash accounts, margin accounts, discretionary accounts, and wrap accounts. Long and short positions are taken, and orders used frequently are market orders, limit orders, and stop orders.

Important investment information is available from individual companies and federal government and Federal Reserve Bank sources. In the private sector, important sources are investment advisory services, newspapers (in particular, *The Wall Street Journal*) and magazines, computer data services, and academic journals.

KEY TERMS
(listed in order of appearance)

financial intermediation	monthly investment plans
financial facilitation	dividend reinvestment plans
underwriting	binding arbitration
underwriting syndicate	litigation
best-effort basis	Securities Act of 1933
private placement	prospectus
primary market	Securities Exchange Act of 1934
secondary market	10-K Report
organized exchange	Maloney Act of 1938
continuous market	Investment Company Act of 1940
capital market	Investment Advisors Act of 1940
money market	Securities Investor Protection Act
commission brokers	cash account
specialists	margin account
floor brokers	discretionary account
floor traders	wrap account
over-the-counter market	long position
NASDAQ	short position
third market	reversing a position
fourth market	market order
full-service firm	limit order
limited-service firm	stop order

REVIEW QUESTIONS

1. Explain how financial facilitation differs from financial intermediation.
2. Compare underwriting to selling on a best-effort basis.
3. Identify market participants and their roles in the transfer-of-funds process.

4. Distinguish between a primary market and a secondary market. Is the first dependent on the second? Explain.

5. Explain an organized exchange, including a definition of a continuous market in your answer. Why is the NYSE called "the Big Board"? Also, identify key organized exchanges in the United States and abroad.

6. What requirements must a company meet to have its stock listed on the NYSE?

7. What is a "seat" on an organized exchange, and how do you get one? Can a seat be looked on as an investment? Explain.

8. Provide a brief narrative describing the execution of an order on the NYSE, including descriptions of commission brokers, specialists, floor brokers, and floor traders.

9. Explain the OTC market and then identify the following: NASDAQ, NASDAQ/NMS, the third market, and the fourth market. What are the "pink sheets"?

10. Indicate some reasons for dealing with a full-service broker; why would an investor deal with a limited-service firm?

11. Explain a monthly investment plan and a dividend reinvestment plan. Do they seem suitable for small investors? Discuss.

12. Suppose you have a dispute with your broker. Explain how you can resolve the matter.

13. Provide a brief discussion of the following legislation: *(a)* the Securities Act of 1933, *(b)* the Securities Exchange Act of 1934, *(c)* the Maloney Act of 1938, *(d)* the Investment Company Act of 1940, *(e)* the Investment Advisors Act of 1940, and *(f)* the Securities Investor Protection Act of 1970.

14. Explain how a cash account, margin account, discretionary account, and wrap account differ. Which would you prefer having? Why?

15. In what sense does a margin account provide leverage? Is this good or bad for investors? Explain.

16. What does it mean to be long or short, and what is "reversing a position"? Identify a "bull" and a "bear."

17. Do stockbrokers impose risks on investors whose shares they have borrowed to complete short sales? Explain.

18. Agree or disagree: Short positions are not advised for dividend-paying stocks because short sellers must pay dividends on all shorted stocks, thereby reducing trading profit.

19. Explain the differences among market orders, limit orders, and stop orders. Give one reason why you might use each.

---

1. The stockbrokerage firm of W. F. Wallace, Inc., utilizes the following commission schedule:

PROBLEMS AND PROJECTS

Value of the Transaction	Commission
A. Under $500	Minimum commission of $25
B. $500–$1,000	$10 plus 3% of the transaction value
C. $1,000–$10,000	$40 plus 1.5% of the transaction value
D. Over $10,000	$190 plus 1.0% of the transaction value

    a. Calculate the commission and express it as a percentage of the transaction in each of the following cases: (1) 100 shares @ $15, (2) 500 shares @ $60, (3) 100 shares @ $4, and (4) 300 shares @ $3.

    b. Compare the commissions above with those of other brokerage firms indicated in this chapter. Does Wallace appear to be a full-service broker or a discounter? Explain.

2. Brian Wade has $5,000 to invest. He intends to use his margin account to buy 100 shares of General Electric at $100 a share. Answer the following questions: (a) What is the initial margin requirement? (b) Assuming the broker has a 25% maintenance margin requirement, at what price of GE will Brian get a margin call? (c) How much additional margin must Brian deposit if the broker insists the account be brought up to the initial margin requirement? (d) How much interest will Brian pay during the first month if the broker charges 0.75% for the month (9% annual rate)?

3. Shirley Han is thinking of short selling 100 shares of Exxon at $50 a share. She will deposit 50% margin to initiate her position. Answer the following questions about this transaction: (a) What will Shirley's profit or loss be if Exxon increases to $60 a share? What if it decreases to $30 a share? (b) Exxon will pay a dividend of $2 a share; how does this affect Shirley? (c) How much equity will Shirley have in the account if Exxon increases to $60 a share? Will she get a margin call if the maintenance margin requirement is 30%? Explain. (d) How long can Shirley maintain the short position?

4. You have placed a limit order to buy 100 shares of Delta Airlines at $60 a share. Your broker indicated Delta was trading at $60\frac{1}{8}$ when the order was taken, but you noticed that Delta never traded higher than $59\frac{3}{4}$ after the order was placed. What price did you pay for the stock? Explain.

5. (Student Project) Call a local company and request a quarterly report, an annual report, and a copy of its 10-K report. Also see if a notice of the annual shareholders' meeting is available.

6. (Student Project) Using your school library, find and review at least one publication in each of the following categories: a federal government publication, a Federal Reserve publication, an investment advisory service, a financial newspaper, an investment-oriented magazine, and an academic journal.

7. (Student Project) Inquire if your school uses a computer data source. If it does, try to obtain fee information. Then determine the annual cost of using a system based on your estimate of usage. Also, you can inquire if a stockbrokerage firm provides computer services and perhaps allows a portion of commissions as a credit against the system's cost.

CASE ANALYSES

2.1 Dustin Hall Selects a Stockbroker

Dustin Hall is a successful civil engineer, earning about $60,000 a year. His hobby is the stock market, although he has not studied investments formally. In fact, most of his readings are from *Money* magazine and various how-to-get-rich books. Dustin often works 60 or more hours a week and travels extensively. Figuring he will save $1,000 a month, he wants to start investing, primarily in common stocks. His investment objective is long-term growth over time, and he has a high tolerance for risk.

Dustin has recently been contacted by a college friend who has just made a career change from chemical sales to retail stock brokering. She is employed by a full-service firm and is working on her licenses. She also is studying in preparation for examinations qualifying her as a certified financial planner. Her firm is highly respected and has excellent research facilities. Dustin is ready to establish an account but first has asked some questions of you. Answer them, indicating your reasons, as they apply in his specific case.

a. Do you feel a full-service broker is more appropriate than a discounter? **Questions**
b. Does a margin account seem appropriate? Would you recommend a discretionary account with his friend?
c. Should Dustin be an active short seller?
d. Do you recommend a monthly investment plan? Explain.

Fran LaBelle has inherited $24,000 from her grandfather and hopes to parlay this sum into a small fortune. To do so, Fran will play the stock market. Fran opened a margin account with a full-service brokerage firm that charges a commission of 1.5% of the value of a transaction. Although her broker has recommended a number of stocks to Fran, she usually ignores his advice and makes her own selections, taking a position in only one stock at a time and utilizing margin almost to the fullest extent possible.

**2.2
Fran LaBelle's
Active Trading**

She started her trading as soon as she received the $24,000 by taking a long position in 400 shares of IBM at $120 a share. A month later, she sold IBM at $125 a share. She then took a long position in 1,000 shares of GM at $48 a share. She sold these shares three months later at $60 a share and immediately shorted 1,000 shares of Eastman Kodak at $69 a share. She has held this position for two months basically because she doesn't want to take a loss, since Kodak has increased to $75 a share. Fran is fairly sure her strategy on Kodak will work out, given enough time. But she is vexed with her trading now that IBM is at $130 a share. She is contemplating closing her Kodak position and buying IBM again.

a. Calculate Fran's commissions to date. Then, calculate her gain or loss on **Questions** each trade and her total gain or loss after considering all commissions. Assume also that Eastman Kodak paid a dividend of $1.40 a share while Fran was short.
b. Assume that Fran's margin account had an average monthly loan amount of $24,000 on the IBM trade, $25,000 on the GM trade, and $35,000 on the Eastman Kodak trade. Assuming an interest rate of 1% a month, calculate Fran's interest on the margin account.

    c. Evaluate Fran's trading success using the following benchmarks: (1) she simply bought and held IBM, and (2) she invested her funds in a six-month certificate of deposit with a guaranteed 8% annual rate.

    d. Suppose Fran holds her current short position. Assuming her initial margin was $34,500, at what price of Eastman Kodak will she receive a margin call, assuming a 30% maintenance margin requirement?

    e. What is your opinion of Fran's investment approach? What specific recommendations do you suggest?

HELPFUL READING

Belsky, Gary. "How Your Broker Makes a Buck." *Money*, June 1992, pp. 142–55.

Carlson, Charles. "A Lot for (Almost) Nothing: The Lure of Dividend Reinvestment Plans." *Barron's*, February 17, 1992, p. 17.

DeCarlo, Scott, and Gilbert Steedly. "Stock Market Lotto." *Forbes,* June 21, 1993, pp. 210–13.

Morgenson, Gretchen. "Here's How the Pros Do It." *Forbes*, June 21, 1993, pp. 222–23.

———. "Fun and Games on the NASDAQ." *Forbes,* August 16, 1993, pp. 74–80.

Raghavan, Anita. "Stock Boom Doesn't Spur Bull Market in Seats." *The Wall Street Journal,* March 20, 1993, p. C1.

Rescigno, Richard. "Brokers vs. Customers: The Business of Deciding Their Disputes Is Booming." *Barron's*, March 23, 1992, pp. 18–19.

Siconofli, Michael. "Paine Webber Is Penalized for Sales Pressure on Brokers." *The Wall Street Journal*, July 27, 1993, p. C1.

Slater, Karen. "Victims of Brokers Have a Powerful Ally." *The Wall Street Journal*, April 16, 1992, p. C1.

APPENDIX: POPULAR INVESTMENT INFORMATION SOURCES

The sources listed below frequently are used by investors. Information is provided for subscribing to magazines or newspapers. Subscription rates change, so you should check current rates before subscribing. Moreover, some publications have special introductory rates or lower rates for students. Category II and III sources are likely to be found in school or public libraries.

I. Newspapers and Magazines		
Publication (Primary Topics)	Frequency	Publisher
Barron's (investments)	Weekly	Dow Jones & Co., Inc. 200 Liberty Street New York, NY 10281

I. Newspapers and Magazines (*continued*)		
Publication (Primary Topics)	**Frequency**	**Publisher**
Better Investing (investments)	Monthly	National Association of Investment Clubs 1515 E. Eleven Mile Road Royal Oak, MI 48067
Changing Times (investments and personal finance)	Monthly	Kiplinger Washington Editors, Inc. 1729 H Street, N.W. Washington, DC 20006
Financial World (investments)	Biweekly	Financial World Partners 1328 Broadway New York, NY 10001
Forbes (investments)	Biweekly	Forbes, Inc. 60 5th Avenue New York, NY 10011
Fortune (company backgrounds, investments)	Biweekly	Time, Inc. Time & Life Bldg. New York, NY 10020–1393
Inc. (small company backgrounds)	Monthly	Inc. Publishing, Inc. 38 Commercial Wharf Boston, MA 02110
Investor's Business Daily (investments and financial news)	Daily	Investor's Business Daily, Inc. 12655 Beatrice Street Los Angeles, CA 90066
Venture (small company backgrounds)	Monthly	Venture Magazine, Inc. 801 Second Avenue New York, NY 10017
The Wall Street Journal (economic and financial markets)	Daily	Dow Jones & Co., Inc. 200 Liberty Street New York, NY 10281

II. Information Services		
Name of Service	**Frequency**	**Information**
A. Standard and Poor's		
1. Corporation Records	Daily	Comprehensive reference material on numerous companies.
2. NYSE Stock Reports	Periodic revisions	Current data and recent developments on NYSE stocks.
3. ASE Stock Reports	Periodic revisions	Current data and recent developments on Amex stocks.

II. Information Services (*continued*)		
Name of Service	Frequency	Information
A. Standard and Poor's (*continued*)		
4. OTC Stock Reports	Periodic revisions	Current data and recent developments on OTC stocks.
5. Dividend Record	Daily Weekly Quarterly	Dividend information on common and preferred stocks.
6. Daily Stock Price Record	Quarterly	Daily prices on over 7,000 issues; 3 volumes—NYSE, Amex, and OTC stocks.
7. Creditweek	Weekly	Reviews credit conditions and evaluates outlook for fixed-income securities.
8. The Outlook	Weekly	Analyzes common stocks and the outlook for equities.
9. Bond Guide	Monthly	Statistical data on numerous bonds (corporates and governments) and preferred stocks.
10. Stock Guide	Monthly	Statistical data on over 5,000 common and preferred stocks.
B. Moody's		
1. Bond Survey	Twice weekly	Analyses and recommendations on various bond issues.
2. Bond Record	Weekly	Prices, ratings, other data on various bond issues.
3. Industrial Manual	Yearly (supplement twice weekly)	Data on earnings, operations, and management activities for industrial firms.
4. Public Utility Manual	Same as 3	Same as 3 for public utilities.
5. Transportation Manual	Same as 3	Same as 3 for transportation companies.
6. OTC Industrial Manual	Same as 3	Same as 3 for OTC companies.
7. Unlisted Manual	Same as 3	Same as 3 for small emerging companies.
8. Bank and Finance News Reports	Same as 3	Data on financial companies.
9. Municipal and Governments Manual	Same as 3	Data and ratings on municipal and foreign bonds.

II.	Information Services (*continued*)		
	Name of Service	Frequency	Information
B.	Moody's (*continued*)		
10.	Handbook of Common Stocks	Quarterly	Statistical data on numerous companies.
C.	Value Line		
1.	Investment Survey	Weekly	Comprehensive data and evaluation of about 1,700 firms.
2.	Options and Convertibles	Weekly	Comprehensive data and evaluation of numerous convertible issues, warrants, and options.
D.	Wiesenberger's		
1.	Investment Companies	Annual	Authoritative statistical review of numerous investment companies.
2.	Current Performance	Monthly	A supplement to 1.
E.	Morningstar		
1.	Mutual Fund Sourcebook	Annual	Similar to D.1. except it is more analytical.
2.	Closed-End Investment Companies	Annual	Similar to E.1.
F.	Dun and Bradstreet Key Business Ratios	Annual	Provides financial ratios for numerous industries.
G.	Robert Morris Associates Annual Statement Studies	Annual	Similar to F. Each is an excellent reference for industry analyses.

III.	Academic and Professional Publications		
	Publication	Frequency	Information
A.	*AAII Journal*	Monthly	Articles related to all forms of investing.
B.	*C.F.A. Digest*	Quarterly	Abstracts of investment articles.
C.	*Financial Analysts Journal*	Bimonthly	Excellent articles covering new developments in investments.

III. Academic and Professional Publications (*continued*)		
Publication	Frequency	Information
D. *Financial Management*	Quarterly	Deals primarily with financial management applications.
E. *Financial Planning*	Monthly	Covers all aspects of financial planning, including investments.
F. *Institutional Investor*	Monthly	Current-trend articles of interest to professional investors.
G. *Journal of the American Society of CLU and ChFC*	Bimonthly	Articles on insurance and financial planning.
H. *Journal of Business*	Quarterly	Theoretical and research-oriented articles on business topics.
I. *Journal of Finance*	Five a year	Theoretical and research-oriented articles on finance topics.
J. *Journal of Financial and Quantitative Analysis*	Quarterly	Similar to H.
K. *Journal of Financial Economics*	Quarterly	Similar to H; considerable economic theory orientation.
L. *Journal of Financial Planning*	Quarterly	Covers all aspects of financial planning, including investments.
M. *Journal of Portfolio Management*	Quarterly	Articles deal with both investment vehicles and portfolio management.
N. *National Real Estate Investor*	Monthly	Covers real estate investing, finance, management.
O. *Real Estate Review*	Quarterly	Articles cover all aspects of real estate investing.
P. *REIT Fact Book*	Annual	Statistical data and other information on the REIT industry.

CHAPTER THREE

Measuring Investment Return

After you finish this chapter, you
will be able to:

- understand the concept of a
  holding period return and why it
  is important to measure the
  average of such returns
  correctly.

- compute the future value of a
  single payment and an annuity.

- compute the current value of a
  single payment and an annuity.

- calculate approximate rates of
  return on investments.

- see historical rates of return on
  key financial assets and how
  these returns have varied over
  time.

- identify certain risk premiums,
  which are additional returns for
  undertaking riskier investments.

- understand how popular market
  indexes are calculated.

I nvestments differ widely in their return and risk characteristics. Some, such as a savings account, offer returns immediately and have little risk, while others—a zero coupon bond, for example—defer your return for many years and have substantial risk. Selecting investments on the basis of their return and risk characteristics is a difficult task, and much of the difficulty arises in simply measuring each. A discussion of investment risk is presented in the next chapter, while investment return is the topic of this one. We'll look first at measuring investment return with a holding period return and then we'll discuss important concepts dealing with time value of money. The chapter continues by looking at historical returns on common stocks and selected debt instruments, and concludes with a discussion of anomalies in stock returns and the use of market indexes.

THE HOLDING PERIOD RETURN

Holding period return: total return of an investment over a period of time

A **holding period return** (HPR) is the total return of an investment for a given period of time. It has three cash flow elements to consider: an amount initially invested (P_0); any periodic distribution received while the investment is held (R); and the amount received when the investment is sold (P_1). The dollar holding period return ($\$HPR$) is calculated as follows:

$$\$HPR = R + (P_1 - P_0) \qquad (3.1)$$

If P_1 is greater than P_0, there is a capital gain; if it is negative, there is a capital loss.

An HPR is most often expressed as a ratio in relation to the initial investment, P_0. This relationship is shown below:

$$HPR = \frac{[R + (P_1 - P_0)]}{P_0} \qquad (3.2)$$

As an example, suppose $P_0 = \$50$, $P_1 = \$60$, and $R = \$4$; then,

$$HPR = \frac{[\$4 + (\$60 - \$50)]}{\$50}$$

$$= \frac{[\$4 + \$10]}{\$50}$$

$$= \frac{\$14}{\$50} = 0.28, \text{ or } 28.0\%$$

Frequently in discussion, an HPR is presented as a percentage; however, the calculation always gives the decimal.

BOX 3.1   INVESTMENT INSIGHTS

How Important Are Dividends to Investors?

This is a strange question: why wouldn't dividends be important? Actually, a deeper issue is involved here. Paying a dividend is expensive for several reasons. First, the shareholders give up an opportunity to invest the funds within the business, where investment rates might be higher than elsewhere. Second, the tax law doesn't allow a corporation to deduct dividends in figuring its income tax liability. In effect, this means each dollar of corporate income paid out as a dividend is taxed twice—once at the corporate level and again at the individual investor's level—before it can be reinvested. True, you eventually want to receive funds from the corporation (or to sell your shares at a profit), and taxes must be paid on those funds; but if a dividend is not paid, taxes at least can be deferred, which by itself is a big advantage. Considering the drawbacks, it's a wonder any corporation ever pays a dividend, and some financial theorists have argued that they shouldn't.

But most corporations do, and many have specific policies about how much to pay and how often. Their officers point out that shareholders want and expect dividends with the same intensity that employees want to be paid. Are shareholders nearsighted, or ignorant of the tax law? Perhaps, but risk and uncertainty might better explain their behavior. After all, a dividend is the bird in hand, while price appreciation might be the two in the bush. In a risky and uncertain world, this behavior is definitely not irrational.

But can you as an investor profit from it? All things considered, wouldn't companies that pay low or no dividends be better picks than the more generous ones? Probably not, because each dividend-paying policy will attract investors who favor that approach, which is called the clientele effect. As investors seek out their preferences, they will bid stock prices up to a point where any extraordinary gain is eliminated. So, your selection should be guided by your investment objectives for current or future return and not by believing one approach is better than others.

Current Return

The *R* term above represents an investment's **current return.** In many investments, it is what you expect to receive on a regular basis: each quarter or each month, for example. The most common types of current return are interest and dividends, but there are others.

Current return: cash payments or other advantages an investment offers on a regular basis

Interest   Many debt instruments pay interest on a routine basis. Bonds, for example, pay interest every six months. A savings account, on the other hand, may pay interest quarterly, monthly, or even daily. Some debt instruments, such as mortgage-backed passthroughs (explained in Chapter 10),

make payments that include both interest and return of the initial investment. The total received can be treated as current return because the security's ending value will be lower by the amount of principal repayments.

Dividends   Many common stocks and practically all preferred stocks pay
dividends (unless the preferred dividends are in arrears), usually on a quarterly basis. Keep in mind, though, we are considering only cash dividends and
not stock dividends. Stock dividends are distributions of additional shares of
the issuing company's common stock and do not involve cash.

Other Cash Distribution   Some investments offer cash distribution other
than interest or dividends. A partnership, for example, might simply distribute available cash to the partners. As another example, a corporation may
have a share repurchase plan that periodically allows you to sell some of your
shares back to the corporation. As an investor, you might look on such
redemptions more as a cash distribution than as a reduction in the size of
your holdings in the company.

Income Tax Savings   If you are a part owner of a partnership or a sole pro-
prietor, the business operations may result in a tax loss. This loss is reported
by you on your individual tax return and, in effect, reduces other taxable
income you might have. Under current tax law, if you are active in managing
the business and if you have other income not in excess of $100,000, you can
deduct up to $25,000 of losses from such income. (For each $1 of income
above $100,000, you lose $0.50 of the deduction until the entire $25,000 is
eliminated. Also, the deduction limitation does not apply to losses in oil and
gas ventures.) This tax loss has value, the amount depending on your marginal tax rate: the higher your rate, the greater the value of the tax loss.

Commissions and the HPR   Most investors incur costs in their investing
activities and view such costs as a reduction of their return. Any commissions you pay should be deducted from the sales proceeds when you sell
securities and added to the purchase outlay when you buy them; that is, P_0
and P_1 should be adjusted for commissions. (Other kinds of costs, such as
interest on a margin account or dividends paid on stock sold short, should
also be considered in certain situations.)

Returning to the previous example, suppose that a commission of $1
applied at both the purchase and the sale of the asset. Then, the new HPR
can be determined.

$$\text{HPR} = \frac{[\$4.00 + (\$59.00 - \$51.00)]}{\$51.00} = \frac{\$12.00}{\$51.00} = 0.235$$

As you see, considering these additional outlays reduces the HPR substantially, from 28.0% to 23.5%.

Future Return

An investment's appreciation in value is referred to as its **future return.** Keep in mind that a security's historical price appreciation is always known with certainty and measured with little difficulty. Securities, however, are purchased on the basis of expected future appreciation, which usually is difficult to estimate and never known with certainty. Two estimating techniques discussed in later chapters are the earnings approach and the dividends approach.

Future return: appreciation in an investment's value over time

An earnings approach assumes a security's future price will be some known multiple of its future earnings per share. For example, if a stock is expected to sell at 10 times next year's earnings and if earnings are estimated at $3 a share, next year's stock price will be $30 a share. As you probably guess, the trick is to estimate next year's earnings and then hope the earnings multiplier doesn't change.

A dividend approach takes the view that a security's price appreciation—in percentage terms—will be the same as its percentage increase in dividends, again on a per-share basis. Thus, if dividends grow 10% next year, the stock's price will also increase by 10%. For example, ABC, Inc. pays $2 a share in dividends this year and its stock sells for $25 a share. Its dividend next year is expected to increase to $2.20 a share—a 10% increase. So, the stock's price should increase to $27.50 (1.10 × $25.00). If you follow this method, your task is to make a good estimate of dividend growth and then hope the relation of price growth to dividend growth stays the same.

Measuring the HPR Over Time

An HPR is a simple, easily understood calculation if the holding period in question is exactly one year. When the holding period is less or longer than a year, confusion can—and often does—result. As an example, suppose a friend of yours boasts of an investment he made, claiming he earned an "average" annual rate of return of 26.1% over a three-year period. You are impressed but ask to see his actual investment results, which are shown in Exhibit 3.1. Are you still impressed? Let us look at his "average" a bit more closely.

Calculating Average Returns　　We see now how he got the 26.1 figure: it's the arithmetic average of each year's HPR. But does that give us a clear idea of his investment performance? If you look closely, you can see that he invested $100 and three years later received $100 when he sold. Meanwhile, he received $10 in dividends each year. You and I might be more inclined to think that his return was exactly 10% each year and, so, "averaged" 10% for the three years.

The problem with the **arithmetic average** is that it has a built-in bias favoring gains over losses. For example, if you invest $100 and it's worth $200

Arithmetic average: simple average found by adding the values of occurrences and dividing by their number

EXHIBIT 3.1
Calculating the arithmetic and geometric average rates of return

(1) Time	(2) Security's Price	(3) Dividend Received	(4) Each Period's Total Return	(5) Each Period's HPR (ratio)	(6) Column (5) Plus 1.0
zero	$100	$—	$—	—	—
1 year later	60	10	−30	−0.300[a]	0.700
2 years later	120	10	+70	+1.167[b]	2.167
3 years later	100	10	−10	−0.083[c]	0.917
Sum				0.784	—
Arithmetic average (divide sum by 3) =				0.261	—
Cumulative total return = (0.700 × 2.167 × 0.917)				—	1.391
Geometric average ($\bar{X}_g$) =				—	0.116[d]

NOTES:

$$a\left[\frac{10 + (60 - 100)}{100}\right] = -0.300$$

$$b\left[\frac{10 + (120 - 60)}{60}\right] = +1.167$$

$$c\left[\frac{10 + (100 - 120)}{120}\right] = -0.083$$

$$d(1.391)^{\frac{1}{3}} - 1.0 = 1.11629 - 1.0 = 0.1163$$

a year later, you have a 100% gain, but if it falls back to $100 by the end of the second year, you have only a 50% loss. Clearly, if the base period for calculating percentage gains and losses is the first period, gains always have an edge over losses. This problem can be avoided by using the **geometric average** ($\bar{X}_g$). Its calculation is lengthier but worth the effort. The appropriate formula is shown below, where n = number of periods the investment is held:

Geometric average: complex average that eliminates the upward bias involved with an arithmetic average

$$\bar{X}_g = [(HPR_1 + 1.0)(HPR_2 + 1.0) \ldots (HPR_n + 1.0)]^{\frac{1}{n}} - 1.0 \qquad (3.3)$$

The expression within the parentheses is called the *cumulative total return* (see Exhibit 3.1), which is easy enough to calculate. Finding the geometric average can be a simple task as well, thanks to the availability of relatively inexpensive calculators. Many of these have a so-called y^x (read as y to the x) key. This key makes it possible to raise a number to any power, such as the ⅓ power in the example. Uses of the financial calculator are illustrated throughout the text. Our presentation is for the Hewlett-Packard 12C (a popular model), although the steps are similar for other calculators. Exhibit 3.2 shows each step to calculate the geometric mean.

The data in Exhibit 3.1 indicate a geometric average of 11.6%, quite a bit less than the arithmetic average of 26.1%. The difference between the two average values is always larger when periodic returns are more volatile; in the current example, returns vary considerably over the three years.

Using Average Returns   An important lesson should be learned here: if you are examining the performance of an investment over time and if the annual returns vary considerably, don't rely on the arithmetic average to measure performance. You will get a biased view. A more fundamental question to ask is whether or not an average should be used in the first place. Returning to our example, we can see that even the geometric average gives a different answer than our commonsense feel of the 10% annual return over the three years. Which of these two is correct?

There is no mathematical answer to this question because it depends on your perspective. If you believe that year-by-year performance measurement is important, then the geometric average is preferred. On the other hand, if your concern is only with return over the entire period, then the commonsense figure is appropriate. Actually, we shouldn't rely too heavily on intuitive feelings. The example above is a simple one, insofar as the ending value is the same as the beginning value. If these differed, common sense may not tell us how to handle the gain or loss. In this situation, we need the investment's rate of return—a concept to be developed shortly.

Step	Enter	Depress Key(s)	Function
1	—	[f][CLX]	Clears registers
2	1.39100	[ENTER]	Enters cumulative total return
3	0.33333	y^x	Enters exponent (1/3 = 0.33333)
4	—	—	Read answer: 1.11629
5	1.00000	[—]	Subtracts 1
6	—	—	Read final answer: 0.11629

EXHIBIT 3.2
Using the financial calculator to find the geometric average

TIME VALUE OF MONEY

All things considered, we prefer investments that offer returns sooner rather than later. If you have a choice between receiving $100 today or $100 a year from today, you would be foolish not to take the current payment. The reason for your choice is simple; $100 invested at any positive rate of interest will grow to an amount greater than $100 in a year. If you could invest at, say, 10%, the $100 would grow to $110. Similar reasoning tells us that with a 10% inflation rate, $110 received one year from today is no better than $100 today. When we think in these terms, we are considering the time value of money.

A time-value-of-money problem can be viewed in one of two ways: a future-value application or a present-value application. Each is discussed below.

Determining Future Values

Future value: value of an investment at a future point in time

A **future value** is the amount an investment made today will grow to at the end of a given period, assuming it is invested at a given rate of interest *and* further assuming that all periodic interest earned on the investment is also invested at the *same rate* of interest. You can find the future value of a single payment or of a series of equal payments, which is called an **annuity.**

Annuity: series of equal payments

Future Value of a Single Payment   Suppose you could buy a three-year certificate of deposit (CD) at a bank that is advertising a 10% rate on such CDs. How much would you get back at the end of three years if you invested $1,000 today? Before jumping to a solution, consider the time line in Exhibit 3.3. It is helpful in setting up time-value-of-money problems. As you move along the line away from the point t_0, assume you are moving forward in time. Each of the points—t_1, t_2, and t_3—represent separate periods of time, usually one year, although other periods can be represented. Any line pointing below the time line indicates an outflow (payment) of cash; any line pointing above the time line indicates an inflow (receipt) of cash. You see, then, the CD involves a $1,000 outflow at t_0 and leads to an unknown inflow

EXHIBIT 3.3
A time line: Finding the future value of a single payment

$PV = \$1,000$

t_0 t_1 t_2 t_3 Time

$? = FV$

$FV = \$1,331$
if $i = 10\%$

three years later. (A problem this simple doesn't require a diagram to help solve it, but diagrams can be useful when more complex investments are evaluated.)

An easy way to find a future value (FV) is to use the formula below:

$$FV = (1.0 + i)^n \times PV \tag{3.4}$$

where PV = present value, or amount invested today,
         i = interest rate earned on the investment, and
         n = number of periods the investment is held.

We then can solve:

$$\begin{aligned} FV &= (1.0 + 0.10)^3 \times \$1{,}000 \\ &= (1.10)^3 \times \$1{,}000 \\ &= (1.331) \times \$1{,}000 \\ &= \$1{,}331 \end{aligned}$$

The solution above is also an easy one with a financial calculator. Exhibit 3.4 indicates the steps to solve the problem above. As you see, we get the same answer as above.

Another solution approach is to use a future value of $1 table, a portion of which is shown in Exhibit 3.5. The entire table (and tables for all other future and present values) can be found in Appendix A at the end of the text. Going down the table to the third period row and then over to the 10% column gives the value 1.3310. Multiply this by the initial investment to arrive at the future value of $1,331.00.

Whatever method is used, it is important to understand the process. It should be seen, for example, that the calculation above does indeed assume that periodic interest earned is reinvested at 10%. We can show this more concretely by determining the amounts on hand at the end of each period:

Step	Enter	Depress Keys	Function
1	—	[f] [CLX]	Clears registers.
2	1000	[CHS] [PV]	Enters present value as a negative number.
3	3	[n]	Enters number of periods.
4	10	[i]	Enters interest rate.
5	—	[FV]	Provides answer: 1,331.00.

*The Hewlett-Packard 12C. Other calculators operate on a similar basis. You should review the owner's manual for instructions on clearing registers and setting up a financial mode.

EXHIBIT 3.4
Using a financial calculator* to find the future value of an investment

EXHIBIT 3.5
Portion of a future value of $1 table. (Note: See Appendix A.1 for the complete table.)
The number boxed is the one illustrated in the text.

Periods (n)	8%	9%	10%	12%	14%	15%
1	1.0800	1.0900	1.1000	1.1200	1.1400	1.1500
2	1.1664	1.1881	1.2100	1.2544	1.2996	1.3225
3	1.2597	1.2950	1.3310	1.4049	1.4815	1.5209
4	1.3605	1.4116	1.4641	1.5735	1.6890	1.7490
5	1.4693	1.5386	1.6105	1.7623	1.9254	2.0114
6	1.5869	1.6771	1.7716	1.9738	2.1950	2.3131
7	1.7138	1.8280	1.9487	2.2107	2.5023	2.6600
8	1.8509	1.9926	2.1436	2.4760	2.8526	3.0590
9	1.9990	2.1719	2,3579	2.7731	3.2519	3.5179
10	2.1589	2.3674	2.5937	3.1058	3.7072	4.0456

The column header group is labeled *(i)*.

Illustrated in text example: 1.331 × $1,000 = $1,331

Period 1	$1,100 = $1,000 + 0.10($1,000)
Period 2	$1,210 = $1,100 + 0.10($1,100)
Period 3	$1,331 = $1,210 + 0.10($1,210)

A future value is also called a *compound value*, and the process of finding a compound value is called *compounding*, which involves *compound interest*. These terms are often used by financial institutions in describing their financial products.

Future Value of an Annuity Rather than investing a single amount at the beginning of the investment period, suppose you are considering an investment that calls for an even payment each period. Exhibit 3.6 shows a time

EXHIBIT 3.6
A time line: Finding the future value of an ordinary annuity (FVOA)

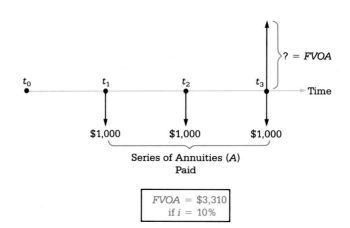

line for an investment requiring a payment of $1,000 a year for a three-year period, the payments being made at the end of each year and the interest rate being 10%. What is the future value of this annuity, called an **ordinary annuity (OA)**?

Ordinary annuity: series of equal payments occurring at the end of each period

Exhibit 3.7 shows a solution using a financial calculator, and Exhibit 3.8 finds the answer with a future value of a $1 annuity table (see Appendix A.2 for a larger table).

Some annuities call for annuity payments to be made at the beginning of each period rather than at the end. This type of annuity is called an **annuity due (AD).** Exhibit 3.9 shows the time line for an annuity due, illustrating the same problem discussed for the ordinary annuity. You can solve an AD with a financial calculator by simply indicating that payments take place at the beginning of periods. Referring to Exhibit 3.7, change step 2 to [g] [BEG] and follow the other steps as indicated. The answer will be 3,641.00.

Annuity due: series of equal payments occurring at the beginning of each period

Step	Enter	Depress Keys	Function
1	—	[f] [CLX]	Clears registers.
2	—	[g] [END]	Indicates payments occur at end of periods.
3	1000	[CHS] [PMT]	Changes sign and enters annuity.
4	3	[n]	Enters number of periods.
5	10	[i]	Enters interest rate
6	—	[FV]	Provides answer: 3,310.00

EXHIBIT 3.7
Using a financial calculator to find the future value of an annuity

EXHIBIT 3.8
Portion of a future value of $1 annuity table. (Note: See Appendix A.2 for the complete table.) The number boxed is the one illustrated in the text.

Number of Periods	8%	9%	10%	12%	14%	15%
1	1.0000	1.0000	1.0000	1.0000	1.0000	1.0000
2	2.0800	2.0900	2.1000	2.1200	2.1400	2.1500
3	3.2464	3.2781	3.3100	3.3744	3.4396	3.4725
4	4.5061	4.5731	4.6410	4.7793	4.9211	4.9934
5	5.8666	5.9847	6.1051	6.3528	6.6101	6.7424
6	7.3359	7.5233	7.7156	8.1152	8.5355	8.7537
7	8.9228	9.2004	9.4872	10.089	10.730	11.066
8	10.636	11.028	11.435	12.299	13.232	13.726
9	12.487	13.021	13.579	14.775	16.085	16.785
10	14.486	15.192	15.937	17.548	19.337	20.303

(*i*)

Illustrated in text example: 3.3100 × $1,000 = $3,310

EXHIBIT 3.9
A time line: Finding
the future value of an
annuity due (FVAD)

The larger value comes about because of one extra compounding period, which is shown in the following equation:

$$FVAD = (1.0 + i)FVOA \qquad (3.5)$$

Applying this to the current problem confirms the calculator solution:

$$FVAD = (1.0 + 0.10) \$3,310 = (1.10) \$3,310 = \$3,641$$

Determining Present Values

Present value: today's
value of a payment
made in the future

In finding a future value, we are moving forward in time to determine the accumulation of an investment or series of investments. In finding a **present value,** we reverse the process by asking, how much are amounts received in the future worth today? The arithmetic of finding an answer is called *discounting.*

Present Value of a Single Payment We can rearrange equation 3.4 to find a present value of a single payment. Now, the unknown is PV, while FV is known. For example, how much must you invest today to receive $1,000 three years from now, assuming an interest rate of 10%? Exhibit 3.10 shows a time line, and a solution appears below.

$$PV = \frac{FV}{(1.0 + i)^n} = \frac{1.0}{(1.0 + i)^n} \times FV$$

$$= \frac{1.0}{(1.10)^3} \times \$1,000 = \frac{1.0}{1.331} \times \$1,000 \qquad (3.6)$$

$$= 0.7513 \times \$1,000 = \$751.30$$

EXHIBIT 3.10
A time line: Finding
the present value of a
single payment

EXHIBIT 3.10
A time line: Finding
the present value of a
single payment

You can also find the present value of a single payment by using the financial calculator. Referring to Exhibit 3.4, after entering 1,000, depress [FV] at step 2 instead of [PV] and do not depress [CHS]; then, depress [PV] at step 5 instead of [FV]. Read the answer: −751.30. The minus sign indicates an outlay. Exhibit 3.11 shows a solution using a present value of $1 table to solve the problem. (A larger table is found in Appendix A.3.)

Present Value of an Annuity   Just as we have a future value of an annuity, we also have a present value of an annuity. A time line illustrating an example is shown in Exhibit 3.12. As you see, the problem is to calculate the present value of $1,000 received at the end of each year for the next five years, assuming an interest rate of 10%. Because the receipt takes place at the end

EXHIBIT 3.11
Portion of a present value of $1 table. (Note: See Appendix A.3 for the complete table.) The number boxed is the one illustrated in the text.

Period	8%	9%	10%	(i) 12%	14%	15%	16%
1	.9295	.9174	.9091	.8929	.8772	.8696	.8621
2	.8573	.8417	.8264	.7972	.7695	.7561	.7432
3	.7938	.7722	.7513	.7118	.6750	.6575	.6407
4	.7350	.7084	.6830	.6355	.5921	.5718	.5523
5	.6806	.6499	.6209	.5674	.5194	.4972	.4761
6	.6302	.5963	.5645	.5066	.4556	.4323	.4104
7	.5835	.5470	.5132	.4523	.3996	.3759	.3538
8	.5403	.5019	.4665	.4039	.3506	.3269	.3050
9	.5002	.4604	.4241	.3606	.3075	.2843	.2630
10	.4632	.4224	.3855	.3220	.2697	.2472	.2267

Illustrated in text example: 0.7513 × $1,000 = $751.30

EXHIBIT 3.12

A time line: Finding
the present value of an
ordinary annuity
(PVOA)

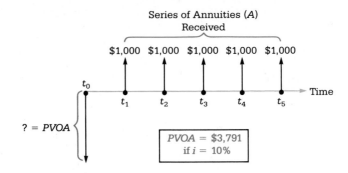

of the year, this is an ordinary annuity. If you use a financial calculator to
solve the problem, refer to Exhibit 3.7 and make the following changes:

> at step 3, do not depress [CHS],
> at step 4, enter 5 instead of 3,
> at step 6, depress [PV] instead of [FV] and read −3,790.80.

The negative sign indicates an outflow. A present value annuity table
(Appendix A.4) can also be used to find the solution, as shown in Exhibit
3.13.

    If the cash inflows took place at the beginning—rather than the end—of
each year, we would have an annuity due, as shown in Exhibit 3.14. To find
the present value of an annuity due (PVAD) using the financial calculator, go
through the same steps for finding a PVOA except at step 2, indicate pay-

EXHIBIT 3.13

Portion of a present value of $1 annuity table. (Note: See Appendix A.4 for the com-
plete table.) The number boxed is the one illustrated in the text.

Illustrated in text
example: 3.7908 ×
$1,000 = $3,790.80

Number of Periods	8%	9%	10%	12%	14%	15%
1	0.9259	0.9174	0.9091	0.8929	0.8772	0.8696
2	1.7833	1.7591	1.7355	1.6901	1.6467	1.6257
3	2.5771	2.5313	2.4869	2.4018	2.3216	2.2832
4	3,3121	3.2397	3.1699	3.0373	2.9137	2.8550
5	3.9927	3.8897	3.7908	3.6048	3.4331	3.3522
6	4.6229	4.4859	4.3553	4.1114	3.8887	3.7845
7	5.2064	5.0330	4.8684	4.5638	4.2883	4.1604
8	5.7466	5.5348	5.3349	4.9676	4.6389	4.4873
9	6.2469	5.9952	5.7590	5.3282	4.9464	4.7716
10	6.7101	6.4177	6.1446	5.6502	5.2161	5.0188

_(i)_ heads the interest-rate columns.

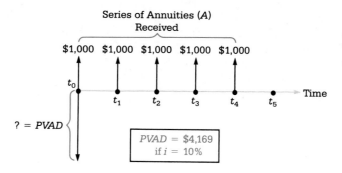

ments take place at the beginning of periods by depressing [g] [BEG]. Making this change, you will read the answer, $-4,169.87$. Also,

$$\text{PVAD} = (1.0 + i) \text{ PVOA} \qquad (3.7)$$

And,

$$\text{PVAD} = (1.0 + 0.10)3,790.79 = (1.10)3,790.79 = 4,169.87$$

Finding Rates of Return or Annuity Amounts

All the illustrations above assume a known interest rate and number of periods. The problem is to find a future or present value. However, many investment problems are structured in ways that we must calculate the interest rate (more broadly called the rate of return) on an investment or the number of periods an investment must be held to achieve a given target. A discussion of each situation follows.

Finding Rates of Return   The financial calculator makes it easy to solve for any unknown variable; you merely enter what is known and in the last step depress the key for the unknown variable. For example, assume you want to know the rate of return of a $2,000 investment that matures in five years and pays $3,200. Clear the registers and then:

enter 2000	depress [CHS] and [PV],
enter 3200	depress [FV],
enter 5	depress [n],
—	depress [i] and read 9.856.

The investment has an 9.86% return. Finding rates of return this quickly is an invaluable asset of the financial calculator.

   If you do not have a financial calculator, you can use the time value of money tables to approximate a rate of return. In the example above, we have both a present value and a future value of a single payment. First, calculate the ratio of future value to present value: it is 1.60 ($3,200/$2,000). Because the number of periods is five, we refer to the row with five periods in the future value of $1 table in Exhibit 3.5 and go through the columns until we find the number closest to 1.60. The closest number is 1.6105, which indicates a 10% rate of return. Because 1.60 is slightly less than 1.6105, the actual return is slightly less than 10%. You could visually estimate the answer at, say, 9.8%, or go for greater accuracy by interpolating, as shown below:

$$? = 9.00 + [(0.0614/0.0719) \times 1\%]$$
$$= 9.00 + [0.854 \times 1\%] = 9.854\%$$

The approximation method can also be used with annuities. For example, suppose an insurance company will sell you an annuity contract for $10,000 that will pay you $1,600 at the end of each year for the next 10 years. What rate of interest does the contract offer? In this case, calculate the ratio of present value to the annual payment (the annuity): it is 6.250. Now, refer to the present value of $1 annuity table in Exhibit 3.13. You should see that 6.250 is between a 9% and a 10% return. By interpolating, you should find the answer is 9.61%.

Because the approximation method requires annuity tables and because we have only ordinary annuity tables in the text, our examples involving the approximation method will not include annuities due. Annuity due problems are solved easily with the financial calculator by merely switching to the beginning-of- period mode.

Finding Annuity Amounts   Many investment problems involve a calculation of an annuity amount; retirement planning, for example, requires that you estimate an amount to invest each year to achieve a retirement nest egg. Let's return to the problem immediately above. Suppose the insurance company offers a contract that requires a $10,000 initial outlay and has a 9% annual return. How much will you receive at the end of each of the next 10 years? Referring to Exhibit 3.13, the present value of $1 annuity factor for 9% and 10 years is 6.4177. Divide this number into $10,000 for the answer— $1,558.19.

Solving the problem with the financial calculator has the following steps (after clearing the registers):

enter	10000	depress [CHS] and [PV]
enter	10	depress [n]
enter	9	depress [i]
	—	depress [PMT] and read 1558.19

The Power of Compounding

When interest rates were high in the 1970s and early 1980s, many financial institutions attempted to lure investors with a dramatic promotional tool: values compounded over a long period. For example, how much will just $1,000 grow to if you invest it today at 10% and hold the investment 40 years? Answer: $45,259, which isn't exactly petty cash. Even a 10% return was considered rather paltry in those days when some investments were yielding 16% and more. It wasn't hard to find newspaper and magazine ads showing how you could become a millionaire by investing very little each year until your retirement.

Were the ads true? Of course they were; they simply failed to tell the whole story, which was that if you are earning high rates of return on your investments, you can bet that inflation is also high (which it was) and your real rate of return (an inflation-adjusted return) won't be much higher than its long-term historical average. In other words, your $1,000 will grow to $45,259, but you might pay $20 for a can of Coke and $450,000 for a new car. So, we should avoid drawing unrealistic conclusions from the power of long-term compounding. On the other hand, it isn't unrealistic to see other aspects of the compounding process that might influence our investment decisions.

The Power of Small Additional Yield You might not worry about getting an extra one or two percentage points on your investments, thinking the small extra yield is not worth the aggravation. But consider this: how much would your $1,000 grow to over 40 years if it were invested at 12% rather than 10%? Answer: $93,050. You more than double—$93,050 versus $45,259—the accumulation. (See Exhibit 3.15 for a graphic presentation.) You might want to keep this in mind if you are young and starting an investment program. Getting the extra 1%, 2%, or 3% consistently over 40 years *does* make a difference, even in low interest rate environments such as that of the early 1990s.

The Power of a Few Extra Years Another factor to consider is when to start investing. Let's say your choices are today or 10 years from today. How much difference would it make in your accumulation if you held an investment 30 years instead of 40? You can see the answer in Exhibit 3.15. If your investment earns 10%, the 30-year accumulation is only $17,449, which is $27,810 less than the 40-year accumulation. The last 10 years increases your accumulation 2.6 ($45,259/$17,449) times! The investment moral here is simple to see: the sooner you start investing, the better off you will be. That is why even a small investment, particularly through a tax-deferring arrangement, when you are 25 will be as effective as a much larger investment when you are 45.

BOX 3.2   A QUESTION OF ETHICS

Isn't It Time for a Truth in Giving and Wagering Act?

Back in the 1960s, lenders were so abusive with interest-rate gimmicks, Congress passed a law—The Truth in Lending Act—to protect borrowers. Today, if you buy something and finance it, the lender is required to tell you the true annual percentage rate (APR) of interest on the loan. Unfortunately, if you buy a lottery ticket from your home state, lottery officials are free to lie through their teeth in telling you how much you might win.

The trouble arises from ignoring the time value of money. For example, suppose you buy a lottery ticket on a $1,000,000 jackpot. Somewhere in the fine print on the ticket, you might read that the winner collects the $1,000,000 with 20 annual payments of $50,000 each. Is that a million? Sure. Would you trade it for, say, $700,000 right now? You would be foolish if you didn't. Even at an investment rate as low as 5%, the $700,000 in hand is far better than the annual payments. Actually, the payments are worth about $654,266 at the 5% rate. If you take a more realistic rate of about 7% that could actually be earned in mid-1993 on, say, a 20-year Treasury bond, the present value is only $529,700. So, the $1,000,000 lottery turns out to be the $529,700 lottery.

Not to be outdone by public bureaucrats, some private enterprisers know a good gyp when they see one. When interest rates were higher some years ago, all sorts of giveaway schemes were hatched. A particularly imagi-native one in our area was a realtor who offered to pay you (eventually) the purchase price of certain homes in his listings—if you bought one now. That's right, folks, he'll pay for your home. (More correctly, the home seller paid for it with the realtor acting as an agent.) What's the gimmick? Well, if you buy a home, you get a zero coupon municipal bond that matures in 30 years. Suppose you buy a $100,000 home; you get a $100,000 bond. The bond isn't worth $100,000 until its maturity in 30 years. At the time the realtor was so generous, a bond like this was priced to yield about 10%, which means the realtor paid about $5,700 for it. This also means the $100,000 home cost $94,300, not zero.

Should the government try to legislate more honesty in reporting future monetary amounts when buyers or gamblers rely on them in buying or betting? Surprisingly, there isn't much enthusiasm for change. Some people have little sympathy for gamblers, even though many are from low socioeconomic groups who could use a little help. Other people argue that time-value-of-money concepts are just too hard for the average person to understand, so why bother? (That's a curious argument too. You would think consumer ignorance is a reason to provide protection, not to deny it.) Down deep, maybe the reason support runs low is that all of us like to dream. It's more fun to think of becoming a millionaire than a half-millionaire.

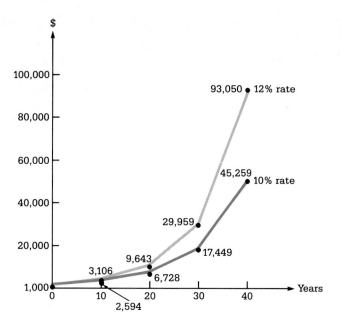

EXHIBIT 3.15
Compounding $1,000
at 10% and 12%

HISTORICAL INVESTMENT RETURNS

The return measurements developed above will be used throughout the text to evaluate investment alternatives. To begin, we can use them to examine the historical returns of broad investment categories. We do so not simply out of curiosity but because the past can provide valuable insights about realistic potential returns in the future. Many first-time investors have grossly exaggerated notions and expectations of investment returns. Some believe that doubling your money in two or three years is what you should get with, say, a common stock investment. Anything less than that is considered a bad investment—one to sell and move into something else. The discussion below is intended to temper that unrealistic view.

Returns from Key Financial Assets

A number of excellent studies have measured historical returns from key financial assets. One of these is published each year by Ibbotson Associates, Inc. in their *Annual Yearbook*. This book is a valuable source of information on return and risk measurements for common stocks, long-term bonds, U.S. Treasury bills, and the Consumer Price Index (CPI).

The Return on Common Stocks   Exhibit 3.16 shows year-by- year returns on common stocks of both large and small companies. The large companies are represented by Standard and Poor's (S&P) 500 Stock Index (explained later in this chapter). The small company index is composed of stocks that make up the fifth (smallest) quintile of stocks listed on the New York Stock Exchange (NYSE). This grouping is adjusted each five-year period to maintain the small size characteristic, and size is measured by total market capitalization, that is, number of shares outstanding times market price per share. Although Exhibit 3.16 speaks for itself, some observations seem particularly warranted.

To start, notice the big difference between the arithmetic and geometric average returns and how this difference is larger for the small company stocks. This observation confirms our earlier comments that the arithmetic average overstates returns and that the bias increases as the variation in returns increases. Second, the positive returns in both series are occasionally remarkable: you more than doubled your money in small stocks in 1933 (143% return); and their annual returns exceeded 50% in nine of the 67 years. The

EXHIBIT 3.16
Historical returns on common stocks. (Source: © *Stocks, Bonds, Bills, and Inflation 1993 Yearbook*™, Ibbotson Associates, Chicago [annual updates by Roger G. Ibbotson and Rex A. Sinquefield]. Used by permission. All rights reserved.)

big company stocks did well too: their returns were over 50% in 1933 and 1954 and in excess of 30% in 14 different years. But poor performances were also present: you lost almost 60% of your investment in small company stocks in 1937 and lost more than 30% with them on five occasions. Meanwhile, big company stocks showed their largest loss (−43%) in 1931 and had yearly losses in excess of 20% four times.

What picture emerges from the data? Unless you knew in advance what each year would bring, the most you could expect to earn were the long-term averages—10.3% in big company stocks each year and 12.2% in small company stocks—and be prepared for a roller coaster ride while earning them. These two percentage returns may seem small to you, but you will see shortly that over a long period, such as 67 years, they produce enormous accumulations of wealth.

The Return on Long-Term Bonds Each bond series assumes a long maturity (20 years) and, as you see in Exhibit 3.17, the average returns on government bonds (4.8%) and corporate bonds (5.5%) are much less than the returns on common stocks, but so are their year-to-year variations in returns. Perhaps the most noteworthy observation about bond returns is their increasing volatility in recent years. High inflation in the 1970s and early 1980s ushered

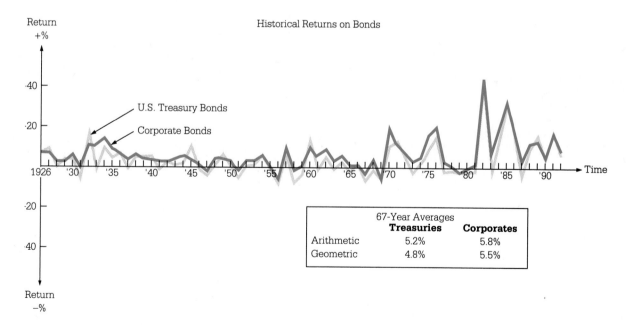

	67-Year Averages	
	Treasuries	**Corporates**
Arithmetic	5.2%	5.8%
Geometric	4.8%	5.5%

EXHIBIT 3.17
Historical returns on bonds. (Source: © *Stocks, Bonds, Bills, and Inflation 1993 Yearbook™*, Ibbotson Associates, Chicago [annual updates by Roger G. Ibbotson and Rex A. Sinquefield]. Used by permission. All rights reserved.)

in high interest rates, and the constantly changing outlook for future inflation led to the wide year-to-year swings in bond returns. By the mid-1980s, the situation seemed to have stabilized somewhat, although large positive returns were then earned as the inflation rate abated. For example, the returns on corporate bonds and Treasury bonds in 1991 were 19.9% and 19.3%, respectively.

U.S. Treasury Bills and the CPI   Exhibit 3.18 shows returns on U.S. Treasury bills and the CPI. The Treasury bills series is an index based on the shortest term bills but with no maturity less than one month. The CPI assumes monthly rates of return. As you would expect, the average return on bills (3.7%) is the lowest of all the investments, but so are the variations in return. You would not have had a negative return in any year, but your highest return was only about 15% (1981). The return on bills also increased substantially during the recent inflationary years.

The average inflation rate for the 67-year period is 3.1%, which is somewhat less than the average return on bills. Comparing these two rates leads to the conclusion that the real rate of return on bills was about 0.6%, which is quite low in comparison to real rates available in recent years. These often have been in the 2% to 4% range.

EXHIBIT 3.18

Historical returns on U.S. Treasury bills. (Source: © *Stocks, Bonds, Bills, and Inflation 1993 Yearbook*™, Ibbotson Associates, Chicago [annual updates by Roger G. Ibbotson and Rex A. Sinquefield]. Used by permission. All rights reserved.)

The Accumulation of Wealth

Given the rates of return indicated in Exhibits 3.16, 3.17, and 3.18, how much wealth could you have accumulated by investing in the various assets? The table in Exhibit 3.19 answers this question. We look first at accumulations over the entire 67-year period and then at shorter holding periods.

Entire Period Accumulations   Going to the bottom line, we find the accumulations over the entire 67-year period. So, for example, if you had invested $1,000 at the beginning of 1926 in the S&P 500 and then immediately reinvested all dividends as they were received, your $1,000 grew to $727,000—a rather remarkable sum! And the $2,279,000 accumulation with small company stocks seems almost unbelievable. But never underestimate the power of compounding and remember from our previous discussion how much an extra 2% return can give you. (Refer to Exhibit 3.16, and notice that the additional return small company stocks earned over the S&P 500 was 1.9%.)

   With those amazing accumulations in stocks, why would you invest anywhere else? The answer is risk. We have seen in the previous exhibits how stock returns were much more volatile from year to year than the returns on bonds, bills, and inflation. The effects of return volatility on wealth accumulation are observable if we look at shorter holding periods.

Accumulations over Shorter Periods   Exhibit 3.19 shows six 10-year holding periods and the 7-year period ending in 1992. Accumulations over these shorter periods show clearly that the road to riches in stocks had a few pitfalls along the way. For example, your $1,000 invested in 1926 in small com-

EXHIBIT 3.19

Accumulation of wealth: End-of-period wealth from $1,000 invested at the beginning of each period indicated

Period	Big Company Stocks (S&P 500)	Small Company Stocks	Corporate Bonds	U.S. Treasury Bonds	U.S. Treasury Bills	Inflation
1926–35	$ 1,774	$ 1,030	$ 1,986	$ 1,629	$ 1,219	$ 768
1936–45	2,240	5,146	1,480	1,553	1,020	1,318
1946–55	4,685	2,917	1,207	1,138	1,116	1,480
1956–65	2,865	4,152	1,293	1,207	1,318	1,184
1966–75	1,384	1,480	1,424	1,344	1,724	1,741
1976–85	3,806	11,623	2,547	2,367	2,367	1,967
1986–92	2,612	1,840	2,156	2,142	1,524	1,298
1926–92	727,000	2,279,000	36,000	24,000	11,400	7,900

(Source: © *Stocks, Bonds, Bills and Inflation 1993 Yearbook*™, Ibbotson Associates, Chicago [annual updates by Roger G. Ibbotson and Rex A. Sinquefield]. Used by permission. All rights reserved.)

pany stocks was worth a paltry $1,030 10 years later; had you invested in corporate bonds, you would have almost doubled your money. Also, each stock group did poorly during the inflationary decade 1966–75, when you were better off in risk-free Treasury bills.

It is somewhat interesting that each asset, except Treasury bonds, was the leader in at least one period: S&P 500 in 1946–55 and 1986–92; small company stocks in 1936–45 and 1976–85; corporate bonds in 1926–35; inflation and Treasury bills (about a tie) in 1966–75. The baton of leadership changed hands frequently.

So much for history. The important question now is what the next decade will bring. Although no one knows for sure or can even make a highly accurate guess, the evidence we have seen so far in this chapter indicates that at the very least, investors were rewarded for taking risks, and the more risk they took, the greater were their rewards. The reward did not always come immediately and often required a decade or longer to be realized. Do you have the patience and adequate cash reserves to wait? If not, be careful of investing most of your funds in stocks.

Risk Premiums

The idea that investors receive extra return for taking extra risk is expressed by the concept of a risk premium. Essentially, a risk premium is simply the difference between the return on a lower-risk investment and the return on one with higher risk. Although risk premiums can be calculated for any pair of investments, the three discussed here are used often and are particularly important.

Market risk premium: return difference between common stocks and U.S. Treasury bills

The Market Risk Premium   The **market risk premium** is defined as the difference in returns between a broad market index, such as the S&P 500, and U.S. Treasury bills. For the total period in question (67 years), this premium is 6.6%, based on geometric averages (10.3% − 3.7%). The investment implication of this premium is extremely important in framing a realistic expectation of a future return in a portfolio of common stocks. For example, if you expect the T-bill rate will average 4% in the future, you could logically expect a 10.6% return on your stock investment. Are you guaranteed to get it? Of course not—that's the essence of risk; but your expectation is not unrealistic. The market risk premium will be discussed and used in Chapters 6 and 7.

Bond maturity premium: return difference between U.S. Treasury bonds and U.S. Treasury bills

Bond Maturity Premium   Another important risk premium is the **bond maturity premium.** It is the difference in returns between long-term U.S. Treasury bonds and U.S. Treasury bills. Over the same 67 years, this premium is 1.1%, based on geometric averages (4.8% − 3.7%). This means investors received a premium for investing in long-term bonds with their greater risks. (The nature of this risk—called interest-rate risk—is explained in Chapter 4.)

Bond Default Risk Premium   The **bond default risk premium** is the difference in returns between corporate bonds and U.S. Treasury bonds. It measures the extra yield bond investors receive by investing in bonds that have default potential. U.S. Treasury bonds are assumed to be free of default risk; that is, you don't have to worry about the Treasury meeting its interest and redemption obligations. Corporate issuers present a different situation. Here, exceptionally difficult economic times could lead to possible bankruptcies and substantial defaults. Anticipating this, investors demand—and usually get—a default risk premium. For the period in question, this premium was 0.7% (5.5% − 4.8%), again using the geometric averages. This premium is discussed in greater depth in Chapter 9.

Seasonality and Anomalies in Stock Returns

Examining historical returns often uncovers interesting relations. Just as buying small stocks gives you a return advantage over buying large stocks, your return might also depend on *when* you buy stocks.

The January Effect   A number of studies have found that stock returns often are higher in January than in the other 11 months. This phenomenon is referred to as the **January effect.** For example, Ibbotson and Associates, our source for the returns we just have examined, indicate that the January effect applies to all size groupings but is particularly strong with small stocks. Indeed, Ibbotson finds that all the extra return small stocks have over large stocks occurs in January.

So, is the small-firm effect really a January effect? We can never disentangle the two because they frequently occur together. Stock market scholars have tried to find explanations for the January effect—such as investors selling in December to take tax losses and then buying back in January—but there are no conclusive findings.

The Monday Effect   Surprisingly, of the five business days in the week, only one—Monday—shows negative historical returns, which is called the **Monday effect.** For example, one study that covered daily returns from July 1962 through December 1978 showed a −0.17% average Monday return; all other days of the week were positive, with Wednesday offering the highest positive return of +0.10%. As with the January effect, explanations of the Monday effect are not completely satisfying.

The Presidential Cycle Effect   Some researchers have found relationships between stock returns and presidential cycles, called the **presidential cycle effect.** One study examined returns from 1947, halfway through the Roosevelt-Truman administration, through 1992, George Bush's last year in office. Surprisingly, the average return for the two parties was almost equal—13.4% for the Democrats and 13.3% for the Republicans. However, when

Bond default risk premium: return difference between corporate bonds and U.S. Treasury bonds

January effect: tendency of stock returns to be higher in January than in the other 11 months

Monday effect: tendency for stock returns to be lower on Mondays than on the other four days of the week

Presidential cycle effect: relation between stock returns and Democratic and Republican years of administration returns are examined by year in office, some differences are apparent. For example, returns in the second year in office for Democrats average only 4.9%; the first year for Republicans is even worse, with an average of 3.4%. Each party enjoys a robust third year—19.0% for Democrats and 21.9% for Republicans—while the fourth year for each comes close to their long-term averages.

Market Anomalies   An anomaly refers to a phenomenon that shouldn't exist but does; in other words, it defies explanation. A number of such unexplainable relationships exist with respect to stock returns. For example, if the winner of the annual Super Bowl is a member of the old NFL, the stock market increases; when an old AFL team wins, the market sinks. At various times, stock returns have been correlated to winning streaks of the New York Mets and the length of women's skirts. Before you fall for any anomalies, remember that although they may show strong correlation with stock returns, if you searched long enough for other oddities, you probably would find them. Who knows: maybe the rate of ice melt at the North Pole predicts stock prices with amazing accuracy. Beware of such spurious correlations because they often end abruptly.

UNDERSTANDING MARKET INDEXES

Ask someone how the market did yesterday and the answer will probably refer to one of the more popular market indexes, most likely the Dow Jones Industrial Average (DJIA), shown in Exhibit 2.10 in Chapter 2. But does the DJIA represent the overall market? And how is it calculated? The answers are provided below, for both the DJIA and the S&P 500.

The DJIA

DJIA: Dow Jones Industrial Index, a price-weighted index of 30 stocks

The **DJIA** is a price-weighted index; in other words, its value is an average of stock prices. Specifically, it is an average of the prices of 30 industrial stocks. The series has been in existence since 1884; however, it has included 30 stocks only since 1928. And it hasn't consisted of the same 30; some companies have been eliminated and others added. An interesting case is IBM: it was added to the list in 1932 but then replaced in 1939 by American Telephone and Telegraph. It reappeared in 1979 as it and Merck & Co. replaced Chrysler and Esmark.

Computing the DJIA would be a simple task if it were not for the fact that companies often have stock splits or declare stock dividends, each of which increases the number of shares outstanding. This in turn leads to price decreases that bias the average unless they are taken into account. Consider the simple example on page 98 that deals with only three stocks.

BOX 3.3   GETTING AN INVESTMENT EDGE

Thinking of Investing in an Index: Which One and How?

Disappointed with their own security-selection skills and those of so-called experts, many investors have thrown in the towel and turned to index investing. If this seems a bit cowardly, understand that many of the towel-throwers are large institutions, such as pension funds. Some estimates have shown that more than $200 billion is now invested in indexes. Although index investing sounds simple, some homework is needed to avoid being in the wrong index.

To begin with, you should know that the most common form of index investing is through mutual funds; so, you need to contact the larger mutual fund families and ask which index funds they offer. The leader in index investing clearly is the Vanguard Group (call 1-800-662-7447), which offers 11 index funds covering a wide range of investment opportunities in stocks and bonds, both U.S. and foreign. Index investing is relatively simple (no high-paid professional managers), which saves money for index funds, which in turn usually leads to higher yields to investors. If you want to avoid mutual funds, you can buy the S&P 500 Index through trust certificates (called "spiders") that trade on the American Stock Exchange. Your broker buys these certificates as you would buy any other shares of stock.

Also, pay close attention to the particular index the fund is tracking because all indexes are not the same. There can be differences even within a category. Suppose you are interested in small companies; which index is appropriate? For example, Vanguard offers the Extended Market Fund that tracks the Wilshire 4500 Index and the Small Capitalization Fund that tracks the Russell 2000 Index. If you really want small companies, then the Small Capitalization Fund is the better choice. The Extended Market Fund is more of a "mid-cap" fund (mid-cap refers to stocks with an aggregate market value of $400 million to $5 billion). Over long periods, the yield differences may not be large, but they can be significant over short periods. For example, from January 1, 1993, through July 27, 1993, the Extended Market Fund had a return of 5.5%, while the Small Capitalization Fund's return was 7.2%, about 30% better.

Finally, granted that index investing is easy, but is it worth it? Considerable evidence suggests that it is. After allowing for commissions, loads, and other costs, the returns on index funds often exceed the returns on professionally managed funds with similar investment goals. It's nice to know that the simple investment life might also be the most profitable.

	Day 1		**Day 2**	
Stock	Price	No. Shares	Price	No. Shares
A	$10	1,000	$10	1,000
B	20	1,000	10	2,000
C	30	2,000	30	2,000
	Total = $60		Total = $50	
	Divisor = 3		Divisor = ?	
	Average price = $20		Average price = $20	
			? = $50/$20 = 2.5	

Stocks A, B, and C have prices of $10, $20, and $30, respectively, on Day 1. On Day 2, Stock B splits two for one, increasing its total shares outstanding to 2,000 and reducing its price to $10 a share. In effect, then, its price was unchanged from Day 1, as were Stocks A and B. However, the aggregate value of the three stocks is only $50. Clearly, if we divided by three we would get an average price of $16.67, indicating a drop in the index. But the drop is due solely to the stock split. A new divisor is needed—one that would give an average price equal to what it would have been had the split not taken place. You must solve for this divisor, and in the example, it is 2.5.

Over the years, the DJIA has been adjusted often for stock splits and stock dividends. This is reflected in the current low value of its divisor. In early 1994, this value was 0.4442, which is substantially less than 30 (the beginning number).

Problems with the DJIA   Although the DJIA is the most often watched barometer of the overall market, it does have limitations. First, it is heavily influenced by stocks with high prices. In the example above, if each stock increased by the same percentage amount, Stock C's influence on the index would be three times greater than Stock A's or B's (after the split). Second, because it consists of only 30 issues, you might question whether this is a large enough sample to be representative of the entire stock market. From a statistical point of view, it probably is not. Third, apart from the small size, the sample is clearly biased in favor of large, blue-chip stocks because the 30 companies are among the largest in the world. The DJIA is considered a fair indicator of this market segment but not necessarily of the entire market.

Other Dow Jones Averages   In addition to the DJIA, Dow Jones compiles a transportation average consisting of 20 stocks and a utility average consisting of 15 stocks. The averages are calculated in an identical manner to the DJIA, so the same criticisms apply to them. One big advantage with all three is that they are reported, both graphically and numerically, in each issue of *The Wall Street Journal*. This high visibility makes them convenient.

The S&P 500 Stock Index

The **S&P 500** differs from the DJIA in several important ways. First, it is a value-weighted, rather than price-weighted, index. This means the index considers not only the price of a stock but the number of shares outstanding as well. Consider the example below.

S&P 500: value-weighted index of 500 stocks compiled by the Standard and Poor's Corporation

	Day 1			Day 2		
Stock	No. Shares	Price	Market Value	No. Shares	Price	Market Value
A	1,000	$10	$10,000	1,000	$ 9	$ 9,000
B	1,000	20	20,000	2,000	10	20,000
C	2,000	30	60,000	2,000	33	66,000
Totals			$90,000			$95,000

Day 1 = base period = $90,000/$90,000 = 1.000
Day 2 index value = $95,000/$90,000 = 1.056

As you see, a value-weighted index is based on the aggregate market value of the stock—that is, price times number of shares. An obvious advantage to this index is that stock splits and stock dividends do not affect the index value. Stock *B's* split had no influence on the Day 2 value of the index because the larger number of shares were multiplied by the lower price. (Price was assumed to be unchanged to simplify the example.) Perhaps a disadvantage to this index is that large capitalization stocks—those with a large number of shares outstanding—heavily influence the index value. In the example above, the index is up 5.6% on the strength of the 10% increase in Stock *C's* price. *A's* price decline and *B's* unchanged price exert less influence on the index value because of their fewer shares outstanding.

The S&P 500 consists of four separate indexes: the 400 industrials, the 40 utilities, the 20 transportation, and the 40 financial. Each index is value-weighted, as illustrated above. The base period is 1941–43, and the base number was arbitrarily set at 10. As of late March 1993, the value of the S&P 500 was about 448, which means the index has increased almost 45-fold since the base period.

Although the S&P 500 is a more comprehensive index than the Dow Jones averages, it is heavily influenced by the large companies it includes. As a result, it, too, does not reasonably measure changes in smaller capitalization stocks.

Other Indexes

There are numerous other indexes reported regularly. We will mention just a few. The Wilshire 5000 Equity Index is published by Wilshire Associates, Inc. in Santa Monica, California. It includes all stocks on the NYSE and the American Stock Exchange (Amex), plus active over-the-counter (OTC)

issues—some 5,000 stocks in all. It is a value-weighted series and is reported each week in *Barron's* and in each issue of *Forbes*.

Both the NYSE and the Amex have value-weighted indexes that include all issues traded on their respective boards. The NASDAQ Series consists of six separate indexes (all value-weighted) covering industrials, banks, insurance, other financial firms, transportation, and utilities, and a composite index of the six categories. In total, about 2,400 OTC stocks are reported daily. Each issue of *The Wall Street Journal* and *Investor's Business Daily* reports the NYSE, Amex, and OTC (industrials, insurance, banks, and composite) indexes as well as many other indexes.

Value Line Index: index of 1,700 large and small companies followed by the *Value Line Investment Survey*

Another widely watched index is the **Value Line Index.** Its popularity arises from the popularity of the *Value Line Investment Survey*. The Value Line Index is an equally weighted geometric average of the returns of 1,700 companies. The index is broad-based in the sense that it includes both large and relatively small firms.

SUMMARY

Investment profitability often is measured with an HPR, which takes into consideration current return items (interest, dividends, and others) and price appreciation (or depreciation). If HPRs are calculated for a number of periods, an average HPR value can be determined using an arithmetic average or a geometric average. The latter measurement is the more accurate because the arithmetic average can be biased to favor more volatile investments.

Most investment analysis requires understanding of time-value-of-money concepts. The future value of a single payment and the future value of an ordinary annuity or an annuity due can be calculated using appropriate formulas, financial calculators, or tables. The present value of a single payment and the present value of an ordinary annuity or an annuity due can be calculated in a similar manner. Compounding over long periods produces substantial future values.

Historical returns on key financial assets show higher returns for stock investments than for bond investments or U.S. Treasury bills. Various risk premiums can be determined and used in selecting or evaluating investments. The market risk premium is the difference in returns between stocks and Treasury bills; the bond maturity premium is the difference in returns between Treasury bonds and Treasury bills; the bond default premium is the difference in returns between Treasury bonds and corporate bonds. Some market analysts have identified seasonal factors in historical returns. These include the January effect, the Monday effect, and the presidential cycle effect. There also are market anomalies, such as the Super Bowl effect. Many investors follow the market by watching a market index. Although the most popular index is the DJIA, it is rather narrow in scope and may not be representative of the overall market. Accordingly, other indexes are used, such as the S&P 500, the Wilshire 5000, and those for the NYSE, Amex, and OTC markets.

KEY TERMS
(listed in order
of appearance)

holding period return
current return
future return
arithmetic average
geometric average
future value
annuity
ordinary annuity
annuity due
present value

market risk premium
bond maturity premium
bond default risk premium
January effect
Monday effect
presidential cycle effect
DJIA
S&P 500
Value Line Index

REVIEW
QUESTIONS

1. Explain a holding period return and show how it is calculated. Also, indicate how commissions should be treated.
2. Identify and explain sources of current return. Explain future return.
3. What is the difference between an arithmetic mean and a geometric mean? Use the following data on XYZ stock in discussing your answer: 1993 price = $25; 1994 price = $50; 1995 price = $25. (Calculate each mean return for the years 1994 and 1995.)
4. Indicate what is meant by a future value of a single payment and indicate how one is determined.
5. Define an annuity. Explain the difference between an ordinary annuity and an annuity due.
6. Explain how the future value of an ordinary annuity can be determined.
7. Explain the concept of a present value and indicate how a present value of a single payment is determined.
8. Explain how the present value of an ordinary annuity can be determined.
9. Indicate how compounding differs from discounting.
10. At least four factors are involved in every time-value-of-money problem, and there may be a fifth. Indicate the five factors.
11. Explain the "power" of a small additional yield and a few extra years. Consider 8% and 10%, and 30 and 40 years.
12. Discuss historical returns on key financial assets and the accumulation of wealth with each.
13. Explain the following terms and provide amounts for each based on historical return data: (a) the market risk premium, (b) the bond maturity premium, and (c) the bond default risk premium.
14. Explain if the following strategies may be effective: (a) buying stocks on December 31, (b) buying stocks near the close of trading on Friday, and (c) buying stocks at the beginning of the first year of a Republican administration and the beginning of the second year of a Democratic administration.
15. Explain a stock market anomaly, giving an example of one.
16. Answer the following questions concerning the DJIA: (a) How many stocks are in it? (b) Is it price-weighted or value-weighted? (c) What factor causes changes in its divisor? (d) Has it included the same companies since its inception? Briefly explain two of its limitations.
17. (a) In what important ways does the S&P 500 differ from the DJIA? (b) What is a possible disadvantage with the S&P 500?

1. Ed Mason bought 100 shares of Cindy's at 5½ a year ago. Over the year, he received a dividend of $0.20 a share and the stock closed recently at 7¼.
    a. Calculate Ed's HPR for the year.
    b. Suppose Ed paid commissions of $20 to buy the stock and would pay $25 if he were to sell it now. Calculate the new HPR, assuming Ed sells the 100 shares.

2. Juanita Perez is trying to evaluate an investment she made. She paid $20 for a share of stock two years ago. Today its price is $24, but it has varied considerably while Juanita held it. At the end of the first year, for example, it was $16. It also paid a $1.00 dividend each year and Juanita has just received the second year's dividend.
    Calculate Juanita's average rate of return in the stock, using both the arithmetic and the geometric average. Discuss your results with Juanita.

3. You recently have reviewed the performance of one of your stocks since you purchased 200 shares of it four years ago at $50 a share. Here is your information:

Year	Price One Year Later	Dividends Per Share
1	$45.00	$2.00
2	70.00	3.00
3	53.00	1.00
4	60.00	1.00

    Calculate the arithmetic and geometric average returns on your investment.

4. Determine the following future values:
    a. $100 invested at 15% for 20 years.
    b. $200 invested at the end of each of the next 10 years at 9%.
    c. $450 invested at the beginning of each of the next 5 years at 8%.

5. Determine the following present values:
    a. $10,000 received at the end of 13 years; $i = 10\%$.
    b. $800 received at the end of each of the next 11 years; $i = 14\%$.
    c. $300 received at the beginning of each of the next 4 years; $i = 12\%$.

6. Determine the following rates of return:
    a. $4,000 invested today that grows to $6,000 in 8 years.
    b. $1,800 invested at the end of each of the next 12 years that accumulates to $40,000.
    c. $7,000 invested in an annuity contract today that pays $1,400 at the end of each of the next 7 years.

7. Determine the following ordinary annuity amounts:
    a. to accumulate $20,000 in 8 years with a rate of 6%.
    b. for an annuity payout contract that requires a $13,000 immediate outlay and guarantees a rate of 4% annually.

8. Josey Wells is considering making an investment in a tax shelter. The investment requires a cash payment of $5,000 today, and the shelter promoter is sure Josey will double her money in about five years. What is Josey's rate of return on the investment? Construct a time line to help you solve this problem.

9. You have a portfolio consisting of 300 shares of X, 200 shares of Y, and 100 shares of Z; their current market prices are $12, $15, and $18, respectively. Suppose their prices next week are $10, $17, and $21, respectively. Then, calculate the percentage of increase or decrease in the index.

a. Construct a price-weighted index, showing the current index value and the value next week.
b. Construct a value-weighted index and show index values for the two points in time.
c. Which index gives you the best measurement of your portfolio's performance for the week? Discuss, using your answers from parts *a* and *b*.
d. Suppose one of the stocks split during the week. Would each index require an adjustment to reflect the split? Explain.

10. *(Student Project)* You have recently been hired as a marketing specialist of a major commercial bank. The bank is attempting to increase deposits in its tax sheltering devices, such as IRAs. It also wants to gain better penetration in the young-depositor market segment. Prepare a promotional piece that might appeal in this situation. Be sure to include an example, or examples.

   As a side task, management wants you to consider how it might promote a new certificate of deposit it is introducing, called the "Super CD." It guarantees a rate two percentage points higher than the bank's rate on savings accounts for as long as the depositor holds the CD. Management is concerned that potential customers will not get excited about only two percentage points. They want you to write a promotional piece that really sells the product.

11. *(Student Project)* Call or visit a commercial bank or savings and loan and ask if they have any literature on IRAs, Keoghs, or other tax sheltering devices. See if time-value-of-money concepts are covered. If they are, analyze them.

CASE ANALYSES

Phil and Janet Hines are awaiting the birth of their first child. Neither Phil nor Janet carries life insurance, but they are concerned now that an untimely death of either or both of them would create economic hardships in supporting the child. Consequently, they are considering buying two whole life insurance policies (one for each) that pay $200,000 to a beneficiary in the event of Phil's or Janet's death ($400,000 if both die). Combined premiums will be $5,000 annually, beginning in one year.

**3.1
The Hineses
Evaluate Life
Insurance
Policies**

Although the Hineses recognize the need for life insurance, they are concerned over its relatively high cost. An insurance agent has told them the policies they are considering are whole life policies, which accumulate cash value. This means the Hineses could cash in the policies in the future if they no longer wanted insurance. The agent further explained that rather than cashing in, the Hineses could choose to convert the policies to annuity contracts that would provide them with retirement income. Moreover, he indicated life insurance investment has an edge over other investments insofar as cash value accumulates on a tax-deferred basis. To illustrate his points, the agent provides the following information, which is based on an assumption that both policies would be carried for 30 years and then either cashed in or converted to annuity contracts.

Questions

1. Guaranteed cash value—$332,194 (lump sum).
2. Annuity contracts with guaranteed payments for 10 years—$47,297 (annually) with payments beginning one year after the policy conversion.

    a. Determine the implicit rate of return on the policies.
    b. Determine the implicit rate of return on the annuity contracts.
    c. Suppose the Hineses feel inflation will average 4% annually over the next 30 years. Do you regard the policies as attractive investments? Discuss, indicating the real rate of return on the policies.
    d. Would you recommend the insurance policies? Explain.

3.2 Amy Burke Plans for College

Amy Burke is an ambitious young lady. Although she just turned 10 years of age, she has a paper route and works at other odd jobs. She plans to save from the income she earns to help pay her college costs in the future, but she may need help from her parents. Amy's dad has explained that one year in college currently costs about $8,000 at the university Amy is considering, but he expects this cost to increase 7% a year indefinitely in the future. He also explained that he and Amy's mom invested $5,000 in a College-Bound Savings Program at Amy's birth. This program guarantees an 8% annual rate for 18 years. Although Amy expects to earn $3,000 a year for the next 8 years, she wonders if that will be sufficient to meet 4 years of college costs.

Questions

    a. Determine each year's college cost, assuming Amy's dad's inflation estimate is correct and that Amy starts college in 8 years.
    b. Determine how much will be available from her parents' savings program when Amy starts college.
    c. Regardless of your answer to question *a*, assume that Amy wants to accumulate $54,980 by the beginning of the first year. After paying first-year costs, she will invest the remainder to earn 7%, thereby assuring adequate funds for the 3 remaining years. Now, considering your response to question *b*, how much must Amy save each year, assuming the savings are invested at the end of each year in a vehicle that earns 10%? Will her annual earnings of $3,000 be sufficient? Explain.
    d. Do you believe Amy can earn a rate as high as 10% on her savings? Explain.

HELPFUL READING

Cohen, Laurie P. "That Frightening Month Is Here Again." *The Wall Street Journal,* October 5, 1992, p. C1.

Goodman, Jordan E. "Building Your Assets on Autopilot." *Money,* February 1993, pp. 82–83.

Granito, Barbara Donnelly. "For Investing in Small Stocks, No Single Index Will Do." *The Wall Street Journal,* March 17, 1993, p. C1.

Siegel, Jeremy J. "The Equity Premium: Stock and Bond Returns Since 1802." *Financial Analysts Journal*, January-February 1992, pp. 28–38.

Smith, Keith V. "The Stock Market Doesn't Mind Democrats." *The Wall Street Journal*, July 20, 1992, p. C1.

Stovall, Robert H. "Forecasting Stock Market Performance via the Presidential Cycle." *Financial Analysts Journal*, May-June 1992, pp. 5–8.

CHAPTER FOUR

Measuring Investment Risk

After you finish this chapter, you will be able to:

- calculate and understand risk statistics: the variance, standard deviation, and coefficient of variation.

- see historical risk statistics on key financial assets.

- understand the nature of diversification and how it reduces investment risk.

- recognize that asset correlations affect portfolio risk, and you will see historical correlations among key financial assets.

- calculate a beta value and understand its use in designing a portfolio.

- identify the major sources of investment risk.

Most people have a general idea of risk but usually find the concept difficult to explain in concrete terms. We often think of risk as a possibility of something bad happening to us. Taking a difficult course, such as investments, is risky because your grade may not be as high as you could earn in an easier course. Betting on a sporting event is risky because there is a good chance of picking a loser. But risk must have a bright side along with the gloomy one, or we would always take Basket Weaving 101 and never place a bet. As we will see in this chapter, investment risk is most properly understood when it is expressed in statistical terms that consider the entire range of an investment's possible returns. Moreover, risk often depends on the number of individual assets held. In general, you can reduce it by holding a reasonably diversified portfolio of individual assets. To understand how a portfolio reduces risk, we must begin by looking at the risk of individual assets.

INDIVIDUAL ASSET RISK

You can measure an investment's risk with several commonly used statistics: the *variance,* the *standard deviation,* and the *coefficient of variation.* To determine these statistics, you must first calculate an investment's *expected return.* If your investment is limited to a single asset, your consideration of risk does not have to extend beyond that asset's risk statistics. This is the simplest case and a good place to begin our discussion.

The Expected Return

Expected return: investment's weighted average return, which considers payoffs and probabilities

An investment's **expected return ($\bar{R}$)** is a weighted average return determined by multiplying each of its possible returns by the probability of each return occurring. Let's consider an example. Suppose you are planning a relatively safe investment in a bank savings account currently paying 8%. You plan to hold the investment one year, but you aren't sure that your annual return will actually be 8% because market interest rates could increase or decrease during the year, and your account is the kind that adjusts its interest to market rates. To keep things simple, if rates increase, you believe your rate for the year will average 10%; if rates decrease, it will average 6%. As an alternative to this investment, you are also considering investing in a long-term bond. It currently yields 10%, but if interest rates change, so will its market price and so will your holding period return for the year. If rates rise, the bond's price will fall, and your return will fall to zero; if rates fall, the bond's price will rise, and your return jumps to 20%. (Bond prices and market interest rates are inversely related. We'll discuss this relationship in greater depth in Chapter 9.)

Before you can choose between the two investments, you must have some idea about market rates of interest in the upcoming year. Suppose your strongest feeling is that rates will be unchanged, but you believe there is a slightly better chance they will fall rather than rise. You could express these feelings in terms of probability estimates, such as you think there is a 50% chance for unchanged rates, a 30% chance for a fall, and a 20% chance for a rise. With this information, along with the possible returns indicated above, we can calculate each investment's expected return. This is done in Exhibit 4.1, which indicates an expected return of 7.8% for the savings account and 11.0% for the bond.

Dispersion of Returns

In statistics, an average is a measurement of central tendency—that is, how values of the observed events cluster together. Along with averages, we often calculate dispersion statistics—the variance, standard deviation, and coefficient of variation—which measure how the observed values are spread out. These statistics indicate investment risk.

The Variance   Exhibit 4.2 shows how each dispersion statistic is calculated. You start with the **variance** (σ^2). To calculate it, first subtract the expected return from each possible return (column 2); square the answer (column 3); then multiply this number by the probability of the actual return (in column 1) occurring; finally, add the numbers in column 4 and the sum is the variance. As Exhibit 4.2 shows, the wider the range of possible returns and/or the greater the spread of probability estimates, the larger will be the value of the variance. In the reverse case, the variance is smaller. An investment with a zero variance, for example, has only one possible return. It's a sure thing, and there is no risk. Any number other than zero (they all will be positive) means some degree of risk, with larger values meaning greater risk. In this example, the bond is clearly the riskier investment because its variance is 49.0 versus 1.96 for the savings account.

Variance: measurement of dispersion that reflects differences between possible returns and the expected return

EXHIBIT 4.1
Calculating an expected return ($\bar{R}$)

| | Percentage Returns If Market Interest Rates: | | | |
	Rise	Stay the Same	Fall	Expected Returns ($\bar{R}$)*
Probability of Event Occurring	.2	.5	.3	
Investment Alternatives:				
Savings Account	10	8	6	(.2 × 10) + (.5 × 8) + (.3 × 6) = 7.8
Long-Term Bond	0	10	20	(.2 × 0) + (.5 × 10) + (.3 × 20) = 11.0

*Letting R_1 = a possible return and Pr_1 = the probability of the return occurring, then the expected return ($\bar{R}$) is calculated:
$$\bar{R} = (R_1 \cdot Pr_1) + (R_2 \cdot Pr_2) + \ldots + (R_n \cdot Pr_n)$$

EXHIBIT 4.2
Calculating risk mea-
surements: The vari-
ance (σ^2), standard
deviation (σ), and coefficient of variation (C)

(1) Possible Returns R_1	(2) $(R_1 - \bar{R})$	(3) $(R_1 - \bar{R})^2$	(4) $(R_1 - \bar{R})^2 \times Pr$
Savings Account:			
10	$10 - 7.8 =$ 2.2	4.84	$4.84 \times .2 = 0.968$
8	$8 - 7.8 =$ 0.2	0.04	$0.04 \times .5 = 0.020$
6	$6 - 7.8 = -1.8$	3.24	$3.24 \times .3 = \underline{0.972}$
			$\sigma^2 = 1.960$
			$\sigma = \sqrt{\sigma^2} = 1.400$
			$C = 1.400/7.8 = 0.180$
Bond:			
0	$0 - 11.0 = -11.0$	121.0	$121.0 \times .2 = 24.200$
10	$10 - 11.0 = - 1.0$	1.0	$1.0 \times .5 =$ 0.500
20	$20 - 11.0 =$ 9.0	81.0	$81.0 \times .3 = \underline{24.300}$
			$\sigma^2 = 49.000$
			$\sigma = \sqrt{\sigma^2} =$ 7.000
			$C = 7.0/11.0 =$ 0.640

Standard deviation:
square root of the vari-
ance

The Standard Deviation   An often-used statistic is the **standard deviation** (σ), which is simply the square root of the variance. The bond's standard
deviation is 7.0 and the savings account's is 1.4. By itself, the standard deviation gives no greater information than does the variance. It is used, however,
in analytical statistics to form probability estimates about future events
occurring. The standard deviation is important to us because we need it to
find the coefficient of variation.

Coefficient of variation:
measurement of risk rel-
ative to return, calculated as standard devia-
tion/expected return

The Coefficient of Variation   The **coefficient of variation (C)** is simply
the ratio of the standard deviation to the expected return $(\sigma/\bar{R})$. It is called a
risk-to-reward ratio because it shows the amount of risk per unit of return.
The savings account, for example, has 0.18% risk per 1.0% of return, while
the bond has 0.64% risk per 1.0% of return. The bond is riskier not only in
absolute terms, but also in relative terms—that is, risk relative to return.

The coefficient of variation is the better risk statistic to use when you
compare investments with different expected returns. The investment with
the higher expected return might also show a higher variance and standard
deviation. Does this mean it is riskier? Not necessarily—at least not in relation to expected return.

Historical Risk Statistics on Key Financial Assets

In Chapter 3, we saw rates of return on important financial assets: common
stocks, long-term bonds, and U.S. Treasury bills. Using the risk statistics we

EXHIBIT 4.3
Risk measurements on
key financial assets:
1926–92

Asset	Arithmetic Mean Return	Standard Deviation of Returns	Coefficient of Variation
Common stocks:			
S&P 500`	12.4	20.6	1.66
Small company	17.6	35.0	2.00
Long-term bonds:			
Corporates	5.8	8.5	1.47
U.S. Treasuries	5.2	8.6	1.65
Short-term:			
Treasury bills	3.8	3.3	0.87
CPI	3.2	4.7	1.47

SOURCE: © *Stocks, Bonds, Bills, and Inflation 1993 Yearbook*™, Ibbotson Associates, Chicago (annual updates by Roger G. Ibbotson and Rex A. Sinquefield). Used by permission. All rights reserved.

have just learned, we can turn our attention to the degree of risk an investor faced in holding these assets. Exhibit 4.3 shows the standard deviation and coefficient of variation for each asset and the Consumer Price Index (CPI). The overall results are not surprising: the high-yielding common stocks have the most risk and the low-yielding Treasury bills have the least. We expect return and risk to go together; that is, the higher the asset's return, the greater its risk.

Somewhat surprising perhaps is the poor performance of Treasury bonds relative to corporate bonds. As you see, Treasuries were slightly riskier than corporates, based on their standard deviation values, and they had a somewhat larger coefficient of variation. In retrospect, most investors probably would have preferred the corporates with their extra return.

PORTFOLIO RISK

Suppose you could hold only one asset: would you select the investment with the highest return, or the one with the least risk? You must choose one or the other. In the previous example, you must pick either the bond with its expected return of 11% and high risk, or the savings account with its expected 7.8% return and low risk. Other investment alternatives often present different return-and-risk characteristics. Some may represent better alternatives than the two being considered; that is, they might offer a higher return with the same or less risk. If such a situation exists, we say the one asset *dominates* the other, and so we would drop the inferior asset and consider only the better one. But even after we make these eliminations, we are left with individual assets and their unique risk characteristics.

Fortunately, we are free to hold as many specific assets as we choose. When we combine assets, we create a portfolio with its own return-and-risk

BOX 4.1   INVESTMENT INSIGHTS

Do Investors Make Adequate Risk-Return Assessments?

Do you make investment decisions as most people do? And do you and other investors deal with risk and return adequately in selecting investments? How about a short quiz before we tackle these questions? Respond to them as you would *actually* make choices, not as you think you ought to make them.

1. You have just won $3,000 in a contest and are given two choices. Which will you take?
    a. Keep the $3,000.
    b. Exchange the $3,000 for an 80% chance to win $4,000.
2. You are invited to participate in a game of chance involving the flip of a fair coin. You must play heads, and each time a head appears, you win $150; if a tail appears, you must pay $100. You will:
    a. not play the game.
    b. play the game.
3. Which lottery ticket would you rather have:
    a. one with a 2% chance of winning $3,000?
    b. one with a 1% chance of winning $6,000?
4. Given a choice, which do you prefer:
    a. a sure loss of $3,000?
    b. an 80% chance of losing $4,000 and a 20% chance of losing nothing?

If you chose response a to questions 1 and 2, you are in the company of most respondents. You realize your choices are not the better ones, mathematically speaking; nevertheless, you are unwilling to take the risk alternatives for the compensations indicated. Also, did you take alternative b to question 4? Most people do, which is indeed interesting because it doesn't fit with their answers to questions 1 and 2. In question 4, they take the risk alternative even though it is likely to be the cost-

lier one. Finally, if you picked b to question 3, you are with the majority. About two out of three respondents choose b even though the expected reward ($60) is the same each way.

Now that you know if you are in the majority or not, you might ask what any of this has to do with investing; surprisingly, some people believe that a lot is involved. All types of foolish investing behavior stem from our psychological quirks. Our risk aversion pushes us to accept mediocre, fairly safe returns, rather than take some risks for much better ones (questions 1 and 2). For example, we prefer IBM to a lesser-known company that might be just as safe and more profitable. Our abhorrence of losses often forces us to take bad risks when we do take them (question 4). We hold on to a disaster, hoping to recoup losses when the better choice would be to cut them by dumping it. Moreover, most of us have difficulty assessing risk and return situations unfamiliar to us (question 3) and so tend to overestimate benefits and underestimate costs. We buy stocks like Genentech because we think they will make us rich with some esoteric technology and because we have no way of reasonably assessing their potential rewards.

Now that we know what's the matter with us—psychologically—how do we break loose? The answer is simple: go against the majority. Avoid big-name companies and technology all-stars, and buy the lesser-knowns and the out-of-favor stocks. Bucking the trend could cause us emotional stress, so a better alternative might be to let computers make our investment choices. This strategy is not so far-fetched: artificial intelligence systems are already being used for that purpose.

characteristics. The important quality of a portfolio is that it can reduce investment risk without necessarily reducing expected return. It is perhaps the only sure thing investors will ever find.

Diversification

Diversification is the process of combining assets for the purpose of reducing risk. As we shall see, its effectiveness depends on two factors: how asset returns are correlated and the number of assets held.

Diversification: process of combining assets to reduce risk

How Diversification Works   We can illustrate diversification by returning to our bond and savings account example. Suppose that after you examine the risk and return characteristics of each, you find it almost impossible to make a choice. You really cannot favor one over the other. Because you aren't restricted to investing in only one, you could consider investing a portion of your total funds in each. In this situation, it might make sense to allocate half of your investment dollars to each.

You now have a new asset—the portfolio—with its own return-and-risk characteristics. Exhibit 4.4 shows how these characteristics are calculated. As you see, the portfolio offers an expected return of 9.4% and a standard deviation of 2.8%; its coefficient of variation is 0.298. Is this portfolio better than either of the individual assets? The answer depends on the investor's perspective. If we compare it with the bond, we can say that it offers a lower return but it also has substantially less risk. The investor still must choose

---

I.   Calculate Possible Portfolio Returns (R_i):

Interest Rates Rise: $R_1 = (.5 \times 10) + (.5 \times \ 0) = 5 + \ 0 = \ 5$

Interest Rates Stay
Same: $R_2 = (.5 \times \ 8) + (.5 \times 10) = 4 + \ 5 = \ 9$

Interest Rates Fall: $R_3 = (.5 \times \ 6) + (.5 \times 20) = 3 + 10 = 13$

II. Calculate Expected Portfolio Return ($\bar{R}$):

$\bar{R} = (.2 \times 5) + (.5 \times 9) + (.3 \times 13) = 1.0 + 4.5 + 3.9 = 9.4$

III. Calculate Risk Statistics (σ^2, σ, and C):

$(R_i - \bar{R})$	$(R_i - \bar{R})^2$	$(R_i - \bar{R})^2 \times \mathbf{Pr}$
−4.4	19.36	$19.36 \times .2 = 3.872$
−0.4	0.16	$0.16 \times .5 = 0.080$
3.6	12.96	$12.96 \times .3 = \underline{3.888}$
		$\sigma^2 = \overline{7.840}$
		$\sigma = \sqrt{\sigma^2} = 2.800$
		$C = 2.8/9.4 = 0.298$

EXHIBIT 4.4
Evaluating a portfolio invested evenly in a savings account and a bond

between higher return or less risk, but this portfolio might be an attractive alternative to either the bond or the savings account alone. Although we can't generalize about the investor's preference for the portfolio, we can say that it represents a third alternative. To that end, diversification was effective.

Correlated Returns and Effective Diversification   The portfolio above is an effective alternative because of the negative correlation between the bond's return and the return on the savings account. If interest rates rise, the savings account return also rises but the bond return falls, and the reverse happens when interest rates fall. Negative correlation enhances the risk-reducing power of a portfolio. In fact, if returns are perfectly negatively correlated—meaning they *always* move in opposite directions—you can arrange a portfolio to eliminate risk altogether. On the other hand, if returns are positively correlated, risk reduction is more difficult.

To see this, suppose the bond's return moved in the same direction as the return on the savings account. Adding the two returns together would compound the variations in return, rather than offset them. At the extreme, if assets are perfectly positively correlated, a portfolio will not reduce risk. Exhibit 4.5 illustrates the risk implications of holding correlated assets. The **correlation coefficient** is a statistical measurement of the degree of correlation between two variables. It ranges in value from +1.0 to −1.0. (You may want to read the first major section of Chapter 17 to review correlation analysis, although it is not necessary for an understanding of this chapter.)

Over long periods, most investment returns are either positively correlated or uncorrelated. Strong negative correlations are rare, unless you get into hedging situations. Exhibit 4.6 shows correlations among the key financial assets. As this exhibit shows, there are some negative correlations, but they are rather weak. Strong positive correlations exist between the S&P 500 and small company stocks and between corporate and Treasury bonds. Treasury bills and the CPI are moderately correlated, while all other correla-

Correlation coefficient: statistical measurement of the correlation between two variables

EXHIBIT 4.5
Correlation of asset returns and reduction of risk

If Assets Are:	Value of Correlation Coefficient Is:	Combining Assets Will:
Perfectly positively correlated	+1.0	Not reduce risk at all
Positively correlated	Between zero and +1.0	Reduce risk slightly; the lower the value, the more the reduction
Uncorrelated	0.0	Reduce risk considerably
Negatively correlated	Between zero and −1.0	Virtually eliminate risk
Perfectly negatively correlated	−1.0	Completely eliminate risk

EXHIBIT 4.6

Correlations among key financial assets: Historical correlation coefficient values

	S&P 500	Small Companies	Corporate Bonds	Treasury Bonds	Treasury Bills	CPI
S&P 500	—	+0.81	+0.22	+0.14	−0.05	−0.02
Small companies	—	—	+0.09	+0.00	−0.10	+0.04
Corporate bonds	—	—	—	+0.93	+0.22	−0.15
Treasury bonds	—	—	—	—	+0.25	−0.15
Treasury bills	—	—	—	—	—	+0.42
CPI	—	—	—	—	—	—

SOURCE: © *Stocks, Bonds, Bills, and Inflation 1993 Yearbook*™, Ibbotson Associates, Chicago (annual updates by Roger G. Ibbotson and Rex A. Sinquefield). Used by permission. All rights reserved.

tions are weak. Various portfolios of the five assets—such as one composed of the S&P 500 (or small company stocks), corporate (or Treasury) bonds, and Treasury bills—would have offered effective reduction of risk while maintaining a reasonable return.

The Number of Securities and Diversification How many securities must an investor hold to be adequately diversified? Suppose we are considering a broad universe of similar securities, such as the common stocks in the S&P 500. Suppose further we select individual stocks from the 500 in some random manner, such as by throwing darts at a page that has each of their names on it. Each stock a dart hits is then added to our portfolio. Exhibit 4.7 shows what happens to the portfolio risk as we increase the number of securities.

As you see, adding only a few securities reduces risk considerably. By the time you hold 15 to 20, you have practically eliminated all the risk that can be eliminated. This risk is called **random,** or **diversifiable, risk.** Random risk is the risk associated with a specific asset. For example, the national concern over controlling health care costs sent a shock wave through the medical care industry in 1993; so, a firm such as U.S. Surgical had its price knocked from about $120 to $26 a share. Fortunately, you can get rid of random risk through a portfolio. You cannot eliminate all risk, however. The remaining portion is the amount of risk you would have even if you held the entire 500 stocks in the index. It cannot be eliminated and is therefore called **market,** or **nondiversifiable, risk.**

The reason market risk cannot be eliminated is explained in part by the fact that the returns of most individual stocks are positively correlated, and any sample of sufficient size will include fewer negatively correlated or uncorrelated returns. Thus, combining stocks reduces but does not eliminate total risk. Because some risk remains, the only thing you can do is manage it.

Random, diversifiable risk: risk related to a specific asset; it can be eliminated through diversification

Market, nondiversifiable risk: risk that cannot be eliminated through diversification

EXHIBIT 4.7
Risk and the number of
securities in a portfolio

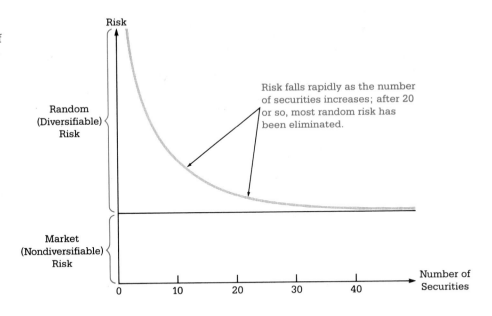

Using the Beta Concept

Portfolios can be managed to meet return-and-risk targets. Doing so involves the use of another risk statistic, called the *beta weight,* or simply *beta.* To understand how beta works, we must first understand what it means.

Beta: measurement of an asset's risk based on its return co-movements with the market's return

Calculating Beta   **Beta** is a statistic that measures changes in an asset's return in relation to changes in the return of a broad portfolio of assets. Although any broad portfolio can be considered, one that is used often is the S&P 500 stock index. Suppose you gather historical data for the annual rate of return on IBM common stock and the S&P 500 for the past 10 years. You could then plot these points, as shown in Exhibit 4.8. Next, fit a line, such as the one shown in Exhibit 4.8, through the scattering of points. (You could use a freehand method to fit the line, but regression programs on a hand calculator or a computer will give a much more accurate fit.) This line is called the asset's characteristic line, and its slope is the asset's beta value. The steeper the line's slope, the greater is beta's value, and the more shallow the slope, the less its value.

Interpreting Beta Values   Exhibit 4.8 should illustrate the idea that a beta value shows how changes in the return of a particular asset will be influenced by changes in returns for the overall market. For example, IBM's beta of 1.30 indicates that if the market's return increases or decreases by 10%, IBM's return will increase or decrease by 13% (1.3 × 10). It has 30% more variation in return than the market. A beta of, say, +0.6, on the other hand, shows a stock with only 60% of the return variation of the market. Beta, then, shows risk; the higher the positive value of beta, the greater the risk, and the

Beta measures changes in the return of a specific stock relative to changes in return of the overall market. It is an index of return sensitivity, with the overall market's index number equalling 1.0. Statistical methods are used to calculate beta. The first step is to gather return data for the stock in question and the market (the S&P 500). In this illustration, ten periods of hypothetical returns for IBM and the S&P 500 are on the left, and a graphic representation of finding beta is on the right.

IBM's Return	S&P 500 Return
15%	10%
7	4
22	15
23	18
−16	−10
12	2
−6	−5
28	20
14	12
6	−2

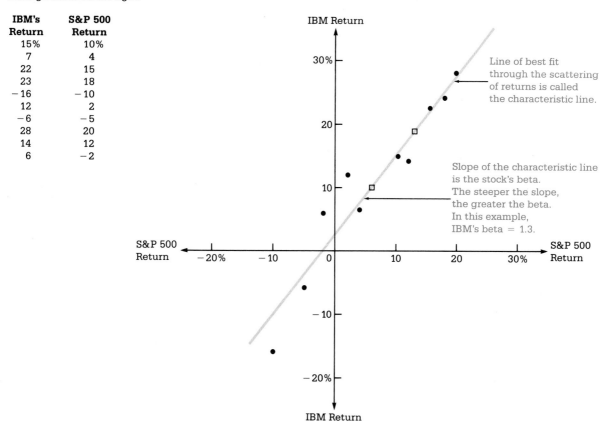

EXHIBIT 4.8
Determining a stock's beta value

lower the positive value, the less the risk. Studies indicate that most assets have positive-valued betas. Negative betas indicate assets with returns that move in opposition to the direction of the market return. Such assets are rare. A negative beta has implications similar to those of negative correlation, discussed earlier, and has the same effect in reducing portfolio risk. A summary of the investment implications of beta values appears in Exhibit 4.9, and a sample of actual betas appears in Exhibit 4.10.

Beta-Designed Portfolios   Because beta indicates nondiversifiable risk, it is useful for designing portfolios that meet individual risk dispositions. For example, if you want a conservative, low-risk portfolio, limit your investments to those with low beta values, keeping in mind that you must hold about 15

EXHIBIT 4.9
Investment implica-
tions of beta values

Beta Value	Investment Implication
Negative	This stock's return moves in the opposite direction of the market; you can reduce risk substantially by holding it along with a market portfolio. Few stocks have negative betas.
Between zero and +1.0	This stock is less risky than the market; a portfolio of low-beta stocks would be a conservative portfolio.
+1.0	The market's beta is +1.0; an individual stock with this value is as risky as the market.
Greater than +1.0	A stock with a beta greater than +1.0 is riskier than the market; a portfolio of these stocks would show considerable variation in return over time.

EXHIBIT 4.10
A sample of beta
values

Company	Major Business	Beta Value
Allegheny Power	Public utility	0.60
Albertson's	Supermarket operation	1.25
Atlantic Richfield	Oil refinery	0.70
Borden, Inc.	Food products	1.10
Bristol Myers	Home products	1.05
Consolidated Edison	Public utility	0.75
Delta Airlines	Airline operation	1.10
Federal Express	Overnight mail delivery	1.15
GTE Corporation	Communications (established company)	0.90
MCI	Communications (new company)	1.35
Merrill Lynch	Stockbrokerage	1.75
PaineWebber	Stockbrokerage	1.75

SOURCE: *Value Line Investment Survey: Summary and Index*, August 20, 1993. Copyright 1993 by Value Line Publishing, Inc. All rights reserved. Reprinted by permission.

Beta-designed portfolio approach: using beta values to design a portfolio with a targeted risk level

to 20 assets to virtually eliminate the diversifiable risk. If you want an aggressive portfolio, reverse your posture and buy 15 to 20 high-beta assets. This **beta-designed portfolio approach** is certainly quick and easy, but it does present problems.

Problems with Beta   The use of betas in constructing portfolios is somewhat limited for several reasons. To begin with, unless you intend to calculate your own betas, you must use published sources, such as the *Value Line Investment Survey*. Although these are readily available for a large number of common stocks, they are generally unavailable for other kinds of assets, such as bonds, preferred stocks, and tangibles.

Second, research has shown that beta values are sensitive to the particular index selected to represent (serve as a proxy for) the market. For example, you might derive a beta of 1.3 for IBM using the S&P 500, whereas another index, say the Wilshire 5000 Equity Index, might give a beta of 0.9. Which do you take? There is no clear answer.

A third problem with betas is they may not remain stable long enough to be useful. This is called the **nonstationarity problem.** Remember that historical data are used to calculate betas. But suppose a company's situation changes; perhaps it increases its business activities in very risky ventures. Its current or future beta would be higher than its past beta, and you would understate the company's risk with the historical beta estimate. There isn't much you can do about this problem, but it might be a mistake to exaggerate it. Many decisions must be guided by historical data and the relationships they provide. There is no reason to believe the problem with historical data is more acute in investment analysis than anywhere else, or that errors are more likely to occur with a beta approach than with another. Nothing short of perfect knowledge of the future will eliminate guesswork in decision making.

Nonstationarity problem: tendency of beta values to change over time, thereby limiting their usefulness

SOURCES OF RISK

Now that we understand risk as variations in return over time, our attention can turn to sources of such variations. One broad source consists of changes in the economic environment. Another has to do with characteristics of the security issuer. An investment's risk might also be affected by its marketability and by changes in the tax law.

Changes in the Economic Environment

We live in an extremely complex economy. Not only do many domestic factors influence an investment's return, but we now must consider international factors as well. The business cycle expands and contracts, interest rates go up and down, some industries grow rapidly while others go into decline, the dollar strengthens and weakens, and other changes take place, all of them influencing the investments we make. Change is the key element in risk. If everything would work out as expected when an investment was made, risk would be minimal. The discussion below emphasizes the important role change plays.

Economic Performance Risk **Economic performance risk** refers to return variability caused by changes in real output of the economy. Asset returns are clearly influenced by the overall performance of the national economy. A sluggish economy over a long period inevitably leads to poor investment returns. The stagnant 1970s is a good example: investors earned better

Economic performance risk: investment return variability caused by changes in real output of the economy returns in savings accounts than they did in many equity investments. If the economy is growing at a meager 1% or 2% annually, the average real return on all assets can hardly be much higher. Economic cycles also create investment risk by creating uncertainty. Even a robust economy, such as most of the 1960s or most of the 1980s, has periods of slow growth. The fear that a recession (or worse a depression) might occur often depresses stock prices; when the economic outlook improves, prices rally.

Inflation risk: loss of purchasing power if an investment's return does not keep pace with inflation

Inflation Risk **Inflation risk** has to do with a loss of purchasing power because an investment's return fails to keep pace with the rate of inflation. During periods of high inflation, this loss can be considerable. You might recall from Chapter 3 that the historical rate of inflation has been about equal to the rate of return on U.S. Treasury bills, which means the bills' real rate of return has been about zero. In recent years, the real rate of return has been high, relative to the long-run historical average. One possible explanation is that investors require a higher risk premium to compensate them for the risk of making greater errors in forecasting inflation rates, which have become both higher and more unstable.

A common theme in the 1970s and early 1980s was to hedge inflation by investing in tangible assets: real estate, jewelry, art works, and, particularly, gold and silver. Tangible assets did indeed show relatively high rates of return during this period, and some investment advisors believe you should always have a portion of your total portfolio in tangibles to serve as the inflation hedge. No doubt, people who come from countries where high inflation is a perennial problem agree with this philosophy.

Also, because inflation-adjusted rates of return are so important, you should see how they are calculated. The equation below solves for the real rate of return (r') on an investment, given its nominal rate of return (r) and the inflation rate (i).

$$r' = [(1.0 + r)/(1.0 + i)] - 1.0$$

As an example, suppose $r = 10\%$ and $i = 5\%$, then

$$r' = [(1.10)/(1.05)] - 1.0$$
$$= 1.0476 - 1.0$$
$$= 0.0476, \text{ or } 4.76\%$$

Notice that your answer is slightly less than if you merely subtracted the inflation rate from the nominal rate (5%), which frequently is done. The difference is trivial if we are talking about compounding an investment's return over a few years, but it can be substantial if the return is compounded over many years, as you might do in the area of retirement planning.

Interest-rate risk: price losses or gains associated with fixed-income securities when overall interest rates change

Interest-Rate Risk **Interest-rate risk** has to do with a loss or gain you might experience on a fixed-income security because interest rates in general rise or fall after you purchase it. Because interest rates and inflation rates often move together, interest-rate risk and inflation risk are considered separate parts of the overall problem of an inflation-biased economy.

It is important to see that interest-rate risk is associated with volatile interest rates—not simply high interest rates. Investors can adjust to high rates, as evidenced by the fact that interest rates vary considerably among different industrialized and economically stable countries of the world. In Switzerland, the rate might be 2%, while in neighboring Italy, it might be 20%. Yet the Swiss and Italian investors seem to adjust to the different interest and inflation rates in designing their investment portfolios. (Keep in mind, also, the real interest rates in each country are probably about the same.) The problem arises when rates become unstable: this instability creates the changes in market prices of debt instruments. We will examine interest-rate risk in more detail in Chapter 9.

International and Political Risks   No sooner had inflation fears begun to subside in the mid-1980s and investors had become disenchanted with tangibles, when a new diversification theme became popular: internationalize your portfolio. Almost overnight, mutual funds began increasing their offerings of international funds to give investors opportunities to play the theme. The same investor who five years earlier was buying gold at the gold store in a shopping center was now trying to invest in Korea, or Japan, or Australia.

What caused such interest? Surely a main cause was the expected decline in the value of the dollar relative to other currencies. It was thought that investments denominated in foreign currencies would benefit because of the weakening of the dollar and, conversely, strengthening of those currencies. Regardless of the eventual outcome for the fickle investor who likes to play themes, the experience does underscore the importance of considering the international situation in designing a portfolio. It appears that a portfolio with international diversification is stabler than one without, and often there is no reduction in return. This topic is covered in greater detail in Chapter 17.

There are different ways to achieve an international portfolio. One of the easiest is to invest in multinational corporations, such as IBM and Exxon. Many large companies that we typically view as American are probably more accurately seen as global because more than 50% of their sales or earnings are outside the United States. If you own a reasonable number of shares in these companies, your portfolio is already internationalized.

Political risks are part of the international investment scene and should not be ignored. The apartheid problem in South Africa, for example, has created an unstable investment environment in that country, as investors in its huge gem- and gold-mining operations will attest. Even stable European or Asian countries frequently scare American investors who hear of increasing socialism or some other "ism" that doesn't look favorably on private property. True, we seem to be enjoying a period of relative economic harmony, but that can change almost overnight. As an investor, you should think twice before you invest a substantial portion of your portfolio in, say, the Mexico Fund or the Korean Fund.

Characteristics of the Security Issuer

Investing means buying individual assets, whose soundness depends on the financial strength of the organizations who issued them. As these organizations gain or lose strength, so do their securities. We can look at the characteristics of security issuers in terms of business risk and financial risk.

Business risk: risk associated with the nature of the business activities of a security issuer

Business Risk   **Business risk** arises because of the nature of the business of the security issuer. We usually think of this risk in relation to common stock, although you can extend it to partnership interests and perhaps other kinds of investments. If you invest in a company that is in a risky industry— the drug and biotechnical industries in 1992–93, for example—you can expect to hold a risky stock. The highest form of business risk usually comes with a company that produces only one product or product line. The company may have played an active role in developing the product's technology and is now trying to market it. The single product makes the company particularly vulnerable to factors such as a slackening of demand, the introduction of a cheaper or better competitive product, or poor inventory management. Diversification is essential if you intend to invest in such companies and want to avoid excessive risk. If you think genetic engineering is the coming thing, for example, try to find at least five or six companies that are in the industry and divide the amount you want to invest in genetic engineering among them, rather than putting all of it in one company.

Financial risk: risk that arises when a business firm finances itself with large amounts of debt

Financial Risk   A security issuer can also increase the amount of risk its investors experience by financing itself with large amounts of borrowing. This **financial risk** is brought about by the company's level of debt obligations. Creditors rank before stockholders in both interest payments and distributions in liquidation. The larger the creditors' position, the less stockholders can expect. Moreover, debt requires the regular payment of interest, which can weaken the company's cash flow and make it difficult to operate the business. Even a company with a well-diversified product line can expose its owners to a high level of risk through excessive borrowing. And if the single-product company borrows heavily, you have about as risky an investment as you might find.

There is a reason business firms use debt in their financing efforts, and you as a shareholder should be aware of it. All things considered, the use of debt—sometimes called leverage—often increases a company's earnings per share of common stock. If the company can earn more on its investments than it must pay in interest to finance those investments, then it will enhance earnings per share by investing. But the enhanced earnings per share depend on a certain level of sales and operating income. If either of these falls to lower levels, the impact on earnings per share is disastrous; naturally, if either goes above the targets, the impact is beneficial. In either case, the volatility of earnings per share is increased, and that is the cause of the added risks.

Other Sources of Risk

With so many kinds of investments available, you can also find many sources of risk. Two other sources that are fairly common are marketability risk and the risk from a changing tax law.

Marketability Risk Some investments prove to be difficult to sell after they are purchased. This difficulty commonly occurs with many tangible investments, but it can also be the case for some stocks, bonds, and, particularly, limited partnership interests. **Marketability risk** arises when there is no effective secondary market for an investment. In an effective market, the investment can not only be sold, but it can also be sold at a competitively determined price and without paying excessive selling costs. There may always be a buyer for the Salvador Dalí print you just bought, but perhaps only at a price the buyer sets and at a commission of 20% of the sale.

Marketability risk: risk that arises when there is no secondary market for an investment

Some stocks and bonds are so thinly traded that you should concern yourself with their marketability risk. Even if you see the stock listed in *The Wall Street Journal* each day, do not assume you will be able to sell it without difficulty. Moreover, you may pay a sizeable difference in the bid-ask spread when you trade, which further reduces your potential investment profit. This, too, should be looked on as a cost of poor marketability.

Risks from a Changing Tax Law A tax law that is in a constant state of flux also poses investment risk. It seems that each year the president and Congress give us a tax reform package that changes the after-tax returns on many investments. Almost immediately, the market prices of these investments change in response to an improved or worsened return picture. A dramatic example is the situation with tax-free securities, such as municipal bonds. Their attraction is based directly on their tax advantage, which in turn reflects the investor's marginal tax rate. If that rate is lowered, for example, municipal bonds lose some of their advantage over taxable issues. This leads to lower market prices on the instruments until their market yields are again competitive with taxable issues. An investor can do little to diversify against the risks of a changing tax law without knowing in advance how the law will be changed. Will capital gains be favored or disfavored this year? Will depreciation be allowed at a rapid or slow rate? No one knows the answers to such questions. Perhaps the only diversification strategy is to hold an array of investment alternatives so that any unfavorable impacts on one type of investment may be offset by favorable impacts on another. To be sure, it's a guessing game—a game that investors are finding less fun to play as tax laws change with increasing frequency.

Risk and Time: Are They Related?

As we discussed earlier in this chapter, adding securities to a portfolio reduces risk and does not necessarily reduce return. Most investors accept this rule, even though they may not adhere to it as much as they should. But what about the length of time an asset is held? Does it have any relationship to risk? Can you, for example, reduce risk by adding more years to your holding period, just as you reduce portfolio risk by adding more securities to a portfolio? Is there **time diversification** as well as security diversification?

Time diversification: decline in risk associated with holding investments for longer periods

The question is intriguing, and some researchers have been looking into it lately. Just as good returns from some securities offset poor returns of others, leaving the overall portfolio stabler, it seems returns in good years offset those in bad years, leaving an asset's average annualized return for a long holding period stabler. In a cursory manner, it appears that lengthening the holding period does indeed reduce return variability, as measured by customarily used risk statistics. As Exhibit 4.11 shows, the standard deviation of common stocks declines from 20.6% when one-year holding periods are used to 6.3% for five-year holding periods. Looking at the coefficient of variation, you would have to conclude that stocks offer a better return-risk situation than Treasury bills for investors who intend to hold each for at least five years.

EXHIBIT 4.11

Average annualized return ($\bar{R}$), standard deviation (σ), and coefficient of variation (C) for various holding period lengths*

	Common Stocks	Treasury Bills
1-Year holding periods		
$\bar{R}$	12.4%	3.8%
σ	20.6	3.3
C	1.7	0.9
3-Year holding periods		
$\bar{R}$	10.7	3.8
σ	11.1	3.2
C	1.0	0.8
5-Year holding periods		
$\bar{R}$	10.3	3.8
σ	6.3	3.1
C	0.6	0.8

*Nonoverlapping periods, 1926 through 1992.

BOX 4.2   GETTING AN INVESTMENT EDGE

What's the Risk of Being Out of the Market?

The risk of investing in common stocks— that is, being *in* the market—is measured in a fairly straightforward manner. We usually look at the market's volatility in terms of a statistic such as the variance. But what is the risk of being *out of* the market? Clearly, this is an opportunity cost in terms of a foregone return.

Consider some of these numbers. During the decade of the 1980s (120 months), the S&P 500 showed an average annual return of 17.5%. But suppose you missed the six best-performing months? Amazingly, your return falls to 6.9! Who would be so unlucky (or dumb) to miss the six best months? Well, judging by the way some people are in and out of the market, it may not be that difficult to do.

A. Gary Shilling provides a different perspective. Over the 45-year period from 1946 through 1991 (540 months), the Dow Jones Industrial Average provided an average annual return of 11.2%. Missing the 50 best months pared the return to 4.5%, but missing the 50 worst months would have increased the return to 19.0%. Shilling concludes that timing the market may pay off.

Not so, concludes Paul A. Samuelson, 1970 winner of the Nobel Memorial Prize in economic science. Using an elegant mathematical proof, he shows that investors without any particular forecasting skills who try to time the market at quarterly intervals in effect give up 11% of their portfolio value each year to indulge in the luxury of playing the game. (See the *Journal of Portfolio Management*, Fall 1989.) Professor Samuelson is skeptical of forecasting acumen and, so, believes that market timing is a waste of time and money.

Time diversification research demonstrates what many investment advisors have urged for a long time. First, identify your investment objectives, which helps formulate how long assets will be held. If these are long periods, you need not be concerned with short-term fluctuations in value, and you have greater flexibility in choosing assets that sometimes are considered inherently risky. Second, having the patience to hold assets for the long run often is the easiest way to success in investing. Along with time diversification, you need security diversification. Otherwise, you might buy one or two stocks and hold them for a long time—while the companies go into bankruptcy.

SUMMARY

The risk associated with holding an individual asset can be measured by using three statistics—the variance, standard deviation, and coefficient of variation—in evaluating the asset's historical returns. The greater the dispersion of returns, the higher the statistics' values and the greater the asset's risk. Examining historical returns of key financial assets shows very low risk for Treasury bills and very high risk for common stocks, with long-term bonds' risks in the middle.

When individual assets are held simultaneously, a portfolio is created that may have a risk characteristic different from that of the assets of which it is composed. This difference results from diversification of assets and the return correlations among them. Poorly or negatively correlated asset returns reduce portfolio risk, while highly correlated returns leave risk unchanged. If securities are picked randomly and added to a portfolio, portfolio risk declines as more securities are added. The risk eliminated is called diversifiable risk. Some risk cannot be eliminated regardless of the number of securities added; this risk is called nondiversifiable risk. Although it cannot be eliminated, it can be managed. A risk statistic used in this effort is a security's beta weight, which measures the responsiveness of a security's return in relation to changes in return for the overall securities market. High beta values indicate high risk, while low beta values show low risk. Although betas are helpful, their usefulness is limited if they are difficult to calculate or do not remain stable over time.

Primary sources of risk are related to changes in the economic environment and to characteristics of the security issuer. Along with risks of an uncertain business cycle, changes in the economic environment create inflation risk, interest-rate risk, and international and political risks. Risks related to the security issuer include business risk and financial risk. Other sources of risk include marketability problems and a changing tax law. Time diversification indicates that longer holding periods reduce securities' risks insofar as standard deviations of annualized returns decline as the holding period increases.

KEY TERMS
(listed in order of appearance)

expected return	beta-designed portfolio approach
variance	nonstationarity problem
standard deviation	economic performance risk
coefficient of variation	inflation risk
diversification	interest-rate risk
correlation coefficient	business risk
random, diversifiable risk	financial risk
market, nondiversifiable risk	marketability risk
beta	time diversification

REVIEW QUESTIONS

1. What is risk? Should it be understood only as a chance of a loss? Explain.
2. What is an expected return and how is it calculated?
3. Explain what is meant by dispersion of asset returns. Indicate the statistics that measure dispersion.

4. What is meant by correlation of asset returns?

5. Discuss the historical risk statistics on key financial assets. Do the data contain any surprises? Explain.

6. How would you interpret the following values for the correlation coefficient relating returns from two assets: $+0.8$, -0.3, 0.0, -1.0, and $+1.0$?

7. How does correlation among asset returns influence the risk of a portfolio? Is it better to hold assets that are positively or negatively correlated? Explain. When can risk be eliminated completely? When can it not be reduced at all?

8. How many stocks (selected randomly from the S&P 500) must you hold to achieve reasonable diversification? Will this portfolio eliminate all risk, or will some remain? Explain.

9. Discuss the historical correlations among key financial assets. Do the values suggest that a portfolio of these assets could be effective in reducing risk? Explain.

10. Answer the following questions about the beta measurement:
    a. What is it?
    b. How is it determined?
    c. How can it be used in designing a portfolio?
    d. What are some problems in its use?

11. NCF Corporation has a beta of 1.8. Your return from the stock last year was 10%. You expect the market to go down 20% this year. What will be your return with NCF this year? What would it be if you expected the market return to increase 20%?

12. Explain economic performance risk and inflation risk. Are these simply different perspectives on the same thing? Explain.

13. Determine an investment's real rate of return if its nominal rate is 20% and inflation is 5%.

14. Explain interest-rate risk. Is this risk related in some way to inflation risk? Explain.

15. Explain international and political risks. How can you avoid such risks?

16. Explain business risk and financial risk. How can you minimize or avoid these risks?

17. Explain marketability risk and risk from a changing tax law. Can either of these risks be minimized or avoided?

18. What is time diversification? Is it a substitute for security diversification? Explain.

---

1. Matt McGuire is thinking of making a stock investment. As he sees it, his return can be zero, 20%, or 40%. If there is an equal probability of each return occurring, calculate (a) the expected return, (b) the variance, (c) the standard deviation, and (d) the coefficient of variation.

    After you have your answers, compare this investment with another Matt is considering. Its statistics are $\overline{R} = 12\%$; $\sigma^2 = 81\%$; $\sigma = 9\%$; $C = 0.75$. Compare the two investments. Does one dominate the other, or must Matt trade off risk for return? Discuss.

PROBLEMS AND PROJECTS

2. The returns from Wing Aircraft Supplies are related to strength in the overall economy, as shown below:

	Economy		
	Weak	So-So	Strong
Wing's Returns	−10%	+12%	+30%

An economic forecaster believes the economy may be headed toward a recession. When asked to be more specific, she indicated the odds of a weak economy are 3 out of 10, while the odds for a strong economy are only 1 in 10. The odds for a so-so economy are then 6 in 10. Given the information above, calculate the expected return, variance, standard deviation, and coefficient of variation for Wing's returns.

3. Suppose you were thinking of investing in Wing Aircraft, the company from problem 2. However, you would combine this investment with a bond investment (50% in each) that is likely to do better in a weak economy than in a strong one. This investment's returns, given the three states of the economy above, are 12%, 9%, and 6%, respectively.

   a. Determine the expected return, variance, standard deviation, and coefficient of variation for this investment.

   b. Discuss the advantages of this portfolio versus investing all your funds in one of the two assets.

4. Shown below is a table of correlation coefficients among four investments. Assuming the returns from the investments are $A = 20\%$, $B = 10\%$, $C = 15\%$, and $D = 30\%$, which two investments would you hold together? Explain your answer.

	A	B	C	D
A	1.0	0.6	0.5	0.9
B	—	1.0	0.8	−0.5
C	—	—	1.0	0.9
D	—	—	—	1.0

5. You are planning an investment portfolio for your eventual retirement in 40 years. You believe that the portfolio will show an average annual return of 12%. You also think inflation will average 5% a year.

   a. Calculate your expected real rate of return.

   b. Assuming you invest $10,000 in the portfolio, determine its future *real* value.

   c. Determine the future *real* value using the approximate real rate of return of 7%. Compare this answer with part (b).

6. *(Student Project)*   Locate the *Value Line Investment Survey* at your school library and review five companies familiar to you. Find the beta for each. Are their values what you might have expected from your general knowledge of the companies? Explain.

7. *(Student Project)*   Contact a financial officer of a small company in your hometown whose stock trades in the OTC market and is reported in *The Wall Street Journal*. Ask the officer if he would be interested in having the stock's beta determined. If so, gather daily price data for, say, 31 days. Based on daily price changes, determine HPRs for 30 days. At the same time, record daily closing values for the S&P 500 and calculate 30 HPRs for it. (Ignore dividends in both cases.)

Do not annualize the data, and be careful with decimal points. For example, if a stock price goes from 30 to 30 1/8, record the return as +0.004167 (+0.125/30.0). When you finish, discuss your results with the officer.

CASE ANALYSES

Janine Ricardo is considering investing in the construction industry. She believes the industry will do well over time but realizes its short-run performance may not be spectacular. Janine has narrowed her investment selections to three possible companies: (1) Home Builders, Inc. (HBI), a company that constructs single-family detached homes; (2) Home Repairs, Inc. (HRI), a company specializing in home remodeling and repair projects; and (3) National Tool Company (NTC), a firm that manufactures tools used in the construction industry.

4.1
Janine Ricardo
Considers
Investment
Correlations

Janine thinks a robust economy bodes well for both HMI and NTC, to varying degrees, but poorly for HRI. Although Janine's investment strategy is to hold a portfolio over time, rather than to frequently trade securities, she is concerned about excessive variations in portfolio value. Before investing, she plans to analyze the portfolio implications of the three companies. Accordingly, she also has developed probability estimates for changes in the economy for the upcoming year. Additionally, she has estimated returns from the three companies, given changes in the economy. Her data appear in the following table.

	Condition of Economy		
	Weak	Average	Strong
Probability	0.25	0.50	0.25
Likely returns (%):			
HBI	−20	+18	+44
HRI	+12	+ 8	+ 4
NTC	−32	+16	+56

a. Explain why Janine probably should not invest in NTC.
b. Calculate the expected return, variance, standard deviation, and coefficient of variation for HBI and HRI. Then, discuss which is the riskier.
c. Suppose that Janine decides to invest 90% of her funds in HRI and 10% in HBI. Calculate the expected return for this portfolio.
d. Janine believes she has a reasonable tolerance toward risk and describes herself as a moderate risk averter. Suppose that in the upcoming year, Janine could invest in a savings account guaranteed to pay a sure return of 8% for the year. Considering your work in question c above, what advice might you offer Janine? Explain.

Questions

4.2
Lenny Young
Needs Beta

Lenny Young has been watching the stock of Dayton Dynamics (DDY), a small high-tech company that provides specialized engineering services to firms in the defense industry. The firm's shares are traded in the OTC market, but Lenny has been unable to obtain data about the company, other than last year's annual report to shareholders. He is sure the company represents a high-risk situation and would feel more comfortable investing in its shares if he could assess the magnitude of that risk.

After searching a number of library sources, Lenny has given up hope of finding any information bearing on DDY's riskiness. Consequently, he will undertake his own study. Going back over the past 10 weeks, he has recorded the weekly returns for both DDY and the S&P 500. The data appear below.

Week	DDY	Market
1	8%	5%
2	16	8
3	−20	−10
4	− 5	4
5	40	25
6	25	20
7	12	8
8	− 5	− 4
9	30	10
10	39	24

a. Calculate DDY's beta. (Use any method. If you have studied regression analysis, use its methods. Otherwise, use a graphic approach and fit in the characteristic line with a visual approximation.)
b. Comment on DDY's beta. How risky is the stock in relation to the market? Suppose the market declines 12% in the upcoming year; what is DDY likely to do?
c. Lenny is considering investing most of his funds in DDY if the return-risk situation of its stock seems attractive. Considering Lenny's approach, do you believe beta is an appropriate statistic for measuring risk? Explain.

HELPFUL
READING

Holton, Glyn A. "Time: The Second Dimension of Risk." *Financial Analysts Journal*, November-December 1992, pp. 39–45.
Kreiger, Andrew J. "To Hedge or Not to Hedge." *Forbes*, January 4, 1993, p. 91.
Kritzman, Mark. "What Practitioners Need to Know About Estimating Volatility: Part 1." *Financial Analysts Journal,* July-August 1992, pp. 22–25.

CHAPTER FIVE

Investments in the Overall Financial Plan

After you finish this chapter, you will be able to:

- understand what is meant by liquidity and why investors hold liquid assets.
- identify the various financial institutions that offer checking and savings deposits.
- understand and evaluate the different types of checking and savings deposits offered by financial institutions and various other securities.
- structure a liquidity management strategy that considers the possibility of borrowing.
- analyze the investment aspects of life insurance and decide whether to buy expensive whole life insurance or inexpensive term insurance, investing the saved premiums in other assets.
- understand the importance of retirement planning and how it shapes the investment portfolio before and after retirement.

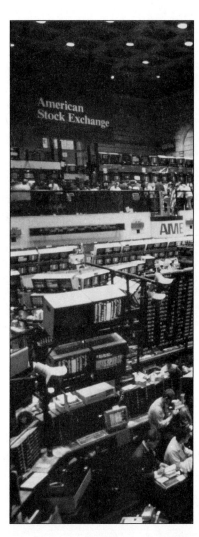

In Chapter 1, we introduced the theme that investors should have objectives to guide their investment decisions. By having specific goals, we are in a position to measure our success objectively by simply determining if the goals are being achieved. Moreover, our investment goals reflect a broader issue in terms of what we are trying to achieve in life, such as educating our children or eventually purchasing a new home. So, investing should not take place in a vacuum but rather should be an important part of our overall family financial plan. Important investment-related components of this plan include maintaining adequate liquidity, selecting the proper life insurance policy to meet our needs, and preparing for our eventual retirement. These activities are the topics of this chapter.

LIQUIDITY MANAGEMENT

Liquid assets are the first investments many people make. Indeed, they are often called savings, rather than investments. Regardless of what they are called, they are a necessary and important part of anyone's portfolio. Investing in liquid assets is simple because every financial depository institution in the country offers them. A trip to your neighborhood bank or savings and loan can usually satisfy your entire liquidity need. However, if you are trying to increase your yield or want to be a bit more aggressive in managing your liquid assets, you might have to shop outside the neighborhood. Thanks to deregulation of the financial institutions industry, these shopping trips are now possible and often worthwhile.

Liquidity management:
strategy for determining how much liquidity to hold, in what forms, and in which institutions

     Liquidity management (also called *cash management*) is best understood as a strategy for determining how much liquidity you will hold, in what forms, and in which financial institutions. There are many strategies, ranging from the ultraconservative, where you hold virtually nothing other than a checking account, to the aggressive, where you hold assets that are more difficult to convert to cash and, possibly, even use tax shelters such as IRAs to enhance your return.

Why Hold Liquid Assets?

An asset is said to be liquid when it can be converted to cash easily and with little or no loss in value. Coins and currency are the most liquid of all assets. They are legal tender, which means they cannot be refused if you offer them to pay a debt. Unfortunately, currency and coins offer no positive return and pose the problems of easy theft and misplacement. Moving away from coins and currency, assets become less liquid. Your personal check may be accepted in most places in your hometown, but it may be turned down somewhere else; thus, it has less liquidity. Your savings account is even less liquid because you must go through the inconvenience of making a withdrawal each time you need money. Much further down on the liquidity list is a certifi-

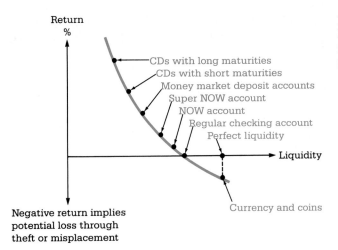

EXHIBIT 5.1
Liquidity-return curve
for cash and federally
insured deposits

cate of deposit (CD); with it, you may pay a penalty for withdrawing funds before maturity.

As liquidity increases, asset return decreases, as Exhibit 5.1 shows. The deposits indicated will be explained shortly. We would prefer to have both return and liquidity, but most often it does not work that way. We must choose: either more liquidity or greater return. How much liquidity often depends on our reasons for wanting liquidity in the first place. These reasons are to undertake transactions, to have emergency reserves, and to have a store of value.

Undertake Transactions   We must hold some liquid assets for undertaking transactions. Our cash inflows and outflows are often irregular and somewhat unpredictable. You might get paid twice a month. Out of those payments you must make recurrent living expenditures. Your paycheck might go directly into your checking account, where checks are then issued to pay bills and to get needed currency for small items. Your balance will be relatively high twice a month and gradually diminish in the two weeks after you are paid. So, you will have an average balance for the month—a necessary investment in a liquid asset. As you might guess, this average balance depends on various factors.

First, the larger your income and monthly expenses, the larger the average balance. If your income is $3,000 a month, you will have a larger average balance than if it is $1,000 a month. Second, the more infrequently you are paid, the larger the average balance. Someone paid weekly will have less in the checking account, on average, than someone paid monthly. Third, the more uncertain and irregular your cash flows, the larger the average required balance to protect against a possible shortage of funds. These factors are summarized in Exhibit 5.2.

EXHIBIT 5.2

Reasons for holding liq-uid assets

Reason	Important Factors Determining Amounts Held
A. Undertake transactions	1. Amount of monthly expenses 2. Frequency of pay periods 3. Degree of uncertainty of future income and expenses
B. Hold emergency reserves	1. Amount of monthly expenses 2. Disability income protection 3. Disposition toward taking risks
C. Keep a store of value	1. Good investment vehicle 2. Temporary parking place

Emergency reserve: liquid assets held to pro-tect against unforseen expenses or loss of income

Emergency Reserves   An **emergency reserve** means liquid assets held to protect against unforeseen expenses or unexpected loss of income. Financial planners often recommend that you keep between three and six months of living expenses in emergency reserves. So, if your budget shows monthly expenditures of $2,000, you need about $6,000 to $12,000, according to their advice. If you have adequate disability income insurance, you can take the lower figure; if you don't, you should plan to hold the higher amount.

For many people, this reserve represents a sizeable investment in rela-tion to their incomes. Many question whether it's really needed, and we prob-ably will not know the answer unless we experience a financial emergency. The danger in lacking sufficient reserves is that you may have to deal with an emergency by selling other assets that you would prefer to hold. These assets could be your home, your car, even an engagement or a wedding ring. In addition to having poor liquidity, these assets often hold irreplaceable senti-mental value. You be the judge of the size of your emergency fund, but give it sufficient thought before you decide.

Because the emergency fund is not used for transactions, you can extend your portfolio to hold assets other than a checking account. Taking some risk to achieve higher yields is not out of the question so long as the risk is minimal. Stocks and most bonds would be poor choices, but CDs would be acceptable in most cases.

Store of value: holding liquid assets because they are expected to provide the highest returns

Temporary parking place: suggests that the store-of-value feature of liquid assets lasts for only a short time

Store of Value   Liquid assets may be held simply because you believe that they are the best **store of value;** in other words, your wealth will increase the most—or erode the least—with them. In this sense, liquid assets are selected because they are the best investments to hold. When liquid assets are selected for this reason, we describe the investor as looking for a **tempo-rary parking place** for her money. *Temporary* is the key word because the investor would prefer investing in less liquid assets and will do so when the investment horizon improves. As in the case of the emergency fund, a wider array of assets can be selected for store-of-value purposes. In many cases, investors can look for the highest-yielding liquid assets because losses or some inconveniences can be tolerated. Indeed, during periods of high rates, some investors limit their entire investment activities to selecting and managing liquid assets. They often move all their deposits to another bank or a money market mutual fund (which will be explained later in the chapter) to capture a half-percent greater yield for a period as short as a week. Although such cases are extreme, high short-term rates make investors more aware of the importance of sound liquidity management. As we saw in Chapter 3, a small extra yield over a long period leads to substantial increases in wealth.

Financial Institutions

As mentioned above, many alternative financial institutions offer liquid assets. We often deal with these institutions without giving much thought to whether or not they are the most appropriate to meet our needs or if our deposits have adequate protection. Depositors in Ohio, for example, learned painfully that so-called state insurance on deposits provided virtually no protection in the wake of a large, failing institution. Had the state government not intervened in the crisis caused by the failure of a large savings and loan (S&L; Home State Savings), depositor losses would have been substantial. Before investing, then, determine if federal insurance protection is provided. If it is not, select another institution.

The Federal Deposit Insurance Corporation (FDIC) insures commercial banks; the Savings Association Insurance Fund (SAIF) insures savings institutions; and the National Credit Union Administration (NCUA) insures credit unions. Each depositor in any of these institutions has $100,000 insurance. Notice: the insurance is per depositor, *not* per deposit. So, if your family has more than $100,000 to invest, you should either use multiple accounts (in different family members' names) at the same institution or use different institutions.

Commercial Banks   Most commercial banks are all-purpose financial institutions, which means they offer a wide array of financial products and services. You probably have a checking or savings account with one, and you may also have a loan, either directly or through Visa or MasterCard. Commercial banks also offer trust services that are used to achieve a number of objectives. Despite competition within the financial institutions industry, most people still want to maintain some form of business with a commercial bank. Most bank deposits are insured with FDIC, but make sure of this before you invest.

Savings and Loans and Savings Banks   S&Ls and savings banks are savings institutions that historically limited their lending to mortgage loans. Many still do, although others have become much more aggressive in their lending policies (Home State, mentioned previously, was extremely aggressive, doing repurchase agreements with ESM Securities, a government bond

BOX 5.1 INVESTMENT INSIGHTS

Is Cash "Trash"?

The sharp drop in short-term interest rates over the past several years has led many investors to adopt a cash-is-trash perspective in managing their portfolios. That could be a tragic mistake. Cash satisfies our perpetual need for liquidity. When short-term rates are high, not only do we get liquidity, but cash returns often exceed returns on stocks or long-term bonds. That's the best of both worlds, but don't expect this situation to last long—in the more common case we must choose between liquidity and return.

But investors seem not to understand or appreciate the trade-off. Billions of dollars have recently been pulled out of maturing, short-term CDs and rechanneled into various inappropriate alternatives. For example, stock and long-term bond funds are price volatile; although you can quickly convert your shares to cash, you may take large losses in the process if stock and bond prices fall.

Another dubious alternative is a variable annuity contract. Brokers often give these a big push because of their tax-deferral advantage to you (and the high commission to them), which makes their yields attractive even if you continue allocating funds to cash investments. But taking money out of a contract could lead to a 10% tax penalty and a surrender charge. Factor these two items into the yield calculation, and it's doubtful that you gain an edge over straight cash investments. The broker might tell you that you incur these charges only if you withdraw funds. Wait a minute: isn't that exactly why we hold cash—in case we need funds quickly?

Interestingly, cash isn't as trashy as some people might think. Keeping your money exclusively in stocks over a 30-year period (1963–92) provided an annual compounded return of 10.9%. Putting 20% of your money into U.S. Treasury bills would have lowered the portfolio return to 10.1%—a mere 0.8% difference. Investment advisors often stress the importance of managing risk by maintaining a balanced portfolio over time. When you convert cash assets into stocks or bonds, in effect you are trying to time the market. Hope for good luck because you'll need it.

dealer that eventually went bankrupt). Many S&Ls have experienced financial problems in recent years, making it all the more important to determine if your deposit is SAIF-insured.

Credit Unions Investors often overlook their credit unions as a place to hold their liquid deposits. This is unfortunate because many offer competitive interest rates—both when you invest and when you borrow—along with NCUA protection. The credit union also may be the most convenient place to do business because there may be an office at your place of work. But once again, be careful if NCUA protection is not provided.

Consumer Banks   A consumer bank is any financial institution that limits its lending or depositing activities to individuals and excludes businesses. Large S&Ls and commercial banks are attempting to expand their business over state lines by setting up consumer banks. To investors, this expansion provides new opportunities to earn higher rates. Accept nothing less than federal insurance protection.

Stockbrokerage Firms   Your stockbroker can also provide liquid instruments. Many offer money market mutual funds (explained later in this chapter) and they can purchase other instruments, such as Treasury bills or commercial paper. Probably one advantage of using your broker is that cash balances in your securities account can be transferred immediately to liquid assets. Not only is this convenient, but your funds are invested for longer periods because you avoid mail delays. Merrill Lynch was the originator of so-called sweep accounts with its cash management account, a type of all-purpose checking, saving, borrowing, and investing account. Despite a high initial investment of $20,000, this account is exceptionally popular with investors. Other brokerage firms and other financial institutions have entered the market with similar accounts. If you are interested in using a sweep account, you should make comparisons because there are differences in annual costs, minimum balances, and other features.

ALTERNATIVE TYPES OF LIQUID ASSETS

The array of liquid assets offered today is indeed very wide. Many investors are not familiar with them, and the best advice someone might offer at the outset is to shop around. Federal regulation of financial institutions has virtually ended with respect to maximum interest rates and minimum deposit amounts, so any remaining restrictions are set by the institution.

Accounts at Financial Institutions

Many investors limit their liquid investments to deposits at financial institutions. They may do so because deposit rates often are competitive with rates on other liquid assets but require smaller minimum investments, or because they are convenient and federally insured, or because inertia keeps them from searching for alternatives. Exhibit 5.3 shows an array of liquid assets, which includes the most popular ones at financial institutions.

Checking and NOW Accounts   Most of us understand a checking account, but a **NOW account** often is less familiar. NOW stands for *negotiated order of withdrawal*, a term used to describe checks issued by institutions other than commercial banks. That distinction is meaningless today, and it is better to understand a NOW account simply as a checking account that pays

NOW account: checking account that pays interest

EXHIBIT 5.3
Currency and popular
deposits at financial
institutions

	Average March Balances (billions)	
	1992	1991
Currency	$ 292.3	$ 267.2
Checking accounts at commercial banks	340.9	290.5
NOW accounts at all financial institutions	385.2	333.8
Savings deposits, including MMDAs	1,186.0	1,042.5
Nonnegotiable (small) CDs	870.5	1,168.7

SOURCE: *Federal Reserve Bulletin*, May 1993.

interest. You may have heard of a super-NOW account. This is a NOW account that pays more interest than a regular NOW and probably has a higher minimum balance requirement.

Each is a checking account in every respect. Their advantage is obvious: your balances held for transactions purposes earn interest. This is not a trivial advantage, but it must be weighed against a possible disadvantage if the minimum balance requirement forces you to keep more in the account than you would otherwise. If this is the case and if you could earn a higher rate on the excess amount somewhere else, then you should consider holding a regular checking account with a lower minimum requirement and investing the difference elsewhere. For example, suppose you normally keep an average balance of $400 in your regular checking account. You are considering opening a super-NOW account that pays 4% interest and has a $2,500 minimum average balance requirement. Assuming your balance would average the $2,500 minimum means the account would earn $100 interest a year. However, if you could invest the extra $2,100 at, say, 10%, you would be $110 a year better off maintaining a regular checking account and investing the difference.

Savings Accounts   A number of different kinds of savings accounts are available, as Exhibit 5.3 shows. The simplest is the **passbook account,** so named because a passbook often is used to record activity in the account. This savings account allows an unlimited number of withdrawals each period but usually pays the lowest rate of interest. The passbook account is rapidly being replaced by statement accounts. Instead of a passbook, you receive monthly statements, as with a checking account.

Passbook account: savings account using a passbook; today it refers more to an account with the fewest restrictions but offering the lowest rate of interest

Money market deposit account: savings account with floating interest rate pegged to market rates of interest

Money market deposit accounts (MMDAs) are savings accounts that pay money market rates, which means the rates change over time in step with interest-rate changes in the money markets. To investors with limited funds, this feature is attractive. It allows them to participate in the money market, which usually excludes them because of high minimum investment amounts. (Another alternative is the money market mutual fund [MMMF].)

MMDAs have minimum balance requirements, usually around $2,500, and offer limited access to funds, with perhaps only three withdrawals or other transfers a month.

Another attractive savings vehicle is the **certificate of deposit (CD).** These are available in practically any amount and with a wide array of maturities, ranging from 1 week to more than 10 years. A CD is quite different from an MMDA. An interest rate is locked in for the CD's maturity; that is, it has a fixed rate of return. If you think that interest rates will decline in the future, you would prefer the CD to an MMDA; but if you think that they will increase, you would pick the MMDA. Because long-term yields are generally higher than short-term yields, CDs usually offer higher rates than MMDAs. You would expect this to be the usual case because CDs tie up your funds for a given maturity. They should offer a higher return to compensate you for accepting the risk involved in possible interest-rate fluctuations. But suppose you want to cash in the CD before its maturity. Be prepared to pay a penalty for early redemption. The amount of the penalty will be at the discretion of the issuing financial institution. Make sure you ask about such penalties before investing in CDs.

Certificate of deposit: savings account with a maturity and penalties for early withdrawal

Know How Your Savings Account Earns Interest Surprising as it may seem, there is no established pattern of paying interest that all financial institutions follow. Some compound interest quarterly or annually, while others compound it daily or even continuously. Some require that your funds be invested for an entire month or quarter before interest is paid; others credit your account daily. Are these differences trivial? Often they are not.

For example, Exhibit 5.4 shows the accumulation of $1,000 invested for various periods assuming an 8% stated annual rate and compounding at different intervals. At the end of 16 years, daily compounding adds $170.19 ($3,596.13 − $3,425.94) more to your account—and remember, you invested only $1,000 at the start.

Frequency of Compounding	Years Deposit Is Held				
	1	2	4	8	16
Annually	$1,080.00	$1,166.40	$1,360.49	$1,850.93	$3,425.94
Semiannually	1,081.60	1,169.86	1,368.57	1,872.98	3,508.06
Quarterly	1,082.43	1,171.66	1,372.79	1,884.54	3,551.49
Weekly	1,083.22	1,173.37	1,376.79	1,895.55	3,593.11
Daily	1,083.28	1,173.49	1,377.08	1,896.35	3,596.13
Continuously	1,083.30	1,173.51	1,377.13	1,896.48	3,596.62

EXHIBIT 5.4
Funds accumulated at 8% interest ($1,000 invested)

Also, the method the institution uses to determine what balances qualify to earn interest has a considerable effect on the amount of interest earned. Exhibit 5.5 shows four widely used methods applied to assumed quarterly activity.

Day of Deposit to Day of Withdrawal   This method means interest is earned on each day's balance. Notice that this is not the same as daily compounding, in which each day's interest is added to your account to earn future interest (compound interest). The calculations in Exhibit 5.5 actually assume simple interest calculations, where interest earned (I) equals principal (P) times rate (r) times time (T); that is,

$$I = P \times r \times T$$

Minimum Balance   This method pays interest only on the minimum balance in the account for the period. As you see in Exhibit 5.5, this method can lead to little interest if you make withdrawals during the period. Moreover,

EXHIBIT 5.5
Determining savings balances that qualify for interest

Activity in the Account		
Day	Deposit (Withdrawal)	Balance
1	$1,000	$1,000
30	1,000	2,000
60	(900)	1,100
90	Closing	1,100
Interest Calculations		

1. Day of deposit to day of withdrawal:
    a. $1,000 × 30/360 × .06 = $ 5.00
    b. $2,000 × 30/360 × .06 = $10.00
    c. $1,100 × 30/360 × .06 = $ 5.50
                          Total $20.50

2. Minimum balance:
         $1,000 × 90/360 × .06 = $15.00

3. FIFO:
    a. $ 100 × 90/360 × .06 = $ 1.50
    b. $1,000 × 60/360 × .06 = $10.00
                          Total $11.50

4. LIFO:
    a. $1,000 × 90/360 × .06 = $15.00
    b. $ 100 × 60/360 × .06 = $ 1.00
                          Total $16.00

deposits made during the period usually must be received before a given date—such as before the 10th day of the 1st month of the quarter—to earn interest for the quarter. This method does not benefit depositors.

FIFO FIFO means first-in, first-out. It assumes that withdrawals you make during the period reduce your earliest balances—another assumption in the bank's favor. So, the $900 withdrawal made two months after the quarter began is assumed to reduce the opening balance of $1,000.

LIFO LIFO means last-in, first-out. In contrast to FIFO, it assumes that withdrawals reduce your later, rather than earlier, balances. Here, the $900 withdrawal is assumed to reduce the $1,000 deposit made on the 30th day.

LIFO is more to your advantage than FIFO but is still less generous than the day-of-deposit-to-day-of-withdrawal method. If you think that some activity will occur in your savings account fairly often, you should probably try to select an institution offering the day-of-deposit-to-day-of-withdrawal method over those offering the minimum balance, FIFO, or LIFO method.

U.S. Treasury Securities

Because they are free of default risk, Treasury securities often are favored by investors seeking safety of principal. There is little difference between Treasury securities and currency itself; the former is interest-bearing debt of the Treasury, while the latter is non–interest-bearing debt. The non–interest-bearing type is preferred only when perfect liquidity is more important than earnings. The instruments shown in Exhibit 5.6 and discussed below are popular Treasury securities held for liquidity.

	End-of-Year Amounts (billions)		
	1992	1991	1990
Treasury debt:			
Bills	$657.7	$590.4	$527.4
Savings bonds	155.0	135.9	124.1
Non-Treasury issuers			
Commercial paper	549.4	531.7	562.7
Negotiable (jumbo) CDs[a]	357.5	424.7	494.9
Money market mutual funds[a,b]	342.3	363.9	348.9

EXHIBIT 5.6
Popular short-term investments other than deposits at financial institutions

[a]Average daily balance.

[b]Excludes funds that are offered only to businesses or other institutional owners.

SOURCE: *Federal Reserve Bulletin*, May 1993.

Treasury bills: discount securities of the U.S. Treasury with maturities ranging from 3 to 12 months

Treasury Bills   **Treasury bills** are debt obligations of the U.S. Treasury sold on a discount basis with maturities ranging from three months to one year. At the beginning of 1993, about $658 billion of Treasury bills were outstanding. Bills are issued in minimum denominations of $10,000, and they are actively traded in the secondary market. Treasury bills can be purchased through commercial banks or stockbrokerage firms. Buying them directly from the Treasury is just as easy, however, and avoids commissions. All that is needed is a tender form, available from 37 Treasury Direct Servicing Offices. This is a simple form that you complete and submit to the Federal Reserve Bank in your area. You also must establish a Treasury Direct Account that will be connected with your checking or savings account. All payments from the Treasury are wired directly to the account. Active T-bill investors, however, usually roll over maturing bills into new issues.

Bills are now sold only in "book entry" form, which means buyers must have accounts with the Treasury. New issues of bills with less than one year maturity are sold at auction every Monday morning (those with one year maturity are auctioned only once a month). Both stock market and credit analysts frequently watch the outcomes in these auctions in an effort to gauge future interest rates. Whether these observations are of much help is another matter, but we do know the T-bill rate is volatile and sensitive to changes in the supply and demand for credit.

Bonds and Notes with Short Remaining Maturities   Treasury bonds and notes are explained in greater detail in Chapter 10, but for now, let us recognize that they can also serve as liquid instruments. There is also an active secondary market for bonds and notes, again making it possible to buy them with varying maturities. Buying a T-bond with three months remaining to its maturity is little different from buying a three-month T-bill. In fact, investors will prefer the bond if its yield to maturity is better. As you guess, the active secondary market keeps the yields to maturity about equal on all Treasury debt of equal maturity. You can purchase Treasury bonds and notes in the same ways you purchase Treasury bills, including direct purchase from the Treasury.

U.S. Series EE bonds: called savings bonds, they are offered in small denominations and have numerous advantages, particularly to small investors; sold in discount form.

U.S. Series EE Bonds   **U.S. Series EE bonds,** usually called savings bonds, are nonnegotiable instruments of the Treasury sold on a discount basis and issued primarily for the benefit of small investors. They are replacing the old Series E bond, considered in the past as an investment "dog" because its yield was low in relation to yields elsewhere. But the Series EE bond has changed the "dog" image, and many investment advisors now view savings bonds as good short-term vehicles. About $155 billion was invested in EE bonds at the start of 1993.

Exhibit 5.7 summarizes the most important characteristics of savings bonds. Notice that their yields are indexed to other Treasury securities; specifically, they yield 85% of the actual average interest earned on an index of Treasury securities for the five-year period before their redemption. The

EXHIBIT 5.7

Important facts about U.S. Series EE savings bonds

PURCHASE PRICE	☐ $25 to $5,000, maximum investment is $30,000 per person
YOUR RETURN	☐ No less than 4.0% if held five years or longer
	☐ Actual return after five years indexed to returns on U.S. Treasury securities (six-month annualized yield beginning May 1, 1993 = 4.78%; this rate changes every six months)
WHERE TO BUY	☐ Through payroll deduction plans
	☐ At most banks and other financial institutions
	☐ Through the mail from Bureau of Public Debt, Washington, DC 20226
REDEMPTION	☐ Must wait six months, unless there is an emergency
	☐ Redeem at any bank, but be careful not to redeem immediately before an interest date (there are two a year) because you can lose several months' interest even if you redeem only several days too early
OTHER ADVANTAGES	☐ No buying or selling charges, fees, or commissions
	☐ Federal income taxes can be deferred until redemption or possibly be avoided altogether if bond interest is used for a child's education
	☐ No state or local income taxes

yield is changed every six months, and the 4.78% yield that began May 1, 1993, was quite good in relation to other short-term rates available then. Other features that appeal to some investors are federal income tax deferral on the interest until you redeem the bond and no state or local income taxes. Moreover, federal income taxes may be avoided altogether if interest on the bond is used to pay for a child's college or vocational education. Single people earning $40,000 or less and married couples jointly earning $60,000 or less earn a full exclusion of all Series EE bond interest. For incomes from $40,000 to $50,000 (single return) and $60,000 to $90,000 (joint return), partial exclusion is available; for incomes over $50,000 and $90,000, no exclusion is allowed. This possible avoidance of taxes on Series EE bonds makes them attractive and highly competitive with all other debt instruments—those with long maturities as well as those with short maturities. So, savings bonds may not have the same conveniences as savings accounts, but their other advantages should be considered carefully in constructing the investment portfolio. To obtain current rates on the bonds, call the Series EE Bond Information Center at 1-800-872-6637.

U.S. Series HH bonds:
acquired by conversion
of Series EE bonds, they
pay semiannual interest

U.S. Series HH Bonds **U.S. Series HH bonds** are also issued by the Treasury. You cannot buy them, however; you can acquire them only by exchanging Series EE bonds (or series E bonds, an older version of Series EE). The HH series differs from the EE series in that interest is paid semiannually at a fixed 4% rate and the bonds mature in 10 years (but can be extended to 30 years). An appealing feature of HH bonds is that deferred interest on EE bonds can be continued by the exchange. However, semiannual interest is taxable.

Non–Treasury-Issued Securities

Although the Treasury is considered the safest insurer of securities, there are other issuers. Corporations such as GM and IBM often sell commercial paper as a means of borrowing on a short-term basis, and commercial banks sell negotiable CDs.

Commercial paper:
unsecured debt obliga-
tion of a corpration with
a maturity of 270 days or
less

Commercial Paper **Commercial paper** is a short-term, unsecured debt obligation of a corporation. About 1,000 corporations issue commercial paper in denominations usually starting at $25,000 and with maturities ranging from one to six months. Because of Security and Exchange Commission restrictions, commercial paper's maturity is limited to 270 days or less. The high minimum investment puts commercial paper out of reach to many investors, although some banks and S&Ls may have a program that allows you to participate with smaller amounts in pooled weekly purchases. Commercial paper is also sold on a discount basis, and its issuers must have strong credit histories, but even so, they are not as safe as the Treasury. Thus, commercial paper rates are higher than T-bill rates. Investing on your own, you may not be able to have a reasonably diversified portfolio of commercial paper, but many MMMFs are buyers. Investing in them opens the market to you and allows you to earn the higher rates without taking considerable extra risk. About $549 billion of commercial paper was outstanding at January 1, 1993.

Negotiable CDs: issued
by commercial banks
with maturities less
than one year and tai-
lored to individual cus-
tomers' needs

Negotiable CDs **Negotiable CDs** are bank debt instruments sold to investors who negotiate both yield and maturity. They are also negotiable instruments; if you own one, you can sell it directly to someone else. This feature makes them different from the CDs previously discussed, and there are other important differences. The minimum denomination of a negotiable CD is $100,000, and maturities usually range from one month to one year. Their yields are also higher than T-bill rates and tend to be on a par with commercial paper rates. The high minimum investment means that most of us will own negotiable CDs the same way we will own commercial paper—that is, through a pooling arrangement such as the MMMF. Negotiable CDs had an average daily balance of about $358 billion at the beginning of 1993.

Money Market Mutual Funds An **MMMF** is a pooling arrangement; specifically, it is a mutual fund that invests in short-term debt instruments, primarily of the type discussed above. MMMFs are easy to establish, either with your broker or directly with the fund. You can find convenient listings of most funds, including addresses and phone numbers, in various issues of *Forbes and* Money magazines, which also evaluate fund performance. All funds have a minimum initial investment, which can range from $500 to over $10,000. Subsequent deposits can be much smaller, and you typically access your funds by writing a check, which usually also has a minimum amount requirement. The funds that require larger initial investments often allow unlimited check-writing privileges that in effect make the account a NOW account.

There are different kinds of MMMFs, ranging from those that invest only in short-term Treasury securities to those that invest in so-called junk paper. This paper usually consists of commercial paper with a low quality rating or negotiable CDs issued by lesser-known banks. Some MMMFs invest in municipal bonds with short maturities. These provide tax-free income to investors, but their yields usually are below MMMFs that invest in taxable securities. If you have a high marginal tax rate, they may provide a better after-tax return.

The MMMF industry points out that no MMMF has ever defaulted. Some have faced illiquidity crises in the past because they had overextended the maturity of their portfolio, but they were rescued by other MMMFs. True, the record has been excellent. But does this mean it will continue to be so in the future? If the trend continues to "junk," then investors must be cautious. The situation is not unlike having a loaded gun in the house: the fact that it has never accidentally fired in no way lessens its potential danger. Finally, the single most important factor influencing the yields on MMMFs is the size of the management fee. Some funds have fees as low as 0.25% of assets, while others are as high as 1.5%. All things considered, you should search for a low-cost fund because it probably will offer a relatively better yield.

Money market mutual fund: pooling arrangement that invests in money market instruments and makes its shares available to small investors

BORROWING AND LIQUIDITY MANAGEMENT

We think of investment borrowing as being undertaken to acquire long-term investments from which, it usually is assumed, you will earn a higher rate than the rate of interest on the borrowed funds. If investors hold both short- and long-term investments, it is purely arbitrary to say they borrow to invest long because they could just as easily sell the short-term investments and avoid borrowing altogether. We could, in fact, raise the issue that they really borrow to invest in short-term assets. The situation is illustrated in Exhibit 5.8.

Because interest rates on short-term loans usually are higher than interest rates on short-term investments, the more interesting question is why

EXHIBIT 5.8
Borrowing and
investing

A. Traditional view often sees short-term borrowing
   financing long-term investments.

B. But many investors hold both short- and long-term
   investments; thus, short-term borrowing finances both.

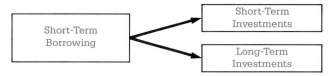

C. This arrangement is often more desirable than
   converting short-term investments to long-term
   and holding little or no funds for an emergency.

D. With no short-term investments, a future emergency
   would dictate selling long-term investments at possible
   losses or borrowing under unfavorable conditions.

investors are willing to pay this differential. Why not forget the emergency reserve and use the funds to reduce any short-term debt we might be carrying, whether it was used to buy securities or finance a new car or for another purpose? If an emergency does arise in the future, we can always borrow then, as we need the funds. Many investors do not follow that approach, however, preferring instead to maintain rather permanent amounts of short-term debt.

Avoiding Future Borrowing

Borrowing *today* to keep short-term investments means you might avoid borrowing in the *future,* a course of action that would be dictated if an emergency did arise and if you had sold your short-term investments. Waiting until an emergency arises is the riskier approach in two ways: First, you face a possibility that funds might not be available. Suppose you have a good income now and are viewed as a good credit risk. Borrowing is easy. But if the emergency in some way impairs your credit standing—you lose your job, for example—obtaining credit may become more difficult or more expensive. Second, even if your credit standing is unchanged, you face the risk of unknown future interest rates: they might be lower, but they could be higher. In either event, your risk is greater because you face a greater array of possible outcomes. The interest differential, then, is the price investors must pay if they want to invest in long-term assets and simultaneously reduce risk. Managed effectively, it may not be an exorbitant cost to pay.

Frequently Used Sources of Investment Credit

Investors who use borrowed funds usually favor sources that are relatively cheap or convenient. The loan sources below are used frequently.

The Margin Account   The mechanics of a margin account were explained in Chapter 2. It was noted there that a margin account is easy to establish and that you typically pay the prime rate of interest plus one or two percentage points on amounts actually borrowed. Also, you need not borrow with a margin account; instead, you can put up the full value of securities purchased and retain borrowing power for later, if it is needed. Our attention below is on the **leverage** aspect of margin investing.

Exhibit 5.9 shows a situation in which an investor is considering borrowing $10,000 to invest in long-term securities. We assume she does not want to sell her short-term securities to do so, although that would be a possibility. It is also assumed the short-term assets will yield a certain 4%, while the long-term investment could show a +30% return or a −30% return. If she doesn't use margin, her rate of return is simply 4%. If she margins, she can leverage the return on her invested capital to +26% if the +30% return is achieved on the long-term investment. If the −30% return occurs, leverage works the other way: now her portfolio return falls to a −34%. This analysis ignores taxes, which would dampen the differences somewhat, but it serves to show that leverage is a two-edged sword, cutting both for and against us.

Leverage: using borrowed funds to increase the size of an investment

	No Leverage	Leverage Proftit	Leverage Loss
Amount invested in short-term assets	$10,000	$10,000	$10,000
Amount invested in long-term assets	-0-	10,000	10,000
Total invested in assets	$10,000	$20,000	$20,000
Less amount borrowed	-0-	10,000	10,000
Net invested capital	$10,000	$10,000	$10,000
Short-term return (4%)	$ 400	$ 400	$ 400
Long-term return (+30%, −30%)	-0-	3,000	−3,000
Interest on $10,000 borrowed (8%)	-0-	−800	−800
Total return	$ 400	$ 2,600	$−3,400
Rate of return on invested capital	+4%	+26%	−34%

EXHIBIT 5.9
Leverage illustrated

Using Securities as Loan Collateral   The example above illustrates what takes place in a margin account with the broker acting as an intermediary. You can arrange your own loans, however, by taking your securities to a bank and pledging them as collateral. You probably will pay the same interest, so why not use the broker and avoid the trouble? Indeed, most people do just that. But if you prefer holding your certificates rather than leaving them with the broker, using your securities as collateral might appeal to you.

Borrowing on Whole Life Insurance Policies   A whole life insurance policy may be the cheapest source of funds anywhere, particularly if you bought the policy some time ago. The policy will have loan values printed within it, making it possible to determine how much you might borrow. It also will specify a guaranteed borrowing rate that could be considerably below current market rates. If that's true, it makes virtually no sense to borrow anywhere else, assuming you have made up your mind to borrow. Don't be dissuaded by an insurance representative's arguments that you are robbing your beneficiaries. If that's true, a loan that must be repaid after your death is robbing your beneficiaries. The simple truth is that if you can borrow at a low rate, say 4%, it makes sense to do so.

Be careful with some new insurance policies that are being marketed as though they offer short-term liquidity. They also allow policyholders to borrow and at rates that seem attractive. However, a policy loan then means that earnings on the policy fall from high market rates (the ones touted when the policies are promoted) to much smaller guaranteed rates.

It is not advisable to buy life insurance specifically for its ability to provide liquidity. It does not accomplish that goal effectively. If you already have a policy with loan features, then carefully examine the policy in comparing it with other loan sources, if you are seeking a loan.

Borrowing from Retirement Plans   Borrowing from a retirement plan sounds almost as terrible as robbing beneficiaries. It isn't, unless you want to assume the borrower takes the money and loses it in reckless abandon. Assuming contrarily that you are intelligent and not prone to childish behavior, why, then, borrow somewhere else at higher rates or, far worse, never establish a tax-deferred plan in the first place because the money might be needed in the future?

Tax-deferred investing is one of the best techniques for accumulating wealth (as we shall discuss shortly). If you are investing in an employer-provided 401(k) plan or a tax-deferred annuity or if you have your own Keogh plan, you will have borrowing privileges. There are restrictions that you should understand before borrowing, but these are not particularly burdensome. By all means, ask your employer or tax advisor for details before you undertake major debt obligations elsewhere.

Consumer Credit   Although we don't usually associate consumer credit with investing because both go on simultaneously with many investors, it would be a mistake to ignore it. Several observations seem particularly important.

First, consumer credit is expensive credit, and interest cannot be deducted for income tax purposes. Visa and MasterCard arrangements can exceed 20% interest even in today's low-interest environment. In this situation, you would be better off trying to reduce the debt by selling short-term assets or to look for alternative sources of debt.

Second, using credit simply as a shopping convenience and paying your monthly bill on a timely basis to avoid interest makes sense. In fact, it's like an interest-free loan for the amount of your average monthly charges. Surely, take the loan and invest it. With some cards, however, interest is charged from the day a purchase is made, which eliminates this advantage.

INVESTING IN LIFE INSURANCE

You may not consider life insurance part of your investment portfolio, but that would be a mistake if you are thinking of buying whole life or universal life policies. In either case, your annual premiums can be large and may well consume most of your funds that could be invested elsewhere. Many insurance agents now stress the investment aspects of their policies, so it makes sense for investors to evaluate them as investments.

Life Insurance and Your Estate

Not everyone needs life insurance. Indeed, its primary purpose is to provide resources (an estate) for those who might need them in the event of your death. This observation raises two points: First, if you have no survivors who would be burdened by your untimely demise, then there is no need for an estate. This is why children and young adults have little need for life insurance. Second, if resources are available elsewhere, then life insurance is again not needed. For most younger investors, this situation is not likely.

Exhibit 5.10 shows how life insurance should be integrated within the overall estate plan. When a family is formed and then begins to develop, its needs soar, usually in response to desires for decent housing, medical care, and future education of the children. As these goals are gradually accomplished, family needs diminish over time and finally end with an amount a husband and wife want to leave to their heirs. Meanwhile, investment assets start to accumulate and increase in value. In the beginning, they are far less than the family's needs, thus creating a need for life insurance: it fills the gap between needs and available resources. At some point, the value of investment assets is enough to meet needs and life insurance is no longer necessary. Exhibit 5.10 represents a hypothetical—perhaps idealized—estate plan, but it is a useful guide to follow.

Determining a specific amount of needed life insurance requires a careful and comprehensive review of future family expenditures and income,

EXHIBIT 5.10
Needs, investment
assets, and life
insurance required

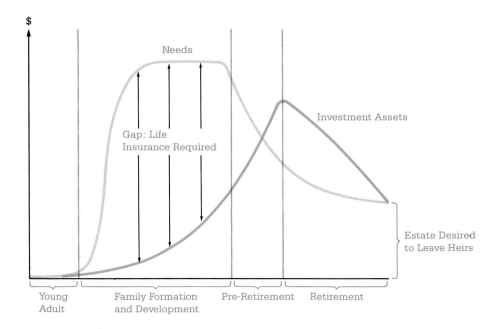

assuming the insured's death. Exhibit 5.11 shows estimated insurance requirements to replace 75% of earnings after taxes to the insured's age of 65. For example, if you are 25 years old and have a gross pay of $30,000, you need $390,000 (13 × $30,000) of life insurance. The amounts in Exhibit 5.11 are only rough approximations, which should be refined by considering your particular needs. For instance, a family with two spouses and six dependents clearly needs more than a family with only two dependents (the assumed number in the table).

EXHIBIT 5.11
Insurance
requirements to
replace 75% of
earnings after taxes to
insured's age 65 (as a
multiple of gross
annual pay)*

Gross Annual Pay	25	30	35	40	45	50	55
$ 20,000	14	13	12	10	9	7	6
30,000	14	13	12	10	9	7	5
40,000	13	12	11	10	9	7	5
60,000	12	12	11	9	8	6	5
80,000	12	11	10	9	8	6	4
100,000	11	10	9	8	7	5	4
150,000	10	10	9	8	7	5	4
200,000	9	9	8	7	6	5	5

*After-tax income varies among individuals. Factors such as investment rate of return, inflation rate, and individual debt, needs, goals, and retirement benefits should be determined on a personal basis.
SOURCE: The Principal Financial Group.

As you review the estimates in Exhibit 5.11, you might conclude that the amounts are high and that most families are terribly underinsured. This would be a correct perception. Because so much life insurance may be needed, the next question is, what kind?

Popular Forms of Life Insurance

A number of life insurance contracts are available, and the trend is to tailor policies to meet unique family needs. The most popular forms are term, whole life, universal life, and variable life.

Term Life Insurance **Term life insurance** provides protection for a given period—1, 5, 10, 20, or any number of years—without building asset value. In other words, it is pure insurance: you pay premiums and you receive protection. In this regard, it is similar to auto or homeowner's insurance. Term is the simplest life insurance to understand, but there are policy variations. For example, constant term provides a constant level of protection over the policy's life, while decreasing term allows the face value of the policy to decline over time. Some policies allow you to convert to whole life insurance if you wish, while others do not.

Term life insurance: provides protection for a given period but does not build asset value

Premiums on term insurance are low for young people, but they increase over time and eventually become prohibitively high for elderly people. If you are in your mid-20s and in good health and don't smoke, you should be able to buy $100,000 of insurance for a five-year period for about $200 a year; if you are in your early 60s, the annual premium will be about $2,000—if you are insurable. (Premiums vary considerably among insurers, making comparative shopping important.)

Despite its low cost, term insurance is less popular than whole life insurance. The lack of appeal might be explained by the buyers' fear of not being able to buy insurance later in life, but it also probably reflects the desire of most insureds to build an estate. Then, too, term insurance is not promoted heartily by insurance salespeople.

Whole Life Insurance **Whole life insurance** provides protection for the insured's entire life, but more important, it also builds up asset value over time, as Exhibit 5.12 shows. This latter feature makes whole life a hybrid of insurance and investment. The important question, then, is, how good an investment is it?

Whole life insurance: provides protection for an insured's entire life and builds growing asset value over time

As you suspect, the annual premiums for whole life are considerably greater than for term insurance for a given level of protection. You should view the additional premiums as you would any other investment you could make; in other words, if a term policy provides the same coverage at lower cost, then you should invest in a whole life policy only if the additional investment offers a satisfactory rate of return. Exhibit 5.13 presents an analysis of this decision for Megan Duffy. Megan has decided that her family will need

EXHIBIT 5.12
Buildup of cash value
of a typical $100,000
face value whole life
policy with dividends
applied to premiums

Year	Cash Value
1	$ -0-
2	-0-
3	2,748
4	5,278
5	7,962
6	10,648
7	13,332
8	16,017
9	18,872
10	21,728

$100,000 of additional protection over the next 10 years. She has obtained
premium information for a whole life policy and a term policy, which are similar in all respects except for premiums and cash value at the end of 10 years.

Megan determines the amount she could save each year with term
compared with whole life and assumes she will invest it to earn 8% each year

EXHIBIT 5.13
Investment analysis of
whole life versus term
insurance

Insured: female, age 35
Term of insurance: 10 years
Dividends on whole life: applied to premiums

(1)	(2) Premiums		(3)	(4)
Year	Whole-Life	Term		Savings with Term
1	$2,182	$253		$1,929
2	2,182	264		1,918
3	2,041	283		1,758
4	2,020	290		1,730
5	1,999	298		1,701
6	1,978	309		1,669
7	1,957	324		1,633
8	1,936	337		1,599
9	1,913	353		1,560
10	1,885	371		1,514

Compound value (CV) of column 4, assuming saving takes place at the beginning
of each year and is invested to earn 8% each year until maturity:

CV = $27,060

Cash value of whole life policy at the end of 10 years = _21,728_ (from Exhibit 5.12)

Advantage of term insurance $ 5,332

until the end of the 10 years. She then compares the future value of this series of investments with the cash value of the whole life policy at the end of 10 years. If the future value is greater, she will buy the term policy; if it is less, she will buy the whole life policy. As you see in Exhibit 5.13, the term insurance approach accumulates to $27,060, which is $5,332 more than the cash value of the whole life policy, making term the better alternative. Further analysis indicates that the whole life policy offers about a 5% annual rate of return. If Megan can invest elsewhere at a rate better than this, she should choose the term insurance alternative. Because this decision is important, investors must consider the following factors:

- ☐ Make sure the policies are almost identical. An important consideration is that the term policy must be renewable each year without a medical examination.
- ☐ Consider the impact of federal income taxes. The cash buildup with the whole life policy is tax-deferred; you pay no tax until your withdrawals from the policy exceed what you have invested in it. Megan's assumed 8% investment rate should not be a pre-tax rate; rather, it should also be a tax-deferred rate. Using an IRA for the side investment would accomplish that end, although some differences might arise.
- ☐ You must, in fact, invest the premium savings. Agents who push whole life (and many do because their commissions are higher) stress the forced-savings element in whole life policies. They argue that if you buy term, you probably will spend your savings, rather than invest them. (You might find this argument nonrelevant if you have discipline in managing your financial activities.)
- ☐ Whole life policies allow for borrowing. You can borrow easily and perhaps at an attractive fixed rate. This gives you immediate liquidity. You can also borrow with the term approach, using the side investments as collateral for a margin account, for instance. But rates are volatile and may be much higher. At the very least, determine borrowing arrangements with whole life and then evaluate their importance in the decision.

Universal Life Insurance As many consumers began evaluating their insurance needs in the manner just described and as they concluded that term insurance was the more attractive alternative, insurance companies began to realize that unless they designed more attractive life insurance, their business would suffer. The answer was the **universal life policy.**

A universal life policy is nothing more than a combination of term insurance and an investment account on the side. In other words, the insurer is doing for you what you should be able to do for yourself. There might be some justification in this if the insurer could earn higher returns or save you a lot of time and aggravation, but that appears not to be true. Moreover, you will pay high management fees, such as 7% to 10% on the annual premium plus 1% to 2% for annual maintenance. The side assets often are nothing more than

Universal life policy: policy that combines term insurance and an investment side account money market instruments, which means you are paying, say, a 7% load to invest in a money market fund. That is not effective investing. Review thoroughly any universal life policy being considered: Determine the fees, and then review the rates of return previously issued policies have earned in the past, comparing them with other market rates earned elsewhere during the same period. While considering returns, keep in mind that universal life policies also provide borrowing privileges and that income is earned on a tax-deferred basis.

Variable life insurance: similar to universal life but often only one initial premium is paid

Variable Life and Variable Annuities   **Variable life insurance** is similar to universal life in that typical insurance protection is combined with investment growth. Perhaps the major difference is in how premiums are paid. Many variable life policies are paid with a single premium at the time they are purchased, rather than with annual premiums. Variable annuities are actually not insurance policies, although they often are sold by insurance companies (along with many stockbrokerage firms). The most popular contract requires a single or several payments into the contract; then, the investor can make initial and periodic allocations among various mutual funds, such as stock, bond, or money market funds. In contrast to variable life, which might offer death benefits at two to three times the amount of the initial investment, a variable annuity has no insurance protection.

As with universal life, variable life and variable annuities often have high annual maintenance fees and/or a high initial load. These have lowered the returns on most contracts in relation to returns you could have earned investing in similar assets on your own. Despite poor returns, these contracts have become exceptionally popular because they offer tax-deferring advantages. Such advantages will be explained later in this chapter.

DESIGNING THE PORTFOLIO FOR RETIREMENT

For many investors, their most important investment goal is to have sufficient funds to help them *enjoy* their retirement years. *The* word *enjoy* is emphasized for a reason: many people today no longer look on retirement as a time to diminish their interests and activities in preparation for death. Indeed, today's elderly people see retirement as an opportunity to accomplish goals previously unattainable because of work's demands. Retirees in the past might have been willing to accept whatever Social Security and the company pension provided them and to scale down living standards if those amounts were inadequate to maintain them, but not so today. Living a comfortable and enriched life in retirement takes funds—and careful planning during the work years to make sure those funds are available.

Planning for Retirement

Planning for retirement involves three steps: First, you must estimate your living expenses in retirement; second, you must determine the proportion of

BOX 5.2   GETTING AN INVESTMENT EDGE

Retirement Planning: How Much Will You Need and When Should You Start Saving?

Let's consider the second question—When should you start saving?—first. The answer is, as soon as possible, even if you can afford only a modest amount and have only a hazy idea about how much will be needed in retirement. Starting early puts the power of compounding on your side, which never should be taken lightly. For example, suppose you are 25 and you want to accumulate $200,000 by age 65. Starting a savings program immediately and investing at, say, a 10% rate requires a monthly investment of a mere $31.63. But waiting until you are age 45 to begin will then require $263.38 a month. That's almost nine times as much; true, your needs between ages 45 and 65 should be less than between 25 and 45, but it's doubtful they will be nine times less.

How much you will need in retirement depends on how you want to live. If you are fairly typical, the budget information in the accompanying table (based on Census Bureau data) should be helpful. Most people need about 70% to 80% of their preretirement income, but don't rule out the possibility that you will have a different situation that could require more. Along this line, notice the sharp increase in health care costs. These expenses can vary considerably from one family to another.

Retirement Living Expenses	How They Change in Retirement: Percentage of Preretirement Expenses	As a Percentage of the Retiree's Budget
Housing	57%	32%
Food	59	17
Transportation	43	17
Health care	158	12
Clothing	41	4
Entertainment	38	4
Other (includes personal care, insurance, and contributions)	43	15
Total	—	100%

those expenses that will be met by Social Security and employer-provided plans; and third, you must build a portfolio to provide additional retirement funds, if they are needed. These steps are explained below, using Martin and Francine Dixon as an example. The Dixons have recently prepared retirement plans, even though they are quite young. They recognize that investing for retirement is a long process, and the sooner it is begun, the better are its chances for success.

Retirement Living Expenses   To estimate retirement living expenses, you first must decide how you want to live in retirement. The Dixons have chosen to maintain a lifestyle similar to their current situation, which requires a budget of about $60,000 a year. Because of certain savings, such as somewhat lower income taxes and the fact that their home mortgage will be paid off, they think that $50,000 a year will be adequate. This estimate is the first input on the worksheet shown in Exhibit 5.14.

The Dixons are in their early 30s and won't start retirement for another 30 years. Any inflation over their working years will require a higher budget estimate. Column 5 shows the impact of an estimated annual rate of inflation of 4%. To maintain a $50,000 budget in current dollars will take $162,170 in future dollars. The 4% estimate seems realistic to the Dixons; it could prove completely wrong, but at least it's a start and it provides a benchmark to reference portfolio returns that must be estimated later in the process.

Social Security and Employer-Provided Income   The next step is to estimate annual retirement income provided by Social Security and employer-provided retirement plans. As Exhibit 5.14 shows, the Dixons begin by determining how much would be available if retirement took place immediately; as you see, their estimates are $15,000 for Social Security and $18,000 for employer plans. Each of these must also consider future inflation.

Social Security benefit computations are indexed to the Consumer Price Index and, so, will increase at the 4% inflation rate. The Dixons are less sure of their employer plans. These plans have beaten past inflation rates by an average of two percentage points, leading the Dixons to assume the same performance in the future. This means the annual retirement income from the two sources are $48,650 and $103,382, totalling $152,032. Subtracting this total from the required retirement income of $162,170 leaves an annual income shortage of $10,138. This is the retirement income gap the Dixons must provide for by themselves.

Designing the Portfolio to Meet Retirement Needs   The $10,138 gap must be closed either with income earned by holding retirement assets or by gradually liquidating the assets during retirement. This choice brings into focus another aspect of retirement planning: the amount you want to leave your heirs at death. Although not the most pleasant of topics, it nevertheless must be addressed or the retirement portfolio cannot be estimated. Some people

EXHIBIT 5.14

A retirement plan for Martin and Francine Dixon

Current ages: early 30s
Planned retirement date: 30 years in future

(1) Item	(2) Current Amount	(3) Assumed Annual Growth Rate	(4) Compound Value Factor*	(5) Amount at Retirement (2) × (4)
1. Living expenses	$50,000	4%	3.2434	$162,170
Income				
2. Social Security	15,000	4%	3.2434	48,650
3. Employer-provided plans	18,000	6%	5.7434	103,382
				152,032
4. The "gap" = (1) − [(2) + (3)]	—	—	—	$ 10,138
5. Expected rate of return on assets held during retirement years				0.06
6. Retirement assets needed = (4) ÷ (5)				$168,967
7. Expected rate of return on assets held before retirement = 10%				
8. Future value annuity factor (ordinary annuity) at 10% for 30 years*				164.49
9. Annual investment required = (6) ÷ (8)				$ 1,027

*See Chapter 3 for a discussion of future value techniques.

hope to build a portfolio of sufficient size so they can live from its income in retirement and then pass it intact at death. There are many different wishes here, but this one makes planning convenient because you then do not have to consider depleting (or possibly increasing) the portfolio during the retirement years. The Dixons have made that assumption, as Exhibit 5.14 shows.

Beginning with the $10,138 requirement, they first estimate the rate of return they expect to earn on the retirement portfolio. As you see, this is 6%. Dividing $10,138 by 0.06 indicates the portfolio must have a value of $168,967. The Dixons have 30 years to achieve this target—this fact is certain. They are unsure, though, of what they will earn each year on their investments before retirement, so they must estimate a figure, and their estimate is 10%. Using the future value of an annuity approach (see Chapter 3 and assume an ordinary annuity OA), the annual investment the Dixons must make is $1,027. Their comprehensive investment plan, then, must allocate this amount each year for retirement.

You must choose investment assets that will meet your return objective. If you select a return that is not guaranteed, then an element of risk enters the picture. For example, at the time the Dixons were planning, a 10% rate was not guaranteed, although it seemed realistic in light of their estimate of inflation. Specifically, they intended to invest in equity mutual funds, using any tax-sheltering or tax-deferring arrangements available. They are aware that a retirement plan requires periodic monitoring to determine if its assumptions are still appropriate or if they require revising. A change in the inflation rate or portfolio rate of return could lead to substantial changes in the annual required investment. A serious investor includes an annual retirement portfolio review as an important part of his or her investment approach.

Using Self-Directed Investment Plans

A key to successful self-directed investment plans is to use tax-favored arrangements. These can increase investment accumulations substantially over the years before retirement, as we will see below. The three most popular devices are IRAs, Keogh Plans, and 401(k) plans.

Individual retirement account: easy-to-establish self-directed retirement plan that can defer taxes

The IRA   The **individual retirement account—IRA**—has been called the perfect tax shelter. Although this might be stretching it a bit, an IRA is a quick and effective way to save and invest for retirement. You set up an IRA by simply signing a form at the financial institution where you plan to invest—a bank, S&L, stockbrokerage firm, insurance company, or others— and your investment becomes an IRA; specifically, it allows up to $2,000 to be deducted in computing your taxable income. Notice that an IRA is not an investment itself, as some people mistakenly believe.

Although IRAs are simple to start and maintain, they have several limitations. First, you can invest no more than $2,000 a year or the amount of your earned income (usually wages or salaries), whichever is the smaller; also, you can invest up to $250 for a spouse with no earned income. Second, the maximum tax deduction is allowed only if income does not exceed $40,000 on a joint return or $25,000 for a single filer. You gradually lose the deduction as income exceeds these limits; however, you still can use IRAs for tax deferral.

Keogh plan: self-directed retirement plan available to self-employed people

Keogh Plans   A **Keogh plan** is like an IRA except that it is based on self-employment income and allows far greater annual deductions, up to $30,000. You also can borrow from a Keogh, which is a useful way of getting money out of the account without paying a penalty. For these reasons, a Keogh is probably a better deal than the IRA, and if you have self-employment income, you should investigate its possibilities. Many financial institutions will be helpful in providing information on establishing and maintaining a Keogh plan, and they also will serve as the plan's trustee.

401(k) plan: employer-provided retirement plan made available to employees on an optional basis

A 401(k) Plan   In contrast to an IRA or Keogh, **a 401(k) plan** is made available on an optional basis by an employer. The amount you choose to invest is taken out of pre-tax dollars, so a 401(k) has the same tax advantages as the other two. Moreover, because many employers will match your contribution, either partially or fully, the 401(k) can become the best of the three. It also allows for substantial annual contributions ($8,475 for the 1991 tax year, but the amount is indexed to inflation each year) and borrowing without penalty. By all means, determine if your employer has a 401(k), and if so, obtain as much information as you can about the plan.

Investment Accumulations   Choosing not to use a retirement plan could be a costly mistake, as Exhibit 5.15 shows. Column 6 indicates how much a $1,000 initial investment grows over time, assuming no retirement plan is used. As you see, the accumulation is $8,051 after 30 years, assuming a 10% pre-tax return and 7.2% after-tax and all annual earnings reinvested at the latter rate.

Columns 2 and 3 indicate accumulations under the assumption that an investor uses a retirement technique that allows a deduction for the initial

EXHIBIT 5.15
Amounts accumulated from a $1,000 investment assuming three tax situations: (1) investment is deductible and earnings are deferred, (2) investment is not deductible but earnings are deferred, and (3) no deduction and no deferral

Assumptions:	Funds earn a pre-tax return of 10%. Marginal tax rate is 28%. Marginal tax rate does not change over time.				
	(2) Situation 1	(3)	(4) Situation 2	(5)	
(1) Year	Before Tax on Withdrawals	After Tax on Withdrawals	Before Tax on Withdrawals	After Tax on Withdrawals	(6) Situation 3
0	$ 1,280	$ 922	$ 1,000	$1,000	$1,000
1	1,408	1,014	1,100	1,072	1,072
2	1,540	1,109	1,210	1,151	1,149
3	1,704	1,227	1,331	1,238	1,232
.					
.					
.					
10	3,320	2,390	2,594	2,147	2,004
.					
.					
20	8,611	6,200	6,728	5,124	4,007
.					
.					
30	22,335	16,081	17,449	12,843	8,051

investment and further allows all annual earnings to be reinvested at the pre-tax rate. The plan could be a Keogh, 401(k), or IRA (assuming the maximum income limitation is not exceeded). Column 2 indicates accumulations before considering taxes that would apply when funds are withdrawn, while Column 3 allows for such taxes. As you see, even after making the allowance, the accumulation after 30 years is almost twice that of using no retirement plan.

Columns 4 and 5 show accumulations assuming a situation that allows reinvested earnings to be tax-deferred but does not allow a deduction for the initial investment. This situation describes the use of an IRA after income exceeds the maximum limitation for a deduction. Also, other tax-deferred annuities—not necessarily associated with retirement—would be applicable here. As you see, the 30-year accumulation in column 5 is less than in situation 1 but still exceeds that in situation 3 by a considerable amount. Finally, you should note the long-term nature of retirement investing. Tax advantages become meaningful only after long periods. As Exhibit 5.15 indicates, even after a period as long as 10 years, the advantages are slight and probably not worth the illiquidity the tax shelters impose. After 20 or 30 years, however, the differences seem well worth the disadvantages.

Investment Planning in Retirement

Investment planning *in* retirement involves a different set of considerations than planning *for* retirement. To begin with, the process of budgeting and living within one's means becomes a reality rather than a plan. Inflation still must be considered during the retirement years, particularly if it accelerates and strains the resources accumulated for retirement. Also, the portfolio usually is restructured, with riskier assets being replaced by those with less risk. Finally, estate planning becomes a more important factor, although, as we noted above, it must be considered early in planning for retirement.

Budgeting in the Retirement Years   As retirement begins, many retirees find that a relatively large portion of their income becomes fixed. The fixed income is a consideration among many employer-provided pensions, and it also arises when whole life insurance policies are converted to annuities. As long as inflation remains relatively tolerable (perhaps 3% a year or less), the loss of purchasing power is not dramatic, although it can be serious if the retiree has a long life. At high inflation rates, you are forced to either reduce your living standards considerably or deplete retirement assets, thereby reducing your estate. It is important to understand that the retirement planning discussed above and expressed in Exhibit 5.14 assumes no change in inflation during the retirement years. The inflation factor must be included in the analysis if inflation appears to be a serious problem. We will not rework the example to show inflation's impact, but the Dixons could have a problem

BOX 5.3   A QUESTION OF ETHICS

Are We Heading Toward a National Crisis in Planning for Retirement?

A subtle but dramatic change is taking place in employee retirement plans: they are being converted from the defined-benefit form to the defined-contribution variety. With the former, employers guarantee retirement benefits to employees according to a particular formula that considers length of service and level of compensation. Employees make no contributions to such plans, and they typically are thought of as a major fringe benefit. In contrast, a defined-contribution plan usually is jointly funded by employees and employer and jointly contributed funds are invested in various vehicles, usually stock, bond, and MMMFs. These plans do not guarantee benefit levels because the amount of funds available to pay retirement benefits depends on how well (or poorly) the funds perform.

Over a three-year period (1990 through 1992), more than 30,000 U.S. employers terminated defined-benefit plans. In 1990, almost 40% of the terminated plans were not replaced, and of the 60% that did replace, the replacement was a defined-contribution plan. Experts believe that the trend will continue, perhaps even accelerating. So, what are the problems?

The primary concern is that many employees must now make decisions on how to invest the contributions. By itself, this is probably desirable because it provides for more individual choice. But how many employees have sufficient investment knowledge to make intelligent choices? Poor choices over time—being too conservative, for example—can lead to meager accumulations. Although some companies try to help employees by holding investment and financial planning seminars, all too often the seminar leaders present a biased view because they also sell financial products.

Another critical concern is that employees often are free to withdraw funds from a plan when they leave an employer. When you are a typical 30-year-old with a high-consumption living standard and you have the choice of, say, withdrawing $10,000 from a plan or rolling it over into another tax-deferred retirement plan, the incentive to take the cash is strong, despite tax penalties. Some job changers aren't even fully aware that they were contributing to a retirement plan, and for them, the immediate cash is like "found money."

Should we hold employers more accountable for future employee retirement benefits? Or should the federal government intervene in the process and perhaps strengthen Social Security retirement benefits and, of course, taxes to pay for them? Or do we let employees take the responsibility and, if they act irresponsibly, suffer a low-consumption retirement? There is no easy solution to this one.

with their employer-provided income, forcing them either to accumulate more than $168,967 or to reduce the final estate they pass to their heirs.

The Portfolio in Retirement   There is no simple answer to the inflation problem. Perhaps being aware of it and then attempting to select assets that provide inflation-indexed income is the only solution. For example, retirees might choose to take the cash value of their life insurance policies, rather than convert them to annuities, and do their own investing. We saw in Chapter 3 that Treasury bills offered returns that about equaled the inflation rate over a long period. Although there is no assurance this will continue— that is, the bill return is not contractually indexed to inflation—it is quite likely to do so. Or U.S. Series EE bonds might be an appropriate choice for funds not needed immediately. These are indexed by contract to rates of return on Treasury securities.

If you choose short-term assets with variable returns, you often must forgo the potentially higher returns with fixed-income assets. Moreover, your income will fluctuate—a situation many retirees want to avoid. Investing in retirement is no different from investing at other times: we cannot have our cake and eat it too. If we want to protect against escalating inflation, we must accept both variable income and lower returns if the inflation rate diminishes, which it did substantially in the early 1990s and which caused considerable anguish to retirees who had become accustomed to high rates on their CDs.

Estate planning: strategies designed to minimize the federal estate tax

Investments and the Estate Plan   At some point, we must address the prospect of arranging our portfolios for our heirs' convenience rather than for our own. To meet this objective, we try to organize our assets in a manner that makes transfer easy and minimizes the amount of estate tax. Doing so might call for another complete restructuring of the portfolio, with the two factors above being the primary considerations. **Estate planning** is a complex subject, involving both legal and tax factors. Therefore, generalization is difficult. However, there usually are advantages in beginning to distribute assets before death. These advantages derive from the tax law that allows credits to each spouse in determining the estate tax liability and also allows deductions of annual gifts up to $20,000 (each spouse consenting) for each child or other donee. These substantial estate tax savings should not be overlooked.

The larger the estate, perhaps the larger the potential savings. But even estates as small as $600,000 can benefit from effective planning. Although this amount might seem large to you, actually it isn't. Inflation has elevated most investors' incomes and estates, and a home worth half the amount above is not uncommon today in many parts of the United States. Even modest inflation rates over the next 20 to 30 years will put many families above the threshold level when estate taxes begin, although the government may increase the estate tax credit to adjust for inflation.

SUMMARY

Liquid assets are held to undertake transactions or to serve as emergency reserves or a store of value. Financial institutions offer many liquid assets to investors. Such institutions include commercial banks, S&Ls and savings banks, credit unions, consumer banks, and stockbrokerage firms.

Accounts at financial institutions include checking and NOW accounts as well as savings accounts, which may be passbook accounts, MMDAs, and CDs. Financial institutions determine interest on savings accounts in many ways. Liquid assets also include U.S. Treasury securities (bills and bonds, or notes with short maturities); U.S. Series EE and HH bonds; and non–Treasury-issued securities, such as commercial paper, negotiable CDs, and MMMFs.

Liquidity management must consider the possibility of borrowing to meet liquidity needs. The advantage of holding both short-term assets and debt is that it avoids the possibility of borrowing in the future. Frequently used sources of credit are margin accounts, bank loans (using securities as collateral), whole life insurance policies, retirement plans, and consumer credit such as Visa and MasterCard.

Life insurance often is considered when investment choices are made because it is part of an investor's total estate. Popular forms of life insurance are term life, whole life, universal life, and variable life. Choosing between term and whole life often involves an estimate of the results of buying term and investing the difference.

Considering retirement requires both planning for retirement and planning during retirement. In the case of the former, it is necessary to estimate retirement living expenses and income from Social Security and employer-provided plans. If such income is inadequate, the gap must be managed by the investor through self-directed plans. These investments should be made using the advantages of tax shelters such as IRAs, Keogh plans, and 401(k) plans. The portfolio during retirement often is adjusted to increase safety of principal and plan for its eventual transfer to heirs. At this point, estate planning becomes important.

KEY TERMS
(listed in order of appearance)

liquidity management
emergency reserve
store of value
temporary parking place
NOW account
passbook account
money market deposit account
certificate of deposit
Treasury bills
U.S. Series EE bonds
U.S. Series HH bonds
commercial paper
negotiable CDs
money market mutual fund
leverage
term life insurance
whole life insurance
universal life policy
variable life insurance
individual retirement account
Keogh plan
401(k) plan
estate planning

1.   Discuss what is meant by liquidity management. Include in your discussion the meaning of liquidity and the relationship between liquidity and asset return.

2.   Explain three reasons why investors want to hold liquid assets. If your monthly expenditures are $3,000, about how much should you hold in an emergency fund? When would short-term investments be used as a temporary parking place?

3.   Describe the five kinds of financial institutions discussed in this chapter. Explain whether it is worth your time to shop around if you are looking for one.

4.   Identify the key characteristics of the following deposits: *(a)* checking, NOW, and super-NOW accounts; *(b)* passbook account; *(c)* MMDA; and *(d)* CD.

5.   Does it matter how often interest is compounded on a savings account? Explain.

6.   Indicate four methods savings institutions use to determine interest on a savings account. Indicate which is the best method for investors.

7.   Identify the key characteristics of U.S. Treasury bills, including a discussion of how you might purchase them.

8.   Identify the key characteristics of U.S. Series EE bonds. What feature enhances their appeal to investors concerned about inflation and rising interest rates?

9.   Explain commercial paper and negotiable CDs. Are these popular securities with small investors? Explain.

10. Discuss MMMFs, describing their characteristics, varieties, and safety record. Do you think that they are as safe as MMDAs? Indicate your personal preference for one over the other, explaining the reason for your choice.

11. If you examine balance sheets of many investors, you find that some have both long- and short-term investments and some form of short-term debt, such as a margin account or installment loans. Is it correct, then, to argue that borrowed funds are used to acquire long-term investments? Discuss.

12. Can a margin account be used as a source of loan funds? Is this similar to borrowing from a bank, pledging securities as collateral? Explain.

13. Are life insurance policies a source of loan funds? Explain, discussing the implication of "robbing from your beneficiaries."

14. What form of borrowing "robs from your retirement"? Explain, indicating whether you think that this source of funds should be used.

15. Should consumer credit sources, such as Visa and MasterCard, ever be used? Explain.

16. What justifications are there for considering life insurance as an investment? Explain.

17. Discuss how your life insurance needs can change throughout your life. Discuss the "gap" as it applies to life insurance planning.

18. Compare and contrast: term life insurance, whole life insurance, universal life insurance, and variable life insurance.

19. Suppose you are considering either a whole life or a term policy. How should you analyze the decision? Discuss important factors that should be considered.

20. How does planning *for* retirement differ from planning *in* retirement? Also, what role does inflation play in each case? Discuss.

21. Discuss three steps in planning for retirement.

22. Explain the "gap" in retirement planning and how it is closed.

23. Explain IRAs, Keoghs, and 401(k) plans; then discuss the advantages of accumulating funds with an IRA, investing in a tax-deferral plan, and investing with no deduction and no deferral.

24. Explain why and how you might restructure your portfolio, given considerations of estate planning.

PROBLEMS AND PROJECTS

1. Which is the better savings account: one offering a 4.25% rate compounded annually or another offering a 4.0% rate compounded quarterly? Indicate the total accumulation with each account after 5 years, 10 years, and 40 years.

2. Tito Francola has a savings account that determines interest quarterly. It offers an 8% rate computed on an annual basis and determines interest quarterly. Qualifying balances for interest are based on the minimum balance method. Activity in Tito's account last quarter was as follows:

Opening balance at day 1	$1,000
Deposit, 60 days after day 1	500
Withdrawal, 75 days after day 1	600
Balance at end of the quarter	900

Calculate Tito's interest and compare it with the amount he would have earned with other methods of determining interest: *(a)* day of deposit to day of withdrawal, *(b)* FIFO, and *(c)* LIFO.

3. Tom Lustie's investment portfolio now consists of $5,000 of short-term investments that yield about 10% a year. He is considering opening a margin account and using it to borrow $5,000 to invest in common stocks that he expects will appreciate 20% in value next year. He estimates his margin interest at 12% and does admit the stocks have an equal chance of declining 20% in value. Determine Tom's possible rates of return on his invested capital if he goes ahead with his plan. Compare your answers with his rate of return if he does not. What would you advise Tom to do? What would you do personally?

4. Barry Beavis has a gross pay of $40,000. Barry is 30 years old and has two dependents. How much life insurance does he need? How much would he need if his income increased to $60,000? How much would he need if he was 50 instead of 30?

5. Flora Luckett is trying to decide if she should purchase term life insurance or a whole life policy. Each insurance would last for five years. The annual premiums on the policies are $200 for term and $1,500 for whole life. The cash value of the whole life policy at its maturity is $8,000.
   a. If Flora can earn 10% on her other investments (comparable in risk and tax treatment to the whole life policy), which is the better alternative? Show your calculations.
   b. What other factors should Flora consider before making a choice? Explain.

6. Assume you are 25 years old and plan to retire at age 65. Based on today's prices, you figure that you will need $40,000 annually to enjoy your retirement, and if you retired today, you could expect to receive $8,000 a year from Social

Security and $5,000 a year from an employer-provided plan, which has shown an annual growth rate of 5% a year that you think will continue in the future. You also think inflation will be 3% annually until and during retirement.

a. If $40,000 is adequate today, how much will you need at age 65?

b. Determine the annual income from Social Security and the retirement plan when you retire.

c. Assuming your portfolio will match the inflation rate during the retirement years and your portfolio held for retirement will earn 8%, determine how much you must invest each year to achieve your retirement goals. (Assume that you want to pass your retirement portfolio intact to your heirs.)

7. Lars and Greta Oyens' parents are advancing in age but are in good health. The senior Oyenses have been successful in farming and own an estate worth $2 million. The farm property is worth $1 million and the balance is invested in a portfolio of growth stocks and long-term bonds. Lars and Greta are concerned that their parents could die unexpectedly. A $2 million estate would be taxed heavily, and they lack sufficient funds to pay such taxes. However, there is a good chance the folks could live another 20 years. Both Lars and Greta have successful careers of their own, and neither is interested in running the farm.

a. What step could the elder Oyenses take now to reduce the estate tax? Assuming each lives 20 years, how much of the estate could be passed to Lars and Greta?

b. What estate planning steps might be appropriate in the Oyens' situation?

8. *(Student Project)* Obtain a current copy of Money magazine and a copy that is two years old. Find the sections (usually in the first 50 pages) describing returns on many of the investments explained in this chapter. Compare rates on the investments between the two time periods and discuss your findings.

9. *(Student Project)* Contact a Federal Reserve Bank in your area and ask for a tender form for 13-week bills. You also can contact the U.S. Treasury Bureau of the Public Debt at 1-202-287-4113 for information.

10. *(Student Project)* Call the Series EE Bond Information Center at the number given in the text and obtain current rate information. Also, present an argument favoring investment in such bonds.

11. *(Student Project)* Contact a local insurance agent and ask him or her to describe briefly a whole life policy and a universal life policy that could be written specifically for you. Assume you want $100,000 of protection. Then, ask for cost and other details of a term policy for the same amount. Assume you are interested in constant-level term and wish to maintain coverage until age 60.

CASE ANALYSES

5.1 The Hamiltons Consider a Short-Term Portfolio

Melanie and Frank Hamilton are a professional couple with two young children. Their combined income is $72,000 a year, consisting mostly of salaries and dividends from their stock investments. The Hamiltons are avid investors and enjoy a stock and bond portfolio (about equally weighted) worth about $81,000; however, they have no short-term investments other than a checking account that has an average balance of around $800. Frank thinks short-term investments are not suitable for their goals, which consist primarily of an educational fund for their children and a retirement fund. Moreover, Frank argues that stocks can always be sold if a cash emergency arises.

Melanie disagrees. Her casual reading of investment literature suggests that most investment advisors recommend that some short-term investments be held all the time. Accordingly, she has prepared the following list of vehicles, along with current rates, to consider as possible additions to their portfolio. The Hamiltons have a low risk tolerance with respect to achieving their major goals. Also, the Hamiltons do not have particularly good disability insurance, although they do have excellent life insurance coverage.

1. U.S. Treasury bills (3.0%)
2. U.S. Series EE bonds (4.0%)
3. MMDA (2.5%)
4. MMMF—low risk (3.5%)
5. Three-year CDs (5.0%)
6. Ten-year CDs (5.5%)
7. Commercial paper (3.3%)
8. Negotiable CDs (3.2%)
9. Money market life insurance policy (current rate of 6% but guaranteed rate of 2.5%; policy loans—up to a maximum of $10,000—are available at 5.5%, but policy then earns the guaranteed rate)

a. Do you agree with Frank that short-term investments are not suitable for their investment goals? Explain.
b. What portion, if any, of the Hamiltons' portfolio would you recommend be invested in short-term securities? Would you sell stocks, bonds, or both to rearrange the portfolio?
c. Select short-term securities for the Hamiltons, indicating a total investment and a breakdown of amounts to be invested in the vehicles you think are appropriate.

Questions

Leo and Maria Tiant are expecting their first child shortly. Maria will resign her position as a personnel director and devote full time to managing the household. Leo will continue his position as an agricultural economist with a large seed company where he earned $60,000 last year. The Tiants will need considerably more insurance on Leo's life when the baby arrives. They have been reviewing policies with an agent but are having difficulty making a decision. They regard themselves as having a low tolerance for risk and preferring a high-consumption lifestyle. Their attempts at budgeting in the past have not been successful.

The agent favors a whole life policy with a $300,000 face value (an amount paid to Maria, or other beneficiary, in the event of Leo's death). Annual premiums would be $5,000 and the policy would have a guaranteed cash value of $292,000 at the end of 25 years—the length of time the Tiants believe insurance is most needed. The agent also indicated that term insurance for $300,000 could be written with a level annual premium of $1,400.

**5.2
The Tiants
Consider Life
Insurance**

Questions
a. Assume the Tiants have a 30% marginal tax rate and could earn 10% on their investments over the next 25 years; which form of insurance is the better investment? Show how you arrive at your answer.
b. Which form would you recommend for the Tiants? Explain your selection.

5.3
The Markleys
Plan for
Retirement

Delbert and Florence Markley have operated a motel on a major interstate highway for the past 15 years. The business has been quite successful, enabling the Markleys to enjoy a high standard of living while educating their three children. They have accumulated a modest amount of savings—$15,000—that is invested in CDs. However, Del and Flo, now in their early 40s, have not done any retirement planning. Because they are self-employed, their retirement years could be a disaster if they can't sell the motel at a reasonable price, or if their children intend to operate the business. Recognizing potential future problems, the Markleys have decided to draft a retirement plan and adhere to it over the next 20 years.

   If they retired today, Del and Flo would need $40,000 a year to enjoy the lifestyle they desire. Considerably more will be needed in 20 years if inflation averages 3% a year, as they anticipate. Flo called Social Security to determine the amount a retiring couple in a situation similar to theirs would receive if retirement occurred today. This amount was $12,000. The Markleys plan to live off the current income their retirement nest egg will provide, and they will pass the principal amount to their children as part of their will. Moreover, they intend to invest in securities that will match inflation, thereby covering rising living costs during the retirement years. Flo is somewhat familiar with time-value-of-money concepts, although she has not worked with them for many years. Neither she nor Del understands possible income tax implications of retirement planning. Flo had intended to rough out an amount they need to save and invest each year, based on an assumption their investments would yield 12% before taxes and 9% after taxes. They also believe their investments will yield 4% after taxes during their retirement years. The Markleys would like you to assist and advise them in drafting a retirement plan.

Questions
a. Determine the amount needed to meet annual living expenses in retirement. Also, determine the amount covered by Social Security and the "gap." Finally, indicate the retirement assets needed during the retirement years.
b. What portion of the "gap" will their current savings of $15,000 provide, assuming it is invested at the after-tax rate?
c. Considering your response to questions *a* and *b*, determine how much the Markleys must invest each year before retirement, again assuming the after-tax rate applies.
d. Suppose the Markleys can use a tax-sheltering arrangement that would allow them a $15,000 tax deduction immediately if the funds are invested under the shelter. How much would this accumulate over the 20-year

period, also assuming reinvested earnings are tax deferred? How much would accumulate if a tax deduction could not be taken at the time of investing but all reinvestments are tax-deferred? Compare these amounts (after allowing for taxes on withdrawals) with your response to question *c*. (Point of concern: Tax-deferred investing involves certain complexities in the Markleys' case because they do not anticipate reducing the principal accumulated at the time of retirement. This approach could lead to eventual problems because withdrawals are now required after a certain age, and it complicates any estate plan they may draw up later.)

HELPFUL READING

Clements, Jonathon. "Getting Growth and Income Once You Retire." *The Wall Street Journal,* December 13, 1992, p. C1.

Fenner, Elizabeth. "The Best Way to Save for Retirement." *Money*, November 1992, pp. 92–109.

Fried, Carla A. "Questions to Ask Your Agent." *Money*, January 1993, pp. 96–101.

Gottschalk, Earl C., Jr. "Beware of 'Pension Max' Insurance Sales Pitch." *The Wall Street Journal*, August 6, 1993, p. C1.

Greer, Carolyn T. "Coming to Terms with Term." *Forbes*, August 2, 1993, pp. 44–45.

Schultz, Ellen E. "Taking the Confusion Out of Options for Withdrawals from Retirement Plans." *The Wall Street Journal*, August 25, 1992, p. C1.

———. "Raiding Pension Money Now May Leave You Without Piggy Bank for Retirement." *The Wall Street Journal*, April 7, 1993, p. C1.

———. "Variable Annuity Buyers Warned to Check the Underlying Funds." *The Wall Street Journal*, July 13, 1993, p. C1.

Simon, Ruth. "How to Retire with All the Money You Will Ever Need." *Money*, June 1993, pp. 102–13.

Slater, Karen. "Term Insurance or Cash Value? No Easy Answer." *The Wall Street Journal*, June 28, 1991, p. C1.

Updegrave, Walter L. "Saving on Life Insurance." *Money*, June 1992, pp. 86–90.

PART ONE

CFA EXAMINATION QUESTIONS

1. A securities market characterized by individuals or organizations that buy and sell securities for their own inventories is called:

   a. a primary market.
   b. a secondary market.
   c. an over-the-counter market.
   d. an institutional market.

2. Specialists on stock exchanges do all of the following *except:*

   a. act as dealers for their own accounts.
   b. monitor compliance with margin requirements.
   c. provide liquidity to the market.
   d. monitor and execute unfilled limit orders.

3. The over-the-counter market for exchange-listed securities is called the:

   a. third market.
   b. fourth market.
   c. after-market.
   d. block market.

4. Assume you purchase 100 shares of common stock on margin for $50 per share. Also assume the initial margin is 50% and the stock pays no dividend. What would be your rate of return if you sell the stock one year later for $60 per share? Ignore interest on margin and assume you did not remove any money from the account prior to selling the stock.

   a. 16.7%
   b. 20.0%
   c. 33.3%
   d. 40.0%

5. Assume you sell short 100 shares of common stock at $50 per share. With initial margin at 50%, what would be your rate of return if you repurchase the stock at $40 per share? The stock paid no dividends during the period, and you did not remove any money from the account before making the offsetting transaction.

   a. 20%
   b. 25%
   c. 40%
   d. 50%

6. You are considering acquiring a common stock that you would like to hold for one year. You expect to receive both $1.50 in dividends and $26 from the sale of stock at the end of the year. What is the maximum price you would pay for the stock today if you wanted to earn a 15% return?

   a. $23.91
   b. $24.11
   c. $27.30
   d. $27.50

7. The difference between an arithmetic average and a geometric average of returns:

   a. increases as the variability of the returns increases.
   b. increases as the variability of the returns decreases.

c. is always negative.

d. depends on the specific returns being averaged but is not necessarily sensitive to their variability.

8. If the market prices of each of the 30 stocks in the Dow Jones Industrial Average (DJIA) all change by the same percentage amount during a given day, which stock will have the greatest impact on the DJIA?

a. The one whose stock trades at the highest dollar price per share.

b. The one whose total equity has the highest market value.

c. The one having the greatest amount of equity in its capital structure.

d. The one having the lowest volatility.

9. The Value Line index is an equally weighted geometric average of the return of about 1,700 firms. What is the value of an index based on the geometric average returns of three stocks, where the returns on the three stocks during a given period were 20%, 10%, and 5%?

a. 4.3

b. 5.0

c. 11.7

d. 13.4

10. What is the present value of the following stream of year-end payments discounted at 12% per year?

Year 1	Year 2	Year 3	Year 4
−$100	−$200	−$100	$450

a. −$53.37

b. −$44.65

c. −$33.92

d. −$13.06

11. If $1,500 is invested today and $1,500 is invested one year from today both at the annual interest rate of 12% compounded annually, what will be the total amount in the account two years from today?

a. $3,180

b. $3,360

c. $3,382

d. $3,562

12. An investment of $232 will increase in value to $268 in three years. What is the annual compound growth rate?

a. 3.0%

b. 4.0%

c. 5.0%

d. 6.0%

13. You are buying a $100,000 house with a 30-year mortgage requiring payments to be made at the end of each year. The interest rate is 10% and the first payment is due one year from today. How much will your annual payment be?

a. $10,608
b. $10,672
c. $12,343
d. $13,303

14. You are creating a charitable trust to provide six annual payments of $20,000 each, beginning today. How much money must you set aside now at 10% interest compounded annually to meet the required disbursements?

a. $75,815
b. $78,815
c. $83,397
d. $95,816

15. Given $100,000 to invest, what is the expected risk premium in dollars of investing in equities versus risk-free T-Bills (U.S. Treasury bills) based on the following table?

Action	Probability	Expected Return
Invest in	.6 ———	$50,000
equities	.4 ———	−$30,000
Invest in		
risk-free T-bill	1.0	$ 5,000

a. $13,000
b. $15,000
c. $18,000
d. $20,000

16. Based on the scenarios below, what is the expected return for a portfolio with the following return profile?

	Market Condition		
	Bear	Normal	Bull
Probability	.2	.3	.5
Rate of return	−25%	10%	24%

a. 4%
b. 10%
c. 20%
d. 25%

17. Empirical evidence from the past 60 years indicates there is a high positive correlation between the returns on 30-day U.S. Treasury bills and the:

    a. return on long-term U.S. Treasury bonds.
    b. inflation rate in the United States.
    c. return on U.S. common stock.
    d. return on U.S. corporate bonds.

18. Historical data suggest that stocks are most likely to produce positive returns if the investor's time horizon is:

    a. one year.
    b. three years.
    c. five years.
    d. ten years.

19. Standard deviation and beta both measure risk, but they are different in that:

    a. Beta measures both systematic and unsystematic risk, while standard deviation measures only unsystematic risk.
    b. Beta measures only systematic risk, while standard deviation is a measure of total risk.
    c. Beta measures only unsystematic risk, while standard deviation is a measure of total risk.
    d. Beta measures both systematic and unsystematic risk, while standard deviation measures only systematic risk.

20. Which *one* of the following is *not* a criticism of beta?

    a. Different calculation methods yield differing beta numbers.
    b. Estimated betas on individual stocks are unstable.
    c. In some periods, low beta stocks outperform high beta stocks.
    d. Wide-scale usage has reduced the effectiveness of the beta measure.

21. Which statement about portfolio diversification is correct?

    a. Proper diversification can reduce or eliminate systematic risk.
    b. The risk-reducing benefits of diversification do not occur meaningfully until at least 10 to 15 individual securities have been purchased.
    c. Because diversification reduces a portfolio's total risk, it necessarily reduces the portfolio's expected return.
    d. Typically, as more securities are added to a portfolio, total risk would be expected to fall at a decreasing rate.

Investing in Common Stocks

Common stocks provide ownership interests in the corporations that issue them. If you buy common stock, you are a partial owner of the business, and your return will depend directly on its success—or failure.

Chapter 6 explains return and risk characteristics of common stock investing. It identifies different opportunities in common stocks and categorizes risk into diversifiable and nondiversifiable sources, explaining how investors can deal with each. It also discusses how required rates of return can be derived for common stocks and how earnings and dividend approaches are used to select securities.

Chapter 7 explains the tools of fundamental analysis of common stock. It identifies key components of a company's balance sheet and income statement and shows how ratio analysis is useful in measuring financial strength and earnings performance. It also indicates how changes in the overall economy or a particular industry affect specific firms.

Chapter 8 discusses and evaluates technical analysis, viewing selected technical indicators in depth. It introduces the topic of efficient security markets. Also, the efficient market hypothesis is explained, and empirical tests of the hypothesis are reviewed.

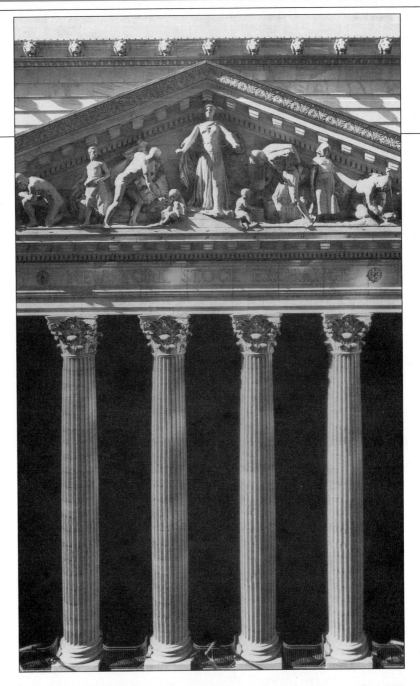

CHAPTER SIX

Return and Risk
in Common Stocks

After you finish this chapter, you
will be able to:

- identify the basic rights of common stockholders, and understand what it means to have a
residual interest

- recognize different return opportunities in common stocks that
are provided through cash dividends or price appreciation.

- recognize the risks of common
stock investing, including firm-
specific, industry, and market
risks.

- determine a required rate of
return to evaluate stock opportunities by constructing and using
a securities market line.

- understand and apply the earnings approach and the dividend
approach to stock evaluation
and selection.

- apply the dividend model with
multiple growth rates.

- identify other valuation methods, based on asset approaches,
break-up value, and rules of
thumb.

To many people, investment and common stock mean the same thing. All funds not needed for liquidity are invested in common stocks. For these investors, "playing the market" is an obsession not terribly different from "playing the horses," and they know less about the stocks they trade than racing enthusiasts know about horses they bet on. The lure is the super return. Most of us have read that $1,000 invested in Microsoft 10 years ago or McDonald's 25 years ago would have made us rich, and we saw in Chapter 3 that simply investing $1,000 in the smallest companies on the New York Stock Exchange 67 years ago would have made us millionaires today. With profits this high and so easily earned, who can resist?

To be sure, common stocks do offer the potential for returns higher than those usually available on money market instruments and long-term bonds. Earning these returns, though, is not easy and demands that you take risks. Risk means variability of return: the chances of taking substantial losses with common stocks are high even if you do your homework and invest intelligently. And if you plan to be an investor who "plays the market," rather than "invests in the market," your losses can be extraordinary. The intent of this chapter and the next two is to help you be an intelligent common stock investor.

COMMON STOCK CHARACTERISTICS

Common stock: represents an ownership interest in a corporation and entitles its owner to certain rights

A share of **common stock** represents an ownership interest in the issuing corporation. When you invest in common stocks, you acquire certain ownership rights, and you are looking for various return opportunities. Before investing, you should understand these rights and opportunities.

Stockholders' Rights

Suppose you are thinking of investing in Mead Corporation—a paper and forest products company with other diversified interests—by buying 100 shares of its common stock at $40 a share. Along with receiving a stock certificate (such as the one shown in Exhibit 6.1) evidencing your ownership, you will become one of about 18,000 other investors who own some 59 million shares of Mead common stock. Your 100 shares will give you a 0.00000170 (100/59,000,000) interest in the company. Although your holding is minuscule, you are an owner. True, you have far less power than someone who owns 1 million shares, but you have identical privileges. Each of you has the right to vote for members of the board of directors or in other matters affecting the company, the right to maintain a proportionate interest in the company, and the right to share in its distributions of assets or earnings.

Voting right: allows a shareholder to cast a vote in corporate matters; usually each share has one vote, except in the case of cumulative voting

The Right to Vote   Your **voting right** means one vote for each share of stock. A corporation is not a democracy that allows one vote for each shareholder. The person who holds 1 million shares to your 100 has 10,000 times

EXHIBIT 6.1

A share of Mead common stock (Courtesy of the Mead Corporation.)

more say in the business than you do. Some corporations, however, have a system of voting—called cumulative voting—that gives more power to shareholders with a minority interest. Suppose nine members are to be elected to nine seats on a corporation's board of directors. With traditional voting, if you own 100 shares, you can cast 100 votes for each seat; but with cumulative voting, you could cast 900 votes for only one director, giving up your right to vote for the other eight seats. With this method, minority interests might be able to pool their votes to elect at least one or several directors.

The Preemptive Right   As small as it is, you still have a right to maintain your proportionate interest in Mead. This is called a **preemptive right.** Without such a right, your ownership interest could be diluted by simply selling more shares to others and not to you. If Mead wanted to sell 10 million more shares to raise capital, you would have a right to buy 17 (0.00000170 × 10,000,000) more shares. Most investors do not put a great deal of emphasis

Preemptive right: allows shareholders to maintain their proportionate ownership interests

on the preemptive right, and many corporate charters (the document that creates the corporation) are amended to allow investors to give up the right so
that management has greater financing flexibility.

Right to share: allows shareholders to participate, under particular conditions, in earnings or asset distributions

The Right to Share in Earnings or Asset Distributions   The **right to share** in earnings or other distributions is the right that appeals most to investors. With common stock you have the right to participate (in proportion to the number of shares you own) in the distribution of earnings or assets. This right is limited, however. For example, most states prohibit any distribution that would impair the firm's capital and subject its creditors to greater risk. In addition, if the corporation has preferred stock outstanding, all current or past unpaid dividends must be paid on it before any cash distributions can be made to common stockholders. As a common stockholder, therefore, you stand last in the distribution line, behind both bondholders and preferred stockholders. You are said to have a **residual claim;** that is, you get what is left. Although this sounds dismal, getting what is left is why you buy common stock in the first place. Although bondholders and preferred stockholders have prior claims, the amounts they are entitled to usually are fixed each year, which means that regardless of how well (or poorly) the company does, the amount they get is the same. In contrast, the amounts available to common stockholders vary in direct proportion to the company's profits. Exhibit 6.2 illustrates this situation.

Residual claim: means that shareholders' claim to asset distributions ranks behind the claims of creditors and preferred shareholders

EXHIBIT 6.2

Illustration of common stock's residual interest

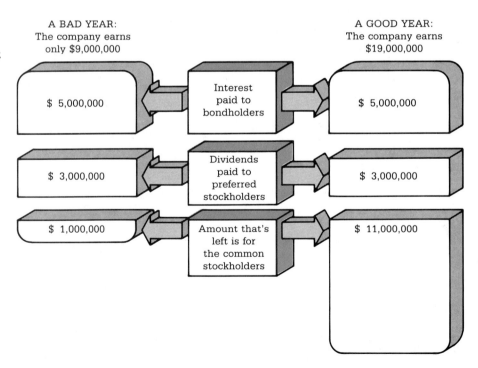

A BAD YEAR: The company earns only $9,000,000		A GOOD YEAR: The company earns $19,000,000
$ 5,000,000	Interest paid to bondholders	$ 5,000,000
$ 3,000,000	Dividends paid to preferred stockholders	$ 3,000,000
$ 1,000,000	Amount that's left is for the common stockholders	$ 11,000,000

The company has bonds outstanding requiring $5 million a year in interest and preferred stock requiring $3 million a year in dividends. This represents $8 million of fixed obligations that must be paid before any earnings are available to common stockholders. Thus, in a bad year, when profits are only $9 million, common stockholders' claims on earnings would be $1 million; but in a good year, when profits jump to $19 million, they are entitled to $11 million. The corporation may not pay all the common stockholders' claims in dividends. Indeed, it is more common to retain a large portion of earnings for reinvestment in the business. The proportion of earnings (E) paid in dividends (D) is called the **payout ratio;** that is,

$$\text{payout ratio} = D/E$$

We will use this ratio later and in Chapter 7, but you can see now that companies with high ratios usually represent poor growth opportunities. It is difficult for the company to grow when it pays out a large proportion of its earnings in dividends.

Payout ratio: amount of earnings paid in dividends to common shareholders, calculated as dividends/earnings

Corporate Distributions

Although cash dividends are by far the most common form of distributions to shareholders, there are other forms. Each is explained below.

Cash Dividends   Many corporations have policies of paying regular, quarterly **cash dividends.** Successful corporations have the capacity to make the dividends grow significantly over time. For example, if you had bought Ennis Business Forms, Inc., in 1967, your annual dividend alone in 1992 would have been 1.7 times its then current price; in other words, using 1967's price, your dividend yield was 166.7%! As an investor, you must choose between high current yield and high dividend growth. Later in this chapter, each factor is considered in a valuation approach. For now, let us focus on important dividend dates.

Cash dividends: dividends paid in cash

Date of Record   The company's board of directors sets the **date of record.** If your name appears in the firm's stock ledger on this date, you are entitled to receive the dividend. As an example, assume this date is October 10.

Date of record: date you must own shares to be entitled to a dividend

Ex-Dividend Date   The stock exchanges set the **ex-dividend date,** usually four business days before the date of record, or October 6 in our example. Beginning with the ex-dividend date, a stock sells without ("ex") the dividend. For example, if ABC, Inc., closes at $50 a share on October 5 and a $2 dividend has been declared, on October 6, its stock will open at $48 a share. If you buy it on that date or later, you do not get the dividend.

Ex-dividend date: date set by stock exchanges to determine who actually receives a dividend

Payment Date   The date the company will mail dividend checks is called the **payment date,** and it is also set by the board of directors. The date selected might be October 31.

Payment date: date the company mails dividend checks

Liquidating dividends: capital distributions that reduce the corporation's size; not true dividends

Liquidating Dividends **Liquidating dividends** are not true dividends but rather distributions of capital. In effect, the company is reducing its size, or going out of business altogether, and is selling assets and distributing cash to shareholders. These distributions may or may not be taxable, depending on your investment in the stock. If you receive them, you will probably need help in filing a tax return.

Stock repurchases: company buys back shares from investors; not a true dividend but has the same effect as one

Stock Repurchases Although **stock repurchases** aren't true dividends either, they probably have the same effect: you receive cash by selling a portion of your shares back to the company. So, you have cash but fewer shares, which, on the surface, looks like a wash; however, the market price of the stock typically increases with fewer shares outstanding. You might have the cash plus no loss in *the value* of your investment.

Stock dividend: dividend paid in shares of a company's stock

Stock Dividends and Stock Splits When we speak of a distribution to common stockholders, we do not include stock dividends or stock splits. A **stock dividend** is a distribution of additional shares of the company's own common stock. For example, Mead might declare a 10% stock dividend, which means every stockholder would receive shares totaling 10% of the amount owned. Your 100 shares would thus entitle you to 10 more. You seem wealthier because your ownership has gone up 10%; unfortunately, the price per share will go down 10%, leaving your wealth unchanged. Neither you nor any other shareholder can be made wealthier simply by increasing the number of shares outstanding.

Stock split: produces same effect as a stock dividend except more new shares usually are issued

A **stock split** works like a stock dividend except more new shares usually are issued. For example, the most popular stock split is two-for-one, which means you receive one additional share for each share held. Stock splits also have no impact on your wealth. Why, then, do so many companies have stock dividends and stock splits? There is probably no simple or single answer to this question. It commonly is believed that a stock's price should be kept within a popular range—say, $30 to $60—to make the shares more marketable. A high price, for example, might exclude some investors who lack sufficient capital. So, if price increases beyond this range, a stock dividend or split will return it. Along this line, sometimes you will see a reverse split, such as 1-for-10. Now, the stock's price has decreased too much, suggesting a deteriorated company. Most academic researchers doubt the argument of an optimal price range because it supports the notion of increasing shareholder wealth by increasing or decreasing the number of shares outstanding.

Another argument advanced in favor of stock dividends is that they let shareholders know that earnings are good, but the company wants to retain cash for internal investment rather than paying a dividend. It is extremely doubtful, however, that shareholders require a stock dividend to provide them with information.

Opportunities in Common Stocks

Unlike conventional bonds and money market instruments that have a rather narrow investment purpose, common stocks offer an array of investment opportunities. The more important of these opportunities are discussed below.

Growth Stocks   All of us like to get in on the ground floor of a company we think has a bright future. We are looking for growth in such an opportunity. A **growth stock** is one investors believe will show greater growth in earnings than the expected growth in the overall economy. There are all sorts of growth companies: Pfizer is one, Novell is another. Pfizer has a proven track record of growth, and its position in the health industry gives rather good assurance that it will enjoy future growth. Novell, on the other hand, is a newcomer. It has had remarkable success with its software, but it is in an extremely competitive industry where fortunes are made—and then lost—almost overnight. The more rapid the expected growth, the riskier the company. Moreover, the mere presence of growth should not be seen as a guarantee of a good investment. The market price of the stock might be so high that even if the expected growth materializes, you still have a bad investment.

Growth stock: stock whose price is expected to increase at a greater rate than the growth in the overall economy

Although growth can be measured in a number of ways, probably the most frequently used measurement is the growth of **earnings per share (EPS),** which is a company's total earnings divided by the total number of common stock shares outstanding. Generally, the more rapid the growth of a company's EPS over time, the larger the periodic increases in its stock price. But don't expect this relationship to hold every period. For example, Exhibit 6.3 shows the trends of EPS and year-end market prices for Pfizer. As you see, Pfizer enjoyed dramatic growth in EPS over the period, going from $1.05 in 1982 to $3.25 in 1992 (an average annual growth rate of 12%). In turn, the market price of the stock rose even more dramatically from $17.22 in 1982 to $72.50 in 1992 (an average annual growth rate of 15.5%). Notice, though, the sharp decline in price from $84 in 1991 to $72.50 in 1992. This downtrend continued into early 1993, when Pfizer was selling at $63. Will Pfizer be a strong performer as the 1990s continue? Many analysts think so, but don't expect super returns each year. Considering such potential return volatility, it is good advice to have a long investment horizon with growth stocks.

Earnings per share: company's total earnings divided by the total number of common stock shares outstanding

Income Stocks   An **income stock** offers a fairly high dividend yield. Public utility stocks stand out as examples. Yields with these stocks often are on a par with yields available on corporate bonds. This appeals to investors who look for good current yield along with some potential for price appreciation. However, don't assume your dividend yield has the same protection as a bond yield. Dividends can be—and frequently are—cut if the company faces a disruptive situation. After the nuclear reactor leak at Three Mile Island, General

Income stock: stock that offers a fairly high dividend yield

EXHIBIT 6.3

Pfizer: EPS and market price—1982–92

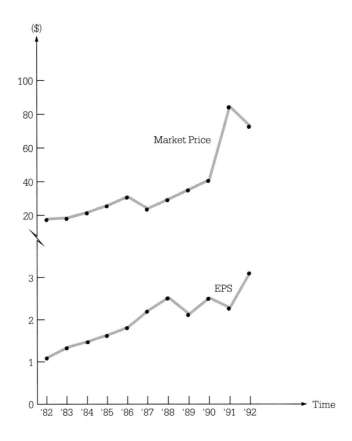

Public Utilities suspended its dividend and the price of its stock fell from $17 to under $5. (The stock has rebounded since then and currently sells above $30.)

Growth and income stock: stock that offers both moderate growth and moderate dividend yield

Growth and Income Stocks A **growth and income stock** offers a reasonable dividend yield—perhaps one that equals the rate you might earn on a passbook savings account—along with good potential for long-term price appreciation, although at a slower rate than that of a growth stock. A public utility in a growing metropolitan area, such as Florida Telephone, is an example.

Blue chip: high-quality stock; one that delivers what is expected of it—growth or income

Blue Chips The term **blue chip** is used to describe a stock that is thought to be of high quality. Again, Pfizer or Xerox easily come to mind. The term itself is ambiguous because high quality can be achieved in various ways. A growth stock can have high quality, but so can an income stock or a stock with any particular characteristic. Perhaps we should think of a blue chip stock as one with a high probability of achieving whatever it promises—growth, income, or something else.

BOX 6.1   A QUESTION OF ETHICS

"Flipping" for Profits in the Hot Issues Market: Who Gets Cut into the Deals?

The IPO (initial public offering) market is no place for weak-kneed investors. Prices immediately after shares are issued are extremely volatile, often changing by 20% or more in the first few hours of trading. A segment of this market, however, called hot issues, is quite a different matter. There are virtually no risks and profits are almost guaranteed.

A hot issue is one with a recognized strong demand before the issuance date. These shares are likely to increase in value, almost ensuring a profit to anyone who owns them. "Flipping" describes the process of quickly selling hot issue shares and pocketing the difference between the sale price and the price guaranteed in the offering. Capital is invested for only a short period, and annualized rates of return are enormous. Forgetting momentarily that this hardly reflects an efficient market, the important question is, who should get cut into the sure money?

The hot issues market offers brokers an opportunity to reward certain customers who generate big commissions or who provide referrals or other benefits. Apparently, one beneficiary was Tom Foley, Speaker of the U.S. House of Representatives. Glenn R. Simpson, a reporter for *Roll Call* (a twice-weekly newspaper covering Capitol Hill), shows that Foley made more than $100,000 over a four-year period, 1989–92. Foley, who admitted that he knew virtually nothing about investments, benefitted through his friendship with Peter De Roetth, a high school classmate and a principal in Account Management Corporation. Foley denied any wrongdoing or lack of ethics on his part or De Roetth's.

Is there an ethical issue in the hot issues market? Should small shareholders with little influence be left out of the action? Who are the losers? Whenever a virtual free profit exists, something is wrong with the marketplace. The short-run losers seem to be existing shareholders who could have received a higher price for the new shares being issued by their corporations. But why don't they demand higher prices from the underwriters? Various financial theories with such imaginative names as "winner's curse" attempt to explain why such underpricing persists. None of these helps us to resolve the ethical issue of who should get the benefits. Perhaps we should let Congress decide the issue. Then, again, maybe that isn't a good idea either.

Cyclical Stocks   **Cyclical stock** is more responsive to changes in the business cycle than other stocks. Companies in the capital goods industries, such as Mead Corporation, experience far greater volatility in earnings than companies in the food or beverage business, such as Heinz or PepsiCo. Other volatile industries are those associated with housing, mining, and transporta-

Cyclical stock: stock that has strong responses to changes in the overall economy tion. The Big Three automakers are fairly cyclical stocks because their dominant product is a consumer durable, the purchase of which is easily postponed in an economic slowdown.

Defensive stock: stock that moves in opposite direction to changes in the overall economy

Defensive Stocks   The return of a **defensive stock** is expected to vary in opposition to the cycles of the overall economy. Defensive stocks' returns are not as volatile as the overall market return. Put more concretely, these are stocks with low betas, as discussed in Chapter 4. (The beta concept is also used later in this chapter.) Holding a defensive stock is a good idea, but defensive stocks are not always easily found. Companies dealing in consumer perishables or consumer services often have betas less than 1.0—meaning they are less risky than the overall market—but it is virtually impossible to find stocks with negative betas. For example, not 1 stock out of 1,700 in the Value Line survey has a negative beta, and less than 2% have betas of 0.5 or less.

It commonly was thought that investors should play an economic cycle by investing in cyclical stocks when an economic expansion was anticipated and then sell these stocks and invest in defensive issues as the cycle moved toward contraction. Surely, many still advocate this approach, but growing evidence indicates that few people can forecast the cycle with recurring accuracy, much less design an investment program to benefit from it.

Speculative stock: any potentially high-risk situation

Speculative Stocks   A **speculative stock** can involve practically any type of situation. The term is about as ambiguous as blue chip and used just as frequently. Most investors probably understand *speculative* to mean an opportunity for a fast profit, such as you might earn in a takeover or merger or the unexpected development of a new product. We also might think of a speculative stock as simply a high-risk stock, one with a high beta or a high absolute measure of risk, such as the standard deviation. Thinking of risk in these more concrete terms is the better way to do it, as we shall see later in this chapter.

American depository receipts: trust certificates issued against a trust holding of a foreign security

Stocks of Foreign Companies   Many large foreign companies, such as Volkswagenwerk (West Germany) or Telefonos de Mexico, S.A. (Mexico), have their shares available in U.S. markets. In most cases, they do so through **American depository receipts (ADRs).** The ADR process works like this: a foreign company places shares in trust with an American bank, which in turn issues depository receipts to U.S. investors. The ADRs, then, are claims to shares of stock and are, for all practical purposes, the same as shares. The trustee bank performs all clerical functions—issuing annual reports, maintaining a stockholder ledger, paying and keeping dividend records, and so on—allowing the ADRs to trade in markets just as other securities trade. The growing popularity of international investing has created a huge demand for ADRs. The number of issues listed on organiz l exchanges has grown from

150 in 1988 to about 250 in 1993. Over that same period, the volume of trading of both listed and over-the-counter ADRs has grown from around $40 billion to more than $180 billion.

You can invest in companies from all parts of the world using ADRs, achieving a high degree of international diversification. However, doing your own research to select companies may be difficult. There is, for one thing, a shortage of data: the annual report may be all that is available, and its reliability is questionable in some instances. With the exception of Australia, Canada, and the United Kingdom, financial reporting and accounting standards are quite different from those accepted in the United States. Although this isn't necessarily bad, it is different. If you are thinking of finding an undiscovered growth company in Spain or Singapore, for example, most advisors will probably tell you to forget it. Financial reporting in each country is poor and unreliable, making analysis difficult even for people with extensive accounting training. On the other hand, if you limit your selections to large, widely recognized companies, your risks are no greater (other than exchange rate and political risks) than they are with most U.S. companies.

Reading Stock Quotations

Many stocks are quoted daily in the financial pages of local and national newspapers. Before investing, you may follow a stock in the paper, and after you make a selection, your curiosity will probably lead you to keep watching it. Exhibit 6.4 shows a typical listing for Mead Corporation and explains how to interpret the data. As you see, quite a bit of information is provided on one line. Pay particular attention to items 5 and 6 because they will be applied later in the chapter.

Mead's stock is traded on the New York Stock Exchange. A listing on the American Stock Exchange is the same. Less information is provided for over-the-counter stocks. If the stock is on the OTC National Market Issues list, you are provided with all the information given on a New York Stock Exchange or American Stock Exchange issue. If the listing is on NASDAQ's Small-Cap Issues, limited data, such as that shown for Brentwood Financial Corporation, are provided.

Name and Indicated Dividend	Sales (100s)	Last	Net Change
BrntwFn .12e	5	14 ½	− ½

Brentwood Financial's dividend is $0.12 a share, although the letter e indicates that this may not be a regular dividend. On the reported day, 500 shares traded and the last price for the day is $14.50. The net change of − ½ indicates a decrease of $0.50 a share from the last price on the reported day versus the last price of the previous trading day.

1. The highest price per share paid in the past year; prices are quoted in dollars and eighths of dollars, so a price of 10⅛ = $10.125 a share. Mead's highest price was $37.

2. The lowest price per share paid in the last year. Mead's lowest price was $18.

3. The company's name, which may be abbreviated. Mead's is not.

4. The indicated regular dividend in the current year based on what the company has paid in the last quarter or six months. Some companies also pay extra dividends in good earnings years, but these are not shown. Mead's regular dividend was estimated at $1 a share.

5. The current yield, which is found by dividing the current year regular dividend by the closing price of the stock. Mead's current yield is 2.7%.

6. The price-earnings ratio, which is the company's earnings over its last fiscal year divided into the closing price of the stock. There is no entry if earnings are negative, as in Mead's case.

7. The number of shares sold on that day in hundreds. For example, 519 means 51,900 shares of Mead stock.

8. The highest price paid for the stock that day. Mead's was 36⅜ ($36.375).

9. The lowest price paid for the stock that day. Mead's was 35¼ ($35.25).

10. The last price paid that day. Mead's was 36⅞.

11. The difference between the closing price that day and the closing price of the previous day. For example, Mead's closing price on Monday was 1⅛ ($1.125) higher than its closing price on Friday.

EXHIBIT 6.4
Typical listing of a common stock in the financial pages of many newspapers

RISKS IN COMMON STOCKS

A groundwork for understanding risk in common stocks was built in Chapter 4. We continue to build on that foundation in this chapter.

Liquidity and Inflation Risks

Practically all common stocks have high degrees of both liquidity and inflation risk. The lack of liquidity is probably clear to you, if you remember that liquidity means not only being able to sell an asset quickly and at low cost, but also being able to sell it with no loss in market value. Common stocks offer no guarantee of price and, so, lack liquidity.

Less clear might be why common stocks are high inflation risks. In fact, you may have heard just the opposite: that you should invest in common stocks to hedge inflation. The logic behind this advice is that business firms can raise prices of their products and services to match the inflation rate, thereby maintaining profit margins on sales and preserving real returns for investors. The logic hasn't always held. Although common stocks did perform well in what was then considered the inflationary 1950s, they did poorly during much of the 1970s and early 1980s, when the inflation rate far exceeded that of the 1950s. The underlying reasons for such a poor performance are not clear. We do know that a high and volatile inflation rate increases business risk within firms and dampens their willingness to expand or make needed investments in new technology or product development. Profitability eventually suffers. Simultaneously, the inflation forces investors to require higher rates of return from common stocks, both to match the higher rates available on alternative investments, particularly tangibles and money market instruments, and to compensate them for what is now perceived as a riskier investment medium. On balance, it is better to hold other assets for inflation hedges and to hold common stocks for other reasons.

Firm-Specific and Industry Risks

When you invest in a common stock, you invest in a specific company with products or services competing in specific industries. If you buy Exxon, you are in the international oil business—for better or worse. We will cover firm and industry analysis in detail in Chapter 7, but an overview of the risk factors is appropriately included here.

Declining Market Position Probably the greatest risk of all arises from a deteriorating market position. An individual firm—such as Chrysler, before its resurgence—can lose its market position when it fails to compete in its industry. An entire industry—the railroads, for example—may decline or become less able to compete with foreign producers, as the U.S. auto industry has suffered from competition with the Japanese auto industry. Whatever the cause, the long-run impacts usually are both a riskier stock and a less profitable one. Although we frequently are told to avoid stocks in declining market situations, following that advice is not easy. Has Chrysler made a sound recovery, and is it no longer in financial danger? Is GM now the high-cost producer? Will the Big Three learn how to control quality and costs and once again resume world leadership in manufacturing automobiles? Perhaps. Perhaps not.

To some extent, any company faces a threat of an eroding market. Even public utilities have seen consumers cut demand through energy conservation and alternative heating sources, such as solar energy, firewood, and

BOX 6.2   GETTING AN INVESTMENT EDGE

Where to Look for Value

With 20,000 or so stocks in the United States, trying to find undervalued ones can be difficult and time-consuming, even with easy access to data. The problem is where to look. Savvy analysts have identified certain "winner" characteristics over the years, and recent academic research, although certainly not conclusive, does offer support for some of them. Here's a limited list you might want to consider.

SMALL COMPANY STOCKS

Over fairly long periods, small company stocks do substantially better than large company stocks. They do so even after taking risk into consideration.

NEGLECTED STOCKS

A neglected stock is one that is not actively followed by many professional analysts or professional investors. The logic here is that a large following draws attention to a stock, which in turn drives up its price. Neglected stocks can be those of both large and small companies, but you probably will find more of the latter.

To help you find small company neglected stocks, you can refer to the "Shadow Stocks" list compiled each year by the *AAII Journal* (see the February issue). To make this list, companies also must meet an earnings criterion and have no more than 15% of their shares owned by institutions.

LARGE INSIDE OWNERSHIP

An insider is someone with a significant interest in a company—for example, someone who owns a large number of shares, is on the board of directors, or is a company officer. When the inside ownership stake is large, stock returns often are higher. The rationale

kerosene. Few companies and industries are free of competition or insulated from economic misfortune. The most recent classic example must be the decline of IBM. Long considered the bluest of the blue chips, its dominance of the computer industry was thought to be beyond challenge and its stock was regarded as almost "permanent" long-term value. However, its reliance on mainframes and inability to adjust to changing market forces in the personal computer industry led to a shocking decline in its market value in 1992 (from more than $100 a share to under $50). Some analysts believe that IBM may stage a strong revival, but many others believe that it will never be the dominant firm it once was.

Given the difficulties of forecasting, the best advice is probably not to attempt to determine which firms or industries will do spectacularly well or poorly, but rather to diversify among firms and across industry lines.

for this factor is old-fashioned self-interest. People who run the company seem to do a better job of it when they have much to gain—or lose.

LOW P/E RATIOS

A P/E ratio is a company's EPS divided into the market price of its stock. Many analysts believe that companies with low P/E ratios do not have good earnings growth opportunities. They might be dull companies selling basic products or services, as opposed to the exciting ones selling esoteric items: Johns Manville and gypsum board versus Genentech and genetically engineered gene splices. Low P/E stocks do better because their prices have not been driven excessively high. They represent a solid return based on actual performance, rather than a hypothetical return based on assumed earnings growth rates that may never be achieved. Be careful,

though: some of the low P/E stocks might represent companies destined for bankruptcy, particularly if the earnings figure is for a past, rather than a current or future, year.

LOW DEBT LEVELS

A small amount of debt reduces the risk in a stock, but there is some evidence that it might also indicate better performance. Again, reasons are unclear here. Perhaps a management that spends too much time on financing, instead of producing and marketing, winds up with less profit for shareholders. But the superior performance might reflect the fact that fewer low-debt companies go bankrupt over time. When you take a total loss in a stock, your portfolio had better contain some exceptional winners or your overall results will be poor.

Inability to Control Costs   Even companies with bright futures can experience difficulties if they can't control costs. The list of bankrupts each year usually includes as many from this category as ones with declining market positions. Young growth firms are especially vulnerable. Their ability to sell products and services often far exceeds their skill at business management. One month you will read of how well things are going, and the next month the company files bankruptcy. Osborne Computer, a leader in the development of personal computers and an eventual bankrupt, is a classic example.

Companies with a heavy dependence on natural resources—public utilities, for example—or with a product line connected to the natural resources industries—manufacturers of oil drilling equipment, for example—are particularly vulnerable to cost changes beyond their control. Although utility rates soared when the world price of oil shot up, it would be a mistake to think that most public utilities simply passed on all the cost increase to consumers. Some of the increases were absorbed by the utilities and the shareholders who owned them. Similarly, when the price of oil fell, manufacturers of oil drilling equipment found their market had largely disappeared as drilling for new oil slowed considerably. Using Value Line or another advisory service, check the earnings reports and the historical movements of the market price of Schlumberger, a leading manufacturer in this industry, and the message will become clear.

Other factors that present cost control problems are an extensive use of unionized labor and special environmental problems. An alleged reason for the auto industry's problems are the high wages and benefits paid to its unionized workers. Costs to control environmental pollution are legendary in some cases. Nuclear power is probably a dead industry because of the enormous costs of meeting pollution control requirements. For example, nuclear reactor facilities have been abandoned by Cincinnati Gas and Electric and Long Island Lighting Company. If you dislike investment risks, you should look closely at firms or industries for particular situations that could lead to uncontrollable cost increases, and avoid these businesses when selecting your stocks.

Excessive Use of Debt   Measuring the impact of a company's borrowing on earnings and risk is much easier than determining similar measurements for many of the factors discussed above. All you need is the firm's current balance sheet. A heavy reliance on debt means a greater number of fixed claims in front of your residual claim. All things being equal, it also means a riskier stock. It is simple to avoid this risk by limiting your investments to companies with little debt or preferred stock outstanding.

Market Risk

Market risk can be understood as the risk of a stock's price increasing or decreasing because of changes in the overall stock market. Over time, the prices of most stocks move in the same direction, up or down. When we speak of the market going up or down, we must remember that the market is merely an aggregation of individual stocks. We usually are referring to a broad index of the market, such as the Dow Jones 30-Stock Industrial Average or the Standard and Poor's (S&P) 500 Stock Index. It is these 30 or 500 stocks, then, that average an increase or decrease.

What Causes Market Risk?   Fundamentally, the strengths, weaknesses, and uncertainties of the economy are the causes of volatile stock prices. As Exhibit 6.5 shows, periods of sharply falling stock prices often are associated with economic recessions, although 1987 was clearly an exception. The poor performance of stocks in the 1970s is probably explained by an equally bad performance of the economy. Per capita real growth in income, for example,

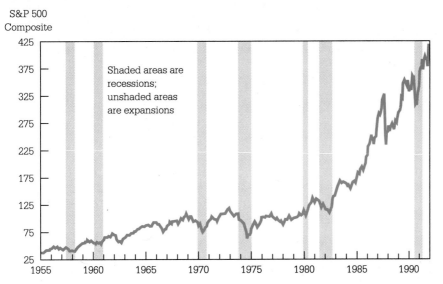

S&P 500
Composite

Shaded areas are recessions; unshaded areas are expansions

EXHIBIT 6.5
The stock market and the economy

lagged far behind similar figures in the 1960s and 1950s. Conversely, the strong performance of stocks during most of the 1980s reflects resurgent strength in the economy. We mentioned the poor performance of stocks during inflationary periods; we should now recognize that the real problem is one of poor economic performance, a situation probably exacerbated by high inflation.

Although changes in the economy lead to changes in stock prices, it is wrong to think there is some simplistic connection between the two. You may hear the evening newscaster make a comment such as, "The government's latest figures on unemployment led to lower prices on Wall Street today." Did the news lead to lower prices? Perhaps, if it was quite unexpected news. By and large, though, most news of this sort is not news to investors. Unemployment figures are anticipated far in advance of news releases, which more often confirm what most analysts expected. So, if you are trying to use economic data to forecast future stock prices, consider this: The Bureau of Economic Analysis does exactly the opposite; they consider stock prices one of their better *leading* indicators of future economic performance.

Managing Market Risk   It should be clear that market risk cannot be eliminated and must be faced if you plan to invest in common stocks. However, it affects stocks differently. Cyclical stocks, as we noted, tend to be influenced more than defensive stocks. The key to managing market risk is to first measure it and then determine how much additional return you require for undertaking it. Our discussion in Chapter 4 of measuring market risk led us to the beta concept. You should recall that beta is a quantitative estimate of the variability of returns of an individual stock in relation to the variability of returns of the overall stock market. Although beta values theoretically can be positive or negative, as noted above, the overwhelming majority are positive, and we will limit our discussion to them. Keep in mind, then, what a beta value means:

From zero to 1.0:   a stock with less return variability than the market; the lower the number, the less the variability and the less risky the stock.

Equal to 1.0:   a stock with return variability and price risk equal to the market's.

Greater than 1.0:   a stock with greater return variability than the market; the higher the number, the greater the variability and the riskier the stock.

We will now use betas to estimate required returns for individual stocks.

ESTIMATING A STOCK'S REQUIRED RETURN

How much return should you get from a stock—15% a year, 20%, or what? Intuitively, you know that your return should be better than what you can receive investing risk-free, such as in Treasury bills. Otherwise, why take the risk of a common stock? But determining how much better it should be is a difficult task. We shall attempt to answer the question by using the **capital asset pricing model (CAPM)** and one of its constructs, the **securities market line (SML).**

Capital asset pricing model: theory explaining how asset prices are determined

Securities market line: construct of the capital asset pricing model; shows the relation between required return and risk

The CAPM and the SML

The CAPM is essentially a theory that attempts to explain how asset returns are determined. An important underpinning to the theory is that returns depend on the degree of risk investors are willing to undertake—the higher the risk, the greater the return. But returns do not depend on total risk; rather, they depend only on market risk. Why is that so? Because, as we discussed in Chapter 4, a diversified portfolio can eliminate firm-specific and industry risks without reducing expected return. The theory argues that the competitive behavior of thousands of investors eventually drives asset returns to a point where investors are compensated only for actual risks assumed. Because industry and firm-specific risks can be eliminated, investors will not be compensated for undertaking them. Thus, market risk is the only risk we need consider in evaluating a stock, and we can limit our assessment of an asset's risk to its market risk indicator—the beta weight.

For example, before you decide to invest in an individual stock, you might consider limiting your investing to two assets: Treasury bills and a pooling arrangement that is a duplicate of the S&P 500 stock index. (Such arrangements actually exist. The simplest offers shares that are ⅟₁₀th the value of the S&P 500 index. These shares, called "spiders," trade on the American Stock Exchange.) If you put all your funds into T-bills, you would have no risk and a certain return; let us assume it is 6.0% for the upcoming investment period. If you put all your funds into the S&P 500 (call it the market), you would have a risk estimated by a beta value of 1.0 and an uncertain return for the period. You could put half your funds in each, thereby giving your portfolio a beta of 0.5 and a return midway between 6.0% and the market return. Let us first estimate the required market return and then look at the required return-and-risk characteristics of many portfolios composed of simply T-bills and/or the market. We'll also allow you to borrow funds to achieve higher returns and greater risks.

What Is a Reasonable Estimate of the Required Market Return? Our primary means of determining a reasonable estimate of the required market return is to look in the past. Rather than finding an absolute number, we should try to determine the amount of excess return over the return on T-bills. This figure is far more useful because both the T-bill rate and the market rate are volatile from one year to the next. The study by Ibbotson Associates, cited in Chapter 3, indicated that over the period 1926–92, the premium of stock returns over the T-bill return—called the market risk premium—was about 6.5%, based on the geometric average return of each. Suppose we want to continue earning this average over an extended number of years in the future. We need to plan a somewhat higher premium on a year-by-year basis to achieve this average. As Ibbotson Associates point out (1993 *Yearbook,* p. 125), we should target the arithmetic average each year. Some years' returns will be over this average, and some years' returns will be under, but setting the arithmetic average as a goal should lead us to earn the geometric average as a long-run return.

So, to determine a required return for an upcoming year, estimate the T-bill rate and add the risk premium based on arithmetic averages—about 8.5% (see Chapter 3). In the current example, the target required return is 14.5% (6.0% + 8.5%). Remember that this is a total return. As such, it will consist of dividends and price appreciation. For example, if dividend yield is estimated at 4.0%, price appreciation is expected to be 10.5%.

Required Returns When Betas Are 1.0 or Less Exhibit 6.6 will help us understand the SML. For the time being, focus your attention on the segment of the line beginning at 6.0% on the *y* axis and going out to the point where beta equals 1.0 on the *x* axis. In effect, the SML is a line that connects the two points: 6.0% and zero beta (point 1) and 14.5% and beta = 1.0 (point 2). There is more than geometry involved, though. Any point on the line—such as point *A*—represents a portfolio of T-bills and the market. The characteristics of three portfolios are shown in Exhibit 6.7.

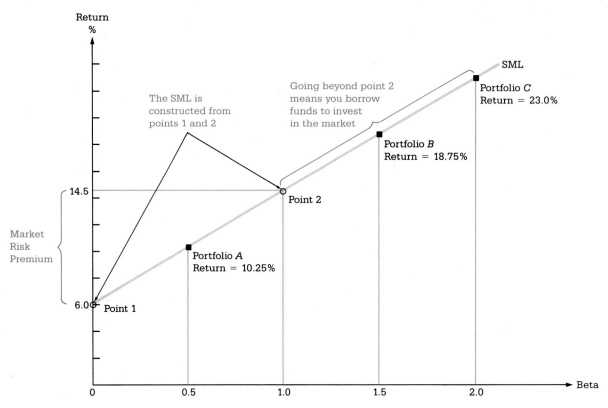

EXHIBIT 6.6
Constructing and using the SML

EXHIBIT 6.7
Characteristics of three
portfolios composed of
T-bills and the market

T-bill return (or cost) = 6.0% Market return = 14.5%			
		Portfolios	
	A	B	C
Percentage invested in T-bills	+50	−50*	−100*
Percentage invested in the market	+50	+150	+200
Required return:			
(+0.5 × 6) + (0.5 × 14.5) =	10.25%	—	—
(−0.5 × 6) + (1.5 × 14.5) =	—	18.75%	—
(−1.0 × 6) + (2.0 × 14.5) =	—	—	23.0%
Portfolio betas	0.5	1.5	2.0

*Minus sign indicates borrowing.

Portfolio A, for example, is invested half in bills and half in the market. Its beta of 0.5 is the weighted average: $(1.0 \times 0.5 + 0.0 \times 0.5)$. Its return of 10.25% is the weighted average: $(6.0 \times 0.5 + 14.5 \times 0.5)$. Another way to determine a portfolio's return (R_1) is to express it in terms of the risk-free rate (R_F), the portfolio beta (β_1), and the market risk premium (MRP), which is the difference between the market return (R_M) and R_F, that is, MRP $= R_M - R_F$. The following relation holds:

$$R_1 = R_F + \beta_1 \text{ (MRP)} \qquad (6.1)$$

As we see in the case of portfolio A:

$$10.25 = 6.0 + 0.5 \text{ (8.5)}$$

Required Returns When Betas Are Greater Than 1.0 The relations above seem simple enough to understand, but you might wonder how an investor could ever construct a portfolio with a beta greater than 1.0 with only T-bills and the market. If you are limited to investing only your own funds, you can't. But suppose you borrow and invest an amount greater than your own funds. To keep things simple for the time being, let's assume you can borrow at the T-bill rate. This assumption allows us to extend the SML beyond point 2 in Exhibit 6.6.

Borrowing has two impacts: it increases our portfolio beta beyond 1.0 and it increases our expected portfolio return. Exhibit 6.8 shows the effects of borrowing different amounts. For example, portfolio B assumes you have $1,000 to invest. But you want to increase your return and are willing to take risks to do so. Thus, you borrow $500 and invest $1,500 in the market. As you see, your net return is an expected $187.50, or 18.75% on your invested funds. Again, you could calculate this return using the weighted average return indicated above.

$$18.75 = -0.5 \text{ (6.0)} + 1.5(14.5) = -3.0 + 21.75$$

	Portfolios	
	B	C
Amount of your funds to invest	$1,000.00	$1,000.00
Amount of funds you borrow	500.00	1,000.00
Total invested in the market	$1,500.00	$2,000.00
Total return (market return = 14.5%)	$ 217.50	$ 290.00
Less interest paid (6%) on borrowed funds	30.00	60.00
Net return	$ 187.50	$ 230.00
Rate of return on your invested funds	18.75%	23.0%

EXHIBIT 6.8
Determining the rate of return on portfolios using borrowed funds

Now, the T-bill return is actually a cost—hence, the negative sign—and the weight (0.5) shows the proportion of borrowed funds to your own funds invested. In this case, you borrow $0.50 for each $1.00 of your own funds.

The portfolio beta is determined by dividing your funds into total funds invested, so 1.5 = $1,500/$1,000. You should be able to see now how the returns and betas for portfolios B and C in Exhibit 6.6 were determined. More important, you should see that the SML is a line that connects points representing all possible risk-and-return combinations from holding a risk-free asset (as a borrower or lender) and the market.

Shifts in the SML   Keep in mind that an SML is constructed at a given point in time. The line isn't set in stone, and we should expect that it will shift over time. Indeed, as the risk-free rate increases or decreases, the SML will shift upward or downward. For example, if the T-bill rate increased to 8.0%, the SML would shift upward, as shown in Exhibit 6.9. This means all rates of return would increase by two percentage points. The market return would be 16.5% and a 0.5-beta portfolio's return would be 12.25%. During much of 1992

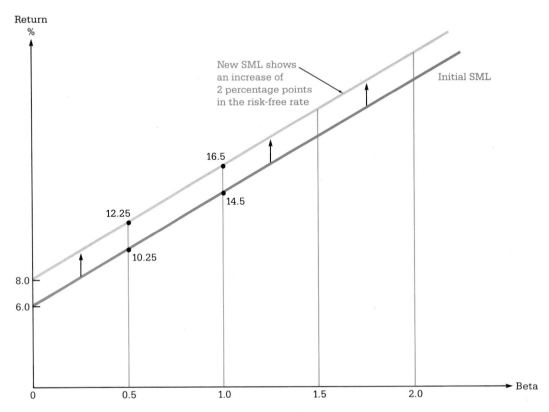

EXHIBIT 6.9
An upward shift in the SML

and through mid-1993, the T-bill rate was around 3%. This means the SML had a considerable downward shift, signaling much lower required returns. You should see, for example, that the required return on the market would have been 11.5%.

The SML could also change its slope, but this implies a changing risk premium. Although a change is possible, we prefer to think of the risk premium as being fairly constant over an extended period. If the scope of our investment is long term, this assumption is reasonably realistic and does not diminish the analysis.

Before moving on, we should discuss the topic of borrowing at the risk-free rate. Is this a realistic assumption? Probably it is not. Although you may have access to some funds at very low rates, such as a life insurance policy, you eventually reach a borrowing point at which interest costs exceed the risk-free rate. Although we won't pursue the implications of this point in greater detail, let us note that a rate higher than the T-bill rate would reduce the slope of the SML for all beta values greater than 1.0. Such a slope is shown in Exhibit 6.10, and the practical application is that portfolios with

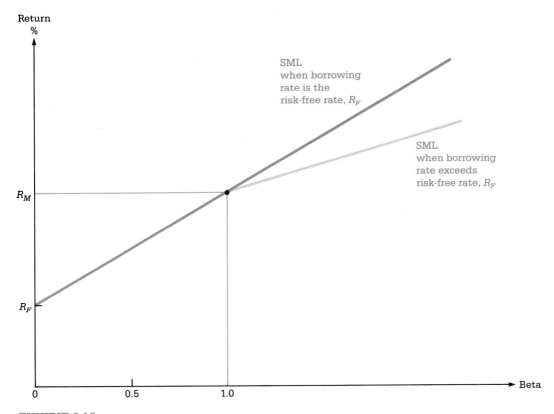

EXHIBIT 6.10
SML under two assumptions of the borrowing rate

betas greater than 1.0 earn proportionately less return in relation to their risk than those with betas of 1.0 or less.

Using the SML

The SML provides us with a clear estimate of the *minimum* return we can require from investing in a specific stock. For example, if you were thinking of investing in a stock that has a beta of 0.5, you should require a return of at least 10.25%. Why should you settle for less when you can easily achieve this much through the simple portfolio of 50% in the market and 50% in T-bills?

Choosing stocks, then, is a straightforward process of comparing their required returns with their expected returns. The process is illustrated for the three stocks shown in Exhibit 6.11. Stock *E* is definitely chosen because its expected return greatly exceeds its required return. Stock *F* is definitely rejected because its expected return is much less than its required return, and stock *G* is a borderline case because its expected return barely exceeds its required return (you might flip a coin to decide this one). A graphic illustration of the selection process is shown in Exhibit 6.12. You can generalize from this graph that any stock represented by a point below the SML is rejected, any above is accepted, and any almost on the line leaves us indifferent between accepting and rejecting.

DETERMINING EXPECTED RETURNS

The next step in the stock selection process is estimating expected returns. There are two widely used approaches: the earnings approach and the dividend approach. The two approaches are similar and better understood as two perspectives on the same process.

Earnings approach: method of determining a stock's expected return based on projected earnings per share

The Earnings Approach

An **earnings approach** consists of estimating future earnings and dividends per share of a selected stock and from them deriving a holding period return.

EXHIBIT 6.11
Selecting stocks by comparing required rates of return with expected rates of return

Stocks	Beta	Required Rate of Return	Expected Rate of Return	Decision
E	0.5	10.25%	14.00%	Definitely accept; expected rate well exceeds required rate
F	1.5	18.75	15.00	Definitely reject; expected rate is far below required rate
G	2.0	23.00	23.25	A borderline case; flip a coin to make your choice

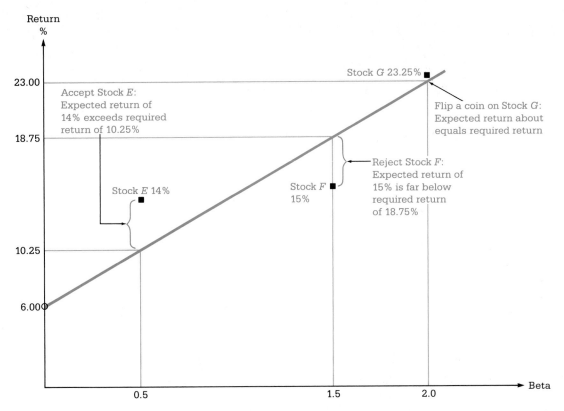

EXHIBIT 6.12
Graphic illustration of selecting stocks using the SML

As an alternative procedure—one that is computationally easier—we can use the stock's required rate of return to calculate the present value of the future cash flows we expect to receive. If this present value exceeds the current market price of the stock, we know its expected rate of return exceeds the required rate, and the stock should be purchased. An example will help illustrate the process.

Suppose we are thinking of investing in the stock of DAX, Inc., a company that has a long history of earnings and dividends. Its stock has a beta of about 0.71. Assume further the risk-free rate is again 6.0% annually. DAX, Inc., then, has a required rate of return of about 12%: 12.0 = 6.0 + 0.71(8.5). For simplicity, we will assume a three-year holding period and a current price of $20 a share for the stock. Exhibit 6.13 summarizes the analysis, and the important steps in the process are discussed below.

Estimate Future EPS The earnings approach begins by estimating the stock's future EPS. With DAX, Inc., EPS in the past year was $2. Assuming EPS will grow at a 10% annual rate will give future EPS amounts of $2.20,

EXHIBIT 6.13

Analysis of DAX, Inc., using the earning approach

Current market price of DAX = $20 a share Current EPS = $2			
	Year 1	Year 2	Year 3
1. Future EPS (10% growth rate)	$2.20	$2.42	$ 2.66
2. Future DPS (50% payout ratio)	1.10	1.21	1.33
3. P/E ratio at end of year 3	—	—	10
4. Market price at end of year 3	—	—	$26.60
5. Annual cash flows (lines 2 + 4)	$1.10	$1.21	$27.93
6. Present value of $1 factors ($i$ = 12%)	0.893	0.797	0.712
7. Present value of future cash flows (line 5 × line 6)	$0.98	$0.96	$19.89

Present value of the stock = $0.98 + $0.96 + $19.89 = $21.83

Decision: buy the stock because its present value of $21.83 exceeds its current market price of $20.00.

Actual rate of return (using HP 12C calculator) = 15.5%. This exceeds the required rate of return of 12% and further confirms the buy decision.

$2.42, and $2.66. Many difficulties are involved in estimating the growth rate, but it is the key to the analysis and you should devote most of your time to this task. Candidly, this is what securities analysts are paid handsomely to do (or, more specifically, to do well). You might get a first guess at future growth by looking at a company's historical rate of growth. If you believe this growth rate will continue, then you can use it to project future earnings.

For example, we noted earlier in this chapter that Pfizer had an EPS growth rate of 12% over the 10-year period ending in 1992. We could use this rate in valuing Pfizer unless we had other information that might indicate a higher or lower rate is more appropriate. In early 1993, there was a cloud hanging over the health care industry in general and pharmaceuticals in particular with respect to impending major changes that might arise from Hillary Rodham-Clinton's task force examining the industry. Although little was known at that time, many observers expected that the industry would be adversely affected through price controls or other legislative requirements. In Pfizer's case, then, the 12% historical rate might be too high, but forecasting a new, lower rate would have been a difficult task.

Estimate the Payout Ratio The payout ratio tells us how much of the future earnings will be distributed to stockholders. There must be a logical connection between the EPS growth rate and the payout ratio in the sense that a high payout ratio dampens EPS growth, and vice versa. Growing companies must retain and invest earnings, rather than pay them out as dividends. So, if you are using a company's historical growth rate in EPS, you should also use its historical payout ratio. It would be a mistake, for example, to assume a high EPS growth rate along with a high payout ratio. On the other hand, a slower growth rate may be associated with a higher payout ratio.

Estimate Dividends per Share The payout ratio applied to EPS gives dividends per share (DPS). Dividends paid represent actual cash inflows to investors. EPS amounts, in contrast, benefit shareholders only indirectly.

Estimate a Future P/E Ratio If you follow an earnings approach, you generally believe stocks will sell at some multiple of their current or future EPS. This multiple is called the P/E ratio. For example, the stock's past year's EPS is $2 and the market price is $20; thus, the P/E ratio is 10 ($20/$2). If you think that ratio will stay the same, the stock's price at the end of three years will be $26.60, or 10 times its EPS of $2.66 in year 3.

Find and Discount the Annual Cash Flows The annual cash flows consist of the dividends received plus the future price of the stock—that is, its price at the end of year 3 in our example. After the cash flows are determined, they must be discounted at the stock's required rate of return: 12% in the example. Discounting involves finding present value of $1 coefficients from Appendix A.3 and multiplying them by the cash flows. Adding the discounted cash flows gives us their present value of $21.83, as indicated in Exhibit 6.13.

Make a Decision Because the present value of the cash flows exceeds the current market price of DAX, Inc., the stock should be purchased. This decision is further confirmed by calculating the internal rate of return on the investment. It is 15.5%, which exceeds the required rate of 12%. Thus, we can do better in DAX, Inc., than we can in a portfolio invested 29% in T-bills and 71% in the market. Assuming we are reasonably diversified to begin with, DAX, Inc., should be bought.

The Dividend Approach

An alternative method for evaluating a stock purchase is a **dividend approach** (also called a dividend growth model). Although this approach can be applied in various ways, the most frequently used is to express the expected total return (TR) of a stock as the sum of its current return and its future return. The current return (CR) is what you expect the stock to yield in the first year you own it—that is, its upcoming annual dividend (D_1) divided by its current price (P_0). Its future return (FR) usually is expressed as the expected percentage growth (g) of dividends in the future. We then have:

Dividend approach: method of determining a stock's expected return based on projected dividend yield and growth

$$TR = CR + FR = \frac{D_1}{P_0} + g \qquad (6.2)$$

BOX 6.3   INVESTMENT INSIGHTS

Why Did the Stock Market Explode in the 1980s?

At the end of 1979, the S&P 500 stood at 107.94; 10 years later it was 353.40, a 227% increase. What caused this explosion? Historically, corporate earnings growth and declining interest rates usually have explained stock market booms. But a study by Barry Wigmore at Goldman Sachs suggested that these familiar factors could explain only 35% of 1980's growth. Wigmore reached this conclusion by noting that the S&P 500's EPS growth was only 54% and the decline in interest rates (U.S. Treasury 10-year notes) was only 25%. Add these two together (79%) and divide by the 227% and you get the 35%. So, where did the other 65% come from?

There was no other explanations, according to John W. Peavy III, professor of financial investments at Southern Methodist University. Peavy notes (in the *Financial Analysts Journal,* June 1992) that Wigmore does not handle the two factors correctly; he assumes a linear relationship when in fact the relationship is nonlinear. The nonlinearity arises from the dividend growth model that Peavy uses in his explanation.

Peavy estimated a required 1989 dividend yield on the S&P 500 of 0.032, which, because of falling interest rates, was considerably lower than the 0.052 required rate in 1979. Dividing 1979's dividend of $5.66 by 0.032 tells us that the index should have risen to 176.88 simply because of lower rates. This factor alone explains 64% of the change in the S&P 500.

The other factor—EPS growth—explains almost all the rest. Peavy divides the 1989 dividend per share of $11 by 0.032 to arrive at a 1989 estimated index value of 343.75. Because the actual value was 353.40, he accounts for more than 97% of the change during the 1980s.

So, there really wasn't much dramatically different in the 1980s from other decades. Over the long haul, solid economic growth coupled with declining interest rates make stock investments very profitable.

Return to DAX, Inc., as an example of this approach. If we thought that its EPS growth rate would stay at 10% and its payout ratio would remain 50%, then its dividend growth rate would also be a constant 10%. With these assumptions, we can find its *TR:*

$$TR = \frac{\$1.10}{\$20.00} + 0.10 = 0.55 + 0.100$$

$$= 0.155, \text{ or } 15.5\%$$

You should see that its upcoming annual dividend is $1.10 and the current price is $20. Notice also this return is the same as the one determined using the earnings approach. This result is no coincidence because the assumption we made regarding a constant rate of dividend growth assures this outcome. Each method, in effect, determines a present value as a function of future dividends and the discount rate. If we discounted the cash flows in Exhibit 6.13 at 15.5%, the present value would be the stock's current price, $20. Equation 6.2 can be rearranged also to solve for current price; that is,

$$P_0 = \frac{D_1}{(TR - g)} \tag{6.3}$$

And,

$$\$20 = \frac{\$1.10}{(0.155 - 0.10)} = \frac{\$1.10}{(0.055)}$$

Equation 6.2 assumes a constant dividend growth rate forever, which may or may not be realistic. If you have reason to believe the growth rate would change, then more extensive methods would be needed to determine a stock's present value. One such approach is presented in the next section.

Valuation with Multiple Growth Rates

The earnings or dividend models can be modified to accommodate various earnings or dividend growth rates over time. Computer spreadsheet programs make it relatively easy to change any of the valuation variables and then determine the change's impact on the value of the stock. To illustrate the impact of different growth rates, let us rework the DAX, Inc., case.

An Example Instead of assuming that DAX's dividends will grow at a 10% rate forever, suppose that after three years the growth rate falls to 5%, which is then expected to continue forever. What impact does this have on share value? To solve the problem, we break it down into two parts: First, determine the present value of dividends received *during* the higher growth period; second, determine the present value of the expected market value of the stock *at the end of* the higher growth period.

Calculations for the first part follow. The discount rate is 12%, which is the assumed required rate of return as in previous examples with DAX.

Year	Dividend	Present Value of $1 Factor	Present Value
1	$1.10	0.893	$0.98
2	1.21	0.797	0.96
3	1.33	0.712	0.95
Present value of dividends			$2.89

These are the same calculations (with the exception of year 3) as those in Exhibit 6.13.

To determine the market value of the stock at the end of the higher growth period, we apply equation 6.3 with some modifications. First, the value will be at the end of a future year, not at the present time, and second, instead of using total return (*TR*), we use required return (*RR*). This gives us the following

$$P_t = \frac{D_{t+1}}{(RR - g)}$$
(6.4)

which is applied in the present example.

$$P_3 = \frac{D_4}{(RR - g)}$$

$$P = \frac{\$1.33 \times 1.05}{(0.12 - 0.05)} = \frac{\$1.40}{0.07} = \$20.00$$

So, DAX, Inc., stock will be worth $20 a share at the end of year 3. (Notice that the dividend in year 4 is determined by increasing year 3's dividend by 5%.) However, we are interested in the present value of that future value. Thus, we discount, using the appropriate present value of $1 factor; that is,

Present Value of P_3 = $20.00 × 0.712 = $14.24

The last step is to add $14.24 and $2.89 to arrive at the present value of the stock—$17.13. According to this approach, investors should be willing to pay up to $17.13 for a share of DAX common stock.

Discussion   Notice that DAX is worth less, given the new assumption of lower dividend growth after year 3. All things held constant, this is what you might expect because a lower growth rate implies lower future dividends. You should note also that we did not make a new assumption about DAX's payout ratio after the higher-growth period is over. A more realistic assumption would be that the payout ratio increases as earnings growth decreases. In that event, the dividend in year 4 would be greater than $1.40. Assume the payout ratio increases to 60%. Because earnings in year 4 is $2.80 (5% increase over year 3), the dividend would be $1.68 (0.60 × $2.80). This implies a share value of $24 at the end of year 3 ($1.68/0.07) instead of $20. The present value of $24 is $17.09. Adding this to $2.89 gives a total present value of $20.98, which is greater than $17.13, although it is still slightly less than the $21.83 associated with the constant 10% growth.

Multistage growth model: extends the basic earnings approach by allowing for various rates of EPS growth over time

The **multistage growth model** is particularly useful in evaluating growth stocks, which typically have high earnings growth rates. Surely, these rates cannot continue forever, and the analyst must consider that at some future date, or dates, the growth rates will fall. Failure to make this consideration can lead to inflated stock values. Although our example considers only one change in the growth rate, it is fairly straightforward to consider more changes using the same method.

Other Valuation Methods

The earnings and dividend models are used extensively to evaluate stocks. However, other approaches are also used. Some of the more popular alternatives are explained here.

Multiple-of-Earnings (or Cash-Flow) Approaches A **multiple-of-earnings approach** argues that the price of a company's stock should be some multiple of its EPS. We have used this method in a mechanical manner in determining the terminal year's share price in the earnings approach shown in Exhibit 6.13. Although the method itself is quite simple, a number of problems need to be addressed.

Multiple-of-earnings approach: valuation method that bases a stock's value as a multiple of its EPS

First, what is an appropriate multiplier—that is, P/E ratio? Should we use a historical average? a forecasted value? or what? Some analysts argue that the P/E ratio should equal a company's historical rate of growth of EPS. Returning to our discussion of Pfizer, we noted its average annual growth rate was 12%; so, its P/E ratio should be 12. However, Pfizer's ratio was in this range in only 2 of the 11 years in the 1982–92 period (11.4 in 1987 and 12.3 in 1988); it was 39.4 in 1991 and had an 11-year average of 17.6 (see Exhibit 6.3). So, if you felt comfortable with the estimate of 12, you should have avoided Pfizer in early 1993. That may have been the right decision at that time, but this method probably would have kept you out of Pfizer during most of the 1980s and early 1990s; and that would have been a mistake because Pfizer was an excellent performer.

A second issue in using a multiple-of-earnings approach is what EPS to use. Should it be last year's? or forecasted next year's? or the forecast two years out? or what? Clearly, there is no overwhelming consensus of opinion here, although most analysts would prefer a forecasted figure.

Finally, because EPS can be so volatile from year to year, some analysts prefer using a multiple-of-cash-flow approach. Cash flow will be explained in the next chapter, so we will defer our discussion until then. Let us note here, though, that future cash flow per share (CFS) may be more predictable than future EPS. Furthermore, the price of the stock might show a more reliable historical connection to CFS than to EPS.

Asset Approaches Rather than focusing on earnings and dividends, some methods focus on asset values. One of the oldest approaches is the **Ben Graham NCAV** (net current asset value) **rule.** This rule argues that any stock with a market value less than the company's net current assets per share is a good buy. Graham's net current assets are simply current assets minus total liabilities. An asset is current if it is cash or will convert to cash

Ben Graham NCAV rule: old valuation method that bases a company's share price on its net current assets within a year, while liabilities are a company's debt obligation. (These are explained and used in greater detail in Chapter 7.) Clearly, this is a simple rule to follow, but in recent years, relatively few companies have sold below net current assets.

Break-up value: valuation method that assumes a company is worth more broken into various pieces than as a whole

Break-Up Value Some analysts attempt to determine **break-up value,** which arises with companies that supposedly are worth more broken up than left intact. Such companies may have divisions that do not mesh well with their overall operations, or business interests that cannot be managed well because of inexperience or lack of expertise. Other reasons may increase a company's break-up value, such as a more favorable tax situation to other companies. Such undervalued companies become targets for either friendly or unfriendly takeovers. The raider hopes to acquire the stock at a price below break-up value per share and then turn a profit from breaking the company apart. Small investors can hardly become corporate raiders; however, by buying takeover candidates, they can realize substantial price appreciation when a raider begins to act. The raider typically drives up the market price of the stock in trying to gain control. The situation becomes profitable for small investors if a bidding war between two (or more) raiders begins. The theory is good, and there have been a number of good applications. Unfortunately, determining break-up value is difficult, and there is no guarantee a raider will show interest in a potential target.

Rules of Thumb There are numerous rules of thumb for determining value, but we will discuss only one: it argues that stocks in general are good buys whenever dividend yields are high relative to Treasury bill yields. For example, when stock yields are, say, 75% of bill yields, they should be purchased. Conversely, if their yields fall to, say, 50% of bill yields, they should be sold. This rule of thumb can be modified and applied to specific companies, taking into consideration their growth characteristics. Is it worth the effort, though? Again, applying an earnings or dividend approach is relatively simple and usually provides far better insights on the valuation process. For example, as we have already seen, if Treasury bill yields change, so will required rates of return, which in turn influence the present values of stocks. It makes more sense to work with these relations directly, rather than indirectly through rules of thumb.

SUMMARY

Common stock provides investors with a right to vote, a right to maintain their proportionate interest in the corporation, and a right to share in earnings or asset distributions. Investors have various opportunities in common stocks: growth (price appreciation), current income, a combination of growth and income, blue chips (considered high-quality stocks), cyclical price behavior, defensive (countercyclical) price behavior, and speculative situations. Price and other information on common stocks are reported daily in the financial pages of many newspapers.

Common stocks have liquidity and inflation risks, firm-specific and industry risks, and market risk. Market risk often is measured by a stock's beta weight, which allows investors to manage market risk by framing required rates of return.

A required rate of return can be derived from an SML, which is constructed by using a risk-free rate of return and an estimate of the market's rate of return. Once established, points on the SML indicate required asset returns given their beta weights. The SML can be used to evaluate specific investments by comparing their required rates of return with their expected rates of return. Assets with expected rates greater than required rates should be purchased or held; assets with expected rates less than required should not be bought or should be sold.

Expected rates of return can be estimated using an earnings approach or a dividend approach. The former requires estimates of future earnings per share, the payout ratio, and future P/E ratios. The latter uses a current return percentage and an estimate of dividend growth infinitely into the future. Although the two approaches can be different, in many applications they are virtually identical and lead to similar expected rates of return. The methods can be used also under an assumption of multiple growth rates. Other approaches can be used to determine stock value; these include asset approaches, break-up value, and rules of thumb.

KEY TERMS
(listed in order
of appearance)

common stock
voting right
preemptive right
right to share
residual claim
payout ratio
cash dividends
date of record
ex-dividend date
payment date
liquidating dividends
stock repurchases
stock dividend
stock split
growth stock
earnings per share

income stock
growth and income stock
blue chip
cyclical stock
defensive stock
speculative stock
American depository receipts
capital asset pricing model
securities market line
earnings approach
dividend approach
multistage growth model
multiple-of-earnings approach
Ben Graham NCAV rule
break-up value

REVIEW
QUESTIONS

1. As an owner of common stock, you have three basic rights. Identify and explain each, indicating which of the three you think is most important to most investors.
2. How does a stock dividend differ from a cash dividend? How are stock dividends and stock splits similar, and why do companies have them? Does either increase your wealth? Explain.
3. Indicate three important dates with respect to a cash dividend.
4. Explain liquidating dividends and stock repurchases. As a shareholder, do you receive cash with each of these? Are they true dividends in the sense that they distribute earnings? Explain.
5. Explain the investment opportunities offered by the following kinds of stocks: (a) growth stock, (b) income stock, (c) growth and income stock, (d) blue chip, (e) cyclical stock, (f) defensive stock, and (g) speculative stock.
6. What are liquidity and inflation risks? Explain whether or not stocks have been good hedges against inflation.
7. What are firm-specific and industry risks? Explain specific sources of such risks.
8. Define market risk and explain its causes. Also explain how market risk can be managed.
9. How can you construct an SML; that is, what information is necessary to construct it?
10. If the risk-free rate changes, what changes might occur to (a) the slope of the SML, (b) the position of the SML, and (c) the value of the market risk premium? Explain your responses.
11. An SML provides required rates of return: Explain what this statement means.
12. Suppose investors cannot borrow at the risk-free rate. Explain the implication of this limitation on the SML.
13. What is an expected return? Indicate how it differs from a required return.
14. Indicate six steps in utilizing an earnings approach to stock valuation.
15. Provide the basic formula for the dividend approach. How does it differ from an earnings approach? Does each lead to a similar decision regarding a stock, if a constant dividend growth rate is assumed?
16. What implications does a situation of multiple growth rates have on stock valuation? Is such a situation a realistic approach for growth stocks? Explain.
17. Identify and briefly explain other methods of stock valuation.

PROBLEMS
AND PROJECTS

1. You are looking at a quotation of AB&C in the morning newspaper. You see:

    25⅜   19⅞   AB&C   1.20   5.6   16   40387   21⅝   21⅛   21½   −⅜

    Explain what each entry means.
2. Construct an SML assuming the risk-free rate (T-bill rate) is 6% and the market risk premium is 8.5%. Then, calculate the return for a stock with a 0.75 beta value and explain the implication of this return in terms of deciding to invest in the stock.
3. Referring to problem 2, construct a new SML under the assumption the risk-free rate increases to 10%. What implication does such an increase have in terms of investing in specific stocks?

4. Again referring to problem 2, suppose investors can lend at the T-bill rate of 6% but borrow at an 8% rate. Construct a new SML to reflect this situation. Does it influence the selection of the 0.75 beta stock? Would it influence the selection of a stock with a 1.5 beta? Explain.

5. You are thinking of investing in one or possibly all three stocks listed below. Assuming a risk-free rate of 8.8% and a market risk premium of 8.5%, explain which, if any, of the stocks should be purchased.

	Ace Co.	King Inc.	Queen Inc.
Beta values	0.400	0.612	1.800
Expected rates of return (%)	11.5	16.6	19.0

6. In addition to the information provided in problem 5, you have other data for King, Inc. You know the current market price of the stock is $15 a share and last year's EPS was $1.50. The company's payout ratio was—and will be in the future—60%, and EPS is expected to grow at a 10% rate each year. Determine the present value of a share of King, Inc., stock, assuming a three-year holding period. Does your answer confirm your decision about the stock in problem 5? Explain.

7. Using information provided in problems 5 and 6, use the dividend approach to show that King, Inc.'s, expected rate of return is in fact 16.6%.

8. Suppose you uncover additional information about Queen, Inc. Specifically, you find that its EPS last year was $2 and is forecasted to be $2.30 in the upcoming year. The average annual rate of growth of EPS is 15% over the past five years, while the average P/E ratio is 20. Using a multiple-of-earnings approach, determine four possible values of the stock's price.

9. (Student Project) P/E ratios are published in each issue of The Wall Street Journal and Barron's. From the library, reference an issue of either one and draw a sample of 20 companies: 10 with very low P/E ratios and 10 with very high ratios. Do not select companies with negative earnings or a company whose price performance over the year is known to you. Now, with a current issue of either paper, obtain current prices and evaluate performances of the two groups. Write a brief essay describing your experiment.

CASE ANALYSES

Larry and Barb Zumwalt are a young couple in relatively strong financial shape. Each has a professional career and earns around $40,000 annually. In addition, they have accumulated about $20,000 that can be earmarked for speculative investing. They intend to develop a common stock portfolio, making their own security selections rather than utilizing pooling arrangements. The Zumwalts have done a reasonable amount of reading on the topic of common stock investing, although they hardly consider themselves experts. They admit they have no idea what kinds of stocks to buy or what amounts of return they should expect from their investments.

**6.1
The Zumwalts'
Interest in
Common Stocks**

To illustrate their problems, Barb believes that they should invest heavily in public utility stocks because their dividend yields are good at around 9%. She does not favor growth stocks because of their low yields and because they seem difficult to find. Barb likes the three public utilities operating in their region of the state, and she would invest at least $5,000 in each of them. Larry disagrees with Barb. He favors growth stocks and believes that yearly returns of 30% are likely if the right stocks can be found. Larry hopes to find the right stocks by subscribing to an investment advisory service that claims a successful past history. Larry sees little risk in this strategy, but he admits that Barb's utility stocks are probably less risky.

Questions

a. The Zumwalts indicate a willingness to undertake speculative investing. However, do they have concrete investment plans? Discuss.

b. Explain whether the Zumwalts comprehend risk and return possibilities from common stock investing. Suppose they ask you to advise them in this regard. Indicate specific risks and discuss how these risks might be managed. Then explain how sensible estimates of required return can be generated, given an understanding of risk.

c. Do either public utility stocks or growth stocks seem appropriate for the Zumwalts? Discuss.

d. How would you advise Larry and Barb as to specific selections of stocks? Explain.

**6.2
Analytical
Evaluation of
the Darden Tool
Company**

The Darden Tool Company had an initial public offering of its common stock last year. The company produces specialized tools and components used in manufacturing cellular telephones. The spectacular growth of this industry has created exciting opportunities for Darden, and the price of its stock reflects this potential. Its current price is $40 a share, which is 25 times its EPS in the previous year. EPS has grown at a 20% annual rate for the past four years, and analysts anticipate this rate will continue for at least four more years. They also believe the current P/E ratio will continue for four more years. Darden's management does not favor a large dividend, preferring instead to reinvest earnings; the current payout ratio is 40%. At present, the risk-free rate is 6.0%, the market risk premium is 8.0%, and the company's beta is 1.5.

Questions

a. Determine the present value of the stock, using the earnings approach. Does the stock represent a good purchase? Explain.

b. Calculate the stock's total return, using the dividend approach. Does this approach indicate a good buy? Explain.

c. Determine the stock's present value assuming the following: *(i)* after four years, earnings and dividend growth fall to a 12% annual rate, which will continue indefinitely; and *(ii)* the payout ratio increases to 60%, beginning in the fifth year. Do these new assumptions change your recommendations in parts *i* and *ii*? Explain.

Antilla, Susan. "New Shaker in the A.D.R. Business." *New York Times,* August 1, 1993, p. 13.

Durand, David. "What Price Growth?" *The Journal of Portfolio Management,* Fall 1992, pp. 84–91.

Gottschalk, Earl C., Jr. "Compounding Power of Regular Dividend Boosts." *The Wall Street Journal,* August 12, 1992, p. C1.

Harris, Dianne. "Stocks with Goodies for All." *Money,* May 1992, pp. 134–41.

Newman, Anne. "Sleuthing for Small Stocks Meant for Stardom." *The Wall Street Journal,* October 22, 1991, p. C3.

Palmer, Jay. "Europe's for Sale: Should You Buy?" *Barron's,* June 14, 1993, p. 16.

Peavy, John W., III. "Stock Prices: Do Interest Rates and Earnings Really Matter?" *Financial Analysts Journal,* May/June 1992, pp. 10–12.

HELPFUL
READING

CHAPTER SEVEN

Fundamental Analysis of Common Stocks

After you finish this chapter, you will be able to:

- understand a business balance sheet, including what it does and does not show.

- understand an income statement in terms of what it shows and what its limitations are.

- evaluate balance sheet strength by understanding liquidity and solvency ratios.

- evaluate earnings strength by understanding earnings ratios.

- see how earnings and dividend growth relate to the market price of a common stock.

- grasp how economic performance moves in cycles and realize the importance of forecasting future economic activity.

- understand the nature of industry analysis.

I f the key to successful investing is finding undervalued securities, the important question is, how is it done? Various approaches were explained in Chapter 6. They are a part of securities analysis called fundamental analysis, and someone working in this area is referred to as a fundamentalist. Fundamentalists believe that it is possible to determine the intrinsic value of common stock. This value may reflect factors such as a company's earning power, its asset structure, the quality of its management or product lines, or its potential for being acquired in a merger or other takeover.

Fundamental analysis:
method of determining a stock's value that examines a firm's underlying strengths, such as its earning power or asset structure

Fundamental analysis typically follows a three-stage approach: analyses of the firm, industry, and overall economy. It is not important when each stage is considered, but it is vital that all three components link together. A cyclical firm such as the Mead Corporation, our illustrative company in this chapter, has operations that are sensitive to overall economic changes. Analysts attempting to forecast Mead's future earnings must first make an assessment of future economic growth in the forecast period. Then, they must determine how the paper industry will respond to the forecasted growth and, finally, how firms in the paper industry, such as Mead, will be affected. Our presentation in this chapter begins with the firm; then, we consider the overall economy and, finally, the industry.

FINANCIAL STATEMENTS

Any financial analysis of a firm requires data, and a good starting point for obtaining data is a company's annual financial report, particularly the financial statements. As an investor, you should be familiar with the two most important of these—the balance sheet (also called a statement of financial condition) and the income statement.

The Balance Sheet

Business balance sheet:
statement showing assets a business owns, its liabilities, and the difference between the two—net worth

A **business balance sheet** shows the assets and liabilities of a business and the difference between the two, which is referred to broadly as net worth. Assets are things of value to a business: its cash, accounts receivable, inventories, machinery and equipment, land and buildings, and many others, including intangible items such as patents and copyrights. Liabilities are amounts a business owes its creditors over both the long and the short term. Net worth, as the difference between assets and liabilities, indicates what the business is worth, in an accounting sense. If the business is a corporation, net worth usually is referred to as shareholders' (or shareowners') equity.

Exhibit 7.1 shows the balance sheet for Mead Corporation for the two years ended December 31, 1992 and 1991. Mead, one of the world's largest manufacturers of paper, produces more than 1.2 million tons annually. It has a strong position in coated paper board and multiple packaging and is the largest maker of paper-based school and home office supplies. Through its

Mead Data Central (MDC) Division, the company developed the world's lead-ing electronic information retrieval services for law, patents, accounting, finance, news, and business information. You may be more familiar with Mead and its MDC Division through its information retrieval trade names, LEXIS and NEXIS. A securities analyst would probably describe Mead as a cyclical company with interesting above-average growth potential in its elec-tronic publishing area. At December 31, 1992, Mead had about 18,000 share-holders who held about 59,000,000 shares of common stock. The company also had 20,400 employees.

Mead's 1992 financial report is comprehensive, complete with an 11-year review of important financial data that we use later in a ratio analysis. To provide additional insights on Mead, we show at the end of this chapter a complete research report prepared by Standard and Poor's Corporation. (These reports, available for a large number of listed and over-the-counter stocks, can be purchased from Standard and Poor's for $9.00 each.) You should find the report informative and a useful supplement in determining Mead's intrinsic value.

Assets, Liabilities, and Shareholders' Equity   Most of the assets, liabilities, and shareholders' equity accounts are probably clear to you and do not require elaboration. As you can see, Mead had total assets of $4.03 billion at the end of 1992. About 58%, or $2.35 billion, was invested in property, plant, and equipment; about 28%, or $1.13 billion, was invested in current assets; the balance—14%, or $0.55 billion—represented long-term investments and other assets. Any notes to a financial statement are important and should be reviewed. For example, note D associated with "other assets" indicates vari-ous items, the most important of which is goodwill ($237 million). Goodwill, as used here, is an accounting concept; it tells us that Mead acquired inter-ests in other businesses and paid an amount greater than so-called book value (to be defined shortly).

As you probably know, the "balance" in a balance sheet refers to the fact that the total value of all assets ($4,031.4 million) equals the total value of all liabilities, deferred items, and shareholders' equity ($4,031.4 million). Although liabilities and shareholders' equity are easily understood, if you lack a strong background in accounting, you may not know the nature of deferred items. These do not represent amounts that are currently and contractually owed to creditors, as are liabilities, but rather potential future obligations of the corporation. For example, the postretirement benefits represent the pre-sent value, net of income taxes, of estimated benefits Mead will pay to cur-rent and future retirees. So, although $98.3 million is not actually owed retirees, it is a reasonable estimate of the present value of future contingent payments.

What the Balance Sheet Shows   The main function of the balance sheet is to show what a company is worth at some point in time, using accounting

EXHIBIT 7.1

Mead Corporation's balance sheet. (Source: *Mead Annual Shareholders' Report,*
1992. Courtesy of Mead.)

December 31	1992	1991
Assets		
Current assets:		
Cash and cash equivalents	$ 18.4	$ 24.6
Accounts receivable, less allowance for doubtful accounts		
of $24.9 in 1992 and $27.9 in 1991	582.1	533.3
Receivable from sale of business		45.0
Inventories (Note B)	425.9	454.6
Deferred tax asset (Note L)	51.3	
Prepaid expenses	51.7	35.4
Total current assets	1,129.4	1,092.9
Investments and other assets:		
Investments in and advances to investees (Note C)	58.9	67.8
Other assets (Note D)	493.0	460.4
	551.9	528.2
Property, plant and equipment, at cost (Notes E and P):		
Land and land improvements	128.2	125.1
Buildings	602.6	595.7
Machinery and equipment	3,113.5	2,971.3
Construction in progress	78.2	71.8
	3,922.5	3,763.9
Less accumulated amortization and depreciation	(1,785.5)	(1,611.4)
	2,137.0	2,152.5
Timber and timberlands, net of timber depletion	213.1	212.6
Property, plant and equipment—net	2,350.1	2,365.1
Total assets	$4,031.4	$3,986.2

All dollar amounts in millions

concepts to measure worth. The worth of a business corporation is shown by
the value of shareholders' equity. Mead was worth $1,495,400,000 at
December 31, 1992. If we divide this figure by the number of shares of common stock outstanding on that date, we then have shareholders' equity per
share, more commonly referred to as **book value per share;** that is,

Book value per share:
value measurement cal-
culated as shareholders'
equity divided by the
number of common
shares outstanding

$$\text{book value/share} = \frac{\$1,495,400,000}{59,000,000} = \$25.35$$

Was each share of Mead's stock really worth $25.35? Because the mar-
ket price of each share at that time was about $40, we could conclude that
something was wrong: either investors were paying too much or book value is
not a good measurement of true value. Although both alternatives could be

EXHIBIT 7.1
Continued

December 31	1992	1991
Liabilities and Shareowners' Equity		
Current liabilities:		
Notes payable	$	$ 45.0
Accounts payable:		
Trade	256.5	237.8
Affiliated companies	27.0	28.5
Outstanding checks	81.2	81.4
Accrued wages	92.5	88.4
Taxes, other than income	58.0	57.4
Other current liabilities	204.0	196.4
Current maturities of long-term debt	10.7	11.4
Total current liabilities	729.9	746.3
Long-term debt (Note E)	1,332.3	1,315.7
Deferred Items:		
Income tax liability (Note L)	275.2	248.8
Postretirement benefits (Note O)	98.3	94.4
Other	100.3	102.6
	473.8	445.8
Shareowners' equity (Notes G and H):		
Common shares	175.2	174.0
Additional paid-in capital	12.3	1.5
Foreign currency translation adjustment	(.8)	7.2
Retained earnings	1,308.7	1,295.7
	1,495.4	1,478.4
Total liabilities and shareowners' equity	$4,031.4	$3,986.2

See notes to financial statements

true, keep in mind that book value is purely an accounting concept. As such, it depends on certain accounting conventions and regulations for determining value. One of the most important of these is the use of historical cost as a basis for measuring asset values; in effect, companies show the values of most of their assets at the price paid for them less any depreciation the companies have taken to allow for loss of productivity or obsolescence. But is cost the same as value? Not in most cases, and in some, there are huge differences. When you begin fundamental analysis, book value can be a starting point, but you must go beyond it in almost every situation for a more comprehensive view of value.

What the Balance Sheet Doesn't Show Apart from the problem of reporting values that are more appropriately described as historical costs, a balance sheet may not even list all of a company's assets or its potential liabilities. For example, unless a company actually purchases an asset or expends funds to develop and produce it, the asset will not be shown on the balance sheet. Furthermore, increases in value attributable to inflation or increased demand are also ignored. This means Coke's and PepsiCo's formulas, trademarks, copyrights, and many other intangible assets are not even shown. Walt Disney's library of films, reportedly worth hundreds of millions of dollars, is shown at a tiny fraction of that figure, and there are many other examples. In Mead's case, an interesting question is, what is the market value of the timber and timberlands shown on the balance sheet at a value of $213.1 million at December 31, 1992? Timber prices were exceptionally high at that time, and the true market value of those properties may have been substantially higher. If so, Mead certainly was worth more than $25.35 a share.

Hidden assets: things of value to a company that may not appear (or may be undervalued) on its balance sheet

   Hidden assets are, in some cases, worth far more than assets revealed on the balance sheet. Fundamentalists have devoted considerable research time looking for **hidden asset plays.** A *play* is Wall Street jargon for finding a way to profit from an undervalued or overvalued situation. If the market price of a company's stock is far below its book value, which includes values of the hidden assets, then the company may be a good candidate for a takeover. Buying the stock now and waiting for the takeover is the play.

Hidden asset plays: strategies based on hidden assets and the expectation of a firm takeover

   Certain potential losses might also not appear on a company's balance sheet. Although certified public accountants must indicate potential losses and contingent liabilities when reasonable evidence suggests they will occur, it is not cut and dried as to what makes up reasonable evidence, or how much the future amounts will be. As noted above, it is extremely important to read all parts of a company's financial report, including the footnotes, because expected future adversities may be reported there and no place else.

The Income Statement

Income statement: listing of a company's revenues and expenses over time

The **income statement** is a listing of revenue and expense accounts that show the results of a company's operations over some period. Because the generation of income is the primary function of most businesses, the income statement is regarded as the most important statement the company prepares. Exhibit 7.2 shows Mead's income statements for the years ended December 31, 1992, 1991, and 1990. The term *consolidated* indicates Mead has income from its subsidiary corporations that has been incorporated into these statements.

What the Income Statement Shows   The objective of the income statement is to show the amount of net income (or net loss) the company earned for the period indicated. (Mead's statement refers to net income as net earnings; they have the same meaning.) As you see, Mead's net income in 1992 was $71,600,000, up from $6,900,000 in 1991. Investors are less interested in total earnings than they are in earnings per share of common stock (EPS). Exhibit 7.2 shows each EPS, which in 1992 was $1.21, up from $0.12 in 1991.

EXHIBIT 7.2

Mead Corporation's income statement. (Source: *Mead Annual Shareholders' Report,* 1992. Courtesy of Mead.)

Year Ended December 31	1992	1991	1990
Net sales	$4,703.2	$4,579.3	$4,772.4
Cost of products sold	3,779.4	3,712.2	3,850.4
Gross profit	923.8	867.1	922.0
Selling, administrative and research expenses	671.7	634.7	617.6
Other expenses (Note J)	95.0	34.5	88.5
Earnings from operations	157.1	197.9	215.9
Other revenues (expenses)—net (Note K)	(.5)	64.5	23.7
Interest and debt expense	(101.1)	(114.4)	(92.6)
Earnings from continuing operations before income taxes	55.5	148.0	147.0
Income taxes (Note L)	23.9	54.3	52.3
Earnings from continuing operations before equity in net earnings (loss) of investees	31.6	93.7	94.7
Equity in net earnings (loss) of investees (Note C)	6.0	(18.1)	11.7
Earnings from continuing operations	37.6	75.6	106.4
Loss from discontinued operations (Note M)		(10.0)	(74.8)
Earnings before extraordinary item and cumulative effect of change in accounting principle	37.6	65.6	31.6
Extraordinary item, gain on retirement of debt			6.9
Cumulative effect of change in accounting principle (Notes L and O)	34.0	(58.7)	
Net earnings	$ 71.6	$ 6.9	$ 38.5
Per common and common equivalent share (Note A):			
Earnings from continuing operations	$ .63	$ 1.29	$ 1.71
Loss from discontinued operations		(.17)	(1.20)
Earnings before extraordinary item and cumulative effect of change in accounting principle	.63	1.12	.51
Extraordinary item			.11
Cumulative effect of change in accounting principle	.58	(1.00)	
Net earnings	$ 1.21	$ .12	$ .62

All dollar amounts in millions, except per share amounts

See notes to financial statements

Limitations of the Income Statement   Like the balance sheet, the income statement should not be relied on as the absolute truth of a company's earnings performance. Keep in mind that net income is an accounting concept, shaped and formed by accounting rules, regulations, and conventions. Some of these make a great deal of sense for determining value, while others are more controversial.

For example, we mentioned previously the accountant's insistence that historical cost be used to state asset values. These same historical costs, then, form the basis for depreciation, which is taken as an expense on the income statement. No one questions that depreciation is an economic reality that must be recognized in measuring earnings. But should the annual allocation be based on what an asset actually cost when it was purchased, or what it could be sold for today, or how much it would cost today to replace it? Depending on your view, you could have three substantially different depreciation figures. Even if we agree on what basis to depreciate, we may then disagree on our estimates of the asset's life, which also gives us different depreciation amounts. Many financial analysts have become so skeptical of depreciation figures that they have chosen to ignore them altogether by calculating cash flows. A **cash flow** is net income plus depreciation (or depletion); that is,

Cash flow: measurement of a firm's ability to generate cash

$$\text{cash flow} = \text{net income} + \text{depreciation}$$

It has become an important concept, so you should be familiar with it. Like earnings, it often is shown on a per share basis.

Mead does not list its depreciation (and depletion) on the income statement. It is found elsewhere in the report, however, and the amounts, along with cash flow figures, are as follows:

	1992	**1991**	**1990**
Depreciation	$299,600,000	$288,400,000	$247,500,000
Net income	71,600,000	6,900,000	38,500,000
Total cash flow	$371,200,000	$295,300,000	$286,000,000
Cash flow per share	$6.29	$5.04	$4.60

As you can tell, the depreciation amounts are extremely large in relation to net income.

Do cash flow figures help in determining a company's value? Some analysts strongly believe they do, while others are less convinced. Cash flow figures are more useful in comparing one company with another than in looking at a single company's historical data because companies may differ considerably in using depreciation methods. In effect, cash flows remove these differences.

Along with depreciation, there are other areas in which accounting principles often are applied differently. Important differences arise in valuing inventories, with some companies choosing to value them at their more recent purchase prices, while others value them at older prices. It often takes an expert to unravel the differences in income produced by these different valuation methods. During periods of stable prices, the differences are not large.

Accounting-determined net income is not perfect, and in some situations, you should go beyond it to judge a company's capacity to generate earnings. But ignoring net income altogether would be a mistake. In the overwhelming majority of cases, it provides a reasonable estimate of a company's earnings strength.

EVALUATING FINANCIAL PERFORMANCE

The balance sheet and income statement by themselves provide a good overview of a company's financial strengths and weaknesses. If you have reviewed Exhibits 7.1 and 7.2 closely, you probably have formed an impression of Mead. You can sharpen that impression by examining the data more extensively and critically through ratio analysis, which is a technique of looking at one account value in relation to another. It often provides insights that are missed when looking at accounts independently.

Ratio analysis often is performed by looking at the historical data of one company over a period of time. With this method, called *historical analysis*, trends and averages are used to evaluate a given year's performance. Another approach, called *cross-sectional analysis,* compares one company's ratios with those of others or to industry averages. A thorough financial review includes both approaches, although we will limit our discussion to historical analysis. (You can find industry comparisons in Standard & Poor's *Research Report* presented at the end of this chapter.) Data for the historical analysis comes from Mead's *1992 Annual Report*.

Measuring Balance Sheet Strength

Is Mead a financially strong company, a candidate for bankruptcy, or somewhere in the middle of these extremes? Is it sufficiently liquid to pay its bills on an ongoing basis, or is it burdened by excessive short-term debt? Ratio analysis can shed light on these questions.

Liquidity   One balance sheet strength is adequate liquidity. A company is liquid when it has sufficient current assets to pay its current liabilities. The term *current* usually means the asset can be converted to cash within the firm's normal operating cycle, usually presumed to be one year; a current liability is one that must be paid within one year. Total liquidity is measured by net working capital (NWC), defined as current assets minus current liabilities. Exhibit 7.1 shows Mead's net working capital in 1992 was $399.5 million ($1,129.4 − $729.9) at year's end. Given current assets, current liabilities, and NWC, two liquidity ratios can then be calculated.

NWC/Sales   NWC typically must increase as sales increase. Mead could not be expected to run its business with no more NWC than the corner grocer. If NWC lags considerably behind sales growth, the company could face a future liquidity problem. Mead's **NWC/sales ratio** was 0.085 ($395.0/$4,703.2) in 1992. Exhibit 7.3 indicates this ratio is above the 11-year average value of 0.060.

NWC/sales ratio: measurement of a firm's liquidity

EXHIBIT 7.3
Mead's liquidity ratios

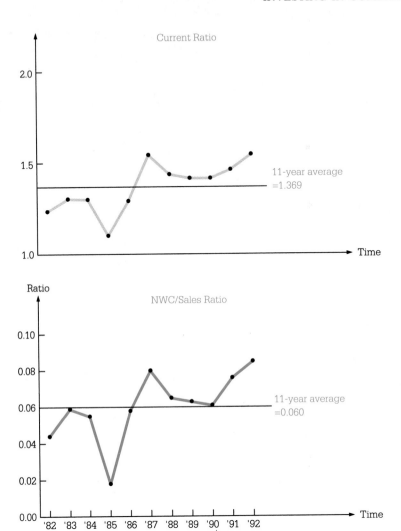

Current ratio: liquidity
measurement defined as
current assets divided
by current liabilities

The Current Ratio   The **current ratio** is current assets divided by current liabilities; that is,

$$\text{current ratio} = \frac{\text{current assets}}{\text{current liabilities}}$$

Mead's 1992 current ratio is

$$\frac{\$1,129.4}{\$729.9} = 1.55$$

A current ratio of 1.55 means Mead had $1.55 in current assets for each $1 of current liabilities. Exhibit 7.3 indicates this is also above the 11-year average of 1.37.

Liquidity is an elusive quality to measure. The previous two ratios suggest an improving position, although they do not show a liquidity surplus. To gain further insights at this point, an analyst would consider using industry comparisons to determine how Mead's liquidity position compares with that of other firms in the paper industry. An unfavorable comparison would be considered in determining the intrinsic value of the company's stock.

Solvency   Solvency is different from liquidity: liquidity is a short-term concept, while solvency takes a longer view. Each has to do with evaluating a company's debt position. Solvency is particularly important to a company's bondholders. They are concerned that interest and principal payments can be met over the bond issue's life and that the company is not forced into bankruptcy. In the latter case, the bondholders' claims are more likely to be paid if there is a small amount of debt in relation to assets. Two ratios often are used to measure the firm's debt structure: the total debt ratio and the debt/equity ratio.

The Total Debt Ratio   The **total debt ratio** shows total liabilities divided by total assets; that is,

$$\text{total debt ratio} = \frac{\text{total liabilities}}{\text{total assets}}$$

Total debt ratio: measurement of a firm's solvency defined as total liabilities divided by total assets

The following equation shows Mead's 1992 total debt ratio:

$$\frac{\$729.9 + \$1,332.3}{\$4,031.4} = \frac{\$2,062.2}{\$4,031.4} = 0.512$$

At the end of 1992, Mead's total liabilities were about 51% of its total assets; thus, asset values could shrink 49% before creditors would face a potential loss in selling assets to cover their claims. This assumes assets could be sold at book values, which may not be true. Exhibit 7.4 shows Mead's debt ratio has remained fairly stable since 1982 but was above its 11-year average in 1992.

The Debt/Equity Ratio   Because the total debt ratio includes current liabilities in the calculation, it duplicates some information available with the current ratio. To measure the long-term financial structure, analysts use the **debt/equity ratio.** Its calculation is shown below:

$$\text{debt/equity ratio} = \frac{\text{long-term debt}}{\text{total shareholders' equity}}$$

Debt/equity ratio: solvency measurement defined as long-term debt divided by total shareholders' equity

EXHIBIT 7.4
Mead's solvency ratios

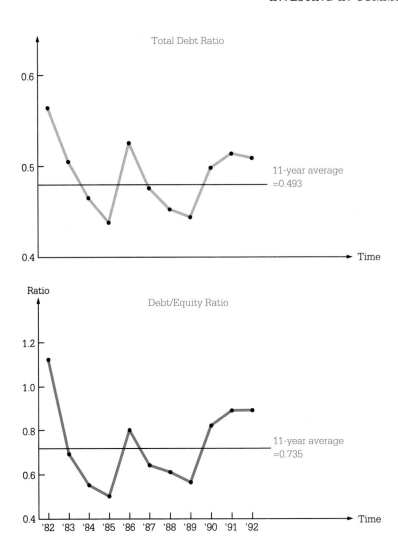

Mead's 1992 figure is determined as follows:

$$\frac{\$1,332.3}{\$1,495.4} = 0.891$$

Exhibit 7.4 indicates this ratio is above its 11-year average of 0.735 and has risen rather sharply since 1989. This trend clearly shows how Mead has increased its use of long-term debt relative to owners' equity. Although the company's solvency position has deteriorated somewhat, one might argue that it was too strong in the past. EPS often can be increased by using borrowed money. If so, the shareholders' position is not enhanced by low levels of debt; in effect, they are better off if borrowed funds are used to invest in earning assets. Clearly, though, adding debt to the capital structure increases the company's risk. At some point, investors may consider that risk excessive.

Measuring Earnings Strength

Although balance sheet strength is important, earnings strength is even more so. In fact, balance sheet strength usually arises from earnings strength. Despite how strong a company might be to start with, it cannot sustain constant losses without eventually facing bankruptcy. You can measure earnings strength by examining profit margins, key earnings ratios, and earnings and dividend growth rates.

Profit Margins   A **profit margin** shows a particular profit measurement divided by revenues (sales). Analysts consider the following three as important:

Profit margin: ratio of a particular profit measurement divided by sales

$$\text{gross profit margin} = \frac{\text{gross profit}}{\text{sales}}$$

$$\text{operating income margin} = \frac{\text{operating income}}{\text{sales}}$$

$$\text{net income margin} = \frac{\text{net income}}{\text{sales}}$$

In 1992, Mead had the following values:

$$\text{gross profit margin} = \frac{\$923.8}{\$4,703.2} = 0.196, \text{ or } 19.6\%$$

$$\text{operating income margin} = \frac{\$157.1}{\$4,703.2} = 0.033, \text{ or } 3.3\%$$

$$\text{net income margin} = \frac{\$71.6}{\$4,703.2} = 0.015, \text{ or } 1.5\%$$

Exhibit 7.5 shows annual values for the three margins above over the period 1982–92.

The gross profit margin is the beginning point of all profits. The cost of acquiring or manufacturing the products a firm sells must be kept in line with product prices or profits will erode. Mead's gross profit margin has been fairly constant at around 20% since 1984. This is a favorable showing, in the sense that Mead has been able to maintain its margin during periods of economic slack; a negative is that margins didn't improve during the boom years in the mid-1980s.

The operating income margin extends the gross profit margin by measuring profits after operating expenses such as selling, administrative, and

EXHIBIT 7.5

Mead's profit margins

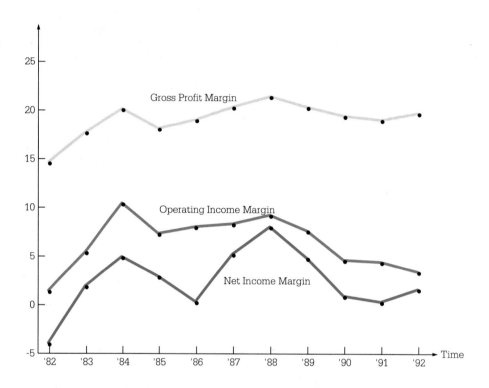

research have been considered. Mead's 11-year history with this margin is far less favorable. As you see in Exhibit 7.5, the 3.3% showing in 1992 is far below the 11-year average of 6.3% and is showing a definite downtrend in recent years. It seems that Mead must bring operating expenses more in line with revenues before the company can show significant progress in profits, even if economic growth accelerates.

The net income margin measures profitability after all expenses and other revenues have been considered. Exhibit 7.5 indicates the high degree of volatility in this margin over the 11 years. This is typical of cyclical companies, although in Mead's case, the volatility was enhanced by discontinuing certain operations and by major changes in accounting methods.

Earnings Ratios   Earnings ratios indicate profitability in relation to certain charges that must be covered each year—such as interest—and to funds invested in the business. Three often-watched ratios are the times-interest-earned figure and the returns on investment and on equity.

Times-Interest-Earned Ratio   A company's earnings must be used first to pay bond interest. Only after it is paid can the company pay dividends to shareholders or retain any funds for reinvestment. The **times-interest-earned ratio** indicates the adequacy of earnings to pay interest and is calculated as follows:

Times-interest-earned ratio: profitability measurement that shows a firm's ability to cover its interest obligations

$$\text{times-interest-earned ratio} = \frac{\text{earnings from operations}}{\text{interest}}$$

Mead's 1992 times-interest-earned ratio is

$$\frac{\$157.1}{\$101.1} = 1.55$$

In 1992, Mead had $1.55 of earnings from operations for each $1 of interest, which is rather weak coverage. Exhibit 7.6 shows that coverage is substantially below the 11-year average of 2.96. If earnings fall in the future, Mead

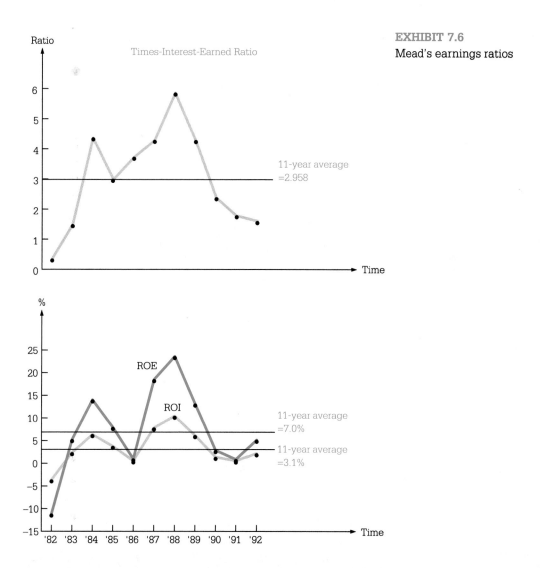

EXHIBIT 7.6

Mead's earnings ratios

may have difficulty meeting its interest obligations. However, we should recall that Mead's cash flow was very strong in relation to earnings.

Return on investment: profitability measurement that relates profit to total assets

Return on Investment **Return on investment (ROI)** indicates the company's ability to generate profits from its assets. The ratio is shown below:

$$ROI = \frac{\text{net income}}{\text{asset investment}}$$

Asset investment often is measured by the year-end value of total assets. However, if total assets increase or decrease substantially from one year to the next, it would be better to use the average of the two years. Mead's total assets did not change very much from 1991 to 1992. Mead's 1992 ROI is

$$\frac{\$71.6}{\$4,031.4} = 0.018, \text{ or } 1.8\%$$

Mead earned about 1.8% in 1992 on its asset investments. Is this a good return? Relative to the 11-year average of 3.1%, it is not. Moreover, ROI is an after-tax return, and you might compare it with similar returns, such as those on long-term municipal bonds. Using this yardstick, we would conclude it was very poor because municipal bonds yielded about 5.5% for most of 1992 and offered less risk. Moreover, Exhibit 7.6 shows that ROI has never been above 10.0% and has been somewhat volatile over the 11-year period. The most likely explanation for this poor performance is that Mead was reinvesting much of its profits to make assets and earnings grow. Many of these investments were in product research and development—areas that do not immediately show high returns. If these investments ultimately prove profitable, Mead's ROIs in the future could be much higher.

Return on equity: profitability measurement that relates profit to shareholders' equity

Return on Equity ROI does not consider how the company's assets were financed; as such, it measures the return to total investment, not the return to the stockholders' investment. A direct measurement of this latter item is the **return on equity (ROE).** It is calculated in the following way:

$$ROE = \frac{\text{net income}}{\text{average shareholders' equity}}$$

where average shareholders' equity is the year-end value. Mead's ROE in 1992 is

$$\frac{\$71,600}{\$1,495.4} = 0.048, \text{ or } 4.8\%$$

Exhibit 7.6 shows the 11-year history of this ratio and indicates that 1992's value is substantially below the average of 7.0%. Mead's ROE figures are more impressive than its ROIs, illustrating the beneficial effect of using borrowed funds to enhance the return to owners.

Earnings and Dividend Growth   Exhibit 7.7 shows Mead's EPS, dividends per share (DPS), cash flow per share (CFS), and market price (average of high price and low price each year) for the period 1982–92; also shown are values for the price-earnings (P/E) and price-cash flow (P/CF) ratios. The cyclical nature of Mead's operations are clearly visible here with respect to the high volatility of EPS. From a deficit of $1.60 in 1982 (a recession year), EPS grew to $5.37 in 1988 and then declined sharply to $0.12 in 1991 (another recession year). A turnaround seems to have begun in 1992, when EPS rebounded to $1.21.

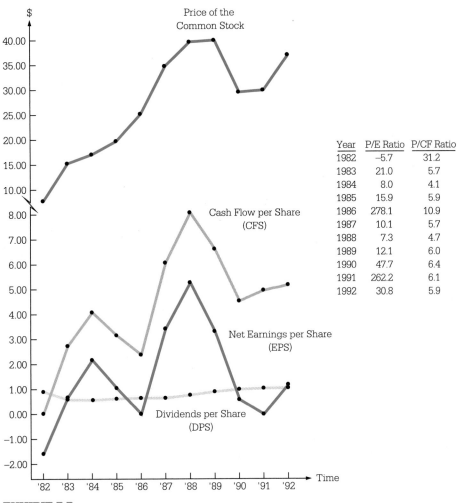

Year	P/E Ratio	P/CF Ratio
1982	−5.7	31.2
1983	21.0	5.7
1984	8.0	4.1
1985	15.9	5.9
1986	278.1	10.9
1987	10.1	5.7
1988	7.3	4.7
1989	12.1	6.0
1990	47.7	6.4
1991	262.2	6.1
1992	30.8	5.9

EXHIBIT 7.7
Mead's performance over time

Determining historical growth rates for cyclical companies presents a problem, in that the answer you get is sensitive to the period you select as a starting point. Consider DPS as an example: If we select 1982 as the base year, there has been little growth—an annual rate of about 1.3%—for the next 10 years (1983–92). But if we take 1987 as the base year, the rate jumps to 9% for the following five-year period (1988–92).

So, what is the best estimate of future DPS growth? Most analysts would look not only at historical rates, but also at anticipated future rates. In Mead's case, the elimination of several marginally profitable ventures, the expected above-average growth of its electronic publishing division, coupled with the expectation of an improving economy suggest that Mead might sustain an annual dividend growth rate of 10% in the future. We will use this assumption in the next section.

Was Mead a Fairly Valued Security?

In early 1993, Mead was selling at about $40 a share. At this price, is Mead fairly valued? Or is it overvalued or undervalued? We examine this issue with two valuation methods from Chapter 6—the dividend approach and the multiple-of-earnings (or cash flow) approach.

Applying the Dividend Approach   Applying the dividend approach, some preliminary steps are necessary. First, calculate the expected total return (ETR). The total return (TR) formula is:

$$TR = \text{current return} + \text{future return} = \frac{D}{P} + g$$

where D = the dividend expected in the upcoming year (1993),

P = the current price of the stock ($40), and

g = the expected growth of dividends in the future (10%, as discussed above)

D can be estimated by multiplying the 1992 dividend of $1 per share by 1.10, which assumes the 1993 dividend will increase by 10.0%. Then D = $1.10. Now,

$$ETR = (\$1.10/\$40) + 0.10 = 0.028 + 0.100 = 0.128, \text{ or } 12.8\%$$

The next step is to calculate the required return *(RR)*. To do this, we need Mead's beta value (β_i), the market risk premium *(MRP)*, and an estimate of the risk-free rate (R_F) available in early 1993. These are fitted into the equation:

$$RR = R_F + \beta_i(MRP)$$

BOX 7.1 GETTING AN INVESTMENT EDGE

Should PSRs Replace P/E Ratios?

According to one investment advisor, Kenneth Fisher, PSRs should replace P/E ratios. Why? Because earnings are influenced too heavily by management discretion (or indiscretion). Different accounting methods among companies or changes in methods within a company over time can cause huge distortions in corporate earnings, making true profitability in an economic sense virtually impossible to determine. Fisher's point has merit. Even financial analysts often err badly in forecasting earnings, caused as much by accounting problems as by the difficulty of the task.

So what is a PSR, and why is it better? PSR stands for price-to-sales ratio. You calculate it by multiplying the market price of a company's stock by all its shares outstanding and dividing this product by its sales. For example, suppose XYZ stock is selling at $8 a share, there are 2 million shares outstanding, and its sales are $20 million. Its PSR is 0.80 ($8 × 2,000,000 = $16,000,000; $16,000,000/$20,000,000 = 0.80). Fisher believes sales are less easily influenced by accounting assumptions and conventions, making the ratio more indicative of a company's underlying financial strength. He advises using the ratio contrarily; that is, companies with low PSRs are the most desirable. Fisher recommends avoiding stocks with PSRs over

1.5 and definitely selling a stock when the PSR is between 3 and 6.

Fisher writes a column regularly in *Forbes*, so it is easy to read about PSR applications and to track the performance of his recommendations. Evan Sturza recently has suggested several modifications to the basic PSR to make it more effective. First, Sturza believes a company's debt should also be included in the calculation. He proposes doing this by adding debt to the market value of the stock. So, if XYZ had $8 million in debt, its total capitalization is $24 million and its PSR increases to 1.2 ($24,000,000/$20,000,000). Sturza's second point is that a company's industry should be considered because PSRs vary so much among industries. To accommodate this factor, he suggests that a PSR be divided by the average PSR of the industry. If XYZ's industry average PSR is 2.0, then its relative PSR is 0.6 (1.2/2.0). Finally, investors should select stocks on the basis of relative PSRs.

Should you use PSRs—the basic or the improved version—to select securities? Probably not, if you intend to limit your analysis to this single factor. Investment value is a complex concept that seldom is captured in one perspective on a company. Use all the tools, P/E ratios *and* PSRs, and all other ratios that pinpoint strengths and weaknesses.

Mead's beta was estimated at 1.4. U.S. Treasury securities with a 90-day maturity were yielding about 3%. Assuming an *MRP* of 8.5% (the 67-year arithmetic average) gives the following value for *RR*:

$$RR = 0.03 + 1.4(.085) = 0.03 + 0.119 = 0.149, \text{ or } 14.9\%$$

Because a fairly valued security is one that has an expected return equal to its required return, we conclude Mead was overvalued because its required return exceeded its expected return. The difference of 2.1% (14.9% − 12.8%) is rather large, indicating Mead would have been a poor investment. However, we should not automatically reject a company because it does not measure up to the standard of one approach. The earnings approach and dividend approach discussed in Chapter 6 work most effectively with companies that exhibit reasonably stable growth patterns. A cyclical company such as Mead does not fit these models as nicely as we might want and, so, is more difficult to value. On the other hand, if we cannot find a sustainable rate of earnings and dividend growth to justify the risks inherent in a stock, then we should be cautious before investing.

Applying the Multiple-of-Earnings (Cash-Flow) Approach   We noted in Chapter 6 that many analysts attempt to forecast EPS for upcoming periods and then apply a P/E ratio to forecast future price. In Mead's case, a consensus of forecasts indicated an average EPS of $2.50 and a P/E ratio of 18.3 for 1993 (see page 3 of Standard and Poor's report at the end of this chapter). Assuming these forecasts are correct, Mead's price should reach $45.75 ($2.50 × 18.3) by the end of 1993. That would mean a price appreciation of $5.75 for the year and a total return of $6.85, assuming a dividend of $1.10. The 1993 holding period return (HPR) would be 0.144 ($5.75/$40), or 14.4%. This is fairly close to the required return of 14.9%, so we might conclude that Mead is fairly valued.

But we also can question the forecasts of $2.50 for EPS and 18.3 for the P/E ratio. In the case of the latter, if you refer to Exhibit 7.7, you see that Mead's P/E ratio has varied considerably over time. When EPS was negative in 1982 and extremely small in 1986 and 1991, the P/E values are meaningless. And even in the other years, the variation is considerable, ranging from 47.7 in 1990 to 7.3 in 1988. How the experts derive their estimate of 18.3 for 1993 is anybody's guess.

If you refer again to Exhibit 7.7, notice that the cash flow multiplier (P/CF) is much stabler, although it, too, shows quite a bit of variation. But if we eliminate 1982, the variation is much smaller—from 4.1 to 10.9—and the average for the 10-year period 1983–92 is 6.14. A reasonable estimate of CFS for 1993, based on the consensus forecast of $2.50 for EPS, is $7.75. Given these two estimates, we forecast Mead's end-of-1993 price to be $47.28 (6.1 × $7.50). This figure leads to a 1993 HPR of about 21% [($7.28 + $1.10)/$40], again assuming a $1.10 DPS for the year. This method shows that Mead was somewhat undervalued.

What Do We Conclude About Mead?   So, we use three methods and arrive at three answers: one says Mead is overvalued (sell shares if you own them, or perhaps short-sell if you don't), the second says fairly valued (hold shares if you own them but no compelling reason to buy), and the third indicates undervalued (buy shares). Now, what should we do? This type of dilemma is fairly common in security valuation, underscoring the fact that the process is as much art as science. In early 1993, we might have agreed that Mead was no superbargain at prices above $40 a share, given what we knew about the company, the economy, and the industry; but at prices under $40, its appeal increases. As new information became available, though, we might have revised our opinion.

By mid-May 1993, Mead's price had increased to about $45 a share, which put it a bit ahead of where it should have been according to the forecasts above. Interestingly, securities analysts were revising their estimates of Mead's earnings slightly downward, which should have had a negative effect on the price. Based on fundamentals, the $5 increase in share value seemed excessive. Another factor entered the scene in the form of investor enthusiasm (fad?) for cyclicals of all sorts. When fads take hold, don't expect any method to forecast accurately. Now the investment becomes a gambling situation. If you want to play, forget fundamentals and brush up on the theory of mob behavior and probability theory.

Using Ratio Analysis

Ratio analysis has been in use for a number of years, and its application in investments was pioneered by Ben Graham, who was mentioned in Chapter 6. Until the advent of the personal computer and easily accessible data bases, only professional investment advisors made widespread use of the techniques. Today, for a rather modest investment, amateurs also can perform ratio analysis on a wide array of companies. Selecting companies often is done by screening, using so-called **filters**.

Filters: selected value characteristic used in a screening process

Screening with Filters   The first step is to access a data base, such as the Compustat Tapes. Then, you must decide which ratios are important. After your selection, the data base is screened to select companies that meet criteria imposed by your ratio selections. This process is called **screening with filters**.

For example, suppose you are a cautious investor and do not want to invest in a company with a debt ratio greater than 0.50. By entering this requirement as a command, you might find that, say, 3,000 firms of the total on the data set meet this requirement. Next, you also want to invest in companies with good earnings records. So, of the 3,000 initial firms, you impose a second requirement that annual growth in EPS over the past 10 years must equal or exceed 20%. This might screen out 2,500 firms, narrowing the list to 500. Because this is still too large and because you also like some div-

Screening with filters: computer-based technique that uses several (or many) filters to select undervalued companies idend income, your last command might be that only firms with dividend yields of 4% or better are desired. The last ratio might leave only 12 firms, from which you make your selections. Success with the method depends on the usefulness of the filters selected and the bold assumption that selected firms will continue their desired characteristics in the future. There are obvious problems and risks that should be considered before you start a screening program.

The Usefulness of Ratios   Clearly, ratios help us understand the financial characteristics of a firm. Do you believe that you understand Mead better as a result of the simple ratio analysis in this chapter? And do you now have a basic understanding of which ratios might be important in a screening operation? Few people argue that ratios are not helpful in such efforts. Unfortunately, some people believe that a single ratio, or some simplistic use of ratios, can distinguish "good" stocks from "bad" ones. At best, ratios are rough indicators of financial strength. In some respects, they are similar to various tests a medical doctor might use to measure your body strength or health. If your temperature exceeds 98.6 degrees, or if your blood pressure is above 120/80, or if your cholesterol count exceeds 200, you have a greater risk of encountering a physical problem. Do these measurements mean you are unhealthy? Or, do they tell a doctor specifically what's wrong with you if you complained of not feeling well? Not necessarily. Similarly, financial ratios can only indicate greater potential risks; they seldom can tell us what is fundamentally wrong or right with a company.

EVALUATING THE ECONOMY AND THE INDUSTRY

Top-to-bottom approach: indicates that fundamental analysis considers three investigative channels: overall economy (top), the industry, and the firm (bottom)

As indicated previously, determining how well an individual company might do in the future often requires a prior assessment of the likely performances of the overall economy and the company's industry. This **top-to-bottom approach** is shown in Exhibit 7.8 and is discussed throughout the following sections.

Brief History of U.S. Cycles

Business cycle: persistent and somewhat rhythmic ups and downs of economic activity over time

The history of the U.S. economy is one of uneven growth. Changes in economic activity over time—referred to as the **business cycle**—have been persistent, sometimes taking place at moderate and reasonably predictable rates, other times changing so wildly that all you can do is guess about the future. The business cycle influences the economic fortunes of the industries and firms that are part of it. Few of them escape the misfortunes of a recession, and many of them prosper during the upswings. Exhibit 7.9 demonstrates one aspect of this correlation.

Fundamental analysis involves:

I. Economic Analysis
Assessing the future
performance of the
overall economy

II. Industry Analysis
Determining the business
cycle's impact on specific
industries *and* evaluating
how new developments might
influence an industry

III. Firm Analysis
Analyzing how specific
companies might perform
given industry changes and
considering their individual
operating and financial
characteristics

EXHIBIT 7.8
A top-to-bottom
evaluation approach

The exhibit shows that since 1952, the economy has been in a period of expansion; however, there have been eight recessions with varying degrees of intensity. As you see, business profits are sensitive to the economic cycle, declining measurably as the economy falters. Few firms escape the downward drag of the cycle, although some feel it far worse than others. Particularly sensitive to the cycle are industries that produce capital goods (machinery, equipment, and so forth) or consumer durables (autos, housing, and major appliances). Less sensitive are industries that provide services or produce perishable consumer goods. We noted earlier that Mead's earnings were particularly sensitive to the business cycle.

Forecasting Economic Cycles

Although the cycle may cause serious economic harm, it actually represents good purchase or sale opportunities to investors. Good, that is, if investors could forecast coming cyclical changes with a fair degree of accuracy. Investors, economists, and practically everyone else have been trying to do so almost from the time a business cycle was first observed. Although forecasting techniques have improved considerably over the years, not even professional forecasters have a high degree of accuracy. Forecast errors are still large, particularly those pertaining to cyclical turning points, which are unquestionably the most difficult parts of the cycle to forecast. Despite these problems, if you are doing fundamental analysis, you must consider the economy's impact on the firm you are reviewing. To keep abreast of the economy,

EXHIBIT 7.9

Economic activity.
(Source: *Survey of
Current Business,*
February 1993.)

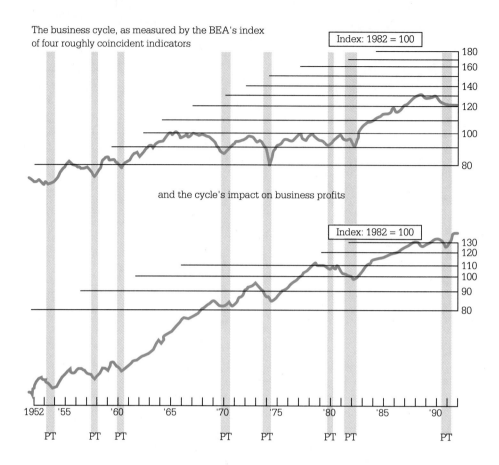

get in the habit of reading financial publications to gain a general awareness
of where the economy is and perhaps where many of the experts think it may
go. Two methods will help in this effort: following the government's publication of its leading economic indicators and determining the nature of the consensus among experts.

The Leading Indicator Series   Each month, the Bureau of Economic
Analysis (BEA) publishes its comprehensive list of economic indicators in
Survey of Current Business, which is available in many public and school
libraries. Of particular importance is a list of 11 indicators, called the leading
indicators. The **leading indicator series (LIS)** includes 11 variables that
have tended to change direction before changes in the business cycle; thus,
they lead the cycle. The 11 were chosen from among hundreds that were
tested to perform this function. Exhibit 7.10 shows how the LIS has tracked
the business cycle. As you see, it usually turns down before the peak of an
economic cycle is reached and turns up before the trough of a recession
occurs. Notice, however, that the number of months elapsing between the

**Leading indicator
series:** composite of 11
economic time series
that supposedly lead the
business cycle

BOX 7.2   INVESTMENT INSIGHTS

Artificial Intelligence and Neural Nets: Machine Replacements for the Security Analyst?

These days, hardly a securities analyst works without the benefit of a computer. It is indispensable—and until recently so was the securities analyst. But if some of the math geniuses keep improving their computer models, that may not be true in the future. Two new methods, artificial intelligence and neural nets, may have profound effects on the securities analysis business.

In its most basic form, artificial intelligence attempts to simulate the decision-making processes of humans. It has been applied to a wide range of activities, such as the decision of a loan officer to make (or deny) a loan application. By loading the computer with the same data loan officers use and, more important, with a program that models their decision-making processes, several studies have shown that the computer usually makes the same accept-reject decisions as loan officers. But why use computer models if they do no better than humans? Because they are a lot cheaper. Analyzing a security is similar to analyzing a loan: in the final analysis, you must also make an affirmative (buy)-negative (don't buy) decision. Moreover, the data securities analysts and loan officers use are similar.

A neural net is an extension of basic artificial intelligence but takes it one important step further. Rather than merely mimicking human decision making, a neural net strives to improve it. Again, huge amounts of data are fed into the computer. The programming, though, does not necessarily point out key factors but lets the computer seek them out. Just as a human begins a task, makes mistakes, learns from his mistakes, and keeps repeating the process until an optimal endpoint is reached, so does the computer. Now, however, the machine replaces the person not only because it's cheaper, but also because it can do the process more effectively. The computer may find data relationships that would escape human analysts; moreover, it recognizes how these relationships strengthen or weaken over time and constantly incorporates this new information in its forecasts.

A strong proponent of neural nets is Avner Mandelman, president of Cereus Investments. Writing in *Barron's* (December 14, 1992), Mandelman describes neural net programs and indicates sources of software. He also indicates that the most important forecasting factors (at the time of his article) are (1) the rate of change in the S&P 500 from the previous year, (2) the ratio of 91-day T-bill rates to the S&P 500's dividend yield, (3) the change in the 10-year bond from the previous year, and (4) the change in the dividend payout ratio (DPS/EPS) over the past six months. Writing in mid-December of 1992, Mandelman's model flashed a strong buy signal for 1993. But 1993 was only a so-so year for the S&P 500 with a 10% return.

EXHIBIT 7.10
The BEA's index of 11
leading indicators.
(Source: *Survey of
Current Business,*
February 1993.)

This series is the most widely watched index forecasting future
economic activity. It has consistently turned down before the
peak of the cycle and turned up before the trough. However,
the lead times (in months) have been erratic, ranging from
20 months in advance of 1957's peak to 1 month in
advance of 1969's and 1974's troughs.

cue given by the LIS and the eventual peak or trough varies considerably.
This wide variation in lead times has serious implications for using the LIS to
profit from forecasting, but we think you will understand this point better in
an investment setting. We will, therefore, defer discussion to Chapter 8,
where technical market indicators are explained and evaluated.

Changes in the LIS usually are headline news, particularly when they
change direction, foreshadowing a downturn or upturn. If you are even a
casual viewer of the evening news or reader of the newspaper, you will catch
the announcements. Naturally, so will everyone else. This publicity means
that even if the forecasts are correct, you probably will find it difficult to take
an investment action that other investors are not also taking. Therefore, trying to "market time" purchases or sales in anticipation of changes in the
business cycle will not increase your investment return; in fact, the increased
commissions will probably lower it.

Consensus of Experts   In one respect, following the LIS is a form of using
expert opinion because the list itself has been prepared by experts. It does
not offer interpretation, however, nor does it provide estimates of future activity. These functions are undertaken by many professional forecasters who are
more than willing to share their results and opinions with us. Most full-service brokerage houses and many commercial banks have economic forecasters on their staffs. If you are a client, you can get their advice immediately
through your representative. If you are not a client, you must wait until it is
made available to the public.

The key to using forecasts is getting a **consensus of experts** because individual forecasters have been so terribly incorrect at various times. Even the well-known Henry Kaufman from Salomon Brothers—considered the most accurate interest-rate forecaster—has had huge errors. In 1982, he forecasted sharp increases in interest rates, even though they were already at historically high levels. His forecast sent the stock market reeling but eventually proved incorrect because interest rates then entered a period of dramatic declines. Several institutions have attempted to formalize the consensus approach by obtaining forecasts from an array of well-known forecasters. For example, *The Wall Street Journal* undertakes a consensus forecast each December and June and publishes the results in one of its issues. The National Association of Business Economists obtains a consensus among its members bimonthly and publishes the results in its newsletter, *NABE News*. This consensus is growing in stature, and many newspapers and TV stations are now reporting the results.

Perhaps the best-known consensus forecast is **The Blue Chip Indicators,** published by Robert Egger in Sedona, Arizona. Egger polls some 40 economists on various cyclical issues. Distinct advantages of his series are that it is available monthly and that it provides not only the average forecast, but also the variations about the average. Thus, you can see if there is reasonable agreement or disagreement among the forecasters. A wide variation alerts us to wide differences of opinion and probably indicates greater risk in accepting the average. Unfortunately, Egger's series is rather expensive for small investors, at about $330 a year. It has a large circulation—more than 1,000 clients, most of whom are businesses—indicating that many find the consensus approach appealing.

Industry Analysis

An industry links the individual firm to the overall economy. The financial analyst often develops industry outlooks and forecasts that shape her projections for the firm. As an example, page 6 of Standard and Poor's research report on Mead at the end of this chapter provides a brief discussion and outlook for the paper industry. If you want a more comprehensive survey of this industry and others, you can consult Standard and Poor's *Industry Surveys*. These include in-depth analyses of major industries, such as Mead's industry—building and forest products, including paper. Value Line, another popular advisory service, also performs industry evaluations and presents them in its *Investment Survey* publication. **Industry analysis** usually consists of three activities: correlating industry performance to performance of the overall economy, finding new developments within the industry, and correlating industry performance to performance of the firm.

The Industry and the Business Cycle We mentioned earlier that few industries are immune from variations in the business cycle. Particularly sen-

---

Consensus of experts: forecasting method that relies on a consensus (average) of forecasts made by many forecasters

The Blue Chip Indicators: publication of a well-known forecasting service that relies on the consensus method

Industry analysis: analyzes how the overall economy affects an industry, how the industry affects a specific firm, and new technological developments likely to emerge in an industry sitive industries are those with activities in some way dependent on interest rates. Housing is a classic example because interest payments typically constitute the single largest expense of home ownership. The sale of new homes is very dependent on changes in interest rates on mortgage loans, as Exhibit 7.11 shows. Changes in the housing industry induce repercussions in many other industries, such as home appliances and financial lending. High real rates of interest also influence activities of business firms, who often curtail their capital spending programs; so, industries producing capital goods are also heavily influenced by the cycle.

In contrast to cyclical industries, other areas of the economy commonly go through the cycle without experiencing its forces to a large extent. The food and beverage industries, for example, do not show wide variations in sales. Nor do many service industries, such as health and life insurance. Some industries may even be countercyclical; that is, their sales increase during economic slowdowns. Home gardening and other do-it-yourself industries supposedly perform this way.

Whether the analyst uses sophisticated statistical tools or simple, back-of-the-envelope calculations, he must express quantitatively an estimate of the expected change in industry performance, given a change in the overall economy. For example, if the economy is expected to grow at a 3% real rate in 19XX, what will be the percentage of change in this industry's sales that *result from* this growth? An answer to this question completes the first part of industry analysis. The analysis can grow more complex as you try to link

EXHIBIT 7.11
Housing construction and interest rates. (Source: *Statistical Abstract of the United States, 1992.*)

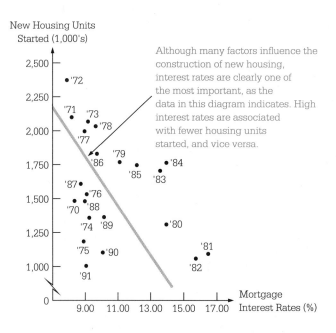

Although many factors influence the construction of new housing, interest rates are clearly one of the most important, as the data in this diagram indicates. High interest rates are associated with fewer housing units started, and vice versa.

industry sales to specific components of the economy, such as interest rates, or changes in the money supply.

New Developments in the Industry   Apart from cycle-induced changes, new developments may be taking place within the industry that would lead analysts to increase or decrease their estimates of industry performance. New developments, such as the introduction of the personal computer in the early 1980s, may influence analysts to increase their sales estimates. Other developments may lead them to revise profit estimates; an example is the auto industry's conversion to greater use of robotics and other capital-intensive production techniques. New developments also include favorable or unfavorable legislation, including the impact of federal income tax legislation. Changes in the tax law in 1986 have been particularly hard on industries requiring heavy capital investment, because one of the changes repealed the investment tax credit. Also, any material changes in union contracts or increase in unionization of the work force could lead to significant cost changes.

Uncovering all new trends in an industry may be a difficult task. And measuring their impacts on industry performance may be far less accurate than measuring the impacts of the business cycle. Despite the problems, you cannot ignore emerging trends. Although they often lead to higher rates of return, they also increase risk, particularly in the formative stages.

Linking the Industry to the Firm   Just as all industries do not march in perfect step with the economy, all firms will not keep exact pace with the industry. There are various explanations for the differences. For one thing, firms have different cost structures, some relying heavily on fixed costs, with others having higher variable costs. Public utilities, for example, have different cost configurations, depending on whether their generating equipment uses hydroelectric or nuclear power, with their high fixed costs, or coal or oil, with their high variable costs. A decline in industry demand will have much more devastating results on profit for firms with high fixed costs than it will for those with high variable costs.

Another factor to consider is each firm's product mix. Some might offer top-of-the-line items that do well when the economy is operating robustly, while others might offer more basic product lines that sell better when the economy is in modest growth. Then, too, you need to consider geographic differences. A firm servicing one geographic region of the country might show booming sales, while firms located in other regions do poorly. The housing market, for example, was booming in Boston in the mid-1980s, driving the median price of a home to the highest in the nation, while in Houston, the housing industry declined as a result of a slump in the oil industry brought about by the sharp drop in oil prices. Five years earlier, the situation was just the reverse. And at the end of the 1980s, the California market replaced the

BOX 7.3   A QUESTION OF ETHICS

Why Are There So Few Sell Recommendations?

If you selected 100 stocks randomly at any point in time, what proportion do you think are undervalued or overvalued? Common sense tells us the answer is 50% for each, unless markets are somehow inefficiently biased in one direction. It's surprising, then, when we read securities analysts' recommendations and find that the number of buy recommendations (undervalued companies) greatly exceeds the number of sell recommendations.

In a study done by Maureen McNichols, professor at Stanford University's Graduate School of Business, and Hsiou-wei-Lin, a graduate student, the number of buy recommendations of brokerage firms not involved in underwriting a company's stock is about eight times greater than the number of sell recommendations (56% versus 7.1%; hold recommendations were 37.0%). The real shocker comes when analysts' brokerage firms are involved in underwriting: then the breakdown is 71.5% buys, 27.8% holds, and 0.7% sells.

Results such as these raise serious questions about the professionalism of securities analysts, particularly those associated with stockbrokerage firms. It generally is understood that buy recommendations can generate far more commissions than sell recommendations. Moreover, more than one analyst has faced management's wrath by panning a company that could generate huge underwriting fees.

Arguments can be advanced to explain the preponderance of buy recommendations. For example, analysts don't select stocks randomly for evaluation; they might already have a favorable predisposition before a formal analysis is undertaken. A similar argument could be made with respect to underwriting; a brokerage firm is not likely to try underwriting a company that it believes will sink. Also, because stock prices are more often rising than falling over time on balance, bullish emotion should outweigh the bearish. Although security analysis is supposed to transcend emotions, as long as people are involved in the process, don't expect cold, machine-like rationality.

Still, the numbers above seem too large to indicate a lack of bias. If true, how seriously can investors rely on analysts' recommendations? One might argue that experienced investors have learned to deal with the bias by tempering the analysts' findings. That's fine for them, but what about amateur investors who have yet to learn the game? Should they be expected to pay their dues as they learn to distinguish analysis from "puffery"? Such a solution does not speak well for a group who aspires to professionalism. A strong set of standards and stiff fines for violating them seem a better alternative, and redress in the courts may be appropriate in the more flagrant cases. If CPAs can be sued for misconduct, why not CFAs?

Northeast as the booming market; however, it softened considerably in the early 1990s.

Determining how the individual firm will respond to industry changes completes industry analysis; you could also make the point that it is the beginning of firm analysis. Whatever the perspective, it is important to focus your attention on how changes in the industry lead to changes in a firm's earnings. Exhibit 7.12 shows how GM's EPS has been influenced by changes in activity in the auto industry. GM is a major part of the industry; the high correlation between its EPS and industry sales is not surprising. Similarly high correlations are found in many other industry-firm relationships.

Most of the large stockbrokerage firms and the independent advisory services, such as Standard and Poor's, Moody's, and Value Line, employ security analysts who specialize in specific industries. Along with becoming knowledgeable about an industry, they increase their understanding of the industry's individual firms. This background enables them to make specific recommendations for purchases or sales. As an individual investor, you might find it difficult to do your own research on a level comparable to theirs, and it is to your advantage to use these sources.

SUMMARY

The key financial statements of a business are the balance sheet and the income statement. The balance sheet shows assets, liabilities, and shareholders' equity. Items not shown on the balance sheet can be important also. These include hidden assets and contingent liabilities. An income statement shows the company's earnings and dividends. The major limitation in using income statements is a lack of uniformity in presenting such items as depreciation and inventory costs. Investors often prefer a cash flow concept that attempts to measure the company's ability to generate cash.

Ratio analysis is a technique for evaluating a company's economic performance. Balance sheet strength is measured by liquidity and solvency ratios. Earnings strength is measured by the ability to cover interest charges, the ROI, the ROE, and earnings and dividends growth.

Evaluating a security requires an assessment of future economic activity overall and in specific industry sectors. A leading indicator series and the consensus of experts are used to forecast economic cycles. Industry analysis begins by relating changes in the industry to changes in the overall economy. It then looks for new developments in the industry that might accelerate or reduce its historical growth patterns. The final step in industry analysis is to link the industry with specific firms in it. The analyst attempts to determine how specific firms will respond to anticipated industry changes.

EXHIBIT 7.12
New automobile sales
and GM's EPS

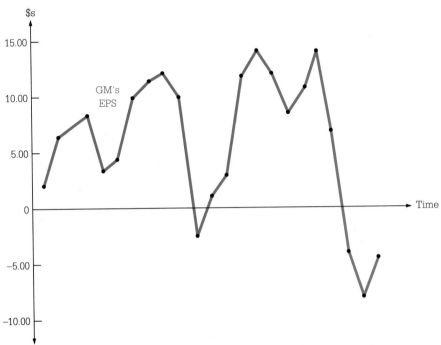

KEY TERMS
(listed in order
of appearance)

**REVIEW
QUESTIONS**

1. Briefly explain items typically listed on a balance sheet.
2. Explain the following items that, although not common, might be found on a business balance sheet: *(a)* goodwill, net of amortization; *(b)* customers' deposits and deferred service revenue; *(c)* minority interests; *(d)* accumulated translation adjustments; and *(e)* treasury stock.
3. Define book value per share and then explain if you believe it is a good estimate of the true value of a common stock.
4. Explain why a balance sheet might not show all items of value to a company. Also, what is a hidden asset and a hidden asset play?
5. What is the objective of the income statement? Briefly explain items typically found on the statement.
6. Discuss several limitations of an income statement.
7. What is cash flow, and how does cash flow per share differ from EPS?
8. Offer a brief debate on the topic "Is EPS an ideal indicator of a firm's earning performance?" Take the side favoring the issue.
9. Define net working capital. Indicate two ratios that measure a company's liquidity position.
10. In what way does solvency differ from liquidity? Indicate two ratios that measure a company's solvency position.
11. What is a profit margin? Briefly explain three margins.
12. Indicate three ratios that measure a company's earnings strength. Which of the three is the best measurement from the perspective of a *shareholder's* investment?
13. The growth rates of which variables usually influence the growth rate of a company's common stock price?
14. What is meant by screening with filters, and how are ratios used in the process? Suppose you are a growth-oriented investor but want to avoid excessively risky companies. Select three screening ratios that you would apply to a data base. Explain your selections.
15. Briefly describe the performance of the overall economy since 1952 and its implication for business profitability. Also, explain the LIS and its relation to the overall economy.

16. What is meant by the consensus of experts? Explain the advantages of such an approach.
17. Explain three aspects of industry analysis. Which aspect do you think is the most difficult to do? Explain.

| PROBLEMS AND PROJECTS | 1. Given the following data (in millions of dollars), what evaluation do you have for the Endicott Company's liquidity and solvency positions? Explain. |

	1995	1994	1995 Industry Average
Current assets	$478	$532	$236
Fixed assets	489	346	513
Total assets	$967	$878	$749
Current liabilities	$341	$327	$104
Long-term debt	225	174	251
Shareholders' equity	401	377	394
Total liabilities and shareholders' equity	$967	$878	$749
Sales	$879	$843	$815
Interest expense	23	14	25
Net income	38	36	43
Dividends	14	10	17
Depreciation	20	16	15

2. Given the data in problem 1, evaluate the Endicott Company's earnings strength, comparing it with the industry average.
3. In addition to the data in problem 1, you also know the Endicott Company had 10 million shares of common stock outstanding during each year; the industry average number of shares outstanding was 11 million during each year. Determine EPS and cash flow per share; then, evaluate the company relative to the industry average. Do you believe the market price of Endicott's stock is higher or lower than the average stock price of its industry competitors? Explain your reasoning.
4. Financial data for Blunt Enterprises appear in the following table, arranged in alphabetical order.

Account	1995	1994
Common stock (100,000 shares)	$ 200,000	$ 200,000
Cost of products sold	9,270,000	8,850,000
Current assets	456,000	421,000
Current liabilities	282,000	205,000
Dividends	181,000	161,000
Income taxes	200,000	190,000
Interest expense	22,000	24,000
Long-term debt	180,000	200,000

Operating expenses	1,042,000	993,000
Plant and equipment, net	810,000	683,000
Retained earnings	604,000	499,000
Sales	14,080,000	13,290,000
Selling expenses	3,260,000	2,980,000

a. Rearrange the data to produce the balance sheet and the income statement for each year.

b. Discuss the company's liquidity position and solvency position using appropriate ratios for each.

c. Calculate the following margins in each year: gross profit, operating income, and net income. Discuss your results.

d. Using appropriate ratios, discuss the company's earnings strengths, comparing the two years.

e. Calculate the percentage of increases in EPS and DPS and, assuming the DPS percentage growth continues in the future, explain if Blunt is overvalued or undervalued if its market price is $60 a share. (Assume: Blunt's beta = 1.7, $R_F = 8\%$, and $MRP = 8.5\%$.)

f. Calculate Blunt's 1995 book value per share and discuss it in relation to the market price of $60.

5. Selected data for the DNQ Company appear below:

Year	Net Profit	Depreciation	Stock Price	Dividends
1990	$4,000,000	$2,000,000	$24	$500,000
1991	2,600,000	2,100,000	11	550,000
1992	200,000	2,200,000	12	550,000
1993	1,300,000	2,400,000	28	550,000
1994	6,400,000	2,800,000	37	780,000
1995 (est.)	6,000,000	3,000,000	?	900,000

a. If the company had 2 million shares of common stock outstanding in each of the years above, for each year calculate EPS, CFS, DPS, the P/E ratio, and the P/CF ratio.

b. Calculate the five-year average P/E and P/CF. Using each average, forecast the stock price for the end of 1995. Which forecast seems more realistic? Discuss.

c. Assume the 1994 year-end price was $37 and the required return for the stock is 15%. Then, using the forecast from question *b* that you think is the more realistic, discuss if DNQ's stock is fairly valued.

6. *(Student Project)* Obtain a financial report for a company of interest to you. Reports often are kept at university libraries, or you can call a local company and request one. Then, using the ratios developed in this chapter, evaluate the company. If possible, find its beta value (try Value Line's *Investment Survey*) and make a comparison between the company's expected return and its required return. Check the return on Treasury securities for your R_F rate.

7. *(Student Project)* Make sure you read Box 7.1, "Should PSRs Replace P/E Ratios?" Then, utilizing 1992 data available for Mead, calculate its basic PSR and the adjusted PSR that considers debt. Work with total debt, as reported on the balance sheet.

8. *(Student Project)* Obtain the most recent issue of *Survey of Current Business* from your school library. Reviewing the LIS, determine where the economy is headed six months in the future. Prepare a brief report on your findings.

CASE ANALYSES

**7.1
Rob Dexter
Looks for the
Right Stock**

Rob Dexter is a conservative investor who is greatly concerned with preservation of capital. However, he does seek growth as an investment objective. Two companies have come to his attention lately, and he is considering investing in one of them. Both are in the same industry. Consider the following ratios and recommend one of the companies to Rob, explaining the reasoning for your selection.

	Fleet, Inc.	Dirge, Inc.
Current ratio	1.8	1.9
NWC/sales	0.5	0.6
Debt ratio	0.6	0.3
Debt/equity ratio	1.5	0.4
ROI	8%	10%
ROE	20%	14%
Times interest earned	4.5	7.2
10-year growth rates:		
Earnings per share	15%	12%
Dividends per share	17%	11%
Price of common stock	14%	9%
Current share price of stock	$50	$99
Last year dividend per share	$ 2	$ 6
Beta	1.5	0.8

Risk-free rate = 8%
Market risk premium = 8.5%

**7.2
Allison
Demming
Undertakes an
Industry
Analysis**

Allison Demming is considering investing in Precision Tools, a leading firm in the machine tool industry. Her research leads Allison to believe that Precision is a sound company with reasonably good earnings possibilities. However, she is concerned about the machine tool industry, which tends to be somewhat volatile. Allison has gathered quarterly data for Precision, the machine tool industry, and the overall economy. She hopes the data might reveal certain linkages that can help her plan an investment strategy. The data appear in the accompanying table. The industry sales index, the economic activity index, and Precision Tool's per-share stock price are values at the beginning of each quarter.

Year Quarter	Precision Tool's EPS	Industry Sales Index	Economic Activity Index	Precision Tool's Stock Price
1992: I	$1.62	125	108	$83.50
II	1.98	133	114	78.25
III	2.09	136	118	60.00
IV	2.17	142	125	67.38
1993: I	1.27	140	127	46.88
II	1.66	135	124	39.13
III	0.81	121	120	40.13
IV	0.65	113	116	32.50
1994: I	−0.10	103	111	34.75
II	1.05	106	113	45.38
III	1.54	112	118	62.50
IV	2.12	126	122	77.25
1995: I	2.33	142	133	91.63
II	1.55	152	145	73.75
III	1.23	158	148	83.50
IV	3.06	165	155	92.13
1996: I	—	—	—	88.75

Questions

a. Calculate Precision Tool's EPS for each of the years above and determine a P/E ratio based on the stock price (1) at the beginning of the year, (2) at the end of the year, and (3) average for the year.

b. Plot the time series above on graph paper. Explain any correlations you observe.

c. Do the time series indicate a trading strategy Allison might use? Explain.

d. What advice might you offer Allison with respect to her intended investment?

HELPFUL READING

Bajkowski, John. "Creating Stock Screens That Make Practical Sense." *AAII Journal,* July 1993, pp. 34–37.

Hirshey, Mark. "Size Effects in the Market Valuation of Fundamental Factors." *Financial Analysts Journal*, March-April 1992, pp. 91–95.

Leibowitz, Martin L., and Stanley Kogelman. "Franchise Value and the Growth Process." *Financial Analysts Journal*, January-February 1992, pp. 53–62.

Magnet, Myron. "How to Grow in a Cyclical Business." *Fortune*, September 6, 1993, pp. 78–82.

Markese, John. "A Fundamental Guide to Common Stock Valuation." *AAII Journal*, January 1993, pp. 30–33.

Reinganum, Marc R. "A Revival of the Small-Firm Effect." *The Journal of Portfolio Management*, Spring 1992, pp. 55–62.

Sorensen, Eric H., and Chee Y. Thum. "The Use and Misuse of Value Investing." *Financial Analysts Journal*, March-April 1992, pp. 53–57.

Zipser, Andy. "Goodwill Games." *Barron's*, August 9, 1993, p. 12.

Standard & Poor's

RESEARCH REPORT

To order S&P Research Reports call 1-800-642-2858

Prepared from Database and Satellite Sources
Thu., May. 13, 1993 05:16pm ET

Mead Corp*

*An S&P 500 Company

Exchange: NYSE
Symbol: MEA
Primary business: Mfr paper,lumber,wood prod
Number of Employees: 21,600
Incorporated in Ohio in 1930
Headquarters:
Courthouse Plaza N.E.
Dayton OH 45463
(513) 495-6323

Chrmn & CEO: S. C. Mason
Pres: S. S. Benedict
Secy: J. L. Hayman
VP & CFO: W. A. Enouen
Investor Relations: Fred Houck

ANALYSTS' CONSENSUS   " Buy/Hold "

Consensus Breakdown		As of 05/12/93
■ By National Firms	=	Buy/Hold
■ By Regional Firms	=	Hold
■ By Nonbroker	=	Hold

S&P INVESTMENT OVERVIEW

Sales for 1993 should show moderate progress as the general economy stages a recovery. Prices for market pulp are firming, but softness is evident in coated and uncoated papers. The strong coated natural kraft market, where MEA has recently expanded, should bolster results as the year progresses.

CONSENSUS EARNINGS FORECAST   (05/12/93)

	FY 1992 (Actual)	Wall Street Consensus Ests. FY 1993	FY 1994
■ Earnings Per Share ($)	0.63	2.50	3.52
■ Price-Earnings Ratio	71.4	18.3	13.0
■ Next Qtr. (Jun) EPS ($)	-.59	0.80	1.01

May include discontinued operations.

FISCAL YEAR ENDS December 31

Next Earnings Report Expected: 07/14/93

PRICE/VOLUME TRENDS   (05/11/93)

■ Price/Volume

Current Price ($)	45.625
40-Day Avg. Daily Volume	149,562
Beta	1.3488
S&P 500 Composite	444.360
S&P MidCap 400	164.000

KEY STATISTICS AT A GLANCE

■ Price Performance   (05/07/93)

12-Month High	47.37
12-Month Low	33.12
% Change in Price Last 12 Mos.	+18
12 Month Price Rel. to S&P 500	1.09
Value of $10,000 Invested 12/31/87	15,256

STOCK SPLITS DURING LAST FIVE YEARS: None

■ Earnings/P-E Trends

Actual EPS FY 1992 ($)	0.63
Trailing 12-Mos. EPS ($)	0.75
5-Year Earnings Growth (%)	NM
Current P-E	60.0
5-Year P-E High	77.5
5-Year P-E Low	5.4

■ Dividends

Indicated Annual Dividend Rate ($)	1.000
Current Yield (%)	2.2
5-Year Dividend Growth Rate (%)	9.7
Dividends as % of 12 Month EPS	133.3
Ex-Dividend Date	02/02

DIVIDEND HISTORY: Dividends have been paid since 1940. A dividend reinvestment plan is available. A poison pill' stock purchase right was adopted in 1986.

■ Other

Book Value Per Share ($)	21.32
Market Capitalization (Mil. $)	2,641
Shares Outstanding (000)	58703
% Held by Institutions	79.0
Insider Sentiment	POSITIVE

Mead Corp

BUSINESS SUMMARY

25-FEB-93 Mead is a major integrated producer of white papers, coated paperboard, packaging systems and school and office supplies, and operates large paper distribution and electronic publishing businesses. Industry segment contributions in 1991:

	Sales	Profits
Paper	24%	34%
Packaging & paperboard	22%	40%
Distribution & other	44%	11%
Electronic publishing	10%	15%

The company makes white papers, including bond and writing papers, technical papers, and grades used in the printing and publishing fields. A wide range of specialty and industrial paperboard items, packaging systems, corrugated containers and school supplies are also produced. Mead also operates electronic publishing services.

MEA affiliates make pulp, lumber, and other building materials. The acquisition of Crown Zellerbach's distribution group in September 1986 greatly expanded Mead's distribution business.

At December 31, 1991, some 1,267,000 acres of timberland in the U.S. were owned and another 106,000 controlled. Affiliates held cutting rights on additional acreage in Canada. MEA obtained 17% of its 1991 wood requirements from its own land.

IMPORTANT DEVELOPMENTS

Jan 93 - The company said fourth quarter earnings had been reduced by $0.10 a share by temporary operating problems at its Alabama coated board mill. Strong performances were registered in the coated board, containerboard and electronic publishing businesses. Mead's jointly-owned Northwood affiliate benefited from improved pulp mill productivity, as well as prices for pulp and wood products and a weaker Canadian dollar. Mead's paper businesses continued to suffer from weak prices.

Jul 92 - Mead said it would invest $34.1 million to expand recycling capabilities at the company's coated paper board mill in Alabama. The mill produces some 800,000 tons of coated natural kraft annually for beer and soft drink carriers.

EARNINGS ESTIMATES & TRENDS   (05/12/93)

Current Analyst Consensus Estimates (ACE)

Fiscal Years	Average	High	Low	No. of Ests.	Deviation	P-E Ratio
1993	2.50	3.00	1.00	21	0.26	18.3
1994	3.52	4.40	2.75	16	0.29	13.0
2Q 1993	0.80	0.95	0.60	4	0.10	—

Analyst Consensus Estimates (ACE) History

	Average	Number of Analysts Changes During Month	Percent Change
Estimates for fiscal 1993			
April	2.52	4	-1%
March	2.54	4	-1%
Feb.	2.56	4	0%
Jan.	2.57	11	-8%
Dec.	2.78	3	-2%
Nov.	2.83	5	-2%
Oct.	2.88	9	-3%
Estimates for fiscal 1994			
April	3.52	0	-1%
March	3.54	1	-1%
Feb.	3.58	0	-4%
Jan.	3.73	1	-11%
Dec.	4.20	0	-14%
Nov.	4.90	0	0%

Additions or deletions to coverage may cause % change in average estimates without any analyst changes.

Mead Corp

PRICE HISTORY

Source for chart: Standard & Poor's Trendline

MEA	ANNUAL PRICE RANGES	52 - WEEK PRICE HISTORY

TECHNICAL EVALUATION

	1992								1993			
	May	Jun	Jul	Aug	Sep	Oct	Nov	Dec	Jan	Feb	Mar	Apr	May
Rel. Str.	97	96	108	97	93	107	97	99	97	112	96	111	

Short-Term	↑	Support	43.5
Med.-Term	↑	Resistance	45.9
Long-Term	↑		

Volume Ths. Shs.
- 180
- 120
- 60

ANALYSTS' CONSENSUS – "Buy/Hold" (05/12/93)

	No. of Ratings	% of Total	One Month Prior	Three Mos. Prior	By Source		
					National	Regional	Non-broker
Buy	5	23	5	6	4	1	0
Buy/Hold	4	18	4	3	1	2	1
Hold	10	45	10	10	6	1	3
Weak Hold	0	0	0	0	0	0	0
Sell	0	0	0	0	0	0	0
No Opinion	3	14	3	3	1	2	0
Total	22	100	22	22	12	6	4

Average Qualitative Opinion = 0.86

S&P STOCK EVALUATION MEASURES

Wall Street Consensus	Buy =	>1.00
Average Qualitative Opinion (AQO) = **0.86**	Buy/Hold =	>.75 & <1.00
	Hold =	>.35 & <.749
Copyright © S&P 1993	Weak Hold =	>.0 & <.349
	Sell =	<.0

Standard & Poor's STARS	★★★★★	**Buy**
	★★★★	**Accumulate**
Stock Appreciation Ranking System (STARS) = ★★★	★★★	**Hold**
	★★	**Avoid**
Copyright © S&P 1993	★	**Sell**

Standard & Poor's	A+ Highest	B Below Average
Earnings & Dividend Ranking = **B-**	A High	B- Low
	A- Above Avg.	C Lowest
Copyright © S&P 1993	B+ Average	D In Reorg.

COMPANIES OFFERING COVERAGE

Standard & Poor's Corp
A G Edwards & Sons Inc
Babson United Invst Advisors
Bear Stearns & Co
Brown Brothers Harriman
Dean Witter Reynolds Inc
Donaldson Lufkin & Jenrette
Goldman Sachs & Co
Kidder Peabody & Co Inc
Merrill Lynch Research
Nomura Research Inst
Oppenheimer & Co Inc
PaineWebber
Pershing, Division of DLJ Sec.
Prudential Securities
S G Warburg & Co Inc
Salomon Brothers Inc
Shearson Lehman Brothers
Smith Barney Harris Upham
Swiss American Securities
The First Boston Corporation
Value Line Securities Inc

Mead Corp

QUARTERLY EARNINGS HISTORY (05/07/93)

Fiscal Year Ending December 31

	1Q	2Q	3Q	4Q	Year
Revenue (Million $)					
1993	1135.50	–	–	–	–
1992	1088.20	1225.40	1254.50	1135.10	4703.20
1991	1097.20	1176.50	1210.80	1094.80	4579.30
1990	1141.00	1227.90	1267.90	1135.60	4772.40
1989	1128.90	1207.40	1197.50	1078.30	4612.10
1988	1085.30	1159.90	1174.10	1044.60	4463.90
After Tax Profit Margin (%)					
1993	2.25	–	–	–	–
1992	1.63	NM	2.99	1.51	0.79
1991	1.22	1.59	2.09	0.75	1.43
1990	3.46	3.75	3.13	NM	0.66
1989	4.66	5.15	5.82	2.90	4.67
1988	6.06	6.29	14.52	4.15	7.90
Net Income (Million $)					
1993	25.60	–	–	–	–
1992	17.70	-34.70	37.50	17.10	37.60
1991	13.40	18.70	25.30	8.20	65.60
1990	39.50	46.10	39.70	-93.70	31.60
1989	52.60	62.20	69.70	31.30	215.80
1988	65.80	73.00	170.50	43.40	352.70
Earnings Per Share ($)					
1993	0.43	–	–	–	–
1992	0.30	-.59	0.63	0.29	0.63
1991	0.23	0.32	0.43	0.14	1.12
1990	0.62	0.73	0.63	-1.54	0.51
1989	0.81	0.96	1.06	0.50	3.33
1988	1.01	1.12	2.56	0.68	5.37
Dividends Paid ($)					
1993	0.25	–	–	–	–
1992	0.25	0.25	0.25	0.25	1.00
1991	0.25	0.25	0.25	0.25	1.00
1990	0.22	0.25	0.25	0.25	0.97
1989	0.19	0.22	0.22	0.22	0.85
1988	0.165	0.19	0.19	0.19	0.735

May include discontinued operations.

CAPITALIZATION (05/07/93)

Long Term Debt: $1,332,300,000 (12/92).
Common Stock: 58,703,000 shs. (no par).
Shareholders of record: 20,300.

INCOME COMPONENT ANALYSIS (05/07/93)

Fiscal Year Ending December 31

	1987	1988	1989	1990	1991
Return on Equity (%)	18.9	25.8	13.5	6.9	5.0
Return on Assets (%)	7.7	11.2	5.9	2.9	1.9
Operating Margin (%)	12.0	12.3	10.2	10.4	10.2
Effective Tax Rate (%)	43.3	37.5	31.7	33.0	41.8
Cash Flow (Mil. $)	360.0	534.0	416.0	300.0	312.0
Interest as % of Cash Flow	22.8	13.9	24.3	37.7	38.1
Capital Expenditures as % of Cash Flow	48.6	NM	NM	NM	85.3
Dividends as % of Cash Flow	11.3	9.3	13.8	20.1	18.8

Calendar Years Ending December 31

	1989	1990	1991	1992	1993
Stock Price					
High	46.62	39.50	37.25	41.62	47.37
Low	34.25	19.50	24.50	33.12	37.50
P E Ratio					
High	14.0	77.5	33.3	66.1	–
Low	10.3	38.2	21.9	52.6	–

BALANCE SHEET STATISTICS (05/07/93)

Fiscal Year Ending December 31

	1989	1990	1991
Assets (Million $)			
Cash	21.0	21.0	25.0
Non-Cash	964.0	961.0	1068.0
Total Current	985.0	982.0	1093.0
Noncurrent	2765.0	2907.0	2893.0
Total Assets	3750.0	3889.0	3986.0
Liabilities (Million $)			
Current	700.0	693.0	746.0
Noncurrent	1369.0	1665.0	1762.0
Total Liabilities	2069.0	2358.0	2508.0
Equity (Million $)			
Shareholders' Equity	1681.0	1531.0	1478.0
Total Equity & Liabilities	3750.0	3889.0	3986.0

Mead Corp

INDUSTRY COMPARISON (05/07/93)

Most Recent Fiscal Year		
	Mead Corp	Paper, Diversified
Ratio Analysis		
Price/Earnings Ratio	60.0	40.1
Return on Equity (%)	5.0	6.9
After Tax Profit Margin (%)	0.79	3.02
Return on Assets (%)	1.9	3.2
Debt/Equity Ratio (%)	89.0	70.0
Sales Per Employee ($)	211,990	169,432
Coverage Analysis		
Interest Coverage	2.7	1.5
Interest as % of Debt	9.0	9.2
Growth Rate Analysis		
5-year Revenue Growth (%)	1.9	5.0
5-year Earnings Growth (%)	NM	–
5-year Dividend Growth (%)	9.7	11.2

INDUSTRY PARTICIPANTS (05/12/93)

Company	Stock Symbol	Current AQO
Mead Corp	(MEA)	0.86
Albany Int'A'	(AIN)	0.18
Bowater Incorporated	(BOW)	0.38
Champion Int'l	(CHA)	0.36
Chesapeake Corp	(CSK)	0.44
Glatfelter (P. H.)	(GLT)	0.44
International Paper	(IP)	0.78
Temple-Inland	(TIN)	0.84
Union Camp	(UCC)	0.57
Westvaco Corp	(W)	0.35

INDUSTRY OUTLOOK

Patience is the operative word for the paper industry. As with the general economy, the long-predicted and long-awaited recovery seems always fixed on the horizon. An industry recovery is still expected, but the consensus now foresees a later and slower upturn than had previously been expected. Many paper companies are looking toward at least the fall of 1993 for a significant turn in pricing, which has been pressured by overcapacity and weak conditions for industries of key customers. Also adding to pressure on the industry is economic weakness overseas, particularly in Europe where currency fluctuations have made U.S. products less competitive.

Although many paper products continue to face weak markets, demand has picked up for coated groundwood papers, used in magazines, catalogs and inserts, and several major companies recently instituted a price increase of approximately 7% in the list price for such paper.

Despite the problems presently encountered by U.S. companies looking to expand in foreign markets, these markets offer enormous potential. The U.S. forest products industry has the technical know-how, capital, state-of-the-art manufacturing base and wood fiber resources to dominate the world forest products industry. Already, companies such as Scott Paper, James River, International Paper and Kimberly-Clark are moving rapidly to position themselves as truly global operations. The U.S. domestic market may be nearing saturation in the use of paper products, but developing markets overseas are very attractive areas for expansion in this industry.

The wood products side of the Paper and Forest Products industry is leading the paper side with sharp improvements in earnings. This is likely to continue because the politically induced wood shortage is unlikely to go away or in any way be resolved near term, despite the Clinton Administration's timber summit and well-publicized interest in reaching a solution. Millions of acres of Pacific Northwest timberlands will remain off limits to loggers. Companies such as Weyerhaeuser and Longview Fibre, with large private timber holdings, stand to gain from current environmental concerns. Producers of alternative building materials such as oriented strand board also stand to benefit; Louisiana-Pacific is a prime example.

Mead Corp

■ **05/03/93** Union Camp Corp. announced that it plans to sell the equipment and inventory of its School Supplies & Stationery Division to Mead Corp. and discontinue all of that division's operations in Birmingham, Ala., Franklin, Ohio, and Houston, Tex. The division has approximately 280 employees.

■ **04/20/93** 3 months earnings per share, $0.43 vs $0.31 for the same period a year ago. Results are based on average Com. & Com. equivalent shares. Results for '92 exclude gain of $0.55 per share to reflect adoption of FASB 109. Results for '92 have been restated.

■ **02/02/93** Goldman, Sachs & Co., J.P. Morgan Securities Inc. and Smith Barney, Harris Upham & Co. Inc. offered $150,000,000 of 8.125% Debs., due Feb. 1, 2023, for public sale at 99.23 plus accrued interest from Feb. 1, 1993. The Debs. are redeemable at Co.'s option, in whole or in part, on or after Feb. 1, 2003, upon not less than 30 nor more than 60 days notice at prices commencing at 103.68 on Feb. 1, 2003, and decreasing annually to 100 on Feb. 1, 2013, and thereafter, all plus accrued interest to the redemption date. The offering was made pursuant to a shelf registration filed under SEC Rule 415 covering up to $400,000,000 of debt securities issuable under an indenture dated July 15, 1982, as amended. Underwriting discount: 0.875%; proceeds to Co., $147,532,500. Net proceeds will be used to repay short-term debt. Standard & Poor's Corp. announced that a final rating of BBB+ was assigned to Co.'s 8.125% Debs., due Feb. 1, 2023. UP 3/4... Merrill upgrades to near term above average from neutral, long term buy from above average... Co. unavailable... 10:35 am... MEAD CORP. (MEA 42 5/8) UP 1 3/8, MERRILL UPGRADES TO NEAR TERM ABOVE AVERAGE FROM NEUTRAL, LONG TERM BUY FROM ABOVE AVERAGE... Analyst Sherman Chao tells salesforce at current prices MEA valued at one of lowest multiples of EPS and cash flows among paper and forest products stocks... says EPS growth over next couple of years not dependent on sharply higher prices, but rather on cost reductions, improved mix... expects MEA to be rediscovered by investors seeking cyclical ideas outside of straight linerboard and wood products plays... Maintains $2.50 '93 EPS estimate, $3.50 '94 EPS estimate./L.M. Barrett

■ **01/29/93** Fourth quarter earnings per share, $0.29 vs $0.14 for the prior year. 12 months earnings, $0.63 vs $1.12 for the prior year. Results for 12-months '92 period exclude gain of $0.58 per share to reflect adoption of FASB 109 & include charges of $1.00 per share from corporate-wide performace improvement program & $0.30 per share from sale of Ampad Corp.

■ **01/04/93** Mead Data Central Inc., subsidiary, announced that it acquired Folio Corp., Provo, Utah, a producer of 'infobase' software. Co. added that an infobase is analogous to a database, but much more effective at managing the free-format and semi-structured kinds of information that people deal with most often.'

■ **11/09/92** UP 1 1/8... Kidder, Morgan Stanley reiterate buys... Co. unavailable...

■ **10/14/92** 3 months earnings per share, $0.63 vs $0.43 for the same period a year ago. 9 months earnings, $0.35 vs $0.98 for the same period a year ago. Results are based on av-

erage Com. & Com. equivalent shares. Results for nine-month periods excludes gain of $0.57 per share for '92 & loss of $1.00 per share for '91 from an accounting change. Results for '91 have been restated to reflect accounting change.

■ **07/15/92** 3 months loss per share, $0.59 vs earnings of $0.32 for the same period a year ago. 6 months loss, $0.29 vs earnings of $0.55 for the same period a year ago. Results are based on average Com. & Com. equivalent shares. Results for '92 periods include charges of $1.00 per share from reserve for corporate-wide performance improvement program & $0.30 per share from sale of office products business. Results for six-month '92 period exclude credit of $0.58 per share from adoption of FASB 109. Results for six-month '91 period exclude loss of $1.00 per share from adoption of FASB 106. Results for '91 have been restated.

■ **07/06/92** UP 1 3/8... Witter upgrades to buy/hold from swap... Bear Stearns raises estimates... Shearson reiterates buy... 11:40 am... MEAD CORP (MEA 38) UP 1 3/8... WITTER UPGRADES TO BUY/HOLD FROM SWAP; RAISES ESTIMATES... Analyst Evadna Lynn says upgraded stock in response to co's 2nd quarter forecast of $0.70 vs. $0.32... notes stock has upside potential due to MEA's apparent success in lowering costs, effectively selling out of commercial office products business, continuous cost reduction efforts, including 5% reduction in work force... Raises $1.50 '92 EPS estimate to $2.15, $2.35 '93 EPS estimate to $3.25... Sets $42-$45 price target./L.M. Barrett

■ **07/02/92** UP 7/8... Co. sees 2Q EPS reduced by $1.30 due to reserve to cover performance improvement program, sale of Ampad unit... sees $0.70 EPS before charges.

Mead Corp

CHAPTER EIGHT

Technical Analysis, Market Timing, and Efficient Markets

After you finish this chapter, you will be able to:

- understand pressure indicators that show who is buying and selling securities, that measure market activity, or that reveal investor psychology.

- evaluate pressure indicators, judging their reliability, accuracy, and timeliness.

- understand the graphic approach to technical analysis.

- evaluate the graphic approach to technical analysis by understanding the nature of randomness.

- determine what is meant by efficient markets and review evidence in support of the efficient market hypothesis.

As we have just seen, fundamental analysis attempts to discover underlying strengths and weaknesses in the overall economy and its component industries and firms. It involves considerable work with no assurance of investment success, even if the work is done well. Indeed, a market technician (someone who uses technical analysis) might argue that you are wasting your time with fundamental analysis. After all, you probably are using published information available to anyone. If you are successful at finding an undervalued security, isn't it likely that many others will find it too? Thousands of investors are using the same data as you and using the same analytical techniques. If they all come to the conclusion that a security is undervalued, won't they quickly rush to buy it, thereby pushing up its price so that eventually it is no longer undervalued?

The arguments above have been made by technicians and others for quite some time. To them, finding undervalued securities must be done with other methods. This chapter explains and discusses some of these methods. We also evaluate both technical and fundamental analysis within the framework of a body of investment literature that is called *the efficient market hypothesis.*

USING PRESSURE INDICATORS

Technical analysis: valuation techniques unrelated to underlying financial strengths of a firm or overall market

To begin, let us define **technical analysis** very broadly as any security selection method that does *not* look at investment fundamentals. Supposedly, one of the large stockbrokerage firms employs a technician who refuses any information about a particular company or industry or the economy overall. He works in a shuttered room, alone with his graphs and other forecasting devices, to protect against "alien fundamental information" that might influence his chart readings. If you watch the immensely popular *Wall Street Week* on PBS, you will hear the host, Louis Rukeyser, refer to the gnomes, or "cave-dwelling" technicians who prepare the technical market indicators used on the show. This abhorrence of fundamentals is typical of many market technicians, although some feel more strongly about recommendations that are supported by positive conclusions from fundamental analyses.

Pressure indicator: comparison of economic time series to reflect the strength and weakness of demand for stocks

A **pressure indicator** is any economic time series, or combination of economic time series, that reflects the underlying strength or weakness—relative pressure—of some demand element for an individual stock or for the overall market. In using pressure indicators, technicians are usually attempting to forecast the future direction for the overall market, even though some of their indicators can be applied to forecast future prices of specific securities. There are three popular sets of indicators: those that show what kinds of investors are buying or selling stocks, those that measure market activity, and those that reveal investor psychology.

Who Is Buying or Selling?

If you have reason to believe some buyers are smarter than others, then you might want to time your purchases and sales in conjunction with those of the smart investors—if they can be identified. Also, if you notice the smart buyers are not buying but choosing instead to increase their liquidity positions, then you might want to do the same. This approach involves two steps: first, you must decide who are smart investors; second, you must find information that reveals what they are doing.

The Odd-Lot Ratio   The **odd-lot ratio** shows the ratio of odd-lot purchases to odd-lot sales; that is,

$$\text{odd-lot ratio} \ = \ \frac{\text{odd-lot sales}}{\text{odd-lot purchases}}$$

Odd-lot ratio: ratio of odd-lot sales to odd-lot purchases; reflects the role of unsophisticated investors

Remember that an odd lot is an order for less than 100 shares. What can such a ratio reveal? If you take the view that odd-lot traders are probably unsophisticated investors with little capital to invest, while round-lot traders are just the opposite, then an increase in the ratio indicates greater selling activity among unsophisticated buyers. And if you are willing to assume the unsophisticated buyer is generally *wrong* about the market, then you should be buying, or at least not selling. Conversely, a decrease in the ratio would be interpreted as a selling signal.

Of course, if you bought or sold every time the indicator changed direction, you might be buying and selling constantly. Most technicians believe that minor changes in an indicator are not meaningful and should not be acted on immediately. Rather, they believe a time series of the indicator—such as the one shown in Exhibit 8.1—should be constructed and trading cues taken from significant changes in the series. But how do you measure a

*Measured in shares or dollars.

EXHIBIT 8.1

The odd-lot ratio

significant change? Although many technicians believe that it is a subjective skill, they do use some objective criteria, such as looking for trend reversals. To help in this effort, **moving averages** are often determined.

Moving averages: time series smoothing technique used to determine buy and sell points

To calculate a moving average, you first must decide on a meaningful length of time for establishing trading rules. Assuming, for example, that we work with weekly odd-lot data available in *Barron's,* we might decide that five weeks is a reasonable time period. The moving average is then calculated by adding a new value each week and subtracting the value that is then five weeks old. To illustrate, a five-period moving average is calculated in Exhibit 8.2. With a moving average line, we are then in a position to derive trading rules based on the series performance in relation to the moving average. Rule 1, for example, might be to buy stocks whenever the time series has been below its moving average but has just crossed over it, moving upward. Rule 2 could be to sell stocks when the series has been above the moving average but has just crossed over, moving downward. These trading rules are illustrated in Exhibit 8.3.

Five periods are usually not enough for establishing moving-average trading rules because frequent trend reversals will occur, which in turn lead to frequent buying and selling. Working with daily observations, most technicians use 30- to 270-day moving averages to reveal what they call minor and major trends. We will not comment on the usefulness of this approach at this point, but we should note that the moving-average technique can be applied to any time series, not just that of the odd-lot ratio.

Odd-lot short sales: pressure indicator showing the volume of short selling done by unsophisticated investors

Odd-Lot Short Sales   Because short selling is generally left to investment professionals, **odd-lot short sales** are supposed to show the very worst of odd-lotters' decisions: when they sell short. A persistent increase in their short selling is interpreted as practically a sure sign the market is headed

EXHIBIT 8.2

Calculating a five-period moving average for the odd-lot ratio

Period	Value	Moving Average Calculation
1	2.0	—
2	1.8	—
3	1.9	—
4	1.7	—
5	1.2	(2.0 + 1.8 + 1.9 + 1.7 + 1.2)/5 = 8.6/5 = 1.72
6	1.0	(1.8 + 1.9 + 1.7 + 1.2 + 1.0)/5 = 7.6/5 = 1.52
7	0.6	(1.9 + 1.7 + 1.2 + 1.0 + 0.6)/5 = 6.4/5 = 1.28
8	0.8	(1.7 + 1.2 + 1.0 + 0.6 + 0.8)/5 = 5.3/5 = 1.06
9	1.2	(1.2 + 1.0 + 0.6 + 0.8 + 1.2)/5 = 4.8/5 = 0.96
10	1.6	(1.0 + 0.6 + 0.8 + 1.2 + 1.6)/5 = 5.2/5 = 1.04
11	1.8	(0.6 + 0.8 + 1.2 + 1.6 + 1.8)/5 = 6.0/5 = 1.20
12	1.2	(0.8 + 1.2 + 1.6 + 1.8 + 1.2)/5 = 6.6/5 = 1.32
13	0.6	(1.2 + 1.6 + 1.8 + 1.2 + 0.6)/5 = 6.4/5 = 1.28
14	1.4	(1.6 + 1.8 + 1.2 + 0.6 + 1.4)/5 = 6.6/5 = 1.32

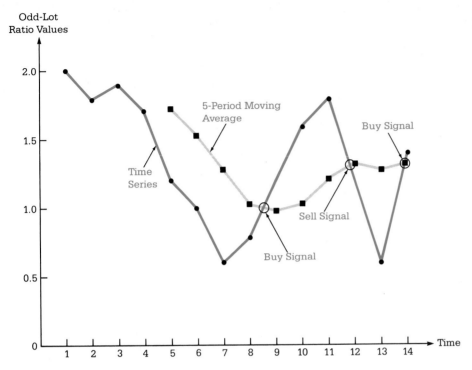

EXHIBIT 8.3
The odd-lot ratio. Time series and five-period moving average

upward—the opposite direction from what the odd-lotters think—while decreases signal a bear market. Again, to measure this pressure indicator, you could construct a time series, such as the one shown in Exhibit 8.4.

Institutions' Cash Positions   Rather than doing the opposite of what odd-lotters are doing, which is actually an indirect approach, why not try to identify intelligent investors and follow their leads directly? Of course, we must be able to identify smart investors and also find objective indicators of their trading activities. Who are smart investors? One answer might be professional money managers, people who manage the portfolios of pension funds, mutual funds, and other investment pools.

Mutual funds, for example, report their cash positions each month; that is, they indicate the proportion of their investment portfolio held in cash and marketable securities. By watching this information over time, you could determine if the managers were making significant changes in their cash positions. Increasing them would be interpreted as a sign managers were becoming more pessimistic about the market, while decreases in cash positions would indicate optimism.

Insider Activity   Portfolio managers may be smart, but surely the smartest investor of all should be a company insider, someone who knows firsthand

EXHIBIT 8.4
Odd-lot short sales

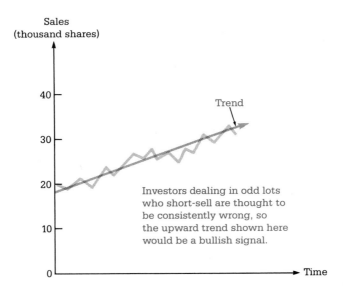

Investors dealing in odd lots who short-sell are thought to be consistently wrong, so the upward trend shown here would be a bullish signal.

what the company plans to do in the future. Corporate directors, officers, and stockholders with significant ownership interests in the corporation must report any purchases or sales of their company's stock to the Securities and Exchange Commission (SEC), which makes this information publicly available. With it, you can trade exactly as the insiders do: if they are buying, so can you, and you can sell when they sell. The information, however, may be several months old by the time it is released, which diminishes its timeliness. Another shortcoming occurs if insiders are both buying and selling. Then investors must establish some way to discern which influence is the stronger.

Interpreting Market Activity

Along with attempting to identify buyer and seller groups, many technicians believe that it is important to gauge buying and selling pressures for the overall market. To do this, they often look at the Dow theory, trading volume, the advance/decline index, and the new highs/new lows index.

Dow theory: method of measuring market strength based on the performances of the Dow Jones Industrial Averages and the Dow Jones Transportation Index

The Dow Theory   The **Dow theory** is probably the oldest formal technical approach to the market. In broad terms, the theory holds that a market's strength is measured by the relative performance of two averages: the industrials and the railroads (now broadened and called the transportation average). A strong market—bullish or bearish—is one in which both averages are moving in the same direction. A weak or indecisive market exists when they are moving in opposite directions. People who still hold to the Dow theory are looking for movements in the two averages that will confirm a broad market trend. For example, if the industrials were in an uptrend while the transportation average was waffling up and down with no clear pattern, a sudden, persistent upward movement in the latter average would confirm that a major bull market was under way.

Volume and Price-Related Volume Substantial price increases and decreases are often accompanied by heavy trading activity. To a technician, the volume of shares traded over a particular period might be as important as the change in a market index (such as the Dow Jones 30 Industrials). Suppose that over the past four weeks the index increased 5% each week, but the number of shares traded each week consistently declined. The technician sees this as a sign of weakness and would be less enthusiastic about future price increases than would be the case had volume increased each week.

Some technicians link volume to price by noting the specific number of shares traded when the price of a stock increased, when it decreased, and when it was unchanged. Exhibit 8.5 shows how this data might be used to

Period	Price of Stock	Shares Traded	Volume +	Volume −	On-Balance Volume	
1	$ 10	10,000	—	—	—	**EXHIBIT 8.5**
2	9	12,000	—	12,000	− 12,000	Volume indicators
3	8⅛	30,000	—	42,000	− 42,000	
4	9⅛	16,000	16,000	—	− 26,000	
5	9	20,000	—	20,000	− 46,000	
6	9¼	60,000	60,000	—	+ 14,000	
7	10	40,000	40,000	—	+ 54,000	
8	10	25,000	—	—	+ 54,000	

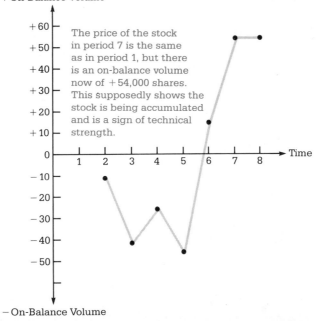

+ On-Balance Volume

The price of the stock in period 7 is the same as in period 1, but there is an on-balance volume now of + 54,000 shares. This supposedly shows the stock is being accumulated and is a sign of technical strength.

− On-Balance Volume

BOX 8.1   GETTING AN INVESTMENT EDGE

Do Insiders Really Beat the Market? And Can Outsiders Following Insiders Do As Well?

You would think if there is one group of investors who might have an edge, it would be corporate insiders: officers, directors, and people who own a lot of the company's stock. If they don't know what's going on in their own companies and, more important, what's likely to happen in the future, then there is little hope for the rest of us. Although the proposition that corporate insiders do indeed earn superior investment returns seems obvious and might be taken as an act of faith, market analysts have said, "No, it needs to be tested, as do all other theories suggesting some investors beat the market."

There has been no shortage of tests because information is readily available by virtue of the SEC requirement that insiders report transactions in their companies' stocks by the 10th day of the month after the transactions. The information is then published in the SEC *Official Summary*. It is also available through private newsletters that often devise methods of interpreting trading activity to rate stocks as to the extent of inside buying or selling.

So what does the research tell us? On balance, it confirms what we thought: insiders apparently do earn abnormally high returns, meaning they beat the market on a risk-adjusted basis. Although not overwhelming, the evidence is strong enough to suggest that if insiders can do it, outsiders can follow their trading cues and do it too. This proposition is far more interesting because, if true, it offers us all an opportunity to improve our investment performance.

Before you rush out to look at the *Official Summary* or buy one of the newsletters, be cautious. The evidence is far less convincing that we can mimic insiders to earn returns as high as theirs. A study by Gary A. Benesh and Robert A. Pari indicates the problem.* They tested investment performance of both insiders and outsiders, using the Consensus of Insiders (COI) newsletters published by Perry Wysong as the source of information outsiders used to determine insider trading. Each month the COI provides its subscribers a list of the 20 highest-rated stocks, based on insider trading over the previous four months. How well would you have done following the

---

*Benesh, Gary A., and R. A. Pari, "Performance of Stocks Recommended on the Basis of Insider Trading," *The Financial Review 22*, February 1987, pp. 145–58.

On-balance volume index: measures relative strength by linking volume to price changes

construct an index. Joseph Granville, probably the best-known technician, first popularized this method by constructing the **on-balance volume index,** such as the one shown in Exhibit 8.5. He also developed specific trading rules based on the index. Generally, a consistent upward trend in the index is bullish, while a downward trend is bearish.

monthly lists? The accompanying figure shows the answer.

Adjusting for market performance and risk, outsiders earned a monthly cumulative superior return of about 4.7% over a 13-month period from the time the insider trading took place. Not bad, except that none of the monthly superior returns was significant in a statistical sense. In other words, the 4.7% cumulative figure could be due to luck or any other random event. Luck is not the explanation for superior insider returns, though. They clearly beat the market (with statistical significance). Unfortunately for us, they did it in the four months before trades were published in the COI.

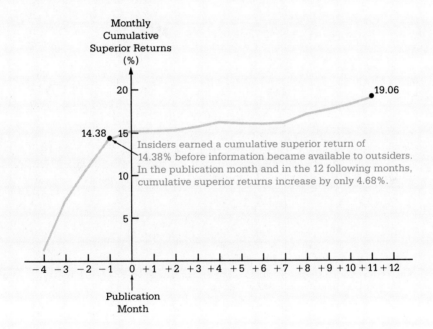

The *Advance/Decline Index* The **advance/decline index** plots the number of issues advancing in price divided by the number declining in price each day (or other period). As long as the series remains in an uptrend, many technicians would remain bullish about the market, while a downtrend calls for bearishness. Exhibit 8.6 illustrates the advance/decline index. Issues

Advance/decline index: shows number of stocks increasing in price relative to those decreasing in price

EXHIBIT 8.6
The advance/decline
index

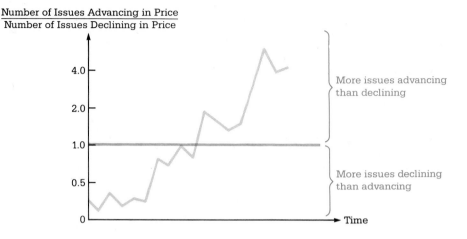

Number of Issues Advancing in Price
———————————————————
Number of Issues Declining in Price

More issues advancing
than declining

More issues declining
than advancing

EXHIBIT 8.7
New highs/new lows
index*

Number of Issues at 52-Week Highest Price
————————————————————————
Number of Issues at 52-Week Lowest Price

More new highs
than new lows

More new lows
than new highs

*To show the magnitude of new highs and new lows, this series is
sometimes shown as new highs minus new lows. The graph must
then allow for negative values.

advancing and declining are reported daily in *The Wall Street Journal*, which
provides a source of data to construct the index.

**New highs/new lows
index:** shows number of
stocks hitting 52-week
high prices relative to
the number hitting 52-
week lows

The New Highs/New Lows Index   The **new highs/new lows index** is
constructed from periodic data that show the number of new issues that traded at their highest 52-week price divided by the number of issues that traded
at their lowest 52-week price. Exhibit 8.7 illustrates this index, which is often
used as a companion to the advance/decline index and is interpreted in the
same manner.

Investor Psychology

Some technicians believe that investor psychology is the dominant force in the market. If investors are cautious and conservative, the market will not do well. Conversely, investor optimism will eventually lead to higher prices and a robust market. The trick is to measure optimism and pessimism. Three indexes are used often: Barron's Confidence Index, the slope of the yield curve, and activity in low-priced stocks.

Barron's Confidence Index   **Barron's Confidence Index** is calculated by dividing the yields of the best-grade bonds by the yields of intermediate-grade bonds; that is,

$$\text{Barron's Confidence Index} = \frac{\text{Yield: Best-Grade Bonds}}{\text{Yield: Intermediate-Grade Bonds}}$$

You would expect the index to always have a value less than 1.0, but the amount less indicates the degree of bond market enthusiasm. A downward trend in the index, such as that shown in Exhibit 8.8, might show that investors are demanding greater yields to compensate them for the higher risk associated with poorer-quality bonds. This demand for higher yields in turn shows growing investor pessimism and perhaps a future decline in the stock market as this pessimism spills out of the bond market. On the other hand, an upward trend in the index indicates optimism and potential future market strength.

Slope of the Yield Curve   The yield curve will be explained in Chapter 9. You will learn that it shows the relation between debt instrument yields to

Barron's Confidence Index: shows the yield on best-grade bonds relative to the yield on intermediate-grade bonds

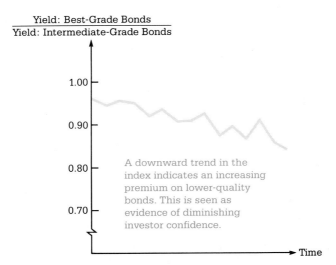

$$\frac{\text{Yield: Best-Grade Bonds}}{\text{Yield: Intermediate-Grade Bonds}}$$

A downward trend in the index indicates an increasing premium on lower-quality bonds. This is seen as evidence of diminishing investor confidence.

EXHIBIT 8.8
Barron's Confidence Index

maturity and maturity. A normal yield curve is one that has positive slope; that is, the longer an instrument's maturity, the greater its yield to maturity. Occasionally, though, yield curves become inverted, as shown in Exhibit 8.9. On the surface, an inverted yield curve seems an anomaly: why should investors receive lower yields on debt instruments with longer maturities, which are clearly riskier than those with short maturities? The answer lies in the fact that investors expect interest rates to fall, and as they do, investors will earn greater price appreciation with longer maturities.

Market technicians believe that bond investors are smart investors, and their belief that interest rates will fall is a cue to begin buying stocks. Some technicians also believe that a steeply sloped positive yield curve can provide evidence that interest rates will rise in the future. Although not as strong a signal, such a curve is seen as a selling cue.

Activity in Low-Priced Stocks   The activity in low-priced stocks supposedly heats up as a bull market comes to an end. Why is this so? Again, because it indicates increased activity of small investors, who are attracted to low-priced stocks. It also shows that all investors are disregarding fundamentals in favor of securities that have low prices because investors see better percentage gains in low-priced issues as opposed to high-priced issues. *Barron's* constructs an index of low-priced stocks and reports it each week in its statistics section.

EXHIBIT 8.9
Yield curves and future interest rates

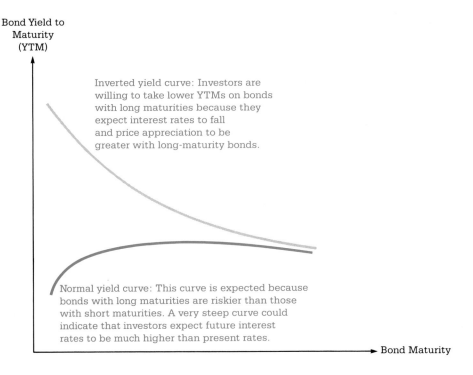

Bond Yield to Maturity (YTM)

Inverted yield curve: Investors are willing to take lower YTMs on bonds with long maturities because they expect interest rates to fall and price appreciation to be greater with long-maturity bonds.

Normal yield curve: This curve is expected because bonds with long maturities are riskier than those with short maturities. A very steep curve could indicate that investors expect future interest rates to be much higher than present rates.

Bond Maturity

Evaluating Pressure Indicators

You might be interested in using indicators as a forecasting method, but before you do, consider some questions about their effectiveness. Pressure indicators are similar in use to the leading economic indicators discussed in Chapter 7. To be effective, a leading indicator must (1) give a correct signal, (2) give the signal with sufficient lead time for appropriate action, and (3) have consistent lead times. Exhibit 8.10 shows how a perfect market indicator would work. Notice that it gave four correct signals—two increases and two decreases—with a consistent one-month lead time, which would have been enough time for an investor to take action. This perfect market indicator is a pure fiction, existing only in theory. Actual indicators show a much more confused picture.

Correct Signals   Many indicators do not consistently give correct signals; that is, they might signal a market increase, but the market subsequently

EXHIBIT 8.10
Illustration of a perfect market indicator

goes down. Exhibit 8.11 shows how most market indicators actually work. As you see, the pattern of relationships between the two time series is very hazy. True, a quick or casual glance gives the impression of a close correlation between them, but a more detailed examination might show the indicator is virtually useless as a forecasting tool. If you look closely, you can see that a false signal was given from the middle of February to late February. The indicator was showing a market increase that never came, or at least did not come until the middle of March. The indicator fell sharply in late February and early March, leaving us to wonder whether the increase or the decrease was appropriate.

Sufficient Lead Time   Even if an indicator provides a correct signal, by the time it is interpreted, the market may have already moved. Is it clear that the upward January trend in the indicator was recognizable in sufficient time to

EXHIBIT 8.11

Illustration of most market indicators

get in the market? Notice that the indicator's trend wasn't established clearly until the last week or so in January. By then, the market was also moving up sharply. If you hesitated a day or so, you probably missed most of the gains.

Consistent Lead Times   Exhibit 8.11 shows inconsistent lead times between the indicator and the market. Indeed, the pattern is so confusing that you could just as easily argue that the market leads the indicator, rather than the indicator leading the market. For example, the market clearly turned up in mid-March before the indicator and seems to have done so in mid-April as well. The false signal in mid-February mentioned earlier could also be interpreted as the market signaling a downturn in the indicator. If we analyzed the two series with mathematical techniques, we probably would find they tend to move together rather than one leading the other. If this is true, the market indicator is best described as a coincident, rather than a leading, indicator. Coincident indicators have little value in forecasting.

An Appraisal   Can pressure indicators help you make better investment decisions? Consider this: If you plan to use them, you also intend to time your purchases and sales of securities to what you believe are market cycles. However, the investment literature contains strong evidence that timing often does no better than a simple buy-and-hold approach and that when commissions are considered, it usually does worse.

To the uninitiated investor, the technician's pressure indicators and price graphs (these are covered in the next section) often appear to be highly mathematical and complex constructs that must be good because they are impossible to understand. Most are not that mathematical, nor are they complex. If we can't understand them, it probably reflects a lack of substance on their part rather than our ignorance. The underlying rationale for many of the indicators does not exist. For example, there is no clear evidence showing odd-lot traders are worse—or better—than their round-lot counterparts. Moreover, the record of mutual fund managers is hardly one of superior performance; in fact, mutual funds so often perform more poorly than an unmanaged market index that you might be better off doing the opposite of what the managers do.

Even when an indicator's underlying logic seems more substantial, there are still problems to consider. For example, it is true that all inverted yield curves have been followed by falling interest rates and rising stock prices. But the lead times between when the curve became inverted and when interest rates and stock prices moved have been highly unpredictable. Using the yield curve to forecast would have been no more effective than using some simple, naive approach, such as always buying stocks whenever their prices have fallen 30% and selling them after they increase 50%.

BOX 8.2   INVESTMENT INSIGHTS

Watch the Super Bowl and Be a Super Forecaster

Want to get your portfolio started right each year? Forget technical analysis, fundamental analysis, expert advice, and anything else that takes a lot of work and might have some connection to the stock market. Instead, enjoy a football game. Specifically, watch the Super Bowl each January and if one of the old NFL teams wins, buy; if one of the expansion AFL teams wins, don't buy (for even better results, go short). Sounds crazy, right? Well, the accompanying table shows how you would have done with this strategy since the Super Bowl began. You would have missed the market direction in only 3 of 27 years, which is remarkable. (And the misses were so close that a few points change at year's end could have given a perfect record.) Indeed, the chances of doing this well by luck are about 4 in 1,000. With performance this good, why use anything else?

Let's be serious. Stock market performance and the Super Bowl are definitely independent events. The fact that they appear not to be is unusual. But if you looked at an endless number of independent events, you eventually should find one that forecasts the market as well as or better than the Super Bowl. If you understand the point here, you should also understand why some supposedly more sophisticated forecasters show remarkable forecasting results. Keep this in mind: with thousands of professionals forecasting, the odds are excellent that we can find one or two who do it almost perfectly. Are they lucky, or are they good? You make the decision.

SUPER BOWL FORECAST RESULTS

Year	Winner	League	Change in the Market
1967	Green Bay Packers	NFL	+20.09%
1968	Green Bay Packers	NFL	+ 7.66
1969	New York Jets	AFL	−11.42

SUPER BOWL FORECAST RESULTS (*Continued*)

Year	Winner	League	° Change in the Market
1970	Kansas City Chiefs	AFL	+ 0.16*
1971	Baltimore Colts	NFL	+10.79
1972	Dallas Cowboys	NFL	+15.63
1973	Miami Dolphins	AFL	−17.37
1974	Miami Dolphins	AFL	−29.72
1975	Pittsburgh Steelers	NFL	+31.55
1976	Pittsburgh Steelers	NFL	+19.15
1977	Oakland Raiders	AFL	−11.50
1978	Dallas Cowboys	NFL	+ 1.06
1979	Pittsburgh Steelers	NFL	+12.31
1980	Pittsburgh Steelers	NFL	+25.77
1981	Oakland Raiders	AFL	− 9.72
1982	San Francisco 49ers	NFL	+14.76
1983	Washington Redskins	NFL	+17.27
1984	Los Angeles Raiders	AFL	+ 1.39*
1985	San Francisco 49ers	NFL	+26.34
1986	Chicago Bears	NFL	+14.63
1987	New York Giants	NFL	+ 2.03
1988	Washington Redskins	NFL	+12.41
1989	San Francisco 49ers	NFL	+27.50
1990	San Francisco 49ers	NFL	− 6.56*
1991	New York Giants	NFL	+26.31
1992	Washington Redskins	NFL	+ 4.46
1993	Dallas Cowboys	NFL	+ 9.98
1994	Dallas Cowboys	NFL	?

*Incorrect forecasts

USING CHARTS AND GRAPHS

Not all technicians employ pressure indicators as their primary forecasting devices. Many prefer using price charts and graphs. Even if you are not a technician, you might find that a price graph helps you to understand a security's historical price movements. Apart from its use as a forecasting tool, a price graph provides some indication of a security's price volatility and, thus, its risk. The discussion below focuses on the forecasting aspect of price graphs.

EXHIBIT 8.12
Price graphs

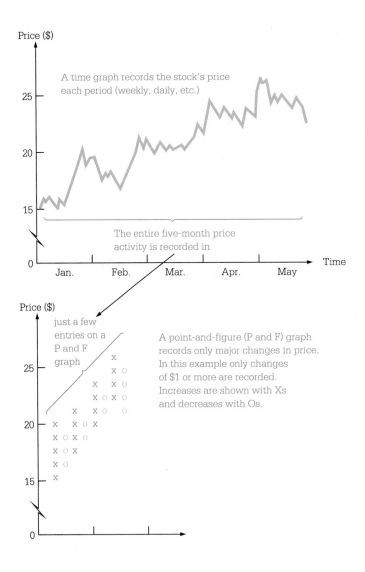

Constructing Graphs

The most popular price graph is a **time graph,** which plots the periodic (daily, weekly, quarterly, or whatever) price of a security over time. The top graph in Exhibit 8.12 shows a typical time graph. The analyst appears to be recording the price of the stock every other or every third day. As we see, price has shown an up-down pattern, gradually increasing from $15 to $26 a share and then declining to $21. Constructing a time graph is simple and can be done by anyone.

Many of the price changes over the five months are inconsequential: up a half or a quarter, down a half or a quarter, and so forth. Some analysts think that it is unnecessary to record all prices and that a more effective use of time would be to record only important changes. Defining important is arbitrary; in the case of a stock selling at $15, you might decide any price change of $1 or more is important and will be recorded. You ignore, then, any change less than this amount. The lower graph in Exhibit 8.12 shows the construction of a graph using this approach. It is called a **point-and-figure (P and F) graph.**

Assuming you start the graph when the price is $15, no entries are made until the middle of January, when the price reaches $16. You then enter an X to show an increase of $1. As you see, price continues increasing until $20 is reached toward the end of January. So keep entering Xs up to $20 on the P and F graph. Then in late January, price begins to fall and continues falling until mid-February, eventually reaching $16.50. These decreases are recorded with three Os. Using the same methods, you record and condense the entire five months of price activity on the P and F chart. As you see, P and F charts require less time to maintain, which enhances their appeal to technicians who are watching many individual stocks. Excellent computer software packages can now automatically record and analyze data available from various data banks, so saving time is no longer a problem. You might think, then, that P and F graphs would become obsolete; that has not been the case. Indeed, you can buy software that constructs P and F graphs.

Interpreting Graphs

Whether a time or a P and F graph is used, the price movements must be interpreted. There are probably as many interpretation methods as there are technicians using them, so attempting to explain even a small portion of them would take the rest of this text. We will discuss two methods that are widely used: support and resistance lines, and the head-and-shoulders pattern. Interpretation methods are usually the same for time and P and F graphs.

Support and Resistance Lines **Support and resistance lines** are trend lines drawn through a series of high and low prices. The top graph in Exhibit 8.13 provides an illustration. As you see, this stock's price has been trending upward, reaching a string of highs and lows along the way. By drawing lines through the highs and lows, you create the support and resistance lines. Why use these names? Notice that as price reached its highs, selling pressures increased (technicians might describe this as "investors taking their profits") and price fell; that is, there was resistance to greater price increases. Each time the support line was reached, buying pressures mounted, giving support to the price.

A logical question to ask is, "So what?" What do support and resistance lines have to tell us about future price? Many technicians believe that as long as price remains within its support and resistance lines, it is safe to hold the stock, but there are no compelling reasons to either buy or sell it. However, if the resistance line is penetrated from below, a buying situation exists; if the

EXHIBIT 8.13
Interpreting price graphs

support line is penetrated from above, a selling situation exists. Exhibit 8.13 shows the latter, and the interpretation is that price is headed much lower. Most technicians also watch volume. If a breakthrough is accompanied by heavy volume (as shown in Exhibit 8.13), the signal is considered even stronger.

A Head-and-Shoulders Pattern   A **head-and-shoulders pattern** is a price pattern that looks like a head and two shoulders, such as the one shown in the lower part of Exhibit 8.13. Many stock prices exhibit such patterns, although sometimes it takes a vivid imagination to see them. Technicians revel when they see a head-and-shoulders pattern because it is thought to be one of the strongest technical price indicators. The interpretation is about the same as it is for support and resistance lines. In the example, price has again gone through the support line, indicating continued price weakness. Had it not penetrated the support line but instead increased above the resistance line—formed by passing a line through the tips of the two shoulders—the technician would probably believe that price would continue to increase, eventually going above the head. Because a head-and-shoulders pattern is considered a stronger pattern than simple support and resistance lines, the technician probably would have greater confidence in his or her forecast.

Head-and-shoulders pattern: price movements that trace out a pattern resembling a head and two shoulders

Moving Averages   A moving average was introduced and explained earlier in this chapter. While moving averages can be used to evaluate any time series, they play a very important role in the technical analysis of price graphs. The graph shown in Exhibit 8.3 can represent a price time series instead of an odd-lot ratio (imagine the vertical axis shows prices). In this case, the buy and sell signals would be the same. The effectiveness of using moving averages depends very much on the price movements of the market. A rather flat market with a repeating up-down pattern generates numerous signals, leading to frequent buying and selling, large commissions, and large investor losses. The method is used more successfully when longer trends take place.

Price Momentum   Many technical analysts evaluate a stock's **price momentum,** which refers to the relative speed of its price increases or decreases. Momentum can be measured in numerous ways. One method involves calculating percentage changes each period (usually weekly or quarterly). For example, suppose over the past three weeks a stock price goes from $10 to $11 to $12⅛ to $13⅜. Calculating percentage changes indicates price is rising at about a constant 10% rate, which is its momentum. Increasing momentum—considered desirable—would be reflected in a series such as $10 to $11 to $13¼ to $17⅛, which shows first a 10% increase, then a 20% increase, and finally a 30% increase. Rather than calculating percentage increases, some analysts weight each period's return, giving more weight to more recent periods. These are called *relative strength* indicators. Suppose price over three weeks goes from $10.00 to $10.50 to $11.00 to $12.00, and the

Price momentum: measurement of the relative speed of price increases or decreases analyst weights the most recent week at 0.6 and the two previous weeks at 0.2 each. Then, weighted weekly performance is shown below:

$$
\begin{array}{lllll}
\text{week 1:} & + & \$0.50 \times 0.2 & = & + \ \$0.1 \\
\text{week 2:} & + & 0.50 \times 0.2 & = & + \ \ \ 0.1 \\
\text{week 3:} & + & 1.00 \times 0.6 & = & + \ \ \ 0.6 \\
& & & \text{total} = & + \ \$0.8
\end{array}
$$

Price increased $2 over the three weeks, and the relative strength of the third week is 0.667 ($0.6/$0.8).

Trading rules are then established based on recent periods' relative strengths. A buy signal in the example above might be a relative strength of 0.6 or better. As with a moving average technique, the analyst hopes to find a stock on the verge of a sustained upward trend in price.

Relative strength ratios can also compare the price movement of one stock to its industry average, or the relative strength of an industry to the overall market. The calculations for these comparisons are similar to those illustrated for comparing performances during different periods. The purpose of the comparisons is the same.

Evaluating the Use of Graphs

There is a mystique about price graphs that appeals to many investors. How can you not be impressed by the patterns often seen in the graphs? Surely, all you need to do is find the interpretation key to unlock the mystery the graphs hold. Support and resistance lines are one of the keys, but there might be others that are even more effective. Believe it or not (and most technicians don't), most of the patterns you are likely to see are easily explained by random processes.

What Is Randomness?   You can understand randomness better by creating your own price chart. Take a coin and flip it 250 times, recording each time the head or tail that results. (This experiment goes much faster if you can find a few friends to help you.) Now, on a piece of graph paper, assume you are watching a stock that is currently selling at $25. Assume each flip of the coin represents one day. Each time you get a head, assume price increases by $1; if you get a tail, assume it decreases by $1. For example, if the first flip was a head, you assume price increased to $26 on the first day; if the second flip is a tail, price falls back to $25 on the second day. After 250 flips, you will have about a year's price graph (allowing days off for weekends and holidays).

What do you think this graph might look like? You probably agree that flipping a coin is a random process, and the graph should then show randomness. Would randomness appear as a series of up $1 and down $1 on a rotating basis, such as the top graph in Exhibit 8.14? That would be almost math-

EXHIBIT 8.14
Hypothetical price
graphs

ematically impossible. Instead, you are likely to have series of ups and downs called *runs,* and your graph more likely will look like the one at the bottom of Exhibit 8.14. Such a time series is often called a **random walk.** You might get three or four heads in a row, followed by a couple of tails, and then two or three more heads, and so forth. In short, you surely would expect a series of runs, and some might be quite long. When you are finished, you might be amazed at how closely your graph resembles many actual price graphs. Indeed, you may turn up a head-and-shoulders pattern or two, and you probably will have little trouble finding some support and resistance lines. And consider that coin flipping is only one of many randomizing techniques that could be used to create the price graph. A more complicated one might provide an even better facsimile.

Random walk: changes in a variable over time that reveal no identifiable pattern

The Implications of Randomness   If a price graph can be explained by random processes, is it likely there are any predictive patterns in the time series

BOX 8.3   INVESTMENT INSIGHTS

Can Candlesticks Shed Some Light on Technical Analysis?

In the never-ending search for the ultimate price forecaster, technicians have come up with a new tool—candlestick charts. Candlesticks actually are quite old, supposedly going back to the 17th century, when they were used by the Japanese to trade rice futures contracts on the Osaka futures exchange. A candlestick is a way of recording a security's prices—high, low, open, close—for a trading period. Figure 1 in the chart indicates candlesticks when the closing price is lower than the open price (the thick part is shaded black) and when the close is higher than the open (the thick part is unshaded). The thin lines above and below the body are called shadows; they show the high and low prices for the trading period.

Each charting method develops its own techniques to interpret a chart, such as the one shown in Figure 2. You hardly need candlestick art to tell you that price decreased over the period. However, there are two key clues that supposedly foreshadow the drop. First, a black candlestick encloses a white one, which is called a bearish engulfing pattern. Second, there is a window, which means there were no trades between a previous session's low and this session's high.

Its long history and oriental origin add a certain mystique to candlestick charting, but that doesn't necessarily make it any better than other charting techniques. As with any method, learn it well first and then try it out in a simulated manner before you put up real money.

that can be used to forecast future prices? The answer is no. As you begin your coin-flipping experiment, what is your best guess for the stock's price one year later? The right answer is $25 because you logically expect about an equal number of heads and tails after 250 flips. It would be unlikely, however, that you would get exactly 125 heads and 125 tails. Rather than picking one specific future price, you would prefer to think in terms of a likely price range. For example, the odds are fairly good the future price will be somewhere between $20 and $30.

Unfortunately, our conclusion about the effectiveness of price graphs to improve investment performance is they are no better than pressure indicators. You can do as well with most simple random methods—something to consider before you pay several hundred dollars or more a year for a chart service.

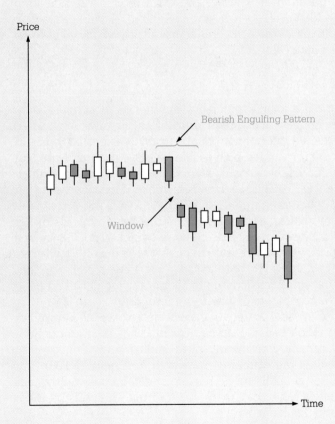

EFFICIENT MARKETS

We have discussed the two broad approaches to security evaluation and selection: the fundamental approach and the technical approach. Proponents for each contend their methods allow them to identify undervalued and overvalued securities and, over time, to earn returns in excess of what might be earned by buying a random portfolio of securities or by buying a broad market index such as the S&P 500. Earning this extra return is referred to as **beating the market.** In the sections to follow, we'll look at the empirical evidence that relates to these beating-the-market claims. First, we must understand that comparing performances is legitimately undertaken only when risk is held constant; that is, if an analyst consistently recommends securities far riskier than the market, you should expect a return in excess of the market return. The important question is whether the extra return was adequate compensation for the added risk. As we saw in Chapter 6 with respect to common stocks, this means earning a return above that which you would expect, given the stock's beta value.

Beating the market: expression related to stock-picking success (or failure) that takes risk into consideration

What Are Efficient Markets?

There are several definitions of market efficiency, but the one most appropriate for investment purposes defines an **efficient market** as one in which a security's price reflects all existing information that bears on its expected return in the future. This information includes both technical data, such as historical prices and volume, and fundamental data, such as past or projected earnings and balance sheet strength. Assuming investors make decisions based on such information, and further assuming a sufficient number of investors in the market so that no single investor can influence market price with his or her trading, then a market price is described as being in equilibrium. This means it is a relatively stable price with no pressure to push it either up or down. This stability may be short-lived, however, because new information can arise that might change investor expectations, leading to greater buying or selling pressures that push price to a new higher or lower equilibrium.

Efficient market: market that investors cannot beat, on a risk-adjusted basis

In such a market, an investor can earn excess profits only by knowing in advance the new information causing an equilibrium shift. Market analysts who believe investors cannot consistently have such information express their view in what is called the **efficient market hypothesis (EMH).** Put simply, those who hold to the EMH argue that no one can consistently beat the market, and they have conducted many tests to determine if the EMH can be supported by factual evidence.

Efficient market hypothesis: argument that markets are efficient

The Weak Form of the EMH   The EMH was first tested by evaluating the effectiveness of technical analysis, primarily charting techniques. As we saw, chartists believe that historical price patterns offer clues to future price movements. With the aid of the computer, testing charting techniques is relatively easy because most trading strategies can be expressed in a mathematical format. For example, support and resistance lines can be found, and trades based on their penetrations can be determined and evaluated. Many such tests have been conducted, and the overwhelming evidence indicates charting techniques do *not* beat the market. You will do just as well with a simple buy-and-hold strategy, selecting securities randomly.

The failure of technical approaches to beat the market is described as weak support for the EMH, or the **weak form of the EMH.** The adjective *weak* suggests that merely showing the failure of technical analysis does not provide a strong argument in favor of efficient markets. Most sophisticated fundamentalists thought that technical analysis was closer to voodoo forecasting than genuine security analysis, anyway. So it came as no surprise to learn that what they long suspected was indeed true. However, they felt much stronger evidence was needed to sustain the EMH.

Weak form of the EMH: argument that methods of technical analysis cannot be used to beat the market

The Semistrong Form of the EMH   Such evidence was not long in coming, and much of it was directed against fundamental techniques. Several studies showed that buying securities because their shares were to be split (a favorite technique in years past and still occasionally heard of today) was a complete waste of time. So, too, were strategies based on changes in certain macroeconomic variables, such as interest rates, GNP, or the money supply. Other studies showed that earnings announcements by managements had virtually no effect on their firms' stock prices. First-time investors are often surprised when the stock market, or an individual stock, fails to react to good (or bad) news about the economy or about the company. For example: IBM announces record earnings, and the stock falls in price. Investors must learn (some the hard way) that current prices already reflect the expected news. Indeed, it is only "news" if the information is different from what had been anticipated.

The **semistrong form of the EMH** argues that any public information—not only historical prices—cannot be used to earn above-expected returns. This means that fundamental analysis using, for example, a company's financial report as a data source is as much a waste of time as drawing a chart of its price history. Although the early studies supported the semistrong form, recent studies offer mixed evidence. Buying stocks with low P/E ratios has been found to produce above-expected returns. Also, there appears to be an advantage in buying small company stocks. We saw in Chapter 3 that small companies did show much greater returns than the S&P 500, although they also showed greater risk. In effect, the current research seems to indicate the added return was worth the added risk. You would have been better off buying them than leveraging the S&P 500 to achieve an equivalent degree of risk (beta).

Semistrong form of the EMH: argument that methods of fundamental analysis cannot be used to beat the market

The Strong Form of the EMH   The **strong form of the EMH** argues that investors cannot consistently earn above-expected profits using *any* information—public or private. This form does not mean that someone with privileged information cannot make an occasional windfall; many corporate insiders have possessed such information and used it to their advantage. What the strong form does say is that even insiders cannot consistently earn superior

Strong form of the EMH: argument that no method of analysis or any type of information can be used to beat the market returns by virtue of their information monopoly. Because federal law requires directors, officers, and important shareholders (those owning 10% or more of a company's total stock) to report transactions in their companies' stocks to the SEC, there is ample information to test the strong form. The results of such tests are mixed, although the evidence leans mostly in the direction that insiders do earn superior returns on a risk-adjusted basis. The strong form of the EMH must therefore be rejected. Can other investors—outsiders—also earn superior returns by following the trading patterns of insiders? This issue has also been tested, and although evidence again is mixed, it leans most heavily in the direction that outsiders cannot earn superior returns.

Another test of the strong form determined whether professional money managers could beat the market. On the surface, it is logical to expect that they could. They have extensive research facilities and probably are the first to receive information about a company. So what is their performance record? Surprisingly, a large majority show below-expected returns for their clientele when commissions and administrative expenses are considered. In fact, their performance has been so poor over the years that many institutional investors have given up on them and turned their money over to funds that simply buy the market. These are called index funds. They make no pretense to earn superior returns, and their success is measured strictly by how well they correlate with a market index such as the S&P 500. A high correlation guarantees the fund will earn at least as much as the index and have the same degree of risk. An index fund doesn't beat the market, but it doesn't lose to it either. Over $100 billion is invested in such funds, and the total grows larger each year.

Implications of the EMH

Is the evidence supporting the EMH strong enough to encourage you to abandon your effort to find undervalued securities or superior-performing mutual funds and instead put your money in an index fund? There may not be a simple yes-or-no answer to this question. The following points are worth considering.

1. The evidence appears sufficiently strong to discourage the use of graphing and other technical approaches. In fact, strategies based on them typically involve such frequent trading that you probably will do much worse than the market and enrich only your broker.

2. The evidence also seems strong enough to discourage your use of fundamental analysis if it is based exclusively on public information and uses techniques used by everyone else. This advice is particularly appropriate if you are analyzing large companies thousands of other analysts are watching. Being realistic, what can we hope to find, for example, in IBM's financial report that other analysts will not find? You also should give little attention to research reports prepared by professional analysts if their analysis goes no further than reworking the company's financial report or repeating information management has made available to the

public. Surprisingly, many such reports are limited to these activities with perhaps a broad overview of the effectiveness of the company's management or its position in the industry. Few investors show superior returns with these reports.

3. Your best hope is to concentrate on small companies, trying to find information other investors do not have. Your odds might be better if you limit your investigations to companies in your home area (where you might have an advantage in getting information) or to those in an industry in which you have a particular expertise. If several such firms interest you, then prepare a fundamental analysis, using the tools highlighted in Chapter 7 and risk analyses explained in Chapter 4. And by all means, make sure you have adequate diversification. If you can find only one or two companies that appeal to you, consider investing only a limited portion of your available funds in them. Is this approach risky? Indeed it is; in a sense, you are becoming as entrepreneurial as the people who founded the company and possibly still hold a large portion of its common stock. But this may be what it takes to beat the market.

SUMMARY

Technical analysis attempts to discover profitable investments using methods that do not rely on measuring the intrinsic strengths of a company, industry, or overall economy. It uses pressure indicators that show who is buying or selling, levels of market activity, and investor psychology. Specific indicators include the odd-lot ratio, odd-lot short sales, institutions' cash positions, insider activity, the Dow theory, volume and price-related volume, the advance/decline index, the new highs/new lows index, Barron's Confidence Index, slope of the yield curve, and activity in low-priced stocks. There is little evidence to show that using pressure indicators leads to better investment decisions. Indicators often give false signals, signal too late to be effective, or have inconsistent lead times.

Market technicians also use charts and graphs. These can be time graphs or P and F graphs. Interpreting graphs is not a precise science and often involves subjective evaluation. There is little evidence to show that using graphs or charts helps improve investment decisions. Many so-called chart patterns are actually random patterns.

An efficient market is one in which a security's price reflects all existing information that bears on its expected future return. An efficient market hypothesis implies that investors cannot consistently outperform the overall market on a risk-adjusted basis. The hypothesis has been tested in various settings and has been supported in some and rejected in others. Implications of the tests for investors include a general rejection of technical analysis for security selection; a rejection of fundamental analysis, if it is performed on companies with a large following; and some support for fundamental analysis when it is applied to small companies with few followers.

KEY TERMS
(listed in order
of appearance)

technical analysis
pressure indicator
odd-lot ratio
moving averages
odd-lot short sales
Dow theory
on-balance volume index
advance/decline index
new highs/new lows index
Barron's Confidence Index
time graph

point-and-figure (P and F) graph
support and resistance lines
head-and-shoulders pattern
price momentum
random walk
beating the market
efficient market
efficient market hypothesis (EMH)
weak form of the EMH
semistrong form of the EMH
strong form of the EMH

REVIEW
QUESTIONS

1. Explain the following: (a) the odd-lot ratio, (b) odd-lot short sales, (c) institutions' cash positions, and (d) insider activity. Discuss how these indicators are supposed to help you make better investment decisions.
2. Explain how a moving average line is constructed, and discuss its purpose in time series analysis.
3. Explain the following: (a) the Dow theory, (b) on-balance volume index, (c) advance/decline index, and (d) new highs/new lows index. What investment implications do these indicators have? Explain.
4. Explain the following: (a) Barron's Confidence Index, (b) slope of the yield curve, and (c) activity in low-priced stocks. Indicate the rationale behind these indicators.
5. Discuss three important attributes of a successful leading indicator. Is it likely that you will find technical indicators with all three? Explain.
6. Explain a time graph and a P and F graph, comparing the two with respect to construction and interpretation.
7. Explain support and resistance lines.
8. Explain a head-and-shoulders pattern.
9. Discuss how moving averages are used in interpreting a price graph.
10. What is meant by momentum? How is it measured?
11. Explain the nature of randomness. Construct a line showing a random walk.
12. Discuss what is meant by an efficient market and what it means to beat the market.
13. Explain the EMH and evidence supporting it. Classify the evidence in the weak form, semistrong form, and strong form.
14. Given the research supporting (or failing to support) the EMH, discuss some investment implications arising from such evidence.

PROBLEMS
AND PROJECTS

1. You have recorded the following prices for a stock over the past 25 days:

1	$17	6	$23	11	$24	16	$24	21	$23
2	18	7	26	12	22	17	22	22	25
3	20	8	24	13	20	18	25	23	27
4	20	9	21	14	21	19	26	24	26
5	22	10	23	15	23	20	22	25	23

a. Construct a time graph for the stock. Also, construct a five-day moving average line and indicate buy and sell points.

b. Given the cues from your answer to question (a), determine your profit or loss assuming you bought 100 shares on day 1 and followed the trading cues thereafter. Assume commissions were 1% of the trade amount. Compare your performance with this trading strategy versus buying 100 shares on day 1 and holding them through day 25.

2. For the past five days, you have recorded the price of a particular stock and volume of shares traded. Below are the data:

Day	Price	Volume
1	$54	28,000
2	52	34,000
3	51	22,000
4	52	51,000
5	53	97,000

a. Determine on-balance volume for days 2 through 5.

b. Do you think the stock should be bought or sold? Explain.

3. Monsanto's price was $45 a share one year ago. End-of-quarter prices since then are (Q1) $46, (Q2) $48, (Q3) $52, and (Q4) $60.

a. Determine price momentum by calculating quarterly percentage changes. Is momentum increasing? Explain.

b. Suppose you weight quarterly changes as follows: 40% for the most recent quarter and 20% for the three other quarters. If you require a relative strength of 0.65 as a condition for purchase, is Monsanto a buy? Illustrate your answer.

4. Be sure to read Box 8.2, "Watch the Super Bowl and Be a Super Forecaster." Using the market return data, evaluate the following trading strategy: buy stocks the year before an election year and hold them until the election year is over. Election years were 1988, 1984, 1980, 1976, 1972, and 1968. Compare the returns from this strategy versus the one of being guided by the Super Bowl winner. For simplicity, assume you buy when an NFL team wins and hold for the year. If an AFL team wins, assume you invest in a savings account that pays 7%. Also use the geometric progression and geometric mean as an evaluation method. (See Chapter 3 if you need a review.) Finally, compare performances of the election-year strategy and the Super Bowl strategy to a buy-and-hold approach.

5. (Student Project) Simulate the price movement of a stock with a deck of cards. Here are the rules: current stock price = $30; each card represents one trading week; price changes as follows:

> any diamond—up 2 points
> any heart except the king—up 1 point
> king of hearts—up 20 points
> any club—down 2 points
> any spade except the queen—down 1 point
> queen of spades—down 13 points

Shuffle, go through the entire deck and then answer the following.

a. Prepare a time graph and indicate interesting patterns.

b. What must be the closing price of the stock one year from now? Explain.

6. *(Student Project)* Select a random sample of 10 stocks from Value Line's *Investment Survey.* For a four-year period before the most current year, determine for each the ratio of market value per share to book value per share, the number of shares of stock outstanding, the percentage increase (decrease) in earnings per share, and price momentum. Rank each stock for each performance indicator and then determine an aggregate rank. Finally, see if the aggregate rank correlates well with price appreciation or depreciation in the most current year.

CASE ANALYSES

8.1
Agnes Wade:
Junior
Technician

Agnes Wade is employed by ABC, Inc., a firm involved in hauling hazardous materials. Although Agnes does not have any privileged information about the company, she does know business is brisk and expected to remain so in the foreseeable future. Agnes has saved some money and is considering investing it in ABC's common stock. She does not understand financial statement data, but she has read material about technical analysis and thinks she can use some of the simpler methods to determine if the stock is a good buy. Accordingly, she has collected price and volume data for the company for the past 20 days.

Day	Price	Volume	Day	Price	Volume
1	9.50	3,000	11	12.00	8,000
2	9.75	2,000	12	11.88	6,000
3	10.13	6,000	13	11.25	9,000
4	10.13	4,000	14	11.38	4,000
5	10.00	7,000	15	11.00	10,000
6	10.25	5,000	16	11.25	5,000
7	10.75	9,000	17	10.50	16,000
8	11.63	12,000	18	10.38	9,000
9	11.50	7,000	19	10.25	14,000
10	11.75	15,000	20	11.50	7,000

With the data, Agnes will construct the following graphs: *(a)* a time graph of price, *(b)* a five-day moving average of price (show on graph to *a*), *(c)* an on-balance volume graph, and *(d)* a P and F graph, assuming an important price movement is $0.50.

Questions

a. Construct the graphs indicated above.
b. Agnes thinks ABC is a good stock to buy. Explain whether you agree with her.

Troy Darnell believes he can invest successfully if he can discover a way to determine how the overall market is likely to perform. He recalls from his college investments course that technical analysis deals with the topic of market forecasting, and he is considering using some of its methods. He has accumulated a substantial amount of monthly data, which he will analyze. The data appear in the accompanying table. Bond yields are based on high-grade and intermediate-grade corporate issues and on Treasury issues with maturities of over 20 years (long) and 3 months (short).

8.2
Troy Darnell
Looks at the
Indicators

a. What technical indicators are the series in the table intended to reflect? Discuss each briefly and *how* each is supposed to work.
b. Suppose Troy is attempting to forecast the index for the industrials. How well does each of the indicators perform this task? Discuss.
c. Is it clear that each indicator leads the industrials, or do the industrials lead the indicator? Explain.
d. Using whatever method(s) you believe are suitable, forecast the industrials for each of the first three months of year 3. How strongly do you feel about your forecasts? Discuss.

Questions

| Year/ Month | Market Indexes | | | Bond Yields | | | |
| | Indus- trials | Trans- portation | New Highs/ New Lows | High Grade | Int. Grade | Maturities | |
						Long	Short
1/1	100	100	8.5	9.0%	12.0%	8.0%	6.0%
2	104	102	9.2	9.5	12.1	8.2	6.4
3	106	101	7.2	9.7	12.6	8.3	6.7
4	108	103	6.3	10.3	13.7	8.8	6.5
5	107	103	6.7	10.1	13.8	8.8	7.1
6	104	101	2.1	9.8	13.9	8.9	7.7
7	102	102	1.5	10.3	14.6	9.4	8.3
8	96	98	1.7	10.6	14.8	9.7	9.1
9	92	99	0.4	10.8	14.7	9.9	10.2
10	93	96	0.5	10.5	14.2	9.5	10.4
11	91	96	0.6	10.2	14.0	9.2	10.5
12	95	95	1.3	10.1	13.5	9.0	10.2
2/1	98	100	4.2	9.8	12.7	8.9	9.1
2	104	102	3.8	9.6	12.1	8.8	8.6
3	109	106	2.7	9.1	12.0	8.4	8.8
4	116	109	3.1	8.7	11.3	8.1	8.6
5	123	107	2.8	8.4	10.4	7.8	7.6
6	120	112	4.8	8.1	9.6	7.3	6.8
7	126	114	3.9	8.0	9.5	7.4	6.2
8	124	116	5.3	8.2	9.5	7.5	5.9
9	127	122	6.9	8.3	9.4	7.6	5.3
10	127	124	8.2	8.5	9.6	7.5	5.1
11	131	125	8.5	8.6	9.6	8.1	5.1
12	124	120	2.6	8.9	10.8	8.3	5.2

HELPFUL
READING

Coghlan, Richard. "The Wave Is Your Friend." *Barron's*, June 7, 1993, p. 18.

Dorfman, John, R. "Luck or Logic? Debate Rages on Over 'Efficient Market' Theory," *The Wall Street Journal*, November 14, 1993, p. C1.

Engel, Charles, and Charles S. Morris. "Challenges to Stock Market Efficiency." *Economic Review*, Federal Reserve Bank of Kansas City, September/October 1991, pp. 21–35.

Lynch, Peter. "Beating the Street." *Money*, March 1993, pp. 120–35.

Raghavan, Anita. "CRB Futures Index Gets Suprisingly High Marks as a Barometer for Forecasting Inflation." *The Wall Street Journal*, October 12, 1992, p. C1.

Schultz, John. "The Giant Hedge." *Barron's*, August 9, 1993, p. 26.

Sheeline, Bill. "Knowing When to Take Your Profits." *Money*, April 1993, pp. 140–41.

PART TWO

CFA EXAMINATION QUESTIONS

1. What is the expected return of a zero-beta security?

   a. The market rate of return
   b. Zero rate of return
   c. A negative rate of return
   d. The risk-free rate of return

2. According to the CAPM, the risk premium an investor expects to receive on any stock or portfolio increases:

   a. directly with alpha.
   b. inversely with alpha.
   c. directly with beta.
   d. inversely with beta.

3. Which *one* of the following would best explain a situation where the ratio of "net income to total equity" for a firm is higher than the industry average, while the ratio of "net income to total assets" is lower than the industry average?

   a. Net profit margin is higher than the industry average.
   b. Debt ratio is higher than the industry average.
   c. Asset turnover is higher than the industry average.
   d. Equity multiplier must be lower than the industry average.

Reprinted with permission of the Association for Investment Management and Research. All questions are Level I Examination Questions, unless noted otherwise. Material related to questions 1 and 2 can be found in Chapter 6, questions 3 and 4 in Chapter 7, and questions 5–9 in Chapter 8. Material related to the problems can be found in Chapters 6 and 7.

4. Fundamental analysis uses the following technique:

    a. earnings and dividends prospects
    b. relative strength
    c. price momentum
    d. moving averages

5. Two basic assumptions of technical analysis are that security prices adjust:

    a. rapidly to new information and market prices are determined by the interaction of supply and demand.
    b. rapidly to new information and liquidity is provided by securities dealers.
    c. gradually to new information and prices are determined by the interaction of supply and demand.
    d. gradually to new information and liquidity is provided by securities dealers.

6. A support level is the price range at which a technical analyst would expect the:

    a. supply of a stock to increase substantially.
    b. supply of a stock to decrease substantially.
    c. demand for a stock to increase substantially.
    d. demand for a stock to decrease substantially.

7. When technical analysts say a stock has good "relative strength," they mean the:

    a. stock has performed well compared to other stocks in the same industry.
    b. total return on the stock has exceeded the total return on other stocks in the same industry.
    c. recent trading volume in the stock has exceeded the normal trading volume.
    d. ratio of the price of the stock to a market index has trended upward.

8. "Random walk" occurs when:

    a. past information is used in predicting future prices.
    b. future price changes are uncorrelated with past price changes.
    c. stock prices respond slowly to both new and old information.
    d. stock price changes are random but predictable.

9. An efficient market is one in which:

    a. transactions costs are low and liquidity is high.
    b. good fundamental analysis consistently produces superior portfolios.
    c. information is rapidly disseminated and reflected in prices.
    d. modern electronic communications speed trading.

PROBLEMS

Eastover Company (EO) is a large, diversified forest products company. Approximately 75% of its sales are from paper and forest products, with the remainder from financial services and real estate. The company owns 5.6 million acres of timberland, which is carried at very low historical cost on the balance sheet.

Peggy Mulroney, CFA, is an analyst at the investment counseling firm of Centurion Investments. She is assigned the task of assessing the outlook for Eastover, which is being considered for purchase, and comparing it with another forest products company in Centurion's portfolios, Southampton Corporation (SHC). SHC is a major producer of lumber products in the United States. Building products, primarily lumber and plywood, account for 89% of SHC's sales, with pulp accounting for the remainder. SHC owns 1.4 million acres of timberland, which is also carried at historical cost on the balance sheet. In SHC's case, however, that cost is not as far below current market as Eastover's.

I. Mulroney recalled from her CFA studies that the constant-growth discounted dividend model (DDM) was one way to arrive at a valuation for a company's common stock. She collected current dividend and stock price data for Eastover and Southampton, shown in Table 1 below.
   A. Using 11% as the required rate of return (i.e., discount rate) and a projected growth rate of 8%, **compute** a constant-growth DDM value for Eastover's stock and **compare** the computed value for Eastover to its stock price indicated in Table 1. Show calculations.

Mulroney's supervisor commented that a two-stage (DDM) may be more appropriate for companies such as Eastover and Southampton. Mulroney believes that Eastover and Southampton could grow more rapidly over the next three years and then settle in at a lower but sustainable rate of growth beyond 1994. Her estimates are indicated in Table 2 below.
   B. Using 11% as the required rate of return, **compute** the two-stage DDM value of Eastover's stock and **compare** that value to its stock price indicated in Table 1. Show calculations.

TABLE 1
Current Information

	Current Share Price	Current Dividends Per Share	1992 EPS Estimate	Current Book Value Per Share
Eastover (EO)	$ 28	$ 1.20	$ 1.60	$ 17.32
Southampton (SHC)	48	1.08	3.00	32.21
S&P 500	415	12.00	20.54	159.83

II. In addition to the discounted dividend model (DDM) approach, Mulroney decided to look at the price/earnings ratio and price/book ratio, relative to the S&P 500, for *both* Eastover and Southampton. Mulroney elected to perform this analysis using 1987–1991 and current data.

A. Using the data in Tables 1 and 3, **compute** *both* the current and the 5-year (1987–1991) average relative price/earnings ratios and relative price/book ratios for Eastover and Southampton. **Discuss** *each* company's current relative price/earnings ratio as compared to its 5-year average relative price/earnings ratio and *each* company's current relative price/book ratio as compared to its 5-year average relative price/book ratio.

B. **Briefly discuss** *one* disadvantage for *each* of the relative price/earnings and relative price/book approaches to valuation.

TABLE 2
Projected Growth Rates

	Next 3 Years (1992, 1993, 1994)	Growth Beyond 1994
Eastover (EO)	12%	8%
Southampton (SHC)	13%	7%

TABLE 3
Eastover Company (EO)

	1986	1987	1988	1989	1990	1991
Earnings per share	$ 1.27	$ 2.12	$ 2.68	$ 1.56	$ 1.87	$ 0.90
Dividends per share	0.87	0.90	1.15	1.20	1.20	1.20
Book value per share	14.82	16.54	18.14	18.55	19.21	17.21
Stock price						
–High	28	40	30	33	28	30
–Low	20	20	23	25	18	20
–Close	25	26	25	28	22	27
Average P/E	18.9x	14.2x	9.9x	18.6x	12.3x	27.8x
Average price/book	1.6x	1.8x	1.5x	1.6x	1.2x	1.5x

Southampton Corporation (SHC)

	1986	1987	1988	1989	1990	1991
Earnings per share	$ 1.66	$ 3.13	$ 3.55	$ 5.08	$ 2.46	$ 1.75
Dividends per share	0.77	0.79	0.89	0.98	1.04	1.08
Book value per share	24.84	27.47	29.92	30.95	31.54	32.21

TABLE 3
Continued

	1986	1987	1988	1989	1990	1991
Stock price						
–High	34	40	38	43	45	46
–Low	21	22	26	28	20	26
–Close	31	27	28	39	27	44
Average P/E	16.6x	9.9x	9.0x	7.0x	13.2x	20.6x
Average price/book	1.1x	1.1x	1.1x	1.2x	1.0x	1.1x

S&P 500

	1986	1987	1988	1989	1990	1991	5-Year Average (1987-1991)
Average P/E	15.8x	16.0x	11.1x	13.9x	15.6x	19.2x	15.2x
Average price/book	1.8x	2.1x	1.9x	2.2x	2.1x	2.3x	2.1x

Investing in Fixed-Income Securities

F ixed-income securities are important portfolio components for most investors. They are held primarily to accumulate funds for future expenditures, such as making a large purchase or living in retirement. On balance, they are safer than common stocks and many other assets, although recent volatile interest rates have increased their risks substantially. This change makes it important to understand the nature of debt instruments before you invest in them.

Chapter 9 uses the concepts developed in Chapter 3 to explain how returns on debt instruments are determined. It also analyzes interest-rate risk, explaining how this risk is measured and discussing its importance in selecting specific debt securities. Also covered is default risk, which is mea-sured with ratings prepared by ratings agencies.

Chapter 10 explains bondholder rights with respect to interest payments, claims on assets in liquidation, and other preferences. It identifies various forms of long-term debt, distinguishing among Treasury, federal agency, corporate, and local government debt instruments and indicating advantages and disadvantages of each. It also explains preferred stock, highlighting its characteristics and potential use in long-term portfolios.

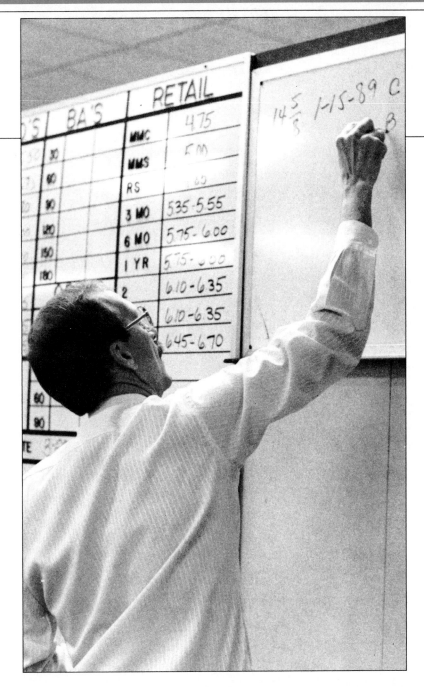

CHAPTER NINE

Risk and Return with Fixed-Income Securities

After you finish this chapter, you will be able to:

- understand the cash flows with both zero coupon and interest-bearing bonds and how to calculate current yield and yield to maturity for each.

- see what investors expect to receive from an interest rate.

- identify the interest-rate risk with a bond and see how it is measured with an interest elasticity coefficient or Macaulay's duration coefficient.

- understand the reinvestment problem with its reinvestment risk and rollover risk.

- recognize default risk and become familiar with quality ratings published by Moody's and Standard and Poor's.

- see that interest rates have a history of volatility and that forecasting future rates is virtually impossible.

- identify the pattern of short-versus long-term rates and understand the concept of a yield curve.

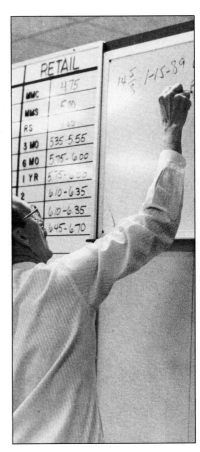

A fixed-income security, commonly called a bond, represents an obligation by its issuer to pay interest (if interest is promised) on a timely basis and to repay the loan at its maturity. This is a legally binding obligation giving you the right to seek remedies in court if the issuer reneges. Despite legal protection, bonds can be risky. To begin with, a promise to pay interest and principal is one thing and actually paying it is another. Issuers do default, leaving their creditors with partially or totally worthless claims. Then, even if the creditor meets all the obligations, you may still hold a risky investment if it has a long maturity and if interest rates in general are volatile.

In Chapters 3 and 4, we saw the historical returns and risks from key debt instruments: U.S. Treasury bills, U.S. Treasury bonds, and corporate bonds. In this chapter, we examine in greater detail how the returns from bonds are calculated and why bonds are risky. We also consider the historical volatility of interest rates and raise the issue of whether interest rates can be forecasted.

RETURN WITH BONDS

Zero coupon bonds: bonds that pay no periodic interest

Bonds offer returns in two ways: First, many pay periodic interest, called *coupon interest*. A bond, for example, usually pays interest twice a year. Second, some bonds are redeemed at prices greater than their purchase prices. These latter bonds are called **zero coupon bonds,** while the former are called **interest-bearing bonds,** or **coupon bonds.** Your cash flows from each are a bit different, as is the method of calculating their yields.

Interest-bearing bonds: bonds that pay periodic (usually semiannual) interest

Cash Flows

A cash flow refers to cash you pay out or cash you receive from an investment. The timelines presented in Chapter 3 showed cash flows in a format that helped us determine present and future values. This approach is continued, but our emphasis now is on measuring investment rate of return, or yield.

Zero Coupon Bonds   Because a zero coupon bond pays no periodic interest, your entire return consists of the discount. Recalling that an investment's dollar holding period return (HPR) is

$$\$HPR = R + (P_1 - P_0)$$

and because $R = 0$, the return is simply $(P_1 - P_0)$. Exhibit 9.1 shows a timeline for a 10-year zero coupon bond.

Zero coupon bonds—zeros, for short—are issued by both governments and corporations. They have become popular with investors who are accumulating funds for retirement. Because they pay no periodic interest, you don't

EXHIBIT 9.1

Cash flows from a zero coupon bond

have to worry about how to reinvest such interest to accumulate a retirement nest egg. In striking contrast to bills, their maturities are much longer. Many zeros have maturities of 10 years or longer, and some go as long as 40 years. The zero shown in Exhibit 9.1 has a 10-year maturity. If you bought it for $385 and the issuer redeemed it for $1,000 (the most common redemption value, or face value), your return would be $615.

Interest-Bearing Bonds   Most long-term bonds are not zeros; in contrast, they pay interest on a regular basis. The amount of interest paid each year is determined by their coupon rate and face value. The coupon rate is expressed as a percent, which is then applied to the face value to determine interest dollars. The bond shown in Exhibit 9.2, for example, has a 10% coupon rate and a $1,000 face value. Interest each year will be $100 (0.10 × $1,000). Because most bonds pay interest semiannually, you would get an interest

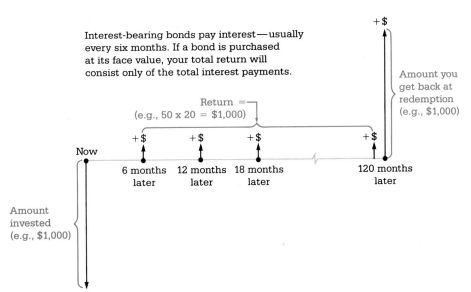

EXHIBIT 9.2

Interest-bearing bond purchased and redeemed at face value

payment of $50 every six months. Exhibit 9.2 assumes you buy the bond at its face value, which means your return consists of the 20 interest payments, or $1,000 in total.

When bonds are issued, they often are priced at face value. However, bonds also can be purchased in the secondary market, where their prices usually are quite different from face value: either lower or higher, depending on credit ease or tightness after issuance. Exhibit 9.3 shows a 10-year bond bought at $750. Assuming a redemption price of $1,000 means your total return consists of both the 20 interest payments of $50 each and the discount of $250. Total return, then, is $1,250.

Interest-bearing bonds may also trade in the secondary market at premiums to face value. For example, the 10-year bond we are discussing might have been purchased at, say, $1,100, rather than $750. Because a premium is the opposite of a discount, we will not show a separate timeline; however, you should understand that the $HPR would be only $900—$1,000 in coupon interest less the $100 premium above face value. Before going on, we should also note that bonds trading at discounts from their face values are called **discount bonds** and those trading at premiums are called **premium bonds.**

Discount bond: bond selling at a price less than its face value

Premium bond: bond selling at a price greater than its face value

Calculating Yields

A statement about an investment's yield considers its dollar return in relation to the amount invested and the length of time the investment is held. For ease of calculation, the latter item often is ignored, and we refer to the yield

EXHIBIT 9.3
Interest-bearing bond purchased at a discount and redeemed at face value

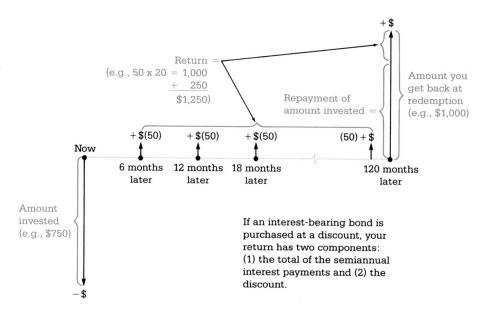

EXHIBIT 9.4

Calculating the current yield for interest-bearing bonds

Panel A: A Bond Bought at Face Value

$$CY = \frac{I}{P_0}$$

I = annual interest
P_0 = market value (also amount invested)

↑ current yield

↑ ratio of annual interest to market value

Illustration assuming: I = $ 100
P_0 = $1,000

$$CY = \frac{\$100}{\$1,000} = 0.1000 \text{ or } 10.000\%$$

Panel B: A Bond Bought at Less Than Face Value

Same formula as above

Illustration assuming: I = $100
P_0 = $750

$$CY = \frac{\$100}{\$750} = 0.13333 \quad \text{or} \quad 13.333\%$$

as a **current yield.** In many instances, it is a somewhat imprecise measurement, and a more accurate yield is yield to maturity. Each of these yields should be understood.

Current Yield The current yield (CY) for zeros is a meaningless concept because they offer no current return. Thus, CY applies only to interest-bearing bonds. The CY for an interest-bearing bond bought at face value is shown in Panel *A* of Exhibit 9.4. As you see, maturity is ignored. The bond illustrated has a CY of 10%. The CY for an interest-bearing bond bought at less than face value is shown in Panel *B* of Exhibit 9.4. In this example, the CY is greater than 10%—it's 13.333%—because the bond's purchase price was $750, not $1,000. Also, the CY for the premium bond mentioned above is 0.091, or 9.1% ($100/$1,100).

Yield to Maturity In precise terms, the **yield to maturity (YTM)** is a specific rate that causes the present value of the debt instrument's discounted cash inflows to equal its cash outflow (the purchase price). You must remember the present value concept explained in Chapter 3 for this definition to make sense. Finding a YTM means finding present values of the periodic interest and the redemption price and adding the two together to equal the

Current yield: yield measurement that does not consider the amount of time a bond is held; calculated by dividing a bond's price into its annual interest

Yield to maturity: specific rate that equates the sum of discounted future cash flows of a bond to its current price instrument's purchase price. This procedure is shown in Exhibit 9.5, using the 10% bond purchased at face value as an example. The present value of the coupon interest payments is $623.11 and the present value of the future redemption value is $376.89. Adding the two together equals the bond's current price of $1,000.

The YTM for a zero coupon bond can be calculated with a financial calculator. For example, if you are using the HP 12C, input the following: current price (−$385) as the present value, redemption value ($1,000) as the future value, and years to maturity (10) as n. Depress the i key and read the answer of 10.0%.

You can also use the future value of $1 table to approximate the YTM. First, find the ratio of future value to present value: it is 2.5974 ($1,000/$385). Then, go down to the 10th period on the table (Appendix A.1) and over to the column value that is closest to 2.5974. You should find this number is 2.5937, which is in the 10% column; so, the YTM is 10%. In this case, the two numbers—2.5974 and 2.5937—are close. This may not always be true, which means you have to interpolate to find a reasonably close approximation of the YTM.

Exhibit 9.6 shows YTM calculations for interest-bearing bonds. Panel A shows that YTM is the same as CY if the bond is bought at face value. If the bond's price is more or less than face value, YTM must be calculated. Panel B shows the steps you take with a financial calculator. Notice that 20 (not 10) periods are involved because coupon interest is paid semiannually. Notice also that the answer is a semiannual rate of return. YTM usually is expressed

EXHIBIT 9.5
YTM illustrated

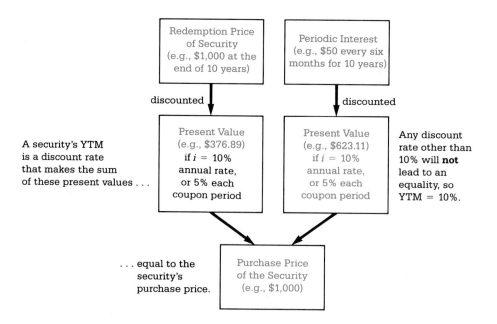

EXHIBIT 9.6
Calculating YTM for interest-bearing bonds

Panel A: A Bond Bought at Face Value

Same amount as current yield; see Panel *A* of Exhibit 9.4

Panel B: A Bond Bought at Less or More Than Face Value

I. Solution using a financial calculator (the HP 12C) and assuming a bond with a 10% coupon rate, 10-year maturity, and selling at $750; that is,

$$P_1 = \text{redemption value} = FV = \$1,000$$
$$P_0 = \text{current market price} = PV = \$750$$
$$I = \text{coupon interest} = PMT = \$50$$
$$n = \text{number of periods} = 20$$

Enter	Depress Keys	Operation
—	[f] [CLX]	Clears registers
1000	[FV]	Enters redemption value
750	[CHS] [PV]	Enters market price as an outlay (a negative number)
50	[PMT]	Enters semiannual coupon interest
20	[*n*]	Enters number of interest periods
—	[*i*]	Read YTM of 7.4414%. This can be annualized by multiplying by 2: $2 \times 7.4414 = 14.883\%$.

II. Short-Cut Approach

$$YTM = \frac{\text{annual interest } + \text{ average capital gain (loss)}}{\text{average investment}}$$

$$YTM = \frac{I + \dfrac{P_1 - P_0}{n}}{\dfrac{P_1 + P_0}{2}}$$

Illustration assuming same values as above:

$$YTM = \frac{\$100 + \dfrac{\$1,000 - \$750}{10}}{\dfrac{\$1,000 + \$750}{2}}$$

$$YTM = \frac{\$100 + \dfrac{\$250}{10}}{\dfrac{\$1,750}{2}}$$

$$YTM = \frac{\$100 + \$25}{\$875} = \frac{\$125}{\$875} = .14286 \text{ or } 14.286\%$$

as an annual equivalent, so multiply the answer by 2. As you see, the annual return for the example bond is 14.883%.

Without a financial calculator, a solution is lengthy and less accurate. Present value tables can be used with a series of trial discount rates until the sum of the discounted interest payments and discounted redemption value equal the bond's price. This is time-consuming. A short-cut approach—also shown in Panel *B* of Exhibit 9.6—is sometimes used, even though its approximation of YTM can be inaccurate. As you see, 14.286% is quite a bit less than 14.883%.

If you need to make YTM calculations frequently, using a financial calculator such as the HP 12C is a must. Before buying a financial calculator, make sure it will perform such calculations. Most of the inexpensive ones do not.

What Does the YTM Imply?   As mentioned above, YTM makes the sum of discounted cash inflows equal purchase price. But in the case of an interest-bearing bond, this also implies that its periodic interest payments are reinvested at the YTM. Is this a reasonable assumption? It may or may not be, depending on your assessment of future investment opportunities. If interest rates are expected to fall, you may not reinvest at rates as high as the YTM; if interest rates rise, you are likely to earn higher rates. YTM is a measurement of profitability, and it should not be relied on to determine future cash flows arising from reinvested interest.

For example, suppose you bought the 10-year coupon bond we have been discussing with a YTM of 10%. Assume further that you think you also can invest the $50 interest each six-month period at 10% (5% per interest period). As shown in Exhibit 9.7, your accumulated funds at the end of 10 years is $2,653, of which $653 is interest on interest. The calculations below show how these amounts are determined.

Future value interest factor for a $1 annuity compounded at 5% for 20 periods (from Appendix A.2) = 33.066; thus, $50 × 33.066 = $1,653. If we subtract the total coupon interest of $1,000 (20 × $50), we arrive at the interest on interest of $653. The total future value, then, has three components:

Coupon interest	$1,000
Interest on interest	653
Redemption value	1,000
Total	$2,653

Suppose, though, you reinvested at some other annual rate—say, 14% (7% per interest period); now, the interest on interest is $1,050 [(40.995 × $50) − $1,000]. The point is, your accumulated funds depend on both reinvestment rates and the accumulation period, and neither has anything to do with a calculated YTM. The accumulation period (maturity) may have a greater

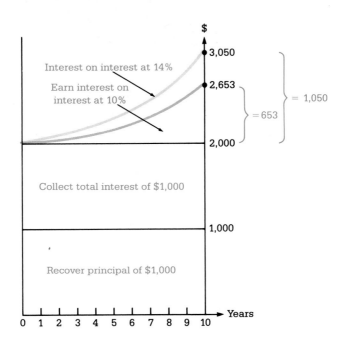

EXHIBIT 9.7
Future value of a
10-year 10% bond,
assuming interest
payments are
reinvested at 10% or
14% annual rate

impact on the interest-on-interest factor than does the reinvestment rate. This point is underscored emphatically in Exhibit 9.8, which shows the future value of a 20-year, 10% bond. As you see, at the end of 20 years, interest on interest is $4,040, more than six times as much as it is at the end of 10 years!

Relation Between YTM and Bond Price It is important to understand the relationship between YTM and bond price. Specifically, as YTM increases (decreases), bond price decreases (increases); that is, YTM and bond price are

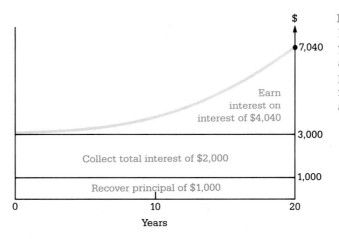

EXHIBIT 9.8
Future value of a 20-year 10% bond, assuming interest payments are reinvested at 10% annual rate

inversely related. To illustrate, let's find the price of the 10% bond, assuming semiannual interest and annual YTMs of first 12% and then 8%.

At 12%:

> (a) Present value of the coupon interest:
> Present value of $1 annuity (from Appendix A.4) at
> 6% for 20 periods = 11.4699
> 11.4699 × $50 = $573.50
>
> (b) Present value of the redemption value:
> Present value of $1 (from Appendix A.3)
> at 6% for 20 years = 0.3118
> 0.3118 × $1,000 = $311.80
>
> (c) Present value = $573.50 + $311.80 = $885.30

At 8%:

> (a) Present value of the coupon interest:
> Present value of $1 annuity (from Appendix A.4) at
> 4% for 20 periods = 13.5903
> 13.5903 × $50 = $679.52
>
> (b) Present value of the redemption value:
> Present value of $1 (from Appendix A.3)
> at 4% for 20 years = 0.4564
> 0.4564 × $1,000 = $456.40
>
> (c) Present value = $679.52 + $456.40 = $1,135.92

The inverse relationship between YTM and price is an important factor in measuring a bond's riskiness, a topic to be covered shortly.

What Investors Expect in an Interest Rate

Under what conditions would you be willing to loan money to borrowers, and how much interest must they pay to make the investment attractive? To answer these questions, you would have to consider your preferences for current versus future consumption, the expected inflation rate during the term of the loan, your need for liquidity, and the probability the lender will make timely interest and principal payments.

Preference for Current Consumption   Given a choice between consuming goods and services today versus consuming them in the future, most of us will choose current consumption. Why not? Why should we defer consumption enjoyment unless we are compensated for doing so? Most people will not, which explains why lenders demand a reward for giving up current consumption. This reward is interest. With it, you can consume *more* in the future than you can today, making abstinence worthwhile.

Real Versus Nominal Return   A nominal return means the actual dollars (or percent) an investor receives; a real return adjusts the nominal return to allow for price changes taking place during the investment period. If you made a $100, one-year loan at 10% interest, you would get back $110 a year later. If prices rose 5% during the year, it would cost $105 to buy the same amount of goods and services you gave up a year earlier. Your real return is not $10; it is $5. Your real rate of return using current (not last year's) prices is about 4.76%. You should recall this calculation from Chapter 4 where the real rate of return *(r′)* was compared with a nominal rate *(r)* and the inflation rate *(i)*:

$$r' = \frac{1.0 + r}{1.0 + i} - 1.0$$

Compensation for Giving Up Liquidity   Investing means giving up holding cash, the most liquid of all assets. Because the future is uncertain, we can never be sure the cash we invest will not be needed during the investment period. Even if we can convert the investment back to cash, there usually are transaction costs and personal inconveniences involved, and we may even take a loss in selling the instrument. All other things the same, most investors prefer liquidity and demand a premium if they must forgo it. The poorer the liquidity, the greater the premium.

Compensation for Assuming Default Risk   If there is a question about a borrower's ability to meet her financial obligations, lenders will also demand a premium for this added risk, and the greater the doubt, the greater the premium. As we explained in Chapter 4, ability to handle debt is determined by both the nature of the borrower's business and the total amount of debt outstanding. If you buy the bonds of a wildcatting oil company loaded with debt, you should expect a high premium for assuming default risk.

Putting It Together   An expected interest rate must take all the factors above into consideration, as Exhibit 9.9 shows. You begin with an estimate of your required real rate of return. The next step is to estimate the period's inflation (deflation) rate to arrive at a nominal rate. This rate must be high enough to induce you to be a lender. After this is done, you add premiums for illiquidity and potential default to arrive at the total returns you need from specific debt instruments. If actual returns available in the marketplace are less than these, you will not invest; on the other hand, if some or all of the market rates exceed your required rates, you will invest.

　　Do investors actually go through such detailed procedures before investing? There is good evidence suggesting many do, although they don't neces-

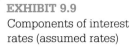
EXHIBIT 9.9
Components of interest
rates (assumed rates)

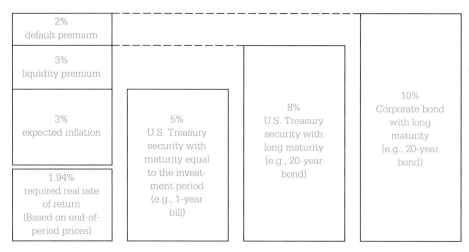

sarily think in terms of specific risk premiums or adjust for inflation in the same mechanical way. Keep in mind, we are talking about *expected* rates of return at the beginning of a period, not *realized* rates after the period is over. You may expect a real rate of 1.94%, for example, but if inflation is greater than 3%, your realized rate will be less. Such a situation seemed to exist during the inflationary period 1966–82. Investors apparently consistently underestimated inflation, leading to very low and even negative real rates of return on debt instruments in some of those years. However, the situation reversed in the period 1982–90 when investors overestimated inflation. Real rates of return were exceptionally high during that period. Since 1990, real rates have been close to their long-run historical averages, particularly for short- and intermediate-term securities.

RISKS WITH BONDS

Both liquidity and default risks must be measured in specific debt instruments. Ideally, we want to have a quantitative estimate or qualitative ranking for each risk component. With these, it is then possible to determine if a debt instrument's expected return is large enough to warrant our investment. We must also consider risks associated with reinvesting periodic coupon interest.

Bond Prices and Changing Interest Rates

A number of forces influence securities markets. They include actions of the federal government (the Treasury) and the federal reserve system (the Fed), investors' rational and emotional reactions, the need for funds by business firms, and international influences. All these are important in debt markets because their combined impacts determine the level of interest rates and the volume of credit during a period. Moreover, the network of cause-and-effect relations among interest rates and financial variables is indeed complex and not fully understood by anyone. By practicing a policy of tight money, for example, the Fed may both lower and raise interest rates simultaneously. Tightness usually has its initial impact on short-term debt instruments, increasing their rates. These higher rates in turn are thought to spill over into long-term markets, increasing rates there as well. But if the Fed's policy is seen as lowering the long-term inflation rate, this could lead to a greater demand for long-term debt instruments, thereby decreasing their rates. Disentangling those separate influences may be impossible.

Regardless of what causes interest rates to change, the heart of the problem, from an investor's perspective, is what happens to the prices of previously purchased debt instruments while changes take place. Look at it this way: Suppose you bought a 10-year bond such as one we have been discussing, the 10% bond with a 10% YTM. You thought the bond was a good investment and planned to hold it until your retirement in 10 years when it matures. Now, imagine the day after you bought it, some extraordinary event takes place, causing all interest rates to rise one full percentage point, which is a 10% increase in rates. Newly issued bonds that are identical to yours now pay investors $110 a year in interest, while yours still pays only $100. Who would buy your bond for the price you paid—$1,000? No one. To sell it, you would have to lower the price so that its YTM would also be 11%. This loss in value was the liquidity risk you faced when you bought the bond.

You might argue that if you don't sell the bond, you really won't have a loss. This is *not* so. If you don't sell, your loss is in the form of an opportunity cost. Had you waited one day, you could have bought, for the same price, a bond that provided $10 more interest each year for the next 10 years. This is no less a loss than your direct cash loss from selling. Your only decision is when to take the loss: you can take it quickly by selling, or slowly over 10 years by holding. True, interest rates might go back down to 10% in the future, which means the price of the bond goes back up to $1,000. But you would have a similar price increase with the 11% bond.

Changes in debt instruments' prices resulting from changes in interest rates is called interest-rate risk, a topic introduced in Chapter 4. In reality, this risk is part of liquidity risk. But in addition to potential loss of capital, liquidity risk includes marketability risk: factors that might make selling an instrument difficult, such as a poor resale market or high transactions costs. For securities that do not have these impediments, liquidity risk and interest-rate risk are the same thing. In the material below, we will use the narrower expression—interest-rate risk—to clearly identify the topic of concern to us.

The Importance of Maturity   We showed earlier, in the discussion of reinvesting periodic interest payments, the sensitivity of a future value to the interest-on-interest accumulation factor. You should recall that extending maturity increases appreciably the importance of interest-on-interest. You

BOX 9.1   INVESTMENT INSIGHTS

Does Your Bond Portfolio Need to Be Immunized?

Before responding to this question, we ought to ask, what disease can our bond portfolio catch? The answer is that it may not achieve our investment objective, if that objective is to accumulate a certain sum of money by a certain date. You should understand that the most popular bonds—those paying coupon interest—involve reinvestment risk; that is, after you receive coupon interest and then reinvest it, if reinvestment interest rates fall after you buy the bonds, your accumulation will also fall short of the target, even though the bonds' value will increase. The problem is that the value increase does not offset the shortfall with the reinvested coupon interest.

The trick to avoiding this potential problem is to select bonds using their duration coefficients as a guide, rather than their maturities. So, if the investment horizon is 10 years, don't buy 10-year bonds; rather, buy bonds with a 10-year duration coefficient. This simple procedure immunizes your portfolio in many cases. Now, price appreciation equals lost reinvested interest and your target accumulation is preserved. Immunization works the other way as well: if interest rates go up, price depreciation is offset by enhanced reinvested interest.

As you probably have guessed, something this simple has to have a catch. The problem here is that duration coefficients will change every time reinvestment rates change, which means you must constantly monitor and adjust your portfolio to keep its duration coefficient equal to the holding period. For example, if reinvestment rates rise, the existing portfolio duration coefficient falls. You could then restore the previous duration coefficient by selling some bonds and replacing them with other bonds that have longer maturities. Moreover, the mere passage of time changes duration coefficients and also necessitates adjustments.

All this hassle can be avoided by using zero coupon bonds, which have no reinvestment risk. But zeros also have problems. First, there is an income tax flaw because you must accrue interest each year even though you don't receive it; second, there are far fewer zeros (particularly in corporate issues) than coupon bonds, which limits your choice; and third, zeros might have lower yields. When these factors are considered, the extra work with immunization may prove profitable.

should see, too, that if the reinvestment rate changes, its greatest impact will be on securities with long maturities. The longer the maturity, everything else the same, the riskier the security. Keep in mind, the interest-on-interest concept is simply a way of analyzing the situation. Even securities that do not pay periodic interest—zeros, for example—also have maturity risk. In fact, they are the riskiest of all bonds, as we will see below.

The Importance of Coupon Rate Why do zeros have a greater price risk than interest-bearing bonds? Because you must wait until maturity to recover any of your investment. This is not the case with interest-bearing bonds. If interest rates rise while you hold them, you will at least gradually recover your investment through the periodic interest payments, which are available to invest at the existing higher rates; with a zero, you recover nothing until the end. This means your opportunity costs are highest, and the longer the maturity, the greater they are.

Coupon rate and maturity, then, work together to produce interest-rate risk. Low coupon rates and long maturities mean considerable risk, while high coupons and short maturities mean less. For example, if you buy a zero coupon bond with a 40-year maturity, you have about the riskiest debt instrument available, not considering default risk.

Determining Interest-Rate Risk

Interest-rate risk can be determined by measuring the sensitivity of changes in a debt instrument's price in relation to changes in its YTM. There are two measurement concepts, the interest elasticity coefficient (also called bond price elasticity coefficient) and Macaulay's duration coefficient.

Calculating the Interest Elasticity Coefficient The **interest elasticity coefficient, E**, is defined as

$$E = \frac{\text{(Percentage Change in Bond Price)}}{\text{(Percentage Change in YTM)}}$$

Interest elasticity coefficient: measurement of the percentage of change in a bond's price relative to a percentage of change in its yield to maturity

Because price and YTM always move in opposite directions, the sign of E is always negative. That being the case, the negative sign usually is ignored in discussion. Exhibit 9.10 shows elasticity calculations for securities discussed above (numbers 1, 2, and 3). The other security (4) has been added to provide an additional example.

Imagine that one day after you make a selection, the security's YTM increases by 10%. (This is a rather extreme jump for one day and not likely to happen. In the past, though, 10% increases have not been uncommon for periods as short as two or three weeks.) Column 2 shows the first YTM, while column 3 shows the second, which is 10% higher than the first. The YTMs shown in column 2 are those calculated earlier for securities 1 through 3; security 4's YTM is assumed to be the same as security 1's. The arithmetic in Exhibit 9.10 is straightforward. Notice that averages for prices and YTMs are used to determine the bases for calculating percentage changes. This is necessary to avoid the bias favoring percentage increases over percentage decreases when the base is the first value. (See Chapter 3 for additional discussion of this topic.)

EXHIBIT 9.10
Calculating interest elasticity coefficients assuming a 10% increase in YTM

| Security (1) | YTMs (%) | | Prices | | Elasticity Coefficient* (6) |
	First (2)	Second (3)	First (4)	Second (5)	
1. 10-year zero	10.00	11.00	385	352	−0.94
2. 10-year, 10% bond selling at face value	10.00	11.00	1,000	940	−0.65
3. 10-year, 10% bond selling at $750	14.88	16.37	750	692	−0.85
4. 20-year zero	10.00	11.00	149	124	−1.92

*NOTE: To avoid bias in selecting a base to determine percentage changes, the averages of the two YTMs and two prices are used. Thus, the formula is:

$$E = \frac{\dfrac{\text{Change in Price}}{(P_1 + P_2)/2}}{\dfrac{\text{Change in YTM}}{(\text{YTM}_1 + - \text{YTM}_2)/2}}$$

Applying the formula to security 1 gives the results below:

$$E = \frac{\dfrac{385 - 352}{(385 + 352)/2}}{\dfrac{10.00 - 11.00}{(10.00 + 11.00)/2}} = \frac{\dfrac{33}{368.5}}{\dfrac{-1.00}{10.5}} = \frac{0.0896}{-0.0952} = -0.94$$

Interpreting Elasticity Coefficients   The absolute value of E (that is, ignore the negative sign) tells us how sensitive a debt instrument's price is to changes in interest rates. In doing this, it ranks debt instruments according to interest-rate risk. The elasticity numbers in column 6 of Exhibit 9.10 clearly rank the securities shown there. Security 4, the 20-year zero, is the riskiest; it is twice as risky as security 1, the 10-year zero, and almost three times riskier than security 2, the 10% bond selling at face value. Notice also that by comparing security 1 with security 4, we have an example of the point made earlier that longer maturity means greater risk. Comparing security 1 with security 2 confirms that a lower coupon rate adds to risk.

Macaulay's duration concept: bond risk measurement that considers the length of time needed to recover a bond's principal and coupon interest

Macaulay's Duration Concept   Like elasticity, **Macaulay's duration concept** (named after F. R. Macaulay) is an attempt to measure risk in a debt instrument. It is defined as the weighted average time required to recover principal and all interest payments. On a first reading, this statement seems confusing because we assume it takes the entire term to maturity to recover principal and all interest. The 10%, 10-year bond, for example, will pay $1,000 in total interest ($100 a year) and is redeemed for $1,000. Don't you have to hold the bond 10 years to recover this $2,000? No. If you can reinvest the periodic interest payments you receive at *any* positive rate of interest, it will take less time, how much less depending on the reinvestment rate. The answer to the apparent riddle is the interest-on-interest concept explained earlier.

To see this, let's assume an extreme example: suppose you could reinvest the periodic interest payments at a 50% annual rate. The first year's interest of $100 would grow to $3,844 nine years later! You could forget the other nine years of interest and principal and have $1,844 left over. So, the three important factors determining how quickly interest and principal are recovered are maturity, coupon rate, and the assumed reinvestment rate.

Calculating the Duration Coefficient   Unlike the interest elasticity coefficient, the **duration coefficient, D,** is not calculated quickly, although the calculations are simple. Exhibit 9.11 shows the procedure for the 10%, 10-year bond selling at face value. The assumed reinvestment rate is the bond's YTM of 10%. The value of the duration coefficient, D, is 6.7644, which is the weighted average number of years it takes to recover the $2,000 of interest and principal. Also unlike interest elasticity, which is a "pure" number, duration is dimensioned in particular units—years.

Duration coefficient: measurement of Macaulay's duration

Interpreting and Using D Values   What does a D value imply in terms of risk? As you might guess, the higher the value, the greater the risk because it

EXHIBIT 9.11
Calculating a duration coefficient, D

(1) Year	(2) Cash Flow*	(3) PV Factor (YTM = 10%)	(4) PV of Cash Flow	(5) PV/Price	(6) (1) × (5)
1	100	0.909	90.90	0.0909	0.0909
2	100	0.826	82.60	0.0826	0.1652
3	100	0.751	75.10	0.0751	0.2253
4	100	0.683	68.30	0.0683	0.2732
5	100	0.621	62.10	0.0621	0.3105
6	100	0.565	56.50	0.0565	0.3390
7	100	0.513	51.30	0.0513	0.3591
8	100	0.467	46.70	0.0467	0.3736
9	100	0.424	42.40	0.0424	0.3816
10	1,100	0.386	424.60	0.4246	4.2460
Totals	2,000	—	1,000.00	1.0000	6.7644
				Duration Coefficient, D = 6.7644	

*Annual interest is assumed for case of presentation.

implies a longer recovery period. Exhibit 9.12 shows D values for the four securities shown in Exhibit 9.10. As you see, the 20-year zero is the riskiest, while the 10% coupon bond selling at $750 is the least risky.

A duration coefficient allows us to estimate how much a bond's price will change, given a change in its YTM. The steps to make the estimate are as follows:

1. Calculate an adjusted D value, which is called the modified duration coefficient. This is done by dividing the known D value by (1.0 + new YTM), expressing YTM as a decimal. For the 10% bond selling at face value, we have

    $$\text{adjusted } D = 6.7644/(1.0 + 0.11) = 6.7644/(1.11) = 6.0941$$

2. Multiply the adjusted D by the absolute change in YTM, expressing the change in decimal form. Such change for the 10% bond is 0.01. Then, the

    $$\text{percentage change in price} = 6.0941 \times 0.01 = 0.060941$$

3. Multiply the percent change in price by the initial price to determine the absolute change in price:

    $$\text{absolute change in price} = 0.060941 \times \$1,000 = \$60.94$$

Duration coefficients, then, estimate risk and provide estimates of potential losses (or gains) if interest rates happen to rise (or fall) after they are purchased. If you want to have a low-risk bond portfolio, you should select bonds with low D (or E) values; if you want risk, expecting rates to fall, then select bonds with high values. Finally, you should note in Exhibit 9.12 the zero coupon bonds have D values equal to their terms to maturity: 10 and 20 years. This is the case with all zeros.

EXHIBIT 9.12
Risk rankings with D value

Security	D Value	Rank*
1. 10-year, zero coupon bond	10.0000	3
2. 10-year, 10% bond selling at face value	6.7644	2
3. 10-year, 10% bond selling at $750	6.2266	1
4. 20-year, zero coupon bond	20.0000	4

*1 = lowest risk.

The Reinvestment Problem

Our discussion of interest-rate risk thus far has focused on the relation of a bond's price to changes in its YTM. There is another aspect of changing interest rates that concerns investors. It has to do with the problem of reinvesting periodic interest payments that will be received over the bond's remaining life. Suppose interest rates rise immediately after you buy the 10% bond that we have been discussing. The undesirable effect is the bond's price will fall. There also is a desirable effect insofar as you now will be able to reinvest all remaining coupon interest at higher rates. The situation works in reverse if interest rates decline; then, the desirable effect of a price increase accompanies the undesirable effect of lower reinvestment rates.

Reinvestment Risk   Because future reinvestment rates are unknown, the uncertainty surrounding the accumulation of funds over a given period is referred to as **reinvestment risk.** Interestingly, zero coupon bonds, which have the highest price risk, also have the lowest reinvestment risk. In fact, because they have no interest to reinvest, there is no risk. That is why zeros make ideal instruments for investment goals designed to accumulate specific sums of money. In contrast, bonds with high coupon rates present greater risks because there are greater interest amounts to reinvest. Also interesting is the fact that within this context, even short-term debt instruments are risky because each time they mature you must reinvest their redemption amounts into new issues of the same type of security or into other kinds of securities. When maturing instruments are replaced with new instruments of the same type of security—Treasury bills, for example—the risk of reinvesting at lower rates is called **rollover risk.**

Reinvestment risk: risk associated with the uncertainty of future investment rates

Rollover risk: assumes that as an instrument matures, funds received are reinvested in a newer issue of the same instrument

A Reinvestment Example   To illustrate the problem of reinvesting future coupon interest, let's consider an example. Suppose you intend to accumulate $20,000 at the end of 10 years. If you select zeros, then you can lock in the future amount by simply buying 20 10-year bonds. At maturity, each bond is worth $1,000, and so, you meet the target. Assuming a YTM of 10%, which means a price of $385 per bond, you need to invest $7,700 (20 × $385) today.

Rather than selecting zeros, assume that you invested $7,700 in the 10% coupon bonds, presumed also to have a YTM of 10% and thus selling at $1,000 per bond. (Assume you can purchase 7.7 bonds.) Now, imagine that immediately after purchase, interest rates fall drastically and remain low over the next 10 years, so that you reinvest periodic interest at an average annual rate of only 4%. In this case, you will accumulate only $2,215 per bond and only $17,056 in total ($2,215 × 7.7). The $2,215 has the following components:

$$
\begin{array}{lr}
\text{Coupon interest} = \$50 \times 20 = & \$1,000 \\
\text{Interest on interest} = & 215 \\
\text{Redemption value} & \underline{1,000} \\
\text{Total} & \$2,215
\end{array}
$$

You should recall our previous presentation for determining accumulations. In the present example, you are using a future value of $1 annuity factor for 2% for 20 periods (24.297 from Appendix A.2); then, 24.297 × $50 = $1,215.

With the coupon bonds, you miss the target by $2,944 ($20,000 − $17,056). How important is the miss? That depends on how important was the goal. At any rate, you should now understand the nature of reinvestment risk.

Managing Reinvestment Risk   As noted above, managing reinvestment risk can be simple if the investor selects only zeros. There may be instances, however, when yields are better with coupon issues. So, the bond manager needs to consider each in designing a portfolio. Managing reinvestment risk is simply one aspect of managing the total bond portfolio. Professional bond managers are concerned with both yield and adequate liquidity. For example, suppose you manage a bond portfolio for the benefit of a company's retirement program. Over time, you must have sufficient cash to meet retirement obligations, but concurrently, you want to invest funds to earn high rates of return. Balancing the two requires considerable skill and an understanding of methods and tools that go beyond this introductory text.

Default Risk

Default risk: possibility of not receiving a debt instrument's promised cash flows

Default risk is understood as the possibility of not receiving a debt instrument's promised cash flows. The higher this probability, the greater is default risk. Unlike interest-rate risk, which affects all debt instruments, default risk applies when the issuer's financial strength is in question. The only securities without default risk are those issued by the U.S. Treasury, which has access to the currency printing press, if that is ever needed.

Estimating default risk is a difficult task, particularly as it applies to evaluating the chances of receiving a timely and full redemption, which may take place many years in the future. Despite the difficulties, estimates must be made. Fortunately, we need not develop our own figures; professional rating agencies do the job for us. Our tasks are first to understand what their ratings mean and then to have a realistic understanding of how yields vary among debt instruments with different quality ratings.

The Rating Agencies   The two best-known rating agencies are Moody's and Standard and Poor's. Each has its own formula for determining quality ratings. These formulas consider a variety of factors that measure a borrower's capacity to meet its debt obligations, the most important being its liquidity, debt-carrying capacity, and earnings (these were explained in Chapter 6). Each agency evaluates proposed new debt issues and gives them a rating. These ratings are letter grades, which range from Aaa to C for Moody's and from AAA to D for Standard and Poor's. Exhibit 9.13 shows these ratings. Within each letter grade, the agencies further refine the grade: Standard and Poor's uses + or − to show that an issue is in the higher or lower end of a grade, while Moody's uses numbers. For example, an A+ or A1 rating means an issue is at the top of the A class; an A− or A3 puts it at the bottom. Incidentally, a bond with one of the first four ratings is referred to in the investment community as *investment grade*, whereas one with a lower rating is called *speculative*. These descriptions arise from requirements imposed on many trust fund managers to limit their client purchases to securities with ratings in the first four categories. This rule serves as a screening device to minimize portfolio risk.

In addition to rating new issues, the agencies also evaluate outstanding debt issues and report them in their advisory services, which can be found in most major libraries. Not infrequently, an issue's rating changes because its financial strength has weakened or improved. When such a change is downward, indicating poorer quality, the market price of the issue declines substantially, if the rating change was unexpected.

Moody's and Standard and Poor's rate debt issues of both state and local governments and corporations. In addition to rating bond issues, the agencies rate commercial paper and other short-term debt instruments.

Yield and Rating   It is probably obvious that a debt issue's yield depends on its rating—the lower the rating, the higher the yield—all other things held constant. Exhibit 9.14 shows how yields varied by rating class (including Treasuries, assumed to have no default risk) at three points in time. The data show that yields and ratings are indeed inversely related, but they also show that yield differences (in these examples called quality spreads) are not constant over time. For example, spreads were lowest in 1992, while the spread between Treasuries and Aaa-rated issues was highest in 1990.

The data indicate that you will be compensated for investing in poorer quality issues, but you can expect this compensation to vary (unpredictably) over time. Whether it is high enough to adequately reward you for carrying such risk is a decision you must make. Some people view the yield differences as more than adequate reward, while others confine their bond investments to Treasury issues.

HISTORICAL INTEREST-RATE VOLATILITY

To say that interest rates vary over time grossly understates the situation. In truth, they have been extremely volatile, creating an investment environment as risky as that of many common stocks. If this volatility continues—and

EXHIBIT 9.13

Bond quality ratings (Sources: Moody's *Industrial Manual* and Standard and Poor's *Creditweek*).

Moody's

Aaa   Bonds which are rated Aaa are judged to be of the best quality. They carry the smallest degree of investment risk and are generally referred to as "gilt edge." Interest payments are protected by a large or by an exceptionally stable margin and principal is secure. While the various protective elements are likely to change, such changes as can be visualized are most unlikely to impair the fundamentally strong position of such issues.

Aa   Bonds which are rated Aa are judged to be of high quality by all standards. Together with the Aaa group they comprise what are generally known as high grade bonds. They are rated lower than the best bonds because margins of protection may not be as large as in Aaa securities or fluctuation of protective elements may be of greater amplitude or there may be other elements present which make the long term risks appear somewhat larger than in Aaa securities.

A   Bonds which are rated A possess many favorable investment attributes and are to be considered as upper medium grade obligations. Factors giving security to principal and interest are considered adequate but elements may be present which suggest a susceptibility to impairment sometime in the future.

Baa   Bonds which are rated Baa are considered as medium grade obligations, *i.e.*, they are neither highly protected nor poorly secured. Interest payments and principal security appear adequate for the present but certain protective elements may be lacking or may be characteristically unreliable over any great length of time. Such bonds lack outstanding investment characteristics and in fact have speculative characteristics as well.

Ba   Bonds which are rated Ba are judged to have speculative elements; their future cannot be considered as well assured. Often the protection of interest and principal payments may be very moderate and thereby not well safeguarded during both good and bad times over the future. Uncertainty of position characterizes bonds in this class.

B   Bonds which are rated B generally lack characteristics of the desirable investment. Assurance of interest and principal payments or of maintenance of other terms of the contract over any long period of time may be small.

Caa   Bonds which are rated Caa are of poor standing. Such issues may be in default or there

---

many credit analysts think it will—you should give your bond investments the same concern you give common stock investment.

Short- and Long-Term Rates

Exhibit 9.15 compares current yields on short-term debt instruments—Treasury bills and long-term Treasury bonds. Some observations seem important. First, it is clear that both yields have increased considerably in recent years. As we saw earlier, this is to be expected because inflation has also increased. Second, although bills show greater yield variability, this does not mean they are riskier. Risk is measured by HPRs, which in turn are heavily influenced by price changes; as we have seen, a 10% yield change for long-term bonds will have a far greater price impact than a similar change for may be present elements of danger with respect to principal or interest.

Ca   Bonds which are rated Ca represent obligations which are speculative in a high degree. Such issues are often in default or have other marked shortcomings.

C   Bonds which are rated C are the lowest rated class of bonds and issues so rated can be regarded as having extremely poor prospects of ever attaining any real investment standing.

Standard and Poor's

AAA   Debt rated AAA has the highest rating assigned by Standard & Poor's. Capacity to pay interest and repay principal is extremely strong.

AA   Debt rated AA has a very strong capacity to pay interest and repay principal and differs from the higher rated issues only in small degree.

A   Debt rated A has a strong capacity to pay interest and repay principal although it is somewhat more susceptible to the adverse effects of changes in circumstances and economic conditions than debt in higher rated categories.

BBB   Debt rated BBB is regarded as having an adequate capacity to pay interest and repay principal. Whereas it normally exhibits adequate protection parameters, adverse economic conditions or changing circumstances are more likely to lead to a weakened capacity to pay interest and repay principal for debt in this category than in higher rated categories.

BB, B, CCC, CC   Debt rated BB, B, CCC and CC is regarded, on balance, as predominently speculative with respect to capacity to pay interest and repay principal in accordance with the terms of the obligation. BB indicates the lowest degree of speculation and CC the highest degree of speculation. While such debt will likely have some quality and protective characteristics, these are outweighed by large uncertainties or major risk exposures to adverse conditions.

C   The rating C is reserved for income bonds on which no interest is being paid.

D   Debt rated D is in default, and payment of interest and/or repayment of principal is in arrears.

Plus (+) or Minus (-)   The ratings from "AA" to "B" may be modified by the addition of a plus or minus sign to show relative standing within the major rating categories.

---

bills. Third, in most years, the bond yield is greater than the bill yield. This might not surprise you because bonds are riskier. What might surprise you are the few years when bill yields exceeded bond yields. Bill yields were higher in four years (three since 1969) and equal to bond yields in two years. Were these periods of investor irrationality? Probably not, as we now explain.

The Yield Curve   The concept of a yield curve can help in the explanation. A **yield curve** shows YTM in relation to maturity for debt instruments that are alike in all other respects. Such curves usually are drawn for Treasury securities because they differ only in maturity, and the yield-curve pattern we most often find is the one represented by the April 1993 curve in Exhibit 9.16. As you see, long-term yields exceeded short-term yields, and the curve slopes upward. This upward-sloping yield curve is considered normal in that it illus-

Yield curve: graphic presentation showing the relation between bonds' yields to maturity and their maturities

EXHIBIT 9.14

Yields on long-term bonds and quality spreads

	1992		1991		1990	
Grade	Yields	Spreads	Yields	Spreads	Yields	Spreads
U.S. Treasury	7.61		7.67		8.14	
		0.53		1.10		1.18
Aaa	8.14		8.77		9.32	
		0.32		0.28		0.24
Aa	8.46		9.05		9.56	
		0.16		0.25		0.26
A	8.62		9.30		9.82	
		0.36		0.50		0.54
Baa	8.98		9.80		10.36	

SOURCE: *Federal Reserve Bulletin*, various issues

trates the growing liquidity risk investors face with longer maturities and shows they demand higher rates for undertaking such risk. The very steeply upward-sloping curve also reflected another factor in 1993—the expectation of investors that interest rates would probably rise in the future. Expectations play a large part in shaping current bond prices and yields.

Flat and Inverted Yield Curves When yields on short-term securities are about the same as those on long-term securities, the yield curve becomes flat—the situation in December 1988 for maturities from 1 to 30 years. If short-term yields exceed long-term yields, the yield curve is said to be inverted, as in February 1989 for maturities from 2 to 30 years. Flat and inverted curves have appeared increasingly in recent years. Their presence is associated with high rates in general. As you see, rates were substantially higher in

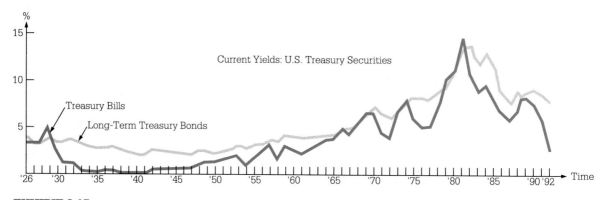

EXHIBIT 9.15

Current yields: U.S. Treasury securities (Source: Various Federal Reserve publications.)

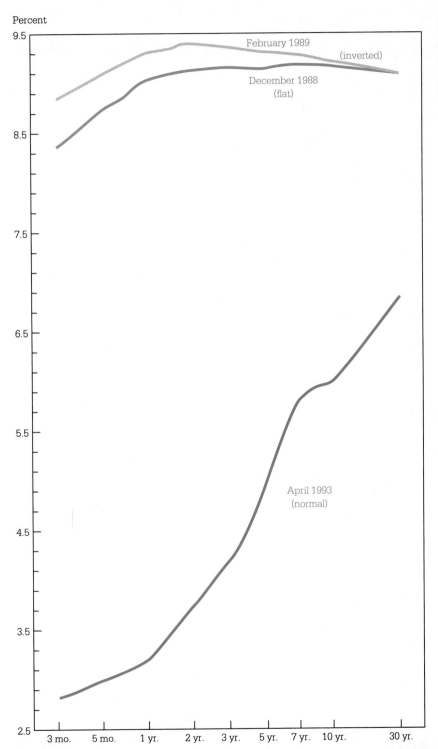

Percent

February 1989

(inverted)

December 1988
(flat)

April 1993
(normal)

9.5

8.5

7.5

6.5

5.5

4.5

3.5

2.5

3 mo. 5 mo. 1 yr. 2 yr. 3 yr. 5 yr. 7 yr. 10 yr. 30 yr.

EXHIBIT 9.16
Yield curves for
Treasury securities
(Source: various
Federal Reserve
publications.)

BOX 9.2   GETTING AN INVESTMENT EDGE

Is There a Message in the Yield Curve?

Investors look for omens in practically any situation, and one that has gotten a lot of press lately is the yield curve. As curves go, the yield curve is one of the easiest to find. All you need is any issue of *The Wall Street Journal* and the skill to find the curves, which are located in the financial pages (part C).

Now that you have it, what does it tell you? Well, all you will see is how interest rates on Treasury issues stacked up against their maturities on the particular day reported. But some analysts see much more. For example, if the curve is flat or slopes downward, this supposedly indicates that smart investors expect rates will fall in the future. If the curve slopes upward very sharply, the message is that rates will be rising.

Do the signs work? Some analysts think so, but the evidence is hardly conclusive. Perhaps the better way to use yield curves is in forecasting the overall economy. As the accompanying graph indicates, the onset of recessions since 1953 have been preceded by flat and inverted curves. (A zero yield spread is a flat curve, while negative spreads indicate inverted curves.) Unfortunately, investors can't make money with this information, unless someone concocts a way to take short positions on the economy.

Wait a minute, though: if it's true that flat and negative yield curves forecast a recession, can't we put such information to use? How about this approach: when the economy is at the depths of a recession, forecast that yield curves will eventually become upward-sloping. The graph shows that ought to work. If you're under 25, however, you might want to wait until you live through your first recession as an adult. You will be amazed at how difficult it is to be optimistic when gloom and doom abound. Remember, you are looking at only eight recessions, which hardly make a large data base. The ninth one might be totally different.

December 1988 and February 1989 than they were in April 1993. Again, expectations are an explanation for such curves is that both investors and debt issuers believe yields will probably fall in the future. Assuming this to be true, you can see why short-term yields will be higher.

For example, if you thought yields would decline, which of the four securities shown in Exhibit 9.10 would you want to hold? Your answer should be the 20-year zero. It offers the greatest price-appreciation potential. If many investors think as you do, market pressures should force prices of long-term bonds up in relation to prices of short-term instruments; and because yields move inversely to prices, long-term yields will fall relative to short-term yields. (Keep in mind that both yields are at historically high levels.) Not only will market pressures develop on the demand side of debt markets, but they will also emerge on the supply side. Business firms that can choose between

YIELD SPREAD CYCLES

Percent

[a]Spread is the difference between the Treasury 10-year and one-year constant-maturity yield. Shaded areas represent periods of recession. Last date plotted is February 1993.
SOURCE: *Federal Reserve Bulletin*, various issues.

issuing long-term or short-term debt will choose the latter even though its CY (cost to them) is higher. They will pay these high yields only for a short period, whereas if they issued long-term debt they would be saddled with high rates for many years. Thus, the supply of long-term debt decreases relative to the supply of short-term debt, which adds pressure to increase its relative price.

Forecasting Interest Rates

An appropriate final topic for this chapter is a consideration of whether interest rates can be forecasted with reasonable accuracy. The importance of the topic is obvious: if you can forecast, you can profit handsomely from future changes in interest rates. During earlier times, when interest rates were stable, forecasting was more or less taken for granted. "Experts" usually gave us their pronouncements about where they thought rates were headed, and most investors followed the line. In truth, rates changed so little that few people bothered to go back to see if the forecasts were as accurate as everyone thought them to be. In an age of volatile rates, however, fortunes are made or lost by swift and sharp changes in interest rates. As we entered this age, it became increasingly clear that no forecaster—at least no one who made his forecasts public information—could predict rates with any greater accuracy than the average person could achieve with naive methods. In other words, the "experts" often could not beat a simple forecasting method such as "next month's interest rate will equal this month's interest rate."

Ironically, despite such poor forecasting performances, there is no shortage of professional forecasters; indeed, their number has grown, probably because investors now feel a far greater need for their services. Most large banks have professional forecasters, as do the large stockbrokerage firms, along with independent forecasting firms such as Evans Economics or the Wharton Econometric Forecasting Associates. In late 1992, many "experts" were predicting an upward surge in interest rates, arguing that the era of low rates was coming to an end. What happened? Rates continued to fall, with the 30-year Treasury bond setting all-time lows (rates).

If you plan to invest in long-term debt instruments, probably the best advice is to do so as part of an overall investment strategy that does not call for forecasting interest rates. Moreover, avoid the temptation to allocate a larger portion of your portfolio to long-term instruments, at the expense of short-term instruments, when interest rates have fallen and are relatively low. You should always maintain adequate liquidity—the topic discussed in Chapter 5—and not sacrifice it for higher yields.

SUMMARY

Return from a debt instrument consists of periodic interest and/or price appreciation. Discount securities offer only price appreciation, while interest-bearing securities pay interest and may have price appreciation. The CY of a debt instrument is its interest divided by its market value; a YTM is a rate that causes the present value of its cash flows to equal its market value. A YTM assumes periodic interest earned is subsequently invested at the calculated YTM. An interest rate includes elements to allow for giving up current consumption and liquidity and to cover expected inflation and possible defaults.

Bonds may have high liquidity and default risks, which are positively related to a bond's maturity, coupon interest rate, and the level of interest rates. Liquidity risk is measured by an interest elasticity coefficient or Macaulay's duration coefficient. Reinvestment risk and rollover risk are associated with reinvesting interest and redemption amounts. Default risk is measured by quality grades provided by rating agencies such as Moody's and Standard and Poor's. Bonds with higher default risk offer higher yields.

Interest rates have been volatile in recent years. Short-term interest rates usually are lower than long-term rates, and a yield curve shows the relation of rates to maturity. Yield curves typically slope upward—indicating that rates increase with maturity—but on occasion are inverted, meaning rates fall as maturity increases, or are flat, meaning yields are about the same on short- and long-term securities. Forecasting interest rates is a difficult task that has not been done accurately in the past.

KEY TERMS
(listed in order
of appearance)

zero coupon bonds
interest-bearing bonds
discount bond
premium bond
current yield
yield to maturity
interest elasticity coefficient

Macaulay's duration concept
duration coefficient
reinvestment risk
rollover risk
default risk
yield curve

**REVIEW
QUESTIONS**

1. Distinguish between a zero coupon bond and a coupon bond. Then, construct timelines for each, making up your own dollar amounts and maturities.
2. Define current yield.
3. Explain the concept of YTM. What is implied in a YTM calculation? Include interest-on-interest in your response.
4. What factors do investors consider in evaluating an interest rate? Explain, using different types of fixed-income securities in your answer.
5. Suppose you recently purchased a bond and interest rates in general rose sharply immediately thereafter. Should this be a concern to you? Explain.
6. How is a bond's price risk related to its coupon rate and term to maturity?
7. Explain how the interest elasticity coefficient is calculated and what information it provides. How would you interpret an E value of -0.40?
8. Explain Macaulay's duration concept and interpret the following D values: $D = 0.20$; 1.00; 5.00; and 20.00. Suppose each of these is a discount security; does this information help to understand another aspect of each? Explain.
9. What is reinvestment risk? What type of security eliminates such risk? Explain. Also, identify rollover risk.
10. What is default risk? Explain whether it can be measured.
11. You plan to limit your bond investments to those with a Moody's rating of no less than Aaa. Your friend will select only Baa-rated bonds. Explain who will earn the higher yield and if you expect the yield differential to remain the same over time.
12. What is a yield curve? How would you construct one? Explain.
13. Using appropriate graphics, illustrate normal, flat, and inverted yield curves.
14. Why is the normal curve called normal? Explain how yield curves might be used to forecast future interest rates.
15. Is there evidence indicating certain individuals forecast interest rates accurately? Discuss.

PROBLEMS AND PROJECTS

1. C. C. Lee is thinking of investing in one of the following two securities: an 8% bond currently selling for $700 with 20 years to maturity, when it will be redeemed for $1,000; or a zero coupon bond maturing in 20 years for $1,000 and currently selling for $200. How would you advise C. C.? Be sure to use YTMs in your discussion.

2. Calculate the CY and YTMs for the following:
   a. a 12% corporate bond that matures in 8 years, selling at face value.
   b. a 10% Treasury bond that matures in 12 years, selling at $900.

3. What is meant by interest on interest? Explain the concept, using a 20-year, 12% bond, selling initially at face value and with an assumed reinvestment rate of 12%. Then, assume a reinvestment rate of 16%.

4. Determine prices for a 6%, 20-year bond assuming the following YTMs: 4%, 6%, 10%.

5. Calculate interest elasticity coefficients for each bond below, assuming each is currently selling at face value when interest rates rise by 25%. Also, discuss which is the riskier bond.
   a. a 20-year, 8% bond.
   b. a 10-year, 8% bond.

6. Calculate duration coefficients for each of the following bonds and then rank them according to risk (each has a YTM of 10%):
   a. a 3-year, 10% bond, selling at par.
   b. a 3-year, 20% bond, selling at $1,249.
   c. a 3-year zero, selling at $751.

7. You are evaluating a bond with a D value of 6.25, which was calculated assuming a YTM of 9%. You expect the YTM to increase to 10%. How much will the bond's price change (and in what direction) if the current price is $1,000?

8. *(Student Project)* Obtain a current issue of *The Wall Street Journal* and find the yield curve graphs in the financial pages. Interpret the patterns shown.

9. *(Student Project)* Write or call a large city bank, such as Chase Manhattan, and ask if they provide interest rate forecasts to their business clients or the general public. If they do, try to get back issues, and then determine the accuracy of their forecasts.

CASE ANALYSES

9.1 The Bradys Face Reinvestment Problems

Ian and Karen Brady are a married couple in their mid-30s with two children. Their combined incomes of $82,000 provide for a comfortable living, but they face substantial costs when their children begin college in 10 years. They have about $20,000 to invest now and are considering investing in fixed-income securities. Ian thinks that they should limit their portfolio to 10-year, zero coupon issues with yields to maturity of about 7%. Karen disagrees. She thinks the portfolio should include coupon bonds with YTMs of about 9%. Her bonds have a BBB rating, while Ian's are AAA-rated. Karen believes Ian is too conservative. She argues that if interest rates fall, as each expects will happen, her strategy will be better because she will have locked in the higher rates. She also thinks her strategy is better if, by some chance, interest rates rise; in that event, the larger losses will be with Ian's zeros.

The Bradys have some liquidity apart from the $20,000 earmarked for the children, but it is not considerable. They would like your advice on the matter. Before meeting with them, you have gathered yield data for selected Treasury issues:

90-day bills	3.0
5-year notes	5.0
10-year bonds	6.0
20-year bonds	6.5

Questions

a. What will the bond portfolio be worth 10 years from now if Ian's approach is followed? Is it possible to know what it will be worth if Karen's approach is followed? Explain.

b. Do you think that Karen has a correct risk perspective on their investment problem? Has she actually locked in higher rates? Discuss.

c. Does it seem likely that interest rates will fall in the future? Discuss your conclusion. How important to the Bradys' investment objective are interest rate movements? Explain.

d. How would you advise the Bradys? If you prefer Ian's or Karen's approach, explain why.

9.2 Felix Minoso's Bond Strategy

Felix Minoso has recently read that bonds have become almost as risky as common stocks. He doesn't understand why that should be the case, but it doesn't disappoint him because Felix likes to actively trade securities. He is particularly attracted to U.S. Treasury issues because there is no default risk. Considering some of the bankrupts he has encountered in common stock investing, that feature is a welcome relief.

Felix's broker has explained that bond prices go up when investors think that interest rates will fall, and vice versa. The broker sent Felix a newspaper article that highlighted economists' interest-rate forecasts for the upcoming year. Most thought that interest rates would decline from present levels. The broker argued that, given Felix's objective, he should invest his funds in 30-year T-bonds, currently yielding 9%. She specifically recommends zero coupon bonds. Felix was cool to this approach. For one thing, he didn't like the idea of receiving no interest; and for another, CYs were much higher on one-year T-bills (12%) and five-year notes (10%). Felix decided to follow his instincts by investing $30,000 in each of the three securities, rather than investing all $90,000 in the zeros. He purchased all the securities at their face values and intends to sell them after he realizes a sufficient gain in each.

Questions   a. Suppose interest rates fell shortly after Felix invested, and new yields are 5% on the bills, 6% on the notes, and 7% on the bonds. Determine Felix's portfolio gain. Then, determine the portfolio gain if Felix had listened to his broker. Assume that no securities were sold in either case.

b. Calculate elasticity coefficients for the three securities. How could these values have helped Felix in developing his investment strategy? Would they have been applicable if interest rates had risen instead of fallen? Explain.

c. Were Felix's reasons for rejecting his broker's advice sensible, given his investment objective? Explain.

d. What roles, if any, should reinvestment risk and rollover risk play in Felix's approach? Discuss.

HELPFUL READING

Asinof, Lynn. "But Just How Risky Are Bonds for You?" *The Wall Street Journal*, May 17, 1993, p. C1.

Bernstein, Peter L. "Who Needs Bonds?" *Forbes*, February 1, 1993, p. 113.

Clements, Jonathan. "T-Bill Trauma and the Meaning of Risk." *The Wall Street Journal*, February 12, 1993, p. C1.

Kritzman, Mark. "What Practitioners Need to Know About Duration and Convexity." *Financial Analysts Journal*, November-December 1992, pp. 17–19.

Lehn, Kenneth. "The Lessons of Marriott." *The Wall Street Journal*, March 11, 1993, p. A16.

CHAPTER TEN

Bonds and Preferred Stock Characteristics

CORPORATE BONDS

Bondholders' Rights

Special Bond Features

The Mechanics of Buying Corporate Bonds

International Bond Investment

U.S. TREASURY AND AGENCY ISSUES

Treasury Debt

Federal Agency Bonds

MUNICIPAL BONDS

The Income Tax Advantage

Kinds of Municipal Bonds

Default Risk in Municipal Bonds

PREFERRED STOCK

Basic Stockholder Rights

Other Features of Preferred Stock

Preferred Stock Returns

Risks in Preferred Stocks

After you finish this chapter, you will be able to:

* understand the nature of a corporate bond, recognizing what rights you possess as a bondholder and how these rights are protected.

* see the various features of corporate bonds and read corporate bond quotations in the financial pages.

* understand the characteristics of Treasury bonds and notes and read their quotations in the financial pages.

* recognize the important characteristics of preferred stocks, understanding how they differ from bonds and common stocks.

* calculate the return from a perpetuity and the yield to call.

* compare preferred stock returns with bond returns.

* identify and measure interest-rate risk and use ratings guides to assess default risk in preferred stocks.

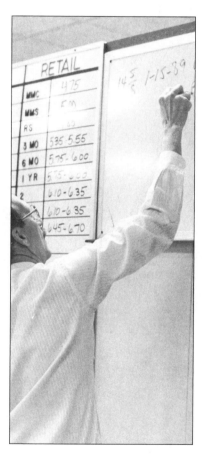

Why invest in bonds? In some respects they are the worst of all possible worlds: they lack the potential for capital appreciation that many common stocks offer; yet they involve considerable risk. So why not construct a portfolio of stocks and short-term investments and forget bonds altogether? In fact, many investors moved in that direction in the 1970s and early 1980s, as fluctuating interest rates put bond prices on a roller coaster and persistently increasing inflation drove their prices to all-time lows.

But as the 1980s moved on and into the 1990s, bonds made a remarkable recovery. Declining inflation and interest rates sent bond prices soaring. Undoubtedly, some investors turned to bonds in an effort to improve their portfolio return, which suffered when short-term yields fell. Perhaps they saw bonds as substitutes for short-term debt, which they definitely are not. But why not invest exclusively in higher-return common stocks if you are going for the long term? The answer, put simply, is that bonds are less risky. There is far less risk of losing most of your investment through default, and there is, overall, less price risk. Perhaps the most important advantage of a bond is that you have a much better idea of what your cash flows will be if you hold the bond until maturity. With common stock, you are never guaranteed future cash flows. Which would you rather have if you are investing to achieve a future goal that is extremely important to you? If you consider the alternatives, you will understand why bonds play a key role in investing.

This chapter explains important characteristics of both corporate and government bonds. It also explains preferred stock, which is another form of fixed-income security and often a bond substitute for certain investors.

CORPORATE BONDS

Corporate bond: debt obligation—IOU—of a corporation

A **corporate bond** is essentially a debt obligation (an IOU) of the corporation that issued it. When a business borrows large sums of money, corporate bonds are created in the process. The amount borrowed is far too large for any one creditor to handle, so the business cannot simply go to a bank or some other financial institution to take care of its needs. A bond, then, is a fractional part of a large business loan the issuer has with many creditors, rather than just one. In this sense, a bond is similar to a single share of common stock, except it probably has a much higher market price. Its more important differences are legal in nature.

Bondholders' Rights

If you own a bond, such as the one shown in Exhibit 10.1, you are a creditor. As such, you enjoy a far better legal position than does an owner of common stock. You also rank ahead of preferred stockholders. The coupon rate of interest—6.75% in Exhibit 10.1—is a legal obligation of the issuer and must be paid. If it isn't, you can take legal action to force payment. Common or preferred stock dividends, on the other hand, are paid at the discretion of the company.

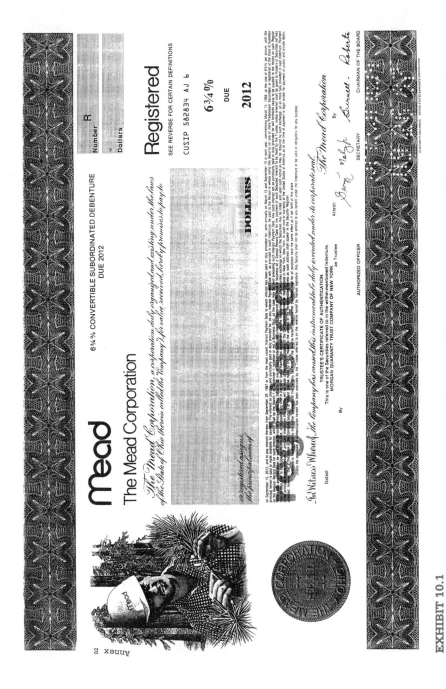

EXHIBIT 10.1

Mead's corporate bond. (Courtesy of The Mead Corporation.)

335

Additionally, the company is legally bound to redeem your bond at its face value, which is also called the bond principal and is almost always $1,000 for a corporate bond. And if the issuer faces financial difficulties and is forced to sell assets in bankruptcy proceedings, the amount owed you for either interest or principal must be paid before any payments are made to common and preferred stockholders. The right to receive interest and timely redemption of principal and the right to share first in asset distributions are basic bondholder rights. These are discussed in greater detail below.

Bond indenture: contract between the corporation issuing bonds and the investors who purchased them

The Bond Indenture   The **bond indenture** is a legal agreement between the issuer and the bondholders. It provides details about the basic bondholder rights, such as the coupon rate, when interest will be paid, how redemption will take place, and others. It also usually places restrictions on the issuer's future activities. These restrictions serve to strengthen the bondholders' position and include such items as (1) a limitation on issuing future debt, (2) a limitation on paying dividends on common or preferred stock, and (3) a provision that prevents the company from selling fixed assets, merging with another company, or undertaking an activity that would materially change the nature of the business. These restrictions are extremely important in preserving the issuer's solvency.

Despite them, many issuers do fail and are forced into liquidation. If the company fails to pay interest or principal on a debt issue, it is in default. Most bond indentures will also require that a default on another issue leads to default on the one under this specific indenture. Liquidation in bankruptcy seldom provides bondholders with a 100% recovery of their investments. Settlements are more likely to range from 30 to 40 cents on the dollar and often are less. Default risk was discussed in Chapter 9, but you should be mindful of it as we move through this chapter. If you buy low-rated bonds, you will carry more risk than with high-rated bonds. It is important to review a bond's rating in Moody's or Standard and Poor's before investing.

Trustee: institution, usually a commercial bank, that represents the bond investors and safeguards their interests

The Trustee   The issuer would find it impossible to have a separate contract with each bondholder. Instead, the indenture covers all bondholders. But who enforces the indenture on behalf of the bondholders? That is the function of the **trustee,** which typically is a large commercial bank. The trustee's primary function is to seek legal action if the issuer fails to meet the indenture's terms.

Mortgage bond: bond issue supported with collateral that consists of real property

Mortgage Bonds   Corporations often pledge collateral to strengthen a bond issue. When this is done, the bond is called a **mortgage bond.** An announcement of a mortgage bond issue is shown in Exhibit 10.2. The corporation might choose this type of issue in an effort to get a lower interest rate or simply out of necessity because it cannot borrow on the strength of its general credit standing. Collateral can consist of real estate, such as land, buildings, and factories, and personal property, including machinery, equip-

New Issue   May 14, 1993

$275,000,000

Showboat, Inc.

9¼% First Mortgage Bonds due 2008

Price 100%

Donaldson, Lufkin & Jenrette
Securities Corporation   **Lehman Brothers**

EXHIBIT 10.2
Announcement of a mortgage bond issue appearing in *The Wall Street Journal.*

ment, and anything else not permanently attached to buildings. Although corporations of all kinds issue mortgage bonds, the public utility industry is unquestionably the largest issuer. This is partially explained by the fact that public utility property usually will hold its value for many years in the future, which may not be true of many other businesses. The collateral for the mortgage bond in Exhibit 10.2 is a steamboat (or steamboats). What is a steamboat worth if Showboat, Inc., was forced into bankruptcy? Your guess might be as good as anybody else's.

BOX 10.1   INVESTMENT INSIGHTS

Are Bonds Bad Investments?

With so much money invested in so many types of bonds, the question above is either rhetorical or a grave indictment of investor intelligence. Can thousands of investors—both professional and amateur—be so misdirected? Apparently so, according to Peter L. Bernstein, noted investment advisor and founding editor of the *The Journal of Portfolio Management,* a sort of bible for professional money managers.

In the February 1, 1992, issue of *Forbes* magazine ("Who Needs Bonds?"), Bernstein cites three arguments in making his case against bonds: First, bond returns historically are substantially lower than stock returns—around 5% a year on average since 1925. Second, bond returns and stock returns are highly positively correlated; so, diversification advantages are rather small in a stock-bond portfolio. Third, the boom in derivative instruments has provided new opportunities for managing equity risk, thereby eliminating the need for bonds to temper portfolio risk. Bernstein, then, believes that investors can achieve better portfolio results by ignoring bonds and limiting their portfolios to stocks, money market securities, and perhaps hedge instruments, such as options and futures.

O that life were so simple! Many other observers might disagree with Bernstein. For example, it isn't true that bond and stock returns are highly correlated. Ibbotson and Associates show a correlation coefficient of only +0.14 between stocks and long-term Treasury bonds over the period 1926–92. That's not a strong correlation, which means

there should be significant diversification advantages in holding each.

It is true that stock and bond returns have moved together and have been good during most of the 1980s and early 1990s as the economy wrenched out high inflation. But at other times their returns have diverged. During the 1930s, bonds averaged about 5% a year, while stocks averaged about zero. Bonds clearly are the vehicle of choice in a weak economy with low inflation. Although stocks have performed relatively well in the early 1990s, another recession following closely on the heels of the 1990–91 recession might tell a different story for stocks; if inflation remains low, bonds should do quite well.

Moreover, Bernstein may be minimizing the cost of managing equity risk through derivative instruments. Although such management is clearly possible and often used, it typically requires a sacrifice of return. Sure, we can reduce our downside risk in stocks, for example, by buying put options. But that could be an expensive strategy and perhaps no more effective than if we held a portfolio of stocks and bonds.

Finally, there is a feeling that the 5% spread between bond and stock returns is likely to be smaller in the future. Bond returns were terrible during the 1970s because bond investors seemed to consistently underestimate inflation. There is some evidence to propose that bond investors will be inflation-smarter in the future; if they are, the yield spread should shrink and investors should hold more—not fewer—bonds in their portfolios.

A bond that is not supported by collateral is called an unsecured bond, or a **debenture.** You will find a large number of both mortgage bonds and debentures outstanding. On the surface, a mortgage bond seems the safer of the two; after all, with specific collateral to support the loan, if the issuer goes into liquidation, any proceeds from the sale of the collateral must be used first to pay off the mortgage bonds. In general, they are safer but not always. If the collateral is poor and the corporation has financial weaknesses, the bond's strength is diminished accordingly. You would be better off with debentures of a financially strong company rather than mortgage bonds issued by Fly-by-Night Airlines using its dilapidated hangars and World War II–vintage aircraft as collateral.

Debenture: bond not secured by collateral

Equipment Trust Certificates A particular type of mortgage bond is called an **equipment trust certificate.** Such certificates are issued by companies that are financing transportation equipment, such as railroad cars, jet airplanes, and containers used on oceangoing and inland water vessels. In the past, this collateral was referred to as rolling stock because the only equipment was railroad boxcars. Such items often make excellent collateral: they are durable and can be taken over easily if the borrower defaults, and because their construction is so standardized, they have a good resale market.

Equipment trust certificate: particular type of mortgage bond used extensively in the transportation industry

Subordinated Debentures As mentioned above, most indentures will restrict the corporation's future borrowing activities in an effort to protect the bondholders' position. The more debt a corporation issues, the riskier it is. Without such a provision, bondholders would be in serious trouble whenever the issuer decided it needed more capital.

To overcome the restriction against future borrowing, the indenture might allow the corporation to sell additional bonds if the position of the new bondholders is subordinated (made inferior) to the position of the existing bondholders. The additional bonds issued under such a condition are called **subordinated debentures.** (A bond issue also can be subordinated to other debt claims, such as commercial paper.) The Mead bond in Exhibit 10.1 is a subordinated debenture. The investor's position is materially weakened with this type of bond. Exhibit 10.3 shows how subordination works. The corporation has two bond issues outstanding: the debentures and the subordinated debentures. Each has total principal of $4 million and there are $2 million of general creditor claims. If the company's assets are sold for $6 million, the debentures would be paid in full because they are entitled to their own share plus the subordinated debentures' share. In contrast, the subordinated debenture holders receive only $800,000, a loss of $3.2 million, or $0.80 on each $1.

Subordinated debenture: bond that assigns to another debt claimant its right to share in a liquidation

Because of the greater potential default risk, yields on subordinated debentures are higher than those on mortgage bonds and debentures, all other things held constant. Indeed, the lower-quality issues (referred to as

EXHIBIT 10.3
How subordination
works

	Debt Outstanding			
	Debentures	Subordinated Debentures	General Creditors	Total Debt
Amount	$4,000,000	$4,000,000	$2,000,000	$10,000,000
Percentage of total	40%	40%	20%	100%
Percentages applied to amount received from sale of assets	$2,400,000	$2,400,000	$1,200,000	$ 6,000,000
Subordination allocation	+ 1,600,000	− 1,600,000		
Final distribution	$4,000,000	$ 800,000	$1,200,000	$ 6,000,000

junk) often have yields rivaling those on common stocks. Some analysts think that such bonds are more closely related to equity than to debt. Their market prices, for example, are strongly influenced by events affecting the issuers as well as by changes in market rates of interest. This is reasonable because any factor that strengthens or weakens an issuer will clearly help or hurt the prospect of receiving the subordinated debentures' promised interest payments and redemptions.

Registered bonds: bonds with their owners' names registered by the issuing corporation; interest paid directly to owners

Payment of Interest All corporate bonds issued today are **registered bonds,** which means the bonds are registered in the name of their owners. If you wish, you can receive a bond certificate such as the one shown in Exhibit 10.1. Interest is mailed to you, usually every six months. In the past, many corporate bonds were **bearer bonds.** These bonds were not registered, and ownership was transferred by simply exchanging the bonds with someone else. To receive interest, you clipped an appropriate coupon attached to the bond and presented it to the bank acting as trustee. Corporate bearer bonds are no longer issued because of the Internal Revenue Service's ruling that interest is subject to withholding; many are still in existence, however, and will remain outstanding until their eventual redemption.

Bearer bonds: nonregistered bonds; owners receive interest by "clipping" coupons and presenting them to a bank

Income bond: bond that pays interest only if the corporation achieves a certain level of profit

We noted before that bond interest payments are a legal liability of the issuer. There is one exception: an **income bond** pays interest only if the issuer has sufficient earnings to make such payments. Income bonds seldom are issued by corporations except when reorganizations are brought about by financial difficulties. A type of income bond called a revenue bond frequently is issued by municipalities. Revenue bonds are discussed later in this chapter.

PIK bond: bond that allows its issuer to pay interest by issuing additional bonds, rather than cash

Another unique bond, with respect to interest payments, is a payment-in-kind bond, called a **PIK bond.** Interest from this bond may not be paid in cash; rather, the issuer has the option of paying cash or paying in additional bonds. For example, suppose a PIK issue has a 15% annual coupon rate and semiannual interest is due. The company can choose to pay the $75 in cash, or it can choose to issue 0.075 of an additional bond. The PIK interest period typically is for a limited number of years (usually 5 to 10), after which cash interest is paid.

PIK bonds were expected to grow in popularity, but that has not happened. A possible explanation is that the restructuring movement, so popular in the 1980s, has slowed considerably.

Redemption Provisions   All bonds issued in the United States have finite maturities; that is, issuers are obligated to redeem them. (Interestingly, since the Napoleonic Wars, Great Britain has issued bonds, called consols, that never mature.) However, because maturity often is so far in the future, bond investors are rightfully concerned about the issuer's ability to make good on the redemption promise. To safeguard their interest, some bond issues require a **sinking fund,** which means the corporation must set aside funds (usually with the trustee) for the exclusive use of redeeming the bonds. This is done by calling (this term will be explained shortly) a portion of the bonds each year or by buying them in the secondary market. Also, some bond issues are divided into a series of redemption dates, in which case retirement is called **serial redemption.**

Sinking fund: arrangement that requires the bond issuer to set aside funds for the redemption of a bond issue

An issuer's liability to pay interest ceases once a bond is called for redemption. If you fail to offer a called bond, you cannot collect interest after the call date, although the issuer is obligated to pay the principal. If you delay for a long period, the loss of interest could be substantial. Bond investors must watch serial redemptions closely, both for corporate and for municipal bonds.

Serial redemption: redeeming bonds by their serial numbers before the bond issue's stated maturity

Special Bond Features

The supply of and demand for bonds are in a constant state of flux. To attract investors, bond issuers often must add certain features, called sweeteners, to make the bonds more saleable. At other times, an issuer's market exists, and sellers then take away the sweeteners or add features that are of greater benefit to them. Let us see what some of these sweeteners and features are.

Convertibility   A **convertible bond** is one that can be converted into shares of the common stock of the issuing corporation. The Mead bond in Exhibit 10.1 is a convertible bond. Another type of convertible bond that is used infrequently is one that converts into the common stock of another company. These bonds are called **exchangeable bonds.** For example, General Cinema Corporation has a bond issue that converts into the common stock of RJR Nabisco. A holder of this bond presents it to General Cinema, which

Convertible bond: bond that can be converted into shares of common stock of the bond issuer

Exchangeable bonds: bonds issued by one corporation that can be converted into shares of common stock of another corporation makes the exchange from shares of RJR Nabisco that it owns. Sometimes the convertible feature is viewed as the ultimate sweetener because you enjoy the safety and high yield of a bond while simultaneously having a stake in the company's future growth. But you pay for this sweetener, as we shall see in more detail in Chapter 11.

A unique form of a convertible bond is the so-called LYON, which stands for *liquid yield option note*. Created by Merrill Lynch, LYONs are corporate bonds issued in zero coupon form that are both callable and putable (these terms are explained immediately below) and that can be exchanged for shares of the issuing corporation. Well-known companies, such as Disney, have issued LYONS; in early 1993, however, the LYONs market cooled as issuers began exercising their call rights to redeem the bonds. Apparently, investors didn't believe that this would happen, and many took losses as a result of the redemptions.

Floating rate bond: bond that has its interest payments pegged to market interest rates

Floating Rate Bonds   A **floating rate bond** has its periodic interest payments indexed to some broad market interest-rate index. As the rate on this index goes up or down, so do the interest payments on the floating rate bond. As you can see, a bond such as this will protect you against interest-rate risk. Most of these bonds have been issued by commercial banks and other kinds of financial institutions, although some industrial concerns have also issued them. On balance, they have not been exceptionally popular with investors, probably because their yields are not exceptionally generous. Yields commonly are set one or two percentage points above the 90-day Treasury bill rate, which is a rather modest premium for undertaking the potential default risk. The slowing-down of inflation has further reduced the public's interest in the protection offered by floaters, but if prices and interest rates heat up again, they may regain popularity.

Put bond: bond that allows its owner to sell it back to the issuer at a set price

Put Bonds   A **put bond** allows the holder to sell ("put") the bond back to the issuer at a set price. In other words, you have a guaranteed redemption price that you can exercise any time. Puts of this sort are most popular in municipal bond issues, although nongovernmental issuers have also used them. The put option again eliminates interest-rate risk. If rates rise, forcing down bond prices, you can avoid a loss by exercising your put right; in effect, you bail out. A sweetener this good also comes with a price, which is a substantially reduced yield. Investors, then, must determine if they are better off owning an instrument such as this versus owning short-term instruments. Most corporate issuers are not fond of put bonds because they disrupt financing operations. Corporate treasurers must consider the possibility of being forced to redeem a bond issue through puts, probably at a time when they would be forced to borrow at increasingly higher interest rates.

Super poison put: provision in the bond indenture that requires a corporation to redeem an entire bond issue in the event of a buyout or other form of restructuring

A new kind of put was introduced into bond indentures in 1989 as a result of an upheaval in the corporate bond market brought about by the takeover movement. The new put, called a **super poison put,** forces a company to redeem a bond issue in the event of a buyout, takeover, or other massive recapitalization. Bondholder fears motivating the new put were well founded. A number of takeovers around that time led to substantial declines in the market values of existing bonds because the takeovers relied so heavily on additional debt. Unfortunately, there were no provisions in existing indentures prohibiting shareholders from selling their shares to other buyers, who purchased them almost entirely with borrowed funds. The situation was so bad that a new form of risk was introduced into the investment literature— **event risk.** This risk refers to the potential weakening of current bondholder claims by virtue of a takeover or other recapitalization. The super poison put is designed to protect bondholders from event risk.

Event risk: potential weakening of a bond issue as a result of a corporate restructuring

The Right to Call   Most corporate bond issues give the issuer the right to call the bonds for an early redemption. Whereas the put feature benefited bondholders, the call feature benefits the issuer. Why do issuers want the call option? Very simple: it gives them greater flexibility in future financing. For example, a corporation may have issued 20-year bonds at 12% interest in 1990. Suppose the total issue was for $20 million. This means the corporation must pay $2.4 million each year in bond interest. Now it's 1994, and 16-year bonds of the same quality are yielding only 8%. The company would clearly benefit—to the tune of $800,000 each year—if it would issue new bonds and use the proceeds to retire the old bond issue. This is called refunding, and it's an ongoing function in most large corporations.

If a call benefits the issuer, it obviously works against the investor. You may have purchased the 12% bond and then were looking for $120 interest each year for the next 20 years. Now you find the bond being taken away from you. Because this is undesirable, bonds with call features typically have a **call premium** for some time after the issuance. For example, the bond above might be callable at $1,100 for five years after issuance, the $100 being a premium you receive for an early redemption. If you buy a bond that is selling at a price above its call value, you must consider the risk that a call will take place. If you assume the market price quickly adjusts to the call price, you will take a capital loss that could exceed the call premium. It is dangerous to pay more than the call price, even though some issuers seldom exercise their calls.

Call premium: difference between the call price of a bond and its face value

The Mechanics of Buying Corporate Bonds

Most corporate bonds can be purchased as easily as you buy common stocks. There is an active secondary market for bonds, although many issues are thinly traded, meaning they have little trading volume. Such issues are more sensitive to changes in demand and supply and usually are more price-volatile. Bonds are traded on the New York Bond Exchange (part of the New York Stock Exchange), the American Bond Exchange (part of the American Stock Exchange), and the over-the-counter market. By far, the largest volume of bond trading is done in the over-the-counter market because all governmental issues and many corporate issues are traded there.

BOX 10.2   A QUESTION OF ETHICS

The Marriott Case: Should Bondholders Have Extracontractual Rights?

Many people have little sympathy for bondholders, who typically are professional money managers who should know what they are doing. That's true, but keep in mind that the pros aren't buying bonds for their own portfolios. They manage other people's money; so, when they get burned, its our pension plan that takes the hit.

A recent case draws attention to ethical issues in bond financing. In 1992, Marriott Corporation proposed to split itself into two corporations. One (to be called Marriott International) would operate its hotel and food management activities—a highly profitable area—while the other (to be called Host Marriott) would own its real estate holdings, somewhat of a loser in recent years. The problem arises in that the real estate segment would assume most of Marriott's debt, about $3 billion at the time of the proposal, while the profitable division goes debt-free. Is that legal, and if so, is it fair?

The legality will be settled in the courts because Marriott's bondholders have filed claims against the restructuring. A key point at issue is that Marriott bondholders could easily have protected themselves against such an event by having appropriate covenants included in the bond indenture. Surely, the numerous restructurings, leveraged buyouts, and other corporate goings-on during the 1980s should have alerted bond investors to potential event risk. Professional investors could hardly claim ignorance.

Are bondholders, then, entitled to rights outside the contract based on ethical issues?

In short, was Marriott's action a fair one? Like most ethical issues, an answer is difficult and sure to placate one party at the expense of another. Kenneth Lehn, professor of business administration at the University of Pittsburgh, raises some legitimate points against giving extracontractual benefits to bondholders (see *Barron's*, March 11, 1993).

First, by accepting weaker covenants, bondholders receive higher interest rates than would otherwise be available. Second, spin-offs often create efficiency by providing better information on divisional performance and by focusing management attention more acutely on its core businesses. Lehn also thinks that if the courts favor bondholders in the case, it sets a precedent for other corporate stakeholders: why shouldn't employees also seek compensation in the courts if a restructuring hurts them?

It is hard to fault Lehn's arguments; still, to what extent do we expect corporate leaders to live up to the spirit of a contract? Clearly, Marriott's bondholders had reason to believe that the full resources of the corporation would support the bond issue. Surely, that spirit could be preserved even in a restructuring by simply having Marriott International in effect cosign the obligations. And talk about setting a bad precedent—why shouldn't any business creditor, not just bondholders, dodge its obligations by splitting the company and unevenly shifting the debt? Further, how voluminous must contracts become to avoid any and all potential hazards? No wonder we need so many lawyers.

Bonds can be owned in a margin account and used as collateral for a broker's loan, just as you might use stocks for that purpose. In fact, the margin requirement for some bonds may be less than it is for stocks. You should ask your broker for details and also determine his commissions. Before investing in corporate bonds, you should understand their price quotations.

Reading Corporate Bond Quotations   Bond prices, along with other information, are reported in the financial pages of many newspapers, local and national. The Wall Street Journal reports information daily on bonds traded on the New York and American exchanges. Exhibit 10.4 shows two typical listings. (The Mead bond is the same one shown in Exhibit 10.1.)

Exhibit 10.4 requires little elaboration, but you might note the current yield calculation is the same one explained in Chapter 9. We indicated there that current yield often is not the most appropriate yield measurement and that yield to maturity (YTM) should also be considered in evaluating a potential bond purchase. Using a financial calculator to find YTM, we can determine that Navistar's is 11%. There were 11 years (assumed) remaining to maturity when the calculation was made (in early 1993). As you see, this is somewhat higher than the current yield of 10.3%.

Corporate Bond Commissions and Spreads   Most major brokerage houses charge corporate bond commissions on a sliding scale on which the commission per bond declines as more bonds are purchased. The scale below is typical:

Number of Bonds Purchased	Commission
First 5 bonds, or $5,000 of par value	$10 per bond, or per $1,000 of par value
Next 20 bonds, or $20,000 of par value	$7.50 per bond, or per $1,000 of par value
Amounts above 25 bonds or $25,000 of par value	$5 per bond, or per $1,000 of par value

If you purchased 27 bonds, the commission would be $210 [(5 × $10) + (20 × $7.50) + (2 × $5) = $50 + $150 + $10 = $210]. Assuming you paid $1,000 for each bond would make the commission percentage equal to 0.7% ($210/$27,000), which is relatively inexpensive. However, you should determine if there is a minimum commission per transaction. Many discount brokers charge a minimum that usually is no less than $25. A purchase of only one bond, then, would involve a 2.5% ($25/$1,000) commission rate in this case.

Although commissions are reasonable, you also pay a spread for bonds purchased in the over-the-counter market, where about 90% of all bond

EXHIBIT 10.4

Reading corporate bond quotations

Corporate bond prices are reported in the financial pages of many newspapers. Typical listings and explanations are shown below. Quotations were in mid-April 1993.

Bond			Cur Yld	Vol	Close	Net Chg
Mead	6¾	12	cv.	51	100½	−½
Nav Str	9	04	10.3	245	87½	+1⅝
Off Dep	Zr	07	—	40	51	+⅛
(1)	(2)	(3)	(4)	(5)	(6)	(7)

(1) Name of the issuer: Nav Str is Navistar and Off Dep is Office Depot.
(2) Coupon rate of interest: 6¾ tells us the bond pays $67.50 a year interest.
(3) The year the bond matures: Mead's bond matures in 2012.
(4) *Cur Yld* means the bond's current yield: Navistar's current yield of 10.3% is determined by dividing the annual interest of $90 by the bond's closing price of $875. The symbol *cv.* in the Cur Yld column tells us the bond is a convertible, and current yields are not calculated for convertibles. The Mead bond is a convertible and the Office Depot bond is a zero coupon.
(5) *Vol* means the number of bonds traded: 51 Mead bonds traded on the day being reported.
(6) *Close* is the last price the bond traded at during the day: Mead's closing price is 100½. This reported price is one-tenth the actual price; to get the actual price, you must multiply the reported price by 10:

$$\text{actual price} = 10 \times \text{reported price}$$
$$= 10 \times 100\tfrac{1}{2}$$
$$= 10 \times 100.5$$
$$= 1{,}005$$

(7) *Net Chg* means the difference between the closing price of the day being reported and the closing price of the previous day: Navistar's price increased (+) by 1⅝, which means the price was up $16.25 (10 × 1⅝ = 10 × 1.625 = 16.25) for the day.

trading occurs. The spread is the difference between the bid and the asked prices, and because many bonds are thinly traded, spreads can be relatively large. In some cases, they can be as much as $50 a bond, although $10 to $20 spreads are more common. Even these smaller amounts add substantially to transactions costs and make frequent bond trading an expensive activity.

International Bond Investment

Just as you can invest in foreign stocks, you also can invest in foreign bonds. Although many foreign companies issue less debt than their U.S. counterparts, foreign governments issue considerable amounts and in a wide array of forms and maturities. Investing in foreign bonds became popular in the early 1990s because interest rates on foreign debt were much higher than rates on comparable domestic bonds. As a result, the number of international bond mutual funds and money market mutual funds grew rapidly.

You can invest directly in foreign bonds, although the number traded in the United States is small. By far, the more popular alternative is to invest in international bond mutual funds. Regardless of the approach, it is important to understand that a foreign bond is one denominated in the currency of a foreign country. If Honda sells bonds in the United States denominated in dollars (which would be called a Yankee bond), this is no different than if GM sold bonds in the United States, and neither are foreign bonds. But if Honda sells bonds denominated in yen, then we have foreign bonds. Although such bonds typically would be sold in Japan, in today's multinational financial marketplace, they may be sold throughout the world. Often such bonds are called Eurobonds; technically, this term refers to any bond sold outside the country in which the issuer is located and denominated in a currency different from the issuer's country.

Exchange-Rate Risk   The key aspect of denomination in a foreign currency is that the bond then takes on exchange-rate risk. Discussed more thoroughly in Chapter 17, this risk arises when the exchange rate between two currencies changes over time. When this happens, your return can either increase or decrease, depending on the nature of the change. If the dollar strengthens against the yen, for example, the interest on a Honda bond paid in yen converts to fewer dollars than it would have converted into at the previous exchange rate. As a result, your effective yield is less than what you might have anticipated. This situation did in fact occur in the early 1990s; so, many investors lured to international bond funds touting yields of 10% to 12% (when 8% was available domestically) were sadly disappointed when a strengthening dollar wiped out most of the extra return.

Several studies have shown that over time, a bond portfolio weighted with domestic and foreign issues usually offers less price volatility and perhaps a slightly higher return than a portfolio that consists of only domestic bonds. As is usually the case, the patient investor is rewarded, while the short-term speculator may or may not reap an advantage.

A Unique Foreign Bond—Brady Bond   A somewhat interesting foreign bond is a **Brady bond.** Brady bonds are issued by developing nations (in minimum denominations of $250,000) under guidelines established by former

Brady bond: bonds issued by foreign countries under guidelines established by the federal government

Treasury Secretary Nicholas Brady. These bonds offer high yields but are extremely price volatile because of potential default risk. Salomon Brothers maintains a Brady Bond Index, which showed a 40% total return in 1991 but less than 5% in 1992 as a result of political problems in Venezuela. At $250,000 a bond, it is unlikely that small investors will invest in Brady Bonds directly; however, they are available through pooling arrangements (see Chapter 14).

U.S. TREASURY AND AGENCY ISSUES

The federal government, through the Treasury and its various agencies, issues a considerable amount of debt, as Exhibit 10.5 shows. There is a strong demand for government debt because it is considered the safest to hold. Treasury bills were explained in Chapter 5; our attention now is on Treasury notes and bonds. Notes and bonds are similar in that each has a coupon rate of interest and pays interest semiannually. They differ in that notes have maturities of 2 to 10 years, while bonds have maturities greater than 10 years. These are maturities at the time of issuance. Because many bonds and notes were issued in the past and are in the process of maturing, you can buy them in the secondary market to achieve practically any maturity you want. We will discuss important aspects of government debt in the sections below.

EXHIBIT 10.5
U.S. Treasury and federal agency debt outstanding

	End-of-Year Balances (Billions)		
	1992	1991	1990
Treasury debt:			
Bills	$ 657.7	$ 590.4	$ 527.4
Notes	1,608.9	1,430.5	1,166.2
Bonds	472.5	435.5	388.2
Total	$2,739.1	$2,456.4	$2,081.8
Federally sponsored agency debt:			
Federal Home Loan Banks	$114.7	$107.5	$117.9
Federal Home Loan Mortgage Corporation	29.6	30.3	30.9
Federal National Mortgage Association	166.3	133.9	123.4
Farm Credit Banks	51.9	52.2	53.6
Student Loan Marketing Association	39.7	38.3	34.2
Financing Corporation	8.2	8.2	8.2
Resolution Funding Corporation	23.1	30.0	30.0
Farm Credit Financial Assistance Corporation	1.3	1.3	1.3
Total	$442.1	$401.7	$392.5

Treasury Debt

As we indicated in Chapter 9, Treasury debt is considered the safest of all debt and in fact is as safe as currency because it is also backed by the full faith and credit of the U.S. government. Although some cynics might regard such faith as ill-founded, it has served us well in the past. In addition, if the Treasury ever defaults on its debt, few other investments will be worth holding. Gold or other tangibles perhaps, but even they aren't sure bets if the federal government is bankrupt.

One advantage of investing in Treasury securities is that interest is exempt from state and local income taxes. If you live in an area with high local taxes, this advantage will not be trivial. For example, suppose the local tax has a marginal rate of 10% and you have a 28% marginal federal rate. Assume further that you could earn 6% on a Treasury bond and 8% on a corporate. The pre-tax difference is two percentage points, but as Exhibit 10.6 shows, the after-tax difference is only 1.01% (5.33% − 4.32%). The added risk with the corporate may not be worth a spread as small as this; thus, you should consider both your federal and local income tax situations in deciding between treasuries and corporates.

Reading Quotations on Treasuries   With more than $2 trillion of Treasury notes and bonds outstanding, investors have a wide array of coupon rates and maturities to consider. Information on price and YTM is reported in the

	Treasury Bond	Corporate Bond
Assumed amount invested	$ 1,000	$ 1,000
Pretax interest earned (6%, 8%)	60.00	80.00
State and local income tax (10% rate)	-0-	−5.93*
Federal income tax (28% rate)	−16.80	−20.74*
After-tax return	$ 43.20	$ 53.33
After-tax rate of return	4.32%	5.33%

EXHIBIT 10.6
Comparing after-tax returns of Treasury and corporate bonds

*State and local taxes can be deducted in determining the federal tax liability and federal taxes can be deducted in determining the state and local tax liability. If L = the local tax liability and F = the federal tax liability, we then have the following equations:

$$L = .10\,(80 - F) \quad \text{and} \quad F = .28\,(80 - L)$$

$$
\begin{aligned}
\text{Solving,} \quad L &= .10[80 - .28(80 - L)] \\
L &= .10\,[80 - 22.4 + .28L] \\
L &= 8 - 2.24 + .028L \\
.972L &= 5.76 \\
L &= 5.93 \\
F &= .28(80.00 - 5.93) = 20.74
\end{aligned}
$$

financial pages of many newspapers in the format shown in Exhibit 10.7. The reported information is similar to that of corporate bonds, except fractional parts are in thirty-seconds rather than in eighths. The colon in front of the fractional part is a bit confusing to the first-time reader: you automatically assume the quote is in decimals, which it is not. You should also notice that YTM is reported, rather than current yield, as in the case of corporate bonds. As mentioned before, YTM is the more useful yield figure. Having it readily available makes the evaluation of specific bonds much simpler.

Buying Treasury Bonds   Treasury bonds can be purchased through your broker or directly from a Federal Reserve bank. The latter approach saves commissions but does take some effort. Purchases can be handled through the mail, and if you want to buy a Treasury security in this manner, you can begin with a call to the Federal Reserve bank closest to you or write the Bureau of the Public Debt, Department F, Washington, DC 20239–0001, for more information.

Stripped Treasury Securities   All sales of bonds and notes made by the Treasury are of the interest-bearing (coupon) variety. However, beginning in

EXHIBIT 10.7
A sample listing of Treasury notes and bonds at mid-April 1993

Rate	Maturity	Bid	Asked	Bid Change	Yield
7	Sep 96n	105:22	105:24	+6	5.23
15¾	Nov 01	161:10	161:14	+4	6.48
7¼	Aug 22	98:29	98:31	+2	7.34
(1)	(2)	(3)	(4)	(5)	(6)

(1)   *Rate* refers to the coupon rate. Notice the high coupon rate of 15 ¾% for the second bond; this bond was issued many years ago when interest rates were high.

(2)   *Maturity* refers to the month and year when the bond matures; the first bond matures in September 1996. The symbol *n* indicates a note rather than a bond.

(3)   *Bid* is the highest price bond dealers were offering to buy the bond. Fractional parts are thirty-seconds, and actual prices are 10 times the quotation. Thus, the second bond's bid price is $1,613.13 [(161 + 10/32) × 10].

(4)   *Asked* is the lowest price dealers were accepting.

(5)   *Bid Change* shows the difference between the bid price on the quotation day and the bid price of the previous day. The change of +6 points for the first bond means its bid price was up $1.88 (6/32 × 10).

(6)   *Yield* means yield to maturity. Notice that the first two securities have coupon rates substantially higher than their yields and, so, are selling at premiums to face value. In contrast, the third security is selling at a yield slightly higher than its coupon rate; so, it is selling at a discount.

the early 1980s, to meet the huge demand investors had for a default risk-free bond, several large stockbrokerage houses began to offer so-called **stripped Treasury securities (STRIPS,** for short). They would buy a large number of Treasury securities and then create pools with various maturities. The pools consisted of both coupon interest and redemption payments. The securities were placed in a trust with a commercial bank, and certificates to the various pools—all issued in zero coupon form—were sold to investors. It was an ingenious technique to transform coupon bonds into zero coupon bonds with a wide array of maturities.

The brokerage houses gave the certificates rather imaginative acronyms, such as CATs (Certificates of Accrual on Treasury Securities) and TIGRs (Treasury Investment Growth Receipts), and these bonds are still available today. Beginning in 1985, however, the Treasury initiated a program of Separate Trading of Registered Interest and Principal of Securities, from which the acronym STRIPS is derived. The Treasury does not issue STRIPs but rather facilitates stripping, which still is initiated by large banks and stockbrokerage houses. So, you must buy STRIPs through a broker, who adds a commission—usually 1% to 2% of the purchase. After purchase, the STRIPs are registered with the Federal Reserve in your name and are direct obligations of the federal government.

STRIPS are by far the most popular zero coupon bond. They are quoted each day in the financial newspapers, and typical listings are shown in Exhibit 10.8. As with coupon Treasuries, prices are quoted in thirty-seconds; so, the zero maturing in November of 2022 has a bid price of $112.50 [(11 + 8/32) × 10].

One final comment on STRIPS. The Internal Revenue Service gives them an unfavorable tax treatment. You must accrue interest each year and report it as taxable income even though you don't actually receive it. Although this tax treatment appears as a major disadvantage, it is not if you own the STRIPS in an IRA where your tax is deferred. Surely, many investors hold them in this form. If you don't, it makes more sense to own coupon Treasury securities. You would pay the same amount of tax on the earned interest, but because you actually receive the interest, your after-tax rate of return over the security's life would be greater.

Stripped Treasury securities: zero coupon Treasury bonds created by separating interest and principal payments of various coupon issues

Maturity	Type	Bid	Asked	Chg.	Ask Yld.
Nov. 1996	np	81:18	81:21	+5	5.40
Nov. 2007	ci	33:12	33:17	+1	7.51
Nov. 2022	bp	11:08	11:11	+1	7.44

np = Treasury note stripped principal.

ci = Stripped coupon interest (bond or note).

bp = Treasury bond stripped principal.

EXHIBIT 10.8
A sample of quotations of U.S. Treasury STRIPS at mid-April 1993

Federal Agency Bonds

Federal agency bond:
bond issued by an
agency of the federal
government

A **federal agency bond** is issued by an agency of the federal government. To carry out its objectives, the federal government has many separate agencies, some of which become involved directly and indirectly in various financing arrangements. Such financing creates agency bonds. Agency bonds are also backed by the full faith and credit of the Treasury (with the exception of most passthrough securities, which will be explained shortly). Because the yield on agency debt is slightly higher than the yield on Treasury debt, you might improve your portfolio return by making a substitution, either partially or completely. You should consider the items below, however, before investing in agency debt.

Characteristics of Agency Debt   With some exceptions, agency debt is similar to Treasury debt. The minimum denomination varies from $1,000 to $50,000, depending on the particular security. Maturities at issuance also vary from 9 months to 40 years. Agency debt quotations are identical to Treasury quotations, and you can find them daily in *The Wall Street Journal*.

**Mortgage-backed
passthrough participa-
tion units:** agency
bonds that pay
investors interest and
principal on mortgage
loans

Many investors have considerable interest in agency issues that are quite different from Treasury bonds and notes. These securities are **mortgage-backed passthrough participation units** issued by the Government National Mortgage Association (Ginnie Mae), the Federal National Mortgage Association (Fannie Mae), and the Federal Home Loan Mortgage Corporation (Freddie Mac). Participation units are created when an agency buys mortgages from savings and loans, commercial banks, or other lenders and packages them in a large pool; then, individual units are sold that "pass through" mortgagee payments of interest and principal to investors. If you buy one of these units, you are acting indirectly as a mortgage lender. You will receive monthly payments of both interest and principal, and your entire investment eventually is recovered as all the mortgages in the pool are repaid.

Even though the individual mortgages in the pool may have maturities of 25 and 30 years, the pool's life is unlikely to be that long because most mortgages are repaid well before their maturities. A 12-year average often is used in evaluating passthroughs, but shorter maturities are possible and likely if interest rates fall substantially because borrowers will refinance their existing mortgages. Thus, you will be disappointed if you buy a high-yielding passthrough, expecting to enjoy this return for 25 years or longer, and then find most of the mortgages are repaid within 3 to 4 years.

Ginnie Mae passthroughs are backed by the full faith and credit of the U.S. Treasury, but other passthroughs are not. There are no particular tax advantages to passthrough issues. Any amounts you receive that are designated as principal payments represent a return of your capital and are therefore nontaxable. But this is true of any investment. Interest payments are fully taxable at the federal, state, and local levels, which means passthroughs are taxed like corporate debt. (Most other agency debt is free of state and local tax.)

Investment Appeal of Agency Issues Other than the higher yield of agency issues versus Treasury issues, little justification exists for the unusual public interest in agency debt, specifically the passthrough units. Moreover, this yield advantage may diminish if you live in an area with high local taxes on income. Also, be cautious of ads, such as the one shown in Exhibit 10.9, that create an impression of virtually no risk with agency debt. The ad tells you that prices and yields fluctuate, but the message comes after "Ready liquidity" and is situated to look more like an advantage than a disadvantage. This fund would have considerable interest-rate risk; you could be in for a real shock if you had to sell your shares on short notice and if interest rates had increased since you purchased the shares.

MUNICIPAL BONDS

Technically, a municipality is an incorporated political subdivision within 1 of the 50 states. The term **municipal bond** refers to a debt instrument of practically any political unit—city, village, school district, water district, pollution control district, county, or state—other than one of the federal government. The right to tax and borrow is a state right, one often exercised by the states and their political subdivisions in myriad ways.

Municipal bond: bond issued by a political unit within a state

The Income Tax Advantage

The popularity of municipal bonds arises primarily from the fact that the interest they pay escapes federal income taxation, although capital gains and losses resulting from trading such bonds are considered in determining taxable income. Being tax-free is no small advantage, as Exhibit 10.10 shows. An investor in a 31% bracket must earn a pre-tax return about 1.5 times the amount of the municipal's return to do as well in a taxable bond. And if you are in a 39.6% bracket, municipal bonds may well be your best investment.

This advantage can turn to a disadvantage, however, whenever Congress decides to lower marginal tax rates. (Naturally, it becomes an even bigger advantage when rates are increased.) By referring to the formula in Exhibit 10.10, you can see that the pre-tax yield equivalent would fall as the marginal tax rate falls. Other bonds would thus become more attractive relative to municipals, and to remain competitively priced with other bonds, municipal bond prices would also fall. On balance, the threat of a changing federal tax rate structure increases the overall price volatility of municipals.

Although all municipal bond interest is free of federal income tax, it may be subject to state or local income taxes if you own bonds issued by political subdivisions outside your home state or city. In response to investor demand to lower taxes, some mutual funds are offering double and triple tax-free bonds to investors residing in certain states (New York, Ohio, and Michigan, for example). Investing in these funds is one way to pay no tax whatsoever on interest earned.

EXHIBIT 10.9

Advertisement for a
Ginnie Mae mutual
fund appearing in
*The Wall Street
Journal.* (Courtesy
Dreyfus Corp.)

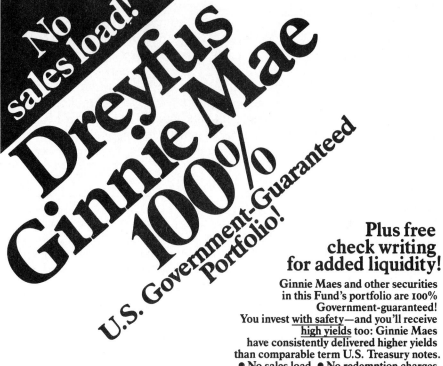

EXHIBIT 10.10
The income tax advantage of municipal bonds

The formula below is used to determine the pretax yield equivalent of a municipal bond assuming a yield of Y% and a marginal tax rate of *MTR:*

$$\text{Pretax yield equivalent (\%)} = \frac{Y\%}{(1.0 - MTR)}$$

If *Y = 8%* and *MRT = 0.31*, then

$$\text{Pretax yield equivalent (\%)} = \frac{8\%}{(1.0 - 0.31)} = \frac{8\%}{0.69} = 11.59\%$$

Sample calculated values (%)

	Bond Yield (Y)%						
MTR	4%	5%	6%	7%	8%	9%	10%
0.150	4.71	5.88	7.06	8.24	9.41	10.59	11.77
0.280	5.56	6.94	8.33	9.72	11.11	12.50	13.89
0.310	5.80	7.25	8.70	10.15	11.59	13.04	14.49
0.360	6.25	7.81	9.38	10.94	12.50	14.06	15.63
0.396	6.62	8.28	9.93	11.59	13.25	14.90	16.56

Kinds of Municipal Bonds

Almost all municipal bonds are issued in $5,000 denominations. They are purchased in registered form and have various features. Some of the more important ones are discussed below.

General Obligation Versus Revenue Bonds   A **general obligation bond** is backed by the full taxing authority of the issuer. A **revenue bond** is issued to finance a specific revenue-generating project, such as a highway or a hospital. It is backed only by the revenues the project generates. All things considered, a general obligation bond is a far stronger bond than a revenue bond. Nevertheless, new municipal bond issues are predominantly the latter by a margin of almost three to one. Practically all general obligation bonds are retired serially, while revenue bonds have a set term to maturity.

General obligation bond: municipal bond backed by the full taxing authority of the issuer

Revenue bond: municipal bond whose interest and principal can be paid only by revenues of the project for which it was issued

Zero Coupon   Many recent municipal bond offerings have been in zero coupon form. The popularity of Treasury STRIPs has not gone unnoticed by promoters of new security issues, and a zero coupon municipal bond overcomes the disadvantage of paying taxes on accrued interest on a taxable zero. So, you need not limit your purchases of zeros to those you will hold in an IRA.

It is particularly important to be aware of any call feature on a zero coupon municipal bond because interest does not accrue after the call date. With a zero coupon municipal, this could be disastrous. For example, suppose you bought a $5,000 par value, 20-year zero for $1,559 (priced to yield 6%).

BOX 10.3   GETTING AN INVESTMENT EDGE

These Floaters Aren't for Fishing

The financial engineers on Wall Street lack no imagination in devising securities to meet customer demand. With the number of municipal offerings shrinking, a new product has been hatched—inverse floaters, an ingenious creation that plays well with both sides of the interest-rate forecasting gang. Through mid-1993, more than $10 billion had been sold. Here's how they work.

Large municipal bond dealers buy a number of fixed-coupon municipals in the secondary market and then place them in a trust. Counting the fixed interest and the redemption amounts, there will be a fixed sum of money over the life of the trust. Two classes of certificates that will share the fixed sum are issued against the trust. The first class are floating-rate notes tied to an index of short-term rates. Buy these if you think interest rates will go up in the future. The second class are zero coupon notes that at the termi-

nation of the trust get all the funds left in it. Will there be anything left? Yes, if interest rates fall during the trust's life. Because the first class receives floating interest, the more rates fall, the less they get and the more funds left to the second class. So, buy the second class if you think interest rates will fall. Of course, if interest rates rise sharply, rather than fall, the second class could lose substantially, perhaps everything invested in them.

Sounds risky for the second class, doesn't it? Apparently not risky enough for crap-shooting investors. Some of the new floaters now are leveraged. Leverage is created by *not* sharing evenly the funds in the trust. For example, suppose 75% of the total is allocated to the floating-rate notes and then the gain (loss) to the second class is doubled if rates fall (increase). With this much volatility and risk, who needs Las Vegas?

You put it away until your retirement in 20 years. Unknown to you, the bond was called 10 years after issuance at $2,792. When you present the bond for redemption at your retirement date, you receive $2,792—not the expected $5,000! Unless you are willing to be an alert investor, it is better to do your municipal bond investing through pooling arrangements. Most investment advisors probably agree that this is good advice for all bond investment.

The Put Feature   In recent years, we have also seen the introduction of the adjustable-rate option bond. These are municipal bonds that give holders an option each year to sell back the bond at its face value to the issuer. The adjustable rate feature means the interest rate is also adjusted each year in step with changing market rates of interest. Such a bond provides excellent protection against interest-rate risk but, as you expect, offers considerably lower yields than conventional municipals with long maturities.

Default Risk in Municipal Bonds

Municipals, like corporate bonds, carry default risk. That fact was brought home dramatically when the Washington Public Power Supply System (WPPSS) defaulted on $2.25 billion of bonds that had been issued to finance the construction of two new plants. The failure gave WPPSS its nickname of Woops and caught investors—large and small—by surprise. Some cases were tragic, as families lost much of the life savings they had invested for eventual retirement. Two important lessons should be learned from this tragedy.

First, municipal bonds are evaluated by Moody's and Standard and Poor's (see Chapter 9) in the same manner as corporate bonds. If you invest without consulting these ratings, you are ignoring an important step in the evaluation process. Don't assume the words *government* and *safety* mean the same thing. They don't.

Second, regardless of a bond's rating, never limit your investments to a few individual issues. A portfolio is essential to eliminate random risk. Considering how many local governmental units are now issuing revenue bonds—and even general obligation bonds—of dubious quality, you should expect defaults to occur. If you can't diversify adequately on your own, you should consider buying an insured municipal bond. There are two municipal bond insurers: the American Municipal Bond Assurance Company and the Municipal Bond Insurance Association. Each of these companies is rated triple-A by Moody's and Standard and Poor's, which means the bonds they insure also carry that rating. In the municipal bond investment community, this insurance is called "sleep insurance." The fact that about one-fourth of all new long-term issues carry such insurance probably tells us that investors place a premium on sleeping. Of course, a good night's sleep costs something—a lower yield than what you could get with a poorer-rated issue.

PREFERRED STOCK

Preferred stock often is called a hybrid security because it has characteristics of both common stock and bonds. It is similar to a bond in that it usually pays a fixed dividend each year, but from a legal perspective, it is considered equity. Your rights as a preferred stockholder are stronger than those of the common stockholders but considerably weaker than bondholder rights. In the event of a forced liquidation, the lowest-ranking subordinated debenture's claim must be satisfied in full before any distribution is allowed to even the highest-ranking preferred stock. This feature alone would seem to be enough to discourage most investors, but when you consider that yields on preferred stock often are less than yields on bonds, it is a wonder anyone buys them. They do have some appealing features, however, that we will study in this chapter.

Many corporations issue preferred stock by default: they would prefer to issue bonds, but their financial position may be too weak to support a bond

Preferred stock: stock issued by corporations that has characteristics of both debt and equity issue or there may be restrictions from an existing bond indenture that pro-hibits it. Why is preferred the second choice? Very simple: bond interest can be deducted in determining taxable income and dividends cannot. Consider, then, a corporation facing a marginal tax rate of 34%. If it issues preferred stock, it must earn about $1.52 for each $1 of dividends it pays ($1.00/.66), but it must earn only $1 to pay $1 of interest. With a penalty this severe, cor-porate financial officers clearly prefer to issue bonds.

Basic Stockholder Rights

Preferred stockholders have certain basic rights, including conditional voting rights, the right to receive dividends, and the right to share in asset distribu-tions in liquidation. These rights are explained below.

Voting Rights   Unless specified to the contrary in the articles of incorpora-tion, preferred stock is nonvoting stock; however, the trend toward greater shareholder representation in corporate matters has led some issuers to extend voting rights to the preferred. This right may take the form of absolute voting rights, with the preferred shareholders voting along with the common shareholders whenever a vote is taken; or, it may be conditional on certain events taking place. These events include not paying a dividend (called **pass-ing the dividend**), or proposing a new long-term debt issue or a new pre-ferred offering, or a potential merger.

Passing the dividend: expression referring to a corporation not paying a dividend on preferred stock

A Right to Dividend Distributions   Preferred holders have a right to receive their indicated dividends. This right is legally contingent on the board of directors actually declaring them. In contrast to bond interest, which becomes a legal liability of the corporation the moment it is due, preferred dividends require a specific declaration by the board.

Until the late 1970s and early 1980s, most preferred stock was issued with a $100 par value. Since then, there has been a trend toward issuing pre-ferreds with smaller par values, probably to increase their marketability. Dividends may be expressed in dollars or as a percentage of par. In the latter case, par must be known to determine the dollar amount. Once issued, the yield on a preferred will be determined by the dollar dividend and its market price, as we will discuss later in this chapter.

Cumulative: feature stipulating that all passed dividends on preferred stock must be paid before a dividend can be paid to common stockholders

Cumulative Versus Noncumulative Dividends   If dividends are **cumula-tive,** all passed dividends must be paid before any dividend can be paid to common stockholders. If dividends are noncumulative, any passed dividend is lost forever. Allowing the corporation to pass a dividend and never be con-cerned about repaying would create an almost intolerable situation for the preferred holders. Therefore, practically all preferred is cumulative. Exhibit 10.11 shows a share of preferred stock issued by the Mead Corporation, which has been redeemed and is no longer outstanding. You should notice

EXHIBIT 10.11
A share of Mead Corporation preferred stock. (Courtesy of the Mead Corporation.)

that it is cumulative and voting. It is also convertible into shares of the common stock, and it pays an annual dividend of $2.80 a share.

Participating Versus Nonparticipating Most preferred stock receives a fixed dividend each quarter. If the preferred is nonparticipating, it receives no more than its stated amount, but if it is **participating,** it receives an additional dividend after an initial dividend is paid to the common stockholders. The participating feature was needed in the 1930s to help sell preferred during very depressed market periods. You are no longer likely to encounter a participating preferred except, possibly, in closely held corporations where stock issues can be shaped to meet unique circumstances. No participating preferred is traded on the New York Stock Exchange, the last having been retired in the early 1960s. Participating preferred, though, is often used in closely held corporations as part of the family estate plan.

Participating: feature that allows preferred stock to receive an extra dividend in certain situations

Adjustable rate preferred stock: preferred stock with dividends pegged to market rates of interest

Adjustable Rate Preferred   A new form of preferred stock was introduced in 1982—**adjustable rate preferred stock.** Rather than a fixed dividend rate, this stock has an adjustable rate, which is determined either by an index of yields on Treasury securities or through a so-called Dutch auction. The intent of either type is to offer a security that, it is hoped, has little price fluctuation and, so, appeals to investors seeking a high degree of liquidity. As we shall see shortly, practically all such investors are corporate cash managers because corporations have a strong tax incentive to earn income in the form of dividends rather than interest.

PIK preferred: preferred stock that allows its issuer to pay dividends in additional preferred shares, rather than cash

Payment-in-Kind (PIK) Preferred   We described earlier PIK bonds. With these instruments, borrowers have the option of paying interest either in cash or in additional bonds. Similar preferred stock, called **PIK preferred,** has been issued, usually as part of a financing package for a leveraged buyout. The issuer can choose to pay quarterly dividends either in cash or in additional preferred shares.

A Right to Assets in Liquidation   Preferred stockholders stand between bondholders and common stockholders when assets are distributed in liquidation. Because bonds are debt instruments, they must be paid first, including all principal and accrued interest. If corporate assets are adequate to meet these claims, then remaining funds are distributed to the preferred shareholders before distributions are made on the common. Because in the overwhelming majority of failures, assets are insufficient to meet creditor claims, it is unlikely that preferred stockholders receive anything in a forced liquidation. Thus, the advantage of ranking ahead of the common should not be viewed as a valuable one.

Some preferred stock is being referenced as *preference stock*. Such stock is a weaker form of preferred in that it ranks behind regular preferred issues with respect to both dividend and asset distributions. However, it still ranks before the common.

Other Features of Preferred Stock

A public issue of preferred stock is accompanied by a prospectus, which details shareholder rights and specifies corporate obligations. The prospectus can be viewed as an agreement between shareholders and the issuer. Some of the more important features of the agreement are explained below.

Dividend Payments   The agreement details when dividends will be paid. It also specifies the amounts or how the amount is to be calculated, if the dividend is participating or adjustable. The agreement also explains the cumulative feature and indicates when passed dividends must be paid. Because dividends are the primary reason investors buy preferreds, provisions dealing with dividends should be understood thoroughly before investing.

Retirement, Call, or Convertible   Until recently, most preferred stock was issued in perpetuity, which means it is never retired. Current trends are toward preferred with a call feature, or a convertible feature coupled with a call. The call feature gives the corporation an option to retire the issue if it so chooses. It typically does choose to do so when interest rates have fallen below the preferred's rate. If you bought preferred with a high yield and expected that yield to continue, you might be disappointed if the corporation calls the stock. The company may establish a sinking fund to retire a portion of the issue each year, either by exercising the call or through purchases in the open market. Sinking funds are not mandatory, however, and must be provided in the agreement.

Much preferred stock is convertible into shares of common stock. The preferred stock agreement must specify conversion terms, the most important being the number of common shares into which each share of preferred converts. Frequently, this conversion ratio decreases over time. Also, to force eventual conversion, the issuer must attach a call feature. Otherwise, investors might hold the preferred to receive a larger dividend than they could earn on the common, knowing the price of their preferred will increase if the common increases because it can always be converted into the common. The investment opportunities and risks of convertible securities are discussed later in this chapter.

Restrictive Covenants   Preferred stock agreements are similar to bond indentures in placing restrictions on certain company activities. These restrictions often ban the company from issuing more bonds or preferred stock; they might require that a minimum level of working capital be maintained; they might restrict dividends on the common stock; or they might call for voting rights, as we saw earlier. These covenants attempt to keep the issuer in strong financial condition, thereby safeguarding the preferred shareholders' interests.

It is important to recognize, however, that legal recourses available to preferred stockholders in the event the issuer fails to meet terms of the agreement are quite different from those available to bondholders. Preferred holders' rights derive ultimately from the articles of incorporation creating the company, not from a legal contract, such as the bond indenture. Moreover, taking action against the issuer could force it into bankruptcy—a situation in which preferred holders seldom gain an advantage.

Preferred Stock Returns

Many preferred stocks are reported in the financial pages of most newspapers. You can identify the preferred stock with the symbol pf after the company's name; for example, USX pf indicates the preferred stock of USX corporation. The return from a straight preferred is measured with the same time-value-of-money techniques explained in Chapter 3. The calculations depend

EXHIBIT 10.12

Cash flows from a perpetuity

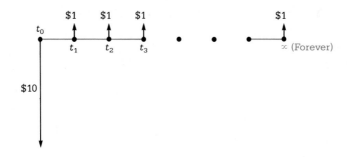

on whether the preferred is issued in perpetuity or if it has a call that is likely to be exercised.

A Perpetuity   If the preferred is a perpetuity, its cash flows would appear as indicated by the example in Exhibit 10.12. Assuming the investor pays $10 for a share of preferred that promises to pay a $1 a year dividend forever, the current yield *(CY)* is found with the formula below:

$$CY = \frac{D}{P}$$

where D = the annual dividend, and
           P = the current price of the preferred

This is the same formula you use to determine the CY on a savings account. In effect, a perpetuity is identical to a savings account (assuming interest, but not principal, is withdrawn each period). When you put your money in a savings account, you expect to receive the indicated interest rate for as long as the funds are deposited—forever, if you never withdraw principal.

Yield to Call   If a call seems likely, a more appropriate yield calculation is **yield to call (YTC).** This yield involves finding the discount rate that equates the present value of the future dividends and the call price to the current market price. Exhibit 10.13 provides two examples. Preferred *A* is selling at a price below the call. In this case, the investor believes interest rates will fall, thereby increasing the preferred's price up to the call value. Preferred *B* is selling at a price in excess of its call value. If the investor expected the issue not to be called until the end of three years (the preferred agreement might indicate this is the case), then the YTC calculation would be a realistic one to use in deciding whether or not to buy the stock. However, paying a price in excess of call value can be risky if the issue is immediately callable. The YTC figure shown for preferred *B* could be a fiction if the call takes place sooner.

Yield to call: yield calculation that assumes an issue will be called

Preferred *A*: selling at less than its call price of $9 and expected to be called at the end of three years

Preferred *B*: selling at more than its call price of $9 and not expected to be called until the end of three years

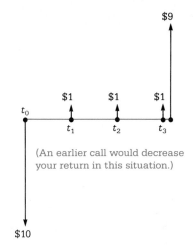

$$\$8 = \left\{ \frac{\$1}{(1 + YTC)^1} + \frac{\$1}{(1 + YTC)^2} + \frac{\$10}{(1 + YTC)^3} \right\}$$

Solve for *YTC*
YTC = .1606, or 16.06%

$$\$10 = \left\{ \frac{\$1}{(1 + YTC)^1} + \frac{\$1}{(1 + YTC)^2} + \frac{\$10}{(1 + YTC)^3} \right\}$$

Solve for *YTC*
YTC = .0689, or 6.89%

EXHIBIT 10.13
YTC calculations

YTC calculations may also be appropriate for bonds, if a call seems likely. Considering that many bond issues are callable, investors should consider the possibility of a call and calculate a YTC, rather than the YTM discussed in Chapter 9.

Comparison to Bond Yields   Exhibit 10.14 shows that yields on straight preferreds are closely correlated to bond yields. You expect this correlation because both are fixed-income securities. What you might not expect is that preferred stocks offer lower yields than bonds. Considering their lower ranking in asset distributions, most people guess that preferred yields should be higher—not lower—than bond yields. The tax law again explains the riddle. Under the present code, corporations are allowed to exclude 70% of most dividend income they receive, while they cannot exclude any interest income. The impact of this law on after-tax income and rate of return is considerable.

Because of the after-tax yield advantage of preferred, many corporate investors favor preferred over bonds, which explains why pre-tax preferred yields are less than bond yields. You must consider carefully whether you, as an individual investor, want to compete with corporate investors in the pre-

[a]Standard and Poor's Preferred Stock Index: Consists of ten high quality straight preferreds.
[b]Standard and Poor's Composite Bond Index of A-rated issues.

EXHIBIT 10.14
Preferred stock and bond yields. (Source: Standard and Poor's *Statistical Service,*
April 1993. Standard and Poor's, a division of McGraw-Hill, Inc., 25 Broadway, New
York, NY 10014.)

ferred markets. If you are interested in straight preferreds, you should be
advised not to invest because you receive no preferential tax treatment on
dividend income. However, if you have your own corporation or are associated with your family's corporation, or if you manage corporate funds, preferred
stock may be a desirable investment.

Risks in Preferred Stocks

If you invest in straight preferred stocks, you will have a risk situation almost
identical to that involved in bond investing. You must be concerned with both
interest-rate risk and default risk.

Interest-Rate Risk   Because preferred stocks are fixed-income securities,
their market prices are affected by changes in the overall level of interest
rates. It is important to measure the degree of interest-rate risk. You should
remember from Chapter 9 that two measurement tools are used: the interest
elasticity coefficient (*E*) and Macaulay's duration coefficient (*D*). We will limit

the current discussion to the interest elasticity approach. To calculate the interest elasticity coefficient for a perpetuity, we can use the formula:

$$E = \frac{\text{percentage change in preferred's price}}{\text{percentage change in preferred's CY}}$$

The elasticity formula requires two price-CY points. Returning to the example of a preferred that pays a $1 annual dividend and is currently selling for $10, by selecting a second point we can find an E value. Let's assume interest rates rise by 10%, which causes this preferred's CY also to increase by 10%, going from 10% to 11%. For CY to increase, price must decrease. To find the new price, we simply rearrange the CY formula and solve for it:

$$CY = \frac{D}{P} \quad \text{or} \quad P = \frac{D}{CY}$$

Because the new CY = 0.11, the new P = $9.09 ($1.00/0.11). The change in P is −$0.91, which is a 9.1% ($0.91/$10.00) decrease in price. Therefore, E = −.91:

$$E = \frac{-9.1}{+10.0} = -0.91$$

Suppose we go the other way and assume CY declines to 9%—a 10% decrease. Now, price increases to $11.11 ($1.00/0.09), which is an 11.11% increase ($1.11/$10.00); and:

$$E = \frac{+11.11}{-10.00} = -1.11$$

As you see, you get a different value, depending on whether CY increases or decreases. What causes the difference is the way we normally measure percentage changes. As pointed out in Chapter 9, to avoid the problem, simply average the two. By doing so, we obtain the approximate value of −1.0 [(0.91 + 1.11)/2].

The elasticity value of −1.0 is important because it applies to any perpetuity, regardless of its price, so long as current yield is held constant. For example, suppose we had a preferred that paid a $2 dividend and was currently selling for $20 a share. Going through the calculations above again would show that its elasticity is also −1.0. Exhibit 10.15 shows graphically the relation between CY and price for both securities.

If you buy a preferred stock perpetuity, then you can expect its percentage changes in price to be about the same as percentage changes in long-term bond yields. This implies considerable price risk—something to be considered carefully in making your investment selections.

EXHIBIT 10.15
Elasticity of a
perpetuity

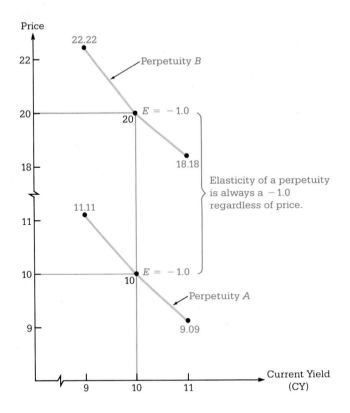

Default Risk   Investors in preferred stock must be concerned with the issuer's ability to meet future dividend payments and to retire the issue if it is not a perpetuity. You should expect that serious financial difficulties in the firm will in all likelihood lead to passed dividends. This does not mean most issuers pass the preferred dividend at the drop of a hat, but in a financial crisis, they have no choice. As a result, you can find some issues with dividends in arrears, an expression that means unpaid dividends have accumulated with the cumulative feature. Before investing, then, you should consult a rating agency to determine the quality of the issue you are considering.

Both Moody's and Standard and Poor's rate preferred issues. Their rating systems are similar to those used in rating bonds, although there are some differences. Exhibit 10.16 shows Standard and Poor's rating guide. The individual ratings reflect Standard and Poor's estimate of both the issuer's asset protection (ability to avoid bankruptcy) and its ability to pay dividends in the future. The value of such a rating guide should not be underestimated. The individual investor seldom is in a position, or skillful enough, to do her own ratings of preferred issues. Moreover, these services also provide information on individual preferred issues that you usually need if you are a potential buyer. They indicate any dividend arrearages, information certain investors find vital to their investment strategy.

"AAA"   This is the highest rating that may be assigned by Standard & Poor's to a preferred stock issue and indicates an extremely strong capacity to pay the preferred stock obligations.

"AA"   A preferred stock issue rated "AA" also qualifies as a high-quality fixed income security. The capacity to pay preferred stock obligations is very strong, although not as overwhelming as for issues rated "AAA."

"A"   An issue rated "A" is backed by a sound capacity to pay the preferred stock obligations, although it is somewhat more susceptible to the adverse effects of changes in circumstances and economic conditions.

"BBB"   An issue rated "BBB" is regarded as backed by an adequate capacity to pay the preferred stock obligations. Whereas it normally exhibits adequate protection parameters, adverse economic conditions or changing circumstances are more likely to lead to a weakened capacity to make payments for a preferred stock in this category than for issues in the "A" category.

"BB," "B," "CCC"   Preferred stock rated "BB," "B," and "CCC" are regarded, on balance, as predominately speculative with respect to the issuer's capacity to pay preferred stock obligations. "BB" indicates the lowest degree of speculation and "CCC" the highest degree of speculation. While such issues will likely have some quality and protective characteristics, these are outweighed by large uncertainties or major risk exposures to adverse conditions.

"CC"   The rating "CC" is reserved for a preferred stock issue in arrears on dividends or sinking fund payments but that is currently paying.

"C"   A preferred stock rated "C" is a nonpaying issue.

"D"   A preferred stock rated "D" is a nonpaying issue with the issuer in default on debt instruments.

NR indicates that no rating has been requested, that there is insufficient information on which to base a rating, or that S&P does not rate a particular type of obligation as a matter of policy.

EXHIBIT 10.16
Standard and Poor's preferred stock ratings. (Source: Standard and Poor's *Stock Guide*, July 1993. Standard and Poor's, a division of McGraw-Hill, Inc., 25 Broadway, New York, NY 10014.)

SUMMARY

Corporate bonds offer certain bondholder rights, which are detailed in the bond indenture. A trustee is appointed to make sure the issuing corporation meets the terms of the indenture. A mortgage bond is backed by specific real property, while a debenture is not supported by collateral. An equipment trust certificate is a mortgage bond, backed by transportation equipment. Subordinated debentures have positions inferior to straight debentures. All U.S. corporation bonds are registered (rather than held in bearer form) and have finite maturities; some have special redemption provisions that include sinking funds and serial redemption. Special bond features include convertibility into common stock, floating rates, and put options; a feature favoring the issuer is a right to call the bond before its maturity. Bonds are purchased on organized exchanges or in the over-the-counter market, and their prices are reported daily in the financial pages of many newspapers. Commissions on bonds can be relatively high, particularly if bid-asked spreads are involved. Investing in foreign bonds has become popular in recent years, although it involves an added risk called exchange-rate risk.

Treasury bonds are considered free of default risk. They can be purchased through a broker or directly from a Federal Reserve bank. Although all Treasury bonds and notes are issued in coupon form, the Treasury has a system that provides so-called STRIPS, which are the equivalent of zero coupon bonds. Agency bonds are issued by agencies of the federal government. Passthrough certificates—a type of agency issue—are also popular because of their apparent high yields; these yields may not be realized, though, because mortgages are prepaid.

Municipal bonds are issued by state and local governments. Their primary investment appeal is the lack of federal taxation on their interest. Municipal bonds can be general obligation bonds or revenue bonds. Most are interest-bearing, although zero coupon issues are becoming popular. Some offer put features to minimize interest-rate risk. Investors should be aware of default risks in municipal bonds and use quality ratings in making selections.

Preferred stock is an alternative fixed-income security, although the tax law makes it more appealing to corporate—rather than individual—investors. Preferred stockholders usually do not vote, but they do have dividend rights that usually are cumulative and nonparticipating. They also have a right to assets in liquidation, which rank ahead of common stockholder rights but are inferior to those of bondholders. A preferred stock agreement indicates dividend payments and other characteristics of the issue. It also details restrictive covenant features. The return from a straight preferred is determined using a perpetuity formula if the issue is not callable; in the event it is callable, a YTC calculation is more appropriate. Yields on preferreds often are below bond yields, which seems unusual because preferreds have a weaker position. The explanation is that corporate investors favor preferreds over bonds because of a dividend exclusion allowed in determining corporate taxable income. Risks in preferred stocks include interest-rate risk and default risk. The latter risk is estimated by rating agencies: Standard and Poor's and Moody's.

KEY TERMS (listed in order of appearance)		
	corporate bond	income bond
	bond indenture	PIK bond
	trustee	sinking fund
	mortgage bond	serial redemption
	debenture	convertible bond
	equipment trust certificate	exchangeable bond
	subordinated debenture	floating rate bond
	registered bonds	put bond
	bearer bonds	super poison put

event risk
call premium
Brady bond
stripped Treasury securities
federal agency bond
mortgage-backed passthrough
  participation units
municipal bond
general obligation bond

revenue bond
preferred stock
passing the dividend
cumulative
participating
adjustable rate preferred stock
PIK preferred
yield to call

1. What is a corporate bond? What basic rights do bondholders have and how are these rights protected?

2. How does a mortgage bond differ from a debenture? Explain which kind of bond is an equipment trust certificate.

3. What is a subordinated debenture? Discuss the risks associated with this type of bond.

4. Identify and explain the following bond characteristics: *(a)* registered bond versus bearer bond; *(b)* sinking fund and serial redemption; *(c)* convertible bond; *(d)* floating rate versus put bond; *(e)* the right to call and the call premium.

5. Explain an income bond, indicating the circumstances usually associated with its issuance.

6. Explain a PIK bond and discuss possible risks associated with it.

7. Explain event risk and discuss how a super poison put deals with it.

8. You are thinking of buying seven bonds issued by Duke Power. They have a face value of $1,000 and a market price of $800. How much commission can you expect to pay on the purchase?

9. Explain why you might want to invest in foreign bonds. How can you make such investments, and what added risk do you assume? What are Brady bonds?

10. Briefly explain Treasury debt, indicating your opinion of its safety and adequacy of return (include taxes in your response).

11. Explain a STRIP, indicating its possible investment appeal.

12. What are agency issues? Are these good substitutes for Treasury issues? Discuss.

13. What are mortgage-backed passthrough participation units, such as Ginnie Maes? Explain why falling interest rates might be a concern if you own such units. Finally, do you regard a mutual fund investing in Ginnie Maes to be about as safe as a money market fund? Explain.

14. How does a general obligation municipal bond differ from a municipal revenue bond? Which one is safer? Which is more popular?

15. Is there an advantage in owning a zero coupon municipal or an adjustable-rate option municipal? Explain each.

16. Because municipalities are governments, is it necessary to exercise precautions in selecting municipal bonds? Explain, indicating what precautions, if any, you might take. Include in your answer a discussion of "sleep insurance."

17. Explain why preferred stock is called a hybrid security and why most corporations prefer not to issue preferreds, choosing bonds instead.

18. Briefly explain the basic rights of preferred stockholders, comparing their rights with those of common stockholders and bondholders.
19. Compare the following: cumulative versus noncumulative; participating versus nonparticipating.
20. Explain PIK preferred and adjustable rate preferred.
21. Explain three ways a preferred stock may be terminated—that is, not have a perpetual life.
22. Indicate similarities between preferred stock and bonds with respect to requirements imposed on the corporation. Explain whether preferred holders have equal legal recourses if issuers fail to meet the requirements.
23. A perpetuity formula often is used to evaluate a preferred stock. What is the assumption when such a formula is used? Explain when it might be inappropriate, and indicate a more appropriate valuation formula in these instances.
24. Why are yields on preferred stocks often less than bond yields, even though they typically represent greater investment risk? Also, indicate if the yields on bonds and preferred stocks move together or in opposite directions.
25. What is the elasticity value for a perpetuity? Explain how to interpret this value and use it in making investment decisions.

PROBLEMS AND PROJECTS

1. You purchased three subordinated debentures and two debentures ($1,000 face value for each) of Dekline Corporation several years ago. The company has recently gone into bankruptcy and all its assets have been sold for $3 million. You have learned the company issued $2 million of subordinated debentures and $2 million of debentures and has $4 million of general creditor claims. Assuming you paid face value for your bonds, how much will you lose in the bankruptcy?

2. You are reading a bond quotation in the morning newspaper:

   Ace   9s   11   9.7   25   93⅛   92⅛   92¼   +1¼

   a. Briefly explain what each item above means, putting prices in dollars and cents.
   b. Using a financial calculator, determine the bond's YTM and compare it with its current yield. Assume it is 1991.

3. Interpret the following Treasury quotation (put prices in dollars and cents):

   10s   2010   Feb   102:8   102:24   +.4   9.92

4. You can invest in a municipal bond yielding 8% or a corporate bond yielding 10%. Show which one is the better of the two, assuming marginal tax rates of 15%, 28%, and 33%.

5. Assume the yield on AAA-rated corporate bonds is 8.5% while Treasuries with similar maturities are yielding 7.9%. If you have a 33% federal income tax rate and a 12% combined state and local income tax rate, which bond offers the higher after-tax yield?

6. Blant Corporation has a cumulative preferred issue outstanding with an indicated annual dividend of $2 a share. There are 50,000 shares issued and 150,000 shares of common stock outstanding.

a. Assuming Blant declares a total dividend of $200,000, indicate the per share distribution to the preferred and the common. Indicate amounts for each if dividends of $80,000 or $400,000 were declared.

b. Assume Blant was forced to pass dividends for two full years. Things have improved, and it wants to resume paying dividends. In the first quarter that dividends resume, how much must be paid the preferred before distribution is made to the common?

7. Determine the CY for a perpetuity that pays $4 a year in dividends and has a price of $50 a share. Suppose the issue has a call at $48 a share that can be exercised by the company at any time. However, you think that it will not be called for two years. Estimate your YTC in this case. Suppose your assumption is wrong and the issue is called one year later. What is your actual return?

8. *(Student Project)* Obtain a recent issue of *The Wall Street Journal*, and in the third section, find the column indicating yields on corporates, Treasuries, and municipals. Discuss the yield situation.

9. *(Student Project)* Public utilities usually have complex capital structures. If one is located in your area, contact the public relations department and request the most recent financial report. Then, determine the different bond issues the company has outstanding. Look for key differences among the issues.

CASE ANALYSES

Florence Mims has recently been divorced. The divorce settlement has provided her with a $90,000 portfolio, invested heavily in growth stocks. Florence is in her late 30s. She has a good income as an independent accountant but lacks a retirement plan. She intends to establish one and believes that bonds should occupy a key position in it. She is unfamiliar with bond investment, however, and has turned to you for advice. Her future marginal tax rate for federal income tax is 33%, and she lives in a state with no state or local income taxes. Before your meeting with Florence, you have jotted down a number of bonds and their current YTMs (see the following list). Some, or possibly all, of these bonds may not be appropriate for her situation. Your assignment is to develop a $60,000 bond portfolio for Florence. This assumes she will leave $30,000 invested in growth stocks. Also, you can assume that Florence will manage her portfolio in the future and that she doesn't mind the related work.

**10.1
Florence Mims
Seeks a Bond
Portfolio**

Bond Sample *(all have long maturities; assume 20 years)*

(a) Florida Power and Light mortgage bond 7%

(b) Coca-Cola subordinated debentures 8.5%

(c) Frionics, Inc., (growth company) subordinated debenture 12%

(d) RJR Holdings Capital Corporation PIK subordinated debenture 12%

(e) Treasury bond 6%

(f) Federal agency bond 6.5%

(g) GMAC debentures 7.5%

(h) State of New York general obligation bonds 5.5%

(i) Collateralized Treasury receipts 5.8%

(j) Ginnie Mae passthrough certificates 7%

(k) State of California revenue bonds (zero coupon) 6.1%

Questions

a. Indicate those bonds you think are most appropriate for Florence.

b. Design a bond portfolio, indicating specific bonds selected and amounts invested in each.

10.2 Arnold Savain Considers Straight Preferreds

Arnold Savain is considering investing to establish a retirement nest egg. He knows little about stocks or bonds but believes that following a conservative investment program should reduce his portfolio risk to reasonable levels. His Uncle Mort has told him that preferred stocks are better and safer investments than common stocks. As Mort says, "That's why they're called preferred." Mort shows Arnold stock listings in the newspaper and indicates that many preferred issues have 8% and 9% yields, while yields on most common stocks are under 3%. Mort has picked three preferreds that he particularly likes and recommends that Arnold invest all his funds in them. Details for these stocks follow.

	Consolidated Retailers	Pacific Utilities	Southern Telephone
1. Par value	$100	$25	$75
2. Dividend yield	10%	8%	6%
3. Maturity	10 years	20 years	perpetuity
4. Callable	immediately	3 years	no
5. Call price	par	$30	—
6. Current market price	$105	$24	$48
7. Advisory service rank	AA	BBB	B

Although Arnold appreciates Uncle Mort's advice, he thinks a second opinion is needed. For one thing, Mort's strategy seems too simple, and for another, he notices that yields on U.S. Treasury bonds are quoted in the newspaper at 8%. As Arnold sees it, a yield this high is as good as Pacific Utilities' and better than Southern Telephone's. So, if he decides to invest in preferreds, Consolidated Retailers seems the only logical selection.

Questions

a. Calculate CYs for each security.

b. Calculate YTMs for Consolidated Retailers and Pacific Utilities. Is it likely each issuer will allow the preferreds to remain outstanding until maturity? Explain.

c. Calculate YTCs for Consolidated Retailers and Pacific Utilities, assuming the former is called in one year and the latter is called in three years.

d. What is the interest elasticity for the Southern Telephone preferred? Explain your answer.

e. Do you agree with Uncle Mort's advice? Discuss, indicating specific points of agreement or disagreement.

f. Assuming that Arnold wants to invest some of his funds in one of the three securities, which do you recommend? Explain reasons for your choice.

Gregory, Deborah W., and Miles Livingston. "Development of the Market for U.S. Treasury Strips." *Financial Analysts Journal*, March-April 1992, pp. 68–74.

Mahar, Maggie. "How Sallie Will Survive." *Barron's*, June 14, 1993, p. 10.

Schifrin, Matthew, with Lisa Coleman. "Hello, Sucker." *Forbes*, February 1, 1993, pp. 40–42.

Stein, Benjamin. "Stacked Deck." *Barron's*, June 21, 1993, p. 14.

Vogel, Thomas T., Jr. "New Unit Trust Gives Small Investors a Play on Volatile Developing-Nation Brady Bonds." *The Wall Street Journal*, June 20, 1993, p. C19.

_____. "Investors' Search for Higher Yields Has Spawned More-Volatile Inverse Floaters in Muni Realm." *The Wall Street Journal*, July 9, 1993, p. C15.

_____. "Disney Amazes Investors with Sale of 100-Year Bonds." *The Wall Street Journal,* July 21, 1993, p. C1.

HELPFUL READING

PART THREE

CFA EXAMINATION QUESTIONS

1. An investment in a coupon bond will provide the investor with a return equal to the bond's yield to maturity at the time of purchase if:

    a. the bond is not called for redemption at a price that exceeds its par value.

    b. all sinking fund payments are made in a prompt and timely fashion over the life of the issue.

    c. the reinvestment rate is the same as the bond's yield to maturity.

    d. all of the above.

Reprinted with permission of the Association for Investment Management and Research. All questions are Level I Examination Questions, unless noted otherwise. Material related to questions 1–7 can be found in Chapter 9, questions 8–11 in Chapter 10, and material related to the problems is in Chapters 9 and 10.

2. The interest rate risk of a bond normally is:

   a. greater for shorter maturities.
   b. lower for longer duration.
   c. lower for higher coupons.
   d. none of the above.

3. An 8%, 20-year corporate bond is priced to yield 9%. The Macaulay duration for this bond is 8.85 years. Given this information, the bond's modified duration is:

   a. 8.12
   b. 8.47
   c. 8.51
   d. 9.25

4. A 9-year bond has a yield-to-maturity of 10% and a modified duration of 6.54 years. If the market yield changes by 50 basis points, the bond's expected price change is:

   a. 3.27%
   b. 3.66%
   c. 5.00%
   d. 6.54%

5. When interest rates decline, the duration of a 30-year bond selling at a premium:

   a. increases.
   b. decreases.
   c. remains the same.
   d. increases at first, then declines.

6. Yield to maturity and current yield on a bond are equal:

   a. when market interest rates begin to level off.
   b. if the bond sells at a price in excess of its par value.
   c. when the expected holding period is greater than one year.
   d. if the coupon and market interest rate are equal.

7. Which bond has the longest duration?

   a. 8-year maturity, 6% coupon
   b. 8-year maturity, 11% coupon
   c. 15-year maturity, 6% coupon
   d. 15-year maturity, 11% coupon

8. A firm's preferred stock often sells at yields below its bonds because:

   a. owners of preferred stock have a prior claim on the firm's earnings.
   b. preferred stock generally carries a higher agency rating.
   c. corporations owning stock may exclude from income taxes most of the dividend income they receive.
   d. owners of preferred stock have a prior claim on a firm's assets in the event of liquidation.

9. Any bond issued by an agency of the U.S. government:
   a. is exempt from the federal income tax on interest.
   b. becomes a direct obligation of the U.S. Treasury in case of default.
   c. is secured by assets held by the agency.
   d. none of the above.

10. All else being equal, which *one* of the following bonds *most likely* would sell for the highest price (or lowest yield)?
    a. Callable debenture
    b. Putable mortgage bond
    c. Callable mortgage bond
    d. Putable debenture

11. A municipal bond carries a coupon of 6 3/4% and is trading at par; to a taxpayer in the 34% tax bracket, this bond would provide a taxable equivalent yield of:
    a. 4.5%
    b. 10.2%
    c. 13.4%
    d. 19.9%

PROBLEMS (Level II Examination)

Barney Gray, CFA, is Director of Fixed-Income Securities at Piedmont Security Advisors. In a recent meeting, one of his major endowment clients suggested investing in corporate bonds yielding 9%, rather than U.S. government bonds yielding 8%. Two bond issues—one U.S. Treasury and one corporate—were compared to illustrate the point.

U.S. Treasury bond	8% due 6/15/2010	Priced at 100
AJAX Manufacturing	9.5% due 6/15/2015	Priced at 105
Rated AAA		
Callable @ 107.5 on 6/15/1995		

Gray wants to prepare a response based upon his expectation that long-term U.S. Treasury interest rates will fall sharply (at least 100 basis points) over the next three months.

   a. **Evaluate** the return expectations for *each* bond under this scenario, and **support** an evaluation of which bond would be the superior performer. **Discuss** the price-yield measures that affect your conclusion.

Following Gray's response in Part *a* above, his client wanted to know why a collateralized mortgage obligation, which is AAA rated and composed of only government-guaranteed bonds, should yield 9.5% when U.S. Treasury bonds yield only 8%. Both bonds have modified durations of seven years.

   b. Justify the yield spread between these two securities that appear to have similar quality characteristics. Discuss the differences in return behavior in these two types of bonds.

Using Leverage-Inherent Investments

Leverage-inherent investments provide opportunities to shape investment portfolios in ways otherwise unattainable. They can be used to increase potential return *or* to reduce risk. In this latter capacity, they often perform an insurance function—guaranteeing certain outcomes, but at a cost. Leverage-inherent investments are also called derivative instruments because their value derives from that of the underlying securities to which they have claims.

Chapter 11 explains the nature of an option security. It indicates how the market value of an option depends on its specific characteristics and on certain market factors. Warrants, rights, and convertibles are explained and discussed in detail, with emphasis placed on their investment advantages and disadvantages.

Chapter 12 extends option analysis to put and call options. It identifies their unique characteristics and how they are used in speculative and hedging situations. Covered option writing is also explained and evaluated in terms of its risk and potential for increasing return.

Chapter 13 discusses uses of commodity and financial futures in investment portfolios. It indicates their hedging and speculating opportunities and describes how they can be used in place of other investments, such as common stocks and bonds.

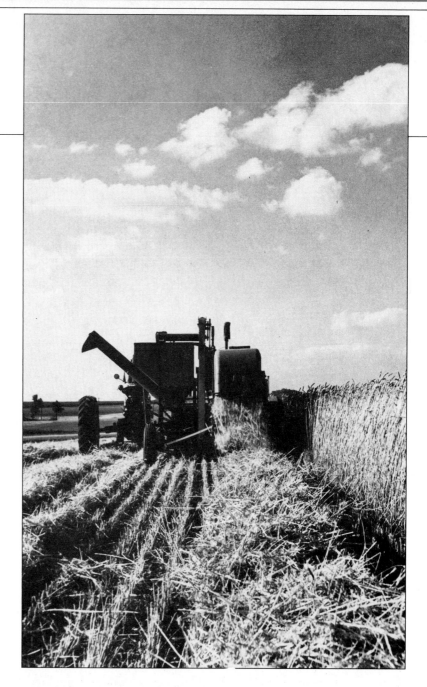

CHAPTER ELEVEN

Warrants, Rights, and Convertibles

After you finish this chapter, you will be able to:

- understand the nature of an option security and identify its key characteristics.

- determine an option security's formula value and option premium.

- recognize and understand the factors that influence the market value of an option.

- understand the characteristics of warrants and reasons for investing in them.

- understand the characteristics of rights and recognize why it is important to take action within rights' maturities.

- understand the characteristics of convertibles, comparing and contrasting them with warrants.

- use a method that helps to evaluate a convertible issue and judge its investment suitability.

W̲arrants, rights, and convertibles (covered in this chapter) and put and call options (covered in Chapter 12) share a common characteristic: they give you the right to buy or sell an underlying security. You may have heard of options being used in other areas, such as someone holding an option to purchase a parcel of land, or a professional sporting team having an option to acquire the contract of a certain player. Although options have many uses, they are most prevalent in financial markets, where their trading has become highly standardized and extremely efficient. The beginning investor often sees option securities as nothing more than wagering tickets, but that perception is not completely accurate. Surprisingly, options can be used both to increase and to decrease investment risk, as we shall see.

OPTION VALUE

Option security: instrument that gives its
owner a right to buy or
sell an underlying asset

An **option security** (or option, for short) is any instrument that gives its owner a right to buy or sell an underlying asset at a set price over a given period of time. An option derives its value exclusively from the value of the underlying asset to which it has a claim. Exhibit 11.1 shows the relation with a hypothetical ADM option. This option is referred to as a call because it gives its holder the right to buy ("call") the underlying security from someone else. In contrast to calls, there are put options, which allow holders to sell ("put") shares of the underlying security to others. For ease of presentation, the discussion in this section is limited to call options; also, we are discussing option value in general and not specific options. The general principles, however, apply to all types of option securities.

Derivative instrument:
option that focuses on
the value of the option's
underlying asset

Because of the value relation between an option and its underlying security, options are called **derivative instruments.** Moreover, changes in their value correlate almost perfectly with changes in value of the underlying security. Suppose the option in Exhibit 11.1 allowed its holder to buy one

EXHIBIT 11.1
Example of an option
security

* Standard option contracts (explained in Chapter 12) deal with 100 shares of the underlying stock. However, it is usually easier for beginners to understand option principles by considering one share for one option.

share of ADM stock at $150 a share anytime within the next six months. The value of this option would depend on the market price of ADM.

Exhibit 11.2 shows the **minimum** (or **formula**) **value** of the option, given different prices of the stock. The minimum value is the lowest possible market value of an option: the formula for determining this value will be discussed shortly. In this example, if the stock's price is $160, the minimum value of the option should be $10. Why can't it be less? Suppose it were $5: you could make an easy, risk-free profit by buying the option and using it to buy one share of ADM at $150. Your total investment would be only $155, and you could immediately sell the share for $160 to net $5 on the deal. Of course, everyone is free to do this, and buying pressures should arise to push the price of the option up to its formula value of $10. Indeed, some investors might think so highly of the option they would bid its price beyond the formula value. For example, if ADM's price is $149, its formula value is zero. But would you be willing to pay something for an option that allows you to buy a share at the fixed price of $150 anytime you want within the next six months? You almost certainly would! Clearly, the formula value is simply a starting point to estimate an option's market value. Before examining market value, we need to understand very well the important features of an option.

Minimum (formula) value: option's lowest theoretical value

Option Features

The important features of an option are its nature as a right, its strike price, and its maturity. These are explained below.

A Right, Not an Obligation An option provides a *right* to buy or sell the underlying security. There is no obligation to do so. You are not forced to buy

Formula Value of the Option ($)

A formula value is the lowest price at which an option can sell; however, actual market price is usually much higher than this minimum.

Formula Value

Market Value of the Underlying Stock ($)

Strike Price

EXHIBIT 11.2

Illustration of an option's formula value

ADM at $150 a share. If its market price is less than this at the end of the option's life, you will discard the option as you would a losing lottery ticket. Any amount you paid for it is a total loss.

Strike price: price at which an option's underlying asset can be purchased

The Strike Price The **strike price** (also called exercise price) is the price you must pay to acquire the underlying security. It is fixed for the life of the option, so you know in advance how much it will cost to acquire the security. Without an option, you must endure the risk of a changing price. Suppose it is important that you pay no more than $150 for ADM: without the option, there is no guarantee, and you run the risk of being unable to make the purchase. As you see, this aspect of an option reduces risk.

The strike price in relation to the market price of the underlying security determines an option's formula value. Specifically, for a call option:

$$\text{formula value} = (\text{market price of stock} - \text{strike price})$$

Formula values can be positive or negative, although the latter has no economic relevance.

In the money: option has positive formula value

Out of the money: option has negative formula value

At the money: option has approximately zero formula value

Maturity Maturity refers to an option's life, which is the length of time available to exercise it. If a call option is about to expire, and if its strike price is below the underlying security's market price—a situation called **"in the money"**—you would choose to exercise the option even if you did not want the underlying security. You can always sell it at the market price and earn the profit the option provides. However, if the option is **"out of the money"**—strike price is greater than the underlying security's market price—you discard the option and let it expire worthless. The expression **"at the money"** means the strike price is equal to the market price. If this occurs at maturity, the option is still worthless.

Options and Leverage

Leverage-inherent investments: options that focus on their ability to magnify price volatility

In addition to being called derivative investments, options are called **leverage-inherent investments.** An option investment by itself can allow you to control many more shares of the underlying security than you could by investing the same amount directly in the security. This leverage is illustrated with the example in Exhibit 11.3.

Suppose you have $16,000 to invest and you are thinking of buying 100 shares of ADM currently selling at $160 a share. As an alternative, you also are considering buying 1,600 of the six-month, $150-strike-price options at $10 each. Assuming you hold the options until their maturity and then either exercise or discard them, you will lose the entire $16,000 if ADM's last price is $150 or less; if it is $160, you break even; and at $170, you make $16,000 profit. With the stock itself, your profit or loss is much less—only $1,000. In effect, the options give the price action of 1,600 shares, rather than only 100,

	Closing Price of ADM Stock		
	150	160	170
1. $16,000 invested in 100 shares of common stock	$ (1,000)	$-0-	$ 1,000
2. $16,000 invested in 1,600 options with a $150 strike price	$(16,000)	$-0-	$16,000

EXHIBIT 11.3
Profit (losses) from investing in ADM stock versus investing in ADM options

over the six-month period. This is an exceptionally high degree of leverage that often appeals to risk-seeking investors. We'll see later that leverage has value to investors, and the more leverage embedded in an option, the greater the option's value, all other things held constant.

Determinants of Market Value

Five factors determine the market value of an option: (1) the number of shares it controls, (2) its strike price in relation to the market price of the underlying stock, (3) its maturity, (4) the price volatility of the underlying stock, and (5) the level of interest rates. Factors (1) and (2) determine the option's formula value, while factors (3), (4), and (5) determine its time premium, a concept to be explained shortly. A discussion of each of the five factors follows.

Number of Shares Controlled   Our example so far has assumed a one-to-one relation between an option and the underlying stock; that is, one option controls one share of stock. However, the relation is not always one to one. Some warrants, for example, call more or less than one share. The standardized put and call contracts that we will discuss in Chapter 12 have a relation of 100 shares per contract. The greater the number of shares controlled, the greater the option's formula and market values.

Strike Price and Underlying Stock's Market Price   As we have shown, the formula value of an option depends directly on the price of the underlying stock. As formula value changes, the market value of the option must change by at least an equal amount. If the company splits the stock or declares a stock dividend, the strike price of the option is automatically adjusted proportionately. So, if ADM declared a two-for-one stock split, the option's new strike price would be $75 per share.

Maturity   All things the same, the longer the maturity of an option, the greater its market value. For an option to have value at its maturity, it must be in the money; and the longer the period before maturity, the greater the probability this price movement will take place. Suppose ADM is selling at

BOX 11.1   INVESTMENT INSIGHTS

Exotic Options: When Will the Variations End?

An option contract seems simple enough: you pay a premium for the right to buy or sell some asset at a fixed price over a given period. The simplicity of this "plain vanilla" option is deceptive, however, because it can be held in so many different configurations. If you have struggled to understand strategies such as hedges, spreads, covered option writing, synthetic securities, and others, you probably wonder why anyone would want an option flavor other than plain vanilla.

Well, you would be wrong. The growing interest in risk management uncovered new potential-loss situations and stimulated the demand for new derivative instruments to control their risks. Enter the exotic options. Here are a few of the new varieties.

☐ *All-or-Nothing Option*   An option that pays a fixed amount—say, $1,000—if it is in the money. It doesn't matter how deeply it is in the money; $1 is as good as $100.

☐ *Look-Back Option*   This option allows its holder to buy at the minimum price (call) or sell at the maximum price (put) that existed over a previous (look-back) period. Of course, the option is bought at the beginning of the period.

☐ *Compound Option*   An option on an option; for example, a call on a put.

The three new flavors above are perhaps the more popular ones, although it is difficult to imagine specific risk situations that they would help control. Actually, any type of option can be created if it satisfies a buyer and a seller. For example, one contract was created that defined the payoff as a multiple of the difference in the exchange rate between two currencies over a period of time; another pegged the payoff in relation to the difference between short-term and long-term interest rates.

We don't read much about exotic options because they are traded in the over-the-counter market and are not standardized as are the exchange-traded puts and calls. Moreover, the action usually is limited to big players, mostly financial institutions. The fact that you and I may never trade the exotics does not diminish their importance to us. It's our money in those institutions. Supposedly, the exotics help their managers manage our risk exposure more effectively. Let's hope they know what they are doing.

$140 and you are considering the option with the $150 strike price. You might not pay much for one that matures in a week, realizing there is little remaining time for ADM to gain $10 or more. On the other hand, you might pay quite a bit for a six-month option because ADM has a good chance of increasing by $10 over such a long period.

Price Volatility of the Underlying Security   If you were considering the six-month option just mentioned, you would also be concerned about the price volatility of ADM's stock. The greater the volatility of the stock, the greater the probability your option will be in the money. So, options on volatile stocks are worth more than similar options on stable ones. Some beginning investors find this relation confusing because they associate greater volatility with greater risk and less—not more—value. An option, though, presents a different situation. Keep in mind that you are not taking a downside price risk beyond the amount you pay for the option. If you paid, say, $15 for the option above and ADM fell to $100 a share, your loss is still only $15. Someone who bought the stock would lose $40. Options allow investors to play volatile stocks with limited and known risks. Investors are willing to pay for this advantage, and the riskier the stock, the more they are willing to pay.

Level of Interest Rates   It is not intuitively clear why interest rates should have a bearing on the market prices of options, but they do. The connection arises from the leverage-inherent nature of options. The simplest way to see this connection is to view options as an alternative to other leverage techniques, such as buying securities with a margin account. Suppose you are considering the two alternatives: margin or options. If the interest rate on the margin account is high, you should prefer options, and you also should be willing to pay more for them than if margin interest was low. Thus, high interest rates are associated with high option prices, and vice versa.

Exhibit 11.4 can help you remember the five important factors influencing option value. The exhibit assumes an increase in each factor, so you should realize that a decrease would have the opposite effect of the one shown.

Predicting Market Values

Considerable research has been done in the area of determining market values for options. Given the factors discussed above, it is possible to construct a model that indicates what the market price of an option should be. The most widely used such model is one developed by Fischer Black and Myron

	Change in Factor	Change in Option Value
1. Number of options to acquire one share of the underlying stock	+	−
2. Market price of the underlying stock	+	+
3. Option's maturity	+	+
4. Price volatility of the underlying stock	+	+
5. The overall level of interest rates	+	+

EXHIBIT 11.4

Factors influencing an option's market value

Black-Scholes Model:
technique for estimating
the market value of an
option

Scholes, called the **Black-Scholes Model (BSM).** Exhibit 11.5 shows theoretically predicted market values for the $150 ADM option, along with the formula values. Note that the market value of the option is $15 when the market price of the stock is $160.

Also, notice the option has value even when the stock's market price is far below the strike price of $150. As long as there is even a small possibility that ADM's price could increase sufficiently within six months to put the option in the money, investors would be willing to pay some amount for the option. Also, you can see that the spread between an option's market value and its formula value decreases as the stock's price increases. This spread is called the **time premium,** and the relation below shows how it is determined:

Time premium: difference between an option's market value and its formula value; premium decays over time

$$\text{time premium} = (\text{market value of option} - \text{formula value of option})$$

So, the time premium is $5 ($15 − $10) when the price of the stock is $160. (The graph does not show negative formula values because they have no practical application.) Also, all options should have a positive time premium, as shown in Exhibit 11.5.

Do market prices of options actually behave in the manner predicted by the BSM? On balance, they appear to, making the BSM one of the most useful theoretical constructs to come from the field of finance. Its worth is dra-

EXHIBIT 11.5

Market value of an option and option premium

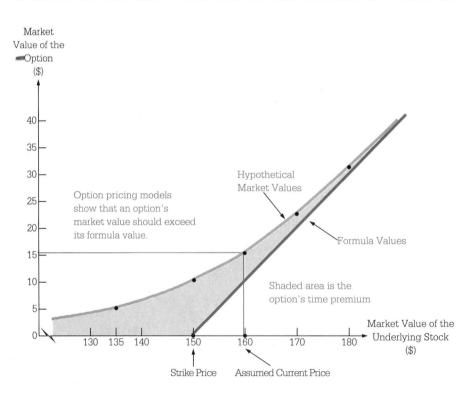

matically shown by the fact that practically every option specialist uses it to look for overvalued or undervalued options. You can buy BSM software for your computer, and there are programmed hand calculators that use the model. The important point to recognize is that option trading is a highly specialized and sophisticated area—not one in which you trade on the basis of guesswork and hunches.

What Determines Time Premium?

The willingness of investors to pay a time premium depends on the option's formula value and its maturity, all other factors held constant. Let's see why.

The Loss of Leverage   If you look closely at Exhibit 11.5, you should notice that time premium becomes smaller as the price of the stock (and formula value) increases. The explanation of this relation is that leverage becomes less important as formula value increases, and investors will pay less for it. For example, if ADM's price increased to $200 a share, the option now has a formula value of $50; thus, it takes more than three times the investment to control one share than when ADM's price was $150. Leverage is slipping. To really see the relation, suppose ADM went to $1,000 a share; now the option's formula value is $850, and you pay almost as much for the option as you do for the stock. Now, leverage is completely lost, as is time premium.

The Loss of Time   As we noted earlier, an option's maturity determines its market value. We can say more specifically that as time passes, time premium decays. Surprisingly, the **decay rate** is not constant per unit of time but is more like the figure shown in Exhibit 11.6. As you see, the decay rate moves rather slowly early in an option's life but quickly speeds up as the option gets close to maturity. This rate of decay has important implications to option traders. For example, suppose you bought ADM's option when it was first sold. Your intention was a quick speculation that ADM would jump in price within a week for some particular reason. But suppose you guessed wrong, and ADM remains flat. You might be better off selling your option quickly to recover a relatively large portion of your cost rather than waiting too long until the option's value decays sharply.

Decay rate: rate at which an option loses value over time

WARRANTS AND RIGHTS

Warrants and rights are issued by corporations as part of their financing plans. They are typical option securities insofar as they entitle their owners to acquire other securities at a fixed price for a given period. However, there are similarities and dissimilarities between them, which are explained in the sections that follow.

EXHIBIT 11.6
An option's time
premium decay rate

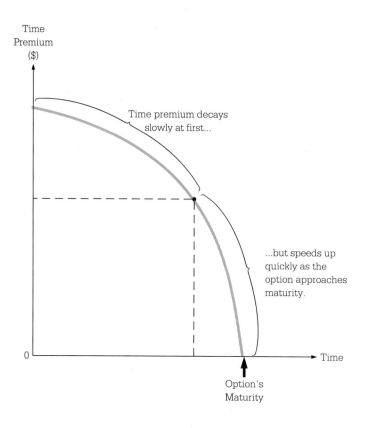

Time
Premium
($)

Time premium decays
slowly at first...

...but speeds up
quickly as the
option approaches
maturity.

0   Time

Option's
Maturity

Characteristics of Warrants

Warrants: call option
securities issued by cor-
porations as part of their
financing plans

Warrants typically come into existence as "sweeteners" as part of a corporate financing plan. They often are attached with bonds or common stock. An
example of the latter is shown in Exhibit 11.7, which shows an announcement of an offering made by the Stratosphere Corporation. The offer is a unit
consisting of one share of common stock and one warrant; however, the
tombstone ad does not tell us the number of warrants needed to buy one
share of common stock or the strike price.

Trading Warrants   Within a specified time after purchasing a unit, you may
strip the warrants and do with them as you please; that is, you can choose to
hold or sell them. They have their own investment lives and often are traded
on the organized exchanges or in the over-the-counter market. If you look at
stock quotations in the financial pages of a newspaper, you will find them
listed in the same place you find stocks, and you identify them with the symbol *wt* after the issuer's name. Commissions on warrants usually follow the
same schedules brokers use for common stocks.

New Issue

Own a piece of THE TOWER

11,700,000 Units
7,000,050 Units Minimum

STRATOSPHERE CORPORATION
LAS VEGAS, NV

PRICE $5.00 PER UNIT

The Company is developing and currently constructing, and upon completion will own and operate, the 1,012 foot Stratosphere Tower and its attendant entertainment facilities. The Stratosphere Tower (America's tallest observation tower) will be located on the Las Vegas Strip next to Bob Stupak's Vegas World Hotel & Casino.

The Company is making a public offering of Units, each Unit consisting of one share of common stock and one redeemable common stock purchase warrant. The public offering price is $5.00 per Unit, minimum purchase 300 Units.

A Prospectus describing the Company and its offering may be obtained from:

YAEGER SECURITIES, INC.
ENCINO, CA

COHIG & ASSOCIATES, INC.
DENVER, CO

ROBERT TODD FINANCIAL CORPORATION
NEW YORK, NY

STUART, COLEMAN & COMPANY, INC.
NEW YORK, NY

UNION EQUITY PARTNERS
LAS VEGAS, NV

BARABAN SECURITIES, INC.
LONG BEACH, CA

CAMELOT INVESTMENT CORPORATION
HAUPPAUGE, NY

HAYNE MILLER & FARNI, INC.
MINNEAPOLIS, MN

MATHEWS, HOLMQUIST & ASSOCIATES, INC.
MINNEAPOLIS, MN

MARCHÉ SECURITIES, INC.
MINNEAPOLIS, MN

DUKE & COMPANY, INC.
NEW YORK, NY

SCHNEIDER SECURITIES, INC.
DENVER, CO

TAMARON INVESTMENTS, INC.
ENGLEWOOD, CO

VSR FINANCIAL SERVICES, INC.
LEAWOOD, KS

Or send your name and address to: Yaeger Securities, Inc., 16633 Ventura Blvd., Suite 1220c, Encino, CA 91436

EXHIBIT 11.7
Announcement of a stock issue with detachable warrants

At the time of issuance, warrants usually have maturities between 3 and 10 years, but there are exceptions, and you can even find a few perpetual warrants. Strike prices typically are fixed over the warrants' lives, although increasing strike prices are not uncommon. This feature often forces investors to use their warrants to acquire the common stock, if the warrant is in the money. Practically every warrant calls common stock; however, in a few instances, warrants might call a corporation's preferred stock or one of its bonds.

A Sample of Warrants   Exhibit 11.8 provides a small sample of warrants. The information was provided by *Value Line Options and Convertibles*, the weekly survey published May 24, 1993. Value Line is an excellent reference source for all option securities. The five issues shown were selected to show diversity in characteristics, rather than to support some argument. However, you should notice that the plus or minus sign in column 5 indicates whether an issue is in the money (+) or out of the money (−) and the dollar amount shows by how much. Notice further that issues 4 and 5—Immunex Corporation and Tyco Toys—are deepest in the money and have the lowest time premiums on an adjusted basis (which is necessary because the issues differ considerably in strike price).

Examining the five warrants, which one would you prefer to buy? Buying Immunex's is similar to buying the stock outright. It is a sizeable investment because of the high price of the warrant. In contrast, you pay only $0.03 (3 cents) for a Hotel Investors' warrant, but you are probably asking for a miracle if you expect the price of the stock to increase from $1.50 to $16.95. It's a risky proposition but one a risk-seeking investor might be inclined to take. Your preference for an option security should begin with your preference for the underlying stock. To this extent, you cannot divorce option analysis from stock analysis. However, once you have pinpointed a company that appeals to you, then it is necessary to decide whether to invest directly in the stock or indirectly through an option security. Now, option analysis, such as that provided by the BMS, can be used to determine if the warrant is overvalued or undervalued.

Characteristics of Rights

Rights: call option securities that allow a company's shareholders to acquire additional shares

Rights are also created in connection with corporate financing plans. They are issued to investors who own a company's common stock, allowing them an opportunity to acquire additional shares of stock at a price below the current market price. So, rights are always in the money, at least when they are issued. In contrast to warrants, rights have short lives—usually only several weeks.

Trading Rights   After rights have been issued, they trade in securities markets as any other option security. If you are a shareholder of a company issu-

EXHIBIT 11.8

A sample of warrants

(1) Issuer	(2) Ratio: Stock to Warrant[a]	(3) Strike Price	(4) Market Price of the Common Stock	(5) Formula Value[b]	(6) Market Price of the Warrant	(7) Premium[c]	(8) Adjusted Premium[d]	(9) Months to Maturity	(10) Price Volatility[e]
1. Bank of New York	1.00	$62.00	$51.75	$-11.25	$8.56	$19.81	.320	53	125%
2. Genesco	1.00	10.65	10.13	-.52	.63	1.15	.108	5	135
3. Hotel Investors	1.00	16.95	1.50	-18.45	0.03	18.48	1.090	39	85
4. Immunex Corporation	1.00	20.35	48.25	+27.90	29.25	1.35	.066	31	115
5. Tyco Toys	2.00	8.25	12.00	+7.50	7.75	0.25	.030	½	155

[a]The conversion ratio: for example, 2.00 means one warrant buys 2.00 shares of stock.

[b]Formula value = column (2) × [column (4) − column (3)].

[c]Premium = column (6) − column (5).

[d]Adjusted premium takes into consideration differences in strike prices; it is column (7) divided by column (3).

[e]This volatility measurement is calculated by Value Line. It is the standard deviation of the security's price relative to the standard deviation of the average common stock covered by Value Line.

SOURCE: Securities' details are from *Value Line Convertibles*, May 24, 1993. Copyright 1993 by Value Line, Inc. All rights reserved; reprinted with permission. All calculations of return, premia, or value are those of the authors.

ing rights, you must decide whether you will use them to acquire additional shares or sell them before they expire. It is important that you act within the right's maturity because if you fail to do so, the right will expire and you will suffer a loss if the right is in the money, which it usually is. Many shareholders in the past have ignored their rights for whatever reason and have suffered unnecessary losses. An advantage in exercising rights is that you save commissions in acquiring additional shares of stock. However, there is no advantage in using your rights to buy at the lower strike price. Although this may seem an advantage, it isn't because you give up the opportunity to sell your rights. Because of their short lives, rights have limited uses as option instruments.

Formula Value of a Right   Because you may come in contact with rights as a shareholder, it is useful to understand how the formula value of a right is determined. This value depends essentially on two factors: the number of rights *(N)* it takes to acquire one new share of the common stock and the subscription (strike) price *(SP)* of the rights offering. Suppose you have learned that Ralston Purina is planning a rights offering to raise $500 million. You know there are 40 million shares of common stock outstanding, so 40 million rights will be issued; each share always receives one right. You determine the company will set a subscription price at $25 a share, and the current market price *(MP)* of the stock is $35 a share.

Before calculating the formula value for each right, you must determine how many rights will be required to buy one new share. You can do this by first dividing the amount of funds to be raised by the subscription price to determine the number of new shares to be issued. The answer is 20 million ($500,000,000/$25); then, because 40 million rights will be issued, it will take two rights (plus $25) to buy one new share. The formula value *(V)* for each right is:

$$V = \frac{(MP - SP)}{(N + 1)} = \frac{(\$35 - \$25)}{(2 + 1)} = \frac{\$10}{3} = \$3.33$$

Assuming you own 100 shares, you would receive 100 rights with a total value of $333.33. Although this seems like a good deal, the company is not providing a gift. After the rights are issued, the market price of the stock will fall by the value of each right. In our example, the price will fall to $31.67 ($35 minus $3.33). Suppose you decide to sell your rights. You will then have $333.33 plus stock worth $3,166.67; you are no better or worse off after the rights offering.

Exercising the rights won't increase your net worth, either. The following calculations demonstrate this point by comparing the two alternatives.

	Exercise Rights	Sell Rights
Number of rights granted	100	100
Number of new shares purchased	50	-0-
Cash used to buy new shares @ $25 each	$1,250	-0-
Market value of stock owned:		
150 shares @ $31.67	$4,750	—
100 shares @ $31.67	—	$3,167
Cash from selling rights	—	333
Cash retained by not buying new shares	—	1,250
New worth after taking action	$4,750	$4,750

This comparison shows there is no particular advantage in either selling or exercising rights. If you care to increase your investment on a commission-free basis, then you should exercise; if that is not important, then sell the rights. What is important is taking action within the rights' maturity. Failure to do so in the example above leads to an unnecessary loss of $333.33.

CONVERTIBLES

A **convertible security** usually is one that can be exchanged for shares of common stock of the issuer; however, there are a few convertibles that exchange into preferred stock or bonds. Convertibles are an important financing medium for many corporations, and they are used extensively. There are both convertible preferred stocks and convertible bonds. Listings of each can be found in the financial pages where other preferred stocks and other bonds are listed. The symbol *cv* appears after the name of the issuer if it is a convertible bond; convertible preferreds have no identifying symbol.

Convertible security: company's bond or preferred stock that owners can convert into its common stock

Characteristics of Convertibles

Convertibles are complex financial instruments. In contrast to a bond with detachable warrants that allow investors to strip the option value from the debt security, a convertible's option value is permanently fixed to it and embedded in its market price. Investors, then, must evaluate both debt and option characteristics of convertibles in forming portfolios.

Debt Characteristics   Exhibit 11.9 shows an announcement of a convertible bond issued some time ago by Dreyer's Grand Ice Cream. If you were thinking of buying this bond, you would want to know its coupon rate (6.5%), its maturity (May 25, 2011), and any other debt characteristic—such as quality rating, call provisions, sinking fund availability, and more—that might help you evaluate the instrument as a debt security. Because these have been cov-

EXHIBIT 11.9

Announcement of a convertible bond issue appearing in *The Wall Street Journal*. (Courtesy Dreyer's Grand Ice Cream.)

This advertisement is neither an offer to sell nor a solicitation of an offer to buy these securities. The offering is made only by the Prospectus. These securities are redeemable prior to maturity as set forth in the Prospectus.

<u>NEW ISSUE</u>

$50,000,000

6½% CONVERTIBLE SUBORDINATED DEBENTURES DUE 2011

The Debentures are convertible into Common Stock of the Company at any time on or before May 25, 2011, unless previously redeemed, at a conversion price of $32 per share, subject to adjustment under certain conditions.

Price 100%

(Interest payable June 1 and December 1 in each year)

Copies of the Prospectus may be obtained in any State only from the undersigned as may lawfully offer these securities in such State.

HAMBRECHT & QUIST
INCORPORATED

---

ered in Chapter 10, we will not repeat them here. In evaluating the Dreyer's bond, we will assume a 25-year maturity, although it is likely to be far less than this as you read the discussion.

A first point of interest to the convertible investor is how much interest return he is giving up by buying a convertible rather than a straight bond. At the time the Dreyer's issue came to market, 25-year Treasury bonds were yielding about 7.5%. Without the convertible feature, the Dreyer's bond would yield much more than 6.5%; it might yield, say, 9.5%. Thus, you give up about $30 a year on each bond to hold the convertible option. However, you hold a debt instrument with whatever protections it provides in the event of default. This issue might have greater appeal than Dreyer's common stock with its far greater bankruptcy risk.

Option Characteristics The most important option characteristic is the instrument's **conversion ratio.** This ratio tells us the number of common shares into which the instrument converts. The announcement in Exhibit 11.9 does not give the conversion ratio, but it does show a conversion price of $32 (conversion price is the same as strike price). Knowing that, we can determine the conversion ratio by also knowing that most bonds have a face value of $1,000. The calculation is shown below:

$$\text{conversion ratio} = \frac{\$1,000}{\text{conversion price}} = \frac{\$1,000}{\$32} = 31.25$$

Conversion ratio: number of common shares acquired by converting one convertible bond or one preferred share

The Dreyer's convertible converts into 31.25 shares of Dreyer's common stock. Although practically all bonds have both conversion ratios and conversion prices, many convertible preferred stocks have only conversion ratios. For example, Delta Airlines has a convertible preferred that converts into 0.760 shares of the common. The lack of a conversion price is not a material item because it does not have any influence on conversion value.

Along with the conversion ratio, other important information would be how long the conversion right lasts (25 years in Dreyer's case) and whether or not the conversion ratio is fixed over the life of the issue. This ratio frequently decreases over time, serving as an incentive to investors to convert into the common earlier rather than later. Call provisions on the bond are also important because a call could shorten the option period, thereby lowering the option value.

Investment Opportunities in Convertibles

Sometimes convertibles are called the best of both worlds. This lavish praise arises from the fact that as a bond, a convertible offers a relatively safe investment, while at the same time providing participation in the issuer's growth through the convertible feature. True, a convertible does possess these features, but you pay for them through its higher market price. As with every investment, there is the inevitable trade-off of risk and return.

Convertible Values Illustrated Given its particular debt and option characteristics, the value of a convertible at any time depends primarily on the market price of the underlying common stock and the general level of interest rates. The influence of these factors for the Dreyer's bond is shown in Exhibit 11.10.

Value as Straight Debt If you bought the bond, you might argue the worst that could happen (short of bankruptcy) would be a sharp drop in the price of the common stock. Even if that happened, you would still hold a bond paying 6.5% interest each year, or $32.50 every six months. Assuming it will be redeemed at $1,000 at the end of 25 years and also assuming an opportunity investment rate (what you could earn by investing in a similar

EXHIBIT 11.10

Dreyer's Grand Ice Cream convertible bond

bond without a conversion option) of 9.5% allows us to determine the bond's **value as straight debt.** We do this by calculating its present value, using the methods explained in Chapter 9. This value is $715.23. The Dreyer's bond, then, should have a market price at least this high, as long as interest rates don't change. In Exhibit 11.10, the value as straight debt is shown as a horizontal line that implies this value is not influenced by the price of the common stock. At low prices of the common stock, this value dominates other values, which is indicated by the color portion of the line. At high prices of the common stock, the value as straight debt is unimportant because conversion value becomes dominant.

Value as straight debt: value of a convertible bond without considering its conversion option

Conversion Value   A convertible's **conversion value** is its value as a common stock. To determine this value, you multiply the price of the common stock by the conversion ratio. If the common stock price is zero, conversion value is also zero; as the price increases, conversion value increases in proportion to the conversion ratio, as shown in Exhibit 11.10. Notice that when the price of the common stock is $26 a share—the actual market price of Dreyer's common when the convertible was issued—conversion value is $812.50 (31.25 × $26). As you see in Exhibit 11.10, when conversion value reaches $715.23, at a price of $22.89 for the common ($715.23/31.25), it dominates the value as straight debt. The color portion of the line indicates that conversion value dominates. The entire color line, then, represents minimum values for the convertible. It should never sell below these prices in efficient markets.

Conversion value: value of the number of shares of common stock into which the convertible converts

Theoretical Market Value   Using an option pricing model, such as the BSM, you could generate theoretical market values similar to those shown in Exhibit 11.10. As we have seen before in this chapter in discussing time premium, the **conversion premium**—the difference between market value and

Conversion premium: difference between the market value of a convertible and its conversion value conversion value—becomes smaller as the price of the underlying stock increases. At high prices of the stock, owning the convertible is much like owning the stock outright: interest yield will be low and price risk will be about the same as with the stock. At low prices of the stock, the conversion premium has little value and owning the convertible is similar to owning a straight bond: interest yield is high and price risk is connected more closely with changes in interest rates (not demonstrated in the diagram) than with changes in the price of the stock (except for large increases in price).

Investors must weigh each of these situations in selecting convertibles. Many prefer to buy convertibles that are in price situations similar to the Dreyer's bond; they want a bond with a conversion price about 20% to 30% above the current market price of the stock. They hope the price will increase sufficiently over time to produce capital gains; meanwhile, they enjoy an interest yield that usually is much better than what could be earned in dividends with the common stock. Investors such as these often use a payback method to evaluate a convertible.

Using a Payback Method to Evaluate a Convertible   Suppose you thought that Dreyer's was a good investment opportunity and you planned to invest in it. However, you wondered: should the investment be in the common stock or in the convertible? If you chose to buy 31.25 shares of stock, your investment would have been the conversion value of $812.50; you would have saved the conversion premium of $187.50. But Dreyer's common stock did not pay a cash dividend at the time the convertible was issued. Looking at the situation this way, one might argue that the bond's interest each year eventually will recoup the premium. From that point on, you are better off with the bond because of the greater current return each year. How many years will it take to recover the convertible's premium? The answer to this question is called the **payback period,** or break-even time. The formula below calculates the payback period *(N):*

Payback period: length of time needed to recover the conversion premium through greater current return

$$N = \frac{\text{conversion premium}}{(CR \text{ convertible} - CR \text{ common stock})}$$

where: conversion premium = market value of the convertible minus conversion value,

CR convertible = the current return in dollars of the convertible, and

CR common = the current return in dollars on the number of common shares into which the convertible converts.

The payback period for Dreyer's is:

$$N = \frac{\$187.50}{(\$65 - \$0)} = 2.89 \text{ years}$$

Is 2.89 years good, bad, or indifferent? Although convertible investors surely look at many other factors in making a decision, any payback period of less than four years is considered a fairly quick payback. So, an argument could be made to buy the convertible rather than the stock. Given its better position in the event of financial trouble, this advice seems even more appropriate. Dreyer's might represent an excellent growth company, and at the end of 2.89 years, you may have wished that you invested the entire $1,000 in the common stock to buy 38.46 shares ($1,000/$26). On the other hand, if the price of the common stock falls, you will take less loss with the convertible, and by then, you will have recovered the entire conversion premium. As you see, a convertible represents an interesting investment alternative but is not quite the *best* of both worlds.

The Problem of an Early Call   We noted earlier that if a convertible is called, investors may not earn the return they had anticipated. Most convertibles have calls and many companies exercise the call as soon as it is to their advantage to do so. Indeed, convertibles often are issued at times when managements believe their firms' common stocks are undervalued or long-term interest rates are too high, or both. Their intent is to call as soon as economic conditions turn more favorable.

To understand the implications of an early call, let us assume that Dreyer's common stock increases to $35 a share shortly after issuance of the convertible and that the convertible is callable—say, at $1,050—at any time. The market value of the convertible when the price of the common is $35 should be about $1,175 (you can see this in Exhibit 11.10). However, the conversion value is $1,093.75 (31.25 × $35); if the bond is called, investors clearly would choose to convert to the common rather than honor the call because this provides $43.75 ($1,093.75 − $1,050.00) more. Either alternative is substantially below the theoretical market value of $1,175. If that value did in fact exist and if investors purchased bonds at that price, they would lose $81.25 ($1,175.00 − $1,093.75) as a result of the call. It is highly unlikely a price of $1,175 would exist unless investors felt strongly that the bond issue would not be called. Given the trend toward early calls, this possibility is remote.

Thus, the bond's price probably would be close to $1,093.75. Now, suppose you bought the bond at its initial offering in preference to the common stock and a call takes place, say, one year after issuance. How does your choice compare with the alternative of investing directly in the stock? The gain on the bond is $93.75 ($1,093.75 − $1,000.00). Adding this to one year's interest of $65 gives a total gain of $158.75. But had you invested $1,000 and bought 38.46 shares of the common, your gain would have been $346 [($35 × 38.46) − $1,000]—more than twice as much. Although our example is hypothetical, the message is clear: investors should examine call provisions closely before investing. Payback periods have little meaning if an issue is likely to be called sooner.

BOX 11.2   GETTING AN INVESTMENT EDGE

Percs and Decs: Definitely Not the Best of Both Worlds

Convertible buyers often think that they have the best of both worlds—a high current yield and a play on the common stock. They pay for this advantage because the convertible's price usually has a premium over its conversion value. Some of the new convertible preferreds coming to market, though, should cause us to look more closely at what we're getting for our investment.

In 1991, Morgan Stanley & Co. introduced Percs, an acronym for *preference equity redemption cumulative stock*, and in 1993, Salomon Brothers introduced Decs—*dividend enhanced convertible security*. Each of these has a major disadvantage from the investor's perspective: you can be forced to convert into the common stock. In addition to forcing conversion, Percs also put a cap on the amount of price appreciation, a feature that ultimately proved unpopular with investors.

Although Decs do not impose a cap, they automatically convert into the common after a specified period. For example, MascoTech, Inc., sold an issue in late June (1993) at $20 a share, which also was the approximate price of the common stock at that time. The dividend yield was 6% (the common's yield was 0.4%) and the issue is not callable for three years. But at the end of that time, each convertible share automatically converts into one common share. That's great if the common has appreciated in value—not so great if it hasn't.

By having conversion forced on them, investors lose the opportunity to sit on the preferred and reap the dividend, which usually exceeds what the common pays for a comparable amount of funds invested. Although you might not like it if a conventional preferred's price goes down, your disappointment is softened by the high yield. So, you can be patient, perhaps for many years, and wait until the common's price rebounds. With a Decs, your high yield lasts for only three years.

Still, if you were thinking of investing in MascoTech anyway, the Decs should be a more attractive alternative than buying the common outright. Many investors apparently thought so because the company was able to sell a $200 million issue—twice the amount it initially thought it could sell. Because there are certain advantages to corporations in issuing convertible preferreds as opposed to convertible bonds, we should be seeing many more Decs in the future. Convertible preferreds already account for almost 50% of the total convertible market, almost twice the amount they had in the early 1990s.

Convertibles as Defensive Issues   In the example above, the common stock increased in value. Suppose, though, it declines. For example, assume Dreyer's price falls to $20 a share at the end of one year. The bond's price declines to about $900 (again, inspect Exhibit 11.10), leading to a loss of $100 a bond. This is partially offset by the $65 of interest, resulting in a net loss of

$35 for the year. But buying 38.46 shares of the common would have led to a far greater loss of $231 [$1,000 − (38.46 × $20)]. Convertibles, then, are the better choice if price declines seem likely. In this sense, they are viewed as defensive issues.

Return Volatility with Convertibles   Because upside potential is poorer with convertibles vis-à-vis the common stock, while downside protection is better, convertibles should exhibit historical return patterns that are less volatile than those of common stocks. In short, they are less risky. Given this situation, over time, their returns also should be less. Assuming investors hold portfolios of convertibles, they should determine whether that strategy is better than an alternative of simply holding a portfolio consisting of equities and debt instruments that might achieve a similar risk exposure. There is little evidence indicating a portfolio of convertibles is the better choice.

Another factor to consider in determining the price volatility of a convertible is that it may exhibit considerable price reactions in relation to changes in interest rates. So, even if common stock prices are fairly stable, changes in interest rates could cause reverse changes in convertibles' prices. For example, suppose interest rates rose after you bought Dreyer's bond and an appropriate rate to value the bond as straight debt is now 12.0% instead of 9.5%, the previous opportunity rate. The value of the bond as debt is now $566.55 instead of $715.23. Although the market price of the bond is not likely to decline by the difference in these prices ($148.68) because the conversion value and time premium must still be considered, it will suffer some price loss.

As a potential convertible investor, then, you must be aware that your convertibles are likely to have beta values less than 1.0, particularly if you invest in convertible mutual funds, but they may show as much price volatility as the overall stock market. The lower beta means the volatility is not completely dependent on stock price volatility. As we noted, some of the volatility reflects bond market volatility.

A Sample of Convertibles

Before leaving convertibles, it is instructive to examine a small sample to see their diversity. Exhibit 11.11 shows two convertible preferreds and two convertible bonds. Part *A* provides basic information about the convertible and the underlying stock, while Part *B* prepares a payback analysis for each issue. As you see, Unisys has the quickest payback, while Olsten Corporation has the longest. Also, current yields were reasonably attractive, considering that intermediate-term Treasury bonds were yielding about 5.7% at the time.

Unisys has a relatively small conversion premium and a relatively quick payback period. However, the issue was callable within about two years. So, it is unlikely the conversion premium will go much higher in the immediate

EXHIBIT 11.11

A sample of convertible issues

	Preferred Stocks		Bonds	
	Alco Std.	Delta Airlines	Olsten Corporation	Unisys
Part A: Basic Information:				
1. Conversion price	$ 0	$ 0	$ 34.80	$ 10.24
2. Conversion ratio	1.120	.760	28.74	97.68
3. Annual dividend or interest	$ 2.375	$ 3.50	$ 48.75	$ 82.50
4. Maturity	—	—	2003	2000
5. Market price of the convertible	$61.38	$56.75	$995.00	$1,360.00
6. Price of the common stock	$47.75	$58.38	$ 24.63	$ 12.13
7. Annual dividend per share on the common stock	$ 0.96	$ 0.18	$ 0.25	$0
8. Total dividends = line 7 × line 2	$ 1.08	$ 0.13	$ 7.19	$0
Part B: Payback Analysis:				
9. Conversion value = line 2 × line 6	$53.48	$44.37	$707.87	$1,184.86
10. Conversion premium = line 5 − line 9	$ 7.90	$12.38	$287.13	$ 175.14
11. Extra current return with the convertible = line 3 − line 8	$ 1.30	$ 3.37	$ 41.56	$ 82.50
12. Payback years = line 10 ÷ line 11	6.08	3.67	6.91	2.12
13. Current yield on the convertible (percent) = line 3 ÷ line 5	3.87	6.17	4.90	6.07

SOURCE: Securities' details are from *Value Line Options*, May 24, 1993. Copyright 1993 by Value Line, Inc. All rights reserved; reprinted with permission. All calculations of return, premia, or value are those of the authors.

future. As previously discussed, the existence of a call—and most convertibles are callable—imposes a constraint on conversion premium whenever a call seems likely. Would Unisys call the issue at the first possible call date? That is difficult to say. The current yield on the convertible of 6.07% was rather generous for a convertible at that time. If the issue was to be refinanced, it is likely the new issue would offer a yield less than that. So, if interest rates did not change, refinancing would seem likely. Of course, with two years remaining to the first call, anything could happen in the bond markets. However, if financing could take place at, say, 5.5%, a call would seem likely.

SUMMARY

An option security provides a right to buy or sell an underlying security and derives its value from the value of that underlying security. An option must have a strike price and most have fixed maturities. Options provide leverage, an appealing feature to some investors. The value of an option is determined by the number of shares it controls, its strike price in relation to the underlying security's market price, its maturity, the price volatility of the underlying security, and the level of interest rates. Option market values often are predicted with the BSM.

A warrant is created as part of a corporate financing package. Warrants are traded on organized exchanges and in the over-the-counter market. Rights are created as part of a stock offering. They have short lives, and their market values tend to follow their formula values.

A convertible security has both debt and option characteristics. As such, it offers unique investment opportunities. Its market value is determined in light of its value as common stock or straight debt. The BSM can be used to predict its market values. Convertibles often are evaluated by using a payback method that compares owning them with owning the underlying stock directly. Convertibles often are called defensive issues, but their overall price volatility may be as great as common stocks'.

**KEY TERMS
(listed in order
of appearance)**

option security	decay rate
derivative instrument	warrants
minimum (formula) value	rights
strike price	convertible security
in the money	conversion ratio
out of the money	value as straight debt
at the money	conversion value
leverage-inherent investments	conversion premium
Black-Scholes Model	payback period
time premium	

**REVIEW
QUESTIONS**

1. Explain why an option is called a derivative instrument.
2. What is meant by the formula value of an option? What assurance do we have that option prices must always equal or exceed their formula values?
3. Identify three key features of an option security.
4. Explain why options are considered leverage-inherent securities.
5. Identify five factors that determine an option's market value. Working with each individually, indicate what effect, if any, a *decrease* in the value of the factor would have on the market value of the option.
6. Why should the general level of interest rates have any bearing on an option's market value? Explain, creating your own example.
7. How does the time premium of an option decay over time?
8. Explain the nature of warrants and some aspects of trading them. Do the warrants shown in Exhibit 11.8 show characteristics of option securities? Explain.

9. What is a right? How are rights created? Do they represent long-term investment vehicles? Explain.

10. What is a convertible security? Explain some of its characteristics, such as conversion ratio, conversion price, conversion value, conversion premium, value as straight debt, and theoretical market value.

11. Indicate several advantages of investing in a convertible security as opposed to investing directly in the underlying stock.

12. How is a payback method used to evaluate a convertible?

13. Most convertibles have calls that allow their issuers to retire them before maturity. Explain how a call influences your evaluation of a convertible.

14. Do convertibles offer protection against downside risk? Explain.

15. Over time, convertibles should have *greater* price volatility than their underlying stocks. Explain your agreement or disagreement with this statement.

---

1. You are thinking of investing $10,000 by purchasing 100 shares of XYZ, Inc., at $100 a share. As an alternative, you are considering buying 1,000 options that would allow you to acquire XYZ at $90 a share anytime within the next six months. Each option costs $10. Assuming the price of XYZ's shares is $90, $100, or $110 six months from now, indicate your profit or loss with each alternative. Then explain why an option is described as leverage-inherent.

2. Using your best judgment, complete the following table. (First, find the option's strike price.)

PROBLEMS AND PROJECTS

Price of the Common Stock	Formula Value	Expected Market Value	Time Premium
$40	$ ____	$20.50	$ 0.50
35	____	____	____
30	____	11.00	____
25	5.00	____	2.00
20	____	4.00	____
15	____	____	8.00
10	____	0.13	____
5	−15.00	____	____
0	____	-0-	20.00

3. Suppose you own 100 shares of ABC Company, which has just announced a rights offering. You will be able to purchase one share of common stock at $20 a share plus four rights. The current market price of the stock is $25 a share.
   a. What will each right be worth after the rights are issued and begin trading?
   b. Is it to your advantage to sell the rights, use the rights to buy more shares, or discard the rights? Explain your answer, using a numeric example.

4. You own an option with a market price of $30 and a formula value of $20. Assuming that it has four months to maturity, construct a diagram that shows its time premium over the four months. Make a reasonable estimate for the curve.

5. You are thinking of buying a convertible bond issued by Lancer Industries. The bond matures in 10 years, has a coupon rate of 6% (interest paid semiannually), and is currently selling at its face value of $1,000. You notice that similar bonds without a convertible feature currently have a yield to maturity of 9%. The Lancer bond has a conversion price of $40 a share. Lancer's common stock is currently selling at $30 a share and pays an annual dividend of $0.20 a share. You believe the dividend will increase substantially in the distant future but do not anticipate any increases over the next five years. The stock has considerable price risk, as indicated by its beta value of 1.6.

    a. Determine the bond's current conversion value, conversion premium, value as straight debt, and payback period.

    b. Discuss whether you would prefer investing in the convertible bond or the common stock.

6. You are thinking of buying a convertible preferred stock (a perpetuity) that has a conversion ratio of four (four shares of common for one share of preferred). The preferred currently has a market price of $28 a share and pays an annual dividend of $1.50 a share. The common stock has a market price of $5 a share and pays a dividend of $0.20 a share. Similar preferred stock without a convertible feature yields 8%.

    a. Construct a diagram showing the preferred's value as straight debt and conversion value. Also, "rough in" a curve that approximates its market value.

    b. Evaluate the preferred using a payback method.

7. Pete Martinez is thinking of investing in the convertible bond of United Conglomerates, Inc., currently selling at par. The conversion price is $100, the coupon rate is 8%, and the bond is callable in one year at $1,100. United's common stock currently sells at $80 a share, but it is fairly risky, having a beta of 1.2. Pete anticipates the common will rise in value to $100 a share by year end, but he agrees there is an equal chance it could fall to $60 a share. His broker has given him Black-Scholes theoretical values for the bond in both cases: $1,120 and $900. United pays no dividends on its common stock.

    a. Outline the profit/loss situation for the upcoming year with both the bond and an equal investment in the common stock, assuming United calls the bond if the common increases in value as anticipated.

    b. Suppose the bond is callable at $1,200 instead of $1,100 and after three years instead of one. Assume further that the price of the common stock after three years is projected to be $110 a share. With these new conditions, how would you advise Pete with respect to buying the bond or the stock? Explain, using time value of money and a 10% discount rate (Pete's assumed opportunity investment rate).

8. *(Student Project)* Review current issues of *The Wall Street Journal* until an ad for a convertible appears. Contact a brokerage firm that is part of the underwriting syndicate and request a prospectus. Read the provisions concerning conversion feature and call provisions. Then, find information on the common stock—its price and expected dividend—and evaluate the convertible.

CASE ANALYSES

Ken Loggia invested $10,000 in one-year certificates of deposit (CDs) that are about to mature. Ken can roll over the CDs at an 8% rate, but he is hesitant to do so because he believes the stock of DNX Pharmaceuticals is primed for a major price increase. The company has recently developed a new over-the-counter pain reliever that has considerable profit potential. Ken is willing to take some risk in playing his feeling about DNX, but he doesn't want to lose the entire amount.

DNX common stock is currently selling at $50 a share. Several years ago the company issued warrants that allow a holder to buy one share of the common at $40 a share. The current market price of the warrants is $14 each, and they mature in four years. Also, put and call options on DNX are available. A call option with a six-month maturity and $55 strike price is available for $2.00 a share, or $200 per 100-share contract.

Ken is somewhat familiar with common stocks, but he has little understanding of options and warrants. His first thought was to invest the entire $10,000 by buying 200 shares of the common stock. The stock should pay a quarterly dividend of $0.50 a share, and Ken hopes its price will increase to $58 a share by midyear. Ken realizes his price appreciation estimates could be at least 20% off the mark—higher or lower—depending on first-year sales of the new product. The warrants and options alternatives were suggested to Ken by a friend who, unfortunately, also knew little about their mechanics. Ken believes he can make a better decision if he could determine potential profit or loss from each alternative, given his most likely price estimates *and* the possible 20% variations.

11.1
Ken Loggia
Thinks That His
Options Warrant
Consideration

a. Developing profit/loss estimates first requires estimating the market values of the options and warrants at the end of six months. The following table presents alternative values, given the three possible stock prices. You must select the most realistic price in each case.

Questions

		Price of the Common Stock		
		$46.40	**$58.00**	**$69.60**
Possible values of the call options (per share):	(1)	−8.60	3.00	-0-
	(2)	-0-	8.00	19.60
	(3)	−3.60	-0-	14.60
Possible values of the warrants (per warrant):	(1)	6.40	17.00	32.00
	(2)	−3.60	21.00	40.00
	(3)	11.00	25.00	50.00

b. With your value selections from question a, develop profit/loss estimates, assuming $10,000 is invested in the common stock, or in warrants, or in call options.

c. Which alternative do you recommend for Ken? Explain.

d. Suppose you could allocate the $10,000 among the three alternatives. Develop a portfolio of the three for Ken, explaining your rationale.

11.2
Mona Giles Looks at a Convertible

Mona Giles has decided to invest in Parkhurst Industries, a company that Mona believes will do well in the years ahead. She was ready to purchase 100 shares of the common stock at $20 a share when her broker told her that she might consider buying two 25-year convertible subordinated debentures the company was about to issue at par. The convertible issue has a conversion price of $25 a share and an 8% coupon rate. The bonds have a call price of $1,100, but they cannot be called for three years.

The company currently pays a dividend of $1 a share on the common stock. Dividends are not likely to increase in the near future because the company needs cash to complete an expansion project. Parkhurst issued the convertibles as an alternative to issuing straight subordinated debentures that would have carried a 12% coupon rate.

Mona is finding it difficult to choose between the two alternatives. She believes that interest rates will remain stable in the years ahead but the price of Parkhurst's common stock will be volatile, ranging from a possible low of $10 a share to a possible high of $40 a share. Her best estimate is that price will increase 10% a year. Mona needs help in determining profit/loss estimates for the convertibles, and she needs advice in making a selection. She describes herself as a definite risk averter.

Questions

a. Given Mona's high and low estimates for the price of the common stock, determine profit or loss amounts from investing $2,000 in each investment alternative—the common stock or the convertibles. Assume a three-year holding period and consider dividends and interest. To determine the price of the convertibles, consider the alternatives listed in the following table. Select the most realistic alternative given each possible price of the common stock. (Do not consider time value of money in your work and assume Mona would hold either securities at the end of three years.)

		Prices of the Common Stock		
		$ 10.00	$ 26.62	$ 40.00
Possible prices of				
a convertible:	(1)	400.00	1,000.00	1,620.00
	(2)	690.00	1,300.00	1,000.00
	(3)	1,000.00	1,100.00	2,000.00

b. Calculate the payback period for the convertible.

c. Which security do you recommend for Mona? Give reasons for your choice.

Granito, Barbara Donnelly. "New Derivative Products Are Surprisingly Complex." *The Wall Street Journal*, April 12, 1993, p. C1.

Granito, Barbara Donnelly, and Craig Torres. "Portfolio Surprise: Many Americans Run Hidden Financial Risk from 'Derivatives'." *The Wall Street Journal*, August 10, 1993, p. A1.

Harlan, Christi. "SEC Studies Risks of 'Exotic' Derivatives." *The Wall Street Journal,* April 29, 1993, p. C1.

Lenzner, Robert, and William Hueslein. "The Age of Digital Capitalism." *Forbes*, March 29, 1993, pp. 62–72.

Lipin, Steven. "Banks Try to Avoid Rules on Derivatives." *The Wall Street Journal*, July 22, 1993, p. C1.

HELPFUL
READING

Put and Call Options

After you finish this chapter, you will be able to:

- understand the characteristics of standardized put and call contracts and why investors use them.

- understand what is involved in contract settlement and recognize the importance of commissions in option trading.

- identify profit opportunities and risks in various trading strategies involving naked positions, hedges, spreads, and arbitrage.

- understand profit opportunities and risks in covered option writing.

- recognize advantages and disadvantages of using market index options in an option-bills portfolio or as a hedge against market risk.

Option writing: refers to selling options

Warrants, rights, and convertibles are issued by corporations as part of their financing plans. In contrast, put and call options can be created by anyone. As an individual, you can create a put or call by calling your broker and giving the instruction to sell a contract, which is called **option writing.** One usually can be sold within minutes, and you will be wealthier, at least for the moment, by the amount the buyer agrees to pay. Just as IBM can raise funds by selling option securities, so can you; and just as IBM incurs risks and gives up certain rights in the process, so will you.

In addition to selling options, you can buy them. Indeed, buying is probably more often undertaken by beginning investors. In this chapter, we will examine the investment uses of puts and calls from both buyers' and sellers' perspectives.

PUT AND CALL CHARACTERISTICS

Call option: provides the right to buy an underlying asset

Put option: provides the right to sell an underlying asset

A **call option** is the type of option examined in detail in Chapter 11. The term *call* means a right to buy the underlying asset at the strike price anytime during the option's life. A **put option** is new to us: it gives the right to sell the underlying asset at the strike price anytime during the option's life. Like a call, a put can be used to increase investment return and risk or to reduce each.

Trading Puts and Calls

Puts and calls are traded on organized exchanges in a manner similar to that for stock and bond trading. There are five major exchanges: the Chicago Board Options Exchange and the American Exchange are the two largest, with the smaller ones being the Pacific Exchange, the Philadelphia Exchange, and the New York Exchange. As Exhibit 12.1 shows, contracts are

EXHIBIT 12.1
Put and call options available

Underlying Assets	Example	Number of Different Contracts
Individual common stocks	IBM	over 300
Stock indexes	the S&P 500	23
Foreign currencies	the British pound	15
Futures:		
commodity contracts	gold	33
interest-rate contracts	T-bonds	10
foreign currencies	Japanese yen	6
stock indexes	Nikkei 225	5

available for individual stocks (such as IBM), stock indexes (such as the S&P 500), foreign currencies (such as the British pound), and a large array of futures contracts on various commodities and financial instruments (such as soybeans, gold, and Eurodollars). Option contracts have proliferated so rapidly in the 1980s and early 1990s that even experienced investors find it difficult to be familiar with all of them. Fortunately, all options work on the same general principles discussed in Chapter 11 and in this chapter. It is more important to understand these principles than to memorize details about specific contracts.

Reading Put and Call Quotations

Puts and calls are reported in a separate section of the financial pages of many newspapers. Typical quotations are shown in Exhibit 12.2. The underlying securities are IBM common stock and Sears common stock. IBM options are popular and actively traded. As you see, options are available with maturities in three separate months. Sears options are less popular and more representative of the majority of options on individual stocks. Their maturities are on a three-month basis.

Each contract involves 100 shares. You must multiply the prices shown, which are on a per-share basis, by 100 to determine the contract's value. For example, the IBM February 60 call is worth $75 ($¾ × 100): a buyer pays this amount and a seller receives it. The prices shown in Exhibit 12.2 once again demonstrate that option prices are influenced by how deeply they are in the money (or far out of it) and by maturity. We find the IBM February 50 call is

	Strike		Calls			Puts	
IBM	Price	Feb.	March	Apr.	Feb.	March	Apr.
55	50	5¼	7⅜	8⅞	1³⁄₁₆	2⁹⁄₁₆	3⅝
55	55	2³⁄₁₆	4½	6¼	3⅜	4¾	5⅝
55	60	¾	2⁷⁄₁₆	3⅞	6⅞	8	8½
Sears		March	June	Sept.	March	June	Sept.
40⅛	35	5¼	5½	6⅜	³⁄₁₆	½	⅞
40⅛	40	1⁵⁄₁₆	2⅜	3⅛	1¼	2¹⁄₁₆	2⅞
40⅛	45	³⁄₁₆	¾	1³⁄₁₆	r	6¼	r

The symbol *r* means the option did not trade that day.

Closing prices of the underlying stocks

Closing prices of the option contract. Quoted price is per share of the underlying stock. Because the standard contract requires delivery of 100 shares, multiply by 100 to determine a contract's total value.

EXHIBIT 12.2
Typical newspaper listings of option quotations

worth more than the February 60 call (5¼ versus ¾); and the March 60 call is worth more than the February 60 call (2⁷⁄₁₆ versus ¾).

Notice that put values move in the opposite direction of call values in the sense that as the underlying stock's price increases (decreases), a put's value decreases (increases). A right to sell IBM at 60 is worth more than the right to sell it at 50, and each increases in value as the price of IBM falls.

Because many examples in this chapter involve formula values, let us recall that the formula value for a call (illustrated in Chapter 11) is market price of the stock minus strike price of the option. The formula value of a put is the opposite; that is, formula value equals strike price of the put minus market price of the stock. Also, the standardized put and call contracts involve the delivery of 100 shares of the underlying stock, and the index options pay off at 100 times the index. Taking this information into consideration, we then express the following formulas for the formula values of a call and a put:

Formula value (call contract) = 100(market price of stock − strike price)

Formula value (put contract) = 100(strike price − market price of stock)

So, all the IBM 50 call contracts (maturity is irrelevant) have a formula value of +$500 and all the IBM 50 put contracts have a formula value of −$500, as calculated below.

Formula value (call contract) = 100($55.00 − $50.00) = $500.00

Formula value (put contract) = 100($50.00 − $55.00) = −$500.00

Finally, using the formulas, you should be able to determine that the 60 call contracts have a formula value of −$500, while the 60 put contracts' formula value is +$500.

Buyers and Sellers

Put and call options help shape a portfolio's risk exposure and potential return. Options can make it more flexible by allowing investors to take many positions in different securities at relatively low cost. They also serve as a form of insurance by converting unknown and potentially huge losses into known, manageable costs.

Who Buys Options, and Why?   Option buyers fall into two groups. The first group seeks higher investment returns through the leverage quality of options. We reviewed leverage in Chapter 11 and can note here that it works the same way with puts and calls. The standard option contract on individual stocks involves 100 shares of the underlying security, which means you control quite a few shares with a relatively small investment. The second group of option buyers is looking for the insurance protection of options.

The insurance aspect comes into play when an investor wants to lock in a known price for a security. For example, suppose you bought 100 shares of IBM at $40 a share. It is now $55, and you have a $1,500 profit that you are happy with, but you think that IBM might increase further in price. Not willing to risk the loss of most of your profit, you buy the 55 April put for $562.50 ($5⅝ × 100). This move gives you about 10 weeks of protection (assuming this is the first week in February); if IBM is above $55 at maturity, you discard the option as you would an expired insurance policy on your car, but if it is below $55, you can exercise the option and sell your shares at that price. Paying about $56 a week to insure the value of your stock might seem stiff insurance, but the alternative of losing a substantial sum of money might be far less appealing.

Although locking in selling prices with puts is the most common form of option insurance, you also can lock in a buying price by buying a call. This insurance could be important if you sold a stock short and have a profit that you want to protect. In this situation, the call performs the same function as a put for a long position.

Who Sells Options, and Why?   Option sellers also fall into two groups. The first group is made up of speculators who sell options for the income provided. They believe the options will expire out of the money, freeing them of the obligation to sell or buy shares at strike prices. Keep in mind it is the seller's responsibility to make good on the option, which can be expensive. For example, suppose you sold an IBM April 50 call for $887.50 ($8⅞ × 100; see Exhibit 12.2). April's maturity now arrives and IBM is selling at $70. You have an obligation to deliver 100 shares at a price of $50, and assuming you must buy them in the market, you will lose $2,000 [($70 − $50) × 100] meeting the obligation. Your net loss would be $1,112.50 ($2,000.00 − $887.50).

The second group of option sellers consists of investors seeking additional income from shares they own. These sellers are called **covered option writers,** and their plan is to sell the options as an alternative either to selling their shares immediately or to holding them uncovered—that is, without offsetting options. Covered option writing is popular, and it will be covered in greater detail later in this chapter.

Covered option writers: investors who sell call (put) options on stocks they own (or have shorted)

Contract Settlement

As an option approaches and eventually reaches its maturity, some action must be taken. There are three ways to settle a contract: reverse a position, take or make delivery of the underlying security, or receive (pay) cash.

Reverse a Position   **Reversing a position** means you take action opposite to your initial action before the contract expires. For example, suppose you bought an option that is now considerably in the money and has a high market value. You don't want the underlying security and are content with the

Reversing a position: offsetting an existing position in an option contract before its maturity profit in the option. So, you sell the option, reversing your original long position. It is likely that more than 90% of all option contracts are settled in this manner. The option, having performed its function, is eliminated from the portfolio and perhaps replaced with another having a longer maturity or a different strike price.

Take or Make Delivery   If an option is in the money, you might want to **take (make) delivery.** For example, you might exercise an IBM put and choose to sell your shares at the strike price; or, you might exercise a call and take delivery of the shares at the strike price. Option trading has become highly organized and efficient. Your contract is actually with a central clearing organization called the Options Clearing Corporation (OCC), formed by the option exchanges to facilitate trading. An important function of the OCC is to simplify settlement. Without going into details, let us simply note two important implications for option traders: First, you are assured of performance on your contract; if you have a call, for example, you need not worry about another party being able to deliver 100 shares of the underlying stock when you want them. Second, as an option writer, you face the risk the OCC might call your number, so to speak, to honor your obligation before an option's maturity. To honor option holder demands, a random process of allocating performance responsibilities to writers is used. As a writer, you could be forced to sell or buy shares far ahead of the time you anticipated you would have to act, if your anticipation date was the option's maturity. Option writers must be aware of this provision in the option contract.

Take (make) delivery: option writer exercizing his right to buy (sell) shares at the strike price

Sometimes beginning option investors worry that if they fail to take action with an in-the-money option before maturity, they will lose whatever it might be worth, just as you take losses when you fail to act with stock rights. This is not true with options. If you take no action before maturity, your broker automatically buys or sells shares to complete the option contract. So, if you bought a call option with a strike price of $50 and then forgot about it, when the option expires, your broker will notify you that you bought 100 shares of the stock at $50. The confirmation slip will also show that you paid a commission to buy the shares. This commission could be far more than the commission to reverse a position, and if you didn't want the shares, it would be foolish to let the option expire. If you trade options, you must be an alert investor.

Cash settlement: payment of cash at an option's maturity

Cash Settlement   In a **cash settlement,** no underlying security is delivered; rather, you receive (or pay) cash equal to the difference between the strike price and the market price of the underlying instrument at maturity. For example, suppose you bought a call on the S&P 500 index with a strike price of 400. At maturity, the index stands at 450, giving you a 50-point profit. Because this contract requires payment at 100 times the index value, you receive a cash settlement of $5,000 ($50 × 100). Someone selling the call under the same circumstances would pay $5,000.

Option Cost/Share	Number of Option Contracts Traded			
	1	5	10	15
$ ¼	$ 5.89(a)	$14.45	$ 27.82	$ 41.20
½	8.56	27.82	54.57	81.32
1	26.75	58.15(b)	101.12	132.31
5	26.75	88.76	150.55	209.65(c)

Commission as a percentage of contract value:

(a) $\dfrac{\$5.89}{(\$0.25 \times 100 \times 1)} = \dfrac{\$5.89}{\$25.00} = 0.236\ (23.6\%)$

(b) $\dfrac{\$58.15}{(\$1.00 \times 100 \times 5)} = \dfrac{\$58.15}{\$500.00} = 0.116\ (11.6\%)$

(c) $\dfrac{\$209.65}{(\$5.00 \times 100 \times 15)} = \dfrac{\$209.65}{\$7,500.00} = 0.282\ (2.8\%)$

EXHIBIT 12.3
Illustrative put and call commissions of a full-service stockbroker

Cash settlement is more efficient than share delivery and is characteristic of a mature options market. It is necessary for instruments that could not possibly be delivered, such as the S&P 500 index. Actually, there is no reason why it cannot be used for individual stocks, even though delivery is possible.

Brokerage Commissions

Trading options can be expensive if you deal in small quantities or low-priced options. Exhibit 12.3 indicates a small sample of option commissions and shows how they depend on the number of contracts involved and the market price of the option. The important point to see is not the absolute dollar amount, but rather the commission as a percentage of funds invested. Buying one contract at a price of $0.25 a share leads to a commission of only $5.89, which seems reasonable. However, it is actually about 24% of invested funds. Keep in mind, too, that option trading may involve two transactions if the option is in the money; for example, you may reverse a position and pay another option commission, or you may take delivery and pay a stock commission. And if you don't want the stock and eventually sell it, a third commission comes into play. Small wonder most stockbrokers are enthusiastic about option trading.

PUT AND CALL TRADING STRATEGIES

Investors use puts and calls in an almost endless variety of techniques. There are three basic approaches: naked positions, hedges, and spreads. Each is explained in the sections that follow.

Naked Positions

Naked position: owning or writing an option without holding other related positions

Although it sounds exciting, a **naked position** is nothing more than owning or writing a put or call without having an offsetting position in another security. Naked positions are the riskiest of all positions, particularly to put and call sellers, although buyers face risks as well.

Calls: Buyer's and Seller's Perspectives   Exhibit 12.4 illustrates a profit-loss graph with a call from the perspective of both the buyer and the seller. The amounts shown are based on the formula value of an option, which implies we are looking at the situation at the option's maturity, when there is zero time premium. It is assumed the call is traded at a price of $600 and has a strike price of $50.

From the buyer's perspective, the most he can lose is $600; he will lose this much if the price of the underlying stock at maturity is $50 or less. As the price of the stock increases above $50, he begins to earn a contribution to profit. At a price of $56, he breaks even, the profit on the option being just enough to offset its cost. At prices greater than $56, positive trading profit appears. At $70, for example, he makes a profit of $1,400.

The seller's perspective is directly opposite to that of the buyer. She earns her maximum profit whenever the stock's market price is less than the strike price. As the market price increases, her profit diminishes: she also breaks even at $56 and begins taking losses for prices beyond that figure. At $70, her loss is $1,400. As you examine the graph, you should see that the seller has a great deal to lose if the stock's price increases dramatically. Many

EXHIBIT 12.4
Profit-loss graph:
Naked position in a call

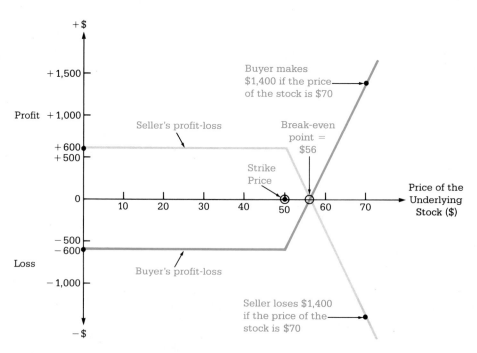

writers deal with this problem by setting maximum loss limits and immediately reversing a position whenever the maximum is reached.

Puts: Buyer's-Seller's Perspectives A put option has identical implications to the call option. Now, however, the buyer's profit increases as the price of the stock falls, while the seller's profit decreases. Exhibit 12.5 shows the profit-loss graph for a put. Again, the most the buyer can lose is $600, while the seller's losses can be much greater.

Hedge Positions

A **hedge** usually is viewed as taking two positions simultaneously in two assets to reduce risk. We discussed earlier in this chapter how options serve as insurance. Insurance is a hedge in the sense that it will reduce your portfolio's return by the cost of the insurance, but it simultaneously reduces risk. If you own a house or a car, you can look at the asset itself and the insurance policy covering it as a combination of assets; not insuring would be cheaper but riskier. So it is with stock ownership, and Exhibit 12.6 shows changes in your net worth that would result from straight ownership (the solid line) or the combination of stock plus the put option (the dashed line). The put illustrated is the same one shown in Exhibit 12.5. As you see, with the put, your

Hedge: holding two positions simultaneously to reduce risk

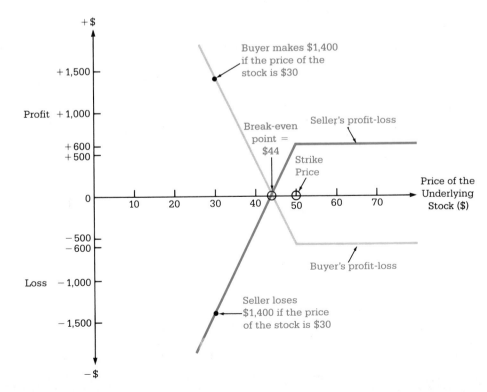

EXHIBIT 12.5
Profit-loss graph:
Naked position in a put

EXHIBIT 12.6

Illustration of a put
hedge to ensure a
minimum net worth

net worth will never go lower than the cost of the put ($4,400), while straight
ownership of the stock could lead to a zero net worth.

Spreads

Spread: holding simulta-
neous positions in an
effort to make a profit

Spreads are similar to hedges insofar as several positions are taken in different securities, but they differ in that their intent is to earn profit rather than to
simply reduce risk. Spreads are less risky than naked positions and, consequently, have less profit potential. Put and call traders devise many spread
situations involving different maturities or different strike prices. (Our discussion does not distinguish between spreads, straddles, and other names used
to identify different situations.) What they hope to create is a low-risk profit
opportunity. Let us consider a number of examples.

A Maturity Spread   Suppose you see a call with a three-month maturity
selling for $200. You also see another call with a six-month maturity selling
for $400. Assume each has a strike price of $40 a share, and the current market price of the stock is also $40 a share. So, you think: "Why not sell the
longer maturity and use the money to buy two of the shorter maturities? If the
price of the stock jumps, I should earn about twice as much on my long position as I will lose on my short position. Even a little additional gain is worth it
because I have virtually no investment in the deal." This is an example of a
maturity spread, which involves offsetting positions in options with the
same strike price but with different maturities. It sounds good, and on rare
occasions, you might actually find a price structure, such as in this example,
that makes maturity spreading attractive. There is risk in this spread, though.
Suppose the stock's price fell and the two shorter maturity calls expire worth-

Maturity spread: selling
options with longer
maturities while simul-
taneously buying a
greater number of
options with shorter
maturities

less. You still hold—now, naked—the short position in the longer maturity. You probably would reverse this position, but that involves a cost and means you lose on the hedge. Then, too, don't forget commissions that must be paid on each transaction.

A Neutral Spread   Suppose you are neither bullish nor bearish about a particular stock. In fact, you think its price will be flat over the near term. Given such a feeling, you might consider selling a **neutral spread**. This means you sell both a put and a call on the same stock at the same strike price and with the same maturity. Exhibit 12.7 shows a profit-loss graph for such a spread involving a put and a call with strike prices of $50 for each.

> **Neutral spread:** selling both a call and a put option simultaneously in the belief the stock's price will be stable

If the stock's price at maturity is exactly $50, each option expires worthless and you are free to pocket the amount received from selling the two—assumed to be $500 each, or $1,000 in total. Now, if the stock's price is higher or lower than $50, one of the options will be in the money and the other will be worthless. You will earn some profit on this spread for all stock prices between $40 and $60, which are the two break-even prices. If price exceeds $60 or goes below $40, you will suffer losses, as shown in Exhibit 12.7. At a price of $70, for example, the call will be worth $2,000, which offsets the $1,000 you received from selling both options, leaving you with a $1,000 loss.

A Volatile Spread   If you reverse the assumption of a neutral spread and assume instead that a stock's price will move dramatically either up or down, then you *buy* both the put and the call rather than selling them. The profit-loss graph for this spread would be the exact opposite of the one shown in Exhibit 12.7. You show losses where the neutral spreader shows profits, and vice versa. A **volatile spread** might be appropriate for a stock that has been the subject of takeover rumors and has run up in price. If one of the rumors proves correct, its price might jump still higher; if all the rumors are false, prices might fall sharply.

> **Volatile spread:** buying both a call and a put option simultaneously in the belief the stock's price will be volatile

Bull and Bear Spreads   A **bull or bear spread** assumes you have definite feelings about the future price of a stock, but your feelings are not strong enough to take naked positions. For example, you might feel reasonably sure a stock will make a move, but that it has a better chance of increasing in price than decreasing. In this situation, a spreader might buy two calls and one put. This is a bull spread, and it is illustrated with the profit-loss graph shown in Exhibit 12.8. As you might guess, a bear spread might consist of buying two puts and one call. You can reinforce your understanding of a profit-loss graph by constructing one for this bear spread.

> **Bull or bear spread:** buying both calls and puts simultaneously but not in an equal proportion

Arbitrage Opportunities

An **arbitrage** usually is understood as taking offsetting positions in an investment situation in an attempt to exploit unusual price disparities without taking risk. At the beginning of Chapter 11, we noted that options must

> **Arbitrage:** taking offsetting positions in an effort to exploit unusual price disparities

BOX 12.1   GETTING AN INVESTMENT EDGE

Synthetic Fabrics, Synthetic Fuels, and Now, Synthetic Stocks

If your tastes run toward the real thing, you aren't going to like a synthetic stock, but here it is. How do you get the imitation? First, find the stock you are thinking of buying and see if options are traded on it. If they are, *buy* a call and *sell* a put. Presto—instant stock!

Put and call options give their buyers rights to buy or sell stocks at set prices over set periods. If you own a call, you have a right to buy the stock, while a put gives you the right to sell it. To create the synthetic, you buy the call, which gives you any price appreciation the stock makes above the call price. That's also what you get when you own the stock. When you sell the put, you must make good to its buyer any price depreciation below the put price. You lose on this end, which is also what happens when the stock falls in price. As you see, there's no difference between holding the stock and the synthetic creation, as far as price changes are concerned. That being the case, why not own the stock outright and save time and effort—*and* commissions? Because there are times when owning the synthetic is cheaper than owning the stock.

The accompanying table illustrates a synthetic stock based on the prices of Borland Industries in mid-July 1993. Borland closed on July 22 at $19.50 a share. To create the synthetic, you should look for options with strike prices about the same as the price of the stock, and you need an appropriate account with a broker and sufficient equity to support the shorted put. Assuming you deposited $9,750 worth of Treasury bills, which yielded about 3.0% at the time, you would have earned interest of the amounts shown in the table. On the same day, put and call options closed at the prices shown. Three commissions will apply: one to open each position and another to close one of the two. (One of the options must close in the money, and the assumption is you would buy it back before its maturity. The other option expires out of the money.)

Everything now considered, the September synthetic provides a $116 advantage over owning the stock outright ($696 annualized; you would repeat the deal every two months.)

Although this example appears attractive, other factors must be considered. If the stock pays a dividend, the synthetic may be

sell at prices equal to or greater than their formula values, or potential arbitrage profits arise. Another example of an arbitrage profit might involve a maturity spread, as discussed previously in this chapter. Suppose the price of an April call option is $400, while a July call is $350. This is a price disparity that can be exploited: sell the April option and buy the July. If the stock price increases, each option should increase about the same amount; if price less desirable. For that reason, non- or low-paying stocks like Borland often are selected. Also, you might have to deliver shares on the put if your number is called by the option clearing house, which adds another commission cost. To lower this probability, you should close positions before the options mature. But doing so also increases the annual cost by increasing the number of deals you need to transact in a year. To reduce this cost, it is helpful to have maturities as long as possible, which also saves annual commission costs.

Is creating a synthetic worth it? Perhaps, if you have a lot of time to watch for option prices that enhance the deal—high put price and low call price—and if you can reduce commissions through a discounter or by trading in larger volumes. Otherwise, you are probably better off directly in the stock.

Cost of Creating 500 Shares of Synthetic Borland Industries Stock

	September Maturities	
	Price	Amount
Buy 5 calls (strike price = ($20)	$1\frac{5}{8}$	$(813)
Sell 5 puts (strike price = $20)	2	1,000
Estimated commissions		(120)
Estimated interest earned		49
Net advantage		$116
Net advantage annualized		$696

decreases and both options expire worthless, you still net $50 (before commissions) with no risk.

Such opportunities are virtually nonexistent with individual securities, but index options and the securities represented by an index occasionally show such possibilities. Let us note also that the expression *arbitrage* has now been extended to include price disparities that may not offer risk-free

EXHIBIT 12.7
Profit-loss graph for a
neutral spread

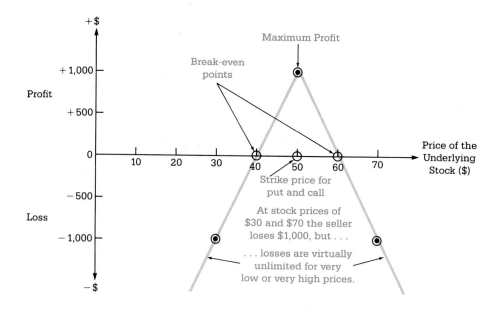

EXHIBIT 12.8
A bull spread: Buy two
calls and one put

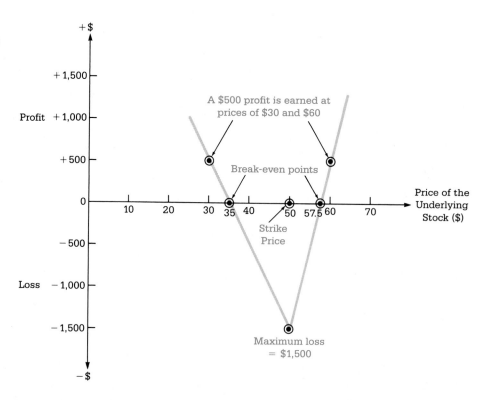

BOX 12.2   INVESTMENT INSIGHTS

Will Stock Markets in the Future Be Stabler?

The casual meandering of the stock market during much of 1992 and 1993 (through July) raises the question of whether or not the market is becoming stabler. One observer apparently thinks that that may be the case. John W. Schulz, managing director of Brean Murray Foster Securities, finds evidence supporting his view in the trading ratio of put options to call options (see "The Giant Hedge," *Barron's*, August 9, 1993, pp. 26–27). The put/call ratio for options traded on the Chicago Board Options Exchange has been compiled for some time and frequently is used by technicians as an indicator to gauge investor sentiment. Schultz, though, thinks that it might also tell us something about market volatility.

For starters, he notes that since 1983, the ratio has been rising and the trend seems to have accelerated since the 1990 bear market. Increased trading in puts relative to calls by itself, however, is clueless if most trading reflects naked positions. Schultz doubts that is the case. Rather, he believes that the overwhelming majority of outstanding contracts reflects hedged positions. Why do hedged positions tell us something that naked positions do not? Because in a hedged position, you effectively have already sold or bought shares.

For example, suppose you own 100 shares of a stock you think is fully valued at $20 a share and not likely to go higher in price. Without options, you would sell the stock; but now, instead of selling, you hedge your position by buying a put option that protects against a possible loss. Suppose further that the seller of the option, although bullish on its outlook, also hedges her position by short-selling 100 shares. Now, if the price of the stock does indeed fall and is below the option's strike price, you may choose to deliver your 100 shares; in turn, the option seller closes her position by delivering your shares.

Apart from any profit considerations in the trades above, Schultz's main point is that your 100 shares do not come to the market when the stock's price is falling and under pressure because they were presold at the time the put contract was traded. Theoretically, preselling of this type serves to smooth supply-demand forces over time, leading to less price volatility.

Schultz notes, however, that a smoother market does not imply the elimination of market cycles or even the possibility of market panics. Is he right? The proof of the pudding, so to speak, will be to observe market volatility in the future. A declining variance over time, although not proving that he is correct, will at least not contradict his thesis. It is interesting that immediately after the market crash in 1987, a hot research question was whether or not the market was becoming more volatile. Oddly, derivative instruments—options and futures—were getting some of the blame then because they were integral parts of defensive strategies that didn't work. In six years, they go from villain to hero!

opportunities but do offer favorable opportunities in relation to hypothetically correct prices. These "correct" values typically are those derived from option pricing models, such as Black-Scholes. To illustrate with the previous example, assume the correct prices are $400 for the April call and $420 for the July. Suppose the July's actual price is $410; thus, it is undervalued and should be bought. The trader in this case arbitrages the deal by selling the April. Doing so is less risky than holding the July naked but also has far less profit potential. Indeed, the trader anticipates profiting only to the extent that other investors eventually recognize the July underpricing and bid its price up to the "correct" value, whereupon the positions are reversed and arbitrage profits taken.

Today's dynamic trading looks for arbitrage situations in futures contracts as well as options. We will therefore return to this topic in Chapter 13.

OTHER PUT AND CALL USES

As mentioned earlier, puts and calls provide many investment opportunities to investors. Covered option writing became popular as the standard option contract was developed and the organized options exchanges were created in the early 1970s. Moreover, the creation of numerous index options challenged investors to devise new investment strategies—and they responded. The index options became the most actively traded of all options. In early 1993, option contracts based on 23 indexes were available. As Exhibit 12.9 shows, these ranged from broad stock indexes, such as the S&P 500, to rather specialized indexes, such as biotech and oil. You should notice the substantial volume in the index options, particularly the S&P 100. On the day reported, this one index option accounted for almost 30% of the total call volume for all options and more than 42% of the total put volume. There is little doubt that many professional money managers are using index options in various trading strategies, some of which are explained below. (In Chapter 17, we provide additional discussion of the use of derivative instruments in a portfolio-management setting.)

Covered Option Writing

Covered option writing means that you sell call options against securities you own. (Short sellers can also sell puts against stocks they have shorted; however, this activity is far less popular.) The idea is to improve your investment performance by receiving income from the sale of the option. However, there are risks the covered option writer should know. These risks are best understood by looking at an example.

An Example   If an investor plans to hold a security in the long term but does not believe that its price will increase much in the near future, then writing a call option against it can be advantageous. This is illustrated in Exhibit 12.9. Assume you own 100 shares of ADM, currently selling at $155 a

Exchange	Total Call Volume	Total Put Volume	Call Open Interest	Put Open Interest
Chicago	337,736	248,859	4,249,310	2,895,823
American	102,439	46,684	2,949,719	1,508,413
Pacific	42,684	18,003	839,999	368,501
Philadelphia	52,085	32,047	1,742,689	1,017,567
New York	7,327	1,843	376,476	159,192
Totals	542,271	347,436	10,158,193	5,949,496
Indexes				
CBOE S&P 100	158,077	147,118	399,447	549,156
NSX500	1,857	995	95,413	184,796
SPX500	31,904	38,203	469,403	597,871
SP500EOQ	0	43	0	288
Rus2000	2,648	721	12,958	10,783
BioT	113	0	1,336	1,150
FT–SE100	70	121	1,156	2,096
MajMkt	2,902	2,825	47,604	56,429
MajMEOQ	0	0	0	0
AMEX Computer Technology	135	30	354	239
AMEX Oil	107	99	1,055	427
InstOpen	205	25	13,630	4,919
AMEX Japan Index	773	1,179	34,559	34,070
AMEX S&P 400 MidCap	197	219	13,236	62,855
Phrmldx	1,699	569	6,880	7,379
BioTch	270	45	3,331	2,653
Eurotop	23	0	29	132
Wilshldx	171	30	3,819	4,687
Phil Gold/Silver	1,062	66	8,842	1,349
Phil Value Line	105	5	9,131	2,386
Phil NATIONAL OTC 100	94	211	3,982	5,659
Bankldx	88	204	702	1,001
NY Idx o	12	29	2,540	5,446

EXHIBIT 12.9
Index options and total option trading

SOURCE: With the permission of *Investor's Business Daily*, March 12, 1993, p. 24.

share. You regard ADM as a permanent part of your portfolio, but you do not believe its price will increase much over the next 10 weeks. Because you can sell a $155 call option for $625, you see no reason not to and so earn this extra income. You face two problems, however: first, if you guess wrong about ADM's price, you must buy back the option; second, you must pay at least one commission and possibly two.

Exhibit 12.10 compares the alternatives of writing versus not writing the option. Because you probably would reverse your option position before maturity, we must assume you will pay more than formula value for the option. For simplicity, we assume a $50 time premium for the $160 and $165

EXHIBIT 12.10

An example of covered option writing

Assumptions:

1. Investor owns 100 shares of ADM with a current price of $155.
2. A call option that expires in 10 weeks can be sold for $625; the option's strike price is $155.
3. If the option is in the money, the position is reversed.

	Closing Price of ADM ($)				
	145	150	155	160	165
Income from selling option	$ 625	$625	$625	$625	$ 625
Less commissions:					
Selling the option	27	27	27	27	27
Reversing the position	—	—	—	30	30
Less cost of option repurchased	—	—	—	550*	$1050**
Net option income (loss)	$ 598	$598	$598	$ 18	($ 482)
Gain (loss) in stock's price	(1000)	(500)	-0-	500	1000
Net gain (loss) from covered option writing	($ 402)	$ 98	$598	$518	$ 518
Net gain (loss) from holding ADM uncovered	(1000)	(500)	-0-	500	1000

*Assumes the investor pays a 10% time premium to repurchase the option and reverse the position.

**Assumes a 5% time premium.

closing prices when the option would be in the money. The comparisons are straightforward: as you see, writing the option is to your advantage if the price of the stock is around $160 or less. At higher prices, you would do better owning the stock uncovered.

Generalizations on Covered Option Writing From the previous example, you should see that covered option writing improves investment return only under certain conditions. It does not guarantee greater returns or less risk all the time. Moreover, trying to time option sales because you think you can forecast the short-run price of a stock often is a mistake. Few people can forecast this accurately. Moreover, it could be a mistake to buy a stock if your sole intent is to write options against it. Exhibit 12.10 shows that if ADM's price falls below $150, your losses will be substantial. Meanwhile, the most you can gain is $598.

All things considered, the best stocks to write options against usually are those that have little expected price variation and that pay high dividends. You might want to hold these stocks for the long run and you don't expect their prices to be volatile. Unfortunately, options on such stocks have market values less than those on volatile stocks, which lowers the net option income. Finally, although we illustrated covered option writing by using an example of a single stock (ADM) and its call option, it is probably more common today to use index call options as covered writing hedges against a whole portfolio of stocks. This involves less risk than when you hold only one (or a few) covered individual stocks.

An Option-Bills Portfolio

A market index option can be used conveniently to create an **option-bills portfolio.** Such a portfolio consists of investing most of your funds in Treasury bills (or other fixed-income security) and a small portion in a call option on a market index. For example, suppose you have $30,000 earmarked for stock investment. However, you know stocks are risky and you could lose a substantial portion of your funds if you invested directly in them. On the other hand, you are aware of the growth potential of stocks over time, and you want to participate in that growth, if it takes place. In other words, you want to have your cake and eat it too. A possible solution: put most of the funds in Treasury bills and use a portion periodically to buy call options on the market. If the market jumps during some period, your long position in the calls will ensure that you participate in the jump. On the other hand, if the market is flat or declines, you discard the options and appreciate the wisdom of investing only a fraction of your funds in them.

Option-bills portfolio: holding a combination of Treasury bills and index call options as an alternative to holding stocks

The Cost of an Option-Bills Portfolio   In investments, you can almost never have your cake and eat it too, and an option-bills portfolio is no exception to this rule. Index options are relatively expensive, as Exhibit 12.11 shows. The index in this case is the S&P 100, which includes 100 active stocks from the S&P 500. You can see that buying about 10 weeks of coverage (the May maturity) costs $662.50 ($6$\frac{5}{8}$ × 100) for the 460 call. An investor with about $30,000 to invest could have considered placing about $29,338 in T-bills and $662 in the option.

Over an extended period, total outlays on the options will be considerable, and the net return from the option-bills portfolio is likely to be less than that from a portfolio consisting of stocks only. The strategy seems more appropriate, then, in a short-run setting where safety of principal is important but the investor believes that a market jump is imminent.

Strike Price	Calls			Puts		
	March	April	May	March	April	May
450	6$\frac{1}{8}$	9$\frac{5}{8}$	13$\frac{1}{4}$	1$^{11}\!\!\diagup\!\!_{16}$	5$\frac{1}{8}$	8$\frac{1}{4}$
455	2$\frac{1}{2}$	6$\frac{5}{8}$	9$\frac{1}{2}$	3$\frac{1}{2}$	7$\frac{1}{8}$	9$\frac{3}{4}$
460	$\frac{3}{4}$	4$\frac{1}{2}$	6$\frac{5}{8}$	5$\frac{3}{8}$	9$\frac{7}{8}$	11$\frac{1}{4}$

EXHIBIT 12.11
A sample of price quotations on the S&P 100 index. (Source: With the permission of *Investor's Business Daily*, March 12, 1993, p. 24.)

Closing value of the index on day of the quotes = 453.72

Market value of an option = 100 × quoted price

**Market-indexed certifi-
cate of deposit:** savings
account with an index
option attached

Market-Indexed Certificates of Deposit   An innovation in an option-bills
portfolio plan is a **market-indexed certificate of deposit** (CD). Although
these CDs were introduced by commercial banks in the mid-1980s, they have
become popular in recent years and now are being issued by stockbrokerage
firms as well as commercial banks. For example, Merrill Lynch introduced a
product, referred to as "Mitts," that pays $10 *plus* 115% of the price gain of
the S&P 500 between July 1992 and August 1997. The minimum return then
is zero (you get back your $10 investment) if the market is unchanged or
declines over the five-year period. In contrast to similar CDs issued by commercial banks, Mitts trade on the New York Stock Exchange.

   Market-indexed CDs are designed for smaller investors and, unfortunately, sometimes for those poorly informed about option value. It sounds
great that you can't lose any money—many of the advertisements trumpet
"zero risk to capital"—but you should realize that you give up any interest or
dividends that could be earned with a traditional investment. The important
question is whether you are better off in an indexed CD or simply investing in
a similar manner on your own—for example, buying a five-year zero coupon
bond along with a call option on a market index. When option-pricing formulas, such as Black-Scholes, are used to determine the option value embedded
in the indexed CDs, they appear overpriced. In effect, you pay rather high
administrative costs to the financial institution for creating the option-bills
portfolio.

Hedging Market Risk

Market risk hedge:
technique of buying an
index put option while
simultaneously buying
selected stocks

Index options also make it possible to use a **market risk hedge.** To see an
application of this type of hedge, suppose you believe you can select stocks
that will outperform the overall market. Even if you are successful, you may
still show investment losses if the overall market moves against you during
an investment period. In a major market cycle, most stock prices move in the
same direction. So, a decline in the market will probably drag your stocks
along with it. But if you are capable of picking superior stocks, their price
declines should be less than the overall market's, just as you would expect
them to increase more rapidly than the market in an upswing.

   Because you cannot control the market, your strategy is to hedge it by
buying an index put. If the market does poorly, the put should increase in
value to partially offset some of the losses you might take on your stocks. If
the market does well, you discard the put and enjoy the superior returns on
your stocks. In either case, the return you realize should be as good as—or
better than—the return if you simply invested in the stocks alone. This put
hedge is shown in Exhibit 12.12. The example assumes you can always do
twice as well as the market. If it declines by 10%, your stocks will fall only
5%; if it increases 10%, your stocks will jump 20%. The three assumed
changes in the market show how this hedge affects portfolio returns. It is
true that you will have positive profits *before* considering the cost of the

	$20,000 Invested in:	
	Stocks Alone	Stocks Hedged
Market Declines 10%		
Change in portfolio (−5%)	$−1,000	$−1,000
Change in the put's value (+10%)	—	+2,000
Cost of the put	—	− 750
Profit or loss	$−1,000	$+ 250
Market Declines 2%		
Change in portfolio (−1%)	$− 200	$− 200
Change in put's value	—	+ 400
Cost of the put	—	− 750
Profit or loss	$− 200	$− 550
Market Increases 10%		
Change in portfolio (+20%)	$+4,000	$+4,000
Change in put's value	—	—
Cost of the put	—	− 750
Profit or loss	$+4,000	$+3,250

EXHIBIT 12.12
Example of a market risk hedge

option. However, when this cost is considered, minor changes in the market will lead to insufficient changes in your stocks to cover the option cost. In such a situation, you would have been better off simply holding the stocks unhedged.

Options on Futures Contracts

Standardized put and call contracts are available on futures contracts. Because we have not yet covered futures contracts, you must wait until Chapter 13 to become familiar with the underlying assets of such option contracts. What you will learn is that futures contracts are widely used by professional money managers and having option contracts available on them makes risk management more flexible and cost-effective. In some respects, delivering a position in a futures contract is easier than delivering a hard asset, such as gold.

In a futures contract, you can take either a long position or a short position (explained in Chapter 13). If you buy a call on a gold futures contract, you have the right to take a long position, which means you think the price of gold will go up in the future. If you buy a put contract, you have the right to take a short position—you think gold's price will go down. Finally, it is important to remember that these are option contracts, which means you are under no obligation to enter into the futures contract if that were to prove unprofitable. So, if you bought a call with a strike price of gold of $360 and if gold was under this amount at the option's maturity, you simply discard the futures option as you would any other out-of-the-money option.

BOX 12.3   A QUESTION OF ETHICS

Be Wary of CDs Bearing Gifts

Wouldn't it be great if you could invest in the market and get a guarantee never to lose any money? And wouldn't it be great if you could do this right at the neighborhood bank and not pay commissions or deal with a pushy stockbroker? Well, you probably can, if your bank is like many others that offer market-indexed CDs. A good example is Citicorp's Stock Index Insured Account—a five-year CD that, as promoted in full-page ads, promises stock market returns along with zero risk to principal. How can they make such promises?

Read their literature more closely, and you will find the answer. First and most important, you do not receive any interest on the CD. In effect, what Citicorp does is take the interest you could earn on a five-year traditional CD and use it to buy call options on the market. This leads to the second point: do you get a good option value? This is a difficult question to answer because of the way the CD's return is calculated. Here's the deal: record each month-end value of the S&P 500 for the next 60 months after the CD is purchased; then, find the average and subtract from it the value at the time of purchase; express the difference as a percentage of the beginning value, then double that number to get your return. If, by some chance, the percentage difference is negative, you get back the initial investment—your capital is preserved.

Are you having a hard time trying to figure this one out? Most people do. For example, the return depends not only on how much the S&P 500 increases over the five years, but also on how the increases take place month to month. Consider this weird possibility: The index is at 500 when you buy the CD and remains at 500 for the next 59 months. On the 60th month, it jumps to 1,000. The average for 60 months is 508.33, leading to a 1.67% gain. Your total return is 3.33% (2 × 1.67%). So, your $10,000 grows to $10,330 for an annualized compound return of a mere 0.65%. In contrast, if you invested $10,000 directly in the index and received only $300 a year in dividends, your compounded return is 17.2%!

You could argue that the scenario above is unlikely to occur. Still, it points out the problem of evaluating the CD. As these products become more abstruse, we will need experts in option valuation to separate the good from the bad. Without such a professional opinion, it might be better to invest elsewhere. Finally, wouldn't depositors interests be served better with simpler products.

SUMMARY

A put or call option provides its holder with a right to sell or buy an underlying asset at a given price over a given period. Anyone—including individual investors—can both buy and sell such options. Option buyers try to either increase a portfolio's return or lower its risk. Option sellers are seeking speculative profits or additional income through covered option writing. Buyers and sellers must settle option contracts by reversing their positions, taking or making delivery of underlying shares, or transferring cash. They must be aware of commissions in determining option strategies.

These strategies include naked positions, hedge positions, spreads, and arbitrage positions. Naked positions offer the most profit potential but also are the riskiest; hedges are designed primarily to reduce risk; spreads have a variety of risk and return opportunities; and arbitrage positions exploit temporary price disparities.

Covered option writing is a popular practice that involves selling call options on stocks an investor owns. The intent is to earn option income that exceeds possible price appreciation of the underlying security while the option is held. An option-bills portfolio holds market index call options along with Treasury bills as an alternative to holding stocks. Index options are used to hedge market risk. In this activity, an investor buys securities he thinks will outperform the market and hedges against an adverse movement of the market by purchasing a market index put. The put reduces risk but also reduces potential profit. Options are available on futures contracts, which makes risk management more flexible and cost-effective.

KEY TERMS (listed in order of appearance)

option writing
call option
put option
covered option writers
reversing a position
take (make) delivery
cash settlement
naked position
hedge

spread
maturity spread
neutral spread
volatile spread
bull or bear spread
arbitrage
option-bills portfolio
market-indexed certificate of deposit
market risk hedge

REVIEW QUESTIONS

1. What is meant by "writing" an option? Do option writers take more or fewer risks than option buyers? Explain.
2. How does a put differ from a call? What types of underlying securities do puts and calls cover, and how are they traded?
3. Discuss two groups of put and call buyers and sellers.
4. Explain how put options can be used as portfolio insurance.
5. Explain three methods of settling an option contract. Discuss if you must take action or run the risk of suffering losses when an in-the-money contract expires.
6. What is a naked position? Who has the greater risk—buyer or seller—in such a position? Discuss your answer.
7. What is a hedge position, and what is its primary intention?
8. What is a spread, and what is its primary intention? Briefly explain the following spreads: (a) maturity, (b) neutral, (c) volatile, (d) bull, and (e) bear.

9. What is an arbitrage position? Give several examples of arbitrage opportunities with options.
10. How is covered option writing accomplished, and what is its primary purpose?
11. Explain generalizations that seem appropriate to covered option writing. Explain whether risk-averse investors should engage in this activity.
12. Discuss how an option-bills portfolio works and when it may be an appropriate investment strategy.
13. How can you use an index option to hedge market risk? When should you consider using such a hedge, and is it true that this hedge can assure a profit regardless of changes in the stock market? Explain.
14. Explain an option on a futures contract.

PROBLEMS AND PROJECTS

1. Interpret the put and call quotations below, indicating which set is associated with each type of option.

KLM	Strike Price	Dec.	March	June
$52\frac{1}{8}$	45	$7\frac{3}{4}$	$9\frac{1}{8}$	$10\frac{1}{4}$
	50	$2\frac{7}{8}$	$4\frac{3}{8}$	$6\frac{1}{4}$
	55	$\frac{7}{8}$	$1\frac{3}{4}$	$2\frac{1}{2}$
$52\frac{1}{8}$	45	$\frac{1}{4}$	$\frac{7}{8}$	$1\frac{3}{8}$
	50	$1\frac{1}{8}$	$2\frac{1}{8}$	$3\frac{1}{4}$
	55	$3\frac{1}{4}$	$5\frac{1}{8}$	$6\frac{7}{8}$

2. Referring to problem 1, determine your brokerage commission if you bought a December 45 put (one contract); then, explain whether you think this commission is reasonable or expensive.
3. Referring to problem 1, construct a profit-loss graph for the June 50 call from both the buyer's and the seller's perspective (naked positions). What is the profit or loss for each for stock prices of $40, $45, $50, $55, and $60? What is the break-even price?
4. Referring to problem 1, construct a profit-loss graph for the June 50 put. Respond to the same questions asked in problem 3.
5. Referring to problem 1, construct profit-loss graphs for the following strategies: (a) a neutral spread—June maturity, 50 strike, (b) a volatile spread—June maturity, 50 strike, (c) a bull spread—June maturity, 55 strike, and (d) a bear spread—June maturity, 55 strike. Find break-even points.
6. Do you see any arbitrage profits in the data of problem 1? Discuss. Change one of the prices to create an arbitrage opportunity.
7. Referring to problem 1, suppose you own 100 shares of the stock in question and plan to keep it in your portfolio. However, you are concerned the price of the stock might fall. Explain how you can "insure" against potential losses, using an appropriate option (use a 55 strike price and June maturity). Show your response graphically.
8. Referring to problem 1, suppose you own 100 shares of the stock in question and plan to keep it in your portfolio. However, you are considering writing a call

option against it. Assuming you write the June 50 and pay a $30 commission for each option transaction, evaluate the decision to write the option. Assume stock prices of $40, $45, $50, $55, and $60 and a 10% premium above formula value if the option is repurchased.

9. *(Student Project)* Evaluate your skill in making profits from daily forecasts of the stock market. Each day, forecast the market and then buy 10 appropriate options on the S&P 100. Assume you reverse your position at the end of the day. Do this daily for 10 days, recording your gain or loss each day. Also, charge commissions of $150 on each transaction. Report your trading performance at the end of the period.

CASE ANALYSES

The Hendersons, Robert and Angela, are nearing retirement. Bob will leave his employer in a year and they will move to St. Petersburg, Florida. Bob has about $400,000 in a retirement plan where he works, and the funds currently are invested in a broad portfolio of common stocks. The plan is a so-called money purchase plan (also called a defined contribution plan); it allows Bob the flexibility of deciding how his funds should be invested, such as in a stock fund, bond fund, or money market fund.

The stock market crash of October 19, 1987, has scared the Hendersons enormously. They shudder to think how their retirement nest egg could be depleted by a prolonged bear market. On the other hand, another robust year could add substantially to their retirement funds. Angela thinks the prudent course of action is to transfer all amounts to the money market fund. Although Bob shares this view, he wonders whether other courses of action might be available. For example, he has read how some investors use options as insurance protection. The Hendersons are in a quandary and have asked your advice. The S&P 100 is now at 453.72.

**12.1
The Hendersons
Hedge Their
Retirement Fund**

a. Explain how an option-bills portfolio might work in the Hendersons' case. You can assume that Bob would transfer his retirement funds into a money market fund and that he would trade options on his own.
b. Refer to the option quotations in Exhibit 12.11, and assume they would be representative of the situation facing the Hendersons for the upcoming year. Assume the May contract has 10 weeks before maturity. Determine the number of contracts needed and the cost of engaging in an option-bills portfolio, assuming the 460 strike was selected. Then, determine the net cost, assuming the money market fund earns 4% for the year.
c. Suppose the Hendersons decided to leave their funds invested in the stock fund, but to hedge the situation, they will buy puts on the S&P 100.

Questions

Assuming the May 460s are selected, how much will this insurance cost the Hendersons for the year? Assume the stock fund pays a 3% dividend and correlates closely with the S&P 100 with respect to price changes.

d. Considering each approach, make a recommendation to the Hendersons. Do you believe either plan is appropriate, or would they be better off putting the $400,000 in the money market fund? To answer this question, you should assume different possible outcomes for the market over a 10-week period, such as down 4%, down 2%, unchanged, up 2%, up 4%, and up 6%.

12.2 Rachel Elliot Considers a Market Risk Hedge

Rachel Elliot seems to have a unique skill at finding undervalued stocks. Her picks always seem to beat the market on a risk-adjusted basis, but she always seems to find them when the market heads south. Investment patience is not one of Rachel's better traits, so she usually sells before the market recovers and takes losses in the process. Rachel has done well in bull markets, but she is looking for a way to improve her performance in bear markets.

An examination of her past trades reveals that she usually does five percentage points better than the overall market. So, if the market goes up 10%, Rachel's portfolio is likely to go up 15%; if the market goes down 10%, her portfolio will go down only 5%; and she would show a 5% return if the market is unchanged. Rachel has $61,000 to invest. She is considering using a market risk hedge because she is concerned that the market may perform rather poorly in the months ahead. Rachel describes her tolerance for risk as fairly low.

Questions

a. Using the option prices shown in Exhibit 12.11 (May maturities and 460 strike price), evaluate a market risk hedge. Assume the following possibilities for the market: down 10%, unchanged, and up 10%. Also, assume the closing value of the index on the day of the quotes is 453.72.

b. Do you recommend a market risk hedge for Rachel? Explain your response.

HELPFUL READING

Feldman, Amy. "CDs for CPAs." *Forbes*, July 19, 1993, pp. 92–94.

Laing, Jonathan R. "The Next Meltdown?" *Barron's*, June 7, 1993, p. 10.

Schultz, John W. "The Giant Hedge: It Explains This Market, a Money Manager Says." *Barron's*, August 9, 1993, pp. 26–27.

Schwartz, Jonathan P. "An Upward Bias." *Barron's*, March 22, 1993, p. 19.

Scism, Leslie. "Variants of Convertible Preferred Stock Can Leave Investors with a Bad Taste." *The Wall Street Journal*, July 27, 1993, p. C1.

Strong, Robert A. *Speculative Markets*. Chicago: Longman Financial Services Publishing, 1989.

Teitelbaum, Richard S. "Is This CD All That It Promises to Be?" *Fortune*, May 3, 1993, pp. 30–31.

CHAPTER THIRTEEN

Commodity and Financial Futures

After you finish this chapter, you will be able to:

- understand the characteristics of futures contracts and how to read commodity futures quotations.

- identify important aspects of trading futures contracts, including the use of margin and selecting a broker.

- see the uses of commodity futures and distinguish among trading strategies that are speculative, hedging, or investment-oriented.

- appreciate that speculative trading involves substantial risks and seldom is conducted profitably by either amateurs or professionals.

- evaluate the uses of financial futures in speculative, hedging, or investment applications.

- understand quotations of financial futures, with particular emphasis on Treasury bond and bills futures quotations.

Like options, commodity and financial futures can make investment port-folios more flexible by broadening the array of assets from which to choose and by providing new opportunities for managing risk. Although futures have a long history in the United States, going back to the early part of the nineteenth century, many investors ignored them until very recently. Looking for ways to hedge inflation and to deal with volatile interest rates, investors turned their attention to the futures markets in the 1970s. What they found was a remarkably efficient and sophisticated trading system, very similar to the more familiar stock and bond markets. With the inflation rate subsiding considerably by the mid-1980s, some of the appeal of futures was gone, and so were many of the trend-following investors. A few were wealthi-er, but the majority probably paid their dues to learn that futures trading is not for the novice investor unwilling to learn its fundamentals or appreciate its risks. This chapter attempts to explain each.

CHARACTERISTICS OF FUTURES

Investing in futures is, in a sense, investing in the future. Suppose your business is milling wheat, corn, and other grains into flour. You need a constant supply of these grains to continue operating, and because you are a prudent person, you are concerned about their future availability and future price. Without a **futures market**—a market in which futures contracts are trad-ed—all you could do is worry about the future. You must buy the grains in the **cash market** (a market in which actual commodities are traded; a grain elevator, for example) when the need arises and pay the prevailing prices. However, a futures market allows you to negotiate for the future delivery of the needed grains.

> **Futures market:** market in which futures contracts are traded

> **Cash market:** market in which commodities are traded

Now, suppose you entered into an agreement in January for deliveries in April, but when April arrives, you find there is an ample supply of grains available for purchase at lower prices than those negotiated. Can you simply discard your agreement, as you would an option that expires valueless? The answer is an emphatic no, and that is the major difference between owning an option and entering into a futures contract: An option is a right, not an obligation; a futures contract is an obligation to perform. You buy an option, but you do not buy a futures contract. If you buy an option, your potential losses are known and limited; if you take a naked position in a futures contract, your potential losses are virtually unknown and unlimited. Under-standing a futures contract is essential before you consider trading futures.

The Futures Contract

> **Commodity futures contract:** involves the future delivery of a tangible commodity or a financial instrument

A **commodity futures contract** involves the future delivery of a tangible commodity or financial instrument. It has specific terms and conditions that must be met.

Contract Specifications   A futures contract must clearly specify the rights and obligations given each party to the contract. The following provisions are important:

☐ The commodity must be defined precisely in terms of quality, purity, weight, or any other characteristic that might influence market value.
☐ The time and place of delivery must be certain.
☐ The quantity of the commodity or amount of the financial instrument must be indicated.
☐ The price at which delivery will take place must be established.

The flour miller in our previous example would be concerned with each of the provisions above because he or she would probably intend to take delivery of the grains per the conditions of the contract. That would be a rare occurrence, however, because the overwhelming majority of contracts never involve delivery.

As in the case of options, most futures contracts are closed by reversing a position. This procedure is used even more often with futures trading, in which it is estimated at least 97% of all positions are reversed. Even the miller who needs the grains often finds it more convenient to buy them in the cash markets rather than by a futures contract delivery. The contract served its function during the uncertain period, and when it is over, it can be eliminated through reversal.

Reading a Futures Quotation   Exhibit 13.1 shows a typical commodity quotation. Commodity quotes can be found in the financial pages of many newspapers, although they are not reported as extensively as stocks, bonds, and options. *The Wall Street Journal, New York Times,* and *Investor's Business Daily* have comprehensive daily listings, and *Barron's* has one each week.

The commodity illustrated is corn, and although Exhibit 13.1 is self-explanatory, it is important to realize that the total value of a contract is not reported. To determine total value, multiply the contract quantity—in this case, 5,000 bushels—by the settle price. For example, the July contract closed at $2.375 a bushel; multiplying this by 5,000 gives a total market value of $11,875. Sometimes this figure is called your **money at risk.** If you traded one July contract, you should look at your investment—your money at risk—as $11,875, regardless of how much or little of your own funds were used to trade the contract. As you see, one contract involves a substantial sum of money.

Money at risk: total market value of a futures contract

Buyer—A Long Position   As we mentioned earlier, you do not actually buy a contract, although the terms *buy* and buyer often are used. A buyer takes a long position, which means she will *accept* delivery of the commodity according to the contract provisions. Because buyers accept delivery at the established contract price, they are of the opinion that the actual price in the cash

EXHIBIT 13.1 Explanation of a typical commodity futures quotation

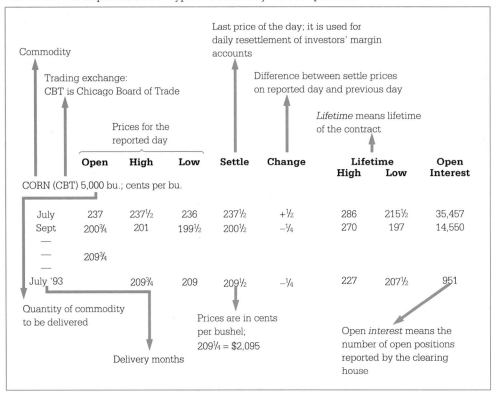

market at the time of delivery will be higher. If true, they could exercise their right to buy at the lower contract price and immediately sell the commodity at the higher market price to earn a profit. Viewed more simply, buyers expect the commodity's price to increase in the future. If it does, the value of the futures contract—like the value of a call option—will increase right along with it, as Exhibit 13.2 indicates. The buyer probably has no intention of holding the contract to maturity and may reverse her position at a profit (or loss) five minutes after it is opened.

Seller—A Short Position   A "seller" (again, a misnomer) agrees to make delivery of the commodity. The seller expects the price of the commodity to fall in the future, in which case the commodity could be purchased at the lower cash market price for a quick profit. Few sellers will hold contracts on the settlement day; they, like buyers, will reverse their positions. As with put and call options, one investor's profit is another's loss, as Exhibit 13.2 shows. Keep in mind, though, with a futures contract, the buyer's potential losses are virtually unlimited, whereas for the buyer of an option, the maximum loss is the cost of the option.

One helpful way to view a futures contract is to visualize it as a wager between two investors about a future price of the commodity. One bets it will

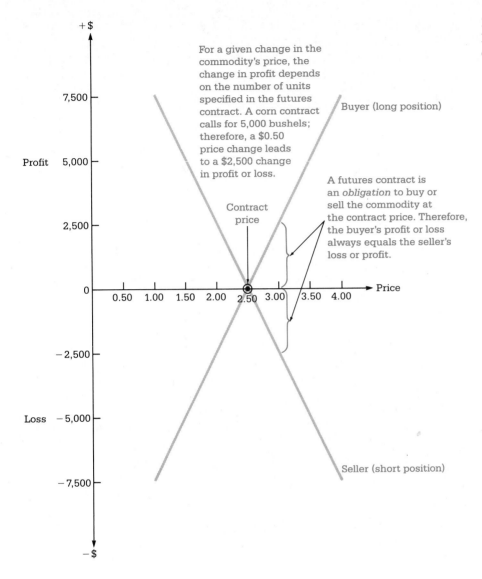

EXHIBIT 13.2
Profit-loss graph for a
corn futures contract

increase and the other bets it will decrease. The loser then pays the winner the contract quantity times the difference between the contract price and the actual market price at the end of the trading period, which is every day (as we will see shortly).

Trading Futures

Trading futures is relatively easy to do. All you need are sufficient funds and a commodity account with a broker. Trading is similar to stock trading, with the same orders—market, limit, and stop-loss—and margin being used.

Opening an Account Because futures are inherently risky, most brokers require that you meet certain net worth or income requirements before you can open a commodity trading account. Assuming you meet these requirements, most brokers then require an initial deposit (margin) that must be maintained as long as the account is open. This deposit varies among brokers but usually is $5,000 or more. Keep in mind, this is an idle, nonproductive investment. Many brokers will allow the deposit of Treasury bills, but they may then insist on a larger deposit, say, $20,000.

In addition to the initial deposit, each contract you trade has its own margin requirements. For example, a corn contract has an initial margin requirement of $1,000, which is low in relation to the contract's total value. Small margin requirements are characteristic of all futures contracts, as Exhibit 13.3 indicates. Along with the initial margin requirement, brokers impose their own maintenance margin requirements. In the case of corn, this requirement might be set at $750. If you took a position in corn with the minimum margin of $1,000 and price moved against you by only five cents ($250/5,000) a bushel, you would get a margin call. Because margins often are slim in futures trading, margin calls are frequent. If you can't make the call, your broker will immediately close the position with you taking the loss.

As a point of information, margin in futures trading is not actually margin in the sense that it represents your equity in the purchase of an asset; as we have seen, you do not buy or sell an asset. Margin in futures trading is more in the nature of a performance bond: if you do not live up to the terms of the futures contract, your broker is free to use the funds in settlement of a deficiency. The term *margin*, though, is used extensively in futures trading, and most investors view it no differently than they view margin to trade stocks or other securities.

EXHIBIT 13.3
Illustrative futures contracts and initial margin requirements

Commodity or Financial Instrument	Initial Margin
Cocoa	$1,000
Corn	1,000
Cotton	1,000
Gold	3,500
Live cattle	1,500
Lumber	1,200
Japanese yen	1,800
Pork bellies	1,500
Soybeans	1,500
S&P 500 stock index	7,500
Treasury bills	2,500

Selecting a Broker   Full-service stockbrokers also provide commodity brokerage services. You probably will deal with the same representative who
handles your other securities. Commissions with full-service brokers vary but
are in the neighborhood of $80 a "round turn." This means you pay one com-
mission to open and close a position. Some brokerage firms specialize in
commodity trading, and these firms often discount commissions, with
charges of $40 a round turn being fairly common. To attract you as a cus-
tomer, many of the discounters will offer very low commissions for a limited
period or for a limited number of orders.

Of course, each broker claims to be the best or the most economical or
to offer some other advantage. The full-service (expensive) brokers usually
provide research reports on various commodities, which are supposed to
improve your trading profits. Whether they do or do not can be argued, but
any broker worth dealing with should carefully explain the risks of futures
trading. For every one successful trader who made a fortune starting with a
shoestring, there are probably nine failures. A failure often is a sad story of
someone who trades a few contracts successfully and thinks he cannot lose.
But losses come quickly and heavily in this market segment, and no one is
perfect, or even very good.

Investor Protection   Commodity trading is regulated to some degree,
although your protections are not as strong as with stocks and bonds. The
Commodity Exchange Authority, a division of the Department of Agriculture,
is responsible for enforcing federal regulations that pertain to commodity
transactions and commodity exchanges. These regulations have more to do
with establishing uniform trading standards than with protecting investors.

In 1974, Congress created the Commodity Futures Trading Commission
(CFTC), which was intended to be a regulatory commission, enforcing federal
laws in the futures and options markets. It has come under fire in recent
years for failing to prevent abusive practices to some investors. In 1989, the
Federal Bureau of Investigation made public the details of a sting operation
in the commodities exchanges, which indicated some floor traders were
arranging trades in a manner that benefited them at the expense of their
clients. Such illegal practices were supposed to be monitored by the CFTC.
An in-depth review of the commission was ordered by the House Agriculture
Committee, with the key issue being why the CFTC failed to curb trading
abuses. A number of changes have resulted from the review, although some
observers believe that the industry has acted on its own accord to avoid similar abuses in the future.

Organized Exchanges and the Clearinghouse

An organized futures exchange is similar to an organized stock or bond
exchange. It is owned and operated (on a nonprofit basis) by its members,
who hold seats on the exchange. Its primary function is to provide an arena

EXHIBIT 13.4
Important commodity
exchanges in the
United States and
Canada

Chicago Mercantile Exchange (CME)
Chicago Board of Trade
International Monetary Market of the CME
Commodity Exchange, Inc.
Mid-America Commodity Exchange
Minneapolis Grain Exchange
New Orleans Commodity Exchange
Kansas City Board of Trade
New York Cotton Exchange
New York Futures Exchange (a division of the New York Stock Exchange)
New York Mercantile Exchange
Winnipeg Commodity Exchange

for the orderly and efficient trading of futures contracts. The largest in the
United States is the Chicago Board of Trade, but there are quite a few important other exchanges, as Exhibit 13.4 indicates.

Clearinghouse: system
that facilitates futures
trading

Each exchange has a clearing system that involves a **clearinghouse.**
The clearinghouse facilitates trading by eliminating the need for buyers and
sellers to deal directly with each other. Instead, each deals with the clearinghouse. So, if you buy or sell a futures contract, your obligation is to the clearinghouse and you can expect contract performance from it, not from a person
on the other side of the contract. The clearinghouse in turn must take steps
to make sure each trader can meet his obligations. It does so through the
margin requirements and through daily resettlement of accounts. This reset-

Marking to market:
process of updating
trading accounts daily

tlement is also called **marking to market,** and it means that at the end of
the trading day, each one of your futures positions is updated using the commodity's settlement price given for the day. For example, suppose you bought
a corn contract at $2.50 in the morning and the settlement price at the end of
trading was $2.55; your account would show the day's profit of $250 ($0.05 ×
5,000).

You are free to withdraw this gain in cash. However, if price moved
against you, it would be necessary to deposit additional margin equal to the
loss. In effect, with futures trading, there is no such thing as a paper loss, or a
paper profit, although many traders do not make daily withdrawals or daily
deposits. (They have excess margin as a buffer.)

COMMODITY FUTURES

Commodity futures have been in existence longer than any other futures contract. Exhibit 13.5 provides a list of the major commodities for which futures
contracts are available; as you see, the list is quite extensive. Investors deal
in commodity futures for reasons similar to those for using options—to either

EXHIBIT 13.5
Commodity futures
contracts available

Commodity Group	Specific Commodities
Grains and oilseeds	Corn, oats, soybeans, soybean meal, soybean oil, wheat, barley, flaxseed, rapeseed, and rye
Livestock and meat	Feeder cattle, live cattle, hogs, and pork bellies (bacon)
Food and fiber	Cocoa, coffee, cotton, orange juice, world sugar, and domestic sugar
Metals and petroleum	Copper, gold, platinum, palladium, silver, crude oil, heating oil, gas oil, and NY gasoline—leaded regular and unleaded regular
Wood	Lumber

speculate or to hedge against risks inherent in production or merchandising activities that require commodities. Additionally, commodity futures have been used to protect portfolios against inflation and to reduce overall portfolio risk.

Speculative Trading

Commodity futures have considerable speculative appeal. As with options, traders can take naked positions or spreads (see Chapter 12). The extremely low margin requirements allow many people to participate in the market with relatively high risk exposure. Where else, for an initial ante of $10,000 or so, can you control $50,000 to $100,000 worth of investments? And where else, if you guess right, can you make as much as $1,000 to $2,000 a day on your $10,000 ante—and withdraw it at the end of the day? Finally, where else can you compete on a reasonably fair footing with most other "players," who probably don't know any better than you what will be the future price of corn or pork bellies (bacon)? The speculative appeal of commodity futures is great, but there are facts you should consider before you attempt to trade.

Most Individual Speculators Lose   Studies of the trading performances of individual speculators are not encouraging. In fact, the overwhelming majority—as high as 90%—lose in futures trading and many lose heavily. Most engage in frequent trading, opening and closing positions daily and even several times during the day. As you suspect, commissions eventually consume most of the profit of those fortunate enough to show any before commissions. Despite such frequent trading, speculators often stay with one position that they are convinced will make a big profit. More often than not, price moves against them, and their losses become enormous and eventually wipe out their margin balances.

The beginning speculator should be advised also that trading based on reaction to a natural calamity is exceptionally risky. You may hear that Florida

BOX 13.1   INVESTMENT INSIGHTS

Earn 50% More in Commodities Than in Stocks: Is There a Gimmick?

You know the answer to this question must be yes, but who would propose such an opportunity? None other than one of Wall Street's most prestigious firms, Goldman, Sachs & Co. (GS). Several years ago, the firm introduced with much fanfare the Goldman Sachs Commodity Index. It did this not as a gesture of goodwill to help commodity traders track prices but in an effort to cut into the lucrative trading of derivative instruments based on indexes. The strategy had two key steps: First, create the index, thereby gaining informational monopoly power; second, stimulate the demand for commodities by showing their profitability.

The demand stimulator was a study done by GS that showed the GS Commodity Index returned 15.22% over a 20-year period beginning in 1970, while the S&P 500 showed a measly 10.26% return. Did the time period selected account for the huge difference (a favorite trick whenever you want to prove a point)? Only partially; other factors were also at work.

For starters, the index components changed over time. Apart from the problem created for measuring historical returns reliably, this makes it almost ludicrous to use such a changing index in a forecasting sense. Also, the investment method assumed that investors would use U.S. Treasury bills for margin. Although this is a realistic assumption, we should recall that T bills showed rather good returns over the study period—an average of 7.6%. But this return is unlikely in the future; 1993's average is close to 3%.

Finally, almost one-third of the 15.22% is attributable to roll yield. This yield arises when long positions are maintained through time and when more distant futures contracts are cheaper than more current contracts—a situation referred to as an inverted basis curve. As with inverted yield curves for debt instruments, inverted basis curves are considered somewhat unusual and not likely to dominate normal curves in the future.

Take away the interest on T bills and roll yield—that is, focus on price changes only—and the 15.22% return falls to a bit less than 4%. This didn't even match the average inflation rate of around 6% over the period. Let's hope the people managing our pension and retirement plans (the likely market for derivatives based on the GS Index) aren't overly impressed.

has just been hit by a cold wave, freezing the entire orange crop. Now is a good time to buy orange juice futures because price must increase. The problem is that everyone is hearing the same news and reacting the same way. By the time you enter the market, price may have already peaked. Later, when the news indicates the cold wave wasn't as bad as first feared, you are still holding a long position when price plummets. Before you trade on the basis of rumor or news, or for any other reason, you should take the time to first trade on paper only. Be honest with yourself as you record trades executed, and measure your performance. Put everything in writing *before* you trade, and don't forget commissions. Do this for a while—perhaps a year or longer— and if you are not discouraged at the end of this time, then you can consider trading for keeps.

Many Professional Traders Also Lose Individual investors can take heart that professional traders' performances are not much better than theirs. Many commodity pooling arrangements, such as limited partnerships, were begun in the late 1970s when interest in commodity trading heightened. Their trading performances are a matter of public record and were, for a while, reported regularly in *Barron's*. What does the record show? It is not one of overwhelming success; indeed, professionals do not perform much better than rank amateurs. There are some with exceptionally high returns, but there are many more with very low and negative returns. Many of the professional traders base their trading systems on technical analysis, which was described in Chapter 8. Trading signals based on moving averages, for example, are popular. However, these mechanical systems apparently work no better here than they do in trading common stocks.

Hedging

Earlier in this chapter, we saw an example of a miller who might want to use futures contracts to remove uncertainties from the business. Many businesses and individuals face similar risks. For example, a farmer with corn growing in the field has no choice but to have a long position in corn. Many jewelers have natural long positions in gold or silver, while a building contractor who has sold a house that is yet to be built has a natural short position in lumber. That these people want to hedge is not surprising; indeed, you wonder why hedging doesn't always take place. Why wouldn't farmers hedge their crops at planting time? And if the futures price is not high enough to make a profit on the crop, why even bother to plant? Commodity hedging sounds simple, but there are risks to consider.

Mechanics of a Hedge Suppose it is April and a farmer has just planted enough seed to harvest 10,000 bushels of corn in September. Not willing to take risks, he sees that a September corn futures is selling at $2 a bushel and immediately sells two contracts (10,000 bushels). As the growing season moves along, suppose corn shortages appear likely because of a poor growing season and the price of corn rises to $3 a bushel by September. This is bad luck for the farmer, who now wishes he had not hedged in April. The crop is harvested and sold for $30,000, but he must then close his short position in the futures market at a loss of $10,000. His net gain from the crop is $20,000.

But suppose the price of corn fell to $1 a bushel by September. Now the crop is sold for only $10,000, but the futures contract provides an additional profit of $10,000. Again, the net gain is $20,000. As you see, the hedge locks in the price of the commodity on the futures contract; in this case, $2 a bushel. This example also illustrates a **perfect hedge,** which means a gain or loss in the cash market is offset *exactly* by loss or gain in the futures market. (Gain or loss is measured by the difference in price between when the futures position is opened and when it is closed. Gain or loss in the cash market assumes the commodity could be sold in the cash market at the time the futures position is taken. In the case of the farmer with unharvested corn, this is obviously an assumption.)

Perfect hedge: losses (gains) in a cash market position are offset perfectly by gains (losses) in futures positions

Hedging Problems   People who must use hedges often argue that hedges work better in textbooks than they do in the real world. They think perfect hedges seldom are found. The farmer, for example, hopes to harvest 10,000 bushels, but he may not. His fields may yield more or less, which means he may have underhedged or overhedged, either of which exposes him to risk. For example, suppose the yield is 5,000 bushels and corn's September price is $3 a bushel. The crop is sold for $15,000, but the loss of $10,000 on the two futures contracts reduces the net gain to only $5,000.

Another problem confronting short-term hedgers is a divergence of prices in the futures and cash markets. One assumes that the price of a commodity in the futures market should be almost identical to its price in the cash market. That may not be true because they are two different markets. The price of corn on a September futures contract need not be the same as the cash price of corn in April. For example, suppose the cash price for corn in April was $1.90 a bushel. Instead of a farmer growing corn, let us now assume a grain elevator operator holding 10,000 bushels in inventory. To hedge her position, she also shorted corn at $2 for September delivery. Much to her surprise, a week later she receives a big order to ship 10,000 bushels immediately to a customer. Her price—the cash market price—has fallen to $1.85 a bushel; but when she reverses her position in the futures contracts, she finds the September price has risen to $2.05 a bushel. Price decreased in the cash market and increased in the futures market.

Basis: futures price of a commodity subtracted from its cash price

Basis   In this case, basis moved against the hedger. **Basis** is the difference between the cash price and the futures price. Adverse changes in basis are common in commodity hedging, with risk being greater as the two prices are more separated in time. As a contract reaches its maturity, basis converges to zero, as Exhibit 13.6 shows. Why zero? Any positive or negative basis would set up a virtual risk-free trading opportunity: buy at the low price and immediately resell at the high one. For example, suppose that one day before the September corn contract expires, the futures price is $2, while the cash price is $1.95. You immediately sell a futures contract and at the same time call a grain elevator and buy 5,000 bushels in the cash market. You then deliver

EXHIBIT 13.6
Basis illustrated

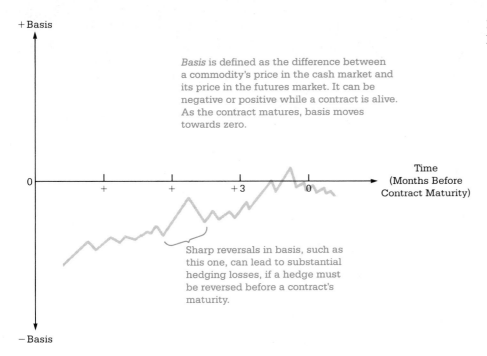

+ Basis

Basis is defined as the difference between a commodity's price in the cash market and its price in the futures market. It can be negative or positive while a contract is alive. As the contract matures, basis moves towards zero.

Time
(Months Before
Contract Maturity)

Sharp reversals in basis, such as this one, can lead to substantial hedging losses, if a hedge must be reversed before a contract's maturity.

− Basis

these bushels to fulfill the futures contract and pocket $250 ($0.05 × 5,000) in profit. Efficiency in the futures markets makes such opportunities almost impossible.

Basis Management   Professional hedgers attempt to manage basis in the sense of trying to determine its trends, cycles, or seasonal changes. Basis most often should have a negative value. Why? Because it must reflect the so-called **cost of carry,** which is the total cost of holding a commodity until an expiration date of a futures contract based on that commodity. In the example above, we can suppose for the moment that cost of carry from April through September was $0.10 ($2.00 − $1.90) a bushel of corn. This cost includes storing and insuring one bushel of corn for five months as well as the opportunity cost of funds needed to buy the bushel at $1.90. The following cost items per bushel might apply in our case:

Cost of carry: total cost of holding a commodity until the expiration of a futures contract on that commodity

Storage costs	$0.0425
Insurance costs	0.0100
Cost of funds (0.06 × $1.90 × 5/12)	0.0475
Total cost of carry	$0.1000

So, with a futures price of $2.00 a bushel in April, you could short one contract for $10,000. However, if you then simultaneously bought 5,000 bushels in the cash market and held them until the September expiration date of the futures contract, you would incur total costs of $10,000 ($9,500 to buy the corn and $500 to carry it) and, so, would break even. Why, then, go through the aggravation?

You wouldn't if all you hoped for was breaking even. But suppose the futures price was $2.20 a bushel instead of $2.00; couldn't we then go through the same procedure and make a profit of $0.20 a bushel? The answer is yes—but don't expect such arbitrage profits to be readily available. What we can do, so can everybody else, and quickly the two prices—spot and futures—should be brought back into alignment. In short, all of us will be trying to short the futures contract, driving down its price, while buying in the cash market, driving up the cash price. The final equilibrium price should be one that has a negative $0.10 per bushel basis. Although equilibrium usually is restored quickly, it may not be quick enough to help the hedger, such as the grain elevator operator in the example above.

Inverted Basis Curve   Because cost of carry is always some positive number, you might wonder how basis can ever be positive; that is, how can a futures price ever be less than the cash price? This situation, although not common, can occur when traders believe that prices in the future will be much lower than their current levels. For example, suppose corn supplies currently are very low because of a big grain deal with Russia, leading to tight market conditions and high current prices. However, the current growing crop is bountiful and should lead to large supplies—and low prices—in the future; thus, we get futures prices lower than cash prices, which is called an **inverted basis curve.** Can this odd relation be exploited in an arbitrage process? Unfortunately, no; so, it persists until supplies are restored to normal levels.

Inverted basis curve: basis is positive rather than negative, converging to zero at the contract's maturity

Investing in Commodity Futures

Investing in commodity futures represents a third general use of these instruments. Investing differs from trading or hedging in several respects. First, it implies a perpetual long position because your intent is really to invest directly in commodities, but the futures contract is used as a more efficient substitute. Second, far less leverage is used even though it is available.

Advantages   Investing a portion of your portfolio in tangible assets is considered advantageous during inflationary periods. Prices of many tangibles keep pace with inflation. Because a long position in a futures contract allows you to own tangibles indirectly at relatively low cost, a perpetual long position may be a more attractive alternative than owning tangibles directly. Even gold and silver, which are the easiest tangibles to own, present the ownership problems of safe storage, insurance, and eventual resale.

Futures contracts allow for possible greater diversification among commodities. If you try to hedge inflation with a single commodity such as gold, you could be frustrated if gold's price is upset by other events. Excess production in Russia or South Africa, for example, might depress price. Moreover, diversifying among an array of actual tangibles may be impossible or undesirable. Where would you store 5,000 bushels of corn or 15,000 pounds of orange juice?

A third advantage of investing in futures is revealed by several studies that have shown their returns to be poorly correlated to returns from common stocks. Poor correlation is an advantage if you are considering holding the assets in portfolio because it leads to lower portfolio risk. Portfolios of stocks and futures have been shown to be less risky and about as profitable (over time) as holding each separately. Thus, you can argue that an efficient portfolio should include both.

Disadvantages　　There are problems with using commodity futures. To begin with, unless you are quite wealthy or want to use considerable leverage, adequate diversification among an array of contracts may be difficult. Few investors could afford to have unleveraged positions in, say, 10 contracts. You would need well over $100,000, depending on the contracts chosen. The pooling arrangements mentioned earlier are helpful here, but you must be sure their investment objective is inflation hedging. If it is speculating, they are unsuitable to meet your goal. Second, there are some costs to consider. Although commissions are not high, they may be frequent if you select contracts with short maturities, and if your initial margin is not in the form of Treasury bills, you forgo interest that could be earned elsewhere.

Perhaps the biggest disadvantage in hedging inflation is that most investors are not prepared to take the losses that must come if disinflation occurs, as it did beginning in the early 1980s. Most commodity prices fell sharply, leading to substantial losses for holders of long positions. You might argue that the inflation hedge worked exactly as it should have—stock and bond prices increased while commodity prices decreased—but few investors were prepared to take such losses. What they actually wanted was inflation protection *and* stock price appreciation and high interest rates on their bonds. What they wanted was impossible or at least unlikely to happen. An attempt to have all three requires buying options, not futures contracts. But as we saw in Chapter 12, this is tantamount to buying insurance and paying the heavy premiums.

FINANCIAL FUTURES

Financial futures are identical to commodity futures in most respects, except the underlying asset is an intangible financial asset rather than a tangible commodity. Although currency futures have been in existence for some time, interest-rate futures first made their appearance in late 1975, and index futures were not available until 1982. Today, financial futures are as popular

EXHIBIT 13.7
Financial futures con-
tracts available

Financial Group	Specific Financial Instruments
Currencies	British pound, Canadian dollar, Japanese yen, Swiss franc, German mark, and U.S. dollar index
Interest-Rate Securities	Eurodollars, Treasury bonds, Treasury bills, Treasury notes, GNMA passthroughs, bank certificates of deposit, and stripped Treasuries
Indexes	Municipal bond index, S&P 500 index, New York Stock Exchange composite index, Kansas City Value Line index, major market index, and the Commodity Research Bureau index

and as widely used as commodity futures. Exhibit 13.7 shows a partial listing of contracts available.

Measured by money at risk, the financial futures now dominate futures trading. Exhibit 13.8 shows graphs of key financial futures and indicates the open interest of each. Some of the open interests are extremely large—for example, about 279,000 U.S. Treasury bond contracts and more than 311,000 Eurodollar contracts. You will learn shortly that each T bond contract has a face value of $100,000, which means the money at risk is $27.9 billion; each Eurodollar contract has a face value of $1 million, leading to a money-at-risk amount of $311 billion! This truly is high finance. In contrast, on the same reporting day, corn had the largest open interest—244,524 contracts—of the commodities. The money at risk, however, was $2.6 billion (using the closest contract's settle price). Although this isn't exactly petty cash, it doesn't even come close to many of the financial futures.

Currency Futures

**Currency futures con-
tract:** specifies the
exchange of one curren-
cy for another

A **currency futures contract** calls for delivery of a specified number of units of a given currency: pounds, francs, yen, and others. Exhibit 13.9 shows a quotation for British pounds. At the settle price, the pound cost $1.4895 for September delivery of 62,500 pounds; so, the contract was worth $93,093.75.

Who cares to trade currency futures? Again, there are three interested parties: speculators, hedgers, and investors. The speculator hopes to profit by guessing correctly the future prices of currencies. For example, she might anticipate future economic problems in Great Britain that will weaken the pound. Given this conviction, shorting the pound is the correct strategy because the speculator believes its value will fall relative to the dollar. If you thought the dollar would weaken relative to the pound, you would take a long position in the pound, expecting its price to increase. If these are naked positions, they will be extremely risky, as are naked positions in commodity futures.

EXHIBIT 13.8

Graphics of popular financial futures contracts (Source: Reproduced with the permission of *Investor's Business Daily*, March 12, 1993, p. 24.)

EXHIBIT 13.9
Explanation of a typical currency futures quotation. (See Exhibit 13.1 for previously explained items.)

	Open	High	Low	Settle	Change	Lifetime High	Lifetime Low	Open Interest
BRITISH POUND (IMM)—62,500 pounds; $ per pound								
Sept	1.4785	1.4950	1.4760	1.4895	+.0135	1.5430	1.3240	24,453

Price is in dollars per pound;
1.4895 means each pound
costs $1.4895

Hedgers in currencies hope to manage risks that arise in connection with their business activities. If you own a business in Great Britain, your profits are earned in pounds, not dollars. You ultimately want dollars and perhaps will convert the pound earnings to dollars at a future date for transfer to the United States. Until the transfer takes place, you are at the risk of a weakening pound. You may have £62,500 earnings when the pound is worth $1.50, but if it falls to $1.45 in the interim, you will lose $3,125 ($0.05 × 62,500). To hedge this risk, you short one futures contract. If the pound does fall, your position will show a profit to offset the loss in holding the pound.

Investors might consider using currency futures to internationalize their portfolios. As the dollar weakened in the mid-1980s, it became fashionable to add an international flavor to one's portfolio to reduce risk. There is merit in the effort; however, using foreign currencies to accomplish the task is both difficult and risky. For most investors, it would be more efficient to use mutual funds specializing in foreign investment, or to invest in companies that are international in scope, such as IBM or Exxon.

Interest-Rate Futures

Interest-rate futures contract: specifies the delivery of a debt instrument

An **interest-rate futures contract** also has the same features as a commodity contract, except the underlying asset is a debt instrument. You should notice that contracts are available for an array of Treasury securities—bonds, notes, and bills—all of which are popular.

Reading Quotations   Exhibit 13.10 shows how to interpret a typical quotation for a Treasury bond futures contract. This contract assumes delivery of $100,000 face value of Treasury bonds with an 8% coupon rate (paid semiannually) and a maturity of 20 years. Actual settlement can be made with many different Treasury bonds. (The details are rather complicated and not essential to our understanding of the futures contracts.) Once again, the most common form of settlement is position reversal.

BOX 13.2   A QUESTION OF ETHICS

Do the Derivative Markets Need Greater Regulation?

Measured by any standard, the growth in derivatives over the past 20 years has been explosive, and virtually no area of investment activity has escaped their influence. Consider the following items:

☐ The Chicago Mercantile Exchange alone typically trades $12 billion of stock index futures a day—almost twice as much as the actual stocks traded on the New York Stock Exchange.

☐ The Chicago Board of Trade trades $12 trillion of futures and options on U.S. Treasury debt in a year—about four times the outstanding total of all Treasury debt.

☐ In 1992, the lead banks of the 50 largest bank holding companies held derivatives with a face value of $6.3 trillion—an amount 50% greater than the national debt.

☐ Profits related to proprietary trading (which often involves derivatives) are enormous, accounting for 70% of Salomon Brothers pre-tax earnings from 1990 through the second quarter of 1993; Lawrence E. Hillibrand, who headed Salomon's bond-arbitrage unit, made $23 million in 1990 (he was 31 years of age).

With such huge markets and profit opportunities, there is little doubt that growth will continue, in terms of both traditional instruments and new, exotic creations. The latter are worrying many observers. Futures and options traded on the major exchanges are subject to strict guidelines in terms of adequate protection to investors. If your call option bought through a broker is deep in the money, you can be assured a seller will be able to make good on delivery if you choose to exercise. The same is true for a futures contract. But how safe is a commercial bank that has entered into agreements to swap currencies or interest payments on debt obligations?

Some market analysts contend that we don't know—and that could be disastrous in the event of some major financial calamity. The Securities and Exchange Commission (SEC) has entered the picture by being empowered to examine the capital requirements of the affiliates of stockbrokerage firms that deal in exotic securities. Previously, its regulation did not extend to such affiliates. Although the SEC's beginning activities will be limited to factfinding, there is no doubt that any regulative action will influence not only securities firms, but also all financial institutions, including large commercial banks. Also, in the international banking area, an industry think tank group, called the Group of Thirty, has published a study that offers a number of suggestions for improvement. An important one is to use accounting procedures that clearly disclose the risk in derivative positions.

No one questions for a minute the important role derivatives now play in helping all types of investors and borrowers manage their wealth positions and future cash flows. But the public has a stake in all this in terms of preserving the safety of our commercial banks, insurance companies, and other financial institutions. The great crash of October 1987, which some observers think was aggravated by heavy derivative trading in index options and futures, should be a lesson for the future.

EXHIBIT 13.10

Explanation of a typical Treasury bond futures quotation (see Exhibit 13.1 for previously explained items)

As you read Exhibit 13.10, notice the settle price of $96,438. This amount is the present value you find by discounting (at an annual rate of 0.08370) the (a) $4,000 semiannual coupon interest for 40 periods and (b) the redemption value of $100,000 at the end of the 40th period.

Exhibit 13.11 shows a typical quotation for a Treasury bill futures contract. Its reporting features are somewhat different from those for bonds. The most confusing aspect is the reported price, which really isn't a price. It is an index number, and to determine price, you must apply the mathematical manipulation shown in the exhibit. The contract illustrated has a price (market value) of $985,475. Notice also that the day's change in yield is the same number as the change in settle price but with the opposite sign. This is always the case because the index number representing price is simply 100.00 minus the yield; that is, 94.19 = 100.00 − 5.81. People who trade bills frequently know that a one-basis-point change in yield leads to an opposite $25 change in contract value. So, the reported yield change of −0.05 means a minus five basis points, which in turn means an increase in contract value of $125 ($25 × 5).

Also, the Eurodollar contract is quoted the same as the Treasury bill contract. As noted earlier, its popularity is amazing. It reflects the popularity

EXHIBIT 13.11

Explanation of a typical Treasury bill futures quotation (see Exhibit 13.1 for previously explained items)

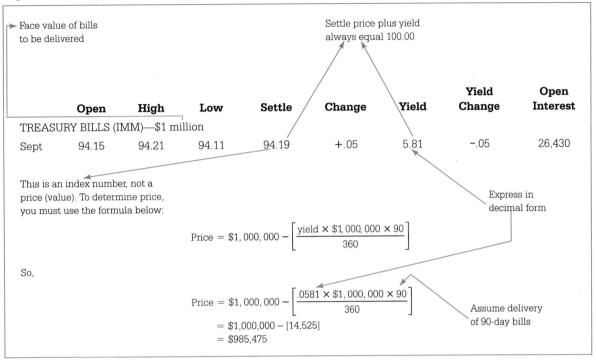

of Eurodollar deposits in general and the willingness of international money managers to hedge, or in other ways manage, these deposits.

Trading Interest-Rate Futures   In relation to contract value, margin requirements for Treasury futures are low, generally in the $2,000-to-$3,000 range. This low margin adds to their speculative appeal. Because we have covered speculative trading in detail already, we will not elaborate further here except to say that interest-rate futures have shown as much price volatility as many commodities. If interest rates in the future continue to vary as much as they have in the past, this volatility should continue. A danger unique to interest-rate futures has to do with believing that someone can forecast future interest rates. Put bluntly, no one can—or at least no one who makes his forecasts public information has demonstrated an ability to do so. Unfortunately, many people act as though they can forecast successfully. You might be skeptical if people tell you they know what corn's price will be next year, but you are more likely to believe a well-dressed banker with an impressive aura who announces authoritatively, "Interest rates will rise next year!"

Don't rush out and short a Treasury bond contract on the basis of such news. Many investors have, and many have lost substantially.

Interest-rate futures also are used extensively in hedging. Suppose you have accumulated $200,000 in 8%, 20-year Treasury bonds in your employer's retirement plan. You will retire in about one year and will receive a lump-sum distribution of the value of the bonds at that time. You are concerned that interest rates might skyrocket during the year, driving down the value of the bonds considerably. What to do? Simple: short two Treasury bond contracts for delivery in one year. If interest rates do rise, your losses in the pension plan should be offset by profits on the futures contracts. And if you guess wrong and interest rates fall, your losses on the futures contracts should be offset by price appreciation of your bonds. The costs of this hedge in terms of a commission and setting up an account with appropriate margin may be relatively high for only two contracts, but the alternative could be even costlier. Hedges such as this by pension plans themselves and by many other types of financial institutions are common. Indeed, the hedging applications of interest-rate futures are only recently being understood and used. One complicating factor involves matching changes in the value of the bond portfolio to changes in the futures contract. Dealing with the problem requires the use of hedge ratios.

Hedge Ratios   The problem confronting an interest-rate hedger arises when the instrument to be hedged does not have an exact counterpart in a futures contract. For example, suppose your retirement fund contains 8% Treasury securities with 6-year maturities instead of those with 20-year maturities. Unfortunately, a futures contract based on six-year Treasuries does not exist. However, you still could consider a hedge using the existing contract, if you realize that price fluctuations of the futures contract will be greater than those of your bonds. This is because a 20-year bond is more volatile than a 6-year bond, all other things held constant. (If you do not understand why, you need to review Chapter 9.)

To illustrate, suppose both 6-year bonds and 20-year bonds are selling at par ($1,000) when interest rates rise, and yields to maturity on each bond increase to 10%. The value of a 6-year bond will fall to $913, while a 20-year bond declines to $830. The ratio of the changes in value (20-year to 6-year) is 1.95 ($170/$87). Thus, to hedge your position, you must short 0.513 (1.0/1.95) of a futures contract for each $100,000 in the retirement fund. With $200,000 invested, you must short 1.026 contracts. Because you can't deal in fractional parts, you must settle for second best, which is to short one contract. The number of futures contracts needed to hedge perfectly an existing position in the cash market is called a **hedge ratio**—0.513, in our example. Hedge ratios usually are not important in commodity futures, but they play critically important roles in certain financial futures, primarily interest-rate and stock index futures.

Hedge ratio: number of futures contracts needed to hedge perfectly an existing position in the cash market

Our example is simplified for ease of presentation. In actual settings, hedge ratios may be more complicated to determine, for several reasons. First, the bonds to be hedged are likely to have coupon rates other than 8%. Second, hedge ratios must be calculated each time interest rates change and as maturities of the underlying instruments change. For example, one year later, your portfolio of bonds will have five-year maturities (not six), and a new hedge ratio will apply. (Keep in mind, the 20-year maturity of the assumed Treasury bond used in the futures contract never changes—it is assumed always to be 20 years.)

Index Futures

An **index futures contract** is based on values of a particular index. As in the case of index options, index futures cannot be settled by delivery. Cash settlement stands in place of delivery, but once again, the most popular form of settlement is position reversal. Exhibit 13.12 shows a typical quotation on the S&P 500 index. The value of the contract is 500 times the index number. So, the settle price of 448.15 means the September contract was worth $224,075 ($448.15 × 500.) As you can tell from the large open interest, the S&P 500 futures is popular.

Index futures contract: futures contract based on an index

Speculative Positions   Anyone who wants to speculate in the stock market might find that it is easier to do so with a stock index futures than by trading stocks directly. Suppose that you had $224,000 to invest in stocks and that you planned to buy stocks similar to those in the S&P 500. Rather than doing this, you deposit $224,000 in Treasury bills with your broker (far more than what is needed to meet a margin requirement, but we do not want to introduce leverage into the example) and then buy one S&P 500 futures that eventually expires. While it is held, your risk exposure is about the same either

EXHIBIT 13.12

Explanation of a typical index futures quotation (see Exhibit 13.1 for previously explained items)

	Open	High	Low	Settle	Change	Lifetime High	Lifetime Low	Open Interest
S&P 500 INDEX (CME) 500 times index								
Sept	446.90	448.20	445.45	448.15	+.80	458.60	391.00	171,903

Settlement is always in cash

Value of a contract = 500 × Index

Therefore,   Value = 500 × $448.15 = $224,075

BOX 13.3   GETTING AN INVESTMENT EDGE

Are Spreads a Low-Risk Way to Play the Market?

The introduction of stock index futures some years ago created a marriage made in the pits, critics say. When the Kansas City Commodity Exchange started trading futures contracts on the Value Line stock index, stock traders learned there was a whole new game to be played—not on the pompous stock exchanges, but amid the yelling, screaming, and unruly behavior of the commodities futures markets. And when other futures contracts on other indexes were created, they learned there wasn't only one new game, but several.

Enter the spread, which is a sort of cross between a naked position (where you can lose your shirt overnight) and a hedge (where you might reduce risk but can't make a profit). Spreads come in many varieties, but in the stock index game, a popular play is to go long in one index while shorting another. On the surface, this seems to be a hedge; you would think that both indexes will move in the same direction. So, how can you make any money on this deal? The trick is that you believe they

will move in the same direction *but not by the same amount.* What you hope to do is guess correctly the change in each.

For example, suppose at the end of January 1993 you thought the market was ready for a big increase. But you are a bit squeamish on your feeling and aren't willing to risk big bucks that you will be right. You reason, though, that if the market jumps, smaller stocks with high betas should increase more than stable stocks with low betas. What to do? Go long on the Value Line index, which consists of about 1,700 small and large stocks, and short on the less volatile S&P 500 index, which contains only the big blue chips. This is an example of a bull spread.

The spread on September contracts at January 22 was 38.60 index points (see the accompanying table). Suppose that seven months later, you reverse the positions. Now the spread is 24.55 and the gain is 14.05 (38.60 − 24.55) points; at 500 times the gain, your profit is $7,025. Even allowing for com-

way. The only relevant factors to consider then are (1) interest on the T bills that you earn with T bills but not with the stocks, (2) dividends earned on the stocks but not with T bills, and (3) commissions each way, which would be a onetime occurrence with the stocks (assuming you buy and hold) but occur periodically with the futures as you renew each expiring contract. In many cases, the futures approach is the better alternative. Unfortunately, it involves a fairly large investment, putting it out of reach for investors with limited funds.

Market timers have become avid users of stock index futures because it gives them far greater flexibility than the alternative of frequently trading in missions of $120 or so, the seven-month profit is great. What's greater is you would have needed only about $1,200 margin to do the spread, versus about $7,000 if you had shorted (or gone long on) one of the index contracts.

While this spread worked, you should realize that many do not. Indeed, during most of the latter half of the 1980s, small stocks underperformed large stocks. Continuous spreading during this period would have produced substantial losses.

Example of a Bull Spread (Spreader Expects Spread to Decrease)

	Price (in points)	
At January 22:		
Buy the Value Line Index	398.90	
Sell the S&P 500 Index	437.50	
Spread	38.60	
At August 20: reverse positions		
The Value Line Index	431.80	32.90 profit
The S&P 500 Index	456.35	18.85 loss
Spread	24.55	
Decrease in spread	14.05	14.05 profit

and out of stocks. They adjust their portfolios easily and at much lower cost by holding Treasury securities and taking long or short futures positions in line with their outlook on the market.

Hedge Positions   Hedge positions are also extremely popular with professional money managers. We noted earlier how a retirement fund invested in bonds can be hedged with interest-rate futures; similarly, one invested in stocks can be hedged with stock index futures. Just as hedge ratios were important before, so are they now. For example, your retirement portfolio might be invested in securities only half as risky as, say, the S&P 500. Instead of hedging on a one-to-one basis, you hedge one-half to one. For example, if the index was 450.00, the value of one contract would be $225,000. If you had $450,000 invested in the retirement fund, you would hedge it by shorting one contract. Assume the market declines 10%: your retirement fund should go down 5%, from $450,000 to $427,500. But your short position should increase 10% in value, assuming the S&P declines to 405.00. The profit here is $22,500 (500 × 45.00 points), which offsets exactly the loss in the retirement fund.

Arbitrage Positions   We discussed in Chapter 12 how options enter into arbitrage opportunities. Similar opportunities exist with index futures. This is because a futures index should have a theoretically correct value in relation to the securities that compose the index. Actual values, however, might be slightly different from the theoretical values. For example, suppose a futures contract on the S&P 500 that will expire in one month is quoted at 451.00 when the index itself has a value of 448.00. In other words, there is negative basis of 3.0 points. Suppose that all 500 stocks in the index, in their proper proportion, could be purchased and held for one month. Assume further that all transactions costs (costs of carry), including an allowance for interest on funds that could have been invested elsewhere, amount to 0.5% of the purchase amount. In relation to the index value of 448.00, transactions costs are 2.24 (448.00 × 0.005). Adding this figure to the index value of 448.00 gives 450.24, which is the theoretically correct value.

Because the futures contract is quoted at 451.00, an arbitrage opportunity is available: buy the stocks and short the index. You lock in a risk-free profit of 0.76 points (451.00 − 450.24), which amounts to $380 per contract (0.76 × 500). On the surface, this procedure seems simple, but in reality, it is difficult to carry out. The major impediment is buying the underlying stocks in an index. Modeling the S&P 500 perfectly would require a considerable amount of money, and trades would have to take place quickly to exploit favorable price differences. An arbitrager must execute trades in both the futures market and the stock market to realize the expected gain. If, in our example, the stock purchases lagged behind the futures sale, stock prices might increase, thereby eliminating the small profit margin. They also could decrease, improving the deal, but in either event, risk increases—a situation arbitragers try to avoid.

Such arbitraging has become popular primarily because large brokerage firms have simplified it by creating *market baskets,* which are smaller versions of stocks in an index. For example, 20 key stocks might show price variations almost identical to those of the S&P 500. If so, this basket can be used as a substitute for the 500 stocks. A further simplification was created with the *designated order turnaround system*, which allows arbitragers to place coordinated buy or sell orders (using computers) for a number of stocks on the floor of an exchange. This form of arbitraging is referred to as **program trading.** It is not completely risk-free because a market basket may not correlate perfectly with its intended index; however, risks are minimal.

Program trading: computerized system of trading stocks on an organized exchange

SUMMARY

A futures contract is an obligation to buy or sell a specific amount of a certain commodity or financial instrument at a set price at some future point in time. The contract must provide specific details about each of these items. Futures information is provided daily in many newspapers. Long and short positions are possible with a futures contract; long means acceptance of future delivery and short means making such delivery. Trading futures is similar to trading stocks or options in that an account is opened with a broker. Most futures traders make extensive use of margin, which is more technically known as a performance bond. There is little investor protection, and trading is conducted through organized exchanges, facilitated by clearinghouses.

Commodity futures are available for a wide variety of commodities, such as corn, soybeans, and pork bellies. Speculative trading is a highly risky activity premised on forecasting future commodity prices. Hedging often is undertaken to reduce risk. There are advantages and disadvantages to both speculative trading and hedging.

Financial futures are available for a wide variety of financial instruments, such as Treasury securities, foreign currencies, and stock indexes. These futures are quoted in the financial pages in a format similar to that of commodity futures and are used by speculators and hedgers in similar trading activities.

KEY TERMS (listed in order of appearance)

futures market
cash market
commodity futures contract
money at risk
clearinghouse
marking to market
perfect hedge
basis

cost of carry
inverted basis curve
currency futures contract
interest-rate futures contract
hedge ratio
index futures contract
program trading

REVIEW QUESTIONS

1. Define a futures market and then compare it with a cash market. If you used wheat in your baking business, in which market would you buy it?
2. List four important provisions of a futures contract.
3. What do the following terms in a futures quotation mean: (a) settle price and (b) open interest? How do you determine your money at risk in a futures contract?
4. Do you actually buy or sell a futures contract? Explain. And, is margin the same type of margin you use in trading stocks? Explain.
5. What role does a clearinghouse play in futures trading? What steps are taken by the clearinghouse to make sure traders can meet their obligations? Explain.

6. What makes speculative trading of commodity futures extremely risky? Does discussion in this chapter encourage speculation? Explain.

7. You operate a grain elevator that currently holds 100,000 bushels of corn. You could sell the corn today for $2.40 a bushel, but you plan to hold it for three months, when you think price will be higher. Discuss how you might hedge this position.

    Suppose a week after you executed a hedge, you want to reverse it, but your broker exclaims, "Your hedge wasn't perfect and basis has moved against you." What does this mean?

8. What is meant by cost of carry? Does it explain the difference between a cash price and a futures price? Discuss.

9. Explain how a yield curve can become inverted.

10. Discuss advantages and disadvantages of investing in commodity futures contracts.

11. Broadly, how do financial futures differ from commodity futures? Also, discuss the relative importance of each.

12. Discuss one hedging example involving each of the following: (a) a currency futures, (b) an interest-rate futures, and (c) an index futures.

13. What is a hedge ratio? Explain its use in hedging situations involving interest-rate futures.

14. The following settle prices were found for futures quotations:
    a. Treasury bonds—98–08
    b. Treasury bills—93.20
    c. S&P 500—250.22
    Determine a contract's market value for each of the above.

15. Why would market timers be interested in stock index futures?

16. Discuss arbitrage opportunities in stock index futures.

17. Explain program trading, including in your discussion an explanation of why stock baskets and the designated order turnaround system are necessary.

PROBLEMS AND PROJECTS

1. Olaf Hilger took a long position in three corn futures contracts at a contract price of $2.20 per bushel. The broker requires $10,000 to open a commodity-trading account, regardless of the number of trades.
    a. Including the initial margin requirement for a corn contract, how much money must Olaf deposit with his broker?
    b. Determine Olaf's profit (loss) if corn futures prices are $2.50 and $1.90. What would profit (loss) be if Olaf took a short position?

2. In mid-June 1993, Andy Metz notices the following settle quotations for an ounce of gold (100 ounces to the contract):

June	361.90
August	365.80
June 94	385.30

    He also saw on the evening news that gold closed on the day of the quotes at $361.19 an ounce.

   a. Determine the amount of basis for each contract. Is basis converging toward zero? Explain.

   b. Suppose Andy shorted the August contract. By the end of July, the price of gold jumped considerably, with the August contract closing at 410. Calculate Andy's gain or loss on his naked position.

   c. Suppose Andy could borrow $36,119 at an interest rate of 8%. He is contemplating the following strategy: Buy 100 ounces of gold now, simultaneously taking a short position in one August 94 gold futures contract. Total commissions would be $100. Evaluate this strategy.

3. Margo Fibber is convinced the dollar will weaken against other currencies over the next six months. The current exchange rate is 1.5000 dollars to the pound. The most recent settle price for a British pound futures contract maturing in six months is 1.4500 dollars to the pound.

   a. Do other investors share Margo's outlook on exchange rates? Explain.

   b. What strategy should Margo follow (given her conviction), assuming she will trade the pound contract? Also, determine her profit or loss if she reverses her position at an exchange rate of 1.5500.

   c. Suppose Margo owned a boutique on Downing Street in London. She anticipates having a cash flow of 185,000 pounds available at the end of six months. Assuming Margo wants to be sure to have the dollar equivalent ($277,500) available for wiring home at that time, what strategy should she pursue? Explain and illustrate.

4. The settle price on a Treasury bond futures contract is 101–16 and its quoted yield is 7.85%.

   a. What is the price in dollars?

   b. Reviewing material from Chapter 9, if necessary, explain how the yield is calculated.

   c. Suppose interest rates rose and the yield increased to 8%. Determine the change in settle price and the amount of change per basis-point change in yield.

5. The settle price on a Treasury bills futures contract is 92.22 and its quoted yield is 7.78%.

   a. What is the price in dollars?

   b. What is the relation between yield and settle price?

   c. Suppose interest rates fall and yield is quoted at 7%. By how much will the futures price (in dollars) rise?

6. Many interest-rate forecasters attempt to forecast changes in the yield curve, rather than changes in interest rates as such. Suppose you thought the yield curve, which is now upward-sloping, would flatten within the next month. Specifically, suppose you thought 90-day Treasury bills would go from 6% to 9%, while 20-year bonds would go from 8% to 9%. Given these assumptions, what spread would you take with futures contracts? Provide specific details in your answer. (Hint: short one contract while going long on another.)

7. *(Student Project)* Select a futures contract and follow its price variations for a 10-day period. To make the exercise more exciting, take a position in the contract at the beginning of the period. Calculate your gain or loss at the end of the period.

8. *(Student Project)* Some commodity traders act on certain unexpected events. For example, a frost might hit Florida, potentially damaging the citrus crop. Follow the news fairly closely for such events—look in particular for international

crises—and if you find one, develop a strategy to play the event with futures contracts. Record daily price quotations and evaluate performance after, say, a 10-day period.

CASE ANALYSES

13.1
Corey Darwin
Seeks Protection
for His
Inheritance

Corey Darwin will inherit within the next year about $600,000 in bonds that are part of his grandmother's estate. Corey intends to sell the bonds, using the proceeds to buy a condominium and a Porsche 928. He is scared that interest rates might rise sharply during the probate period, thereby lowering the bond prices. Afraid that this occurrence could cost him the Porsche, Corey is searching for ways to cope with potential losses in the bonds' values during the waiting period.

    The bonds consist mainly of Treasury securities with an average maturity of eight years, an average coupon rate of 8%, and an average yield to maturity of 8%. A friend of Corey's has suggested that he short sell bonds now as a hedge. If bond prices fall, profit from the short sales will offset losses on the bonds he will inherit. That seemed an ideal approach until Corey learned that he must provide margin for the short sale—both initially and perhaps later if bond prices rise instead of fall. Another friend then suggested that Corey use futures contracts as a hedge. Unfortunately, Corey knows little about this approach.

Questions

a. Does the use of futures contracts seem a viable alternative for Corey? Describe briefly the approach he will take.
b. Must Corey worry about margin and margin calls with this approach? Explain.
c. Reviewing material from Chapter 9, determine the possible loss in Corey's portfolio value if yield to maturity increased to 10%.
d. Determine the decrease in value of a Treasury bond futures contract if its yield to maturity increases from 8% to 10%.
e. Calculate the hedge ratio for Corey's situation, and give him specific instructions on how to use Treasury bond futures to solve his problem.

13.2
Sue Hagan
Considers an
Arbitrage

Sue Hagan follows the stock market fairly closely. Recently, she notices the settle price on the S&P 500 index futures is 460 for a delivery date one month in the future. The actual index value currently is 455. Sue doesn't understand why these two values are different, and she believes the difference represents an arbitrage opportunity.

    Sue believes that she can construct a basket of five stocks that will have price variations closely correlated to movements of the index. Dealing in 100-

share lots and with an average share price of $75, she estimates that $40,000 would be necessary to buy one basket. She believes commissions would be 0.5% on both purchases and sales of the stocks and $80 (round turn) on one futures contract. Sue also estimates the cost of funds at 0.6% a month, although she is not sure this cost is a relevant consideration.

Questions

a. Is Sue correct in her reasoning that the settle price on the futures contract should equal the index value? Would she be correct if there was one day remaining before the contract's maturity? Explain.
b. Can Sue arbitrage successfully? Explain with calculations.
c. What potential risk or problem do you envision in this arbitrage? Explain.

HELPFUL READING

Chicago Board of Trade. *Commodity Trading Manual*, Chicago, 1985.

George, Kathryn E. "New Face, New Force." *Barron's*, August 23, 1993, p. 14.

Getler, Warren. "Some Meteorologists Reap Windfall from Crop Futures Market." *The Wall Street Journal*, July 13, 1993, p. C1.

Lisclo, John. "Pinatubo and the Prairie." *Barron's*, August 23, 1993, p. 8.

Morris, Charles S. "Managing Interest-Rate Risk with Interest-Rate Futures." *Economic Review*, Federal Reserve Bank of Kansas City, March 1989, pp. 3–20.

Taylor, Jeffrey. "O'Connor's Clout: Trading by Numbers." *The Wall Street Journal*, October 12, 1991, p. C1.

_____. "Some Hope to Reap Profit If Grains Rally." *The Wall Street Journal*, September 17, 1993, p. C1.

PART FOUR

CFA EXAMINATION QUESTIONS

1. If a stock is selling for $25, the exercise price of a put option on that stock is $20, and the time to expiration of the option is 90 days, the minimum and maximum prices for the put today are:

    a. $0 and $ 5
    b. $0 and $20
    c. $5 and $20
    d. $5 and $25

---

2. In the Black–Scholes option valuation formula, an increase in a stock's volatility:

   a. increases the associated call option value.
   b. decreases the associated put option value.
   c. increases or decreases the option value, depending on the level of interest rates.
   d. does not change either the put or call option value because put–call parity holds.

3. Stock warrants attached to bonds are usually detachable after a certain date, at which time they begin to trade separately. As a rule, warrants tend to trade at a premium over their respective intrinsic values, with the size of such warrant premiums being largely determined by:

   I. the market's expectations regarding the future price behavior of the underlying common stock.
   II. the dividend yield on the stock (i.e., the lower the dividend yield, the higher the premium).
   III. the length of time the warrant has to go to expiration date.
   IV. the market the warrants are traded in (premiums tend to be larger in the over-the-counter market).

   a. I and II only
   b. I and III only
   c. II and IV only
   d. III and IV only

Use the following data in answering Questions 4, 5, and 6

	Convertible Bond X	Convertible Bond Y
Coupon	4 1/2%	6%
Maturity	18 years	24 years
Market price of convertible	$1,137.50	$885.00
Market price of common stock	$55.625	$32.50
Conversion ratio	18.75	25.00
Dividends per share of common stock	$1.25	$2.10
Yield-to-maturity on the convertible	3.47%	7.00%
Yields on comparably rated nonconvertible bonds	10.25%	10.25%
Dividend yield on the common stock	2.25%	6.46%

4. The common stock conversion price for Convertible Bond Y is:

   a. $27.23
   b. $35.40

    c. $40.00

    d. $81.25

5. The yield sacrifice on Convertible Bond X is:

    a. 1.63%

    b. 2.25%

    c. 5.75%

    d. 6.78%

6. Bond X's break-even time is:

    a. less than one-half of the break-even time of Bond Y.

    b. greater than one-half of the break-even time of Bond Y, but less than that of Bond Y.

    c. greater than Bond Y's break-even time, but less than 2 times as much.

    d. greater than 2 times Bond Y's break-even time.

7. An investor would consider converting a convertible bond into common stock if the bond's:

    a. break-even time exceeds five years.

    b. conversion value exceeds its market price.

    c. conversion premium exceeds its yield-to-maturity.

    d. yield-to-maturity equals that of comparable non-convertible bonds.

8. An at-the-money protective put position (comprised of owning the stock and the put):

    a. protects against loss at any stock price below the strike price of the put.

    b. has limited profit potential when the stock price rises.

    c. returns any increase in the stock's value, dollar for dollar, less the cost of the put.

    d. provides a pattern of returns similar to a stop–loss order at the current stock price.

9. A zero-investment portfolio arises when:

    a. an investor has only downside risk.

    b. the law of prices remains unviolated.

    c. the opportunity set is not tangent to the capital allocation line.

    d. a risk-free arbitrage opportunity exists.

PROBLEM (LEVEL III EXAMINATION)

You have decided to buy protective put options to protect the U.S. stock holdings of one of GAC's portfolios from a potential price decline over the next three months. You have researched the stock index options available in the U.S. and have assembled the following information:

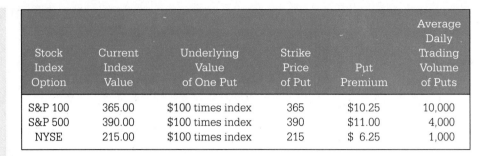

Stock Index Option	Current Index Value	Underlying Value of One Put	Strike Price of Put	Put Premium	Average Daily Trading Volume of Puts
S&P 100	365.00	$100 times index	365	$10.25	10,000
S&P 500	390.00	$100 times index	390	$11.00	4,000
NYSE	215.00	$100 times index	215	$ 6.25	1,000

(For each stock index option, the total cost of one put is the put premium times 100.)

	Beta vs. S&P 500	Correlation with Portfolio
Portfolio	1.05	1.00
S&P 100	0.95	0.86
S&P 500	1.00	0.95
NYSE	1.03	0.91

A. Using all relevant data from the above tables, **calculate** for *each* stock index option *both* the number and cost of puts required to protect a $7,761,700 diversified equity portfolio from loss. **Show** all calculations.

B. **Recommend** and **justify** which stock index option to use to hedge the portfolio, including reference to *two* relevant factors other than cost.

You know that it is very unlikely that the current stock index values will be exactly the same as the put strike prices at the time you make your investment decision.

C. **Explain** the importance of the relationship between the strike price of the puts and the current index values as it affects your investment decision.

D. **Explain** how an option pricing model may help you make an investment decision in this situation.

PART FIVE

Extending the Investment Portfolio

Although stocks, bonds, and derivative instruments are perhaps the core assets in many investors' portfolios, other assets are also important. Indeed, they may be far more important. In this part of the text, we review and analyze other popular investment vehicles.

Chapter 14 covers pooling arrangements. These investments often appeal to investors who cannot achieve adequate diversification on their own or who want to use the professional management pooling arrangements offer. The chapter provides a comprehensive treatment of pooling arrangements but focuses on the most important task—evaluating them for selection purposes.

Chapter 15 examines the advantages and disadvantages of tangible assets. The most important tangible investment for many investors—their personal residences—is thoroughly evaluated. We also examine other real estate investments and the important topic of how they can be financed. The chapter concludes with a discussion of gold and other tangible investments.

CHAPTER FOURTEEN

Investment Companies and Other Pooling Arrangements

After you finish this chapter, you will be able to:

- recognize the differences between closed-end and open-end investment companies (funds).

- understand a fund's net asset value and the investment implications of premiums or discounts on closed-end funds.

- identify the various expenses of investing in open-end mutual funds, including front-end and back-end loads.

- recognize the many different fund objectives and the various services funds provide.

- understand how to evaluate a fund on a risk-adjusted return basis.

- understand the advantages and disadvantages of a unit investment trust.

- understand the nature of a real estate investment trust and recognize its advantages and disadvantages.

- see how a limited partnership differs from other pooling arrangements and whether or not it is an appropriate investment.

- recognize the potential advantages of investment clubs.

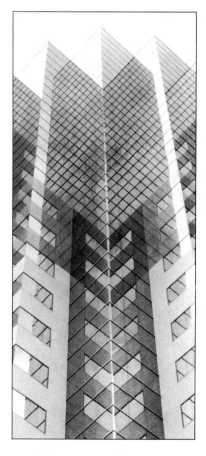

M any investors lack sufficient resources to establish adequately diversified portfolios on their own. Consequently, they turn to pooling arrangements, which not only offer diversification, but also provide professional money management. Moreover, by pooling your resources with those of other investors, you might be encouraged to invest in areas that you otherwise would avoid because of excessive risk or the need for specialized knowledge. How willing are you to go it alone in gas or oil drilling ventures, or in commercial real estate, or even in health and biotech stocks?

We examine pooling arrangements in this chapter, starting with investment companies, included in which is the overwhelmingly most popular pooling arrangement—the mutual fund. After investment companies, we turn our attention to public trusts, limited partnerships, and self-directed plans. Before we begin, you should recognize that putting your money in a pooling arrangement does not eliminate your need to be a wary investor; nor does it eliminate all your investment work. As we shall see, there are important legal and managerial differences among the types of arrangements, and more important, there are vast differences among their performances. Just as you can invest in a bad stock, you also can get into a bad pooling arrangement.

TYPES OF INVESTMENT COMPANIES

Organized investment company (fund): most popular pooling arrangement, often characterized by active portfolio management

An **organized investment company** (often called a **fund**) pools the resources of many individuals to buy securities issued by businesses, governmental units, and others. It is characterized primarily by active portfolio management and a wide range of services offered to its shareholders. The popularity of funds is exceptionally strong, as Exhibit 14.1 indicates.

EXHIBIT 14.1
Total assets of investment companies— selected years (in billions of dollars)

	Open-End Funds		Closed-End Funds
Year	Non–Money Market	Money Market	
1991	$803.0	$442.0	$60.0
1988	426.6	312.4	38.8
1987	453.8	298.6	15.8
1986	424.8	274.7	10.7
1982	76.8	180.5	7.2
1980	66.7	71.6	8.1
1976	47.5	3.6	6.6
1972	59.8	0.0	6.7
1962	22.4	0.0	2.8
1952	3.9	0.0	1.0

SOURCE: CDA/Wiesenberger Investment Company Services. *Investment Companies, 1992*, p. 27. CDA Investment Technologies, Inc., Rockville, MD 20850.

EXHIBIT 14.2
Numbers of funds—
selected years

Year	Open-End	Closed-End
1991	2,240	239
1989	2,150	160
1988	2,111	144
1987	1,782	93
1986	1,356	62
1985	1,071	39

SOURCE: CDA/Wiesenberger Investment Company Services. *Investment Companies, 1992*. CDA Investment Technologies, Inc., Rockville, MD 20850.

The public's interest in non–money market mutual funds, however, seems to rise and fall with the stock market. When the market is strong and bullish, investors turn to funds as a way to participate in the boom. The long bull market that began in 1982 brought with it an explosive increase in investor demand; the decline in non–money market assets in 1988 (after the market crash in late 1987) shows how this demand fades when prices fall. Notice also a similar decline in 1976 relative to 1972, which reflects the severe recession in 1974–75. However, the explosive growth since 1988 suggests that we may have entered a new era of pooled-resource investing. Certainly, there now are many more funds from which to choose, and their diversity of investment objectives is constantly expanding. If there is an investment theme to be played, you probably can find a fund playing it.

Funds can be classified into two broad categories: closed-end funds and open-end funds. A further classification of the open-end funds divides them into load and no-load funds. Exhibit 14.2 indicates how open-end funds dominate the industry.

Closed-End Funds

A **closed-end fund** was the first type of fund created. The key distinction between it and an open-end fund involves their capital structures: a closed-end fund has a relatively fixed capital structure, while an open-end fund's capital structure is changing constantly. This means the number of shares to a closed-end fund is practically constant, while the number to an open-end fund increases or decreases in response to shareholder demand. You buy and sell shares of closed-end funds as you do the shares of any company, and you find their quotations on the same financial pages of your newspaper. Stockbrokers offer the same trading assistance, and commissions are the same as for any trade. In short, trading shares of a closed-end fund such as Adams Express is no different from trading shares of IBM.

Closed-end fund: fund with a relatively fixed capital structure; shares trade in the open market

EXHIBIT 14.3
Illustration of NAV
per share

Shares Held and Market Value per Share	Total
100 IBM @ $150 per share	$15,000
200 Xerox @ $80 per share	16,000
400 GM @a $70 per share	28,000
Total	$59,000
Less fund liabilities	1,000
Total net asset value	$58,000
Shares outstanding to the fund = 1,000	
Net asset value per share (referred to as NAV)	$ 58.00

Determining Net Asset Value   The prices of closed-end fund shares, then, are market-determined; you might pay $20 a share for Adams Express. However, the market price should bear some relation to the market values of the securities Adams holds minus any liabilities it might owe. Indeed, this underlying value usually is the first piece of information an investor wants in evaluating a fund, whether open- or closed-end. It is called a fund's **net asset value (NAV),** and its determination is shown in Exhibit 14.3. In this simplified example, the fund owns common stock shares in three companies. Collectively, the shares are worth $59,000. After deducting the fund's liabilities of $1,000 and then dividing by the 1,000 shares the fund has issued, the NAV of $58 per share is determined. If this is a closed-end fund, you could say its intrinsic value is $58 a share. The market price may be higher than this figure—the shares are then trading at a premium—or lower, in which case the shares trade at a discount. There are investment implications of premiums and discounts that should be considered.

Net asset value: net market value, on a per-share basis, of the securities a fund holds

Discounts and Premiums   A closed-end fund selling at a **discount** seems a good investment opportunity. If you can buy shares in IBM, Xerox, and GM through a fund and pay less for them than if you purchased directly, why not take advantage of it? Indeed, many investors have done so because it is a good opportunity. As Exhibit 14.4 shows, discounts can vary considerably over time, and the reasons for the relatively small discounts from 1982 through 1986 and again in 1991–92 are not clear.

Discount: market price of a closed-end fund's shares is less than NAV

There also are some funds selling at a **premium,** which raises the question, are they worth it? To have a premium, a fund must offer investors something they cannot achieve easily on their own. For example, several closed-end funds, such as the Mexico Fund and the Japan Fund, specialize in foreign investment. You might find it inconvenient and difficult to invest directly in securities of these countries, so you will pay a premium for the advantage of investing indirectly. Other funds might command premiums because they offer leverage opportunities or tax savings of one type or

Premium: marker price of a closed-end fund's shares is greater than NAV

BOX 14.1   INVESTMENT INSIGHTS

Are Discounts on Closed-End Funds Worth Anything?

Closed-end funds selling at discounts are prized by many investors, including Burton Malkiel, a former Wall Street professional, highly respected finance academician, and author of the immensely popular paperback *A Random Walk Down Wall Street,* 5th ed. (New York: W. W. Norton and Company, 1990). With these funds, you can buy well-known stocks at less than their market prices. In this age of computer-assisted investment programs and mathematical trading models, how can something this simple give you an edge? There must be a catch.

Malkiel argues that there really is none. He believes that discounts usually reflect a lack of enthusiastic promotion of closed-end funds, in contrast to the hype that characterizes many open-end funds. The fact that the closed-end fund has a fixed number of shares gives the fund's manager little reason to spend money to promote it. Many investors don't even know such funds exist, much less that they can be bought cheaply.

If a discount is very large, be careful because something other than a lack of promotion is probably at work. For example, the capital shares of a dual fund sell at huge discounts. (Dual funds consist of income shares that receive all the dividends from the portfolio, plus capital shares that take all the capital

appreciation or losses.) The fact that the capital shares of such funds sell at discounts means nothing because the net asset value calculation assumes the fund would be liquidated tomorrow and proceeds used to redeem the income shares. Liquidation, however, will not take place for many years, so the discount shows nothing more than the time value of money. Other large discounts might show unfavorable tax situations, such as a fund having huge unrealized profits that, when taken, will increase shareholders' taxable incomes.

Although Malkiel plays down the importance of some explanations for the discounts, even he would probably advise that you get more information if one fund's discount dwarfs those of its counterparts. In the late 1980s, some of the foreign funds showed rather large discounts (50% for the Brazil Fund, for example). A partial explanation was, supposedly, fear of an adverse move in currency exchange rates. (The dollar was expected to strengthen against other currencies.) What you might see in this situation is not only an opportunity to buy foreign stocks at reduced prices, but also an opportunity to play your hunch on changes in exchange rates. But that's a different game—good luck if you play it.

another. It would be a mistake to pay a premium without determining why it exists. The underlying reason might make sense and work well in your portfolio design. On the other hand, it might not reflect any item of importance to you. If you are not sure, ask your broker or contact the fund and request a prospectus.

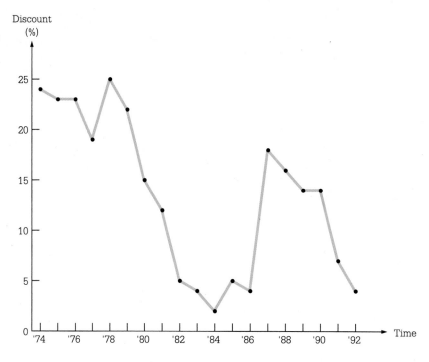

EXHIBIT 14.4
Year-end discounts from NAV: Eight diversified closed-end funds (Source: CDA/Wiesenberger Investment Company Services. *Investment Companies, 1992.* CDA Investment Technologies, Inc., Rockville, MD 20850.)

Open-End (Mutual) Funds

Open-end fund: fund that sells (and redeems) shares to (from) investors directly

An **open-end fund** is appropriately referred to as a mutual fund, although that term is also used to denote closed-end funds. In contrast to the closed-end fund with its fixed number of shares, an open-end fund sells new shares to anyone who wants to buy them. Moreover, it buys back shares from anyone who wants to sell them. All trades take place at the fund's NAV (plus or minus possible commissions), which has the same calculation as that of a closed-end fund. So, with an open-end fund, you usually deal directly with the fund, rather than through a broker (although brokers can be used to trade shares). This feature appeals to many investors who have become disenchanted with their brokers' advice and commissions, but it does mean you must find an open-end fund's address or telephone number to open an account. This inconvenience should be minor because many funds advertise in the popular press, and magazines such as *Forbes* and *Money* provide regular mutual fund evaluations that include such information.

Before an account can be opened, the fund must provide a prospectus that describes the fund and indicates its past performance. It is important to read this document thoroughly to understand the nature of the fund. Of course, its performance history is of interest, but determine also what charges the fund may impose on your account and the nature of its invest-

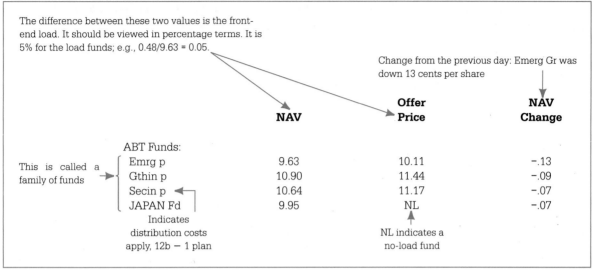

EXHIBIT 14.5
Explanation of an open-end fund quotation

ment objectives. Most local newspapers provide quotations on open-end funds, so you can monitor the fund's progress. Exhibit 14.5 shows how to interpret a typical quotation. You should consider first if the fund charges a purchase commission: if so, this typically is the largest single expense you will pay with the fund.

Front-End Loads As you see in the exhibit, the fund Japan Fd is listed as NL, which means no load. A load is a commission, and in this case, it means no commission is charged to buy shares of the fund. The other three funds have offer prices greater than their NAVs; the differences are purchase commissions. ABT Funds would be referred to as a family of funds. Purchase commissions, or **front-end loads,** are the most common form of investor charge, and about one-third of all open-end funds have a front-end load. Some charge less than 5.0%, while others charge as high as 9.3%. This is hardly a trivial figure, and you should logically wonder why anyone would pay it, given that alternative no-load funds are available. Surely, the load funds must perform better than the no-loads. This is *not* true, as studies on relative performance have shown. By all means, thoroughly review no-loads that meet your investment objectives before considering load funds. There is no reason to spend 9.3% of your investment funds each time you purchase.

The Wall Street Journal has broadened its reporting of mutual fund quotations. Along with offer price and NAV quotes, the *Journal* lists a fund's

Front-end loads: commissions paid when fund shares are bought investment objective and total return performances for various periods. A typical quote for the Japan Fund might show the following:

	Inv. Obj.	NAV	Offer Price	NAV Chg.	Total Return			
					YTD	26 wks	4 yr	R
Japan Fd	ITL	9.95	NL	+.09	+16.5	+21.3	+2.6	D

Japan Fund's objective (ITL) is international equity investment, as we might have guessed from the fund's name. NAV, Offer Price, and NAV Chg. provide the same information as shown in Exhibit 14.5. The total return data, though, are new and quite useful if we are interested in a fund's performance. As we see above, Japan Fund has done well in terms of year-to-date (YTD) and 26-week performances, although its 4-year performance is poor. Finally, the letter R refers to the fund's rank, which is a comparison to other funds with the same investment objective. The comparison period is the longest one indicated (four years in our example), and the D grade tells us that this fund was in the fourth quintile ranking (A = top 20%, B = second 20%, C = third 20%, D = fourth 20%, and F = fifth 20%).

Other Fund Charges   Rather than a front-end load, some funds have charges for redeeming shares, called **back-end loads.** These charges usually are in the 1% to 2% range. Along with loads, funds have begun imposing other kinds of charges. You should determine if the fund has a start-up cost when you open the account or if it has an annual maintenance fee. Another possibility is a deferred sales charge, which means you are charged a commission if you do not hold shares a sufficient length of time. Be particularly alert to any **12b–1 plan** that allows a fund's management to use up to 1.25% of the fund's net assets each year to pay promotion costs that can include commissions to selling agents. In effect, a 12b–1 plan passes on the usual front-end load as an operating cost of the fund. Either way, directly or indirectly, fund shareholders pay the load.

Back-end loads: commissions paid when fund shares are sold

12b-1 plan: charge against existing shareholders that management uses to attract new shareholders

FUND OBJECTIVES AND SERVICES

Investment company selection begins by identifying those funds with investment objectives similar to your own. Next, you consider the importance of various services they might offer.

Fund Objectives

As mentioned earlier, fund objectives are quite diverse. Generally, a fund invests in securities that help achieve its stated objectives, although some funds have not always done so. For example, the collapse of energy stocks several years ago prompted some managers of energy funds to invest elsewhere. At one time, one of these funds—New Era Fund—held as much as

40% of its portfolio outside the energy sector. Had you invested in New Era because you wanted to have part of your portfolio in the energy sector, your effort would have been partially defeated. When you read the fund's prospectus, review its current holdings to determine if they are reasonably supportive of its objectives.

It is important to realize that a fund may not achieve its objectives, just as you, as an individual investor, may not achieve yours. Many growth funds, for example, have selected securities that haven't grown much; on the other hand, some funds that strive for high current income might show remarkable price appreciation if interest rates fall. Also, you must allow a reasonably long period to judge whether or not the fund is fairly successful in achieving its stated goals. A 1-, 2-, or even 10-year evaluation period may be too short. The discussion below focuses on the most common fund objectives.

Growth Funds   A **growth fund** attempts to achieve long-term price appreciation in the shares it purchases. There are two main subgroups: some funds invest primarily in established growth companies, while other funds seek small companies with untested growth results. The latter group is considerably riskier than the former, but as Exhibit 14.6 shows, they don't always provide greater price appreciation. As a group, growth funds are one of the most popular forms of funds. Many investors prefer using growth funds to achieve growth goals in their portfolios, while investing on their own—primarily using deposits at financial institutions—for current income. Finding good growth companies does involve considerable research effort and skills, so shifting the effort to a fund often is a sensible alternative.

Growth fund: fund that seeks long-term price appreciation

Maximum Capital Appreciation Funds   **Maximum capital appreciation funds** seek quick capital gains and use various investment approaches to achieve them. Many search for merger or takeover candidates; others use call options, short sales, margin accounts, and other leverage techniques. For the period shown in Exhibit 14.6, these funds did not perform exceptionally well.

Maximum capital appreciation funds: funds that use various techniques to gain short-term profits

Income Funds   An **income fund** invests primarily in fixed-income securities—bonds and preferred stocks—in an attempt to provide a high current return to its shareholders. Price appreciation is not its target, although it might be achieved in an environment of falling interest rates. Although price depreciation is hardly one of its objectives, that, too, is possible if interest rates rise. In short, an income fund may have considerable interest-rate risk if the maturity of its portfolio is rather long. It might also present default risks if it invests exclusively in high-yielding, low-rated issues. These so-called junk funds became popular as interest rates fell in the early 1980s, appealing to investors who were willing to give up quality to preserve yield. You might note in Exhibit 14.6, however, that corporate high-yield funds actually yielded less than higher-quality corporate bond funds—10.2% versus 11.0%. Risk was *not* rewarded during the 10-year period noted.

Income fund: fund seeking high current return

EXHIBIT 14.6
Mutual funds:
Objectives and perfor-
mance (excludes
money market funds)

Number of Funds	Types of Funds	10-Year Annualized Return 4/1/83–3/31/93
	Equity	
254	Long-term growth	12.4%
68	Small company growth	10.8
101	Maximum capital appreciation	9.8
64	Equity income	12.8
201	Growth and income	13.2
	Specialized	
11	Health care	14.4
16	Energy and natural resources	10.6
16	Technology	9.5
27	Utilities	12.5
167	International/global	13.1
32	Gold and precious metals	−1.6
9	Financial services	16.9
	Income	
195	Corporate bond	11.0
76	Corporate high-yield	10.2
74	Government mortgage	10.6
186	Municipal bond	9.6
70	International bond	13.3
	S&P 500 stock index	15.5

SOURCE: CDA/Wiesenberger, *Mutual Funds Update,* CDA Investment Technologies, Inc., March 31, 1993, p. 3.

Balanced fund: fund
seeking a combination
of growth and current
return

Balanced Funds A **balanced fund,** also called an equity-income or growth-and-income fund (see Exhibit 14.6), is one seeking a combination of current income plus price appreciation. Its portfolio typically includes bonds, preferred stocks, and common stocks in varying proportions, reflecting its relative preferences for income or growth. These often are conservative funds with beta values less than 1.0. Some people question the need for a balanced fund because investors can achieve their own balancing by combining income and growth funds. This alternative approach is worth considering, if you are willing to do the extra work in reviewing two types of funds.

Money market fund:
fund that invests in
highly liquid debt
instruments

Money Market Funds A **money market fund** invests exclusively in short-term debt obligations of businesses and government units. The average maturity of most funds' portfolios is between 10 and 40 days, which means they are very liquid. Most money market funds hold a combination of corporate and government debt instruments, although some specialize. For example, you can find funds that invest exclusively in Treasury issues. Others invest only in federal tax–exempt securities. These money market municipals have lower pre-tax yields than their fully taxable counterparts but often have an after-tax yield advantage to investors in high tax brackets.

Sector Funds A **sector fund,** also called a specialized fund, invests exclusively in one industry. As of April 30, 1993, for example, the Fidelity family had no fewer than 36 sector funds investing in industries such as energy, health care, telecommunications, leisure, and precious metals. Sector funds appeal to investors who think that a particular industry might perform better than the overall economy but lack sufficient resources to diversify within that industry. The idea is appealing, but keep in mind, it rests on the presumption that you can identify the better-performing industries early enough in the investment cycle to be profitable. That may be hard to do. For example, everyone knows that as the economy moves out of recession, the housing industry typically does well. So, why not buy the housing sector? The trouble is that indeed, everyone does know, which means prices of stocks in the housing industry increase well before the industry actually enters recovery. If you want to speculate, you must buy the sector while the economy is in deep recession—a riskier proposition than buying later in the cycle.

> **Sector fund:** fund that invests in only one industry

    Also, keep in mind, a sector fund is riskier than a fund investing in a cross section of industries. A high percentage of your investment funds committed to one industry can be exceptionally dangerous. And if you diversify across sectors, you might question whether that policy is any better than simply investing in a conventional equity fund that could offer lower commissions and operating costs (in relation to assets). You should notice in Exhibit 14.6 that returns varied considerably among the sector funds—16.9% for the financial services sector to −1.6% for gold and precious metals.

International and Global Funds An **international equity fund** is one that invests exclusively in stocks issued by companies outside the United States; in contrast, a **global equity fund** invests in stocks issued by both foreign and U.S. companies. Also, an **international bond fund** invests primarily in fixed-income securities issued by foreign companies or countries. You should see in Exhibit 14.6 that such funds are popular with investors, and their returns were fairly good for the period noted, particularly the international bond funds.

> **International equity fund:** fund that invests exclusively in foreign stocks
>
> **Global equity fund:** fund that invests in both U.S. and foreign stocks
>
> **International bond fund:** fund that invests in fixed-income securities issued by foreign companies and countries

    In Chapter 17, we discuss the advantages of diversifying your portfolio to include international investments; but one of the reasons for doing so can clearly be seen here—potentially greater returns. Surprisingly, such diversification may also provide lower systematic portfolio risk. If we want to diversify internationally, using mutual funds may be the easiest way to do it, particularly if we seek broad diversification to include companies in emerging economies, such as those in China, Malaysia, and Peru. Although many American Depository Receipts (ADRs) (see Chapter 6) are available for large companies in developed countries, such as Honda, they are not available for companies in less-developed countries.

Index fund: fund that invests in securities represented in an index

Index Funds   An **index fund** is one that invests in securities represented in an index. The idea is to provide an investment portfolio that matches a popular index. The best-known such fund is Vanguard's Index Trust. It is a huge fund that is based on the S&P 500 index, and its performance correlates almost perfectly with it. On the surface, an index fund does not seem an appropriate fund in which to invest; surely you would expect a fund manager to do better than an unmanaged index. The popularity of this fund suggests that many investors think otherwise. We'll look at this topic later in this chapter. For now, notice in Exhibit 14.6 that of the equity and specialized fund categories, only one—financial services—outperformed the S&P 500. Many specific funds did better, but many more did worse and some did far worse. This should alert you to the need to evaluate a fund carefully before investing in it.

Dual fund: fund that creates two classes of securities

Dual Funds   A **dual fund** is a unique arrangement that has the appearance of a balanced fund seeking modest growth and reasonable current return. Its uniqueness arises from the fact that two classes of stock are issued to investors when the fund is formed, each representing half the total money raised. The first class—called *income shares*—receives all the dividend and interest from the portfolio and is redeemed at a set price at some future date. The second class—called *capital shares*—receives all the capital appreciation of the portfolio. In effect, each class has a leveraged position with respect to its return objective. For example, the income shares receive twice the dividends and interest as they would if they were to put up all the money to acquire the fund's portfolio. Likewise, the capital shares receive twice the capital appreciation.

Dual funds are closed-end, and there were only four such funds as of July 1993. Some observers thought that they would become more popular, but that has not happened.

Mutual Fund Services

Mutual funds have recently begun offering a wide assortment of services to their shareholders. Fidelity, for example, operates customer service centers that look like combined commercial bank and stockbrokerage offices. The larger fund families seem to be growing even larger, while the smaller individual funds are finding it more difficult to compete. The trend toward the financial supermarket appears prevalent in the mutual fund industry because investors prefer to have most of their investment needs satisfied in one institution. The services discussed below are those most investors find useful.

Telephone Transactions   Although the Fidelity service center appeals to some investors, many more prefer transacting by phone. After you establish an account, all additional purchases or sales can be made in this manner. You must be sent a prospectus for each fund in which you invest, and you need to file a separate application for each, but this takes little time. You also can have funds wired to your bank to avoid a mail lag involved with a check.

Reinvestment of Dividends and Capital Gains You have a number of reinvestment options with a fund. You can choose to have all dividends and capital gains mailed to you, you can take dividends in cash and reinvest capital gains by buying additional shares to the fund, or you can reinvest both in additional shares. Many funds, particularly income funds, allow you to withdraw a given amount each month as an annuity. If the fund's earnings exceed the annuity, the excess is automatically reinvested in the fund; in the reverse situation, shares are automatically sold to make up the annuity amount.

Also, some funds charge loads on reinvestments. This policy seldom is highlighted in the fund's prospectus but is in effect whenever reinvestment takes place at an offer price, rather than NAV.

Fund Switching A fund-switching privilege allows you to sell shares in one fund and reinvest the proceeds in another if each fund is a member of the same family. This service seems to be exceptionally well received by investors, particularly because a number of switches can be made each year without incurring separate charges. However, loads may apply to load funds, and there also may be an annual limit on the number of free switches, so it is important to read the fund's literature to understand the situation. Switching particularly appeals to investors who try to do market timing. You can invest in a growth or other equity fund when you think that the market will be bullish and then switch to a money market fund when your outlook turns bearish. We mentioned earlier playing sector funds to time the business cycle, which is made easier by fund switching. The growing number of investors who use switching services indicates that many people at least think they can time the market successfully; however, as we noted in Chapter 8 and elsewhere, there is little evidence to suggest they can. Although convenient, fund switching also makes it easy to show investment losses if you can't time the market properly.

Adaptability to Retirement Plans Most mutual funds are readily adaptable to individual retirement plans, such as IRAs and Keoghs. Making your investment an IRA, for example, requires nothing more than completing a simple form that allows the fund to serve as a trustee. The set-up cost and annual maintenance fees are competitive with those charged by commercial banks and other financial institutions. Apparently, mutual funds are doing very well competing for IRA deposits; their share of the market has increased rapidly. Finally, a number of investors use fund switching among their IRA accounts because gains escape current taxation. (Unfortunately, losses do not offset other taxable income.)

EVALUATING FUND PERFORMANCE

After you have identified a number of funds that meet your investment objectives, how do you decide which funds are the best? Most investors attempt to find a partial answer to this question by examining the fund's historical performance. You can do this yourself using data from the fund's prospectus and annual financial report or from a library source such as CDA Investment Technologies, Inc.'s *Investment Companies*, or you might rely on evaluations provided in publications such as *Forbes, Money*, and *Business Week*. Even if you take the easy approach, you should understand how evaluations are made. The procedures are explained in the following sections.

Understanding Returns

Most funds make periodic cash distributions designated as dividends from investment income or as distributions from realized gain on investments. Exhibit 14.7 shows a 10-year performance summary for Fidelity Fund, a large growth fund that invests primarily in blue chip issues. This reporting format is standard and used by practically all funds. Notice that lines 4 and 6 show the dividend and capital gain distributions. In 1992, for example, shareholders received $0.48 in dividend distributions and $0.58 in capital gain distributions. Notice also the NAV values at the beginning (line 8) and end (line 9) of each year.

Holding Period Return for a Single Year   As a shareholder, you should be interested in determining a holding period return (HPR). Using the information in Exhibit 14.7, we can calculate the HPR for 1992 as follows:

$$\text{HPR} = \frac{\text{Distributions} + \text{Change in NAV}}{\text{Beginning of Year NAV}}$$

$$= \frac{(\$0.48 + \$0.58) + (\$18.94 - \$18.46)}{\$18.46}$$

$$= \frac{\$1.06 + \$0.48}{\$18.46} = \frac{\$1.54}{\$18.46} = 0.0834, \text{or } 8.34\%$$

Your rate of return in 1992, then, was 8.34%. The calculation above assumes you withdraw the distributions and do not reinvest them in the fund; also, it assumes they are made at the end of the year.

Most fund annual reports show rates of return based on a reinvestment assumption. To calculate this rate, you must know when distributions took place during the year and the NAV at the times distributions were made. Let us assume that Fidelity made its dividend and capital gain distributions

EXHIBIT 14.7

Past performance of Fidelity Fund

	Years Ended December 31									
	1992	1991	1990	1989	1988	1987	1986	1985	1984	1983
1. Investment income	$ .58	$ .66	$ .82	$ .78	$ .65	$ .56	$ .74	$ .81	$ .84	$ .98
2. Expenses	.13	.13	.12	.11	.10	.11	.11	.11	.10	.14
3. Net investment income	.45	.53	.70	.67	.55	.45	.63	.70	.74	.84
4. Distributions from net investment income	(.48)	(.50)	(.74)	(.68)	(.56)	(.48)	(.66)	(.72)	(.71)	(.84)
5. Net realized and unrealized gain (loss) on investments	1.09	3.29	(1.60)	3.69	1.85	.28	2.08	3.33	(.70)	2.96
6. Distributions from net realized gain on investments	(.58)	(1.15)	—	(1.17)	—	(2.72)	(4.08)	(.05)	(4.40)	(1.97)
7. Increase (decrease) in net asset value	.48	2.17	(1.64)	2.51	1.84	(2.47)	(2.03)	3.26	(5.07)	.99
Net asset value:										
8. Beginning of period	18.46	16.29	17.93	15.42	13.58	16.05	18.08	14.82	19.89	18.90
9. End of period	$18.94	$18.46	$16.29	$17.93	$15.42	$13.58	$16.05	$18.08	$14.82	$19.89
10. Ratio of net investment income to average net assets	2.37%	2.84%	4.04%	3.76%	3.69%	2.75%	3.48%	4.25%	5.06%	4.34%
11. Ratio of expenses to average net assets	.67%	.68%	.66%	.64%	.67%	.67%	.60%	.66%	.66%	.71%
12. Portfolio turnover rate	151%	267%	259%	191%	175%	211%	214%	215%	200%	210%
13. Shares outstanding at end of period (in millions)	71,513	71,500	65,319	60,603	57,821	64,053	48,640	42,116	41,671	33,629

SOURCE: Fidelity Fund's 1992 *Annual Report.*

(totaling $1.06) at June 30, 1992; then, the HPR would be calculated as follows:

Date	Activity	Number of Shares Held/Acquired	NAV	Total
1/1/92	Beginning balance	1.000	$18.46	$18.46
6/30/92	Distributions	0.057	18.60	1.06
12/31/92	Ending balance	1.057	18.94	20.02

$$\text{HPR} = (\$20.02 - \$18.46)/\$18.46 = \$1.56/\$18.46 = 0.0845 \ (8.45\%)$$

As you see, this HPR is slightly higher than the 8.34% previously calculated. Although the difference is slight in this case, in other instances it could be much larger. Also, you should know that Fidelity Fund actually made distributions quarterly, rather than only once, at June 30. We made the assumption to simplify the calculations.

HPRs over Time   The year 1992 was selected arbitrarily to illustrate HPR calculation methods for a single year, but you would be interested in HPRs for all years. These can be obtained from various *Annual Reports* of Fidelity Fund or calculated from the data in Exhibit 14.7. Exhibit 14.8 shows Fidelity's HPRs and similar figures for the S&P 500, for each year from 1983 through 1992. The 10-year average returns are geometric, not arithmetic, averages. As you can see, Fidelity Fund did not perform as well as the S&P 500 over the 10-year period—13.8% versus 16.1%.

EXHIBIT 14.8
Historical average returns: Fidelity Fund and the S&P 500

Years Ended 12/31	Fidelity Fund's HPRs	S&P HPRs
1983	22.4%	22.5%
1984	1.5	6.2
1985	27.7	31.6
1986	15.8	18.6
1987	3.3	5.3
1988	17.8	16.6
1989	28.3	31.5
1990	−5.0	−3.2
1991	23.5	30.6
1992	8.5	7.7
Average	13.8	16.1

SOURCE: Fidelity Fund, various *Annual Reports*.

Measuring Risk

A fund's risk can be measured with the techniques explained in Chapter 4. The beta measurement seems particularly appropriate because many funds' returns show a high degree of statistical correlation to the overall market's return. This gives analysts greater confidence in using the statistic to make investment decisions. Along with the beta measurement, we derive a fund's alpha value, which shows if it outperformed the market *on a risk-adjusted basis.*

Determining Alpha and Beta Using the data provided in Exhibit 14.8, the graph in Exhibit 14.9 is prepared. It shows a regression of Fidelity Fund's

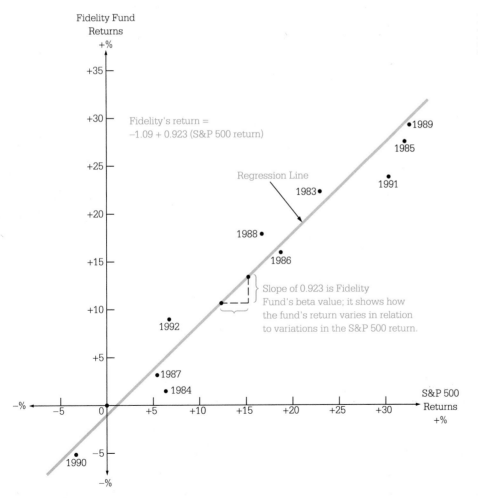

EXHIBIT 14.9
Determining Fidelity Fund's beta value

returns on the S&P 500 returns. The return for each in a given year is one data point on the graph. The regression line is a line of best fit through the 10 data points. You could fit this line freehand, but a more accurate fit is provided by a calculator or computer.

The slope of the regression line is the fund's beta value. As the figure shows, Fidelity's beta was 0.923, which means it was somewhat less risky than the overall market with its beta of 1.0. So, although Fidelity had a lower return than the market over the 10-year period, we are not sure whether this lower return reflects poor fund management or less fund risk. To analyze this issue further, we can determine Fidelity's **alpha value.** Exhibit 14.10 is helpful in this effort.

Over the 10-year period, the average return on short-term Treasury bills was about 7.0%. With this figure and the 16.1% rate of return on the S&P 500, the securities market line (SML) is drawn. You should remember the SML discussion from Chapter 6, but note the line in Exhibit 14.10 has a different shape because use of the SML in the current situation is somewhat different. In Chapter 6, the SML was constructed on the basis of *expectation*; that is, although historical data were used, the thrust of the analysis was to determine expected future returns for all portfolios consisting of different combinations of a risk-free asset and a market asset. These returns then served as

Alpha value: performance measurement representing the difference between a fund's actual and SML-derived returns

EXHIBIT 14.10
Illustration of Fidelity Fund's alpha value

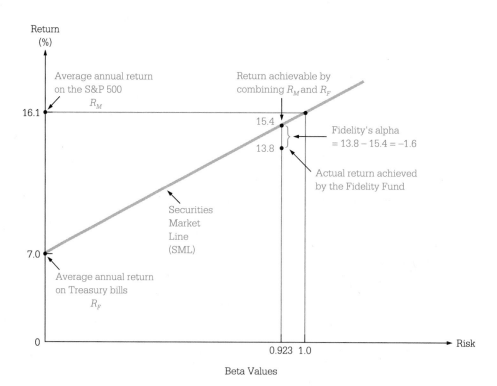

minimum required returns to evaluate specific assets with given beta values. In the current application, the SML is used to evaluate what has *actually happened* over some period of time. It is called an *ex-post* (after-the-fact) SML, while the expectative SML is called *ex-ante* (before the fact).

Although the perspectives are quite different, the mechanical use of the SML is identical. Now, we want to know what return (R_i') could have been achieved by investing in only the two assets—the S&P 500 (R_M) and Treasury bills (R_F)—in a proportion that would have led to a portfolio beta of 0.923. The answer is determined below:

$$R_i' = R_F + \beta_i (R_M - R_F)$$
$$R_i' = 7\% + 0.923 (16.1\% - 7\%)$$
$$R_i' = 7\% + 0.923 (9.1\%)$$
$$R_i' = 7\% + 8.4\%$$
$$R_i' = 15.4\%$$

Because this return is higher than Fidelity's actual return of 13.8%, we conclude its management underperformed the market on a risk-adjusted basis. You would have been better off investing on your own in a market index and Treasury bills. The difference between Fidelity's actual return of 13.8% and the return on the SML of 15.4% is called Fidelity's alpha value: -1.6%. In general, then:

$$\alpha_i = R_i - R_i'$$

Positive α_i means good management, while negative α_i means the opposite; the greater the number, the better (the worse) the performance. There is an expression among professional money managers: "To keep your alphas up and your betas down." You should understand the wisdom of this adage.

Choosing a Fund   As a general rule, you should select funds that show positive alpha values and avoid those with negative alpha values. That is a simple rule to follow, but how do you choose among funds that all have positive alphas, assuming each meets your investment objective? There are a number of responses to this question. One method ranks funds on the basis of alpha and chooses those funds with the higher values. If another fund had an alpha of, say, 2%, it would be a better choice than Fidelity.

Another widely used approach compares a fund's excess return with its beta weight. In this case, excess return is defined as actual return minus the risk-free return. The comparison is called the **Treynor Index (TI),** and it is calculated for Fidelity Fund below.

$$TI = \frac{R_i - R_F}{\beta_i} = \frac{13.8\% - 7.0\%}{0.923} = \frac{6.8\%}{0.923} = 7.37\%$$

Treynor Index: performance measurement that adjusts a fund's return in excess of the risk-free rate by its beta

Fidelity's 7.37% value could be compared with TI values of other funds and a selection made on the basis of the highest value.

Finally, an approach that is used more quickly than the two above compares the fund's beta-adjusted return with the market return. This **risk-adjusted rate of return (RAROR)** is shown below.

Risk-adjusted rate of return: performance measurement that compares a fund's risk-adjusted return with the market return

$$RAROR = \frac{R_i}{\beta_i} - R_M$$

$$= \frac{13.8\%}{0.923} - 16.1\% = 15.0\% - 16.1\% = -1.1\%$$

Funds are then ranked by RAROR values, and those with higher values are favored. The advantage of this approach is that it eliminates the need to use the risk-free rate. From a theoretical perspective, it is less rigorous than either the alpha ranking or the TI.

How Good Are Fund Managers?

If you read fund advertisements in the popular press, you probably conclude that fund managers are geniuses at selecting securities. The advertisements are almost always return-oriented and almost never mention risk in any useful way. Moreover, they are fond of illustrating by how much they beat the S&P 500, but they never tell you what risks they took to do so.

Because performance information is readily available, the subject of evaluating performance has been well researched by finance academicians. Results of earlier studies were fairly uniform and indicated that few funds outperformed the S&P 500 index on a risk-adjusted basis, as we have just explained it (see Exhibit 14.11). And those that did better in one year were not likely to repeat this accomplishment in a following year. In short, they might have been lucky, as you would expect any small set out of a large group of investors to be in any given year. Some newer studies have indicated partially conflicting results. They indicate that some funds have consistently done better than the market. These funds apparently achieve their success by selecting and holding securities that perform well, rather than through clever market-timing techniques. An implication of these studies is that investors should avoid funds with high turnover ratios and rapidly changing beta weights.

Popular Sources of Fund Evaluations

Evaluating mutual funds is a regular feature of some financial magazines. *Forbes* has an annual survey of mutual funds, which includes an evaluation of performance. It attempts to rank funds on the basis of how well they do in both bull and bear markets. Its rankings are given as letter grades, such as A,

BOX 14.2   GETTING AN INVESTMENT EDGE

Focus on Loads and Annual Expenses

Y ou have $1,000 to invest and are considering mutual funds. Two have come to your attention: Fund A has an 8.5% load and typically incurs operating expenses at 2% of net assets; Fund B is a no-load fund with an expense ratio of 0.25%. If each fund manager earns, say, 12% each year before expenses, how much better off are you with Fund B? Answers are below.

B's advantage is anything but trivial, but you probably think this example is stretched to make a point. It is somewhat, but not completely. There are funds with loads as high as 8.5%, and you certainly can find two funds with that much difference in expense ratios.

Saving money, then, is simple: First, ignore all load funds; second, select only those no-load funds with low operating expense ratios. But as with all simple plans, there are a few hitches. First, by eliminating all load funds you cut out a few super performers, such as Fidelity's Magellan Fund— the best performer of all funds over the past 15 years. By relaxing the rule to exclude only high-load funds (loads over 5%), you keep most of the better performers, including Magellan.

Second, many load funds are sold by stockbrokers who also provide investment and portfolio management advice. Notice in the table that the load has far less importance with long holding periods. Paying $820 over 20 years may not be an excessive amount if the broker provides useful advice.

The table clearly shows that operating costs are the real villain in the long run. Indeed, some studies have shown that selecting funds with low cost ratios is the most consistent method of selecting funds that are likely to perform well in the future. One mutual fund family, Vanguard, emphasizes low costs, and its funds typically have the lowest ratios in the industry. Not surprisingly, its funds—particularly its index funds—are consistently among the better performers.

Years After Investment	Accumulations		B's Advantage	Advantage Due to	
	Fund A	Fund B		No Load	Low Costs
1	$1,007	$1,120	$ 113	$ 95	$ 18
10	2,373	3,106	733	265	468
20	6,156	9,646	3,490	820	2,670

EXHIBIT 14.11
Mutual fund per-
formance (Source:
Michael C. Jensen,
"The Performance of
Mutual Funds in the
Period 1945–64."
Journal of Finance,
May 1968, pp.
389–416.)

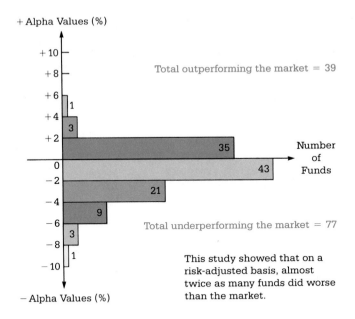

+ Alpha Values (%)

Total outperforming the market = 39

Total underperforming the market = 77

Number of Funds

This study showed that on a risk-adjusted basis, almost twice as many funds did worse than the market.

− Alpha Values (%)

B. This is an attempt to bring risk into the picture, but it falls somewhat short of the ideal because the connection between return and risk is not expressed quantitatively or rigorously. *Money* magazine follows a similar approach in its evaluations and receives the same criticism. If you select your funds by using either of these sources, you should at least review several years (or more) of evaluations to see if their current high-rated funds have performed well in the past.

    Business Week also has an annual fund evaluation appearing in one of the February issues. Its review appears to use the beta approach explained above to rank funds on a return-risk basis. By following its rankings, or those of *Forbes* or *Money*, you can select funds that have performed well and avoid those that have not. However, you still might want to consider other fund characteristics, particularly loads. As noted previously, there is no evidence supporting superior performance by load funds, and it is difficult to justify investing in a fund with a heavy initial load.

    Finally, an exceptionally high-quality source of mutual fund coverage and evaluation is Morningstar's *Mutual Fund Sourcebook*. This comprehensive journal provides evaluation data based on the techniques we have just covered along with its own proprietary method. A sheet for Fidelity Fund from the *Sourcebook* is shown in Exhibit 14.12. Investors could hardly ask for a more comprehensive treatment; notice that the Fidelity Fund received a four-star (above average) ranking for its 10-year performance.

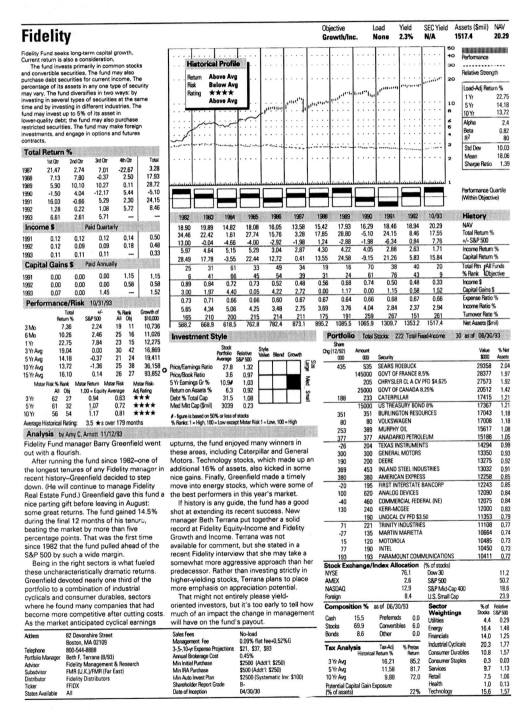

EXHIBIT 14.12

A page from Morningstar's *Mutual Fund Sourcebook*. (Source: "1993 *Morningstar Mutual Funds*, Volume 21, Issue 3, Morningstar, Inc., 225 W. Wacker Dr., IL 60606. (312) 696-6000. Reprinted by permission.)

INVESTMENT TRUSTS

Although the organized investment company is the most common form of pooling arrangement, there are other important forms. Investment trusts are used in various settings to invest in assets ranging from Treasury bills to precious gems.

Trust: legal document that allows one party to manage assets for the benefit of other parties

A **trust** is a legal document that allows one person or institution to hold title to assets and to manage them for the benefit of others. Trusts are common in estate planning, where they often are used in conjunction with wills to help in the process of transferring wealth, both during a person's lifetime and at his death. These "private trusts" differ somewhat from "public trusts" that are used in investing. The private trust has a *grantor*, who transfers assets to a *trustee*, who in turn manages them for the benefit of *beneficiaries*. In an investment trust, the grantor is replaced with a trust originator, who purchases assets and then transfers them to a trustee. The originator in turn sells units to the trust to investors, who stand in place of beneficiaries. The trustee's role is the same in each case.

With a unit investment trust, the ownership instruments are called *units*, but in a real estate investment trust, they are called *shares*. The two types of trusts differ in important ways in addition to terminology, as we shall see.

Unit Investment Trusts

Unit investment trust: public trust created to invest in certain types of assets, usually fixed-income securities

A **unit investment trust (UIT)** usually is formed to invest in intangible assets, the most popular being debt instruments of one type or another. However, some trusts do invest in tangible assets. Units often are priced at $1,000 each, and most trusts require a minimum purchase of two to five units. Most UITs have finite lives that are pegged to the maturities of the assets they own, while others are terminated as of a certain date (with assets being sold and proceeds distributed to unit holders). In most cases, the originator of the trust makes a market in trust units, which means you, as an investor, can sell your units at any time, as you can with an open-end mutual fund. This feature enhances the investment's marketability considerably, but you should understand that units are repurchased at the current market values of trust assets. If these assets are subject to price variability, you run the risk of poor liquidity even though the units are readily marketable. The more common investment trusts are explained below.

Municipal bond trust: UIT that invests in municipal bonds

Municipal Bond Trusts   The **municipal (muni) bond trust** is probably the most popular of all UITs. A muni trust usually is formed by a brokerage house or other originator specializing in them, such as John Nuveen and Company—one of the largest. Exhibit 14.13 shows the formation process. Muni trusts appeal to investors in the highest federal income tax brackets. Some of these trusts have been formed to offer both state and local tax

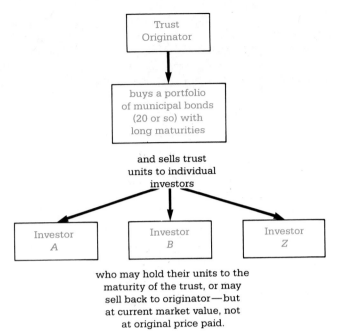

EXHIBIT 14.13
Formation of a municipal bond trust

exemption as well, but these often have lower yields than nationally invested trusts and may not offer a significant after-tax advantage. Moreover, because their portfolios are limited to narrow geographical and taxing regions, they typically involve higher risk because of the shortage of suitable securities available for an adequately diversified portfolio.

As an investor, you face the choice between muni trusts and muni mutual funds, and you also must decide whether either one is more desirable than buying muni bonds on your own. A minimum investment in a trust or fund typically is $1,000 to $5,000, while at least $15,000 is needed to achieve adequate diversification when investing on your own. Exhibit 14.14 compares other aspects of the three investment approaches. Trusts typically have front-end loads of about 4.5% and charge annual operating fees of about 0.2%. These fees are about one-fourth those of the mutual funds. In addition, a trust has a 2.0% spread to sell. Considering these costs together suggests that the longer the holding period, the better alternative a trust will be. With an annual savings of 0.6% (0.8% − 0.2%), it takes almost 11 years (6.5/.06) for the total costs to be the same with each.

The default risk with a trust usually is low. Some originators have taken greater risks recently, however, so it is important to review a trust's prospectus to examine the quality of the portfolio it will hold. If more than, say, 20% of the issues are rated below BBB (Standard and Poor's minimum investment grade) or Baa (Moody's), there is potential for default losses, and you must

EXHIBIT 14.14

Investing in municipal bonds: Three approaches

Item to Consider	On Your Own	Unit Trust	No-Load Mutual Fund
Selecting and holding bonds	Your job: make sure of adequate diversification	Originator picks and holds 15 to 40 issues	Portfolio manager holds and actively manages over 40 issues
Managing the portfolio	Your job: avoid excessive trading	Virtually no management	Considerable: avoid funds with excessive turnovers
Payments	Semiannual payments	Monthly checks, if desired	Monthly checks or reinvestment
Commissions and fees	Commission usually is a 2.0% spread between buying and selling	2% buy-sell spread, plus 4.5% front-end load, plus 0.2% operating costs	No load and no spread, but 0.8% operating costs
Insurance	Yes, a must for a small portfolio	Available, but will reduce yield	Unnecessary because of large portfolio
Investor appeal	Experienced investor with no less than $10,000 to invest in munis	Casual investor willing to hold 10 years or longer	Investor with shorter horizon or one who wants other mutual fund services

decide whether you will be comfortable with this situation. About one-half the trusts being formed in recent years offer default insurance. While reducing risk, insurance also reduces yield by as much as 40 basis points. A muni fund usually has sufficient diversification to eliminate the problem of default risk; however, it may offer higher interest-rate risk if its portfolio includes bonds with longer maturities. A fund's portfolio is constantly changing, so gauging its interest-rate risk is more difficult than it is with a trust with its fixed portfolio. (Actually, a trust's portfolio is not always fixed: it may sell bonds if the trustee judges a deterioration in their quality; however, it is legally prevented from buying additional bonds. Also, if bonds default or are called, the trust's income can change.)

GNMA trusts: UITs that invest in agency passthrough bonds

GNMA Trusts Most large stockbrokerage houses have formed **GNMA trusts** that invest in Ginnie Mae and other agency passthrough securities. These UITs have also been popular because investing directly involves difficulties, primarily the $25,000 face value of a single security. Most trusts pass both interest and principal payments to trust holders each month, thus providing a steady cash flow.

Mutual funds also invest in mortgage-backed securities, so the logical question is whether you are better off with a mutual fund or a UIT. As in the case of a muni trust, it's difficult to generalize, so you must read the prospectus of any fund or trust you are considering. The funds may not have a front-end load, while the trusts usually charge about 4% or 5%. On the other hand, a fund's yearly management fees typically are higher. The funds offer better services involving reinvestment of interest or principal, withdrawals, and fund switching, which might be important if you are investing in other funds within a family.

Other UITs   UITs have been used to achieve a wide variety of investment objectives. Over the years, their holdings have ranged from highly liquid assets—precursors of today's money market mutual funds—to diamonds and other precious gems. Two recent innovations are quite interesting: one offers the opportunity to buy the S&P 500 index and the other puts your money in Brady bonds. In 1993, the American Stock Exchange launched a UIT called *Standard and Poor's Depository Receipts* (**SPDRs,** or **"spiders"**). Each unit in effect represents a 1/10th interest in the S&P 500 stock index. So, if you buy units, your investment should follow the S&P 500 index almost perfectly, including the receipt of quarterly dividends. The trust has a 25-year life and units trade on the American Stock Exchange. Spiders have become popular, with daily trading volume often in excess of 4 million shares.

SPDRs ("spiders"): unique UIT that creates a trust share with 1/10th interest in the S&P 500 index

A potentially very risky UIT was originated by Van Kampen Merritt in mid-1993, which invested in price-volatile Brady bonds. You should recall from Chapter 10 that Brady bonds are issued by developing countries throughout the world under guidelines developed by former Treasury secretary Nicholas Brady. The UIT consists of a number of series, each holding $6 million face value of Brady bonds, and requires a minimum investment of $3,250. Investors will receive both interest and price appreciation and should earn a return of about 9.5% over an approximate 27-year period, *if* none of the bonds default on interest and principal redemptions; this is a very big "if."

Real Estate Investment Trusts

A **real estate investment trust (REIT)** invests in assets related to the real estate industry. Although its legal characteristics make it a trust, investors often view and evaluate a REIT as though it were a closed-end investment company. There are similarities: each has a relatively fixed capital structure with shares traded on the organized exchanges and the over-the-counter market, and each pays most of its earnings in dividends. But there is an important difference: a mutual fund invests exclusively in securities, while REITs invest in both securities and tangible assets.

Real estate investment trust: trust that invests in assets related to the real estate industry

A congressional act in 1960 regulated REITs extensively. To operate as one and to enjoy the federal income tax exemption, the trust must meet five conditions:

1. 75% of its assets must be in real estate, mortgages, cash, or government securities at the end of each quarter;
2. 75% of its gross income must come from real estate or mortgages;
3. it must distribute 90% of its income to beneficiaries (shareholders);
4. it must have at least 100 beneficiaries; and
5. 50% or more of its shares cannot be controlled by any five or fewer beneficiaries.

REITs usually are classified as equity or mortgage trusts.

Types of REITs   There are differences among REITs, and with about 130 from which to choose, it is necessary to identify these differences. They are highlighted in Exhibit 14.15 and discussed in the following sections.

Equity trust: REIT that invests in tangible property

Equity Trusts   An **equity trust** invests in tangible, real property. Some hold interests in a wide variety of real estate assets—commercial and office buildings, shopping centers, warehouses, and more—throughout the United States, while others either specialize in a particular type of property or limit their investing to a small geographical area. The principal assets of Santa Anita Realty, for example, are the Santa Anita racetrack and a 50% interest in an adjacent enclosed shopping center.

EXHIBIT 14.15
Types of REITs

Type	Activity	Investment Appeal
Equity trust	Invests in tangible property, mostly real estate	A convenient way to invest in real estate on a diversified basis
Mortgage trust	Invests in mortgages	Higher yields of commercial loans available to investors with limited funds
Finite-life REIT (FREIT)	Invests in real estate	Properties sold in 10 to 15 years and trust liquidated; REIT shares may not sell at large discount from equity per share
Single-purpose REIT	Invests in properties of a single company	Very attractive return, *if* lessee company remains financially sound
CMO REIT	Buys mortgage-backed passthroughs; sells collateralized securities backed by them	Opportunity to earn a spread between short-term and long-term interest rates

Mortgage Trusts   A **mortgage trust** invests in mortgages backed by real estate. If you invest in one, in effect you are participating in the commercial mortgage-lending business. Commercial lending involves large sums of money and often complex lending arrangements. A small, inexperienced investor cannot enter this area easily without a pooling arrangement.

Mortgage trust: REIT that invests in mortgages

Finite-Life REITs   A **finite-life REIT,** called a **FREIT,** is designed to sell all its properties at the end of 10 or 15 years and distribute any capital gains to the shareholders. The rationale for a FREIT is that it should overcome the tendency for REITs to sell at discounts from the appraised values of the properties they own. With a definite termination point, investors should be willing to pay share prices that reflect the intrinsic value of the FREIT. Investors apparently have been willing to accept the rationale because FREIT shares typically sell at higher multiples of earnings than comparable equity trusts.

Finite-life REIT: REIT with a set maturity date

Single-Purpose REITs   A **single-purpose REIT** is established to buy properties of a single company, such as chains of fast-food restaurants or tire stores. It then leases these properties back to the business. An investment in one of these can be risky because the REIT is dependent on the success of the leasing business.

Single-purpose REIT: REIT that buys properties of a single company

CMO REITs   **CMO REITs** were created in 1985. They do not invest in properties or mortgages but perform a brokering function by buying mortgage-backed passthroughs (see Chapter 9 for a discussion) and then selling to institutional investors debt instruments backed by the mortgage passthroughs. These debt instruments are called collateralized mortgage obligations (CMOs). Investors in a CMO REIT, then, expect to earn income from a spread (called a "residual") between returns on the passthroughs and interest paid on the CMOs.

CMO REIT: REIT that buys mortgage-backed securities and then creates and sells new securities backed by them

Some CMO REITs have become disasters, for several reasons. First, the CMO security essentially offers variable short-term rates, while the passthroughs are relatively long-term fixed rates. Rising short-term rates cause the residuals to disappear. Second, passthrough income is influenced considerably by refinancings. As these occur when interest rates decline, revenue sources are depleted. These factors sent one large CMO REIT—Residential Resources Mortgage Investments Corporation—into a Chapter 11 reorganization and depressed CMO REIT prices. CMO REITs deserve close scrutiny. Their proferred yields, sometimes going as high as 20%, may be illusory.

The Return from a REIT   As noted earlier, 90% of a REIT's earnings must be distributed as dividends. The current return on many REITs is therefore fairly high but also volatile, a factor you should not overlook if a stable return is important to you. Similar to the NAV of a mutual fund, the equity per share

(EqPS) of a REIT can be determined by dividing assets minus liabilities by the number of shares outstanding; that is,

$$EqPS = \frac{(REIT \ asssets - liabilities)}{REIT \ shares \ outstanding}$$

EqPS is an important figure to investors who want to know if the market price of a REIT share is selling at a discount or premium to it. You should understand, however, that assets are measured at their book—rather than appraised—values. If a REIT acquired properties some years ago, there is a good possibility that book value will be substantially below appraised value. So, it is important not to attach excessive importance to the EqPS figure.

Exhibit 14.16 presents a small sample of three equity trusts and three mortgage trusts to illustrate REIT performance and value characteristics. As you see, they vary considerably in realized dividend growth over the past 5- and 10-year periods (columns 5 and 6). Projecting future price appreciation based on the 10-year historical rate and combining it with the current dividend yield leads to some rather pessimistic expected total returns, as shown in column 9. You must be cautious in using these projections because the assumption that past dividend growth will continue in the future may not hold true. This was the case when Exhibit 14.16 was prepared because many analysts were bullish on REITs and many of their prices had increased substantially over the previous year.

The year 1993 was proving to be a banner year for new REITs. By early August, close to $6 billion had been raised with REIT Initial Public Offerings (IPOs). One expert was predicting that another $6 billion would be raised by year end. If true, more money would be raised in 1993 than in all the previous 32 years (since REITs began) combined. If you would like more information

EXHIBIT 14.16

Historical performance of six REITs, May 17, 1993

REIT (1)	BETA (2)	Premium or (Discount) 1992 (3)	Premium or (Discount) 1988 (4)	Div/Share Growth 5 Yr. (5)	Div/Share Growth 10 Yr. (6)	Current DPS $ (7)	Current DPS Yield (8)	Total Return (6) + (8) (9)
BRE Properties	.40	65%	69%	0.0%	5.0%	2.40	6.5%	11.5%
Federal Realty	.75	247	199	6.1	8.3	1.53	5.7	14.0
HRE	.70	−37	−8	−9.6	−5.3	1.16	8.9	3.6
LNH Reit, Inc.	.80	−47	6	−25.0	−14.0	.56	7.4	−6.6
Santa Anita Realty	.55	135	402	−7.8	−2.1	1.36	8.5	6.4
MGI Properties	.70	−21	16	−13.0	−4.6	.80	5.7	1.1

SOURCE: Securities' details are from *Investment Survey: Real Estate Investment Trust Industry*, May 17, 1993. Copyright 1993 by Value Line, Inc. All Rights Reserved; Reprinted with Permission. All Calculations of return, permia, or value are those of the authors.

about REITs, contact the National Association of REITs, 1129 20th Street NW, Suite 705, Washington, DC 20036 (telephone 202–785–8717).

LIMITED PARTNERSHIPS AND INVESTMENT CLUBS

Two other pooling arrangements are quite popular: limited partnerships and investment clubs. Each is explained below.

Limited Partnerships

A **limited partnership** is a legal arrangement that combines features of a corporation and a general partnership (see Exhibit 14.17). It is similar to a corporation in that its investors (called *limited partners*), like corporate shareholders, have limited liability for business losses. They also are inactive in managing the business, preferring instead to turn over these responsibilities to a person called the *general partner*. A limited partnership resembles a general partnership in that profits or losses are passed directly to the partners, rather than being profits or losses of the business.

Before the 1986 Tax Reform Act, the appeal of many limited partnerships was taxpayer ability to deduct partnership losses from other taxable income in filing the individual federal income tax. These deductions could turn mediocre or poor business ventures into rather profitable investments for people with high marginal tax rates. Such deductions are no longer allowed (with some exceptions for oil and gas shelters), and with tax advantages eliminated, limited partnerships have lost some of their investment importance.

Limited partnership: legal arrangement with features of a corporation and a general partnership

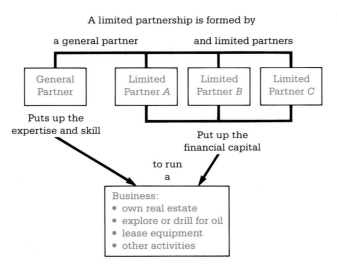

EXHIBIT 14.17
Illustration of a limited partnership

Business Activities   The most important business activities undertaken by limited partnerships are in real estate and energy resources. Others include equipment leasing deals and livestock feeding and breeding programs.

Real estate limited partnership: most popular type of limited partnership; owns and manages properties

Real Estate   **Real estate limited partnerships,** the most popular form, acquire and manage properties of all types. Some emphasize current income and immediate cash flow, while others seek long-term capital appreciation. A limited partnership may be a *public syndicate*, which is marketed much like a new distribution of common stock. *A private syndicate*, on the other hand, restricts the number of limited partners. A public syndicate is often a *blind pool*—totally or partially—which means the properties the partnership will acquire are not known at the time partnership interests are sold. These interests typically are $1,000 each, and in general, you must buy at least five units. In contrast, many private syndicates are formed to buy a specific property, such as a shopping center or an office building, and this property is identified to the prospective partners. Such a limited partnership interest often requires an investment of $25,000 or more.

Energy resources limited partnership: invests in programs related to finding, developing, and selling natural resources

Energy Resources   **Energy resources limited partnerships** are in the business of finding, extracting, and transporting all forms of energy resources. They are most popular in the oil and gas industry, where three types of programs exist. An exploratory program searches for new fields in areas that appear fertile but where strikes have not yet been made. The fact that fewer than 15 out of 100 drillings find oil indicates these programs are extremely risky, but a strike can be very profitable. Investing in one of these programs often is compared to investing in an untested, very small growth company.

A *developmental* program drills wells in areas that already have producing wells. The success rate here is considerably greater, but each well's payoff is much smaller. An investment in a developmental program can be compared to investing in a tested growth company such as General Electric. The third alternative is an *income program*, which buys producing wells with known reserves. This investment is similar to buying a corporate bond. The annual production of crude is fairly uniform over time, just as is the payment of bond interest. Its value, however, is highly unpredictable because it depends on the price of oil, just as the value of a bond is unpredictable because interest reinvestment rates in the future are so volatile.

The return from any energy resource program depends heavily on the price of energy. In the late 1970s and early 1980s, energy prices were very high and programs proliferated, many offering fairly attractive returns. But when the price of oil fell to around $10 a barrel in 1986, these same programs and many like them became disasters. Large originators, such as Petro-Lewis, faced bankruptcy, and most limited partnership interests fell considerably in value.

Other Business Areas   In the past, limited partnerships have been active in other business areas such as equipment leasing and livestock feeding or breeding programs. In an *equipment leasing deal*, the partnership buys

BOX 14.3   A QUESTION OF ETHICS

Do We Need Standards in Reporting Mutual Fund Performance?

Are you surprised by the large number of funds claiming to be #1 in performance? If you're wondering how that can happen, the answer is simple: define the standard by which you measure performance. Some examples: The Newberger and Berman Guardian Fund promoted itself as the #1 growth-and-income fund; but a closer examination of the fine print indicates that it compared itself with only those funds with assets between $500 million and $1 billion. The Kaufman Fund boasts itself as the #1 growth fund (fine print: from both the low and high in 1987 through 1992). And the Blanchard Flexible-Income Fund touted itself as the #1 yielding general bond fund for February (1993) based on statistics compiled by Lipper Analytical Services; the fund looked only at current yield, and when total returns were considered, it finished near the bottom of its group.

This type of puffery raises serious ethical issues for the mutual fund industry. Are we to consider mutual fund advertising analogous to the type we see for consumer products in general, where such puffery is routine? Or, do we consider mutual funds as financial institutions similar to commercial banks, where we set high standards for promotional activities? We don't allow banks to confuse consumers with interest-rate ads (although they did in

the past), so why should mutual funds get away with it?

The Investment Company Institute, a trade group representing the industry, has proposed guidelines to help eliminate some of the more abusive practices, such as those mentioned above. Because it has no legal power, it can only exhort its members. Failure to listen could easily lead to strict legal controls on the part of the Securities and Exchange Commission. Regardless of who sets the rules, given the imagination and creativity of fund promoters, it might make sense to disallow performance measurements developed by a fund. Funds could refer only to measurements developed by credible, independent sources, such as Morningstar.

The enormous popularity of mutual funds has brought many first-time investors into the investment game, and unfortunately, that's how many of them view it. With hundreds of billions of dollars already invested in mutual funds through IRAs, 401(k), and other self-directed retirement plans, investors should have sound return-risk data to help them make intelligent decisions. Instead, they are bombarded with hoopla and half-truths that create a "fund-of-the-month" attitude, where the best strategy is the endless pursuit of #1.

equipment—such as a computer installation—that is needed by a particular business. It then leases the equipment to that business under a standard lease agreement that provides the business an opportunity to buy the equipment at the end of the lease period. In *livestock feeding programs*, a limited partnership is formed to buy stock from farmers or ranchers and to feed the animals until they are ready for market; *breeding programs* operate somewhat differently, holding the stock as a producing asset rather than selling it after a short period.

As previously mentioned, much of the success of these limited partnerships in the past was attributable to the then-existing income tax structure, rather than to any economic advantages of the arrangement. Why shouldn't the business buy its own computer, or ranchers feed their own cattle? It often was desirable for certain corporate entities to shift business expenses or tax credits to individuals because they had much higher marginal tax rates. Limited partnerships were ideal vehicles for making such shifts. The 1986 tax law greatly reduces the marginal rate disparities and does away with other tax incentives to form limited partnerships.

Investment Potential   The tax advantages of limited partnerships once made them particularly attractive investments, but they offer few other advantages to offset their disadvantages. The key disadvantages are high promotion and syndication costs and poor liquidity.

Public syndicates are expensive to form and market. As much as 20% of total funds raised commonly go into areas not related to the actual buying of real estate, drilling of wells, or whatever the business might be. Selling costs run in the 7% to 10% range, the general partner usually takes an acquisition fee of 5% or so, and other items add another 5% to 10%. An investment must offer a fairly good and continuous return to offset an initial burden of this magnitude.

Practically all limited partnership interests have poor liquidity, although a secondary market for some interests exists. Without a strong secondary market, selling your interests becomes difficult. The large brokerage firms that help market the public syndicates might be able to find potential buyers. But determining the intrinsic value of an interest might be impossible, which means you have no way of knowing if the price you are offered is a fair one, and there will be a selling commission. Given these obstacles, you should consider a limited partnership interest as having the poorest marketability and liquidity of practically any intangible investment you will make.

Moreover, another worry with limited partnerships has surfaced in the form of general partners with financial difficulties. Large Southmark Corporation in Dallas, a general partner in numerous arrangements, sought Chapter 11 bankruptcy in late 1988; six months later, Cardinal Industries, Inc., a Columbus, Ohio, general partner, followed suit. Legally, a limited partnership is distinct from the general partner, and its economic viability should continue. As a practical matter, that may not be the case. A general partner wrapped up in protecting itself may prove to be a poor property manager.

Investment Clubs

An **investment club** is an informal association of individual investors who pool their resources for investment purposes. Although clubs often are viewed with disdain by investment professionals, their number is rapidly growing, and some evidence suggests their investment performance is not as bad as the experts might think. For example, Exhibit 14.18 shows that from 1976 through 1983, the clubs beat the S&P 500 every year. Their performance has been about even since then. Many clubs affiliate with the National Association of Investment Clubs (NAIC). As of July 2, 1993, the NAIC reported 10,000 affiliated clubs representing 210,000 individual members. Thomas O'Hara, NAIC's president, indicated that NAIC was enrolling 1,100 new members a week.

Why have investment clubs become popular? First, a long bull market, such as the one that began in 1982, often attracts first-time investors, both to the market and, eventually, to an investment club. Second, many experienced investors have also joined. These people have become disenchanted with the advice of their brokers or the performance of their mutual funds. To illustrate this point, consider that an association called the American Association of Individual Investors (AAII), formed as recently as 1979, now has more than 120,000 members. The AAII takes a serious and professional perspective on

Investment club: informal association of investors who pool resources and talents

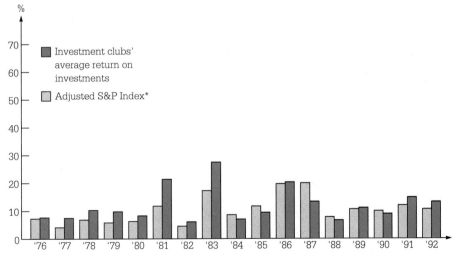

EXHIBIT 14.18
Performance of investment clubs (Source: National Association of Investment Clubs, 1515 East 11 Mile Road, Royal Oak, MI 48067.)

*Adjusted to include dividends as well as appreciation

investments and is active in sponsoring academic research relating to individual investing. Its journal, published 10 times a year, includes many interesting and timely articles that should be helpful in making your investment decisions. The individual investor who joins the AAII often joins an investment club as much to share ideas and research as to pool funds. A third reason for the clubs' popularity is that they help members share investment expenses, such as those incurred in buying magazines, market newsletters, and, particularly, computer software. Many investors now routinely use the computer in their investing activities. Software and data retrieval services are large expenses for a single person to bear.

Organization and Operation   Investment clubs usually are organized by people who have a common interest. They may work together, be members of the same church, or live in the same neighborhood. They typically meet monthly, and members pay monthly dues that can vary considerably. The average is in the $20-to-$25 range. Members often are given research assignments: they are expected to find securities to recommend for purchase. And the total membership reviews the club's portfolio each month to consider possible eliminations and new purchases and to decide the disposition of any interest or dividends received since the last meeting.

The club usually elects officers, and the position that should concern you most is the treasurer. Although fraud is rare, it does exist, and instances have been reported in which club members lost as much as $10,000 to fraudulent operators. You might want the treasurer to be bonded, or at the very least, avoid a club with a careless approach to handling cash or securities. It is also important to understand the club's policy of liquidating your interest if you should want to do so. Some clubs may hesitate to sell securities specifically for the purpose of redeeming a member's interest, which means there may be a waiting period until the club has sufficient cash.

Advantages/Disadvantages   Apart from the advantages of pooling and sharing resources and research efforts, an investment club offers fun and fellowship. These attributes should not be taken lightly; many members thoroughly enjoy the monthly meetings and the challenge of finding attractive investment opportunities. However, there are disadvantages to consider.

To begin with, too much fun often detracts from the main function, which is to invest. If a club worries more about entertainment during the meetings than investing, you may have a good time but a bad investment return. You must decide which is more important. Also, some clubs are dominated by one or two strong-willed persons who shape the club's investing activities. This situation can be fine, but only if they are good investors. Moreover, some clubs degenerate into gambling operations. Their members grow impatient with conservative investments and look for more action. After a while, their portfolios consist mostly of options or futures contracts. Again, you must decide if speculative investing of this sort appeals to you. Finally, investment clubs are not tax-exempt. You must keep a record of your share of all transactions having tax implications. This can be a real aggravation if the club engages in frequent trading or keeps poor records.

SUMMARY

Investment companies are popular pooling arrangements. A closed-end fund has a fixed number of shares that are traded like other stocks. A fund share has a net asset value (NAV), but closed-end fund shares can trade at discounts or premiums to NAV. Open-end funds—which are far more popular than closed-end funds—sell additional fund shares and redeem them (each at NAV) in response to investor demand. These funds may have front-end loads and other charges.

It is important to understand a fund's investment objective: growth, income, money market, sector, specialized, or index. Funds offer many investment conveniences, such as telephone transactions, automatic reinvestment of dividends or capital gains, fund switching, and adaptability to retirement plans.

Investors should evaluate fund performance before making specific selections. HPRs should be used and geometric averages determined. Fund risk often can be measured with a beta weight, and the beta method also indicates superior or inferior performance by the fund in relation to the overall market. Some fund managers tout their performances in the popular press but often neglect to indicate risk. Moreover, fund evaluation in the popular press usually does not link risk and performance in an adequate manner. So, it is important for investors to be capable of making their own evaluations.

A UIT is a pooling arrangement that invests funds in certain types of securities, most often municipal bonds or GNMA passthrough certificates. Some trusts invest in liquid assets, or in corporate bonds in an attempt to mimic a bond index. REITs invest in tangible property (equity trusts) or mortgages (mortgage trusts). Some REITs have finite lives, and some invest in the property of a particular kind of business. The return from a REIT is similar to any stock return, and REITs' historical experience has been mixed. They did poorly in the early and middle 1970s but have improved considerably since then.

A limited partnership is a unique business arrangement that combines features of a corporation and a general partnership. Limited partnerships are active in real estate, energy resources, and other business areas. Without a tax advantage, they are no more appealing than other investments, and high start-up and operating costs put them at a disadvantage. An investment club is a somewhat informal arrangement with some advantages and disadvantages. Although it offers social benefits along with investing, an excessive amount of entertainment defeats the purpose of the club.

KEY TERMS
(listed in order of appearance)

organized investment company	dual fund
closed-end fund	alpha value
net asset value	Treynor Index
discount	risk-adjusted rate of return
premium	trust
open-end fund	unit investment trust
front-end loads	municipal bond trust
back-end loads	GNMA trusts
12b-1 plan	SPDRs ("spiders")
growth fund	real estate investment trust
maximum capital appreciation funds	equity trust
income fund	mortgage trust
balanced fund	finite-life REIT
money market fund	single-purpose REIT
sector fund	CMO REIT
international equity fund	limited partnership
global equity fund	real estate limited partnership
international bond fund	energy resources limited partnership
index fund	investment club

REVIEW QUESTIONS

1. Discuss the current popularity of investment companies. Which form—open-end or closed-end—is more popular?
2. Describe the characteristics of a closed-end fund. Is there any advantage in investing in closed-end funds selling at discounts or premiums? Explain.
3. What is a fund's NAV? How might this differ from its offer price? Explain.
4. Describe the characteristics of an open-end fund. Do you buy its shares in the same manner as you buy shares in a closed-end fund? Explain.
5. Explain the following terms: *(a)* front-end load, *(b)* back-end load, *(c)* 12b–1 plan, and *(d)* fund family.
6. Briefly explain eight fund objectives. Which might be the most important to you personally?
7. How does a dual fund work? Discuss whether it is more or less risky than a traditional fund offering a similar portfolio.
8. Briefly discuss four important fund services. Which might be the most important to you personally?
9. How might an investor measure his or her *annual* return from a fund?
10. How do most funds calculate return measurements reported to shareholders?
11. Explain the terms *beta value* and *alpha value* as they apply in mutual fund evaluations.
12. How does the market risk premium differ in measuring fund performance as opposed to its use in finding undervalued or overvalued securities?
13. Explain the Treynor Index, indicating how it is calculated.
14. What is a RAROR, and how is it calculated?
15. Describe the performance evidence of mutual fund managers and sources of fund evaluations.

16. Describe the characteristics of a UIT. How does one differ from a mutual fund?
17. Discuss advantages and disadvantages of investing in muni UITs as opposed to a no-load muni mutual fund and buying munis on your own.
18. Describe two innovations in UITs.
19. Define a REIT, detailing the conditions it must meet to be exempt from federal income taxation.
20. Explain the following: equity trust, mortgage trust, finite-life REIT, single-purpose REIT, and CMO REIT.
21. Explain a REIT's EqPS.
22. Discuss the investment potential of the six REITs highlighted in this chapter.
23. What is a limited partnership and how do its income tax implications differ from those of other investments?
24. Define the following terms: public syndicate, private syndicate, and blind pool.
25. What three types of programs are available with energy resource limited partnerships? Explain each program, comparing it with another security having a similar return pattern.
26. Discuss the investment potential of limited partnerships.
27. Explain an investment club and discuss advantages and disadvantages of joining one.

PROBLEMS AND PROJECTS

1. The Zoom Fund has 10,000 shares outstanding. It owns 100 shares of DuPont (selling at $80 a share) and 500 shares of Exxon (selling at $50 a share). Calculate its NAV if it also has $500 in liabilities.
2. The Radiant Fund made two distributions last year. The first was a dividend of $1.00 a share and the second was a capital gain of $3.00 a share. NAV was $30 at the beginning of the year, $20 when the dividend was distributed, $15 when the capital gain was distributed, and $25 at year's end.
   a. Calculate Radiant's HPR assuming all distributions took place at year's end and were not reinvested.
   b. Calculate its HPR taking into consideration when dividends were paid and assuming they were reinvested when received. Compare this return with the one calculated in *a* and discuss.
3. Annual returns for the Sun Fund, the Moon Fund, and the S&P 500 are shown below.

Year	Sun	Moon	S&P 500
1	8.0%	4.0%	5.0%
2	−1.0	3.0	2.0
3	27.0	11.0	15.0
4	36.0	12.0	20.0
5	−23.0	−2.0	−10.0

   a. Calculate the arithmetic average return for each. Then determine the geometric accumulation for each. If you have an appropriate calculator, show that the geometric average returns are 7.3%, 5.5%, and 5.9%, respectively. Finally, discuss which is the best-performing fund.

b. Your highest return is with the Sun Fund, but is it high enough to offset its added risk? To answer this question, begin by determining Sun and Moon funds' beta values. Use any method, including a graphic plot of the return of each fund versus the S&P 500's returns. Then determine alpha values (assume the average risk-free return was 2.0%), TI values, and RARORs. Discuss your findings, indicating the best investment: the Sun Fund, the Moon Fund, or a portfolio of the S&P 500 and the risk-free asset.

4. Assume that you have decided to allocate a portion of your portfolio (about $20,000) to municipal bonds; however, you are unsure whether to invest directly in them or to use UITs or mutual funds. The UIT you are considering will have a 20-year life, origination fees at 3% of amounts invested, and annual operating costs of 0.5% of net assets. The mutual fund is a no-load, but its annual operating costs will be 1.0% of net assets. A self-directed portfolio will involve commissions of around 1% on purchases or sales.

a. Determine the amount of funds accumulated over a six-year period with each approach, assuming (1) each earns an 8% rate on invested funds, (2) all annual earnings are withdrawn and reinvested at 6%, and (3) the self-directed portfolio is terminated at the end of the sixth year.

b. Discuss how the following factors should be considered in reaching a decision: the quality of the securities selected, the need for insurance, management of the portfolio over time, and ability to lock in yields.

5. A certain REIT has assets of $226 million, liabilities of $3.2 million, and 20 million shares outstanding. Each share currently sells at a $2 discount. What is the market value of each share?

6. Nick Vlahos is employed by a major oil company as a petroleum engineer. Nick's salary is about $70,000 a year, and he has no dependents. Nick has accumulated $25,000 and has it invested in a money market mutual fund. Of the total, $20,000 is a temporary arrangement while Nick evaluates certain investment alternatives. He thinks that a major concern in selecting new vehicles should be his relatively high marginal tax rate of 40% (federal, state, and local taxes). Nick has not sought professional advice because he likes to make his own investment decisions. Nick believes that he has a relatively high tolerance for risk.

As he sees the picture, there are two alternatives: municipal bonds and limited partnerships. With respect to the former, he has seen an ad in the local newspaper indicating the bonds of a certain hospital in his area will be issued to provide investors with an 8% return free of all taxes. He also noted in an investment magazine that a muni UIT supposedly offers a guaranteed 8.5% return; this return would be subject to the combined state and local tax rate of 7%.

As for limited partnerships, a friend of Nick's recommends a deal being offered by a large stockbrokerage firm. The partnership will invest in office buildings and shopping centers. Nick would be a limited partner and not active in managing the business. The annual return from the partnership is likely to be 15% before considering taxes. Another possible limited partnership is a small deal Nick has heard of in his hometown. The partnership will acquire vacant land near a large university's sports center and develop it into a parking lot. Parking spaces then would be leased to football and basketball fans. The potential annual return here is 20%, although a tax loss of $2,000 (for each $5,000 investment) is expected in the first year of operation. Nick would be active in managing the business.

a. Which of the two municipal bond investments do you recommend for Nick? Give specific reasons for your selection.

b. Which of the two limited partnerships do you recommend for Nick? Give specific reasons for your selection.

c. Recommend a portfolio for Nick. Assume a minimum investment of $5,000 in each case.

7. Sue Markley is considering investing in REITs. She has read that their recent performances have been good, and she thinks they will fit well within her portfolio, which now consists mostly of long-term corporate bonds and a money market mutual fund. She is looking for investments with characteristics different from those she already holds. Sue is not familiar with REITs, and she selected the four shown in the table because they appeared in a newspaper article about REITs. She would like you to advise her in this situation.

REIT	Type	Current Price	Equity Per Share	Current Yield	5-Year Annual Div. Growth
HO Properties	Equity	$22	$14	8%	10%
Van Atta	Mortgage	60	70	14	6
ZMC, Inc.	FREIT*	24	23	10	10
Delaney	CMO	16	43	23	2

*Terminates to five years.

The estimated market value of each REIT's assets varies considerably in relation to per-share equity. ZMC's and HO Properties' market value per share about equal per-share equity; Van Atta's is a bit lower, while Delaney's is substantially lower.

a. Based on total return calculations, which is the most attractive REIT?

b. Indicate other important considerations, and then discuss the investment appeal and risks of each.

c. Which REIT(s) do you recommend for Sue? Explain your response.

8. (Student Project) From a library, request a year of back issues to Forbes, Money, and Business Week. For each publication, find the issue that evaluates mutual funds. Then select a sample of 10 or so funds and compare evaluations. In reviewing the Forbes issue, compare fund operating costs (expressed as a percentage of net assets) and note the wide variations. Does it appear that funds with high ratios have better performance histories? Discuss.

9. (Student Project) From one of the sources indicated in problem 8, find the toll-free numbers of several funds. Call them and request a prospectus, the last annual report, and the most recent quarterly report. When these publications arrive, evaluate each fund, using the methods explained in this chapter. Prepare a report on your findings.

CASE ANALYSES

14.1
Are Mutual
Funds
Appropriate for
the Ankeneys?

The Ankeneys, Nick and Karla, are a recently married couple with two young children. They have a modest combined income but plan to save and invest $1,000 a year to meet future goals. They are seeking a balanced portfolio invested in common stocks, bonds, and money market instruments. Nick and Karla have some understanding of securities and security analysis but hardly consider themselves proficient in the area. Nick is a carpenter and Karla works part-time as a legal assistant. Both are busy right now and have little free time.

They initially planned to do their own security selection, but lately they have been leaning toward investment companies, even though their knowledge of this investment medium is limited. They have been contacted by a representative of a securities firm. She has indicated the firm can service all the Ankeneys' needs, including mutual funds. She also provided literature on various stock funds that indicate rather good performances over the past 20 years.

Questions

a. Which method of investing do you think is more appropriate for the Ankeneys? Explain your answer.
b. Should the Ankeneys consider investing in funds on their own, or should they rely exclusively on the securities firm representative? Cite and discuss specific factors in reaching your conclusion.
c. Assuming the Ankeneys choose to invest in funds on their own, indicate the steps they should take in the process. How should they select appropriate funds, how can they establish accounts, and what decisions should they make with respect to reinvesting dividends? Also, indicate data sources the Ankeneys can consider in evaluating and following fund performances.

14.2
Roger Maltbey
Examines a
Mutual Fund
Report

Roger Maltbey intends to invest in a mutual fund that specializes in investing in the common stock of small companies. The fund seems to have done quite well over the past 10 years, and Roger thinks it also should do well in the future. A popular personal finance magazine gives the fund a high ranking, which is encouraging, but Roger is a bit skeptical because a similar rank is given to many other funds. He requested literature from the fund and received a preliminary report indicating performances for the past two years. Roger doesn't completely understand the data. He has requested your help.

He would like you to advise him on the relative attractiveness of the fund and whether it is suitable for him. He describes his primary investment objective as long-term capital accumulation and indicates that he has an average tolerance for risk. Information on the fund appears in the following table.

	Past Year	Two Years Ago
1. Investment income	$.90	$.97
2. Expenses	.15	.12
3. Investment income—net	.75	.85
4. Dividends from net investment income	(.80)	(.81)
5. Realized and unrealized gain (loss) on investments—net	2.84	1.13
6. Distributions from realized gains	(4.14)	(.28)
7. Net increase (decrease) in net asset value	(1.35)	.89
8. Beginning of year	15.57	14.68
9. End of year	14.22	15.57
10. Ratio of expenses to average net assets	1.57%	1.03%
11. Portfolio turnover	186%	112%

To help in responding to Roger, you did some research and found that yields on 90-day U.S. Treasury bills averaged 7% in the past year and 10% two years ago. Additionally, the overall market showed a return of 18% a year ago and 9% two years ago. You also have found the fund's beta value, which is 1.8.

a. Determine HPRs for each of the two years.
b. Evaluate the fund's performance for each of the two years using alpha values, TI values, and RARORs.
c. Would you advise Roger to invest in the fund? Explain your answer.

HELPFUL READING

Bary, Andrew. "Back in the Dog House?" *Barron's*, September 13, 1993, p. 29.

Brandstrater, J.R. "New Favorites, Old Flaws: Time Hasn't Erased Unit Investment Trusts' Problems." *Barron's*, July 19, 1993, p. 32.

Christopherson, John A., and Andrew L. Turner. "Volatility and Predictability of Manager Alpha." *The Journal of Portfolio Management*, Fall 1991, pp. 5–12.

Clements, Jonathan. "Beefing Up Bond Fund Can Mean Mixing in Junk and Foreign Issues." *The Wall Street Journal*, July 8, 1991, p. C1.

_____. "Mutual Funds for Penny-Pinching Investors." *The Wall Street Journal*, January 15, 1993, p. C1.

Edgerton, Jerry. "Where Index Funds Work Best." *Money*, June 1993, pp. 94–100.

Forsyth, Randall. "Peerless Performance." *Barron's*, September 7, 1992, p. 27.

Grover, Mary Beth. "Funds for Fence Sitters." *Forbes*, January 18, 1993, p. 108.

_____. "The Short Side." *Forbes*, April 26, 1993, pp. 296–97.

Rudnitsky, Howard. "Watch Your Wallet." *Forbes*, May 10, 1993, pp. 44–45.

Simon, Ruth. "How Fund Directors Are Letting You Down." *Money*, September 1993, pp. 104–14.

Teitelbaum, Richard S. "A Safe Way into Munis." *Fortune*, April 19, 1993, pp. 30–31.

Zweig, Jason, and Mary Beth Grover. "Fee Madness." *Forbes*, February 15, 1993, pp. 160–64.

CHAPTER FIFTEEN

Real Estate, Gold, and Other Tangibles

After you finish this chapter, you
will be able to:

- understand why a personal residence has investment appeal
  and how to determine its profitability within a rent-versus-buy
  framework.

- identify different kinds of rental
  properties and determine a
  rental property's rate of return.

- understand why a vacation
  home has potential investment
  appeal.

- understand different methods of
  property valuation.

- evaluate the various types of
  mortgage loans available.

- recognize tangibles' characteristics and relative advantages/dis-
  advantages.

- understand gold's investment
  characteristics and how to
  invest in it.

- identify pros and cons of other
  tangibles.

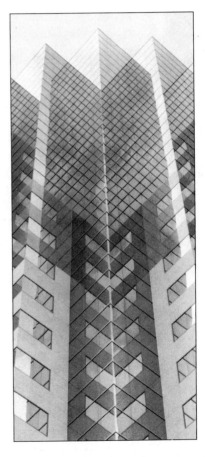

Regardless of how we measure the popularity of investments, real estate tops the list. Far more American families (about 6 out of 10) own homes than common stock (about 2 out of 10), and their investment is much greater. In addition, many own other forms of real estate, such as apartment houses and commercial and industrial properties. Moreover, millions of Americans now own a second home that is used partially for their own pleasure and partially to earn income. Owning a piece of America has been, and still is, the American dream. Sometimes this dream has stood in the way of sound economic decisions in real estate investing. One purpose of this chapter is to keep that from happening. It takes the view that all real estate—even the personal residence—should be evaluated as an investment, using traditional tools of analysis. Moreover, those same tools should be used to evaluate other tangibles, such as gold, silver, diamonds, artwork, hobbies, and collectibles.

THE PERSONAL RESIDENCE

Personal residence: any form of owned dwelling that provides a place in which to live

The **personal residence** is any form of owned dwelling that provides a place in which to live. It is different from all other investments in that you live in it, and a place to live is a necessity. A home typically has emotional appeal: many families enjoy their homes and would keep them even if they were terrible financial investments and even if it meant changing jobs to avoid moving. Such families probably are not in the majority. Indeed, the average family probably stays in a house about seven years, rather than a lifetime, which means the housing investment decision is being made frequently. So, it is important to examine the investment appeal of the personal residence and determine how much to invest in it.

Investment Appeal

A personal residence has three primary investment characteristics that enhance its appeal: price appreciation, tax sheltering of income, and a return variability that is relatively low. These three features are described below.

Price Appreciation   Many observers regard housing as an ideal investment. They point out that housing prices typically increase at least in step with the inflation rate, if not quicker. In addition, they note the return on the housing investment often is on a par with returns from other investments, such as stocks and bonds. Exhibit 15.1 shows evidence supporting this view. The median price of single-family homes jumped from $24,900 in 1971 to $103,600 in 1992, an average annual increase of 7.2% using the arithmetic mean and 7.1% with the geometric mean. These figures exceed the average annual increase of 5.9% in the consumer price index (CPI). The return on common stocks was much better during this period, but the sizeable difference

(1) Year	(2) Median Price 1 Family Existing Units	(3) Annual Percentage Increase	(4) Annual Percentage Increase in the CPI	(5) Annual Rate of Return on the S&P 500
1992	$103,600	3.9%	2.9%	7.7%
1991	99,700	4.7	3.1	30.6
1990	95,200	2.5	6.1	−3.2
1989	92,900	4.1	4.7	31.5
1988	89,200	4.2	4.4	16.8
1987	85,600	6.6	4.4	5.2
1986	80,300	6.5	1.1	18.5
1985	75,400	4.1	3.8	32.2
1984	72,400	3.0	4.0	6.3
1983	70,300	3.7	3.8	22.5
1982	67,800	2.1	3.9	21.4
1981	66,400	6.8	8.9	−4.9
1980	62,200	11.7	12.4	32.4
1979	55,700	14.4	13.3	18.4
1978	48,700	13.5	9.0	6.6
1977	42,900	12.6	6.8	−7.2
1976	38,100	6.4	4.8	23.8
1975	35,800	9.5	7.0	37.2
1974	32,700	10.9	12.2	−26.5
1973	29,500	5.7	8.8	−14.7
1972	27,900	12.1	3.4	18.9
1971	24,900	9.2	3.4	14.3
Averages:				
Arithmetic		7.2	5.9	13.1
Geometric		7.1	5.9	11.8
Housing beta (in relation to S&P 500) = −0.03				

EXHIBIT 15.1
Investment character-istics of the personal residence

between the arithmetic and geometric means shows their greater return volatility. Comparing geometric means shows an edge (11.8% versus 7.1%) in favor of stocks.

Housing prices increased even during the recessionary periods of 1974–75, 1980–82, and 1990–91. The overall growth in housing prices often masks wide disparities among different regions of the country, as Exhibit 15.2 shows. Sections of Washington State had been a hot area in the early 1990s, as evidenced by the sharp increases in Richland, Kennewick, and Pasco counties and in Spokane. These increases contrast in stark fashion with the decreases in other areas, such as Toledo, Ohio. Also interesting are the dra-matic differences in housing prices from one region of the country to another; for example, from Toledo to Providence, RI.

EXHIBIT 15.2
Regional housing price
changes

Location	Price Change First Quarter 1992— First Quarter 1993	Median Sales Price First Quarter, 1993
Hot Markets		
Richland, Kennewick, Pasco counties, WA	+24.5%	$ 96,400
Spokane, WA	+10.9	79,100
Charleston, WV	+10.3	75,400
Fort Meyers, Cape Coral, FL	+10.3	76,400
Madison, WI	+ 9.3	97,700
Cold Markets		
Toledo, OH	−11.1	65,800
Philadelphia, PA	− 9.0	108,900
Los Angeles, CA	− 8.0	199,700
Atlantic City, NJ	− 7.8	101,400
Providence, RI	− 5.0	112,500

SOURCE: *Home Sales: May 1993.* Economics and Research Division, National Association of Realtors, 777 14th Street NW, Washington DC 20005.

Supply and Demand Influences   Exhibit 15.3 indicates the price of housing depends a great deal on supply-and-demand influences. Family preferences for home ownership, population growth, income, and the *real* cost of mortgage funds are the primary demand factors. As preferences, population, and income increase, or real mortgage rates fall, the demand for housing increases, thereby increasing the price of housing (all supply factors held constant). Reverse changes in these factors reduce price. It is important to see that real—not nominal—mortgage rates influence demand. During much of the 1970s, nominal mortgage rates appeared high (in a historical sense); yet when adjusted for inflation, they actually were very low and were negative in several years. As expected, the demand for residential housing was exceptionally strong in this period. But the situation reversed in the early 1990s. Now nominal mortgage rates were very low, but with annual inflation running at about 3%, real mortgage rates were actually higher than in the 1970s. As expected, housing demand was weak.

The level of construction technology, construction costs (wages, prices of materials, the price of land, and others—all again measured in real terms), and the rate at which existing homes are demolished determine the supply of housing. If technology declines or construction costs or the demolition rate increase, the supply of housing falls. Reduction in the supply of housing in turn increases its price (all demand factors held constant). An improvement in technology or a decrease in real construction costs or the demolition rate increases housing supply, thereby depressing price.

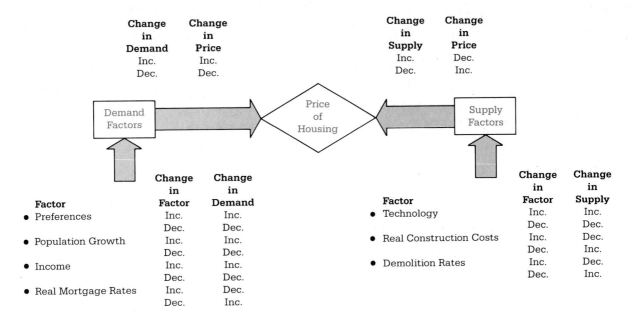

EXHIBIT 15.3
Supply, demand, and the price of housing

Although all supply-and-demand factors are important, the major price influences over the past 20 years seem to have been persistent increases in real construction costs and continually strong family preferences for home ownership. Will these conditions continue in the future? That is impossible to know. Perhaps the technology of manufacturing houses will improve, with greater emphasis on modular housing produced in the factory with production-line techniques. Perhaps family preferences for housing will change, moving away from ownership and toward renting. Few people now expect either of these changes, or any other, will take place, and most observers seem to believe housing prices at least will match inflation in the foreseeable future.

Local Influences Supply and demand can be extended to include many local influences. Accessibility to highways or public transportation, good schools, places of employment, and shopping areas often increases demand, as do neighborhood aesthetics. Indeed, realtors are fond of citing the three most important factors to consider in buying a home: location, location, and location. Although this quip might be an exaggeration, surely, the one feature of a home you cannot change is its location. Finally, characteristics of a house are important: one with a bad floor plan or structural defects or one in run-down condition does not have a market value as high as another similarly situated but in good shape. As a potential investor, you need to evaluate the local situation carefully before investing. This takes time, as does maintaining a home after the purchase, which is another item to consider.

Tax-Sheltering Aspects   The personal residence has important tax-sheltering aspects. First, you can defer any gain on the sale of a home by reinvesting (within two years of the sale) in another of equal or greater value. Second, you can avoid up to $125,000 of gains by selling your house at age 55 or older (if you meet several other conditions). This is unquestionably one of the best tax advantages available. Third, both interest on a home mortgage and state and local property taxes are deductible in determining taxable income.

Under existing tax law, the deductibility of interest creates another indirect advantage of owning a home with a mortgage. Although the mortgage interest is deductible, interest on consumer loans is not. It makes sense, then, to use a mortgage loan as a source of consumer credit. This use is limited, however: you cannot deduct interest on borrowed amounts in excess of the cost of the property plus any improvements. In other words, you can't use appreciation in value as a borrowing base. Exceptions are allowed, if the funds are used to meet medical or educational expenses.

Low Price Volatility   Exhibit 15.1 also indicates the low price volatility of houses. The figures are 12-month averages, which do not reveal volatility on a month-to-month basis, but even considering these data, volatility remains relatively low. Several studies have examined the risk characteristics of housing, using appropriate statistical methods. They have found, for instance, that housing has a low beta (a beta determined by the data in Exhibit 15.1 is -0.03), meaning its price volatility relative to the stock market is low. We will discuss risk perspectives on real estate later in this chapter.

We can say here, that housing is not a short-term investment, as we will see later in this chapter. There are high fixed costs in relation to obtaining a mortgage loan and paying a commission when a property is sold. It usually takes years of price appreciation to offset these costs and eventually show a gain.

Housing Affordability

An important investment decision is how much to invest in housing. If you apply for a mortgage loan, the lending institution will answer the question by applying their suitability rules to your case. For example, many follow a rule that your monthly housing expenses should not exceed some percentage of your monthly income. The Federal National Mortgage Corporation (which insures mortgage loans) recommends that monthly mortgage payments plus other consumer loan payments should not exceed 28% of monthly gross income. Assuming a monthly income of $2,500 and consumer loan monthly

Interest Rate	Loan Maturities (Years)				
	10	15	20	25	30
6%	$45,036	$59,252	$69,790	$77,603	$83,396
8	41,220	52,301	59,809	64,767	68,120
10	37,822	46,512	51,814	55,006	56,976
12	34,843	41,667	45,413	47,483	48,591
14	32,196	37,566	40,193	41,529	42,194

EXHIBIT 15.4
Amount of affordable mortgage for a $500 monthly payment: Various interest rates and loan maturities

payments of $200 gives us the following example for Rita Winfrey, a potential buyer.

Monthly income	$ 2,500
28% of monthly income	$ 700
Less consumer loan payments	200
Recommended monthly mortgage payment	$ 500
Affordable mortgage (see Exhibit 15.4)	$56,976
Plus the down payment	13,024
Affordable home	$70,000

In this case, Rita can afford a $500 monthly mortgage payment. She qualifies for a 30-year loan with a fixed 10% interest rate, which provides $56,976. This amount, along with her down payment of $13,024, means she can afford a $70,000 property.

Kinds of Properties

A number of options are available to home buyers. Your final decision should consider the amenities that appeal to you plus the potential financial return. The three popular forms of home ownership are the detached single-family home, the condominium, and the cooperative.

Detached Single-Family Homes The **detached single-family home** is still the number one choice of most home buyers. Indeed, the demand for this form of housing has withstood the hippie, yuppie, and all other movements. Years ago, when the suburbs were being assailed by sociologists and community planners as cultural wastelands, inner-city families were patiently saving their funds for a down payment on a three-bedroom ranch in the "slurbs." The trend seems equally strong today, judging by how young people respond to opinion polls asking them to rank their aspirations. At the top usually is the desire to own a detached, single-family home in a community with good schools and good police and fire protection.

Detached single-family home: most popular type of personal residence

Condominium housing: housing units that share common areas

Condominiums **Condominium housing** is a blend of apartment living and home ownership. The condo complex includes common areas that unit owners share, both in use and in expense. Keep in mind that you own your individual condo just as you would a detached house. You arrange your own financing and are responsible for its interior upkeep. Expenses of the common areas are met by charging individual owners a monthly maintenance fee, which can be quite high if the complex has a swimming pool, tennis courts, and other amenities. A condo appeals to home buyers who do not want the maintenance demands of a detached house, yet want the tax advantages and price appreciation property ownership has to offer. Although condominiums were slow to be accepted in certain parts of the country, buyer reluctance seems to have faded. You now can find expensive condos being constructed in rather conservative areas. Their price appreciation relative to detached houses, however, may not be as good. This generalization does not apply in all areas, but it makes sense to research your area if you are thinking of buying a condo and if price appreciation is important.

Cooperatives: similar to condominiums, except ownership interest is in the form of unit-entitlement shares

Cooperatives A **cooperative** appears similar to a condominium in that you own a unit that is part of a complex. However, the ownership form is different. A cooperative is a corporation, and you buy shares to it that entitle you to live in your unit. Again, you arrange your own financing to buy the shares and pay monthly maintenance fees. A possible disadvantage of a cooperative is that you must receive approval of the cooperative's board of directors before you can sell your shares. Cooperatives are popular on the East Coast, particularly in New York City, where many apartment complexes are actually cooperatives. Some of these apartments, such as those in the Trump Tower, cost in excess of $3 million for perhaps a unit with no more than 2,000 square feet of space. Your monthly maintenance fee might be about $5,000. Moreover, price appreciation on some of these has been spectacular, averaging 20% a year in some instances.

The Rent-Versus-Buy Decision

Because everyone must live somewhere, the decision to buy a home can be viewed as a decision not to rent. Let us ignore for the moment any nonfinancial motivation in the decision and concentrate strictly on the financial aspects. The steps involved in evaluating a rent-versus-buy decision are explained in the following sections. We will use the example of Rita Winfrey, whom we met earlier.

Cash Flows Before Taxes and Mortgage Payments Renting or owning involves cash outflows. Exhibit 15.5 details these flows in Rita's case. Rita currently pays $500 a month rent; she also must pay for some utilities, insurance, and small amounts of maintenance (mostly interior painting). As you see, she can save $6,000 a year in rentals by buying, but she will incur higher utilities, insurance, and maintenance and pay property taxes of $1,500 each

	(1) Rent	(2) Buy	(3) Difference (1) − (2)
Year 1:			
Rent payments	$6,000	$ -0-	$ 6,000
Utilities	1,200	2,400	−1,200
Insurance	200	500	− 300
Maintenance	100	600	− 500
Property taxes	-0-	1,500	−1,500
Totals	$7,500	$5,000	$ 2,500
Year 2: 1.05 × $2,500			2,685
Year 3: 1.05 × $2,685			2,879
Year 4: 1.05 × $2,879			3,083
Year 5: 1.05 × $3,083			3,297

EXHIBIT 15.5
Rita Winfrey's rent-versus-buy decision: Annual cash flows before taxes and mortgage payments

year. In total, buying saves her $2,500 in the first year. Assuming all items would increase each year by about the same rate (5% in this example), Rita's savings grow over time. For ease of presentation for now, we will extend the analysis only five years, but it is relatively easy to go out further.

Interest and Principal Payments on the Mortgage Exhibit 15.6 details Rita's $6,000 annual mortgage payments ($500 a month, as determined above). As you see, practically all the amounts are for interest. At the end of five years, Rita will have reduced her principal only to $55,024—$1,952 less than the beginning balance.

Income Tax Savings From a tax point of view, paying interest on a mortgage is better than paying principal because interest payments can be taken as an itemized deduction in computing taxable income. So can property tax payments, and combining the two gives Rita annual deductions, as shown in column 4 of Exhibit 15.7. The value of these deductions depends on the tax-

(1) Year	(2) Total Payments	(3) Interest	(4) Principal	(5) Ending Loan Balance*
Start	—	—	—	$56,976
1	$6,000	$5,683	$317	56,659
2	6,000	5,650	350	56,309
3	6,000	5,613	387	55,922
4	6,000	5,573	427	55,495
5	6,000	5,529	471	55,024

EXHIBIT 15.6
Rita Winfrey's rent-versus-buy decision: Mortgage payments

*Ending loan balance equals beginning loan balance minus principal payments; e.g.: 56,309 = 56,659 − 350.

EXHIBIT 15.7
Rita Winfrey's rent-
versus-buy decision:
Income tax savings

(1) Year	(2) Interest	(3) Property Taxes*	(4) Total	(5) Total × 0.28
1	$5,683	$1,500	$7,183	$2,011
2	5,650	1,575	7,225	2,023
3	5,613	1,654	7,267	2,035
4	5,573	1,736	7,309	2,047
5	5,529	1,823	7,352	2,059

*Assumed to grow at a 5% annual rate.

payer's marginal tax rate. Rita expects to pay a marginal rate of 28%; thus, the value of her deductions is shown in column 5. By purchasing a home, she will reduce her tax liabilities by the amounts indicated.

Annual Cash Flows   We now can determine the annual cash flows relevant to the rent-versus-buy decision. In Exhibit 15.8, the tax savings from Exhibit 15.7 and the cash flow savings before taxes from Exhibit 15.5 are combined, and the annual mortgage payment of $6,000 is deducted from the total. The resulting figures are the after-tax cash flows, and as you see, they are negative. This means if she buys the home, Rita must pay additional amounts each year, starting at $1,489 and decreasing to $644 in the fifth year. Rita can view these amounts as additional investments in the property. The final step is to determine the profitability of these investments combined with the initial down payment of $13,024.

Profitability of the Investment   As it now stands, the investment has a negative return. However, an important factor—price appreciation—has yet to be considered. Suppose the property appreciates 5% a year. At the end of five years, it will be worth $89,340. If Rita then decides to sell it, she will pay a realtor's commission of $6,254 (assuming a 7% commission rate), leaving

EXHIBIT 15.8
Rita Winfrey's rent-
versus-buy decision:
Annual cash flows

(1) Year	(2) Cash Flow Savings Before Taxes	(3) Income Tax Savings	(4) Total Savings	(5) Mortgage Payments	(6) Annual Cash Flows (4) − (5)
1	$2,500	$2,011	$4,411	$6,000	$−1,489
2	2,685	2,023	4,708	6,000	−1,292
3	2,879	2,035	4,914	6,000	−1,086
4	3,083	2,047	5,130	6,000	− 870
5	3,297	2,059	5,356	6,000	− 644

Cash Available at the End of Five Years	
Market value of home at the end of five years	$89,340
Less realtor's commission (7% rate)	6,254
Net value	$83,086
Less mortgage balance	55,024
Net cash available	$28,062
Investment Cash Flows	
Year 0 (beginning investment)	$−13,024
Year 1	− 1,489
Year 2	− 1,292
Year 3	− 1,086
Year 4	− 870
Year 5 (−644 + 28,062)	+27,418
	IRR = +10.24%

EXHIBIT 15.9
Rita Winfrey's rent-versus-buy decision: IRR analysis

her with $83,086. Her mortgage balance will be $55,024 (see Exhibit 15.6), and subtracting that from $83,086 leaves her with a final net of $28,062. Exhibit 15.9 shows these steps and presents the final cash flow picture to be evaluated. Using internal rate of return (IRR) methods (see Chapter 3), Rita determines the investment has an IRR of 10.24%. This is an after-tax return that Rita should compare with other after-tax returns. At the time the analysis was made, it was a relatively attractive return.

However, there are several items to keep in mind. First, it is assumed that no tax applies on the price appreciation. Second, the analysis above is sensitive to the assumed annual price increase of the home. An excessively optimistic view will favor the buy decision. Finally, it could be argued that your investment should not be limited to the down payment and annual cash flows but should consider also the annual build-up in equity resulting from price appreciation. This increases the size of the investment base and reduces the IRR, making the investment relatively less attractive. This perspective is appropriate if in fact the equity build-up could be withdrawn and invested elsewhere. However, that often is not the case.

THE RENTAL PROPERTY

A rental property is one that provides periodic income in the form of rentals or other types of revenues. These properties are available in many different forms, ranging from a single dwelling to something as huge as the Empire State Building. In a broad sense, they also include agricultural and mineral lands. Most of the larger property investments are owned by pooling arrangements, such as REITs or limited partnerships. Our present concern, though, is with a direct investment in real estate.

BOX 15.1   INVESTMENT INSIGHTS

The Personal Residence: Your Home *and* Your Business?

Trying to make money in real estate has always been a popular pursuit. In the past, investors focused mainly on traditional income-generating properties such as multi-unit residential rentals, office and commercial buildings, and strip shopping centers. Today, a new breed of investor has entered the game—homeowners who view their homes more as investment vehicles than as places that offer shelter. These people apply real estate's magic equation—profit = sweat equity × leverage × turnover—to the asset they know best, their personal residences.

In a story in *Money* ("The New House Rules," November 1992), Anthony Cook describes a couple (Sam and Jody Malhas) in the San Diego area who bought and sold four personal residences between 1986 and 1990, earning a profit of more than $250,000 in the process. It seems the Malhases enjoyed a combination of skill, hard work, and good fortune by being in a hot market at the right time. Unfortunately, their story has a somewhat sour end. Their fifth rehab involved substantial outlays of both cash and sweat equity, and by the time it finally was sold, they had lost all the previous profits plus $500,000 in home equity.

The Malthases' story typifies the opportunities and risks in "flipping" your personal residence. If housing prices are rising fairly rapidly—say, 10% a year or better—frequent turnover allows you to use built-up equity to support a larger borrowing base. So, you keep trading up, perhaps eventually winding up in a house you can't afford to live in, in terms of meeting mortgage payments and other cash outlays. A downturn in the market ends the spiral and possibly puts you in bankruptcy court.

Is it worth it? Only you can answer that question. If you like remodeling work and can find reliable contractors for the jobs you can't handle, don't mind frequent negotiations with lenders to arrange financing, and can tolerate the drudgery and inconveniences of moving frequently, then go for it. Frankly, there are probably easier ways to make a living or supplement your regular earnings. Moreover, opportunities may be limited in the future. Lenders have become cautious in making loans, and more important, housing prices in most parts of the United States are rising at much lower rates; indeed, in some areas, they are declining. In short, the game seems to be over for now, although it could reopen quickly if inflation heats up.

Residential Properties

Residential rental property: real estate investment that provides housing for others

An investment in a **residential rental property** is one that provides living space to others. A duplex or fourplex, for example, has appealed to many Americans. Some have used such an investment as a starting point from which to build an extensive and profitable portfolio of properties.

Immigrants to the United States often are astounded at the relative ease of becoming a property owner here, since ownership is so difficult in many other countries where land is more scarce and incomes are generally lower.

The fact that residential real estate is relatively easy to own does not mean profiting from its ownership is equally easy. This distinction is often forgotten because of the number of get-rich-quick-in-real-estate hucksters who write books or appear on cable television. Some of their approaches are blatantly erroneous, while others are subtler; all distort the risk and return characteristics of real estate. You should evaluate a real estate investment as you would any other, using realistic assumptions and proper analytical methods that encompass both return and risk.

Evaluating an Investment   An evaluation of a rental property involves the same approach that was used to evaluate the personal residence. However, there are differences in determining the periodic cash flows. To illustrate these differences, we might assume that our hypothetical home buyer, Rita Winfrey, has decided to purchase the property she was considering, but rather than using it as her personal residence, she has decided to make it a rental property. Exhibit 15.10 shows annual cash flow data estimated for the next 10 years. Because of the importance of the decision, Rita has decided to extend the analysis period from 5 years to 10, although she regards a holding period of 6 years to be the most realistic.

Rita believes that she can rent the house for $800 a month, but she is allowing 10% of rentals for vacancies. The operating expenses are the same amounts estimated in Exhibit 15.5, except that she is adding $100 a year for miscellaneous expenses connected with renting: advertising, collecting rents, and so forth. Net rentals minus operating expenses is called net operating income (NOI); as you see, in Rita's case, NOI is $3,540 in the first year and then assumed to grow at a 5% rate each year.

Depreciation and mortgage interest are deducted from NOI to determine taxable income. Depreciation is a non-cash deduction the IRS allows to recover the cost of the property. It can be applied only to the building—not the land on which the building sits—and must be estimated by dividing the building cost by 27.5, which is the current number of years of life the IRS requires you to use. Rita estimates the land's value at $10,000, leaving a value of $60,000 for the building. This gives an annual depreciation amount of $2,181. After deducting this amount and the annual mortgage interest from NOI, Rita determines the property will provide taxable losses in each of the 10 years. Applying her estimated marginal tax rate of 28% to these losses indicates annual reductions in taxes as shown in line 15. Netting these tax reductions against Rita's taxable losses provides after-tax losses (line 16). Annual cash flows, then, are simply after-tax losses minus mortgage principal payments (observe that interest payments are deducted in determining NOI) plus annual depreciation, which was not a cash deduction. Rita's cash flows are negative in all but the last year. This means she must invest the

EXHIBIT 15.10

Cash flows from Rita Winfrey's rental property

						Years					
	1	2	3	4	5	6	7	8	9	10	
1. Rental income	$9,600										
2. Less: allowance for vacancies (10%)	960										
3. Net rentals	$8,640										
4. Less operating expenses:											
5. Utilities	2,400										
6. Insurance	500										
7. Maintenance	600										
8. Property tax	1,500										
9. Miscellaneous	100										
10. Total	5,100										
11. Net operating income	$3,540	$3,717	$3,903	$4,098	$4,303	$4,518	$4,744	$4,981	$5,230	$5,492	
12. Less: depreciation [(70,000 − 10,000)/27.5]	2,181	2,181	2,181	2,181	2,181	2,181	2,181	2,181	2,181	2,181	
13. Mortgage interest	5,683	5,650	5,613	5,573	5,529	5,478	5,425	5,364	5,297	5,224	
14. Taxable income (loss)	($4,324)	($4,114)	($3,891)	($3,656)	($3,407)	($3,141)	($2,862)	($2,564)	($2,248)	($1,913)	
15. Reduction in tax liability (t = .28)	1,211	1,152	1,090	1,024	954	879	801	718	629	536	
16. After-tax income (loss)	($3,113)	($2,962)	($2,802)	($2,632)	($2,453)	($2,261)	($2,061)	($1,846)	($1,618)	($1,378)	
17. Mortgage principal	317	350	387	427	471	522	575	636	703	776	
18. Cash flow = 16 − 17 + 12	($1,249)	($1,131)	($1,008)	($878)	($743)	($602)	($455)	($301)	($140)	$27	
19. Market value (year end)	73,500	77,175	81,034	85,085	89,340	93,807	98,497	103,422	108,593	114,023	
20. Realtor's commission	5,145	5,402	5,672	5,956	6,254	6,566	6,895	7,240	7,602	7,982	
21. Cumulative depreciation	2,181	4,362	6,543	8,724	10,905	13,086	15,267	17,448	19,629	21,810	
22. Taxable gain on sale	536	6,135	11,904	17,853	23,991	30,326	36,869	43,630	50,620	57,851	
23. Tax on gain (t = .28)	150	1,718	3,333	4,999	6,717	8,491	10,323	12,216	14,174	16,198	
24. Cumulative principal payments	317	667	1,054	1,481	1,952	2,474	3,049	3,685	4,388	5,164	
25. Mortgage balance due	56,659	56,309	55,922	55,495	55,024	54,502	53,927	53,291	52,588	51,812	
26. Cash flow on sale	11,546	13,746	16,106	18,635	21,344	24,247	27,352	30,675	34,230	38,031	

amounts shown on line 18 to sustain the investment. (She can withdraw the $27 in year 10.)

Lines 19 through 26 provide data to determine cash flows arising from sale of the property. Taxes on gains are considered because rental property does not enjoy any tax deferral or avoidance. A 5% annual appreciation in market value is assumed in line 19. The final cash flow resulting from sale of the property is shown on line 26.

Single-Point Evaluation   Working with the data in Exhibit 15.10, Rita determines the investment has a return of +5.3% for a six-year holding period. Again, she must consider the after-tax nature of the return. Considering that long-term municipal bonds were also yielding about 7.5% at the time, Rita does not consider the 5.3% attractive, given the possibly greater risk of the property investment and the fact that it would take more of her time to manage. However, she must balance these disadvantages against the advantage that the property might serve as a better hedge against increases in the inflation rate.

Multipoint Evaluation   Because Rita has the data of Exhibit 15.10 on a spreadsheet computer program, she can make different assumptions and easily determine how they will influence cash flows. With new cash flows, she can equally easily determine rates of return. These data are shown in Exhibit 15.11.

Rita first wanted to know how IRR might change if her holding period was shorter or longer than six years. As you see, it declines appreciably to −6.3% if she sells at the end of two years, and it increases to +7.8% if she holds it 10 years. Then, Rita assumed different price appreciation rates—3% and 7%—holding everything else constant. Her return falls to a −1.4% if price appreciates only 3% a year but jumps to +10.8% if growth is 7%. Finally, Rita tested different annual rentals of $8,400 and $10,800; IRR falls to +0.3% in the first case and increases to +10.3% in the second.

These simulations are no substitute for good data or sensible assumptions to begin with, but they do help Rita see what might happen under different circumstances. Rita is still unimpressed with the returns. She thinks that the odds are slim that 7% growth will take place or that she can charge rentals of $10,800 a year; she is discouraged by the fact that return increases only to 10.8% and 10.3%, respectively, even if one or the other does happen.

Tax Limitations   Under the 1986 Tax Reform Act, allowable losses from real estate investing will be limited. If you are active in managing the property (such as Rita would be) and if your income is under $100,000, you will be allowed a maximum loss offset against other income of $25,000. As income exceeds $100,000, a portion of the maximum loss is taken away; specifically, the loss is reduced by 50% of income over $100,000 until the entire $25,000 is eliminated. For example, an income of $130,000 means $15,000 of the maximum deduction is taken away [0.5 × ($130,000 − $100,000)], and only $10,000 can offset other taxable income. This limitation applies to any business you own, not just real estate, and, to repeat, you must be active in the management of the business. Passive investors cannot use losses from any source to offset other taxable income, such as wages, interest, or dividends. However, they can offset losses from one business against profits of others; in effect, they cannot have *net* business losses.

Current Income Versus Price Appreciation   Rental properties are similar to common stock investing in that you can choose between those that provide

Single-point evaluation: estimating one (most likely) rate of return on an investment

Multipoint evaluation: estimating a range of returns arising from changes in assumptions used in the evaluation model

EXHIBIT 15.11
Rita Winfrey's rental
property sensitivity
analysis: Cash flows
and IRRs under
different assumptions

A. Different holding periods: gross rentals and price appreciation held constant.

Year	Holding Periods				
	2 years	4 years	6 years	8 years	10 years
0	$−13,024	$−13,024	$−13,024	$−13,024	$−13,024
1	− 1,249	− 1,249	− 1,249	− 1,249	− 1,249
2	+12,615	− 1,131	− 1,131	− 1,131	− 1,131
3	—	− 1,008	− 1,008	− 1,008	− 1,008
4	—	+17,757	− 878	− 878	− 878
5	—	—	− 743	− 743	− 743
6	—	—	+23,645	− 602	− 602
7	—	—	—	− 455	− 455
8	—	—	—	+30,220	− 301
9	—	—	—	—	− 140
10	—	—	—	—	+38,058
IRR	−6.3%	+2.2%	+5.3%	+6.8%	+7.8%

B. Six-year holding period: different rates of price appreciation and gross rentals.

Year	Annual Price Appreciation		Annual Rentals	
	3%	7%	$8,400	$10,800
0	$−13,024	$−13,024	$−13,024	$−13,024
1	− 1,249	− 1,249	− 2,027	− 472
2	− 1,131	− 1,131	− 1,948	− 315
3	− 1,008	− 1,008	− 1,865	− 150
4	− 878	− 878	− 1,778	+ 22
5	− 743	− 743	− 1,688	+ 202
6	+16,800	+31,174	+22,652	+24,637
IRR	−1.4%	+10.8%	+0.3%	+10.3%

SOURCE: Exhibit 15.10 provides cash flows for Part *A* and the price appreciation columns of Part *B*. Cash flows for the annual rental columns of Part *B* were derived from simulations on Exhibit 15.10.

good current cash flows (but poor price appreciation potential) and others that might appreciate in price (but have relatively poor current cash flows). In short, there are "income" properties and "growth" properties. Under the old tax law, growth properties enjoyed a tax avoidance advantage in the form of long-term capital gains. Although that is no longer true, a growth property—such as the one evaluated above for Rita Winfrey—still provides better tax sheltering through tax deferral. For example, an income property might show smaller taxable losses than those of the growth property. As a result, less tax sheltering takes place each year. When the properties are sold, the growth property will show a larger gain, resulting in more taxes at that time.

However, you have had the use of tax savings earlier with it, so that even if total taxes are the same, you are better off having the savings earlier.

Income properties tend to be found in sections of the community that are not developing or perhaps even declining. Although rentals may not be as high as in the more affluent parts of the community, they may be fairly generous in relation to property prices. Growth properties, on the other hand, often are located in growing sections of town, usually the suburbs. Although price appreciation may be better here, keep in mind that it must be sufficiently high to generate a decent return. The rental property evaluated for Rita Winfrey did not appreciate quickly enough to make the investment worthwhile.

Commercial and Industrial Properties

A **commercial or industrial property** differs from a residential property in that tenants are business firms rather than individuals or families. The properties might also be different, being designed or adapted for commercial or industrial use. Typical examples of such real estate that might be owned by an individual investor include small office buildings and warehouses, small shopping centers, and buildings used by restaurants and other retail or wholesale establishments. Rental periods tend to be longer, and long-term leases are fairly common. You evaluate an investment in such a property no differently than you evaluate a residential property. The objective again is to determine, as completely as possible, the risk and return on the investment.

Because long-term leases are so common with commercial and industrial properties, it is important to examine existing leasehold agreements carefully before purchasing. Specifically, you should understand both your rights and obligations and those of the lessee under the lease agreement. Lessors often are expected to provide services for lessees. In the event these services are not provided or are provided inadequately, lessees may be able to break their leases. Losing tenants could make the investment a disaster because finding others may be exceptionally difficult if the property has specialized uses. A related problem arises when costs of providing services increase rapidly, while rentals are either fixed or rise only moderately. An example can be found in the energy crises in the 1970s. As energy prices soared, many lessors with fixed-lease rentals were caught in a profit bind because their lease agreements required them to provide heat and other utilities to tenants. Ideally, contracts should be written to include escalator clauses or, better yet, to have tenants pay all expenses connected with using the property (except financing costs).

Moreover, with a property of this type, you may have only one, or few, tenants. This is an advantage if tenants are in sound financial shape and willing to pay the leasehold rental. But if they have financial difficulties or are irresponsible in paying rentals, you could easily experience a large negative cash flow that might exhaust your resources and keep you from making time-

Commercial or industrial property: property rented to business firms for commercial uses ly payments on your mortgage. In residential properties, you tend to spread the risk of losing collections among a larger number of tenants.

Considering that many commercial and industrial properties require a fairly large investment and are somewhat specialized in use, they often present a riskier situation than residential properties. The size of the investment means a greater use of leverage and perhaps less property diversification. Specialized use can lead to greater variations in operating income in response to vacancies or changes in costs. These are generalizations; it is possible to find a commercial or industrial property with strong contract protection that makes the investment risk very low. Finally, the same income tax provisions indicated above apply in the case of commercial and industrial properties.

The Vacation Home

Vacation home: property used for both rental and personal-use activities

A **vacation home**—also called a *second home*—is a hybrid of a rental property and a personal residence. Some people buy such homes with the intent of using them part of the year as a vacation place and renting them the rest of the time. Other people purchase them strictly as an investment or strictly as a vacation home. Whatever their intended uses, vacation homes became exceptionally popular investments in the 1970s and 1980s. Areas such as Hilton Head and Kiawah islands along the East Coast, or practically anywhere on Florida's coasts, have seen rapid development of condominium complexes and detached housing projects. Although many of these places have been purchased by permanent residents as first homes, many others represent vacation homes. These same patterns can be found in many other parts of the United States. Practically any part of the country with appealing physical features, such as shorelines, mountains, forests, and favorable climate, attract vacationers and vacation home buyers. Before purchasing a vacation home, buyers need to consider the income tax law.

Income Tax Considerations   The income tax law will influence the investment appeal of a vacation home. Indeed, it may well determine how you use the property. There are three possible situations having to do with how often you use the property.

Situation 1: You rent the property for 14 days or fewer. In this case, the IRS is not concerned with your property as an investment. You need not report any rental income you might earn from renting it 14 or fewer days, but you cannot deduct any expenses other than mortgage interest and property taxes (assuming you file an itemized return).

Situation 2: You use the property for 14 days or fewer (or not more than 10% of the total days it is rented, whichever is greater). Now the property is considered an investment and is treated like any other real estate investment. This means you can deduct *all* business expenses, including depreciation, in determining the rental's profit or loss. However, the same loss limitation rules apply. If you are inactive in managing the property, you cannot deduct losses against other forms of income. If you are active, the maximum loss is $25,000 if your income is less than $100,000. As explained above, you then gradually lose this $25,000 as your income exceeds $100,000.

Situation 3: You use the property 15 days or more (or for more than 10% of the total days it is rented, whichever is greater). Now, the property is a combination of personal residence and investment, and its tax treatment is similar to that of hobbies. This means you must report any net income but cannot deduct any losses, even if you are active in managing the property. The IRS insists that you allocate all expenses on the basis of the property's use as a business and as a personal residence. An example is shown in Exhibit 15.12. Here, the taxpayer used the property 15 days and rented it 30 days, for a total of 45 days. The personal proportion then is one-third (15/45) and the business proportion is two-thirds (30/45). All expenses are allocated on the basis of these proportions. Notice the $200 business loss is not deductible. Moreover, the taxpayer can deduct only $900 of property taxes and mortgage interest, which is the personal allocation.

Notice in particular how much tax difference one day can make. Had the taxpayer stayed one day less, she would have been in situation 2 and total deductions would have been $1,800 (the total net loss), instead of $900! You must become familiar with the tax law before buying a place or deciding how to use it after it has been purchased. Moreover, the law is being challenged in a number of court cases and may change if any of these are successful.

Investment Appeal of Vacation Homes   If the vacation home is used primarily for vacation purposes, it is questionable that it will ever offer a positive rate of return, unless annual price appreciation is dramatic—probably in the range of 15% or more a year. Few properties consistently show increases of this magnitude. Return often is not important because the main reason for owning the property is enjoyment, not profit. Keep in mind that a first home

| | Allocations | | |
	Personal 1/3	Business 2/3	Total
Rentals	$ —	$ 3,000	$ 3,000
Less: taxes and interest	(900)	(1,800)	(2,700)
operating expenses	(400)	(800)	(1,200)
depreciation	(300)	(600)	(900)
Net income (loss)	$(1,600)	$(200)	$(1,800)
Amount deductible for tax purposes	$ 900	$ -0-	$ 900

EXHIBIT 15.12
Allocating expenses of a vacation home for income tax purposes

may be profitable because of the saved rentals, but there are no similar savings here, unless you consider saved vacation expenses.

If the ownership intent is primarily business, then you should evaluate the property as you would any other investment, using the methods detailed previously and being careful again to make realistic assumptions. Despite what a rental agent might tell you, most properties have high vacancy rates. This usually is due to the seasonal nature of vacationing, but it might also reflect a large available supply of rental units. A thorough market research of the area and personal familiarity with it are necessary to do a proper investment evaluation. Also, you must be concerned by the passive-owner aspect of the tax law. If you are inactive in managing the property, which is quite common with vacation homes, no losses will be deductible. This means you must be at least partially active to qualify for tax losses. The extent of this activity is a debatable issue, but it is understood by the IRS as being involved in finding renters, arranging for property upkeep, and performing many other routine chores, either directly or by hiring others. Sham activity, such as "visiting occasionally to make sure everything is OK," is disallowed.

Property Valuation

Regardless of the type of real estate that interests you, a key question to consider as a buyer (or as an eventual seller) is, what is a property worth? It is a difficult question to answer for various reasons. First, each property unit is unique to its owner in that it occupies a particular space unavailable to anyone else. In some instances, this uniqueness of site is the sole source of value, while in others, it amounts to little because equally attractive space is available elsewhere. A property can also be unique in its construction, design, aesthetic appeal, neighborhood effects, or other factors. A second difficulty in evaluating the worth of a property is that it often is accompanied by other conditions, such as availability of owner financing or an assumable mortgage, fully occupied rental units, and a favorable property tax situation. Finally, a property's price may be negotiable, leading to good or bad buys, depending on an owner's disposition to sell. Valuing and then buying a property is quite different from buying 100 shares of IBM stock on the New York Stock Exchange. The valuation isn't necessarily more difficult, but it is different. Three methods are used widely in the process: the cost approach, the comparative sales approach, and the capitalization of income approach.

Cost approach: method of valuing real estate that uses replacement cost adjusted for depreciation

The Cost Approach The **cost approach** bases the value of a property on the cost of its replacement. If you are considering a duplex in a good neighborhood, you might estimate a cost of $200,000 to replace the unit. Adding, say, $50,000 for the value of the land, you estimate the property value at $250,000. If the unit is relatively new, this approach might work well; it is quite unrealistic for older properties. In some cases, you need to make large allowances for economic depreciation of the unit. For example, a newly constructed unit may have a 50-year life, while the existing one will last only 30 more years. The $200,000 replacement cost is then adjusted downward to $120,000 (30/50 × $200,000).

Although most older properties have less value than new ones, there are numerous exceptions arising from uniqueness. An existing unit may have a desirable site that allows its owner to charge rentals above competitive rates. This situation makes the older property worth more than a similar new one. Although it is a starting point, replacement cost seldom is the final estimate of value.

The Comparative Sales Approach   The **comparative sales approach** determines a property's value by examining recent sales of similarly situated properties. This method is particularly important in owner-occupied residential property valuations because there are no cash flows or other profit indicators on which to determine value. Anyone who has bought or sold a home appreciates the information provided by a comparative sales analysis. If several houses similar to the one you are considering buying recently sold for $170,000, you might regard an asking price of $175,000 as realistic. Naturally, the key to this method's usefulness lies in being reasonably sure the target property is in fact similar to the recent sale units. If they are in mint condition and the target is in need of some repairs, a downward adjustment is warranted, at least by an amount equal to fix-up expenses, including an allowance for your own labor if you intend to provide it.

Comparative sales approach: property valuation method that examines recent sales of similar properties

The Capitalization of Income Approach   The **capitalization of income approach** finds the value of a property by capitalizing a stream of future cash flows. This is the method we have used to evaluate Rita Winfrey's target property in the previous examples. By determining the profitability of an investment *at a given price*, we use the same present value techniques as if we discount cash flows at a required rate of return to *determine an intrinsic value*. You should recognize that this overall approach is similar to the techniques used in determining the intrinsic value of common stock (review Chapter 6). Referring back to Exhibit 15.9, the IRR of 10.24% causes the cash flows in years zero through five to equal $0 exactly. If we discounted the cash flows at a lower rate—say, 8%—there would be positive net present value, indicating the purchase is attractive. Contrarily, discounting at a higher rate—say, 12%—would lead to a negative net present value and an unattractive investment.

Capitalization of income approach: property valuation method that capitalizes a property's future cash flows

Although the discounting techniques apply to all property valuations with cash flows, simplified approaches often are used. One such method involves capitalizing NOI by some appropriate rate (r). The formula for this so-called **direct capitalization approach** is:

Direct capitalization approach: simplified income-capitalization method based on a property's net operating income

$$\text{value} = \text{NOI}/r$$

The approach essentially assumes NOI is a correct profit measurement and that it will continue forever (a perpetuity). Each assumption may be inappropriate in many situations. Moreover, the technique fails to address changes in NOI over time. Surely, a property with rising annual NOIs is worth more than one with static NOIs. A parallel example is the difference in valuing a common stock as opposed to a preferred stock.

The method is used widely, and we should illustrate it. To do so, let us return to the example in which Rita Winfrey is considering renting the house. Exhibit 15.10 shows NOI (line 11) in each of 10 years. Working with the midpoint, assumed to be between years 5 and 6, NOI is estimated at $4,411 [($4,303 + $4,518)/2]. Assuming an appropriate capitalization rate is 8%, the property's value is $55,138 ($4,411/0.08). This amount is considerably below the asking price of $70,000, indicating it is excessive.

Risk Perspectives in Real Estate

To some people who have bought and sold homes over the years, almost always at substantial profits, the notion of risk in real estate seems remote. But it's there and it's a factor to reckon with if you plan on being a big-time real estate investor. Below are a few perspectives worth considering.

Is Real Estate Less Risky Than Stocks?   Stacked up against stocks, real estate returns always appear far stabler. Some researchers argue that the way values are measured creates the difference. Stock values reflect market-driven prices, while real estate values often are based on appraisals, which are stabler. One study showed that if you substitute appraisal values for stocks (based on earnings capitalization approaches), their risk declines significantly and is about the same as that of real estate.

What Role Does Leverage Play?   Most real estate investments are highly leveraged. If risk is measured by variations in appraisal value, the actual return volatility is understated because leverage magnifies both positive and negative returns. True, leverage is ignored also in measuring risk for financial assets, but they usually involve considerably less leverage than does real estate.

Consider Portfolio Effects   Some important portfolio effects apply to real estate investment. For example, diversifying across property types—apartment units, industrial facilities, office buildings, retail outlets, and others—tends to reduce overall risk while not sacrificing return. Similar advantages are obtained by diversifying geographically, although not by following the traditional geographical divisions. The new perspective on geographical diversification focuses on economic locations—for example, oil-sensitive regions or coastal regions. Although few individual investors have the means to achieve such extensive diversification, institutional investors often have them.

Moreover, the portfolio approach should be considered by people in selecting real estate pooling arrangements, such as real estate investment trusts and limited partnerships.

Consider Market Inefficiencies Real estate often is viewed as a classic example of an inefficient market. Because property units differ so much in quality, location, financing terms, and other ways, buyers and sellers find it difficult to measure economic value. Enter the opportunity for an ambitious, hard-working person to exploit these market frictions and make a bundle. That's the good side of inefficiencies; the bad side—the risk side—is that you might be the victim and not the victor. Inefficiencies create risk.

Holding Costs Can Create Losses Although many people have never sold a home at a loss, that doesn't necessarily mean all their sales have been profitable. In weak markets, owners hold on to their properties rather than lower prices for quicker sales. But holding is expensive. If an appropriate opportunity interest rate is considered, a so-called profitable sale may actually have been a loss. Suppose you hold a $200,000 home a year longer than you anticipated. At 8%, you can knock $16,000 off of the profit as a holding cost. This cost might be reduced if you continued living in the house for the year.

FINANCING PROPERTY INVESTMENT

Financing a property investment often involves as much time and effort as finding one. The number of financing options available today is considerably greater than in the past, and you should be familiar with the more common forms to decide what is best for your particular situation. The basic forms of mortgages are covered in the following sections, and Exhibit 15.13 provides an overview of the wide array of financing forms that are in frequent use.

Fixed-Rate Mortgage

A **fixed-rate mortgage** has, as its name indicates, a fixed rate of interest over the loan's maturity. This is probably still the most popular loan from the investors' point of view because a known rate of interest is locked in for the length of the loan. Not only does this make cash flow budgeting simpler, but it represents an opportunity to profit from the investment if inflation accelerates after the loan is made. Many real estate buyers in the past negotiated low-interest loans with fixed payments, enabling them to acquire properties that subsequently increased considerably in value through inflation. Their gains were the lenders' losses, and these losses became so huge that they threatened the entire savings and loan industry in the 1980s. As a result, many institutions refused to make fixed-rate loans or would make them only at high rates of interest. The decline in interest rates in the mid-1980s

Fixed-rate mortgage: mortgage loan with a fixed rate of interest

EXHIBIT 15.13

Overview of mortgage financing options

Type	Description	Considerations
Fixed-rate mortgage	Fixed interest rate, usually long-term; equal monthly payments of principal and interest until debt is paid in full.	Offers stability and long-term tax advantages; limited availability. Interest rates may be higher than other types of financing. New fixed-rate mortgages are rarely assumable.
Flexible-rate mortgage	Interest rate changes are based on a financial index, resulting in possible changes in your monthly payments, loan term, and/or principal. Some plans have rate or payment caps.	Readily available. Starting interest rate is slightly below market, but payments can increase sharply and frequently if index increases. Payment caps prevent wide fluctuations in payments but may cause negative amortization. Rate caps, while rare, limit amount total debt can expand.
Renegotiable-rate mortgage (rollover)	Interest rate and monthly payments are constant for several years; changes possible thereafter. Long-term mortgage.	Less frequent changes in interest rate offer some stability.
Balloon mortgage	Monthly payments based on fixed interest rate; usually short-term; payments may cover interest only with principal due in full at term end.	Offers low monthly payments but possibly no equity until loan is fully paid. When due, loan must be paid off or refinanced. Refinancing poses high risk if rates climb.
Graduated-payment mortgage	Lower monthly payments rise gradually (usually over 5 to 10 years) and then level off for duration of term. With flexible interest rate, additional payment changes possible if index changes.	Easier to qualify for. Buyer's income must be able to keep pace with scheduled payment increases. With a flexible rate, payment increases beyond the graduated payments can result in additional negative amortization.
Shared-appreciation mortgage	Below-market interest rate and lower monthly payments, in exchange for a share of profits when property is sold or on a specified date. Many variations.	If home appreciates greatly, total cost of loan jumps. If home fails to appreciate, projected increase in value may still be due, requiring refinancing possibly at higher rates.
Assumable mortgage	Buyer takes over seller's original, below-market rate mortgage.	Lowers monthly payments. May be prohibited if "due on sale" clause is in original mortgage. Not permitted on most new fixed-rate mortgages.
Seller take-back	Seller provides all or part of financing with a first or second mortgage.	May offer a below-market interest rate; may have a balloon payment requiring full payment in a few years or refinancing at market rates, which could sharply increase debt.

EXHIBIT 15.13

Continued

Type	Description	Considerations
Wraparound	Seller keeps original low rate mortgage. Buyer makes payments to seller who forwards a portion to the lender holding original mortgage. Offers lower effective interest rate on total transaction.	Lender may call in old mortgage and require higher rate. If buyer defaults, seller must take legal action to collect debt.
Growing-equity mortgage (rapid-payoff mortgage)	Fixed interest rate but monthly payments may vary according to agreed-on schedule or index.	Permits rapid payoff of debt because payment increases reduce principal. Buyer's income must be able to keep up with payment increases.
Land contract	Seller retains original mortgage. No transfer of title until loan is fully paid. Equal monthly payments based on below-market interest rate with unpaid principal due at loan end.	May offer no equity until loan is fully paid. Buyer has few protections if conflict arises during loan.
Buy-down	Developer (or third party) provides an interest subsidy, which lowers monthly payments during the first few years of the loan. Can have fixed or flexible interest rate.	Offers a break from higher payments during early years. Enables buyer with lower income to qualify. With flexible-rate mortgage, payments may jump substantially at end of subsidy. Developer may increase selling price.
Rent with option	Renter pays "option fee" for right to purchase property at specified time and agreed-on price. Rent may or may not be applied to sales price.	Enables renter to buy time to obtain down payment and decide whether to purchase. Locks in price during inflationary times. Failure to take option means loss of option fee and rental payments.
Reverse-annuity mortgage (equity conversion)	Borrower owns mortgage-free property and needs income. Lender makes monthly payments to borrower, using property as collateral.	Can provide homeowners with needed cash. At end of term, borrower must have money available to avoid selling property or refinancing.
Zero-rate and low-rate mortgage	Appears to be completely or almost interest-free. Large down payment and one-time finance charge, then loan is repaid in fixed monthly payments over short term.	Permits quick ownership. May not lower total cost (because of possibly increased sales price). Doesn't offer long-term tax deductions.

SOURCE: *The Mortgage Money Guide*, The Federal Trade Commission.

BOX 15.2   GETTING AN INVESTMENT EDGE

Don't Forget: You Also Invest in the Mortgage

To many real estate investors, financing an investment often is as difficult as finding the right property to buy. In today's credit environment, the choices are many, and making wrong ones can erode the profit you hope to make. Here are some of the more important factors to consider.

FIXED-RATE VERSUS ADJUSTABLE-RATE LOAN

Most people opt for a fixed-rate loan, but that isn't always the correct choice. A fixed-rate loan carries a higher interest rate, perhaps as much as two to three percentage points higher. By selecting the fixed-rate, you implicitly are betting that interest rates will rise in the future. Or you reason that even if they decline, you can always refinance the fixed-rate loan at a lower rate. Either way, you might be wrong: interest rates don't always go up and refinancing can be expensive.

Focus on the most important factor in the decision—how long you believe you will own the property. If there is a reasonable chance you will own it less than four years, an adjustable-rate loan is likely to be more attractive. If you hold it longer than six years, the fixed-rate loan makes more sense; you might pay more interest, but the extra outlay is worth it as a hedge against rising interest rates.

Because loans differ so much, generalizations are difficult. The best way to make the decision is to project annual interest and other costs each year for different holding lengths for each loan alternative. Then assume different interest-rate changes and see what happens. Does this take time and effort? Yes. Is there an easier way to do it? No.

---

brought renewed activity in fixed-rate lending, although variable-rate loans are still used frequently. There are now two types of fixed-rate loans: those with fixed payments and those with increasing payments.

Fixed Rate–Fixed Payment Loans

Conventional mortgage: mortgage loan with a fixed interest rate and fixed monthly payments

The so-called **conventional mortgage** has a fixed rate and fixed payments. Typically, it is not insured by the Federal Housing Administration (FHA) or Veterans Administration (VA) (both are explained later), and the borrower usually has a down payment of at least 20% of the property's appraised value. We have used a 10%, 30-year mortgage in our previous examples for Rita Winfrey. You should recall this loan had a monthly payment of $500, and you also might remember that Rita borrowed $56,976. You might not realize, though, that over 30 years, Rita will repay $180,000 (360 × $500); because

ONE-YEAR VERSUS THREE-YEAR ADJUSTMENT PERIODS

The same logic and analysis apply here as in deciding between a fixed-rate and adjustable-rate loan. Simply add another column to your worksheet, reflecting another adjustable-rate loan with a different adjustment period.

15-YEAR VERSUS 30-YEAR MORTGAGE

Many buyers seeking a fixed-rate loan have recently chosen a 15-year maturity rather than the traditionally sought longer ones of 25 or 30 years. The lure is a slightly lower rate and considerably less interest over the loan's life. For example, interest on a 7.5%, 15-year loan for $100,000 amounts to $66,862 over the loan life. Although that seems a lot, consider that a 7.5%, 30-year loan for the same amount would total $101,285 in interest ($34,423 more) over 15 years and *still* leave you with an unpaid principal of $75,427.

The key to choosing one over the other rests solely on your marginal tax rate and what you might earn on the monthly payment savings with the 30-year loan. For example, the monthly payment with the 15-year loan is $927; with the 30-year loan, it is $699 ($228 less). Assuming you have a 28% marginal tax rate, if you can invest the monthly savings to earn more than 5.4% (annual rate), you would be better off with the 30-year loan. The 5.4% rate represents the after-tax cost [7.5% × (1.0 − 0.28)] of the mortgage; you also can view it as the opportunity earning rate of investing in the mortgage, which is what you do by choosing a 15-year maturity. So, if you can earn more than 5.4% (after taxes) in other 15-year investments, choose them rather than the shorter mortgage.

she borrowed $56,976, the difference—$123,024—represents total interest over the life of the loan. If the property increases 5% in value each year for the next 30 years, it eventually will be worth $302,535 [$70,000 × $(1.05)^{30}$]. As you see, the numbers become large when compounding over a long period. They are more dramatically appealing than useful in decision making. As we saw, Rita did a return analysis that favored buying. This perspective is more appropriate than focusing on limited information, such as how much interest you pay and what the house is worth at some point in the future.

Growing-Equity Mortgage In response to borrowers' wishes for a fixed interest rate but in an effort to cope with inflation uncertainty, some lenders developed what is known as the **growing-equity mortgage.** This loan fixes the interest rate but requires the borrower to pay off the loan in a much shorter period of time. For example, you might negotiate a 15-year, 10% mortgage.

Growing-equity mortgage: mortgage loan with a fixed interest rate but accelerating loan payments

Rather than paying a fixed monthly amount, your payments will be smaller at the beginning of the loan and gradually increase each year until they are much higher at the end. You might start at $500 a month if you borrowed $56,976, but in the 15th year, the monthly payment might be twice that amount.

You pay considerably less total interest with this type of loan, but that does not necessarily make it a better loan. You must consider the income tax impact and the opportunity investment rates available during the maturity of each loan. In effect, your monthly payments are less for the first 15 years with the fixed-payment loan and higher in the last 15 years (because the growing equity loan is then paid off). After considering these payment differentials and related tax effects, the important final question is, what rates can these differential amounts earn? It is a complex problem, and you might ask the lending institution to help you evaluate it. At the very least, they should provide you with monthly payment information—principal and interest—for both types of mortgages. With these data, you then can apply an IRR or Net Present Value (NPV) analysis, after adjusting for the tax deductibility of interest.

Adjustable-Rate Mortgage

Adjustable-rate mortgage: mortgage loan with an interest rate (and monthly payments) indexed to market interest rates

Although the growing-equity mortgage is one response to the inflation problem, the more popular response has been the **adjustable-rate mortgage (ARM).** This loan does not have a fixed interest rate; instead, the rate varies in response to changes in market rates of interest. This type of loan removes interest-rate risk from the lender and transfers it to the borrower. This is a decided disadvantage to you as an investor; however, there is a consolation in that the loan's initial interest rate is lower than the rate on a fixed-rate loan. For example, the latter might have a 10% rate, while the former is only 8.5%. Your monthly payments will vary over the life of the loan if interest rates vary. Investors with high-interest ARMs were pleasantly surprised by the sharp decreases in monthly payments when interest rates fell in the mid-1980s. Before negotiating an adjustable-rate loan, you should consider the following items.

The Frequency of the Adjustment   Some loans adjust annually, while others adjust less frequently (usually every three years). The more frequently an adjustment takes place, the more variable your monthly payments will be—for better or worse. This increased variability means greater risk, but it also means you get a lower rate. For example, an annually adjusting loan might be offered at 8.5%, while a loan that adjusts every three years might call for a 9.0% rate. Choosing between the two requires a guess as to the future direction of interest rates.

Rate Cap or Minimum   Most ARMs have a rate maximum, or cap. This means the interest rate on the loan cannot exceed this figure. A cap can apply to an adjusting period—one or three years—and/or to the life of the loan. For example, a three-year ARM may have a rate cap of, say, three percentage points each adjustment period and a maximum rate of 16% over the life of the loan. So, if you took out a loan with an initial rate of 9%, its maximum value three years later would be 12%, and the most you would ever pay is 16%. Many ARMs also have minimums that favor lenders. For example, the rate may not decrease more than three percentage points in an adjustment period or ever go lower than, say, 6%.

What Is the Adjustment Index?   ARMs use various interest-rate indexes on which to make loan interest adjustments. These vary from the three-month Treasury bill rate to the National Average Federal Home Loan Bank (FHLB) Mortgage Contract Rate. The key question is, which are the more volatile rates? The Treasury bill rate has been the most volatile in the immediate past (past 10 years), while the FHLB rate has been the least volatile. However, these years have seen extraordinarily volatile short-term rates, and whether this pattern will continue is unclear. Probably the best advice is to avoid any index based on the so-called cost of funds to the institution. Not only might this figure be difficult to measure, but it also might be easy for the institution to manipulate. It is better to stick with a nationally derived index.

Sources of Mortgage Loans

Mortgage loans are provided by a variety of lending institutions. Savings and loans do the most mortgage business, although commercial banks are rapidly increasing their share of the market. Mortgage companies also are active in the business. Although most lending is still done on a local level, some observers believe that in the future, you might negotiate a mortgage with many possible lenders located anywhere in the United States. This will be accomplished through computer networks integrating lenders with real estate salespeople. In other words, the person who helps you buy a property might also arrange for its financing under the most favorable terms to you. The lender might be your neighborhood bank, or it might be a mortgage company located 3,000 miles away.

One feature that increases the liquidity of a mortgage loan is insurance provided by the FHA or the VA. Each establishes standards as to borrowers' suitability, maximum loan amounts, and down payments. If these standards are met, the agency insures the loan, which means it will compensate the lender in the event the borrower does not meet his obligations. This encourages lenders who might otherwise not be willing to make loans.

An advantage to the investor of an **FHA or VA loan** is a much smaller down payment, which can be as low as 5% of the property's purchase price.

FHA or VA loan: mortgage loan supported by the Federal Housing Administration or Veterans Administration

Another advantage is these loans are assumable by third parties. This means if you plan to sell your property, you can pass the mortgage to the buyer. Conventional loans have due-on-sale clauses that prevent such transfers. An FHA or VA loan with a low fixed rate could be a valuable asset in selling your home if interest rates rise above the contract rate. A disadvantage to the FHA loan is that 0.5% interest is added to the loan rate. (The VA loan does not add the differential; moreover, it attempts to establish a maximum rate on the loan for the veteran's benefit.)

GOLD AND OTHER TANGIBLES

Tangible: physical item that can be bought or sold in some market

To begin, let us define a **tangible** as any physical item that can be bought or sold in some market. This is a broad definition that allows us to consider virtually any item. The investment quality of the tangible will depend heavily on how well its market functions. If you own gold in virtually any form, you can find a well-developed market for your sales, guaranteeing you a fair price. On the other hand, if your tangible normally trades through flea markets and garage sales, you may have a problem if you should want to sell. Along with marketability, you need to consider the intrinsic quality of a piece. You may own a coin that has a catalog price of $100, but this price usually presumes the coin is in mint condition. If yours is not, its price will be far less than $100.

There are advantages and disadvantages in investing in tangibles. The most important ones are explained in the following sections.

Tangibles' Advantages

To some, the primary appeal of a tangible is its beauty; any investment characteristics are secondary. In contrast, others have no concern for aesthetic attributes. Indeed, these often are seen as unnecessary complications. Gold held in a distant vault will do just fine for these investors, while the collector wants her gold in the form of jewelry to be worn and enjoyed. Exhibit 15.14 highlights the investment and use characteristics of tangibles.

Use Characteristics   A tangible can be used in a number of ways. Broadly, we can say you enjoy the item for its own sake; or, you enjoy it because it

EXHIBIT 15.14
Tangibles' characteristics

Use Characteristics	Investment Characteristics
Direct enjoyment	Hedge against political risks
A display of wealth	Hedge against inflation risk
Item is needed anyway	Portfolio diversification

reflects your wealth to society; or, you must buy a noncollectible item to serve your needs anyway.

Direct Enjoyment   As mentioned above, many investors enjoy the items they collect. Indeed, perhaps one of life's true pleasures is enjoying the artistic expressions of human endeavor. Also, many people enjoy collections as hobbies. Coin and stamp collecting, for example, have challenged people for years, and other collections have become popular.

A Display of Wealth   Because tangibles can be seen, they serve as an excellent vehicle for displaying wealth. Our society frowns on crass displays of wealth: you aren't likely to take out a newspaper ad announcing when you make your first million, but you might buy a Picasso oil painting. Each approach tells the world you have made it, but the latter also shows you are a connoisseur of fine art. It is socially acceptable, while the ad is in terrible taste. This display function should not be taken lightly. If we look closely, we are likely to find that most of us consider it in much of what we buy—our cars, for example. From an investment perspective, this behavioral pattern supports a market demand for certain tangibles.

The Item Is Needed Anyway   Apart from enjoyment or wealth display, you might consider investing in a tangible if a similar item must be purchased to meet some need. For example, if you are planning an engagement and future marriage, you will probably buy an engagement ring. Now, there are many from which to choose, and rather than just buy a ring, you might devote extra time and spend a bit more to invest in a stone. The same approach can be followed when you set up housekeeping and start buying furniture. A Shaker bench or chair purchased 30 years ago might not have cost more than a laminated plastic alternative. Today, its value has increased at least 10-fold, while the laminated plastic piece is probably in the community dump.

Investment Characteristics   Most investors are interested in tangibles because of the potential returns they offer. However, there are other factors to consider. Because the value of many intangibles is independent of political boundaries, they serve as hedges against political risks. And because tangibles' prices fluctuate, they offer potential investment advantages as inflation hedges or as components to a portfolio.

Tangibles' Returns   Compared with intangibles, the returns on some tangibles have been fairly good, as we will indicate in the following sections. Bear in mind, though, that measuring a tangible's return within the context of an index is considerably more difficult than measuring one for an intangible. The problem is that prices paid for items at auction do not necessarily reflect the value of supposedly similar items not auctioned. For example, if a Van Gogh painting sells for $50 million (as one did), does that mean every Van Gogh painting is worth $50 million? Critics point out that often the most valuable pieces go to auction, while those less valuable are held. So, an upward bias in the index is created. Although the index is far from perfect, it does provide some indication of tangibles' performances, and even allowing for bias, the returns have been rather good.

Hedge Against Political Risks As citizens of the United States, many of us take for granted the reasonable stability of our financial system and the intangible assets it creates. People in quite a few other countries face different situations. To them, holding your wealth in paper assets is foolish because a weak government might allow their value to collapse. Along with real estate, tangibles represent a more sensible wealth-holding alternative. The price of gold, for example, often is thought to reflect worldwide peace or hostility, with the former leading to lower prices and the latter leading to higher.

Hedge Against Inflation Risk Because inflation is a form of political instability, intangibles' prices change in step with inflation rates. However, the positive correlation between inflation and tangibles' returns holds only over relatively long periods of time. Over short intervals, the correlation can be weak or even negative. For example, gold's price fell for most of the period 1983–92; although inflation during this period was modest, it was, nevertheless, positive.

Portfolio Diversification Tangibles can be used to achieve more efficient portfolio diversification than is possible by holding only intangibles. This is so because tangibles' returns often are poorly positively correlated—and sometimes negatively correlated—with intangibles' returns, particularly common stock returns. You should recall from Chapter 4 that such correlations, rather than strong positive correlations, are helpful in reducing risk without giving up return.

Exhibit 15.15 indicates correlations among five asset groups. As you see, the tangibles—paintings, gold, and housing—are moderately positively correlated with one another, with correlations ranging from +0.666 (paintings and gold) to +0.477 (gold and housing) to +0.321 (paintings and housing).

EXHIBIT 15.15
Asset return correlations

	Paintings	Gold	Housing	Stocks	AAA Bonds
Paintings	1.000				
Gold	0.666	1.000			
Housing	0.321	0.477	1.000		
Stocks	0.003	−0.213	0.204	1.000	
AAA Bonds	0.336	0.243	0.307	−0.162	1.000

Perfect positive correlation = 1.000
Perfect negative correlation = −1.000
No correlation = 0.000

NOTE: Data apply to the period 1971–84.

SOURCE: Michael F. Bryan, "Beauty and the Bulls: The Investment Characteristics of Paintings," *Federal Reserve Bank of Cleveland, Economic Review,* 1Q 1985, p. 3.

Combining these assets in portfolio would have reduced risk only moderately. However, combining any one with, say, common stocks would have led to a reasonable reduction in risk. This reduction results from the poorer correlations—from +0.204 (with housing) to +0.003 (with paintings) to −0.213 (with gold). An interesting finding in this study is the correlation between stocks and bonds, which is −0.162. This means a portfolio of gold, stocks, and bonds would have been efficient over the period indicated.

Tangibles' Disadvantages

To this point in the discussion, tangibles seem almost too good to be true: high return, low risk (when held in portfolio), and enjoyment in use. Unfortunately, they have disadvantages that detract from their overall appeal.

High Commissions and Holding Costs Depending on the tangible in question, you may pay commissions ranging from 1% to 2% (gold, for example) to as much as 30% (an art object, for example) on its purchase or sale, or both. As you move to the high end, trading tangibles on a frequent basis will enrich only the dealer, even if price appreciation is excellent.

Holding costs with tangibles can also be high. All tangibles must be stored in safe places to prevent theft, and art objects and other collectibles might deteriorate in quality if they are not treated properly. Insurance and other guardian services, such as safe deposit boxes, home alarm systems, and storage companies, also add to costs. With respect to insurance, make sure your homeowner's policy has an endorsement to insure the market value of your items. If it doesn't, you will receive only the fair value to replace a lost item. Your Shaker chair, for example, will be valued at an amount no greater than that of the laminated plastic alternative, rather than at its market value.

A Need for Specialized Knowledge Anyone who has taken a serious attitude toward collecting knows that considerable time, effort, and skill are needed to develop a valuable collection. Serious collectors usually specialize in a narrow area, which they follow and study in depth, and most experts will probably tell you to do likewise. They also suggest that you should not begin collecting with the objective of making a profit; instead, you should concentrate on the aesthetic characteristics of your collectibles and understand them well. Don't buy something because you heard it is in fashion; rather, buy it because, in your experienced opinion, it is a good piece of work. If you lack an experienced opinion, you must rely on someone who has one. Expert opinion, though, is expensive, which also erodes any price appreciation.

Extremely Volatile Prices Most tangibles' prices are volatile. Gold, for example, went from $36 an ounce in 1970 to almost $900 an ounce in 1980 and down to $360 an ounce by mid-1990. A one-carat, D-flawless diamond could have been purchased for $4,300 in 1974; six years later it was worth

$62,000, and one year after that it was down to $25,000. Such price volatility should serve as a warning not to hold an excessive proportion of your portfolio in tangibles.

No Current Return   Your only return from a tangible is price appreciation. Investing in tangibles means you must forgo dividends, interest, or other regular cash flows that you could receive on alternative investments. In a sense, a tangible is similar to the common stock of an emerging growth company. It, too, usually pays no dividend, and its future price appreciation is uncertain. Some tangibles investors might disagree with this analogy. In their view, certain tangibles are far less risky than most growth stocks; these investors would probably prefer to compare a tangible to a zero coupon bond, with its price appreciation only a little less certain.

Poor Resale Markets   We mentioned earlier that the investment quality of a tangible depends heavily on the existence of an efficient resale market. Efficient means there is a reasonable number of buyers so that price cannot be dictated by anyone. It also means trading takes place at reasonable cost; that is, commissions or other charges do not absorb a large portion of the item's resale value. Many tangibles fail to meet one or both of these criteria. Indeed, unless you limit your tangible investing to gold or other precious metals, you are likely to encounter difficulties. There are varying degrees of difficulty, depending on the popularity of the tangible. Postage stamp and coin collecting are popular hobbies, which means there is an active resale market that is reasonably efficient. On the other hand, if your collectibles are less popular, you may be able to sell only at an annual show (usually held in a distant city) or through limited mail order operations in which prices are set by buyers.

Rampant Fraud   A concern faced by all tangibles investors is the rampant fraud that exists in these markets. Many investors of both moderate and substantial means have been swindled in one way or another by unscrupulous operators. Keep in mind that virtually no regulation exists (other than the law in general) as it does with stocks, bonds, and many other intangibles. Anyone can call himself an expert and set up shop as a coin dealer, an art importer, an antique auction house, or anything else. Moreover, placing a value on a collectible often is a highly subjective judgment, and dealers might overgrade items they sell while undergrading purchases. If you are not an expert in your collectibles area, then the best advice is to find one who is reputable and follow her advice to the letter.

　　You should also be careful about participating in gold and other precious metal ownership plans. Several of these have gone into bankruptcy, leaving investors with virtually worthless certificates to claim gold coins or gold bullion that didn't exist. If you invest in any arrangement that you do not first check thoroughly, including asking for references and even seeking legal advice, you may be asking for trouble.

Investing in Gold

Gold is called the perfect tangible. You can own it in many ways, and over a long period, its price has kept pace with inflation. Some years ago, a financial institution dealing in gold ran a clever advertisement that stated: "Two hundred years ago a good suit of clothing cost 1 ounce of gold—it still does today." This ad appeared when inflation was accelerating and certainly drove home the inflation-protection quality of gold. Salomon Brothers routinely reports returns on both tangibles and intangibles. In the July 5 issue of *Forbes*, an article written by R. S. Salomon ("The Big Picture") indicates the 20-year return on gold (1973–93) was 6.9%. This was a bit higher than the inflation rate of 6.1% for the period but far behind the 12.2% return on common stocks.

  Gold has other advantages. Because it is so valuable, a fairly large investment can be held in a small physical quantity. This facilitates storage and protection; for example, most investors can easily store their gold coins in a bank safe deposit box. Gold also can be purchased in standardized units, making it possible to invest precisely the amount you want. Many other tangibles are not so easily divisible—you either buy a whole painting or none. True, you can buy a lesser work if your funds are limited, but that may be difficult. Also, collecting gold requires no particular skill or effort, unless you choose gold jewelry or other gold artifacts. Finally, gold is exceptionally easy to buy and sell, and commissions are relatively inexpensive. Before you buy gold, though, you should understand its risks and the different forms of ownership.

Gold's Price Volatility Exhibit 15.16 indicates the absolute price volatility (the standard deviation) of gold and selected other household assets, along with the rate of return for each during the period indicated. Using the coefficient of variation (which compares risk with return) to measure risk in a relative sense shows that gold was less risky than common stocks and Chinese

Gold: tangible easiest to own or trade

	(1) Annual Rate of Return	(2) Standard Deviation of Returns	(3) Coefficient of Variation (2) ÷ (1)
Gold	16.2%	31.4%	1.94
Chinese ceramics	14.3	37.7	2.64
Paintings index	10.7	8.2	0.77
Stocks	8.4	19.4	2.31
Housing	6.4	4.3	0.67
AAA bonds	6.1	2.5	0.41

EXHIBIT 15.16
Return and risk measurements on selected household assets

NOTE: Data apply to the period 1970–84.

SOURCE: Michael F. Bryan, "Beauty and the Bulls: The Investment Characteristics of Paintings," The Federal Reserve Bank of Cleveland, *Economic Review* 1Q 1985, p. 5.

ceramics (a popular collectible). However, it was considerably riskier than housing, paintings, and corporate bonds.

Volatility by itself is not necessarily undesirable. As we discussed earlier in this chapter, the important issue is whether gold's price volatility adds to or reduces an investor's overall portfolio volatility. The conclusion you can draw from the study cited in Exhibits 15.15 and 15.16 is that it reduces volatility significantly if it is held in portfolio with common stocks and bonds.

Ways to Own Gold   Gold can be owned in a number of ways. Before choosing one, you should understand the advantages and disadvantages of each. If one of your reasons for owning gold is to enjoy its beauty, then some ownership methods will not be suitable because they involve holding your gold at a financial institution or owning claims to gold, rather than gold itself.

Gold coins: coins minted by various governments

Gold Coins   A number of countries, including Canada, Mexico, the United States, and South Africa, mint **gold coins.** By far the most plentiful and popular is the South African Krugerrand, although the Canadian Maple Leaf is rapidly gaining in popularity because of the unsettled racial situation in South Africa. The most common size is one ounce, but smaller sizes are available. Coins can be purchased through many stockbrokers, coin dealers, and some banks.

Owning gold in coin form has many advantages. The coins are a pleasure to view, conveniently small, and easily transferred to someone else if you should care to sell them. Because the amount of gold embodied in them is known, you don't need to have them assayed on transfer. Coins also have disadvantages. First, most states impose a sales tax on their purchase. Second, coins typically sell at premiums above their gold content. For example, if gold is quoted at $350 an ounce, you might pay $360 for a one-ounce coin. Third, you sell coins at a bid price less than the ask price you pay to buy them: if you sold the coin above, you might get only $356. (Also, prices vary among dealers, making it necessary to shop around for the best deal.) Finally, you will incur some expenses to safeguard your holdings.

Gold bullion: bars of gold assayed as to weight and purity

Bullion and Certificates   **Gold bullion** comes in the form of bars, with the quantity of gold indicated by an assay report. You can buy a bar with as little as one ounce of gold, although most bars contain larger quantities. Brokers, banks, and gold dealers handle bullion and also offer certificate programs. A bar of gold has less aesthetic appeal than a coin, and when you consider both commissions and disposal costs (assaying and others), there is no advantage in owning bullion as opposed to coins, unless you are dealing in a large quantity.

Gold ownership certificate: evidence of ownership of gold stored in a financial institution's vault

Rather than owning bullion directly, you can participate in an ownership program. In this case, you buy gold and receive a **gold ownership certificate.** The gold is stored in a repository somewhere else, usually in a bank vault located in a state without a sales tax—Delaware, for example. You can make purchases over the phone, charging them to your credit card; however, you must present the certificate when you sell.

Certificate programs also have advantages and disadvantages. In most cases, you will buy gold at close to its market price—rather than paying a premium—and you eliminate the storage problem. However, you will pay a commission to buy the gold and a service fee for storage each year. Commissions are usually 3% (or less) of the amount purchased, and annual fees are typically one-quarter of one percent of cost, up to a maximum, such as $60 or $70.

Unquestionably, your chief concern with a certificate program is the integrity of the repository institution. As mentioned above, some nonbank firms have gone bankrupt, forcing huge losses on certificate holders. If you are a conservative person, you will sleep better if you choose coins or bullion bars over certificates.

Gold Jewelry and Works of Art   Gold is a principal element in many pieces of jewelry and works of art. Owning any of these items, then, is also an ownership of gold. However, all things considered, it is not an ideal way to own gold unless you are also enthusiastic about the creation. This is because the gold component of most pieces is quite small; in effect, you usually pay far more for the creative work than you do for the gold. There is quite a bit of bogus advertising about gold jewelry. The expression "solid gold," for example, is virtually meaningless as a description of gold content; all it means is the piece is not hollow. Deal with a reputable jeweler and look for carat ratings: 18 carats indicates 75% gold, and 14 carats means 58% gold. So, if an 18-carat ring weighs one-half ounce and costs $500, you should see that you are buying 0.375 (0.5 × 0.75) of an ounce of gold; if the current price of gold is $380 an ounce, your ring has $142.50 (0.375 × $380) worth of gold in it. You then judge if the creative component is worth $357.50 ($500 − $142.50).

Gold Mining Stocks   An indirect ownership of gold is to purchase common stocks of gold mining companies, such as Campbell Red Lake, Newmont, and Giant Yellowknife. Studies have shown a high degree of correlation between changes in the price of gold and changes in the prices of mining company stocks. They also indicate that stock prices typically are more volatile; that is, if gold's price changes, say, 10%, mining stocks' prices might change 20%. This is desirable when prices increase but not so welcome when they decline. (For more detail, see Box 15.3.)

An advantage of this play on gold is that you probably will earn some dividends on the stocks, the amount depending on the particular companies selected. The main disadvantage is the risk of investing in a company that might not do well, even if gold's price does increase. To overcome this obstacle, you should seek a diversified portfolio of gold mining stocks. Many investors choose mutual funds for this purpose.

Other Tangibles

Investors often consider other tangibles in addition to gold as part of their portfolios. Silver and other precious metals are popular investments and so

BOX 15.3   INVESTMENT INSIGHTS

Gold Versus Gold Stocks

So you're convinced gold is ready to make a move. Fine. Now, how do you play your hunch? There are a number of choices, but an important one is whether you care to invest directly in the metal or indirectly by buying an intangible whose value correlates closely to that of gold. Among the more popular intangibles are the common stocks of gold-mining companies. As the graph below shows, their returns and gold's often move in a locksetp manner. Notice, though, that variations in the stock returns are more pronounced than variations in gold's price. So with the stocks you get a bigger play for your buck. If you guess

correctly, you will magnify your return by buying stocks rather than gold itself, such as gold coins or bullion. If you guess wrong, your losses also will be magnified. An advantage to owning gold-mining stocks is the possibility of earning dividends. Gold itself pays no current return and in fact involves holding costs.

Finally, over the entire period shown in the graph, the average return on gold was around 1%, while the fund's average return was 3%. So you were compensated for taking the greater risks with the funds, although you would have been better off had you invested in risk-free U.S. Treasury bills.

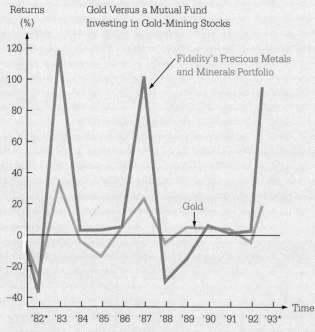

Gold Versus a Mutual Fund Investing in Gold-Mining Stocks

* Partial years

are precious gems and artworks. Also, hobbies and collectibles intrigue many people as much for entertainment as for profit.

Silver   Although gold is clearly the metal of choice to most investors, some are intrigued by other metals, particularly silver and platinum. Investing in silver is at least as risky as investing in gold and frequently more so.

Sometimes **silver** is considered a good substitute tangible for gold. Its price variations over time correlate in a strong, positive manner with those of gold, although silver is believed to be more volatile. When gold peaked at about $900 an ounce in 1980, silver reached its highest-ever price of around $50 an ounce. It subsequently fell to about $5 an ounce and has traded between $5 and $13 since then. The 20-year return on silver from the Salomon article is 2.7%, which is far below gold's return of 6.9%.

Silver: investment tangible sometimes considered a substitute for gold

Silver is in far greater supply than gold and has far more applications because it is used in a number of industrial and commercial processes. Each of these factors explains silver's price volatility. For example, its industrial uses put it in competition with other metals or manufactured items such as plastic. When these items are substituted for silver, its demand falls, leading to lower prices; when silver is substituted for them, the reverse situation takes place.

Silver can be purchased in the same ways as gold. A popular form of silver investment is to hold silver coins. You can buy bags of silver coins through coin dealers. A bag of "junk" silver contains 715 ounces of 90% silver dimes, quarters, or half-dollars minted before 1965. "Clad" silver bags have 295 ounces in 40% silver Kennedy half-dollars minted between 1965 and 1970. A third bag consists of 755 ounces of 1878–1935, 90% silver dollars. You can buy fractional parts of bags and have them stored at a bank. Also, if the bag is unopened, you do not need an assay report if you decide to sell.

Diamonds and Other Precious Gems   **Diamonds** are by far the most popular of all precious gems. Investing in diamonds is quite different from investing in gold. To begin with, judging quality is a serious problem because each diamond has unique characteristics of size, clarity, and ability to refract light. To overcome the problem, the Gemological Institute of America has developed a grading standard that gemologists use to grade stones. More important, you receive a certificate indicating the grade. Grading adds considerably to the cost of an investment, and with commissions, sales and excise taxes, dealer markup, and, possibly, other expenses added, your total purchase costs could range from 30% to 100% of the amount invested.

Diamond: most popular precious gem

Also, you cannot buy or sell diamonds as easily as gold. You must use a dealer who can provide a certificate, and it is important to select one who is reputable. Fraud has been extensive in the precious stone business, with dealers selling low-grade diamonds but charging high-grade prices. It is suggested that you trade only with dealers in Chicago and New York because they have experience with investment programs that your local jeweler can-not offer. Salomon reported a 20-year return of 8.5% on diamonds.

Artwork and Antiques   Perhaps no tangible offers as much difficulty in col-lecting as do **artwork** and **antiques.** Many people believe that any original artwork by even some obscure artist might be worth something someday, if the artist is ever "discovered," and any piece of furniture more than 100 years old automatically becomes a valuable antique. Neither view is correct. Your chances of becoming rich by buying the works of an unknown artist are so slim that you would be better off panning for gold in one of your local streams. Most investors in art do not look for unrecognized artists; rather, they work through art dealers or other experts who guide their purchases in the direction of known artists. True, there are degrees of recognition, and you might prefer the risks of a lesser-known talent to the more assured value with an old master. As with diamonds, acquisition costs are extremely high, and resale is even more difficult.

> **Artwork and antiques:** tangible investments appealing to certain investors (collectors)

The same rule holds for the antique investor. Although age can add to the value of a piece, it does not substitute for workmanship and quality. Indeed, much old, poorly constructed, and tasteless furniture will be worth nothing in normal times and with normal tastes. Admittedly, times and tastes are not always normal, and some outlandishly ugly pieces have had value because of a faddish appeal. You can guess the risks involved in this type of investing.

Collectibles and Hobbies   The distinction between an antique and a col-lectible is tenuous. Historically, antiques referred to furniture and various other household items such as silver service sets. In recent years, practically everything found in the home, shop, or farm was sought after and referred to in general as **collectibles.** Semantics aside, the profits in collectibles often have matched those in antiques. Almost any item you can imagine—depres-sion jewelry, marbles, beer cans, paisley shawls, original battery-operated toys, 1930 watches, and many, many more—have been auctioned in recent years for high prices. Baseball cards—rookie cards in particular—were big winners in the late 1980s. A 1952 Mickey Mantle rookie card was worth $6,000. Some of us are old enough to remember flipping many such cards into a trash can after we tired of them.

> **Hobbies and col-lectibles:** tangibles often associated with the fun of collecting; returns can be quite good

You also have a chance of making a profit with your hobbies: rare coin collecting (numismatics) and stamp collecting (philately). The markets for rare coins and stamps are fairly efficient, although they also are fragmented, consisting of many dealers who trade either directly or through the mail. Quoted prices, markups, and commissions are high and vary among dealers, making comparative shopping important. If collecting is your hobby and if you have skill at it, consider yourself fortunate that you enjoy doing some-thing that might have value; on the other hand, if you know little or nothing about coins or stamps but want to invest in them because you heard they are good inflation hedges, you are better advised to invest elsewhere—gold coins or gold certificates, for example. This investing requires little skill and involves far lower commissions, and you can check the value of your investment each day by finding gold's price in the morning newspaper.

SUMMARY

A personal residence has both emotional and investment appeal. The latter includes price appreciation and tax-sheltering aspects. Price appreciation is influenced by supply-and-demand factors at the national and local levels, while the major tax shelter is the once-in-a-lifetime $125,000 exclusion of all gains resulting from personal residence sales. Housing affordability is determined by a person's income and level of consumer debt, along with the amount of down payment and mortgage interest rate. The most popular personal residence is the detached single-family home, although many people buy condominiums and cooperatives. An important decision for many investors is rent-versus-buy. The economics of the decision can be measured, using rate-of-return analysis.

Rental investment includes residential properties, commercial and industrial properties, and the vacation home. Each should be evaluated with rate-of-return analysis, paying particular attention to aspects of the tax law that might affect profitability. Property valuation uses four methods: the cost approach, the comparative sales approach, the capitalization of income approach with discounting of cash flows, and the direct capitalization approach.

A property investment can be financed with a fixed-rate or adjustable-rate mortgage. If the latter is used, the borrower should determine how the adjustment process will work on a particular loan. Important questions deal with the frequency of adjustment, the existence of rate caps or minimums, and the specific adjustment index used. Mortgage loans are provided by many financial institutions. Some are insured by the FHA or the VA.

Tangibles are physical items that can be bought or sold. They have use advantages in direct enjoyment or as a display of wealth, or they are items, such as an engagement ring, that are needed for some purpose other than investment. They also have investment advantages as hedges against political and inflation risks and to achieve more thorough portfolio diversification. Tangibles' disadvantages include high commissions and holding costs, a need for specialized knowledge, extremely volatile prices, no current return, poor resale markets, and rampant fraud.

Gold is the most popular investment tangible. Its price is volatile, depending on supply-and-demand factors. Gold can be owned directly in the form of coins, bullion, certificates, jewelry, and works of art; indirect ownership of gold is possible through gold mining stocks. Silver is also a popular investment. Diamonds appeal to some investors, as do artwork and antiques. Collecting the latter two items requires considerable experience and knowledge; moreover, transactions and holding costs are exceptionally high. Collectibles and hobbies have become popular. Many people enjoy these activities, apart from any monetary return.

KEY TERMS
(listed in order
of appearance)

personal residence	conventional mortgage
detached single-family home	growing-equity mortgage
condominium housing	adjustable-rate mortgage
cooperatives	FHA or VA loan
residential rental property	tangible
single-point evaluation	gold
multipoint evaluation	gold coins
commercial or industrial property	gold bullion
vacation home	gold ownership certificate
cost approach	silver
comparative sales approach	diamond
capitalization of income approach	artwork and antiques
direct capitalization approach	hobbies and collectibles
fixed-rate mortgage	

REVIEW
QUESTIONS

1. Explain the following investment characteristics of a personal residence: price appreciation, tax-sheltering of income, low return variability. Explain whether recent data indicate the personal residence has been a good investment.
2. Identify factors that determine the demand for and supply of housing. Explain the impact each factor has on demand or supply, and how demand and supply influence the price of new housing.
3. Identify local influences that might be important in determining the price of a specific property.
4. Explain the kinds of properties available to a home buyer. Which do you think will appeal to you? Indicate why.
5. Explain how the following factors are involved in the rent-versus-buy decision: mortgage payments versus rental payments, income tax savings, and price appreciation.
6. Explain various types of rental properties that you might consider investing in; which appeals to you personally?
7. How does the evaluation of a rental property compare with a rent-versus-buy decision? Indicate similarities and differences.
8. Discuss tax limitations as they apply to rental properties.
9. How does a single-point evaluation differ from a multipoint evaluation? Does one input more data than the other? Discuss.

10. What is the investment appeal of a vacation home?

11. With respect to how frequently you rent or use a vacation home personally, explain three situations that influence your taxable income. Is it important to keep a good record of the number of rental and personal-use days? Explain.

12. Explain the following valuation methods: the cost approach and the comparative sales approach. Which method is more appropriate for valuing owner-occupied personal residences? In what type of situation would the cost approach make sense?

13. Explain the capitalization of income approach and the direct capitalization approach. Discuss limitations of the latter method.

14. Explain the following mortgages: fixed-rate, conventional, growing-equity, and adjustable-rate. Which one appeals to you? Explain why.

15. Indicate what the following items mean with respect to an adjustable-rate mortgage: frequency of adjustment, rate cap, adjustment index.

16. What is an FHA or a VA loan? Do they have any advantages over other loans? Explain.

17. Provide a definition of a tangible and then discuss whether you would prefer investing in a diamond ring or gold bullion stored in a distant city.

18. Explain the use characteristics of tangibles. These are important to many investors. Which characteristic, in your view, is the most important? Discuss.

19. Have tangibles provided returns competitive with those of intangibles? Explain.

20. Is an index measuring a tangible's return likely to be as accurate as one that measures an intangible's return? Discuss.

21. Explain investment characteristics of tangibles other than return. Is there a reasonably strong investment rationale for including tangibles in your portfolio, or are tangibles too risky? Explain.

22. Discuss six potential disadvantages of investing in tangibles.

23. In what sense can gold be considered the "perfect" tangible?

24. Indicate and briefly discuss various ways of owning gold. Explain which method you would select if you planned a gold investment.

25. Do you think buying a gold wedding ring is a good way to invest in gold? Explain.

26. Discuss silver as an investment. Explain whether you would prefer owning silver to owning gold.

27. What factors are important to consider before investing in diamonds or other precious gems?

28. Would you advise numismatics or philately for an average investor? Explain.

PROBLEMS AND PROJECTS

1. Lena Klein expects to earn $36,000 next year. Her monthly installment debt payments will be $300. She would like to have a 30-year, 8% loan for the maximum allowable by her savings and loan. How much might she borrow? (Use Exhibit 15.4.) If her monthly payment is more or less than $500, set up a proportion as follows: $X/\$500 = Y/\$68,120$. You will determine a value for X and then solve for Y.)

2. Lorraine French is thinking of buying the condominium she currently rents for $400 a month. Lorraine likes the place and thinks that its value should increase over time because it is situated in a desirable neighborhood. If Lorraine goes ahead with the purchase, she will pay $60,000 for the unit, putting down $3,024 and borrowing $56,976. (Her loan payments would be the same as those shown in Exhbit 15.6.) Property taxes are $600 a year and the condo association fees are $480 a year (nondeductible for income tax purposes). All other ownership expenses—utilities, insurance, telephone, etc.—are not relevant because Lorraine pays them now as a renter. Lorraine has a 28% marginal tax rate.

   a. Calculate the investment's IRR assuming the following: a five-year holding period, 4% annual inflation in property taxes, and annual price appreciation of 8% on the condo.

   b. Evaluate the investment for Lorraine.

3. Allison Zeitle will earn $140,000 in the upcoming year from consulting fees in her engineering firm. Allison also owns and actively manages a rental duplex that will show losses.

   a. Assuming the loss is $2,000, how much can she use to offset other income?

   b. Assume Allison's consulting fees are $80,000. How much can be deducted from rental losses of (a) $2,000 or (b) $30,000?

   c. Assume Allison is inactive in managing the property. How much can she deduct if the loss is $2,000?

4. Steve Grevey is considering purchasing a fourplex at 334 Shaw Avenue, a street near a local hospital. He plans to rent the units to nurses and other medical professionals. The building has been converted from a single residence, and it is located in a suburban area of a major city. His analysis of the property indicates a NOI of $16,000, which seems likely. The buyer is asking $180,000 for the property but will consider lower offers. Steve has talked with some of his friends who have shared financial information with him regarding properties they have recently purchased or sold. Details appear in the following table.

Property	Description	Recent Price	NOI
2100 Park Lane	Duplex in affluent neighborhood	$225,000	$20,000
76 Westbury	Fourplex close to a university in the central city	260,000	35,000
351 Shaw Ave.	Rented single family residence located a block away	70,000	4,000

   a. Assuming Steve uses the direct capitalization approach, discuss what you believe is the most appropriate capitalization rate. Given your estimate, determine the property's value.

   b. Discuss some limitations in this analysis.

5. The correlation coefficient between gold and silver is $+0.8$ and the correlation coefficient between gold and stocks is -0.2. If the expected returns from each asset are the same, which two should be held in a portfolio? Explain why.

6. The following table shows return data for three assets:

	Gold	Art	Bonds
Rate of return	12%	15%	10%
Standard deviation of returns	26	47	4
Correlation coefficients: Gold	1.0	0.8	0.4
Art		1.0	−0.6
Bonds			1.0

a. Which asset is the riskiest, if held by itself?
b. If only two assets are to be held in a portfolio, which two do you recommend? Explain.

7. *(Student Project)* The Sunday newspaper in most communities contains listings of both residential and commercial units. With a recent edition, consider personal residences first. Notice the wide variations in listed prices, depending on neighborhood. If you are familiar with the community, indicate the relationship of listed price to location, citing expensive and inexpensive areas. You should try to control for differences in types of homes. A large, well-appointed home in an inexpensive area might list for more than a small home in an expensive neighborhood.

8. *(Student Project)* Also contained in the Sunday newspaper are listings for rental units. You might consider contacting several realtors to gather financial data for rentals and expenses. Assuming you obtain adequate data for a property, evaluate it. Review credit conditions locally to determine available financing. In this effort, consider contacting a local bank or savings and loan, if available information is inadequate. With all data in hand, evaluate a possible purchase at the seller's asking price.

9. *(Student Project)* Do a search to determine how you might invest in gold in your area. Contact commercial banks, inquiring if they sell gold coins or have gold certificate programs. If this search is not productive, try coin dealers or even pawn shops. Also, look under "gold" in the yellow pages.

CASE ANALYSES

Neil and Jeannie Ryan are a recently married couple with no dependents. Their combined incomes total $57,600, and they have no debts other than a car loan they are paying off at $300 a month. The Ryans are renting an apartment but hope to buy a home in the near future. They have located a place they like very much but are not sure they can afford it, or whether it represents a sound investment. The investment side of the purchase is important to them. They have the funds they would use for a down payment invested in a municipal bond fund that yields about 8%. The Ryans have a rather low tolerance for risk, so they have asked your advice in the matter. You anticipate they will have a 28% marginal tax rate indefinitely in the future.

15.1
The Ryans' First
Home

The home costs $120,000. The Ryans hope to finance the purchase with a 25-year, 10% mortgage for $111,000. Monthly mortgage payments would be $1,000. Expenses in the previous year related to the home and to their apartment are shown in the following table. These expenses are expected to increase 5% each year. Home values in the neighborhood have been increasing about 6% annually, and this rate should continue in the future. Although the Ryans hope to remain in the home for many years, either Neil's or Jeannie's career might require relocation to another city. In this event, the home would be sold and a realtor's commission of 7% (of the market value at the time of the sale) would be paid.

Expense Item	Apartment	New Home
Rent	$9,600	$ —
Utilities	1,400	3,000
Insurance	300	600
Maintenance	200	1,000
Property taxes	—	2,800

Questions

a. Can the Ryans afford the home? Explain.
b. Assume that interest on the mortgage loan is 98% of the annual payment in the first year and then declines by one percentage point in each of the next four years. Considering this information along with appropriate data above, determine a schedule of annual income tax savings associated with the home. Consider a five-year horizon.
c. Considering your work to question *b* and data above, prepare a schedule of annual cash flows.
d. Evaluate the investment by determining an IRR or by calculating the present value of each future cash flow. The latter method is much easier if you do not have a suitable calculator or computer. If you use this approach, discount with an 8% rate and compare the sum of the present values with the down payment of $9,000. Consider a five-year horizon.
e. Do you recommend that the Ryans buy the home? Give specific reasons for your decision.

15.2
The Rosens'
Vacation Home

The Rosens, Milt and Wanda, are thinking of buying a vacation condo at Hilton Head. They enjoy the area and believe that property values will grow about 5% annually in the future. The Rosens plan on retiring there, so by buying now, they will avoid paying a higher price later. In the near future, they anticipate using the condo 20 days a year and hope to rent it another 80 days at $100 a day.

The condo has a cost of $82,500. If depreciation is allowable, it would be based on the total cost and a write-off period of 27.5 years. The Rosens would put up $12,500 and finance $70,000 with a 10%, fixed-rate loan. First-year mortgage payments would total $7,633, of which about $7,000 is interest. Property taxes would be $1,500 annually and other operating expenses would total $2,000 a year. The Rosens would be active in managing the unit, and their taxable income from other sources does not exceed $100,000. They will have a 28% marginal tax rate.

a.   Given the data above, determine the total deductions available to the Rosens. What is the first-year cash flow from the property?

b.   Suppose the Rosens decide to use the property for personal use only 14 days. What is their tax situation—income or loss—with this assumption? What is the cash flow with this situation?

c.   Suppose the Rosens decide to rent the property only 14 days and use it themselves for 36 days. What is their tax situation—income or loss—with this assumption? Estimate the cash flow in this situation.

d.   Evaluate the condo purchase in terms of cash flow per personal-use day. Which is the best alternative?

Brown, Christie. "Resort Art." *Forbes*, January 18, 1993, pp. 100–101.
Cook, Anthony. "The New Rules of Home Buying." *Money*, November 1992, pp. 152–65.
Dingle, Derek T. "The Rules of Trading Up." *Money*, April 1992, pp. 94–111.
Downing, Ned W. "Historic Value." *Barron's*, April 12, 1993, p. 16.
Dubois, Peter C. "Picky, Picky, Picky." *Barron's*, May 24, 1993, p. 15.
Fuhrman, Peter. "Diamonds with Everything." *Forbes*, March 29, 1993, pp. 100–101.
Hannon, Kerry. "What's Ahead for Home Prices?" *Money*, July 1992, pp. 80–99.
Levy, John B. "Crunching Real Estate." *Barron's*, June 7, 1992, p. 12.
Parke, Terrence P. "Buy a Home Downtown." *Fortune*, September 6, 1993, pp. 93–94.
Smith, Marguerite T. "Reaching for a First Home." *Money*, March 1992, pp. 114–29.
_____. "Digging in for Growth." *Money*, March 1992, pp. 144–51.
_____. "Slashing the Taxes on Your Home." *Money*, January 1993, pp. 96–101.
_____. "Tomorrow's Heirlooms." *Money*, May 1993, pp. 174–81.

PART SIX

Maximizing Portfolio Benefits

Investing often appears as disjointed activities: buying stocks, maintaining liquidity, insuring, and so on. The successful investor, though, takes a comprehensive look at his situation and attempts to place all the separate parts into a meaningful whole—the portfolio. A portfolio has a certain synergy, meaning that individual investments often complement one another to produce an end result that is more effective than the sum of their separate influences.

Chapter 16 deals with basic portfolio management. It emphasizes the importance of setting investment goals and selecting specific assets to achieve them. It also stresses the importance of diversification to reduce risk, and it explains how to measure and evaluate portfolio performance. Advantages and disadvantages of market timing are compared with those of a buy-and-hold strategy, with a discussion of how formula plans might be used to accomplish timing goals.

Chapter 17 considers additional topics in portfolio management. It reviews the contributions of modern portfolio theory and explains how derivative instruments can be used to modify portfolios' return-risk profiles. Finally, the important topic of international diversification is discussed.

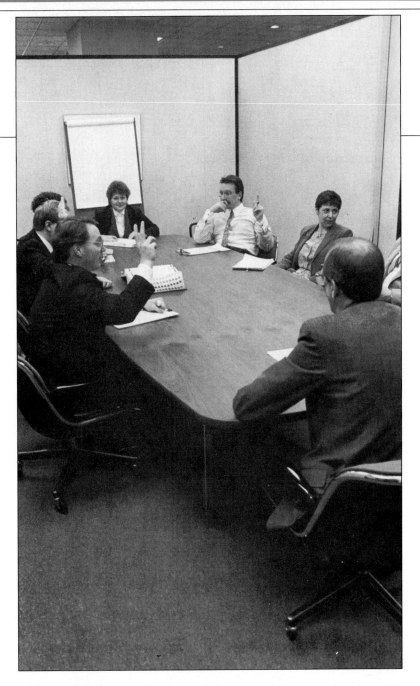

CHAPTER SIXTEEN

Basic Portfolio Management

After you finish this chapter, you
will be able to:

- see the importance of goal setting and forecasting in constructing an investment
  portfolio.

- know how to select specific
  assets to meet your portfolio
  objectives and achieve adequate
  diversification.

- estimate portfolio performance
  by both measuring and evaluating it.

- understand advantages and disadvantages of both buy-and-hold
  and market-timing portfolio
  strategies.

- understand how mechanical
  timing plans work, and their
  advantages and disadvantages.

- identify strategic and tactical
  asset allocation models.

- understand how various defensive techniques are used to protect a portfolio's value.

M ost people realize intuitively that holding one or even several invest-ments is risky. Many still do it, recognizing the risks but hoping their luck will be favorable. Some of the risks these investors take could be avoided by more thoughtful investment selection. The key is to design an effective portfolio—one that eliminates unnecessary risks while simultaneously meeting your investment objectives. To do this, the portfolio must be constructed properly to begin with, monitored closely over time, and modified as circumstances might warrant. This chapter discusses these important tasks.

CONSTRUCTING THE PORTFOLIO

Portfolio: combination of assets held at the same time

A **portfolio** is any combination of assets held at the same time. All assets you own should be considered parts of your portfolio. These would include typical investment assets such as stocks, bonds, mutual fund shares, direct business interests, and personal assets such as your home, automobiles, jewelry, and other important items. As Exhibit 16.1 shows, for purposes of portfolio planning, you also should consider any equity you might have in retirement or profit-sharing plans, even though you may have no control over the manner in which these funds are invested. Constructing a portfolio involves

EXHIBIT 16.1
Suggested portfolio composition in three life stages

A. Couple in Early 30s:
- Family Income = $50,000
- Total Assets = $150,000
- Percentage of Total Assets Invested As Shown

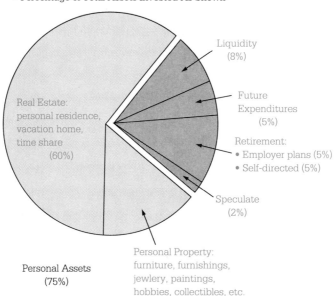

Liquidity (8%)

Future Expenditures (5%)

Retirement:
- Employer plans (5%)
- Self-directed (5%)

Speculate (2%)

Real Estate: personal residence, vacation home, time share (60%)

Personal Assets (75%)

Personal Property: furniture, furnishings, jewelry, paintings, hobbies, collectibles, etc. (15%)

Investment Assets (25%) Include:
- Bank deposits
- Series EE Bonds
- Treasury securities
- Agency debt
- Stocks
- Corporate and municipal bonds
- Mutual fund shares
- Options
- Futures
- Direct business interests
- Investment properties
- Limited partnership interests

B. Couple in Early 50s:
- Family Income = $75,000
- Total Assets = $400,000
- Percentage of Total Assets Invested As Shown

EXHIBIT 16.1
Continued

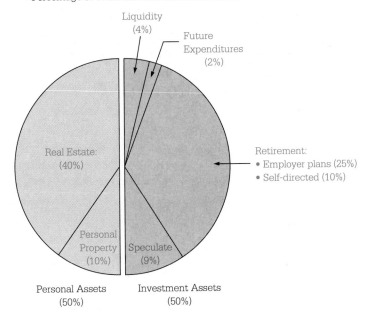

Liquidity
(4%)

Future
Expenditures
(2%)

Real Estate:
(40%)

Retirement:
- Employer plans (25%)
- Self-directed (10%)

Personal
Property
(10%)

Speculate
(9%)

Personal Assets
(50%)

Investment Assets
(50%)

C. Couple in Retirement (Early 60s)
- Family Income = $50,000
- Total Assets = $600,000
- Percentage of Total Assets Invested As Shown

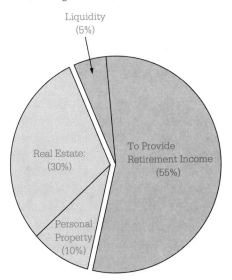

Liquidity
(5%)

Real Estate:
(30%)

To Provide
Retirement Income
(55%)

Personal
Property
(10%)

three steps: first, you must set investment goals; second, you must anticipate the investment environment for the upcoming planning period; and third, you must select specific investment vehicles to achieve your stated goals.

Setting Goals

Investment goals direct and shape the investment portfolio. Specific, tangible goals can guide the investor much more effectively than some nebulous criterion, such as "making as much as you can as fast as you can." Your goals might be to accumulate funds for a future important expenditure, to provide income during retirement years, to build an estate for your heirs, or simply to speculate. Whatever your goals are, they must be identified; otherwise, it is impossible to know which investments are appropriate for the portfolio. Investors' goals differ considerably, which means a portfolio appropriate for one may not be appropriate for another. In setting goals, you establish priorities and define acceptable risk levels.

Investment Priorities   You can think of portfolio construction as analogous to moving through a cafeteria dinner line. In front of you are many offerings, each providing some enjoyment (return) at some cost (risk). In assembling your dinner, you balance the expected enjoyment an item provides with its cost; when you are finished, you hope to have the most enjoyable meal your limited funds can provide. The individual items before you reflect your eating priorities: if you enjoy sweets, you might include a piece of pie; if you are on a diet, the pie might be replaced by fresh fruit.

In the investment cafeteria, you follow the same procedure. If you want to have considerable liquidity, you pick Treasury bills or a money market account; if your priority is inflation protection, you are drawn to real estate or perhaps gold; if you want high current return, you look at Treasury, agency, or corporate bonds; if you want growth over time and don't expect inflation, you move into common stocks; and if you want maximum capital appreciation quickly, you venture into options, or warrants, or even futures contracts. And if you, like most investors, have several priorities simultaneously, you hold a portfolio of several asset groups. Your portfolio, like the cafeteria tray, should represent your best effort to achieve your priorities, given your limited investment funds. A listing of investment objectives for Marita Hapner, an unmarried, young, professional person with no dependents, appears in Exhibit 16.2.

Setting Risk Levels   Your goals also establish tolerable risk levels. For example, if you are investing to accumulate a given sum of money at the end of a given period, and if it is absolutely essential to have that sum available (for a down payment on a house, for example), then you cannot tolerate any investment that might have some price risk. A zero coupon bond maturing on the needed date would be ideal, while a coupon bond with a maturity much beyond that date is inappropriate. As another example, if one of your priori-

BOX 16.1   INVESTMENT INSIGHTS

Integrating All Your Assets into the Portfolio Plan

Over time, many people accumulate a variety of assets and own them in various ways. For example, you have both a 401(k) plan and a defined contribution retirement plan with your employer. You have done some investing on your own and hold the securities with your broker; in addition, you inherited shares of stock when your grandparents died and have these certificates in a safety deposit box. You also have checking and savings accounts. Not only is it important to count all your assets and to periodically value them in the aggregate for financial planning purposes, but it's also a good idea to categorize them to help you manage your portfolio.

The major issue is that we should try to achieve component weights that fit our risk tolerance objective. With assets scattered all over the place, it's easy to go astray. For example, you might not pay much attention to how your retirement plan is funded. Suppose it's 100% in stocks. Coupled with your other stock investments, your equity exposure could be excessive. You should reposition the portfolio by making changes that involve the least cost. The retirement or 401(k) plan may allow you to shift funds into cash or bonds with no transactions costs. If so, this would be the preferred adjusting method.

Looking at the total picture also helps us find the optimal place to own certain assets. For example, mutual funds are appealing for various reasons. However, they have a significant disadvantage from a tax point of view, insofar as all distributions are fully taxable. So, if you own mutual fund shares outright, you lose the advantage of deferring taxes; the simple answer is to own mutual funds in a tax-deferred account such as an IRA or 401(k). Moreover, this is the ideal place to own securities with high current yields—bonds and money market assets. Securities with built-in tax deferral, such as long-term growth stocks or real estate, are more appropriately owned outside tax-deferral shelters.

A spreadsheet program simplifies portfolio analysis considerably, particularly if you update frequently. But for most investors, this is probably more of a luxury than a necessity. The key management activity is the updating and, possibly, reallocating assets. Many investment advisors believe that updating should take place at least quarterly, while reallocation frequency is determined by transactions costs. Assuming external costs (those not including your time) are close to zero, as with many tax-deferral accounts, reallocations should also be as frequent as updates.

ties is maximum capital appreciation, then the risk level you must accept is perhaps the total loss of funds allocated in this direction. If you think that such risk is too much to bear, then your goal is not really a priority, but a wish. But wishes are of no help in effective investing. So, be realistic in establishing priorities and recognizing their related risks. Then, move to the next step.

EXHIBIT 16.2
Marita Hapner's
investment goals

Investor Profile: ☐ Age 23; college graduate; business major.

☐ Marital status: single, no dependents. No change in status is anticipated in the immediate future.

☐ Annual income: $31,000 currently, expected to increase each year.

☐ Investment funds: $20,000 (from inheritance and gifts).

☐ Has adequate funds for liquidity.

☐ Overall risk tolerance: moderate risk averter, although her lack of dependents permits some aggressive investing.

Goal	Discussion	Priority
1. Future expenditure	Must accumulate $10,000 in 10 years for down payment on house or condo	Highest
2. Self-directed retirement	Marita feels Social Security and employer plans may not be adequate	Moderately high
3. Cautious speculation: growth	Because funds are sufficient to meet goals 1 and 2, Marita is willing to take some risks with remaining funds; she wants to invest in common stocks for growth over time	Medium
4. Moderate speculation: inflation hedge	Marita is concerned over loss of purchasing power of her assets; she is willing to invest in assets that can hedge inflation	Low
5. Aggressive speculation	Marita is willing to commit 15% of her funds to very risky assets, even those that might be total losses	Very low

Forecasting the Investment Environment

We can't avoid forecasting, even if we believe no one can do so accurately. To not forecast is actually forecasting by default. The choice, then, is to do it this way or to frame specific forecasts about the upcoming investment environment.

Forecasting by Default   Suppose you say that you have no idea what the investment environment will be next year: interest rates might go up or down; business activity might boom or bust; and the stock market might hit new highs or go into a tailspin. In short, anything is possible. However, would you say that every conceivable event has an equal chance of happening? Do you think inflation at a 100% rate is just as likely as it is at a 4% rate? When pressed this way, most people say that isn't what they mean by not being able to forecast. Rather, they view it as saying essentially that the immediate future will probably look much like the immediate past, and our more distant future will reflect our long-run historical trends. For example, if inflation's rate over the past six months has been 6%, you might guess that that is what it will be for the upcoming month, unless you had reasons to think differently. And if you had to guess inflation's rate over the next 10 years, you might use the long historical U.S. rate of about 3.2%.

There is nothing wrong in forecasting this way; in fact, it may make more sense than using unfounded specific projections. Perhaps the best advice is to realize that you are forecasting even when you might think you are not.

Specific Forecasts   With specific forecasts, you make projections for economic variables influencing your investments' returns. You say, for example, that the inflation rate next year will be 6.3%. It is not necessary that you personally develop these forecasts. You probably will choose instead to use those provided by professional forecasters. The key is to have forecasts and then to link them to expected returns from the investments you are considering. Suppose the 6.3% projected inflation rate is 2.3 percentage points higher than the current inflation rate, which is a fairly sharp increase. Given that projection, you should also project an eventual increase in interest rates, which implies a forecast of falling bond prices. You should avoid buying long-term bonds and perhaps consider selling any you hold.

In a similar manner, you make projections for the business cycle, the overall stock market, specific industries and firms, and the international situation. However, keep in mind our discussions in previous chapters about the accuracy of professional forecasters, which has been poor. Simple trend projections, such as those discussed in projecting by default, might be just as accurate. Recognizing this inaccuracy is not the same as saying, "Why bother?" Our concern is with portfolio planning and not with getting rich on sharp forecasts. There is a distinction between planning and forecasting: forecasting has to do specifically with predicting future events, while planning is concerned with preparing for them. A portfolio is a plan.

Selecting Specific Assets

The plan takes shape as specific assets are selected and as the proportion of the portfolio invested in them is decided. A hypothetical portfolio for Marita Hapner, who was introduced above, is shown in Exhibit 16.3. It serves as an aid in discussing the following topics that are important in actual asset selection.

Conformity to Goals   It is important that assets selected conform to the investor's goals. If you are looking for a high current return, you must select

EXHIBIT 16.3
Marita Hapner's
portfolio at January 1,
19X1

(1) Assets	(2) Units Held	(3) Market Value Per Unit	Total	(4) Percent
1. U.S. Series EE bonds	—	$ —	$ 7,000	35
2. STRIPs maturing in 2011	12 bonds	$181.67	2,180	11
3. Adams Express	200 shares	25.00	5,000	25
4. Lotus Development	100 shares	24.00	2,400	12
5. Canadian Maple Leafs	10 coins	342.00	3,420	17
Totals			$20,000	100

income stocks or bonds, and not growth stocks. Marita has selected five assets that she hopes will achieve her goals. Because she must have $10,000 at the end of 10 years, she is investing $7,000 in U.S. Series EE bonds. At the time she invested, they guaranteed an annual rate of 4.8% if held five years or longer, which means they will be worth about $11,187 at the end of 10 years. The extra $1,187 is necessary to pay income taxes when they are redeemed (she will choose to defer paying taxes each year).

The STRIPs are purchased to satisfy Marita's retirement fund objective. She purchased them using the IRA tax shelter. To participate in future economic growth, Marita wanted about one-third of her portfolio in common stocks. To accomplish this, she purchased Adams Express and Lotus Development. Adams Express is a closed-end mutual fund that invests in blue chip common stocks. It has a beta of about 0.8 and has demonstrated an average annual growth rate of 13% over the previous 10 years. Lotus Development was an extremely successful developer of computer software programs with a bright future. However, its beta of 1.8 indicates a high degree of risk. She realizes this is a speculative investment, but she is impressed with the company. The stock had traded as high as $29 a share in the past year and was selling at $24 when Marita purchased. Finally, to hedge inflation, Marita purchased 10 Canadian Maple Leaf gold coins at a total investment of $3,420.

Adequate Diversification to Eliminate Random Risk   You should hold a sufficient number of securities to eliminate random risk. This usually means at least 15 different common stocks, selected somewhat randomly, and between 5 and 15 different bonds, depending on quality rating. If your funds are not sufficient to acquire this many securities, you should consider mutual funds. Marita's choice of Adams Express makes sense, but investing as much as $2,400 in only one stock (Lotus) is risky because of poor diversification. She might have been better off investing in a mutual fund seeking maximum capital appreciation.

Diversification Among Asset Groups   At various points in the previous chapters, but particularly in Chapters 4 and 15, we discussed the importance of examining asset correlations. We discovered that broad asset groups—stocks, bonds, and tangibles—have poorly correlated returns over time. This is fortunate in designing a portfolio because it means that diversification across asset lines will reduce the portfolio's risk. In this regard, Marita's portfolio is fairly well diversified. The Series EE bonds are indexed to rates on other Treasury issues, giving her some protection against rising interest rates. Meanwhile, if interest rates fall, her STRIPs will increase substantially in market value. If inflation heats up, Marita's gold holdings should do well, although her stocks will probably do poorly; in contrast, if inflation remains moderate and the business cycle continues in the expansion phase, her stocks should do well, while gold may not.

MONITORING THE PORTFOLIO

Once the portfolio is constructed, the next activity is to monitor it. Monitoring involves three separate steps: estimating performance, measuring performance, and evaluating performance. Each of these is now discussed.

Estimating Performance

At the beginning of each planning period, you should estimate the total return—current return and price appreciation—that you expect from each asset in the portfolio. These expectations should follow logically from your projections of the investment environment. Many investors have poorly conceived ideas of investment returns: some think you should get around 50% a year, while others believe 5% is good. Making estimates forces us to look realistically at performance, if we take the task seriously.

Marita Hapner's estimates for the upcoming year are shown in Exhibit 16.4. Marita thought that inflation in 19X1 would be about the same as in the previous year, or down slightly. Thus, she thought interest rates might decline a bit. This projection affects the value of her STRIPs. Their yield to maturity at purchase was 7.06%. At the beginning of 19X2, there would be 24 years to maturity, and Marita sees a yield to maturity then of 6.5%; this means they should be worth $220.60 each. She would enjoy a 21.4% return on her investment, $467 in total.

Marita thought the economy would show moderate growth, and she thought that the stock market would reflect this growth by not showing rapid increases or sharp declines. Adams Express, then, was thought to provide a 15% return, which is slightly better than its 10-year average. The stock pays dividends out of both current income and price appreciation, but Marita chose to reinvest all dividends to acquire additional shares. She expects her holding to be worth $5,750 at the end of the year. Marita was enthusiastic about Lotus, believing a 25% appreciation in price over the year was likely.

EXHIBIT 16.4
Marita Hapner's perfor-
mance estimates for
the year 19X1

(1) Asset	(2) Expected Appreciation		(3) Expected Market Value 1/1/9X2
	$	%	
1. U.S. Series EE bonds	$ 336	4.8%	$ 7,336
2. STRIPs maturing in 25 years	467	21.4	2,647
3. Adams Express	750	15.0	5,750
4. Lotus Development	600	25.0	3,000
5. Canadian Maple Leafs	103	3.0	3,523
Totals	$2,256	11.3%*	$22,256

*Weighted average

She was less enthusiastic about gold. A moderation of inflation and interest rates could lead to lower gold prices. Allowing for this possibility and to be consistent with her estimates for the STRIPs and Adams Express, she foresees only a 3% appreciation in gold's price. With all estimates made, Marita's portfolio is expected to increase 11.3% in value over the year. This is $2,256 of appreciation, which means its market value at 1/1/19X2 will be $22,256.

Measuring Performance

At the end of the planning period—a year in this case—it is necessary to gather data and measure performance. Data gathering consists mostly of finding year-end prices in the newspaper. In the case of mutual funds, you should have a report that shows either the value of your holdings or the number of shares that you hold. In the latter case (which applies to closed-end funds like Adams Express), you must find the market price in the newspaper or through your broker.

Portfolio rate of return: profit measurement that considers withdrawals and new investments over the measurement period

Performance measurement begins by calculating a **portfolio rate of return** (R_P). If new investments are not made during the year—either by depositing additional cash or by reinvesting earned dividends or interest— and if there are no withdrawals, the rate can be calculated as shown below:

$$R_P = \frac{(P_1 - P_0)}{P_0}$$

where P_1 = total portfolio value at the end of the period, and
P_0 = total portfolio value at the beginning of the period.

If activity takes place in the portfolio during the period involving withdrawals (W) or new investments (I), the portfolio rate of return can be approximated with the following formula:

$$R_P = \frac{W + (P_1 - P_0) - I}{P_0 + I(n_1/12) - W(n_2/12)}$$

where I = new investments,
W = with drawals,
n_1 = number of months I is in the portfolio, and
n_2 = number of months W is out of the portfolio.

Exhibit 16.5 shows this calculation for a hypothetical portfolio.

With this calculation, any dividends and interest reinvested in the portfolio are not considered return items when received but are considered additional investments. So, the $100 dividend reinvested on 10/1/19X1 increases the investment base (denominator) by $25, after adjusting for the fractional part of the year the funds are in the portfolio. Keep in mind that dividends and interest reinvested will increase the ending portfolio value (P_1) and will be included in return in this way. Any withdrawals taking place during the year can come from dividends and interest or sale of securities. In either case, the ending portfolio value will be lower by amounts withdrawn. Thus, withdrawals are included (in the numerator) as part of return. Also, the investment base is then reduced to allow for the part of the year funds are not in the portfolio.

Exhibit 16.6 shows what happened in Marita Hapner's case. The Series EE bonds' return was guaranteed. The STRIPs declined in value, rather than increasing as expected. Apparently, interest rates rose. Although the loss was

Item	Symbol	Amount
1. Portfolio value at 1/1/19X1	P_0	$10,000
2. Additional investment at 3/31/19X1	I	1,000
3. Sale of $2,000 of securities on 7/15/19X1	—	—
4. Withdrawal of funds at 7/31/19X1	W	2,000
5. Dividends received on 9/30/19X1	—	—
6. Reinvestment of dividends on 10/1/19X1	I	100
7. Portfolio value at 1/1/19X2	P_1	12,000

$$R_P = \frac{W + (P_1 - P_0) - I}{P_0 + I(n_1/12) - W(n_2/12)}$$

$$R_P = \frac{2,000 + (12,000 - 10,000) - 1,100}{10,000 + 1,000(9/12) + 100(3/12) - 2,000(5/12)}$$

$$R_P = \frac{2,900}{10,000 + 750 + 25 - 833}$$

$$R_P = \frac{2,900}{9,942} = 0.2917, \text{ or } 29.2\%$$

EXHIBIT 16.5
Calculating a portfolio rate of return (R_P) with portfolio activity during the year

EXHIBIT 16.6
Marita Hapner's actual
portfolio performance
in 19X1

(1) Asset	(2) Realized Appreciation $	(3) Realized Appreciation %	(4) Market Value at 1/1/19X2
1. U.S. Series EE bonds	$ 336	5.5%	$7,336
2. STRIPs maturing in 25 years	−65	−3.0	2,115
3. Adams Express	600	12.0	5,600
4. Lotus Development	−500	−20.8	1,900
5. Canadian Maple Leafs	180	5.3	3,600
Totals	$ 551	2.8%*	$20,551

*Weighted average

moderate in an absolute sense, it was considerably below her expectation (see Exhibit 16.4 to compare). Adams Express also performed below expectation, with a realized appreciation of only 12%, and the price of Lotus fell sharply, leading to a $500 loss. Gold's price appreciated more than expected, leading to a gain of $180. In total, Marita's portfolio appreciated only $551, or 2.8%. Thus are the risks of investing; obviously, an evaluation is in order.

Evaluating Performance

Performance can be evaluated in two ways. First, you can evaluate it in an absolute sense, which consists of comparing actual results with the estimates. Second, you can judge performance in a relative sense, which compares actual results with results you might have achieved had you invested differently.

Evaluating Performance in an Absolute Sense If you took the time to make estimates at the beginning of the year, evaluating performance at year's end would consist primarily of asking, "What went wrong—or right?" Marita misguessed the investment environment somewhat, but such errors are to be expected. Moreover, her asset diversification partially buffered the losses she might have taken had she invested most of her funds in only stocks or bonds. Although she is measuring performance annually and planning one year at a time, her investment horizons are actually much longer. Therefore, if 19X1 was not a particularly good year, she is not alarmed by the outcome because there are many more years to follow.

Her biggest concern was investing 12% of her portfolio in one stock—Lotus. Originally convinced it could go no lower in price, Marita learned differently. Although saying the investment was a mistake might be premature—after all, she was willing to speculate with a portion of her funds—her loss does indicate that she must carefully consider whether or not the stock should be held in the future.

Evaluating Performance in a Relative Sense   Evaluating performance in a relative sense requires a yardstick against which comparisons can be made. One yardstick could be the rate of return you might have earned investing on a risk-free basis. If you don't do this well over time, you should ask why you are taking any risks. Instead, why not invest everything in a risk-free asset, such as U.S. Treasury bills? Marita's 2.8% return was below the risk-free rate of around 3.5% for the year.

Another yardstick might be the return on a mutual fund that has characteristics similar to your portfolio. For example, Marita might review how well balanced funds (holding debt and equity instruments) performed during the year. If their returns were well above hers, she might consider investing exclusively with them, rather than relying on her own skills. It should be repeated, though, that making a decision based on only one year's performance is premature.

A third approach could be to use the alpha measurement developed in Chapter 14. This involves first determining a portfolio's beta weight and then deriving an expected return based on both the risk-free rate (R_F) and the rate of return on the market (R_M) over the investment period in question. For example, suppose Marita's portfolio had a beta of 0.5, while $R_F = 3.5\%$ and $R_M = 10\%$. Then, her portfolio return (R_P) should have been:

$$R_P = 3.5\% + 0.5(10\% - 3.5\%) = 3.5\% + 0.5(6.5\%) = 3.5\% + 3.25\% = 6.75\%$$

This return is far better than Marita's 2.8%. This method has the advantage of combining the risk-free rate and a rational allowance for risk in one return measurement. It has a big disadvantage in that you must determine your portfolio's beta weight. If you have a suitable calculator or computer and appropriate software, this is neither a complicated nor time-consuming task. Without these aids, it is unlikely you will make the effort.

MODIFYING THE PORTFOLIO

After the period's results are evaluated, the next step is to decide if the portfolio should be modified. If your investment objectives change, so must the portfolio. If Marita decides that speculation is not appropriate for her, she will probably sell her Lotus shares and invest the funds elsewhere. We normally expect that most investors' goals will change over time. As retirement grows closer, for example, many investors give more priority to preservation of capital and less to its growth. Moving into a higher income tax bracket might also call for portfolio changes: municipal bonds will have greater appeal relative to taxable issues.

Apart from changing the portfolio in response to changing goals, investors also might want to make changes for other reasons. They may hope to profit from their perceptions of a changing investment environment; or they may want to keep asset weights constant, assuming these have changed because of appreciation or depreciation during the previous period. The following discussion focuses on buy-and-hold as a strategy versus proposive portfolio changes.

Buy-and-Hold

Buy-and-hold: simple portfolio approach that advocates portfolio stability unless an investor's goals change

Buy-and-hold is a simple approach. After you decide on specific investments for the portfolio, you buy and hold them. You continue holding them (assuming no changes in your investment goals) despite changes in the investment environment. This approach has advantages and disadvantages.

Advantages   Surely the biggest advantage with a buy-and-hold approach is its simplicity. After the portfolio is constructed, it can be forgotten. Perhaps an equally big advantage is that you don't change investments needlessly or capriciously—a practice common among first-time investors. As a result, commissions are much lower and investment results usually are better. Our discussion of market timing in Chapter 8 indicated that even professionals cannot consistently forecast market changes, much less show profits from trading on such forecasts. Finally, by not trading frequently, you avoid showing taxable gains and thus avoid paying taxes on the gains.

Disadvantages   Although simple to follow, buy-and-hold does not address certain problems. First, and perhaps easiest to deal with, is the problem of reinvesting investment earnings, such as dividends and interest. You might choose to withdraw earnings, thereby eliminating the problem; or, you might reinvest them in the securities that paid them, if that can be done easily and inexpensively. (Mutual funds are ideal in this respect and so are individual companies with reinvestment plans.) You must make some decision, which means buy-and-hold is not free of portfolio management.

A more serious situation arises when asset weights are changed because of relative performance. Exhibit 16.7 illustrates the problem. The investor in this case initially decided to invest an equal amount of funds in common stocks, bonds, and gold. During the year, his stocks have declined somewhat in value, the bonds have remained the same, and gold has appreciated considerably. At year's end, the asset weights are now quite different—about 45% gold, 25% stocks, and 30% bonds. What should the investor do? Under a strict buy-and-hold approach, the answer is to do nothing. However, the question can be raised whether buy-and-hold should apply to specific assets or to specific asset weights. In the latter case, the investor must take end-of-year action. Specifically, he would sell $3,833 of gold and invest $2,667 in common stocks and $1,166 in bonds, thereby restoring the equal proportional weights.

Another serious problem with buy-and-hold is that you do not take advantage of possible tax savings by selling assets with tax losses. Suppose that you hold AAA-rated bonds issued by GMAC, but because interest rates

EXHIBIT 16.7
Nate Bien's portfolio:
Constant ratio invest-
ment objective

(1) Asset	(2) At 1/1/19X1		(3) At 1/1/19X2		(4) Adjustments	(5) Restored Desired Weights 1/1/19X2	
	$	%	$	%		$	%
Common stocks	10,000	33.3	8,500	25.3	+2,667	11,167	33.3
Bonds	10,000	33.3	10,000	29.9	+1,166	11,166	33.3
Gold	10,000	33.3	15,000	44.8	−3,833	11,167	33.3
Totals	30,000	100.0	33,500	100.0	−0−	33,500	100.0

have risen sharply, the value of the bonds is down $2,000. If you are in a 33% tax bracket, you could sell the bonds and save $660 in taxes. Assuming any AAA-rated bonds are as good as the GMAC bonds, it would be foolish not to substitute for them and enjoy the tax savings. True, if the new bonds subsequently appreciate in value, you would have to pay a tax on any gain, assuming they are sold. But this might not happen for many years, and meanwhile you have had the use of current tax savings (less commissions to sell and buy the substitute). Even a hard-core buy-and-hold enthusiast would probably agree that tax swaps, such as the above, should be undertaken.

Market Timing

An alternative to buy-and-hold is to deliberately change the portfolio to accomplish some end. We saw above that deliberate changes are called for in the case of tax swaps or to maintain asset weights. Another purposive change is in anticipation of a changing investment environment. If you feel strongly that stock prices will be rising, for example, or that interest rates will be falling, then it follows that you should adjust your portfolio to achieve the highest potential gain from your projections.

Although purposive portfolio changes can consist of substituting one individual security for another—sell GM and buy Ford, for instance—we are more concerned here with broad changes, such as selling stocks and moving into Treasury bills, or vice versa. Changes of this sort are referred to as **market timing.** Timing models can be simple, as in the case above, or complex, if they involve other asset groups such as bonds, gold, and even foreign securities or currencies. As with the buy-and-hold strategy, timing strategies involve advantages and disadvantages.

Market timing: portfolio approach that attempts to adjust portfolio weights in anticipation of market changes

Potential Advantages and Disadvantages of Timing Timing's biggest potential advantage is a superior investment return. The key word is potential; a superior return is not guaranteed. Another advantage timers frequently

BOX 16.2   INVESTMENT INSIGHTS

Simplifying Asset Allocation by Using Asset Allocation Mutual Funds: Is There an Advantage?

Investing often is done in a faddish manner, and a good case in point is the hot topic of asset allocation. Most experts agree that over a long period, *how* you allocate your investment funds is likely to be the single most important decision you make. But suppose you are uncomfortable making allocation decisions? Not to worry. There are a number of mutual funds designed to do the job for you; all you need to do is find such a fund, invest in it, and relax. A good idea but one that may not prove profitable.

In a study by Anthony Chan and Carl R. Chen that appeared in the Spring 1992 issue of *The Journal of Portfolio Management* ("How Well Do Asset Allocation Mutual Fund Managers Allocate Assets?"), they find, in their words, "some unimpressive evidence." That puts it mildly. Looking at the weekly returns of 19 asset allocation funds, the researchers found that only four showed positive market-timing skills (in a statistically significant manner), in the sense that they correctly adjusted their portfolios in anticipation of market changes. Much more interesting is the fact that 10 funds *incorrectly* made such adjustments (also with statistical significance). In other words, investors would have been better off making asset allocations on their own—by flipping a coin to help them!

Chan and Chen probed a bit more deeply. Because the funds were created at different times and thus had different performance measurement histories, they aggregated the individual funds into grand portfolios for various time periods to evaluate performance as a group. The net result? Same as before—poor timing results. Also, they excluded the weeks of the great market crash (October 19 and 26, 1987) to see if these two weeks influenced the results—they did not. Finally, they used monthly returns on the possibility that managers have longer investment horizons in making allocation decisions. This also proved futile.

Should you put your money in an asset allocation fund? Interestingly, the Chan-Chen study indicates that 8 of the 19 funds had statistically significant alpha values, meaning that they outperformed a benchmark portfolio on a risk-adjusted basis. But they did it with good security-picking skills rather than with good timing techniques. So, if you selected one of these eight funds, you still made money even though it had nothing to do with asset allocation. Luck is nice to have, but you never know when it will end. Although few people doubt the importance of the asset allocation decision, there is little evidence supporting the view that asset allocations should be revised frequently to enhance yield.

cite is that you avoid the calamitous market decline. This sounds encouraging, but "riding the big loss" might not be as bad as taking many small losses that are possible with a timing approach. If you are in and out of the market frequently, your losses can easily grow to a figure as large as the one you would have had by simply holding.

Perhaps the biggest disadvantages with timing are greater commissions and paying possible advisory fees. Moreover, a timing approach may keep you out of the market when it rebounds and starts to rise. Exhibit 16.8 shows this point. The investor in this case is taken through four investment periods. The choices are to buy and hold Treasury bills, buy and hold common stocks, or go back and forth between bills and stocks in an attempt to invest in the security offering the higher return. Column 4 shows return if the investor could guess correctly each period. As you see, the 26% average return is far better than the average return for holding either bills (9%) or stocks (15%). However, as column 5 indicates, the average return is considerably worse (−2%) if incorrect guesses are made each period. Actual return depends on the investor's forecasting ability.

Empirical Analysis of Timing Methods   Numerous studies have been made to determine the effectiveness of timing techniques and the results of market timers, when these are available. The results are mixed. Some timers apparently beat buy-and-hold strategies, but many do not. Exhibit 16.9 shows the results of a study that attempted to determine if persistent seasonal patterns could be identified and used to make timing decisions effectively. The investment choices in this case were (1) buy and hold a portfolio of common stocks; (2) time purchases and sales of common stocks using seasonal indicators, holding Treasury bills when stocks are sold; (3) buy and sell stocks using a random method for making decisions, holding Treasury bills when stocks are sold; and (4) hold Treasury bills. The results are quite interesting: after allowing for transactions costs, the timing strategy shows a poorer return than buy-and-hold, but it also has somewhat less risk. There is no evidence giving

(1) Period	(2) Return on U.S. Treasury Bills	(3) Return on Common Stocks	(4) Return If You Guess Correctly Each Period	(5) Return If You Guess Incorrectly Each Period
1	+10%	+40%	+ 40%	+10%
2	+ 8	−20	+ 8	−20
3	+12	+50	+ 50	+12
4	+ 6	−10	+ 6	−10
Totals	+36%	+60%	+104%	− 8%
Average Return	+ 9%	+15%	+ 26%	− 2%

EXHIBIT 16.8
Illustration of risk with market timing

EXHIBIT 16.9
Portfolio return and
risk: Timing versus
buy-and-hold (transac-
tions costs included)

	(1) Buy and Hold Selected Securities[a]	(2) Timing with Seasonal Indicators	(3) Random Timing	(4) Buy and Hold Treasury Bills
Ten-year-return[b]	206%	152%	43%	93%
Average monthly return	0.94%	0.77%	0.30%	0.55%
Average annual return	11.85%	9.69%	3.60%	6.79%
Standard deviation of monthly returns	5.18%	3.49%	3.54%	0.03%
Beta	0.941	0.554	0.518	—

[a]Portfolio consisted of 18 securities, selected on the basis of having demonstrated significant seasonal patterns in the period 1926–71.

[b]Period was 1972–81.

SOURCE: Pettengill, Glenn N., "Persistent Seasonal Return Patterns," *The Financial Review*, November 1985, pp. 271–86.

a clear edge to either approach, so you must decide between the two, trading off risk and return. Interestingly, the seasonal predictors did much better than the random method, both in increasing return and in reducing risk. (See Chapter 3 for additional discussion of seasonality in stock returns.) Perhaps this offers some hope to those who are looking for timing techniques.

Asset Allocation Models

Market timing, as often practiced, essentially involves a decision to be either in or out of the market. In contrast, asset allocation models are designed to achieve investor goals by holding different kinds of assets at all times. The key decision with these models is the proportional weight each asset group should hold, and the following are popular approaches.

Strategic asset alloca-tion model: broad plan geared toward achiev-ing an investor's long-run goals

Strategic Asset Allocation Models   A **strategic asset allocation (SAA) model** is a broad plan that establishes a model portfolio designed to achieve an investor's long-run goals for return and risk. The major premise of such a plan is that, over the long run, a maximal target real return can be achieved, given the investor's risk tolerance, although this exact return may not be earned each year. A model portfolio is constructed, which calls for certain asset weights expressed as allowable ranges. For example, a portfolio equally weighted in gold, bonds, and common stocks might be appropriate, given an investor's return and risk objectives. These weights are only guidelines, and as market conditions change, they may be modified to take advantage of certain opportunities. Expectations of a robust stock or gold market, for example, might lead the investor to tilt the portfolio weights in favor of these assets without seriously jeopardizing the long-run risk and return goals. Strategic asset allocation plans should not change frequently, however, unless the investor's risk tolerance changes.

Tactical Asset Allocation Models   A **tactical asset allocation (TAA) model** accompanies an SAA model. Essentially, it determines how the short-run asset tilts should be made. The key to tactical asset allocation is making sure funds are not overinvested in risky assets, which would threaten the plan. TAA provides for considerable portfolio management as asset weights are tilted and retilted. However, the investor always maintains a position in each asset as determined by the SAA plan. Considering the previous example, the guideline might be equal weights for stocks, bonds, and gold, but in no event should an asset's weight be less than 20%.

> **Tactical asset allocation model:** accompanies a strategic asset allocation model but addresses short-run return opportunities

Most TAA models contrive asset-shifting schemes based on a comparison of an asset's current performance with its historical long-run trend. Assets with current returns above their trends are invested in more heavily, while those in the reverse situation are sold. Many of the models are computer-driven, with buy and sell signals determined by the computer. This supposedly is an advantage because it eliminates human emotion with its "follow-the-crowd" propensity. Mechanical allocation plans are discussed in the following section.

Mechanical (Formula) Allocation Plans

Realizing the difficulty of accurately forecasting future prices, some advisors recommend following mechanical investment plans, also called formula plans. The underlying premise of these approaches is that you should be a **market contrarian,** which usually means investing in assets that are out of favor. For example, if everybody is buying stocks, you should be selling, and vice versa. But rather than allowing your judgment to decide when an asset is in or out of favor, it is better to establish a trading rule in advance and then allow it to make decisions. Some popular formula plans are explained below.

> **Market contrarian:** person who seeks unpopular investments

Constant Ratio Plan   In a **constant ratio plan,** asset weights are determined in advance and a trigger is set up that calls for action to restore such weights if they are unbalanced by relative price appreciation or depreciation. The illustration in Exhibit 16.7 is an example of a constant ratio plan. In this case, the investor wants one-third of his portfolio invested in common stocks, bonds, and gold. Suppose he sets the trigger at 45% for any of the assets; in other words, as gold's weight hits 45%, some gold is sold automatically and appropriate amounts are invested in the other two assets to restore the target weights. As you see, when you sell gold, you are selling the asset in favor,

> **Constant ratio plan:** approach that periodically rebalances asset weights to achieve a predetermined ratio

and when you buy common stocks and bonds, you are buying the assets out of favor. In the new TAA models, an out-of-favor asset is one whose price has fallen, thereby increasing its potential current return relative to its historical average.

Variable ratio plan: rebalancing approach that takes a contrarian perspective in setting portfolio weights

Variable Ratio Plan A **variable ratio plan** allows the asset weights to vary once action is triggered. In effect, you are increasing your "contrariness." For example, instead of restoring equal weights in the previous example, this plan might call for the most out-of-favor asset's weight to increase to, say, 40%, the next out-of-favor to increase to 35%, and the in-favor asset's weight to decline to 25%. Exhibit 16.10 shows the adjustments for the example shown in Exhibit 16.7.

Do mechanical allocation plans such as these two offer better risk-adjusted returns than those of professional managers using judgmental approaches? A number were effective in avoiding the October 1987 crash, which heightened their appeal. How well they will perform over longer periods remains to be seen.

Dollar cost averaging: method of investing that calls for a constant amount investment at regular time intervals

Dollar Cost Averaging **Dollar cost averaging (DCA)** is a mechanical method of investing initially in securities, rather than one that alters a portfolio's composition. Exhibit 16.11 shows how it works. As you see, the idea is quite simple. You establish an investment plan calling for equal dollar investments at regular intervals. By following the plan, you then buy securities at a wide range of prices, and over time, you will have an average cost somewhere between the highs and the lows. The mechanical nature of the plan keeps investors from using their own judgment to determine buying points or from buying a given number of shares (rather than investing a given number of dollars) at regular intervals. A supporter of this plan believes that investors' judgments usually are wrong.

DCA is a convenient and sensible way to invest. Many investors follow it by reinvesting earnings of their mutual funds and common stocks that allow dividend reinvestment. They also establish investment routines that are regular, rather than being dependent on whether prices are high or low.

EXHIBIT 16.10
Nate Bien's portfolio: Variable ratio investment objective

(1) Asset	(2) At 1/1/19X2 $	(2) At 1/1/19X2 %	(3) Desired %	(4) Adjustments	(5) Restored Portfolio
Common stocks	8,500	25.3	40.0	+4,900	13,400
Bonds	10,000	29.9	35.0	+1,725	11,725
Gold	15,000	44.8	25.0	−6,625	8,375
Totals	33,500	100.0	100.0	−0−	33,500

BOX 16.3 GETTING AN INVESTMENT EDGE

Dollar Cost Averaging: Overrated or Undervalued?

The simpler the investment method, generally the better. Dollar cost averaging (DCA) is definitely simple: allocate a set amount of money to invest at specific time intervals and stick to it. As the years roll by, you get an average price on the investment vehicle, and if the current price is higher than the average, you show a profit. Although simple, is DCA better? Better than what? That's the crucial issue. There appears to be two alternatives to DCA. The first is a definite portfolio plan, while the second is market timing.

To illustrate the first alternative, assume that you inherit $100,000 and think that a portfolio invested 60% in stocks and 40% in U.S. Treasury bills is best for you. There is no reason why you should not immediately invest the funds per your optimal allocations. Investment theory and common sense tell us that it makes no sense to temporarily invest the entire $100,000 in the Treasury bills and then DCA into stocks over time. Until you reach the 60-40 split, your portfolio is suboptimal; in this case, it is too conservative.

But, you might argue, if stock prices are temporarily high, isn't it a big mistake to put the entire $60,000 into them at the outset? Sure it is. But how do you know that prices are temporarily high? What if they are temporarily low? Then why not put the entire $100,000 into stocks and DCA into T bills? In short, when somebody argues that DCA should be used to avoid paying temporarily high prices, the argument is really one of market timing; that is, DCA is a market-timing device, for better or worse.

Why DCA receives so much favorable press is a mystery. Perhaps it reflects investor disenchantment with "expert" market timers who more often are bullish than bearish. DCA is then viewed as a conservative alternative to avoid being burned by incorrect, optimistic market forecasts. In a sense, it is the lesser of two evils. But why take that view? What you should do is determine an asset mix that makes you comfortable and then each time you invest, follow the mix. If you invest $100 a month and if a 60-40 mix feels right, then each month put $60 in your stock fund and $40 in your money market fund. Amazingly, over time, you will get the average price for your stocks and the average yield on the money market fund. You then can boast to your friends that you use DCA methods for *all* your investments.

Finally, a DCA method is inappropriate if it is applied to a single stock. Again, the pro argument for DCA is that you avoid the possibility of paying too high a price. A stock's price is too high only in relation to its underlying fundamentals, which should always be examined before a stock is purchased. Rotely acquiring shares through DCA makes no sense and could lead to tragic results if the stock is a dud.

However, it is a mistake to think DCA can guarantee investment profits, as some promoters tout. It cannot. If a security's price is in a long downtrend, your average cost will always be higher than its current market price. Once the trend is reversed, the current price might jump above the average, but this result is not guaranteed. Be careful of salespersons who supposedly have

EXHIBIT 16.11
Illustration of DCA, assuming $1,000 invested each month

(1) Date	(2) Shares Purchased	(3) Price per Share	(4) Total Shares Held	(5) Total Cost	(6) Average Cost (5)/(4)	(7) Cumulative Profit (Loss) [(3) × (4) − (5)]
1/1	100.00	$10	100.00	$1,000	$10.00	$ –0–
2/1	83.33	12	183.33	2,000	10.91	200
3/1	125.00	8	308.33	3,000	9.73	(533)
4/1	100.00	10	408.33	4,000	9.80	83*
5/1	166.67	6	575.00	5,000	8.70	(1,550)

*Investment hucksters often describe DCA as a "can't miss" investment approach and prove it with an example such as the one above. Notice that when price fell by $2 a share under the starting price (from $10 to $8), you automatically purchased proportionally more shares (25) than the number you cut back (16.67) when price increased by $2 (from $10 to $12). So, over time, the approach should guarantee a profit, such as the $83 above, even if price doesn't increase!

     This argument is based on dollar—rather than percentage—changes. The decline from 10 to 8 is a larger percentage change than an increase from 10 to 12, which explains why more shares are purchased. In other words, the advantage is nothing more than a play on arithmetic. The method is a sensible way to invest in securities, because it eliminates emotional buying or buying because we think we can forecast future prices accurately. But it is certainly no more than that.

a "sure thing" for beating the market. Their advice often is nothing more than DCA, in one form or another.

Defensive Techniques

A defensive technique is designed to limit potential losses. As such, it reduces risk but also limits profits. The limitation on profit might arise because of less exposure to high-profit–high-risk assets or because of costs related to specific strategies. A number of techniques are widely used as defensive strategies; among the more popular methods are portfolio insurance, buying puts or selling deep-in-the-money calls, competitive hedging, and using stop orders.

Portfolio insurance: portfolio technique that attempts to preserve a minimum gain or tolerate only a certain loss

Portfolio Insurance **Portfolio insurance,** the most popular approach by far, is an asset allocation technique that attempts to preserve a minimum gain or tolerate only a predetermined loss. Its starting point is the statement of a maximum loss an investor is willing to endure—for example, 10% of the portfolio value. The trick, then, is balancing investments in both a risky asset and a risk-free asset to assure the loss never exceeds 10%. Assume you have $100,000 to invest, and you intend that the portfolio must never go below $90,000.

     You might begin by putting half your funds in a risk-free asset—say, one-year T-bills—guaranteed to provide an 8% return. The other half goes into the risky asset—say, stocks—with an uncertain return. Then your resolve to sell 60% of the stocks whenever their loss reaches 10%. Suppose after three months, the return on stocks is a loss of 10%, or $5,000. Bills provide their expected 2%, or $1,000, so you are down $3,000 for the quarter. If the next three quarters were similar to the first, you would lose $12,000 for the year— an intolerable outcome. So, you sell $27,000 of the stocks (0.60 × $45,000), investing the proceeds in nine-month bills. Your position starting the second quarter is $18,000 ($45,000 − $27,000) in stocks and $78,000 in bills [$50,000 + $1,000 (interest) + $27,000 (the transfer)]. Suppose stocks then lose another 10%, or $1,800, requiring another transfer, this time of $9,720 [0.60 × ($18,000 − $1,800)]. Now, only $8,280 remains in stocks ($18,000 − $9,720). If then stocks began to increase in value, larger allocations would be made to them, keeping in mind the allocation cannot be so large that a loss of 10% would reduce the overall portfolio below $90,000.

We won't prolong the example because the approach is relatively straightforward, although determining the initial asset weights and the trigger points for selling or buying stocks can be somewhat complicated. Also, if stocks initially increase in value, or subsequently increase the portfolio above $100,000, the target return usually is then increased as well. For example, if stocks increase initially by 10% to $55,000, you might rebalance to $52,500 each and now plan the portfolio never to be less than $94,500 (which is a 10% loss from $105,000).

Although portfolio insurance limits your loss, its disadvantage is that because you reduce your position in stocks during a decline, you have less funds invested to increase in value when the market recovers. Over the course of a stock market cycle, your losses will exceed your gains even if the market ends the cycle unchanged.

Buying Puts or Selling Deep-in-the Money Calls   We discussed in Chapter 12 how each of these methods can be used to reduce or limit losses; a discussion will not be repeated here. We should note, though, that buying puts is the ultimate insurance because it guarantees no losses. Unfortunately, puts are expensive, which seriously reduces portfolio return over time. Also, although selling deep-in-the-money calls buffers any market losses, it also completely shuts out any price appreciation. This defeats one of the main purposes of owning stocks—to realize growth.

Competitive Hedging   **Competitive hedging** allows the investor to invest in the stock of her choice but then tempers the enthusiasm by short-selling another firm within the same industry. The company shorted is one that is expected to perform poorly in relation to the selected company. For example, you think Hewlett-Packard (HP) is a great selection. But suppose the market does poorly and drags HP down with it? To overcome this obstacle, you decide to short-sell IBM, a company that you believe will lag the industry as a whole and surely lag HP.

Competitive hedging: defensive strategy involving the purchase of one stock in an industry while shorting another stock believed to be a weaker performer

This approach is only as good as an investor's ability to identify industry leaders and laggards. If you guess wrong, you can lose on both ends: HP decreases in value, while IBM increases. This method takes the familiar difficulties of finding companies expected to overperform and adds to them the difficulty of finding underperformers. Several large professional money management firms have used the technique with supposedly good results. Again, a final verdict awaits its performance over a long period.

Using Stop Orders   As described in Chapter 2, a stop order is triggered by a market price. For example, you buy a stock at $50 a share; it subsequently rises to $60 a share and you think it will eventually reach $70 a share, but you don't want to lose your profit if it falls back to $50. The solution is to put a stop order (in this case, called a stop-loss) at, say, $58 a share. If the stock continues to rise, your order is never executed, but if price falls to $58, your order becomes a market order to sell the stock. You then take your profit, which as is often pointed out, you can never lose. Some years ago, a how-I-made-a-million-in-the-market book was written that featured only one clever technique: the stop order. The author did indeed make a million—from the book. His profits from the market are less certain to us.

Using stop orders cannot guarantee a profit. To begin with, this strategy has nothing to say about which security to buy in the first place. Moreover, it often leads to excessive trading that absorbs most of your profits in commissions. As you know, many stock prices fluctuate over time. The stock that increased to $60 may show decreases for a while before it advances again. A stop order takes the investor out of the stock and makes repurchase necessary if she wants to hold it again. A double commission such as this is difficult to overcome with future price appreciation, but it probably explains why many stockbrokers favor stop orders.

SUMMARY

In designing an investment portfolio, an important first step is setting goals. Goals establish priorities and indicate tolerable risk levels. Another portfolio activity is forecasting the investment environment. Forecasting by default implies the investor has no preconceived ideas about future prices, which contrasts with making specific forecasts. Assets are selected to conform to investor goals. There would be sufficient diversification to eliminate random risk and to take advantage of poorly correlated returns among broad investment groups, such as stocks, bonds, and tangibles.

After the portfolio is constructed, it must be monitored in three steps: (1) estimate performance in advance of the investment period, (2) measure performance after the period is over, and (3) evaluate performance. Evaluation can be in an absolute sense or relative to performances of other investments or market indicators.

Most portfolios are modified over time in response to changing investment goals or changed perceptions of future investment potentials. A buy-and-hold strategy would make portfolio changes only as investment goals change. Purposive portfolio changes are made in anticipation of changing investment potentials. Methods used to make portfolio changes include market timing, SAA models, and TAA models. Mechanical allocation plans establish investment purchases or sales using predetermined plans, which include constant and variable ratio plans and DCA. To protect portfolio profits, investors use defensive strategies, which include portfolio insurance, buying puts or selling deep-in-the-money calls, industry hedges, and using stop orders.

KEY TERMS (listed in order of appearance)

portfolio
portfolio rate of return
buy-and-hold
market timing
strategic asset allocation model
tactical asset allocation model

market contrarian
constant ratio plan
variable ratio plan
dollar cost averaging
portfolio insurance
competitive hedging

REVIEW QUESTIONS

1. Define a portfolio and explain how goal setting establishes investment priorities and sets tolerable risk levels.
2. In what sense is constructing a portfolio similar to moving through a cafeteria line? Explain.
3. How do you forecast by default? Is it a big mistake to forecast this way? Explain thoroughly.
4. What guidelines should you follow in selecting specific assets for the portfolio? Explain.
5. Identify three separate activities associated with portfolio monitoring.
6. What advantage arises from estimating a portfolio performance? Explain.
7. How is portfolio performance evaluated in (a) an absolute sense and (b) a relative sense? Discuss several standards you might use with respect to the latter activity.
8. Explain advantages and disadvantages of a buy-and-hold investment strategy.
9. Explain what is meant by market timing and then discuss its advantages and disadvantages.
10. Explain an SAA model and a TAA model. Are they alternative or complementary methods?
11. In what sense do formula allocation plans take a contrarian view of the market? Explain several such methods.

12. What is DCA, and what goal does it accomplish?
13. Explain how portfolio insurance works. Is it true insurance in the sense it guarantees no losses? Discuss.
14. Explain the main shortcomings of buying puts or selling deep-in-the-money calls.
15. What is a competitive hedge, and why would you use one?
16. Explain how stop orders are used in a defensive program.

PROBLEMS AND PROJECTS

1. Veronica Larue's portfolio was worth $60,000 at the beginning of the year and $75,000 at year's end. She also received $5,000 in bond interest and $2,000 in dividends and withdrew all interest and dividends when they were received. Given this information, calculate Veronica's portfolio rate of return.

2. Joel Tyler's portfolio had the following transactions last year:

Date	Activity	Amount
1/1	Beginning portfolio value	$50,000
5/31	Received dividends	2,000
6/1	Reinvested dividends	2,000
9/30	Sold securities and withdrew cash	10,000
9/30	Realized profit on securities sold	3,000
12/31	Ending portfolio value	45,000

Calculate Joel's portfolio rate of return.

3. You have decided to invest all your available funds equally weighted in stocks, corporate bonds, and one-year Treasury bills. You will adjust the portfolio at the T bills' maturity using a constant ratio plan. Assume you invested $60,000 initially and the following annual returns were earned: stocks, 20%; bonds, –12% price depreciation and +8% coupon return; T bills, 6%. Indicate the necessary adjustments at year's end, assuming bond interest was withdrawn and T bills were rolled over during the year. Indicate the adjustments if you rebalanced with a variable ratio plan that weights more heavily the poorest-performing asset and most lightly the best-performing asset. Assume weights of 44%, 33%, and 23%.

4. You have $100,000 to invest and have decided to use portfolio insurance as a defensive technique. Your initial allocation was 40% stocks and 60% Treasury bills. Suppose you set a loss limit of $10,000 and resolved to sell half the stocks when half the limit has been lost. Assume the T bills earn a 12% annual return, and after three months, stocks have declined to a point requiring an adjustment. Indicate the value of the stocks at that point and the adjustment that would take place.

5. Larry Ward plans to acquire shares of Exxon by DCA with a stockbroker's monthly investment plan, and he has allocated $100 a month for this purpose. At the purchase date for the past five months, Exxon's price per share was $52, $48, $41, $43, and $45. For each period, determine Larry's cumulative total cost, average cost, and cumulative profit or loss.

6. *(Student Project)* Contact an officer from the trust department of a local bank.

Ask if the bank has any plans that use asset allocation models or portfolio insurance. If so, request information, if it is available.

7. *(Student Project)* Contact a local stockbrokerage firm and ask if they sponsor a mutual fund that uses asset allocation or portfolio insurance techniques. Request a prospectus and a current financial report, and use data contained within them to evaluate the fund. Also, contact the Vanguard Group of mutual funds and request similar information regarding the Vanguard Asset Allocation Fund. The telephone number is 1-800-662-SHIP.

CASE ANALYSES

After several years of unsuccessful investing, Francine and Horace Walker have decided to simplify their future investment activities by holding only three assets: gold, Treasury bonds, and a mutual fund investing in growth stocks. Although they have agreed that no portfolio adjustments will be made during a year, they disagree on how year-end adjustments should be made. Francine favors a constant ratio plan, while Horace thinks that the ratios should be adjusted to favor the asset that performed most poorly in the previous year. As Horace sees it, buying the relatively cheap asset should enhance their return over time. Francine disagrees, arguing that his approach is the same as trying to pick winning stocks.

Initially, the Walkers will invest $8,000 in each asset and will adjust the portfolio at the end of one year. For the upcoming year, they expect to receive $800 interest on the bonds, which they will withdraw, but no dividends from the mutual fund. Based on their forecast of the investment environment, the Walkers think that the mutual fund shares will increase 20%, gold will increase 5%, and bonds will be unchanged.

16.1
The Walkers'
Portfolio Plan

Questions

a. Based on the data above, prepare a portfolio sheet, showing the initial investments, the expected appreciation, and the portfolio rate of return. Also indicate the necessary rebalancing with Francine's approach, assuming the expected returns are realized.

b. The year is now over for the Walkers. Their mutual fund declined 10% in value, the bonds fell 5% in value (but paid the same interest), and gold's price increased 20%. Treasury bills during the year yielded 8%, while the stock market was down 4%. Using research the Walkers conducted before investing, they believe their portfolio has a beta weight of about 0.8. Using the information provided, evaluate performance of the Walkers' portfolio.

c. Indicate how the portfolio will be rebalanced at year's end using Francine's approach. Indicate rebalancing with Horace's approach, assuming his weighting scheme is 40%, 30%, and 30%.

d.   Do the Walkers seem to have clearly defined investment goals? Discuss, indicating how an SAA model might help the Walkers.

16.2
Terri Blair
Considers
Portfolio
Insurance

Terri Blair has accumulated $40,000 in a stock portfolio through successful investing over the past 10 years. Terri was willing to take chances, and she considers herself lucky. She will be married shortly, however, and she wants to reduce her risk tolerance level. Terri's future husband suggests that she put her money in certificates of deposit as a safe haven. Terri is reluctant to do so. For one thing, she is willing to take some risk, and for another, she wants to stay invested in stocks.

Terri's broker has recommended a portfolio insurance plan consisting of two mutual funds—one that is indexed to the market and another that is a money market fund. The broker will manage the plan, and he suggests a maximum tolerable loss of 20% (a so-called 80% floor). All her funds will be invested initially in the index fund; if it declines halfway to the floor, half of the shares will be sold and funds transferred to the money market fund. Another drop of a quarter way to the floor calls for the sale of half the remaining shares, and so on. If the market declines initially and then rebounds, funds are transferred back into the index fund in the same manner, only in reverse.

Questions

a.   Suppose the overall market made two major moves during the year, first declining by 15% and then advancing by 20%. Assuming Terri's stock fund tracked the market perfectly, what is the ending balance in the fund? (Assume for this question that no interest is earned on the money market fund.)

b.   Suppose the 15% stock decline took place on March 31 (10%) and June 30 (5%), while the 20% recovery occurred on July 31 (5%), September 30 (10%), and October 31 (5%). For the purpose of evaluating portfolio insurance, assume that interest earned on money market deposits is withdrawn. Assuming the money market fund offered an 8% annual return while the stock fund paid no dividends, compare Terri's performance for three approaches: (1) buy and hold the stock fund, (2) invest totally in the money market fund, and (3) use portfolio insurance.

c.   Will portfolio insurance reduce Terri's risk exposure? Is it likely to reduce her portfolio return? Discuss.

HELPFUL
READING

Bird, Ron, David Dennis, and Mark Tippett. "A Stop Loss Approach to Portfolio Insurance." *The Journal of Portfolio Management*, Fall 1988, pp. 35–40.

Chan, Anthony, and Carl R. Chen. "How Well Do Asset Allocation Mutual Fund Managers Allocate Assets?" *The Journal of Portfolio Management*, Spring 1992, pp. 81–91.

Clements, Jonathan. "Why It Pays to 'Rebalance' Your Portfolio." *The Wall Street Journal*, June 25, 1993, p. C1.

Hensel, Chris R., D. Don Ezra, and John H. Iikiw. "The Importance of the Asset Allocation Decision." *Financial Analysts Journal*, July-August 1991, pp. 65–72.

Herman, Tom. "The First Rollovers of Spring Bring Advice on Diversification." *The Wall Street Journal*, April 8, 1993, p. C1.

Jacobs, Sheldon. "One Size Doesn't Fit All." *Barron's*, June 28, 1993, p. 33.

Knight, John R., and Lewis Mandell. "Nobody Gains from Dollar Cost Averaging." *Financial Services Review*, 2, no. 1, 1992/1993, pp. 51–62.

Leibowitz, Martin L., and William S. Krasker. "The Persistence of Risk: Stocks versus Bonds over the Long Term." *Financial Analysts Journal*, November-December, 1988, pp. 40–47.

Leibowitz, Martin L., and Stanley Kogelman. "Asset Allocation Under Shortfall Constraints." *The Journal of Portfolio Management*, Winter 1991, pp. 18–23.

Samuelson, Paul A. "The Judgment of Economic Science on Rational Portfolio Management: Indexing, Timing, and Long-Horizon Effects." *The Journal of Portfolio Management*, Fall 1989, pp. 4–12.

Shilling, A. Gary. "Market Timing: Better Than a Buy-and-Hold Strategy." *Financial Analysts Journal*, March-April 1992, pp. 47–50.

CHAPTER SEVENTEEN

Additional Topics in Portfolio Management

MODERN PORTFOLIO THEORY

Return Correlations

The Efficient Frontier

Selecting a Portfolio

MPT and the CAPM

Passive Portfolio Planning
Techniques

MODIFYING PORTFOLIOS WITH
DERIVATIVES

Creating Synthetic Positions

Adjusting Stock Portfolios' Risk
Levels

Adjusting Bond Portfolios' Risk
Levels

INTERNATIONAL
DIVERSIFICATION

Advantages

Disadvantages

After you finish this chapter, you
will be able to:

- recognize the importance of
  return correlations in creating
  an efficient portfolio.

- understand the relationship
  between modern portfolio theory
  (MPT) and the capital asset pricing model (CAPM).

- grasp the simple techniques of
  passive portfolio planning.

- understand how synthetic positions are created and how the
  risk levels of stock or bond portfolios can be adjusted through
  the use of derivatives.

- recognize the advantages and
  disadvantages of diversifying a
  portfolio with foreign securities.

C hapter 16 presented a basic portfolio approach that investors can use to manage their investment funds. It is important to realize that the approach is well founded in investment theory, although we attempted to present it in relatively simple terms. In this chapter, we examine the theoretical underpinning of investment selection, called modern portfolio theory. An understanding of this theory should enhance your appreciation of basic portfolio techniques and might stimulate your interest for further work in investments. After studying modern portfolio theory, we examine some specialized portfolio techniques that are widely used today by professional money managers. These techniques help investors achieve more efficient risk-return portfolios than what might be possible with traditional methods. The chapter ends with a discussion of international diversification.

MODERN PORTFOLIO THEORY

Modern portfolio theory: theory of security selection that focuses on security return correlations

As a formal investment approach, **modern portfolio theory (MPT)** dates back to the early 1950s, when an academician, Harry Markowitz, first developed the theory. The term *modern* was applied to distinguish this new approach from conventional portfolio management, which focused most of its attention on the investor rather than on the behavior of assets when held in portfolio. Today, the knowledgeable investor blends the two approaches to achieve risk-return objectives, much in the way we have studied throughout the text. In fact, the tenets of MPT that involve asset correlations, the securities market line (SML), and the use of beta weights have been brought into our discussions at various points. These tools are widely accepted and often are key factors in making investment decisions. This section explains the underlying rationale of MPT, although it will not go into formal proofs of its basic theorems.

Return Correlations

In Chapter 4, we studied a decision to invest in either a savings account or a long-term bond. The return of each is influenced by changes in the overall level of interest rates: an increase in such rates increases the savings account return but decreases the bond's return. A scenario was then created depicting three possible interest-rate states, the probabilities of each state occurring, and the payoffs to each investment. The results are shown in Exhibit 17.1. As you see, the expected returns are 7.8% for the savings account and 11.0% for the bond.

We then continued the analysis by determining the risk statistics—variance (σ^2), standard deviation (σ), and coefficient of variation (C)—for each investment. These calculations are shown in Exhibit 17.2. Although our discussion at that point considered return correlations, we did not pursue the topic in depth, which is our task now.

EXHIBIT 17.1
Calculating an expected return ($\bar{R}$)

	Percentage Returns If Market Interest Rates:			
	Rise	Stay the Same	Fall	Expected Returns ($\bar{R}$)*
Probability of event occurring	.2	.5	.3	
Investment alternatives:				
Savings account	10	8	6	$(.2 \times 10) + (.5 \times 8) + (.3 \times 6) = 7.8$
Long-term bond	0	10	20	$(.2 \times 0) + (.5 \times 10) + (.3 \times 20) = 11.0$

*Letting R_1 = a possible return and Pr_1 = the probability of the return occurring, then the expected return ($\bar{R}$) is calculated.

$$\bar{R} = (R_1 \cdot Pr_1) + (R_2 \cdot Pr_2) + \cdots + (R_n \cdot Pr_n)$$

The Coefficient of Covariance   In investment analysis, the **coefficient of covariance (Cov)** is based on the interaction of one asset's deviations from its expected return with similar deviations of another asset. These deviations have already been calculated for the savings account (SA) and the bond (B) and are shown in Exhibit 17.2. Calculation of the coefficient of covariance between the two ($Cov: SA, B$) is shown in the following table:

Coefficient of covariance: statistic that measures how two securities' returns vary with each other

(1) $(R_i - \bar{R})$	(2) $(R_i - \bar{R})$	(3) $(1) \times (2)$	(4) Pr	(5) $(4) \times (3)$
2.2	−11.0	−24.2	0.2	−4.84
0.2	− 1.0	− 0.2	0.5	−0.10
−1.8	9.0	−16.2	0.3	−4.86
			$Cov: SA, B =$	−9.80

Although useful in statistical work, this number has little practical meaning to us, making it necessary to calculate the correlation coefficient.

The Correlation Coefficient   The **correlation coefficient (r)** indicates the strength of the correlation and whether it is positive or negative. It is easily calculated once the coefficient of covariance is available, along with the standard deviation of each asset. The correlation between the savings account return and the bond's return ($r: SA, B$) is calculated as follows:

Correlation coefficient: statistic that measures the strength of a correlation between two variables

$$r: SA, B = \frac{Cov: SA, B}{\sigma_{SA} \times \sigma_B} = \frac{-9.8}{1.4 \times 7.0} = \frac{-9.8}{9.8} = -1.0$$

This number tells us the returns are perfectly negatively correlated. Values for r can range from −1.0 to +1.0 (perfect positive correlation). A value of zero

EXHIBIT 17.2
Calculating risk
measurements: The
variance (σ^2),
standard deviation (σ),
and coefficient of
variation (C)

(1) Possible Returns R_i	(2) $(R_i - \bar{R})$	(3) $(R_i - \bar{R})^2$	(4) $(R_i - \bar{R})^2 \times Pr$
Savings Account:			
10	$10 - 7.8 = 2.2$	4.84	$4.84 \times .2 = 0.968$
8	$8 - 7.8 = 0.2$	0.04	$0.04 \times .5 = 0.020$
6	$6 - 7.8 = -1.8$	3.24	$3.24 \times .3 = \underline{0.972}$
			$\sigma^2 = 1.960$
			$\sigma = \sqrt{\sigma^2} = 1.400$
			$C = 1.400/7.8 = 0.180$
Bond:			
0	$0 - 11.0 = -11.0$	121.0	$121.0 \times .2 = 24.200$
10	$10 - 11.0 = -1.0$	1.0	$1.0 \times .5 = 0.500$
20	$20 - 11.0 = 9.9$	81.0	$81.0 \times .3 = \underline{24.300}$
			$\sigma^2 = 49.000$
			$\sigma = \sqrt{\sigma^2} = 7.000$
			$C = 7.0/11.0 = 0.640$

indicates a lack of correlation. As we see, the return from the savings
account is perfectly negatively correlated to the bond's return.

Combining the Two Assets Combining the two assets creates a portfolio,
and the risk of the portfolio depends on the return correlation between the
assets and the proportion of funds invested in each. Exhibit 17.3 shows the
portfolio expected return (8.44%) and standard deviation (0.28%) when funds
are allocated 80% to the savings account and 20% to the bond. The standard
deviation is now so low that for all practical purposes, this portfolio is risk-
free. Using algebraic methods (or trial and error), we can solve for a precise
combination that does indeed provide zero variance; that combination is
0.833 for the savings account and 0.167 for the bond. Holding the assets in
these proportions gives an expected portfolio return of 8.33%.

It is important to see that we have created a risk-free portfolio by combining two risky assets. In short, the portfolio risk, relative to the portfolio
return, is quite different from the risks of the assets held separately, relative
to their returns. This outcome is called a **portfolio effect.** Let us examine
this issue in more detail with another example and with a new concept—the
efficient frontier.

Portfolio effect: efficiency—higher return or
lower risk—from holding
different securities
simultaneously

Efficient frontier: theoretical concept showing
the trade-off between
return and risk

The Efficient Frontier

An **efficient frontier** is a theoretical concept showing the trade-off between
return and risk. It represents all combinations of assets an investor can hold,

I. Calculate Possible Portfolio Returns (R_i):

Interest Rates Rise, $\quad\quad\quad R_1 = (.8 \times 10) + (.2 \times 0)$

$\quad\quad\quad\quad\quad\quad\quad\quad\quad\quad\quad = 8.0 + 0 = 8.0$

Interest Rates Stay the Same, $R_2 = (.8 \times 8) + (.2 \times 10)$

$\quad\quad\quad\quad\quad\quad\quad\quad\quad\quad\quad = 6.4 + 2.0 = 8.4$

Interest Rates Fall, $\quad\quad\quad R_3 = (.8 \times 6) + (.2 \times 20)$

$\quad\quad\quad\quad\quad\quad\quad\quad\quad\quad\quad = 4.8 + 4.0 = 8.8$

II. Calculate Expected Portfolio Return ($\bar{R}$):

$\bar{R} = (.2 \times 8.0) + (.5 \times 8.4) + (.3 \times 8.8) = 1.60 + 4.20 + 2.64 = 8.44$

III. Calculate Risk Statistics (σ^2, σ, and C):

$(R_i - \bar{R})$	$(R_i - \bar{R})^2$	$(R_i - \bar{R})^2 \times Pr$
-0.44	.1936	$.1936 \times .2 = .0387$
-0.04	.0016	$.0016 \times .5 = .0008$
$+0.36$	.1296	$.1296 \times .3 = \underline{.0389}$
		$\sigma^2 = .0784$

$$\sigma = \sqrt{\sigma^2} = .2800$$

$$C = .28/8.44 = .0332$$

when going from one combination to another *always* involves taking more risk to achieve a higher return. Although a simple concept, it does need some explanation.

Another Example   Suppose you could invest in two other assets—*A* and *B*—that have the following characteristics:

	A	B
Expected return, R_i	.10	.16
Expected standard deviation of returns, σ_i	.04	.12

If you could not hold the two together, then it would be necessary to choose between higher return (with *B*) or less risk (with *A*). Removing this restriction opens new possibilities, their value depending again on the correlation of returns between *A* and *B*. We'll consider two possibilities: perfect positive correlation and perfect negative correlation. We also will look at only five combinations of *A* and *B* because that is enough to illustrate the important points. The five combinations (portfolios) are (1) 100% in *A*, 0% in *B*; (2) 75% in *A*, 25% in *B*; (3) 50% in *A*, 50% in *B*; (4) 25% in *A*, 75% in *B*; and (5) 0% in *A*, 100% in *B*.

Column 4 in Exhibit 17.4 shows returns from the five portfolios just described. As you see, the portfolio return is simply the weighted average of the individual returns. For example, portfolio 3 is $(.5 \times .10) + (.5 \times .16) = .05 + .08 = .13$. The risk of each portfolio, though, depends on correlation. Column 5 shows the standard deviation of the portfolios if *A*'s and *B*'s returns

EXHIBIT 17.4
Return and risk characteristics of five portfolios constructed from two securities

(1) Portfolio	(2) Percent in: A	(3) Percent in: B	(4) Portfolio Return (R_P)	(5) Portfolio Risk (σ_P) $r = +1.0$	(6) Portfolio Risk (σ_P) $r = -1.0$
1	100	0	0.100	0.040	0.040
2	75	25	0.115	0.060	0.000
3	50	50	0.130	0.080	0.040
4	25	75	0.145	0.100	0.080
5	0	100	0.160	0.120	0.120

are perfectly positively correlated. As you see, there is no portfolio effect because σ_P is simply the weighted average of A's and B's individual σs. A diagram of σ_P is shown in Exhibit 17.5; however, because there is no portfolio effect, we will not examine this case any further.

Column 6 in Exhibit 17.4 shows each portfolio's standard deviation when A and B are perfectly negatively correlated. A quite different picture now emerges. Not only can risk be reduced, but it can be eliminated with portfolio 2. (Values for σ_P are determined by a formula not discussed in this text.) A diagram of this situation is shown in Exhibit 17.6.

The next step is to show a combination of portfolio returns and standard deviations (σ_P) when $r = -1.0$. This is done in Exhibit 17.7. Focus your attention on portfolio 1, comparing it to portfolio 3. They are equally risky, but portfolio 3 offers a higher return; it is said to dominate 1. A rational investor would never choose 1. So, we can exclude it from consideration. The efficient portfolios—those that involve trading off risk and return—are 2, 3, 4, and 5; a line passed through these points is called the efficient frontier for the portfolios in question.

Generalizing from the Example   Portfolio construction would be simple if we needed to consider only two assets with perfect correlation. Unfortunately,

EXHIBIT 17.5
Portfolio risk (σ_P): Five portfolios of securities A and B with perfectly positively correlated returns ($r = +1.0$)

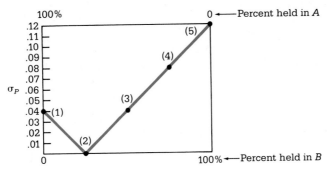

EXHIBIT 17.6
Portfolio risk (σ_P): Five portfolios of securities *A* and *B* with perfectly negatively correlated returns ($r = -1.0$)

life is more difficult. But suppose you could analyze a large number of investments and derive an efficient frontier from your work. Exhibit 17.8 shows an example of how it might appear (temporarily ignore line *IC*). Again, only portfolios not dominated by others form the efficient frontier.

The particular contour of the efficient frontier differs from the one shown in Exhibit 17.7 because it reflects the real-world environment in which perfectly negatively correlated returns among assets seldom, if ever, exist. So, it is impossible to create a zero-risk portfolio. However, we do find low correlations among assets, which still enables us to combine assets efficiently and to create portfolio effects. The mathematical computations needed to derive the efficient frontier become enormous as the number of individual assets increases. Unfortunately, we have to calculate the correlation coefficients between all possible pairs of assets.

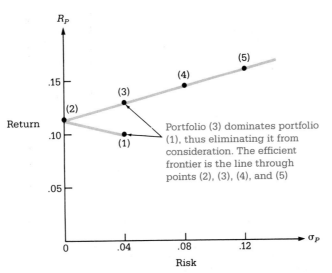

EXHIBIT 17.7
The efficient frontier constructed from portfolios of securities *A* and *B* when $r = -1.0$

BOX 17.1   INVESTMENT INSIGHTS

Do Aggressive Investors Acquire More Wealth?

A cornerstone of modern portfolio theory, including the Capital Asset Pricing Model extension, is that investors with less risk aversion (higher risk tolerance) select portfolios with both greater risk and greater expected return. Over time, these investors should accumulate greater wealth than conservative investors. This is the theory, but is there factual evidence to support it?

Answering the question above in a scientific manner is not as easy as you might think. For one thing, you have to measure investors' risk tolerance levels, which are fundamentally subjective elements. Also, you must control other factors that bear on wealth, such as age, income, and inheritance. An older person, or one with a high income, or a lucky beneficiary may have considerable wealth even though they are very risk-averse.

A particularly enlightening study was done by Thomas H. McInish, Sridhar N. Ramaswami, and Rajendra K. Srivastava ("Do More Risk-Averse Investors Have Lower Net Worth and Income?" *The Financial Review,* February 1993). Using a comprehensive data panel consisting of 3,079 members of upscale households, the researchers did find that lower risk aversion is associated with greater wealth. Risk aversion was measured with a questionnaire that asked respondents to rank four investments with varying levels of risk and expected return. Results were scaled in index form with possible values ranging from 20 (least risk aversion) to 30 (most risk aversion).

The average net worth of a respondent was $335,300, and the average risk-aversion score was 27.7. Regression analysis indicated a negative relation between risk aversion and wealth (as theory predicts), and each index point increase (decrease) reduced (increased) net worth by $10,620. So, if you were average in all respects but aversion to risk, where you showed the least risk aversion (a 20 score), your wealth was considerably more than that of your average counterpart who had the highest risk aversion (a 30 score)—$419,000 versus $311,000.

This finding and others have important implications for portfolio planning. They caution against excessive risk aversion over time. Yet many investors apparently don't get the message, judging by the large amounts invested in long-term, tax-deferred vehicles such as IRAs and 401(k) plans. Some studies have shown that as much as 25% of such investments are in very low risk saving accounts and money market mutual funds. Modern portfolio theory advises against taking unnecessary and foolish risks associated with poor diversification, but that advice should not be interpreted as suggesting excessive risk aversion.

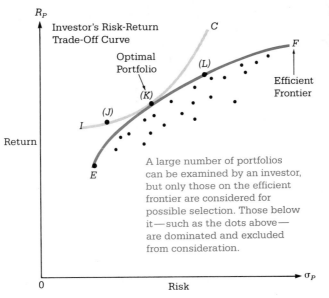

EXHIBIT 17.8
Selecting an optimal
portfolio

Selecting a Portfolio

You cannot select a portfolio only on the basis that it is on the efficient frontier. Many portfolios satisfy that criterion. To choose, you must first determine your willingness to trade off higher return for lower risk. Let's assume you can make such trade-offs, and to see the process visually, let us further assume that you can describe the trade-offs in graphic form as the line *IC* in Exhibit 17.8. Now we have a solution: the point where *IC* touches but does not intersect *EF* indicates the exact portfolio for you. It is portfolio *K*. You would like more return, but you would have to take more risk to get it. Your *IC* line shows that if you went to another portfolio (*L*, for example) to get a better return, you would be dissatisfied. The additional realized return from the *EF* line is less that what you have to earn, as indicated by the *IC* line. So, you would remain at *K* rather than going to *L*. By similar reasoning, you would also refuse portfolio *J*.

MPT and the CAPM

Applying MPT, in the form explained above, to examine an almost infinite number of portfolios that can be created from assets in the real world presents serious mathematical complexities. However, working with broad asset groups—stocks, bonds, gold, and so forth—reduces the problem. Moreover, it isn't necessary that you determine the exact optimal combination of assets to benefit from the lessons MPT has taught us. Even a rough approximation that recognizes asset correlations will provide a better portfolio than one derived without such recognition. In other words, an approximation of the *right* concept is far better than exact use of the *wrong* one.

EXHIBIT 17.9
The Capital Asset
Pricing Model (CAPM)
and portfolio con-
struction

R_P

An efficient portfolio, such as K,
must be on the SML; otherwise,
an investor would reject it and
simply hold the risk-free asset
and the market in portfolio
to achieve the same risk.

Securities Market Line
(SML)

K

Return

R_M

R_M

The SML is constructed by
passing a line through points
R_F (return on a risk-free asset)
and R_M (return on a market
portfolio of securities, given a
beta weight of 1.0).

R_F

1.0

β

Risk

The CAPM uses the
beta weight (β) to
measure risk, rather
than portfolio standard
deviation (σ_p).

Nevertheless, academicians and practitioners wanted an easier
approach. One emerged from a body of ideas after Markowitz's original work,
and it is referred to as the capital asset pricing model (CAPM). The major
thrust of the CAPM is to measure the risk of each asset in terms of how its
return varies in response to changes in the return of the overall market. This
measurement statistic is called the asset's beta value. By determining every
individual asset's beta, you can judge immediately its risk in relation to the
market and in relation to other assets. It is no longer necessary to examine an
infinite number of combinations of thousands of assets to derive an efficient
frontier because combinations of only two assets—one that is risk-free and
one representing the overall market—will accomplish the same end, as
Exhibit 17.9 shows.

We have explained and used the CAPM at various points throughout the
text, particularly Chapters 4, 6, and 7. Although certain fundamental propositions of the CAPM have been the subject of controversy, it nevertheless
remains a useful investment approach that should be understood and used
by individual investors.

**Passive portfolio plan-
ning techniques:** investment selection that uses
only two assets—the mar-
ket and one that is risk-
free

Passive Portfolio Planning Techniques

The widespread acceptance of modern portfolio theory has led many
investors to use **passive portfolio planning techniques,** which holds to

the basic premise of the CAPM that markets are efficient and that investors cannot consistently beat the market on a risk-adjusted basis. Because we cannot beat the market, rather than trying to find undervalued assets, our efforts should be directed toward determining our risk tolerance level and then allocating our investment funds between the risk-free asset and the market.

Returning to Exhibit 17.9, suppose that you believe your risk tolerance is reflected by a beta value of 0.5; that is, you want a portfolio only half as risky as the market. Your portfolio planning, then, is no more complicated than investing half your funds in the risk-free asset and half your funds in the market. As long as your risk-tolerance level doesn't change, you adjust to the 50-50 split at the beginning of each investment period. Although passive portfolio planning seems almost too easy to be effective, consider that possibly as much as several hundred billion dollars is managed using the technique. Consider further that much of this money is invested by large financial institutions. If these investors find it appealing, small investors would do well also to consider its use. There are, however, some problems in implementation, which are discussed below.

What Is the Risk-Free Asset?   The simple answer to this question is that the risk-free asset should be a Treasury security (or insured savings account) that has a maturity equal to the investor's holding period. So, if the holding period is one year, then one-year Treasury securities is the answer. But this answer begs the question because we then must ask, what is the appropriate investment period? If the answer here is a very short period—say, one week—then we will be rebalancing the portfolio quite frequently and incurring transactions costs each time. On the other hand, if the period is very long—say, five years—then we are not likely to hold our desired target mix for much of the period because we will not be rebalancing to the 50-50 split. Because there is no correct answer, each investor must make his own choice. This is a rather minor problem, and many investors find a one-year holding period is workable.

What Is the Market Asset?   Large investors can achieve a market asset by selecting their own securities or other assets, but small investors typically must rely on mutual funds that mimic the market. There are a number of these available, such as the *First Index Trust* (which tracks the S&P 500 stock index) offered by the Vanguard Group of mutual funds. Another issue to resolve is what assets should be included as part of the market asset. Should it consist of stocks only, or should it include other assets, such as long-term bonds and tangibles? Again, there is no right or wrong approach, and investors must follow the one that seems most useful for their situations. Someone who does not own a personal residence might want to include tangibles in the market asset, while a homeowner is likely to want only stocks or stocks and bonds.

Are High Risk Levels Achievable? After the market asset is defined, another issue to resolve is how risk levels greater than the one associated with the market asset can be achieved. Suppose an investor wants a risk level 50% greater than the market asset (a beta of 1.5). How does she get it? A commonly used approach is to borrow money and leverage your investment in the market asset. This procedure was explained in Chapter 6, in which we also noted that investors typically cannot borrow at the low risk-free rate, R_F. Assuming that borrowing is done at a higher rate means the investor cannot achieve the returns indicated by the SML beyond the point R_M; point K, for example, in Exhibit 17.9 would be unachievable.

This problem does not destroy the usefulness of passive investing to aggressive investors, although they may want to consider investing in aggressive mutual funds (those with betas in excess of 1.0) as an alternative to leveraging an investment in the market asset. Another alternative is to use stock index options or futures to shape the portfolio. This possibility is examined in the next section.

MODIFYING PORTFOLIOS WITH DERIVATIVES

The most dramatic and influential change in portfolio management over the past dozen years unquestionably is the increased use of derivative instruments—options and futures contracts—to achieve portfolio goals. You should recall from Chapters 11, 12, and 13 our discussions of how these instruments can be used in risky ways (naked positions) and in ways that potentially reduce risk (hedges and, to a lesser extent, spreads). Because we discussed in these earlier chapters a number of specific strategies involving actual option and futures contracts, our treatment here focuses on general strategies and is limited to market index options and futures. Keep in mind that a large number of index contracts are actually traded; so, our discussion is not simply theoretical.

Creating Synthetic Positions

Synthetic position:
using derivative instruments to mimic stock or bond positions

One of the more intriguing uses of derivatives is their capacity to simulate actual positions in securities, such as stocks or bonds; such a simulated position is called a **synthetic position.** Exhibit 17.10 is provided as a frame of reference to guide our discussion. It shows profits and losses from an actual $250,000 portfolio and from long and short positions in (a) a futures contract that is based on 500 times an index value and (b) long (buyer) and short (seller) positions in 5.0 call or put option contracts that pay off at 100 times the index. We assume each option contract has a strike price of 500 and costs $1,500; also, we assume the futures contracts have a contract price of 500. For simplicity, we assume each derivative has a one-year maturity.

EXHIBIT 17.10
Payoffs with a $250,000
portfolio and various
futures and options

Assumptions:	1. Current index value = 500.
	2. Each option contract costs $1,500
	3. Futures positions are costless
	4. Commissions are not considered

	Index Values		
	400	500	600
1. Portfolio	$−50,000	$ -0-	$+50,000
2. Futures positions			
500 × change in index:			
Long	−50,000	-0-	+50,000
Short	+50,000	-0-	−50,000
3. Call options			
100 × change in index			
× 5 contracts:			
Buyer (long)	− 7,500	− 7,500	+42,500
Seller (short)	+ 7,500	+ 7,500	−42,500
4. Put options			
100 × change in index			
× 5 contracts:			
Buyer (long)	+42,500	− 7,500	− 7,500
Seller (short)	−42,500	+ 7,500	+ 7,500
5. Current yield:			
Portfolio (2%)	+ 5,000	+ 5,000	+ 5,000
Treasury bills (4%)	+10,000	+10,000	+10,000

Synthetic Long Position Assume the index currently has a value of 500. If our portfolio tracks the index perfectly (assume that it is invested in an index fund), as the index increases to 600, we make a profit of $50,000; if it decreases to 400, we lose $50,000. Now, any derivative or combination of derivatives that shows similar gains and losses as the index changes can serve as a substitute for our portfolio. The simplest strategy is to take a long position in the futures contract. This position moves in perfect tandem with our portfolio.

Can you see another strategy using options? Suppose we go long on five call contracts while shorting on five put contracts. Now, what happens if the index goes to 600? As the call option buyer, we make $42,500, and as the put option seller, we make $7,500. The two positions total a $50,000 profit, which is what the portfolio shows.

Which is the better of the two synthetic portfolios? Given our assumptions, they are identical, and one is as good as the other. But in the real world, we may find differences that could make a difference. For example, suppose we could sell the puts for $1,700 while still paying $1,500 for the calls. We then receive $8,500 while paying only $7,500. The options-created synthetic is now better because we make a $1,000 profit. In addition to price disparities, we need to consider such factors as commissions and margin requirements. Indeed, the portfolio manager must constantly examine the situation to determine an optimal approach.

Synthetic Short Positions   Although short positions are not typically an important part of portfolio management, you should see that derivatives can create them as easily as they create long positions. For example, simply take a short position in the futures contract, or, using options, buy five put contracts while selling five call contracts. Presto, instant short positions in a $250,000 portfolio either way.

Is a Synthetic Portfolio Better Than the Real Thing?   Although synthetic positions seem a clever idea, is there any reason why we should prefer them to the real thing? Let's broaden our example. Suppose that if we actually invested in the stock portfolio, our dividend yield would be 2%, or $5,000 a year. Now, if we create a synthetic portfolio, it is essentially costless in the sense that we invest nothing. So, we could put $250,000 in Treasury bills, and assuming they earn 4%, or $10,000, we are $5,000 better off than in the actual portfolio. You should see that as the relation between current yields on stocks and Treasury bills changes, one approach becomes more favorable relative to the other. Again, it is important to remember that we are not considering commissions or other potential costs with derivatives. Bringing them into our present example would diminish the derivatives' advantage, although they are not likely to be so large as to eliminate it.

Adjusting Stock Portfolios' Risk Levels

Let us assume that we want to maintain a $250,000 long position in the market. We can do this with an actual portfolio of stocks that, again, tracks the index perfectly, or by holding $250,000 in T bills plus a long position in 1.0 index futures contract. Assume that we use the latter strategy. Assume further that periodically we feel optimistic or pessimistic about the market's performance in upcoming periods. We might be following a tactical asset allocation model, as discussed in Chapter 16.

Adjusting our synthetic portfolio is extremely easy; for example, if we became bullish, we would want to increase the portfolio beta, say, from 1.0 to 1.5. All that we need to do is take a long position in 1.5 contracts, rather than 1.0 contract. (Assume for simplicity that fractional contracts are possible, or, more realistically, that we have a $500,000 portfolio, in which case we go long on three contracts.)

Exhibit 17.11 shows the case above. As you see, if the index does increase from 500 to 600, the profit on the beta 1.0 portfolio is $50,000, as shown previously. But the beta 1.5 portfolio shows a profit of $75,000.

EXHIBIT 17.11

Using futures contracts
to achieve target
portfolio betas (β)

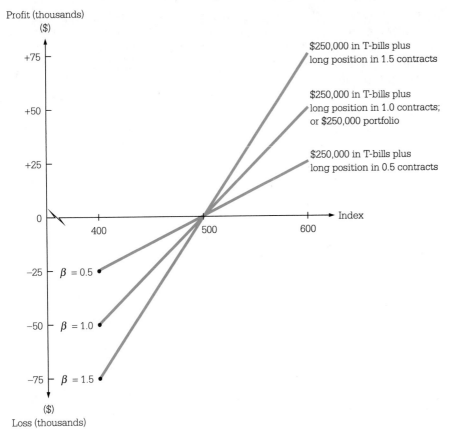

Profit (thousands)
($)

$250,000 in T-bills plus
long position in 1.5 contracts

$250,000 in T-bills plus
long position in 1.0 contracts;
or $250,000 portfolio

$250,000 in T-bills plus
long position in 0.5 contracts

Index

$\beta = 0.5$

$\beta = 1.0$

$\beta = 1.5$

($)
Loss (thousands)

Unfortunately, the sword cuts on both edges, and if the index fell to 400, the beta 1.5 portfolio loses $75,000 rather than $50,000.

Exhibit 17.11 also shows that we can adjust the synthetic portfolio if we become bearish. In this case, we reduce our long position from 1.0 contracts to 0.5 contracts. Now, if the index falls to 400, our loss will be only $25,000 rather than $50,000. Right or wrong in our forecasts, the important point is that adjusting the synthetic portfolio may be easier to do and more cost-effective than making changes in an actual portfolio consisting of stocks and T bills.

Adjusting Bond Portfolios' Risk Levels

Our discussion so far has focused on stock portfolios; bond portfolios should be equally important to us. As we learned in Chapter 9, bond prices can fluctuate considerably in response to changes in the general level of interest rates. We introduced a concept called the interest-rate elasticity coefficient

(E), which measures the changes in a bond's price (present value) relative to changes in its yield to maturity (YTM). Values for E are always negative, and the larger the negative value, the greater the bond's price volatility.

Bond portfolio managers also can become bullish or bearish about future interest-rate environments. Adjusting the bond portfolio in reaction to their sentiments involves changing the average maturity and/or coupon yield of the portfolio. If we thought interest rates would fall, we would seek to increase maturity and/or lower coupon yield; each change would increase the negative elasticity value and, we hope, allow us to benefit through higher bond prices. Contrarily, if we thought interest rates would rise, we would seek a smaller (negative) E value.

Increasing the Portfolio's Risk Exposure To increase the bond portfolio's risk—that is, to raise its E value—we must go long on an appropriate interest-rate futures contract. In Chapter 13, we explain the Treasury bond futures contract in detail. It assumes the delivery of a 20-year Treasury bond with an 8% coupon rate. Suppose, for simplicity, that our portfolio consists entirely of 100 such bonds. The relation between one of these bond's price and its YTM is shown by line (1) in Exhibit 17.12. If YTM is 8%, the bond is priced at par of $1,000. If YTM increases to 10%, price falls to $830; if YTM falls to 6%, price

EXHIBIT 17.12
Using futures to achieve target portfolio interest-rate elasticities (*E)*

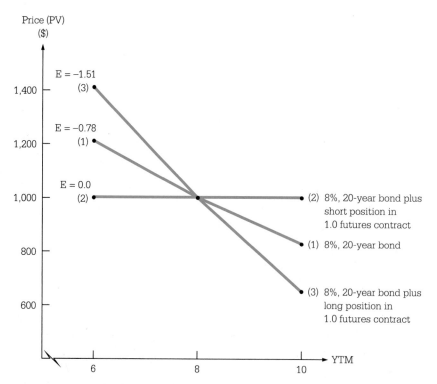

increases to $1,290 (we assume annual interest for simplicity). This bond and our portfolio of 100 such bonds have an E value of −0.78.

If we are bullish about interest rates, we take a long position in the futures contract. In effect, this would double any gains or losses from changes in our bonds' prices. Because we think that they will go up, this doubling is to our advantage. Line (3) in Exhibit 17.12 shows the situation. As you see, long position changes the bonds' elasticity coefficient from −.078 to −1.51. If YTM did indeed fall to 6%, our profit would be $458 per bond (× 100 = $45,800 for the portfolio), rather than $229 ($22,900 for the portfolio). If we guess wrong, we lose $340 per bond, rather than $170.

Decreasing the Portfolio's Risk Exposure (Hedging)   If we thought interest rates would increase, then we would seek a short position in the futures contract, rather than a long one. If we shorted one contract for each 100 bonds that we owned, we would in effect hedge the portfolio perfectly. (One futures contract requires delivery of 100 bonds with a face value of $1,000 per bond.) The perfect hedge means that even if interest rates rise, the value of our bond portfolio remains at $100,000. However, the hedge also eliminates any potential profit if interest rates fall. If we did not want to take this extreme of a position, then we should have shorted less than one full contract for each 100 bonds held.

Finally, we have not addressed real-world problems associated with hedging because these were covered in Chapter 13. A particularly thorny problem with bond portfolios is finding an appropriate hedge instrument. In reality, our bond portfolio is not likely to consist of only 8% bonds with 20-year maturities. Thus, we may need to determine appropriate hedge ratios, as we explained in Chapter 13.

INTERNATIONAL DIVERSIFICATION

As the value of the dollar, relative to other currencies, reached a peak in 1984 and then started to decline, internationalizing the portfolio became a popular investment theme. Many mutual funds specializing in foreign holdings were organized almost overnight, appealing to investors who wanted a convenient vehicle to play the theme. Concurrently, many foreign companies were offering their shares—through American depository receipts (ADRs; see Chapter 6)—to U.S. investors. Actually, the advantages of international diversification had been noted long before this movement began. These advantages, as well as the risks, should be understood by all investors.

Advantages

There are two potential contributions any asset can make to a portfolio: it can increase portfolio return while leaving risk unchanged, or it can reduce port-

EXHIBIT 17.13

Return correlations between the U.S. and three other stock markets

United Kingdom	+0.50
Japan	+0.31
West Germany	+0.38

SOURCE: Gerald P. Dwyer, Jr., and R. W. Hafer, "Are National Stock Markets Linked?" *Review*, Federal Reserve Bank of St. Louis, November/December, 1988, pp. 3–14.

folio risk, leaving return unchanged. There is evidence showing international investing offers such advantages.

Higher Returns   If you limit your investments to one country, then your return over time from a broadly diversified portfolio must be limited to that country's growth. For U.S. citizens, this restriction often has resulted in a relatively poor performance, compared with other countries. For example, Japan's average annual growth rate since the 1960s has been about twice as high as that of the United States. And in recent years, countries such as Hong Kong, South Korea, and Mexico have shown much higher economic growth rates. International investing allows us to participate in these high growth areas and others.

Lower Systematic Risk   As we discussed in Chapter 6, systematic risk cannot be eliminated by adding more securities to a portfolio, but considerable evidence shows that international diversification reduces such risk. This is so because of the relatively poor correlations between returns on U.S. and foreign securities. Exhibit 17.13 indicates correlations found in one study; others show similar results. Although United Kingdom and U.S. returns are moderately correlated, in the other cases, correlations are weak. A U.S. investor, then, could have achieved risk reduction by holding securities in any of the countries along with U.S. securities. This fact is highlighted in Exhibit 17.14, where the internationalized portfolio offers less risk for any given portfolio size.

Disadvantages

The advantage of lower systematic risk just discussed must be balanced against random risks associated with foreign securities. Some investment advisors believe these latter risks are too large to be eliminated through diversification of foreign holdings, and thus, they could influence the internationalized portfolio. Indeed, these advisors doubt the effect shown in Exhibit 17.14 will hold over a long period and believe that internationalizing your portfolio might increase its risk. Critics often single out exchange-rate risk and political risks as the most disturbing influences.

BOX 17.2   A QUESTION OF ETHICS

Is Greater Competition Needed in the ADR Business?

Investing in foreign companies would be virtually impossible for many Americans without ADRs. Created by a mere three New York city banks and, of late, the investment banking firm of Morgan Stanley, ADRs are available on about 250 listed stocks and about the same number traded over the counter. Both individual investors and institutions such as mutual funds use ADRs to achieve an international diversification. That's the good part.

Unfortunately, there is a bad part. The ADR-creating oligopoly apparently has devised a fee structure that one observer described as "price gouging" (Vivian Lewis, editor of *Global Investing,* as quoted in an article by Susan Antilla, "New Shaker in the A.D.R. Business," *The New York Times*, August 1, 1993, Money Section, p. 13). Examples: a fee of 18.5% for distributing dividends of Ashton Mining, an Australian company, and a 10% fee for converting bahts (Thailand currency) to dollars in another distribution. Moreover, the banks charge for issuing certificates and for "rounding off," a practice that adds a cost both when you buy and when you sell.

Several ethical issues are involved with the ADR-creation system. Is price gouging really going on, or, as the banks claim, are high fees necessary to cover the fixed costs associated with a stock issue? Given the almost infinite number of formulas banks might use to allocate general overhead to their ADR services divisions, it is unlikely that any "true" measurement of divisional profit will be forthcoming. And even if it did, what action should be taken? Few people these days favor regulation as a means of lowering prices while simultaneously expanding the market.

To achieve those twin goals, it would be better to create a more competitive environment. Lewis is optimistic that Morgan Stanley's entrance into the industry might have that effect. It is a curiosity that more banks have not tried to become players, if the profits really are so exorbitant. Capital requirements wouldn't appear to create a barrier for many banks; perhaps knowledge and information are the roadblocks, although it's difficult to imagine huge complexities in managing an ADR trust.

Frankly, the government agencies—the Securities and Exchange Commission or the Justice Department—might not perceive the problem as a major one, or that a problem even exists. Smoothing the process whereby foreign companies can more easily tap into American capital is not likely to be on the front burner of any administration—Democratic or Republican. That's unfortunate and one-sided; sure, the foreign company stands to gain, but so does the U.S. investor.

EXHIBIT 17.14

Illustration of risk and portfolio size, holding return constant

Adding securities to any portfolio reduces its risk, but if foreign securities are substituted for U.S. securities, risk is reduced even further.

U.S. Securities

U.S. and Foreign Securities

Number of Securities in the Portfolio

Exchange-Rate Risk   When you invest in a foreign security, your investment return will be determined by two factors. The performance of the security in question is the first determinant. If you purchased bonds of a British firm paying 15% interest, then you will earn that rate, assuming interest is paid. It is paid, however, in pounds, not dollars. As Exhibit 17.15 shows, you must then convert pounds to dollars before the payout has any value to you. But suppose the dollar appreciated 10% against the pound during the year after purchase. (A currency appreciates when acquiring one of its units requires more units of a foreign currency. In the example, initially, 1 pound acquired 1.5 dollars, and later, 1 pound acquired only 1.35 dollars; at the new

EXHIBIT 17.15

Foreign investment return and exchange-rate risk: Dollar appreciation reduces realized yield

	Pounds	Exchange Rate: No. of Dollars to Acquire 1 Pound	Dollars
1/1/19X1: Purchase one British bond with a 15% coupon rate	600.0	1.50 to 1.0	900.0
12/31/19X1: Anticipate interest on bond	90.0	1.50 to 1.0	135.0
Anticipated yield	15%		15%
12/31/19X1: Interest on bond actually received	90.0	1.35 to 1.0	121.5
Realized yield	15%		13.5%

exchange rate, it would take 1.111 [1.5 ÷ 1.35] pounds to acquire 1.5 dollars. Thus, the dollar has appreciated, while the pound has depreciated.) Now, your return realized in dollars is only 13.5%. The adverse movement in the exchange rate—the dollar's *appreciation*—reduced your return.

If exchange rates between the dollar and other currencies showed random movements over time, **exchange-rate risk** would be minimized, with any adverse movement against some currencies being offset by favorable movements against others. However, the historical pattern of rates suggests that most key currencies move together against the dollar, although there are important exceptions. Thus, the strengthening of the dollar in 1989 meant a general *appreciation*, with the implication that most foreign investment returns would be *reduced* (as they were). Exhibit 17.16 shows the dramatic impact changes in exchange rates can have on investment returns. During most of the 1970s, the dollar depreciated relative to most other currencies. As you see, this had the effect of increasing annual rates of return in foreign countries. The rate of return in Switzerland, for example, was boosted from 2.0% to 11.3%.

Exchange-rate risk: risk associated with changes in the value of the dollar relative to the value of foreign currencies

Political Risk   Perhaps most U.S. investors are narrow in their view on world affairs, but the fact remains that many see foreign countries as considerably riskier than the United States. This perception is the biggest deterrent to investing abroad. In some cases, this fear is probably exaggerated, but in others, it may not be. Political instability can arise from a variety of causes, ranging from ineptness at managing internal fiscal affairs to outright confiscation of private property. Surely, diversifying among countries will reduce such risk; nevertheless, a massive change in the world socioeconomic structure could lead to substantial investment losses. (A movement this broad probably would lead to sharp losses in the United States as well.)

With the exception of Japan, those countries with the highest expected growth also offer the highest **political risk**—South Korea, Taiwan, Hong Kong, and other countries in the Pacific basin being good examples. Hong Kong, for instance, becomes part of mainland China in the 1990s. What then?

Political risk: risk associated with political instabilities in countries where investment may otherwise be desirable

EXHIBIT 17.16
Annual returns in six foreign countries and the U.S.

	In National Currency	In U.S. Dollars
United States	5.8%	5.8%
Australia	6.7	7.0
Canada	12.3	11.6
Japan	11.9	16.7
Switzerland	2.0	11.3
United Kingdom	10.1	9.8
West Germany	3.4	10.4

SOURCE: Richard K. Abrams and Donald V. Kimball. "U.S. Investment in Foreign Equity Markets." *Economic Review*, Federal Reserve Bank of Kansas City, April 1981.

No one knows for sure, but the risks of the situation were brought into focus during the student demonstrations in Beijing in 1989. The government's oppressive resistance led many investors to question whether a free enterprise system can coexist with a totalitarian regime.

No one knows the future in a broader perspective. We do know the past, however, and the record is mixed. Many individual and institutional investors have done exceptionally well with foreign investments, but some have not. For example, in the 1970s and early 1980s, massive investments were made by commercial banks in Mexico and other South American countries with mixed performance results. At various times, some observers thought these investments might lead to massive bank failures as countries reneged on their repayment obligations. However, that has not occurred, and interestingly, South America was a "hot" foreign investment market in the early 1990s.

SUMMARY

MPT shows that investors should consider return correlations among assets when forming portfolios. An efficient frontier of portfolios means that investors must give up return in seeking lower risk levels and that only combinations of assets not dominated by other combinations are considered. Combining efficient frontiers with investors' risk-return trade-off curves determines optimal portfolios. MPT led to the development of the CAPM and the SML concept. The SML makes application of MPT much easier and readily available to all investors through passive portfolio planning techniques. There are problems, however, in terms of defining the risk-free asset and the market asset and how high risk levels can be achieved.

Derivative securities—options and futures contracts—based on market indexes provide portfolio managers with greater flexibility in designing and modifying portfolios. Derivatives allow the creation of synthetic positions and portfolios that simulate actual positions and actual portfolios. Synthetic portfolios may be managed more cost-effectively than actual portfolios and, thus, may be more desirable. Synthetic portfolios of stocks and bonds are possible, and each is used to adjust risk levels by adjusting beta values and interest-rate elasticity coefficients.

International diversification may be advantageous by providing both higher returns and, possibly, lower risk than if the portfolio is limited to U.S. securities. Disadvantages include exchange-rate risk and political risk.

KEY TERMS (listed in order of appearance)	modern portfolio theory	passive portfolio planning techniques
	coefficient of covariance	synthetic position
	correlation coefficient	exchange-rate risk
	portfolio effect	political risk
	efficient frontier	

1. In what way does MPT differ from conventional portfolio management?
2. Describe the coefficient of covariance. Is its sign (+ or −) important? Explain.
3. Describe the correlation coefficient. In terms of reducing risk, is it better to have positive or negative values? Explain.
4. What is an efficient frontier? Explain, making sure you indicate what makes it efficient.
5. Explain how an investor can find his optimal portfolio.
6. In what manner does the CAPM simplify MPT? What is the SML?
7. Describe passive portfolio planning techniques. Are these techniques difficult to execute in the real world? Explain.
8. How should the risk-free asset and the market asset be determined? Would these be the same for all investors? Explain.
9. What limitation does passive investing have in terms of achieving portfolios with high risk levels?
10. What is a synthetic position? Explain how you can create a synthetic long position using futures contracts or option contracts. Offer a similar explanation for creating a synthetic short position.
11. Why would investors want to create synthetic portfolios?
12. Explain how you can increase a portfolio's beta with a futures contract. How would you reduce the portfolio's beta?
13. Explain how you can increase a bond portfolio's interest-rate elasticity coefficient? How can you reduce it?
14. Discuss in general several advantages and several disadvantages of international diversification.
15. Explain why foreign diversification can reduce systematic risk.
16. Explain how exchange-rate risk influences a foreign investment.

1. A return matrix from two investments is shown below. Each investment is sensitive to changes in the overall economy.

	Economic Performance		
	Good	So-So	Poor
Probabilities of occurring	0.2	0.6	0.2
Returns: investment A	8%	10%	12%
investment B	30	15	0

   a. For each investment, determine the expected return, variance, and standard deviation.
   b. Determine the coefficient of covariance and correlation coefficient between the two investments' returns.
   c. Explain if the assets are good candidates to be held together in a portfolio.
2. Using the information in problem 1, determine the expected return with a portfolio equally weighted in A and B. Determine the variance and standard deviation for this portfolio.

3. Using the information in problem 1 and using a trial-and-error approach, create an almost risk-free portfolio of A and B. Indicate the proportional portfolio weights of each.

4. With your solutions to problems 2 and 3, explain why you would never invest all your funds in investment A; that is, explain why a portfolio of A and B dominates A.

5. Suppose a market index currently has a value of 200. A futures contract is available and currently quoted also at 200. In addition, put and call options with strike prices of 200 are available, with the put quoted at $800 a contract and the call quoted at $600. The futures contract pays off at 1,000 times the index, while each option contract pays off at 100 times the index. You have $500,000 to invest. You could invest in a mutual fund that mimics the index perfectly and will pay dividends of 3% in the upcoming period. Treasury bills are likely to yield 4% during this period. You believe that the maximum fluctuation of the index is between 160 and 240.

    a. Indicate your holding period return in dollars if you invest in the mutual fund.

    b. Indicate your holding period return if you create a synthetic portfolio using futures contracts. What position will you take in the futures? How many contracts do you need?

6. Given the information in problem 5, determine if a synthetic portfolio created with futures contracts is better than one created with option contracts. Explain how you will use the option contracts, indicating the kind and number needed.

7. You have an investment portfolio of $2 million currently in T bills. Periodically, you have strong feelings that the stock market will perform very well or very poorly in an upcoming period. A market index currently has a value of 500 and a futures contract based on this index is available, which pays off at 500 times the index.

    a. You are bullish about the upcoming period and are considering investing in a portfolio of stocks with a beta of 2.0. Indicate an alternative strategy that should produce similar results.

    b. What would be your portfolio beta if you sold $1 million of bills and invested the funds in (1) the portfolio indicated in question a or (2) a market portfolio with a beta of 1.0.

    c. Using futures contracts, explain how you could create synthetic portfolios to mimic the two in question b.

8. You hold a $4 million portfolio of Treasury bonds with an average coupon rate of 6% and average maturity of 10 years. A futures contract based on this coupon rate and maturity is also available. Assume the contract calls for the delivery of 100 bonds.

    a. Determine the present values of such a bond for YTMs of 6%, 4%, and 8%. (You may need to review Chapter 9 to answer this question and the next.)

    b. Calculate the interest-rate elasticity coefficient from the 4% YTM to the 8% YTM.

    c. Suppose you wanted to double the elasticity value; explain how you can accomplish this goal.

    d. Suppose you wanted to hedge your portfolio so that its value will not change regardless of changes in market interest rates. Explain what you would do.

9. *(Student Project)* Obtain an issue of *The Wall Street Journal*, and find quotations on index futures contracts and index options. Note their specific characteristics.
10. *(Student Project)* Obtain an issue of *Barron's* and find the section that reports on closed-end funds. Prepare a list of the funds that invest in the securities of one country.

CASE ANALYSES

Danielle Boone has accumulated a $5 million portfolio of securities over the past 10 years in a more or less random manner. She owns a hodge-podge of growth stocks, income stocks, and Treasury bonds. Danielle's portfolio took a big hit last year, and she has vowed to get some help to rearrange her holdings so that she has fewer worries and more sleepful nights. She has turned to you in desperation.

17.1
Danielle Boone
Seeks the
Efficient Frontier

You undertook a correlation analysis on your computer and determined the following expected returns, standard deviations, and beta values. This information is shown below. You also interviewed Danielle and determined that she has a relatively high risk tolerance level; specifically, for portfolios with standard deviations of 30%, 25%, 20%, 15%, and 10%, she seeks required returns of 24%, 18%, 14%, 13%, and 12.5%, respectively.

Portfolio	Standard Deviation	Expected Return	Beta
100% GS	30%	16%	2.0
100% IS	20	11	0.8
100% B	10	8	0.0
50% GS + 50% IS	25	13.5	1.4
50% GS + 50% B	15	12	1.0
50% IS + 50% B	15	9.5	0.4
80% GS + 20% B	20	14	1.6
90% GS + 10% B	25	15.2	1.8

a. Determine Danielle's efficient frontier, clearly indicating portfolios on *and* off the frontier.
b. What is the optimum portfolio? Explain.
c. In an SML setting, which portfolio might be considered a risk-free asset? What additional information should you have before making this choice? Which portfolio can be considered a market asset? Explain.
d. Construct an SML. Indicate portfolios that are above, on, or below the SML. Which portfolios are optimal in this setting? Which one do you specifically recommend for Danielle?

Questions

17.2 Danielle Boone Leaves the Frontier and Goes Synthetic

You have been helping Danielle Boone sort out her investments and have recently constructed an optimal portfolio for her (see Case 17.1). You thought that Danielle, after repositioning her assets, would relax and take her investment life easy. Unfortunately, Danielle now thinks she can forecast future market cycles; specifically, she believes that the market will be robust in the upcoming period and is likely to increase by 20%. She is so convinced of this potentiality that she now wants you to recommend strategies that can exploit her feelings. You think that Danielle should also consider the possibility that the market could decrease by 20%.

You are somewhat frustrated with Danielle because she recently incurred commissions when she altered her portfolio, which is currently worth $5 million. You are beginning to think that she will always have a fickle investment attitude and that it might be better for her to put all her money in a risk-free asset and periodically adjust her risk exposure through futures contracts. A contract on a market index is available that pays off at 500 times the index, which currently has a value of 450. (Review the data provided in Case 17.1 before answering the following questions.)

Questions

a. Assume that you will use futures contracts to arrange Danielle's situation to achieve a portfolio beta of 2.0. Explain carefully and in detail what you will do.

b. Explain why the strategy involving futures might be better (or worse) than putting all her $5 million in the growth stock portfolio.

c. Suppose option contracts with a strike price of 450 are also available on the index and are currently quoted at $600 for a put and $500 for a call. The options pay off at 100 times the index. What strategy would you use with these options? Explain if this is a better approach than using the futures contracts.

HELPFUL READING

Antilla, Susan. "New Shaker in the A.D.R. Business." *The New York Times*, August 1, 1993, p. 13.

Booth, David G., and Eugene F. Fama. "Diversification Returns and Asset Contributions." *Financial Analysts Journal*, May-June 1992, pp. 26–32.

Kritzman, Mark. "What Practitioners Need to Know About Optimization." *Financial Analysts Journal*, September-October 1992, pp. 10–13.

McInish, Thomas H., Sridar N. Ramaswami, and Rajendra K. Srivastava. "Do More Risk-Averse Investors Have Lower Net Worth and Income?" *The Financial Review*, February 1993, pp. 91–106.

Ranney, Richard. "Without Portfolio." *Barron's*, April 12, 1993, p. 13.

Riley, William B., Jr., and K. Victor Chow. "Asset Allocation and Individual Risk Aversion." *Financial Analysts Journal*, November-December 1992, pp. 33–37.

Tillery, James A., and Gary Latainer. "A Synthetic Option Framework for Asset Allocation." *Financial Analysts Journal*, May-June 1985, pp. 32–43.

Wyatt, Edward A. "Border Dispute." *Barron's*, May 17, 1993, p. 16.

PARTS FIVE AND SIX

CFA EXAMINATION QUESTIONS

1. A pension plan's real estate holdings consist of:

   ☐ an apartment building in Dallas, Texas;
   ☐ a warehouse in Denver, Colorado; and
   ☐ an office building in Houston, Texas.

   The pension plan would *most likely* invest in which *one* of the following if it wanted to reduce its overall risk?
   a. Shopping center in Greenville, South Carolina
   b. Light industrial center in Arlington, Texas
   c. Apartment building in Boston, Massachusetts
   d. Major office complex in Chicago, Illinois

2. Measuring investment returns provided by real estate as an asset class is complicated by:
   a. the use of leverage that distorts returns.
   b. lack of REIT data.
   c. the fact that REIT valuations understate underlying value.
   d. inaccuracies in appraisal valuations.

3. Study of historical real estate returns is made difficult by:
   a. lack of a real estate market index with a long history.
   b. infrequent transactions of individual properties.
   c. use of appraisals to estimate returns.
   d. all of the above.

4. Both strategic and tactical approaches to asset allocation:
   a. focus on the changing reward-to-variability ratio.
   b. seek to capture market inefficiencies.
   c. require continuing analysis of market circumstances.
   d. deemphasize consideration of changes in investor risk tolerance.

5. A major step in asset allocation is:
   a. assessing risk tolerance.
   b. analyzing company financial statements.
   c. estimating security beta.
   d. identifying market anomalies.

Reprinted with permission of the Association for Investment Management and Research. All are Level I Examination Questions, unless noted otherwise. Material related to questions 1–3 can be found in Chapter 15, questions 4–6 in Chapter 16, and questions 7–13 in Chapter 17.

6. In terms of risk levels, the ultimate result that occurs in a portfolio when part of the equity portion of the portfolio is liquidated and subsequently reinvested in money market instruments is:

   a. a decline in portfolio liquidity.
   b. a dramatic reduction in the beta of the portfolio.
   c. a dramatic reduction in the beta of the equity portion of the portfolio.
   d. an increase in portfolio risk.

7. A measure of how much the returns of two risky assets move together is:

   a. variance.
   b. standard deviation.
   c. covariance.
   d. semi-variance.

8. The standard deviation of variable X is .20. The standard deviation of variable Y is .12. The covariance between X and Y is .0096. The correlation between X and Y is then:

   a. 0.20
   b. 0.24
   c. 0.36
   d. 0.40

9. For a two-stock portfolio, what would be the preferred correlation coefficient between the two stocks?

   a. +1.00
   b. +0.50
   c.   0
   d. −1.00

10. Stocks A, B, and C each have the same expected return and standard deviation. Given the following correlations, which portfolio constructed from these stocks has the lowest risk?

    Correlation Matrix

Stock	A	B	C
A	+1.0		
B	+0.9	+1.0	
C	+0.1	−0.4	+1.0

    a. A portfolio equally invested in stocks A and B
    b. A portfolio equally invested in stocks A and C
    c. A portfolio equally invested in stocks B and C
    d. A portfolio totally invested in stock C

11. Which *one* of the following portfolios cannot lie on the efficient frontier as described by Markowitz?

	Portfolio	Expected Return	Standard Deviation
a.	W	9%	21%
b.	X	5%	7%
c.	Y	15%	36%
d.	Z	12%	15%

12. Portfolio theory as described by Markowitz is most concerned with:

a. the elimination of systematic risk.
b. the effect of diversification on portfolio risk.
c. the identification of unsystematic risk.
d. active portfolio management to enhance return.

13. You are a U.S. investor who purchased British securities for £2,000 one year ago when the British pound cost $1.50. What is your total return based in U.S. dollars if the value of the securities is now £2,400 and the pound is worth $1.75? No dividends or interest were paid during this period.

a. 16.7%
b. 20.0%
c. 28.6%
d. 40.0%

APPENDIX A

Time-Value-of-Money Tables

APPENDIX A.1

Future value of $1 at the end of n periods: $FV = (1.0 + i)^n$

Period	1%	2%	3%	4%	5%	6%	7%	8%	9%	10%	12%	14%	15%	16%	18%	20%	24%	28%	32%	36%
1	1.0100	1.0200	1.0300	1.0400	1.0500	1.0600	1.0700	1.0800	1.0900	1.1000	1.1200	1.1400	1.1500	1.1600	1.1800	1.2000	1.2400	1.2800	1.3200	1.3600
2	1.0201	1.0404	1.0609	1.0816	1.1025	1.1236	1.1449	1.1664	1.1881	1.2100	1.2544	1.2996	1.3225	1.3456	1.3924	1.4400	1.5376	1.6384	1.7424	1.8496
3	1.0303	1.0612	1.0927	1.1249	1.1576	1.1910	1.2250	1.2597	1.2950	1.3310	1.4049	1.4815	1.5209	1.5609	1.6430	1.7280	1.9066	2.0972	2.3000	2.5155
4	1.0406	1.0824	1.1255	1.1699	1.2155	1.2625	1.3108	1.3605	1.4116	1.4641	1.5735	1.6890	1.7490	1.8106	1.9388	2.0736	2.3642	2.6844	3.0360	3.4210
5	1.0510	1.1041	1.1593	1.2167	1.2763	1.3382	1.4026	1.4693	1.5386	1.6105	1.7623	1.9254	2.0114	2.1003	2.2878	2.4883	2.9316	3.4360	4.0075	4.6526
6	1.0615	1.1262	1.1941	1.2653	1.3401	1.4185	1.5007	1.5869	1.6771	1.7716	1.9738	2.1950	2.3131	2.4364	2.6996	2.9860	3.6352	4.3980	5.2899	6.3275
7	1.0721	1.1487	1.2299	1.3159	1.4071	1.5036	1.6058	1.7138	1.8280	1.9487	2.2107	2.5023	2.6600	2.8262	3.1855	3.5832	4.5077	5.6295	6.9826	8.6054
8	1.0829	1.1717	1.2668	1.3686	1.4775	1.5938	1.7182	1.8509	1.9926	2.1436	2.4760	2.8526	3.0590	3.2784	3.7589	4.2998	5.5895	7.2058	9.2170	11.703
9	1.0937	1.1951	1.3048	1.4233	1.5513	1.6895	1.8385	1.9990	2.1719	2.3579	2.7731	3.2519	3.5179	3.8030	4.4355	5.1598	6.9310	9.2234	12.166	15.916
10	1.1046	1.2190	1.3439	1.4802	1.6289	1.7908	1.9672	2.1589	2.3674	2.5937	3.1058	3.7072	4.0456	4.4114	5.2338	6.1917	8.5944	11.805	16.059	21.646
11	1.1157	1.2434	1.3842	1.5395	1.7103	1.8983	2.1049	2.3316	2.5804	2.8531	3.4785	4.2262	4.6524	5.1173	6.1759	7.4301	10.657	15.111	21.198	29.439
12	1.1268	1.2682	1.4258	1.6010	1.7959	2.0122	2.2522	2.5182	2.8127	3.1384	3.8960	4.8179	5.3502	5.9360	7.2876	8.9161	13.214	19.342	27.982	40.037
13	1.1381	1.2936	1.4685	1.6651	1.8856	2.1329	2.4098	2.7196	3.0658	3.4523	4.3635	5.4924	6.1528	6.8858	8.5994	10.699	16.386	24.758	36.937	54.451
14	1.1495	1.3195	1.5126	1.7317	1.9799	2.2609	2.5785	2.9372	3.3417	3.7975	4.8871	6.2613	7.0757	7.9875	10.147	12.839	20.319	31.691	48.756	74.053
15	1.1610	1.3459	1.5580	1.8009	2.0789	2.3966	2.7590	3.1722	3.6425	4.1772	5.4736	7.1379	8.1371	9.2655	11.973	15.407	25.195	40.564	64.358	100.71
16	1.1726	1.3728	1.6047	1.8730	2.1829	2.5404	2.9522	3.4259	3.9703	4.5950	6.1304	8.1372	9.3576	10.748	14.129	18.488	31.242	51.923	84.953	136.96
17	1.1843	1.4002	1.6528	1.9479	2.2920	2.6928	3.1588	3.7000	4.3276	5.0545	6.8660	9.2765	10.761	12.467	16.672	22.186	38.740	66.461	112.13	186.27
18	1.1961	1.4282	1.7024	2.0258	2.4066	2.8543	3.3799	3.9960	4.7171	5.5599	7.6900	10.575	12.375	14.462	19.673	26.623	48.038	85.070	148.02	253.33
19	1.2081	1.4568	1.7535	2.1068	2.5270	3.0256	3.6165	4.3157	5.1417	6.1159	8.6128	12.055	14.231	16.776	23.214	31.948	59.567	108.89	195.39	344.53
20	1.2202	1.4859	1.8061	2.1911	2.6533	3.2071	3.8697	4.6610	5.6044	6.7275	9.6463	13.743	16.366	19.460	27.393	38.337	73.864	139.37	257.91	468.57
21	1.2324	1.5157	1.8603	2.2788	2.7860	3.3996	4.1406	5.0338	6.1088	7.4002	10.803	15.667	18.821	22.574	32.323	46.005	91.591	178.40	340.44	637.26
22	1.2447	1.5460	1.9161	2.3699	2.9253	3.6035	4.4304	5.4365	6.6586	8.1403	12.100	17.861	21.644	26.186	38.142	55.206	113.57	228.35	449.39	866.67
23	1.2572	1.5769	1.9736	2.4647	3.0715	3.8197	4.7405	5.8715	7.2579	8.9543	13.552	20.361	24.891	30.376	45.007	66.247	140.83	292.30	593.19	1178.6
24	1.2697	1.6084	2.0328	2.5633	3.2251	4.0489	5.0724	6.3412	7.9111	9.8497	15.178	23.212	28.625	35.236	53.108	79.496	174.63	374.14	783.02	1602.9
25	1.2824	1.6406	2.0938	2.6658	3.3864	4.2919	5.4274	6.8485	8.6231	10.834	17.000	26.461	32.918	40.874	62.668	95.396	216.54	478.90	1033.5	2180.0
26	1.2953	1.6734	2.1566	2.7725	3.5557	4.5494	5.8074	7.3964	9.3992	11.918	19.040	30.166	37.856	47.414	73.948	114.47	268.51	612.99	1364.3	2964.9
27	1.3082	1.7069	2.2213	2.8834	3.7335	4.8223	6.2139	7.9881	10.245	13.110	21.324	34.389	43.535	55.000	87.259	137.37	332.95	784.63	1800.9	4032.2
28	1.3213	1.7410	2.2879	2.9987	3.9201	5.1117	6.6488	8.6271	11.167	14.421	23.883	39.204	50.065	63.800	102.96	164.84	412.86	1004.3	2377.2	5483.8
29	1.3345	1.7758	2.3566	3.1187	4.1161	5.4184	7.1143	9.3173	12.172	15.863	26.749	44.693	57.575	74.008	121.50	197.81	511.95	1285.5	3137.9	7458.0
30	1.3478	1.8114	2.4273	3.2434	4.3219	5.7435	7.6123	10.062	13.267	17.449	29.959	50.950	66.211	85.849	143.37	237.37	634.81	1645.5	4142.0	10143
40	1.4889	2.2080	3.2620	4.8010	7.0400	10.285	14.974	21.724	31.409	45.259	93.050	188.88	267.86	378.72	750.37	1469.7	5455.9	19426.	66520	*
50	1.6446	2.6916	4.3839	7.1067	11.467	18.420	29.457	46.901	74.357	117.39	289.00	700.23	1083.6	1670.7	3927.3	9100.4	46890.	*	*	*
60	1.8167	3.2810	5.8916	10.519	18.679	32.987	57.946	101.25	176.03	304.48	897.59	2595.9	4383.9	7370.1	20555.	56347.	*	*	*	*

Number of Periods	1%	2%	3%	4%	5%	6%	7%	8%	9%	10%	12%	14%	15%	16%	18%	20%	24%	28%	32%	36%
1	1.0000	1.0000	1.0000	1.0000	1.0000	1.0000	1.0000	1.0000	1.0000	1.0000	1.0000	1.0000	1.0000	1.0000	1.0000	1.0000	1.0000	1.0000	1.0000	1.0000
2	2.0100	2.0200	2.0300	2.0400	2.0500	2.0600	2.0700	2.0800	2.0900	2.1000	2.1200	2.1400	2.1500	2.1600	2.1800	2.2000	2.2400	2.2800	2.3200	2.3600
3	3.0301	3.0604	3.0909	3.1216	3.1525	3.1836	3.2149	3.2464	3.2781	3.3100	3.3744	3.4396	3.4725	3.5056	3.5724	3.6400	3.7776	3.9184	4.0624	4.2096
4	4.0604	4.1216	4.1836	4.2465	4.3101	4.3746	4.4399	4.5061	4.5731	4.6410	4.7793	4.9211	4.9934	5.0665	5.2154	5.3680	5.6842	6.0156	6.3624	6.7251
5	5.1010	5.2040	5.3091	5.4163	5.5256	5.6371	5.7507	5.8666	5.9847	6.1051	6.3528	6.6101	6.7424	6.8771	7.1542	7.4416	8.0484	8.6999	9.3983	10.146
6	6.1520	6.3081	6.4684	6.6330	6.8019	6.9753	7.1533	7.3359	7.5233	7.7156	8.1152	8.5355	8.7537	8.9775	9.4420	9.9299	10.980	12.135	13.405	14.798
7	7.2135	7.4343	7.6625	7.8983	8.1420	8.3938	8.6540	8.9228	9.2004	9.4872	10.089	10.730	11.066	11.413	12.141	12.915	14.615	16.533	18.695	21.126
8	8.2857	8.5830	8.8923	9.2142	9.5491	9.8975	10.259	10.636	11.028	11.435	12.299	13.232	13.726	14.240	15.327	16.499	19.122	22.163	25.678	29.731
9	9.3685	9.7546	10.159	10.582	11.026	11.491	11.978	12.487	13.021	13.579	14.775	16.085	16.785	17.518	19.085	20.798	24.712	29.369	34.895	41.435
10	10.462	10.949	11.463	12.006	12.577	13.180	13.816	14.486	15.192	15.937	17.548	19.337	20.303	21.321	23.521	25.958	31.643	38.592	47.061	57.351
11	11.566	12.168	12.807	13.486	14.206	14.971	15.783	16.645	17.560	18.531	20.654	23.044	24.349	25.732	28.755	32.150	40.237	50.398	63.121	78.998
12	12.682	13.412	14.192	15.025	15.917	16.869	17.888	18.977	20.140	21.384	24.133	27.270	29.001	30.850	34.931	39.580	50.894	65.510	84.320	108.43
13	13.809	14.680	15.617	16.626	17.713	18.882	20.140	21.495	22.953	24.522	28.029	32.088	34.351	36.786	42.218	48.496	64.109	84.852	112.30	148.47
14	14.947	15.973	17.086	18.291	19.598	21.015	22.550	24.214	26.019	27.975	32.392	37.581	40.504	43.672	50.818	59.195	80.496	109.61	149.23	202.92
15	16.096	17.293	18.598	20.023	21.578	23.276	25.129	27.152	29.360	31.772	37.279	43.842	47.580	51.659	60.965	72.035	100.81	141.30	197.99	276.97
16	17.257	18.639	20.156	21.824	23.657	25.672	27.888	30.324	33.003	35.949	42.753	50.980	55.717	60.925	72.939	87.442	126.01	181.86	262.35	377.69
17	18.430	20.012	21.761	23.697	25.840	28.212	30.840	33.750	36.973	40.544	48.883	59.117	65.075	71.673	87.068	105.93	157.25	233.79	347.30	514.66
18	19.614	21.412	23.414	25.645	28.132	30.905	33.999	37.450	41.301	45.599	55.749	68.394	75.836	84.140	103.74	128.11	195.99	300.25	459.44	700.93
19	20.810	22.840	25.116	27.671	30.539	33.760	37.379	41.446	46.018	51.159	63.439	78.969	88.211	98.603	123.41	154.74	244.03	385.32	607.47	954.27
20	22.019	24.297	26.870	29.778	33.066	36.785	40.995	45.762	51.160	57.275	72.052	91.024	102.44	115.37	146.62	186.68	303.60	494.21	802.86	1298.8
21	23.239	25.783	28.676	31.969	35.719	39.992	44.865	50.422	56.764	64.002	81.698	104.76	118.81	134.84	174.02	225.02	377.46	633.59	1060.7	1767.3
22	24.471	27.299	30.536	34.248	38.505	43.392	49.005	55.456	62.873	71.402	92.502	120.43	137.63	157.41	206.34	271.03	469.05	811.99	1401.2	2404.6
23	25.716	28.845	32.452	36.617	41.430	46.995	53.436	60.893	69.531	79.543	104.60	138.29	159.27	183.60	244.48	326.23	582.62	1040.3	1850.6	3271.3
24	26.973	30.421	34.426	39.082	44.502	50.815	58.176	66.764	76.789	88.497	118.15	158.65	184.16	213.97	289.49	392.48	723.46	1332.6	2443.8	4449.9
25	28.243	32.030	36.459	41.645	47.727	54.864	63.249	73.105	84.700	98.347	133.33	181.87	212.79	249.21	342.60	471.98	898.09	1706.8	3226.8	6052.9
26	29.525	33.670	38.553	44.311	51.113	59.156	68.676	79.954	93.323	109.18	150.33	208.33	245.71	290.08	405.27	567.37	1114.6	2185.7	4260.4	8233.0
27	30.820	35.344	40.709	47.084	54.669	63.705	74.483	87.350	102.72	121.09	169.37	238.49	283.56	337.50	479.22	681.85	1383.1	2798.7	5624.7	11197.9
28	32.129	37.051	42.930	49.967	58.402	68.528	80.697	95.338	112.96	134.20	190.69	272.88	327.10	392.50	566.48	819.22	1716.0	3583.3	7425.6	15230.2
29	33.450	38.792	45.218	52.966	62.322	73.639	87.346	103.96	124.13	148.63	214.58	312.09	377.16	456.30	669.44	984.06	2128.9	4587.6	9802.9	20714.1
30	34.784	40.568	47.575	56.084	66.438	79.058	94.460	113.28	136.30	164.49	241.33	356.78	434.74	530.31	790.94	1181.8	2640.9	5873.2	12940.	28172.2
40	48.886	60.402	75.401	95.025	120.79	154.76	199.63	259.05	337.88	442.59	767.09	1342.0	1779.0	2360.7	4163.2	7343.8	22728.	69377.	*	*
50	64.463	84.579	112.79	152.66	209.34	290.33	406.52	573.76	815.08	1163.9	2400.0	4994.5	7217.7	10435.	21813.	45497.	*	*	*	*
60	81.669	114.05	163.05	237.99	353.58	533.12	813.52	1253.2	1944.7	3034.8	7471.6	18535.	29219.	46057.	*	*	*	*	*	*

APPENDIX A.2

Future value of \$1 annuity. $\mathrm{FV} = \left[\dfrac{(1.0 + i)^n - 1.0}{i} \right]$

Period	1%	2%	3%	4%	5%	6%	7%	8%	9%	10%	12%	14%	15%	16%	18%	20%	24%	28%	32%	36%
1	.9901	.9804	.9709	.9615	.9524	.9434	.9346	.9259	.9174	.9091	.8929	.8772	.8696	.8621	.8475	.8333	.8065	.7813	.7576	.7353
2	.9803	.9612	.9426	.9246	.9070	.8900	.8734	.8573	.8417	.8264	.7972	.7695	.7561	.7432	.7182	.6944	.6504	.6104	.5739	.5407
3	.9706	.9423	.9151	.8890	.8638	.8396	.8163	.7938	.7722	.7513	.7118	.6750	.6575	.6407	.6086	.5787	.5245	.4768	.4348	.3975
4	.9610	.9238	.8885	.8548	.8227	.7921	.7629	.7350	.7084	.6830	.6355	.5921	.5718	.5523	.5158	.4823	.4230	.3725	.3294	.2923
5	.9515	.9057	.8626	.8219	.7835	.7473	.7130	.6806	.6499	.6209	.5674	.5194	.4972	.4761	.4371	.4019	.3411	.2910	.2495	.2149
6	.9420	.8880	.8375	.7903	.7462	.7050	.6663	.6302	.5963	.5645	.5066	.4556	.4323	.4104	.3704	.3349	.2751	.2274	.1890	.1580
7	.9327	.8706	.8131	.7599	.7107	.6651	.6227	.5835	.5470	.5132	.4523	.3996	.3759	.3538	.3139	.2791	.2218	.1776	.1432	.1162
8	.9235	.8535	.7894	.7307	.6768	.6274	.5820	.5403	.5019	.4665	.4039	.3506	.3269	.3050	.2660	.2326	.1789	.1388	.1085	.0854
9	.9143	.8368	.7664	.7026	.6446	.5919	.5439	.5002	.4604	.4241	.3606	.3075	.2843	.2630	.2255	.1938	.1443	.1084	.0822	.0628
10	.9053	.8203	.7441	.6756	.6139	.5584	.5083	.4632	.4224	.3855	.3220	.2697	.2472	.2267	.1911	.1615	.1164	.0847	.0623	.0462
11	.8963	.8043	.7224	.6496	.5847	.5268	.4751	.4289	.3875	.3505	.2875	.2366	.2149	.1954	.1619	.1346	.0938	.0662	.0472	.0340
12	.8874	.7885	.7014	.6246	.5568	.4970	.4440	.3971	.3555	.3186	.2567	.2076	.1869	.1685	.1372	.1122	.0757	.0517	.0357	.0250
13	.8787	.7730	.6810	.6006	.5303	.4688	.4150	.3677	.3262	.2897	.2292	.1821	.1625	.1452	.1163	.0935	.0610	.0404	.0271	.0184
14	.8700	.7579	.6611	.5775	.5051	.4423	.3878	.3405	.2992	.2633	.2046	.1597	.1413	.1252	.0985	.0779	.0492	.0316	.0205	.0135
15	.8613	.7430	.6419	.5553	.4810	.4173	.3624	.3152	.2745	.2394	.1827	.1401	.1229	.1079	.0835	.0649	.0397	.0247	.0155	.0099
16	.8528	.7284	.6232	.5339	.4581	.3936	.3387	.2919	.2519	.2176	.1631	.1229	.1069	.0930	.0708	.0541	.0320	.0193	.0118	.0073
17	.8444	.7142	.6050	.5134	.4363	.3714	.3166	.2703	.2311	.1978	.1456	.1078	.0929	.0802	.0600	.0451	.0258	.0150	.0089	.0054
18	.8360	.7002	.5874	.4936	.4155	.3503	.2959	.2502	.2120	.1799	.1300	.0946	.0808	.0691	.0508	.0376	.0208	.0118	.0068	.0039
19	.8277	.6864	.5703	.4746	.3957	.3305	.2765	.2317	.1945	.1635	.1161	.0829	.0703	.0596	.0431	.0313	.0168	.0092	.0051	.0029
20	.8195	.6730	.5537	.4564	.3769	.3118	.2584	.2145	.1784	.1486	.1037	.0728	.0611	.0514	.0365	.0261	.0135	.0072	.0039	.0021
25	.7798	.6095	.4776	.3751	.2953	.2330	.1842	.1460	.1160	.0923	.0588	.0378	.0304	.0245	.0160	.0105	.0046	.0021	.0010	.0005
30	.7419	.5521	.4120	.3083	.2314	.1741	.1314	.0994	.0754	.0573	.0334	.0196	.0151	.0116	.0070	.0042	.0016	.0006	.0002	.0001
40	.6717	.4529	.3066	.2083	.1420	.0972	.0668	.0460	.0318	.0221	.0107	.0053	.0037	.0026	.0013	.0007	.0002	.0001	*	*
50	.6080	.3715	.2281	.1407	.0872	.0543	.0339	.0213	.0134	.0085	.0035	.0014	.0009	.0006	.0003	.0001	*	*	*	*
60	.5504	.3048	.1697	.0951	.0535	.0303	.0173	.0099	.0057	.0033	.0011	.0004	.0002	.0001	*	*	*	*	*	*

APPENDIX A.3

Present value of $1: $PV = \dfrac{1.0}{(1.0 + i)^n}$

Number of Periods	1%	2%	3%	4%	5%	6%	7%	8%	9%	10%	12%	14%	15%	16%	18%	20%	24%	28%	32%
1	0.9901	0.9804	0.9709	0.9615	0.9524	0.9434	0.9346	0.9259	0.9174	0.9091	0.8929	0.8772	0.8696	0.8621	0.8475	0.8333	0.8065	0.7813	0.7576
2	1.9704	1.9416	1.9135	1.8861	1.8594	1.8334	1.8080	1.7833	1.7591	1.7355	1.6901	1.6467	1.6257	1.6052	1.5656	1.5278	1.4568	1.3916	1.3315
3	2.9410	2.8839	2.8286	2.7751	2.7232	2.6730	2.6243	2.5771	2.5313	2.4869	2.4018	2.3216	2.2832	2.2459	2.1743	2.1065	1.9813	1.8684	1.7663
4	3.9020	3.8077	3.7171	3.6299	3.5460	3.4651	3.3872	3.3121	3.2397	3.1699	3.0373	2.9137	2.8550	2.7982	2.6901	2.5887	2.4043	2.2410	2.0957
5	4.8534	4.7135	4.5797	4.4518	4.3295	4.2124	4.1002	3.9927	3.8897	3.7908	3.6048	3.4331	3.3522	3.2743	3.1272	2.9906	2.7454	2.5320	2.3452
6	5.7955	5.6014	5.4172	5.2421	5.0757	4.9173	4.7665	4.6229	4.4859	4.3553	4.1114	3.8887	3.7845	3.6847	3.4976	3.3255	3.0205	2.7594	2.5342
7	6.7282	6.4720	6.2303	6.0021	5.7864	5.5824	5.3893	5.2064	5.0330	4.8684	4.5638	4.2883	4.1604	4.0386	3.8115	3.6046	3.2423	2.9370	2.6775
8	7.6517	7.3255	7.0197	6.7327	6.4632	6.2098	5.9713	5.7466	5.5348	5.3349	4.9676	4.6389	4.4873	4.3436	4.0776	3.8372	3.4212	3.0758	2.7860
9	8.5660	8.1622	7.7861	7.4353	7.1078	6.8017	6.5152	6.2469	5.9952	5.7590	5.3282	4.9464	4.7716	4.6065	4.3030	4.0310	3.5655	3.1842	2.8681
10	9.4713	8.9826	8.5302	8.1109	7.7217	7.3601	7.0236	6.7101	6.4177	6.1446	5.6502	5.2161	5.0188	4.8332	4.4941	4.1925	3.6819	3.2689	2.9304
11	10.3676	9.7868	9.2526	8.7605	8.3064	7.8869	7.4987	7.1390	6.8052	6.4951	5.9377	5.4527	5.2337	5.0286	4.6560	4.3271	3.7757	3.3351	2.9776
12	11.2551	10.5753	9.9540	9.3851	8.8633	8.3838	7.9427	7.5361	7.1607	6.8137	6.1944	5.6603	5.4206	5.1971	4.7932	4.4392	3.8514	3.3868	3.0133
13	12.1337	11.3484	10.6350	9.9856	9.3936	8.8527	8.3577	7.9038	7.4869	7.1034	6.4235	5.8424	5.5831	5.3423	4.9095	4.5327	3.9124	3.4272	3.0404
14	13.0037	12.1062	11.2961	10.5631	9.8986	9.2950	8.7455	8.2442	7.7862	7.3667	6.6282	6.0021	5.7245	5.4675	5.0081	4.6106	3.9616	3.4587	3.0609
15	13.8651	12.8493	11.9379	11.1184	10.3797	9.7122	9.1079	8.5595	8.0607	7.6061	6.8109	6.1422	5.8474	5.5755	5.0916	4.6755	4.0013	3.4834	3.0764
16	14.7179	13.5777	12.5611	11.6523	10.8378	10.1059	9.4466	8.8514	8.3126	7.8237	6.9740	6.2651	5.9542	5.6685	5.1624	4.7296	4.0333	3.5026	3.0882
17	15.5623	14.2919	13.1661	12.1657	11.2741	10.4773	9.7632	9.1216	8.5436	8.0216	7.1196	6.3729	6.0472	5.7487	5.2223	4.7746	4.0591	3.5177	3.0971
18	16.3983	14.9920	13.7535	12.6593	11.6896	10.8276	10.0591	9.3719	8.7556	8.2014	7.2497	6.4674	6.1280	5.8178	5.2732	4.8122	4.0799	3.5294	3.1039
19	17.2260	15.6785	14.3238	13.1339	12.0853	11.1581	10.3356	9.6036	8.9501	8.3649	7.3658	6.5504	6.1982	5.8775	5.3162	4.8435	4.0967	3.5386	3.1090
20	18.0456	16.3514	14.8775	13.5903	12.4622	11.4699	10.5940	9.8181	9.1285	8.5136	7.4694	6.6231	6.2593	5.9288	5.3527	4.8696	4.1103	3.5458	3.1129
25	22.0232	19.5235	17.4131	15.6221	14.0939	12.7834	11.6536	10.6748	9.8226	9.0770	7.8431	6.8729	6.4641	6.0971	5.4669	4.9476	4.1474	3.5640	3.1220
30	25.8077	22.3965	19.6004	17.2920	15.3725	13.7648	12.4090	11.2578	10.2737	9.4269	8.0552	7.0027	6.5660	6.1772	5.5168	4.9789	4.1601	3.5693	3.1242
40	32.8347	27.3555	23.1148	19.7928	17.1591	15.0463	13.3317	11.9246	10.7574	9.7791	8.2438	7.1050	6.6418	6.2335	5.5482	4.9966	4.1659	3.5712	3.1250
50	39.1961	31.4236	25.7298	21.4822	18.2559	15.7619	13.8007	12.2335	10.9617	9.9148	8.3045	7.1327	6.6605	6.2463	5.5541	4.9995	4.1666	3.5714	3.1250
60	44.9550	34.7609	27.6756	22.6235	18.9293	16.1614	14.0392	12.3766	11.0480	9.9672	8.3240	7.1401	6.6651	6.2492	5.5553	4.9999	4.1667	3.5714	3.1250

APPENDIX A.4

Present value of an annuity of $1 per period for n period: $PV = \dfrac{1.0 - \dfrac{1.0}{(1.0 + i)^n}}{i}$

Answers to Chapter-End Problems and Cases and CFA Examination Questions

Chapter 1

1. RI = 8%, RA = 14%, RS = 9.5%.
3. 7.92%.
4. Gains of $70,000 and $150,000 (deferred); taxable gain of $95,000 in 1995.
5. *a:* $4,127. *b:* $17,222. *c:* $47,372. *d:* $139,172. *e:* $139,172.
6. *a:* $3,300. *b:* $9,203. *c:* $29,728. *d:* $57,528. *e:* $95,328.

Case 1.2—*a:* Condo offers $125,000 exclusion while bond fund only defers taxes; condo total taxes = $30,800, bond fund total taxes = $68,600. Condo offers tax advantage *plus* place to live. *b:* after-tax return = 5.04%, muni fund is better.

Chapter 2

1. *a:* 4.17%. *b:* 1.63%. *c:* 6.25%. *d:* 4.11%.
2. *a:* $5,000. *b:* broker's loan is $5,000; minimum securities' value = $6,667. *c:* deposit $1,666.67. *d:* $37.50.
3. *a:* $1,000 loss at $60/share and $2,000 profit at $30/share. *b:* Shirley must pay $200 dividend. *c:* equity = $1,500; at 30% maintenance margin requirement, margin call at $57.69/share.

Case 2.2—*a:* total commissions = $4,125; realized gains of $9,510 and unrealized loss of $8,160. *b:* interest = $1,690. *c:* profit holding IBM (ignores selling commission) = $1,640; T-bill profit = $960; actual trading loss = $340. *d:* margin call @ 79.62/share.

Chapter 3

1. *a:* 0.3546. *b:* 0.2727.
2. arithmetic average = 0.2063, geometric average = 0.1524.
3. arithmetic average = 0.1210, geometric average = 0.0785.
4. *a:* $1,636.65. *b:* $3,038.59. *c:* $2,851.16.
5. *a:* $2,897. *b:* $4,362.16. *c:* $1,020.55.
6. *a:* 5.2%. *b:* 10.64%. *c:* 11.4%.
7. *a:* $2,020.71. *b:* $1,602.78.
8. 14.87%.

9.   *a:* 6.67% increase. *b:* 1.2% increase. *c:* $100 increase.

Case 3.1—*a:* 5%. *b:* 7%. *c:* 1% (reasonable but not great return).

Case 3.2—*a:* year 1 = $13,747, year 2 = $14,708, year 3 = $15,737, year 4 = $16,838. *b:* $19,980. *c:* $54,980, parents' savings = $19,980, annuity of $3,000/yr. at i = 10%, n = 8 yrs. *d:* earning 10% with no risk is impossible given current rates.

Chapter 4

1.   *a:* 20%. *b:* 266.66%. *c:* 16.33%. *d:* 0.8165. Matt must trade off risk and return between the two investments.
2.   mean = 7.2%, var. = 154.56%, st. dev. = 12.43%, C = 1.727
3.   *a:* mean = 9.6%, var. = 3.24%, st. dev. = 1.8%, C = 0.188. *b:* latter portfolio reduces risk and increases return.
4.   D and B should be held together.
5.   *a:* 0.0667. *b:* $132,180. *c:* $149,750.

Case 4.1—*a:* NTC has higher expected return and less risk. *b:* ER = 15.0%, var. = 521.0%, st. dev. = 22.83%, C = 1.52. *c:* possible returns are 8.8%, 9.0%, and 8.0%; ER = 8.7%. *d:* reject 8% and take the combination.

Case 4.2—*a:* beta = 1.65. *b:* DDY will decline 19.8%. *c:* beta is useful only if the portfolio is well diversified.

Chapter 5

1.   effective rate = 4.06%; accumulation on annual 4.25% = 5.285 on quarterly 4% = 4.9138.
2.   *a:* $21.33. *b:* $11.33. *c:* $18.00.
3.   Tom earns 10% if he does nothing; he earns either +30% or −10% if he leverages.
4.   *a:* $480,000. *b:* $720,000. *c:* $280,000.
5.   *a:* difference in premiums = $1,300; FVAD = $8,730, buy term. *b:* consider loan value with whole-life and investment discipline.
6.   *a:* $130,482. *b:* $61,296. *c:* $8,902.
7.   *a:* $800,000. *b:* farm is illiquid and could pose a problem.

Case 5.1—*a:* Frank minimizes possible emergencies. *b:* $36,000 is suggested, $20,000 in stocks and $25,000 in bonds is suggested. *c:* $18,000 in a MMMF and $18,000 in 3-year CDs is suggested.

Case 5.2—*a:* difference in annual premiums is $3,600; after-tax rate of return is 7% (assuming no deferral); FVAD @ 7% = $243,635 and FVAD @ 10% = $389,454; if tax deferral is available, buy term, if not, buy whole life; implicit rate in whole life policy = 8.71%. *b:* Tiants have not been successful at saving and investing in the past, suggesting whole life policy may be a better choice.

Chapter 6

1.   Review appropriate material in text, if help is needed.
2.   Required rate = 12.375%.

3. All required rates are higher; 16.375%.
4. A stock with a beta of 0.75 would not be influenced; stock with 1.5 beta has lower required rate.
5. Required rate: Ace = 12.2%, King = 16.6%, Queen = 19.0%; King is the only stock worth buying.
6. PV of cash inflows = $16.02; buy the stock.
7. Expected current return = 6.6%; expected total return = 16.6%.
8. *a:* $40. *b:* $46.00. *c:* $30.00. *d:* $34.50.

Case 6.1—*a:* They have unclear investment plans; they should express concrete goals and risk-tolerance level. *b:* They have a poor grasp of risk and return. *c:* Difficult to measure "appropriate" because of hazy plans. *d:* Do research before investing.

Case 6.2—*a:* PV = $45.49, buy the stock. *b:* TR = 21.95%. *c:* PV = $21.87, do not buy stock.

Chapter 7

1. Liquidity and solvency have deteriorated.
2. Earnings strength is poor.
3. 1995 EPS = $3.80, 1994 EPS = $3.60, industry EPS = $3.91; 1995 CF/s = $5.80, 1994 CF/s = $5.20, industry CF/s = $5.27.
4. *b:* liquidity has deteriorated a bit, solvency is a bit better. *c:* slight improvements in profit margins. *d:* earnings ratios are excellent but unchanged in 1995. *e:* exp. TR = 15.79%, required return = 22.45%, don't buy the stock. *f:* book value = $8.04.
5. *b:* Avg. *P/E* = 39.0, Avg. *P/CF* = 9.2, cash-flow forecast is more reasonable. *c:* HPR = 13.37%, RR = 15.0%, don't buy.

Case 7.1: RR's: Fleet = 20.75%, Dirge = 14.8%; ER's: Fleet = 21.7%, Dirge = 17.7%; both are buys but Dirge is more undervalued and fits better with Rob's investment goal.

Case 7.2—*a:* annual EPSs = $1.97, $1.10, $0.90, and $2.04; prices reflect expected earnings making beginning-of-year prices more stable in P/E calculations. *b:* graphs. *c:* there is no apparent trading strategy. *d:* buy during recessions and sell during booms in economy/industry.

Chapter 8

1. *a:* sell on day 12, buy on day 18, sell on day 20, buy on day 22. *b:* initial purchase on day 1, overall trading loss = $134.
2. OBV = +92,000, buy stock.
3. *a:* momentum is increasing. *b:* relative strength at Q4 = 0.70; buy, since this exceeds 0.65.
4. Geometric average returns for buy-hold = 6.2%, Super Bowl = 12.4%, election year = 10.6%; election year strategy beats super bowl through 1983 but does less well thereafter.

Case 8.1—*a:* 5-day moving average starts at 9.902 and ends at 10.776. *b:* most recent price of $11.50 penetrates moving average from below, giving a buy signal, however, OBV is negative.

Case 8.2—*c:* it is not clear which indicator leads or lags. *d:* each indicator seems to point down; a decline of about 15% can be estimated, taking the market down to 113.

Chapter 9

1. YTM on 8% bond = 12%, YTM on zero = 8.4%.
2. *a:* CY = YTM = 12%. *b:* CY = 11.11%, YTM = 11.56%.
3. Total accumulations: 12% YTM = $10,286, 16% YTM = $16,543.
4. *a:* $1,273.55. *b:* $1,000. *c:* $656.77.
5. *a:* E = −0.847. *b:* E = −0.601.
6. *D* values for a, b, c = 2.7344, 2.5747, and 3.0000.
7. Adjusted *D* = 5.682 and bond's price falls by $56.82.

Case 9.1—*a:* Zero-coupon portfolio grows to $39,348; coupon-bond portfolio's future value cannot be determined. *b:* reinvestment rates are not locked in. *c:* yield-curve slope suggests rising rates. *d:* falling rates hinder Karen's portfolio but have no effect upon Ian's.

Case 9.2—*a:* Felix's gain = $29,422 while broker's strategy leads to gain of $67,200. *b:* E (T bills) = −.078, E (T notes) = −0.312, E (Zeros) = −2.176. *c:* reasons do not match his objective. *d:* they should play no role since Felix is not a long-term investor.

Chapter 10

1. $1,500,000 to debenture holders and $1,500,000 to general creditors; subordinated debenture holders get nothing.
2. *a:* see related material from text. *b:* *i* = 9.897%.
3. See related material from text.
4. Pre-tax yield = 11.94%.
5. The Treasury after-tax yield = 5.293%; corporate after-tax yield = 5.218%; Treasury is the better choice.
6. *a:* per-share distribution on preferred = $2.00, $1.60, and $2.00; per share common distribution = $0.67, 0, and $5.00. *b:* preferred must receive $4.50.
7. Current yield = 8%, YTC = 6.1%, actual return = 4%.

Case 10.1—*a:* munis seem the best choice. *b:* $30,000 in N.Y. Go's and $30,000 in California Rev's.

Case 10.2—*a:* Co. Retailers = 9.52%, Pac. Utilities = 8.33%, and So. Tel. = 9.38%. *b:* Co. Retailers = 9.21%, So. Tel. = 8.42%. *c:* Co. Retailers = 4.76%, Pac. Utilities = 15.5%. *d:* E = −1.0. *e:* Mort's advice is terrible. *f:* Pac. Utilities seems the best.

Chapter 11

1. $10,000 invested in shares shows −$1,000, –0–, and +$1,000; $10,000 invested in options shows −$10,000, -0–, +$10,000.
2.   At $5 intervals and price range from $40 to $0, the following are suggested time premiums: $0.50, $0.75, $1.00, $2.00, $4.00, $7.00, $10.13, $15.06, $20.00.
3.   *a:* $1.00/right. *b:* makes no difference if rights are exercised or sold.
4.   *y* intercept = $10 and *x* intercept = four months.
5.   *a:* $CV = \$750$, $CP = \$250$, V as debt = $808, $N = 4.55$ years. *b:* choice trades off risk and return—greater upside potential with stock and less risk with convertible.
6.   *a:* at prices of $0, $4, $5, $6, and $8 suggested market values are $15, $18, $24, $27, and $33; value as debt = $15; $CV = 4 \times P$. *b:* extra current return = $0.88, $N = 4.55$ years.
7.   *a:* −2% to +18% is the range of returns for the bond, −25% to +25% is the range for the stock. *b:* bond's present value = $1,100.50 and stock's present value = $1,033.04; bond is better.

Case 11.1—*a:* most realistic values for call options are $–0–, $3.00, and $14.60; realistic values for the warrant are $11, $21, and $32. *b:* profit at stock prices of $46.40, $58.00, and $69.60 are −$720, $1,600, and $3,920 for the stock (200 shares); −$10,000, $5,000, and $63,000 for the options (20 contracts); −$2,142, $4,998, and $12,852 for the warrants (714 warrants). *c:* option strategy is riskiest. *d:* the following mix is suggested: $1,000 in options, $7,500 in stocks, and $1,500 in warrants.

Case 11.2—*a:* most realistic prices are $690, $1,100, and $1,620. *b:* CV/bond = $200, N = five years. *c:* risk aversion suggests the convertibles are better alternative for Mona.

Chapter 12

1.   See related material in text.
2.   Cost = $25/contract; commission is $5.89, or 24%.
3. and 4.   At closing prices of $40 thru $60, buyer's profits/losses on June 50 call are are −$625, −$625, −$625, −$125, +$375; profits on the June 50 put are +$675, +$175, −$325, −$325; reverse signs to get seller's profits/losses; call break-even = $56.25 and put break-even = $46.75.
5.   Break-even points: 40.5 and 59.5 for *a* and *b*; 43.125 and 60.9375 for *c*; 46.875 and 71.25 for *d*.
6.   No arbitrage opportunities are apparent.
7.   At prices of $55 or less, portfolio value = $4,812.50.
8.   See related material in text.

Case 12.1—*a:* transfer $400,000 to MMF and buy call options. *b:* about nine contracts are needed at cost of $5,963; interest is $3,077 and net cost for 10 weeks = $2,886. *c:* total cost = $10,125; dividends are $2,308 and net cost = $7,817. *d:* portfolio insurance strategy is the better approach.

Case 12.2—*a:* two puts are needed at a cost of $2,250; hedge shows more profit at 10% decline and unchanged market; it shows less profit at 10% increase. *b:* the hedge is a matter of choice.

Chapter 13

1. *a:* $13,000. *b:* at price = $2.50, profit = $4,500; at price = $1.90, loss = $4,500; change signs for the short position.

2. *a:* basis for June contract = −0.71, for Aug. contract = −4.61, for June 94 contract = −24.11. *b:* loss = $4,420. *c:* assume zero basis at contract's maturity in August, arbitrage loss = $121.

3. *a:* traders think that the dollar will strengthen. *b:* take long position, reversing at 1.55 gives profit of $6,250/contract. *c:* take short position in three contracts, which should be perfect hedge when contracts mature in six months.

4. *a:* $101,500. *b:* $i = 7.85\%$. *c:* $1,500 change, $100/bp.

5. *a:* $980,550. *b:* settle price = 100.00 − yield. *c:* $982,500, change in price = $1,950, $25/bp.

6. Hedge strategy calls for shorting bills and going long on bonds; assuming one contract in each case and given the expected prices, the hedge loses $1,701; must restructure hedge, such as two bill contracts to one bond contract.

Case 13.1—*a:* futures are better than short selling. *b:* futures also require margin, but probably less than shorting. *c:* possible loss = $74,733. *d:* decrease in value = $17,159. *e:* hedge ratio = 4.36, short 4 (4.36 rounded) T-bond contracts.

Case 13.2—*a:* Sue's reasoning is incorrect. *b:* difference of four points can be arbitraged to lock in $2,000 before carrying costs; Sue must buy $228,000 of stocks (5.7 baskets); carrying costs = $3,728 in total, leading to arbitrage loss. *c:* primary risk is possible poor correlation between index and baskets.

Chapter 14

1. $3.25.

2. *a:* −3.33%. *b:* 5.0%.

3. *a:* Sun—9.4% and 6.3%, Moon—5.6% and 5.5%, S&P 500—6.4% and 5.9%. *b:* Sun's beta = 2.0 and Moon's beta = 0.495; Sun's alpha and TI = −2.5 and −0.80; Moon's alpha and TI = 1.51 and 3.05; Moon is better than Sun and S&P 500.

4. *a:* Accumulations: UIT = $29,549, Fund = $29,765, self-directed = $30,006. *b:* quality should be the same with each vehicle, which may be difficult with self-directed.

5. Eq/s = $11.14, price = $9.14.

6. *a:* after-tax return = 7.91%, other factors must be considered. *b:* after-tax return on public syndication = 9%; return on private deal is enhanced by $2,000 write-off ($800 tax shield) but Nick must be active in business. *c:* suggested allocation and after-tax returns—$5,000 muni UIT (7.91%), $5,000 public LP (9.0%), $10,000 in private LP (14.3%).

7. *a:* Total returns—Delaney = 25%, HO = 18%, Van Atta = 20%, and ZMC = 20%. *c:* Van Atta may duplicate Sue's bond holdings, ZMC's return may not be realistic because it terminates in five years, Delaney may have excessive risks, HO Properties seems best.

Case 14.1—*a:* mutual funds are best for Ankeneys. *b:* spend more time studying mutual funds. *c:* choose a fund family and reinvest all distributions.

Case 14.2—*a:* HPRs = 23.1% and 13.5%. *b:* alpha values = −3.7 and 5.3; TI values = 8.94 and 1.94; RARORs = −5.17 and −1.5. *c:* no superior performances of the fund and it has high risk.

Chapter 15

1. Lena can borrow up to $73,570.
2. *a:* IRR = 49.53%. *b:* investment looks great, but could turn sour if growth is not 8% a year.
3. *a:* $400 can be used as offset. *b:* i) $2,000; ii) $25,000; iii) no offset.
4. *a:* 2100 Park Lane = 8.9%, 76 Westbury = 13.5%, 351 Shaw = 5.7%; none are directly comparable to 334 Shaw; assuming 10% is appropriate return, property is worth $160,000. *b:* it is difficult to determine appropriate capitalization rate.
5. Gold and stocks are the better combination.
6. *a:* art is riskiest as measured by *C* values. *b:* art and bonds represent the best mix.

Case 15.1—*a:* mortgage is affordable. *c:* 5th year cash flow = $40,746. *d:* NPV = $6,192, IRR = 16%. *e:* moving sooner would lower return.

Case 15.2—*a:* $1,700 can offset other income and cash flow = −$2,024. *b:* $5,500 can offset and cash flow = −$960. *c:* cash flow = −$8,100. *d:* cash flow per personal use day = −$101.20, −$68.59, and −$225.00; case 2 seems optimal and Rosens should consider renting somebody else's condo for 6 days if 20 days are desired.

Chapter 16

1. 36.67%.
2. 6.16%.
3. To rebalance equally, sell $3,400 of stocks and buy $600 of T bills and $4,000 of bonds. Rebalance with staggered weights, sell $9,786 of stocks and $806 of T bills and buy $10,592 of bonds.
4. $16,000 of stocks sold and invest in T bills.
5. Cumulative gain/loss by month— − 7.71, − 35.76, − 22.85, − 5.32

Case 16.1—*a:* portfolio return = 11.67%; sell $934 of stocks and buy $267 of gold and $667 of bonds. *b:* portfolio return = 5%; SML return = 4.8%. *c:* Francine's plan—sell $1,467 of gold and buy $533 of stocks and $933 of bonds; Horace's plan—buy $2,560 of stocks and sell $280 of bonds and $2,280 of gold.

Case 16.2—*a:* after decreases, $26,550 is in MMF and $8,550 in stocks; after increases, ending portfolio value = $39,147. *b:* cumulative values—stock fund = $41,476; MMF = $43,200; portfolio insurance = $39,861. *c:* insurance reduces risk exposure because a portion of the portfolio is in risk-free assets, but major disadvantage is limited funds in the market during upswings.

Chapter 17

1. *a:* ER(A) = 10, ER(B) = 15; VAR(A) = 1.6, VAR(B) = 90.0; SD(A) = 1.27, SD(B) = 9.49. *b:* Cov: A, B = −12.0, r = −1.0. *c:* asset combination is perfect insofar as it eliminates risk.
2. ER(P) = 12.5, VAR(P) = 16.9, SD(P) = 4.11
3. Weights of 0.9 for A and 0.1 for B create an almost risk-free portfolio with ER(P) = 10.5.
4. Portfolio offers higher return and less risk than A; thus, it is a better choice than A.
5. *a:* range of payoffs is from −$68,000 to $92,000. *b:* synthetic using futures offers −$64,000, $16,000, $96,000; synthetic using options offers −$60,000, $20,000, $100,000.
6. Options-created synthetic is the better choice, buying 20 calls and selling 20 puts.
7. *a:* number of contracts to gain a beta–2.0 portfolio = 16. *b:* Beta = 1.0 in first instance and 0.5 in second. *c:* go long on eight contracts in the first instance and four contracts in the second.
8. *a:* at YTMs of 4%, 6%, 8%, PVS = $1,164, $1,000, and $864. *b:* E = −0.444. *c:* 40 contracts are needed; holding both the bonds and the contracts achieves an E value of −0.888. *d:* a hedge immunizes the portfolio completely and requires 40 contracts.

Case 17.1—*a:* points *off* the frontier are portfolios 2, 4, and 6. *b:* portfolio 7 is optimum. *c:* portfolio 3 can be viewed as risk-free asset and portfolio 5 can be viewed as the market. *d:* portfolios 3 and 5 are SML anchors and portfolios 8 and 1 are also on the SML; portfolio 1 might be best for Danielle because she has a high risk-tolerance level.

Case 17.2—*a:* invest $5 million in T bonds and go long on 50 futures contracts. *b:* greater flexibility is main advantage with futures. *c:* buy 250 calls and sell 250 puts, earning a profit of $25,000.

Answers to CFA Questions—Multiple Choice

Part I: 1–c, 2–b, 3–a, 4–d, 5–c, 6–a, 7–a, 8–a, 9–a, 10–c, 11–d, 12–c, 13–a, 14–d, 15–a, 16–b, 17–b, 18–d, 19–b, 20–c, 21–d

Part II: 1–d, 2–c, 3–b, 4–a, 5–d, 6–c, 8–b, 9–c

Part III: 1–c, 2–c, 3–b, 4–a, 5–a, 6–d, 7–c, 8–c, 9–d, 10–b, 11–b

Part IV: 1–b, 2–a, 3–b, 4–c, 5–d, 6–a, 7–b, 8–a and c, 9–d

Parts V and VI: 1–a, 2–d, 3–d, 4–d, 5–a, 6–b, 7–c, 8–d, 9–d, 10–c, 11–a, 12–b, 13–d

Brief Answers to CFA Questions—Problems

Part I:
I. *A:* P = $43 (Eastover is undervalued); *B:* P = $48.03 (Eastover is even more undervalued)

II.

A:	EO	SHC	S&P 500
P/E Model			
5-yr. avg.	16.6	11.9	15.2
Relative 5 yr.	1.09	0.78	
Current	17.5	16.0	20.2
Current relative	0.87	0.79	
P/B Model			
5-yr. avg.	1.50	1.10	2.10
Relative 5-yr.	0.71	0.52	
Current	1.62	1.49	2.6
Current relative	0.62	0.57	

EO appears particularly attractive on P/B basis.

B: Review related material in text.

Part II: A: Treasury bond should outperform the corporate bond because of the latter's call feature. *B:* Uncertainty of CMO cash flows (prepayment risk) and somewhat lower quality are primary reasons.

Part IV: A: number of puts for S&P 100 = $[(1.05/0.95) \times 7,761,700]/(365 \times 10) = 235$; cost = $235 \times \$10.25 \times 100 = \$240,875$; using similar methods, number for S&P 500 = 209 and cost = $229,900, number of puts for NYSE = 368 and cost = $230,000. *B:* the S&P 500 offers low cost, good correlation, and good liquidity. *C:* all options are at the money; if otherwise, manager must be concerned with other problems. *D:* See related material in Chapter 13.

Index

STOCK RETURNS(%) AND PRESIDENTIAL TERMS

	Year in Office				Full Term
	1	2	3	4	
1961–64 (D) Kennedy/Johnson	26.6	-8.7	22.5	16.3	64.7
1965–68 (D) Johnson	12.3	-10.0	23.7	10.9	38.6
1969–72 (R) Nixon	-8.3	3.5	14.1	18.7	28.5
1973–76 (R) Nixon/Ford	-14.5	-26.5	36.9	23.6	6.3
1977–80 (D) Carter	-7.2	6.4	18.2	31.5	53.5
1981–84 (R) Reagan 1	-4.9	20.4	22.3	6.0	48.4
1985–88 (R) Reagan 2	31.1	18.5	5.7	16.4	91.1
1989–92 (R) Bush	31.1	-3.2	30.0	7.4	77.2
1993– (D) Clinton	10.0	—	—	—	—
Average (arithmetic) by year:	8.5	0.1	21.7	16.4	—
Average (geometric) by party:	(Democrat)				10.9
	(Republican)				10.1